A-Z SUR

C000283289

CONTENTS

REFERENCE

Motorway	M3
Primary Route	A31
Under Construction	
A Road	A22
Proposed	
B Road	B2236
Dual Carriageway	
One-way Street	
Traffic flow on A Roads is also indicated by a heavy line on the driver's left	
Junction Names	SUNBURY CROSS
Restricted Access	
Pedestrianized Road	
Track & Footpath	
Residential Walkway	
Railway	Level Crossing / Tunnel
Stations: National Rail Network	
Heritage Station	
Underground Station	
Croydon Tramlink	Stop / Tunnel
The boarding of Tramlink trams at stops may be limited to a single direction, indicated by the arrow	
Built-up Area	STATION / VIEW
Local Authority Boundary	
Posttown Boundary	
Postcode Boundary (Within Posttown)	

Map Continuation	86
Large Scale Town Centre	203
Airport	
Car Park (Selected)	P
Church or Chapel	†
Fire Station	■
Hospital	H
House Numbers (A & B Roads only)	69 63
Information Centre	i
National Grid Reference	^{520}
Park & Ride	Artington P+□
Police Station	▲
Post Office	★
Toilet:	
without facilities for the Disabled	▽
with facilities for the Disabled	▽
Disabled facilities only	▽
Viewpoint	
Educational Establishment	
Hospital or Hospice	
Industrial Building	
Leisure or Recreational Facility	
Place of Interest	
Public Building	
Shopping Centre or Market	
Other Selected Buildings	

SCALE

Map Pages 4-199
1:19,000 3⅓ inches (8.47cm) to 1 mile 5.26cm to 1km

0 ¼ ½ ¾ Mile
0 250 500 750 Metres 1 Kilometre

Map Pages 200-203
1:9,051 7 inches (17.78cm) to 1 mile 11.05cm to 1km

0 ⅛ ¼ ⅜ Mile
0 100 200 300 400 500 Metres

Copyright of Geographers' A-Z Map Company Ltd.

Fairfield Road, Borough Green, Sevenoaks, Kent TN15 8PP
Telephone: 01732 781000 (Enquiries & Trade Sales)
01732 783422 (Retail Sales)

www.a-zmaps.co.uk

Copyright © Geographers' A-Z Map Co. Ltd.

Edition 5 2007

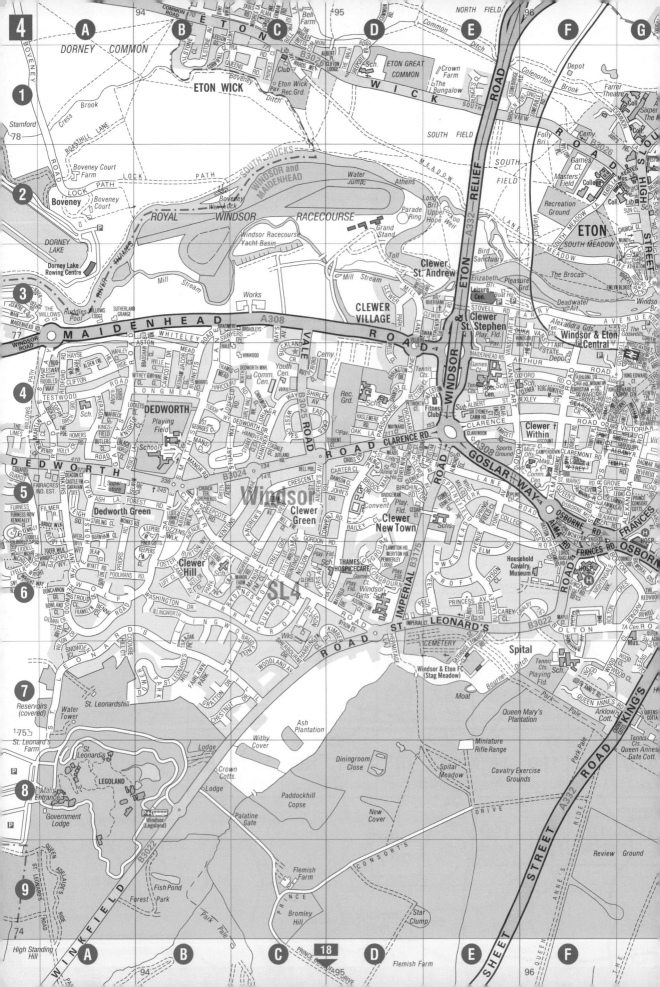

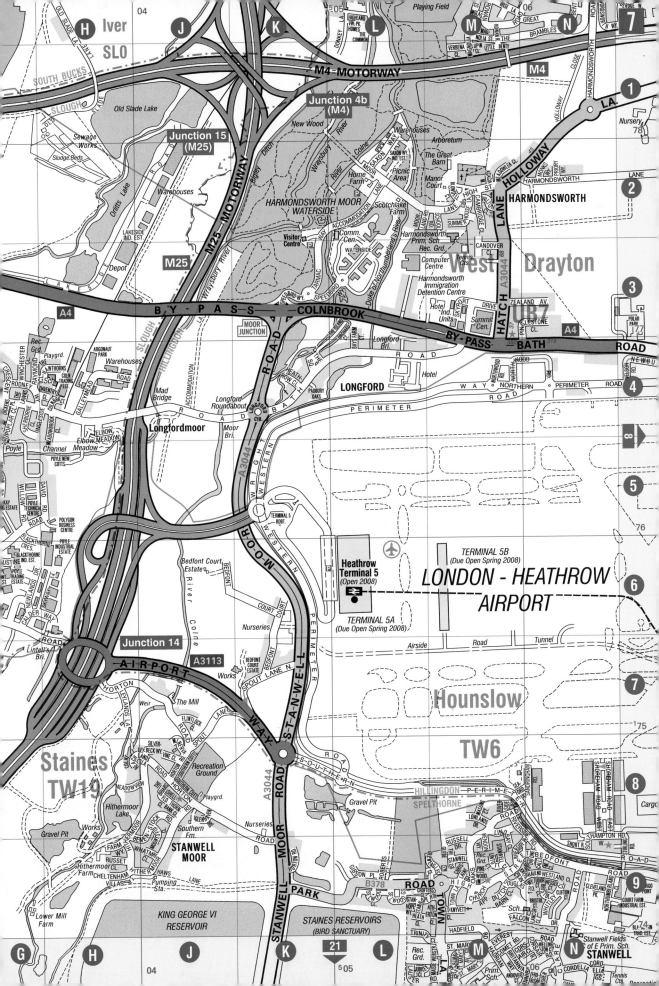

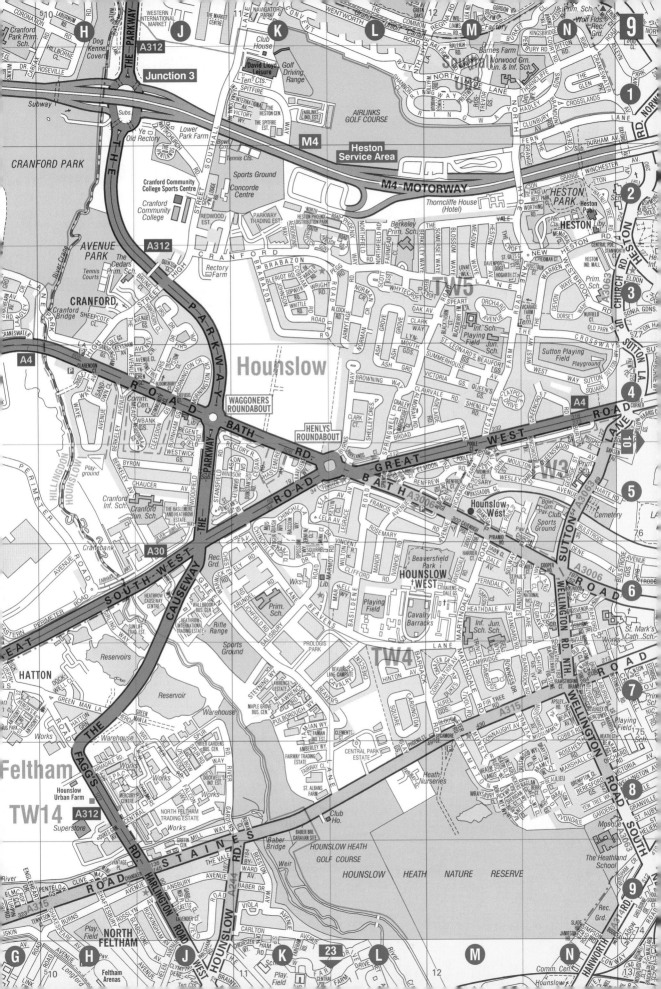

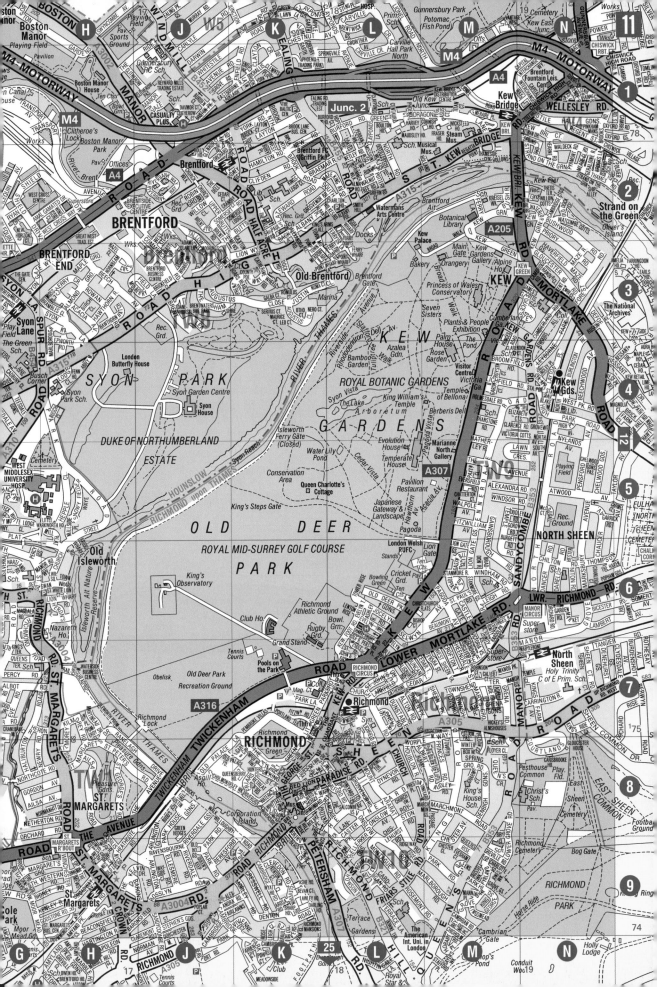

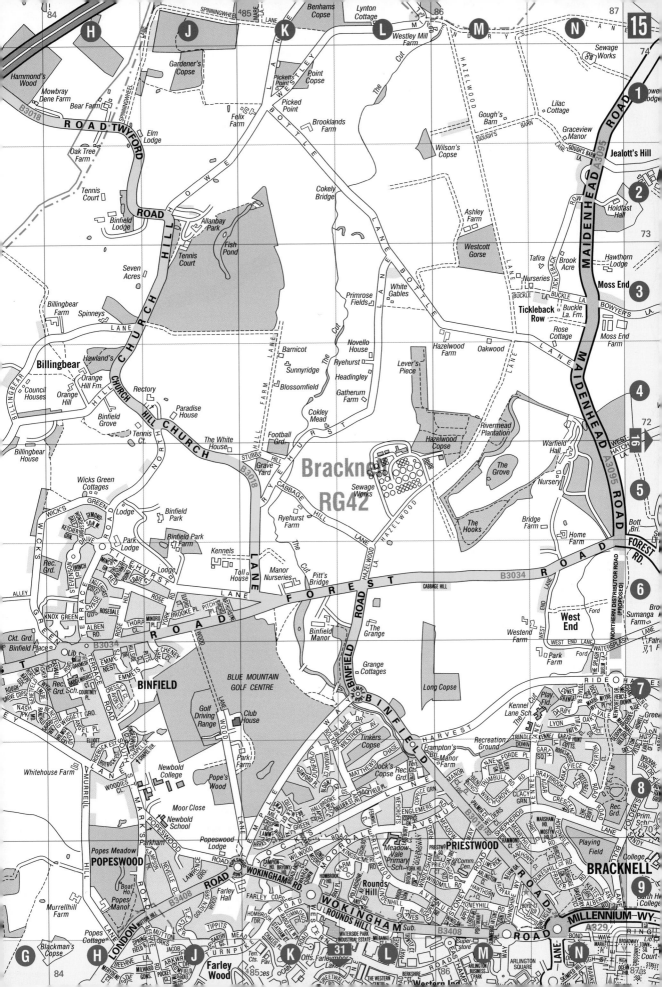

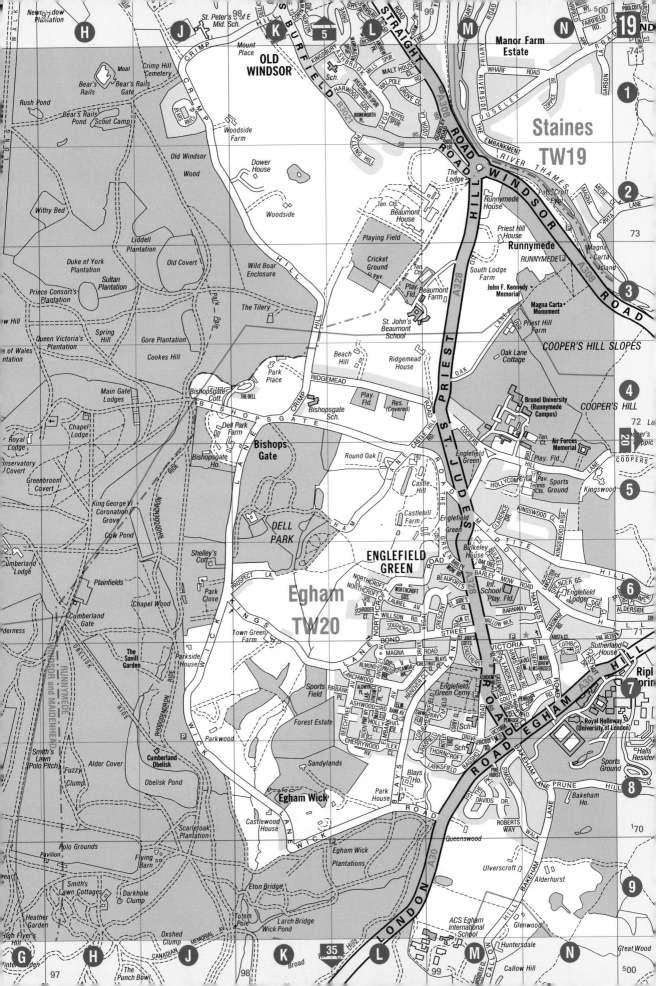

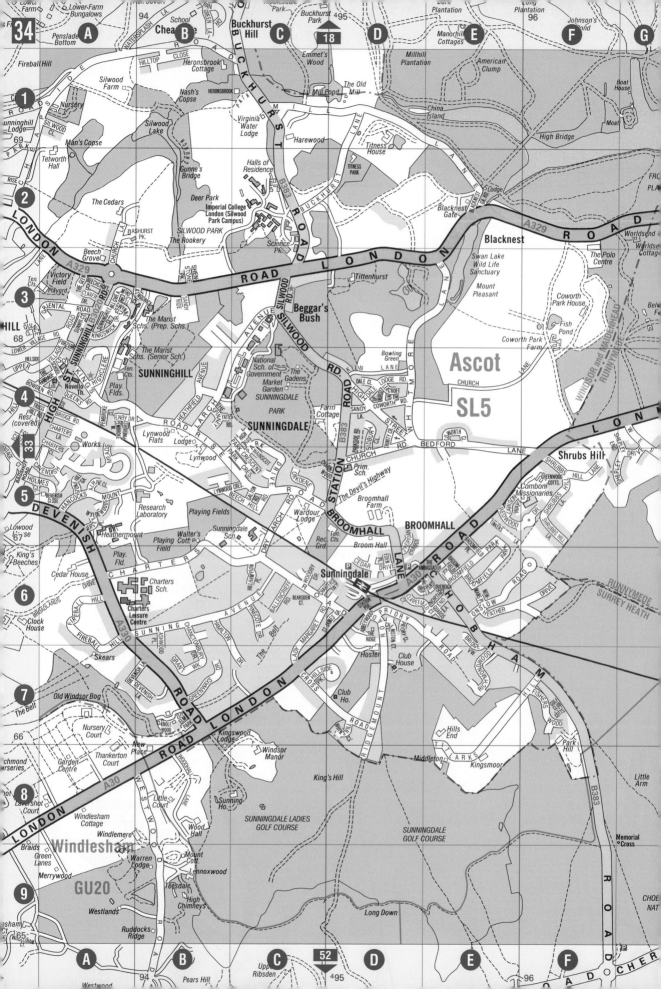

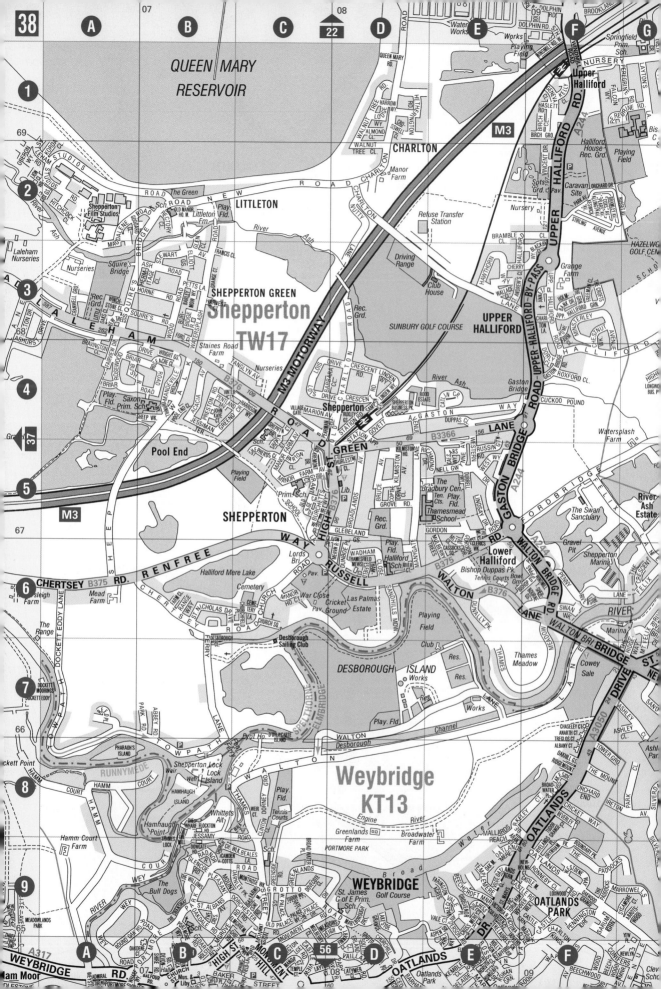

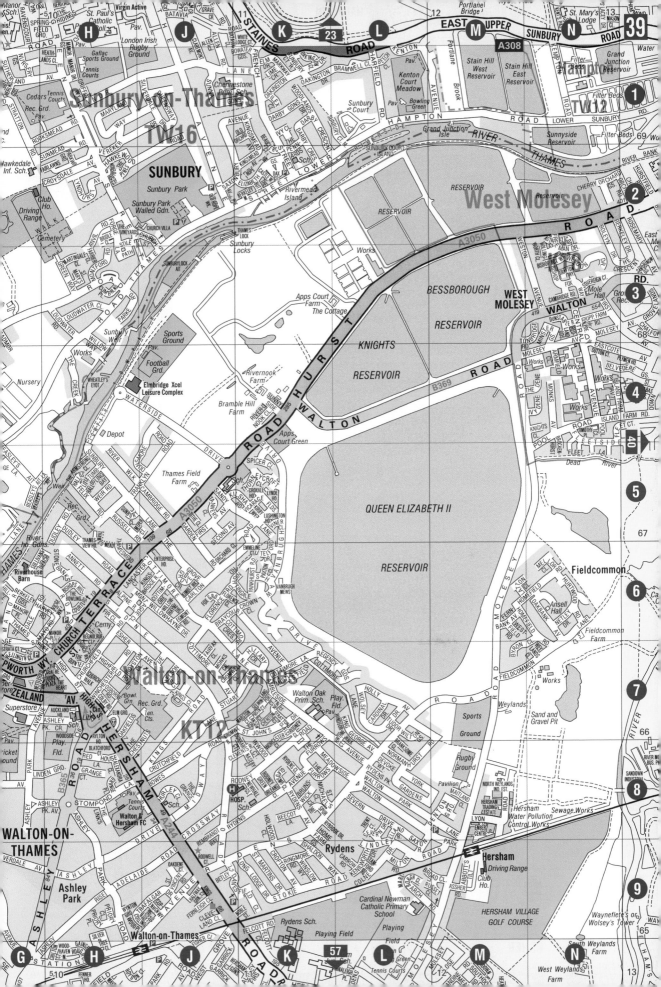

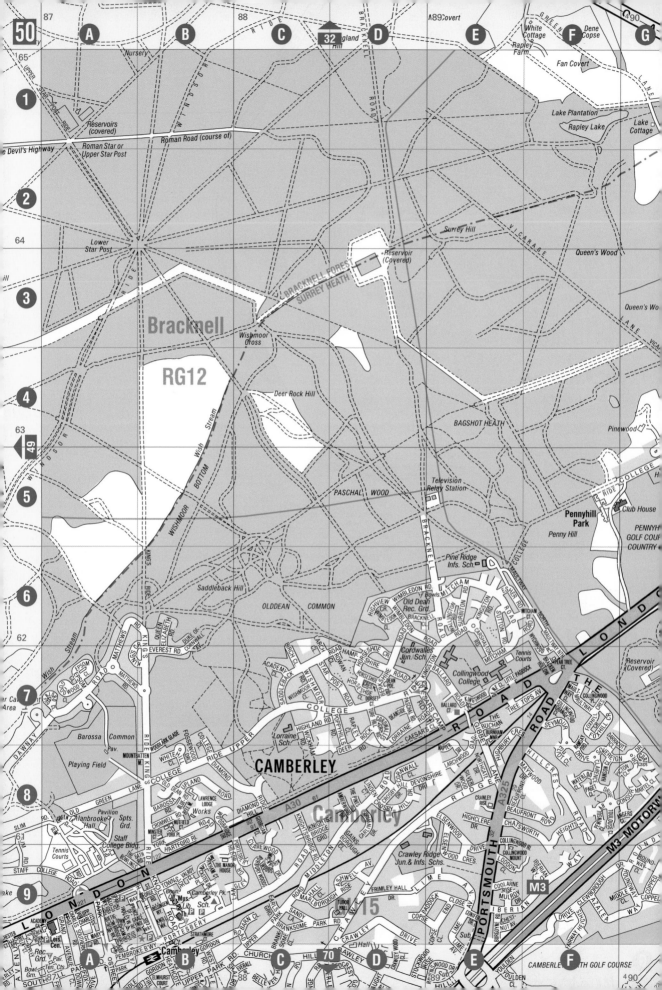

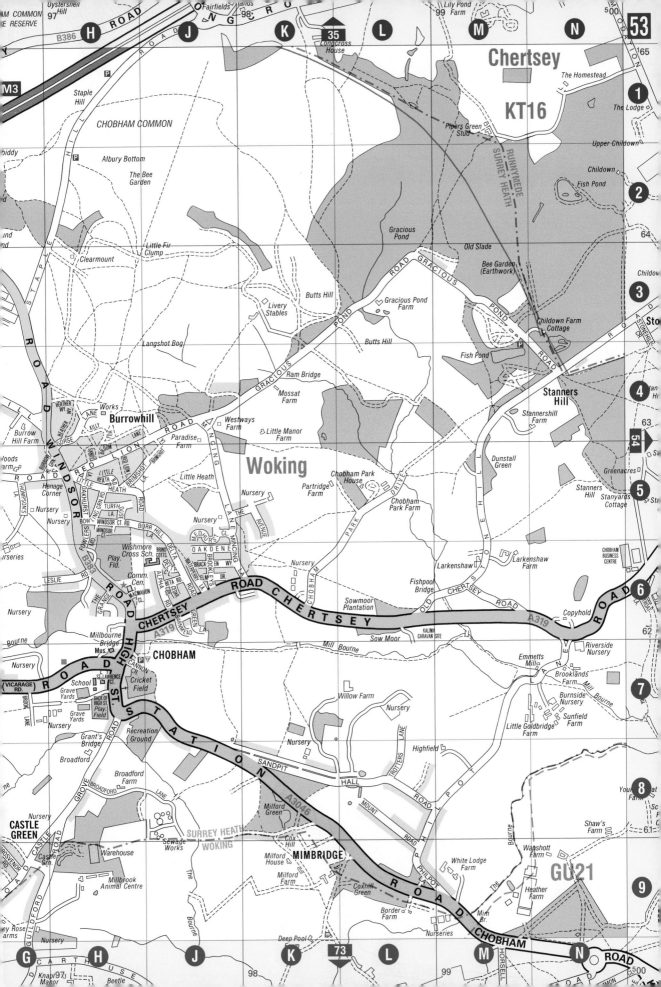

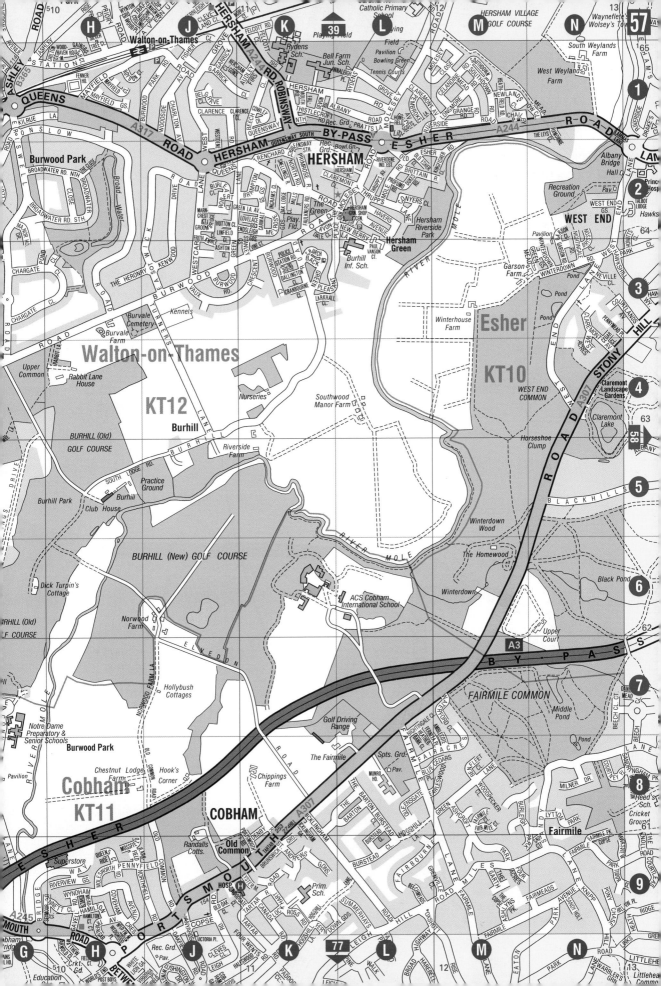

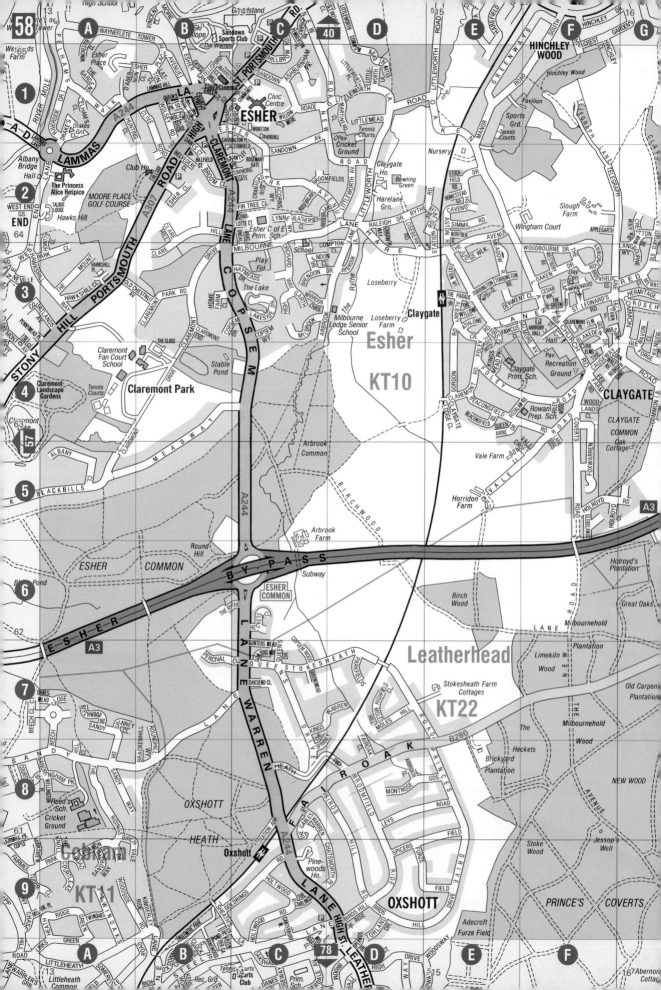

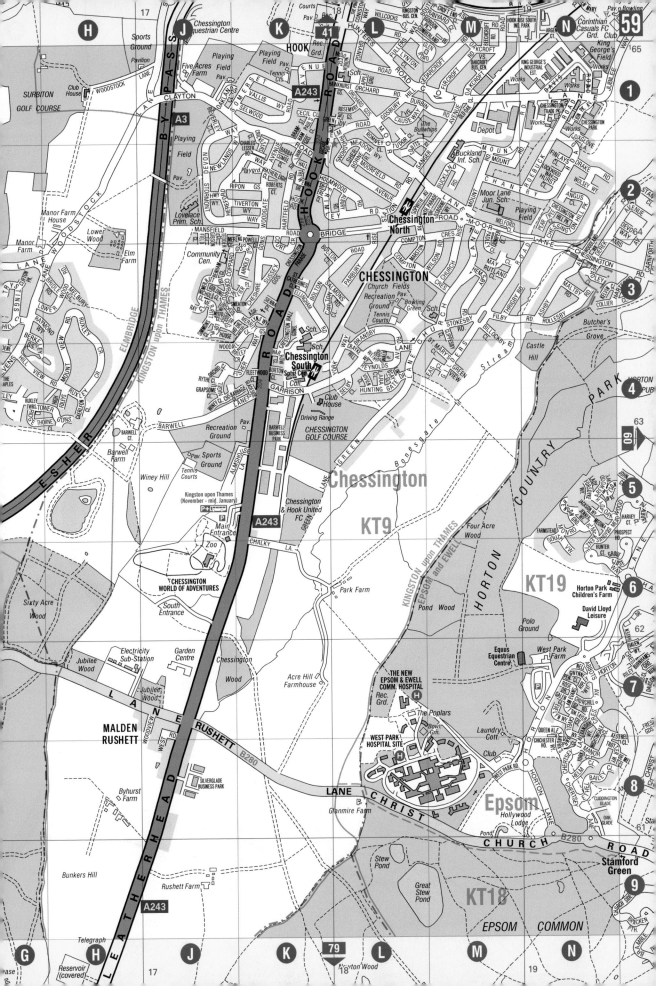

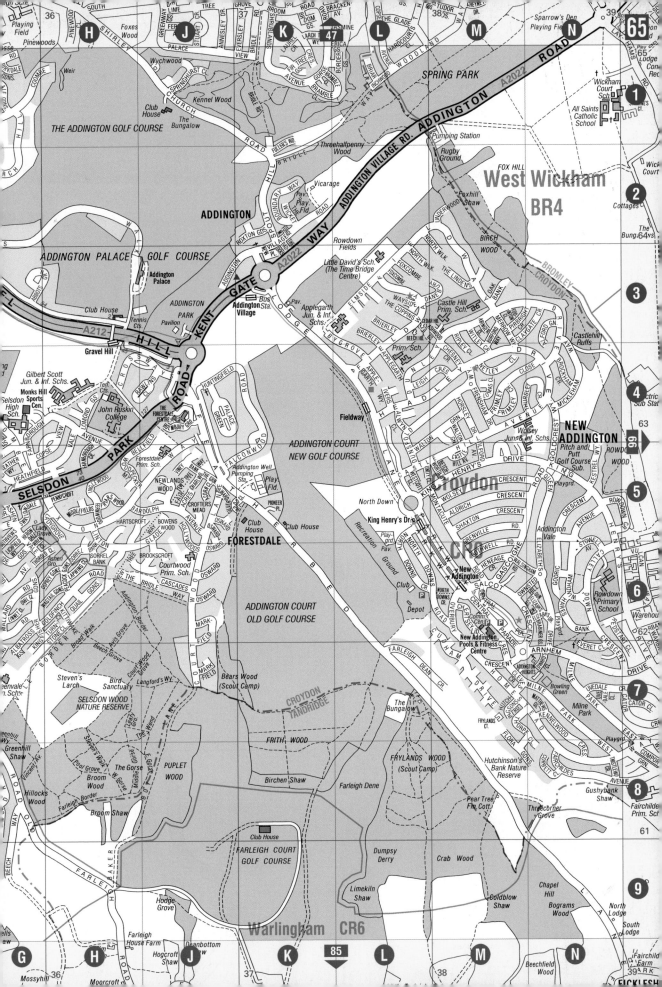

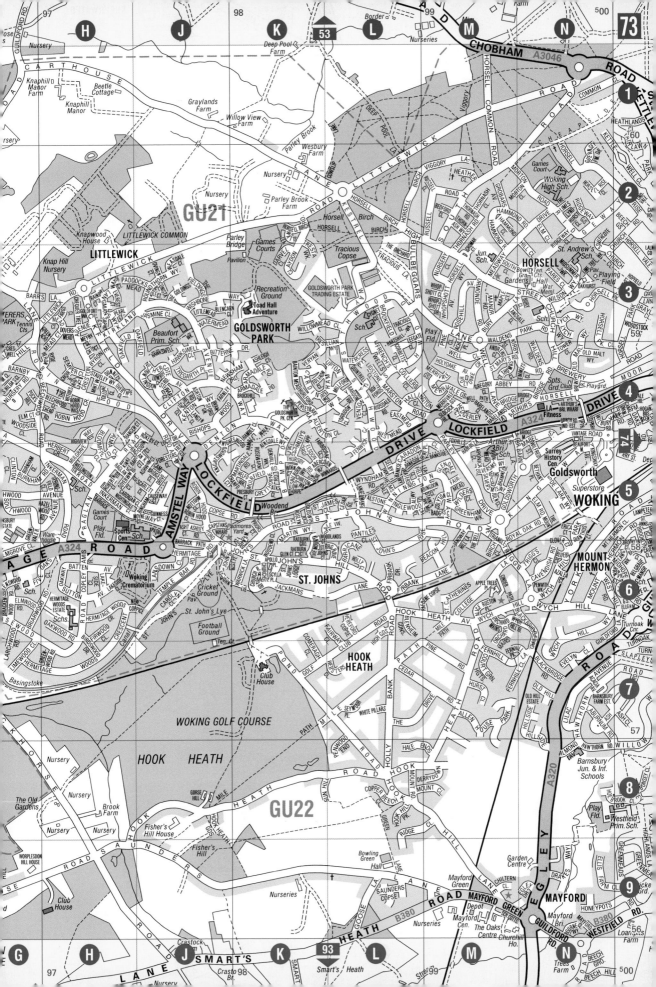

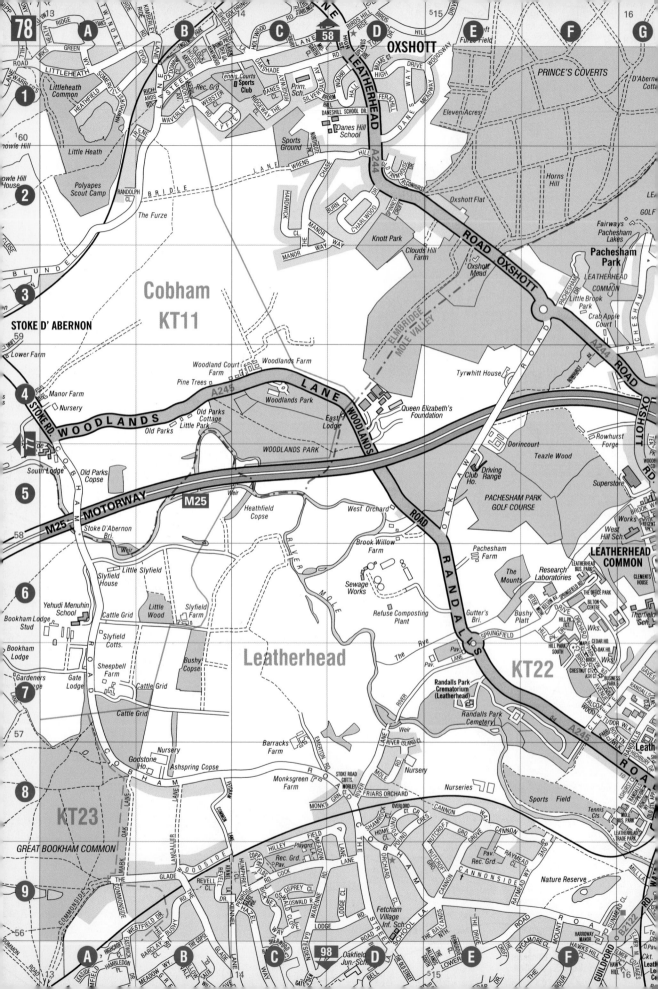

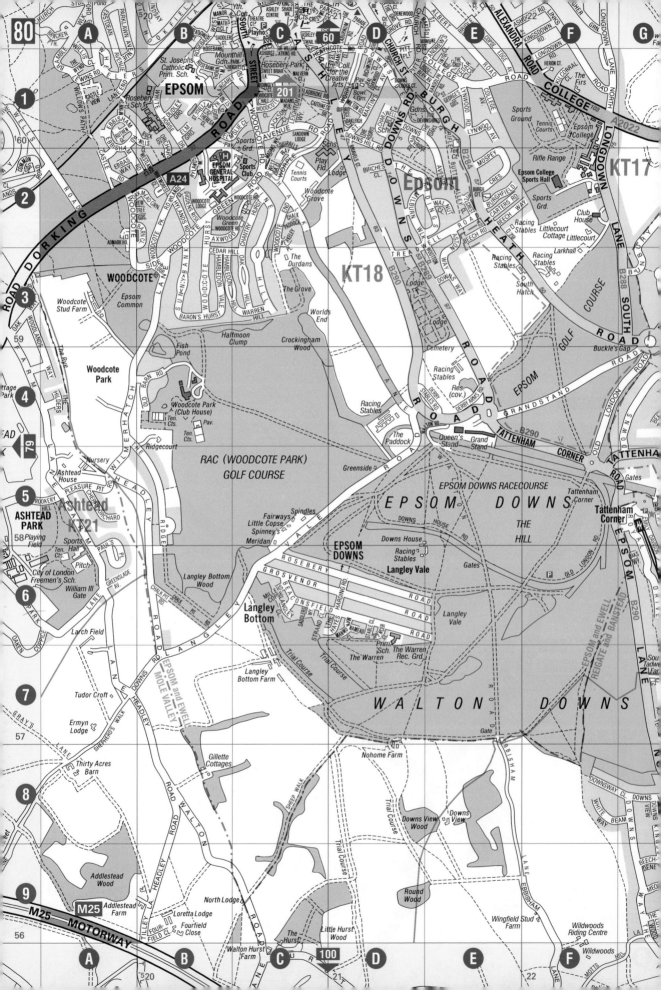

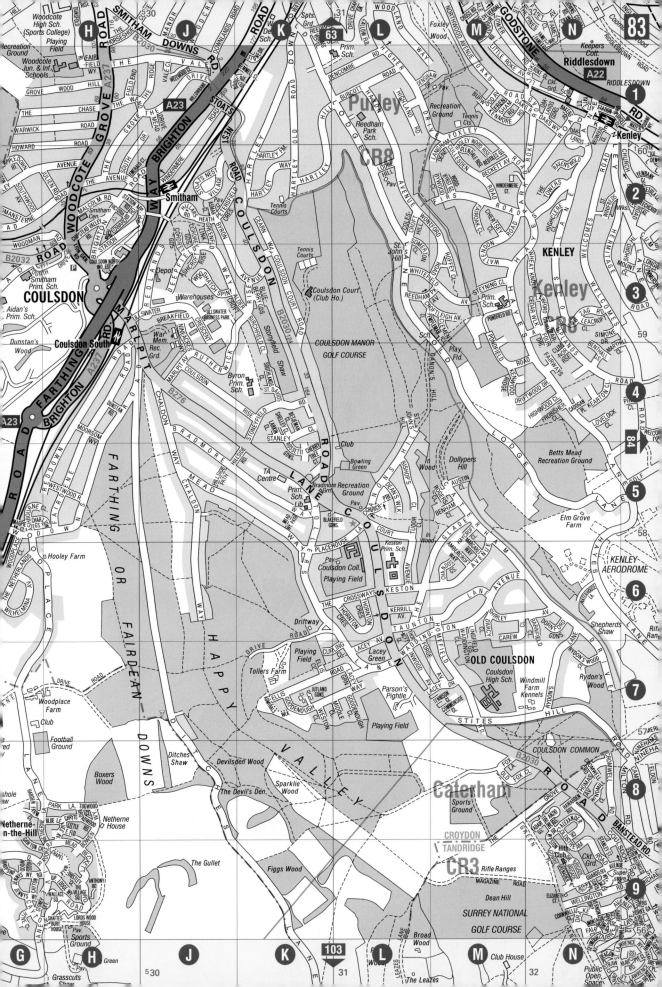

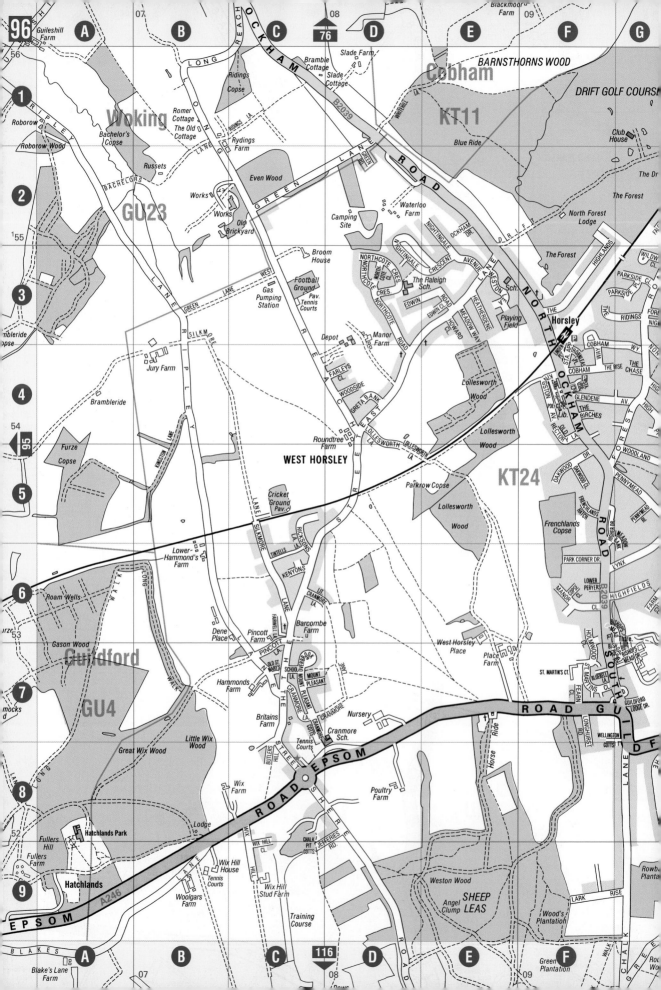

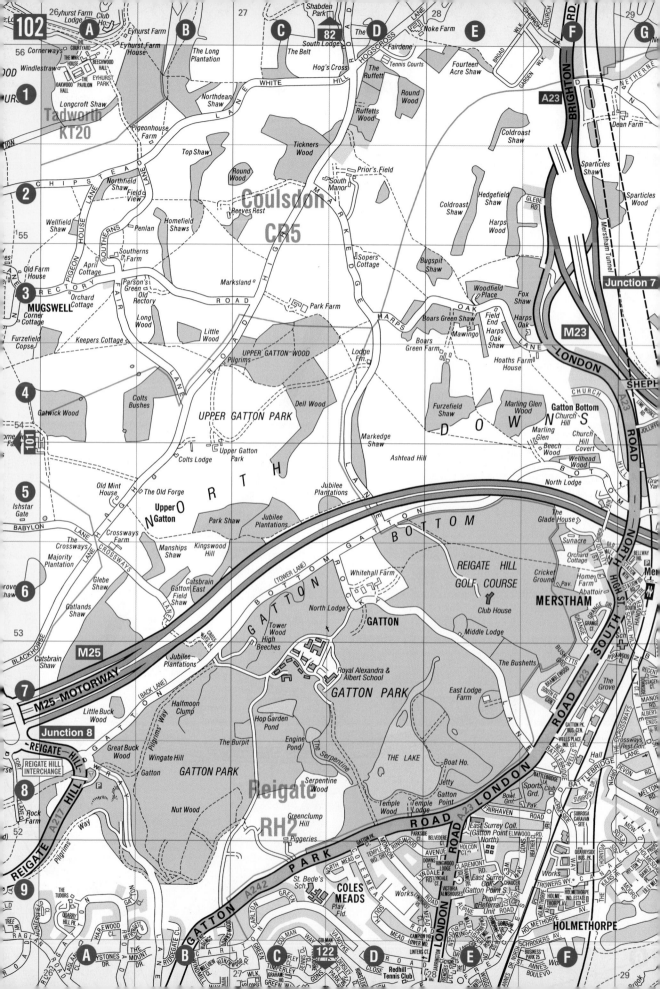

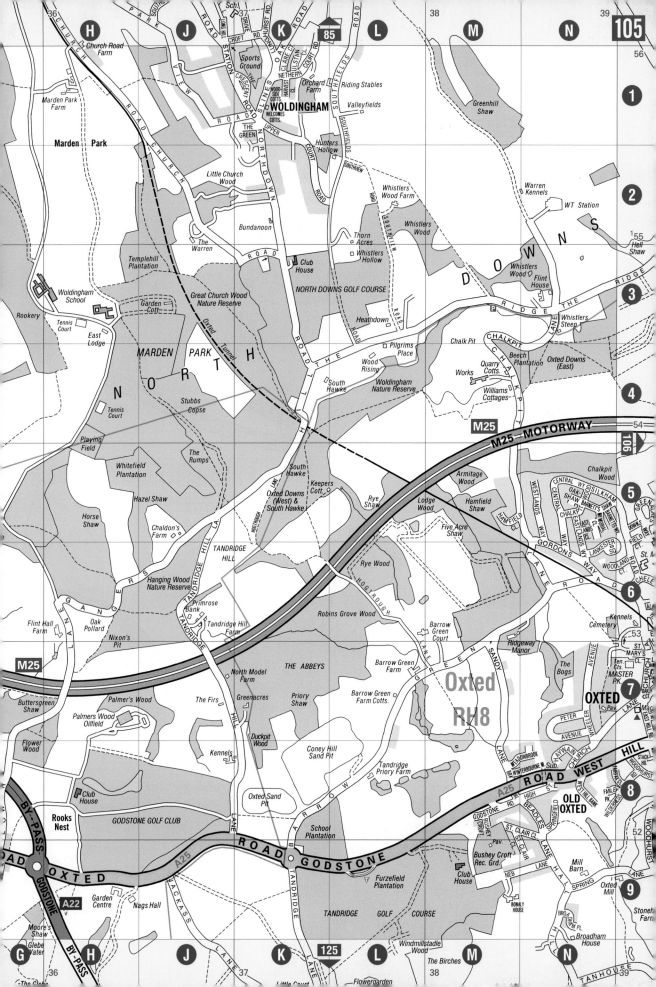

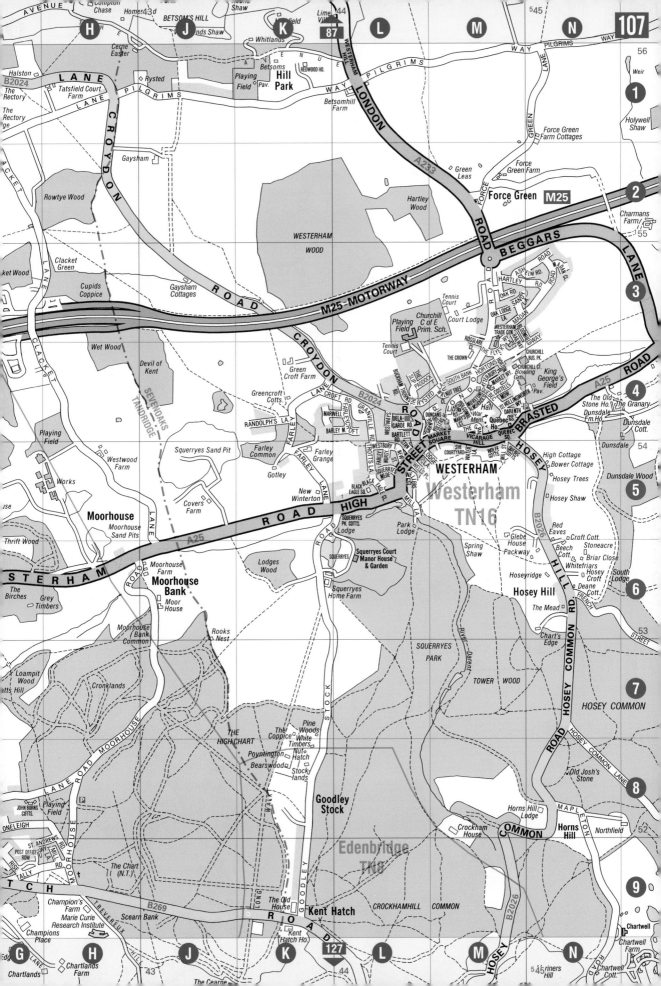

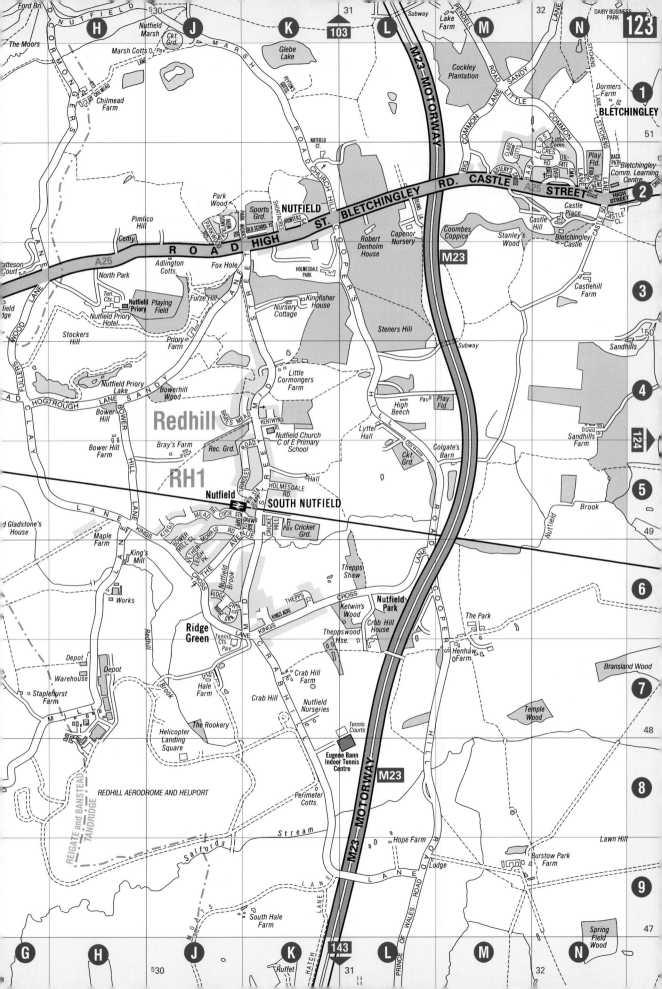

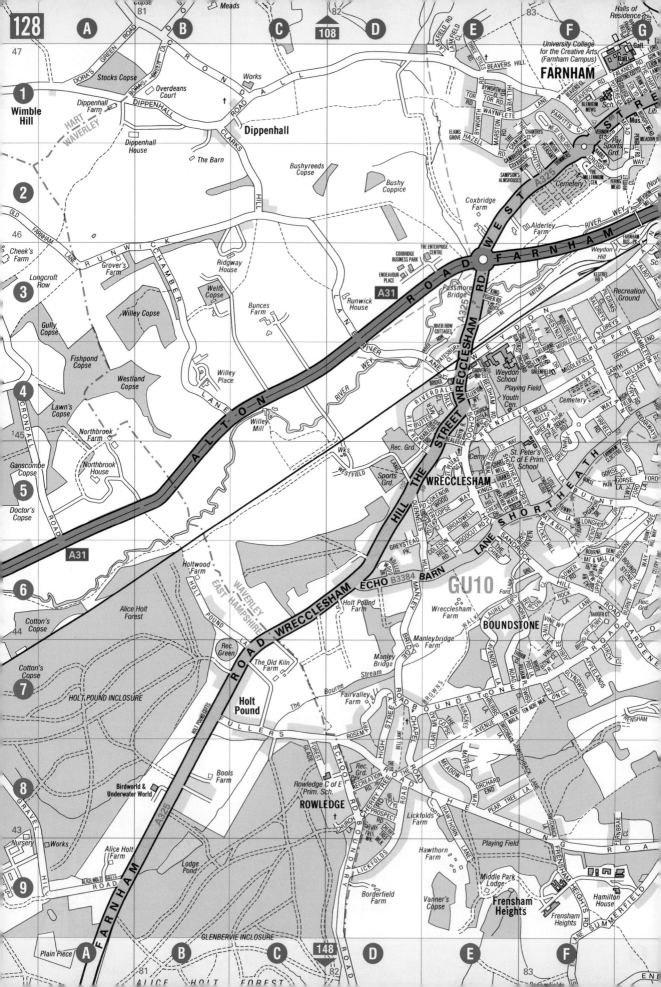

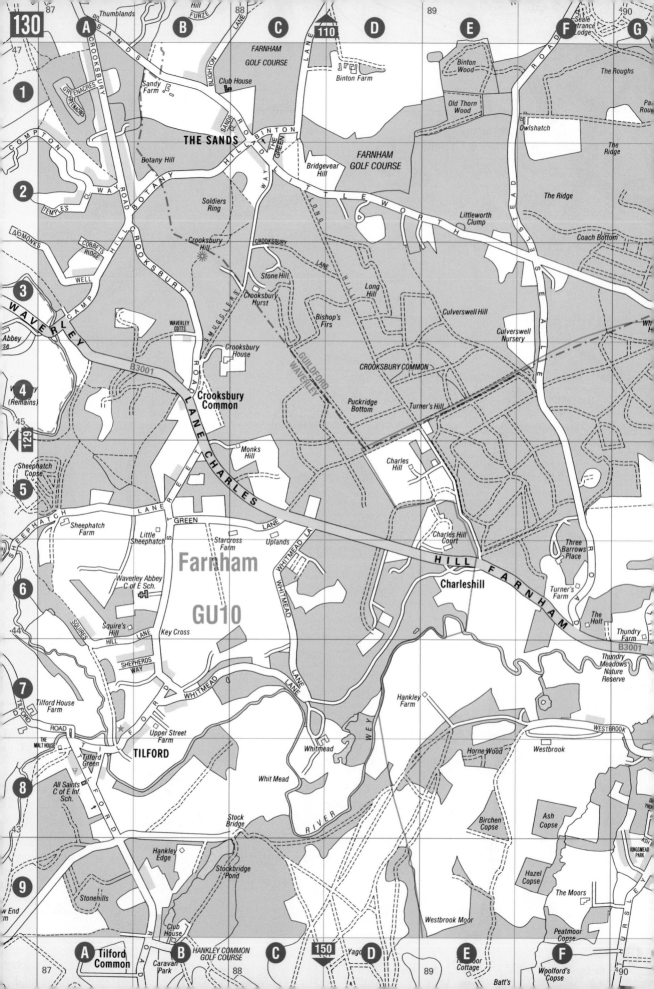

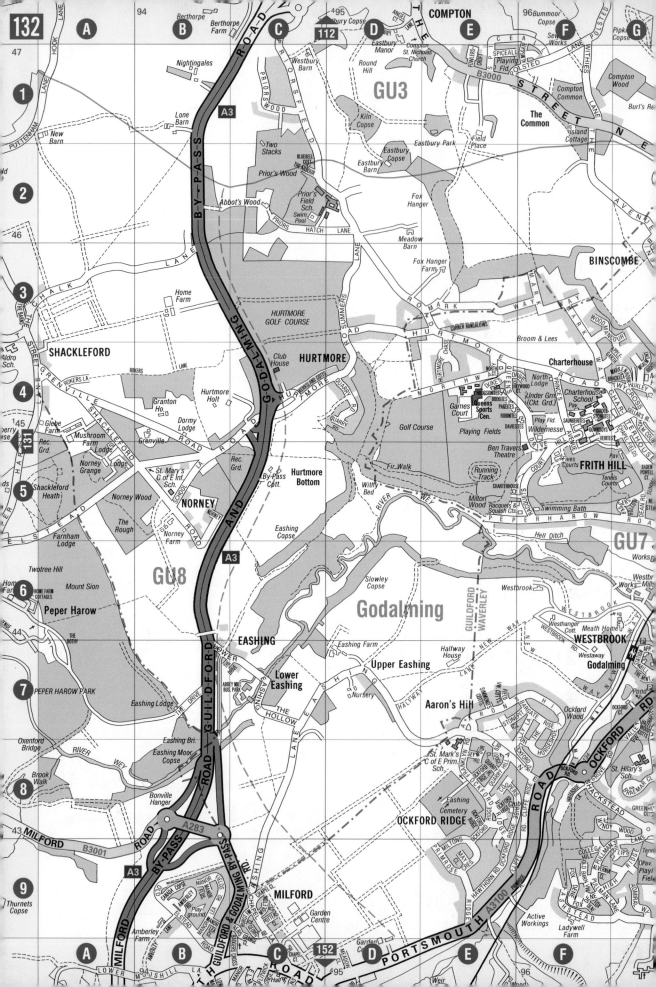

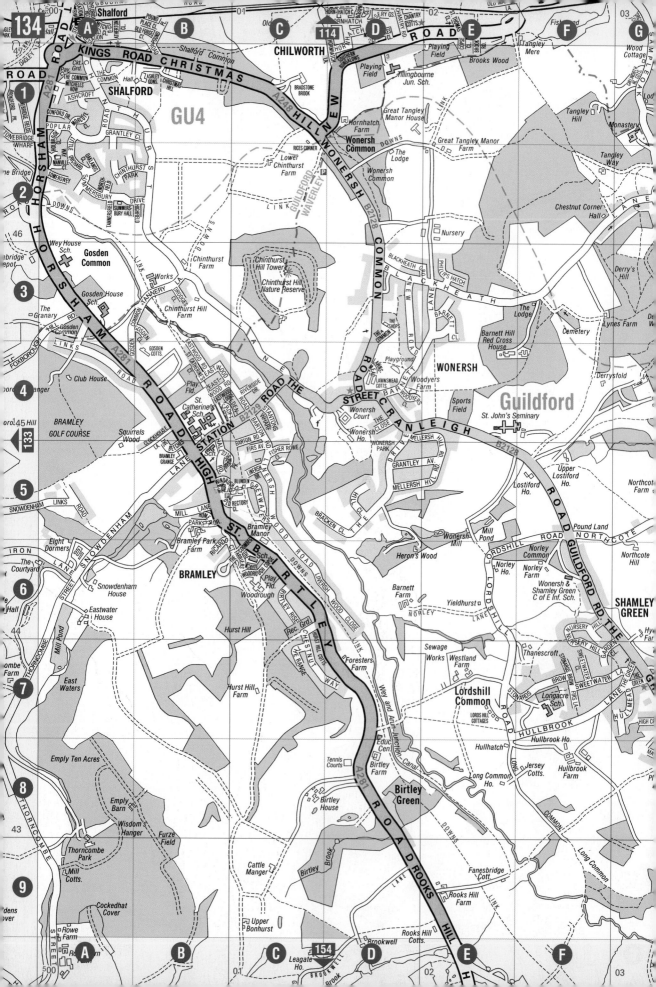

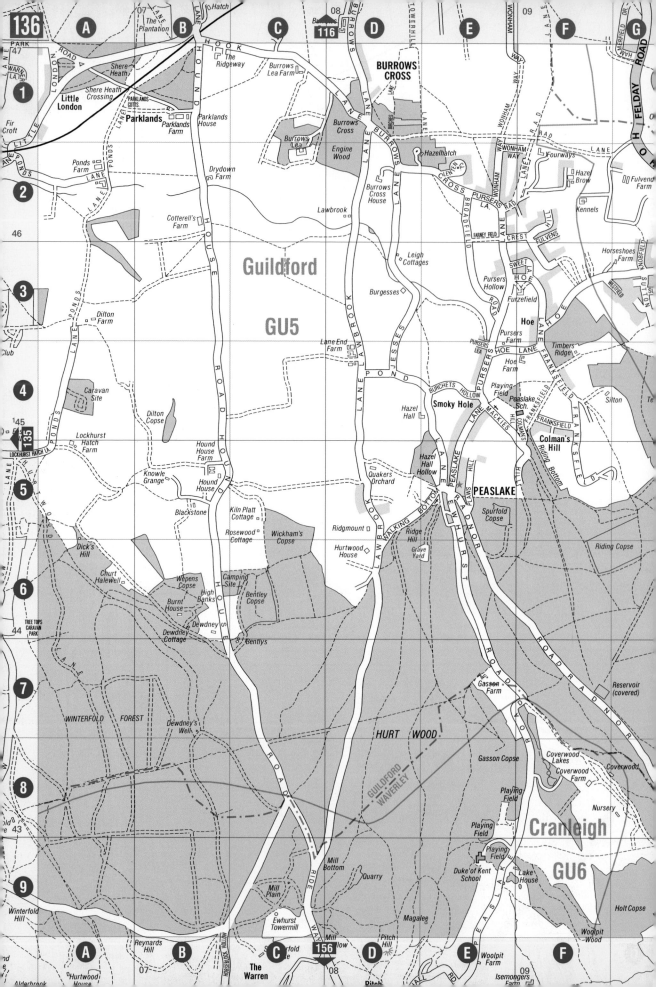

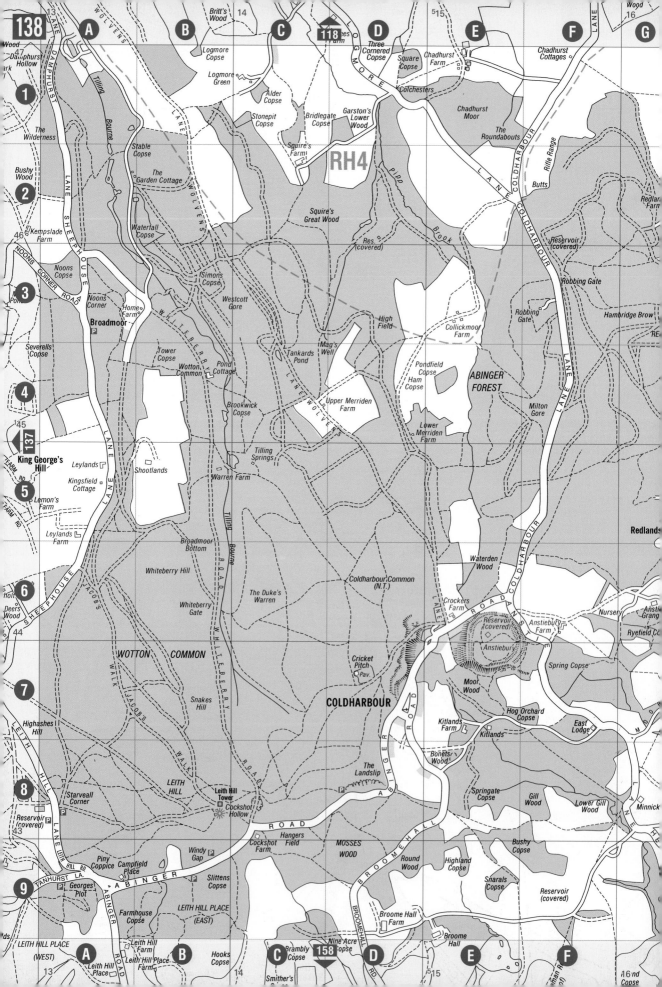

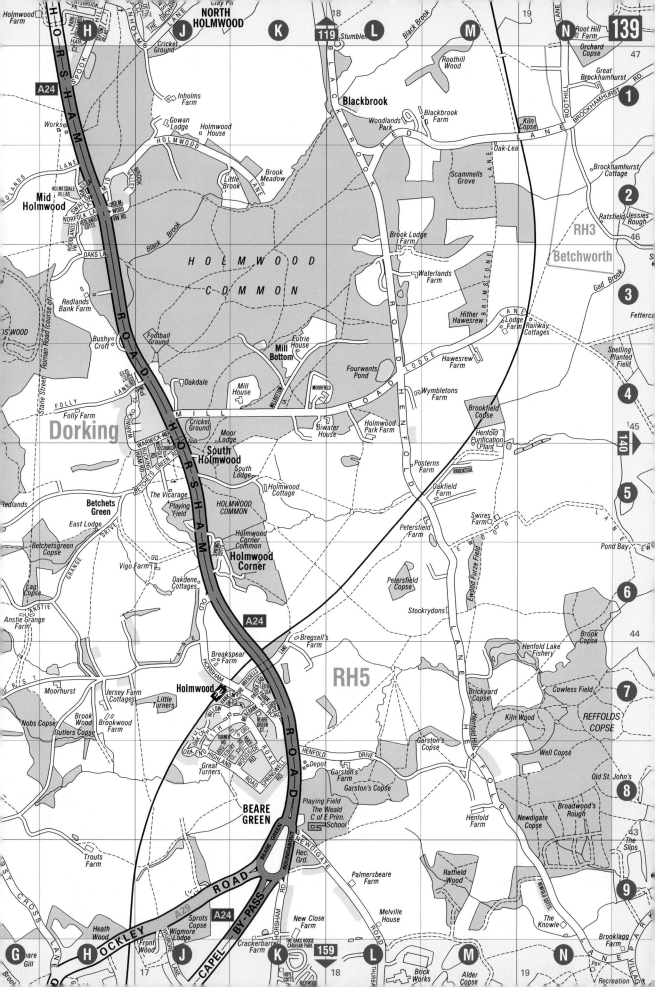

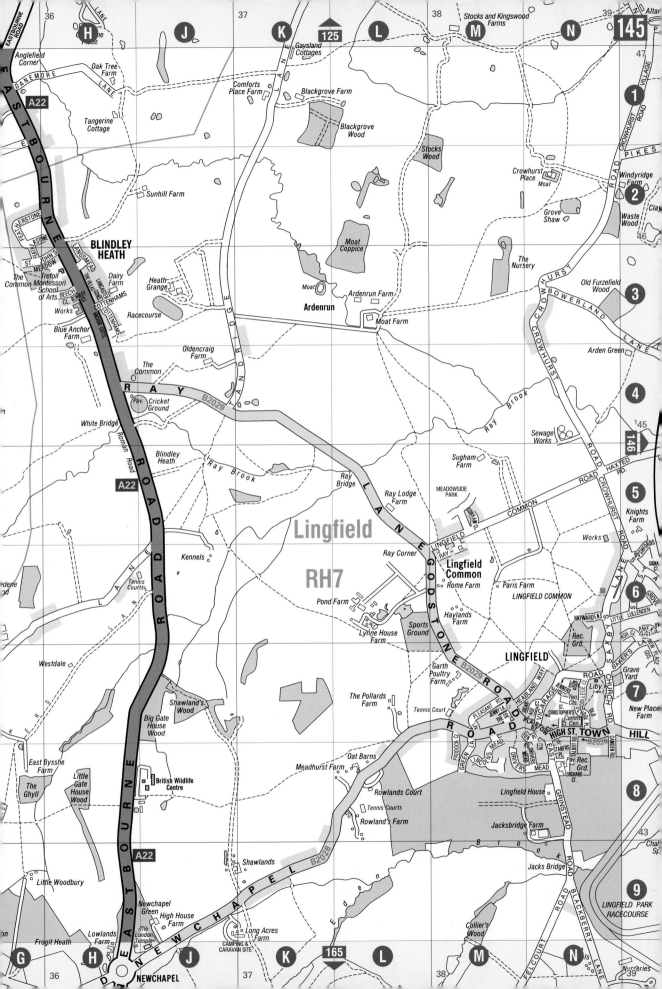

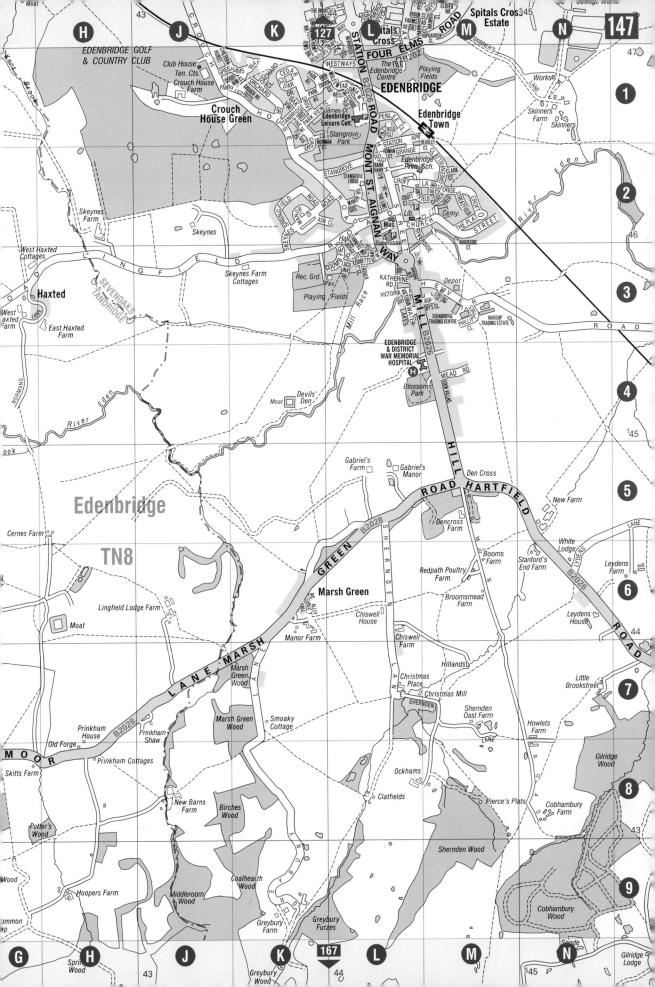

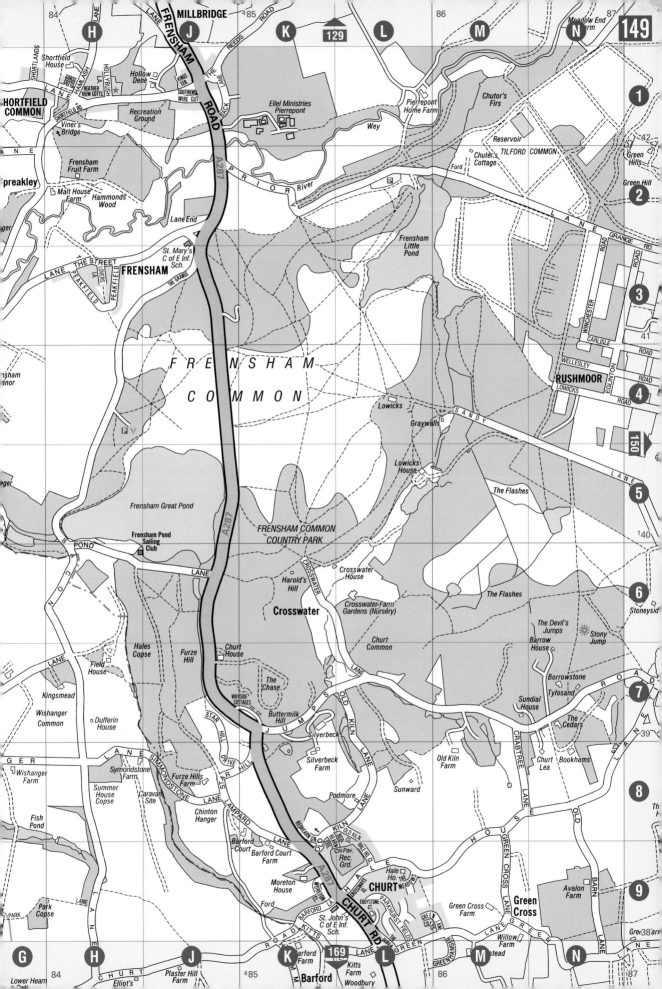

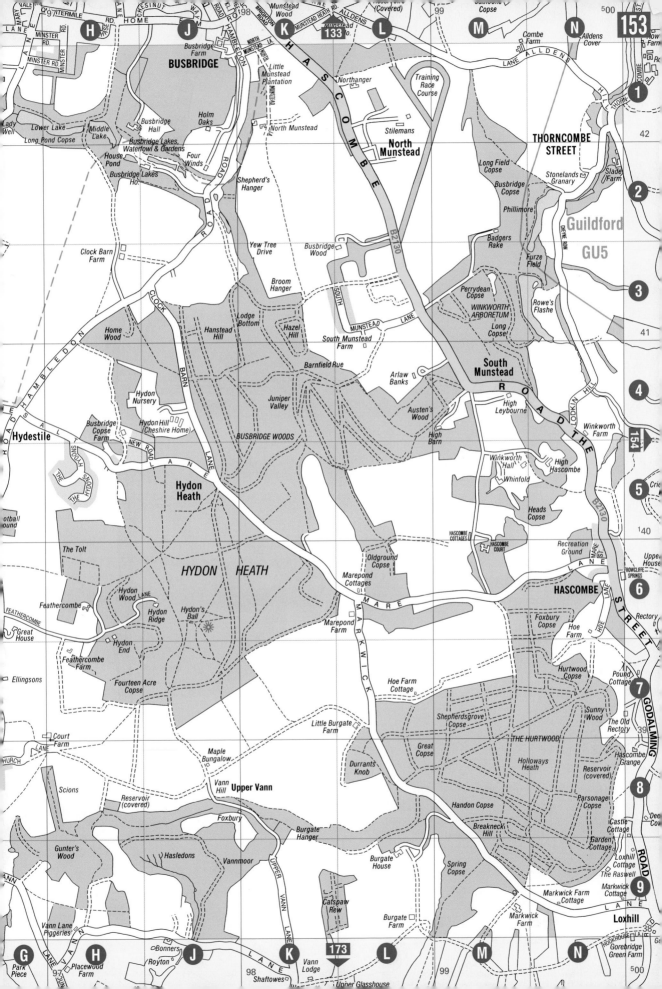

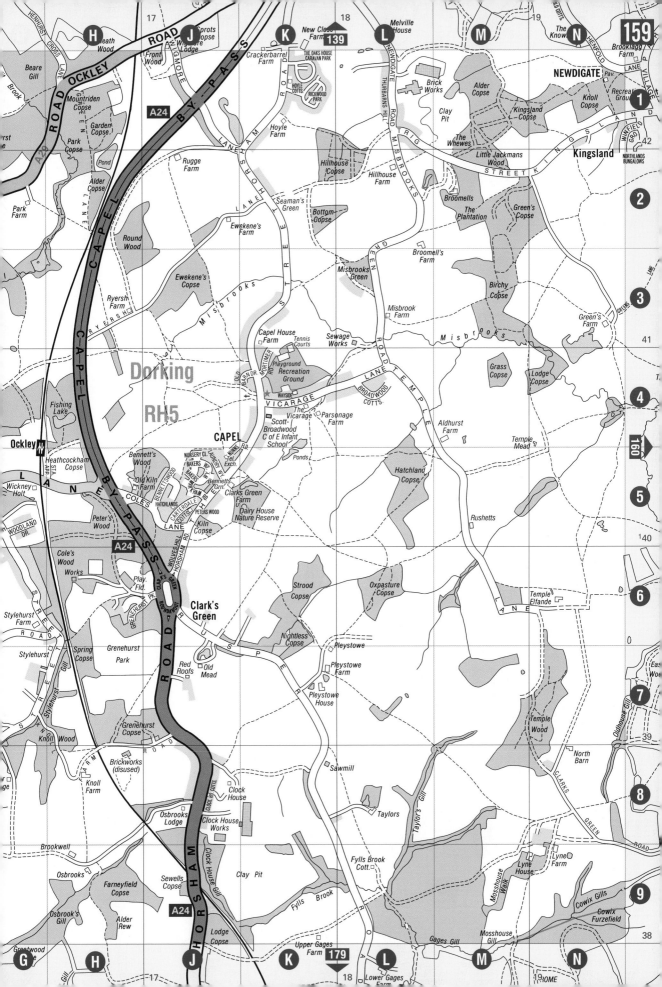

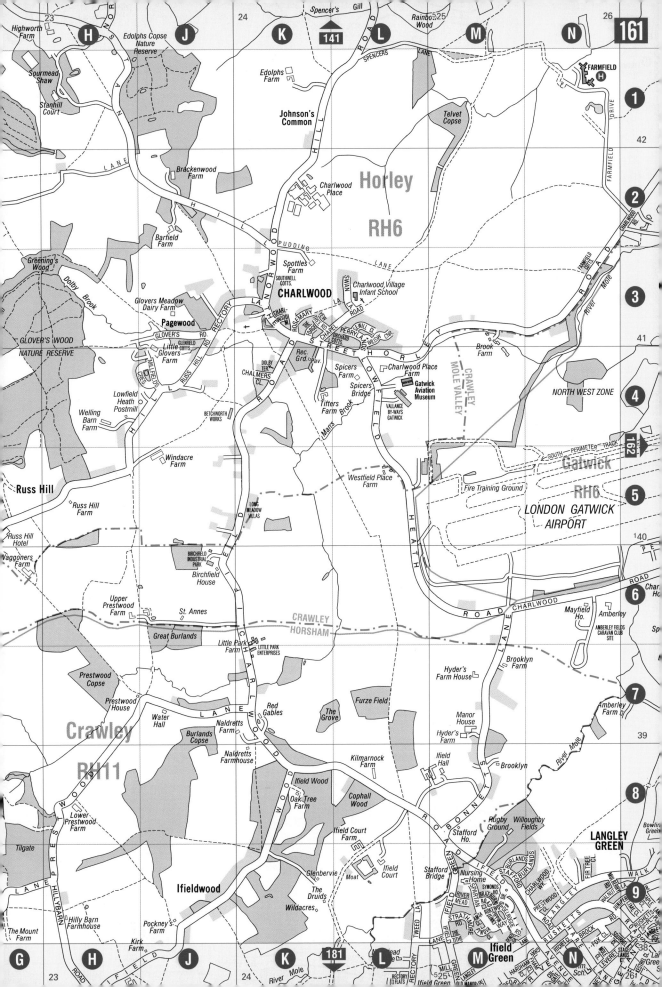

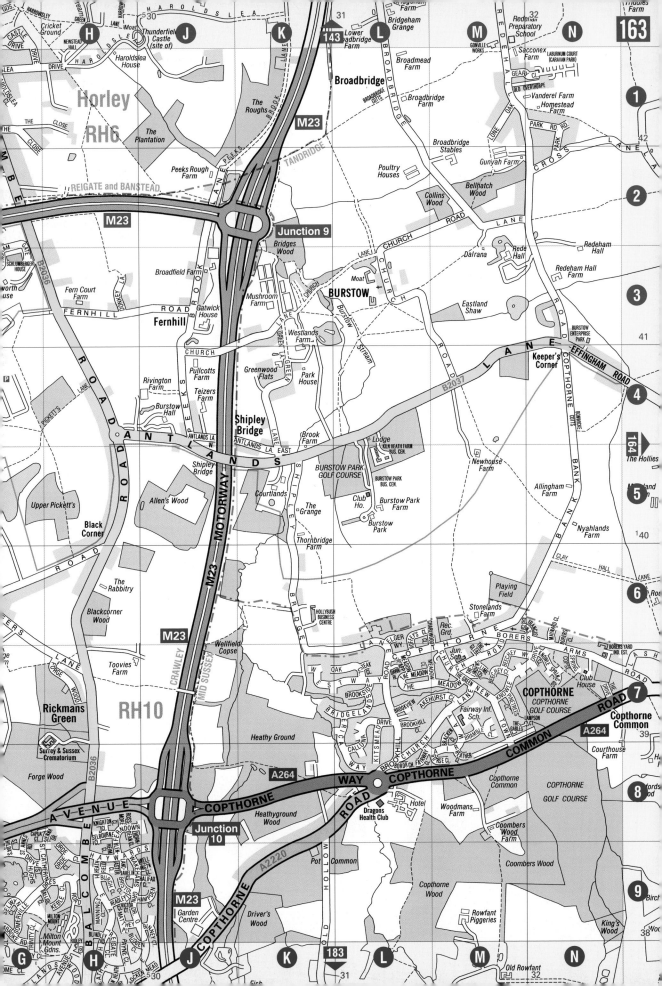

Edenbridge TN8

Spring Wood
Old Plantation
Reynolds Wood
Bowshot Wood
Greybury Farm
Greybury Furzes
Greybury Wood
Greybury Gill
Ash Plantation
Gilridge Lodge
Cobhambury Wood
Spode Farm
Beechenwood Farm
Dry Hill Farm
Jules Wood
Smoky Wood
Ten Acre Wood
Crippenden Manor
Nursery Pits
Long Shaw
Ludwells Farm
Dry Hill Reservoir (covered)
Yorkshire Pit
Willow Bed
Minepit Wood
Leighton Manor Farm
Nappers Wood
Upper Stonehurst Farm
Old Furzefield Wood
Collects
Beeches Farm
Liveroxhill Wood
Clay's Wood
Gouldhurst Gill
Woodlands Farm
Marlpit Shaw
TANDRIDGE SEVENOAKS
Lords Wood
Lower Stonehurst Farm
Drews Rough
Lullenden
The Lodge
Lullenden
Beeches Mead
SHEPHERDS LANE
SMITHERS
Basing and Smithers Farm
Scarletts
Pondtail
SHOE BRIDGES
Furnace Farm
Kent Water
Scarletts Lake
Marlpit Wood
Furnace Pond
Holtye Common
Shepherd's Grove
GROVE LANE
Gotwick Manor Farm
GOTWICK MANOR
Kent Water
Stubbs Wood
Cinder Wood
Cleavers Farm
Mill Wood
Reading's Wood
Bank Farm
Roger's Town
HOLTYE GOLF COURSE
Silver Pines
HOLTYE ROAD
A264
War. Mem.
Ridgeway
Hall
The Vicarage
Steadleaze Wood
Cooper's Wood
Cooper's Wood
Bearwood
Highlands
Holtye
Holmsley Ho.
Keeper's Cottage
Gotwick-Brook
High Meadows
Bower Cottages
Home Farm
Hammerwood
Steadleaze House
Bear Wood
Holtye Croft
FIFTY ACRE WOOD
Brooklands Wood
Beecher Wood
Milton Mount
Cricket Ground
Stubbs Wood
Hammerwood Park
HAMMER WOOD
Southland Wood
Shovelstrode Lodge
Shovelstrode House
Brooklands
Brooklands Cottage
Wet Wood
Cansiron Wood
CANSIRON LANE
Home Wood
Homestall Farm
Homestall Stud
Pond Bay
Little Cansiron Farm
Homestall White Gables
Sewage Works
The Grove
Dog Gate Lodge
Grove Cottage
Water Wood
Dog Cottages
Poultry Farm
Owlett's Farm
Great Cansiron Farm
Lower Owls Croft
Owls Croft
Highfields
Church Wood
BUTCHERFIELD LANE

147
187
ROAD

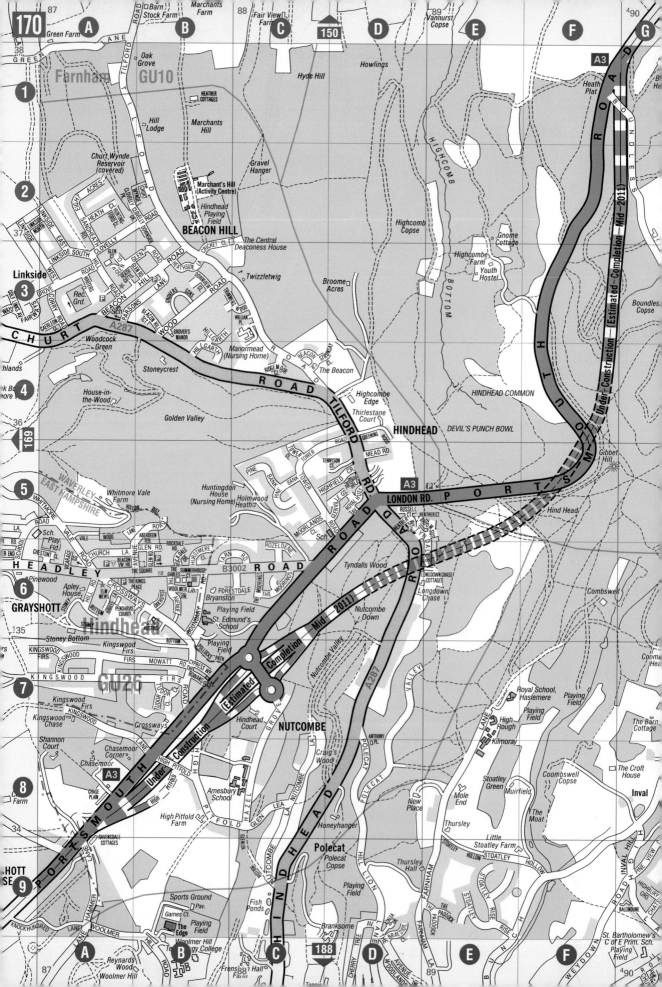

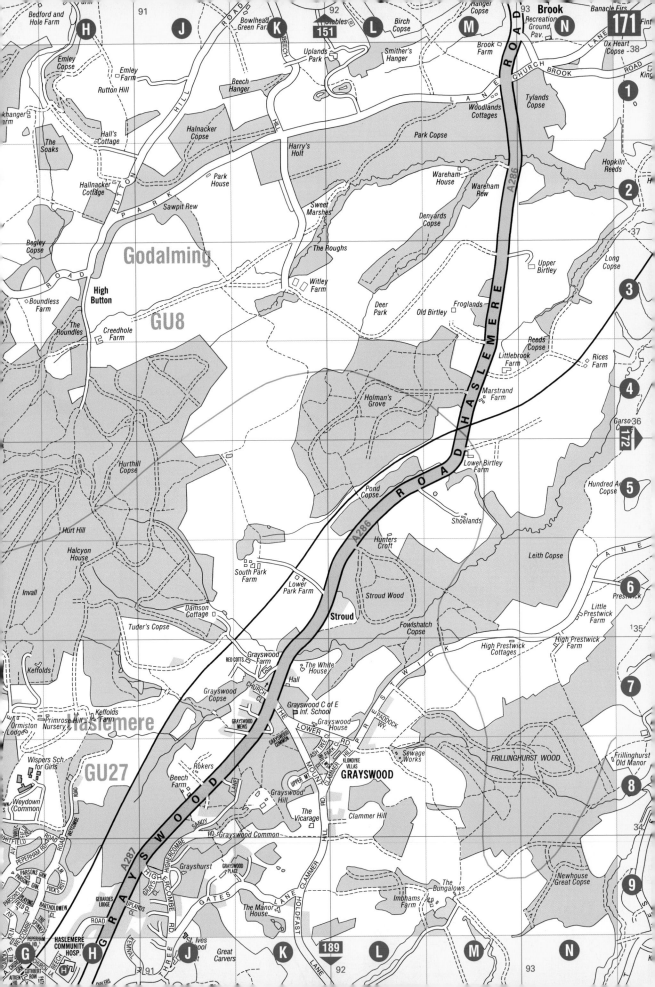

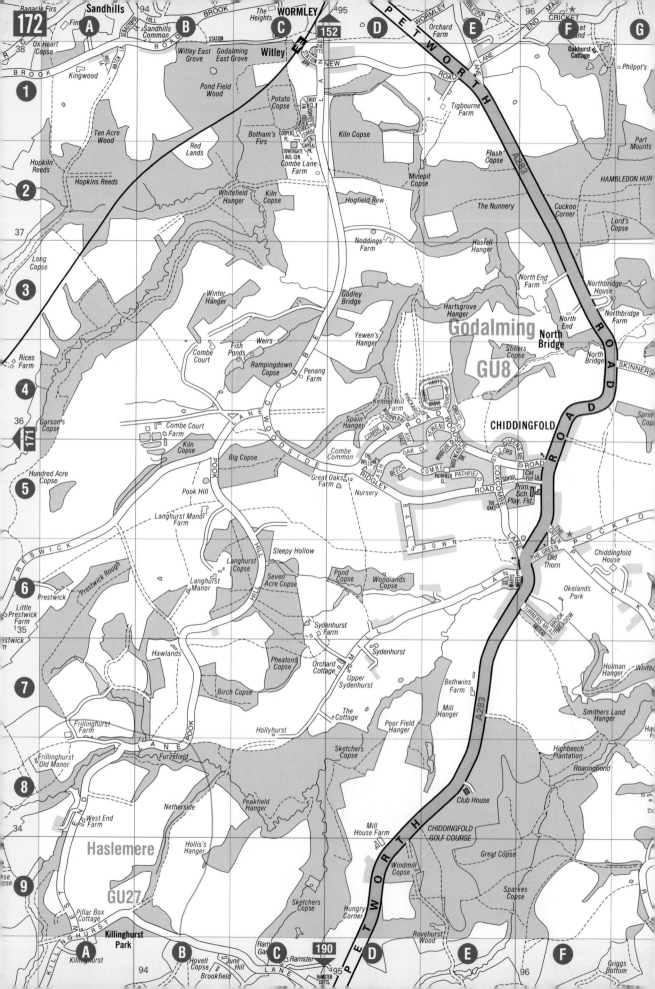

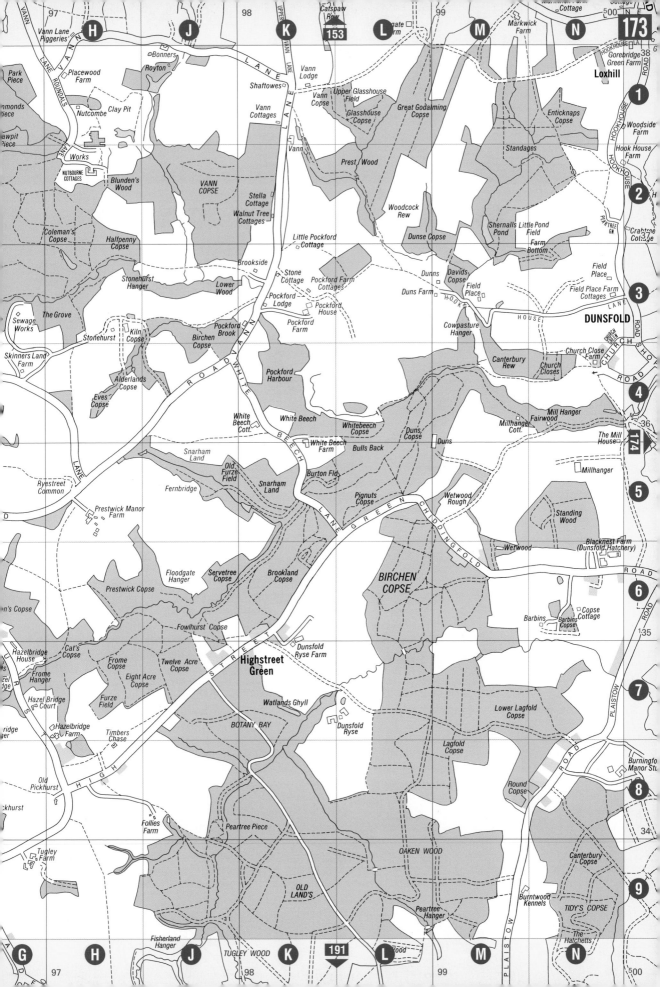

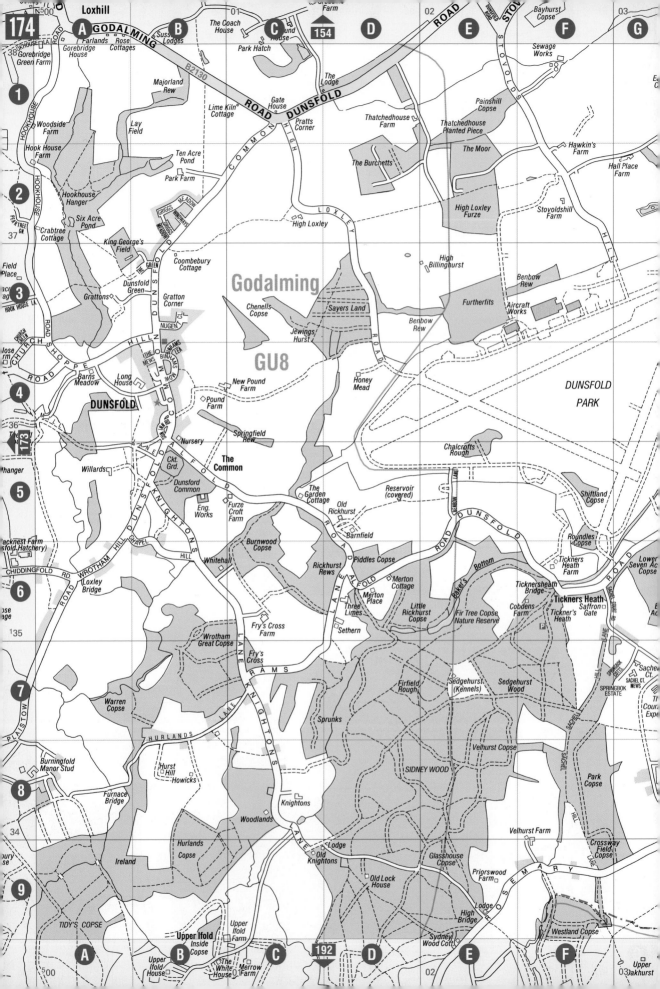

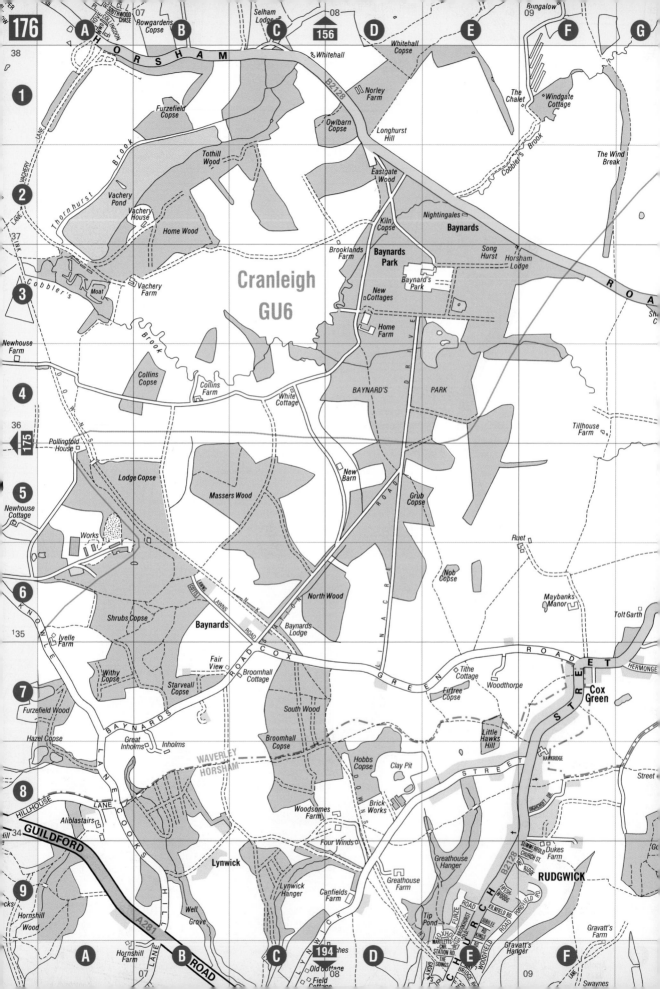

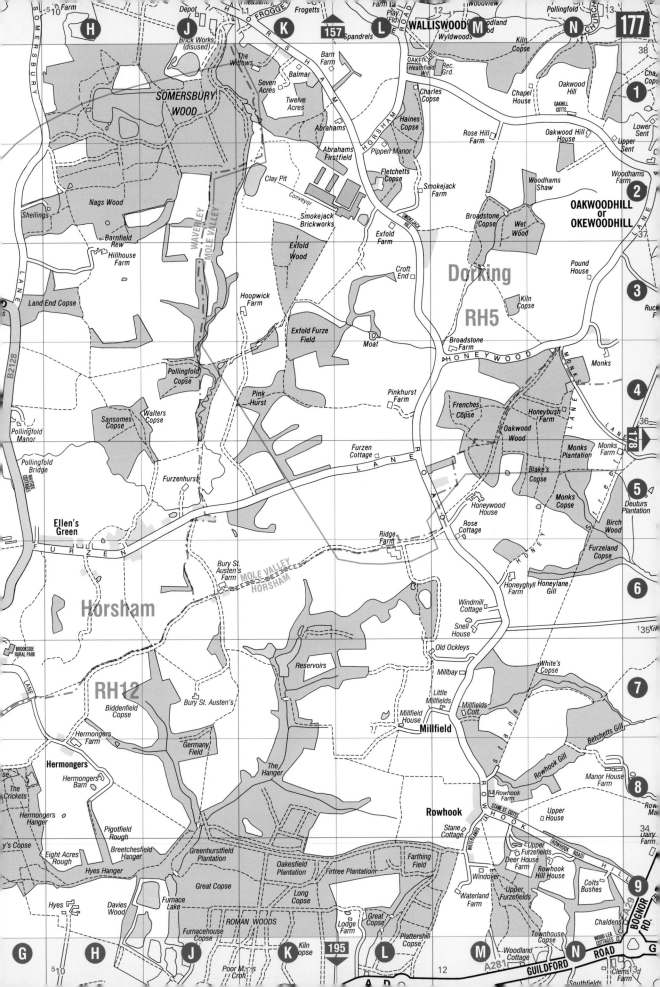

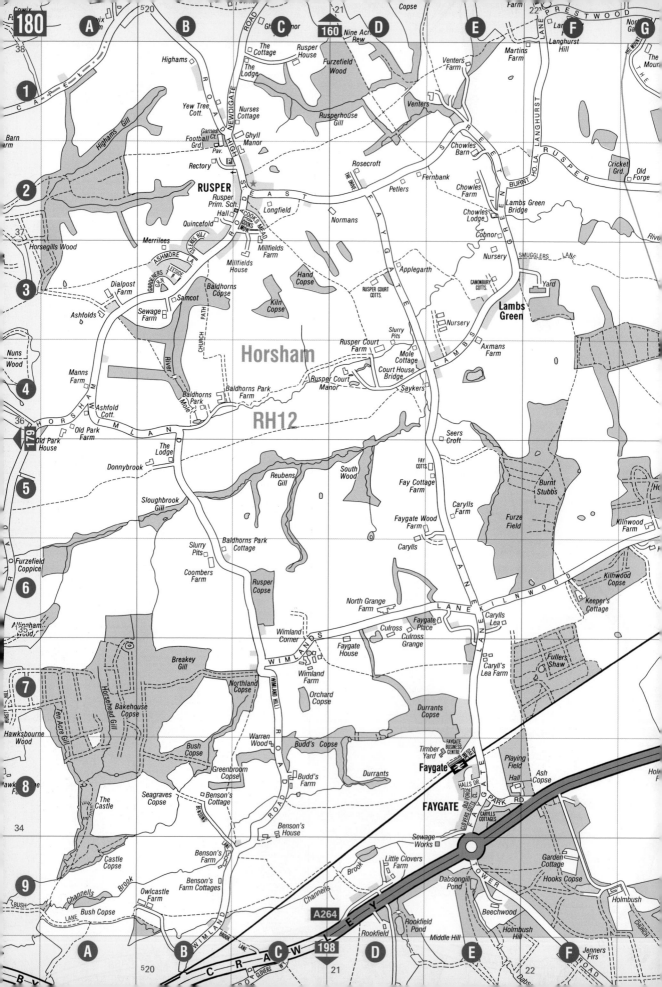

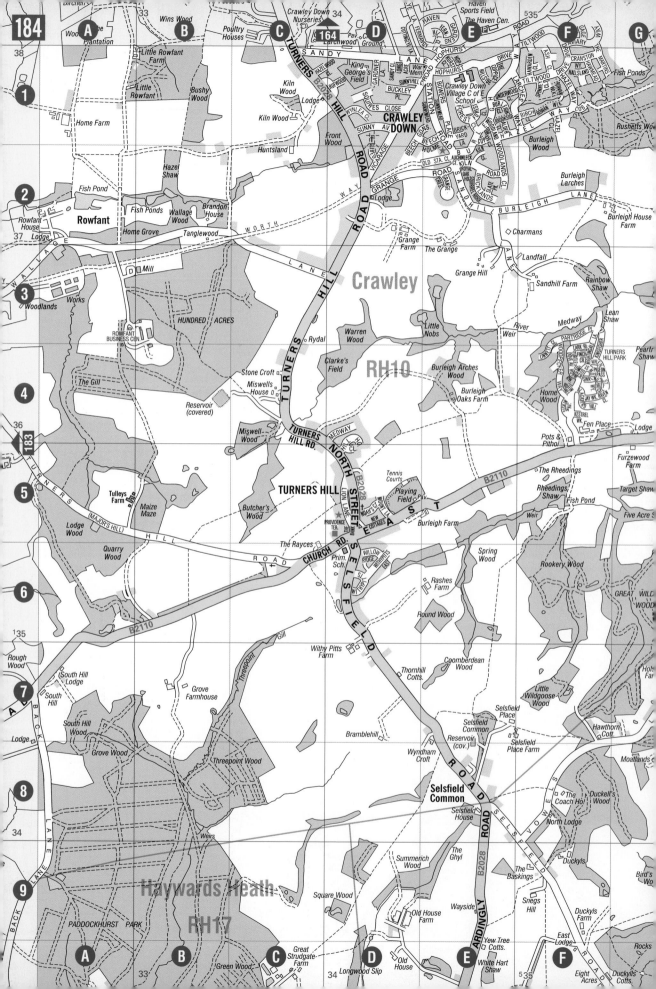

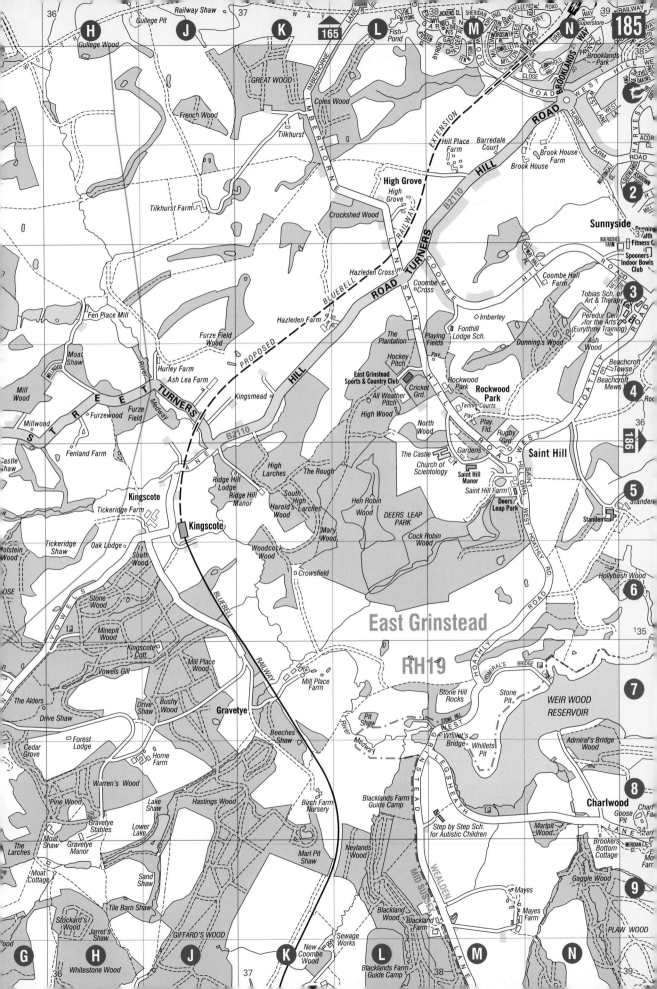

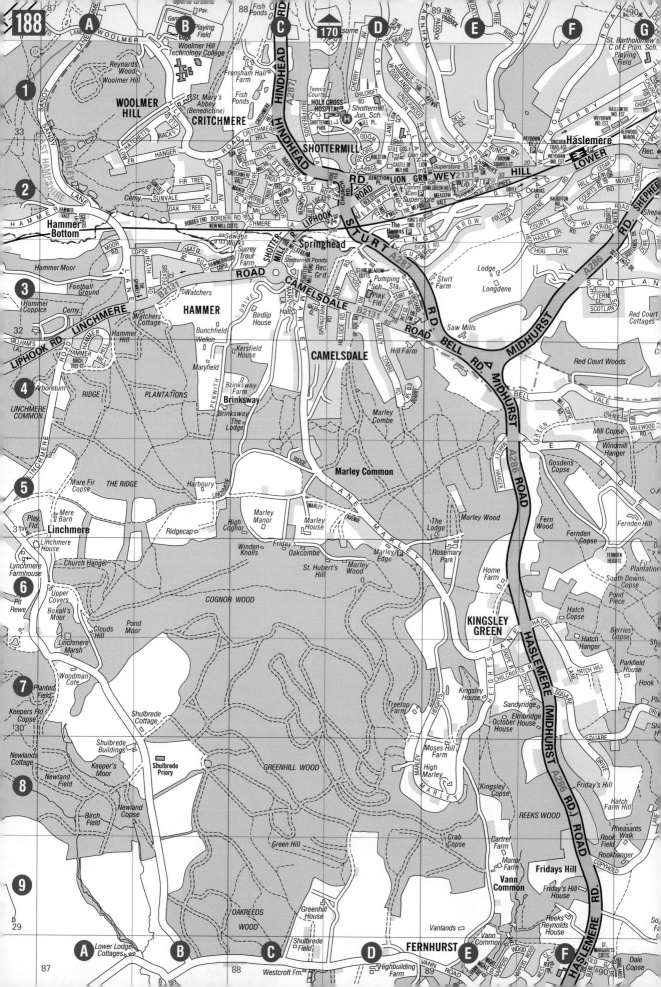

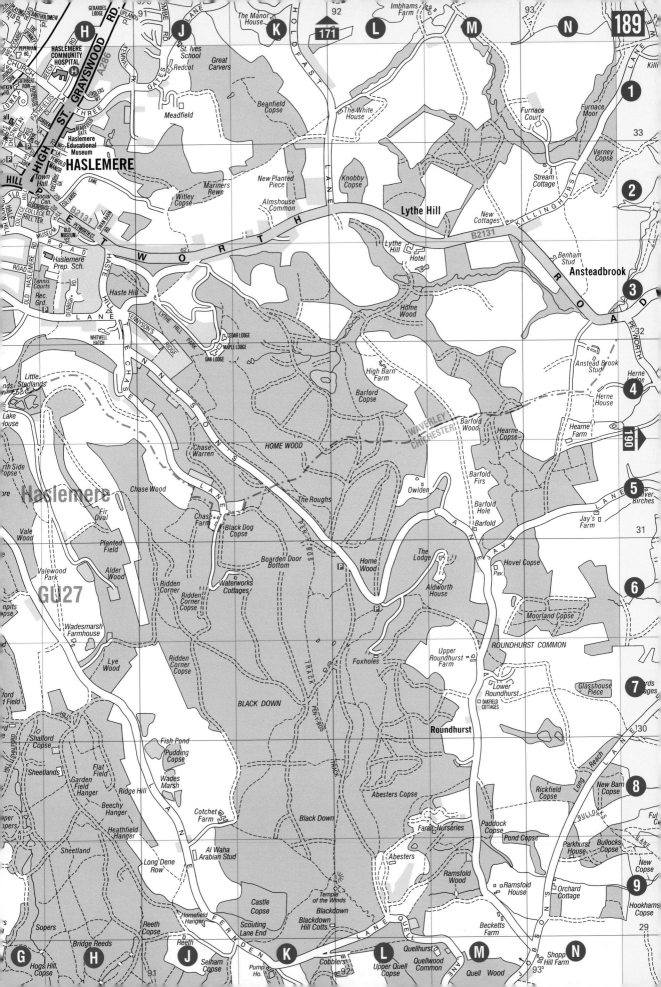

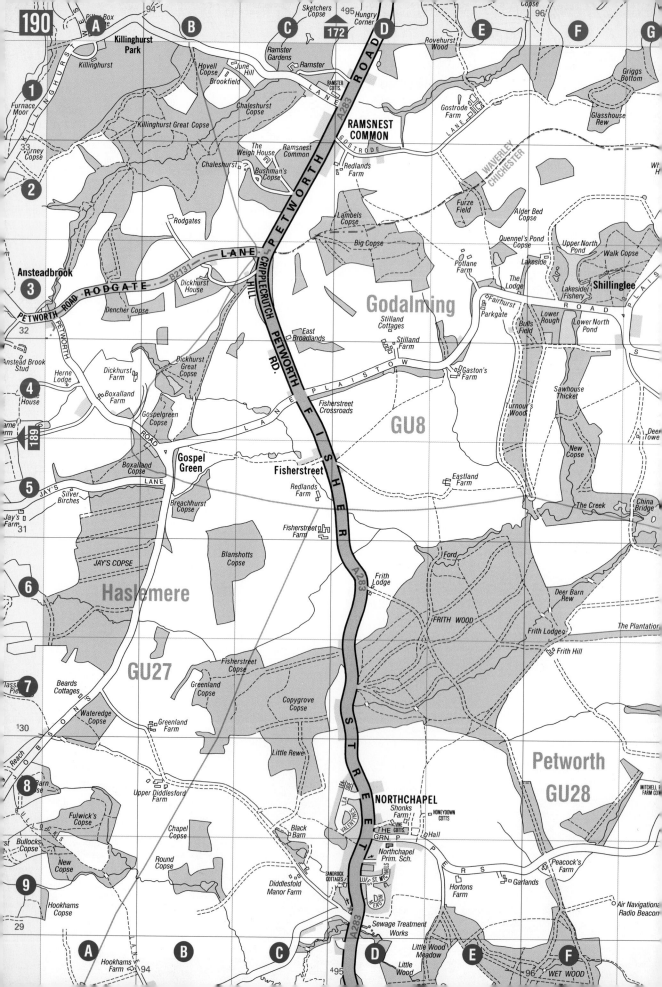

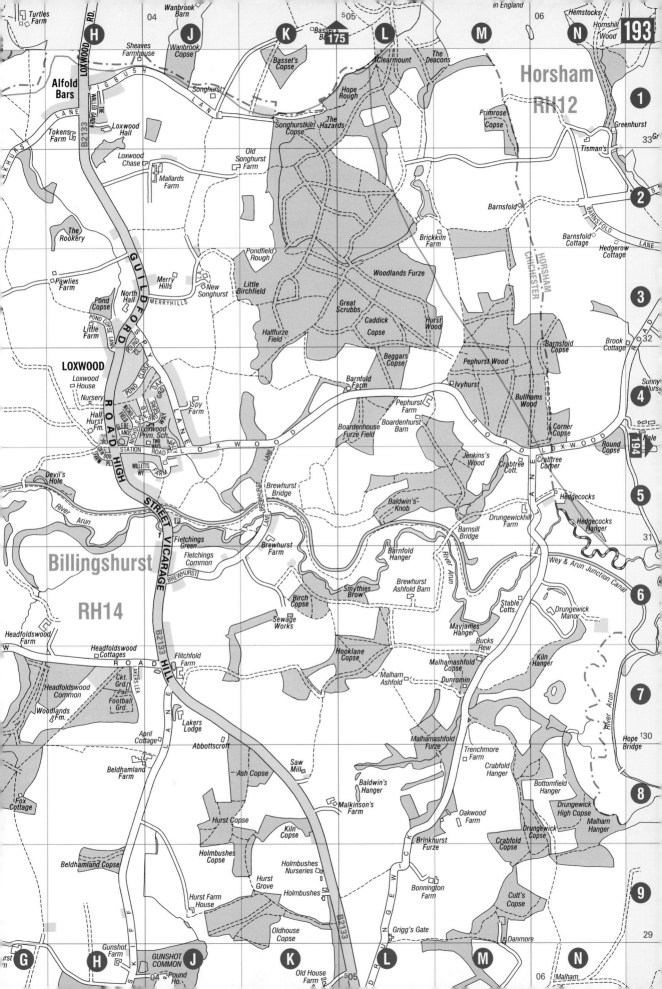

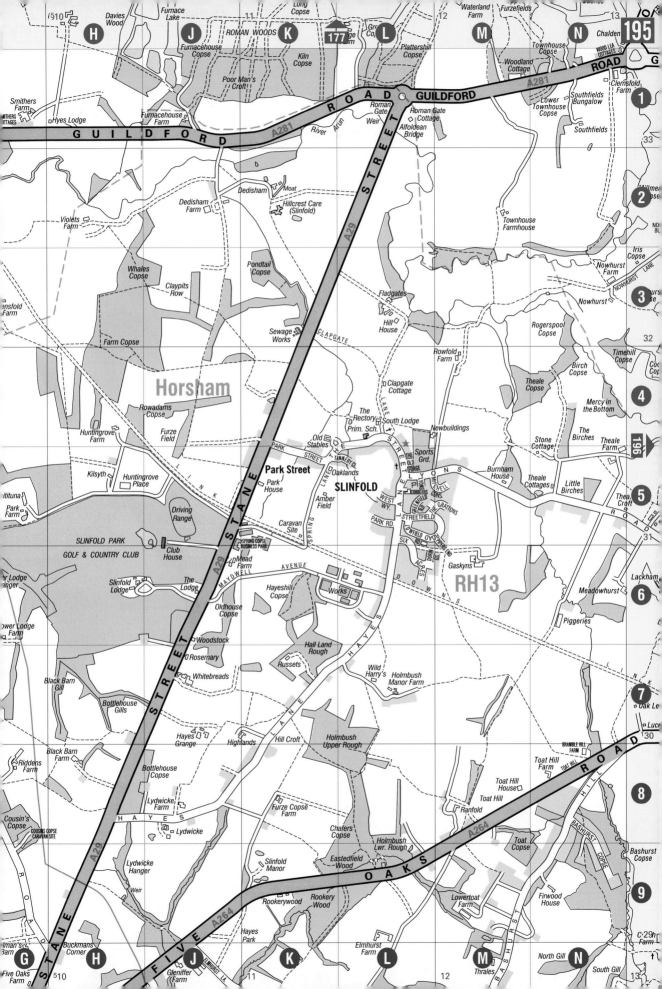

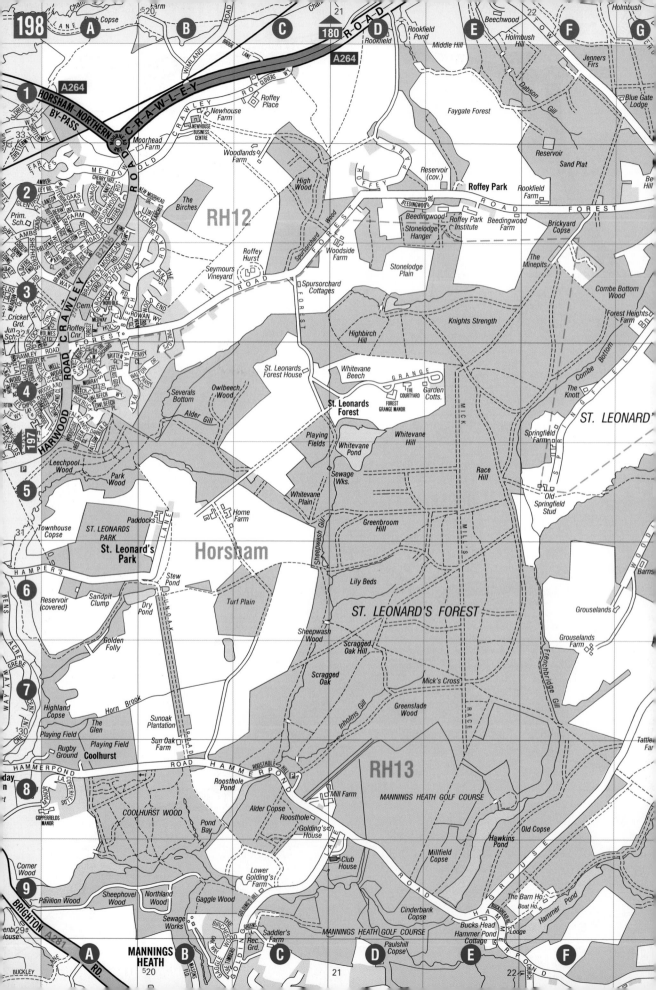

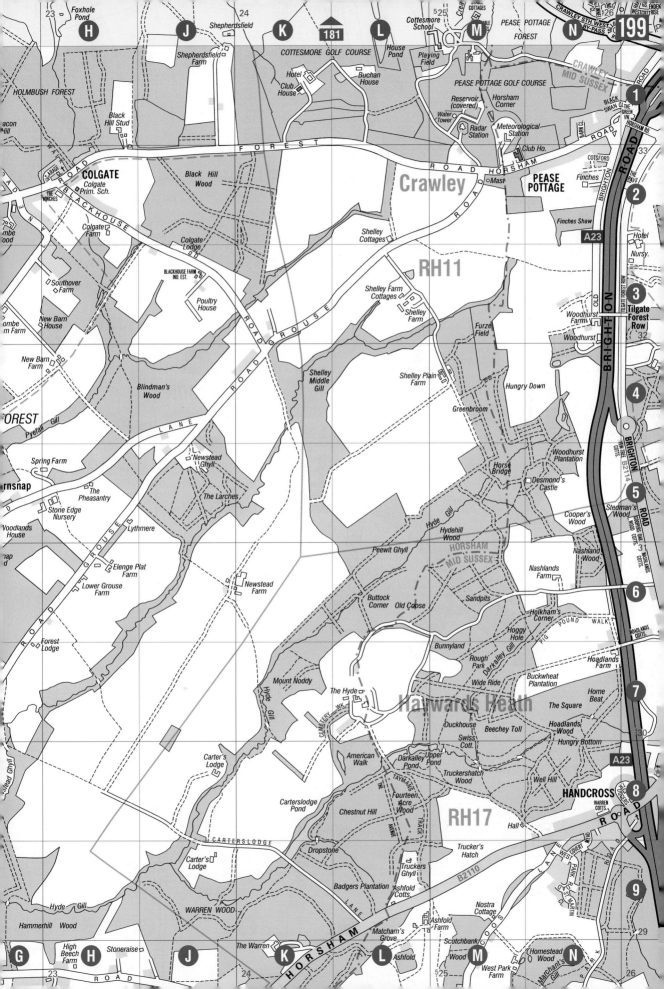

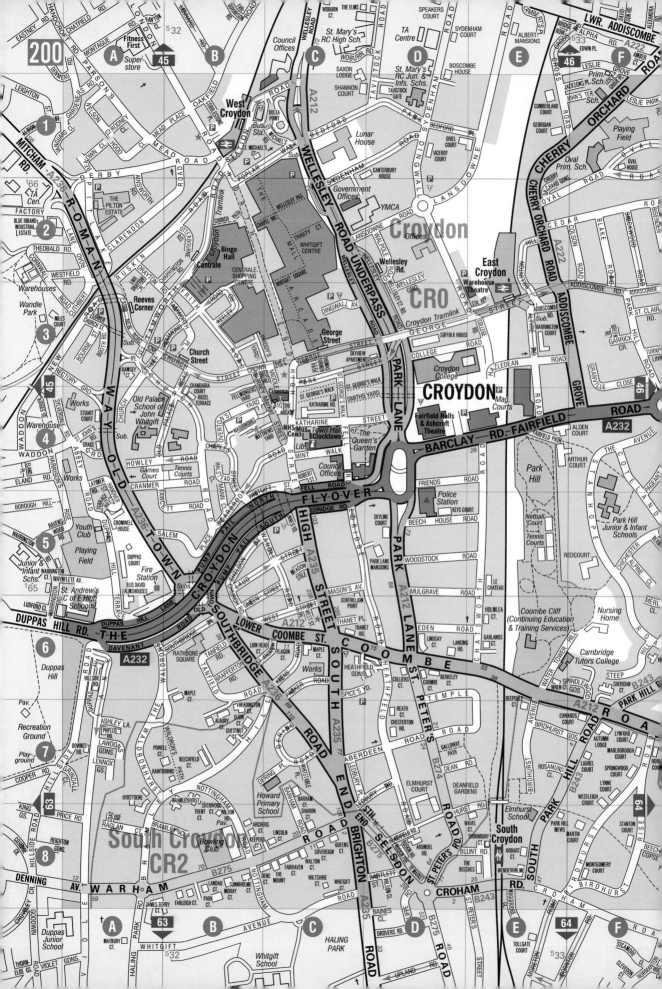

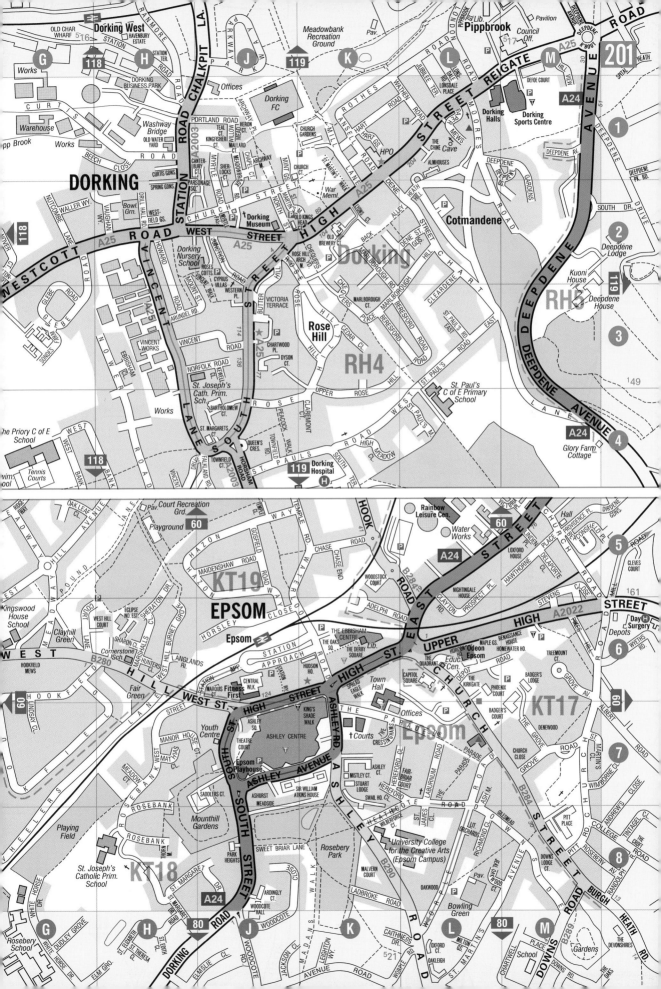

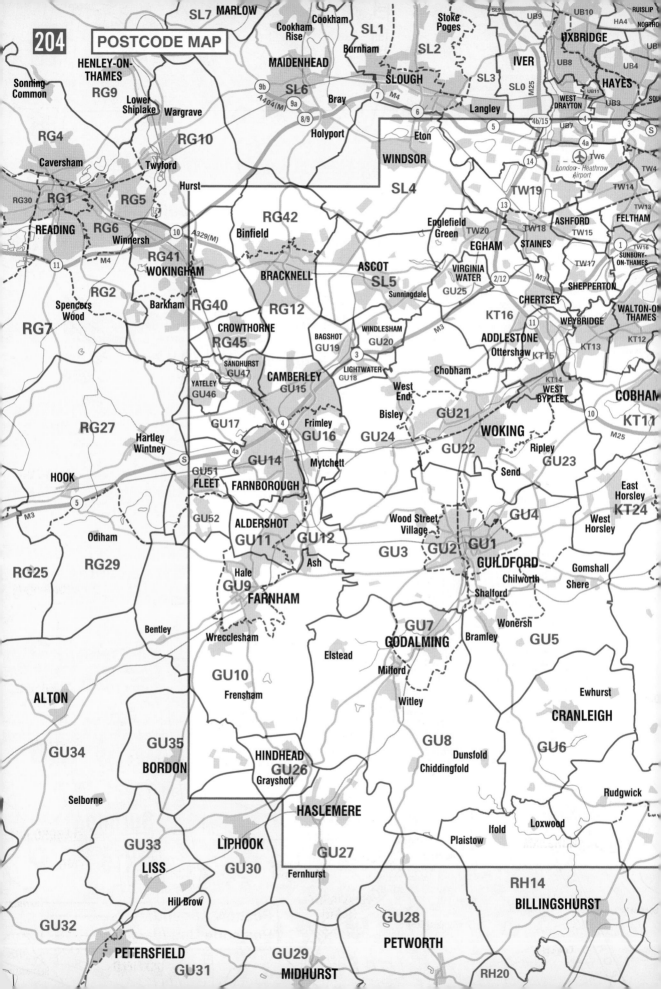

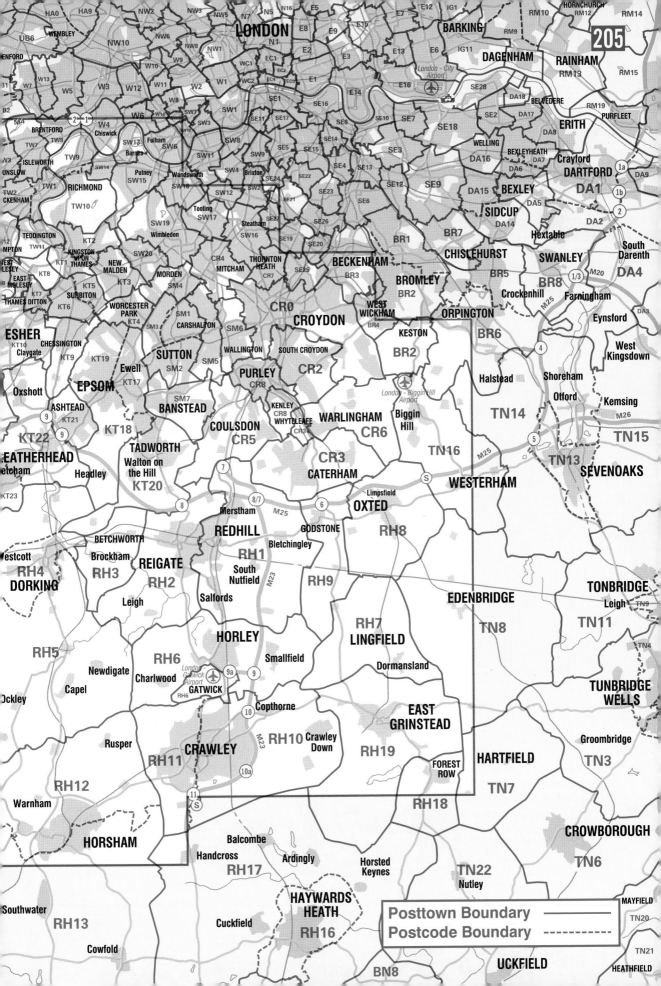

INDEX

Including Streets, Places & Areas, Industrial Estates, Selected Flats & Walkways,
Junction Names, Service Areas, Stations and Selected Places of Interest.

HOW TO USE THIS INDEX

1. Each street name is followed by its Postcode District (or, if outside the London Postcodes, by its Locality abbreviation(s)) and then by its map reference;
   e.g. **Aaron's Hill** GU7: Goda . . . .7E **132** is in the GU7 Postcode District and the Godalming Locality and is to be found in square 7E on page **132**. The page number is shown in bold type.

2. A strict alphabetical order is followed in which Av., Rd., St., etc. (though abbreviated) are read in full and as part of the street name;
   e.g. **Apple Trees Pl.** appears after **Appletree Pl.** but before **Appletree Way**

3. Streets and a selection of flats and walkways too small to be shown on the maps, appear in the index with the thoroughfare to which it is connected shown in brackets;
   e.g. **Abbeyfield** GU1: Guil . . . .4B **114** (off Lwr. Edgeborough Rd.)

4. Addresses that are in more than one part are referred to as not continuous.

5. Places and areas are shown in the index in BLUE TYPE and the map reference is to the actual map square in which the town centre or area is located and not to the place name shown on the map;
   e.g. **ADDLESTONE** 1L **55**

6. An example of a selected place of interest is **Berkshire Yeomanry Mus.** 7G **4**

7. An example of a station is **Addlestone Station (Rail)** 1M **55**
   Included are Rail (**Rail**), Croydon Tramlink (**CT**), Riverbus (**Riverbus**), London Underground Stations (**Tube**) and Park and Ride (**Park & Ride**)

8. Junction names and Service Areas are shown in the index in **BOLD CAPITAL TYPE**; e.g. **APEX CORNER** 4N **23**

9. Map references for entries that appear on large scale pages **200-203** are shown first, with small scale map references shown in brackets; e.g. **Abbey Rd.** CR0: Croy 4A **200** (9M **45**)

GENERAL ABBREVIATIONS

All. : Alley	**Cl.** : Close	**Ga.** : Gate	**Mdws.** : Meadows	**Sth.** : South
App. : Approach	**Coll.** : College	**Gt.** : Great	**M.** : Mews	**Sq.** : Square
Arc. : Arcade	**Comn.** : Common	**Grn.** : Green	**Mt.** : Mount	**Sta.** : Station
Av. : Avenue	**Cnr.** : Corner	**Gro.** : Grove	**Mus.** : Museum	**St.** : Street
Blvd. : Boulevard	**Cott.** : Cottage	**Hgts.** : Heights	**Nth.** : North	**Ter.** : Terrace
Bri. : Bridge	**Cotts.** : Cottages	**Ho.** : House	**Pal.** : Palace	**Twr.** : Tower
B'way. : Broadway	**Ct.** : Court	**Ho's.** : Houses	**Pde.** : Parade	**Trad.** : Trading
Bldg. : Building	**Cres.** : Crescent	**Ind.** : Industrial	**Pk.** : Park	**Up.** : Upper
Bldgs. : Buildings	**Cft.** : Croft	**Info.** : Information	**Pas.** : Passage	**Va.** : Vale
Bungs. : Bungalows	**Dr.** : Drive	**Intl.** : International	**Pl.** : Place	**Vw.** : View
Bus. : Business	**E.** : East	**Junc.** : Junction	**Pct.** : Precinct	**Vs.** : Villas
Cvn. : Caravan	**Ent.** : Enterprise	**La.** : Lane	**Prom.** : Promenade	**Vis.** : Visitors
C'way. : Causeway	**Est.** : Estate	**Lit.** : Little	**Quad.** : Quadrant	**Wlk.** : Walk
Cen. : Centre	**Fld.** : Field	**Lwr.** : Lower	**Res.** : Residential	**W.** : West
Chu. : Church	**Flds.** : Fields	**Mnr.** : Manor	**Ri.** : Rise	**Yd.** : Yard
Chyd. : Churchyard	**Gdn.** : Garden	**Mans.** : Mansions	**Rd.** : Road	
Circ. : Circle	**Gdns.** : Gardens	**Mkt.** : Market	**Rdbt.** : Roundabout	
Cir. : Circus	**Gth.** : Garth	**Mdw.** : Meadow	**Shop.** : Shopping	

LOCALITY ABBREVIATIONS

A Com : Abinger Common	**Char** : Charlwood	**Esh** : Esher	**Horl** : Horley	**North** : Northchapel
A Ham : Abinger Hammer	**Chea** : Cheam	**Eton** : Eton	**Horn** : Horne	**Nth H** : North Holmwood
A'ton : Addington	**Chels** : Chelsfield	**E Wic** : Eton Wick	**Hors** : Horsham	**N Hil** : Norwood Hill
Addl : Addlestone	**Chert** : Chertsey	**Ewe** : Ewell	**Hort** : Horton	**Nut** : Nutfield
Alb : Albury	**Ches** : Chessington	**Ewh** : Ewhurst	**Houn** : Hounslow	**Oak** : Oakwoodhill
Alde : Aldershot	**Chid** : Chiddingfold	**Ews** : Ewshot	**Hurst** : Hurst	**Ockh** : Ockham
Alf : Alfold	**Chil** : Chilworth	**Farnb** : Farnborough	**Hurt** : Hurtmore	**Ockl** : Ockley
Art : Artington	**Chip** : Chipstead	**Farnh** : Farnham	**Ifi** : Ifield	**O Win** : Old Windsor
Asc : Ascot	**Chob** : Chobham	**Fay** : Faygate	**Ifo** : Ifold	**Orp** : Orpington
Ash : Ash	**C Cro** : Church Crookham	**Fel** : Felbridge	**Isle** : Isleworth	**Otter** : Ottershaw
A'ford : Ashford	**Churt** : Churt	**Felc** : Felcourt	**Itch** : Itchingfield	**Out** : Outwood
A Grn : Ash Green	**Clay** : Claygate	**Felt** : Feltham	**J Wel** : Jacobs Well	**Owls** : Owlsmoor
A'tead : Ashtead	**Cob** : Cobham	**Fern** : Fernhurst	**Ken** : Kenley	**Oxs** : Oxshott
Ash W : Ashurst Wood	**Cold** : Coldharbour	**Fetc** : Fetcham	**Kes** : Keston	**Oxt** : Oxted
A Va : Ash Vale	**C Hat** : Coleman's Hatch	**Finch** : Finchampstead	**Kew** : Kew	**P St** : Paley Street
B Lea : Badshot Lea	**Col** : Colgate	**Fleet** : Fleet	**K'fold** : Kingsfold	**Pass** : Passfield
Bag : Bagshot	**C Tow** : College Town	**Flex** : Flexford	**K Grn** : Kingsley Green	**P Pot** : Pease Pottage
Bal : Balcombe	**Coln** : Colnbrook	**For G** : Forest Green	**K Tham** : Kingston upon Thames	**P'lake** : Peaslake
Ban : Banstead	**Comp** : Compton	**F Row** : Forest Row	**K'wood** : Kingswood	**P'marsh** : Peasmarsh
B Grn : Beare Green	**Cop** : Copthorne	**Fren** : Frensham	**Kird** : Kirdford	**P Har** : Peper Harow
Beck : Beckenham	**Coul** : Coulsdon	**Frim** : Frimley	**Knap** : Knaphill	**Pirb** : Pirbright
Bedd : Beddington	**Cove** : Cove	**Frim G** : Frimley Green	**Knoc** : Knockholt	**Plais** : Plaistow
Bedf : Bedfont	**Cow** : Cowden	**Gat** : Gatwick	**Lale** : Laleham	**P Pla** : Plummers Plain
Betch : Betchworth	**C'ford** : Cranford	**Goda** : Godalming	**Lang** : Langley	**Poy** : Poyle
B Hil : Biggin Hill	**Cranl** : Cranleigh	**Gods** : Godstone	**Leat** : Leatherhead	**P Bot** : Pratts Bottom
Bill : Billingshurst	**Craw** : Crawley	**Gorn** : Gomshall	**Leigh** : Leigh	**Pur** : Purley
Bin : Binfield	**Craw D** : Crawley Down	**G'hott** : Grayshott	**Ligh** : Lightwater	**Put** : Puttenham
Bis : Bisley	**C Hil** : Crockham Hill	**G'wood** : Grayswood	**Limp** : Limpsfield	**Pyr** : Pyrford
B'eath : Blackheath	**Cron** : Crondall	**Guil** : Guildford	**Linch** : Linchmere	**Ran C** : Ranmore Common
B'nest : Blacknest	**Crow** : Crowthorne	**Hale** : Hale	**Lind** : Lindford	**Red** : Redhill
B'water : Blackwater	**Croy** : Croydon	**Ham** : Ham	**Ling** : Lingfield	**Reig** : Reigate
Blet : Bletchingley	**Cud** : Cudham	**Hamb** : Hambledon	**Lip** : Liphook	**R Pk** : Richings Park
Blin H : Blindley Heath	**Dat** : Datchet	**Hamm** : Hammerwood	**Lon A** : London Heathrow Airport	**Rich** : Richmond
Book : Bookham	**Deep** : Deepcut	**Hamp** : Hampton	**L'cross** : Longcross	**Rip** : Ripley
Bor : Bordon	**Dip** : Dippenhall	**H Hill** : Hampton Hill	**L'ford** : Longford	**Row** : Rowfant
Bow G : Bowlhead Green	**Dock** : Dockenfield	**H Wic** : Hampton Wick	**L Bou** : Lower Bourne	**Rowh** : Rowhook
Box H : Box Hill	**Dork** : Dorking	**Hand** : Handcross	**Lwr K** : Lower Kingswood	**Rowl** : Rowledge
Brac : Bracknell	**Dorm** : Dormansland	**Hanw** : Hanworth	**L Hea** : Lowfield Heath	**Rudg** : Rudgwick
Braml : Bramley	**D Pk** : Dormans Park	**Harl** : Harlington	**Loxh** : Loxhill	**Run** : Runfold
Brams : Bramshott	**Dorn** : Dorney	**Harm** : Harmondsworth	**Loxw** : Loxwood	**Rush** : Rushmoor
Brast : Brasted	**Dow** : Downe	**Hart** : Hartfield	**Lyne** : Lyne	**Rusp** : Rusper
Brent : Brentford	**Down** : Downside	**Hasc** : Hascombe	**M Hea** : Mannings Heath	**Salf** : Salfords
Bro H : Broadbridge Heath	**Duns** : Dunsfold	**Hasl** : Haslemere	**M Grn** : Marsh Green	**Sande** : Sanderstead
Brock : Brockham	**E Cla** : East Clandon	**Haw** : Hawley	**Mers** : Merstham	**Sandh** : Sandhurst
Brom : Bromley	**E Grin** : East Grinstead	**Hay** : Hayes	**Mick** : Mickleham	**Seal** : Seale
Brook : Brook	**E Hor** : East Horsley	**Head** : Headley	**Mid H** : Mid Holmwood	**Sels** : Selsdon
B'wood : Brookwood	**E Mol** : East Molesey	**H Dwn** : Headley Down	**Mil** : Milford	**Send** : Send
Buck : Buckland	**Eash** : Eashing	**H End** : Heath End	**Min** : Minley	**S'ford** : Shackleford
B Oak : Bucks Horn Oak	**Eden** : Edenbridge	**Hers** : Hersham	**Mit** : Mitcham	**Sha G** : Shamley Green
B'ham : Burpham	**Eff** : Effingham	**Hest** : Heston	**Mord** : Morden	**Sharp** : Sharpthorne
Burs : Burstow	**E Jun** : Effingham Junction	**Hev** : Hever	**Mytc** : Mytchett	**Shep** : Shepperton
Bus : Busbridge	**Egh** : Egham	**H Wood** : Hinchley Wood	**N Add** : New Addington	**Shere** : Shere
Byf : Byfleet	**Els** : Elstead	**Hind** : Hindhead	**Newc** : Newchapel	**S Bri** : Shipley Bridge
Camb : Camberley	**Eng G** : Englefield Green	**H Mary** : Holmbury St Mary	**Newd** : Newdigate	**S Row** : Shurlock Row
Cap : Capel	**Ent G** : Enton Green	**Holm** : Holmwood	**N Haw** : New Haw	**Sid** : Sidlow
Cars : Carshalton	**Eps** : Epsom	**H Pou** : Holt Pound	**N Mal** : New Malden	**Sip** : Sipson
Cate : Caterham	**Eps D** : Epsom Downs	**Hook** : Hookwood	**Norm** : Normandy	**Slea** : Sleaford

10 Pin—Albemarle

Slin : **Slinfold**
Slou : **Slough**
Smal : **Smallfield**
S'hall : **Southall**
S Croy : **South Croydon**
S Gods : **South Godstone**
Sth N : **South Nutfield**
Stain : **Staines**
Stand : **Standford**
Stan : **Stanwell**
Stan M : **Stanwell Moor**
Sto D : **Stoke D'Abernon**
Sunb : **Sunbury**
S'dale : **Sunningdale**
S'hill : **Sunninghill**
Surb : **Surbiton**
Sut : **Sutton**
Sut G : **Sutton Green**
Tad : **Tadworth**
Tand : **Tandridge**
Tats : **Tatsfield**
Tat C : **Tattenham Corner**
Tedd : **Teddington**
T Dit : **Thames Ditton**
Have : **The Haven**
T Hea : **Thornton Heath**
Thor : **Thorpe**
Thur : **Thursley**
Til : **Tilford**
T'sey : **Titsey**
Tong : **Tongham**
T Hil : **Turners Hill**
Twick : **Twickenham**
Twy : **Twyford**
U Hal : **Upper Hale**
U Har : **Upper Hartfield**
V Wat : **Virginia Water**
Wad : **Waddon**
W'ton : **Wallington**
W'wood : **Walliswood**
Wal T : **Walton-on-Thames**
Wal H : **Walton on the Hill**
Wan : **Wanborough**
Warf : **Warfield**
Warl : **Warlingham**
Warn : **Warnham**
W By : **West Byfleet**
W Cla : **West Clandon**
W Dray : **West Drayton**
W End : **West End**
W Hoa : **West Hoathly**
W Hors : **West Horsley**
W Mole : **West Molesey**
W Wick : **West Wickham**
Westc : **Westcott**
Weste : **Westerham**
Westh : **Westhumble**
Weybo : **Weybourne**
Weybr : **Weybridge**
White : **Whitehill**
Whit V : **Whiteley Village**
Whitt : **Whitton**
Whyte : **Whyteleafe**
Windl : **Windlesham**
W'sor : **Windsor**
Wink : **Winkfield**
Wink R : **Winkfield Row**
Win : **Winnersh**
W Grn : **Wisborough Green**
Wis : **Wisley**
Wit : **Witley**
Wok : **Woking**
W'ham : **Wokingham**
Wold : **Woldingham**
Wone : **Wonersh**
Wood : **Woodham**
Wood V : **Wood Street Village**
W Pk : **Worcester Park**
Worm : **Wormley**
Worp : **Worplesdon**
Wor : **Worth**
Wott : **Wotton**
Wray : **Wraysbury**
Wrec : **Wrecclesham**
W Cros : **Wych Cross**
Yate : **Yateley**

10 Pin *4B 74*
(in Big Apple)

A

AARON'S HILL 7E 132
Aaron's Hill GU7: Goda 7E 132
Abbess Cl. SW2 . . . . 2M 29
Abbetts La. GU15: Camb 3N 69
Abbey Bus. Pk.
GU9: Farnh 3M 129
Abbey Chase KT16: Chert 6K 37
Abbey Cl. GU6: Cranl 8H 155
GU22: Pyr 3G 75
RG12: Brac 4B 32
RG40: W'ham 1B 30
Abbey Ct. GU9: Farnh 1H 129
GU15: Camb 1B 70
KT16: Chert 6K 37
TW12: Hamp 8A 24
TW18: Lale 3L 37
Abbeydore Cl.
GU35: Head 4D 168
Abbey Dr. SW17 . . . . 6E 28
TW18: Lale 2L 37
Abbeyfield *GU1: Guil* *4B 114*
(off Lwr. Edgeborough Rd.)
Abbeyfield Cl. CR4: Mit 1C 44
Abbey Fit Sports Cen. 1J 55
Abbey Gdns. KT16: Chert 5J 37
W6 . . . . 2K 13
Abbey Grn. KT16: Chert 5J 37
Abbey Ind. Est. CR4: Mit 4D 44
Abbey Mdws. KT16: Chert 6L 37
Abbey M. RH19: Ash W 3H 187
TW7: Isle 4H 11
TW18: Lale 3L 37
Abbey Mill Bus. Pk.
GU7: Eash 7B 132
Abbey Pde. *SW19* *8A 28*
(off Merton High St.)
Abbey Pl. KT16: Chert 2J 37
RG42: Warf 6A 16
Abbey Rd.
CR0: Croy 4A **200** (9M **45**)
CR2: Sels 6G 64
GU21: Wok 4M 73
GU25: V Wat 4N 35
KT16: Chert 6K 37
SW19 . . . . 8A 28
TW17: Shep 7B 38
Abbey St. GU9: Farnh 1H 129
Abbey Wlk. KT8: W Mole 2B 40
Abbey Way GU14: Farnb 1A 90
Abbeywood GU12: A Va 9F 90
SL5: S'dale 6D 34
Abbot Cl. KT14: Byf 6M 55
TW18: Stain 8M 21
Abbot Rd.
GU1: Guil 7D **202** (5N **113**)
Abbots Av. KT19: Eps 7N 59
Abbotsbury RG12: Brac 4L 31
Abbotsbury Ct. RH13: Hors . . . 5L 197
Abbotsbury Rd. SM4: Mord . . . 4N 43
Abbots Cl. GU2: Guil 6H 113
GU51: Fleet 4B 88
Abbots Dr. GU25: V Wat 4L 35
Abbotsfield Rd. RH11: Ifi 4J 181
Abbotsford Cl. GU22: Wok 4C 74
Abbots Grn. CR0: A'ton 3G 65
Abbots Hospital GU1: Guil 5D 202
Abbots La. CR8: Ken 3N 83
Abbotsleigh Cl. SM2: Sut 4N 61
Abbotsleigh Rd. SW16 . . . . 5G 28
Abbots Mead TW10: Ham 5K 25
Abbotsmede Cl. TW1: Twick . . . 3F 24
Abbots Pk. SW2 . . . . 2L 29
Abbot's Ride GU9: Farnh 3K 129
Abbots Ri. RH1: Red 1E 122
Abbotstone Rd. SW15 . . . . 6H 13
Abbots Wlk. SL4: W'sor 5B 4
Abbots Way BR3: Beck 4H 47
GU1: Guil 2F 114
KT16: Chert 6H 37
ABBOTSWOOD 1B 114
Abbotswood GU1: Guil 1B 114
KT13: Weybr 9G 38
Abbotswood Cl. GU1: Guil 9B 94
Abbotswood Dr.
KT13: Weybr 6E 56
Abbotswood Rd.
SW16 . . . . 4H 29
Abbott Av. SW20 . . . . 9J 27
Abbott Cl. TW12: Hamp 7M 23
Abbotts Cotts.
GU10: Dock 5D 148
Abbotts Rd. CR4: Mit 3G 45
(not continuous)
SM3: Chea 1K 61
Abbott's Tilt KT12: Hers 9M 39
Abbotts Wlk. CR3: Cate 9E 84
Abelia Cl. GU24: W End 9B 52
Abell Ct. KT15: Addl 2K 55
Abercairn Rd. SW16 . . . . 8G 28
Aberconway Rd.
SM4: Mord 3N 43
Abercorn Cl. CR2: Sels 9G 64
Abercorn Ho. GU17: Haw 5K 69
Abercorn M. TW10: Rich 7M 11
Abercorn Way GU21: Wok 5K 73
Aberdare Cl. BR4: W Wick 8M 47
Aberdeen Rd.
CR0: Croy 7C **200** (1N **63**)
Aberdeen Ter.
GU26: G'hott 5B 170
Aberfoyle Rd. SW16 . . . . 7H 29
(not continuous)
Abergavenny Gdns.
RH10: Cop 7A 164
Abingdon *W14* *1L 13*
(off Kensington Village)
Abingdon Cl. GU21: Wok 5M 73
KT4: W Pk 9G 43
RG12: Brac 4C 32
SW19 . . . . 7A 28
Abingdon Ct. GU22: Wok 5B 74
Abingdon Rd. GU47: Sandh . . . 7H 49
SW16 . . . . 1J 45
Abinger Av. SM2: Chea 5H 61
ABINGER BOTTOM 5N 137
Abinger Cl. CR0: N Add 3M 65
RH5: Nth H 9J 119
SM6: W'ton 2J 63
ABINGER COMMON 3L 137
Abinger Comn. Rd.
RH5: A Com 4M 137
Abinger Ct. *SM6: W'ton* *2J 63*
(off Abinger Cl.)
Abinger Dr. RH1: Red 5C 122
Abinger Gdns. TW7: Isle 6E 10
ABINGER HAMMER 9G 116
Abinger Keep *RH6: Horl* *7G 142*
(off Langshott La.)
Abinger La.
RH5: A Com, A Ham 9J 117
Abinger Rd.
RH5: Cold, H Mary, Ockl
. . . . 9A 138
Abinger Way GU4: B'ham 7D 94
Aboyne Dr. SW20 . . . . 1F 42
Aboyne Rd. SW17 . . . . 4B 28
Abrahams Rd.
RH11: Craw 8M 181
Abro Ind. Est. GU11: Alde 9B 90
Abury La. RG12: Brac 5E 32
Acacia Av. GU22: Wok 7N 73
GU47: Owls 6J 49
TW8: Brent 3H 11
TW17: Shep 4B 38
TW19: Wray 7A 6
Acacia Cl. KT15: Wood 6H 55
SE20 . . . . 1D 46
Acacia Ct. RG12: Brac 3N 31
Acacia Dr. KT15: Wood 6H 55
SM3: Sut 7L 43
SM7: Ban 1J 81
Acacia Gdns. BR4: W Wick 8M 47
Acacia Gro. KT3: N Mal 2C 42
Acacia M. UB7: Harm 2M 7
Acacia Rd. BR3: Beck 2J 47
CR4: Mit 1E 44
GU1: Guil 2C **202** (3N **113**)
SW16 . . . . 9J 29
TW12: Hamp 7A 24
TW18: Stain 6K 21
(not continuous)
Academy Cl. GU15: Camb 7C 50
Academy Gdns. CR0: Croy 7C 46
Academy Ga. GU15: Camb 9N 49
Academy Pl. GU47: C Tow 8K 49
Accommodation La.
UB7: Harm 2L 7
UB7: L'ford 4J 7
Accommodation Rd.
KT16: L'cross 9N 35
KT17: Ewe 2F 60
AC Court KT7: T Dit 5G 40
Ace Pde. KT9: Ches 9L 41
Acer Cl. RG42: Warf 9E 16
Acer Dr. GU24: W End 9C 52
Acer Rd. TN16: B Hil 3F 86
Acfold Rd. SW6 . . . . 4N 13
Acheulian Cl. GU9: Farnh 4H 129
Achilles Pl. GU21: Wok 4M 73
Ackmar Rd. SW6 . . . . 4M 13
Ackrells Mead GU47: Sandh . . . 6E 48
Acorn Cl. RH6: Horl 7G 143
RH19: E Grin 1A 186
TW12: Hamp 7B 24
Acorn Dr. RG40: W'ham 1B 30
Acorn Gdns. SE19 . . . . 1C 46
Acorn Gro. GU22: Wok 8A 74
KT20: K'wood 2L 101
UB3: Harl 3G 9
Acorn Keep GU9: H End 4J 109
Acorn M. GU14: Farnb 7M 69
Acorn Rd. GU17: B'water 1G 69
Acorns RH13: Hors 4N 197
Acorns, The RH6: Smal 8M 143
RH11: Craw 8N 181
Acorns Way KT10: Esh 2C 58
Acorn Way BR3: Beck 4M 47
BR6: Farnb 1K 67
Acqua Ho. TW9: Kew 3A 12
Acre La. SM5: Cars 1E 62
SM6: W'ton 1E 62
Acre Pas. SL4: W'sor 4G 4
Acre Rd.
KT2: K Tham 1K **203** (9L **25**)
SW19 . . . . 7B 28
Acres Gdns. KT20: Tad 6J 81
Acres Platt GU6: Cranl 6A 156
Acropolis Ho.
KT1: K Tham 5L 203
Acton La. W3 . . . . 1B 12
Acuba Rd. SW18 . . . . 3N 27
Adair Cl. SE25 . . . . 2E 46
Adair Gdns. CR3: Cate 8N 83
Adair Wlk. GU24: B'wood 8M 71
Adams Cl. KT5: Surb 5M 41
Adams Cft. GU24: B'wood 7N 71
Adams Dr. GU51: Fleet 4C 88
Adams M. SW17 . . . . 3D 28
Adamson Ct. RH11: Craw 8N 181
Adamson Way BR3: Beck 4M 47
Adams Pk. Rd. GU9: Farnh . . . 8J 109
Adams Quarter TW8: Brent 2J 11
Adams Rd. BR3: Beck 4H 47
Adams Wlk.
KT1: K Tham . . . 3J **203** (1L **41**)
Adams Way CR0: Croy 5C 46
SE25 . . . . 4E 46
Adam Wlk. SW6 . . . . 3H 13
Adare Wlk. SW16 . . . . 4K 29
ADDINGTON 2K 65
Addington Bus. Cen.
CR0: N Add 6A 66
Addington Cl. SL4: W'sor 6D 4
Addington Ct. SW14 . . . . 6C 12
Addington Hgts.
CR0: N Add 7M 65
Addington Palace 3J 65
Addington Rd.
BR4: W Wick 1M 65
CR0: Croy 7L 45
CR2: Sande, Sels 7D 64
Addington Village Rd.
CR0: A'ton 3J 65
(not continuous)
Addington Village Stop (CT)
. . . . 3K 65
ADDISCOMBE 7D 46
Addiscombe Av. CR0: Croy 6D 46
Addiscombe Ct. Rd.
CR0: Croy 7B 46
Addiscombe Gro.
CR0: Croy 3E **200** (8B **46**)
Addiscombe Rd.
CR0: Croy 3E **200** (8B **46**)
(not continuous)
RG45: Crow 3H 49
Addiscombe Stop (CT) 7D 46
Addison Av. TW3: Houn 4C 10
Addison Cl. CR3: Cate 9A 84
Addison Ct. GU1: Guil 5B 114
Addison Gdns.
KT5: Surb 8M **203** (3M **41**)
Addison Pl. SE25 . . . . 3D 46
Addison Rd. CR3: Cate 8A 84
GU1: Guil 5F **202** (5A **114**)
GU16: Frim 6C 70
GU21: Wok 4B 74
SE25 . . . . 3D 46
TW11: Tedd 7H 25
Addisons Cl. CR0: Croy 8J 47
ADDLESTONE 1L 55
Addlestone Ho. KT15: Addl 9K 37
ADDLESTONE MOOR 8J 37
Addlestone Moor
KT15: Addl 8L 37
Addlestone Pk. KT15: Addl 2K 55
Addlestone Rd.
KT13: Weybr 1A 56
KT15: Addl 1N 55
Addlestone Station (Rail) 1M 55
Adecroft Way KT8: W Mole 2C 40
Adela Av. KT3: N Mal 4G 42
Adela Ho. *W6* *1H 13*
(off Queen Caroline St.)
Adelaide Cl. RH11: Craw 9B 162
RH12: Hors 4M 197
Adelaide Pl. KT13: Weybr 1E 56
Adelaide Rd.
KT6: Surb 8J **203** (4L **41**)
KT12: Wal T 9H 39
SL4: W'sor 4J 5
SW18 . . . . 8M 13
TW5: Hest 4M 9
TW9: Rich 7M 11
TW11: Tedd 7F 24
TW15: A'ford 6M 21
Adelaide Sq. SL4: W'sor 5G 4
Adelaide Ter. TW8: Brent 1K 11
Adelina M. SW12 . . . . 2H 29
Adeline Genee Theatre 5N 165
Adelphi Cl. RH10: Craw 5H 183
Adelphi Ct. W4 . . . . 2C 12
Adelphi Rd.
KT17: Eps 6K **201** (9C **60**)
Adeney Cl. W6 . . . . 2J 13
Adlers La. RH5: Westh 9G 99
Adlington Pl. GU14: Farnb 3C 90
Admark Ho. KT18: Eps 2A 80
Admiral Ct. SM5: Cars 7C 44
Admiral Ho. TW11: Tedd 5G 25
Admiral Kepple Ct.
SL5: Asc 8J 17
Admiral Rd. RH11: Craw 6M 181
Admiral's Bri. La.
RH19: E Grin 7M 185
Admirals Ct. GU1: Guil 2D 114
Admirals Rd. GU24: Pirb 4K 91
KT22: Fetc 4D 98
KT23: Book 6C 98
Admiral Stirling Ct.
KT13: Weybr 1A 56
Admirals Wlk. CR5: Coul 7K 83
RH5: Ran C 8B 98
Admiralty Rd. TW11: Tedd 7F 24
Admiralty Way GU15: Camb . . . 2L 69
TW11: Tedd 7F 24
Admiral Way GU7: Goda 9G 132
Adrian Ct. RH11: Craw 8N 181
Adrian M. SW10 . . . . 2N 13
Advance Rd. SE27 . . . . 5N 29
Adversane Ct. *RH12: Hors* . . . *4K 197*
(off Blenheim Rd)
Aerodrome Way TW5: Hest 2K 9
Aerospace Blvd.
GU14: Farnb 6L 89
Agar Cl. KT6: Surb 8M 41
Agar Cres. RG42: Brac 8N 15
Agar Ho. KT1: K Tham 6J 203
Agars Pl. SL3: Dat 2K 5
Agate La. RH12: Hors 3L 197
Agates La. KT21: A'tead 5K 79
Agevin Ct. GU51: Fleet 2A 88
Agincourt SL5: Asc 2N 33
Agnes Scott Ct.
KT13: Weybr *9C 38*
(off Palace Dr.)
Agraria Rd. GU2: Guil 4L 113
Agua Ho. KT16: Chert 6L 37
Ailsa Av. TW1: Twick 8G 11
Ailsa Cl. RH11: Craw 6N 181
Ailsa Rd. TW1: Twick 8H 11
Ainger Cl. GU12: Alde 1B 110
Ainsdale Way GU21: Wok 5K 73
Ainslie Wlk. SW12 . . . . 1F 28
Ainsworth Rd.
CR0: Croy 2A **200** (7M **45**)
Aintree Cl. SL3: Poy 4G 6
Aintree Est. *SW6* *3K 13*
(off Aintree St.)
Aintree Rd. RH10: Craw 5E 182
Aintree St. SW6 . . . . 3K 13
Airborne Forces Mus. 8M 89
Airbourne Ho. *SM6: W'ton* *1G 62*
(off Maldon Rd.)
Aircraft Esplanade
GU14: Farnb 4A 90
Airedale Av. W4 . . . . 1E 12
Airedale Av. Sth. W4 . . . . 1E 12
Airedale Rd. SW12 . . . . 1D 28
Air Forces Memorial 5N 19
Air Links Ind. Est.
TW13: Hanw 4M 23
Airlinks Ind. Est. TW5: C'ford . . 1K 9
Air Pk. Way TW13: Felt 3J 23
Airport Bowl *4F 8*
Airport Ga. Bus. Cen.
UB7: Sip 3A 8
Airport Ind. Est. TN16: B Hil . . 2F 86
Airport Way RH6: Gat 2E 162
TW19: Stan M 7H 7
Aisgill Av. W14 . . . . 1L 13
(not continuous)
Aisne Rd. GU16: Deep 5J 71
Aiten Pl. W6 . . . . 1F 12
Aitken Cl. CR4: Mit 6D 44
Aitken Ho. GU27: Hasl 1G 189
Aitman Dr. W4 . . . . 1N 11
Aits Vw. KT8: W Mole 2B 40
Akabusi Cl. CR0: Croy 5D 46
Akehurst Cl. RH10: Cop 7L 163
Akehurst St. SW15 . . . . 9F 12
Akerman Rd. KT6: Surb 5J 41
Alamein Rd. GU11: Alde 2N 109
Alanbrooke Cl. GU21: Knap . . . 5F 72
Alanbrooke Rd. GU11: Alde . . . 7B 90
Alan Hilton Ct. *KT16: Otter* . . . *3F 54*
(off Cheshire Cl.)
Alan Rd. SW19 . . . . 6K 27
Alan Turing Rd. GU2: Guil . . . 3G 113
Albain Cres. TW15: A'ford 3N 21
Alba M. SW18 . . . . 3M 27
Albany Cl. GU51: Fleet 5C 88
KT10: Esh 5A 58
RH2: Reig 9M 101
SW14 . . . . 7A 12
Albany Ct. GU16: Camb 5A 70
GU51: Fleet 4C 88
KT13: Weybr 1C 56
(Hillcrest)
KT13: Weybr 8F 38
(Oatlands Dr.)
TW15: A'ford 8D 22
TW20: Egh 5C 20
Albany Cres. KT10: Clay 3E 58
Albany M. KT2: K Tham 7K 25
SM1: Sut 2N 61
Albany Pde. TW8: Brent 2L 11
Albany Pk. GU16: Camb 5N 69
SL3: Coln 4F 6
Albany Pk. Ind. Est.
GU16: Camb 5A 70
Albany Pk. Rd.
KT2: K Tham 7K 25
KT22: Leat 6G 78
Albany Pas. TW10: Rich 8L 11
Albany Pl. TW8: Brent 2K 11
TW20: Egh 5D 20
Albany Reach KT7: T Dit 4F 40
Albany Rd. GU51: Fleet 5B 88
KT3: N Mal 3C 42
KT12: Hers 1L 57
RH11: Craw 3N 181
SL4: O Win 8K 5
SL4: W'sor 5G 4
SW19 . . . . 6N 27
TW8: Brent 2K 11
TW10: Rich 8M 11
Albany Ter. *TW10: Rich* *8M 11*
(off Albany Pas.)
Albatross Gdns. CR2: Sels 7G 65
Albemarle SW19 . . . . 3J 27

Albemarle Av.—Ambleside Cl.

Albemarle Av. TW2: Whitt ... 2N 23
Albemarle Gdns.
KT3: N Mal ... 3C 42
Albemarle Pk. BR3: Beck ... 1L 47
Albemarle Rd. BR3: Beck ... 1M 47
Alben Rd. RG42: Bin ... 6H 15
Alberta Av. SM1: Sut ... 1K 61
Alberta Dr. RH6: Smal ... 8L 143
Albert Av. KT16: Chert ... 2J 37
Albert Carr Gdns.
SW16 ... 6J 29
Albert Crane Ct.
RH11: Craw ... 1M 181
Albert Dr. GU21: Wok ... 2E 74
SW19 ... 3K 27
TW18: Stain ... 6H 21
Albert Gro. SW20 ... 9J 27
Albertine Cl. KT17: Eps D ... 3G 81
Albert Mans. CR0: Croy ... 1E 200
Albert M. RH1: Red ... 6E 122
Albert Pl. SL4: E Wic ... 1D 4
Albert Rd. CR4: Mit ... 2D 44
CR6: Warl ... 4J 85
GU11: Alde ... 2N 109
GU14: Farnb ... 3A 90
GU15: Camb ... 1A 70
GU19: Bag ... 6J 51
KT1: K Tham ... 3L 203 (1M 41)
KT3: N Mal ... 3E 42
KT15: Addl ... 1M 55
KT17: Eps ... 7M 201 (9E 60)
KT21: A'tead ... 5M 79
RG40: W'ham ... 3A 30
RG42: Brac ... 9N 15
RG45: Crow ... 2G 49
RH1: Mers ... 7G 102
RH6: Horl ... 7E 142
SE25 ... 3D 46
SL4: O Win, W'sor ... 6G 5
SM1: Sut ... 2B 62
TW1: Twick ... 2F 24
TW3: Houn ... 7A 10
TW10: Rich ... 8L 11
TW11: Tedd ... 7F 24
TW12: H Hill ... 6C 24
TW15: A'ford ... 6A 22
TW20: Eng G ... 7N 19
Albert Rd. Nth. RH2: Reig ... 2L 121
Albert St. GU51: Fleet ... 5A 88
SL4: W'sor ... 4E 4
Albert Ter. W6 ... 1F 12
(off Beavor La.)
Albert Wlk. RG45: Crow ... 2G 49
Albery Cl. RH12: Hors ... 4H 197
Albion SL3: Lang ... 1D 6
Albion Cl. RH10: Craw ... 4H 183
Albion Cotts. RH5: H Mary ... 5K 137
Albion Ct. SM2: Sut ... 4B 62
W6 ... 1G 13
(off Albion Pl.)
Albion Ho. GU21: Wok ... 4B 74
Albion M. W6 ... 1G 13
Albion Pl. SE25 ... 2D 46
SL4: W'sor ... 5D 4
W6 ... 1G 13
Albion Rd. GU47: Sandh ... 8G 49
KT2: K Tham ... 9B 26
RH2: Reig ... 4A 122
SM2: Sut ... 3B 62
TW2: Twick ... 2E 24
TW3: Houn ... 7A 10
Albion St.
CR0: Croy ... 1A 200 (7M 45)
Albion Way RH12: Hors ... 6H 197
TN8: Eden ... 8L 127
Albon Ho. SW18 ... 9N 13
(off Neville Gill Cl.)
ALBURY ... 8K 115
Albury Av. SM2: Chea ... 5H 61
TW7: Isle ... 3F 10
Albury Cl. KT16: L'cross ... 9K 35
KT19: Eps ... 5A 60
TW12: Hamp ... 7B 24
Albury Cotts. GU12: Ash ... 2G 111
Albury Ct. CR2: S Croy ... 7B 200
CR4: Mit ... 1B 44
SM1: Sut ... 1A 62
ALBURY HEATH ... 1M 135
Albury Ho. GU1: Guil ... 5B 114
Albury Keep RH6: Horl ... 8F 142
(off Langshott La.)
Albury Pk. GU5: Alb ... 8N 115
Albury Pl. RH1: Mers ... 7G 103
Albury Rd. GU1: Guil ... 4B 114
KT9: Ches ... 2L 59
KT12: Hers ... 3F 56
RH1: Mers ... 7G 102
Alcester Ct. SM6: W'ton ... 1F 62
Alcester Rd. SM6: W'ton ... 1F 62
Alcock Cl. SM6: W'ton ... 4H 63
Alcock Rd. TW5: Hest ... 3L 9
Alcocks Cl. KT20: Tad ... 7K 81
Alcocks La.
KT20: K'wood, Tad ... 8K 81
Alcorn Cl. SM3: Sut ... 8M 43
Alcot Cl. RG45: Crow ... 3G 48
Alcott Cl. TW14: Felt ... 2G 22
Alden Ct.
CR0: Croy ... 4F 200 (9B 46)
Aldenham Ter. RG12: Brac ... 5A 32
Aldenholme KT13: Weybr ... 3F 56
Alden Vw. SL4: W'sor ... 4A 4
Alderbrook Cl. RG45: Crow ... 3D 48
Alderbrook Farm Cotts.
GU6: Cranl ... 3M 155
Alderbrook Rd.
GU6: Cranl ... 2K 155
SW12 ... 1F 28
Alderbury Rd. SW13 ... 2F 12
Alder Cl. GU12: A Va ... 6E 90
RH10: Craw D ... 1E 184
TW20: Eng G ... 6A 20
Aldercombe La.
CR3: Cate ... 5B 104
Alder Copse RH12: Hors ... 8F 196
Aldercroft CR5: Coul ... 3K 83
Alder Gro. GU46: Yate ... 1B 68
Aldergrove Gdns.
TW3: Houn ... 5M 9
Alder Lodge SW6 ... 4H 13
Alderman Judge Mall
KT1: K Tham ... 4J 203
Alderman Willey Cl.
RG41: W'ham ... 2A 30
Alderney Av.
TW5: Hest, Isle ... 3B 10
Alder Rd. GU35: H Dwn ... 3G 168
SW14 ... 6C 12
Alders, The BR4: W Wick ... 7L 47
GU9: B Lea ... 6N 109
KT14: W By ... 8L 55
SW16 ... 5G 29
TW5: Hest ... 2N 9
TW13: Hanw ... 5M 23
Alders Av. RH19: E Grin ... 7N 165
Aldersbrook Dr.
KT2: K Tham ... 7M 25
Aldersey Rd. GU1: Guil ... 3B 114
Alders Gro. KT8: E Mol ... 4D 40
ALDERSHOT ... 2N 109
Aldershot Garrison Sports Cen.
... 7A 90
Aldershot Lodge
GU11: Alde ... 4A 110
Aldershot Military Mus. ... 7A 90
Aldershot Pools & Lido ... 5B 110
Aldershot Rd. GU2: Guil ... 7G 92
GU3: Guil, Norm, Worp ... 8B 92
GU12: Ash ... 3C 110
GU24: Pirb ... 5A 92
GU51: Fleet ... 5B 88
GU52: C Cro ... 9A 88
Aldershot Station (Rail) ... 3N 109
Aldershot Town FC ... 2N 109
Alderside Wlk.
TW20: Eng G ... 6A 20
Aldersmead Av. CR0: Croy ... 5G 47
Alders Rd. RH2: Reig ... 1N 121
ALDERSTEAD HEATH ... 3H 103
Alderstead Heath Cvn. Site
RH1: Mers ... 2H 103
Alderstead La. RH1: Mers ... 3H 103
Alders Vw. Dr.
RH19: E Grin ... 7A 166
Alderton Ct. KT8: W Mole ... 3N 39
(off Walton Rd.)
Alderton Rd. CR0: Croy ... 6C 46
Alderville Rd. SW6 ... 5L 13
Alderwick Dr. TW3: Houn ... 6D 10
Alderwood Cl. CR3: Cate ... 3B 104
Aldingbourne Cl. RH11: Ifi ... 2L 181
Aldis M. SW17 ... 6C 28
Aldis St. SW17 ... 6C 28
Aldren Rd. SW17 ... 4A 28
Aldrich Cres. CR0: N Add ... 5M 65
Aldrich Gdns. SM3: Chea ... 9L 43
Aldrich Ter. SW18 ... 3A 28
Aldridge Pk. RG42: Wink R ... 7F 16
Aldridge Ri. KT3: N Mal ... 6D 42
Aldrington Rd. SW16 ... 6G 29
Aldrin Pl. GU14: Cove ... 1J 89
Aldwick Cl. GU14: Farnb ... 8M 69
Aldwick Rd. CR0: Bedd ... 9K 45
Aldworth Cl. RG12: Brac ... 3M 31
Aldworth Gdns.
RG45: Crow ... 2F 48
Aldwych Cl. RH10: Craw ... 5H 183
Aldwyn Pl. TW20: Eng G ... 7L 19
Alexa Ct. SM2: Sut ... 3M 61
Alexander Cl. TW2: Twick ... 3E 24
Alexander Ct. BR3: Beck ... 1N 47
Alexander Cres. CR3: Cate ... 8N 83
Alexander Fleming Rd.
GU2: Guil ... 4G 113
Alexander Godley Cl.
KT21: A'tead ... 6M 79
Alexander Ho. GU11: Alde ... 2N 109
(off Station Rd.)
KT2: K Tham ... 2J 203
Alexander M. SW16 ... 6G 29
Alexander Pl. RH8: Oxt ... 6A 106
Alexander Raby Mill
KT15: Addl ... 2N 55
(off Bourneside Rd.)
Alexander Rd. CR5: Coul ... 2F 82
GU11: Alde ... 2L 109
RH2: Reig ... 6M 121
TW20: Egh ... 6E 20
(not continuous)
Alexanders Wlk.
CR3: Cate ... 4C 104
Alexander Wlk. RG12: Brac ... 4N 31
Alexandra Av. CR6: Warl ... 4J 85
GU15: Camb ... 1M 69
SM1: Sut ... 9M 43
W4 ... 3C 12
Alexandra Cl. GU47: C Tow ... 8K 49
KT12: Wal T ... 8H 39
TW15: A'ford ... 8E 22
TW18: Stain ... 7M 21
Alexandra Ct. GU14: Farnb ... 4A 90
RG40: W'ham ... 3B 30
RH10: Craw ... 4B 182
SL4: W'sor ... 5G 4
(off Alexandra Rd.)
TW3: Houn ... 5B 10
TW15: A'ford ... 7E 22
Alexandra Dr. KT5: Surb ... 6N 41
Alexandra Gdns.
GU21: Knap ... 5F 72
SM5: Cars ... 4E 62
TW3: Houn ... 5B 10
W4 ... 3D 12
Alexandra Ho. W6 ... 1H 13
(off Queen Caroline St.)
Alexandra Lodge
KT13: Weybr ... 1C 56
(off Monument Hill)
Alexandra Mans. KT17: Eps ... 9E 60
(off Alexandra Rd.)
Alexandra M. SW19 ... 7L 27
Alexandra Pl. CR0: Croy ... 7B 46
GU1: Guil ... 5B 114
SE25 ... 4A 46
Alexandra Rd.
CR0: Croy ... 1F 200 (7B 46)
CR4: Mit ... 8C 28
CR6: Warl ... 4J 85
GU11: Alde ... 2K 109
(not continuous)
GU12: Ash ... 3D 110
GU14: Farnb ... 3A 90
KT2: K Tham ... 8N 25
KT7: T Dit ... 4F 40
KT15: Addl ... 1M 55
(not continuous)
KT17: Eps ... 9E 60
SL4: W'sor ... 5G 4
SW14 ... 6C 12
SW19 ... 7L 27
TN16: B Hil ... 6D 86
TW1: Twick ... 9J 11
TW3: Houn ... 5B 10
TW8: Brent ... 2K 11
TW9: Kew ... 5M 11
TW15: A'ford ... 8E 22
TW20: Eng G ... 7M 19
Alexandra Sq. SM4: Mord ... 4M 43
Alexandra Ter.
GU1: Guil ... 4E 202 (4A 114)
GU11: Alde ... 2M 109
Alexandra Way KT19: Eps ... 7N 59
ALFOLD ... 8H 175
ALFOLD BARS ... 1H 193
Alfold Bus. Cen. GU6: Alf ... 8J 175
ALFOLD CROSSWAYS ... 5J 175
Alfold Rd. GU6: Alf, Cranl ... 7K 155
GU8: Duns ... 5B 174
Alfonso Cl. GU12: Alde ... 4A 110
Alford Cl. GU4: B'ham ... 9B 94
GU47: Sandh ... 8F 48
Alford Grn. CR0: N Add ... 3N 65
Alfred Cl. RH10: Wor ... 4J 183
W4 ... 1C 12
Alfred Rd. GU9: Farnh ... 2H 129
KT1: K Tham ... 6K 203 (2L 41)
SE25 ... 4D 46
SM1: Sut ... 2A 62
TW13: Felt ... 3K 23
Alfreton Cl. SW19 ... 4J 27
Alfriston KT5: Surb ... 5M 41
Alfriston Av. CR0: Croy ... 6J 45
Alfriston Cl. KT5: Surb ... 4M 41
Alfriston Rd. GU16: Deep ... 7G 71
Algar Cl. TW7: Isle ... 6G 10
Algar Rd. TW7: Isle ... 6G 11
Algarve Rd. SW18 ... 2N 27
Alice Crocker Ho.
RH19: E Grin ... 8A 166
Alice Gilliatt Ct. W14 ... 2L 13
(off Star Rd.)
Alice Gough Memorial Homes
RG12: Brac ... 2N 31
Alice Holt Cotts.
GU10: H Pou ... 9A 128
Alice Holt Forest Vis. Cen.
... 2B 148
Alice M. TW11: Tedd ... 6F 24
Alice Rd. GU11: Alde ... 2N 109
Alice Ruston Pl.
GU22: Wok ... 6M 73
Alice Way TW3: Houn ... 7B 10
Alicia Av. RH10: Craw ... 3F 182
Alington Gro. SM6: W'ton ... 5G 63
Alison Cl. CR0: Croy ... 7G 46
GU14: Cove ... 2L 89
GU21: Wok ... 2A 74
Alison Dr. GU15: Camb ... 1D 70
Alison's Rd. GU11: Alde ... 8M 89
Alison Way GU11: Alde ... 2L 109
Alkerden Rd. W4 ... 1D 12
Allan Cl. KT3: N Mal ... 4C 42
Allbrook Cl. TW11: Tedd ... 6E 24
Allcard Cl. RH12: Hors ... 4K 197
Allcot Cl. RH11: Craw ... 6K 181
Allden Av. GU12: Alde ... 5B 110
Allden Cotts. GU7: Goda ... 7E 132
(off Aaron's Hill)
Allden Gdns. GU12: Alde ... 5B 110
Alldens Hill GU5: Braml ... 1N 153
GU8: Bus ... 1N 153
Alldens La. GU8: Bus ... 9L 133
Allder Way CR2: S Croy ... 4M 63
Allenby Av. CR2: S Croy ... 5N 63
Allenby Rd. GU15: Camb ... 9M 49
TN16: B Hil ... 4G 86
Allen Cl. CR4: Mit ... 9F 28
TW16: Sunb ... 9J 23
Allendale Cl. GU47: Sandh ... 5F 48
Allenford Ho. SW15 ... 9E 12
(off Tunworth Cres.)
Allen Ho. Pk. GU22: Wok ... 7M 73
Allen Rd. BR3: Beck ... 1G 46
CR0: Croy ... 7L 45
KT23: Book ... 4B 98
TW16: Sunb ... 9J 23
Allen's Cl. RH19: Ash W ... 3F 186
Allenswood SW19 ... 2K 27
Allen Way SL3: Dat ... 4M 5
Allestree Rd. SW6 ... 3K 13
Alleyn Pk. UB2: S'hall ... 1A 10
Allfarthing La. SW18 ... 9N 13
Allgood Cl. SM4: Mord ... 5J 43
Alliance Cl. TW4: Houn ... 8N 9
Alliance Ct. TW15: A'ford ... 5D 22
Allingham Ct. GU7: Goda ... 4J 133
Allingham Gdns.
RH12: Hors ... 3A 198
Allingham Rd. RH2: Reig ... 6M 121
Allington Av. TW17: Shep ... 2F 38
Allington Cl. SW19 ... 6J 27
Allington Ct. CR0: Croy ... 5F 46
(off Chart Cl.)
Allkins Ct. SL4: W'sor ... 5G 5
Alloway Cl. GU21: Wok ... 5L 73
All Saints Cl. RG40: W'ham ... 1B 30
All Saint's Ct. TW5: Hest ... 4L 9
(off Springwell Rd.)
All Saints Cres. GU14: Cove ... 6K 69
All Saints Dr. CR2: Sande ... 8C 64
All Saints Pas. SW18 ... 8M 13
All Saints Ri. RG42: Warf ... 8B 16
All Saints Rd. GU18: Ligh ... 6N 51
SM1: Sut ... 9N 43
SW19 ... 8A 28
(not continuous)
Allsmoor La. RG12: Brac ... 2D 32
All Souls Rd. SL5: Asc ... 3L 33
Allum Gro. KT20: Tad ... 8G 81
Allyington Way RH10: Wor ... 4H 183
Allyn Cl. TW18: Stain ... 7H 21
Alma Cl. GU12: Alde ... 2B 110
GU21: Knap ... 4H 73
Alma Cotts. GU14: Farnb ... 5A 90
Alma Ct. CR3: Cate ... 8N 83
(off Coulsdon Rd.)
Alma Cres. SM1: Sut ... 2K 61
Alma Gdns. GU16: Deep ... 6H 71
Alma Ho. TW8: Brent ... 2L 11
Alma La.
GU9: H End, U Hal ... 5G 109
Alma Pl. CR7: T Hea ... 4L 45
Alma Rd. GU35: H Dwn ... 4H 169
KT10: Esh ... 7E 40
RH2: Reig ... 2N 121
SL4: E Wic ... 1C 4
SL4: W'sor ... 5F 4
SM5: Cars ... 2C 62
SW18 ... 7N 13
Alma Sq. GU14: Farnb ... 5A 90
Alma Ter. SW18 ... 1B 28
Alma Way GU9: H End ... 5J 109
Almer Rd. SW20 ... 8F 26
Almners Rd. KT16: Lyne ... 7C 36
(not continuous)
Almond Av. GU22: Wok ... 8N 73
SM5: Cars ... 8D 44
Almond Cl. GU1: Guil ... 9N 93
GU14: Farnb ... 7M 69
RH11: Craw ... 4M 181
SL4: W'sor ... 5E 4
TW13: Felt ... 2H 23
TW17: Shep ... 1D 38
TW20: Eng G ... 7L 19
Almond Ct. GU52: C Cro ... 7C 88
Almond Gro. TW8: Brent ... 3H 11
Almond Rd. KT19: Eps ... 7C 60
Almond Way CR4: Mit ... 4H 45
Almorah Rd. TW5: Hest ... 4L 9
Almsgate GU3: Comp ... 1F 132
Alms Heath GU23: Ockh ... 8C 76
Almshouse La. KT9: Ches ... 5J 59
Almshouses GU10: Wrec ... 4E 128
(off Riverdale)
KT16: Chert ... 6J 37
RH4: Dork ... 1L 201 (4H 119)
Alnwick Gro. SM4: Mord ... 3N 43
Aloes, The GU51: Fleet ... 5C 88
Alphabet Gdns. SM5: Cars ... 5B 44
Alpha Ct. CR3: Whyte ... 5D 84
Alpha Ho. RG45: Crow ... 2H 49
Alpha Pl. SM4: Mord ... 7J 43
Alpha Rd.
CR0: Croy ... 1F 200 (7B 46)
GU12: Alde ... 3B 110
GU22: Wok ... 3D 74
GU24: Chob ... 6J 53
KT5: Surb ... 5M 41
RH11: Craw ... 3A 182
TW11: Tedd ... 6D 24
Alpha Way TW20: Thor ... 9E 20
Alphea Cl. SW19 ... 8C 28
Alphington Av. GU16: Frim ... 5C 70
Alphington Grn.
GU16: Frim ... 5C 70
Alpine Av. KT5: Surb ... 8B 42
Alpine Cl.
CR0: Croy ... 5F 200 (9B 46)
GU14: Cove ... 2J 89
SL5: S'hill ... 5A 34
Alpine Rd. KT12: Wal T ... 6H 39
RH1: Red ... 9E 102
Alpine Ski Cen. ... 9A 90
Alpine Vw. SM5: Cars ... 2C 62
Alpine Walks RH11: Craw ... 4A 182
Alresford Rd. GU2: Guil ... 4K 113
Alric Av. KT3: N Mal ... 2D 42
Alsace Wlk. GU15: Camb ... 5N 69
Alsford Cl. GU18: Ligh ... 8K 51
Alsom Av. KT4: W Pk ... 1F 60
Alston Cl. KT7: T Dit ... 6H 41
Alston Rd. SW17 ... 5B 28
Altamont CR6: Warl ... 6E 84
Alterton Cl. GU21: Wok ... 4K 73
Alt Gro. SW19 ... 8L 27
Althea St. SW6 ... 5N 13
Althorne Rd. RH1: Red ... 5E 122
Althorp Rd. SW17 ... 2D 28
Alton Cl. TW7: Isle ... 5F 10
Alton Ct. TW18: Stain ... 9G 21
Alton Gdns. TW2: Whitt ... 1D 24
Alton Ho. RH1: Red ... 1E 122
Alton Ride GU17: B'water ... 9H 49
Alton Rd. CR0: Wad ... 9L 45
GU10: Farnh ... 5B 128
GU51: Fleet ... 4D 88
SW15 ... 2F 26
TW9: Rich ... 7L 11
Altyre Cl. BR3: Beck ... 4J 47
Altyre Rd.
CR0: Croy ... 3E 200 (8A 46)
Altyre Way BR3: Beck ... 4J 47
Alvernia Cl. GU7: Goda ... 9F 132
Alverstoke Gdns.
GU11: Alde ... 3K 109
Alverstone Av. SW19 ... 3M 27
Alverstone Rd. KT3: N Mal ... 3E 42
Alverston Gdns. SE25 ... 4B 46
Alvia Gdns. SM1: Sut ... 1A 62
Alway Av. KT19: Ewe ... 2C 60
Alwin Pl. GU9: U Hal ... 5G 109
Alwyn Av. W4 ... 1C 12
Alwyn Cl. CR0: N Add ... 4L 65
Alwyne Ct. GU21: Wok ... 3A 74
Alwyne Rd. SW19 ... 7L 27
Alwyns Cl. KT16: Chert ... 5J 37
Alwyns La. KT16: Chert ... 5H 37
Amalgamated Dr.
TW8: Brent ... 2H 11
Amanda Ct. TW15: A'ford ... 3A 22
(off Edward Way)
Ambarrow Cres.
GU47: Sandh ... 6E 48
Ambarrow Farm Courtyard
GU47: Sandh ... 5D 48
Ambarrow La. GU47: Sandh ... 5C 48
Ambassador RG12: Brac ... 4L 31
Ambassador, The
SL5: S'dale ... 6E 34
Ambassador Cl. TW3: Houn ... 5M 9
Ambassadors, The
Woking ... 4A 74
Amber Ct.
CR0: Croy ... 1F 200 (7B 46)
GU12: Alde ... 2A 110
KT5: Surb ... 6M 41
TW18: Stain ... 6H 21
(off Laleham Rd.)
Ambercroft Way CR5: Coul ... 6M 83
Amber Hill GU15: Camb ... 2F 70
Amberley Cl. GU23: Send ... 3H 95
RH10: Craw ... 3G 183
RH12: Hors ... 2N 197
Amberley Ct. RH11: Craw ... 7B 162
(off County Oak La.)
Amberley Dr. KT15: Wood ... 6H 55
Amberley Flds. Cvn. Club Site
RH11: L Hea ... 6N 161
Amberley Gdns. KT19: Ewe ... 1E 60
Amberley Grange
GU11: Alde ... 4L 109
Amberley Gro. CR0: Croy ... 6C 46
Amberley La. GU8: Mil ... 1B 152
Amberley Pl. SL4: W'sor ... 4G 4
(off Peascod St.)
Amberley Rd. GU8: Mil ... 9B 132
RH12: Hors ... 2N 197
Amberley Way SM4: Mord ... 6L 43
TW4: Houn ... 8K 9
Amberside Cl. TW7: Isle ... 9D 10
Amberwood Cl. SM6: W'ton ... 2J 63
Amberwood Dr.
GU15: Camb ... 8D 50
Amberwood Ri. KT3: N Mal ... 5D 42
Amblecote KT11: Cob ... 7M 57
Ambleside GU7: Goda ... 6K 133
RG45: Crow ... 3H 49
SW19 ... 2K 27
Ambleside Av. BR3: Beck ... 4H 47
KT12: Wal T ... 7K 39
SW16 ... 5H 29
Ambleside Cl. GU14: Cove ... 1K 89
GU16: Mytc ... 3E 90
RH1: Red ... 8F 122
RH11: Ifi ... 4J 181

Ambleside Cres.
GU9: U Hal 6F 108
Ambleside Dr. TW14: Felt 2G 22
Ambleside Gdns. CR2: Sels . . .5G 64
SM2: Sut 3A 62
SW16 . . . . .6H 29
Ambleside Rd. GU18: Ligh 7K 51
Ambleside Way TW20: Egh . . .8D 20
Ambrey Way SM6: W'ton 5H 63
Ambrose Cl. BR6: Orp 1N 67
Amelia Ho. TW9: Kew 3A 12
W6 . . . . .1H 13
(off Queen Caroline St.)
AMEN CORNER 2J 31
Amen Cnr. SW17 . . . . .7D 28
Amen Cnr. Bus. Pk.
RG12: Brac 2J 31
Amenity Way SM4: Mord 6H 43
American International
University of London, The
. . . . .9L 11
(in Richmond University)
Amerland Rd. SW18 . . . . .8L 13
Amersham Rd. CR0: Croy 5N 45
Amesbury Av. SW2 . . . . .3J 29
Amesbury Cl. KT4: W Pk 7H 43
Amesbury Rd. TW13: Felt 3L 23
Amethyst Ct. BR6: Chels 2N 67
(off Farnborough Hill)
Amey Dr. KT23: Book 2C 98
AMF Bowling
Purley 9K 63
Amhurst Gdns. TW7: Isle 5G 10
Amida Leisure Cen. 4J 47
Amis Av. KT15: N Haw 6J 55
KT19: Ewe 3A 60
Amis Rd. GU21: Wok 6H 73
Amity Gro. SW20 . . . . .9G 27
Amity Way GU15: Camb 1C 70
Amlets La. GU6: Cranl 5M 155
Amorosa Cl. RH11: Ifi 9M 161
Ampere Way CR0: Wad 6J 45
Ampere Way Stop (CT) 7K 45
Amstel Way GU21: Wok 5J 73
Amundsen Rd.
RH12: Hors 2K 197
Amyand Cotts. TW1: Twick 9H 11
Amyand La. TW1: Twick 1H 25
Amyand Pk. Gdns.
TW1: Twick 1H 25
Amyand Pk. Rd.
TW1: Twick 1G 25
Amy Cl. SM6: W'ton 4J 63
Amy Rd. RH8: Oxt 7A 106
Anarth Ct. KT13: Weybr 7F 38
Ancaster Cres. KT3: N Mal 5F 42
Ancaster Dr. SL5: Asc 9J 17
Ancaster M. BR3: Beck 2G 47
Ancaster Rd. BR3: Beck 2G 46
Ancells Bus. Pk.
GU51: Fleet 9D 68
Ancells Farm Nature Reserve
. . . . .2C 88
Ancells Rd. GU51: Fleet 9C 68
Anchor SW18 . . . . .7N 13
Anchorage Cl. SW19 . . . . .6M 27
Anchor Bus. Cen.
CR0: Bedd 9J 45
Anchor Cl. GU3: Norm 9N 91
Anchor Cotts. RH7: Blin H 3H 145
Anchor Ct. RH12: Hors 7J 197
Anchor Cres. GU21: Knap 4G 72
Anchor Hill GU21: Knap 4G 72
Anchor Mdw. GU14: Cove 1L 89
Ancill Cl. W6 . . . . .2K 13
Andermans SL4: W'sor 4A 4
Anders Cnr. RG42: Brac 9L 15
Anderson Cl. GU2: Guil 8L 93
KT19: Eps 8A 60
SM3: Sut 7M 43
Anderson Ct. RH1: Red 6E 122
Anderson Dr. TW15: A'ford 5D 22
Anderson Hgts. SW16 . . . . . . .1K 45
Anderson Ho. SW17 . . . . .6B 28
Anderson Pl. GU19: Bag 3J 51
TW3: Houn 7B 10
Anderson Rd. KT13: Weybr 9E 38
RH10: Craw 7C 182
Andover Cl. KT19: Eps 7C 60
TW14: Felt 2G 23
Andover Ct. TW19: Stan 1M 21
Andover Rd. GU17: B'water 9H 49
TW2: Twick 2D 24
Andover Way GU11: Alde 5N 109
Andreck Ct. BR3: Beck 1M 47
(off Crescent Rd.)
Andrewartha Rd.
GU14: Farnb 3C 90
Andrew Cl. RG40: W'ham 3D 30
Andrewes Ho. SM1: Sut 1M 61
Andrew Reed Ho.
SW18 . . . . .1K 27
(off Linstead Way)
Andrews Cl. GU52: C Cro 7B 88
KT4: W Pk 8J 43
KT17: Eps 8M 201 (1E 80)
Andrew's Ho. CR2: S Croy 3N 63
Andrews Rd. GU14: Cove 9K 69
Andromeda Cl.
RH11: Craw 5K 181
ANERLEY 1E 46
Anerley Pk. SE20 . . . . .1E 46
Anfield Cl. SW12 . . . . .1G 28

Angas Ct. KT13: Weybr 2D 56
Angel Cl. TW12: H Hill 6C 24
Angel Ct. GU3: Comp 9D 112
GU7: Goda 7G 133
Angelfield TW3: Houn 7B 10
Angel Ga.
GU1: Guil 5C 202 (4N 113)
Angel Hill SM1: Sut 9N 43
(not continuous)
Angel Hill Dr. SM1: Sut 9N 43
Angelica Gdns. CR0: Croy 7G 46
Angelica Rd. GU2: Guil 8K 93
GU24: Bis 2D 72
Angell Ct. RH10: Craw 4G 182
Angel M. SW15 . . . . .1F 26
Angelo M. SW16 . . . . .2K 45
Angelo's SL4: Eton 1G 4
(off Common La.)
Angel Pl. RG42: Bin 7H 15
RH2: Reig 6N 121
Angel Rd. KT7: T Dit 6G 41
Angel Wlk. W6 . . . . .1H 13
Angers Cl. GU15: Camb 8G 50
Anglers, The KT1: K Tham 5H 203
Anglers Cl. TW10: Ham 5J 25
Anglers Reach
KT6: Surb 8G 203 (4K 41)
Anglesea Ho.
KT1: K Tham 8H 203
Anglesea Rd.
KT1: K Tham 8H 203 (3K 41)
Anglesey Av. GU14: Cove 7L 69
Anglesey Cl. RH11: Craw 6A 182
TW15: A'ford 4B 22
Anglesey Ct. Rd. SM5: Cars . . .3E 62
Anglesey Gdns. SM5: Cars 3E 62
Anglesey Rd. GU12: Alde 3B 110
Angles Rd. SW16 . . . . .5J 29
Anglo Way RH1: Red 1F 122
Angora Way GU51: Fleet 1C 88
Angus Cl. KT9: Ches 2N 59
RH12: Hors 4K 197
Angus Ho. SW2 . . . . .1H 29
Ankerwycke Priory 3A 20
Anlaby Rd. TW11: Tedd 6E 24
Annadale Ct. RH1: Red 2D 122
(off Warwick Rd.)
Annaleigh Pl. KT12: Hers 1L 57
Annandale Dr.
GU10: L Bou 5J 129
Annandale Rd. CR0: Croy 8D 46
GU2: Guil 5L 113
W4 . . . . .1D 12
Annan Dr. SM5: Cars 5E 62
Anne Armstrong Cl.
GU11: Alde 8B 90
Anne Boleyn's Wlk.
KT2: K Tham 6L 25
SM3: Chea 4J 61
Anne Case M. KT3: N Mal 2C 42
Anneforde Pl. RG42: Brac 8M 15
Anners Cl. TW20: Thor 2E 36
Annesley Dr. CR0: Croy 9J 47
Anne's Wlk. CR3: Cate 7B 84
Annes Way GU52: C Cro 7C 88
Annett Cl. TW17: Shep 3F 38
Annett Rd. KT12: Wal T 6H 39
Anne Way KT8: W Mole 3B 40
Ann Gream Ho.
RH19: E Grin 8A 166
Annie Brookes Cl.
TW18: Stain 4F 20
ANNINGSLEY PARK 6E 54
Anningsley Pk. KT16: Otter 6D 54
Annisdowne Cl.
RH5: A Ham 2G 137
Annsworthy Av. CR7: T Hea 2A 46
Annsworthy Cres.
SE25 . . . . .1A 46
Ansell Gro. SM5: Cars 7E 44
Ansell Rd. GU16: Frim 6C 70
RH4: Dork 1K 201 (4H 119)
SW17 . . . . .4C 28
Anselm Cl. CR0: Croy 9C 46
Anselm Rd. SW6 . . . . .2M 13
Ansley Cl. CR2: Sande 1E 84
Anson Cl. GU11: Alde 1L 109
Anstead GU8: Chid 6F 172
ANSTEADBROOK 3N 189
Anstice Cl. W4 . . . . .3D 12
Anstiebury Cl. RH5: B Grn 8J 139
Anstie Grange Dr.
RH5: Holm 6G 139
Anstie La. RH5: Cold 6E 138
Anston Ct. GU2: Guil 3H 113
Antelope Wlk. KT6: Surb 4K 41
Anthony Ho. CR5: Coul 9H 83
Anthony Pl. GU26: Hind 7D 170
Anthony Rd. SE25 . . . . .5D 46
ANTHONYS 8C 54
Anthony Wall RG42: Warf 9D 16
Anthony W. Ho.
RH3: Brock 5A 120
Antlands La. RH6: S Bri 4J 163
Antlands La. E. RH6: S Bri . . .4K 163
Antlands La. W. RH6: S Bri . . .4J 163
Anton Cres. SM1: Sut 9M 43
Antrobus Cl. SM1: Sut 1L 61
Anvil Cl. SW16 . . . . .8G 28
Anvil La. KT11: Cob 1H 77
Anvil Rd. TW16: Sunb 2H 39
Anyards Rd. KT11: Cob 9J 57
Anzio Cl. GU11: Alde 2M 109

Anzio Gdns. CR3: Cate 8N 83
Apeldoorn Dr. SM6: W'ton 5J 63
Aperdele Rd. KT22: Leat 5G 79
APERFIELD 4G 87
Aperfield Rd. TN16: B Hil 4G 87
Aperfields TN16: B Hil 4G 86
Apers Av. GU22: Wok 8B 74
APEX CORNER 4N 23
Apex Ct. KT14: W By 8K 55
Apex Dr. GU16: Frim 5B 70
Apex Retail Pk.
TW13: Hanw 4N 23
Apley Rd. RH2: Reig 6M 121
Aplin Way GU18: Ligh 7L 51
TW7: Isle 4E 10
Apollo Dr. GU35: Bor 7A 168
Apollo Pl. GU21: Wok 6K 73
Apollo Ri. GU14: Cove 1H 89
Apostle Way CR7: T Hea 1M 45
Apperlie Dr. RH6: Horl 1G 162
Appleby Cl. TW2: Twick 3D 24
Appleby Gdns. TW14: Felt 2G 22
Appleby Ho. KT19: Eps 7C 60
Appledore RG12: Brac 5L 31
Appledore Cl. SW17 . . . . .3D 28
Appledore M. GU14: Farnb 7M 69
Appledown Ri. CR5: Coul 2G 83
Applefield RH10: Craw 2C 182
Apple Gth. TW8: Brent 1K 11
Applegarth CR0: N Add 4L 65
(not continuous)
GU7: Goda 4G 132
KT10: Clay 2F 58
Applegarth Av. GU2: Guil 3G 112
Apple Gro. KT9: Ches 1L 59
Applelands Cl. GU10: Wrec . . .7F 128
Apple Mkt. KT1: K Tham 4H 203
Appleton Gdns. KT3: N Mal 5F 42
Appleton Sq. CR4: Mit 9C 28
Apple Tree Cl. KT22: Fetc 2C 98
Appletree Cl. GU7: Bus 9J 133
Appletree Ct. GU4: Guil 9F 94
Appletree Pl. RG42: Brac 9M 15
Apple Trees Pl. GU22: Wok 6M 73
Appletree Way GU47: Owls 6J 49
Appley Ct. GU15: Camb 1N 69
Appley Dr. GU15: Camb 9N 49
Approach, The KT23: Book 1M 97
RH19: D Pk 4B 166
Approach Rd. CR8: Pur 8L 63
GU9: Farnh 2H 129
KT8: W Mole 4A 40
SW20 . . . . .1H 43
TN16: Tats 1D 106
TW15: A'ford 7D 22
April Cl. BR6: Chels 2N 67
GU15: Camb 4A 70
KT21: A'tead 5M 79
RH12: Hors 4J 197
TW13: Felt 4H 23
Aprilwood Cl. KT15: Wood 7H 55
Apsey Ct. RG42: Bin 8K 15
Apsley Ct. RH11: Craw 5L 181
Apsley Ho. TW4: Houn 7N 9
Apsley Rd. KT3: N Mal 2B 42
SE25 . . . . .3E 46
Aquarius TW1: Twick 2H 25
Aquarius Ct. RH11: Craw 5K 181
Aquila Cl. KT22: Leat 8L 79
Arabella Dr. SW15 . . . . .7D 12
Aragon Av. KT7: T Dit 4F 40
KT17: Ewe 6G 60
Aragon Cl. CR0: N Add 6A 66
TW16: Sunb 7G 22
Aragon Ct. GU21: Knap 4G 72
KT8: E Mol 3C 40
RG12: Brac 3A 32
Aragon Pl. SM4: Mord 6K 43
Aragon Rd. GU46: Yate 2B 68
KT2: K Tham 6L 25
SM4: Mord 5J 43
Aragon Wlk. KT14: Byf 9A 56
Aragorn Ct. GU2: Guil 1L 113
Aram Ct. GU22: Wok 2E 74
Aran Ct. KT13: Weybr 8E 38
Arbor Cl. BR3: Beck 1L 47
Arborfield Cl. SW2 . . . . .2K 29
Arbour, The GU7: Hurt 2C 132
Arbour Cl. KT22: Fetc 1F 98
Arbrook Chase KT10: Esh 3C 58
Arbrook Hall KT10: Clay 3F 58
Arbrook La. KT10: Esh 3C 58
Arbutus Cl. RH1: Red 5A 122
Arbutus Rd. RH1: Red 6A 122
Arcade CR0: Croy 3C 200 (8N 45)
Arcade, The CR0: Croy 4C 200
GU11: Alde 2M 109
RG40: W'ham 2B 30
Arcade Pde. KT9: Ches 2K 59
Arcadia Cl. SM5: Cars 1E 62
Arcadian Pl. SW18 . . . . .1L 27
Archbishop Lanfranc School
Sports Cen. 5J 45
Archbishop's Pl. SW2 . . . . . . .1K 29
Archdale Pl. KT3: N Mal 2A 42
Archel Rd. W14 . . . . .2L 13
Archer Cl. KT2: K Tham 8L 25
Archer M. TW12: H Hill 7C 24
Archer Rd. SE25 . . . . .3E 46
Archers Ct. CR2: S Croy 8B 200
RH1: Red 4D 122
(off Brighton Rd.)
RH10: Craw 1B 182

Archery Pl. GU5: Gorn 8D 116
Arches, The SL4: W'sor 4F 4
(off Goswell Rd.)
Arch Rd. KT12: Hers 9L 39
Archway Cl. SM6: Bedd 9H 45
SW19 . . . . .4N 27
Archway M.
RH4: Dork 1J 201 (4G 119)
SW15 . . . . .7K 13
(off Putney Bri. Rd.)
Archway Pl.
RH4: Dork 1J 201 (4G 119)
Archway St. SW13 . . . . .6D 12
Archway Theatre 9F 142
Arctic Jungle Play Cen. 4C 182
Arcturus Rd. RH11: Craw 6K 181
Arden Cl. RG12: Brac 1D 32
RH2: Reig 7N 121
Arden Gro. BR6: Farnb 1K 67
Arden Rd. RH10: Craw 5D 182
ARDENRUN 3K 145
Ardent Cl. SE25 . . . . .2B 46
Ardesley Wood
KT13: Weybr 1F 56
Ardfern Av. SW16 . . . . .2L 45
Ardingly RG12: Brac 5M 31
Ardingly Cl. CR0: Croy 9G 47
RH11: Craw 1N 181
Ardingly Ct.
KT18: Eps 8J 201 (1C 80)
Ardingly Rd. RH19: W Hoa . . .9E 184
Ardleigh Gdns. SM3: Sut 6M 43
Ardlui Rd. SE27 . . . . .3N 29
Ardmay Gdns.
KT6: Surb 8K 203 (4L 41)
Ardmore Av. GU2: Guil 1L 113
Ardmore Ho. GU2: Guil 1L 113
Ardmore Way GU2: Guil 1L 113
Ardrossan Av. GU15: Camb 2E 70
Ardrossan Gdns. KT4: W Pk 9F 42
Ardshiel Cl. SW15 . . . . .6J 13
Ardshiel Dr. RH1: Red 5C 122
Ardwell Cl. RG45: Crow 2D 48
Ardwell Rd. SW2 . . . . .3J 29
Ardwick Ct. GU14: Farnb 3A 90
(off Sycamore Rd.)
Arena La. GU11: Alde 9J 89
Arenal Dr. RG45: Crow 4G 49
Arena Leisure Cen. 9A 50
Arena Stop (CT) 4F 46
Arethusa Way GU24: Bis 3C 72
ARFORD 3E 168
Arford Comn. GU35: Head . . .3E 168
Arford Rd. GU35: Head 4E 168
Argent Cl. TW20: Egh 7E 20
Argent Ct. KT6: Ches 9N 41
Argente Cl. GU51: Fleet 1C 88
Argent Ter. GU47: C Tow 7K 49
Argonaut Pk. SL3: Poy 4H 7
Argon M. SW6 . . . . .3M 13
Argosy Gdns. TW18: Stain 7H 21
Argosy La. TW19: Stan 1M 21
Argus Wlk. RH11: Craw 6M 181
Argyle Av. TW3: Houn 9A 10
(not continuous)
Argyle Pl. W6 . . . . .1G 13
Argyle Rd. TW3: Houn 8B 10
Argyle St. GU24: B'wood 8L 71
Argyll Ct. GU51: Fleet 4B 88
Ariel Way TW4: Houn 6J 9
Arista Ct. TW20: Eng G 6N 19
Ark, The W6 . . . . .1J 13
(off Talgarth Rd.)
Arkell Gro. SE19 . . . . .8M 29
Arkendale RH19: Fel 6K 165
Arklow M. KT6: Surb 8L 41
Arkwright Dr. RG42: Brac 1J 31
Arkwright Ho. SW2 . . . . .1J 29
(off Streatham Pl.)
Arkwright Rd. CR2: Sande 6C 64
SL3: Poy 5G 6
Arlesey Cl. SW15 . . . . .8K 13
Arlington Bus. Pk.
RG12: Brac 1M 31
Arlington Cl. RG42: Brac 9M 15
SM1: Sut 8M 43
TW1: Twick 9J 11
Arlington Ct. RH2: Reig 1N 121
UB3: Harl 1F 8
Arlington Dr. SM5: Cars 8D 44
Arlington Gdns. W4 . . . . .1B 12
Arlington Ho. TW9: Kew 3A 12
Arlington Lodge
KT13: Weybr 1C 56
Arlington Pk. Mans.
W4 . . . . .1B 12
(off Sutton La. Nth.)
Arlington Pas. TW11: Tedd 5F 24
Arlington Rd. KT6: Surb 5K 41
TW1: Twick 9J 11
TW10: Ham 3K 25
TW11: Tedd 5F 24
TW15: A'ford 6A 22
Arlington Sq. RG12: Brac 1M 31
Arlington Ter. GU11: Alde 2L 109
Armadale Rd. GU21: Wok 4K 73
SW6 . . . . .3M 13
TW14: Felt 8H 9
Armfield Cl. KT8: W Mole 4N 39
Armfield Cres. CR4: Mit 1D 44
Armistice Gdns. SE25 . . . . . . .2D 46
Armitage Ct. SL5: S'hill 5N 33
Armitage Dr. GU16: Frim 5D 70

Armoury La. RG45: Crow 4F 48
Armoury Way SW18 . . . . .8M 13
Armstrong Cl. KT12: Wal T 5H 39
Armstrong Mall GU14: Cove 1J 89
Armstrong Rd.
TW13: Hanw 6M 23
TW20: Eng G 7M 19
Armstrong Way
GU14: Farnb 4G 88
Army Physical Training Corps Mus.
. . . . .8N 89
Armytage Rd. TW5: Hest 3L 9
Arnal Cres. SW18 . . . . .1K 27
Arncliffe RG12: Brac 4M 31
Arndale Wlk. SW18 . . . . .8N 13
Arndale Way TW20: Egh 6C 20
Arne Cl. RH11: Craw 6L 181
Arne Gro. RH6: Horl 6C 142
Arnewood Cl. KT22: Oxs 1B 78
SW15 . . . . .2F 26
Arneys La. CR4: Mit 5E 44
Arnfield Cl. RH11: Ifi 4K 181
Arnhem Cl. GU11: Alde 2N 109
Arnhem Dr. CR0: N Add 7N 65
Arnison Rd. KT8: E Mol 3D 40
Arnold Cres. TW7: Isle 8D 10
Arnold Dr. KT9: Ches 3K 59
Arnold Mans. W14 . . . . .2L 13
(off Queen's Club Gdns.)
Arnold Rd. GU21: Wok 2D 74
SW17 . . . . .8D 28
TW18: Stain 8L 21
Arnott Cl. W4 . . . . .1C 12
Arnulls Rd. SW16 . . . . .7M 29
Arosa Rd. TW1: Twick 9K 11
(not continuous)
Arragon Gdns. BR4: W Wick . . .9L 47
SW16 . . . . .8J 29
Arragon Rd. SW18 . . . . .2M 27
TW1: Twick 1G 24
Arran Cl. RH11: Craw 6N 181
SM6: W'ton 1F 62
Arrancourt RH12: Hors 6G 197
Arran Way KT10: Esh 8B 40
Arras Av. SM4: Mord 4A 44
Arreton Mead GU21: Wok 1B 74
Arrivals Rd. RH6: Gat 2D 162
(not continuous)
Arrol Rd. BR3: Beck 2F 46
Arrow Ind. Est. GU14: Farnb . . .3L 89
Arrow Rd. GU14: Cove 3L 89
Artel Cft. RH10: Craw 3E 182
Artemis Pl. SW18 . . . . .1L 27
Arterberry Rd. SW20 . . . . .8H 27
Arthur Cl. GU9: Farnh 2G 129
GU19: Bag 6J 51
Arthur Ct. CR0: Croy 4F 200
Arthur Henderson Ho.
SW6 . . . . .5L 13
(off Fulham Rd.)
Arthur Rd. GU9: Farnh 2G 129
(not continuous)
KT2: K Tham 8N 25
KT3: N Mal 4G 43
RH11: Ifi 3K 181
RH13: Hors 7K 197
SL4: W'sor 4F 4
SW19 . . . . .6L 27
TN16: B Hil 2E 86
Arthur's Bri. Rd.
GU21: Wok 4M 73
Arthur's Bri. Wharf
GU21: Wok 4N 73
Arthurstone Birches
RG42: Bin 6J 15
Arthur St. GU11: Alde 2N 109
Artillery Rd.
GU1: Guil 4C 202 (4N 113)
GU11: Alde 2N 109
(High St.)
GU11: Alde 6B 90
(North Rd.)
Artillery Ter.
GU1: Guil 3C 202 (3N 113)
ARTINGTON 8M 113
Artington Cl. BR6: Farnb 1L 67
Artington Wlk.
GU2: Guil 8B 202 (6M 113)
Arun Ct. SE25 . . . . .4D 46
Arundale KT1: K Tham 8H 203
Arundel Av. CR2: Sande 6D 64
KT17: Ewe 6G 60
SM4: Mord 3L 43
Arundel Cl. CR0: Wad 9M 45
GU30: Pass 9C 168
GU51: Fleet 5C 88
RH10: Craw 3G 182
TW12: H Hill 6B 24
Arundel Ct. BR2: Brom 1N 47
SW13 . . . . .2G 13
(off Arundel Ter.)
Arundel Ho. CR0: Croy 8D 200
Arundel Mans. SW6 . . . . .4L 13
(off Kelvedon Rd.)
Arundel Pl. GU9: Farnh 1G 128
Arundel Rd. CR0: Croy 5A 46
GU15: Camb 2G 70
KT1: K Tham 1A 42
RH4: Dork 3H 201 (5G 118)
SM2: Chea, Sut 4L 61
TW4: Houn 6K 9
Arundel Ter. SW13 . . . . .2G 13
Arundle Ho. GU1: Guil 4D 202

Arun Ho.—Avenue, The

Arun Ho.
KT2: K Tham 1H **203** (9K **25**)
Arunside RH12: Hors 7G **196**
Arun Way RH13: Hors 7L **197**
Ascent Ho. *KT13: Weybr 2F 56*
(off Ellesmere Rd.)
Aschurch Rd. CR0: Croy 6C **46**
ASCOT 3L **33**
Ascot Ct. GU11: Alde 3M **109**
ASCOT HEATH 1K **33**
Ascot M. SM6: W'ton 5G **63**
Ascot Pk. SL5: Asc 2H **33**
Ascot Racecourse 1K **33**
Ascot Rd. RG42: Warf 1B **16**
SW17 . . . . .7E **28**
TW14: Bedf 2B **22**
Ascot Station (Rail) 3L **33**
Ascot Towers SL5: Asc 1K **33**
ASH 2E **110**
Ashbourne RG12: Brac 5L **31**
Ashbourne Cl. CR5: Coul 5G **83**
GU12: Ash 1G **110**
Ashbourne Ct. GU12: Ash 1G **110**
Ashbourne Gro. W4 . . . . .1D **12**
Ashbourne Ri. BR6: Orp 1N **67**
Ashbourne Rd. CR4: Mit 8E **28**
Ashbourne Ter. SW19 . . . . .8L **27**
Ash Bri. Cvn. Pk.
GU12: Ash 4C **110**
Ashbrook Rd. SL4: O Win 1L **19**
Ashburnham Ct. BR3: Beck . . .1M **47**
Ashburnham Pk. KT10: Esh . . .1C **58**
Ashburnham Rd.
RH10: Craw 5E **182**
TW10: Ham 4H **25**
Ashburton Av. CR0: Croy 7E **46**
Ashburton Cl. CR0: Croy 7D **46**
Ashburton Ent. Cen.
SW15 . . . . .9H **13**
Ashburton Gdns. CR0: Croy . . .8D **46**
Ashburton Memorial Homes
CR0: Croy 6E **46**
Ashburton Rd. CR0: Croy 8D **46**
Ashbury Cres. GU4: Guil 1E **114**
Ashbury Dr. GU17: Haw 5M **69**
Ashbury Pl. SW19 . . . . .7A **28**
Ashby Av. KT9: Ches 3N **59**
Ashby Ct. RH13: Hors 6L **197**
Ashby's Cl. TN8: Eden 3M **147**
Ashby Wlk. CR0: Croy 5N **45**
Ashby Way UB7: Sip 3B **8**
Ash Church M. GU12: Ash 2E **110**
Ash Church Rd. GU12: Ash . . .2F **110**
Ash Cl. GU12: Ash 1F **110**
GU17: B'water 1H **69**
GU22: Pyr 2J **75**
GU22: Wok 7A **74**
KT3: N Mal 1C **42**
KT20: Box H 9B **100**
RH1: Mers 8G **103**
RH7: Ling 6A **146**
RH10: Craw D 1F **184**
SE20 . . . . .1F **46**
SM5: Cars 8D **44**
TN8: Eden 2K **147**
Ash Combe GU8: Chid 5D **172**
Ashcombe Av. KT6: Surb 6K **41**
Ashcombe Cl. TW15: A'ford . . .4N **21**
Ashcombe Dr. TN8: Eden 8K **127**
Ashcombe Pde. *GU22: Wok 7C 74*
(off Kingfield Rd.)
Ashcombe Rd. RH1: Mers 5G **102**
RH4: Dork 3G **118**
SM5: Cars 3E **62**
SW19 . . . . .6M **27**
Ashcombe Sq. KT3: N Mal 2B **42**
Ashcombe St. SW6 . . . . .5N **13**
Ashcombe Ter. KT20: Tad 7G **80**
Ash Ct. KT15: Addl 2K **55**
KT19: Ewe 1B **60**
KT22: Leat 7F **78**
RG40: W'ham 2B **30**
RH19: E Grin 7A **166**
SW19 . . . . .8K **27**
Ashcroft GU4: Chil 1A **134**
Ashcroft Pk. KT11: Cob 8M **57**
Ashcroft Pl. KT22: Leat 8J **79**
Ashcroft Ri. CR5: Coul 3J **83**
Ashcroft Rd. KT9: Ches 9M **41**
Ashcroft Sq. W6 . . . . .1H **13**
Ashcroft Theatre 4D **200**
Ashdale KT23: Book 4C **98**
Ashdale Cl. TW2: Whitt 1C **24**
TW19: Stan 3N **21**
Ashdale Pk. RG40: Finch 1B **48**
Ashdale Way TW2: Whitt 1B **24**
Ashdene Cl. TW15: A'ford 8D **22**
Ashdene Cres. GU12: Ash 1E **110**
Ashdene Ho. TW20: Eng G 7M **19**
Ashdene Rd. GU12: Ash 1E **110**
Ashdown Av. GU14: Farnb 2B **90**
Ashdown Cl. BR3: Beck 1L **47**
GU22: Wok 5A **74**
RG12: Brac 1E **32**
RH2: Reig 7N **121**
RH18: F Row 7J **187**
Ashdown Ct. RH10: Craw 6D **182**
RH13: Hors 4M **197**
SM2: Sut 3A **62**
Ashdown Dr. RH10: Craw 6B **182**
Ashdown Gdns. CR2: Sande . . .2E **84**
Ashdown Ga.
RH19: E Grin 8N **165**
Ashdown Ho. RH6: Gat 3E **162**
Ashdown Pl. KT7: T Dit 6G **40**
KT17: Ewe 4E **60**
RH18: F Row 9G **186**
Ashdown Rd.
KT1: K Tham 4J **203** (1L **41**)
KT17: Eps 9E **60**
RH2: Reig 7N **121**
RH18: F Row 7H **187**
Ashdown Vw.
RH19: E Grin 2A **186**
Ashdown Way SW17 . . . . .3E **28**
Ash Dr. RH1: Red 5E **122**
Ashe Ho. TW1: Twick 9K **11**
Ashenden Rd. GU2: Guil 3J **113**
Ashen Gro. SW19 . . . . .4M **27**
Ashen Va. CR2: Sels 5G **65**
Asher Dr. SL5: Asc 9G **17**
Ashfield RH14: Plais 6A **192**
Ashfield Av. TW13: Felt 2J **23**
Ashfield Cl. TW10: Ham 2L **25**
Ashfield Grn. GU46: Yate 1E **68**
Ashfield Ho. *W14 . . . . .1L 13*
(off W. Cromwell Rd.)
Ashfields Ct. RH2: Reig 1N **121**
ASHFORD 5A **22**
Ashford Av. TW15: A'ford 7C **22**
Ashford Bus. Complex
TW15: A'ford 6D **22**
Ashford Cl. TW15: A'ford 5N **21**
ASHFORD COMMON 8E **22**
Ashford Cres.
TW15: A'ford 4N **21**
Ashford Gdns. KT11: Cob 3L **77**
Ashford Ind. Est.
TW15: A'ford 5D **22**
ASHFORD PARK 5M **21**
Ashford Rd. TW13: Felt 5E **22**
TW15: A'ford 8D **22**
TW18: Lale, Stain 1L **37**
Ashford Sports Cen. 5M **21**
Ashford Station (Rail) 5A **22**
ASH GREEN 4G **111**
Ash Grn. La. E.
GU12: A Grn 4G **111**
Ash Grn. La. W.
GU12: Ash 4D **110**
(not continuous)
Ash Grn. Rd. GU12: A Grn . . .3G **110**
Ash Gro. BR4: W Wick 8M **47**
GU2: Guil 3K **113**
SE20 . . . . .1F **46**
TW5: Hest 4L **9**
TW14: Felt 2F **22**
TW18: Stain 7L **21**
Ashgrove Rd.
TW15: A'ford 6D **22**
Ash Hill Rd. GU12: A Va 9E **90**
Ash Ho. *TW15: A'ford 5A 22*
(off Station Rd.)
Ashington Ct. *RH12: Hors 3K 197*
(off Woodstock Cl.)
Ashington Rd. SW6 . . . . .5L **13**
Ash Keys RH10: Craw 4C **182**
Ashlake Rd. SW16 . . . . .5J **29**
Ash La. GU8: Els 9G **130**
SL4: W'sor 5A **4**
Ashlea Ct. CR6: Warl 5D **84**
Ashleigh Av. TW20: Egh 8E **20**
Ashleigh Cl. RH6: Horl 8D **142**
Ashleigh Cotts.
RH5: Holm 4H **139**
Ashleigh Gdns. SM1: Sut 8N **43**
Ashleigh Rd. RH12: Hors 3J **197**
SE20 . . . . .2E **46**
SW14 . . . . .6D **12**
Ashley Av.
KT18: Eps 7J **201** (9C **60**)
SM4: Mord 4M **43**
Ashley Cen.
KT18: Eps 7J **201** (9C **60**)
Ashley Cl. GU16: Frim G 8E **70**
KT12: Wal T 7G **38**
KT23: Book 3N **97**
Ashley Ct. GU21: Wok 5J **73**
KT18: Eps 7K **201** (9C **60**)
Ashley Dr. GU17: B'water 2H **69**
KT12: Wal T 9H **39**
SM7: Ban 1M **81**
TW2: Whitt 1B **24**
TW7: Isle 2E **10**
Ashley Gdns. BR6: Orp 2N **67**
GU4: Chil 1B **134**
TW10: Ham 3K **25**
Ashley Ho. GU7: Goda 3H **133**
Ashley La.
CR0: Wad 7A **200** (1M **63**)
ASHLEY PARK 9H **39**
Ashley Pk. Av. KT12: Wal T . . .8G **39**
Ashley Pk. Cres.
KT12: Wal T 7H **39**
Ashley Pk. Rd. KT12: Wal T . . .8H **39**
Ashley Pl. *KT12: Wal T 8H 39*
(off Ashley Rd.)
Ashley Ri. KT12: Wal T 1H **57**
Ashley Rd. CR7: T Hea 3K **45**
GU14: Farnb 1B **90**
GU21: Wok 5J **73**
KT7: T Dit 5F **40**
KT12: Wal T 1G **57**
KT18: Eps 1C **80**
KT18: Eps, Eps D
. . . . .7K **201** (9C **60**)
Ashley Rd. RH4: Westc 6C **118**
SW19 . . . . .7N **27**
TW9: Rich 6L **11**
TW12: Hamp 9A **24**
Ashley Sq. KT18: Eps 7J **201**
Ashley Way GU24: W End 9A **52**
Ashling Rd. CR0: Croy 7D **46**
Ash Lodge *TW16: Sunb 8G 22*
(off Forest Dr.)
Ash Lodge Cl. GU12: Ash 3E **110**
Ash Lodge Dr. GU12: Ash 3E **110**
(not continuous)
Ashlone Rd. SW15 . . . . .6H **13**
Ashlyns Pk. KT11: Cob 9M **57**
Ashlyns Way KT9: Ches 3K **59**
Ash Manor Sports Cen. 4D **110**
Ashmead Rd. TW14: Felt 2H **23**
Ashmere Av. BR3: Beck 1N **47**
Ashmere Cl. SM3: Chea 2J **61**
Ash M.
KT18: Eps 7L **201** (9D **60**)
Ashmore Ct. TW5: Hest 2A **10**
Ashmore Ho. RH11: Craw 9B **162**
Ashmore La. BR2: Kes 7E **66**
RH12: Rusp 3B **180**
SL4: Wink 1D **16**
Ashridge GU14: Cove 7L **69**
Ashridge Grn. RG42: Brac 9N **15**
Ashridge Rd. RG40: W'ham 9C **14**
Ashridge Way SM4: Mord 2L **43**
TW16: Sunb 7H **23**
Ash Rd. CR0: Croy 8K **47**
GU12: Alde 3A **110**
GU22: Wok 7N **73**
GU24: Pirb 4C **92**
RH10: Craw 2E **182**
SM3: Sut 6K **43**
TN16: Weste 3M **107**
TW17: Shep 3B **38**
Ash Station (Rail) 2F **110**
Ashstead La. GU7: Goda 9F **132**
Ash St. GU12: Ash 3D **110**
ASHTEAD 5M **79**
Ashtead Common National
Nature Reserve 2J **79**
Ashtead Gap KT22: Leat 3H **79**
ASHTEAD PARK 5N **79**
Ashtead Station (Rail) 4L **79**
Ashtead Woods Rd.
KT21: A'tead 4J **79**
Ashton Cl. KT12: Hers 3J **57**
SM1: Sut 1M **61**
Ashton Gdns. TW4: Houn 7N **9**
Ashton Rd. GU21: Wok 4J **73**
Ashtree Av. CR4: Mit 1B **44**
Ash Tree Cl. CR0: Croy 5H **47**
GU14: Cove 2H **89**
GU27: G'wood 8K **171**
KT6: Surb 8L **41**
Ashtree Cl. BR6: Farnb 1K **67**
Ash Tree Ct. *TW15: A'ford 6C 22*
(off Feltham Hill Rd.)
Ashtrees GU6: Cranl 9N **155**
Ash Tree Way CR0: Croy 4G **47**
Ashurst KT18: Eps . . .7J **201** (1C **80**)
Ashurst Cl. CR8: Ken 2A **84**
KT22: Leat 8G **78**
RH12: Hors 3N **197**
Ashurst Dr. KT20: Box H 8A **100**
RH10: Wor 3H **183**
TW17: Shep 4N **37**
Ashurst Gdns. SW2 . . . . .2L **29**
Ashurst Pk. SL5: S'hill 2B **34**
Ashurst Pl. RH4: Dork 4J **119**
Ashurst Rd. GU12: A Va 9D **90**
KT20: Tad 8G **81**
Ashurst Wlk. CR0: Croy 8E **46**
ASHURSTWOOD 3F **186**
ASH VALE 6E **90**
Ash Va. GU8: Chid 4D **172**
Ashvale Rd. SW17 . . . . .6D **28**
Ash Vale Station (Rail) 6E **90**
Ash Vw. Cl. TW15: A'ford 7N **21**
Ashview Gdns.
TW15: A'ford 6N **21**
Ashville Way RG41: W'ham 3A **30**
Ashway Cen., The
KT2: K Tham 2K **203** (9L **25**)
Ashwell Av. GU15: Camb 9D **50**
Ashwell Ct. TW15: A'ford 3N **21**
Ashwick Cl. CR3: Cate 2D **104**
Ashwindham Ct. GU21: Wok . . .5J **73**
Ashwood CR6: Warl 7F **84**
RH11: Craw 4B **182**
Ashwood Ct. RH18: F Row . . .8H **187**
Ashwood Gdns.
CR0: N Add 3M **65**
Ashwood Pk. GU22: Wok 5C **74**
KT22: Fetc 1C **98**
Ashwood Pl. GU22: Wok 5C **74**
SL5: S'dale 6B **34**
Ashwood Rd. GU22: Wok 5B **74**
TW20: Eng G 7L **19**
Ashworth Est. CR0: Bedd 7J **45**
Ashworth Pl. GU2: Guil 3J **113**
Askill Dr. SW15 . . . . .8K **13**
Aslett St. SW18 . . . . .1N **27**
Asmar Cl. CR5: Coul 2J **83**
Aspects SM1: Sut 2N **61**
Aspen Cl. GU4: Guil 9F **94**
KT11: Sto D 3M **77**
TW18: Stain 4H **21**
Aspen Ct. GU25: V Wat 3A **36**
Aspen Gdns. CR4: Mit 4E **44**
TW15: A'ford 6D **22**
W6 . . . . .1G **13**
Aspen Gro. GU12: Alde 4C **110**
Aspen Ho. CR6: Warl 2L **85**
Aspenlea Rd. W6 . . . . .2J **13**
Aspen Sq. KT13: Weybr 9E **38**
Aspen Va. CR3: Whyte 4C **84**
Aspen Way RH12: Hors 4L **197**
SM7: Ban 1J **81**
TW13: Felt 4J **23**
Aspin Way GU17: B'water 1G **68**
Aspley Rd. SW18 . . . . .8N **13**
Asprey Gro. CR3: Cate 2D **104**
Asprey M. BR3: Beck 4J **47**
Asquith Ho. *SM7: Ban 2L 81*
(off Dunnymans Rd.)
Assembly Wlk. SM5: Cars 6C **44**
Assher Rd. KT12: Hers 9M **39**
Astede Pl. KT21: A'tead 5M **79**
Astleham Rd. TW17: Shep 2N **37**
Astley Ho. *SW13 . . . . .2G 13*
(off Wyatt Dr.)
Astolat Bus. Pk., The
GU3: P'marsh 2M **133**
Astolat Way
GU3: P'marsh 2M **133**
Aston Cl. KT21: A'tead 5J **79**
Aston Ct. RH11: Craw 8N **181**
Aston Grange RG12: Brac 3C **32**
Aston Grn. TW4: C'ford 5K **9**
Aston Mead SL4: W'sor 4B **4**
Aston Pl. SW16 . . . . .7M **29**
Aston Rd. KT10: Clay 2E **58**
SW20 . . . . .1H **43**
Aston Ter. SW12 . . . . .1F **28**
Astonville St. SW18 . . . . .2M **27**
Aston Way KT18: Eps 2E **80**
Astor Cl. KT2: K Tham 7A **26**
KT15: Addl 1M **55**
Astor Ct. *SW6 . . . . .3N 13*
(off Maynard Cl.)
Astoria Ct. *CR8: Pur 7M 63*
(off High St.)
Astoria Mans. SW16 . . . . .4J **29**
Astra Bus. Cen. RH1: Salf 4F **142**
Astral Towers RH10: Craw . . .8B **162**
Astra Mead RG42: Wink R 7F **16**
Astrid Ho. TW13: Felt 3K **23**
Asylum Arch Rd.
RH1: Red 6D **122**
Atalanta Cl. CR8: Pur 6L **63**
Atalanta St. SW6 . . . . .3J **13**
Atbara Rd. GU52: C Cro 9B **88**
TW11: Tedd 7H **25**
Atcham Rd. TW3: Houn 7C **10**
Atfield Gro. GU20: Windl 3A **52**
Atheldene Rd. SW18 . . . . .2N **27**
Athelstan Cl. RH10: Wor 3J **183**
Athelstan Ho.
KT1: K Tham 7M **203**
Athelstan Rd.
KT1: K Tham . . .7M **203** (3M **41**)
Athelstan Way RH13: Hors . . .8L **197**
Athena Cl.
KT1: K Tham . . .5L **203** (2M **41**)
Atherfield Ho. *RH2: Reig 6A 122*
(off Atherfield Rd.)
Atherfield Rd. RH2: Reig 6A **122**
Atherley Way TW4: Houn 1N **23**
Atherton Cl. GU4: Chil 9A **114**
TW19: Stan 9M **7**
Atherton Ct. SL4: Eton 3G **4**
Atherton Dr. SW19 . . . . .5J **27**
Atherton Rd. SW13 . . . . .3F **12**
Athlone KT10: Clay 3E **58**
Athlone Rd. SW2 . . . . .1K **29**
Athlone Sq. SL4: W'sor 4F **4**
Atkins Cl. GU21: Wok 5K **73**
TN16: B Hil 8E **66**
Atkins Dr. BR4: W Wick 8N **47**
Atkinson Ct. RH6: Horl 9F **142**
Atkinson Rd. RH10: Craw 5G **182**
Atkins Rd. SW12 . . . . .1G **28**
Atlanta Ct. CR7: T Hea 2N **45**
Atlantic Ho. RH6: Gat 2E **162**
Atney Rd. SW15 . . . . .7K **13**
Atrebatti Rd. GU47: Sandh 6H **49**
Atrium, The 9A **166**
Atrium, The GU7: Goda 7H **133**
Atrium Ct. RG12: Brac 1A **32**
Atspeed Stadium 7K **197**
Attebrouche Ct. RG12: Brac . . .6B **32**
Atte La. RG42: Warf 7A **16**
Attenborough Cl.
GU51: Fleet 2C **88**
Atterbury Cl. TN16: Weste . . .4M **107**
Attfield Cl. GU12: Ash 3D **110**
Attfield Ct. KT1: K Tham 4L **203**
Attlee Cl. CR7: T Hea 4N **45**
Attlee Gdns. GU52: C Cro 9A **88**
Attlee Ho. RH11: Craw 7N **181**
Attleford La. GU8: S'ford 5K **131**
Attwood Cl. CR2: Sande 1E **84**
Atwater Cl. SW2 . . . . .2L **29**
Atwell Pl. KT7: T Dit 7F **40**
Atwood KT23: Book 2M **97**
Atwood Av. TW9: Kew 5N **11**
Atwoods All. TW9: Kew 4N **11**
Aubyn Hill SE27 . . . . .5N **29**
Aubyn Sq. SW15 . . . . .8F **12**
Auchinleck Ct.
RH10: Craw D 2E **184**
Auchinleck Way
GU11: Alde 2K **109**
Auckland Cl. RH11: Craw 9B **162**
Auckland Gdns. SE19 . . . . .1B **46**
Auckland Hill SE27 . . . . .5N **29**
Auckland Ho. KT12: Wal T 7H **39**
Auckland Rd. CR3: Cate 9B **84**
KT1: K Tham . . .7M **203** (3M **41**)
SE19 . . . . .1C **46**
Auden Pl. SM3: Chea 1H **61**
Audley Cl. KT15: Addl 2K **55**
Audley Ct. TW2: Twick 4D **24**
Audley Dr. CR6: Warl 2F **84**
Audley Firs KT12: Hers 1K **57**
Audley Ho. KT15: Addl 2K **55**
Audley Pl. SM2: Sut 4N **61**
Audley Rd. TW10: Rich 8M **11**
Audley Way SL5: Asc 2H **33**
Audrey Cl. BR3: Beck 5L **47**
Audric Cl. KT2: K Tham 9N **25**
Augur Cl. TW18: Stain 6H **21**
Augusta Cl. KT8: W Mole 2N **39**
Augusta Rd. TW2: Twick 3C **24**
Augustine Cl. SL3: Poy 6G **7**
Augustine Wlk. RG42: Warf . . .8C **16**
August La. GU5: Alb 4M **135**
Augustus Cl. TW8: Brent 3J **11**
Augustus Ct. SW16 . . . . .3H **29**
TW13: Hanw 5N **23**
Augustus Gdns.
GU15: Camb 1G **71**
Augustus Rd. SW19 . . . . .2J **27**
Aultone Way SM1: Sut 8N **43**
SM5: Cars 9D **44**
Aultone Yd. Ind. Est.
SM5: Cars 9D **44**
Aura Ho. TW9: Kew 4A **12**
Aurelia Gdns. CR0: Croy 4K **45**
Aurelia Rd. CR0: Croy 5J **45**
Auriol Cl. KT4: W Pk 9D **42**
Auriol Mans. *W14 . . . . .1K 13*
(off Edith Rd.)
Auriol Pk. Rd. KT4: W Pk 9D **42**
Auriol Rd. W14 . . . . .1K **13**
Aurum Cl. RH6: Horl 9F **142**
Austen Apartments SE20 . . . . .1E **46**
Austen Cl. RH19: E Grin 9L **165**
Austen Ct. *KT22: Leat 8G 78*
(off Highbury Dr.)
Austen Rd. GU1: Guil 4B **114**
GU14: Farnb 8M **69**
Austen Vw. SL3: Lang 2B **6**
Austen Way SL3: Lang 2B **6**
Austin Cl. CR5: Coul 5M **83**
TW1: Twick 8J **11**
Austins Cotts. GU9: Farnh 1G **128**
Austin Way RG12: Brac 3A **32**
Austyn Gdns. KT5: Surb 7A **42**
Austyns Pl. KT17: Ewe 5F **60**
Autumn Cl. RH11: Craw 4A **182**
SW19 . . . . .7A **28**
Autumn Dr. SM2: Sut 5N **61**
Autumn Lodge CR0: Croy 7F **200**
Avalon Cl. SW20 . . . . .1K **43**
Avalon Rd. SW6 . . . . .4N **13**
Avante
KT1: K Tham . . .5H **203** (2K **41**)
Avard Gdns. BR6: Farnb 1L **67**
Avarn Rd. SW17 . . . . .7D **28**
Avebury RG12: Brac 5M **31**
Avebury Cl. RH12: Hors 1N **197**
Avebury Pk. KT6: Surb 6K **41**
Avebury Rd. BR6: Orp 1M **67**
SW19 . . . . .9L **27**
Aveley Cl. GU9: Farnh 4H **129**
Aveley La. GU9: Farnh 5G **129**
Aveling Cl. CR8: Pur 9K **63**
RH10: Craw 5G **182**
Aven Cl. GU6: Cranl 8N **155**
Avening Rd. SW18 . . . . .1M **27**
Avening Ter. SW18 . . . . .1M **27**
Avenue, The BR2: Kes 1F **66**
BR4: W Wick 6M **47**
CR0: Croy 4F **200** (9B **46**)
CR3: Whyte 6D **84**
CR5: Coul 2H **83**
GU3: Comp 1F **132**
GU3: Worp 5H **93**
GU6: Ewh 4F **156**
GU7: Goda 1F **132**
(New Pond Rd.)
GU7: Goda 9H **133**
(The Drive)
GU10: Rowl 8D **128**
(not continuous)
GU12: Alde 5A **110**
GU15: Camb 2N **69**
GU18: Ligh 6L **51**
GU24: Chob 5K **53**
GU26: G'hott 6B **170**
GU27: Hasl 1D **188**
KT4: W Pk 8E **42**
KT5: Surb 5M **41**
KT10: Clay 3E **58**
KT15: N Haw 6J **55**
KT17: Ewe 4G **60**
KT20: Tad 9G **80**
KT22: Oxs 7F **58**
RG40: W'ham 7K **31**
RG45: Crow 1F **48**
RH1: Sth N 6J **123**
RH3: Brock 3N **119**
RH6: Horl 9D **142**

Avenue, The—Barlow Rd.

Avenue, The RH10: Craw 8B 182
RH17: Hand 8L 199
RH19: E Grin 4C 166
SL3: Dat 4L 5
SL4: O Win 8L 5
SL5: Asc 8K 17
SM2: Chea 6L 61
SM3: Chea 4H 61
SM5: Cars 4E 62
SW18 . . . . .1C 28
TN16: Tats, Weste 9H 87
TW1: Twick 8H 11
TW3: Houn 8B 10
TW5: C'ford 3H 9
TW9: Kew 5M 11
TW12: Hamp 7N 23
TW16: Sunb 9J 23
TW18: Stain 9K 21
TW19: Wray 6N 5
TW20: Egh 5D 20
Avenue C KT15: Addl 9N 37
Avenue Cl. KT20: Tad 9G 81
TW5: C'ford 4J 9
Avenue Ct. KT20: Tad 1G 101
Avenue Cres. TW5: C'ford 4J 9
Avenue de Cagny
GU24: Pirb 9C 72
Avenue Elmers
KT6: Surb 8J 203 (4L 41)
Avenue Gdns. RH6: Horl 9G 142
SE25 . . . . .1D 46
SW14 . . . . .6D 12
TW5: C'ford 3J 9
TW11: Tedd 8F 24
Avenue One KT15: Addl 1N 55
Avenue Pde. TW16: Sunb 2J 39
Avenue Pk. Rd. SE27 . . . . . . .3M 29
Avenue Rd. BR3: Beck 1G 46
CR3: Cate 9A 84
GU6: Cranl 9N 155
GU14: Farnb 1B 90
GU26: G'hott 6A 170
GU51: Fleet 3A 88
KT1: K Tham 5K 203 (2L 41)
KT3: N Mal 3D 42
KT11: Cob 3L 77
KT18: Eps 8K 201 (1C 80)
SE20 . . . . .1G 46
SE25 . . . . .1C 46
SM2: Sut 6M 61
SM6: W'ton 4G 62
SM7: Ban 2N 81
SW16 . . . . .1H 45
SW20 . . . . .1G 42
TN16: Tats 7G 87
TW7: Isle 4F 10
TW8: Brent 1J 11
TW11: Tedd 8G 24
TW12: Hamp 9B 24
TW13: Felt 4G 23
TW18: Stain 6F 20
Avenue Road Stop (CT) 1G 47
Avenue Sth. KT5: Surb 6N 41
Avenue Sucy GU15: Camb 2M 69
(not continuous)
Avenue Ter. KT3: N Mal 2B 42
Avenue Three KT15: Addl 9N 37
Avenue Two KT15: Addl 1N 55
Avenue Vs. RH1: Mers 7G 103
Averil Gro. SW16 . . . . .7M 29
Averill St. W6 . . . . .2J 13
Avern Gdns. KT8: W Mole 3B 40
Avern Rd. KT8: W Mole 3B 40
Avery Ct. GU11: Alde 2N 109
(off Alice Rd.)
Aviary Rd. GU22: Pyr 3J 75
Aviary Way RH10: Craw D 9F 164
Aviator Pk. KT15: Addl 9M 37
Aviemore Cl. BR3: Beck 4J 47
Aviemore Way BR3: Beck 4H 47
Avington Cl.
GU1: Guil 2F 202 (3A 114)
Avoca Rd. SW17 . . . . .5E 28
Avocet Cres. GU47: C Tow 7J 49
Avon Cl. GU12: Ash 3D 110
GU14: Cove 7K 69
KT4: W Pk 8F 42
KT15: Addl 3J 55
SM1: Sut 1A 62
Avon Ct. GU9: Farnh 2H 129
RG42: Bin 7H 15
SW15 . . . . .8K 13
Avondale GU12: A Va 6D 90
Avondale Av. KT4: W Pk 7E 42
KT10: H Wood 9G 40
TW18: Stain 8H 21
Avondale Cl. KT12: Hers 2K 57
RH6: Horl 6D 142
Avondale Ct. SM2: Sut 4A 62
(off Brighton Rd.)
Avondale Gdns. TW4: Houn 8N 9
Avondale High CR3: Cate 8E 84
Avondale Rd. CR2: S Croy 3N 63
GU11: Alde 4N 109
GU51: Fleet 3B 88
SW14 . . . . .6D 12
SW19 . . . . .6N 27
TW15: A'ford 4M 21
Avon Gro. RG12: Brac 8A 16
Avon Ho.
KT2: K Tham 1H 203 (9K 25)
W14 . . . . .1L 13
(off Kensington Village)
Avonmead GU21: Wok 5M 73
Avonmore Av. GU1: Guil 2B 114
Avon Path CR2: S Croy 3N 63
Avon Rd. GU9: Farnh 2H 129
TW16: Sunb 8G 22
Avon Wlk. RH11: Craw 4L 181
Avonwick Rd. TW3: Houn 5B 10
Avro Way KT13: Weybr 6N 55
SM6: W'ton 4J 63
Award Rd. GU52: C Cro 8A 88
(not continuous)
Axbridge RG12: Brac 4C 32
Axes La. RH1: Salf 1G 142
Axis Pk. SL3: Lang 1D 6
Axwood KT18: Eps 2B 80
Ayebridges Av. TW20: Egh 8E 20
Ayesgarth GU52: C Cro 8C 88
Ayjay Cl. GU11: Alde 5N 109
Aylesbury Ct. SM1: Sut 9A 44
Aylesford Av. BR3: Beck 4H 47
Aylesham Way GU46: Yate 9A 48
Aylesworth Spur SL4: O Win 1L 19
Aylett Rd. SE25 . . . . .3E 46
TW7: Isle 5E 10
Ayliffe Cl. KT1: K Tham 1N 41
Ayling Ct. GU9: Weybo 5L 109
Ayling Hill GU11: Alde 3L 109
Ayling La. GU11: Alde 4L 109
Aylward Rd. SW20 . . . . .1L 43
Aymer Cl. TW18: Stain 9G 20
Aymer Dr. TW18: Stain 9G 21
Aynscombe Path
SW14 . . . . .5B 12
Ayrshire Gdns. GU51: Fleet 1C 88
Aysgarth RG12: Brac 5L 31
Aysgarth Ct. SM1: Sut 9N 43
Ayshe Ct. Dr. RH13: Hors 6L 197
Azalea Av. GU35: Lind 4B 168
Azalea Ct. GU22: Wok 6N 73
Azalea Dr. GU27: Hasl 9D 170
Azalea Gdns. GU52: C Cro 8C 88
Azalea Ho. TW13: Felt 2J 23
Azalea Way GU15: Camb 9F 50

B

Babbacombe Cl. KT9: Ches 2K 59
Babbage Way RG12: Brac 5M 31
Babbs Mead GU9: Farnh 2F 128
Baber Bri. Cvn. Site
TW14: Felt 8K 9
Baber Dr. TW14: Felt 9K 9
Babington Rd. SW16 . . . . .6H 29
Babylon La. KT20: Lwr K 5M 101
Bachelors Acre SL4: W'sor 4G 4
Bachelors La. GU23: Ockh 2A 96
Back All.
RH4: Dork 2K 201 (5H 119)
Back Dr. RG45: Crow 4G 48
Back Grn. KT12: Hers 3K 57
Back La. GU4: E Cla 9M 95
GU8: Els 7H 131
GU10: B Oak 2A 148
GU10: Fren 1J 149
RH2: Reig 7B 102
RH10: Bal, T Hil 7N 183
RH14: Plais 6A 192
RH17: T Hil 9N 183
TW8: Brent 2K 11
TW10: Ham 4J 25
Backley Gdns. SE25 . . . . .5D 46
Back of High St.
GU24: Chob 7H 53
Back Path RH1: Blet 2N 123
Back Rd. TW11: Tedd 8E 24
Bacon Cl. GU47: C Tow 8J 49
Bacon La. GU10: Churt 6H 149
Badajos Rd. GU11: Alde 1L 109
Baddeley Ho. KT8: W Mole 4A 40
(off Down St.)
Baden Cl. TW18: Stain 8K 21
Baden Dr. RH6: Horl 7C 142
Baden Powell Cl.
KT6: Surb 8M 41
Baden Powell Ct.
GU7: Goda 5G 132
Baden Rd. GU2: Guil 1K 113
Bader Cl. CR8: Ken 2A 84
Bader Ct. GU14: Cove 6L 69
RH10: Craw 1B 182
Badger Cl. GU2: Guil 9L 93
TW4: Houn 6K 9
TW13: Felt 4J 23
Badger Ct. GU10: Wrec 6F 128
Badger Dr. GU18: Ligh 6L 51
Badgersbridge Ride
SL4: Wink 1M 17
Badgers Cl. GU7: Goda 3G 133
GU21: Wok 5M 73
GU52: Fleet 5A 88
RH12: Hors 2M 197
TW15: A'ford 6A 22
Badgers Copse
GU15: Camb 3C 70
KT4: W Pk 8E 42
Badger's Ct.
KT17: Eps 7L 201 (9D 60)
Badgers Cross GU8: Mil 1C 152
Badgers Hill GU25: V Wat 4M 35
Badgers Hole CR0: Croy 1G 64
Badgers Hollow
GU7: Goda 5G 132
Badgers Holt GU46: Yate 1A 68
Badgers La. CR6: Warl 7F 84
Badger's Lodge
KT17: Eps 6M 201 (9D 60)
Badgers Sett RG45: Crow 2E 48
Badgers Wlk. CR3: Whyte 5C 84
CR8: Pur 7G 63
KT3: N Mal 1D 42
Badgers Way RG12: Brac 9D 16
RH14: Loxw 4J 193
RH19: E Grin 8B 166
Badgers Wood CR3: Cate 3A 104
Badger Wlk. GU3: Norm 6N 91
Badger Way GU10: Ews 4C 108
GU12: Alde 1B 110
Badgerwood Dr. GU16: Frim . . .4B 70
Badingham Dr. KT22: Fetc 1E 98
Badminton Rd. SW12 . . . . .1E 28
Badshot Farm La.
GU9: B Lea 7M 109
BADSHOT LEA 7M 109
Badshot Lea Rd.
GU9: B Lea 7L 109
Badshot Pk. GU9: B Lea 6M 109
Bagden Hill RH5: Westh 8D 98
Bagley's La. SW6 . . . . .4N 13
Bagot Cl. KT21: A'tead 3M 79
BAGSHOT 4J 51
Bagshot Grn. GU19: Bag 5J 51
Bagshot Rd. GU3: Worp 1F 92
GU19: Bag 2N 31
GU21: B'wood, Knap 5E 72
GU24: Chob, W End 8B 52
GU24: Wok 8E 72
RG12: Bag, Brac 2N 31
SL5: Asc 8M 33
TW20: Eng G 8M 19
Bagshot Station (Rail) 3J 51
Bahram Rd. KT19: Eps 6C 60
Baigents La. GU20: Windl 3A 52
Bailes La. GU3: Norm 9A 92
Bailey Cl. GU16: Frim 6B 70
RH12: Hors 1M 197
SL4: W'sor 5D 4
Bailey Cres. KT9: Ches 4K 59
Bailey Ho. SW10 . . . . .3N 13
(off Coleridge Gdns.)
Bailey M. W4 . . . . .2A 12
(off Hervert Gdns.)
Bailey Rd. RH4: Westc 6C 118
Baileys Cl. GU17: B'water 2H 69
Bailing Hill RH12: Warn 1E 196
Baillie Rd. GU1: Guil 4B 114
Bain Av. GU15: Camb 4N 69
Bainbridge Cl. TW10: Ham 6L 25
Baines Cl.
CR2: S Croy 8D 200 (2A 64)
Bainton Mead GU21: Wok 4K 73
Baird Cl. RH10: Craw 9E 162
Baird Dr. GU3: Wood V 2E 112
Baird Rd. GU14: Farnb 8A 70
Bakeham La. TW20: Eng G 8N 19
Bakehouse Barn Cl.
RH12: Hors 1L 197
Bakehouse Gdns.
GU52: C Cro 8C 88
Bakehouse M. GU11: Alde . . .2M 109
TW12: Hamp 8A 24
Bakehouse Rd. RH6: Horl 6D 142
Baker Boy La. CR0: Sels 9H 65
Baker Cl. RH10: Craw 5B 182
Baker La. CR4: Mit 1E 44
Bakers Cl. CR8: Ken 1N 83
RH7: Ling 6A 146
Bakers Ct. RH1: Red 4D 122
SE25 . . . . .2B 46
Bakers End SW20 . . . . .1K 43
Bakers Gdns. SM5: Cars 8C 44
Bakersgate Courtyard
GU24: Pirb 4D 92
Bakersgate Gdns.
GU24: Pirb 3D 92
Bakers La. RH7: Ling 7N 145
Bakers Mead RH9: Gods 8F 104
Baker St. KT13: Weybr 1B 56
Bakers Way RH5: Cap 5J 159
Baker's Yd.
GU1: Guil 5D 202 (4N 113)
Bakery M. KT6: Surb 7N 41
Bakewell Way KT3: N Mal 1D 42
Balaam Ho. SM1: Sut 1M 61
Balaclava Rd. KT6: Surb 6J 41
Balchins La. RH4: Westc 7A 118
Balcombe Ct. RH10: Craw 2H 183
Balcombe Gdns.
RH6: Horl 9G 142
Balcombe Rd. RH6: Horl 7F 142
RH10: Craw, Wor 2H 183
Baldreys GU9: Farnh 3F 128
Baldry Gdns. SW16 . . . . .7J 29
Baldwin Cl. RH10: Craw 6G 183
Baldwin Cres. GU4: Guil 1E 114
Baldwin Gdns. TW3: Houn 4C 10
Baldwin Ho. SW2 . . . . .2L 29
Baldwin's Bec SL4: Eton 2G 4
(off Baldwin's Shore)
Baldwins Fld.
RH19: E Grin 6N 165
BALDWINS HILL 7N 165
Baldwins Shore SL4: Eton 2G 4
Balfern Gro. W4 . . . . .1D 12
Balfont Cl. CR2: Sande 9D 64
Balfour Av. GU22: Wok 9A 74
Balfour Cres. RG12: Brac 4N 31
Balfour Gdns.
RH18: F Row 9G 187
Balfour Ho. KT13: Weybr 1B 56
Balfour Pl. SW15 . . . . .7G 12
Balfour Rd. KT13: Weybr 1B 56
SE25 . . . . .4D 46
SM5: Cars 4D 62
SW19 . . . . .8N 27
TW3: Houn 6B 10
Balgowan Cl. KT3: N Mal 4D 42
Balgowan Rd. BR3: Beck 2H 47
BALHAM 2E 28
Balham Continental Mkt.
SW12 . . . . .2F 28
(off Shipka Rd.)
Balham Gro. SW12 . . . . .1E 28
Balham High Rd.
SW12 . . . . .4E 28
SW17 . . . . .4E 28
Balham Hill SW12 . . . . .1F 28
Balham Leisure Cen. 3F 28
Balham New Rd.
SW12 . . . . .1F 28
Balham Pk. Rd. SW12 . . . . . . .2D 28
Balham Station (Rail & Tube)
. . . . .2F 28
Balham Sta. Rd. SW12 . . . . . . .2F 28
Balintore Ct. GU47: C Tow 7J 49
Ballands Nth., The
KT22: Fetc 9E 78
Ballands Sth., The
KT22: Fetc 1E 98
Ball & Wicket La.
GU9: U Hal 5H 109
Ballantine St. SW18 . . . . .7N 13
Ballantyne Dr.
KT20: K'wood 8L 81
Ballantyne Rd.
GU14: Farnb 8M 69
Ballard Cl. KT2: K Tham 8C 26
Ballard Ct. GU15: Camb 7E 50
Ballard Grn. SL4: W'sor 3B 4
Ballard Rd. GU15: Camb 7E 50
Ballards Farm Rd.
CR0: Croy 3E 64
CR2: Croy, S Croy 3D 64
Ballards Grn. KT20: Tad 6K 81
Ballards La. RH8: Limp 7E 106
Ballards Ri. CR2: Sels 3D 64
Ballards Way CR0: Croy 3D 64
CR2: Sels 3D 64
Ballater Rd. CR2: S Croy 2C 64
Ballencrieff Rd. SL5: S'dale . . .6C 34
Ballfield Rd. GU7: Goda 5G 133
Ballindune GU27: Hasl 9G 170
Balliol Cl. RH10: Craw 9G 163
Balliol Way GU47: Owls 6K 49
Ballsdown GU8: Chid 5D 172
Balmain Ct. TW3: Houn 4B 10
Balmain Lodge KT5: Surb 8K 203
Balmoral RH19: E Grin 1C 186
Balmoral Av. BR3: Beck 3H 47
Balmoral Cl. SW15 . . . . .9J 13
Balmoral Ct. KT4: W Pk 8G 42
RH11: Craw 7N 181
SE27 . . . . .5N 29
SM2: Sut 4M 61
Balmoral Cres.
GU9: U Hal 6G 108
KT8: W Mole 2A 40
Balmoral Dr. GU16: Frim 6C 70
GU22: Wok 3E 74
Balmoral Gdns. CR2: Sande 6A 64
SL4: W'sor 6G 4
Balmoral Ho. GU12: A Va 8D 90
Balmoral Rd. GU12: A Va 9E 90
KT1: K Tham . . .7L 203 (3M 41)
KT4: W Pk 9G 42
Balmoral Way SM2: Sut 6M 61
Balmuir Gdns. SW15 . . . . .7H 13
Balquhain Cl. KT21: A'tead 4K 79
Baltic Cen., The TW8: Brent 1K 11
Baltic Cl. SW19 . . . . .8B 28
Balvernie Gro. SW18 . . . . .1L 27
Balvernie M. SW18 . . . . .1M 27
Bampfylde Cl. SM6: W'ton 9G 44
Bampton Way GU21: Wok 5K 73
Banbury RG12: Brac 6C 32
Banbury Cl. GU16: Frim 7D 70
RG41: W'ham 2A 30
Banbury Ct. SM2: Sut 4M 61
Bancroft Cl. TW15: A'ford 6B 22
Bancroft Ct. RH2: Reig 3N 121
Bancroft Rd. RH2: Reig 3M 121
RH10: Craw 4H 183
Banders Ri. GU1: Guil 2E 114
Band La. TW20: Egh 6B 20
BANDONHILL 2H 63
Bandon Ri. SM6: W'ton 2H 63
Banfor Ct. SM6: W'ton 2G 62
Bangalore St. SW15 . . . . .6H 13
Bank, The RH10: T Hil 5D 184
Bank Av. CR4: Mit 1B 44
Bank Bldgs. Rd.
GU6: Cranl 7M 155
Bank Ho. KT15: Addl 1K 55
Bank La. KT2: K Tham 8L 25
RH10: Craw 3B 182
SW15 . . . . .8D 12
Bank M. SM1: Sut 3A 62
Bank Pct. RH10: Craw 9E 162
Bank Rd. GU11: Alde 8B 90
Banksian Wlk. TW7: Isle 4E 10
Bankside CR2: S Croy 3C 64
GU9: Weybo 5L 109
GU21: Wok 5L 73
(not continuous)
Bankside Cl. GU8: Els 8H 131
SM5: Cars 3C 62
TN16: B Hil 5E 86
TW7: Isle 7F 10
Bankside Dr. KT7: T Dit 7H 41
Bank's La. KT24: E Jun 1H 97
Banks Rd. RH10: Craw 3G 182
Banks Way GU4: B'ham 9B 94
Bank Ter. GU5: Shere 8B 116
(off Gomshall La.)
Bannacle Hill Rd.
GU8: Worm 9A 152
Bannister Cl. GU8: Wit 5C 152
SW2 . . . . .2L 29
Bannister Gdns. GU46: Yate 1E 68
Bannister's Rd. GU2: Guil 5J 113
Bannow Cl. KT19: Ewe 1D 60
BANSTEAD 2M 81
Banstead Rd. CR3: Cate 8A 84
CR8: Pur 7L 63
KT17: Ewe 6G 61
SM5: Cars 5B 62
SM7: Ban 6G 61
Banstead Rd. Sth.
SM2: Sut 7A 62
Banstead Sports Cen. 7H 81
Banstead Station (Rail) 1L 81
Banstead Way SM6: W'ton 2J 63
Banstead Wood SM7: Ban 5A 82
Barataria Pk. Cvn. Site
GU23: Rip 7H 75
Barbara Castle Cl.
SW6 . . . . .2L 13
Barbara Cl. GU52: C Cro 7C 88
TW17: Shep 4C 38
Barber Cl. RH10: Craw 7G 182
Barber Dr. GU6: Cranl 6N 155
Barberry Cl. GU52: Fleet 7B 88
Barberry Way GU17: Haw 4L 69
Barbon Cl. GU15: Camb 3H 71
Barchard St. SW18 . . . . .8N 13
Barclay Cl. KT22: Fetc 1B 98
SW6 . . . . .3M 13
Barclay Rd.
CR0: Croy 4D 200 (9A 46)
SW6 . . . . .3M 13
Barcombe Av. SW2 . . . . .3J 29
Bardeen Pl. RG12: Brac 2B 32
Bardney Rd. SM4: Mord 3N 43
Bardolph Av. CR0: Sels 5H 65
Bardolph Rd. TW9: Rich 6M 11
Bardon Wlk. GU21: Wok 4L 73
Bardsley Cl. CR0: Croy 9C 46
Bardsley Dr. GU9: Farnh 3F 128
Barfield Ct. RH1: Red 1E 122
Barfields RH1: Blet 2M 123
Barford Cl. GU51: Fleet 5E 88
Barford La. GU10: Churt 9K 149
Bargate Cl. KT3: N Mal 6F 42
Bargate Ct. GU2: Guil 3H 113
Bargate Ri. GU7: Goda 7F 132
Barge Cl. GU11: Alde 8C 90
Barge Wlk.
KT1: H Wic 5G 203 (2K 41)
KT8: E Mol 2D 40
(Hampton Ct. Cres.)
KT8: E Mol 5G 41
(The Island)
Barham Cl. KT13: Weybr 1D 56
Barham Ct. CR2: S Croy 7C 200
Barham Rd.
CR2: S Croy 7C 200 (1N 63)
SW20 . . . . .8F 26
Barhatch La. GU6: Cranl 5A 156
Barhatch Rd. GU6: Cranl 5A 156
Baring Rd. CR0: Croy 7D 46
Barker Cl. KT3: N Mal 3A 42
KT16: Chert 6G 37
TW9: Rich 5A 12
Barker Grn. RG12: Brac 4N 31
Barker Rd. KT16: Chert 6G 37
Barkers Mdw. SL5: Asc 9H 17
Barker Wlk. SW16 . . . . .4H 29
Barkham Rd. RG41: W'ham 3A 30
Barkhart Dr. RG40: W'ham 1B 30
Barkhart Gdns.
RG40: W'ham 1B 30
Barkis Mead GU47: Owls 5K 49
Barkston Gdns. SW5 . . . . .1N 13
Barkway Dr. BR6: Farnb 1J 67
Barley Cl. RH10: Craw 4B 182
Barley Mead RG42: Warf 8C 16
Barleymead RH6: Horl 7F 142
Barley Mow Cl.
GU21: Knap 4G 72
Barleymow Ct. RH3: Betch . . .3B 120
Barley Mow Hill
GU35: H Dwn 3E 168
Barley Mow La. GU21: Knap . . .3F 72
Barley Mow Pas. W4 . . . . .1C 12
Barley Mow Rd.
TW20: Eng G 6M 19
Barley Mow Way
TW17: Shep 3B 38
Barley Way GU51: Fleet 9C 68
Barlow Cl. SM6: W'ton 3J 63
Barlow Rd. RH11: Craw 6K 181
TW12: Hamp 8A 24

Barmouth Rd.—Beckett Cl.

Barmouth Rd. CR0: Croy 8G 47
SW18 . . . . .1A 28
Barnard Cl. GU16: Frim 6D 70
SM6: W'ton 4H 63
TW16: Sunb 8J 23
Barnard Ct. GU21: Wok 5H 73
Barnard Gdns. KT3: N Mal 3F 42
Barnard Rd. CR4: Mit 2E 44
CR6: Warl 6L 85
Barnards Pl. CR2: S Croy 5M 63
Barnard Way GU11: Alde 1L 109
Barnato Cl. KT14: Byf 8N 55
Barnby Rd. GU21: Knap 4G 73
Barn Cl. GU15: Camb 9C 50
KT18: Eps 2B 80
KT20: Box H 1M 119
RG12: Brac 1B 32
RH11: P Pot 1N 199
SM7: Ban 2B 82
(not continuous)
TW15: A'ford 6C 22
Barn Cres. CR8: Pur 9A 64
Barncroft GU9: Farnh 2H 129
(not continuous)
Barneby Cl. TW2: Twick 2E 24
Barn Elms Athletic Track 4G 13
Barn Elms Pk. SW15 . . . . .6H 13
BARNES 5E 12
Barnes All. TW12: Hamp 1C 40
Barnes Av. SW13 . . . . .3F 12
UB2: S'hall 1N 9
Barnes Bridge Station (Rail)
. . . . .5E 12
Barnes Cl. GU14: Farnb 1B 90
Barnes Common Nature Reserve
. . . . .6F 12
Barnes Ct. CR7: T Hea 2N 45
Barnes End KT3: N Mal 4F 42
Barnes High St. SW13 . . . . . . .5E 12
Barnes M. RH12: Hors 6H 197
Barnes Rd. GU7: Goda 3H 133
GU16: Frim 6C 70
Barnes Station (Rail) 6F 12
Barnes Wallis Av.
RH13: Hors 9D 196
Barnes Wallis Cl. KT24: Eff 5L 97
Barnes Wallis Dr.
KT13: Weybr 7N 55
Barnett Cl. GU5: Wone 3E 134
KT22: Leat 6H 79
Barnett Ct. RG12: Brac 1B 32
Barnett Grn. RG12: Brac 5N 31
Barnett La. GU5: Wone 4D 134
GU18: Ligh 8K 51
Barnett Row GU4: J Wel 7N 93
Barnett's Shaw RH8: Oxt 5N 105
Barnetts Way RH8: Oxt 5N 105
Barnett Wood La.
KT21: A'tead 5J 79
KT22: Leat 7H 79
Barn Fld. GU46: Yate 1C 68
Barnfield GU6: Cranl 7N 155
KT3: N Mal 5D 42
RH6: Horl 9E 142
SM7: Ban 1N 81
Barnfield Av. CR0: Croy 8F 46
CR4: Mit 3F 44
KT2: K Tham 5K 25
Barnfield Cl. CR5: Coul 6N 83
SW17 . . . . .4B 28
Barnfield Cotts.
RH7: Dorm 1C 166
Barnfield Gdns.
KT2: K Tham 5L 25
Barnfield Rd. CR2: Sande 5B 64
RH10: Craw 2B 182
TN16: Tats 7F 86
Barnfield Way RH8: Oxt 2C 126
Barnfield Wood Cl.
BR3: Beck 5N 47
Barnfield Wood Rd.
BR3: Beck 5N 47
Barn Hawe TN8: Eden 2L 147
Barnlea Cl. TW13: Hanw 3M 23
Barnmead GU24: Chob 6J 53
Barn Mdw. Cl.
GU52: C Cro 1A 108
Barn Mdw. La. KT23: Book 2N 97
Barns, The GU8: S'ford 3N 131
Barnsbury Cl. KT3: N Mal 3B 42
Barnsbury Cres. KT5: Surb 7B 42
Barnsbury Farm Est.
GU22: Wok 7N 73
Barnsbury La. KT5: Surb 8A 42
Barnscroft SW20 . . . . .2G 43
Barnsfold La. RH12: Rudg . . .2N 193
Barnsford Cres.
GU24: W End 9D 52
Barnsley Cl. GU12: A Va 3F 90
BARNSNAP 5G 199
Barnsnap Cl. RH12: Hors 2K 197
Barn Theatre, The
Oxted 6A 106
West Molesey 3A 40
Barnway TW20: Eng G 6M 19
Barnwood RH10: Craw 2G 183
Barnwood Cl. GU2: Guil 1H 113
Barnwood Ct. GU2: Guil 1H 113
Barnwood Rd. GU2: Guil 2H 113
Barnyard, The KT20: Wal H . . .2F 100
Baron Cl. SM2: Sut 6N 61
Baron Gro. CR4: Mit 3C 44
Baron Ho. SW19 . . . . .9B 28
Barons, The TW1: Twick 9H 11
BARONS COURT 1K 13
Barons Ct. SM6: Bedd 9H 45
Baron's Ct. Rd. W14 . . . . .1K 13
Barons Court Station (Tube)
. . . . .1K 13
Barons Court Theatre *1K 13*
(off Comeragh Rd.)
Baronsfield Rd. TW1: Twick . . .9H 11
Baron's Hurst KT18: Eps 3B 80
Barons Keep W14 . . . . .1K 13
Baronsmead Rd.
SW13 . . . . .4F 12
Baron's Wlk. CR0: Croy 5H 47
Barons Way RH2: Reig 7M 121
TW20: Egh 7F 20
Baron Wlk. CR4: Mit 3C 44
Baroque Ct. TW3: Houn 6C 10
Barossa Rd. GU15: Camb 8B 50
Barracane Dr. RG45: Crow 2F 48
Barrackfield Wlk.
RH12: Hors 8H 197
Barrack La. SL4: W'sor 4G 5
Barrack Path GU21: Wok 5H 73
(not continuous)
Barrack Rd. GU2: Guil 1K 113
GU11: Alde 2M 109
TW4: Houn 7L 9
Barrens Brae GU22: Wok 5C 74
Barrens Cl. GU22: Wok 6C 74
Barrens Pk. GU22: Wok 5C 74
Barrett Cres. RG40: W'ham . . .2C 30
Barrett Rd. KT22: Fetc 2D 98
Barrhill Rd. SW2 . . . . .3J 29
Barricane GU21: Wok 6L 73
Barrie Cl. CR5: Coul 3G 82
Barrie Ho. KT15: Addl 4J 55
Barrie Rd. GU9: U Hal 5F 108
BARRIHURST 8F 154
Barrihurst La. GU6: Cranl 8F 154
Barringer Sq. SW17 . . . . .5E 28
Barrington Ct. RH1: Red 1E 122
RH4: Dork 6G 119
TW18: Stain 7H 21
(off Thameside)
Barrington Dr. KT22: Fetc 3D 98
Barrington Lodge
KT13: Weybr 2D 56
Barrington Rd. CR8: Pur 8G 63
RH4: Dork 6G 119
RH10: Craw 5B 182
RH13: Hors 6L 197
SM3: Sut 8M 43
Barrow Av. SM5: Cars 4D 62
Barrowgate Rd. W4 . . . . .1B 12
Barrow Grn. Rd. RH8: Oxt . . .8K 105
Barrow Hedges Cl.
SM5: Cars 4C 62
Barrow Hedges Way
SM5: Cars 4C 62
Barrow Hill KT4: W Pk 8D 42
Barrow Hill Cl. KT4: W Pk 8D 42
Barrow Rd. CR0: Wad 2L 63
SW16 . . . . .7H 29
Barrowsfield CR2: Sande 8C 64
Barrow Wlk. TW8: Brent 2J 11
Barrsbrook Farm Rd.
KT16: Chert 7G 37
Barrsbrook Hall
KT16: Chert 7G 37
Barr's La. GU21: Knap 3G 72
(not continuous)
Barry Av. SL4: W'sor 3F 4
Barry Cl. RH10: Craw 6C 182
Barry Sq. RG12: Brac 6B 32
Bars, The
GU1: Guil 4C 202 (4N 113)
Barston Rd. SE27 . . . . .4N 29
Barstow Cres. SW2 . . . . .2K 29
Bartholomew Cl.
GU27: Hasl 9H 171
Bartholomew Ct.
RH4: Dork 4J 201 (6G 119)
Bartholomew Pl.
RG42: Warf 8C 16
Bartholomew Way
RH12: Hors 2N 197
Bartlett Pl. GU16: Frim G 9D 70
Bartlett Rd. TN16: Weste 4L 107
Bartlett St.
CR2: S Croy 8D 200 (2A 64)
Barton, The KT11: Cob 8L 57
Barton Cl. GU11: Alde 3K 109
GU21: Knap 5F 72
KT15: Addl 3J 55
TW17: Shep 5C 38
Barton Ct. *W14 . . . . .1K 13*
(off Baron's Ct. Rd.)
Barton Cres. RH19: E Grin . . .1C 186
Barton Grn. KT3: N Mal 1C 42
Barton Green Theatre 1C 42
Barton Ho. *SW6 . . . . .6N 13*
(off Wandsworth Bri. Rd.)
Barton Pl. GU4: B'ham 9D 94
Barton Rd. GU5: Braml 4C 134
W14 . . . . .1K 13
Bartons Dr. GU46: Yate 2C 68
Bartons Way GU14: Cove 7J 69
Barton Wlk. RH10: Craw 5F 182
Barts Cl. BR3: Beck 4K 47
Barttelot Rd. RH12: Hors 7K 197
Barwell Bus. Pk. KT9: Ches 4K 59
Barwell Cl. RG45: Crow 2E 48
Barwell Ct. KT9: Ches 4H 59
Barwell Cres. TN16: B Hil 8E 66
Barwell La. KT9: Ches 4J 59
Barwood Av. BR4: W Wick 7L 47
Basden Gro. TW13: Hanw 3A 24
Basden Ho. TW13: Hanw 3A 24
Basemoors RG12: Brac 1C 32
Basepoint Bus. Cen.
RH11: Craw 8B 162
Basford Way SL4: W'sor 6A 4
Bashford Way RH10: Craw . . .1H 183
Bashurst Copse
RH13: Itch 8N 195
Bashurst Hill RH13: Itch 9M 195
Basildene Rd. TW4: Houn 6L 9
Basildon Cl. SM2: Sut 5N 61
Basildon Way RH11: Craw . . .6K 181
Basil Gdns. CR0: Croy 7G 46
SE27 . . . . .6N 29
Basingbourne Cl.
GU52: Fleet 7B 88
Basingbourne Rd.
GU52: Fleet 8A 88
Basing Cl. KT7: T Dit 6F 40
Basing Dr. GU11: Alde 5N 109
Basingfield Rd. KT7: T Dit 6F 40
Basinghall Gdns.
SM2: Sut 5N 61
Basing Rd. SM7: Ban 1L 81
Basingstoke Canal Cen. 2E 90
Basing Way KT7: T Dit 6F 40
Baskerville Rd. SW18 . . . . .1C 28
Basset Cl. KT15: N Haw 6K 55
Bassett Cl. GU16: Frim 6C 70
SM2: Sut 5N 61
Bassett Dr. RH2: Reig 2M 121
Bassett Gdns. TW7: Isle 3C 10
Bassett Rd. GU22: Wok 3E 74
RH10: Craw 6H 183
Bassett's Cl. BR6: Farnb 1K 67
Bassetts Hill RH7: Dorm 1C 166
Bassett's Way BR6: Farnb 1K 67
Bassingham Rd.
SW18 . . . . .1A 28
Baston Mnr. Rd.
BR2: Hay, Kes 1D 66
Baston Rd. BR2: Hay 1E 66
Basuto Rd. SW6 . . . . .4M 13
Bat & Ball La. GU10: Wrec 5F 128
(not continuous)
Batavia Cl. TW16: Sunb 9J 23
Batavia Rd. TW16: Sunb 9J 23
Batcombe Mead
RG12: Brac 6C 32
Bateman Ct. RH10: Craw 6E 182
Bateman Gro. GU12: Ash 4D 110
Bates Cres. CR0: Wad 2L 63
SW16 . . . . .8G 29
Bateson Way GU21: Wok 1E 74
Bates Wlk. KT15: Addl 3L 55
Bathgate Rd. SW19 . . . . .4J 27
Bath Ho. Rd. CR0: Bedd 7J 45
Bath Pas.
KT1: K Tham 4H 203 (1K 41)
Bath Pl. *W6 . . . . .1H 13*
(off Peabody Est.)
Bath Rd. GU15: Camb 9B 50
SL3: Coln 3E 6
SL3: Coln, Poy 4G 6
TW3: Houn 5L 9
TW4: Houn 5L 9
TW5: C'ford 4K 9
TW6: Lon A 4F 8
UB3: Harl 4F 8
UB7: Harm, Sip 4N 7
UB7: L'ford 4K 7
Baths App. SW6 . . . . .3L 13
Bathurst Av. SW19 . . . . .9N 27
Batley Cl. CR4: Mit 6D 44
Batsworth Rd. CR4: Mit 2B 44
Batten Av. GU21: Wok 6H 73
Battersea Ct. GU2: Guil 3L 113
Battlebridge La.
RH1: Mers, Red 8F 102
Battle Cl. SW19 . . . . .7A 28
BATT'S CORNER 4C 148
Batts Hill RH1: Red 1C 122
RH2: Reig 1B 122
Batty's Barn Cl.
RG40: W'ham 3C 30
Baulk, The SW18 . . . . .1M 27
Bavant Rd. SW16 . . . . .1J 45
Bawtree Cl. SM2: Sut 6A 62
Bax Cl. GU6: Cranl 8N 155
Baxter Av. RH1: Red 3D 122
Baxter Cl. RH10: Craw 5F 182
Bayards CR6: Warl 5F 84
Bay Cl. RH6: Horl 5C 142
Bay Dr. RG12: Brac 1C 32
Bayeux KT20: Tad 9J 81
Bayfield Av. GU16: Frim 4B 70
Bayfield Rd. RH6: Horl 7C 142
Bayford Cl. GU17: Haw 5M 69
Baygrove M. KT1: H Wic 9J 25
Bayham Rd. SM4: Mord 3N 43
Bayhorne La. RH6: Horl 1G 162
Bay Ho. RG12: Brac 1C 32
Bayleaf Cl. TW12: H Hill 6D 24
Baylis M. TW1: Twick 1G 25
Bayliss Ct.
GU1: Guil 4B 202 (4M 113)
Baylis Wlk. RH11: Craw 8N 181
BAYNARDS 6B 176
BAYNARDS PARK 3D 176
Baynards Rd.
RH12: Rudg 7A 176
Baynton Rd. GU22: Wok 7D 74
Bayonne Rd. W6 . . . . .2K 13
Bay Path RH9: Gods 9F 104
Bay Pond Nature Reserve . . .9F 104
Bay Rd. RG12: Brac 9C 16
Bays Farm Ct. UB7: L'ford 4L 7
Bay Tree Av. KT22: Leat 7G 79
Bay Trees RH8: Oxt 2D 126
Baywood Cl. GU14: Cove 9H 69
Bazalgette Cl. KT3: N Mal 4C 42
Bazalgette Gdns.
KT3: N Mal 4C 42
Beach Gro. TW13: Hanw 3A 24
Beach Ho. *SW5 . . . . .1M 13*
(off Philbeach Gdns.)
TW13: Hanw 3A 24
Beachy Rd. RH11: Craw 8M 181
Beacon Cl. GU10: Wrec 6F 128
SM7: Ban 3J 81
Beacon Ct. RH13: Hors 4N 197
SL3: Coln 3E 6
Beacon Cres.
GU26: Hind 4C 170
Beacon Gro. SM5: Cars 1E 62
BEACON HILL 3A 170
Beacon Hill GU21: Wok 6M 73
RH7: Dorm 2D 166
Beacon Hill Ct.
GU26: Hind 3B 170
Beacon Hill Pk.
GU26: Hind 3N 169
Beacon Hill Rd.
GU10: Ews 5D 108
GU26: Hind 3A 170
GU52: C Cro 8C 88
Beacon Pl. CR0: Bedd 9J 45
Beacon Rd. TW6: Lon A 9B 8
Beaconsfield Cl. W4 . . . . .1B 12
Beaconsfield Gdns.
KT10: Clay 4E 58
Beaconsfield Pl.
KT17: Eps 5M 201 (8D 60)
Beaconsfield Rd. CR0: Croy . . .5A 46
GU22: Wok 7B 74
KT3: N Mal 1C 42
KT5: Surb 6M 41
KT10: Clay 4E 58
KT18: Eps D 6C 80
TW1: Twick 9H 11
Beaconsfield Wlk.
SW6 . . . . .4L 13
Beacon Vw. Ho.
GU26: G'hott 6A 170
Beacon Vw. Rd. GU8: Els 9G 130
Beacon Way SM7: Ban 3J 81
Beadles La. RH8: Oxt 8N 105
Beadlow Cl. SM5: Cars 5B 44
Beadman Pl. SE27 . . . . .5M 29
Beadman St. SE27 . . . . .5M 29
Beadon Rd. W6 . . . . .1H 13
Beaford Gro. SW20 . . . . .2K 43
Beagle Cl. TW13: Felt 5J 23
Beale Cl. RG40: W'ham 1A 30
Beale Ct. RH11: Craw 6M 181
Beales La. GU10: Wrec 4E 128
KT13: Weybr 9C 38
Beales Rd. KT23: Book 5B 98
Bealeswood La.
GU10: Dock 4D 148
Beam Hollow GU9: H End 5H 109
Bean Oak Rd.
RG40: W'ham 2D 30
Beard Rd. KT2: K Tham 6M 25
Beard's Hill TW12: Hamp 9A 24
Beard's Hill Cl.
TW12: Hamp 9A 24
Beard's Rd. TW15: A'ford 7F 22
BEARE GREEN 8K 139
Beare Grn. Ct. RH5: B Grn . . .7K 139
Beare Grn. Rd.
RH5: B Grn 2E 158
Beare Grn. Rdbt.
RH5: B Grn 9K 139
Bearfield Rd.
KT2: K Tham 1J 203 (8L 25)
Bear La. GU9: Farnh 9G 109
Bear Rd. TW13: Hanw 5L 23
Bears Den KT20: K'wood 9L 81
Bearsden Ct. SL5: S'dale 6C 34
Bearsden Way
RH12: Bro H 5D 196
Bears Rails Pk. SL4: O Win . . .1J 19
Bearwood Cl. KT15: Addl 3J 55
Bearwood Cotts.
GU10: Wrec 4E 128
(off The Street)
Bearwood Gdns.
GU51: Fleet 4B 88
Beasley's Ait La.
TW16: Sunb 5G 39
Beatrice Av. SW16 . . . . .2K 45
Beatrice Ho. *W6 . . . . .1H 13*
(off Queen Caroline St.)
Beatrice Rd. RH8: Oxt 7A 106
TW10: Rich 8M 11
Beatrix Ho. *SW5 . . . . .1N 13*
(off Old Brompton Rd.)
Beattie Cl. KT23: Book 2N 97
TW14: Felt 1G 22
Beatty Av. GU1: Guil 2C 114
Beauchamp Rd.
KT8: W Mole, E Mol 4B 40
SE19 . . . . .1A 46
SM1: Sut 1M 61
TW1: Twick 1G 25
Beauchamp Ter. SW15 . . . . . . .6G 13
Beauclare Cl. KT22: Leat 7K 79
Beauclerc Ct. TW16: Sunb 1K 39
Beauclere Ho. SM2: Sut 3A 62
Beauclerk Cl. TW13: Felt 2J 23
Beauclerk Ho. SW16 . . . . .4J 29
Beaufield Ga. GU27: Hasl 1H 189
Beaufort Cl. GU22: Wok 3E 74
RH2: Reig 2L 121
SW15 . . . . .1G 27
Beaufort Ct. SW6 . . . . .2M 13
TW10: Ham 5J 25
Beaufort Gdns. SL5: Asc 9J 17
SW16 . . . . .8K 29
TW5: Hest 4M 9
Beaufort M. GU21: Wok 5N 73
SW6 . . . . .2L 13
Beaufort Rd. GU9: Farnh 9H 109
GU12: A Va 8D 90
GU22: Wok 3E 74
GU52: C Cro 6C 88
KT1: K Tham 8J 203 (3L 41)
RH2: Reig 2L 121
TW1: Twick 1J 25
TW10: Ham 5J 25
Beauforts TW20: Eng G 6M 19
Beaufort Way KT17: Ewe 4F 60
Beaufoy Ho. SE27 . . . . .4M 29
Beaufront Cl. GU15: Camb 8E 50
Beaufront Rd. GU15: Camb 8E 50
Beaulieu Cl. CR4: Mit 9E 28
RG12: Brac 2D 32
SL3: Dat 4L 5
TW1: Twick 9K 11
TW4: Houn 8N 9
Beaulieu Gdns.
GU17: B'water 1H 69
Beaumaris Pde.
GU16: Frim 6D 70
Beaumont *W14 . . . . .1L 13*
(off Kensington Village)
Beaumont Av. TW9: Rich 6M 11
W14 . . . . .1L 13
Beaumont Cl. KT2: K Tham 8N 25
RH11: Ifi 4K 181
Beaumont Ct. *GU51: Fleet 2A 88*
(off Harrow Rd.)
W4 . . . . .1B 12
Beaumont Cres. W14 . . . . .1L 13
Beaumont Dr. KT4: W Pk 6G 43
TW15: A'ford 6E 22
Beaumont Gdns.
RG12: Brac 4C 32
Beaumont Gro.
GU11: Alde 2K 109
Beaumont Pl. TW7: Isle 8F 10
Beaumont Rd. CR8: Pur 9L 63
SE19 . . . . .7N 29
SL4: W'sor 5F 4
SW19 . . . . .1K 27
Beaumonts RH1: Salf 2D 142
Beaumont Sq. GU6: Cranl 7A 156
Beaumont Village
GU11: Alde 2L 109
Beaverbrook Rdbt.
KT22: Leat 1K 99
Beaver Cl. RG41: W'ham 5A 30
RH12: Hors 2L 197
SM4: Mord 6H 43
TW12: Hamp 9B 24
Beaver La. GU46: Yate 1D 68
Beavers Cl. GU3: Guil 2H 113
GU9: Farnh 1F 128
Beavers Cres. TW4: Houn 7K 9
Beavers Hill GU9: Farnh 1E 128
Beavers La. TW4: Houn 5K 9
(not continuous)
Beavers La. Campsite
TW4: Houn 7L 9
Beavers M. GU35: Bor 5A 168
Beavers Rd. GU9: Farnh 1F 128
Beaver Water World 9D 86
Beavor Gro. *W6 . . . . .1F 12*
(off Beavor La.)
Beavor La. W6 . . . . .1F 12
Bechtel Ho. *W6 . . . . .1J 13*
(off Hammersmith Rd.)
Beck Ct. BR3: Beck 2G 46
BECKENHAM 1M 47
Beckenham Crematorium
BR3: Beck 2F 46
Beckenham Gro.
BR2: Brom 1N 47
Beckenham Rd. BR3: Beck 1H 47
BR4: W Wick 6L 47
Beckenham Road Stop (CT)
. . . . .1H 47
Beckenham Theatre Cen., The
. . . . .1L 47
Beckenshaw Gdns.
SM7: Ban 2C 82
Becket Cl. SE25 . . . . .5D 46
SW19 . . . . .9N 27
(off High Path)
Beckett Av. CR8: Ken 2M 83
Beckett Chase SL3: Lang 1B 6
Beckett Cl. RG40: W'ham 2D 30
SW16 . . . . .3H 29

Beckett La. RH11: Craw 9B 162
Beckett Rd. CR5: Coul 9H 83
Becketts Cl. TW14: Felt 9J 9
Becketts Pl.
KT1: H Wic 2G 203 (9K 25)
Beckett Way
RH19: E Grin 1B 186
Becket Wood RH5: Newd 6B 140
Beckford Av. RG12: Brac 5N 31
Beckford Rd. CR0: Croy 5C 46
Beckford Way RH10: Craw 7F 182
Beck Gdns. GU9: U Hal 6G 108
Beckingham Rd.
GU2: Guil 1K 113
Beck La. BR3: Beck 2G 46
Beck Rd. CR4: Mit 5D 44
Beck Way BR3: Beck 2J 47
Beckway Rd. SW16 ....1H 45
Beclands Rd. SW17 ....7E 28
Becmead Av. SW16 ....5H 29
Bective Pl. SW15 ....7L 13
Bective Rd. SW15 ....7L 13
Bedale Cl. RH11: Craw 5A 182
BEDDINGTON 1J 63
BEDDINGTON CORNER 6E 44
Beddington Cross
CR0: Bedd 6H 45
Beddington Farm Rd.
CR0: Bedd 6J 45
Beddington Gdns.
SM5: Cars 3E 62
SM6: W'ton 3E 62
Beddington Gro.
SM6: W'ton 2H 63
Beddington La. CR0: Croy 4G 44
Beddington Lane Stop (CT) 5G 45
Beddington Pk. 8F 44
Beddington Pk. Cotts.
SM6: Bedd 9H 45
Beddington Ter. CR0: Croy 6K 45
Beddington Trad. Est.
CR0: Bedd 7J 45
Beddlestead La. CR6: Warl 4B 86
Bedfont Cl. CR4: Mit 1E 44
TW14: Bedf 9D 8
Bedfont Ct. TW19: Stan M 6J 7
Bedfont Ct. Est.
TW19: Stan M 7K 7
Bedfont Grn. Cl.
TW14: Bedf 2D 22
Bedfont Ind. Pk.
TW15: A'ford 4D 22
Bedfont Ind. Pk. Nth.
TW15: A'ford 4D 22
Bedfont Lakes Country Pk. 3D 22
Bedfont Lakes Country Pk. Vis. Cen.
....4C 22
Bedfont La. TW13: Felt 1G 22
TW14: Felt 1G 22
Bedfont Rd. TW13: Felt 2D 22
TW14: Bedf 2D 22
TW19: Stan 9N 7
Bedfont Trad. Est.
TW14: Bedf 3E 22
Bedford Av. GU16: Frim G 9D 70
Bedford Cl. GU21: Wok 2M 73
W4 ....2D 12
Bedford Ct. *CR0: Croy* *7N 45*
(off Tavistock Rd.)
Bedford Cres. GU16: Frim G 8C 70
Bedford Hill SW12 ....2F 28
SW16 ....2F 28
Bedford La. GU16: Frim G 8D 70
SL5: S'dale 4E 34
Bedford Pk.
CR0: Croy 1C 200 (7N 45)
Bedford Pas. *SW6* *3K 13*
(off Dawes Rd.)
Bedford Pl.
CR0: Croy 1D 200 (7A 46)
Bedford Rd.
GU1: Guil 4B 202 (4M 113)
KT4: W Pk 8H 43
RH13: Hors 7K 197
TW2: Twick 4D 24
Bedfordshire Down
RG42: Warf 7D 16
Bedford Ter. SM2: Sut 3A 62
Bedgebury Gdns.
SW19 ....3K 27
Bedlow Cotts. GU6: Cranl 7A 156
Bedlow La. GU6: Cranl 7A 156
Bedlow Way CR0: Bedd 1K 63
Bedser Cl. CR7: T Hea 2N 45
GU21: Wok 3C 74
Bedster Gdns. KT8: W Mole 1B 40
Bedwell Gdns. UB3: Harl 1F 8
(not continuous)
Beech Av. CR2: Sande 7A 64
GU10: L Bou 6H 129
GU15: Camb 2B 70
KT24: Eff 6L 97
TN16: Tats 6F 86
TW8: Brent 3H 11
Beechbrook Av. GU46: Yate 1D 68
Beech Cl. GU8: Chid 5D 172
GU12: Alde 4C 110
KT11: Cob 8A 58
KT12: Hers 1K 57
KT14: Byf 8N 55
KT24: Eff 6L 97
RH4: Dork 1G 201 (4F 118)
RH7: Blin H 3H 145

Beech Cl. RH19: E Grin 8N 165
SM5: Cars 8D 44
SW15 ....1F 26
SW19 ....7H 27
TW15: A'ford 6E 22
TW16: Sunb 1L 39
TW19: Stan 1M 21
Beech Cl. Ct. KT11: Cob 7N 57
Beech Copse
CR2: S Croy 8F 200 (2B 64)
Beech Ct. *GU1: Guil* *4B 114*
(off Easington Pl.)
KT6: Surb 6K 41
RH19: E Grin 8N 165
Beech Cres. KT20: Box H 8B 100
Beechcroft KT21: A'tead 6M 79
Beechcroft Av. CR8: Ken 2A 84
KT3: N Mal 9B 26
Beechcroft Cl. BR6: Orp 1M 67
SL5: S'hill 3A 34
SW16 ....6K 29
TW5: Hest 3M 9
Beechcroft Ct. RG12: Brac 2N 31
Beechcroft Dr. GU2: Guil 6G 113
Beechcroft Lodge SM2: Sut 4A 62
Beechcroft Mnr.
KT13: Weybr 9E 38
Beechcroft Rd. BR6: Orp 1M 67
KT9: Ches 9M 41
SW14 ....6B 12
SW17 ....3C 28
Beech Dell BR2: Kes 1H 67
Beechdene KT20: Tad 9G 80
Beech Dr. GU17: B'water 2J 69
GU23: Rip 2J 95
KT20: K'wood 9L 81
RH2: Reig 3B 122
Beechen Cliff Way TW7: Isle 5F 10
Beechen La. KT20: K'wood 3L 101
Beechers Cft. TN16: B Hil 4E 86
Beeches, The CR2: S Croy 8D 200
GU5: Braml 5B 134
GU12: A Va 4D 90
KT22: Fetc 2E 98
SM7: Ban 3M 81
TW3: Houn 4B 10
TW18: Stain 6J 21
Beeches Av. SM5: Cars 4C 62
Beeches Cl.
KT20: K'wood 1M 101
SE20 ....1F 46
Beeches Cres.
RH10: Craw 5C 182
Beeches La. RH19: Ash W 3F 186
Beeches Mead
RH19: E Grin 5H 167
Beeches Rd. SM3: Sut 7K 43
SW17 ....4C 28
Beeches Wlk. SM5: Cars 5B 62
Beeches Wood
KT20: K'wood 9M 81
Beechey Cl. RH10: Cop 7M 163
Beechey Way RH10: Cop 7M 163
Beech Farm La.
GU15: Camb 2D 70
Beech Farm Rd. CR6: Warl 7M 85
Beechfield SM7: Ban 9N 61
Beechfield Ct.
CR2: S Croy 7B 200
Beechfields RH19: E Grin 7B 166
Beech Gdns. GU21: Wok 2A 74
RH10: Craw D 2D 184
Beech Glen RG12: Brac 3N 31
Beech Gro. CR3: Cate 4B 104
CR4: Mit 4H 45
(not continuous)
GU2: Guil 3J 113
GU22: Wok 1N 93
GU24: B'wood 7N 71
(not continuous)
KT3: N Mal 2C 42
KT15: Addl 1K 55
KT18: Tat C 4G 80
KT23: Book 5A 98
Beech Hall KT16: Otter 4E 54
Beech Hanger End
GU26: G'hott 6N 169
Beech Hanger Rd.
GU26: G'hott 6N 169
BEECH HILL 3F 168
Beech Hill GU8: Bow G 9K 151
GU22: Wok 1N 93
GU35: H Dwn 5F 168
Beech Hill Rd.
GU35: Head 3E 168
SL5: S'dale 5C 34
Beech Holme
RH10: Craw D 1E 184
Beech Holt KT22: Leat 9J 79
Beech Ho. CR0: N Add 3L 65
RH10: Craw 8B 162
Beech Ho. Rd.
CR0: Croy 5D 200 (9A 46)
Beeching Cl. GU12: Ash 1F 110
Beeching Way
RH19: E Grin 9A 166
Beech La.
GU2: Guil 8A 202 (6M 113)
(not continuous)
GU3: Flex 4L 111
GU26: G'hott 5N 169
Beechlee SM6: W'ton 6G 62
Beech Lawn GU1: Guil 4B 114

Beech Lodge TW18: Stain 6G 21
Beechmeads KT11: Cob 9L 57
Beechmont Av.
GU25: V Wat 4N 35
Beechmore Gdns.
SM3: Chea 8J 43
Beechnut Dr.
GU17: B'water 9G 48
Beechnut Ind. Est.
GU12: Alde 3N 109
Beechnut Rd. GU12: Alde 3N 109
Beecholme SM7: Ban 1K 81
Beecholme Av. CR4: Mit 9F 28
Beech Ride GU47: Sandh 7G 49
GU52: Fleet 6A 88
Beech Rd. GU14: Farnb 7M 69
GU16: Frim G 8D 70
GU27: Hasl 1H 189
KT13: Weybr 1E 56
KT17: Eps 2E 80
RH1: Mers 4G 103
RH2: Reig 9M 101
RH12: Hors 3A 198
SW16 ....1J 45
TN16: B Hil 6D 86
TW14: Bedf 1F 22
Beechrow TW10: Ham 5L 25
Beechside RH10: Craw 4C 182
Beechtree Av. TW20: Eng G 7L 19
Beech Tree Cl.
RH10: Craw 2B 182
Beech Tree Dr.
GU9: B Lea 7M 109
Beech Tree La. TW18: Lale 1K 37
Beech Tree Pl. SM1: Sut 2N 61
Beechvale *GU22: Wok* *5B 74*
(off Fairview Av.)
Beech Wlk. GU20: Windl 3A 52
KT17: Ewe 7F 60
Beech Way CR2: Sels 9G 65
GU7: Goda 8G 133
KT17: Eps 2E 80
TW2: Twick 4A 24
Beechway GU1: Guil 2D 114
Beechwood CR3: Cate 2D 104
Beechwood Av. BR6: Chels 2N 67
CR5: Coul 2F 82
CR7: T Hea 3M 45
KT13: Weybr 1F 56
KT20: K'wood 8M 81
TW9: Kew 4N 11
TW16: Sunb 7H 23
TW18: Stain 7K 21
Beechwood Cl. GU21: Knap 4H 73
KT6: Surb 6J 41
KT13: Weybr 1F 56
SL5: Asc 8J 17
Beechwood Ct. *KT12: Wal T* *9H 39*
(off Station Av.)
SM5: Cars 1D 62
TW16: Sunb 7H 23
W4 ....2C 12
Beechwood Dr. BR2: Kes 1F 66
KT11: Cob 7A 58
Beechwood Gdns.
CR3: Cate 9D 84
Beechwood Gro. KT6: Surb 6J 41
Beechwood Hall
KT20: K'wood 1A 102
Beechwood La. CR6: Warl 6G 85
Beechwood Mnr.
KT13: Weybr 1F 56
Beechwood Pk.
KT20: Box H 9A 100
KT22: Leat 9J 79
Beechwood Rd. CR2: Sande 6B 64
CR3: Cate 9D 84
GU21: Knap 4H 73
GU25: V Wat 6K 35
Beechwood Vs. RH1: Salf 4E 142
Beecot La. KT12: Wal T 8K 39
Beeding Cl. RH12: Hors 3N 197
Beedingwood Dr.
RH12: Col 2D 198
Beedon Dr. RG12: Brac 5K 31
Beehive La. RG12: Bin 1H 31
Beehive Ring Rd.
RH6: Craw 5F 162
Beehive Rd. RG12: Bin 9J 15
TW18: Stain 6H 21
Beehive Way RH2: Reig 7N 121
Beeken Dene BR6: Farnb 1L 67
Beeleigh Rd. SM4: Mord 3N 43
Beemans Row SW18 ....3A 28
Beeston Way TW14: Felt 9K 9
Beeton's Av. GU12: Ash 9E 90
Beggarhouse La.
RH5: Newd 2F 160
RH6: Char, Newd 2F 160
BEGGAR'S BUSH 3C 34
BEGGAR'S HILL 3E 60
Beggar's Hill KT17: Ewe 4E 60
Beggars La. GU24: Chob 7F 52
RH5: A Ham 8F 116
(not continuous)
TN16: Weste 3M 107
Beggars Roost La.
SM1: Sut 3M 61
Begonia Pl. TW12: Hamp 7A 24
Behenna Cl. RH11: Craw 4K 181
Beira St. SW12 ....1F 28
Beldam Bri. Rd.
GU24: Chob, W End 9D 52

Beldham Gdns.
KT8: W Mole 1B 40
Beldham Rd. GU9: Farnh 4E 128
Belfast Rd. SE25 ....3E 46
Belfield Rd. KT19: Ewe 5C 60
Belfry, The RH1: Red 2D 122
Belfry M. GU47: Sandh 7E 48
Belgrade Rd. TW12: Hamp 9B 24
Belgrave Cl. KT12: Hers 1J 57
Belgrave Ct. GU17: Haw 3J 69
W4 ....1B 12
Belgrave Cres. TW16: Sunb 9J 23
Belgrave Mnr. GU22: Wok 6A 74
Belgrave Rd. CR4: Mit 2B 44
SE25 ....3C 46
SW13 ....3E 12
TW4: Houn 6N 9
TW16: Sunb 9J 23
Belgrave Wlk. CR4: Mit 2B 44
Belgrave Walk Stop (CT) 3B 44
Belgravia Ct. *RH6: Horl* *8F 142*
(off St Georges Cl.)
Belgravia M.
KT1: K Tham 8H 203 (3K 41)
Bellamy Cl. W14 ....1L 13
Bellamy Ho. SW17 ....5B 28
TW5: Hest 2A 10
Bellamy Rd. RH10: Craw 7G 182
Bellamy St. SW12 ....1F 28
Belland Dr. GU11: Alde 3K 109
Bel La. TW13: Hanw 4M 23
Bellasis Av. SW2 ....3J 29
Bell Bri. Rd. KT16: Chert 7H 37
Bell Cen., The
RH10: Craw 8D 162
Bell Chase GU11: Alde 2L 109
Bell Cl. GU14: Farnb 8A 70
Bell Cnr. KT16: Chert 6H 37
Bell Cres. CR5: Coul 8F 82
Bell Dr. SW18 ....1K 27
Bellever Hill GU15: Camb 1C 70
Belle Vue Cl. GU12: Alde 2B 110
TW18: Stain 9J 21
Belle Vue Ent. Cen.
GU12: Alde 2C 110
Bellevue Pde. SW17 ....2D 28
Belle Vue Pk. CR7: T Hea 2N 45
Belle Vue Rd. BR6: Dow 6J 67
GU12: Alde 2B 110
Bellevue Rd.
KT1: K Tham 6K 203 (2L 41)
(not continuous)
SW13 ....5F 12
SW17 ....2C 28
Bellew Rd. GU16: Deep 8F 70
Bellew St. SW17 ....4A 28
Bellfield CR0: Sels 5H 65
BELLFIELDS 8M 93
Bellfields Ct. GU1: Guil 8M 93
Bellfields Rd. GU1: Guil 1N 113
Bell Foundry La.
RG40: W'ham 8A 14
Bell Hammer RH19: E Grin 1A 186
Bell Hill
CR0: Croy 3B 200 (8N 45)
Bell Ho. Gdns.
RG41: W'ham 2A 30
(not continuous)
Bellingham Cl.
GU15: Camb 2G 71
Bellingham Dr. RH2: Reig 3L 121
Bell Junc. TW3: Houn 6B 10
Bell La. GU10: Rowl 8D 128
GU17: B'water 1H 69
KT22: Fetc 1D 98
SL4: E Wic 1C 4
TW1: Twick 2G 25
Bell La. Cl. KT22: Fetc 1D 98
Bellmarsh Rd. KT15: Addl 1K 55
Bell Mdw. RH9: Gods 1E 124
Belloc Cl. RH10: Craw 2F 182
Belloc Ct. RH13: Hors 5N 197
Bello Cl. SE24 ....1M 29
Bell Pde. SL4: W'sor 5C 4
Bell Pl. GU19: Bag 4K 51
Bell Rd. GU27: Hasl 4E 188
KT8: E Mol 4D 40
RH12: Warn 9F 178
TW3: Houn 6B 10
Bells All. SW6 ....5M 13
Bellsfield Ct. *SL4: E Wic* *1C 4*
(off Bell La.)
Bells La. SL3: Hort 6D 6
Bell St. RH2: Reig 3M 121
Belltrees Gro.
SW16 ....6K 29
Bell Va. La. GU27: Hasl 4F 188
Bell Vw. SL4: W'sor 6C 4
Bell Vw. Cl. SL4: W'sor 5C 4
Bellway Ho. RH1: Mers 6G 102
Bell Weir Cl. TW19: Stain 3D 20
Bellwether La. RH1: Out 3M 143
BELMONT 6M 61
Belmont KT13: Weybr 3D 56
Belmont Av. GU2: Guil 9J 93
KT3: N Mal 4F 42
Belmont Cl. GU14: Cove 7L 69
Belmont Cotts. *SL3: Coln* *3E 6*
(off High St.)
Belmont Gro. W4 ....1C 12
Belmont M. GU15: Camb 3A 70
SW19 ....3J 27
Belmont Ri. SM2: Sut 4L 61

Belmont Rd. BR3: Beck 1H 47
GU15: Camb 2A 70
KT22: Leat 9G 79
RG45: Crow 1G 49
RH2: Reig 4A 122
SE25 ....4E 46
SM2: Sut 6M 61
SM6: W'ton 2F 62
TW2: Twick 3D 24
W4 ....1C 12
Belmont Station (Rail) 6N 61
Belmont Ter. W4 ....1C 12
Belmore Av. GU22: Pyr 3F 74
Beloe Cl. SW15 ....7F 12
Belsize Gdns. SM1: Sut 1N 61
Belsize Grange KT16: Chert 6L 37
Belstone M. GU14: Farnb 7M 69
Beltane Dr. SW19 ....4J 27
Belthorn Cres. SW12 ....1G 29
Belton Rd. GU15: Camb 1C 70
Beltran Rd. SW6 ....5N 13
Belvedere Av. SW19 ....6K 27
Belvedere Cl. GU2: Guil 1L 113
KT10: Esh 2B 58
KT13: Weybr 2B 56
TW11: Tedd 6E 24
Belvedere Ct. GU17: Haw 3J 69
RH1: Red 8E 102
RH10: Craw 2F 182
SW15 ....7H 13
Belvedere Dr. SW19 ....6K 27
Belvedere Gdns.
KT8: W Mole 4N 39
Belvedere Gro. SW19 ....6K 27
Belvedere Ho. KT13: Weybr 2C 56
Belvedere Rd. GU14: Farnb 3A 90
TN16: B Hil 5H 87
Belvedere Sq. SW19 ....6K 27
Belvoir Cl. GU16: Frim 5D 70
Bembridge Ct. RG45: Crow 3D 48
Bembridge Ho.
KT2: K Tham *3M 203*
(off Coombe Rd.)
SW18 ....*9N 13*
(off Iron Mill Rd.)
Bemish Rd. SW15 ....6J 13
Benbow La. GU8: Duns 5E 174
Benbricke Grn. RG42: Brac 8M 15
Benbrick Rd. GU2: Guil 4K 113
Bence, The TW20: Thor 2D 36
Bench, The TW10: Ham 4J 25
Bench Fld. CR2: S Croy 3C 64
Benchfield Cl.
RH19: E Grin 1D 186
Bencombe Rd. CR8: Pur 1L 83
Bencroft Rd. SW16 ....8G 29
Bencurtis Pk. BR4: W Wick 9N 47
Bendemeer Rd. SW15 ....6J 13
Bendon Valley SW18 ....1N 27
Benedict Cl. BR6: Orp 1N 67
Benedict Dr. TW14: Bedf 1E 22
Benedict Grn. RG42: Warf 8C 16
Benedict Rd. CR4: Mit 2B 44
Benedict Wharf CR4: Mit 2C 44
Benen-Stock Rd.
TW19: Stan M 8J 7
Benetfeld Rd. RG42: Bin 7G 15
Benett Gdns. SW16 ....1J 45
Benfleet Cl. KT11: Cob 8M 57
SM1: Sut 9A 44
Benham Cl. CR5: Coul 5M 83
KT9: Ches 3J 59
Benham Gdns. TW4: Houn 8N 9
Benham Ho. *SW10* *3N 13*
(off Coleridge Gdns.)
Benhams Cl. RH6: Horl 6E 142
Benhams Dr. RH6: Horl 6E 142
Benhill Av. SM1: Sut 1N 61
(not continuous)
Benhill Rd. SM1: Sut 9A 44
Benhill Wood Rd. SM1: Sut 9A 44
BENHILTON 8N 43
Benhilton Gdns. SM1: Sut 9N 43
Benhurst Cl. CR2: Sels 6G 64
Benhurst Ct. SW16 ....6L 29
Benhurst Gdns. CR2: Sels 6F 64
Benhurst La. SW16 ....6L 29
Benjamin Ct. TW15: A'ford 8D 22
Benjamin M. SW12 ....1G 28
Benjamin Rd. RH10: Craw 5H 183
Benland Cotts.
RH12: Warn 7D 178
Benn Cl. RH8: Oxt 3C 126
Benner La. GU24: W End 8C 52
Bennets Courtyard
SW19 ....9A 28
Bennett Cl. KT1: H Wic 9J 25
KT11: Cob 9H 57
RH10: Craw 7F 182
TW4: Houn 8M 9
Bennett Ct. GU15: Camb 1A 70
Bennetts Av. CR0: Croy 8H 47
Bennetts Cl. CR4: Mit 9F 28
Bennetts Farm Pl.
KT23: Book 3N 97
Bennetts Ri. GU11: Alde 4A 110
Bennetts Rd. RH13: Hors 7L 197
Bennett St. W4 ....2D 12
Bennetts Way CR0: Croy 8H 47
Bennetts Wood RH5: Cap 5J 159
Bennett Way GU4: W Cla 7J 95
Benning Cl. SL4: W'sor 6A 4
Bennings Cl. RG42: Brac 8M 15

Benning Way—Bishop Sumner Dr.

Benning Way RG40: W'ham ... 9B 14
Benn's All. TW12: Hamp ... 1B 40
Benns Wlk. TW9: Rich ... 7L 11
(off Michelsdale Dr.)
Bens Acre RH13: Hors ... 6N 197
Bensbury Cl. SW15 ... 1G 27
Bensham Cl. CR7: T Hea ... 3N 45
Bensham Gro. CR7: T Hea ... 1N 45
Bensham La. CR0: Croy ... 6M 45
CR7: T Hea ... 4M 45
Bensham Mnr. Rd.
CR7: T Hea ... 3N 45
Bensham Mnr. Rd. Pas.
CR7: T Hea ... 3N 45
Benson Cl. TW3: Houn ... 7A 10
Benson Rd. CR0: Wad ... 9L 45
RG45: Crow ... 2E 48
Bensons La. RH12: Fay ... 8B 180
Bentalls Cen., The
KT1: K Tham ... 3H 203 (1K 41)
Benthall Gdns. CR8: Ken ... 4N 83
Bentham Av. GU21: Wok ... 2E 74
Bentley Cl. SW19 ... 4M 27
Bentley Copse GU15: Camb ... 2F 70
Bentley Dr. KT13: Weybr ... 5B 56
Bentley Pl. KT13: Weybr ... 1C 56
(off Baker St.)
Bentons La. SE27 ... 5N 29
Benton's Ri. SE27 ... 6N 29
Bentsbrook Cl. RH5: Nth H ... 9H 119
Bentsbrook Cotts.
RH5: Nth H ... 9H 119
Bentsbrook Pk.
RH5: Nth H ... 9H 119
Bentsbrook Rd.
RH5: Nth H ... 9H 119
Benwell Ct. TW16: Sunb ... 9H 23
Benwell Rd. GU24: B'wood ... 6C 72
Benwood Ct. SM1: Sut ... 9A 44
Beomonds KT16: Chert ... 6J 37
Beomonds Row KT16: Chert ... 6J 37
Berberis Cl. GU1: Guil ... 1M 113
(not continuous)
Berberis Ho. TW13: Felt ... 3H 23
Bere Rd. RG12: Brac ... 5C 32
Beresford Av. KT5: Surb ... 7A 42
TW1: Twick ... 9J 11
Beresford Cl. GU16: Frim G ... 8D 70
Beresford Gdns. TW4: Houn ... 8N 9
Beresford Rd.
KT2: K Tham ... 1L 203 (9M 25)
KT3: N Mal ... 3B 42
RH4: Dork ... 3L 201 (5H 119)
SM2: Sut ... 4L 61
Berestede Rd. W6 ... 1E 12
Bergenia Ct. GU24: W End ... 9B 52
Bergenia Ho. TW13: Felt ... 2J 23
Berisford M. SW18 ... 9N 13
Berkeley Av. TW4: C'ford ... 5H 9
Berkeley Cl. GU51: Fleet ... 4C 88
KT2: K Tham ... 8L 25
RH11: Craw ... 7J 181
TW19: Stain ... 3F 20
Berkeley Ct. CR0: Croy ... 6D 200
KT6: Surb ... 6K 41
KT13: Weybr ... 8E 38
KT21: A'tead ... 5M 79
SM6: W'ton ... 9G 44
Berkeley Cres. GU16: Frim ... 6E 70
Berkeley Dr. KT8: W Mole ... 2N 39
SL4: Wink ... 2M 17
Berkeley Gdns. KT10: Clay ... 3G 59
KT12: Wal T ... 6G 39
KT14: W By ... 1H 75
Berkeley Ho. TW8: Brent ... 2K 11
(off Albany Rd.)
Berkeley M. TW16: Sunb ... 2K 39
Berkeley Pl. KT18: Eps ... 2C 80
SW19 ... 7J 27
Berkeley Rd. SW13 ... 4F 12
Berkeleys, The KT22: Fetc ... 2E 98
SE25 ... 3D 46
Berkeley Waye TW5: Hest ... 2L 9
Berkley Cl. TW2: Twick ... 4E 24
(off Wellesley Rd.)
Berkley Ct.
GU1: Guil ... 2F 202 (3A 114)
Berkshire Cl. CR3: Cate ... 9A 84
Berkshire Ct. RG12: Brac ... 1L 31
Berkshire Rd. GU15: Camb ... 7D 50
Berkshire Sq. CR4: Mit ... 3J 45
Berkshire Way CR4: Mit ... 3J 45
RG12: Brac ... 2G 31
RG40: W'ham ... 2G 31
Berkshire Yeomanry Mus. ... 7G 4
Bernadine Cl. RG42: Warf ... 8C 16
Bernard Ct. GU15: Camb ... 2N 69
Bernard Gdns. SW19 ... 6L 27
Bernard Pl. KT17: Ewe ... 6H 61
Bernard Rd. SM6: W'ton ... 1F 62
Bernel Dr. CR0: Croy ... 9J 47
Berne Rd. CR7: T Hea ... 4N 45
Bernersh Cl. GU47: Sandh ... 6H 49
Berney Ho. BR3: Beck ... 4H 47
Berney Rd. CR0: Croy ... 6A 46
Berrington Dr. KT24: E Hor ... 2G 97
Berrybank GU47: C Tow ... 9K 49
Berry Ct. TW4: Houn ... 8N 9
Berrycroft RG12: Brac ... 9B 16
BERRYLANDS ... 5N 41
Berrylands KT5: Surb ... 5M 41
SW20 ... 2H 43
Berrylands Rd. KT5: Surb ... 5M 41
Berrylands Station (Rail) ... 3A 42
Berry La. GU3: Worp ... 3F 92
(not continuous)
GU22: Wok ... 3F 92
KT12: Hers ... 2L 57
(off The Green)
RG42: Warf ... 1D 16
Berry Meade
KT21: A'tead ... 4M 79
Berry Meade Cl.
KT21: A'tead ... 4M 79
Berrymeade Wlk.
RH11: Ifi ... 4K 181
Berrys Ct. KT14: Byf ... 7M 55
Berryscroft Ct. TW18: Stain ... 8L 21
Berryscroft Rd.
TW18: Stain ... 8L 21
BERRY'S GREEN ... 3K 87
Berry's Grn. Rd.
TN16: B Hil ... 3K 87
Berry's Hill TN16: B Hil ... 3K 87
Berry's La. KT14: Byf ... 7M 55
Berry Wlk. KT21: A'tead ... 6M 79
Berstead Wlk. RH11: Craw ... 6L 181
Bertal Rd. SW17 ... 5B 28
Bertram Cotts. SW19 ... 8M 27
Bertram Rd. KT2: K Tham ... 8N 25
Bertrand Ho. SW16 ... 4J 29
(off Leigham Av.)
Bert Rd. CR7: T Hea ... 4N 45
Berwick Cl. TW2: Whitt ... 2A 24
Berwick Gdns. SM1: Sut ... 9A 44
Berwyn Av. TW3: Houn ... 4B 10
Berwyn Rd. SE24 ... 2M 29
TW10: Rich ... 7A 12
Beryl Rd. W6 ... 1J 13
Berystede KT2: K Tham ... 8A 26
Besley St. SW16 ... 7G 29
Bessant Dr. TW9: Kew ... 4N 11
Bessborough Rd.
SW15 ... 2F 26
Bessemer Cl. SL3: Lang ... 1B 6
Beswick Gdns. RG12: Brac ... 9D 16
Beta Rd. GU14: Cove ... 9L 69
GU22: Wok ... 3D 74
GU24: Chob ... 6J 53
Beta Way TW20: Thor ... 9E 20
BETCHETS GREEN ... 5H 139
Betchets Grn. Rd.
RH5: Holm ... 5J 139
Betchley Cl. RH19: E Grin ... 7A 166
BETCHWORTH ... 3C 120
Betchworth Cl. SM1: Sut ... 2B 62
Betchworth Station (Rail) ... 1C 120
Betchworth Way
CR0: N Add ... 5M 65
Betchworth Works
RH6: Char ... 4J 161
Bethany Pl. GU21: Wok ... 5N 73
Bethany Waye TW14: Bedf ... 1F 22
Bethel Cl. GU9: U Hal ... 6J 109
Bethel La. GU9: U Hal ... 5H 109
Bethune Cl. RH10: Wor ... 4H 183
Bethune Rd. RH13: Hors ... 7L 197
Betjeman Cl. CR5: Coul ... 4K 83
Betjeman Wlk. GU46: Yate ... 2A 68
Betley Ct. KT12: Wal T ... 9J 39
Betony Cl. CR0: Croy ... 7G 47
Bettridge Rd. SW6 ... 5L 13
Betts Cl. BR3: Beck ... 1H 47
Betts Way KT6: Surb ... 7H 41
RH10: Craw ... 8B 162
SE20 ... 1E 46
Betula Cl. CR8: Ken ... 2A 84
Between Streets KT11: Cob ... 1H 77
Beulah Av. CR7: T Hea ... 1N 45
Beulah Ct. RH6: Horl ... 8E 142
Beulah Cres. CR7: T Hea ... 1N 45
Beulah Gro. CR0: Croy ... 5N 45
Beulah Hill SE19 ... 7M 29
Beulah Rd. CR7: T Hea ... 2N 45
SM1: Sut ... 1M 61
SW19 ... 8L 27
Beulah Wlk. CR3: Wold ... 7H 85
Bevan Ct. CR0: Wad ... 2L 63
RH11: Craw ... 8N 181
Bevan Ga. RG42: Brac ... 9M 15
Bevan Ho. TW1: Twick ... 9K 11
Bevan Pk. KT17: Ewe ... 6E 60
Beveree Stadium ... 9B 24
Beveren Cl. GU51: Fleet ... 1C 88
Beverley Av. SW20 ... 9E 26
TW4: Houn ... 7N 9
Beverley Cl. GU12: Ash ... 3D 110
GU15: Camb ... 9H 51
KT9: Ches ... 1J 59
KT13: Weybr ... 8F 38
KT15: Addl ... 2M 55
KT17: Ewe ... 7H 61
SW13 ... 5F 12
Beverley Cotts. SW15 ... 4D 26
Beverley Ct. TW4: Houn ... 7N 9
W4 ... 1B 12
Beverley Cres.
GU14: Cove ... 3L 89
Beverley Gdns. KT4: W Pk ... 7F 42
SW13 ... 6E 12
Beverley Hgts. RH2: Reig ... 1N 121
Beverley Hyrst CR0: Croy ... 8C 46
Beverley La. KT2: K Tham ... 8D 26
SW15 ... 4E 26
Beverley M. RH10: Craw ... 4E 182
Beverley Path SW13 ... 5E 12
Beverley Rd. CR3: Whyte ... 3B 84
CR4: Mit ... 3H 45
KT1: H Wic ... 9J 25
KT3: N Mal ... 3F 42
KT4: W Pk ... 8H 43
RG12: Brac ... 2B 32
SE20 ... 1E 46
SW13 ... 6E 12
TW16: Sunb ... 9G 22
W4 ... 1E 12
Beverley Trad. Est.
SM4: Mord ... 6J 43
Beverley Way SW20 ... 9E 26
Beverstone Rd. CR7: T Hea ... 3L 45
Bevill Allen Cl. SW17 ... 6D 28
Bevill Cl. SE25 ... 2D 46
Bevington Rd. BR3: Beck ... 1L 47
Bevin Sq. SW17 ... 4D 28
BEWBUSH ... 6L 181
Bewbush Dr. RH11: Craw ... 6K 181
Bewbush Leisure Cen. ... 7L 181
Bewbush Mnr. Rdbt.
RH11: Craw ... 7K 181
Bewbush Pl. RH11: Craw ... 6K 181
Bewbush Water Garden ... 5J 181
Bewley St. SW19 ... 7A 28
Bewlys Rd. SE27 ... 6M 29
Bexhill Cl. TW13: Felt ... 3M 23
Bexhill Rd. SW14 ... 6B 12
Bexley St. SL4: W'sor ... 4F 4
Beynon Rd. SM5: Cars ... 2D 62
Bicester Rd. TW9: Rich ... 6N 11
Bickersteth Rd. SW17 ... 7D 28
Bickley Ct. RH11: Craw ... 6M 181
Bickley St. SW17 ... 6C 28
Bicknell Cl.
GU1: Guil ... 1C 202 (2M 113)
Bicknell Rd. GU16: Frim ... 4C 70
Bickney Way KT22: Fetc ... 9C 78
Bicknoller Cl. SM2: Sut ... 6N 61
Bicton Cft. GU7: Goda ... 5H 133
Biddulph Rd. CR2: S Croy ... 6N 63
Bideford Cl. GU14: Farnb ... 7M 69
TW13: Hanw ... 4N 23
Bidhams Cres. KT20: Tad ... 8H 81
Bield, The RH2: Reig ... 5M 121
Bietigheim Way
GU15: Camb ... 9A 50
Big All. TN8: M Grn ... 6K 147
Big Apple ... 4B 74
Big Apple Leisure Cen. ... 3A 30
Big Barn Gro. RG42: Warf ... 8B 16
Big Comn. La. RH1: Blet ... 2M 123
Biggin Av. CR4: Mit ... 9D 28
Biggin Cl. RH11: Craw ... 5A 182
BIGGIN HILL ... 4F 86
Biggin Hill SE19 ... 9M 29
BIGGIN HILL AIRPORT ... 8F 66
Biggin Hill Bus. Pk.
TN16: B Hil ... 2F 86
Biggin Hill Cl. KT2: K Tham ... 6J 25
Biggin Way SE19 ... 8M 29
Bigginwood Rd. SW16 ... 8M 29
Biggs Row SW15 ... 6J 13
Bignor Cl. RH12: Hors ... 2N 197
Bilberry Cl. RH11: Craw ... 6N 181
Bilbets RH12: Hors ... 5J 197
(off Rushams Rd.)
Billet Rd. TW18: Stain ... 4J 21
BILL HILL ... 6A 14
BILLINGBEAR ... 4G 15
Billingbear Cvn. Pk.
RG40: W'ham ... 5E 14
Billingbear La.
RG40: W'ham ... 4D 14
RG42: Bin ... 4G 15
Billing Pl. SW10 ... 3N 13
Billing Rd. SW10 ... 3N 13
Billingshurst Rd.
RH12: Bro H ... 5C 196
Billing St. SW10 ... 3N 13
Billington Ct. RH19: E Grin ... 8A 166
Billinton Dr. RH10: Craw ... 3F 182
Billinton Hill
CR0: Croy ... 2E 200 (8A 46)
Billockby Cl. KT9: Ches ... 3M 59
Bilton Cen. KT22: Leat ... 6F 78
Bilton Cl. SL3: Poy ... 5G 7
Bilton Ind. Est. RG12: Brac ... 3K 31
Bindon Grn. SM4: Mord ... 3N 43
BINFIELD ... 7H 15
Binfield Rd. CR2: S Croy ... 2C 64
KT14: Byf ... 8N 55
RG10: S Row ... 1F 14
RG40: W'ham ... 2D 30
RG42: Bin, Brac ... 7L 15
Bingham Dr. GU21: Wok ... 5J 73
TW18: Stain ... 8M 21
Bingham Rd. CR0: Croy ... 7D 46
Bingley Rd. TW16: Sunb ... 8H 23
Binhams Lea GU8: Duns ... 4B 174
Binhams Mdw. GU8: Duns ... 4B 174
Binley Ho. SW15 ... 9E 12
Binney Ct. RH10: Craw ... 9J 163
Binns Rd. W4 ... 1D 12
Binns Ter. W4 ... 1D 12
BINSCOMBE ... 3G 133
Binscombe GU7: Goda ... 3G 132
Binscombe Cres.
GU7: Goda ... 4H 133
Binscombe La. GU7: Goda ... 3G 133
Binstead Cl. RH11: Craw ... 1N 181
Binstead Copse GU52: Fleet ... 6A 88
Binsted Dr. GU17: B'water ... 1J 69
Binton La. GU10: Seal ... 1C 130
Birchanger GU7: Goda ... 7H 133
Birchanger Rd. SE25 ... 4D 46
Birch Av. CR3: Cate ... 2A 104
GU51: Fleet ... 4A 88
KT22: Leat ... 7F 78
Birch Circ. GU7: Goda ... 3J 133
Birch Cl. GU10: Wrec ... 7F 128
GU15: Camb ... 7C 50
GU21: Wok ... 6M 73
GU23: Send ... 3H 95
KT15: N Haw ... 5M 55
RH10: Craw D ... 1F 184
SM7: Ban ... 1K 81
TW3: Houn ... 5D 10
TW8: Brent ... 3H 11
TW11: Tedd ... 6G 25
TW17: Shep ... 1F 38
Birch Ct. KT22: Leat ... 7F 78
RG45: Crow ... 2E 48
SM1: Sut ... 1A 62
SM6: W'ton ... 1F 62
Birchcroft Cl. CR3: Cate ... 3N 103
Birchdale Cl. KT14: W By ... 7L 55
Birch Dr. GU17: Haw ... 3J 69
Birchend Cl. CR2: S Croy ... 3A 64
Birches, The BR6: Farnb ... 1J 67
GU14: Cove ... 1J 89
GU17: B'water ... 1G 69
GU22: Wok ... 5B 74
KT24: E Hor ... 4F 96
RH10: Craw ... 1E 182
RH13: M Hea ... 9B 198
TW4: Houn ... 1N 23
Birches Cl. CR4: Mit ... 2D 44
KT18: Eps ... 2D 80
Birches Ind. Est.
RH19: E Grin ... 7K 165
Birches La. GU5: Gorn ... 1D 136
Birches Rd. RH12: Hors ... 3A 198
Birchett Rd. GU11: Alde ... 2M 109
GU14: Cove ... 9K 69
Birchetts Cl. RG42: Brac ... 9N 15
Birchfield Cl. CR5: Coul ... 3K 83
KT15: Addl ... 1K 55
Birchfield Ct. KT12: Wal T ... 6J 39
(off Grove Cres.)
Birchfield Gro. KT17: Ewe ... 6H 61
Birchfield Ind. Pk.
RH6: Char ... 6J 161
Birchfields GU15: Camb ... 2A 70
BIRCH GREEN ... 5J 21
Birch Grn. TW18: Stain ... 5H 21
Birch Gro. GU1: Guil ... 9M 93
GU22: Pyr ... 2F 74
KT11: Cob ... 1K 77
KT20: K'wood ... 2K 101
SL4: W'sor ... 4A 4
TW17: Shep ... 1F 38
Birchgrove Ho. TW9: Kew ... 3A 12
BIRCH HILL ... 6N 31
Birch Hill CR0: Croy ... 2G 65
Birch Hill Rd. RG12: Brac ... 6N 31
Birch Ho. RH19: E Grin ... 8M 165
SW2 ... 1L 29
(off Tulse Hill)
Birchington Rd. KT5: Surb ... 6M 41
SL4: W'sor ... 5D 4
Birchlands Av. SW12 ... 1D 28
Birchlands Ct.
GU47: Owls ... 5K 49
Birch La. CR8: Pur ... 7J 63
GU24: W End ... 8A 52
SL5: Asc ... 9E 16
Birch Lea RH10: Craw ... 9E 162
Birch Pde. GU51: Fleet ... 4A 88
Birch Platt GU24: W End ... 9A 52
Birch Rd. GU7: Goda ... 3J 133
GU20: Windl ... 3B 52
GU35: H Dwn ... 3F 168
TW13: Hanw ... 6L 23
Birch Side RG45: Crow ... 1E 48
Birch Tree Av. BR4: W Wick ... 2B 66
Birch Tree Ct. GU27: Hasl ... 4A 188
Birch Tree Gdns.
RH19: E Grin ... 7L 165
Birch Tree Vw. GU18: Ligh ... 6L 51
Birch Tree Way CR0: Croy ... 8E 46
Birch Va. KT11: Cob ... 8A 58
Birchview Cl. GU46: Yate ... 2B 68
Birch Wlk. CR4: Mit ... 9F 28
KT14: W By ... 8J 55
(not continuous)
Birch Way CR6: Warl ... 5H 85
GU12: A Va ... 6E 90
Birchway RH1: Red ... 5F 122
Birchwood Av. BR3: Beck ... 3J 47
SM6: W'ton ... 9E 44
Birchwood Cl. RH6: Horl ... 7F 142
RH10: Craw ... 6G 183
RH14: Ifo ... 5F 192
SM4: Mord ... 3N 43
Birchwood Ct. KT13: Weybr ... 2D 56
Birchwood Dr. GU18: Ligh ... 6N 51
KT14: W By ... 8J 55
Birchwood Gro.
TW12: Hamp ... 7A 24
Birchwood La. CR3: Cate ... 3M 103
KT10: Esh ... 5D 58
KT22: Oxs ... 5D 58
Birchwood Rd. KT14: W By ... 8J 55
SW17 ... 6F 28
Birdham Cl. RH11: Craw ... 1N 181
Birdhaven GU10: Wrec ... 5F 128
Birdhouse La. BR6: Dow ... 2J 87
Birdhurst Av.
CR2: S Croy ... 7E 200 (1A 64)
Birdhurst Ct. SM6: W'ton ... 4G 62
(off Woodcote Av.)
Birdhurst Gdns.
CR2: S Croy ... 7E 200 (1A 64)
Birdhurst Ri.
CR2: S Croy ... 8F 200 (2B 64)
Birdhurst Rd.
CR2: S Croy ... 8F 200 (2B 64)
SW19 ... 7C 28
Bird in Hand Path
CR0: Croy ... 6A 46
(off Sydenham Rd.)
Bird M. RG40: W'ham ... 2A 30
Birds Gro. GU21: Knap ... 5E 72
Birds Hill Dr. KT22: Oxs ... 9D 58
Birds Hill Ri. KT22: Oxs ... 9D 58
Birds Hill Rd. KT22: Oxs ... 8D 58
Birdswood Dr. GU21: Wok ... 6H 73
Bird Wlk. TW2: Whitt ... 2N 23
Birdwood Cl. CR2: Sels ... 7F 64
TW11: Tedd ... 5E 24
Birdwood Rd. GU15: Camb ... 9K 49
Birdworld & Underwater World
... 8A 128
Birkbeck Hill SE21 ... 2M 29
Birkbeck Pl. GU47: Owls ... 6K 49
SE21 ... 3N 29
Birkbeck Rd. BR3: Beck ... 1F 46
SW19 ... 6N 27
Birkbeck Station (Rail & CT)
... 2F 46
Birkdale RG12: Brac ... 6K 31
Birkdale Dr. RH11: Ifi ... 4J 181
Birkdale Gdns. CR0: Croy ... 1G 65
Birkenhead Av.
KT2: K Tham ... 3L 203 (1M 41)
Birkenholme Cl.
GU35: H Dwn ... 5H 169
Birkheads Rd. RH2: Reig ... 2M 121
Birkin Ct. KT14: Byf ... 7M 55
Birkwood Cl. SW12 ... 1H 29
Birnam Cl. GU23: Rip ... 2J 95
BIRTLEY GREEN ... 8D 134
Birtley Ri. GU5: Braml ... 6C 134
Birtley Rd. GU5: Braml ... 6C 134
Biscay Rd. W6 ... 1J 13
Biscoe Cl. TW5: Hest ... 2A 10
Bisenden Rd.
CR0: Croy ... 2F 200 (8B 46)
Bisham Cl. RH10: Craw ... 5H 183
SM5: Cars ... 7D 44
Bishams Ct. CR3: Cate ... 2C 104
Bishop Ct. TW9: Rich ... 6L 11
Bishopdale RG12: Brac ... 3M 31
Bishop Duppas Pk.
TW17: Shep ... 6F 38
Bishop Fox Way
KT8: W Mole ... 3N 39
Bishopric RH12: Hors ... 6H 197
Bishopric Ct. RH12: Hors ... 6H 197
Bishop's Av. SW6 ... 5J 13
Bishops Cl. CR5: Coul ... 5L 83
GU52: Fleet ... 7B 88
SM1: Sut ... 9M 43
TW10: Ham ... 4K 25
W4 ... 1B 12
Bishop's Cotts. RH3: Betch ... 2A 120
Bishops Ct. CR0: Croy ... 8C 46
GU2: Guil ... 6B 202
RH12: Hors ... 7J 197
SL5: Asc ... 7K 17
Bishop's Dr. RG40: W'ham ... 1B 30
TW14: Bedf ... 9E 8
Bishopsford Rd. SM4: Mord ... 6A 44
BISHOPS GATE ... 4K 19
Bishopsgate Rd.
TW20: Eng G ... 4J 19
Bishops Gro. GU20: Windl ... 3N 51
TW12: Hamp ... 5N 23
Bishops Gro. Cvn. Site
TW12: Hamp ... 5A 24
Bishop's Hall
KT1: K Tham ... 3H 203 (1K 41)
Bishops Hill KT12: Wal T ... 6H 39
Bishop's La. RG42: Warf ... 2E 16
Bishop's Mans. SW6 ... 5J 13
(not continuous)
Bishops Mead GU9: Farnh ... 1G 128
Bishopsmead Cl.
KT19: Ewe ... 6C 60
KT24: E Hor ... 6F 96
Bishopsmead Ct.
KT19: Ewe ... 6D 60
Bishopsmead Dr.
KT24: E Hor ... 7G 96
Bishopsmead Pde.
KT24: E Hor ... 7F 96
Bishops Pk. Rd. SW6 ... 5J 13
SW16 ... 9J 29
Bishops Pl. SM1: Sut ... 2A 62
Bishops Rd. CR0: Croy ... 6M 45
GU9: U Hal ... 6G 108
SW6 ... 4K 13
Bishops Sq. GU6: Cranl ... 7A 156
Bishopstone Wlk.
RH11: Craw ... 8A 182
Bishop Sumner Dr.
GU9: U Hal ... 6H 109

Bishops Wlk.—Borough Hill

Bishops Wlk. CR0: A'ton 2G 64
Bishops Way TW20: Egh 7F 20
Bishops Wharf GU1: Guil 5A 202
Bishops Wood GU21: Wok 4J 73
BISLEY 2C 72
BISLEY CAMP 6A 72
Bisley Cl. KT4: W Pk 7H 43
Bisley Grn. GU24: Bis 3C 72
Bison Ct. TW14: Felt 1J 23
Bissingen Way GU15: Camb . . .9B 50
Bitmead Cl. RH11: Ifi 4K 181
Bittams La. KT16: Chert 1F 54
Bittern Cl. GU11: Alde 5M 109
GU47: C Tow 7J 49
RH11: Ifi 4J 181
Bitterne Dr. GU21: Wok 4J 73
Bittoms, The
KT1: K Tham 5H 203 (2K 41)
(not continuous)
Bittoms Ct.
KT1: K Tham 5H 203 (2K 41)
Blackberry Cl. GU1: Guil 9L 93
TW17: Shep 3F 38
Blackberry Farm Cl.
TW5: Hest 3M 9
Blackberry La. RH7: Ling 9N 145
Blackberry Rd. RH7: Ling . . .2M 165
RH19: Felc, Ling 2M 165
Blackbird Cl. GU47: C Tow 7J 49
Blackbird Hill RH10: T Hil 4F 184
Blackborough Cl.
RH2: Reig 3A 122
Blackborough Rd.
RH2: Reig 4A 122
Blackbridge Ct.
RH12: Hors 6H 197
Blackbridge La.
RH12: Hors 7G 196
Blackbridge Rd. GU22: Wok . . .6N 73
BLACKBROOK 1L 139
Blackbrook Rd.
RH5: Holm, Nth H 9K 119
Blackburn, The KT23: Book . . .2N 97
Blackburn Trad. Est.
TW19: Stan 9A 8
Blackburn Way GU7: Goda . . .6J 133
TW4: Houn 8M 9
Blackbush Cl. SM2: Sut 4N 61
Blackbushe Bus. Pk.
GU46: Yate 2B 68
Blackbushe Pk. GU46: Yate 1B 68
Blackbushes Rd.
GU51: Fleet 8A 68
Blackcap Cl. RH11: Craw 5A 182
Blackcap Pl. GU47: C Tow 7K 49
BLACK CORNER 5H 163
Black Dog Wlk.
RH10: Craw 1C 182
Black Down 7K 189
Blackdown Av. GU22: Pyr 2G 74
Blackdown Cl. GU22: Pyr 3E 74
Blackdown Rd. GU16: Deep . . .7G 70
Black Eagle Cl.
TN16: Weste 5L 107
Black Eagle Sq.
TN16: Weste 5L 107
Blackett Cl. TW18: Stain 1G 37
Blackett Rd. RH10: Craw 4G 182
Blackett St. SW15 . . . . .6J 13
Blackfold Rd. RH10: Craw 4E 182
Blackford Cl. CR2: S Croy 5M 63
Blackford's Path SW15 . . . . . . .1F 26
BLACKHEATH 2G 135
Blackheath 2H 135
Blackheath RH10: Craw 1H 183
Blackheath Gro.
GU5: Wone 3D 134
Blackheath La.
GU4: B'eath 3D 134
GU5: Alb 2K 135
GU5: Wone 3D 134
Blackheath Rd. GU9: U Hal . . .5F 108
Blackhills KT10: Esh 5N 57
Black Horse Cl. SL4: W'sor 5A 4
Blackhorse La. CR0: Croy 6D 46
KT20: Lwr K 7N 101
Blackhorse Lane Stop (CT) 6D 46
Blackhorse Rd. GU22: Wok . . .7G 72
Blackhorse Way
RH12: Hors 6H 197
Black Horse Yd. SL4: W'sor 4G 5
Blackhouse Farm Ind. Est.
RH13: Col 3J 199
Blackhouse Rd. RH13: Col . . .2H 199
Black Lake Cl. TW20: Egh 9C 20
Blacklands Cres.
RH18: F Row 7H 187
Blacklands Mdw. RH1: Nut . . .2J 123
Black Lion La. W6 . . . . .1F 12
Black Lion M. W6 . . . . .1F 12
Blackman Gdns.
GU11: Alde 4N 109
Blackman's La. CR6: Warl 1A 86
Black Mdws. RG12: Brac 5A 32
Blackmoor Cl. SL5: Asc 1H 33
Blackmoor Wood SL5: Asc 1H 33
Blackmore Cres.
GU21: Wok 2E 74
Blackmore's Gro.
TW11: Tedd 7G 24
Blackness La. BR2: Kes 5F 66
GU22: Wok 6A 74
BLACKNEST 2E 34
Blacknest Ga. Rd.
SL5: S'hill 2E 34
Blacknest Rd.
GU25: V Wat 2G 35
GU34: B'nest 4A 148
SL5: S'hill 2G 35
Black Pond La.
GU10: L Bou 5H 129
Black Prince Cl. KT14: Byf 1A 76
Blackshaw Rd.
SW17 . . . . .5A 28
Blacksmith Cl.
KT21: A'tead 6M 79
Blacksmith La. GU4: Guil 8E 114
Blacksmiths Hill
CR2: Sande 9D 64
Blacksmiths La.
KT16: Chert 6J 37
TW18: Lale 2K 37
Blacks Rd. W6 . . . . .1H 13
Blackstone Cl. GU14: Cove 8J 69
RH1: Red 4C 122
Blackstone Hill RH1: Red 4B 122
Blackstroud La. E.
GU18: Ligh 7A 52
Blackstroud La. W.
GU18: Ligh 7A 52
Black Swan Cl.
RH11: P Pot 1N 199
Blackthorn Cl. RH2: Reig 5A 122
RH11: Craw 1A 182
RH13: Hors 6N 197
Blackthorn Ct. TW5: Hest 3M 9
Blackthorn Cres.
GU14: Cove 6L 69
Blackthorn Dr. GU18: Ligh 8M 51
Blackthorne Av. CR0: Croy 7F 46
Blackthorne Ct.
TW15: A'ford 8D 22
Blackthorne Cres. SL3: Poy 5G 7
Blackthorne Ind. Est.
SL3: Poy 6G 7
Blackthorne Rd.
KT23: Book 4C 98
SL3: Poy 6G 6
Blackthorn Pl. GU1: Guil 9M 93
Blackthorn Rd. RH2: Reig 5A 122
TN16: B Hil 3F 86
BLACKWATER 2J 69
Blackwater Cl. GU12: Ash 3E 110
Blackwater La.
RH10: Craw 4G 183
BLACKWATER PARK 2L 69
Blackwater Pk. GU12: Alde . . .3C 110
Blackwater Station (Rail) 2K 69
Blackwater Trad. Est.
GU12: Alde 4B 110
Blackwater Valley Relief Rd.
GU15: Camb 2L 69
Blackwater Valley Route
GU12: Alde 6C 110
GU14: Farnb 7B 70
Blackwater Vw.
RG40: Finch 5A 48
Blackwater Way
GU12: Alde 4B 110
BLACKWELL 8B 166
Blackwell Av. GU2: Guil 3G 112
Blackwell Farm Rd.
RH19: E Grin 7B 166
Blackwell Hollow
RH19: E Grin 8B 166
Blackwell Ho. SW4 . . . . .1H 29
Blackwell Rd.
RH19: E Grin 8B 166
Blackwood Cl. KT14: W By 8L 55
Blade M. SW15 . . . . .7L 13
Bladen Cl. KT13: Weybr 3E 56
Blades Cl. KT22: Leat 7K 79
Blades Ct. SW15 . . . . .7L 13
W6 . . . .*1G 13*
(off Lower Mall)
Bladon Cl. GU1: Guil 2C 114
Bladon Ct. SW16 . . . . .7J 29
Blagdon Rd. KT3: N Mal 3E 42
(not continuous)
Blagdon Wlk. TW11: Tedd 7J 25
Blair Av. KT10: Esh 8C 40
Blair Ct. BR3: Beck 1L 47
Blairderry Rd. SW2 . . . . .3J 29
Blaire Pk. GU46: Yate 7A 48
Blaise Cl. GU14: Farnb 2B 90
Blake Cl. RG40: W'ham 9D 14
RG45: Crow 3H 49
RH10: Craw 7D 182
SM5: Cars 7C 44
Blakeden Dr. KT10: Clay 3F 58
Blakefield Gdns. CR5: Coul 5K 83
Blake Gdns. SW6 . . . . .4N 13
Blakehall Rd. SM5: Cars 3D 62
Blake M. TW9: Kew 4N 11
Blakemore Gdns.
SW13 . . . . .2G 12
Blakemore Rd. CR7: T Hea 4K 45
SW16 . . . . .4J 29
Blakeney Cl. KT19: Eps 7C 60
Blakenham Rd. SW17 . . . . . . .5D 28
Blake Rd.
CR0: Croy 2F 200 (8B 46)
CR4: Mit 2C 44
Blakes Av. KT3: N Mal 4E 42
Blakes Ct. KT16: Chert 7J 37
Blake's Grn. BR4: W Wick 7M 47
Blakes La. GU4: E Cla 1N 115
KT3: N Mal 4E 42
KT24: W Hors 9A 96
Blakesley Wlk. SW20 . . . . .1L 43
Blakes Ride GU46: Yate 9A 48
Blakes Ter. KT3: N Mal 4F 42
Blakewood Cl. TW13: Hanw . . .5K 23
Blamire Dr. RG42: Bin 7L 15
Blanchard Ho. *TW1: Twick 9K 11*
(off Clevedon Rd.)
Blanchards Hill
GU4: J Wel, Sut G 6A 94
Blanchland Rd. SM4: Mord 4N 43
Blanchman's Rd. CR6: Warl . . .5H 85
Blandfield Rd. SW12 . . . . .1E 28
Blandford Av. BR3: Beck 1H 47
TW2: Whitt 2B 24
Blandford Cl. CR0: Bedd 9J 45
GU22: Wok 4D 74
Blandford Rd. BR3: Beck 1F 46
TW11: Tedd 6D 24
Blane's La. RG12: Brac 7D 32
SL5: Asc 7D 32
Blanford M. RH2: Reig 3B 122
Blanford Rd. RH2: Reig 4A 122
Blanks La. RH5: Newd 8D 140
RH6: Char, Newd 8D 140
Blatchford Cl. RH13: Hors . . .5M 197
Blatchford Ct. KT12: Wal T 8H 39
Blatchford Rd.
RH13: Hors 5M 197
Blays Cl. TW20: Eng G 7M 19
Blay's La. TW20: Eng G 8L 19
Blegborough Rd. SW16 . . . . . .7G 29
Blencarn Cl. GU21: Wok 3J 73
Blendworth Point
SW15 . . . . .2G 26
Blenheim Av. RG12: Brac 2A 32
Blenheim Bus. Cen.
CR4: Mit 1D 44
(off London Rd.)
Blenheim Cl. GU10: Tong 5C 110
KT14: W By 9H 55
RH10: Craw 9H 163
RH19: E Grin 7C 166
SM6: W'ton 4G 63
SW20 . . . . .2H 43
Blenheim Ct. GU14: Farnb 3B 90
SM2: Sut 3A 62
TW18: Stain 5F 20
Blenheim Cres.
CR2: S Croy 4N 63
GU9: U Hal 7F 108
Blenheim Flds.
RH18: F Row 6G 187
Blenheim Gdns.
CR2: Sande 8D 64
GU22: Wok 6L 73
KT2: K Tham 8A 26
SM6: W'ton 3G 62
Blenheim Ho. TW3: Houn 6A 10
Blenheim M. GU9: Farnh 1F 128
Blenheim Pk. GU11: Alde 6A 90
Blenheim Pk. Rd.
CR2: S Croy 5N 63
Blenheim Pl. GU15: Camb 3A 70
TW11: Tedd 6F 24
Blenheim Rd. GU11: Alde 6N 89
KT19: Eps 7C 60
RH12: Hors 3K 197
SL3: Lang 1N 5
SM1: Sut 9M 43
SW20 . . . . .2H 43
Blenheim Way TW7: Isle 4G 10
Blenkarne Rd. SW11 . . . . .1D 28
Bleriot Rd. TW5: Hest 3K 9
BLETCHINGLEY 2A 124
Bletchingley Cl.
CR7: T Hea 3M 45
RH1: Mers 7G 103
Bletchingley Rd.
RH1: Mers 7G 102
RH1: Nut 1L 123
RH9: Gods 9D 104
Bletchmore Cl. UB3: Harl 1E 8
Blewburton Wlk.
RG12: Brac 3C 32
Blewfield GU7: Bus 9J 133
Bligh Cl. RH10: Craw 5D 182
Blighton La. GU10: Run 8B 110
Blincoe Cl. SW19 . . . . .3J 27
Blind La. GU24: Chob 6C 52
RH3: Brock 6B 120
RH8: Oxt 8A 106
SM7: Ban 2C 82
Blindley Ct. RH7: Blin H 3H 145
BLINDLEY HEATH 3H 145
Blindley Rd. RH10: Craw 9H 163
Bloggs Way GU6: Cranl 7M 155
Blomfield Dale RG42: Brac 1J 31
Blondell Cl. UB7: Harm 2M 7
Bloomfield Cl. GU21: Knap 4H 73
Bloomfield Dr. RG12: Brac 8B 16
Bloomfield Rd.
KT1: K Tham 7K 203 (3L 41)
Bloomfield Ter.
TN16: Weste 3M 107
Bloom Gro. SE27 . . . . .4M 29
Bloom Pk. Rd. SW6 . . . . .3L 13
Bloomsbury Cl. KT19: Eps 6C 60
Bloomsbury Ct. *GU1: Guil 5B 114*
(off St Lukes Sq.)
TW5: C'ford 4J 9
Bloomsbury Pl. SW18 . . . . . . .8N 13
Bloomsbury Way
GU17: Haw 3H 69
Bloor Cl. RH12: Hors 1K 197
Blore Ho. *SW10 . . . . .3N 13*
(off Coleridge Gdns.)
Blossom Cl. CR2: S Croy 2C 64
Blossom Waye TW5: Hest 2M 9
Blount Av. RH19: E Grin 9M 165
Blount Cres. RG42: Bin 8K 15
Bloxham Cres.
TW12: Hamp 8N 23
Bloxham Rd. GU6: Cranl 7B 156
Bloxworth Cl. RG12: Brac 3D 32
SM6: W'ton 9G 45
Blue Anchor All. TW9: Rich . . .7L 11
Blue Ball La. TW20: Egh 6B 20
Blue Barn La.
KT13: Weybr 7B 56
Bluebell Cl. RH11: Craw 6N 181
RH12: Hors 3L 197
RH19: E Grin 9L 165
SM6: W'ton 7F 44
Bluebell Cott. GU3: Comp 2C 132
Bluebell Ct. GU22: Wok 6N 73
Bluebell Hill RG12: Brac 9C 16
Bluebell La. KT24: E Hor 7F 96
Bluebell M. GU15: Camb 8B 50
Bluebell Railway
Kingscote Station 6J 185
Bluebell Ri. GU18: Ligh 8M 51
Bluebell Rd. GU35: Lind 4B 168
Bluebell Wlk. GU51: Fleet 3A 88
Blueberry Gdns. CR5: Coul 3K 83
Blue Cedars SM7: Ban 1J 81
Blue Cedars Pl. KT11: Cob 8L 57
Bluecoat Pond RH13: Hors . . .9D 196
Bluecoat Wlk. RG12: Brac 4B 32
Bluefield Cl. TW12: Hamp 6A 24
Bluegates KT17: Ewe 4F 60
Bluehouse Gdns. RH8: Oxt . . .6C 106
Bluehouse La.
RH8: Limp, Oxt 6A 106
Blue Leaves Av. CR5: Coul 8H 83
Blueprint Apartments
SW12 . . . . .1F 28
(off Balham Gro.)
Blue Pryor Ct.
GU52: C Cro 1A 108
Blue Riband Ind. Est.
CR0: Croy 2A 200 (8M 45)
Bluethroat Cl. GU47: C Tow . . .7K 49
Blue Water SW18 . . . . .7N 13
Bluff Cove GU11: Alde 1A 110
Blundel La. KT11: Sto D 3N 77
Blundell Av. RH6: Horl 7D 142
Blunden Ct. GU5: Braml 5C 134
Blunden Rd. GU14: Cove 1L 89
Blunt Rd.
CR2: S Croy 8E 200 (2A 64)
Blunts Av. UB7: Sip 3B 8
Blunts Way RH12: Hors 5J 197
Blyth Cl. TW1: Twick 9F 10
Blytheswood Pl. SW16 . . . . . . .5K 29
Blythewood La. SL5: Asc 2J 33
Blythwood Dr. GU16: Frim 4B 70
Blytons, The RH19: E Grin 9L 165
Board School Rd.
GU21: Wok 3B 74
Boars Head Yd. TW8: Brent 3K 11
Bocketts Farm Pk. 3F 98
Bocketts La. KT22: Fetc 2F 98
Bockhampton Rd.
KT2: K Tham 8M 25
Boddicott Cl. SW19 . . . . .3K 27
Boddington Ho. *SW13 . . . . .2G 13*
(off Wyatt Dr.)
Bodeites GU7: Goda 4E 132
Boden's Ride SL5: Asc 8H 33
(not continuous)
Bodiam Cl. RH10: Craw 3G 183
Bodiam Rd. SW16 . . . . .8H 29
Bodicea M. TW4: Houn 9N 9
Bodley Cl. KT3: N Mal 4D 42
Bodley Mnr. Way SW2 . . . . . . .1L 29
Bodley Rd. KT3: N Mal 5C 42
Bodmin Gro. SM4: Mord 4N 43
Bodmin St. SW18 . . . . .2M 27
Bodnant Gdns. SW20 . . . . .2F 42
Bogey La. BR6: Dow 4J 67
Bog La. RG12: Brac 4D 32
Bognor Rd.
RH12: Oak, Bro H, Warn, Rowh
. . . . .4C 178
Boileau Rd. SW13 . . . . .3F 12
Bois Hall Rd. KT15: Addl 2M 55
Bolderwood Way
BR4: W Wick 8L 47
Bolding Ho. La.
GU24: W End 9C 52
Boleyn Av. KT17: Ewe 6G 60
Boleyn Cl. RH10: Craw 6H 183
TW18: Stain 6G 20
Boleyn Ct. *GU21: Knap 5F 72*
(off Tudor Way)
KT8: E Mol 3D 40
(off Bridge Rd.)
RH1: Red 2E 122
(off St Anne's Ri.)
Boleyn Dr. KT8: W Mole 2N 39
Boleyn Gdns. BR4: W Wick 8L 47
Boleyn Gro. BR4: W Wick 8M 47
Boleyn Wlk. KT22: Leat 7F 78
Bolingbroke Gro.
SW11 . . . . .1D 28
Bolney Ct. RH11: Craw 6L 181
Bolney Way TW13: Hanw 4M 23
Bolsover Gro. RH1: Mers 7J 103
Bolstead Rd. CR4: Mit 9F 28
Bolters La. SM7: Ban 1L 81
Bolters Rd. RH6: Horl 6E 142
Bolters Rd. Sth. RH6: Horl . . .6D 142
Bolton Av. SL4: W'sor 6G 4
Bolton Cl. KT9: Ches 3K 59
SE20 . . . . .1D 46
Bolton Cres. SL4: W'sor 6F 4
Bolton Dr. SM5: Cars 6A 44
Bolton Gdns. SW5 . . . . .1N 13
TW11: Tedd 7G 24
Bolton Gdns. M.
SW10 . . . . .1N 13
Bolton Rd. KT9: Ches 3K 59
RH10: Craw 8F 182
SL4: W'sor 6F 4
W4 . . . . .3B 12
Boltons, The SW10 . . . . .1N 13
Boltons Cl. GU22: Pyr 3J 75
Boltons Ct. *SW5 . . . . .1N 13*
(off Old Brompton Rd.)
Boltons La. GU22: Pyr 3J 75
RG42: Bin 7K 15
UB3: Harl 4D 8
(not continuous)
Boltons Pl. SW5 . . . . .1N 13
Bombers La. TN16: Weste 6M 87
Bomer Cl. UB7: Sip 3B 8
Bonaly Ho. RH8: Oxt 9M 105
Bonchurch Cl. SM2: Sut 4N 61
Bond Gdns. SM6: W'ton 1G 63
Bond Rd. CR4: Mit 1C 44
CR6: Warl 5G 85
KT6: Surb 8M 41
Bond's La. RH5: Mid H 2H 139
Bond St. TW20: Eng G 6L 19
W4 . . . . .1C 12
Bond Way RG12: Brac 9N 15
Bonehurst Rd. RH1: Salf 2E 142
RH6: Horl 2E 142
Bone Mill La. RH9: Gods 3H 125
Bones La. RH6: Horn 7D 144
RH7: Horn, Newc 9E 144
Bonner Hill Rd.
KT1: K Tham . . .4M 203 (1M 41)
(not continuous)
Bonners Cl. GU22: Wok 9B 74
Bonnetts La. RH11: Ifi 8M 161
Bonnys Rd. RH2: Reig 4J 121
Bonser Rd. TW1: Twick 3F 24
Bonsey Cl. GU22: Wok 8A 74
Bonsey La. GU22: Wok 8A 74
Bonseys La. GU24: Chob 5B 54
Bonsor Dr. KT20: K'wood 9K 81
Bonwicke Cotts.
RH10: Cop 4N 163
Bookham Comn. Rd.
KT23: Book 8M 77
Bookham Ct. CR4: Mit 2B 44
KT23: Book 1N 97
Bookham Gro. KT23: Book 4B 98
Bookham Ind. Est.
KT23: Book 1N 97
Bookham Rd. KT11: Down 6K 77
Bookham Station (Rail) 1N 97
Bookhurst Hill GU6: Cranl 7C 156
Bookhurst Rd.
GU6: Cranl, Ewh 6B 156
Boole Hgts. RG12: Brac 5M 31
Booth Dr. TW18: Stain 7M 21
Booth Ho. *TW8: Brent 3J 11*
(off High St.)
Booth Rd.
CR0: Croy 3A 200 (8M 45)
RH11: Craw 6K 181
Booth Way RH13: Hors 5L 197
Borage Cl. RH11: Craw 6M 181
Border Chase RH10: Cop 8L 163
Border Ct. RH19: E Grin 6B 166
Border End GU27: Hasl 2B 188
Border Gdns. CR0: Croy 1L 65
Bordergate CR4: Mit 9C 28
Border Rd. GU27: Hasl 2B 188
Borderside GU46: Yate 9A 48
Bordesley Rd. SM4: Mord 4N 43
Bordeston Ct. *TW8: Brent 3J 11*
(off The Ham)
Bordon Wlk. SW15 . . . . .1F 26
Boreen, The GU35: H Dwn 4G 169
Borelli M. GU9: Farnh 1H 129
Borelli Yd. GU9: Farnh 1H 129
Borers Arms Rd.
RH10: Cop 6M 163
Borers Cl. RH10: Cop 6N 163
Borers Yd. Ind. Est.
RH10: Cop 7N 163
Borkwood Pk. BR6: Orp 1N 67
Borkwood Way BR6: Orp 1N 67
Borland Rd. TW11: Tedd 8H 25
Borley Ct. TW19: Stan 2N 21
Borneo St. SW15 . . . . .6H 13
Borough, The GU9: Farnh 1G 129
RH3: Brock 4N 119
Borough Grange
CR2: Sande 8D 64
Borough Hall Complex 7H 133
Borough Hill
CR0: Wad 5A 200 (9M 45)

Borough Rd.—Bratten Ct.

Borough Rd. CR4: Mit 1C 44
GU7: Goda 6G 133
KT2: K Tham 9N 25
TN16: Tats 8F 86
TW7: Isle 4E 10
Borrodaile Rd. SW18 ....9N 13
Borrowdale Cl.
CR2: Sande 9C 64
RH11: Craw 5N 181
TW20: Egh 8D 20
Borrowdale Dr. CR2: Sande 8C 64
Borrowdale Gdns.
GU15: Camb 1H 71
Boscombe Cl. TW20: Egh 9E 20
Boscombe Gdns.
SW16 ....7J 29
Boscombe Ho. CR0: Croy 1D 200
Boscombe Rd. KT4: W Pk 7H 43
SW17 ....7E 28
SW19 ....9N 27
Bosham Rd. RH10: Craw 6G 183
Boshers Gdns. TW20: Egh 7B 20
Bosman Dr. GU20: Windl 9M 33
Bostock Av. RH12: Hors 4N 197
Bostock Ho. TW5: Hest 2A 10
Boston Ct. SE25 ....3C 46
SM2: Sut 4A 62
Boston Gdns. TW8: Brent 1G 11
W4 ....2D 12
Boston Ho. *SW5 ....1N 13*
(off Collingham Rd.)
BOSTON MANOR 1G 11
Boston Manor House 1H 11
Boston Mnr. Rd.
TW8: Brent 1H 11
Boston Manor Station (Tube)
....1G 11
Boston Pk. Rd. TW8: Brent 1J 11
Boston Rd. CR0: Croy 5K 45
Boswell Ct. KT2: K Tham 1M 203
Boswell Path UB3: Harl 1G 8
Boswell Rd. CR7: T Hea 3N 45
RH10: Craw 6C 182
Boswell Row CR3: Cate 9D 84
Boswood Ct. TW3: Houn 6N 9
Botany Hill GU10: Seal 2B 130
Botery's Cross RH1: Blet 2M 123
Bothwell Rd. CR0: N Add 6M 65
Bothwell St. W6 ....2J 13
Bothy, The GU8: P Har 6A 132
GU22: Pyr 4H 75
SM7: Ban 5A 82
Botsford Rd. SW20 ....1K 43
Bottle La. RG42: Bin, Warf 1K 15
Boucher Cl. TW11: Tedd 6F 24
Boughton Hall Av.
GU23: Send 2H 95
Bouldish Farm Rd.
SL5: Asc 4K 33
Boulevard, The RG12: Brac 2J 31
RH10: Craw 3B 182
(not continuous)
SW17 ....3E 28
SW18 ....7N 13
Boulogne Rd. CR0: Croy 5N 45
Boulters Ho. RG12: Brac 3C 32
Boulter's Rd. GU11: Alde 2N 109
Boulthurst Way RH8: Oxt 1D 126
Boulton Ho. TW8: Brent 1L 11
Boundaries Rd. SW12 ....3D 28
TW13: Felt 2K 23
Boundary Bus. Cen.
GU21: Wok 2C 74
Boundary Bus. Ct. CR4: Mit 2B 44
Boundary Cl. KT1: K Tham 2A 42
RH10: Craw 2C 182
SE20 ....1D 46
UB2: S'hall 1A 10
Boundary Cotts. GU4: Guil 8J 115
Boundary Pk. KT13: Wal T 9F 38
Boundary Rd.
GU10: Dock, Rowl 4C 148
GU14: Farnb 3A 90
GU21: Wok 3C 74
GU26: G'hott 6B 170
RH10: Craw 2C 182
SM5: Cars 3F 62
SM6: W'ton 3F 62
SW19 ....7B 28
TW15: A'ford 6L 21
Boundary Way CR0: A'ton 2K 65
GU21: Wok 2C 74
Boundless Rd.
GU8: Brook 1G 170
BOUNDSTONE 6F 128
Boundstone Cl.
GU10: Wrec 6G 128
Boundstone Rd.
GU10: Fren, Rowl 7E 128
Bourdon Rd. SE20 ....1F 46
Bourg-de-Peage Av.
RH19: E Grin 9C 166
Bourke Cl. SW4 ....1J 29
Bourke Hill CR5: Chip 5D 82
Bourley La. GU10: Ews 2E 108
Bourley Rd. GU11: Alde 2G 108
GU52: C Cro 9D 88
BOURNE, THE 5J 129
Bourne, The GU52: Fleet 7B 88
Bourne Av. KT16: Chert 2J 37
SL4: W'sor 6F 4
Bourne Bus. Pk.
KT15: Addl 1M 55
Bourne Cl. GU4: Guil 9D 114
KT7: T Dit 8F 40
KT14: W By 9K 55
TW7: Isle 6E 10
Bourne Ct. CR3: Cate 1D 104
GU11: Alde 4M 109
RH13: Hors 5L 197
W4 ....2B 12
Bourne Dene GU10: Wrec 6F 128
Bourne Dr. CR4: Mit 1B 44
Bournefield Rd.
CR3: Whyte 5D 84
Bourne Firs GU10: L Bou 6J 129
Bourne Gro. GU10: L Bou 4K 129
KT21: A'tead 6K 79
Bourne Gro. Cl.
GU10: L Bou 4K 129
Bourne Gro. Dr.
GU10: L Bou 4K 129
Bourne Hall Mus. 5E 60
Bourne Hgts. GU9: Farnh 3H 129
Bourne Ho. TW15: A'ford 6B 22
Bourne La. CR3: Cate 8A 84
Bourne Mdw. TW20: Thor 3D 36
Bourne Mill Ind. Est.
GU9: Farnh 9K 109
Bournemouth Rd.
SW19 ....9M 27
Bourne Pk. Cl. CR8: Ken 3B 84
Bourne Pl. KT16: Chert 7J 37
W4 ....1C 12
Bourne Rd. GU7: Goda 3J 133
GU25: V Wat 4N 35
RH1: Mers 8G 103
Bourneside GU25: V Wat 6K 35
Bourneside Rd. KT15: Addl 1M 55
Bourne St.
CR0: Croy 3A 200 (8M 45)
Bournevale Rd. SW16 ....5J 29
Bourne Vw. CR8: Ken 2A 84
Bourne Way GU22: Wok 9N 73
KT15: Addl 2L 55
KT19: Ewe 1B 60
SM1: Sut 2L 61
Bousley Ri. KT16: Otter 3F 54
Bouverie Gdns. CR8: Pur 1K 83
Bouverie Rd. CR5: Chip 5E 82
Bouverie Way SL3: Lang 1A 6
BOVENEY 2A 4
Boveney Ho. *RG12: Brac 3C 32*
(off Segsbury Gro.)
Boveney New Rd. SL4: E Wic 1B 4
Boveney Rd. SL4: Dorn 1A 4
Bovingdon Rd. SW6 ....4N 13
Bovingdon Sq. CR4: Mit 3J 45
Bowater Gdns. TW16: Sunb 1K 39
Bowater Ridge KT13: Weybr 6E 56
Bowater Rd. RH10: Craw 6G 183
Bowcott Hill GU35: Head 4E 168
Bowcroft La. RH12: Rudg 1F 194
Bowden Cl. TW14: Bedf 2F 22
Bowden Rd. SL5: S'hill 4N 33
Bowenhurst Gdns.
GU52: C Cro 9B 88
Bowenhurst Rd.
GU52: C Cro 8B 88
Bowens Wood CR0: Sels 5J 65
Bowen Way CR5: Coul 9H 83
Bower, The RH10: Craw 4G 182
Bower Ct. GU22: Wok 3D 74
Bowerdean St. SW6 ....4N 13
Bower Hill Cl. RH1: Sth N 6J 123
Bower Hill La. RH1: Sth N 4H 123
Bowerland La. RH7: Ling 3N 145
Bower Rd. GU10: Wrec 6F 128
Bowers, The RG40: Finch 7A 30
Bowers Cl. GU4: B'ham 8C 94
Bowers Farm Dr.
GU4: B'ham 8C 94
Bowers La. GU4: B'ham 7C 94
Bowers Pl. RH10: Craw D 1E 184
Bowes Cl. RH13: Hors 5L 197
Bowes Lyon Cl. *SL4: W'sor 4F 4*
(off Alma Rd.)
Bowes Rd. KT12: Wal T 8J 39
TW18: Stain 6G 20
Bowfell Rd. W6 ....2H 13
Bowie Cl. SW4 ....1H 29
Bowland Dr. RG12: Brac 6C 32
Bow La. SM4: Mord 5K 43
BOWLHEAD GREEN 9K 151
Bowlhead Grn. Rd.
GU8: Bow G, Brook 9K 151
Bowling, The KT12: Wal T 6H 39
Bowling Grn. Cl.
SW15 ....1G 27
Bowling Grn. Ct.
GU16: Frim G 7C 70
Bowling Grn. La.
RH12: Hors 5K 197
Bowling Grn. Rd.
GU24: Chob 5H 53
Bowlings, The GU15: Camb 9A 50
Bowman Ct. RG45: Crow 3E 48
RH10: Craw 2B 182
(off London Rd.)
Bowman M. SW18 ....2L 27
Bowmans Mdw. SM6: W'ton 9F 44
Bowness Cl. RH11: Ifi 4J 181
Bowness Cres. SW15 ....6D 26
Bowness Dr. TW4: Houn 7M 9
Bowring Ho. *GU7: Goda 5J 133*
(off St Johns St.)
Bowry Dr. TW19: Wray 9B 6
Bowsley Ct. TW13: Felt 3H 23
Bowsprit, The KT11: Cob 2K 77
Bowyer Cres. RG40: W'ham 9B 14
Bowyers Cl. KT21: A'tead 5M 79
Bowyer's La. RG42: Warf 3N 15
Bowyer Wlk. SL5: Asc 9J 17
Boxall's Gro. GU11: Alde 5M 109
Boxall's La. GU11: Alde 5M 109
Boxall Wlk. RH13: Hors 7K 197
Box Cl. RH11: Craw 8A 182
Boxford Cl. CR2: Sels 8G 65
Boxford Ridge RG12: Brac 2N 31
Boxgrove Av. GU1: Guil 1C 114
Boxgrove La. GU1: Guil 2C 114
Boxgrove Rd. GU1: Guil 2C 114
BOX HILL 9B 100
Boxhill and Westhumble Station
(Rail) 9H 99
Box Hill Country Pk. 1K 119
Box Hill Country Pk. Vis. Cen.
....1K 119
Boxhill Rd. KT20: Box H 1M 119
RH4: Dork 2L 119
Boxhill Way RH3: Brock 7A 120
Box La. RH19: Ash W 3G 186
Boxley Rd. SM4: Mord 3A 44
Box Ridge Av. CR8: Pur 8K 63
Box Tree Wlk. RH1: Red 6A 122
Box Wlk. KT24: E Hor 1F 116
Boxwood Way CR6: Warl 4G 85
Boyce Ho. SW16 ....6G 29
Boyd Cl. KT2: K Tham 8N 25
Boyd Ct. RG42: Brac 9M 15
Boyd Rd. SW19 ....7B 28
Boyle Farm Island
KT7: T Dit 5G 41
Boyle Farm Rd. KT7: T Dit 5G 40
Brabazon Av. SM6: W'ton 4J 63
Brabazon Rd. TW5: Hest 3K 9
Brabiner Gdns. CR0: N Add 6N 65
Brabon Rd. GU14: Cove 9L 69
Brabourne Ri. BR3: Beck 4M 47
Brabrook Ct. SM6: W'ton 1F 62
Bracebridge GU15: Camb 1M 69
Bracewood Gdns.
CR0: Croy 9C 46
Bracken Av. CR0: Croy 9K 47
SW12 ....1E 28
Bracken Bank SL5: Asc 9G 17
Bracken Cl. GU5: Wone 5C 134
GU22: Wok 5B 74
KT23: Book 2N 97
RH10: Cop 7M 163
RH10: Craw 1C 182
TW2: Whitt 1A 24
TW16: Sunb 7G 22
Brackendale Cl.
GU15: Camb 3C 70
TW3: Houn 4B 10
Brackendale Rd.
GU15: Camb 1B 70
Brackendene GU12: Ash 1G 110
Brackendene Cl.
GU21: Wok 2C 74
Bracken End TW7: Isle 8D 10
Bracken Gdns. SW13 ....5F 12
Bracken Gro. RH12: Hors 3A 198
Brackenhill KT11: Cob 8B 58
Bracken Hollow
GU15: Camb 7F 50
Bracken La. GU46: Yate 9A 48
Brackenlea GU7: Goda 4G 132
Bracken Path KT18: Eps 9A 60
Brackens, The RG45: Crow 9F 30
SL5: Asc 2F 32
Brackenside RH6: Horl 7F 142
Bracken Way GU3: Guil 1H 113
GU24: Chob 6J 53
Brackenwood GU15: Camb 1H 71
TW16: Sunb 9H 23
Brackenwood Rd.
GU21: Wok 6G 73
Bracklesham Cl.
GU14: Farnb 7M 69
Brackley KT13: Weybr 2E 56
Brackley Cl. SM6: W'ton 4J 63
Brackley Rd. W4 ....1D 12
Brackley Ter. W4 ....1D 12
Bracklyn Av. RH19: D Pk 5B 166
RH19: Fel 5F 164
BRACKNELL 1N 31
Bracknell Beeches
RG12: Brac 2N 31
Bracknell Cl. GU15: Camb 6D 50
Bracknell Ent. Cen.
RG12: Brac 1M 31
Bracknell Rd. GU15: Camb 5D 50
GU19: Bag 1H 51
RG12: Brac 7D 32
RG42: Warf 6C 16
RG45: Crow 2H 49
Bracknell Sports & Leisure Cen.
....4A 32
Bracknell Station (Rail) 2N 31
Bracknell Wlk.
RH11: Craw 7K 181
Bracondale KT10: Esh 2C 58
Bradbourne St. SW6 ....5M 13
Bradbury Rd. RH10: Craw 6G 182
Braddock Cl. TW7: Isle 5F 10
Braddon Rd. TW9: Rich 6M 11
Bradenhurst Cl. CR3: Cate 4C 104
Bradfield Cl. GU4: B'ham 9C 94
GU22: Wok 5A 74
Bradfields RG12: Brac 4B 32
Bradford Dr. KT19: Ewe 3E 60
Brading Rd. CR0: Croy 5K 45
SW2 ....1K 29
Bradley Cl. SM2: Sut 6M 61
Bradley Hall *TW20: Eng G 4M 19*
(off Coopers Hill La.)
Bradley La. RH4: Dork 1H 119
RH5: Dork 1G 119
Bradley M. SW17 ....2D 28
Bradley Rd. SE19 ....7N 29
Bradmore Way CR5: Coul 4J 83
Bradshaw Cl. SL4: W'sor 4B 4
SW19 ....7M 27
Bradshaws Cl. SE25 ....2D 46
Bradstock Rd. KT17: Ewe 2F 60
Bradstone Brook
GU4: Chil 1C 134
Braeburn Rd. RH11: Ifi 9M 161
Brae Ct. KT2: K Tham 9N 25
Braemar SW15 ....9J 13
Braemar Av. CR2: S Croy 6N 63
CR7: T Hea 2L 45
SW19 ....3M 27
Braemar Cl. GU7: Goda 8G 132
GU16: Frim 6D 70
Braemar Gdns.
BR4: W Wick 7M 47
Braemar Rd. KT4: W Pk 9G 42
TW8: Brent 2K 11
Braeside KT15: N Haw 7K 55
RG12: Bin 1H 31
Braeside Av. SW19 ....9K 27
Braeside Cl. GU27: Hasl 9D 170
Braeside Rd. SW16 ....8G 29
Braes Mead RH1: Sth N 4J 123
Brafferton Rd.
CR0: Croy 6B 200 (1N 63)
Braganza Ct. *GU1: Guil 2C 114*
(off London Rd.)
Bragg Rd. TW11: Tedd 7E 24
Braid Cl. TW13: Hanw 3N 23
Brailsford Cl. CR4: Mit 8C 28
Brain Flowers Hall
SL5: S'hill 2C 34
(off Buckhurst Rd.)
Brainton Av. TW14: Felt 1J 23
Brakes Ri. GU47: C Tow 7K 49
Brakey Hill RH1: Blet 3B 124
Bramber Cl. RH10: Craw 1C 182
RH12: Hors 3A 198
Bramber Ct. *W14 ....2L 13*
(off North End Rd.)
Bramber Ho. KT2: K Tham 2J 203
Bramber Rd. W14 ....2L 13
Bramber Way CR6: Warl 3J 85
Brambleacres Cl. SM2: Sut 4M 61
Bramble Bank GU16: Frim G 8E 70
Bramble Banks SM5: Cars 5E 62
Bramble Cl. BR3: Beck 4M 47
CR0: Croy 1K 65
GU3: Guil 1H 113
RH1: Red 5E 122
RH8: Oxt 2D 126
RH10: Cop 7M 163
TW17: Shep 2E 38
Bramble Ct. GU6: Ewh 4F 156
Brambledene Cl.
GU21: Wok 5M 73
Brambledown TW18: Stain 9K 21
Brambledown Rd.
CR2: Sande 4B 64
SM5: Cars 4E 62
SM6: W'ton 4E 62
Bramblegate RG45: Crow 1F 48
Bramblehall La.
KT20: Box H 1M 119
Bramble Hill Farm
RH13: Slin 8N 195
Bramble La. TW12: Hamp 7N 23
Bramble Ri. KT11: Cob 2K 77
Brambles, The GU7: Goda 4G 133
RG45: Crow 1C 48
SW19 ....6L 27
(off Woodside)
UB7: W Dray 1M 7
Brambles Cl. CR3: Cate 9B 84
GU12: Ash 3F 110
TW7: Isle 3H 11
Brambles Pk. GU5: Braml 5B 134
Brambleton Av.
GU9: Farnh 3G 128
Bramble Twitten
RH19: E Grin 9C 166
Brambletye La.
RH18: F Row 5F 186
Brambletye Pk. Rd.
RH1: Red 5D 122
Brambletye Rd.
RH10: Craw 4E 182
Bramble Wlk. KT18: Eps 1A 80
RH1: Red 5E 122
Bramble Way GU23: Rip 2H 95
Bramblewood RH1: Mers 7F 102
Bramblewood Cl.
SM5: Cars 7C 44
Brambling Cl. RH13: Hors 7N 197
Brambling Rd.
RH13: Hors 7N 197
Bramcote GU15: Camb 1G 71
Bramcote Av. CR4: Mit 3D 44
Bramcote Ct. *CR4: Mit 3D 44*
(off Bramcote Av.)
Bramcote Ho. KT13: Weybr 1D 56
Bramcote Rd. SW15 ....7G 13
Bramerton Rd. BR3: Beck 2J 47
Bramham Gdns. KT9: Ches 1K 59
SW5 ....1N 13
BRAMLEY 5B 134
Bramley Av. CR5: Coul 2G 82
TW17: Shep 2F 38
Bramley Bank Nature Reserve
....3F 64
Bramley Bus. Cen.
GU5: Braml 4B 134
(off Station Rd.)
Bramley Cl.
CR2: S Croy 8A 200 (2N 63)
KT16: Chert 7K 37
RH1: Red 5C 122
RH10: Craw 3D 182
TW2: Whitt 9C 10
TW18: Stain 7L 21
Bramley Ct. CR4: Mit 1B 44
RG45: Crow 2C 48
RH1: Red 1C 122
Bramley Grange
GU5: Braml 5B 134
Bramley Gro. KT21: A'tead 6L 79
RG45: Crow 2C 48
Bramley Hill
CR2: S Croy 8A 200 (2M 63)
Bramley Ho. RH1: Red 4E 122
SW15 ....9E 12
(off Tunworth Cres.)
TW4: Houn 7N 9
Bramleyhyrst CR2: S Croy 7B 200
Bramley La. GU17: B'water 1G 69
Bramley Rd. GU15: Camb 4N 69
SM1: Sut 2B 62
SM2: Chea 5J 61
Bramley Wlk. RH6: Horl 8G 143
Bramley Way BR4: W Wick 8L 47
KT21: A'tead 4M 79
TW4: Houn 8N 9
Bramling Av. GU46: Yate 9A 48
Brampton Gdns. KT12: Hers 2K 57
Brampton Rd. CR0: Croy 6C 46
Bramshaw Ri. KT3: N Mal 5D 42
Bramshot Dr. GU51: Fleet 3B 88
Bramshot La. GU14: Cove 8H 69
GU51: Fleet 1F 88
Bramshot Rd. GU14: Farnb 3F 88
BRAMSHOTT CHASE 9N 169
Bramshott Ct.
GU30: Brams 9F 168
Bramshott Rd. GU30: Pass 8E 168
Bramston Rd. SW17 ....4A 28
Bramswell Rd. GU7: Goda 5J 133
Bramwell Cl. TW16: Sunb 1L 39
Brancaster La. CR8: Pur 6N 63
Brancaster Rd. SW16 ....4J 29
Brandlehow Rd. SW15 ....7L 13
Brandon Cl. GU15: Camb 2H 71
RH10: Craw 5H 183
Brandon Mans. *W14 ....2K 13*
(off Queen's Club Gdns.)
Brandon Rd. GU52: C Cro 1A 108
SM1: Sut 1N 61
UB2: S'hall 1N 9
Brandreth Rd. SW17 ....3F 28
Brandries, The SM6: Bedd 9H 45
BRANDS HILL 2D 6
Brandsland RH2: Reig 7N 121
Brands Rd. SL3: Lang 2D 6
Brandy Way SM2: Sut 4M 61
Brangwyn Cres. SW19 ....9A 28
Branksea St. SW6 ....3K 13
Branksome *KT13: Weybr 3E 56*
(off Gower Rd.)
Branksome Cl. GU15: Camb 9C 50
KT12: Wal T 8L 39
TW11: Tedd 5D 24
Branksome Hill Rd.
GU47: C Tow 8K 49
Branksome Pk. Rd.
GU15: Camb 9C 50
Branksome Rd. SW19 ....9M 27
Branksome Way KT3: N Mal 9B 26
Branksomewood Rd.
GU51: Fleet 3A 88
Bransby Rd. KT9: Ches 3L 59
Branstone Rd. TW9: Kew 4M 11
Brantridge Rd.
RH10: Craw 5D 182
Brants Bri. RG12: Brac 1C 32
Brantwood Av. TW7: Isle 7G 10
Brantwood Cl. KT14: W By 9J 55
Brantwood Ct. *KT14: W By 9H 55*
(off Brantwood Dr.)
Brantwood Dr. KT14: W By 9H 55
Brantwood Gdns.
KT14: W By 9H 55
Brantwood Rd. CR2: S Croy 5N 63
Brasenose Dr. SW13 ....2H 13
Brassey Cl. RH8: Oxt 7C 106
TW14: Felt 2H 23
Brassey Hill RH8: Oxt 8C 106
Brassey Rd. RH8: Oxt 8B 106
Brasted Cl. SM2: Sut 6M 61
Brasted Rd. TN16: Weste 4N 107
Brathway Rd. SW18 ....1M 27
Brattain Ct. RG12: Brac 2B 32
Bratten Ct. CR0: Croy 5A 46

Broadway Chambers—Bucklands Rd.

Broadway Chambers
W6 1H 13
(off Hammersmith B'way.)
Broadway Cl. CR2: Sande 1E 84
Broadway Ct. BR3: Beck 2M 47
GU21: Knap 4F 72
SW19 7M 27
Broadway Gdns. CR4: Mit 3C 44
Broadway Ho. GU21: Knap 5F 72
Broadway Mans. *SW6 3M 13*
(off Fulham Rd.)
Broadway Mkt. SW17 5D 28
Broadway Pl. SW19 7L 27
Broadway Rd. GU18: Ligh 6N 51
GU20: Windl 6N 51
Broadwell Ct. *TW5: Hest 4L 9*
(off Springwell Rd.)
Broadwell Rd. GU10: Wrec 5E 128
Broadwood Cl.
RH12: Hors 3N 197
Broadwood Cotts.
RH5: Cap 4L 159
Broadwood Ri.
RH11: Craw 8M 181
Broadwood Rd. CR5: Coul 8H 83
Brocas St. SL4: Eton 3G 4
Brocas Ter. SL4: Eton 3G 4
Brockbridge Ho. SW15 9E 12
Brock Cl. GU16: Deep 6H 71
Brockdene Dr. BR2: Kes 1F 66
Brockenhurst KT8: W Mole 4N 39
Brockenhurst Av. KT4: W Pk 7D 42
Brockenhurst Cl.
GU21: Wok 1B 74
Brockenhurst Dr.
GU46: Yate 2C 68
Brockenhurst Rd. CR0: Croy 6E 46
GU11: Alde 4N 109
RG12: Brac 2D 32
SL5: Asc 3L 33
Brockenhurst Way
SW16 1H 45
BROCKHAM 5A 120
Brockham Cl. SW19 6L 27
Brockham Cres.
CR0: N Add 4N 65
Brockham Dr. SW2 1K 29
Brockham Grn.
RH3: Brock 4A 120
Brockham Hill
KT20: Box H 9B 100
(off Boxhill Rd.)
Brockham Hill Pk.
KT20: Box H 9B 100
Brockham Ho. *SW2 1K 29*
(off Brockham Dr.)
Brockhamhurst Rd.
RH3: Betch 1N 139
Brockham Keep *RH6: Horl 7G 142*
(off Langshott La.)
Brockham La. RH3: Brock 3N 119
Brockham Pk. 8B 120
Brockham Pk. Ho.
RH3: Betch 9B 120
BROCK HILL 5E 16
Brockhill GU21: Wok 4K 73
Brockhurst Cl. RH12: Hors 7F 196
Brockhurst Cotts. GU6: Alf 5H 175
Brocklands GU46: Yate 2A 68
Brocklebank Ct.
CR3: Whyte 5D 84
Brocklebank Rd.
SW18 1A 28
Brocklesby Rd. SE25 3E 46
Brockley Combe
KT13: Weybr 1E 56
Brock Rd. RH11: Craw 9N 161
Brocks Cl. GU7: Goda 6K 133
Brocks Dr. GU3: Worp 8F 92
SM3: Chea 9K 43
Brockshot Cl. TW8: Brent 1K 11
Brock Way GU25: V Wat 4M 35
Brockway SL3: Lang 1D 6
Brockway Cl. GU1: Guil 2D 114
Brockwell Av. BR3: Beck 4L 47
Brockwell Pk. 1M 29
Brockwell Pk. Gdns.
SE24 1L 29
Brockwell Pk. Row
SW2 1L 29
Broderick Gro. KT23: Book 4A 98
Brodie Rd.
GU1: Guil 5E 202 (4A 114)
Brodrick Rd. SW17 3C 28
Brograve Gdns. BR3: Beck 1L 47
Broke Ct. GU4: Guil 9E 94
Broken Furlong SL4: Eton 1E 4
Brokes Cres. RH2: Reig 1M 121
Brokes Rd. RH2: Reig 1M 121
Bromford Cl. RH8: Oxt 2C 126
Bromley Gro. BR2: Brom 1N 47
Bromley Rd. BR2: Brom 1L 47
BR3: Beck 1L 47
Brompton Cl. SE20 1D 46
TW4: Houn 8N 9
Brompton Pk. Cres.
SW6 2N 13
Brompton Vs. *SW6 2M 13*
(off Ongar Rd.)
Bronsart Rd. SW6 3K 13
Bronson Rd. SW20 1J 43
Bronte Ct. *RH1: Red 2E 122*
(off St Anne's Ri.)
Bronte Ho. SW4 1G 29
Brontes, The RH19: E Grin 9N 165
BROOK
GU5 2N 135
GU8 9N 151
Brook, The RH10: Craw 2B 182
Brook Av. GU9: Weybo 5L 109
Brook Cl. GU12: Ash 1F 110
GU47: Owls 6K 49
GU51: Fleet 5B 88
KT19: Ewe 5D 60
RH4: Dork 3J 119
RH19: E Grin 9D 166
SW17 3E 28
SW20 2G 43
TW19: Stan 1A 22
Brook Cotts. GU46: Yate 9B 48
Brook Ct. *GU14: Cove 9H 69*
(off Melrose Av.)
RH12: Hors 3H 197
TN8: Eden 9L 127
Brook Dr. RG12: Brac 3C 32
Brooke Ct. GU16: Frim G 8D 70
Brooke Forest GU3: Worp 8F 92
Brooke Pl. RG42: Bin 6J 15
Brookers Cl. KT21: A'tead 4J 79
Brookers Cnr. RG45: Crow 2H 49
Brookers Row RG45: Crow 1H 49
Brook Farm Rd. KT11: Cob 2L 77
Brookfield GU7: Goda 3K 133
GU21: Wok 3L 73
Brookfield Av. SM1: Sut 1B 62
Brookfield Cl. KT16: Otter 3F 54
KT21: A'tead 7L 79
RH1: Red 9E 122
Brookfield Gdns. KT10: Clay 3F 58
Brookfield Pl. KT11: Cob 2M 77
Brookfield Rd. GU12: Alde 1C 110
Brookfields Av. CR4: Mit 4C 44
Brook Gdns. GU14: Cove 3L 89
KT2: K Tham 9B 26
SW13 6E 12
Brook Grn. *GU24: Chob 6J 53*
(off Chertsey Rd.)
RG42: Brac 9L 15
(not continuous)
Brook Hill GU5: Alb 3M 135
RH8: Oxt 8M 105
Brookhill Cl. RH10: Cop 7L 163
Brookhill Rd. RH10: Cop 8L 163
Brook Ho. *GU6: Cranl 6A 156*
(off Park Dr.)
GU9: Hale 6J 109
(off Fairview Gdns.)
Brookhouse Rd.
GU14: Cove 2L 89
Brookhurst Fld.
RH12: Rudg 9E 176
Brookhurst Rd. KT15: Addl 3K 55
Brookland Ct. RH2: Reig 1N 121
BROOKLANDS 6A 56
Brooklands GU11: Alde 3K 109
RH9: S Gods 1E 144
Brooklands, The TW7: Isle 4D 10
Brooklands Av. SW19 3N 27
Brooklands Bus. Pk.
KT13: Weybr 7N 55
Brooklands Cl. GU9: H End 5J 109
KT11: Cob 2M 77
TW16: Sunb 9F 22
Brooklands Ct. CR4: Mit 1B 44
KT1: K Tham 7H 203
KT15: N Haw 6M 55
Brooklands Dr.
KT13: Weybr 6A 56
Brooklands Ind. Est.
KT13: Weybr 6N 55
Brooklands La.
KT13: Weybr 3A 56
Brooklands Mus. 5A 56
Brooklands Pl. TW12: H Hill 6B 24
Brooklands Rd.
GU9: H End 5K 109
KT7: T Dit 7F 40
KT13: Weybr 7B 56
RH11: Craw 8A 182
Brooklands Way
GU9: H End 5K 109
RH1: Red 1C 122
RH19: E Grin 1N 185
Brook La. GU5: Alb 2N 135
GU23: Send 9G 74
GU24: Chob 7G 53
RH12: Fay 9B 180
Brook La. Bus. Cen.
TW8: Brent 1K 11
Brook La. Nth. TW8: Brent 1K 11
(not continuous)
Brookley Cl. GU10: Run 9A 110
Brookleys GU24: Chob 6J 53
Brookly Gdns. GU51: Fleet 3C 88
Brooklyn Av. SE25 3E 46
Brooklyn Cl. GU22: Wok 6A 74
SM5: Cars 8C 44
Brooklyn Ct. GU22: Wok 6A 74
Brooklyn Gro. SE25 3E 46
Brooklyn Rd. GU22: Wok 5A 74
SE25 3E 46
Brook Mead GU8: Mil 2C 152
KT19: Ewe 3D 60
Brookmead CR0: Bedd 5G 45
Brookmead Ct. GU6: Cranl 8N 155
GU9: Farnh 2G 128
Brookmead Ind. Est.
CR0: Bedd 5G 45
Brook Mdw. GU8: Chid 6F 172
Brookmead Rd. CR0: Croy 5G 45
Brook Rd. CR7: T Hea 3N 45
GU4: Guil 1E 134
GU8: Brook, Worm 1N 171
GU15: Camb 2N 69
GU19: Bag 5J 51
KT6: Surb 8L 41
RH1: Mers 7G 102
RH1: Red 4D 122
RH12: Hors 2L 197
TW1: Twick 9G 11
Brook Rd. Sth. TW8: Brent 2K 11
Brooksby Cl.
GU17: B'water 1G 68
Brooks Cl. KT13: Weybr 6B 56
Brookscroft CR0: Sels 6J 65
BROOKSIDE 7K 17
Brookside GU4: J Wel 7N 93
GU6: Cranl 7N 155
(Ewhurst Rd.)
GU6: Cranl 9N 155
(Northdowns)
GU9: Hale 6H 109
GU47: Sandh 8H 49
KT16: Chert 6G 37
RH5: B Grn 5M 139
RH9: S Gods 7G 124
RH10: Cop 7L 163
RH10: Craw 2D 182
RH10: Craw D 1E 184
SL3: Coln 3E 6
SM5: Cars 2E 62
Brookside Av. TW15: A'ford 6L 21
TW19: Wray 6A 6
Brookside Cl. TW13: Felt 4H 23
Brookside Cres. KT4: W Pk 7F 42
Brookside Res. Pk. Homes
GU14: Farnb 5M 69
Brookside Rural Pk.
RH12: Rudg 7G 177
Brookside Way CR0: Croy 5G 46
Brooks La. W4 2N 11
Brooks Rd. W4 1N 11
Brook St.
KT1: K Tham 4J 203 (1L 41)
SL4: W'sor 5G 5
Brook Trad. Est., The
GU12: Alde 2C 110
Brook Valley RH5: Mid H 2H 139
Brookview RH10: Cop 7L 163
Brookview Rd. SW16 6G 28
Brookville Rd. SW6 3L 13
Brook Way KT22: Leat 5G 78
Brookwell La. GU5: Braml 1C 154
BROOKWOOD 7D 72
Brookwood RH6: Horl 7F 142
Brookwood Av. SW13 5E 12
Brookwood Ho. *RH6: Horl 5F 142*
(off Skipton Way)
Brookwood Lye Rd.
GU24: B'wood 7E 72
Brookwood Pk. RH6: Horl 9F 142
Brookwood Rd.
GU14: Farnb 1B 90
SW18 2L 27
TW3: Houn 5B 10
Brookwood Station (Rail) 8D 72
Broom Acres GU47: Sandh 7G 49
GU52: Fleet 7A 88
Broom Cl. KT10: Esh 2B 58
TW11: Tedd 8K 25
Broomcroft Cl. GU22: Pyr 3F 74
Broomcroft Dr. GU22: Pyr 2F 74
Broomdashers Rd.
RH10: Craw 2D 182
Broome Cl. GU46: Yate 8B 48
KT18: Head 4B 100
RH12: Hors 3K 197
Broome Cotts. RH4: Dork 4J 119
Broome Ct. KT20: Tad 6K 81
RG12: Brac 2N 31
Broomehall Rd.
RH5: Cold, Ockl 9D 138
Broome Lodge *TW18: Stain 6K 21*
(off Kingston Rd.)
Broome Rd. TW12: Hamp 8N 23
Broomers La. GU6: Ewh 5F 156
Broom Fld. GU18: Ligh 8L 51
Broomfield GU2: Guil 2H 113
GU8: Els 7J 131
TW16: Sunb 9H 23
TW18: Stain 7J 21
Broomfield Cl. GU3: Guil 1H 113
SL5: S'dale 6E 34
Broomfield Ct. KT13: Weybr 3C 56
Broomfield Pk.
RH4: Westc 6C 118
SL5: S'dale 5E 34
Broomfield Ride KT22: Oxs 8D 58
Broomfield Rd. BR3: Beck 2H 47
KT5: Surb 7M 41
KT15: N Haw 7K 55
TW9: Kew 4M 11
TW11: Tedd 7J 25
Broomfields KT10: Esh 2C 58
Broom Gdns. CR0: Croy 9K 47
BROOMHALL 5D 34
Broom Hall KT22: Oxs 1D 78
Broomhall End *GU21: Wok 3A 74*
(off Broomhall La.)
Broomhall La. GU21: Wok 3A 74
SL5: S'dale 5D 34
Broomhall Rd. CR2: Sande 5A 64
GU21: Wok 3A 74
Broomhill GU10: Ews 4C 108
Broomhill Rd. GU14: Cove 9J 69
SW18 8M 13
Broomhouse La. SW6 5M 13
(not continuous)
Broomhouse Rd. SW6 5M 13
Broomhurst Ct. RH4: Dork 7H 119
Broomlands La.
RH8: Limp, T'sey 4F 106
Broom La. GU24: Chob 5H 53
Broomleaf Cnr. GU9: Farnh 1J 129
Broomleaf Rd. GU9: Farnh 1J 129
Broomloan La. SM1: Sut 8M 43
Broom Lock TW11: Tedd 7J 25
Broom Pk.
TW11: Tedd 1G 203 (8K 25)
Broom Rd. CR0: Croy 9K 47
TW11: Tedd 6H 25
Broom Squires GU26: Hind 5E 170
Broom Squires Ct.
GU27: Hasl 2E 188
Broomsquires Rd.
GU19: Bag 5K 51
Broom Water TW11: Tedd 7J 25
Broom Water W.
TW11: Tedd 6J 25
Broom Way GU17: Haw 2K 69
KT13: Weybr 1F 56
Broomwicks Pl.
RH12: Bro H 5E 196
(off Sullington Mead)
Broomwood Cl. CR0: Croy 4G 47
Broomwood Way
GU10: L Bou 5H 129
Broster Gdns. SE25 2C 46
Brougham Pl. GU9: U Hal 5G 108
Brough Cl. KT2: K Tham 6K 25
Broughton Av. TW10: Ham 4H 25
Broughton M. GU16: Frim 5D 70
Broughton Rd. CR7: T Hea 5L 45
SW6 5N 13
Brow, The RH1: Red 8E 122
Browell Ho. *GU1: Guil 2F 114*
(off Merrow St.)
Browells La. TW13: Felt 3J 23
(not continuous)
Brown Bear Ct.
TW13: Hanw 5L 23
Brown Cl. SM6: W'ton 4J 63
Browne Cl. GU22: Wok 7D 74
Browngraves Rd. UB3: Harl 3D 8
Browning Av. KT4: W Pk 7G 42
SM1: Sut 1C 62
Browning Cl. GU15: Camb 2G 70
RH10: Craw 2G 182
TW12: Hamp 5N 23
Browning Ct. *W14 2L 13*
(off Turneville Rd.)
Browning Rd. KT22: Fetc 3D 98
Brownings TN8: Eden 8L 127
Brownings, The
RH19: E Grin 9M 165
Browning Way TW5: Hest 4L 9
Brownjohn Ct. RH10: Craw 2E 182
Brownlow Dr. RG42: Brac 8A 16
Brownlow Rd. CR0: Croy 1B 64
RH1: Red 3C 122
Brownrigg Cres.
RG12: Brac 9C 16
Brownrigg Rd. TW15: A'ford 5B 22
Brown's Hill RH1: Out 1A 144
Browns La. KT24: Eff 5L 97
Brownsover Rd.
GU14: Cove 1H 89
Brown's Rd. KT5: Surb 6M 41
Browns Wlk. GU10: Rowl 7E 128
Browns Wood
RH19: E Grin 6A 166
BROX 4E 54
Broxhead Common (Nature Reserve) 2A 168
Broxhead Farm Rd.
GU35: Lind 2A 168
Broxhead Trad. Est.
GU35: Lind 3A 168
Broxholme Cl. SE25 3A 46
Broxholme Ho. *SW6 4N 13*
(off Harwood Rd.)
Broxholm Rd. SE27 4L 29
Brox La. KT15: Addl 4E 54
KT16: Otter 4E 54
Brox M. KT16: Otter 3E 54
Brox Rd. KT16: Otter 3E 54
Bruce Av. TW17: Shep 5D 38
Bruce Cl. KT14: Byf 9M 55
Bruce Dr. CR2: Sels 5G 64
Bruce Hall M. SW17 5E 28
Bruce Rd. CR4: Mit 8E 28
SE25 3A 46
Bruce Wlk. SL4: W'sor 5A 4
Brudenell SL4: W'sor 6C 4
Brudenell Rd. SW17 4D 28
Brumana Cl. KT13: Weybr 3C 56
Brumfield Rd. KT19: Ewe 2B 60
Brunel Cen., The
RH10: Craw 8D 162
Brunel Cl. TW5: C'ford 3J 9
Brunel Dr. RG45: Crow 8H 31
Brunel Pl. RH10: Craw 4C 182
Brunel University
Runnymede Campus 4N 19
Brunel Wlk. TW2: Whitt 1A 24
Brunner Ct. KT16: Otter 2E 54
Brunswick RG12: Brac 6M 31
Brunswick Cl. KT7: T Dit 7F 40
KT12: Wal T 8K 39
RH10: Craw 5E 182
TW2: Twick 4D 24
Brunswick Ct.
RH10: Craw 5E 182
(off Brunswick Cl.)
SM1: Sut 1N 61
Brunswick Dr.
GU24: B'wood 7A 72
Brunswick Gro. KT11: Cob 9K 57
Brunswick M. SW16 7H 29
Brunswick Rd. GU16: Deep 8G 71
GU24: B'wood 8L 71
(not continuous)
KT2: K Tham 9N 25
SM1: Sut 1N 61
Brunswick Ter. BR3: Beck 1L 47
Bruntile Cl. GU14: Farnb 4B 90
Brushfield Way GU21: Knap 6F 72
Brushwood Rd.
RH12: Hors 2A 198
Bruton Rd. SM4: Mord 3A 44
Bruton Way RG12: Brac 6C 32
Bryan Cl. TW16: Sunb 8H 23
Bryan's All. SW6 5N 13
Bryanston Av. TW2: Whitt 2B 24
Bryanstone Av. GU2: Guil 8J 93
Bryanstone Cl. GU2: Guil 9J 93
GU52: C Cro 7B 88
Bryanstone Ct. SM1: Sut 9A 44
Bryanstone Gro. GU2: Guil 8J 93
Bryce Cl. RH12: Hors 3N 197
Bryce Gdns. GU11: Alde 5A 110
Bryer Pl. SL4: W'sor 6A 4
Brympton Cl. RH4: Dork 7G 119
Brynford Cl. GU21: Wok 2A 74
Bryn Rd. GU10: Wrec 4E 128
Bryony Ho. RG42: Brac 9K 15
Bryony Rd. GU1: Guil 9D 94
Bryony Way TW16: Sunb 7H 23
Buccaneer Way
GU14: Farnb 5G 89
Buccleuch Rd. SL3: Dat 3K 5
Buchan, The GU15: Camb 7E 50
Buchan Country Pk. 7K 181
BUCHAN HILL 9M 181
Buchan Pk. RH11: Craw 7L 181
Buchans Lawn
RH11: Craw 7N 181
Bucharest Rd. SW18 1A 28
Buckfast Rd. SM4: Mord 3N 43
Buckham Thorns Rd.
TN16: Weste 4L 107
Buckhold Rd. SW18 9M 13
Buckhurst Av. SM5: Cars 7C 44
Buckhurst Cl. RH1: Red 1C 122
RH19: E Grin 7M 165
Buckhurst Gro.
RG40: W'ham 3E 30
BUCKHURST HILL 9C 18
Buckhurst Hill RG12: Brac 3D 32
Buckhurst La. SL5: S'hill 2C 34
Buckhurst Mead
RH19: E Grin 6M 165
Buckhurst Rd.
GU16: Frim G 8D 70
SL5: Asc, S'hill 9C 18
TN16: Weste 8J 87
Buckhurst Way
RH19: E Grin 7M 165
Buckingham Av. CR7: T Hea 9L 29
KT8: W Mole 1B 40
TW14: Felt 9J 9
Buckingham Cl. GU1: Guil 2B 114
TW12: Hamp 6N 23
Buckingham Ct.
RH11: Craw 7N 181
SM2: Sut 5M 61
TW18: Stain 5J 21
(off Kingston Rd.)
Buckingham Dr.
RH19: E Grin 1C 186
Buckingham Gdns.
CR7: T Hea 1L 45
KT8: W Mole 1B 40
Buckingham Ga. RH6: Gat 3G 162
Buckingham Rd. CR4: Mit 3J 45
KT1: K Tham 7L 203 (3M 41)
RH5: Holm 5J 139
TW10: Ham 3K 25
TW12: Hamp 5N 23
Buckingham Way
GU16: Frim 5D 70
SM6: W'ton 5G 63
BUCKLAND 2F 120
Buckland Cl. GU14: Farnb 7A 70
Buckland Ct. Gdns.
RH3: Buck 2F 120
Buckland Cres. SL4: W'sor 4C 4
Buckland La. KT20: Wal H 6F 100
RH3: Buck 8F 100
Buckland Rd. BR6: Orp 1N 67
KT9: Ches 2M 59
KT20: Lwr K 7L 101
RH2: Reig 2J 121
SM2: Chea 6H 61
Bucklands Rd. TW11: Tedd 7J 25

Buckland's Wharf—Byron Gro.

Buckland's Wharf KT1: K Tham ... 3G 203 (1K 41)
Buckland Wlk. SM4: Mord ... 3A 44
Buckland Way KT4: W Pk ... 7H 43
Bucklebury RG12: Brac ... 6M 31
Buckleigh Av. SW20 ... 2K 43
Buckleigh Rd. SW16 ... 7H 29
Buckle La. RG42: Warf ... 3M 15
Bucklers All. SW6 ... 2L 13 (not continuous)
Buckler's Way SM5: Cars ... 9D 44
Buckles Way SM7: Ban ... 3K 81
Buckley La. RH13: Hors, M Hea ... 9N 197
Buckley Pl. RH10: Craw D ... 1D 184
Buckmans Rd. RH11: Craw ... 2B 182
Bucknall Way BR3: Beck ... 3L 47
Bucknills Cl. KT18: Eps ... 1B 80
Bucks Cl. KT14: W By ... 1K 75
Bucks Copse RG41: W'ham ... 3A 30
BUCKS GREEN ... 1E 194
Buckshead Hill RH13: P Pla ... 9E 198
BUCKS HORN OAK ... 2A 148
Bucks Horn Oak Rd. GU34: B'nest ... 2A 148
Buckswood Dr. RH11: Craw ... 5M 181
Buckthorn Cl. RG40: W'ham ... 1D 30
Buckthorns RG42: Brac ... 8K 15
Buddleia Ho. TW13: Felt ... 2H 23
Budd's All. TW1: Twick ... 8J 11
Budebury Rd. TW18: Stain ... 6J 21
Budge La. CR4: Mit ... 6D 44
Budgen Cl. RH10: Craw ... 9H 163
Budgen Dr. RH1: Red ... 9E 102
Budge's Gdns. RG40: W'ham ... 1C 30
Budge's Rd. RG40: W'ham ... 1C 30
Budham Way RG12: Brac ... 5N 31
Buer Rd. SW6 ... 5K 13
Buff Av. SM7: Ban ... 1N 81
Buffbeards La. GU27: Hasl ... 1C 188
Buffers La. KT22: Leat ... 6G 79
Bug Hill CR3: Wold ... 7G 84
CR6: Wold ... 7G 84
Buick Ho. KT2: K Tham ... 3M 203 (1N 41)
Bulbeggars La. RH9: Gods ... 1F 124
Bulganak Rd. CR7: T Hea ... 3N 45
Bulkeley Av. SL4: W'sor ... 6E 4
Bulkeley Cl. TW20: Eng G ... 6M 19
Bullard Cotts. GU4: W Cla ... 1H 115
Bullard Rd. TW11: Tedd ... 7E 24
Bullbeggars La. GU21: Wok ... 3L 73
BULLBROOK ... 1C 32
Bullbrook Dr. RG12: Brac ... 9C 16
Bullbrook Row RG12: Brac ... 1C 32
Buller Ct. GU14: Farnb ... 4A 90
Buller Rd. CR7: T Hea ... 1A 46
Bullers Rd. GU9: Weybo ... 6K 109
Bullfinch Cl. GU47: C Tow ... 7K 49
RH6: Horl ... 7C 142
RH12: Hors ... 1J 197
Bullfinch Rd. CR2: Sels ... 6G 64
Bull Hill KT22: Leat ... 8G 79
Bull La. RG42: Brac ... 9N 15
Bullocks La. GU27: Hasl ... 9N 189
GU28: Hasl ... 8N 189
Bullrush Cl. CR0: Croy ... 5B 46
SM5: Cars ... 8C 44
Bull's All. SW14 ... 5C 12
Bulls Head Row RH9: Gods ... 9E 104
BULLSWATER COMMON ... 3D 92
Bullswater Comn. Rd. GU24: Pirb ... 4D 92
Bullswater La. GU24: Pirb ... 3D 92
Bulmer Cotts. RH5: H Mary ... 6K 137
Bulow Est. SW6 ... 4N 13 (off Pearscroft Rd.)
Bulrushes Farm RH19: E Grin ... 2N 185
Bulstrode Av. TW3: Houn ... 5N 9
Bulstrode Gdns. TW3: Houn ... 6A 10
Bulstrode Rd. TW3: Houn ... 6A 10
Bunbury Way KT17: Eps D ... 3G 80
BUNCE COMMON ... 1C 140
Bunce Comn. Rd. RH2: Leigh ... 1C 140
Bunce Dr. CR3: Cate ... 1A 104
Bunce's Cl. SL4: E Wic ... 1E 4
Bunch La. GU27: Hasl ... 1E 188
Bunch Way GU27: Hasl ... 2E 188
Bundy's Way TW18: Stain ... 7H 21
Bungalow Rd. SE25 ... 3B 46
Bungalows, The GU2: Guil ... 7J 93
SM6: W'ton ... 2F 62
SW16 ... 8F 28
Bunting Cl. CR4: Mit ... 4D 44
RH13: Hors ... 5M 197
Buntings, The GU9: Farnh ... 3E 128
Bunyan Cl. RH11: Craw ... 6K 181
Bunyan's La. GU24: Chob ... 1F 72
Bunyard Dr. GU21: Wok ... 1E 74
Burbage Grn. RG12: Brac ... 4D 32
Burbage Rd. SE24 ... 1N 29
Burbeach Cl. RH11: Craw ... 6N 181
Burberry Cl. KT3: N Mal ... 1D 42
Burbidge Rd. TW17: Shep ... 3B 38
Burbury Woods GU15: Camb ... 9C 50
Burchets Hollow GU5: P'lake ... 4E 136
Burchetts Way TW17: Shep ... 5C 38
Burcote KT13: Weybr ... 3E 56
Burcote Rd. SW18 ... 1B 28
Burcott Gdns. KT15: Addl ... 3L 55
Burcott Rd. CR8: Pur ... 1L 83
Burden Cl. TW8: Brent ... 1J 11
Burdenshot Hill GU3: Worp ... 3K 93
Burdenshott Av. TW10: Rich ... 7A 12
Burdenshott Rd. GU3: Worp ... 3K 93
Burden Way GU2: Guil ... 7L 93
Burdett Av. SW20 ... 9F 26
Burdett Cl. RH10: Wor ... 4H 183
Burdett Rd. CR0: Croy ... 5A 46
TW9: Rich ... 5M 11
Burdock Cl. CR0: Croy ... 7G 47
GU18: Ligh ... 7M 51
RH11: Craw ... 7M 181
Burdon La. SM2: Chea ... 4K 61
Burdon Pk. SM2: Chea ... 5L 61
Burfield Cl. SW17 ... 5B 28
Burfield Dr. CR6: Warl ... 6F 84
Burfield Rd. SL4: O Win ... 9K 5
Burford Bri. Rdbt. RH5: Mick ... 9J 99
Burford Ct. RG40: W'ham ... 3D 30
Burford Ho. KT17: Ewe ... 7H 61
TW8: Brent ... 1K 11
Burford La. KT17: Ewe ... 7H 61
Burford Lea GU8: Els ... 7J 131
Burford Rd. GU15: Camb ... 2N 69
KT4: W Pk ... 6E 42
RH13: Hors ... 6L 197
SM1: Sut ... 8M 43
TW8: Brent ... 1L 11
Burford Wlk. SW6 ... 3N 13
Burford Way CR0: N Add ... 3M 65
Burge Cl. GU14: Cove ... 1H 89
Burges Gro. SW13 ... 3G 13
Burgess Cl. TW13: Hanw ... 5M 23
Burgess M. SW19 ... 7N 27
Burgess Rd. SM1: Sut ... 1N 61
Burgess Way TW18: Stain ... 6J 21
Burgh Cl. RH10: Craw ... 9H 163
Burgh Cft. KT17: Eps ... 2E 80
Burghead Cl. GU47: C Tow ... 8J 49
Burghfield KT17: Eps ... 2E 80
BURGH HEATH ... 6K 81
Burgh Heath Rd. KT17: Eps, Eps D ... 8M 201 (1E 80)
Burghley Av. KT3: N Mal ... 9C 26
Burghley Hall Cl. SW19 ... 2K 27
Burghley Ho. SW19 ... 4K 27
Burghley Pl. CR4: Mit ... 4D 44
Burghley Rd. SW19 ... 5J 27
Burgh Mt. SM7: Ban ... 2L 81
Burgh Wood SM7: Ban ... 2K 81
Burgoine Quay KT1: H Wic ... 2G 203 (9K 25)
Burgos Cl. CR0: Wad ... 3L 63
Burgoyne Rd. GU15: Camb ... 9E 50
SE25 ... 3C 46
TW16: Sunb ... 7G 22
BURHILL ... 5J 57
Burhill Rd. KT12: Hers ... 5J 57
Burke Cl. SW15 ... 7D 12
Burket Cl. UB2: S'hall ... 1M 9
Burlands RH11: Craw ... 9M 161
Burlea Cl. KT12: Hers ... 2J 57
BURLEIGH ... 9K 17
Burleigh Av. SM6: W'ton ... 9E 44
Burleigh Cl. KT15: Addl ... 2K 55
RH10: Craw D ... 1E 184
Burleigh Gdns. GU21: Wok ... 4B 74
TW15: A'ford ... 6D 22
Burleigh La. RH10: Craw D ... 2E 184
SL5: Asc ... 9J 17
Burleigh Pk. KT11: Cob ... 8M 57
Burleigh Pl. SW15 ... 8J 13
Burleigh Rd. GU16: Frim ... 6B 70
KT15: Addl ... 2K 55
SL5: Asc ... 1J 33
SM3: Sut ... 7K 43
Burleigh Way RH10: Craw D ... 1E 184
Burley Cl. RH14: Loxw ... 4J 193
SW16 ... 1H 45
Burley Orchard KT16: Chert ... 5J 37
Burleys Rd. RH10: Craw ... 3G 183
Burley Way GU17: B'water ... 9H 49
Burlingham Cl. GU4: Guil ... 1F 114
Burlings, The SL5: Asc ... 1J 33
Burlington Av. TW9: Kew ... 4N 11
Burlington Cl. TW14: Bedf ... 1E 22
Burlington Ct. GU11: Alde ... 3M 109
GU17: Haw ... 3J 69
RH1: Red ... 2D 122 (off Station Rd.)
Burlington Gdns. SW6 ... 5K 13
W4 ... 1B 12
Burlington La. W4 ... 3B 12
Burlington M. SW15 ... 8L 13
Burlington Pl. RH2: Reig ... 2M 121
SW6 ... 5K 13
Burlington Rd. CR7: T Hea ... 1N 45
KT3: N Mal ... 3E 42
SW6 ... 5K 13
TW7: Isle ... 4D 10
W4 ... 1B 12
Burlsdon Way RG12: Brac ... 9C 16
Burma Rd. GU24: Chob ... 9J 35
Burmarsh Ct. SE20 ... 1F 46
Burmester Rd. SW17 ... 4A 28
Burnaby Cres. W4 ... 2B 12
Burnaby Gdns. W4 ... 2A 12
Burnbury Rd. SW12 ... 2G 29
Burn Cl. KT15: Addl ... 1M 55
KT22: Oxs ... 2D 78
Burne-Jones Dr. GU47: C Tow ... 9J 49
Burnell Av. TW10: Ham ... 6J 25
Burnell Rd. SM1: Sut ... 1N 61
Burnet Av. GU1: Guil ... 9D 94
Burnet Cl. GU24: W End ... 9B 52
Burnet Gro. KT19: Eps ... 6H 201 (9B 60)
Burnetts Rd. SL4: W'sor ... 4B 4
Burney Av. KT5: Surb ... 8M 203 (4M 41)
Burney Cl. KT22: Fetc ... 3C 98
Burney Ct. RH11: Craw ... 6M 181
Burney Ho. KT22: Leat ... 8G 78 (off Highbury Dr.)
Burney Rd. RH5: Westh ... 9G 99
Burnfoot Av. SW6 ... 4K 13
Burnham Cl. GU21: Knap ... 5G 73
SL4: W'sor ... 5A 4
Burnham Dr. KT4: W Pk ... 8J 43
RH2: Reig ... 2M 121
Burnham Gdns. CR0: Croy ... 6C 46
TW4: C'ford ... 4J 9
Burnham Ga. GU1: Guil ... 2C 202 (3N 113)
Burnham Gro. RG42: Brac ... 8A 16
Burnham Mnr. GU15: Camb ... 7E 50
Burnham Pl. RH13: Hors ... 7K 197
Burnham Rd. GU21: Knap ... 5G 73
SM4: Mord ... 3N 43
Burnhams Gro. KT19: Eps ... 7A 60
Burnhams Rd. KT23: Book ... 2M 97
Burnham St. KT2: K Tham ... 9N 25
Burnhill Rd. BR3: Beck ... 1K 47
Burn Moor Chase RG12: Brac ... 6C 32
Burnsall Cl. GU14: Farnb ... 8N 69
Burns Av. GU52: C Cro ... 7C 88
TW14: Felt ... 9H 9
Burns Cl. GU14: Farnb ... 8L 69
RH12: Hors ... 1L 197
SM5: Cars ... 5E 62
SW19 ... 7B 28
Burns Dr. SM7: Ban ... 1K 81
Burnside GU51: Fleet ... 4B 88
KT21: A'tead ... 5M 79
Burnside Cl. TW1: Twick ... 9G 10
Burnside Ct. SM5: Cars ... 9E 44
Burns Rd. RH10: Craw ... 1G 182
Burns Way RH12: Fay ... 8H 181
RH19: E Grin ... 9M 165
TW5: Hest ... 5L 9
BURNTCOMMON ... 3H 95
Burnt Comn. Cl. GU23: Rip ... 3H 95
Burnt Comn. La. GU23: Rip ... 3J 95
Burnt Hill Rd. GU10: L Bou, Wrec ... 5F 128
Burnt Hill Way GU10: Wrec ... 6G 128 (not continuous)
Burnt Ho. Gdns. RG42: Warf ... 8C 16
Burnt Ho. La. RH12: Rusp ... 2E 180
Burnthouse Ride RG12: Brac ... 3J 31
Burnthwaite Rd. SW6 ... 3L 13
Burntoak La. RH5: Newd ... 2D 160
Burnt Pollard La. GU18: Ligh ... 6B 52
Burntwood Cl. CR3: Cate ... 8D 84
SW18 ... 2C 28
Burntwood Grange Rd. SW18 ... 2B 28
Burntwood La. CR3: Cate ... 9B 84
SW17 ... 4A 28
BURPHAM ... 9D 94
Burpham Court Farm Pk. ... 7B 94
Burpham La. GU4: B'ham ... 7C 94
Burrell, The RH4: Westc ... 6C 118
Burrell Cl. CR0: Croy ... 5H 47
Burrell Ct. RH11: Craw ... 5L 181
Burrell Rd. GU16: Frim ... 6A 70
Burrell Row BR3: Beck ... 1K 47
Burrells, The KT16: Chert ... 7K 37
Burr Hill La. GU24: Chob ... 5J 53
Burritt Rd. KT1: K Tham ... 1N 41
BURROW HILL ... 9B 72
BURROWHILL ... 5H 53
Burrow Hill Grn. GU24: Chob ... 5G 53
Burrows Cl. GU2: Guil ... 2J 113
KT23: Book ... 2N 97
BURROWS CROSS ... 1D 136
Burrows Cross GU5: Gorn, P'lake ... 1D 136
Burrows La. GU5: Gorn ... 1D 136
Burrow Wlk. SE21 ... 1N 29
Burr Rd. SW18 ... 2M 27
Burrwood Gdns. GU12: A Va ... 9E 90
Burstead Cl. KT11: Cob ... 8L 57
Burstock Rd. SW15 ... 7K 13
Burston Gdns. RH19: E Grin ... 6N 165
Burston Rd. SW15 ... 8J 13
Burston Vs. SW15 ... 8J 13 (off St John's Av.)
BURSTOW ... 3L 163
Burstow Ent. Pk. RH6: Smal ... 3N 163
Burstow Lodge Bus. Cen. RH6: Smal ... 6M 143
Burstow Pk. Bus. Cen. RH6: S Bri ... 5L 163
Burstow Rd. SW20 ... 9K 27
Burtenshaw Rd. KT7: T Dit ... 6G 41
Burton Cl. CR7: T Hea ... 2A 46
GU20: Windl ... 3A 52
KT9: Ches ... 4K 59
RH6: Horl ... 9E 142
Burton Ct. KT7: T Dit ... 5G 40
SE20 ... 1F 46
Burton Dr. GU3: Worp ... 7D 92
Burton Gdns. TW5: Houn ... 4N 9
Burton Rd. KT2: K Tham ... 1K 203 (8L 25)
Burtons Ct. RH12: Hors ... 6J 197
Burton's Rd. TW12: H Hill ... 5B 24
Burton Way SL4: W'sor ... 6B 4
Burtop Rd. Est. SW17 ... 4A 28
Burwash Rd. RH10: Craw ... 4E 182
Burway Cres. KT16: Chert ... 3J 37
Burwell KT1: K Tham ... 4M 203
Burwood Av. CR8: Ken ... 1M 83
Burwood Cl. GU1: Guil ... 2F 114
KT6: Surb ... 7N 41
KT12: Hers ... 3K 57
RH2: Reig ... 3B 122
Burwood Pde. KT16: Chert ... 6J 37 (off Guildford St.)
BURWOOD PARK
KT11 ... 8H 57
KT12 ... 2G 57
Burwood Pk. Rd. KT12: Hers ... 1J 57
Burwood Rd. KT12: Hers ... 4F 56
Bury Cl. GU21: Wok ... 3N 73
Bury Flds. GU2: Guil ... 7B 202 (5M 113)
Bury Gro. SM4: Mord ... 4N 43
Bury La. GU21: Wok ... 3M 73
Bury M. GU2: Guil ... 7B 202
Burys, The GU7: Goda ... 6H 133
Bury St. GU2: Guil ... 7B 202 (5M 113)
Burywood Hill RH5: Ockl ... 3E 158
BUSBRIDGE ... 9J 133
Busbridge Lakes, Waterfowl & Gardens ... 1H 153
Busbridge La. GU7: Goda ... 8G 133
Busby Ho. SW16 ... 5G 29
Busch Cl. TW7: Isle ... 4H 11
Busdens Cl. GU8: Mil ... 2C 152
Busdens La. GU8: Mil ... 2C 152
Busdens Way GU8: Mil ... 2C 152
Bushbury Rd. RH3: Betch, Brock ... 8N 119
Bush Cl. KT15: Addl ... 2L 55
Bush Cotts. SW18 ... 8M 13
Bushell Cl. SW2 ... 3K 29
Bushetts Gro. RH1: Mers ... 7F 102
Bushey Cl. CR8: Ken ... 3C 84
Bushey Ct. SW20 ... 2G 43
Bushey Cft. RH8: Oxt ... 8M 105
Bushey Down SW12 ... 3F 28
Bushey La. SM1: Sut ... 1M 61
BUSHEY MEAD ... 1J 43
Bushey Rd. CR0: Croy ... 8K 47
SM1: Sut ... 1M 61
SW20 ... 2G 42
Bushey Shaw KT21: A'tead ... 4H 79
Bushey Way BR3: Beck ... 5N 47
Bushfield RH14: Plais ... 6B 192
Bushfield Dr. RH1: Red ... 8E 122
Bush La. GU23: Send ... 2F 94
RH12: Hors ... 9N 179
Bushnell Rd. SW17 ... 3F 28
Bush Rd. TW9: Kew ... 2M 11
TW17: Shep ... 4A 38
Bush Wlk. RG40: W'ham ... 2B 30
Bushwood Rd. TW9: Kew ... 2N 11
Bushy Ct. KT1: H Wic ... 9J 25 (off Up. Teddington Rd.)
BUSHY HILL ... 2F 114
Bushy Hill Dr. GU1: Guil ... 1D 114
Bushy Pk. Gdns. TW11: Tedd ... 6D 24
Bushy Pk. Rd. TW11: Tedd ... 8H 25 (not continuous)
Bushy Rd. KT22: Fetc ... 9B 78
TW11: Tedd ... 7F 24
Business Cen., The RG41: W'ham ... 4A 30
Business Pk. 5 KT22: Leat ... 7F 78
Business Pk. 8 KT22: Leat ... 6H 79
Business Pk. 25 RH1: Red ... 1F 122
Busk Cres. GU14: Cove ... 2L 89
Butcherfield La. TN7: Hart ... 1N 187
Butchers Yd. BR6: Dow ... 7J 67 (off High St.)
Bute Av. TW10: Ham ... 3L 25
Bute Ct. SM6: W'ton ... 2G 62
Bute Gdns. SM6: W'ton ... 2G 63
TW10: Ham ... 2L 25
Bute Gdns. W. SM6: W'ton ... 2G 62
Bute Rd. CR0: Croy ... 7L 45
SM6: W'ton ... 1G 62
Butler Rd. GU19: Bag ... 5K 51
RG45: Crow ... 1G 48
Butlers Cl. SL4: W'sor ... 4A 4
TW3: Houn ... 6N 9
Butlers Dene Rd. CR3: Wold ... 7J 85
Butlers Hill KT24: W Hors ... 8C 96
Butler's Pl. GU8: Mil ... 1D 152
Butlers Rd. RH13: Hors ... 4N 197
Butt Cl. GU6: Cranl ... 6N 155
Buttercup Cl. GU35: Lind ... 4B 168
RG40: W'ham ... 2E 30
Buttercup Sq. TW19: Stan ... 2M 21
Butterfield RH19: E Grin ... 7L 165
Butterfield Cl. TW1: Twick ... 9F 10
Butterfields GU15: Camb ... 2N 69
Butterfly Wlk. CR6: Warl, Wold ... 7F 84
Butter Hill RH4: Dork ... 3J 201 (5G 119)
SM5: Cars ... 9E 44
SM6: W'ton ... 9E 44
Buttermer Cl. GU10: Wrec ... 4D 128
Buttermere Cl. GU14: Cove ... 1K 89
RH12: Hors ... 2A 198
SM4: Mord ... 5J 43
TW14: Felt ... 2G 22
Buttermere Ct. GU12: A Va ... 9D 90 (off Lakeside Cl.)
Buttermere Dr. GU15: Camb ... 1H 71
SW15 ... 8K 13
Buttermere Gdns. CR8: Pur ... 9A 64
RG12: Brac ... 2A 32
Buttermere Way TW20: Egh ... 8D 20
Buttersteep Ri. SL5: Asc ... 7G 33
Butterwick W6 ... 1J 13
Butt La. GU3: Put ... 7L 111
Butts, The TW8: Brent ... 2J 11
TW16: Sunb ... 2K 39
Butts Cl. RH11: Craw ... 2N 181
Butts Cres. TW13: Hanw ... 4A 24
Butts La. GU7: Goda ... 7G 133 (not continuous)
Butts Rd. GU21: Wok ... 4A 74
Buxton Av. CR3: Cate ... 8B 84
Buxton Cl. KT19: Eps ... 7A 60
Buxton Cres. SM3: Chea ... 1K 61
Buxton Dr. KT3: N Mal ... 1C 42
Buxton La. CR3: Cate ... 7A 84
Buxton Pl. CR3: Cate ... 7A 84
Buxton Rd. CR7: T Hea ... 4M 45
SW14 ... 6D 12
TW15: A'ford ... 6M 21
Byam St. SW6 ... 5N 13
Byards Cft. SW16 ... 9H 29
Byatt Wlk. TW12: Hamp ... 7M 23
Bychurch End TW11: Tedd ... 6F 24
Bycroft Way RH10: Craw ... 1F 182
Byegrove Rd. SW19 ... 7B 28
Byerley Way RH10: Craw ... 2H 183
Byers La. RH9: S Gods ... 4F 144
Byeway, The SW14 ... 6B 12
Byeways TW2: Twick ... 4B 24
Byeways, The KT5: Surb ... 4N 41
Byfeld Gdns. SW13 ... 4F 12
Byfield Rd. TW7: Isle ... 6G 10
BYFLEET ... 8N 55
Byfleet Ind. Est. KT14: Byf ... 6M 55
Byfleet Lawn Tennis Club ... 1J 75
Byfleet & New Haw Station (Rail) ... 6M 55
Byfleet Rd. KT11: Cob ... 8B 56
KT14: Byf ... 8B 56
KT15: N Haw ... 4M 55
Byfleets La. RH12: Bro H, Warn ... 2D 196
Byfleet Technical Cen. KT14: Byf ... 7M 55
Bygrove CR0: N Add ... 3L 65
Byland Cl. SM5: Cars ... 6A 44
Bylands GU22: Wok ... 6C 74
Byne Rd. SM5: Cars ... 8C 44
Bynes Rd. CR2: S Croy ... 4A 64
By-Pass Rd. KT22: Leat ... 7H 79
Byrd Rd. RH11: Craw ... 6L 181
Byrefield Rd. GU2: Guil ... 9J 93
Byrne Rd. SW12 ... 2F 28
Byron SL3: Lang ... 1D 6
Byron Av. CR5: Coul ... 2J 83
GU15: Camb ... 3F 70
KT3: N Mal ... 4F 42
SM1: Sut ... 1B 62
TW4: C'ford ... 5H 9
Byron Av. E. SM1: Sut ... 1B 62
Byron Cl. GU21: Knap ... 4H 73
GU46: Yate ... 2A 68
GU51: Fleet ... 5B 88
KT12: Wal T ... 7M 39
RH10: Craw ... 2F 182
RH12: Hors ... 2L 197
SE20 ... 2E 46
SW16 ... 7J 29
TW12: Hamp ... 5N 23
Byron Ct. SL4: W'sor ... 6D 4
Byron Dr. RG45: Crow ... 4G 48
Byron Gdns. SM1: Sut ... 1B 62
Byron Gro. RH19: E Grin ... 1M 185

Byron Pl.—Carlson Ct.

Byron Pl. KT22: Leat 9H 79
Byron Rd. CR2: Sels 6E 64
KT15: Addl 1N 55
Byton Rd. SW17 . . . . .7D 28
Byttom Hill RH5: Mick 4J 99
Byward Av. TW14: Felt 9K 9
Byway, The KT19: Ewe 1E 60
SM2: Sut 5B 62
Byways GU46: Yate 1A 68
Byways, The KT21: A'tead 5K 79
Bywood RG12: Brac 6M 31
Bywood Av. CR0: Croy 5F 46
Bywood Cl. CR8: Ken 2M 83
SM7: Ban 4L 81
Byworth Cl. GU9: Farnh 1E 128
Byworth Rd. GU9: Farnh 1E 128

C

Cabbage Hill RG42: Warf 6L 15
Cabbage Hill La. RG42: Bin . . .5K 15
Cabbel Pl. KT15: Addl 1L 55
Cabell Rd. GU2: Guil 2G 113
Caberfeigh Cl. RH1: Red 3B 122
Cabin Moss RG12: Brac 6C 32
Cable Ho. Ct. GU21: Wok 2A 74
Cabrera Av. GU25: V Wat 5M 35
Cabrera Cl. GU25: V Wat 5N 35
Cabrol Rd. GU14: Farnb 9M 69
Caburn Ct. RH11: Craw 5A 182
Caburn Hgts. RH11: Craw 5A 182
Caci Ho. *W14 . . . . .1L 13*
(off Kensington Village)
Cacket's La. TN14: Cud 2M 87
Cackstones, The
RH10: Craw 1H 183
Cadbury Cl. TW7: Isle 4G 11
TW16: Sunb 8F 22
Cadbury Rd. TW16: Sunb 8F 22
Caddy Cl. TW20: Egh 6C 20
Cader Rd. SW18 . . . . .1A 28
Cadet Way GU52: C Cro 9C 88
Cadman Ct. *W4 . . . . .1A 12*
(off Chaseley Dr.)
Cadmer Cl. KT3: N Mal 3D 42
Cadnam Cl. GU11: Alde 6A 110
Cadnam Point SW15 . . . . .2G 26
Cadogan Cl. BR3: Beck 1N 47
TW11: Tedd 6E 24
Cadogan Ct. GU15: Camb 3C 70
GU51: Fleet 4A 88
SM2: Sut 3N 61
Cadogan Ho. *GU1: Guil 4B 114*
(off St Lukes Sq.)
Cadogan Pl. CR8: Ken 4N 83
Cadogan Rd. GU11: Alde 6B 90
KT6: Surb 4K 41
Caenshill Ho. KT13: Weybr . . .4B 56
Caenshill Pl. KT13: Weybr 4B 56
Caenshill Rd. KT13: Weybr . . .4B 56
Caenswood Hill
KT13: Weybr 6B 56
Caenwood Cl. KT13: Weybr . . .3B 56
Caen Wood Rd.
KT21: A'tead 5J 79
Caerleon Cl. GU26: Hind 3A 170
KT10: Clay 4H 59
Caernarvon GU16: Frim 6D 70
Caernarvon Cl. CR4: Mit 2J 45
Caesar Ct. GU11: Alde 2K 109
Caesars Camp Rd.
GU15: Camb 7D 50
Caesar's Cl. GU15: Camb 7D 50
Caesars Ct. GU9: U Hal 6H 109
Caesars Ga. RG42: Warf 8C 16
Caesars Wlk. CR4: Mit 4D 44
Caesars Way TW17: Shep 5E 38
Caffins Cl. RH10: Craw 1C 182
Cage Yd. RH2: Reig 3M 121
Caillard Rd. KT14: Byf 7N 55
Cain Rd. RG12: Brac 1J 31
Cain's La. TW14: Felt 8F 8
Cairn Cl. GU15: Camb 3F 70
Cairn Ct. KT17: Ewe 6E 60
Cairngorm Cl. TW11: Tedd 6G 24
Cairngorm Pl. GU14: Cove 7K 69
Cairo New Rd.
CR0: Croy 3A **200** (8M 45)
Caistor M. SW12 . . . . .1F 28
Caistor Rd. SW12 . . . . .1F 28
Caithness Dr.
KT18: Eps 8K **201** (1C 80)
Caithness Rd. CR4: Mit 8F 28
Calbourne Rd. SW12 . . . . .1D 28
Calcott Pk. GU46: Yate 9B 48
Caldbeck Av. KT4: W Pk 8F 42
Caldbeck Ho. *RH11: Craw 6L 181*
(off Salvington Rd.)
Caldecote KT1: K Tham 4M 203
Calder Ct. SL3: Lang 1B 6
Calderdale Cl.
RH11: Craw 5N 181
Calder Rd. SM4: Mord 4A 44
Calder Way SL3: Poy 6G 7
Caldwell Ho. *SW13 . . . . .3H 13*
(off Trinity Chu. Rd.)
Caldwell Rd. GU20: Windl 2A 52
Caledonian Ho.
RH10: Craw 1B 182
(off Barnfield Rd.)
Caledonian Way RH6: Gat 3F 162
Caledonia Rd. TW19: Stan 2N 21
Caledon Pl. GU4: B'ham 9C 94
Caledon Rd. SM6: W'ton 1E 62
Calfridus Way RG12: Brac 2C 32
California Cl. SM2: Sut 6M 61
California Rd.
KT3: N Mal 3A 42
Callender Ct. *CR0: Croy 5N 45*
(off Harry Cl.)
Calley Down Cres.
CR0: N Add 6N 65
Callis Farm Cl. TW19: Stan 9N 7
Callisto Cl. RH11: Craw 6K 181
Callow Fld. CR8: Pur 9L 63
Callow Hill GU25: V Wat 2M 35
Calluna Ct. GU22: Wok 5B 74
Calluna Dr. RH10: Cop 8L 163
Calonne Rd. SW19 . . . . .5J 27
Calshot Rd. TW6: Lon A 5B 8
(not continuous)
Calshot Way GU16: Frim 7E 70
TW6: Lon A 5B 8
(not continuous)
Calthorpe Gdns. SM1: Sut 9A 44
Calton Gdns. GU11: Alde 5A 110
Calverley Ct. KT19: Ewe 1C 60
Calverley Rd. KT17: Ewe 3F 60
Calvert Cl. GU12: Alde 3B 110
KT19: Eps 6A 60
Calvert Ct. TW9: Rich 7M 11
Calvert Cres. RH4: Dork 3H 119
Calvert Rd. KT24: Eff 6J 97
RH4: Dork 3H 119
Calvin Cl. GU15: Camb 2F 70
Calvin Wlk. RH11: Craw 6K 181
Camac Rd. TW2: Twick 2D 24
Camargue Pl. GU7: Goda 7J 133
Cambalt Rd. SW15 . . . . .8J 13
Camber Cl. RH10: Craw 3G 183
CAMBERLEY 9B 50
Camberley Av. SW20 . . . . .1G 42
Camberley Bus. Cen.
GU15: Camb 1M 69
Camberley Cl. SM3: Chea 9J 43
Camberley Indoor Bowling Club
. . . . .3N 69
Camberley Rd. TW6: Lon A 6B 8
Camberley Station (Rail) . . .1B 70
Camberley Theatre, The 9B 50
Camberley Towers
GU15: Camb 1B 70
(off Up. Gordon Rd.)
Camborne Cl. TW6: Lon A 6B 8
Camborne Cres. TW6: Lon A . . .6B 8
Camborne M. SW18 . . . . .1M 27
Camborne Rd. CR0: Croy 6D 46
SM2: Sut 4M 61
SM4: Mord 4J 43
SW18 . . . . .1M 27
TW6: Lon A 6B 8
Camborne Way TW5: Hest 4A 10
TW6: Lon A 6B 8
Cambourne Wlk.
TW10: Rich 9K 11
Cambray Rd. SW12 . . . . .2G 29
Cambria Cl. TW3: Houn 7A 10
Cambria Ct. TW14: Felt 1J 23
TW18: Stain 5G 20
Cambria Gdns. TW19: Stan . . .1N 21
(not continuous)
Cambrian Cl. GU15: Camb 1N 69
SE27 . . . . .4M 29
Cambrian Rd. GU14: Cove 7J 69
TW10: Rich 9M 11
Cambrian Way RG40: Finch . . .8A 30
Cambria St. SW6 . . . . .3N 13
Cambridge Av. KT3: N Mal 2D 42
(not continuous)
Cambridge Cl. GU21: Wok 5J 73
SW20 . . . . .9G 26
TW4: Houn 7M 9
UB7: Harm 2M 7
Cambridge Cotts.
TW9: Kew 2N 11
Cambridge Cres.
TW11: Tedd 6G 24
Cambridge Gdns.
KT1: K Tham 1N 41
Cambridge Gro. W6 . . . . .1G 13
Cambridge Gro. Rd.
KT1: K Tham 2N 41
(not continuous)
Cambridge Ho. SL4: W'sor 4F 4
Cambridge Lodge Mobile Home Pk.
RH6: Horl 5E 142
Cambridge Mdws.
GU9: Farnh 2E 128
Cambridge Pk. TW1: Twick 9J 11
Cambridge Pk. Ct.
TW1: Twick 1K 25
Cambridge Pl. GU9: Farnh . . .1H 129
Cambridge Rd. CR4: Mit 2G 44
GU11: Alde 2L 109
GU47: Owls 6K 49
KT1: K Tham . . .3M **203** (1M 41)
KT3: N Mal 3C 42
KT8: W Mole 3N 39
KT12: Wal T 5J 39
RG45: Crow 3H 49
RH13: Hors 6K 197
SE20 . . . . .2E 46
SM5: Cars 3C 62
SW13 . . . . .5E 12
SW20 . . . . .9F 26
Cambridge Rd. TW1: Twick . . .9K 11
TW4: Houn 7M 9
TW9: Kew 3N 11
TW11: Tedd 5F 24
TW12: Hamp 8N 23
TW15: A'ford 8D 22
Cambridge Rd. E.
GU14: Farnb 4A 90
(not continuous)
Cambridge Rd. Nth.
W4 . . . . .1A 12
Cambridge Rd. Sth.
W4 . . . . .1A 12
Cambridge Rd. W.
GU14: Farnb 4A 90
(not continuous)
Cambridgeshire Cl.
RG42: Warf 8D 16
Cambridge Sq.
GU15: Camb 9A 50
(off Cambridge Wlk.)
RH1: Red 6E 122
Cambridge Wlk.
GU15: Camb 9A 50
Camden Av. TW13: Felt 2K 23
Camden Cotts.
KT13: Weybr 9B 38
Camden Gdns. CR7: T Hea 2M 45
SM1: Sut 2N 61
Camden Rd. RH7: Ling 8N 145
SM1: Sut 2N 61
SM5: Cars 1D 62
Camden Wlk. GU51: Fleet 4D 88
Camden Way CR7: T Hea 2M 45
Cameford Ct. SW2 . . . . .1J 29
Camel Gro. KT2: K Tham 6K 25
Camellia Ct. GU24: W End 9C 52
Camellia Ho. *TW13: Felt 2H 23*
(off Tilley Rd.)
Camellia Pl. TW2: Whitt 1B 24
Camelot Cl. SW19 . . . . .5L 27
TN16: B Hil 3E 86
Camelot Ct. RH11: Ifi 3K 181
CAMELSDALE 3D 188
Camelsdale Rd.
GU27: Hasl 3C 188
Cameron Cl. GU6: Cranl 9N 155
Cameron Pl. SW16 . . . . .3L 29
Cameron Rd. CR0: Croy 5M 45
GU11: Alde 6B 90
Cameron Sq. CR4: Mit 9C 28
Camgate Cen., The
TW19: Stan 9A 8
Camilla Cl. KT23: Book 3B 98
TW16: Sunb 7G 22
Camilla Dr. RH5: Westh 8G 98
Camille Cl. SE25 . . . . .2D 46
Camm Av. SL4: W'sor 6B 4
Camm Gdns.
KT1: K Tham . . .4M **203** (1M 41)
KT7: T Dit 6F 40
Camomile Av. CR4: Mit 9D 28
Campana Rd. SW6 . . . . .4M 13
Campaspe Bus. Pk.
TW16: Sunb 4G 38
Campbell Av. GU22: Wok 8B 74
Campbell Cir. KT13: Weybr 6A 56
Campbell Cl. GU11: Alde 5A 110
GU46: Yate 9E 48
GU51: Fleet 4A 88
KT14: Byf 8M 55
SW16 . . . . .5H 29
TW2: Twick 2D 24
Campbell Cres.
RH19: E Grin 9L 165
Campbell Flds.
GU11: Alde 3N 109
Campbell Pl. GU16: Frim 3D 70
Campbell Rd. CR0: Croy 6M 45
CR3: Cate 8A 84
GU11: Alde 1M 109
KT8: E Mol 2E 40
KT13: Weybr 4B 56
RH10: Craw 5G 182
TW2: Twick 3D 24
Campden Rd. CR2: S Croy 2B 64
Campen Cl. SW19 . . . . .3K 27
Camp End Rd. KT13: Weybr . . .8D 56
Camperdown Ho. SL4: W'sor . . .5F 4
Camp Farm Rd. GU11: Alde 8B 90
Camp Hill GU10: Farnh 3A 130
Camphill Ct. KT14: W By 8J 55
Camphill Ind. Est.
KT14: W By 7K 55
Camphill Rd. KT14: W By 8J 55
Camping & Cvn. Site
RH7: Ling 1J 165
Campion Cl. CR0: Croy 1B 64
GU17: Haw 3L 69
GU35: Lind 5B 168
Campion Dr. KT20: Tad 7G 81
Campion Ho. RG42: Brac 9K 15
RH1: Red 9D 102
Campion Rd. RH12: Hors 3L 197
SW15 . . . . .7H 13
TW7: Isle 4F 10
Campion Way
RG40: W'ham 1D 30
Camp Rd. CR3: Wold 7H 85
GU14: Farnb 5A 90
SW19 . . . . .6G 26
(not continuous)
Camp Vw. SW19 . . . . .6G 27
Camrose Av. TW13: Felt 5K 23
Camrose Cl. CR0: Croy 6H 47
SM4: Mord 3M 43
Canada Av. RH1: Red 7E 122
Canada Copse GU8: Mil 9B 132
Canada Dr. RH1: Red 7E 122
Canada Rd. GU16: Deep 6H 71
KT11: Cob 9K 57
KT14: Byf 7M 55
Canadian Memorial Av.
TW20: Eng G 1J 35
Canal Bank GU12: A Va 9E 90
KT15: Addl 3M 55
Canal Bank M. GU21: Wok 4A 74
Canal Bri. KT15: Addl 4M 55
Canal Cl. GU11: Alde 8B 90
Canal Cotts. GU12: A Va 9E 90
Canalside RH1: Mers, Red . . .9F 102
Canal Wlk. CR0 . . . . .5B 46
Canberra Cl. GU46: Yate 7A 48
RH11: Craw 9B 162
Canberra Pl. RH12: Hors 4M 197
Canberra Rd. TW6: Lon A 6B 8
Canbury Av.
KT2: K Tham . . .1L **203** (9M 25)
Canbury Bus. Cen.
KT2: K Tham . . .2K **203** (9L 25)
Canbury Bus. Pk.
KT2: K Tham 2K 203
Canbury Ct. KT2: K Tham 8K 25
Canbury Pk. Rd.
KT2: K Tham . . .2K **203** (9L 25)
Canbury Pas.
KT2: K Tham . . .2H **203** (9K 25)
Candleford Cl. RG12: Brac 8A 16
Candler M. TW1: Twick 1G 25
Candlerush Cl. GU22: Wok 4D 74
Candover Cl. UB7: Harm 3M 7
Candy Cft. KT23: Book 4B 98
Canes La. GU35: Lind 4A 168
Canewdon Cl. GU22: Wok 6A 74
Canford Dr. KT15: Addl 8K 37
Canford Gdns. KT3: N Mal 5D 42
Canford Pl. TW11: Tedd 7J 25
Canham Rd. SE25 . . . . .2B 46
Can Hatch KT20: Tad 5K 81
Canmore Gdns. SW16 . . . . . . .8G 29
Canning Rd. CR0: Croy 8C 46
GU12: Alde 2B 110
Cannizaro Rd. SW19 . . . . .7H 27
Cannon Cl. GU47: C Tow 7L 49
SW20 . . . . .2H 43
TW12: Hamp 7B 24
Cannon Cres. GU24: Chob 7H 53
Cannon Gro. KT22: Fetc 9E 78
Cannon Hill RG12: Brac 5A 32
Cannon Hill La. SW20 . . . . . . .4J 43
Cannon M. SL5: Asc 9F 16
Cannons Health Club
Crabbet Park 2K 183
Fulham 4J 13
Norbury 1K 45
Sutton 3M 61
Twickenham 1E 24
West Byfleet 1K 75
Cannonside KT22: Fetc 9E 78
Cannon Way KT8: W Mole 3A 40
KT22: Fetc 8E 78
Canonbury Cotts.
RH12: Rusp 3E 180
Canons Cl. RH2: Reig 2L 121
Canon's Hill CR5: Coul, Pur . . .4M 83
Canons La. KT20: Tad 5K 81
Canons Leisure Cen., The . . .3D 44
Canon's Wlk. CR0: Croy 9G 46
Canons Yd. RH2: Reig 6N 121
Canopus Way TW19: Stan 1N 21
Cansiron La.
RH19: Ash W 3H 187
TN8: Ash W, Cow, Hart
. . . . .7N 167
Cantelupe M.
RH19: E Grin 9B 166
(off Cantelupe Rd.)
Cantelupe Rd.
RH19: E Grin 9B 166
Canter, The RH10: Craw 2J 183
Canterbury Cl. KT4: W Pk 8J 43
Canterbury Ct. *CR2: S Croy . . .4N 63*
(off St Augustines Av.)
GU14: Farnb 3B 90
(off Canterbury Gdns.)
RH4: Dork 1J 201
TW15: A'ford 5A 22
Canterbury Gdns.
GU14: Farnb 3B 90
Canterbury Gro. SE27 . . . . . . .5L 29
Canterbury Hall KT4: W Pk 6G 43
Canterbury Ho. CR0: Croy . . .1D 200
KT19: Eps 7N 59
(off Queen Alexandra's Way)
Canterbury M. KT22: Oxs 9C 58
SL4: W'sor 5D 4
Canterbury Rd. CR0: Croy 6K 45
GU2: Guil 1J 113
GU12: Ash 1E 110
GU14: Farnb 3B 90
RH10: Craw 7C 182
SM4: Mord 6N 43
TW13: Hanw 3M 23
Canterbury Wlk.
GU14: Farnb 3B 90
CANTLEY 9B 14
Cantley Cres.
RG41: W'ham 9A 14
Cantley Gdns. SE19 . . . . .1C 46
Canvas Ct. GU27: Hasl 2F 188
Canvey Cl. RH11: Craw 6A 182
Cape Copse RH12: Rudg 1E 194
CAPEL 4K 159
Capel Av. SM6: W'ton 2K 63
Capel By-Pass
RH5: B Grn, Cap, Ockl . . .3H 159
Capel La. RH11: Craw 4L 181
Capel Rd. RH12: Rusp 2M 179
Capercaillie Cl. RG12 Brac 3J 31
Capern Rd. SW18 . . . . .2A 28
Capital Bus. Cen.
CR2: S Croy 4A 64
Capital Ind. Est. CR4: Mit 4D 44
Capital Interchange Way
TW8: Brent 1N 11
Capital Pk. GU8: Worm 2C 172
GU22: Wok 8D 74
Capitol, The 6K 197
Capitol Sq.
KT18: Eps 6L **201** (9D 60)
Capricorn Cl. RH11: Craw 5K 181
Capri Rd. CR0: Croy 7C 46
Capsey Rd. RH11: Ifi 3K 181
Capstans Wharf GU21: Wok 5J 73
Captains Wlk. RH11: Craw . . .5A 182
Capua Ct. RH10: Craw 8G 163
Caradon Cl. GU21: Wok 5L 73
Caraway Cl. RH11: Craw 7N 181
Caraway Pl. GU2: Guil 7K 93
SM6: W'ton 9F 44
Carbery La. SL5: Asc 2M 33
Cardamom Cl. GU2: Guil 8K 93
Card Hill RH18: F Row 8H 187
Cardigan Cl. GU21: Wok 5H 73
Cardigan Rd. SW13 . . . . .5F 12
SW19 . . . . .7A 28
TW10: Rich 9L 11
Cardinal Av. KT2: K Tham 6L 25
SM4: Mord 5K 43
Cardinal Cl. CR2: Sande 9D 64
KT4: W Pk 1F 60
SM4: Mord 5K 43
Cardinal Cres. KT3: N Mal 1B 42
Cardinal Dr. KT12: Wal T 7L 39
Cardinal Ho. *GU14: Farnb 1A 90*
(off Jubilee Hall Rd.)
Cardinal Pl. SW15 . . . . .7J 13
Cardinal Rd. TW13: Felt 2J 23
CARDINALS, THE 5E 110
Cardinals, The
GU10: Tong 5D 110
(off South Side)
RG12: Brac 3N 31
Cardinals Wlk.
TW12: Hamp 8C 24
TW16: Sunb 7F 22
Cardingham GU21: Wok 4K 73
Cardington Sq. TW4: Houn 7L 9
Cardwell Cres. SL5: S'hill 4N 33
Cardwells Keep GU2: Guil 9K 93
Carew Cl. CR5: Coul 6M 83
Carew Ct. SM2: Sut 5N 61
Carew Manor & Dovecote 9G 45
Carew Mnr. Cotts.
SM6: Bedd 9H 45
Carew Rd. CR4: Mit 1E 44
CR7: T Hea 3M 45
SM6: W'ton 3G 63
TW15: A'ford 7D 22
Carey Cl. SL4: W'sor 6E 4
Carey Ho. RH11: Craw 3A 182
Carey Rd. RG40: W'ham 3B 30
Careys Copse RH6: Smal 8M 143
Carey's Wood RH6: Smal 8M 143
Carfax RH12: Hors 6J 197
Carfax Av. GU10: Tong 4D 110
Carfax Rd. UB3: Harl 1G 9
Cargate Av. GU11: Alde 3M 109
Cargate Gro. GU11: Alde 3M 109
Cargate Hill GU11: Alde 3L 109
Cargate Ter. GU11: Alde 3L 109
Cargill Rd. SW18 . . . . .2N 27
Cargo Forecourt Rd.
RH6: Gat 3B 162
Cargo Point TW19: Stan 9A 8
Cargo Rd. RH6: Gat 2B 162
Cargreen Pl. SE25 . . . . .3C 46
Cargreen Rd. SE25 . . . . .3C 46
Carisbrooke GU16: Frim 6D 70
Carisbrooke Cl. TW4: Houn . . .1M 23
Carisbrooke Ct. SM2: Chea 4L 61
Carisbrooke Ho.
KT2: K Tham 2J 203
TW10: Rich 8N 11
Carisbrooke Rd. CR4: Mit 3H 45
Carleton Av. SM6: W'ton 5H 63
Carleton Cl. KT10: Esh 7D 40
Carlingford Gdns. CR4: Mit 8D 28
Carlingford Rd. SM4: Mord 5J 43
Carlin Pl. GU15: Camb 2A 70
Carlinwark Dr. GU15: Camb 8D 50
Carlisle Cl. KT2: K Tham 9N 25
Carlisle M. KT2: K Tham 9N 25
Carlisle Rd. GU10: Rush 3N 149
SM1: Sut 3L 61
TW12: Hamp 8B 24
Carlisle Way SW17 . . . . .6E 28
Carlos St. GU7: Goda 7H 133
Carlson Ct. SW15 . . . . .7L 13

Carlton Av.—Central Wlk.

Carlton Av. CR2: S Croy 4B 64
TW14: Felt 9K 9
UB3: Harl 1F 8
Carlton Cl. GU15: Camb 3F 70
GU21: Wok 1B 74
KT9: Ches 3K 59
RH10: Craw 4C 182
Carlton Ct. RH6: Horl 6E 142
TW18: Stain 6J 21
Carlton Cres. GU52: C Cro 7C 88
SM3: Chea 1K 61
Carlton Dr. SW15 . . . . .8J 13
Carlton Grn. RH1: Red 9C 102
Carlton Ho. TW3: Houn 9A 10
TW14: Felt 9G 8
Carlton Pk. Av.
SW20 . . . . .1J 43
Carlton Pl. *KT13: Weybr 1C 56*
(off Castle Vw. Rd.)
Carlton Rd. CR2: S Croy 3A 64
GU21: Wok 1C 74
GU35: H Dwn 5H 169
KT3: N Mal 1D 42
KT12: Wal T 6J 39
RH1: Red 1B 122
RH2: Reig 1B 122
RH9: S Gods 1F 144
SW14 . . . . .6B 12
TW16: Sunb 8G 22
Carlton Towers
SM5: Cars 9D 44
Carlton Tye RH6: Horl 8G 142
Carlton Vs. SW15 . . . . .8K 13
Carlwell St. SW17 . . . . .6C 28
Carlyle Cl. KT8: W Mole 1B 40
Carlyle Ct. RG45: Crow 3H 49
SW6 . . . . .4N 13
(off Imperial Rd.)
Carlyle Ho. *KT8: W Mole 4A 40*
(off Down St.)
Carlyle Pl. SW15 . . . . .7J 13
Carlyle Rd. CR0: Croy 8D 46
TW18: Stain 8J 21
W5 . . . . .1J 11
Carlyon Cl. GU14: Farnb 1A 90
GU16: Mytc 1D 90
Carlys Cl. BR3: Beck 1G 47
Carmalt Gdns. KT12: Hers 2K 57
SW15 . . . . .7H 13
Carman Wlk. RH11: Craw 8N 181
Carmarthen Cl.
GU14: Farnb 7L 69
Carmel Cl. GU22: Wok 5A 74
TW9: Rich 5A 12
Carmel Lodge *SW6 . . . . .2M 13*
(off Lillie Rd.)
Carmichael Ct. *SW13 . . . . .5E 12*
(off Grove Rd.)
Carmichael M. SW18 . . . . .1B 28
Carmichael Rd. SE25 . . . . .4C 46
Carminia Rd. SW17 . . . . .3F 28
Carnation Cl. RG45: Crow 8G 30
Carnation Dr. RG42: Wink R . . .7E 16
Carnegie Cl. KT6: Surb 8M 41
Carnegie Pl. SW19 . . . . .4J 27
Carnforth Cl. KT19: Ewe 3A 60
Carnforth Rd. SW16 . . . . .8H 29
(not continuous)
Carnie Lodge SW17 . . . . .4F 28
Carnival Pool 3A 30
Carnival Sq. GU51: Fleet 4A 88
Carnoustie RG12: Brac 6K 31
Carnwath Rd. SW6 . . . . .6M 13
Carolina Rd. CR7: T Hea 1M 45
Caroline Cl. CR0: Croy 1B 64
SW16 . . . . .4K 29
TW7: Isle 3D 10
Caroline Ct. RH11: Craw 4B 182
TW15: A'ford 7C 22
Caroline Ho. *W6 . . . . .1H 13*
(off Queen Caroline St.)
Caroline Pl. UB3: Harl 3F 8
Caroline Rd. SW19 . . . . .8L 27
Caroline Wlk. *W6 . . . . .2K 13*
(off Lillie Rd.)
Caroline Way GU16: Frim 5D 70
Carolyn Cl. GU21: Wok 6J 73
Carpenter Cl. KT17: Ewe 5E 60
Carpenters Ct. TW2: Twick 3E 24
Carrara Wharf SW6 . . . . .6K 13
Carriage Pl. SW16 . . . . .6G 29
Carrick Cl. TW7: Isle 6G 10
Carrick Ga. KT10: Esh 9C 40
Carrick La. GU46: Yate 9D 48
Carrier Bus. Pk.
RH10: Craw 2F 182
Carrigshaun KT13: Weybr 2E 56
Carrington Av. TW3: Houn 8B 10
Carrington Cl. CR0: Croy 6H 47
KT2: K Tham 6B 26
RH1: Red 2D 122
Carrington La. GU12: A Va 5E 90
Carrington Pl. KT10: Esh 1B 58
Carrington Rd. TW10: Rich 7N 11
Carroll Av. GU1: Guil 3D 114
Carroll Cres. SL5: Asc 4K 33
Carrow Rd. KT12: Wal T 9L 39
CARSHALTON 1E 62
Carshalton Athletic FC 9C 44
CARSHALTON BEECHES 5C 62
Carshalton Beeches Station (Rail)
. . . . .3D 62
Carshalton Gro. SM1: Sut 1B 62
Carshalton Lodge
KT13: Weybr 9E 38
(off Oatlands Dr.)
CARSHALTON ON THE HILL . . .4E 62
Carshalton Pk. Rd.
SM5: Cars 2D 62
Carshalton Pl. SM5: Cars 2E 62
Carshalton Rd. CR4: Mit 3E 44
GU15: Camb 6E 50
SM1: Sut 2A 62
SM5: Cars 2A 62
SM7: Ban 1D 82
Carshalton Station (Rail) 1D 62
Carslake Rd. SW15 . . . . .9H 13
Carson Rd. SE21 . . . . .3N 29
CARTBRIDGE 9D 74
Cartbridge Cl. GU23: Send 1D 94
Carter Cl. SL4: W'sor 5D 4
SM6: W'ton 4H 63
Carterdale Cotts.
RH5: Cap 5J 159
Carter Rd. RH10: Craw 6H 183
SW19 . . . . .7B 28
Carters Cl. GU1: Guil 8A 94
KT4: W Pk 8J 43
Carter's Cotts. RH1: Red 5C 122
Carter's Hill RG40: W'ham 5F 14
RG42: Bin 5F 14
Carters Hill Pk.
RG40: W'ham 5E 14
Carters La. GU22: Wok 7E 74
Carterslodge La.
RH17: Hand 9J 199
Cartersmead Cl. RH6: Horl . . .7F 142
Carters Rd. KT17: Eps 2E 80
Carters Wlk. GU9: H End 4J 109
Carter's Yd. SW18 . . . . .8M 13
Carthona Dr. GU52: Fleet 6A 88
Carthouse Cotts. GU4: Guil . . .9E 94
Carthouse La. GU21: Wok 1H 73
Cartmel Cl. RH2: Reig 1C 122
Cartmel Gdns. SM4: Mord 4A 44
Cartwright Way SW13 . . . . . . .3G 13
Carville Cres. TW8: Brent 1L 11
Carylls Cotts. RH12: Fay 8E 180
Cascades CR0: Sels 6J 65
Cascades Ct. SW19 . . . . .8L 27
Caselden Cl. KT15: Addl 2L 55
Casewick Rd. SE27 . . . . .6L 29
Casher Rd. RH10: Craw 6G 183
Cassidy Rd. SW6 . . . . .3M 13
(not continuous)
Cassilis Rd. TW1: Twick 8H 11
Cassino Cl. GU11: Alde 2N 109
Cassiobury Av. TW14: Felt 1G 22
Cassland Rd. CR7: T Hea 3A 46
Cassocks Sq. TW17: Shep 6E 38
Castello Av. SW15 . . . . .8H 13
CASTELNAU 2G 12
Castelnau SW13 . . . . .4F 12
Castelnau Gdns.
SW13 . . . . .2G 13
Castelnau Mans.
SW13 . . . . .2G 13
(off Castelnau, not continuous)
Castelnau Row SW13 . . . . .2G 12
Castle, The RH12: Hors 1L 197
Castle Av. KT17: Ewe 5F 60
SL3: Dat 2K 5
Castle Bus. Cen.
TW12: Hamp 9B 24
(off Castle M.)
Castle Cl. BR2: Brom 2N 47
GU14: Farnb 3C 90
GU15: Camb 2D 70
RH1: Blet 2N 123
RH2: Reig 7N 121
SW19 . . . . .4J 27
TW16: Sunb 8F 22
Castlecombe Dr. SW19 . . . . . . .1J 27
Castle Ct. GU9: Farnh 9G 108
Castlecraig Ct. GU47: C Tow . . .8J 49
Castle Dr. RH2: Reig 7M 121
RH6: Horl 1G 162
Castle Farm Cvn. Site
SL4: W'sor 5A 4
Castle Fld. GU9: Farnh 9G 108
Castlefield Ct. RH2: Reig 3N 121
Castlefield Rd. RH2: Reig 3M 121
Castle Gdns. RH4: Dork 3M 119
Castlegate TW9: Rich 6M 11
CASTLE GREEN 9G 53
Castle Grn. KT13: Weybr 9F 38
Castle Gro. Rd.
GU24: Chob 9G 53
Castle Hill
GU1: Guil 7C **202** (5N 113)
GU9: Farnh 9G 108
SL4: W'sor 4G 5
Castle Hill Av. CR0: N Add 5L 65
Castle Hill Rd.
TW20: Eng G 5L 19
Castle Ho. SM2: Sut 3M 61
Castlemaine Av.
CR2: S Croy 2C 64
KT17: Ewe 5G 61
Castle M. KT13: Weybr 9F 38
SW17 . . . . .5C 28
TW12: Hamp 9B 24
(not continuous)
Castle of Mey Ho.
GU27: Hasl 2D 188
Castle Pde. KT17: Ewe 4F 60
Castle Rd. CR5: Chip 7C 82
GU11: Alde 9K 89
GU15: Camb 2C 70
GU21: Wok 1B 74
KT13: Weybr 9E 38
KT18: Eps 2A 80
RH12: Bro H 5D 196
TW7: Isle 5F 10
Castle Row W4 . . . . .1C 12
Castle Sq.
GU1: Guil 6D **202** (5N 113)
RH1: Blet 2N 123
Castle St.
GU1: Guil 6C **202** (5N 113)
GU9: Farnh 9G 109
GU52: Fleet 6A 88
KT1: K Tham 3J **203** (1L 41)
RH1: Blet 2M 123
Castleton Cl. CR0: Croy 5H 47
SM7: Ban 2M 81
Castleton Dr. SM7: Ban 2M 81
Castleton Rd. CR4: Mit 3H 45
(not continuous)
Castletown Rd. W14 . . . . .1K 13
Castle Vw. KT18: Eps 1A 80
Castle Vw. Rd.
KT13: Weybr 1C 56
Castleview Rd. SL3: Lang 1M 5
Castle Wlk. RH2: Reig 3M 121
TW16: Sunb 2K 39
Castle Way KT17: Ewe 6F 60
SW19 . . . . .4J 27
TW13: Hanw 5K 23
Castle Yd. TW10: Rich 8K 11
Castor Ct. GU46: Yate 8A 48
GU52: C Cro 8C 88
Caswall Cl. RG42: Bin 7H 15
Caswall Ride GU46: Yate 1D 68
Caswell Cl. GU14: Farnb 8L 69
Catalina Rd. TW6: Lon A 5C 8
Catalpa Cl. GU1: Guil 1M 113
Catena Ri. GU18: Ligh 6L 51
Caterfield La. RH7: Ling 1B 146
RH8: Ling, Oxt 8C 126
Cater Gdns. GU2: Guil 1J 113
CATERHAM 2D 104
Caterham By-Pass
CR3: Cate 8E 84
Caterham Cl. CR3: Cate 7B 84
(not continuous)
GU24: Pirb 8B 72
Caterham Dr. CR5: Coul 5M 83
CATERHAM-ON-THE-HILL 9B 84
Caterham Station (Rail) 2D 104
Caterways RH12: Hors 5G 197
Cathcart Rd. SW10 . . . . .2N 13
Cathedral Cl. GU2: Guil 4L 113
Cathedral Ct. GU2: Guil 3K 113
Cathedral Hill GU2: Guil 2K 113
Cathedral Hill Ind. Est.
GU2: Guil 2K 113
Cathedral Pl. *GU1: Guil 2C 202*
(off Old School Cl.)
Cathedral Vw. GU2: Guil 3J 113
Catherine Cl. KT14: Byf 1N 75
Catherine Ct. SW19 . . . . .6L 27
Catherine Dr. TW9: Rich 7L 11
TW16: Sunb 7G 22
Catherine Gdns.
TW3: Houn 7D 10
Catherine Howard Ct.
KT13: Weybr 9C 38
(off Old Palace Rd.)
Catherine Rd.
KT6: Surb 8G **203** (4K 41)
Catherine Wheel Rd.
TW8: Brent 3K 11
Cat Hill RH5: Ockl 7B 158
Cathill La. RH5: Ockl 7B 158
Cathles Rd. SW12 . . . . .1F 28
Catlin Cres. TW17: Shep 4E 38
Catlin Gdns. RH9: Gods 8E 104
Cator Cl. CR0: N Add 7A 66
Cator Cres. CR0: N Add 7A 66
Cator La. BR3: Beck 1J 47
Cator Rd. SM5: Cars 2D 62
Cato's Hill KT10: Esh 1B 58
Cat St. TN7: C Hat, U Har 9N 187
CATTESHALL 6K 133
Catteshall Hatch
GU7: Goda 5K 133
Catteshall La. GU7: Goda 7H 133
Catteshall Rd. GU7: Goda 5K 133
(not continuous)
Catteshall Ter. *GU7: Goda 6K 133*
(off Catteshall Rd.)
Causeway RH12: Hors 7J 197
Causeway, The KT9: Ches 1L 59
KT10: Clay 4F 58
SM2: Sut 5A 62
SM5: Cars 9E 44
SW18 . . . . .8N 13
(not continuous)
SW19 . . . . .6H 27
TW4: Houn 7H 9
TW11: Tedd 7F 24
TW14: Felt, Houn 7H 9
TW18: Stain 5E 20
Causeway Corporate Cen.
TW18: Stain 5E 20
Causeway Ct. GU21: Wok 5J 73
Causewayside *GU27: Hasl . . .1H 189*
(off High St.)
Cavalier Ct. KT5: Surb 5M 41
Cavalier Way
RH19: E Grin 2B 186
Cavalry Ct. GU11: Alde 2K 109
Cavalry Cres. SL4: W'sor 6F 4
TW4: Houn 7L 9
Cavalry Gdns. SW15 . . . . .8L 13
Cavan's Rd. GU11: Alde 7A 90
Cavell Way GU21: Knap 6F 72
KT19: Eps 7N 59
RH10: Craw 4G 182
Cavendish Av. KT3: N Mal 4F 42
Cavendish Cl. RH12: Hors . . .1K 197
TW16: Sunb 7G 22
Cavendish Ct. GU17: Haw 3J 69
KT13: Weybr 3D 56
KT16: Chert 7J 37
(off Victory Rd.)
SL3: Poy 4G 6
SM6: W'ton 3F 62
TW16: Sunb 7G 22
Cavendish Dr. KT10: Clay 2E 58
Cavendish Gdns.
GU52: C Cro 8A 88
RH1: Red 2E 122
Cavendish Meads
SL5: S'hill 5N 33
Cavendish M. GU11: Alde . . .3M 109
Cavendish Pde. TW4: Houn 5M 9
Cavendish Pk. Cvn. Site
GU47: C Tow 9K 49
Cavendish Rd. CR0: Croy 7M 45
GU11: Alde 3M 109
GU22: Wok 6N 73
GU52: C Cro 9A 88
KT3: N Mal 3E 42
KT13: Weybr 5C 56
RH1: Red 3E 122
SM2: Sut 4A 62
SW12 . . . . .1G 28
SW19 . . . . .8B 28
TW16: Sunb 7G 22
W4 . . . . .4B 12
Cavendish Ter. TW13: Felt 3H 23
Cavendish Wlk. KT19: Eps 7A 60
Cavendish Way
BR4: W Wick 7L 47
Cavenham Cl. GU22: Wok 6A 74
Caverleigh Way KT4: W Pk 7F 42
Cave Rd. TW10: Ham 5J 25
Caversham Av. SM3: Chea 8K 43
Caversham Ho.
KT1: K Tham 4J 203
Caversham Rd.
KT1: K Tham . . .3L **203** (1M 41)
Caves Farm Cl.
GU47: Sandh 7F 48
Cawcott Dr. SL4: W'sor 4B 4
Cawsey Way GU21: Wok 4A 74
Caxton Av. KT15: Addl 3J 55
Caxton Cl. RH10: Craw 6B 182
Caxton Gdns. GU2: Guil 1J 113
Caxton La. RH8: Limp 9G 106
Caxton M. TW8: Brent 2K 11
Caxton Ri. RH1: Red 2E 122
Caxton Rd. SW19 . . . . .6A 28
Cayton Rd. CR5: Coul 9G 83
Cearn Way CR5: Coul 2K 83
Cecil Cl. KT9: Ches 1K 59
TW15: A'ford 8D 22
Cecil Ct. CR0: Croy 8C 46
SW10 . . . . .2N 13
(off Fawcett St.)
Cecil Pl. CR4: Mit 4D 44
Cecil Rd. CR0: Croy 5J 45
SM1: Sut 3L 61
SW19 . . . . .8N 27
TW3: Houn 5C 10
TW15: A'ford 8D 22
Cedar Av. GU17: B'water 1J 69
KT11: Cob 2K 77
TW2: Whitt 9B 10
Cedar Cl. CR6: Warl 6H 85
GU12: Alde 4C 110
GU19: Bag 4J 51
KT8: E Mol 3E 40
KT10: Esh 3N 57
KT17: Eps 1E 80
RG40: W'ham 2B 30
RH2: Reig 5A 122
RH4: Dork 3K **201** (5H 119)
RH11: Craw 9A 162
RH12: Hors 5H 197
SE21 . . . . .2N 29
SM5: Cars 3D 62
SW15 . . . . .5C 26
TW18: Lale 2L 37
Cedar Ct. GU27: Hasl 2F 188
KT15: Addl 1L 55
KT16: Otter 2E 54
KT22: Fetc 9G 78
SL4: W'sor 5D 4
SM2: Sut 3A 62
SW19 . . . . .4J 27
TW8: Brent 2J 11
TW20: Egh 5C 20
Cedarcroft Rd. KT9: Ches 1M 59
Cedar Dr. GU51: Fleet 4D 88
KT22: Fetc 1E 98
RG42: Brac 8A 16
SL5: S'dale 6D 34
SL5: S'hill 3G 35
TN8: Eden 1K 147
Cedar Gdns. GU21: Wok 5L 73
GU24: Chob 6J 53
SM2: Sut 3A 62
Cedar Gro. GU24: Bis 2D 72
KT13: Weybr 1D 56
Cedar Hgts. TW10: Ham 2L 25
Cedar Hill KT18: Eps 3B 80
Cedar Ho. GU4: Guil 1E 114
KT22: Leat 6F 78
TW9: Kew 4A 12
TW16: Sunb 8G 22
(off Spelthorne Gro.)
Cedarland Ter. SW20 . . . . .8G 27
Cedar La. GU16: Frim 6B 70
Cedar Lodge GU27: Hasl 3J 189
RH10: Craw 5B 182
Cedarne Rd. SW6 . . . . .3N 13
Cedar Pk. CR3: Cate 8B 84
Cedar Rd.
CR0: Croy 2E **200** (8A 46)
GU14: Farnb 2A 90
GU22: Wok 7L 73
KT8: E Mol 3E 40
KT11: Cob 1J 77
KT13: Weybr 1B 56
SM2: Sut 3A 62
TW4: C'ford 5K 9
TW11: Tedd 6G 24
TW14: Bedf 2E 22
Cedars RG12: Brac 3D 32
SM7: Ban 1D 82
Cedars, The GU1: B'ham 9C 94
GU8: Mil 2B 152
GU24: Pirb 9A 72
GU51: Fleet 5C 88
KT14: Byf 8A 56
KT22: Leat 8K 79
KT23: Book 4C 98
RH2: Reig 3B 122
RH3: Brock 3N 119
SM6: W'ton 1G 63
TW11: Tedd 7F 24
Cedars Av. CR4: Mit 3E 44
Cedars Cl. GU47: Sandh 7E 48
Cedars Ct. GU1: B'ham 9C 94
Cedars Rd. BR3: Beck 1H 47
CR0: Bedd 9J 45
KT1: H Wic 9J 25
SM4: Mord 3M 43
SW13 . . . . .5F 12
W4 . . . . .1B 12
Cedar Ter. TW9: Rich 7L 11
Cedar Tree Gro. SE27 . . . . . . .6M 29
Cedar Vw. GU52: C Cro 7C 88
KT1: K Tham 6H 203
Cedarville Gdns.
SW16 . . . . .7K 29
Cedar Wlk. CR8: Ken 3N 83
KT10: Clay 3F 58
KT20: Tad 7K 81
Cedar Way GU1: Guil 1M 113
SL3: Lang 1A 6
TW16: Sunb 8F 22
Cedarways GU9: Farnh 4G 128
Celandine Cl. RG45: Crow 1H 49
RH11: Craw 6N 181
Celandine Ct. GU46: Yate 8A 48
Celandine Rd. KT12: Hers 1M 57
Celery La. GU10: Wrec 6G 128
Celia Cres. TW15: A'ford 7M 21
Cell Farm Av. SL4: O Win 8L 5
Celtic Rd. KT14: Byf 1N 75
Cemetery La. TW17: Shep 6C 38
Cemetery Pales
GU24: B'wood 9C 72
Cemetery Wlk.
RH17: Hand 7K 199
Centaur Ct. TW8: Brent 1L 11
Centaurs Bus. Pk.
TW7: Isle 2G 10
Centenary Ct. *RH1: Red 2D 122*
(off Warwick Rd.)
Centennial Ct. RG12: Brac 1M 31
Central Av. KT8: W Mole 3N 39
SM6: W'ton 2J 63
TW3: Houn 7C 10
Central Ct. KT15: Addl 1L 55
Centrale Shop. Cen.
CR0: Croy 2B **200** (8N 45)
Centrale Stop (CT)
. . . . .2B **200** (8N 45)
Central Gdns. SM4: Mord 4N 43
Central Hill SE19 . . . . .6N 29
Central La. SL4: Wink 2M 17
Central Mall *SW18 . . . . .9N 13*
(off South Mall)
Central Pde. CR0: N Add 6M 65
KT6: Surb 5L 41
KT8: W Mole 3N 39
RH1: Red 2D 122
RH6: Horl 9E 142
TW5: Hest 3N 9
TW14: Felt 1K 23
Central Pk. Est. TW4: Houn 8L 9
Central Pl. SE25 . . . . .4D 46
Central Rd. KT4: W Pk 7F 42
SM4: Mord 5M 43
Central School Path
SW14 . . . . .6B 12
Central Ter. BR3: Beck 2G 46
Central Wlk.
KT19: Eps 6J **201** (9C 60)
RG40: W'ham 2B 30

Central Way—Chaucer Cl.

Central Way RH8: Oxt 5N 105
SL4: Wink 2M 17
SM5: Cars 4C 62
TW14: Felt 8H 9
Centre, The KT12: Wal T 7H 39
TW3: Houn 6B 10
TW13: Felt 2H 23
Centre Ct. Shop. Cen.
SW19 ....7L 27
Centre Rd. SL4: W'sor 3A 4
Centre Sq. *SW18 ....8M 13*
(off Buckhold Rd.)
Centrillion Point
CR0: Croy 6C 200
Centrium GU22: Wok 4B 74
Centurion Cl. GU47: C Tow 7J 49
Centurion Ct. SM6: W'ton 8F 44
Century Ct. GU21: Wok 3B 74
Century Ho. SM7: Ban 2N 81
SW15 ....7J 13
Century Rd. TW18: Stain 6E 20
Century Way GU24: B'wood ...6A 72
Cerne Rd. SM4: Mord 5A 44
Cerotus Pl. KT16: Chert 6H 37
Chadacre Rd. KT17: Ewe 3G 60
Chadhurst Cl. RH5: Nth H 8K 119
Chadwick Av. SW19 ....7M 27
Chadwick Cl. RH11: Craw 8N 181
SW15 ....1E 26
TW11: Tedd 7G 25
Chadwick M. W4 ....2A 12
Chadwick Pl. KT6: Surb 6J 41
Chadworth Way KT10: Clay 2D 58
Chaffers Mead
KT21: A'tead 3M 79
Chaffinch Av. CR0: Croy 5G 46
Chaffinch Bus. Pk.
BR3: Beck 3G 47
Chaffinch Cl. CR0: Croy 4G 46
GU47: C Tow 7J 49
KT6: Surb 9N 41
RH11: Craw 1B 182
RH12: Hors 1K 197
Chaffinch Rd. BR3: Beck 1H 47
Chaffinch Way RH6: Horl 7C 142
Chailey Cl. RH11: Craw 6M 181
TW5: Hest 4L 9
Chailey Pl. KT12: Hers 1M 57
Chalcot Cl. SM2: Sut 4M 61
Chalcot M. SW16 ....4J 29
Chalcott Gdns. KT6: Surb 7J 41
CHALDON 2L 103
Chaldon Cl. RH1: Red 5C 122
Chaldon Comn. Rd.
CR3: Cate 2N 103
Chaldon Ct. SE19 ....1A 46
Chaldon Path CR7: T Hea 3M 45
Chaldon Rd. CR3: Cate 2A 104
RH11: Craw 8A 182
SW6 ....3K 13
Chaldon Way CR5: Coul 4J 83
Chale Rd. SW2 ....1J 29
Chalet Ct. CR7: T Hea 4N 45
Chale Wlk. SM2: Sut 5N 61
Chalfont Dr. GU14: Farnb 3A 90
Chalfont Rd. SE25 ....2C 46
Chalford Cl. KT8: W Mole 3A 40
Chalgrove Av. SM4: Mord 4M 43
Chalgrove Rd. SM2: Sut 4B 62
Chalice Cl. SM6: W'ton 3H 63
CHALKER'S CORNER 6A 12
Chalk Hill Rd. W6 ....1J 13
Chalk La. GU8: S'ford 3A 132
KT18: Eps, Eps D 2C 80
(not continuous)
KT21: A'tead 6M 79
KT24: E Hor 1G 116
Chalkley Cl. CR4: Mit 1D 44
Chalkmead RH1: Mers 8G 103
Chalk Paddock KT18: Eps 2C 80
Chalk Pit Cotts.
KT24: W Hors 8C 96
Chalkpit La. KT23: Book 5N 97
RH3: Betch 2A 120
RH4: Dork 1J 201 (4G 119)
RH8: Oxt 3M 105
Chalk Pit Rd. KT18: Eps D 6B 80
SM7: Ban 4M 81
Chalkpit Ter. RH4: Dork 3G 118
Chalk Pit Way SM1: Sut 2A 62
Chalkpit Wood RH8: Oxt 5N 105
Chalk Rd. GU7: Goda 6G 133
RH14: Ifo 6E 192
Chalky La. KT9: Ches 6K 59
Challen Ct. RH12: Hors 5H 197
Challenge Ct. KT22: Leat 6H 79
TW2: Twick 1E 24
Challenge Rd. TW15: A'ford ...4E 22
Challice Way SW2 ....2K 29
Challis Pl. RG42: Brac 9K 15
Challis Rd. TW8: Brent 1K 11
Challock Cl. TN16: B Hil 3E 86
Challoner Ct. BR2: Brom 1N 47
W14 ....1L 13
(off Challoner St.)
Challoner Cres. W14 ....1L 13
Challoner Mans. *W14 ....1L 13*
(off Challoner St.)
Challoners Cl. KT8: E Mol 3D 40
Challoner St. W14 ....1L 13
Chalmers Cl. RH6: Char 4K 161
Chalmers Rd. SM7: Ban 2B 82
TW15: A'ford 6C 22
Chalmers Rd. E.
TW15: A'ford 5C 22
Chalmers Way TW14: Felt 8J 9
Chamberlain Cres.
BR4: W Wick 7L 47
Chamberlain Gdns.
TW3: Houn 4C 10
Chamberlain Wlk.
TW13: Hanw 5M 23
(off Swift Rd.)
Chamberlain Way
KT6: Surb 6L 41
Chamber La.
GU10: Farnh 3B 128
Chamberlens Garages
W6 ....1G 12
(off Dalling Rd.)
Chambers Bus. Pk.
UB7: Sip 2B 8
Chambers Pl. CR2: S Croy 4A 64
Chambers Rd. GU12: A Va 8F 90
Chambon Pl. W6 ....1F 12
Chamomile Gdns.
GU14: Cove 9H 69
Champion Down KT24: Eff 6M 97
Champions Dr. TN8: Eden 9K 127
Champion Way
GU52: C Cro 8B 88
Champney Cl. SL3: Hort 6C 6
Champneys Cl. SM2: Chea 4L 61
Chancellor Ct. GU2: Guil 4G 113
(not continuous)
Chancellor Gdns.
CR2: S Croy 5M 63
Chancellor Gro. SE21 ....3N 29
Chancellor's Rd. W6 ....1H 13
Chancellor's St. W6 ....1H 13
Chancellors Wharf W6 ....1H 13
Chancel Mans. RG42: Warf ...7A 16
Chancery La. BR3: Beck 1L 47
Chancery M. SW17 ....3C 28
Chanctonbury Chase
RH1: Red 3E 122
Chanctonbury Dr.
SL5: S'dale 6B 34
Chanctonbury Gdns.
SM2: Sut 4N 61
Chanctonbury Way
RH11: Craw 5A 182
Chandaria Ct. *CR0: Croy 3B 200*
(off Church Rd.)
Chandler Cl. RH10: Craw 5B 182
TW12: Hamp 9A 24
Chandler Ct. RH6: Horl 8F 142
TW14: Felt 9H 9
Chandlers Cl.
KT8: W Mole 4B 40
TW14: Felt 1G 22
Chandlers La. GU46: Yate 8B 48
Chandlers Rd. GU12: A Va 9F 90
Chandlers Way SW2 ....1L 29
Chandler Way RH5: Dork 7J 119
Chandon Lodge SM2: Sut 4A 62
Chandos Gdns. CR5: Coul 6M 83
Chandos Rd. TW18: Stain 6F 20
Channel Cl. TW5: Hest 4A 10
Channings GU21: Wok 2A 74
Channon Ct. KT6: Surb 8J 203
Chantilly Way KT19: Eps 6A 60
Chantlers Cl.
RH19: E Grin 8M 165
Chanton Dr. KT17: Chea 6H 61
Chantrey Rd. RH10: Craw 6C 182
Chantry Cl. KT21: A'tead 6J 79
RH6: Horl 7D 142
SL4: W'sor 4D 4
TW16: Sunb 8H 23
Chantry Cotts. GU4: Guil 9D 114
Chantry Ct. *GU16: Frim 5B 70*
(off Church Rd.)
SM5: Cars 9C 44
Chantry Ho.
KT1: K Tham 8K 203 (3L 41)
Chantry Hurst KT18: Eps 2C 80
Chantry La. GU5: Shere 8A 116
Chantry Rd. GU4: Guil 9D 114
GU19: Bag 5H 51
KT9: Ches 2M 59
KT16: Chert 6L 37
Chantrys, The GU9: Farnh 1E 128
Chantrys Ct. *GU9: Farnh 1F 128*
(off The Chantrys)
Chantry Vw. Rd. GU1: Guil
.....8D 202 & 8F 202 (6N 113)
Chantry Way CR4: Mit 2B 44
Chapel Av. KT15: Addl 1K 55
Chapel Cl. GU8: Mil 9C 132
Chapel Ct. GU8: Mil 1C 152
RH4: Dork 1J 201 (4G 119)
Chapel Farm Animal Trail 8G 98
Chapel Farm Mobile Home Pk.
GU3: Norm 9B 92
Chapel Flds. GU7: Goda 4G 132
Chapel Gdns. GU35: Lind 4A 168
CHAPEL GREEN 4A 30
Chapel Grn. CR8: Pur 9L 63
Chapel Gro. KT15: Addl 1K 55
KT18: Tat C 6H 81
Chapel Hill GU8: Duns 6B 174
KT24: Eff 5L 97
Chapelhouse Cl.
GU2: Guil 3H 113
Chapelier Ho. SW18 ....7M 13
Chapel La. GU8: Mil 9C 132
GU14: Cove 6L 69
GU19: Bag 5H 51
GU24: Pirb 9D 72
KT23: Book, Westh 6C 98
RG42: Bin 8H 15
RH4: Westc 6C 118
RH5: Westh 8E 98
RH10: Craw D 7C 164
RH18: F Row 8H 187
RH19: Ash W 3F 186
Chapel La. Works
RH4: Westc 6C 118
(off Chapel La.)
Chapel Mill Rd.
KT1: K Tham ...6M 203 (2M 41)
Chapel Pk. Rd. KT15: Addl 1K 55
Chapel Rd. CR6: Warl 5G 84
GU10: Rowl 7D 128
GU15: Camb 1N 69
KT20: Tad 1H 101
RH1: Red 3D 122
RH6: Char 3K 161
RH6: Smal 8M 143
RH8: Limp 8E 106
SE27 ....5M 29
TW1: Twick 1H 25
TW3: Houn 6B 10
Chapel Sq. GU15: Camb 9L 49
GU25: V Wat 3A 36
Chapel St.
GU1: Guil 6C 202 (5N 113)
GU14: Farnb 8B 70
GU21: Wok 4B 74
Chapel Ter. RG42: Bin 8H 15
Chapel Vw. CR2: Sels 3F 64
Chapel Wlk.
CR0: Croy 2B 200 (8N 45)
CR5: Coul 9H 83
Chapel Way KT18: Tat C 6H 81
Chapel Yd. *SW18 ....8N 13*
(off Wandsworth High St.)
Chaplain's Hill RG45: Crow 3J 49
Chaplin Cres. TW16: Sunb 7F 22
Chaplin M. SL3: Lang 1B 6
Chapman Rd. CR0: Croy 7L 45
RH10: Craw 7G 182
Chapman's La.
RH19: E Grin 9L 165
(not continuous)
Chapman Sq. SW19 ....3J 27
Chapter Ho. *GU14: Farnb 1A 90*
(off Jubilee Hall Rd.)
Chapter M. SL4: W'sor 3G 5
Chapter Way SW19 ....9B 28
TW12: Hamp 5A 24
Chara Pl. W4 ....2C 12
Charcot Ho. SW15 ....9E 12
Chardin Rd. W4 ....1D 12
Chard Rd. TW6: Lon A 5C 8
Chargate Cl. KT12: Hers 3G 57
Charing Cl. BR6: Orp 1N 67
Charing Ct. BR2: Brom 1N 47
Charing Cross Sports Club 2J 13
Chariotts Pl. SL4: W'sor 4G 4
Charlbury Cl. RG12: Brac 3D 32
Charlecombe Ct.
TW18: Stain 6K 21
Charlecote Cl. GU14: Farnb ...2B 90
Charles Babbage Cl.
KT9: Ches 4J 59
Charles Cobb Gdns.
CR0: Wad 2L 63
Charlesfield Rd.
RH6: Horl 7D 142
Charles Haller St.
SW2 ....1L 29
Charles Harrod Ct.
SW13 ....2H 13
(off Somerville Av.)
CHARLESHILL 6E 130
Charles Hill GU10: Til 5B 130
Charles Ho. *KT16: Chert 7H 37*
(off Sth. Guildford St.)
SL4: W'sor 4F 4
Charles Lesser Ho.
KT9: Ches 2K 59
Charles Nex M. SE21 ....3N 29
Charles Rd. SW19 ....9M 27
TW18: Stain 7M 21
Charles Sq. RG12: Brac 1A 32
Charles St.
CR0: Croy 4B 200 (9N 45)
KT16: Chert 7H 37
SL4: W'sor 4F 4
SW13 ....5D 12
TW3: Houn 5N 9
Charleston Cl. TW13: Felt 4H 23
Charleston Ct. RH10: Craw ...6F 182
Charlesworth Pl.
SW13 ....6D 12
Charleville Ct. *W14 ....1L 13*
(off Charleville Rd.)
Charleville Mans.
W14 ....1K 13
(off Charleville Rd.)
Charleville M. TW7: Isle 7H 11
Charleville Rd. W14 ....1K 13
Charlmont Rd. SW17 ....7C 28
Charlock Cl. RH11: Craw 7M 181
Charlock Way GU1: Guil 9D 94
Charlotte Cl. GU9: H End 4J 109
KT21: A'tead 5L 79
Charlotte Ct. GU1: Guil 5B 114
KT10: Esh 2C 58
RH11: Craw 3A 182
(off Leopold Rd.)
Charlotte Gro. RH6: Smal 7L 143
Charlotte Ho. *W6 ....1H 13*
(off Queen Caroline St.)
Charlotte M. GU14: Farnb 9B 70
KT10: Esh 1B 58
(off Heather Pl.)
Charlotte Rd. SM6: W'ton 3G 63
SW13 ....4E 12
Charlotte Sq. TW10: Rich 9M 11
CHARLOTTEVILLE 5B 114
CHARLTON 2D 38
Charlton Av. KT12: Hers 1J 57
Charlton Ct. GU47: Owls 6J 49
Charlton Dr. TN16: B Hil 4F 86
Charlton Gdns. CR5: Coul 5G 83
Charlton Ho. TW8: Brent 2L 11
Charlton Kings
KT13: Weybr 9F 38
Charlton La. TW17: Shep 2D 38
(not continuous)
Charlton Rd. TW17: Shep 2D 38
Charlton Sq. *SL4: W'sor 5A 4*
(off Guards Rd.)
CHARLWOOD
RH6 ....3K 161
RH19 ....8A 186
Charlwood CR0: Sels 5J 65
Charlwood Cl. KT23: Book 2B 98
RH10: Cop 6L 163
Charlwood Dr. KT22: Oxs 2D 78
Charlwood Ho. TW9: Kew 3A 12
Charlwood La.
RH5: Newd 5F 160
Charlwood M. RH6: Char 3K 161
Charlwood Pl. RH2: Reig 3L 121
Charlwood Rd. RH6: Gat 2A 162
RH11: Ifi 7K 161
RH11: L Hea 6N 161
SW15 ....7J 13
Charlwoods Bus. Cen.
RH19: E Grin 7N 165
Charlwoods Pl.
RH19: E Grin 7A 166
Charlwoods Rd.
RH19: E Grin 8N 165
Charlwood Ter. SW15 ....7J 13
Charlwood Wlk.
RH11: Craw 9N 161
Charman Rd. RH1: Red 3C 122
Charmans Cl. RH12: Hors 3A 198
Charm Cl. RH6: Horl 7C 142
Charminster Av.
SW19 ....1M 43
Charminster Ct. KT6: Surb 6K 41
Charminster Rd. KT4: W Pk ...7J 43
Charmouth Ct. TW10: Rich 8M 11
Charnwood SL5: S'dale 5C 34
Charnwood Av. SW19 ....1M 43
Charnwood Cl. KT3: N Mal 3D 42
Charnwood Rd. SE25 ....4A 46
Charrington Bowl 8A 42
Charrington Rd.
CR0: Croy 2B 200 (8N 45)
Charrington Way
RH12: Bro H 5C 196
Charta Rd. TW20: Egh 6E 20
Chart Cl. CR0: Croy 5F 46
CR4: Mit 3D 44
RH5: Dork 7K 119
Chart Downs RH5: Dork 7J 119
Charter Ct. KT3: N Mal 2D 42
Charter Cres. TW4: Houn 7M 9
CHARTERHOUSE 4F 132
Charter Ho. *SM2: Sut 3N 61*
(off Mulgrave Rd.)
Charterhouse GU7: Goda 5E 132
Charterhouse Cl.
RG12: Brac 4C 32
Charterhouse Rd.
GU7: Goda 4G 132
Charter Pl. TW18: Stain 7J 21
Charter Quay KT1: K Tham ...4H 203
Charter Rd. KT1: K Tham 2A 42
Charters Cl. SL5: S'hill 4A 34
Charters La. SL5: S'hill 4A 34
Charters Leisure Cen. 6A 34
Charter Sq. KT1: K Tham 1A 42
Charters Rd. SL5: S'dale 6A 34
Charters Way SL5: S'dale 6C 34
Charter Wlk. *GU27: Hasl 2G 189*
(off West St.)
Chartfield Av. SW15 ....8G 13
Chartfield Pl. KT13: Weybr 2C 56
Chartfield Rd. RH2: Reig 4A 122
Chartfield Sq. SW15 ....8J 13
Chart Gdns. RH5: Dork 8J 119
Chartham Gro. SE27 ....4M 29
Chartham Rd. SE25 ....2E 46
Chart Ho. CR4: Mit 1D 44
Chart Ho. Rd. GU12: A Va 6E 90
Chart La. RH2: Reig 3N 121
RH4: Dork 2L 201 (5H 119)
Chart La. Sth.
RH5: Dork, Nth H 7J 119
Chart, The (NT) 9H 107
Charts Cl. GU6: Cranl 8N 155
Chart Way RH12: Hors 6J 197
Chartway RH2: Reig 2N 121
Chartwell 9N 107
Chartwell GU9: Farnh 5E 128
GU16: Frim G 9C 70
GU22: Wok 5A 74
(off Mt. Hermon Rd.)
Chartwell Cl. CR0: Croy 7A 46
Chartwell Ct. Grange
RH4: Dork 8H 119
Chartwell Dr. BR6: Farnb 2M 67
Chartwell Gdns. GU11: Alde ...6A 90
SM3: Chea 1K 61
Chartwell Lodge
RH5: Nth H 9H 119
Chartwell Pl.
KT18: Eps 8M 201 (1D 80)
SM3: Chea 1K 61
Chartwood Pl. RH4: Dork 3J 201
Charwood SW16 ....5L 29
Charwood Rd.
RG40: W'ham 2D 30
Chase, The CR5: Coul 1G 83
GU2: Guil 4K 113
GU14: Farnb 8B 70
KT20: K'wood 9M 81
KT21: A'tead 5J 79
KT22: Oxs 2C 78
KT24: E Hor 4G 96
RG45: Crow 1F 48
RH2: Reig 4B 122
RH10: Craw 4E 182
SL5: Asc 8L 17
SM6: W'ton 2J 63
SW16 ....8K 29
SW20 ....9K 27
TW16: Sunb 9J 23
Chase Ct. SW20 ....1K 43
TW7: Isle 5G 10
Chase End
KT19: Eps 5K 201 (8C 60)
Chasefield Cl. GU4: B'ham 9C 94
Chasefield Rd. SW17 ....5D 28
Chase Gdns. RG42: Bin 6H 15
TW2: Whitt 1D 24
Chase La. GU27: Hasl 4H 189
Chaseley Ct. KT13: Weybr 7F 38
Chaseley Dr. CR2: Sande 6A 64
W4 ....1A 12
Chasemore Cl. CR4: Mit 6D 44
Chasemore Gdns.
CR0: Wad 2L 63
Chasemore Ho. *SW6 ....3K 13*
(off Williams Cl.)
Chase Plain GU26: Hind 8A 170
Chase Rd. GU35: Lind 5A 168
KT19: Eps 5K 201 (8C 60)
Chaseside Av. SW20 ....9K 27
Chaseside Gdns.
KT16: Chert 6K 37
Chasewater Ct.
GU11: Alde 3M 109
Chatelet Cl. RH6: Horl 7F 142
Chatfield Cl. GU14: Farnb 3A 90
Chatfield Ct. CR3: Cate 9A 84
Chatfield Dr. GU4: Guil 1E 114
Chatfield Rd.
CR0: Croy 1A 200 (7M 45)
Chatfields RH11: Craw 5N 181
Chatham Cl. SM3: Sut 6L 43
Chatham Ho. *SM6: W'ton 2F 62*
(off Melbourne Rd.)
Chatham M. GU2: Guil 9K 93
Chatham Rd.
KT1: K Tham ...3M 203 (1N 41)
CHATHILL 6L 125
Chatley Heath Semaphore Tower
...........................4E 76
Chatsfield KT17: Ewe 6F 60
Chatsworth Av.
GU27: Hasl 9G 170
SW20 ....9K 27
Chatsworth Cl. W4 ....2B 12
Chatsworth Ct. SW16 ....2K 45
Chatsworth Cres.
TW3: Houn 7D 10
Chatsworth Gdns.
KT3: N Mal 4E 42
Chatsworth Gro.
GU9: U Hal 6G 108
Chatsworth Hgts.
GU15: Camb 8E 50
Chatsworth Lodge *W4 ....1C 12*
(off Bourne Pl.)
Chatsworth Pk. SM7: Ban 4N 81
Chatsworth Pl. CR4: Mit 2D 44
KT22: Oxs 9D 58
TW11: Tedd 5G 24
Chatsworth Rd.
CR0: Croy 6E 200 (1A 64)
GU14: Farnb 2C 90
SM3: Chea 2J 61
W4 ....2B 12
Chatsworth Way SE27 ....4M 29
CHATTERN HILL 5C 22
Chattern Hill TW15: A'ford 5C 22
Chattern Rd. TW15: A'ford 5D 22
Chatterton Ct. TW9: Kew 5M 11
Chatton Row GU24: Bis 4D 72
Chaucer Av. KT13: Weybr 4B 56
RH19: E Grin 1M 185
TW4: C'ford 5J 9
TW9: Rich 6N 11
Chaucer Cl. RG40: W'ham 2E 30
SL4: W'sor 6G 4
SM7: Ban 1K 81

Chaucer Ct.—Chilton Ct.

Chaucer Ct.
GU2: Guil 7B 202 (5M 113)
RH1: Red 9E 102
Chaucer Gdns. SM1: Sut 9M 43
(not continuous)
Chaucer Grn. CR0: Croy 6E 46
Chaucer Gro. GU15: Camb 1B 70
Chaucer Ho. SM1: Sut 9M 43
(off Chaucer Gdns.)
Chaucer Mans. W14 . . . . .2K 13
(off Queen's Club Gdns.)
Chaucer Rd. GU14: Farnb 8L 69
RG45: Crow 4G 48
RH10: Craw 1F 182
SM1: Sut 1M 61
TW15: A'ford 5N 21
Chaucer Way KT15: Addl 3J 55
SW19 . . . . .6B 28
Chavasse Way GU14: Cove 9J 69
Chave Cft. KT18: Tat C 6H 81
Chavecroft Ter. KT18: Tat C . . .6H 81
CHAVEY DOWN 9F 16
Chavey Down Rd.
RG42: Wink R 6F 16
Chaworth Cl. KT16: Otter 3E 54
Chaworth Rd. KT16: Otter 3E 54
Chawridge La. SL4: Wink 2G 16
Cheals Rdbt. RH11: Craw 5N 181
CHEAM 3K 61
Cheam Cl. KT20: Tad 8G 81
RG12: Brac 4B 32
Cheam Comn. Rd.
KT4: W Pk 8G 43
Cheam Leisure Cen. 1J 61
Cheam Mans. SM3: Chea 4K 61
Cheam Pk. Way SM3: Chea . . .3K 61
Cheam Rd. KT17: Ewe 6F 60
SM1: Sut 3L 61
SM2: Chea 6F 60
Cheam Sports Club 4J 61
Cheam Station (Rail) 4K 61
CHEAM VILLAGE 3K 61
CHEAPSIDE 9B 18
Cheapside GU21: Wok 1N 73
Cheapside Rd. SL5: Asc 2N 33
Cheeseman Cl.
RG40: W'ham 1C 30
TW12: Hamp 7M 23
Cheesemans Ter. W14 . . . . . . .1L 13
(not continuous)
Cheffery Ct. TW15: A'ford 7C 22
Chellows La. RH7: Ling 1B 146
Chelmsford Cl. SM2: Sut 5M 61
W6 . . . . .2J 13
Chelsea Cl. KT4: W Pk 6F 42
TW12: H Hill 6C 24
Chelsea FC 3N 13
Chelsea Flds. SW19 . . . . .9B 28
Chelsea Gdns. SM3: Chea 1K 61
Chelsea Studios SW6 . . . . .3N 13
(off Fulham Rd.)
Chelsea Village SW6 . . . . .3N 13
(off Fulham Rd.)
CHELSHAM 4K 85
Chelsham Cl. CR6: Warl 5H 85
CHELSHAM COMMON 3L 85
Chelsham Comn. Rd.
CR6: Warl 4K 85
Chelsham Ct. Rd.
CR6: Warl 5N 85
Chelsham Rd. CR2: S Croy 4A 64
CR6: Warl 5J 85
Cheltenham Av. TW1: Twick . . .1G 25
Cheltenham Cl. KT3: N Mal . . .2B 42
Cheltenham Vs.
TW19: Stan M 9H 7
Chelverton Rd. SW15 . . . . .7J 13
Chelwood Cl. CR5: Coul 6G 82
KT17: Eps 8E 60
RH10: Craw 5D 182
Chelwood Dr. GU47: Sandh . . .6E 48
Chelwood Gdns. TW9: Kew . . .5N 11
Chelwood Gdns. Pas.
TW9: Kew 5N 11
Cheney Cl. RG42: Bin 7J 15
Cheney Ct. RG45: Crow 2H 49
(off Pinewood Av.)
Chenies Cotts. RH5: Oak 2A 178
Chenies Ho. W4 . . . . .3E 12
(off Corney Reach Way)
Cheniston Cl. KT14: W By 9J 55
Cheniston Ct. SL5: S'dale 6D 34
Chennells Brook Cotts.
RH12: Hors 1M 197
(off Giblets La.)
Chennells Way
RH12: Hors 3K 197
Chepstow Cl. RH10: Craw 3J 183
SW15 . . . . .8K 13
Chepstow Ri. CR0: Croy 9B 46
Chepstow Rd. CR0: Croy 9B 46
Chequer Grange
RH18: F Row 8G 187
Chequer Mead Theatre & Arts Cen.
. . . . .9B 166
Chequer Rd. RH19: E Grin 9B 166
Chequers Cl. KT20: Wal H 3F 100
RH6: Horl 7E 142
Chequers Ct. RH13: Hors 5L 197
Chequers Dr. RH6: Horl 7E 142
Chequers La. KT20: Wal H . . .3F 100
Chequers Pl.
RH4: Dork 3K 201 (5H 119)
Chequers Yd.
RH4: Dork 2K 201 (5H 119)
Chequer Tree Cl.
GU21: Knap 3H 73
Cherberry Cl. GU51: Fleet 1C 88
Cherbury Cl. RG12: Brac 2C 32
Cherimoya Gdns.
KT8: W Mole 2B 40
Cherington Way SL5: Asc 1J 33
Cheriton Ct. KT12: Wal T 7K 39
Cheriton Sq. SW17 . . . . .3E 28
Cheriton Way
GU17: B'water 1J 69
Cherkley Hill KT22: Leat 4J 99
Cherrimans Orchard
GU27: Hasl 2D 188
Cherry Bank Cotts.
RH5: H Mary 6K 137
Cherry Cl. SM4: Mord 3K 43
SM5: Cars 8D 44
SM7: Ban 1J 81
SW2 . . . . .1L 29
Cherrycot Hill BR6: Farnb 1L 67
Cherrycot Ri. BR6: Farnb 1L 67
Cherry Cotts. KT20: Wal H 2G 100
Cherry Ct. RH13: Hors 7K 197
Cherry Cres. TW8: Brent 3H 11
Cherrydale Rd.
GU15: Camb 1H 71
Cherry Gth. TW8: Brent 1K 11
Cherry Grn. Cl. RH1: Red 5F 122
Cherry Hill Gdns.
CR0: Wad 1K 63
Cherryhill Gro. GU11: Alde . . .3L 109
Cherryhurst GU8: Worm 9E 152
Cherry La. RH11: Craw 9A 162
Cherry Laurel Wlk.
SW2 . . . . .1K 29
Cherry Lodge GU12: Alde 3N 109
Cherry Orchard
KT21: A'tead 5A 80
TW18: Stain 6J 21
Cherry Orchard Gdns.
CR0: Croy 2E 200 (7A 46)
KT8: W Mole 2N 39
Cherry Orchard Rd.
CR0: Croy 1E 200 (8A 46)
KT8: W Mole 2A 40
Cherry St. GU21: Wok 5A 74
Cherry Tree Av. GU2: Guil 3J 113
GU27: Hasl 1D 188
TW18: Stain 7K 21
Cherry Tree Cl.
GU9: Farnh 9H 109
GU14: Cove 9H 69
GU47: Owls 6J 49
RH10: Craw 1H 183
Cherry Tree Ct. CR5: Coul 5K 83
KT22: Leat 7F 78
(off Park Vw. Rd.)
Cherry Tree Dr. RG12: Brac 2B 32
SW16 . . . . .4J 29
Cherry Tree Grn.
CR2: Sande 1E 84
Cherry Tree La.
GU7: Goda 3G 133
Cherry Tree Rd. GU8: Mil 1B 152
GU10: Rowl 8D 128
Cherrytrees CR5: Coul 8H 83
Cherry Tree Wlk.
BR3: Beck 3J 47
BR4: W Wick 1B 66
GU10: Rowl 8D 128
(not continuous)
RH12: Hors 2A 198
Cherry Way KT19: Ewe 3C 60
SL3: Hort 6E 6
TW17: Shep 3E 38
Cherrywood Av.
TW20: Eng G 8L 19
Cherrywood Cl.
KT2: K Tham 8N 25
Cherrywood Ct. TW11: Tedd . . .6G 24
Cherrywood Dr. SW15 . . . . .8J 13
Cherrywood La. SM4: Mord 3K 43
Cherrywood Rd.
GU14: Farnb 7M 69
CHERTSEY 6J 37
Chertsey Abbey (Remains of)
. . . . .5J 37
Chertsey Bri. Rd.
KT16: Chert 6M 37
Chertsey Cl. CR8: Ken 2M 83
Chertsey Ct. SW14 . . . . .6A 12
Chertsey Cres. CR0: N Add . . .6M 65
Chertsey Dr. SM3: Chea 8K 43
Chertsey Ho. KT16: Chert 7L 37
Chertsey La. KT19: Eps 8N 59
TW18: Stain 6G 20
CHERTSEY LOCK 6L 37
CHERTSEY MEADS 7N 37
Chertsey Meads
KT16: Chert 7M 37
Chertsey Mus. 5J 37
Chertsey Rd. GU20: Windl 3A 52
GU21: Wok 4B 74
GU24: Chob 6J 53
(Alpha Rd.)
GU24: Chob 3A 52
(Windsor Rd.)
KT14: Byf 7M 55
KT15: Addl 8K 37
TW1: Twick 9F 10
Chertsey Rd. TW2: Twick 3B 24
TW13: Felt 4F 22
TW15: A'ford 8E 22
TW16: Sunb 8E 22
TW17: Shep 6N 37
CHERTSEY SOUTH 9G 36
Chertsey Station (Rail) 7H 37
Chertsey St.
GU1: Guil 5D 202 (4N 113)
SW17 . . . . .6E 28
Chertsey Wlk. KT16: Chert 6J 37
Chervil Cl. TW13: Felt 4H 23
Cherwell Cl. SL3: Lang 2D 6
Cherwell Ct. KT19: Ewe 1B 60
Cherwell Wlk. RH11: Craw . . .4L 181
Cheryls Cl. SW6 . . . . .4N 13
Cheselden Rd.
GU1: Guil 5E 202 (4A 114)
Chesfield Rd. KT2: K Tham 8L 25
Chesham Cl. SM2: Chea 6K 61
Chesham Cres. SE20 . . . . .1F 46
Chesham M.
GU1: Guil 5F 202 (4A 114)
Chesham Rd. GU1: Guil 4B 114
KT1: K Tham 1N 41
SE20 . . . . .1F 46
SW19 . . . . .6B 28
Cheshire Cl. CR4: Mit 2J 45
KT16: Otter 3E 54
Cheshire Gdns. KT9: Ches 3K 59
Cheshire Ho. KT16: Otter 3F 54
(off Cheshire Cl.)
SM4: Mord 6N 43
Cheshire Pk. RG42: Warf 7C 16
Chesilton Cres.
GU52: C Cro 8B 88
Chesilton Rd. SW6 . . . . .4L 13
Chesney Cres. CR0: N Add 4M 65
Chessell Cl. CR7: T Hea 3M 45
Chessholme Ct.
TW16: Sunb 8F 22
(off Scotts Av.)
Chessholme Rd.
TW15: A'ford 7D 22
CHESSINGTON 2M 59
Chessington Cl. KT19: Ewe 3B 60
Chessington Hall Gdns.
KT9: Ches 4K 59
Chessington Hill Pk.
KT9: Ches 2N 59
Chessington Ho. KT17: Ewe 5E 60
(off Spring St.)
Chessington North Station (Rail)
. . . . .2L 59
Chessington Pde.
KT9: Ches 3K 59
Chessington Pk. KT9: Ches 1N 59
Chessington Rd. KT17: Ewe . . .5C 60
KT19: Ewe 3N 59
Chessington South Station (Rail)
. . . . .4K 59
Chessington Sports Cen. 4K 59
Chessington Trade Pk.
KT9: Ches 1N 59
Chessington Way
BR4: W Wick 8L 47
Chessington World of Adventures
. . . . .6J 59
Chesson Rd. W14 . . . . .2L 13
Chester Av. TW2: Whitt 2N 23
TW10: Rich 9M 11
Chesterblade La.
RG12: Brac 6B 32
Chester Cl. GU2: Guil 1J 113
GU12: Ash 2F 110
RH4: Dork 3J 119
SM1: Sut 8M 43
SW13 . . . . .6G 13
TW10: Rich 9M 11
TW15: A'ford 6E 22
Chesterfield Cl. RH19: Fel . . .6F 164
Chesterfield Ct.
KT5: Surb 8K 203
Chesterfield Dr.
KT10: H Wood 8G 40
Chesterfield M.
TW15: A'ford 5N 21
Chesterfield Rd. KT19: Ewe . . .4C 60
TW15: A'ford 5N 21
W4 . . . . .2B 12
Chester Gdns. SM4: Mord 5A 44
Chesterman Ct. W4 . . . . .3D 12
(off Corney Reach Way)
Chester Rd. GU12: Ash 1F 110
KT24: Eff 6J 97
SW19 . . . . .7H 27
TW4: Houn 6J 9
TW6: Lon A 6B 8
Chesters RH6: Horl 6C 142
Chesters, The KT3: N Mal 9D 26
Chesters Rd. GU15: Camb 1F 70
Chesterton Cl.
RH19: E Grin 2B 186
SW18 . . . . .8M 13
Chesterton Ct.
RH13: Hors 4N 197
Chesterton Dr. RH1: Mers 6J 103
TW19: Stan 2A 22
Chesterton Ho. CR0: Croy 7D 200
Chesterton Ter.
KT1: K Tham . . .4M 203 (1N 41)
Chester Way GU10: Tong 6D 110
Chestnut All. SW6 . . . . .2L 13
Chestnut Av. BR4: W Wick 2A 66
GU2: Guil 6M 113
GU9: Farnh 3F 128
GU12: Alde 5C 110
GU15: Camb 9E 50
GU25: V Wat 3J 35
GU27: Hasl 1G 189
KT8: E Mol 2F 40
KT10: Esh 6D 40
KT12: Whit V 5F 56
KT13: Weybr 4D 56
KT19: Ewe 1D 60
SW14 . . . . .6C 12
TN16: Tats, Weste 9F 86
TW8: Brent 1K 11
TW11: Tedd 1F 40
TW12: Hamp 8A 24
Chestnut Chase
RG42: Warf 8E 16
Chestnut Cl. GU17: B'water 2K 69
GU23: Rip 3H 95
GU26: G'hott 6A 170
GU51: Fleet 1D 88
KT15: Addl 2M 55
KT20: K'wood 1M 101
RH1: Red 5F 122
RH19: E Grin 9C 166
SM5: Cars 7D 44
SW16 . . . . .5L 29
TN8: Eden 1K 147
TW15: A'ford 5C 22
TW16: Sunb 7G 22
TW20: Eng G 7L 19
UB7: Harl, Sip 3C 8
Chestnut Copse RH8: Oxt 1D 126
Chestnut Ct. CR2: S Croy 7B 200
GU12: Alde 2B 110
KT22: Leat 7F 78
RH1: Red 5D 122
RH13: Hors 6L 197
SW6 . . . . .2L 13
TW13: Hanw 6L 23
Chestnut Cres.
KT12: Whit V 5F 56
(not continuous)
Chestnut Dr. SL4: W'sor 7B 4
TW20: Egh 7N 19
Chestnut End
GU35: Head 5F 168
Chestnut Gdns.
RH12: Hors 3J 197
Chestnut Gro. CR2: Sels 4E 64
CR4: Mit 4H 45
GU22: Wok 7A 74
GU51: Fleet 3C 88
KT3: N Mal 2C 42
SW12 . . . . .1E 28
TW7: Isle 7G 10
TW18: Stain 7L 21
Chestnut La. GU24: Chob 2F 52
KT13: Weybr 2C 56
Chestnut Mnr. Cl.
TW18: Stain 6K 21
Chestnut Mead RH1: Red 2C 122
Chestnut Pl. KT13: Weybr 2C 56
(off Pine Gro.)
KT17: Ewe 7F 60
KT21: A'tead 6L 79
Chestnut Rd.
GU1: Guil 2C 202 (3N 113)
GU14: Farnb 9M 69
KT2: K Tham 1J 203 (8L 25)
RH6: Horl 6F 142
SE27 . . . . .4M 29
SW20 . . . . .1J 43
TW2: Twick 3E 24
TW15: A'ford 5C 22
Chestnuts, The KT12: Wal T . . .8H 39
RH6: Horl 6F 142
Chestnut Ter. SM1: Sut 1N 61
Chestnut Tree Gro.
GU14: Cove 9H 69
Chestnut Vw. GU14: Farnb 4A 90
(off Alexandra Rd.)
Chestnut Wlk. KT12: Whit V . . .5F 56
KT14: Byf 8N 55
RH11: Craw 9A 162
RH19: Felc 2M 165
TW17: Shep 3F 38
Chestnut Way GU5: Braml 6C 134
GU7: Bus 9J 133
TW13: Felt 4J 23
Cheston Av. CR0: Croy 8H 47
Chesworth Cl. RH13: Hors 8J 197
Chesworth Cres.
RH13: Hors 7J 197
Chesworth Gdns.
RH13: Hors 7J 197
Chesworth La. RH13: Hors 7J 197
Chetnole RH19: E Grin 8N 165
Chetwode Cl.
RG40: W'ham 2D 30
Chetwode Dr. KT18: Tat C 5J 81
Chetwode Pl. GU12: Alde 5A 110
Chetwode Rd. KT20: Tad 6H 81
SW17 . . . . .4D 28
Chetwode Ter. GU11: Alde . . .3K 109
Chetwoode Rd.
RH11: Craw 7J 181
Chevening Cl. RH11: Craw . . .8A 182
Chevening Rd. SE19 . . . . .7N 29
CHEVERELLS 9A 86
Chevington Vs. RH1: Blet 1B 124
Cheviot Cl. GU14: Cove 7K 69
GU15: Camb 2G 71
SM2: Sut 5B 62
SM7: Ban 2N 81
UB3: Harl 3E 8
Cheviot Dr. GU51: Fleet 1C 88
Cheviot Gdns. SE27 . . . . .5M 29
Cheviot Rd. GU47: Sandh 5E 48
SE27 . . . . .6L 29
SL3: Lang 1C 6
Cheviot Wlk. RH11: Craw 3N 181
Chevremont
GU1: Guil 5F 202 (4A 114)
Chewter Cl. GU19: Bag 4K 51
Chewter La. GU20: Windl 1M 51
Cheyham Gdns.
SM2: Chea 6J 61
Cheyham Way SM2: Chea 6K 61
Cheylesmore Dr.
GU16: Frim 3H 71
Cheyne Av. TW2: Whitt 2N 23
Cheyne Ct. SM7: Ban 2N 81
Cheyne Hill
KT5: Surb 8L 203 (3M 41)
Cheynell Wlk. RH11: Craw 5L 181
Cheyne Pk. Dr.
BR4: W Wick 9M 47
Cheyne Rd. TW15: A'ford 8E 22
Cheyne Row GU5: Braml 2N 153
Cheyne Wlk. CR0: Croy 8D 46
RH6: Horl 1D 162
Cheyne Way GU14: Cove 7L 69
Chichele Gdns. CR0: Croy 1B 64
Chichele Rd. RH8: Oxt 6A 106
Chicheley Ct. GU14: Farnb 8M 69
Chichester Cl. GU8: Wit 5B 152
RH4: Dork 3H 119
RH10: Craw 7C 182
TW12: Hamp 7N 23
Chichester Ct. KT17: Ewe 5E 60
TW19: Stan 2N 21
Chichester Dr. CR8: Pur 8K 63
Chichester Ho. KT19: Eps 8N 59
Chichester M. SE27 . . . . .5L 29
Chichester Rd.
CR0: Croy 5F 200 (9B 46)
GU12: Ash 1E 110
RH4: Dork 2H 119
Chichester Ter.
RH12: Hors 6K 197
Chichester Way TW14: Felt 1K 23
CHIDDINGFOLD 5F 172
Chiddingfold Rd.
GU8: Duns 5L 173
Chiddingly Cl. RH10: Craw 4E 182
Chiddingstone Cl.
SM2: Sut 6M 61
Chiddingstone St.
SW6 . . . . .5M 13
Chilberton Dr. RH1: Mers 8G 103
Chilbolton TW20: Egh 6A 20
Chilbrook Rd. KT11: Down 5H 77
Chilcombe Ho. SW15 . . . . .1F 26
(off Fontley Way)
Chilcroft La. GU27: K Grn 7F 188
Chilcroft Rd. GU27: Hasl 1D 188
Chilcrofts Rd. GU27: K Grn . . .7E 188
Child Cl. RG40: W'ham 9C 14
Childebert Rd. SW17 . . . . .3F 28
Childerley KT1: K Tham 2N 41
(off Burritt Rd.)
Childerley St. SW6 . . . . .4K 13
Childs Hall Cl. KT23: Book 3N 97
Childs Hall Dr. KT23: Book 3N 97
Childs Hall Rd. KT23: Book 3N 97
Chilham Cl. GU16: Frim 6D 70
Chillerton Rd. SW17 . . . . .6E 28
Chillingford Ho. SW17 . . . . . . .5A 28
Chillingham Way
GU15: Camb 2A 70
Chillingworth Gdns.
TW1: Twick 4F 24
Chilmans Dr. KT23: Book 3B 98
Chilmark Gdns. KT3: N Mal 5F 42
RH1: Mers 7J 103
Chilmark Rd. SW16 . . . . .1H 45
Chilmead RH1: Red 2D 122
Chilmead La. RH1: Nut 1H 123
Chilsey Grn. Rd.
KT16: Chert 5G 37
Chiltern Av. GU14: Cove 1J 89
TW2: Whitt 2A 24
Chiltern Cl. CR0: Croy 9B 46
GU14: Cove 1H 89
GU22: Wok 9M 73
GU27: Hasl 3F 188
GU52: C Cro 7C 88
KT4: W Pk 7H 43
RH11: Craw 3N 181
TW18: Stain 6J 21
Chiltern Ct. SL4: W'sor 4E 4
(off Fawcett Rd.)
Chiltern Ct. M. SL4: W'sor 4E 4
(off Fawcett Rd.)
Chiltern Dr. KT5: Surb 5N 41
Chiltern Hurst TN8: Eden 1J 147
Chiltern Rd. GU47: Sandh 6E 48
SM2: Sut 5N 61
Chilterns, The SM2: Sut 5N 61
Chiltington Ct. RH12: Hors . . .4K 197
(off Blenheim Rd.)
Chilton Cl. GU6: Alf 7H 175
Chilton Ct. KT12: Wal T 1H 57

Chilton Farm Pk.—Church Wlk.

Chilton Farm Pk.
GU14: Cove ... 1H 89
Chilton Rd. TW9: Rich ... 6N 11
Chiltons Cl. SM7: Ban ... 2N 81
Chilvers Cl. TW2: Twick ... 3E 24
CHILWORTH ... 9E 114
Chilworth Ct. SW19 ... 2J 27
Chilworth Gdns. SM1: Sut ... 9A 44
Chilworth Hill Cotts.
GU4: Guil ... 1G 134
Chilworth Manor ... 8F 114
Chilworth Rd. GU5: Alb ... 8J 115
Chilworth Station (Rail) ... 9G 114
China M. SW2 ... 1K 29
Chinchilla Dr. TW4: Houn ... 5K 9
Chine, The GU10: Wrec ... 6E 128
RH4: Dork ... 1L 201 (4H 119)
Chingford Av. GU14: Farnb ... 9A 70
Chinnock Cl. GU52: Fleet ... 6A 88
Chinthurst Hill Nature Reserve ... 3C 134
Chinthurst Hill Tower ... 3C 134
Chinthurst La. GU4: Chil ... 1A 134
GU5: Braml, Wone ... 1A 134
Chinthurst M. CR5: Coul ... 3E 82
Chinthurst Pk. GU4: Chil ... 2A 134
Chiphouse Wood Nature Reserve ... 7A 82
Chippendale Cl.
GU17: Haw ... 2K 69
Chippendale Rd.
RH11: Craw ... 8N 181
Chippenham KT1: K Tham ... 4M 203
CHIPSTEAD ... 5D 82
Chipstead Av. CR7: T Hea ... 3M 45
CHIPSTEAD BOTTOM ... 8B 82
Chipstead Cl. CR5: Coul ... 3E 82
RH1: Red ... 4D 122
SM2: Sut ... 5N 61
Chipstead Ct. GU21: Knap ... 4H 73
Chipstead La.
CR5: Chip, Coul ... 2A 102
KT20: K'wood ... 3L 101
Chipstead Rd. SM7: Ban ... 4L 81
(not continuous)
Chipstead Station (Rail) ... 5D 82
Chipstead Sta. Pde.
CR5: Chip ... 5D 82
Chipstead St. SW6 ... 4M 13
Chipstead Valley Rd.
CR5: Coul ... 3E 82
Chipstead Way SM7: Ban ... 3D 82
Chirton Wlk. GU21: Wok ... 5K 73
Chisbury Cl. RG12: Brac ... 5C 32
Chisholm Ct. W6 ... 1F 12
Chisholm Rd. CR0: Croy ... 8B 46
TW10: Rich ... 9M 11
Chislehurst Rd. TW10: Rich ... 8L 11
Chislett Gdns. GU47: Sandh ... 7E 48
CHISWICK ... 1C 12
Chiswick Bri. W4 ... 5B 12
Chiswick Cl. CR0: Bedd ... 9K 45
Chiswick Comn. Rd.
W4 ... 1C 12
Chiswick Community Sports Hall ... 3C 12
Chiswick Ct. W4 ... 1A 12
Chiswick High Rd.
TW8: Brent ... 1N 11
(not continuous)
Chiswick House ... 2D 12
Chiswick La. W4 ... 1D 12
Chiswick La. Sth. W4 ... 2E 12
Chiswick Mall W4 ... 2E 12
W6 ... 1F 12
Chiswick Plaza W4 ... 2B 12
Chiswick Quay W4 ... 4B 12
CHISWICK RDBT. ... 1N 11
Chiswick Sq. W4 ... 2D 12
Chiswick Staithe W4 ... 4B 12
Chiswick Station (Rail) ... 3B 12
Chiswick Ter. *W4 ... 1B 12*
(off Chiswick Rd.)
Chiswick Village W4 ... 2N 11
Chiswick Wharf W4 ... 2E 12
Chithurst La. RH6: Horn ... 8B 144
Chittenden Cotts.
GU23: Wis ... 3N 75
Chitterfield Ga. UB7: Sip ... 3B 8
CHITTYS COMMON ... 8J 93
Chittys Wlk. GU3: Guil ... 8J 93
Chive Ct. GU14: Cove ... 1H 89
Chivelston SW19 ... 2J 27
Chivenor Gro. KT2: K Tham ... 6K 25
Chives Pl. RG42: Warf ... 8B 16
CHOBHAM ... 7H 53
Chobham Bus. Cen.
GU24: Chob ... 6N 53
Chobham Cl. KT16: Otter ... 3D 54
Chobham Common Memorial Cross ... 8G 34
Chobham Common Nature Reserve ... 9G 34
Chobham Gdns. SW19 ... 3J 27
Chobham La. GU24: Chob ... 9J 35
GU25: V Wat ... 9J 35
Chobham Mus. ... 7H 53
Chobham Pk. Dr.
GU24: Chob ... 6K 53
Chobham Rd. GU16: Frim ... 5C 70
GU21: Knap, Wok ... 5E 72
GU21: Wok ... 3A 74
(Brewery Rd., not continuous)
Chobham Rd. GU21: Wok ... 9M 53
(Horsell Comn. Rd.)
GU21: Wok ... 4B 74
(The Broadway)
GU24: Chob ... 6E 34
KT16: Otter ... 4C 54
SL5: S'dale ... 6E 34
Choda Ct. RH10: Craw ... 4D 182
Choir Grn. GU21: Knap ... 4H 73
Cholmley Rd. KT7: T Dit ... 5H 41
Cholmley Ter. *KT7: T Dit ... 6H 41*
(off Portsmouth Rd.)
Cholmley Vs. *KT7: T Dit ... 5H 41*
(off Portsmouth Rd.)
Cholmondeley Wlk.
TW9: Rich ... 8J 11
(not continuous)
Chrislaine Cl. TW19: Stan ... 9M 7
Chrismas Av. GU12: Alde ... 3A 110
Chrismas Pl. GU12: Alde ... 3A 110
Christabel Cl. TW7: Isle ... 6E 10
Christchurch Av.
TW11: Tedd ... 6G 24
Christchurch Cl.
GU52: C Cro ... 9A 88
SW19 ... 8B 28
Christchurch Dr.
GU17: B'water ... 9H 49
Christchurch Flats
TW9: Rich ... 6L 11
Christchurch Gdns.
KT19: Eps ... 7A 60
Christchurch Ho. *SW2 ... 2K 29*
(off Christchurch Rd.)
Christ Church Mt.
KT19: Eps ... 8A 60
(not continuous)
Christchurch Pk. SM2: Sut ... 4A 62
Christchurch Pl. KT19: Eps ... 7A 60
Christ Chu. Rd. BR3: Beck ... 1K 47
KT19: Eps ... 8L 59
SW14 ... 8A 12
Christchurch Rd. CR8: Pur ... 7M 63
GU25: V Wat ... 2K 35
KT5: Surb ... 5M 41
SW2 ... 2K 29
SW19 ... 8B 28
Christchurch Way
GU21: Wok ... 4B 74
Christian Flds. SW16 ... 8L 29
Christian Sq. SL4: W'sor ... 4F 4
Christie Cl. GU1: Guil ... 9N 93
GU18: Ligh ... 6N 51
KT23: Book ... 3N 97
Christie Dr. CR0: Croy ... 4D 46
Christies RH19: E Grin ... 1N 185
Christie Wlk. CR3: Cate ... 9A 84
GU46: Yate ... 2B 68
Christine Cl. GU12: Ash ... 3D 110
Christmas Hill GU4: Chil ... 1B 134
(not continuous)
Christmas Pie Av.
GU3: Flex ... 3M 111
Christmas Tree Farm ... 8J 67
Christopher Ct. KT20: Tad ... 1H 101
TW15: A'ford ... 6N 21
Christopher Rd.
RH19: E Grin ... 9A 166
Christ's College Ski Cen. ... 9L 93
Christ's Hospital Rd.
RH13: Hors ... 9D 196
RH13: Itch ... 9B 196
(not continuous)
Christs Hospital Station (Rail) ... 9D 196
Christy Ind. Est.
GU12: Alde ... 2B 110
Christy Rd. TN16: B Hil ... 2E 86
Chrystie La. KT23: Book ... 4B 98
Chuchlands Way KT4: W Pk ... 8J 43
Chucks La. KT20: Wal H ... 2G 101
Chudleigh Ct. GU14: Farnb ... 1N 89
Chudleigh Gdns. SM1: Sut ... 9A 44
Chudleigh Rd. TW2: Twick ... 9E 10
(not continuous)
Chuff Cnr. RG42: Warf ... 7B 16
Chumleigh Wlk.
KT5: Surb ... 8L 203 (3M 41)
Church All. CR0: Croy ... 7L 45
Church App. TN14: Cud ... 2L 87
TW19: Stan ... 9M 7
TW20: Thor ... 2E 36
Church Av. BR3: Beck ... 1K 47
GU14: Farnb ... 1A 90
SW14 ... 6C 12
Church Bungs. RH14: Plais ... 5A 192
Church Circ. GU14: Farnb ... 3A 90
Church Cl. GU4: Chil ... 8N 113
GU8: Mil ... 1C 152
GU21: Wok ... 3N 73
GU24: B'wood ... 8C 72
GU27: G'wood ... 7K 171
KT15: Addl ... 1K 55
KT17: Eps ... 7M 201 (9D 60)
KT20: Lwr K ... 5L 101
KT22: Fetc ... 2D 98
SL4: Eton ... 2G 4
TW3: Houn ... 5M 9
TW18: Lale ... 2L 37
Church Cotts. GU9: B Lea ... 6M 109
KT15: Addl ... 9N 37
RH11: Ifi ... 1L 181
(off Ifield St.)
Church Ct. *GU51: Fleet ... 4A 88*
(Branksomewood Rd.)
GU51: Fleet ... 4A 88
(Church Rd.)
RH2: Reig ... 3N 121
RH4: Dork ... 1K 201
TW9: Rich ... 8K 11
Churchcroft Cl. SW12 ... 1E 28
CHURCH CROOKHAM ... 8B 88
Church Dr. BR4: W Wick ... 1A 66
CHURCH END ... 8A 76
Church Est. Almshouses
TW9: Rich ... 7M 11
(off Sheen Rd.)
Church Farm La.
SM3: Chea ... 3K 61
Churchfield TN8: Eden ... 2M 147
Churchfield Ct. RH2: Reig ... 3N 121
Churchfield Ho. *KT11: Cob ... 1J 77*
(off Lushington Dr.)
Churchfield Mans.
SW6 ... 5L 13
(off New Kings Rd.)
Churchfield Pl. KT13: Weybr ... 1B 56
TW17: Shep ... 6C 38
Churchfield Rd.
KT12: Wal T ... 7H 39
KT13: Weybr ... 1B 56
RH2: Reig ... 2L 121
Church Flds. GU35: Head ... 4C 168
Churchfields GU4: B'ham ... 7C 94
GU8: Wit ... 6B 152
GU21: Wok ... 3A 74
KT8: W Mole ... 2A 40
Churchfields Av.
KT13: Weybr ... 1C 56
TW13: Hanw ... 4N 23
Churchfields Rd. BR3: Beck ... 1G 47
Church Gdns. KT22: Leat ... 7H 79
RH4: Dork ... 1K 201 (4H 119)
Church Ga. SW6 ... 6K 13
Church Grn. GU8: Duns ... 3N 173
GU27: Hasl ... 1G 189
KT12: Hers ... 3K 57
KT20: Wal H ... 2F 100
Church Gro. GU51: Fleet ... 4A 88
KT1: H Wic ... 9J 25
Church Hill CR3: Cate ... 2C 104
CR8: Pur ... 6L 63
GU5: Sha G ... 7G 135
GU5: Shere ... 8B 116
GU12: Alde ... 4N 109
GU15: Camb ... 1C 70
GU21: Wok ... 3N 73
GU22: Pyr ... 4H 75
GU27: Hasl ... 1G 189
RG42: Bin ... 4H 15
RH1: Mers ... 4F 102
RH1: Nut ... 2K 123
RH7: Dorm ... 2C 166
SM5: Cars ... 2D 62
SW19 ... 6L 27
TN14: B Hil ... 2L 87
TN16: Tats ... 9F 86
Church Hill Rd. KT6: Surb ... 4L 41
SM3: Chea ... 9J 43
Churchill Av. GU12: Alde ... 4A 110
RH12: Hors ... 5H 197
Churchill Bus. Pk.
TN16: Weste ... 4N 107
Churchill Cl. CR6: Warl ... 4F 84
GU14: Farnb ... 6N 69
KT22: Fetc ... 1E 98
TW14: Felt ... 2G 23
Churchill Ct. BR6: Farnb ... 2L 67
RH10: Craw ... 9E 162
TN16: Weste ... 4M 107
TW18: Stain ... 7K 21
Churchill Cres.
GU14: Farnb ... 6N 69
GU35: Head ... 5E 168
GU46: Yate ... 1C 68
Churchill Dr. KT13: Weybr ... 1D 56
Churchill Ho. *SM7: Ban ... 1L 81*
(off Dunnymans Rd.)
Churchill Rd. CR2: S Croy ... 5N 63
GU1: Guil ... 4F 202 (4A 114)
KT19: Eps ... 7N 59
RH6: Smal ... 8M 143
SL3: Lang ... 1B 6
SL5: Asc ... 1K 33
Churchill Way TN16: B Hil ... 2F 86
TW16: Sunb ... 6H 23
CHURCH LAMMAS ... 5G 20
Churchlands GU11: Alde ... 4N 109
Church La. CR3: Cate ... 2L 103
CR5: Coul ... 9E 82
CR6: Warl ... 4G 84
(Church Rd.)
CR6: Warl ... 3L 85
(Ledgers Rd.)
GU3: Worp ... 5H 93
GU5: Alb ... 8K 115
GU5: Shere ... 8B 116
GU6: Cranl ... 7N 155
GU8: Brook, Wit ... 1N 171
GU8: Hamb ... 8G 153
GU10: Ews ... 3C 108
GU10: Rowl ... 8D 128
GU10: Wrec ... 4E 128
GU12: Ash ... 2F 110
GU14: Cove ... 1K 89
GU23: Send ... 4D 94
Church La. GU24: Bis ... 2D 72
GU24: Pirb ... 9A 72
GU26: G'hott ... 6A 170
GU27: Hasl ... 1G 189
GU35: Head ... 3C 168
KT7: T Dit ... 5F 40
KT9: Ches ... 3M 59
KT13: Weybr ... 1B 56
KT18: Head ... 2B 100
KT18: Tad ... 4J 81
RG42: Bin ... 4J 15
RG42: Warf ... 4B 16
RH1: Blet ... 2A 124
RH5: Newd ... 1A 160
RH5: Oak ... 9N 157
RH6: Burs ... 3K 163
RH6: Horl ... 4J 163
RH8: Oxt ... 8N 105
RH9: Gods ... 1G 124
RH10: Cop ... 8L 163
RH10: Craw ... 2D 182
RH12: Bro H ... 5D 196
RH13: P Pla ... 9F 198
RH19: E Grin ... 9B 166
SL4: W'sor ... 4G 5
SL5: S'dale ... 4E 34
SL5: S'hill ... 3A 34
SM6: Bedd ... 9H 45
(not continuous)
SW17 ... 6D 28
SW19 ... 9L 27
TW1: Twick ... 2G 25
TW10: Ham ... 2L 25
TW11: Tedd ... 6F 24
Church La. Av. CR5: Coul ... 9F 82
Church La. Dr. CR5: Coul ... 9F 82
Church La. E. GU11: Alde ... 3M 109
Church La. W. GU11: Alde ... 3L 109
Church Mdw. KT6: Surb ... 8J 41
Church M. GU46: Yate ... 8C 48
KT15: Addl ... 1L 55
Churchmore Rd.
SW16 ... 9G 29
Church Paddock Ct.
SM6: Bedd ... 9H 45
Church Pde. TW15: A'ford ... 5A 22
Church Pk. RH11: L Hea ... 5C 162
Church Pas. GU9: Farnh ... 1G 129
KT6: Surb ... 4L 41
TW1: Twick ... 2H 25
Church Path
CR0: Croy ... 2B 200 (8N 45)
CR4: Mit ... 2C 44
(not continuous)
CR5: Coul ... 5L 83
GU12: A Va ... 9E 90
GU12: Ash ... 1F 110
GU14: Cove ... 1K 89
GU14: Farnb ... 5A 90
(Queen's Rd.)
GU14: Farnb ... 1A 90
(Rectory Rd.)
GU21: Wok ... 4B 74
KT11: Cob ... 1J 77
RH1: Mers ... 5F 102
RH12: Rusp ... 4B 180
SL5: Asc, S'hill ... 2B 34
SW14 ... 6C 12
(not continuous)
SW19 ... 1L 43
(not continuous)
Church Pl. CR4: Mit ... 2C 44
Church Ri. KT9: Ches ... 3M 59
Church Rd. BR2: Brom ... 2N 47
BR2: Kes ... 4F 66
BR6: Farnb ... 2L 67
CR0: Croy ... 3A 200 (9N 45)
(not continuous)
CR3: Cate ... 1C 104
CR3: Whyte ... 5C 84
CR3: Wold ... 9G 85
CR4: Mit ... 1B 44
CR6: Warl ... 4G 84
CR8: Ken ... 2A 84
CR8: Pur ... 6J 63
GU1: Guil ... 4C 202 (4N 113)
GU8: Duns ... 4N 173
GU8: Hasc ... 7A 154
GU8: Mil ... 2C 152
GU11: Alde ... 5A 110
GU16: Frim ... 5B 70
GU19: Bag ... 4H 51
GU20: Windl ... 3M 51
GU21: Wok ... 2A 74
(Beech Gdns.)
GU21: Wok ... 6K 73
(St John's Hill Rd.)
GU24: W End ... 8C 52
GU27: Hasl ... 1G 188
(Derby Rd.)
GU27: Hasl ... 2D 188
(Liphook Rd.)
GU47: Owls ... 6K 49
GU47: Sandh ... 6E 48
GU51: Fleet ... 3A 88
KT1: K Tham ... 3L 203 (1M 41)
KT4: W Pk ... 7D 42
KT6: Surb ... 7J 41
KT8: E Mol ... 3D 40
KT10: Clay ... 3F 58
KT14: Byf ... 1N 75
KT15: Addl ... 2J 55
KT17: Eps ... 5M 201 (8D 60)
Church Rd. KT19: Ewe ... 4C 60
KT21: A'tead ... 5K 79
KT22: Leat ... 9H 79
KT23: Book ... 1N 97
RG12: Brac ... 1A 32
RH1: Red ... 5C 122
RH2: Reig ... 5M 121
RH6: Burs, Smal, S Bri ... 3L 163
RH6: Horl ... 9D 142
(not continuous)
RH6: Horn ... 5C 144
RH7: Ling ... 7N 145
RH10: Cop ... 7M 163
RH10: T Hil ... 6C 184
RH10: Wor ... 3J 183
RH11: L Hea ... 5C 162
RH12: Bro H ... 5D 196
RH12: Hors ... 3A 198
SL4: O Win ... 8L 5
SL4: Wink ... 4G 16
SL5: Asc ... 3L 33
(Lyndhurst Rd.)
SL5: Asc ... 9F 16
(Priory Rd.)
SL5: S'dale ... 5D 34
SM3: Chea ... 3K 61
SM6: Bedd ... 9H 45
SW13 ... 5E 12
SW19 ... 6K 27
(High St. Wimbledon)
SW19 ... 9B 28
(Western Rd.)
TN16: B Hil ... 4F 86
TW5: C'ford ... 1J 9
TW5: Hest ... 3A 10
TW7: Isle ... 4D 10
TW9: Rich ... 7L 11
TW10: Ham ... 5K 25
TW10: Rich ... 8L 11
TW11: Tedd ... 5E 24
TW13: Hanw ... 6L 23
TW15: A'ford ... 4A 22
TW17: Shep ... 6C 38
TW20: Egh ... 6B 20
Church Rd. E. GU14: Farnb ... 4B 90
RG45: Crow ... 2G 49
Church Rd. Ind. Est.
RH11: L Hea ... 5D 162
Church Rd. W. GU14: Farnb ... 4A 90
RG45: Crow ... 3G 48
Church Row *SW6 ... 3N 13*
(off Park Rd.)
Church Side KT18: Eps ... 9A 60
Churchside Cl. TN16: B Hil ... 4E 86
Church Sq. TW17: Shep ... 6C 38
Church St.
CR0: Croy ... 4A 200 (9M 45)
GU7: Goda ... 7G 132
GU11: Alde ... 2L 109
GU22: Wok ... 8E 74
KT1: K Tham ... 3H 203 (1K 41)
KT10: Esh ... 1B 58
KT11: Cob ... 2J 77
KT12: Wal T ... 7H 39
KT13: Weybr ... 1B 56
KT17: Eps ... 6L 201 (9D 60)
KT17: Ewe ... 5F 60
KT22: Leat ... 9H 79
(not continuous)
KT24: Eff ... 5L 97
RG45: Crow ... 2G 48
RH2: Reig ... 3M 121
RH3: Betch ... 4D 120
RH4: Dork ... 2J 201 (5G 119)
RH11: Craw ... 3A 182
RH12: Rudg ... 1D 194
RH12: Warn ... 1F 196
SL4: W'sor ... 4G 5
SM1: Sut ... 2N 61
TN8: Eden ... 2L 147
TW1: Twick ... 2G 25
TW7: Isle ... 6H 11
TW12: Hamp ... 9C 24
TW16: Sunb ... 2J 39
TW18: Stain ... 5F 20
W4 ... 2E 12
Church St. E. GU21: Wok ... 4B 74
Church Street Stop (CT) ... 3B 200 (8N 45)
Church St. W. GU21: Wok ... 4A 74
Church Stretton Rd.
TW3: Houn ... 8C 10
Church Ter. RH5: Holm ... 5J 139
SL4: W'sor ... 5B 4
TW10: Rich ... 8K 11
CHURCH TOWN ... 1G 124
Church Vw. GU12: Ash ... 2E 110
(not continuous)
GU46: Yate ... 8C 48
TW10: Rich ... 8L 11
Church Vw. Cl. RH6: Horl ... 9D 142
Churchview Rd. TW2: Twick ... 2D 24
Church Villa TW16: Sunb ... 2J 39
Church Wlk. CR3: Cate ... 2D 104
GU7: Goda ... 5J 133
(not continuous)
KT7: T Dit ... 5F 40
KT12: Wal T ... 7H 39
(not continuous)
KT13: Weybr ... 9B 38
KT16: Chert ... 5J 37
KT22: Leat ... 9H 79

Church Wlk.—Clovelly Ct.

Church Wlk. RH1: Blet 2A **124**
RH2: Reig 3N **121**
(not continuous)
RH6: Horl 9D **142**
RH10: Craw 3B **182**
RH12: Col 9G **180**
SW13 . . . . .4F **12**
SW15 . . . . .8G **13**
SW16 . . . . .1G **45**
SW20 . . . . .2H **43**
TW8: Brent 2J **11**
(not continuous)
TW9: Rich 8K **11**
Churchward Ho. *W14 . . . . .1L 13*
(off Ivatt Pl.)
Church Way CR2: Sande 6C **64**
RH8: Oxt 1B **126**
Churston Cl. SW2 . . . . .2L **29**
Churston Dr. SM4: Mord 4J **43**
CHURT **9L 149**
Churt Rd. GU10: Churt 9L **149**
GU26: Hind 9L **149**
GU35: H Dwn 3F **168**
Churt Wynde GU26: Hind 2B **170**
Chuter Ede Ho. *SW6 . . . . .2L 13*
(off North End Rd.)
Chuters Cl. KT14: Byf 8N **55**
Chuters Gro. KT17: Eps 8E **60**
Cinder Path GU22: Wok 6M **73**
Cinema, The 7A **106**
Cineworld Cinema
Crawley 2B **182**
Feltham 3J **23**
Hammersmith 1G **12**
Wandsworth 8N **13**
Cinnamon Cl. CR0: Croy 6J **45**
SL4: W'sor 4C **4**
Cinnamon Gdns. GU2: Guil 7K **93**
Circle, The GU7: Goda 5J **133**
Circle Gdns. KT14: Byf 9A **56**
SW19 . . . . .1M **43**
Circle Hill Rd. RG45: Crow 2H **49**
Circle Rd. KT12: Whit V 5F **56**
Circuit Cen. KT13: Weybr 7N **55**
Circus, The *KT22: Leat 7H 79*
(off Kingston Rd.)
Cirrus Cl. SM6: W'ton 4J **63**
Cissbury Cl. RH12: Hors 2N **197**
Cissbury Hill RH11: Craw 5A **182**
City Bus. Cen. RH13: Hors 7K **197**
City Bus. Cen., The
RH11: Craw 8B **162**
City Limits
Croydon 3L 63
(off Purley Way)
City Pl. RH6: Craw 5F **162**
City Wharf Ho. KT7: T Dit 5H **41**
Civic Cen. 4A **74**
Clacket La. TN16: Weste 2G **107**
CLACKET LANE SERVICE AREA
. . . .**3G 106**
Clacy Grn. RG42: Brac 8M **15**
Claireville Ct. RH2: Reig 3B **122**
Clairvale Rd. TW5: Hest 4L **9**
Clairview Rd. SW16 . . . . .6F **28**
Clammer Hill
GU27: G'wood 8K **171**
Clammer Hill Rd.
GU27: G'wood 9K **171**
Clancarty Rd. SW6 . . . . .5M **13**
Clandon Av. TW20: Egh 8E **20**
Clandon Cl. KT17: Ewe 3E **60**
Clandon Ct. GU14: Farnb 2B **90**
Clandon Ho. GU1: Guil 5C **114**
Clandon M. RH4: Dork 8H **119**
CLANDON PARK **1J 115**
Clandon Pk. 1J **115**
Clandon Pk. House 1J **115**
Clandon Rd.
GU1: Guil 4F **202** (4A **114**)
GU4: W Cla 3H **95**
GU23: Send 3H **95**
Clandon Station (Rail) 7K **95**
Clandon Ter. SW20 . . . . .1J **43**
Clanfield Ride GU17: B'water . . .1J **69**
Clapgate La. RH13: Slin 3K **195**
CLAPHAM PARK **1H 29**
Clapham Pk. Est. SW4 . . . . . . .1H **29**
Clappers Ga. RH10: Craw 2B **182**
Clappers La. GU24: Chob 7F **52**
Clappers Mdw. GU6: Alf 6J **175**
Clappers Orchard GU6: Alf . . .6H **175**
Clare Av. RG40: W'ham 1B **30**
Clare Cl. KT14: W By 9J **55**
RH10: Craw 9G **162**
Clare Cotts. RH1: Blet 2M **123**
Clare Ct. CR3: Wold 1K **105**
GU51: Fleet 4B **88**
Clare Cres. KT22: Leat 5G **79**
Claredale GU22: Wok 6A **74**
Clarefield Ct. SL5: S'dale 6D **34**
Clare Gdns. TW20: Egh 6C **20**
Clare Hill KT10: Esh 2B **58**
Clare Lawn Av. SW14 . . . . .8B **12**
Clare Mead GU10: Rowl 8E **128**
Clare M. SW6 . . . . .3N **13**
Claremont *TW17: Shep 5C 38*
(off Laleham Rd.)
Claremont Av. GU15: Camb . . .1D **70**
GU22: Wok 6A **74**
KT3: N Mal 4F **42**
KT10: Esh 3N **57**
KT12: Hers 1L **57**
Claremont Av. TW16: Sunb 9J **23**
Claremont Cl. BR6: Farnb 1J **67**
CR2: Sande 2E **84**
KT12: Hers 2K **57**
SW2 . . . . .2J **29**
Claremont Ct.
RH4: Dork 4K **201** (6H **119**)
Claremont Dr. GU22: Wok 6A **74**
KT10: Esh 5A **58**
TW17: Shep 5C **38**
Claremont End KT10: Esh 3B **58**
Claremont Gdns.
KT6: Surb 8J **203** (4L **41**)
Claremont Gro. W4 . . . . .3D **12**
Claremont Ho. SM2: Sut 4N **61**
Claremont Landscape Gdns.
. . . . .4N **57**
Claremont La. KT10: Esh 2B **58**
CLAREMONT PARK **4A 58**
Claremont Pk. Rd.
KT10: Esh 3B **58**
Claremont Pl. GU17: Haw 3L **69**
KT10: Clay 3F **58**
Claremont Rd. CR0: Croy 7D **46**
KT6: Surb 8J **203** (4L **41**)
KT10: Clay 4E **58**
KT14: W By 8J **55**
RH1: Red 9E **102**
SL4: W'sor 5F **4**
TW1: Twick 1H **25**
TW11: Tedd 6F **24**
TW18: Stain 6F **20**
Claremont Ter. KT7: T Dit 6H **41**
Claremount Cl. KT18: Tat C . . .4H **81**
Claremount Gdns.
KT18: Tat C 4H **81**
Clarence Av. KT3: N Mal 1B **42**
SW4 . . . . .1H **29**
Clarence Cl. GU12: Alde 2A **110**
KT12: Hers 1J **57**
Clarence Ct. GU51: Fleet 4B **88**
RH6: Horl 7H **143**
SL4: W'sor 4E **4**
TW20: Egh 6B 20
(off Clarence St.)
W6 . . . . .1G 13
(off Cambridge Gro.)
Clarence Cres. SL4: W'sor 4F **4**
SW4 . . . . .1H **29**
Clarence Dr. GU15: Camb 8F **50**
RH19: E Grin 2B **186**
TW20: Eng G 5M **19**
Clarence Ho. *KT12: Hers 2J 57*
(off Queens Rd.)
Clarence La. SW15 . . . . .9D **12**
Clarence M. SW12 . . . . .1F **28**
Clarence Rd. CR0: Croy 6A **46**
GU51: Fleet 5A **88**
KT12: Hers 1J **57**
RH1: Red 6B **122**
RH13: Hors 7K **197**
SL4: W'sor 5D **4**
SM1: Sut 2N **61**
SM6: W'ton 2F **62**
SW19 . . . . .7N **27**
TN16: B Hil 5H **87**
TW9: Kew 4M **11**
TW11: Tedd 7F **24**
W4 . . . . .1N **11**
Clarence St.
KT1: K Tham . . .3H **203** (1K **41**)
(not continuous)
TW9: Rich 7L **11**
TW18: Stain 5G **21**
TW20: Egh 7B **20**
Clarence Ter. TW3: Houn 7B **10**
Clarence Wlk. RH1: Red 6B **122**
Clarence Way RH6: Horl 7H **143**
Clarendon Ct. GU17: Haw 3J **69**
GU51: Fleet 4A **88**
SL4: W'sor 4E **4**
TW5: C'ford 4H **9**
TW9: Kew 4M **11**
Clarendon Cres.
TW2: Twick 4D **24**
Clarendon Dr. SW15 . . . . .7H **13**
Clarendon Ga. KT16: Otter 3F **54**
Clarendon Gro. CR4: Mit 2D **44**
Clarendon M. *KT21: A'tead . . .6M 79*
(off Parker's La.)
Clarendon Rd.
CR0: Croy 2A **200** (8M **45**)
RH1: Red 2D **122**
SM6: W'ton 3G **62**
SW19 . . . . .8C **28**
TW15: A'ford 5A **22**
Clare Pl. SW15 . . . . .1E **26**
Clare Rd. TW4: Houn 6N **9**
TW19: Stan 2M **21**
Clares, The CR3: Cate 2D **104**
Claret Gdns. SE25 . . . . .2B **46**
Clareville Rd. CR3: Cate 2D **104**
Clare Wood KT22: Leat 5H **79**
Clarewood Dr. GU15: Camb 9C **50**
Clarice Way SM6: W'ton 5J **63**
Claridge Ct. SW6 . . . . .5L **13**
Claridge Gdns. RH7: Dorm 9C **146**
Claridges Mead RH7: Dorm . . .9C **146**
Clarke Cl. CR0: Croy 5N **45**
Clarke Cres. GU15: Camb 8K **49**
Clarkes Av. KT4: W Pk 7J **43**
Clark Ho. *SW10 . . . . .3N 13*
(off Coleridge Gdns.)
Clark Pl. GU6: Cranl 8H **155**
Clark Rd. RH11: Craw 8M **181**
CLARK'S GREEN **6J 159**
Clarks Grn. Rd.
RH5: Cap, Newd, Rusp
. . . . .8N **159**
Clark's Grn. Rdbt.
RH5: Cap 6J **159**
Clarks Hill GU10: Dip 1B **128**
Clarks La. RH8: Warl 1C **106**
TN16: Tats 1F **106**
Clark Way TW5: Hest 3L **9**
Claudia Pl. SW19 . . . . .2K **27**
Claverdale Rd. SW2 . . . . .1K **29**
Claverdon RG12: Brac 6M **31**
Claver Dr. SL5: S'hill 3A **34**
Clavering Av. SW13 . . . . .2G **13**
Clavering Cl. TW1: Twick 5G **24**
Claverton KT21: A'tead 4L **79**
Claxton Gro. W6 . . . . .1J **13**
Clay Av. CR4: Mit 1F **44**
Claybrook Rd. W6 . . . . .2J **13**
Claycart Rd. GU11: Alde 9J **89**
(not continuous)
Clay Cl. *KT15: Addl 2K 55*
(off Monks Cres.)
Clay Cnr. KT16: Chert 7K **37**
Claydon Ct. *TW18: Stain 5J 21*
(off Kingston Rd.)
Claydon Dr. CR0: Bedd 1J **63**
Claydon Gdns. GU17: Haw 5M **69**
Claydon Rd. GU21: Wok 3K **73**
Clayford RH7: Dorm 9C **146**
CLAYGATE **3F 58**
Claygate Cres. CR0: N Add . . .3M **65**
Claygate La. KT7: T Dit 7G **40**
KT10: Clay, H Wood 8G **40**
Claygate Lodge Cl.
KT10: Clay 4E **58**
Claygate Rd. RH4: Dork 7H **119**
Claygate Station (Rail) 3E **58**
Clayhall Ho. *RH2: Reig 2M 121*
(off Somers Cl.)
Clay Hall La. RH10: Cop 6N **163**
Clayhall La. RH2: Reig 7J **121**
SL4: O Win 8J **5**
(not continuous)
Clayhanger GU4: Guil 1E **114**
Clayhill
KT5: Surb 8M **203** (4N **41**)
Clayhill Cl. RG12: Brac 2D **32**
RH2: Leigh 1F **140**
Clayhill Rd. RH2: Leigh 3D **140**
Clay La. GU4: B'ham, J Wel . . .6N **93**
KT18: Head 2A **100**
RG40: W'ham 2E **30**
RH1: Sth N 4G **123**
RH7: Newc 9G **144**
TW19: Stan 1A **22**
Claymore Cl. SM4: Mord 6M **43**
Claypole Dr. TW5: Hest 4M **9**
Clayponds Av. TW8 . . . . .1L **11**
Clayponds Gdns. W5 . . . . .1K **11**
(not continuous)
Clayponds La. TW8: Brent 1L **11**
(not continuous)
Clays Cl. RH19: E Grin 1A **186**
Clayton Cres. TW8: Brent 1K **11**
Clayton Dr. GU2: Guil 9J **93**
Clayton Gro. RG12: Brac 9C **16**
Clayton Hill RH11: Craw 5A **182**
Clayton Ho. KT7: T Dit 7H **41**
SW13 . . . . .3H 13
(off Trinity Church Rd.)
Clayton Mead RH9: Gods 8E **104**
Clayton Rd. GU14: Cove 5L **69**
KT9: Ches 1J **59**
KT17: Eps 6L **201** (8D **60**)
TW7: Isle 6E **10**
Cleardene
RH4: Dork 3L **201** (5H **119**)
Cleardown GU22: Wok 5D **74**
Clears, The RH2: Reig 1K **121**
Clears Cotts. RH2: Reig 1K **121**
Clearsprings GU18: Ligh 6L **51**
Clearwater Pl. KT6: Surb 5J **41**
Clearway Ct. CR3: Cate 9D **84**
Cleave Av. BR6: Chels 3N **67**
UB3: Harl 1F **8**
Cleaveland Rd. KT6: Surb 4K **41**
Cleave Prior CR5: Chip 6C **82**
Cleaverholme Cl.
SE25 . . . . .5E **46**
Cleaves Almshouses
KT2: K Tham 3K **203**
Cleeve, The GU1: Guil 3C **114**
Cleeve Ct. TW14: Bedf 2F **22**
Cleeve Rd. KT22: Leat 7F **78**
Cleeves Ct. *RH1: Red 2E 122*
(off St Anne's Mt.)
Cleeve Way SM1: Sut 7N **43**
SW15 . . . . .1E **26**
Clem Attlee Ct. SW6 . . . . .2L **13**
Clem Attlee Pde. *SW6 . . . . .2L 13*
(off North End Rd.)
Clement Cl. CR8: Pur 3M **83**
Clement Gdns. UB3: Harl 1F **8**
Clement Rd. BR3: Beck 1G **47**
SW19 . . . . .6K **27**
Clements Ct. TW4: Houn 7L **9**
Clements Ho. KT22: Leat 6G **78**
Clements Mead KT22: Leat 6G **79**
Clements Pl. TW8: Brent 1K **11**
Clements Rd. KT12: Wal T 8J **39**
Clensham Ct. SM1: Sut 8M **43**
Clensham La. SM1: Sut 8M **43**
Cleopatra Pl. RG42: Warf 8C **16**
Clerics Wlk. TW17: Shep 6E **38**
Clerks Cft. RH1: Blet 2A **124**
Clevedon KT13: Weybr 2E **56**
Clevedon Ct.
CR2: S Croy 8F **200** (2B **64**)
GU14: Farnb 2B **90**
GU16: Frim 6E **70**
Clevedon Gdns. TW5: C'ford 4J **9**
Clevedon Ho. SM1: Sut 1A **62**
Clevedon Rd. KT1: K Tham 1N **41**
TW1: Twick 9K **11**
(not continuous)
Cleve Ho. RG12: Brac 3C **32**
Cleveland Av. SW20 . . . . .1L **43**
TW12: Hamp 8N **23**
W4 . . . . .1E **12**
Cleveland Cl. KT12: Wal T 9J **39**
Cleveland Dr. TW18: Stain 1K **37**
Cleveland Gdns. KT4: W Pk . . .8D **42**
SW13 . . . . .5E **12**
Cleveland Pk. TW19: Stan 9N **7**
Cleveland Ri. SM4: Mord 6J **43**
Cleveland Rd. KT3: N Mal 3D **42**
KT4: W Pk 8D **42**
SW13 . . . . .5E **12**
TW7: Isle 7G **10**
Cleve Pl. KT13: Weybr 2E **56**
Cleves Av. KT17: Ewe 5G **61**
Cleves Cl. KT11: Cob 1J **77**
Cleves Ct.
KT17: Eps 5M **201** (8E **60**)
SL4: W'sor 6C **4**
Cleves Cres. CR0: N Add 7M **65**
Cleves Rd. TW10: Ham 4J **25**
Cleves Way TW12: Hamp 8N **23**
TW16: Sunb 7G **22**
Cleves Wood KT13: Weybr 1F **56**
Clewborough Dr.
GU15: Camb 9F **50**
Clewer Av. SL4: W'sor 5D **4**
Clewer Ct. Rd. SL4: W'sor 3E **4**
Clewer Flds. SL4: W'sor 4F **4**
CLEWER GREEN **5C 4**
CLEWER HILL **6B 4**
Clewer Hill Rd. SL4: W'sor 5B **4**
CLEWER NEW TOWN **5E 4**
Clewer New Town
SL4: W'sor 5D **4**
Clewer Pk. SL4: W'sor 3D **4**
CLEWER ST ANDREW **3D 4**
CLEWER ST STEPHEN **3E 4**
CLEWER VILLAGE **4D 4**
CLEWER WITHIN **4F 4**
Clew's La. GU24: Bis 3D **72**
Clifden Rd. TW1: Twick 2F **24**
TW8: Brent 2K **11**
Cliff End CR8: Pur 8M **63**
Cliffe Ri. GU7: Goda 8F **132**
Cliffe Rd.
CR2: S Croy 8D **200** (2A **64**)
GU7: Goda 9E **132**
Cliffe Wlk. *SM1: Sut 2A 62*
(off Greyhound Rd.)
Clifford Av. SM6: W'ton 1G **62**
SW14 . . . . .6A **12**
(not continuous)
Clifford Gro. TW15: A'ford 5B **22**
Clifford Haigh Ho.
SW6 . . . . .3J **13**
Clifford Ho. *W14 . . . . .1L 13*
(off Edith Vs.)
Clifford Mnr. Rd.
GU4: Guil 7A **114**
Clifford Rd. SE25 . . . . .3D **46**
TW4: Houn 6L **9**
TW10: Ham 3K **25**
Clifton Av. SM2: Sut 7N **61**
TW13: Felt 4K **23**
Clifton Cl. BR6: Farnb 2L **67**
CR3: Cate 1A **104**
GU10: Wrec 7F **128**
KT15: Addl 8K **37**
RH6: Horl 8H **143**
Clifton Ct. KT5: Surb 6M **41**
TW19: Stan 9N **7**
Clifton Gdns. GU16: Frim G 8D **70**
W4 . . . . .1C **12**
(not continuous)
Clifton Lodge SL4: E Wic 1D **4**
Clifton M. SE25 . . . . .3B **46**
Clifton Pde. TW13: Felt 4K **23**
Clifton Pk. Av. SW20 . . . . .1H **43**
Clifton Pl. SM7: Ban 2M **81**
Clifton Ri. SL4: W'sor 4A **4**
Clifton Rd. CR5: Coul 2F **82**
KT2: K Tham 1M **203** (8M **25**)
RG41: W'ham 1A **30**
RH10: Craw 4G **183**
SE25 . . . . .3B **46**
SM6: W'ton 2F **62**
SW19 . . . . .7J **27**
TW7: Isle 5E **10**
TW11: Tedd 5E **24**
Clifton's La. RH2: Reig 1J **121**
Clifton Ter. *RH4: Dork 6H 119*
(off Cliftonville)
Cliftonville RH4: Dork 6H **119**
Clifton Wlk. *W6 . . . . .1G 13*
(off King St.)
Clifton Way GU21: Wok 4J **73**
TW6: Lon A 6B **8**
Climping Rd. RH11: Craw 1N **181**
Cline Rd. GU1: Guil 5B **114**
Clinton Av. KT8: E Mol 3C **40**
Clinton Cl. GU21: Knap 5G **73**
KT13: Weybr 8C **38**
Clinton Hill RH7: Dorm 1C **166**
Clinton Ho. *KT6: Surb 6K 41*
(off Lovelace Gdns)
Clinton Rd. KT22: Leat 1J **99**
Clintons Grn. RG42: Brac 9M **15**
Clippesby Cl. KT9: Ches 3M **59**
Clipstone Rd. TW3: Houn 6A **10**
Clitheroe Rd. GU17: Min 5E **68**
Clitherow Ct. TW8: Brent 1J **11**
Clitherow Gdns.
RH10: Craw 4C **182**
Clitherow Pas. TW8: Brent 1J **11**
Clitherow Rd. TW8: Brent 1H **11**
Cliveden Pl. TW17: Shep 5D **38**
Cliveden Rd. SW19 . . . . .9L **27**
Clive Grn. RG12: Brac 4N **31**
(not continuous)
Clive Rd. GU12: Alde 3B **110**
KT10: Esh 1B **58**
SW19 . . . . .7C **28**
TW1: Twick 5F **24**
TW14: Felt 9H **9**
Clive Way RH10: Craw 3G **182**
Clock Barn La. GU8: Bus 3J **153**
CLOCK HOUSE **1F 82**
Clockhouse, The
SW19 . . . . .4H **27**
Clock Ho. Cl. KT14: Byf 8A **56**
Clockhouse Cl. SW19 . . . . .3H **27**
Clock Ho. Cotts. RH5: Cap . . .8J **159**
Clockhouse Ct. BR3: Beck 1H **47**
GU1: Guil 8M **93**
GU27: Hasl 2G **189**
Clockhouse La.
GU5: Braml 5B **134**
TW14: Bedf 5B **22**
TW15: A'ford 5B **22**
Clockhouse La. E.
TW20: Egh 8D **20**
Clockhouse La. W.
TW20: Egh 8C **20**
Clock Ho. Mead KT22: Oxs 1B **78**
Clockhouse Pl. SW15 . . . . .9K **13**
Clock Ho. Rd. BR3: Beck 2H **47**
Clockhouse Rd.
GU14: Farnb 1N **89**
CLOCKHOUSE RDBT. **2C 22**
Clockhouse Rdbt.
GU14: Farnb 1N **89**
Clock House Station (Rail) . . .1H **47**
Clock Twr. Ind. Est.
TW7: Isle 6F **10**
Clock Twr. Rd. TW7: Isle 6F **10**
Clodhouse Hill
GU22: Wok 9G **73**
Cloister Cl. TW11: Tedd 6H **25**
Cloister Gdns. SE25 . . . . .5E **46**
Cloisters, The GU4: B'ham 9C **94**
GU16: Frim 5B **70**
GU22: Wok 8D **74**
TW7: Isle 6G 10
(off Pulteney Cl.)
Cloisters Mall
KT1: K Tham 3H **203** (1L **41**)
Cloncurry St. SW6 . . . . .5J **13**
Clonmel Rd. SW6 . . . . .3L **13**
TW11: Tedd 5D **24**
Clonmore St. SW18 . . . . .2L **27**
Close, The BR3: Beck 3H **47**
CR4: Mit 3D **44**
CR8: Pur 6M **63**
(Pampisford Rd.)
CR8: Pur 6K **63**
(Russell Hill)
GU5: Wone 4D **134**
GU7: Goda 8J **133**
GU9: Farnh 2J **129**
GU16: Frim 6A **70**
GU18: Ligh 6L **51**
GU25: V Wat 4N **35**
GU47: C Tow 7K **49**
KT3: N Mal 1B **42**
KT6: Surb 5L **41**
KT10: Esh 3B **58**
KT12: Hers 2H **57**
KT14: W By 9J **55**
RH2: Reig 4N **121**
RH3: Brock 7B **120**
RH6: Horl 1G **163**
RH14: Ifo 5E **192**
RH19: E Grin 1N **185**
SE25 . . . . .5D **46**
SL5: Asc 1H **33**
SM3: Sut 6L **43**
SM5: Cars 5C **62**
TN16: B Hil 3K **87**
TW7: Isle 5D **10**
TW9: Rich 6A **12**
Closeworth Rd.
GU14: Farnb 5C **90**
Cloudesdale Rd. SW17 . . . . . . .3F **28**
Clouston Cl. SM6: W'ton 2J **63**
Clouston Rd. GU14: Cove 9L **69**
Clovelly Av. CR6: Warl 6E **84**
Clovelly Ct. *KT17: Eps 9E 60*
(off Alexandra Rd.)

Cricket Ct.—Curtis Gdns.

Cricket Ct. RH19: E Grin 7A 166
Cricketers Cl. KT9: Ches 1K 59
RH5: Ockl 6C 158
Cricketers La.
GU20: Windl 2A 52
RG42: Warf 6E 16
Cricketers M. SW18 ....8N 13
Cricketers Ter. SM5: Cars 9C 44
Cricket Fld. Gro.
RG45: Crow 3J 49
Cricketfield Rd.
RH12: Hors 7H 197
Cricket Grn. CR4: Mit 2D 44
GU8: Hamb 9F 152
CRICKET HILL 1C 68
Cricket Hill GU46: Yate 3D 68
RH1: Sth N 5K 123
Cricket Hill La. GU46: Yate 3C 68
Cricket La. GU10: L Bou 5J 129
Cricket Lea GU35: Lind 4A 168
CRICKETS HILL 3D 94
Cricketts Hill GU5: Shere 8B 116
Cricket Vw. KT13: Weybr 2C 56
Cricket Way KT13: Weybr 8F 38
Cricklade Av. SW2 ....3J 29
Crieff Ct. TW11: Tedd 8J 25
Crieff Rd. SW18 ....1A 28
Criffel Av. SW2 ....3H 29
Crimea Rd. GU11: Alde 2N 109
(not continuous)
Crimp Hill
SL4: Eng G, O Win 1J 19
TW20: Eng G 4K 19
Cripley Rd. GU14: Cove 8J 69
Cripplecrutch Hill
GU8: Chid 3C 190
Cripps Ho. RH11: Craw 7N 181
Crispen Rd. TW13: Hanw 5M 23
Crisp Gdns. RG42: Bin 8K 15
Crispin Cl. CR0: Bedd 8J 45
KT21: A'tead 5M 79
Crispin Cres. CR0: Bedd 9H 45
Crisp Rd. W6 ....1H 13
Cristowe Rd. SW6 ....5L 13
CRITCHMERE 1C 188
Critchmere Hill
GU27: Hasl 1C 188
Critchmere La. GU27: Hasl ...2C 188
Critchmere Va.
GU27: Hasl 2C 188
Criterion Bldgs. *KT7: T Dit* *6H 41*
(off Portsmouth Rd.)
Critten La. RH5: Ran C 3L 117
Crocker Cl. SL5: Asc 9K 17
Crockers La. RH7: Ling 7G 144
Crockerton Rd. SW17 ....3D 28
Crockery La. GU4: E Cla 7M 95
Crockford Cl. KT15: Addl 1L 55
Crockford Pk. Rd.
KT15: Addl 2L 55
Crockford Pl. RG42: Bin 8L 15
Crockham Cl. RH11: Craw 5A 182
CROCKHAM HILL 2L 127
Crocknorth Rd.
KT24: E Hor 1G 117
(not continuous)
RH5: Ran C 1G 117
Crocus Cl. CR0: Croy 7G 47
Croffets KT20: Tad 8J 81
Croft, The CR0: Croy 9C 46
GU8: Els 8J 131
GU46: Yate 8C 48
KT17: Eps 8M 201 (1E 80)
KT22: Fetc 1E 98
RG40: W'ham 3C 30
RG42: Brac 8N 15
RH11: Craw 3M 181
TW5: Hest 2M 9
Croft Av. BR4: W Wick 7M 47
RH4: Dork 3H 119
Croft Cl. UB3: Harl 3D 8
Croft Cnr. SL4: O Win 8L 5
Croft Ct. TN8: Eden 2L 147
Croft End Cl. KT9: Ches 9M 41
Crofters SL4: O Win 9K 5
Crofters Cl. GU16: Deep 5H 71
GU47: Sandh 7F 48
RH1: Red 5F 122
TW7: Isle 8D 10
TW19: Stan 9L 7
Crofters Mead CR0: Sels 5J 65
Croft La. GU46: Yate 8B 48
TN8: Eden 2L 147
Croftleigh Av. CR8: Pur 3L 83
Crofton KT21: A'tead 5L 79
Crofton Av. KT12: Wal T 9K 39
W4 ....3B 12
Crofton Cl. KT16: Otter 4E 54
RG12: Brac 4C 32
Crofton M. GU1: Guil 4B 114
Crofton Rd. BR6: Farnb, Orp ...1J 67
Crofton Ter. TW9: Rich 7M 11
Croft Rd. CR3: Wold 9K 85
GU7: Goda 7G 133
GU8: Wit 5B 152
GU11: Alde 4N 109
SM1: Sut 2C 62
SW16 ....9L 29
SW19 ....8A 28
TN16: Weste 4K 107
Crofts, The TW17: Shep 3F 38
Crofts Cl. GU8: Chid 4E 172
Croftside, The SE25 ....2D 46
Croft Way GU16: Frim 4D 70
RH12: Hors 5G 196
Croftway TW10: Ham 4H 25
Croham Cl. CR2: S Croy 4B 64
Croham Mnr. Rd.
CR2: S Croy 4B 64
Croham Mt. CR2: S Croy 4B 64
Croham Pk. Av.
CR2: S Croy 2B 64
Croham Rd.
CR2: S Croy 8D 200 (2B 64)
Croham Valley Rd.
CR2: Sels 3D 64
Croindene Rd. SW16 ....9J 29
Cromar Ct. GU21: Wok 3M 73
Cromerhyde SM4: Mord 4N 43
Cromer Rd. SE25 ....2E 46
SW17 ....7E 28
TW6: Lon A 5B 8
Cromer Vs. Rd.
SW18 ....9L 13
Cromford Cl. BR6: Orp 1N 67
Cromford Rd. SW18 ....8M 13
Cromford Way KT3: N Mal 9C 26
Crompton Flds.
RH10: Craw 9C 162
Crompton Way
RH10: Craw 1C 182
Cromwell Av. KT3: N Mal 4E 42
W6 ....1G 12
Cromwell Cl. KT12: Wal T 7J 39
Cromwell Ct. *GU21: Knap* *6F 72*
(off Tudor Way)
Cromwell Gro. CR3: Cate 8N 83
Cromwell Ho.
CR0: Croy 5A 200 (9M 45)
Cromwell Pl. GU6: Cranl 9A 156
RH19: E Grin 2B 186
SW14 ....6B 12
Cromwell Rd. BR3: Beck 1H 47
CR0: Croy 6A 46
CR3: Cate 8N 83
GU15: Camb 8B 50
KT2: K Tham ...2K 203 (9L 25)
KT4: W Pk 9C 42
KT12: Wal T 7J 39
RH1: Red 3D 122
SL5: Asc 3M 33
SW19 ....6M 27
TW3: Houn 7A 10
TW11: Tedd 7G 24
TW13: Felt 2J 23
Cromwell St. TW3: Houn 7A 10
Cromwell Wlk. RH1: Red 3D 122
Cromwell Way GU14: Farnb 7N 69
Crondace Rd. SW6 ....4M 13
Crondall Ct. GU15: Camb 2N 69
Crondall End GU46: Yate 8B 48
Crondall Ho. SW15 ....1F 26
Crondall La. GU9: Farnh 1B 128
GU10: Dip 1B 128
Crondall Rd. GU10: Farnh 4A 128
Cronks Hill RH1: Red 5B 122
RH2: Reig 5A 122
Cronks Hill Cl. RH1: Red 5B 122
Cronks Hill Rd. RH1: Red 5B 122
Crooked Billet SW19 ....7H 27
CROOKED BILLET RDBT. 5J 21
Crookham Rd. GU51: C Cro 4A 88
SW6 ....4L 13
CROOKSBURY COMMON ...4B 130
Crooksbury La. GU10: Seal ..2C 130
Crooksbury Rd.
GU10: Farnh, Run, Til ..9N 109
Crosby Cl. TW13: Hanw 4M 23
Crosby Gdns. GU46: Yate 8A 48
Crosby Hill Dr. GU15: Camb ...8D 50
Crosby Wlk. SW2 ....1L 29
Crosby Way GU9: Farnh 2F 128
SW2 ....1L 29
Crossacres GU22: Pyr 3G 75
Cross Deep TW1: Twick 3F 24
Cross Deep Gdns.
TW1: Twick 3F 24
Crossfell RG12: Brac 3M 31
Crossfield Pl. KT13: Weybr 4C 56
Cross Gdns. GU16: Frim G 8D 70
Cross Gates Cl. RG12: Brac 2D 32
Cross Keys RH10: Craw 3B 182
Cross Lances Rd.
TW3: Houn 7B 10
Crossland Ho. *GU25: V Wat* ...*3A 36*
(off Holloway Dr.)
Crossland Rd. CR7: T Hea 5M 45
RH1: Red 3E 122
Crosslands KT16: Chert 1G 55
Crosslands Av. UB2: S'hall 1N 9
Crosslands Rd. KT19: Ewe 3C 60
Cross La. GU16: Frim G 8D 70
KT16: Otter 3D 54
RH6: Smal 2N 163
Cross Lanes
GU1: Guil 3F 202 (3B 114)
Crossley Cl. TN16: B Hil 2F 86
Crossman Ct. RH11: Craw ...8M 181
Cross Oak SL4: W'sor 5D 4
Crossoak La. RH1: Salf 4F 142
Crosspath RH10: Craw 2C 182
Cross Rd.
CR0: Croy 1E 200 (7A 46)
CR8: Pur 9M 63
GU12: A Va 1F 110
KT2: K Tham 8M 25
Cross Rd. KT13: Weybr 9E 38
KT20: Tad 9H 81
SL5: S'dale 7C 34
SM1: Sut 2B 62
SM2: Sut 6M 61
SW19 ....8M 27
TW13: Hanw 5M 23
Crossroads, The KT24: Eff 6L 97
Cross St. GU11: Alde 2M 109
GU14: Farnb 5A 90
RG40: W'ham 2B 30
SW13 ....5D 12
TW12: H Hill 6C 24
CROSSWATER 6K 149
Crosswater Farm Gdns. 6L 149
Crosswater La.
GU10: Churt 6K 149
Crossway KT12: Wal T 8J 39
RG12: Brac 1A 32
RH6: Gat 2D 162
SW20 ....3H 43
Crossways CR2: Sels 4H 65
GU12: Alde 3A 110
KT24: Eff 5L 97
RH10: Craw 2D 182
SM2: Sut 5B 62
TN16: Tats 7E 86
TW16: Sunb 8G 23
TW20: Egh 7F 20
Crossways, The CR5: Coul 6K 83
GU2: Guil 5J 113
KT5: Surb 7A 42
RH1: Mers 7G 102
TW5: Hest 3N 9
Crossways Av.
RH19: E Grin 9M 165
Crossways Cl.
GU10: Churt 9L 149
RH10: Craw 2D 182
Crossways Ct. *SL4: W'sor* *5F 4*
(off Osbourne Rd.)
Crossways La. RH2: Reig 6A 102
(not continuous)
Crossways Rd. BR3: Beck 3K 47
CR4: Mit 2F 44
GU26: G'hott 6A 170
Crosswell Cl. TW17: Shep 1D 38
Crouchfield RH4: Dork 8J 119
Crouch Ho. Cotts.
TN8: Eden 1K 147
CROUCH HOUSE GREEN 1K 147
Crouch Ho. Rd. TN8: Eden ...9J 127
Crouch La. SL4: Wink 1J 17
Crouch Oak La. KT15: Addl 1L 55
Crowberry Cl. RH11: Craw ...7M 181
Crowborough Cl. CR6: Warl ...5H 85
Crowborough Dr. CR6: Warl ...5H 85
Crowborough Rd.
SW17 ....7E 28
Crowcroft Cl. GU2: Guil 8L 93
Crowhill BR6: Dow 6J 67
Crowholt *GU10: Wrec* *6E 128*
(off Echo Barn La.)
CROWHURST 9A 126
Crowhurst Cl. RH10: Wor 3J 183
Crowhurst Keep
RH10: Wor 3J 183
Crowhurst La. RH7: Ling 7L 125
RH8: Ling 7L 125
CROWHURST LANE END 7L 125
Crowhurst Mead
RH9: Gods 8F 104
Crowhurst Rd. RH7: Ling 3N 145
Crowhurst Village Rd.
RH7: Ling 1A 146
Crowland Rd. CR7: T Hea 3A 46
Crowland Wlk. SM4: Mord 5N 43
Crowley Cres.
CR0: Wad 8A 200 (2L 63)
Crown, The TN16: Weste 4M 107
Crown All. *RH12: Hors* *6J 197*
(off Carfax)
Crown Arc.
KT1: K Tham 4H 203 (1K 41)
Crown Ash Hill TN16: B Hil ...1D 86
Crown Ash La. CR6: Warl 3C 86
TN16: B Hil, Warl 3C 86
Crownbourne Ct. *SM1: Sut* *1N 61*
(off St Nicholas Way)
Crown Cl. KT12: Wal T 6K 39
SL3: Coln 3E 6
Crown Cotts. SL4: W'sor 7G 4
Crown Ct. GU7: Goda 7H 133
Crown Dale SE19 ....7M 29
Crown Dr. GU9: B Lea 7M 109
Crown Gdns. GU51: Fleet 5C 88
Crown Hgts.
GU1: Guil 8E 202 (6A 114)
Crown Hill
CR0: Croy 3B 200 (8N 45)
Crown Hill Ct. SL5: Asc 4M 33
Crown Ho. KT3: N Mal 2B 42
Crown La. GU9: B Lea 7L 109
GU25: V Wat 5N 35
SM4: Mord 3M 43
SW16 ....6L 29
Crown La. Gdns.
SW16 ....6L 29
Crown Mdw. SL3: Coln 3D 6
Crown Pde. SM4: Mord 2M 43
Crown Pas. *KT1: K Tham* *4H 203*
(off Church St.)
CROWNPITS 8J 133
Crownpits La. GU7: Goda 8H 133
Crown Pl. GU47: Owls 6K 49
Crown Point SE19 ....7M 29
Crown Ri. KT16: Chert 7H 37
Crown Rd. GU25: V Wat 5M 35
KT3: N Mal 9B 26
SM1: Sut 1N 61
SM4: Mord 3N 43
TN8: Eden 9M 127
TW1: Twick 9H 11
Crown Row RG12: Brac 5B 32
Crown Sq. GU21: Wok 4B 74
Crown St. TW20: Egh 5C 20
Crown Ter. TW9: Rich 7M 11
Crowntree Cl. TW7: Isle 2F 10
Crown Wlk. GU7: Goda 7H 133
CROWN WOOD 5B 32
Crown Yd. TW3: Houn 6C 10
Crowther Av. TW8: Brent 1L 11
Crowther Cl. *SW6* *2L 13*
(off Bucklers All.)
Crowther Rd. SE25 ....4D 46
CROWTHORNE 2H 49
Crowthorne Bus. Est.
RG45: Crow 9H 31
Crowthorne Cl. SW18 ....1L 27
Crowthorne Lodge
RG12: Brac *3N 31*
(off Crowthorne Rd.)
Crowthorne Rd.
GU47: Sandh 7F 48
RG12: Brac 8K 31
(Nine Mile Ride)
RG12: Brac 4M 31
(Threshfield)
RG45: Crow 1J 49
Crowthorne Rd. Nth.
RG12: Brac 2N 31
Crowthorne Station (Rail) 3D 48
Croxall Ho. KT12: Wal T 5K 39
Croxden Wlk. SM4: Mord 5A 44
Croxted Cl. SE21 ....1N 29
Croxted M. SE24 ....1N 29
Croxted Rd. SE21 ....1N 29
SE24 ....1N 29
Croyde Av. UB3: Harl 1F 8
Croyde Cl. GU14: Farnb 8M 69
CROYDON 4C 200 (9N 45)
Croydon Airport Ind. Est.
CR0: Wad 3K 63
Croydon Airport Vis. Cen. 3L 63
Croydon Barn La.
RH6: Horn 7C 144
RH9: S Gods 7C 144
Croydon Clocktower *4C 200*
(off Katherine St.)
Croydon Crematorium
CR0: Croy 4K 45
Croydon Flyover, The
CR0: Croy 6A 200 (1M 63)
Croydon Gro. CR0: Croy 7M 45
Croydon La. SM7: Ban 1A 82
Croydon La. Sth. SM7: Ban ...1A 82
Croydon Rd. BR2: Hay, Kes 1E 66
BR2: Kes 1E 66
BR3: Beck 3G 46
BR4: Hay, W Wick 1C 66
CR0: Bedd, Wad 1F 62
CR0: Croy 3E 44
CR3: Cate 1D 104
CR4: Mit 3E 44
RH2: Reig 3N 121
SE20 ....1E 46
SM6: Bedd, W'ton 1F 62
TN16: Weste 1H 107
TW6: Lon A 5C 8
Croydon Rd. Ind. Est.
BR3: Beck 3G 46
Croydon Sports Arena 4F 46
Croydon Sports Club 7F 64
Croylands Dr. KT6: Surb 6L 41
Croysdale Av. TW16: Sunb 2H 39
Crozier Dr. CR2: Sels 6E 64
Cruch La. SL6: P St 1B 16
Cruikshank Lea
GU47: C Tow 9K 49
Crunden Rd. CR2: S Croy 4A 64
Crundwell Ct. GU9: Farnh 9J 109
Crusader Gdns. CR0: Croy 9B 46
Crusoe Rd. CR4: Mit 8D 28
Crutchfield La. KT12: Wal T ...8J 39
RH6: Sid 5M 141
Crutchley Rd. RG40: W'ham ..1C 30
Crystal Palace FC 3B 46
Cubitt Ho. GU6: Cranl 6L 155
SW4 ....1G 28
Cubitt Way GU21: Knap 5G 72
Cuckfield Cl. RH11: Craw 6L 181
Cuckmere Cres.
RH11: Craw 4L 181
Cuckoo La. GU24: W End 9A 52
Cuckoo Pound TW17: Shep 4F 38
Cuckoo Va. GU24: W End 9A 52
Cudas Cl. KT19: Ewe 1E 60
Cuddington Av. KT4: W Pk 9E 42
Cuddington Ct. KT20: Tad 7H 81
Cuddington Cl. SM2: Chea 5J 61
Cuddington Glade
KT19: Eps 8N 59
Cuddington Pk. Cl.
SM7: Ban 9L 61
Cuddington Way SM2: Chea ...8J 61
CUDHAM 2M 87
Cudham Cl. SM2: Sut 6M 61
Cudham Dr. CR0: N Add 6M 65
Cudham La. Nth. BR6: Dow ...6N 67
TN14: Cud 1L 87
Cudham La. Sth.
TN14: Cud, Knoc 2L 87
Cudham Pk. Rd. TN14: Cud ...6N 67
Cudham Rd. BR6: Dow 7J 67
TN16: Tats 6G 86
CUDWORTH 2D 160
Cudworth La. RH5: Newd 1B 160
Cudworth Pk. RH5: Newd 2E 160
Culdrose Ho. *GU11: Alde* *2M 109*
(off Frederick St.)
Culham Ho. RG12: Brac 3C 32
Cullen Cl. GU46: Yate 1B 68
Cullens M. GU11: Alde 3M 109
Cullerne Cl. KT17: Ewe 6E 60
Cullesden Rd. CR8: Ken 2M 83
Cull's Rd. GU3: Flex 3M 111
CULMER 8C 152
Culmer Hill GU8: Worm 8C 152
Culmer La. GU8: Worm 7C 152
Culmington Rd.
CR2: S Croy 5N 63
Culsac Rd. KT6: Surb 8L 41
Culvercroft RG42: Bin 8K 15
Culverden Ct. *KT13: Weybr* *9E 38*
(off Oatlands Dr.)
Culverden Rd. SW12 ....3G 28
Culverden Ter. KT13: Weybr ...9E 38
Culver Dr. RH8: Oxt 8A 106
Culverhay KT21: A'tead 3L 79
Culverhouse Gdns.
SW16 ....4K 29
Culverlands Cres.
GU12: Ash 1D 110
Culver Rd. GU47: Owls 6J 49
Culvers Av. SM5: Cars 8D 44
Culvers Retreat SM5: Cars 7D 44
Culvers Way SM5: Cars 8D 44
Culworth Ho.
GU1: Guil 5F 202 (4A 114)
Culzean Cl. SE27 ....4M 29
Cumberland Av. GU2: Guil 7K 93
Cumberland Cl. KT19: Ewe 6D 60
SW20 ....8J 27
TW1: Twick 9H 11
Cumberland Ct.
CR0: Croy 1E 200 (7A 46)
Cumberland Dr. KT9: Ches 9L 41
KT10: H Wood 8G 40
RG12: Brac 9B 16
Cumberland Ho.
KT2: K Tham 8A 26
Cumberland Obelisk 8J 19
Cumberland Pl.
TW16: Sunb 3H 39
Cumberland Rd.
GU15: Camb 1G 70
SE25 ....5E 46
SW13 ....4E 12
TW9: Kew 3N 11
TW15: A'ford 4M 21
Cumberlands CR8: Ken 2A 84
Cumberland St.
TW18: Stain 6F 20
Cumberlow Av. SE25 ....2C 46
Cumbernauld Gdns.
TW16: Sunb 6G 22
Cumbernauld Wlk.
RH11: Craw 7K 181
Cumbrae Gdns. KT6: Surb 8K 41
Cumbria Ct. GU14: Farnb 4C 90
RH2: Reig 2B 122
Cumnor Gdns. KT17: Ewe 3F 60
Cumnor Ri. CR8: Ken 4N 83
Cumnor Rd. SM2: Sut 3A 62
Cumnor Way RG12: Brac 3C 32
Cunliffe Cl. KT18: Head 2A 100
Cunliffe Pde. KT19: Ewe 1E 60
Cunliffe Rd. KT19: Ewe 1E 60
Cunliffe St. SW16 ....7G 29
Cunningham Av. GU1: Guil ...2C 114
Cunningham Cl.
BR4: W Wick 8L 47
Cunningham Rd. SM7: Ban 2B 82
Cunnington Rd.
GU14: Farnb 3C 90
Cunworth Ct. RG12: Brac 5L 31
Curchin Cl. TN16: B Hil 8E 66
Curfew Bell Rd.
KT16: Chert 6H 37
Curfew Yd. SL4: W'sor 3G 4
Curlew Cl. CR2: Sels 7G 64
Curlew Ct. *GU11: Alde* *5M 109*
(off Boxhalls La.)
KT6: Surb 9N 41
Curlew Gdns. GU4: Guil 1F 114
Curley Hill Rd. GU18: Ligh 8J 51
Curling Cl. CR5: Coul 7K 83
Curling Va. GU2: Guil 5K 113
Curly Bri. Cl. GU14: Cove 6L 69
Curnick's La. SE27 ....5N 29
Curran Av. SM6: W'ton 9E 44
Currie Hill Cl. SW19 ....5L 27
Curteys Wlk. RH11: Craw 6L 181
Curtis Cl. GU15: Camb 8G 50
GU35: Head 3D 168
Curtis Ct. GU52: C Cro 8B 88
Curtis Fld. Rd. SW16 ....5K 29
Curtis Gdns.
RH4: Dork 1H 201 (4G 118)

Curtis La.—Delft Ho.

Curtis La. GU35: Head ...3C 168
Curtis Rd. KT19: Ewe ...1B 60
RH4: Dork ...1G 201 (4F 118)
TW4: Houn ...1N 23
Curtis's Cotts. RH12: Hors ...5M 179
Curvan Cl. KT17: Ewe ...6E 60
Curzon Av. RH12: Hors ...5H 197
Curzon Cl. BR6: Orp ...1M 67
KT13: Weybr ...1B 56
Curzon Ct. *SW6* ...*4N 13*
(off Imperial Rd.)
Curzon Dr. GU52: C Cro ...8C 88
Curzon Rd. CR7: T Hea ...5L 45
KT13: Weybr ...2B 56
Cusack Cl. TW1: Twick ...5F 24
Cuthbert Gdns. SE25 ...2B 46
Cuthbert Rd.
CR0: Croy ...3A 200 (8M 45)
GU12: A Va ...7F 90
Cuthbert Row GU27: Hasl ...1G 189
Cutthroat All. TW10: Ham ...3J 25
Cutting, The RH1: Red ...5D 122
Cuttinglye La.
RH10: Craw D ...9D 164
Cuttinglye Rd.
RH10: Craw D ...8E 164
CUTTINGLYE WOOD ...8F 164
Cutts Rd. GU11: Alde ...6B 90
Cyclamen Cl. TW12: Hamp ...7A 24
Cyclamen Way KT19: Ewe ...2B 60
Cygmus Ct. *CR8: Pur* ...*7M 63*
(off Brighton Rd.)
Cygnet Av. TW14: Felt ...1K 23
Cygnet Cl. GU21: Wok ...3L 73
Cygnet Ct. GU51: Fleet ...2C 88
Cygnets, The
TW13: Hanw ...5M 23
TW18: Stain ...6H 21
Cygnets Cl. RH1: Red ...1E 122
Cypress Av. TW2: Whitt ...1C 24
Cypress Cl. RG40: Finch ...8A 30
Cypress Ct. GU25: V Wat ...3A 36
SM1: Sut ...2M 61
Cypress Dr. GU51: Fleet ...4E 88
Cypress Gro. GU12: A Va ...6D 90
Cypress Hill Ct.
GU14: Cove ...5L 69
Cypress Ho. SL3: Lang ...1D 6
Cypress Rd. GU1: Guil ...1M 113
SE25 ...1B 46
Cypress Wlk. TW20: Eng G ...7L 19
Cypress Way GU17: B'water ...1G 68
GU26: Hind ...7B 170
SM7: Ban ...1J 81
Cyprus Rd. GU16: Deep ...6H 71
Cyprus Vs. RH4: Dork ...2J 201

D

D'Abernon Chase
KT22: Oxs ...1G 79
D'Abernon Cl. KT10: Esh ...1A 58
D'Abernon Dr. KT11: Sto D ...3M 77
Dacre Rd. CR0: Croy ...6J 45
Dade Way UB2: S'hall ...1N 9
Daffodil Cl. CR0: Croy ...7G 47
Daffodil Dr. GU24: Bis ...3D 72
Daffodil Pl. TW12: Hamp ...7A 24
Dafforne Rd. SW17 ...4E 28
Dagden Rd. GU4: Chil ...9A 114
Dagley Farm Pk. Homes
GU4: Chil ...9N 113
Dagley La. GU4: Chil ...8N 113
Dagmar Rd.
KT2: K Tham ...1M 203 (9M 25)
SE25 ...4B 46
SL4: W'sor ...5G 4
Dagnall Pk. SE25 ...5B 46
Dagnall Rd. SE25 ...4B 46
Dagnan Rd. SW12 ...1F 28
Dahlia Gdns. CR4: Mit ...3H 45
Dahomey Rd. SW16 ...7G 28
Daimler Way SM6: W'ton ...4J 63
Dairy Bus. Pk. RH1: Blet ...9N 103
Dairy Cl. CR7: T Hea ...1N 45
RH4: Westc ...6C 118
Dairyfields RH11: Craw ...4M 181
Dairy House Nature Reserve
...5K 159
Dairy La. TN8: C Hil ...3J 127
Dairyman's Wlk.
GU4: B'ham ...7D 94
Dairy Wlk. SW19 ...5K 27
Daisy Cl. CR0: Croy ...7G 47
Daisy La. SW6 ...6M 13
Daisy Mdw. TW20: Egh ...6C 20
Dakin Cl. RH10: Craw ...7G 183
Dakins, The RH19: E Grin ...1A 186
Dakota Cl. SM6: W'ton ...4K 63
Dalby Rd. SW18 ...7N 13
Dalcross RG12: Brac ...5C 32
Dalcross Rd. TW4: Houn ...5M 9
Dale, The BR2: Kes ...1F 66
Dale Av. TW4: Houn ...6M 9
Dalebury Rd. SW17 ...3D 28
Dale Cl. GU10: Wrec ...4E 128
KT15: Addl ...2K 55
RH12: Hors ...3M 197
SL5: S'dale ...4D 34
Dale Copse *GU27: Fern* ...*9F 188*
(off Old Glebe)
Dale Ct. KT2: K Tham ...1M 203
Daledene *RH19: E Grin* ...*1B 186*
(off Lewes Rd.)
Dale Gdns. GU47: Sandh ...7F 48
Dalegarth Gdns. CR8: Pur ...9A 64
Daleham Av. TW20: Egh ...7C 20
Dale Lodge Rd.
SL5: S'dale ...4D 34
Dale Pk. Av. SM5: Cars ...8D 44
Dale Pk. Rd. SE19 ...9N 29
Dale Rd. CR8: Pur ...8L 63
KT12: Wal T ...6G 39
RH18: F Row ...8H 187
SM1: Sut ...1L 61
TW16: Sunb ...8G 22
Daleside Rd. KT19: Ewe ...3C 60
SW16 ...6F 28
Dale St. W4 ...1D 12
Dale Vw. GU21: Wok ...5L 73
GU27: Hasl ...3E 188
KT18: Head ...1A 100
Dalewood Gdns. KT4: W Pk ...8G 43
RH10: Craw ...1D 182
Dalkeith Rd. SE21 ...2N 29
Dallas Rd. SM3: Chea ...3K 61
Dallaway Gdns.
RH19: E Grin ...9A 166
Dalley Ct. GU47: C Tow ...8J 49
Dalling Rd. W6 ...1G 12
Dallington Cl. KT12: Hers ...3K 57
Dalmally Rd. CR0: Croy ...6C 46
Dalmany Pas. CR0: Croy ...6C 46
Dalmeny Av. SW16 ...1L 45
Dalmeny Cres. TW3: Houn ...7D 10
Dalmeny Rd. KT4: W Pk ...9G 42
SM5: Cars ...4E 62
Dalmore Av. KT10: Clay ...3F 58
Dalmore Rd. SE21 ...3N 29
Dalston Cl. GU15: Camb ...3H 71
Dalton Av. CR4: Mit ...1C 44
Dalton Cl. CR8: Pur ...8N 63
RH11: Craw ...8M 181
Dalton Grn. SL3: Lang ...2B 6
Dalton St. SE27 ...3M 29
Damascene Wlk. SE21 ...2N 29
Damask Cl. GU24: W End ...9B 52
Damask Ct. SM1: Sut ...7N 43
Damphurst La.
RH5: A Com, Wott ...1A 138
Dampier Wlk. RH11: Craw ...8N 181
Damson Way SM5: Cars ...5D 62
Danbrook Rd. SW16 ...9J 29
Danbury M. SM6: W'ton ...1F 62
Danby Ct. RH6: Horl ...6E 142
Dancer Rd. SW6 ...4L 13
TW9: Rich ...6N 11
Danebury CR0: N Add ...3M 65
Danebury Av. SW15 ...9D 12
(not continuous)
Danebury Wlk. GU16: Frim ...6D 70
Dane Cl. BR6: Farnb ...2M 67
Dane Ct. GU22: Pyr ...2H 75
Danecourt Gdns. CR0: Croy ...9C 46
Danehurst TW8: Brent ...3J 11
Danehurst Cl. TW20: Egh ...7A 20
Danehurst Ct. KT17: Eps ...9E 60
Danehurst Cres.
RH13: Hors ...6M 197
Danehurst St. SW6 ...4K 13
Danemere St. SW15 ...6H 13
Danemore La.
RH9: S Gods ...1G 145
Dane Rd. CR6: Warl ...4G 84
SW19 ...9A 28
TW15: A'ford ...7D 22
Danesbury Rd. TW13: Felt ...2J 23
Danes Cl. KT22: Oxs ...1C 78
Danescourt Cres. SM1: Sut ...8A 44
Danesfield GU23: Rip, Send ...1H 95
Danesfield Cl. KT12: Wal T ...9J 39
Danes Hill GU22: Wok ...5C 74
Daneshill RH1: Red ...2C 122
Daneshill Cl. RH1: Red ...2C 122
Daneshill School Dr.
KT22: Oxs ...1D 78
Danesmead KT11: Cob ...7A 58
Danesrood GU1: Guil ...4B 114
Danes Way KT22: Oxs ...1D 78
Daneswood Cl.
KT13: Weybr ...2C 56
Danetree Cl. KT19: Ewe ...4B 60
Danetree Rd. KT19: Ewe ...4B 60
Daniel Cl. SW17 ...7C 28
TW4: Houn ...1N 23
Daniel Lambert Mill
KT15: Addl ...*2N 55*
(off Bourneside Rd.)
Daniell Way CR0: Wad ...7J 45
Daniels Ho. *RH10: Craw* ...*2F 182*
(off Trafalgar Gdns.)
Daniels La. CR6: Warl ...3J 85
Daniel Way SM7: Ban ...1N 81
Dan Leno Wlk. SW6 ...3N 13
Dan Mason Dr. W4 ...5B 12
Danone Ct. *GU1: Guil* ...*3C 202*
(off Park Rd.)
Danses Cl. GU4: Guil ...1F 114
Danvers Way CR3: Cate ...1N 103
Da Palma Ct. *SW6* ...*2M 13*
(off Anselm Rd.)
Dapdune Ct.
GU1: Guil ...3B 202 (3M 113)
Dapdune Rd.
GU1: Guil ...3C 202 (3N 113)
Dapdune Wharf ...2A 202 (3M 113)
Dapdune Wharf Vis. Cen.
...3B 202 (3M 113)
Daphne Ct. KT4: W Pk ...8D 42
Daphne Jackson Rd.
GU2: Guil ...4H 113
Daphne St. SW18 ...9N 13
Darby Cl. CR3: Cate ...9N 83
Darby Cres. TW16: Sunb ...1K 39
Darby Gdns. TW16: Sunb ...1K 39
DARBY GREEN ...9F 48
Darby Grn. La.
GU17: B'water ...1F 68
Darby Grn. Rd.
GU17: B'water ...1F 68
Darby Va. RG42: Warf ...7N 15
Darcy Av. SM6: W'ton ...1G 63
Darcy Cl. CR5: Coul ...6M 83
D'Arcy Pl. KT21: A'tead ...4M 79
Darcy Rd. KT21: A'tead ...4M 79
SM3: Chea ...1J 61
SW16 ...1J 45
TW7: Isle ...4G 11
Darell Rd. TW9: Rich ...6N 11
Darenth Gdns.
TN16: Weste ...4M 107
Darenth Way RH6: Horl ...6D 142
Dare's La. GU10: Ews ...3A 108
Darfield Rd. GU4: B'ham ...9C 94
Darfur St. SW15 ...6J 13
Dark Dale SL5: Asc ...4E 32
Dark La. GU3: Put ...8M 111
GU5: Shere ...8A 116
GU20: Windl ...3M 51
Darlan Rd. SW6 ...3L 13
Darlaston Rd. SW19 ...8J 27
Darley Cl. CR0: Croy ...5H 47
KT15: Addl ...2L 55
Darleydale RH11: Craw ...6A 182
Darleydale Cl. GU47: Owls ...5J 49
Darley Dene Ct.
KT15: Addl ...1L 55
Darley Dr. KT3: N Mal ...1C 42
Darley Gdns. SM4: Mord ...5A 44
Darling Ho. TW1: Twick ...9K 11
Darlington Rd. SE27 ...6M 29
Darmaine Cl. CR2: S Croy ...4N 63
Darnley Pk. KT13: Weybr ...9C 38
Darracott Cl. GU15: Camb ...7F 50
Darrick Wood School Sports Cen.
...1L 67
Darset Av. GU51: Fleet ...3B 88
Dart Cl. SL3: Lang ...1D 6
Dart Ct. RH19: E Grin ...7C 166
Dartmouth Av. GU21: Wok ...1E 74
Dartmouth Cl. RG12: Brac ...2C 32
Dartmouth Grn. GU21: Wok ...1F 74
Dartmouth Ho.
KT2: K Tham ...2J 203
Dartmouth Path
GU21: Wok ...1F 74
Dartmouth Pl. W4 ...2D 12
Dartnell Av. KT14: W By ...8K 55
Dartnell Cl. KT14: W By ...8K 55
Dartnell Ct. KT14: W By ...8L 55
Dartnell Cres. KT14: W By ...8K 55
DARTNELL PARK ...8L 55
Dartnell Pk. Rd.
KT14: W By ...8K 55
Dartnell Pl. KT14: W By ...8K 55
Dartnell Rd. CR0: Croy ...6C 46
Dart Rd. GU14: Cove ...8J 69
Darvel Cl. GU21: Wok ...3K 73
Darvills La. GU9: Farnh ...1H 129
RG10: S Row ...1E 14
Darwall Dr. SL5: Asc ...1H 33
Darwin Cl. BR6: Farnb ...2M 67
RH12: Hors ...4M 197
Darwin Ct. *GU15: Camb* ...*3N 69*
(off Watchetts Rd.)
Darwin Gro. GU11: Alde ...1A 110
Darwin Leisure Cen. ...2H 87
Darwin Pl. RG12: Brac ...3A 32
Darwin Rd. W5 ...1J 11
Daryngton Dr. GU1: Guil ...3D 114
Dashwood Cl.
KT14: W By ...8L 55
RG12: Brac ...9B 16
Dashwood Lang Rd.
KT15: Addl ...1M 55
Dassett Rd. SE27 ...6M 29
DATCHET ...3L 5
DATCHET COMMON ...4N 5
Datchet Pl. SL3: Dat ...4L 5
Datchet Rd. SL3: Hort ...6B 6
SL3: Slou ...1J 5
SL4: O Win ...7K 5
SL4: W'sor ...3G 5
Datchet Station (Rail) ...4L 5
Daubeney Pl. *TW12: Hamp* ...*9C 24*
(off High St.)
Daux Hill RH12: Warn ...1H 197
Davenant Rd.
CR0: Croy ...6A 200 (1M 63)
Davenport Cl. TW11: Tedd ...7G 24
Davenport Lodge
TW5: Hest ...3M 9
Davenport Rd. RG12: Brac ...9C 16
Daventry Cl. SL3: Poy ...4H 7
Daventry Ct. RG42: Brac ...9N 15
David Cl. RH6: Horl ...7F 142
UB3: Harl ...3F 8
David Lean Cinema ...4C 200
David Lloyd Leisure
Brooklands ...6B 56
Cheam ...4J 61
Epsom ...6N 59
Fulham Broadway ...*3M 13*
(within Fulham Broadway Shop. Cen.)
Hounslow ...1K 9
Kingfield Green ...7B 74
Kingston upon Thames
...*3K 203*
(in The Rotunda Cen.)
Merton ...2J 43
David Rd. SL3: Poy ...5H 7
Davidson Rd.
CR0: Croy ...1F 200 (7B 46)
David Twigg Cl.
KT2: K Tham ...1K 203 (9L 25)
Davies Cl. CR0: Croy ...5D 46
GU7: Goda ...4G 133
Daviesites GU7: Goda ...4E 132
Davies Wlk. TW7: Isle ...4D 10
Davis Cl. RH11: Craw ...8M 181
Davis Gdns. GU47: C Tow ...8K 49
Davison Cl. KT19: Eps ...7A 60
Davison Rd. SL3: Lang ...1B 6
Davis Rd. KT9: Ches ...1N 59
KT13: Weybr ...6A 56
Davmor Ct. TW8: Brent ...1J 11
Davos Cl. GU22: Wok ...6A 74
Davy Cl. RG40: W'ham ...3B 30
Dawell Dr. TN16: B Hil ...4E 86
Dawes Av. TW7: Isle ...8G 10
Dawes Ct. KT10: Esh ...1B 58
DAWESGREEN ...9E 120
Dawes Pl. RH1: Mers ...9G 102
Dawes Rd. SW6 ...3K 13
Dawley Ride SL3: Poy ...4G 6
Dawlish Av. SW18 ...3N 27
Dawnay Cl. SL5: Asc ...9K 17
Dawnay Gdns. SW18 ...3B 28
Dawnay Rd. GU15: Camb ...7N 49
(not continuous)
KT23: Book ...4B 98
SW18 ...3A 28
Dawn Cl. TW4: Houn ...6M 9
Dawney Hill GU24: Pirb ...8B 72
Dawneys Rd. GU24: Pirb ...9B 72
Dawn Redwood Cl.
SL3: Hort ...6C 6
Dawn Ri. RH10: Cop ...7L 163
Dawsmere Cl. GU15: Camb ...1G 71
Dawson Cl. SL4: W'sor ...5D 4
Dawson Rd.
KT1: K Tham ...5M 203 (2M 41)
KT14: Byf ...7M 55
Dax Ct. TW16: Sunb ...2K 39
Daybrook Rd. SW19 ...1N 43
Day Ct. GU6: Cranl ...8H 155
Daylesford Av. SW15 ...7F 12
Daymerslea Ridge
KT22: Leat ...8J 79
Days Acre CR2: Sande ...6C 64
Daysbrook Rd. SW2 ...2K 29
Dayseys Hill RH1: Out ...3L 143
Dayspring GU2: Guil ...8L 93
Deacon Cl. CR8: Pur ...5J 63
KT11: Down ...6J 77
RG40: W'ham ...9B 14
Deacon Ct. SL4: W'sor ...5A 4
Deacon Fld. GU2: Guil ...2K 113
Deacon Pl. CR3: Cate ...1N 103
Deacon Rd.
KT2: K Tham ...2L 203 (9M 25)
Deacons Ct. TW1: Twick ...3F 24
Deacons Leas BR6: Orp ...1M 67
Deacons Wlk. TW12: Hamp ...5A 24
Deadbrook La. GU12: Alde ...1B 110
DEADWATER ...5A 168
Deal M. W5 ...1K 11
Deal Rd. SW17 ...7E 28
Dealtry Rd. SW15 ...7H 13
Dean Cl. GU12: Ash ...2G 110
GU22: Pyr ...2G 74
SL4: W'sor ...6A 4
Deanery Pl. *GU7: Goda* ...*7G 133*
(off Church St.)
Deanery Rd. GU7: Goda ...6G 133
TN8: C Hil ...2L 127
Deanfield Gdns.
CR0: Croy ...7D 200 (1A 64)
Dean Gro. RG40: W'ham ...1B 30
Deanhill Ct. SW14 ...7A 12
Deanhill Rd. SW14 ...7A 12
Dean La. RH1: Mers ...1F 102
Deanoak La. RH2: Leigh ...4H 141
Dean Pde. GU15: Camb ...7D 50
Dean Rd.
CR0: Croy ...7D 200 (1A 64)
GU7: Goda ...5G 132
TW3: Houn ...8B 10
TW12: Hamp ...6A 24
Deans Cl. CR0: Croy ...9C 46
KT20: Wal H ...2G 100
W4 ...2A 12
Deans Ct. GU20: Windl ...4A 52
Deansfield CR3: Cate ...3C 104
Deansgate RG12: Brac ...6N 31
Deanside GU15: Camb ...7D 50
Deans La. KT20: Wal H ...2G 101
RH1: Nut ...2L 123
W4 ...*2A 12*
(off Deans Cl.)
Deans Rd. RH1: Mers ...8G 102
SM1: Sut ...9N 43
Dean's Wlk. CR5: Coul ...5L 83
Dean Wlk. KT23: Book ...4B 98
Dearn Gdns. CR4: Mit ...2C 44
Debden Cl. KT2: K Tham ...6K 25
Deborah Cl. TW7: Isle ...4E 10
De Brome Rd. TW13: Felt ...2K 23
De Burgh Gdns. KT20: Tad ...6J 81
De Burgh Pk. SM7: Ban ...2N 81
Deburgh Rd. SW19 ...8A 28
Decimus Cl. CR7: T Hea ...3A 46
Dedisham Cl. RH10: Craw ...4E 182
Dedswell Dr. GU4: W Cla ...7J 95
DEDWORTH ...5B 4
Dedworth Dr. SL4: W'sor ...4C 4
DEDWORTH GREEN ...6A 4
Dedworth Mnr. SL4: W'sor ...4C 4
Dedworth Rd. SL4: W'sor ...5A 4
Deedman Cl. GU12: Ash ...2E 110
Dee Ho. KT2: K Tham ...1H 203
Deen City Farm ...1A 44
DEEPCUT ...7G 71
Deepcut Bri. Rd.
GU16: Deep ...8G 70
Deepdale RG12: Brac ...3M 31
SW19 ...5J 27
Deepdale Ct. CR0: Croy ...6E 200
Deepdene GU10: L Bou ...5J 129
GU27: Hasl ...2C 188
Deepdene Av. CR0: Croy ...9C 46
RH4: Dork ...1M 201 (3J 119)
RH5: Dork ...3M 201 (8J 119)
Deepdene Av. Rd.
RH4: Dork ...3J 119
Deepdene Dr.
RH5: Dork ...1M 201 (4J 119)
Deepdene Gdns.
RH4: Dork ...1L 201 (4H 119)
SW2 ...1K 29
Deepdene Pk. Rd.
RH5: Dork ...1M 201 (4J 119)
Deepdene Rdbt.
RH4: Dork ...1M 201 (4J 119)
Deepdene Va. RH4: Dork ...4J 119
Deepdene Wood
RH5: Dork ...5J 119
Deep Fld. SL3: Dat ...3L 5
Deepfield Rd. RG12: Brac ...1B 32
Deepfields RH6: Horl ...6D 142
Deepfield Way CR5: Coul ...3J 83
Deep Pool La. GU24: Wok ...1L 73
Deeprose Cl. GU2: Guil ...8L 93
Deepwell Cl. TW7: Isle ...4G 10
Deep Well Dr. GU15: Camb ...1C 70
Deerbarn Rd. GU2: Guil ...2L 113
Deerbrook Rd. SE24 ...2M 29
Deerhurst Cl. TW13: Felt ...5J 23
Deerhurst Cres. TW12: H Hill ...6C 24
Deerhurst Pk. RH18: F Row ...7J 187
Deerhurst Rd. SW16 ...6K 29
Deerings Rd. RH2: Reig ...3N 121
Deer Leap GU18: Ligh ...7L 51
Deerleap GU35: H Dwn ...5H 169
Deerleap Rd. RH4: Westc ...6B 118
Dee Rd. SL4: W'sor ...3A 4
TW9: Rich ...7M 11
Deer Pk. Cl. KT2: K Tham ...8A 26
Deer Pk. Gdns. CR4: Mit ...3B 44
Deer Pk. Rd. SW19 ...1N 43
Deer Rock Hill RG12: Brac ...5A 32
Deer Rock Rd. GU15: Camb ...8D 50
Deers Farm Cl. GU23: Wis ...3N 75
Deers Leap Pk. ...5M 185
Deerswood Cl. CR3: Cate ...2D 104
RH11: Craw ...2N 181
Deerswood Ct.
RH11: Craw ...2M 181
Deerswood Rd.
RH11: Craw ...3N 181
Deer Way RH12: Hors ...7G 196
Deeside Rd. SW17 ...4B 28
Dee Way KT19: Ewe ...6D 60
Defiant Way SM6: W'ton ...4J 63
Defoe Av. TW9: Kew ...3N 11
Defoe Cl. SW17 ...7C 28
Defoe Ct.
RH4: Dork ...1M 201 (4J 119)
Defoe Pl. SW17 ...5D 28
De Havilland Dr.
KT13: Weybr ...7N 55
De Havilland Rd. TW5: Hest ...3K 9
De Havilland Way
TW19: Stan ...9M 7
Delabole Rd. RH1: Mers ...7J 103
Delacy Ct. SM2: Sut ...7M 61
Delaford St. SW6 ...3K 13
Delagarde Rd.
TN16: Weste ...4L 107
Delamare Cres. CR0: Croy ...5F 46
Delamere Rd. RH2: Reig ...7N 121
SW20 ...9J 27
Delancey Ct. *RH12: Hors* ...*4J 197*
(off Wimblehurst Rd.)
Delaporte Cl.
KT17: Eps ...5M 201 (8D 60)
De Lara Way GU21: Wok ...5N 73
De La Warr Rd.
RH19: E Grin ...9B 166
Delcombe Av. KT4: W Pk ...7H 43
Delderfield KT22: Leat ...7K 79
Delfont Cl. RH10: Craw ...5H 183
Delft Ho. KT2: K Tham ...1L 203

Delia St.—Dorchester Ct.

Delia St. SW18 . . . . .1N 27
Delius Gdns. RH13: Hors 4A 198
Dell, The GU9: H End 5J 109
GU21: Wok 6M 73
GU46: Yate 1B 68
KT20: Tad 8H 81
RH2: Reig 2M 121
RH6: Horl 7F 142
RH19: E Grin 9D 166
TW8: Brent 2J 11
TW14: Felt 1J 23
TW20: Eng G 4K 19
Dellbow Rd. TW14: Felt 8J 9
Dell Cl. GU27: Hasl 1E 188
KT22: Fetc 1D 98
RH5: Mick 5J 99
SM6: W'ton 1G 63
Dell Cnr. RG12: Brac 1K 31
Deller St. RG42: Bin 8L 15
Dell Gro. GU16: Frim 4D 70
Dell La. KT17: Ewe 2F 60
Dell Rd. KT17: Ewe 3F 60
RG40: Finch 5A 48
Dells Cl. TW11: Tedd 7F 24
Dell Wlk. KT3: N Mal 1D 42
Delmey Cl. CR0: Croy 9C 46
Delorme St. W6 . . . . .2J 13
Delrogue Rd. RH11: Ifi 9M 161
Delta Bungs. RH6: Horl 1E 162
(off Delta Dr.)
Delta Cl. GU24: Chob 6J 53
KT4: W Pk 9E 42
Delta Dr. RH6: Horl 1E 162
Delta Ho. KT16: Chert 6L 37
RH6: Horl 1E 162
(off Delta Dr.)
Delta Pk. SW18 . . . . .7N 13
Delta Point CR0: Croy 1C 200
Delta Rd. GU21: Wok 3C 74
GU24: Chob 6J 53
KT4: W Pk 9D 42
Delta Way TW20: Thor 9E 20
Delves KT20: Tad 8J 81
Delville Cl. GU14: Cove 2J 89
Delvino Rd. SW6 . . . . .4M 13
De Mel Cl. KT19: Eps 8A 60
Demesne Rd. SM6: W'ton 1H 63
De Montfort Pde.
SW16 . . . . .4J 29
De Montfort Rd. SW16 . . . . . . .4J 29
De Morgan Cen., The 8M 13
De Morgan Rd. SW6 . . . . .6N 13
Dempsey Wlk. RH11: Craw . . .1M 181
Dempster Cl. KT6: Surb 7J 41
Denbies Dr. RH5: Dork 1H 119
Denbies Wine Estate, Winery & Vis. Cen. 1H 119
Denbigh Cl. SM1: Sut 2L 61
Denbigh Gdns. TW10: Rich . . .8M 11
Denbigh Rd. GU27: Hasl 3H 189
TW3: Houn 5B 10
Denby Dene GU12: Ash 2F 110
Denby Rd. KT11: Cob 8K 57
Denchers Plat RH11: Craw . . .9B 162
Dencliffe TW15: A'ford 6B 22
Den Cl. BR3: Beck 2N 47
Dene, The CR0: Croy 1G 64
KT8: W Mole 4N 39
RH5: A Ham 9J 117
SM2: Chea 7L 61
Dene Av. TW3: Houn 6N 9
Dene Cl. CR5: Chip 6C 82
GU10: L Bou 5K 129
GU15: Camb 7E 50
GU27: Hasl 3G 188
KT4: W Pk 8E 42
RG12: Brac 8A 16
RH6: Horl 6C 142
Dene Ct. CR2: S Croy 8C 200
GU4: Guil 9D 94
Denefield Dr. CR8: Ken 2A 84
Dene Gdns. KT7: T Dit 8G 40
Denehurst Gdns.
TW2: Twick 1D 24
TW10: Rich 7N 11
Denehyrst Ct. GU1: Guil 4F 202
Dene La. GU10: L Bou 5J 129
Dene La. W. GU10: L Bou 6K 129
Dene Pl. GU21: Wok 5M 73
Dene Rd.
GU1: Guil 4E 202 (4A 114)
GU14: Cove 2L 89
KT21: A'tead 6M 79
Dene St.
RH4: Dork 2K 201 (5H 119)
Dene St. Gdns.
RH4: Dork 2L 201 (5H 119)
Dene Tye RH10: Craw 2H 183
Dene Wlk. GU10: L Bou 5J 129
Denewood
KT17: Eps 7M 201 (9D 60)
Denfield RH4: Dork 7H 119
Denham Cres. CR4: Mit 3D 44
Denham Dr. GU46: Yate 1C 68
Denham Gro. RG12: Brac 5A 32
Denham Pl. RH5: B'wth 7K 139
(off Old Horsham Rd.)
Denham Rd. KT17: Eps 8E 60
TW14: Felt 1K 23
TW20: Egh 5C 20
Denholm Gdns. GU4: B'ham . . .9C 94
Denison Rd. SW19 . . . . .7B 28
TW13: Felt 5G 23
Denleigh Gdns. KT7: T Dit 5E 40
Denly Way GU18: Ligh 6N 51
Denman Cl. GU51: Fleet 4D 88
Denman Dr. KT10: Clay 2G 58
TW15: A'ford 7C 22
Denmans RH10: Craw 2H 183
Denmark Av. SW19 . . . . .8K 27
Denmark Ct. KT13: Weybr 9C 38
(off Grotto Rd.)
SM4: Mord 5M 43
Denmark Gdns.
SM5: Cars 9D 44
Denmark Path SE25 . . . . .4E 46
Denmark Rd.
GU1: Guil 4E 202 (4A 114)
KT1: K Tham 5J 203 (2L 41)
SE25 . . . . .4D 46
SM5: Cars 9D 44
SW19 . . . . .7J 27
TW2: Twick 4D 24
Denmark Sq. GU12: Alde 2B 110
Denmark St. GU12: Alde 2B 110
RG40: W'ham 3B 30
Denmark Wlk. SE27 . . . . .5N 29
Denmead Ct. RG12: Brac 5C 32
Denmead Ho. SW15 . . . . .9E 12
(off Highcliffe Dr.)
Denmead Rd.
CR0: Croy 1A 200 (7M 45)
Denmore Ct. SM6: W'ton 2F 62
Dennan Rd. KT6: Surb 7M 41
Dennard Way BR6: Farnb 1K 67
Denne Pde. RH12: Hors 7J 197
DENNE PARK 7J 197
Denne Rd. RH11: Craw 4B 182
RH12: Hors 7J 197
Dennett Rd. CR0: Croy 7L 45
Dennettsland Rd.
TN8: C Hil 3L 127
Denning Av.
CR0: Wad 8A 200 (1L 63)
Denning Cl. TW12: Hamp 6N 23
Denningtons, The
KT4: W Pk 8D 42
Dennis Cl. RH1: Red 1C 122
TW15: A'ford 8E 22
Dennis Ho. SM1: Sut 1N 61
Dennis Pk. Cres.
SW20 . . . . .9K 27
Dennis Reeve Cl. CR4: Mit 9D 28
Dennis Rd. KT8: E Mol 3C 40
DENNISVILLE 4K 113
Dennis Way GU1: Guil 7A 94
Den Rd. BR2: Brom 2N 47
Densham Dr. CR8: Pur 1L 83
Denton Cl. RH1: Red 8E 122
Denton Gro. KT12: Wal T 8M 39
Denton Rd. RG40: W'ham 2B 30
TW1: Twick 9K 11
Denton St. SW18 . . . . .9N 13
Denton Way GU16: Frim 4B 70
GU21: Wok 4J 73
Dents Gro. KT20: Lwr K 6L 101
Dents Rd. SW11 . . . . .1D 28
Den Vale Trad. Pk.
RH10: Craw 4C 182
Denvale Wlk. GU21: Wok 5K 73
Denzil Rd.
GU2: Guil 5A 202 (4L 113)
Deodar Rd. SW15 . . . . .7K 13
Departures Rd. RH6: Gat 2D 162
Depot Rd.
KT17: Eps 6L 201 (9D 60)
RH11: Craw 9B 162
RH13: Hors 6L 197
TW3: Houn 6D 10
Derby Arms Rd. KT18: Eps D . . .4E 80
Derby Cl. KT18: Tat C 6G 81
Derby Rd.
CR0: Croy 1A 200 (7M 45)
GU2: Guil 3J 113
GU27: Hasl 1F 188
KT5: Surb 7N 41
SM1: Sut 3L 61
SW14 . . . . .7A 12
SW19 . . . . .8M 27
TW3: Houn 7B 10
Derby Rd. Ind. Est.
TW3: Houn 7B 10
Derbyshire Grn. RG42: Warf . . .8D 16
Derby Sq., The KT19: Eps 6K 201
Derby Stables Rd.
KT18: Eps D 4E 80
Derek Av. KT19: Ewe 3N 59
SM6: W'ton 1F 62
Derek Cl. KT19: Ewe 2A 60
Derek Horn Ct. GU15: Camb . . .9N 49
Deri Dene Cl. TW19: Stan 9N 7
Dering Pl.
CR0: Croy 7C 200 (1N 63)
Dering Rd.
CR0: Croy 7C 200 (1N 63)
Derinton Rd. SW17 . . . . .5D 28
Deronda Rd. SE24 . . . . .2M 29
De Ros Pl. TW20: Egh 7C 20
Deroy Cl. SM5: Cars 3D 62
Derrick Av. CR2: Sande 6N 63
Derrick Rd. BR3: Beck 2J 47
Derry Cl. GU12: A Va 8D 90
Derrydown GU22: Wok 8M 73
Derry Rd. CR0: Bedd 9J 45
GU14: Cove 6L 69
Derwent Av. GU12: A Va 9D 90
SW15 . . . . .5D 26
Derwent Cl. GU9: U Hal 6F 108
GU14: Cove 1K 89
KT10: Clay 3E 58
KT15: Addl 2M 55
RH11: Craw 4L 181
RH12: Hors 2A 198
TW14: Felt 2G 22
Derwent Dr. CR8: Pur 9A 64
Derwent Ho. KT2: K Tham 1H 203
SE20 . . . . .1E 46
(off Derwent Rd.)
Derwent Lodge KT4: W Pk 8G 42
TW7: Isle 5D 10
Derwent Rd. GU18: Ligh 7M 51
SE20 . . . . .1D 46
SW20 . . . . .5J 43
TW2: Whitt 9B 10
TW20: Egh 8D 20
Derwent Wlk. SM6: W'ton 4F 62
Desborough Cl. TW17: Shep . . .6B 38
Desborough Ho. W14 . . . . .2L 13
(off North End Rd.)
Desborough Sailing Club 6C 38
Desford Ct. TW15: A'ford 3B 22
Desford Way TW15: A'ford 3A 22
De Stafford Sports Cen. 8C 84
Detillens La. RH8: Limp 7C 106
Detling Rd. RH11: Craw 8A 182
Dettingen Cres. GU16: Deep . . .6H 71
Dettingen Rd. GU16: Deep 6J 71
Devana End SM5: Cars 9D 44
Devas Rd. SW20 . . . . .9H 27
Devenish Cl. SL5: S'hill 5A 34
Devenish La. SL5: S'dale 7A 34
Devenish Rd.
SL5: S'dale, S'hill 5N 33
Deveraux Cl. BR3: Beck 4M 47
De Vere Cl. SM6: W'ton 4J 63
Devereux La. SW13 . . . . .3G 12
Devereux Rd. SL4: W'sor 5G 4
SW11 . . . . .1D 28
Devey Cl. KT2: K Tham 8E 26
Devil's Highway, The
RG45: Crow 2D 48
Devil's Jumps, The 6N 149
Devil's La. TW18: Stain 8F 20
TW20: Egh 7E 20
Devil's Punch Bowl 4E 170
De Vitre Grn. RG40: W'ham 1E 30
Devitt Cl. KT21: A'tead 3N 79
Devoil Cl. GU4: B'ham 8D 94
Devoke Way KT12: Wal T 8L 39
Devon Av. TW2: Twick 2C 24
Devon Bank
GU2: Guil 8B 202 (6M 113)
Devon Chase RG42: Warf 7C 16
Devon Cl. CR8: Ken 3C 84
GU47: C Tow 8J 49
GU51: Fleet 1C 88
Devon Ct. TW12: Hamp 8A 24
Devon Cres. RH1: Red 3B 122
Devoncroft Gdns.
TW1: Twick 1G 25
Devon Ho. CR3: Cate 2C 104
Devonhurst Pl. W4 . . . . .1C 12
Devon Rd. KT12: Hers 1K 57
RH1: Mers 8G 102
SM2: Chea 5K 61
Devonshire Av. GU21: Wok 1E 74
KT20: Box H 9B 100
SM2: Sut 4A 62
Devonshire Dr.
GU15: Camb 8D 50
KT6: Surb 7K 41
Devonshire Gdns. W4 . . . . .3B 12
Devonshire Ho. SM2: Sut 4A 62
Devonshire M. W4 . . . . .1D 12
Devonshire Pas. W4 . . . . .1D 12
Devonshire Pl. GU11: Alde . . .3L 109
Devonshire Point
TW15: A'ford 4D 22
Devonshire Rd. CR0: Croy 6A 46
KT13: Weybr 1B 56
RH13: Hors 6K 197
SM2: Sut 4A 62
SM5: Cars 1E 62
SW19 . . . . .8C 28
TW13: Hanw 4M 23
W4 . . . . .1D 12
Devonshires, The
KT18: Eps 8M 201 (1E 80)
Devonshire St. W4 . . . . .1D 12
Devonshire Way CR0: Croy 8H 47
Devon Way KT9: Ches 2J 59
KT19: Ewe 2A 60
Devon Waye TW5: Hest 3N 9
Dewar Cl. RH11: Ifi 4K 181
Dewar Spur SL3: Lang 2B 6
Dewey St. SW17 . . . . .6D 28
Dewlands RH9: Gods 9F 104
(not continuous)
Dewlands Cl. GU6: Cranl 7N 155
Dewlands La. GU6: Cranl 7N 155
Dewlands Rd. RH9: Gods 9F 104
Dew Pond Cl. RH13: Hors 5M 197
Dewsbury Gdns. KT4: W Pk 9F 42
Dexter Dr. RH19: E Grin 1A 186
Dexter Way GU51: Fleet 1C 88
Diamedes Av. TW19: Stan 1M 21
Diamond Ct. RH1: Red 2E 122
(off St Anne's Mt.)
Diamond Est. SW17 . . . . .4C 28
Diamond Hill GU15: Camb 8C 50
Diamond Pl. RH2: Reig 2N 121
Diamond Ridge
GU15: Camb 8B 50
Diana Cotts. GU10: Seal 8J 111
Diana Gdns. KT6: Surb 8M 41
Diana Ho. SW13 . . . . .4E 12
Diana Wlk. RH6: Horl 8F 142
(off High St.)
Dianthus Cl. KT16: Chert 6G 37
Dianthus Ct. GU22: Wok 5N 73
Dianthus Pl. RG42: Wink R 7F 16
Dibdene La. GU5: Sha G 7H 135
Dibdin Cl. SM1: Sut 9M 43
Dibdin Rd. SM1: Sut 9M 43
Diceland Rd. SM7: Ban 3L 81
Dickens Cl. RH19: E Grin 9M 165
TW10: Ham 3L 25
UB3: Harl 1F 8
Dickens Ct. RG41: W'ham 2A 30
Dickens Dr. KT15: Addl 3H 55
Dickenson Rd. TW13: Hanw . . .6K 23
Dickensons La. SE25 . . . . .4D 46
(not continuous)
Dickensons Pl. SE25 . . . . .5D 46
Dickens Pl. SL3: Poy 4G 7
Dickens Rd. RH10: Craw 6B 182
Dickens Way GU46: Yate 1B 68
Dickenswood Cl.
SE19 . . . . .8M 29
Dickerage La. KT3: N Mal 2B 42
Dickerage Rd. KT1: K Tham . . .9B 26
KT3: N Mal 1B 42
Dickins Way RH13: Hors 8M 197
Dick Turpin Way TW14: Felt 7G 9
Dieppe Cl. W14 . . . . .1L 13
Digby Mans. W6 . . . . .1G 13
(off Hammersmith Bri. Rd.)
Digby Pl. CR0: Croy 9C 46
Digby Way KT14: Byf 8A 56
Digdens Ri. KT18: Eps 2B 80
Dighton Rd. SW18 . . . . .8N 13
Dillon Cotts. GU4: B'ham 7E 94
Dilston Rd. KT22: Leat 6G 79
Dilton Gdns. SW15 . . . . .2F 26
Dimes Pl. W6 . . . . .1G 13
Dingle, The RH11: Craw 3N 181
Dingle Cl. RH11: Craw 2N 181
Dingle Rd. TW15: A'ford 6C 22
Dingley La. SW16 . . . . .3H 29
Dingwall Av.
CR0: Croy 3C 200 (8N 45)
Dingwall Rd.
CR0: Croy 1D 200 (7A 46)
SM5: Cars 5D 62
SW18 . . . . .1A 28
Dinorben Av. GU52: Fleet 6A 88
Dinorben Beeches
GU52: Fleet 6A 88
Dinorben Cl. GU52: Fleet 6A 88
Dinsdale Cl. GU22: Wok 5C 74
Dinsdale Gdns. SE25 . . . . .4B 46
Dinsmore Rd. SW12 . . . . .1F 28
Dinton Rd. KT2: K Tham 8M 25
SW19 . . . . .7B 28
Dione Wlk. RH11: Craw 6K 181
DIPPENHALL 1B 128
Dippenhall Rd. GU10: Dip 1B 128
Diprose Lodge SW17 . . . . .5B 28
Dirdene Cl. KT17: Eps 8E 60
Dirdene Gdns.
KT17: Eps 5M 201 (8E 60)
Dirdene Gro. KT17: Eps 8D 60
Dirtham La. KT24: Eff 6J 97
(not continuous)
Dirty La. RH19: Ash W 3G 187
Disbrowe Rd. W6 . . . . .2K 13
Discovery Pk. RH10: Craw 7E 162
Disraeli Ct. SL3: Lang 2D 6
Disraeli Gdns. SW15 . . . . .7L 13
Disraeli Rd. SW15 . . . . .7K 13
Distillery La. W6 . . . . .1H 13
Distillery Rd. W6 . . . . .1H 13
Distillery Wlk. TW8: Brent 2L 11
Ditches Grn. Cotts.
RH5: Ockl 8M 157
Ditches La. CR3: Cate, Coul 7J 83
CR5: Coul 7J 83
Ditchling RG12: Brac 6M 31
Ditchling Hill RH11: Craw 6A 182
Ditton Cl. KT7: T Dit 6G 40
Dittoncroft Cl. CR0: Croy 1B 64
Ditton Grange Cl. KT6: Surb . . .7K 41
Ditton Grange Dr. KT6: Surb . . .7K 41
Ditton Hill KT6: Surb 7J 41
Ditton Hill Rd. KT6: Surb 7J 41
Ditton Lawn KT7: T Dit 7G 40
Ditton Pk. Rd. SL3: Lang 2A 6
Ditton Reach KT7: T Dit 5H 41
Ditton Rd. KT6: Surb 8K 41
SL3: Dat 4N 5
SL3: Lang 1B 6
UB2: S'hall 1N 9
Divis Way SW15 . . . . .9G 13
(off Dover Pk. Dr.)
Dixon Dr. KT13: Weybr 6A 56
Dixon Pl. BR4: W Wick 7L 47
Dixon Rd. SE25 . . . . .2B 46
Dobbins Pl. RH11: Ifi 4J 181
Doble Ct. CR2: Sande 8D 64
Dobson Rd. RH11: Craw 9B 162
DOCKENFIELD 4D 148
Dockenfield St.
GU10: Dock 2A 148
Dockett Eddy KT16: Chert 7N 37
Dockett Eddy La.
TW17: Shep 7A 38
Dockett Moorings
KT16: Chert 7N 37
Dock Rd. TW8: Brent 3K 11
Dockwell Cl. TW14: Felt 7H 9
Dockwell's Ind. Est.
TW14: Felt 8J 9
Doctor Johnson Av.
SW17 . . . . .4F 28
Doctors La. CR3: Cate 1L 103
Dodbrooke Rd. SE27 . . . . .4L 29
Dodds Cres. KT14: W By 1K 75
Dodd's La. GU22: Pyr 1J 75
Dodds Pk. RH3: Brock 5A 120
Doel Cl. SW19 . . . . .8A 28
Dogflud Way GU9: Farnh 9H 109
Doggetts Cl. TN8: Eden 3L 147
Doghurst Av. UB3: Harl 3C 8
Doghurst Dr. UB7: Sip 3C 8
Doghurst La. CR5: Chip 7D 82
DOGKENNEL GREEN 3L 117
Dogkennel Grn.
RH5: Ran C 3L 117
Dolby Rd. SW6 . . . . .5L 13
Dolby Ter. RH6: Char 4K 161
Dollary Pde. KT1: K Tham 2A 42
(off Kingston Rd.)
Dolleyshill Cvn. Pk.
GU3: Norm 8K 91
Dolliffe Cl. CR4: Mit 1C 44
Dollis Cl. RH10: Craw 4G 182
Dollis Dr. GU9: Farnh 9J 109
DOLLY'S HILL 2K 109
Dolphin Cl. GU27: Hasl 2C 188
KT6: Surb 4K 41
Dolphin Ct. RG12: Brac 3A 32
TW18: Stain 4J 21
Dolphin Ct. Nth.
TW18: Stain 4J 21
Dolphin Est. TW16: Sunb 9F 22
Dolphin Rd. SW18 . . . . .7N 13
Dolphin Rd. TW16: Sunb 9F 22
Dolphin Rd. Nth.
TW16: Sunb 9F 22
Dolphin Rd. Sth.
TW16: Sunb 9E 22
Dolphin Rd. W. TW16: Sunb . . .9F 22
Dolphin Sq. W4 . . . . .3D 12
Dolphin St.
KT1: K Tham 3J 203 (1L 41)
Doman Rd. GU15: Camb 2L 69
Dome, The RH1: Red 2D 122
Dome Hill CR3: Cate 5B 104
Dome Hill Peak CR3: Cate 4B 104
Domelton Ho. SW18 . . . . .9N 13
(off Iron Mill Rd.)
Dome Way RH1: Red 2D 122
DOMEWOOD 5D 164
Dominion Cl. TW3: Houn 5D 10
Dominion Rd. CR0: Croy 6C 46
Donald Rd. CR0: Croy 6L 45
Donald Woods Gdns.
KT5: Surb 8A 42
Doncaster Wlk.
RH10: Craw 5E 182
Doncastle Rd. RG12: Brac 2K 31
Doneraile St. SW6 . . . . .5J 13
Donkey La. RH5: A Com 3L 137
RH6: Horl 3H 163
UB7: W Dray 1L 7
DONKEY TOWN 9A 52
Donnafields GU24: Bis 3D 72
Donne Cl. RH10: Craw 1F 182
Donne Gdns. GU22: Pyr 2G 74
Donnelly Ct. SW6 . . . . .3K 13
(off Dawes Rd.)
Donne Pl. CR4: Mit 3F 44
Donnington Cl.
GU15: Camb 2N 69
Donnington Ct.
RH11: Craw 6L 181
Donnington Rd. KT4: W Pk 8F 42
Donnybrook RG12: Brac 6M 31
Donnybrook Rd. SW16 . . . . . . .8G 29
Donovan Cl. KT19: Eps 6C 60
Donyngs Recreation Cen. 2C 122
Doods Pk. Rd. RH2: Reig 2A 122
Doods Pl. RH2: Reig 2B 122
Doods Rd. RH2: Reig 2A 122
Doods Way RH2: Reig 2B 122
Doomsday Gdn.
RH13: Hors 7N 197
DOOMSDAY GREEN 8N 197
Doomsday La. RH13: Hors . . .8N 197
Doone Cl. TW11: Tedd 7G 24
Doral Way SM5: Cars 2D 62
Doran Ct. RH1: Red 3B 122
Doran Dr. RH1: Red 3B 122
Doran Gdns. RH1: Red 3B 122
Dora Rd. SW19 . . . . .6M 27
DORA'S GREEN 7B 108
Dora's Grn. La.
GU10: Ews 5C 108
Dora's Grn. Rd. GU10: Dip . . .1A 128
Dorcas Ct. GU15: Camb 3N 69
Dorchester Ct. GU15: Camb . . .9N 49
GU22: Wok 3C 74
RH2: Reig 2B 122
TW18: Stain 5J 21

Dorchester Dr.—Dukes Rd.

Dorchester Dr. TW14: Bedf . . . 9F 8
Dorchester Gro. W4 . . . 1D 12
Dorchester Ho. TW9: Kew . . . 3A 12
Dorchester M. KT3: N Mal . . . 3C 42
TW1: Twick . . . 9J 11
Dorchester Rd. KT4: W Pk . . . 7H 43
KT13: Weybr . . . 9C 38
SM4: Mord . . . 6N 43
Doreen Cl. GU14: Cove . . . 7K 69
Dore Gdns. SM4: Mord . . . 6N 43
Dorey Ho. TW8: Brent . . . 3J 11
(off High St.)
Dorian Dr. SL5: Asc . . . 9B 18
Doria Rd. SW6 . . . 5L 13
Doric Dr. KT20: Tad . . . 7L 81
Dorien Rd. SW20 . . . 1J 43
Dorin Ct. CR6: Warl . . . 7E 84
GU22: Pyr . . . 2G 74
Doris Rd. TW15: A'ford . . . 7E 22
DORKING . . . 2J 201 (5G 119)
Dorking Bus. Pk.
RH4: Dork . . . 1H 201 (4F 118)
Dorking Cl. KT4: W Pk . . . 8J 43
Dorking (Deepdene) Station (Rail)
. . . 3J 119
Dorking Halls . . . 1L 201 (4H 119)
Dorking Lawn Tennis & Squash Club
. . . 7G 119
Dorking Mus. . . . 2J 201 (5G 119)
Dorking Rd. GU4: Guil . . . 9F 114
(not continuous)
GU5: Gorn . . . 8E 116
KT18: Eps . . . 8H 201 (3N 79)
KT20: Tad, Wal H . . . 7D 100
KT22: Leat . . . 9H 79
KT23: Book . . . 4B 98
RH5: A Ham . . . 8E 116
RH12: K'fold, Warn . . . 8G 178
Dorking Sports Cen.
. . . 1M 201 (4J 119)
Dorking Station (Rail) . . . 3J 119
Dorking Vs. GU21: Knap . . . 4G 72
Dorking West Station (Rail)
. . . 1H 201 (4F 118)
Dorlcote GU8: Wit . . . 5B 152
Dorlcote Rd. SW18 . . . 1C 28
Dorling Dr. KT17: Eps . . . 8E 60
Dorly Cl. TW17: Shep . . . 4F 38
Dormans RH11: Craw . . . 4M 181
Dormans Av.
RH7: Dorm . . . 9C 146
Dormans Cl. RH7: Dorm . . . 2C 166
Dormans Gdns.
RH19: D Pk . . . 4A 166
Dormans High St.
RH7: Dorm . . . 2C 166
DORMANSLAND . . . 1C 166
DORMANS PARK . . . 4A 166
Dormans Pk. Rd.
RH19: D Pk . . . 3A 166
RH19: E Grin . . . 7N 165
Dormans Rd. RH7: Dorm . . . 9C 146
Dormans Station (Rail) . . . 2B 166
Dormans Sta. Rd.
RH7: Dorm . . . 3B 166
Dormay St. SW18 . . . 8N 13
Dormer Cl. RG45: Crow . . . 2F 48
Dormers Cl. GU7: Goda . . . 4G 133
Dorncliffe Rd. SW6 . . . 5K 13
Dorney Gro. KT13: Weybr . . . 8C 38
Dorney Lake Rowing Cen. . . . 3A 4
Dorney Way TW4: Houn . . . 8M 9
Dornford Gdns. CR5: Coul . . . 6N 83
Dornton Rd.
CR2: S Croy . . . 8E 200 (3A 64)
SW12 . . . 3F 28
Dorothy Pettingell Ho.
SM1: Sut . . . 9N 43
(off Angel Hill)
Dorrien Wlk. SW16 . . . 3H 29
Dorrington Ct. SE25 . . . 1B 46
Dorrington Way
BR3: Beck . . . 4M 47
Dorrit Cres. GU3: Guil . . . 1H 113
Dorset Av. RH19: E Grin . . . 7M 165
Dorset Ct. GU15: Camb . . . 7D 50
KT17: Eps . . . 8E 60
Dorset Dr. GU22: Wok . . . 4D 74
Dorset Gdns. CR4: Mit . . . 3K 45
RH19: E Grin . . . 7M 165
Dorset Rd. BR3: Beck . . . 2G 46
CR4: Mit . . . 1C 44
GU12: A Va . . . 8F 90
SL4: W'sor . . . 5F 4
SM2: Sut . . . 6M 61
SW19 . . . 9M 27
TW15: A'ford . . . 4M 21
Dorset Sq. KT19: Ewe . . . 6C 60
Dorset Va. RG42: Warf . . . 7C 16
Dorset Way KT14: Byf . . . 6M 55
TW2: Twick . . . 2D 24
Dorset Waye TW5: Hest . . . 3N 9
Dorset Wharf W6 . . . 3H 13
(off Rainville Rd.)
Dorsten Pl. RH11: Craw . . . 6K 181
Dorsten Sq. RH11: Craw . . . 6L 181
Dorton Vs. UB7: Sip . . . 3B 8
Dorton Way GU23: Rip . . . 8K 75
Douai Cl. GU14: Farnb . . . 1A 90
Douai Gro. TW12: Hamp . . . 9C 24
Douglas Av. KT3: N Mal . . . 3G 42
Douglas Cl. GU4: J Wel . . . 6N 93
SM6: W'ton . . . 3J 63
Douglas Ct. CR3: Cate . . . 9N 83
GU51: Fleet . . . 2B 88
(off Fleet Rd.)
KT1: K Tham . . . 7K 203
TN16: B Hil . . . 4G 86
Douglas Dr. CR0: Croy . . . 9K 47
GU7: Goda . . . 6J 133
Douglas Gro. GU10: L Bou . . . 6H 129
Douglas Ho. KT6: Surb . . . 7M 41
RH2: Reig . . . 2M 121
Douglas Ho's. KT23: Book . . . 2A 98
Douglas Johnstone Ho.
SW6 . . . 2L 13
(off Clem Attlee Ct.)
Douglas La. TW19: Wray . . . 8B 6
Douglas Mans. TW3: Houn . . . 6B 10
Douglas M. SM7: Ban . . . 3L 81
Douglas Pl. GU14: Cove . . . 9M 69
Douglas Rd. KT1: K Tham . . . 1A 42
KT6: Surb . . . 8M 41
KT10: Esh . . . 8B 40
KT15: Addl . . . 9K 37
RH2: Reig . . . 2M 121
TW3: Houn . . . 6B 10
TW19: Stan . . . 9M 7
Douglas Robinson Ct.
SW16 . . . 8J 29
(off Streatham High Rd.)
Douglas Sq. SM4: Mord . . . 5M 43
Doultons, The TW18: Stain . . . 8J 21
Dounesforth Gdns.
SW18 . . . 2N 27
Dove Cl. CR2: Sels . . . 7G 64
RH11: Craw . . . 1B 182
SM6: W'ton . . . 4K 63
Dovecote Cl. KT13: Weybr . . . 9C 38
Dovecote Gdns. SW14 . . . 6C 12
Dovedale Cl. GU4: B'ham . . . 9C 94
GU47: Owls . . . 5J 49
Dovedale Cres.
RH11: Craw . . . 5N 181
Dovedale Ri. CR4: Mit . . . 8D 28
Dovehouse Grn.
KT13: Weybr . . . 9E 38
Dover Ct. GU6: Cranl . . . 7B 156
Dovercourt Av. CR7: T Hea . . . 4L 45
Dovercourt La. SM1: Sut . . . 9A 44
Doverfield Rd. GU4: B'ham . . . 9C 94
SW2 . . . 1J 29
Dover Gdns. SM5: Cars . . . 9D 44
Dover Ho. Rd. SW15 . . . 7F 12
Dover Pk. Dr. SW15 . . . 9G 12
DOVERSGREEN . . . 7N 121
Dovers Grn. Rd.
RH2: Reig . . . 6N 121
Doversmead GU21: Knap . . . 3H 73
Dover Ter. TW9: Rich . . . 5M 11
(off Sandycombe Rd.)
Doveton Rd. CR2: S Croy . . . 2A 64
Dowdeswell Cl. SW15 . . . 7D 12
Dowding Ct. RG45: Crow . . . 1H 49
Dowding Rd. TN16: B Hil . . . 2F 86
Dower Av. SM6: W'ton . . . 5F 62
Dower Pk. SL4: W'sor . . . 7B 4
Dower Wlk. RH11: Craw . . . 4M 181
Dowes Ho. SW16 . . . 4J 29
Dowgate Ho. KT13: Weybr . . . 9B 38
Dowlands La. RH6: Smal . . . 8A 144
RH10: Cop . . . 8A 144
Dowlans Cl. KT23: Book . . . 5A 98
Dowlans Rd. KT23: Book . . . 5B 98
Dowler Ct.
KT2: K Tham . . . 1K 203 (9L 25)
DOWLESGREEN . . . 1D 30
Dowles Grn. RG40: W'ham . . . 9D 14
Dowman Cl. SW19 . . . 8N 27
Downbury M. SW18 . . . 8M 13
DOWNE . . . 7J 67
Downe Av. TN14: Cud . . . 8M 67
Downe Bank Nature Reserve
. . . 9K 67
Downe Cl. RH6: Horl . . . 6C 142
Downer Mdw. GU7: Goda . . . 3H 133
Downe Rd. BR2: Kes . . . 5F 66
CR4: Mit . . . 1D 44
TN14: Cud . . . 9L 67
Downes Cl. TW1: Twick . . . 9H 11
Downes Ho. CR0: Wad . . . 7A 200
Downe Ter. TW10: Rich . . . 9L 11
Downfield KT4: W Pk . . . 7E 42
Down Hall Rd.
KT2: K Tham . . . 2H 203 (9K 25)
Downham Ct. KT12: Wal T . . . 9K 39
(off Long Lodge Dr.)
Down House and Darwin Mus.
. . . 8J 67
Downhurst Rd. GU6: Ewh . . . 4F 156
Downing Av. GU2: Guil . . . 4J 113
Downing St. GU9: Farnh . . . 1G 129
Downland Cl. KT18: Tat C . . . 5G 81
Downland Ct. RH11: Craw . . . 5A 182
Downland Dr. RH11: Craw . . . 5A 182
Downland Gdns.
KT18: Tat C . . . 5G 81
Downland Pl. RH11: Craw . . . 5A 182
Downlands Cl. CR5: Coul . . . 1F 82
Downlands Rd. CR8: Pur . . . 9J 63
Downland Way KT18: Tat C . . . 5G 81
Down La. GU2: Guil . . . 6G 112
GU3: Comp . . . 9E 112
Downmill Rd. RG12: Brac . . . 1L 31
DOWN PARK . . . 9D 164
Down Pl. W6 . . . 1G 13
Down Rd. GU1: Guil . . . 3D 114
TW11: Tedd . . . 7H 25
Downs, The KT22: Leat . . . 3J 99
SW20 . . . 8J 27
Downs Av. KT18: Eps . . . 1D 80
Downsbridge Rd.
BR3: Beck . . . 1N 47
Downs Cl. GU14: Cove . . . 7K 69
Downs Ct. RH1: Red . . . 9E 102
Downs Ct. Rd. CR8: Pur . . . 8M 63
Downsend Lodge
KT22: Leat . . . 8J 79
(off Epsom Rd.)
Downs Hill Rd. KT18: Eps . . . 1D 80
Downshire Way
RG12: Brac . . . 1M 31
RG42: Brac . . . 9M 15
Downs Ho. Rd.
KT18: Eps D . . . 5D 80
DOWNSIDE . . . 5J 77
Downside GU26: Hind . . . 2B 170
KT16: Chert . . . 7H 37
KT18: Eps . . . 8L 201 (1D 80)
RG12: Brac . . . 2N 31
TW1: Twick . . . 4F 24
TW16: Sunb . . . 9H 23
Downside Bri. Rd.
KT11: Cob . . . 1J 77
Downside Cl. SW19 . . . 7A 28
Downside Comn.
KT11: Down . . . 5J 77
Downside Comn. Rd.
KT11: Down . . . 5J 77
Downside Ct. RH1: Mers . . . 7G 102
Downside Orchard
GU22: Wok . . . 4C 74
Downside Rd. GU4: Guil . . . 4D 114
KT11: Down . . . 3J 77
SM2: Sut . . . 3B 62
Downside Wlk. TW8: Brent . . . 2K 11
(off Windmill Rd.)
Downs La. KT22: Leat . . . 1H 99
Downs Link GU4: Guil . . . 8F 114
GU5: Braml . . . 2A 134
GU5: Braml, Chil, Wone
. . . 3B 134
GU5: Wone . . . 2D 134
GU6: Cranl . . . 4H 155
RH12: Cranl . . . 8M 155
RH12: Rudg, Slin . . . 8D 176
RH13: Slin, Itch . . . 2F 194
Downs Lodge Ct.
KT17: Eps . . . 8M 201 (1D 80)
Downsman Ct.
RH10: Craw . . . 6B 182
Downs Res. Site, The
CR3: Cate . . . 5E 104
Downs Rd. BR3: Beck . . . 1L 47
(not continuous)
CR5: Coul . . . 5H 83
CR7: T Hea . . . 9N 29
CR8: Pur . . . 7M 63
KT18: Eps D . . . 7B 80
KT18: Eps, Eps D
. . . 8M 201 (2D 80)
RH5: Mick . . . 6J 99
SM2: Sut . . . 6N 61
Downs Side SM2: Chea . . . 7L 61
Down St. KT8: W Mole . . . 4A 40
Downs Vw. KT20: Tad . . . 8G 80
RH4: Dork . . . 3K 119
TW7: Isle . . . 4F 10
Downsview Av. GU22: Wok . . . 8B 74
Downsview Cl. KT11: Down . . . 6J 77
Downsview Ct. GU1: Guil . . . 8M 93
Downsview Gdns.
RH4: Dork . . . 6H 119
SE19 . . . 8M 29
Downs Vw. Rd.
KT23: Book . . . 5C 98
Downsview Rd.
GU35: H Dwn . . . 4H 169
RH12: Hors . . . 2A 198
SE19 . . . 8N 29
Downs Way KT18: Eps . . . 3E 80
KT20: Tad . . . 8G 80
KT23: Book . . . 4C 98
RH8: Oxt . . . 5A 106
Downsway BR6: Orp . . . 2N 67
CR2: Sande . . . 7B 64
CR3: Whyte . . . 3C 84
GU1: Guil . . . 3G 114
Downsway, The SM2: Sut . . . 5A 62
Downsway Cl. KT20: Tad . . . 8F 80
Downs Wood KT18: Tat C . . . 4G 80
Downswood RH2: Reig . . . 9B 102
Downton Av. SW2 . . . 3J 29
Downview Cl. GU26: Hind . . . 3B 170
Down Yhonda GU8: Els . . . 8G 131
Doyle Ct. GU27: Hasl . . . 2E 188
Doyle Gdns. GU46: Yate . . . 2B 68
Doyle Ho. SW13 . . . 3H 13
(off Trinity Chu. Rd.)
Doyle Rd. SE25 . . . 3D 46
D'Oyly Carte Island
KT13: Weybr . . . 7C 38
Draco Ga. SW15 . . . 6H 13
Dragon La. KT13: Weybr . . . 7B 56
Dragons Health Club
Copthorne . . . 8L 163
Epsom . . . 1C 60
Purley . . . 4L 63
Dragoon Ct. GU11: Alde . . . 2K 109
Drake Av. CR3: Cate . . . 9N 83
GU16: Mytc . . . 4E 90
TW18: Stain . . . 6H 21
Drake Cl. RG12: Brac . . . 4N 31
RH12: Hors . . . 2L 197
Drake Ct. KT5: Surb . . . 8K 203
Drakefield Rd. SW17 . . . 4E 28
Drake Rd. CR0: Croy . . . 6K 45
CR4: Mit . . . 5E 44
KT9: Ches . . . 2N 59
RH6: Horl . . . 8C 142
RH10: Craw . . . 5C 182
Drakes Cl. GU6: Cranl . . . 7N 155
KT10: Esh . . . 1A 58
Drakes Way GU22: Wok . . . 9N 73
Drakewood Rd. SW16 . . . 8H 29
Draper Cl. TW7: Isle . . . 5D 10
Drapers Cres. KT12: Whit V . . . 6G 56
Drax Av. SW20 . . . 8F 26
Draxmont SW19 . . . 7K 27
Draycot Rd. KT6: Surb . . . 7N 41
Draycott RG12: Brac . . . 4C 32
Draycott M. SW6 . . . 5L 13
(off Laurel Bank Gdns.)
Dray Ct. GU2: Guil . . . 4L 113
Drayhorse Dr. GU19: Bag . . . 5J 51
Draymans Way TW7: Isle . . . 6F 10
Drayton Cl. KT22: Fetc . . . 2E 98
RG12: Brac . . . 1B 32
TW4: Houn . . . 8N 9
Drayton Rd.
CR0: Croy . . . 2A 200 (8M 45)
Dreadnought Cl. SW19 . . . 9A 28
(off Nelson Gro. Rd.)
SW19 . . . 1B 44
(Brangwyn Cres.)
Dresden Way KT13: Weybr . . . 2D 56
Drew Ho. SW16 . . . 4J 29
Drewitts Ct. KT12: Wal T . . . 7G 39
Drew Pl. CR3: Cate . . . 1A 104
Drewstead La. SW16 . . . 3H 29
Drewstead Rd. SW16 . . . 3H 29
Drey Ct. KT4: W Pk . . . 7E 42
Drift, The BR2: Brom . . . 1F 66
DRIFT BRIDGE . . . 1H 81
Drifters Dr. GU16: Deep . . . 5H 71
Drift La. KT11: Sto D . . . 3N 77
Drift Rd. KT24: E Jun . . . 2E 96
SL4: Wink . . . 1L 17
Drift Way SL3: Coln . . . 4E 6
Driftway, The CR4: Mit . . . 9E 28
KT22: Leat . . . 1H 99
(not continuous)
RH11: Craw . . . 2B 182
SM7: Ban . . . 2H 81
Driftways GU46: Yate . . . 8C 48
(off White Lion Way)
Driftwood Dr. CR8: Ken . . . 4M 83
Drill Hall Rd. KT16: Chert . . . 6J 37
RH4: Dork . . . 2H 201 (5G 118)
Drive, The BR3: Beck . . . 1K 47
BR4: W Wick . . . 6N 47
CR5: Coul . . . 1J 83
CR7: T Hea . . . 3A 46
GU2: Guil . . . 3J 113
(Beech Gro.)
GU2: Guil . . . 5J 113
(Crossways, The)
GU3: Art . . . 7L 113
GU5: Wone . . . 5D 134
GU6: Cranl . . . 8N 155
GU7: Eash . . . 7B 132
GU7: Goda . . . 9H 133
GU8: P Har . . . 7B 132
(not continuous)
GU9: Farnh . . . 4G 129
GU22: Wok . . . 7L 73
GU25: V Wat . . . 4B 36
KT2: K Tham . . . 8B 26
KT6: Surb . . . 6L 41
KT10: Esh . . . 7C 40
KT11: Cob . . . 1M 77
KT18: Head . . . 1L 99
KT19: Ewe . . . 3E 60
KT20: Lwr K . . . 4L 101
KT22: Fetc . . . 9E 78
KT22: Leat . . . 1L 99
RH6: Horl . . . 9F 142
RH10: Cop . . . 7N 163
RH12: Rusp . . . 2D 180
RH14: Ifo . . . 5F 192
SL3: Dat . . . 4L 5
SM2: Chea . . . 8L 61
SM4: Mord . . . 4A 44
SM5: Cars . . . 5D 62
SM6: W'ton . . . 6G 62
SM7: Ban . . . 4K 81
SW6 . . . 5K 13
SW20 . . . 8H 27
TW3: Houn . . . 5D 10
TW7: Isle . . . 5D 10
TW14: Felt . . . 1K 23
TW15: A'ford . . . 8E 22
TW19: Wray . . . 8N 5
Drive Mans. SW6 . . . 5K 13
(off Fulham Rd.)
Drive Mead CR5: Coul . . . 1J 83
Drive Rd. CR5: Coul . . . 7H 83
(not continuous)
Drivers Mead RH7: Ling . . . 8M 145
Drive Spur KT20: K'wood . . . 8N 81
Drodges Cl. GU5: Braml . . . 3B 134
Droitwich Cl. RG12: Brac . . . 2B 32
Dromore Rd. SW15 . . . 9K 13
Drove Rd. GU4: Guil . . . 5H 115
(not continuous)
GU5: Gorn, Shere . . . 4C 116
GU5: Shere . . . 5N 115
RH5: Ran C . . . 5J 117
Drovers Ct. KT1: K Tham . . . 3K 203
Drovers End GU51: Fleet . . . 1D 88
Drovers Rd.
CR2: S Croy . . . 8D 200 (2A 64)
Drovers Way GU9: U Hal . . . 6F 108
GU12: A Grn . . . 3G 111
(not continuous)
RG12: Brac . . . 2D 32
Druce Wood SL5: Asc . . . 9J 17
Druids Cl. KT21: A'tead . . . 7M 79
Druids Way BR2: Brom . . . 3N 47
Drumaline Ridge
KT4: W Pk . . . 8D 42
Drummond Cl. RG12: Brac . . . 9D 16
Drummond Ct.
GU1: Guil . . . 3C 202 (3N 113)
Drummond Gdns.
KT19: Eps . . . 7B 60
Drummond Ho. SL4: W'sor . . . 6G 4
(off Balmoral Gdns.)
Drummond Pl. TW1: Twick . . . 1H 25
Drummond Rd.
CR0: Croy . . . 3B 200 (8N 45)
(not continuous)
GU1: Guil . . . 3C 202 (3N 113)
RH11: Ifi . . . 4K 181
Drummonds Pl. TW9: Rich . . . 7L 11
Drungewick La.
RH14: W Grn . . . 9L 193
Drury Cl. RH10: Craw . . . 5H 183
Drury Cres. CR0: Wad . . . 8L 45
Dryad St. SW15 . . . 6J 13
Dry Arch Rd. SL5: S'dale . . . 5C 34
Dryburgh Rd. SW15 . . . 6G 13
Dryden RG12: Brac . . . 6M 31
Dryden Mans. W14 . . . 2K 13
(off Queen's Club Gdns.)
Dryden Rd. GU14: Farnb . . . 8L 69
SW19 . . . 7A 28
Drynham Pk. KT13: Weybr . . . 9F 38
Du Cane Ct. SW17 . . . 2E 28
Ducavel Ho. SW2 . . . 2K 29
Duchess Cl. RG45: Crow . . . 9G 30
SM1: Sut . . . 1A 62
Duchess Ct. KT13: Weybr . . . 9E 38
Duchess of Kent Cl.
GU2: Guil . . . 8L 93
Ducks Wlk. TW1: Twick . . . 8J 11
Dudley Cl. KT15: Addl . . . 9L 37
Dudley Ct. GU52: C Cro . . . 7B 88
Dudley Dr. SM4: Mord . . . 7K 43
Dudley Gro.
KT18: Eps . . . 8G 201 (1B 80)
Dudley Pl. TW19: Stan . . . 9A 8
Dudley Rd.
KT1: K Tham . . . 5L 203 (2M 41)
KT12: Wal T . . . 5H 39
SW19 . . . 7M 27
TW9: Rich . . . 5M 11
TW14: Bedf . . . 2D 22
TW15: A'ford . . . 6A 22
Dudset La. TW5: C'ford . . . 4H 9
Duett Ct. TW5: Hest . . . 3M 9
Duffield Rd. KT20: Wal H . . . 2G 100
Duffins Orchard KT16: Otter . . . 4E 54
Duffins Orchard Mobile Homes
KT16: Otter . . . 4E 54
Dugdale Ho. TW20: Egh . . . 6E 20
(off Pooley Grn. Rd.)
Duke Cl. RH10: Craw . . . 7G 182
Duke of Cambridge Cl.
TW2: Whitt . . . 9D 10
Duke of Cornwall Av.
GU15: Camb . . . 6B 50
Duke of Edinburgh Rd.
SM1: Sut . . . 8B 44
Duke Rd. W4 . . . 1C 12
Dukes Av. KT2: K Tham . . . 5J 25
KT3: N Mal . . . 2D 42
TW4: Houn . . . 7M 9
TW10: Ham . . . 5J 25
W4 . . . 1C 12
Dukes Cl. GU6: Cranl . . . 8B 156
GU9: U Hal . . . 6F 108
TW12: Hamp . . . 6N 23
TW15: A'ford . . . 5D 22
Dukes Ct. GU21: Wok . . . 4B 74
KT15: Addl . . . 1L 55
KT19: Ewe . . . 5D 60
SW14 . . . 5C 12
Dukes Covert GU19: Bag . . . 1J 51
Duke's Dr. GU7: Goda . . . 4E 132
Dukes Ga. W4 . . . 1B 12
Dukes Grn. Av. TW14: Felt . . . 8H 9
Dukes Head RH10: Craw D . . . 7B 164
Dukes Head Pas.
TW12: Hamp . . . 8C 24
Dukes Hill CR3: Wold . . . 7H 85
GU19: Bag . . . 1J 51
Dukeshill Rd. RG42: Brac . . . 9N 15
Dukes La. SL4: W'sor . . . 8D 18
SL5: Asc . . . 8D 18
Dukes Pk. GU11: Alde . . . 7B 90
Dukes Ride RG45: Crow . . . 3D 48
RH5: Nth H . . . 8K 119
Dukes Rd. KT12: Hers . . . 2L 57
RH5: Newd . . . 4A 160

Dukes Sq.—Edgehill Ct.

Dukes Sq. RH12: Hors 7J **197**
Dukes Ter. GU11: Alde 1N **109**
Duke St. GU21: Wok 4B **74**
SL4: W'sor 3F **4**
SM1: Sut 1B **62**
TW9: Rich 7K **11**
Dukes Wlk. GU9: U Hal 6F **108**
Dukes Wood RG45: Crow 1G **49**
(not continuous)
Dulverton Rd. CR2: Sels 6F **64**
Dumas Cl. GU46: Yate 1B **68**
Dumbarton Ct. SW2 . . . . .1J **29**
Dumbarton Rd. SW2 . . . . .1J **29**
Dumbleton Cl. KT1: K Tham . . .3P **25**
Dump Rd. GU14: Farnb 4K **89**
Dumsey Eyot KT16: Chert 6N **37**
Dumville Dr. RH9: Gods 9E **104**
Dunally Pk. TW17: Shep 6E **38**
Dunbar Av. BR3: Beck 3H **47**
SW16 . . . . .1L **45**
Dunbar Ct. KT12: Wal T 7K **39**
SM1: Sut 2B **62**
Dunbar Rd. GU16: Frim 7D **70**
KT3: N Mal 3B **42**
Dunbar St. SE27 . . . . .4N **29**
Dunboe Pl. TW17: Shep 6D **38**
Dunboyne Pl. SL4: O Win 7K **5**
Dunbridge Ho. *SW15* *9E **12***
(off Highcliffe Dr.)
Duncan Dr. GU1: Guil 2C **114**
RG40: W'ham 3C **30**
Duncan Gdns. TW18: Stain 7J **21**
Duncannon Cres. SL4: W'sor . . .6A **4**
Duncan Rd. KT20: Tad 6K **81**
TW9: Rich 7L **11**
Duncans Yd. TN16: Weste 4M **107**
Duncombe Ct. TW18: Stain 8H **21**
Duncombe Rd. GU7: Goda . . .9G **133**
Duncroft SL4: W'sor 6C **4**
Duncroft Cl. RH2: Reig 3L **121**
Duncroft Mnr. TW18: Stain . . .5G **20**
Duncton Cl. RH11: Craw 1N **181**
Dundaff Cl. GU15: Camb 1E **70**
Dundas Cl. RG12: Brac 3N **31**
Dundas Gdns. KT8: W Mole . . .2B **40**
Dundee Rd. SE25 . . . . .4E **46**
Dundela Gdns. KT4: W Pk 1G **61**
Dundonald Rd. SW19 . . . . .8K **27**
(not continuous)
Dundonald Road Stop (CT) 8L **27**
Dundrey Cres. RH1: Mers 7J **103**
Dunedin Dr. CR3: Cate 3B **104**
Dunelm Gro. SE27 . . . . .4N **29**
Dunfee Way KT14: Byf 8N **55**
Dunford Pl. RG42: Bin 8K **15**
Dungarvan Av. SW15 . . . . .7F **12**
Dungates La. RH3: Buck 2F **120**
Dungells Farm Cl.
GU46: Yate 2C **68**
Dungells La. GU46: Yate 2B **68**
Dunheved Cl. CR7: T Hea 5L **45**
Dunheved Rd. Nth.
CR7: T Hea 5L **45**
Dunheved Rd. Sth.
CR7: T Hea 5L **45**
Dunheved Rd. W.
CR7: T Hea 5L **45**
Dunhill Point SW15 . . . . .2F **26**
Dunkeld Rd. SE25 . . . . .3A **46**
Dunkirk St. SE27 . . . . .5N **29**
Dunleary Cl. TW4: Houn 1N **23**
Dunley Dr. CR0: N Add 4L **65**
Dunlin Cl. RH1: Red 8C **122**
Dunlin Ri. GU4: Guil 1F **114**
Dunmail Dr. CR8: Pur 1B **84**
Dunmore GU2: Guil 2G **113**
Dunmore Rd. SW20 . . . . .9H **27**
Dunmow Cl. TW13: Hanw 4M **23**
Dunmow Hill GU51: Fleet 3B **88**
Dunmow Ho. KT14: Byf 9N **55**
Dunnets GU21: Knap 4H **73**
Dunnings Health & Fitness Club
. . . . .2A **186**
Dunning's Rd. RH19: E Grin . . .3A **186**
Dunnymans Rd. SM7: Ban 2L **81**
Dunottar Cl. RH1: Red 5B **122**
Dunraven Av. RH1: Salf 1F **142**
DUNSBOROUGH PARK 7L **75**
Dunsbury Cl. SM2: Sut 5N **61**
Dunsdon Av. GU2: Guil 4L **113**
DUNSFOLD 4B **174**
Dunsfold Cl. RH11: Craw 4M **181**
*SM2: Sut 4N **61***
(off Blackbush Cl.)
Dunsfold Comn.
GU8: Duns, Loxh 5B **174**
Dunsfold Ri. CR5: Coul 9H **63**
Dunsfold Rd.
GU6: Alf, Duns 5E **174**
GU6: Cranl 1C **174**
GU8: Loxh 1C **174**
RH14: Plais 2N **191**
Dunsfold Way CR0: N Add 5L **65**
Dunsford Way SW15 . . . . .9G **13**
Dunsmore Rd. KT12: Wal T 5J **39**
Dunstable Rd. KT8: W Mole . . .3N **39**
TW9: Rich 7L **11**
Dunstall Pk. GU14: Farnb 7M **69**
Dunstall Rd. SW20 . . . . .7G **27**
Dunstall Way KT8: W Mole 2B **40**
Dunstan Rd. CR5: Coul 4H **83**
Dunster Av. SM4: Mord 7J **43**
Dunster Way SM6: W'ton 7E **44**
Dunston Ct. TW18: Stain 5J **21**
Dunton Cl. KT6: Surb 7L **41**
Duntshill Rd. SW18 . . . . .2N **27**
Dunvegan Cl. KT8: W Mole 3B **40**
Dunvegan Ho. RH1: Red 3D **122**
Dupont Rd. SW20 . . . . .1J **43**
Duppas Av.
CR0: Wad 7A **200** (1M **63**)
Duppas Cl. TW17: Shep 4E **38**
Duppas Ct. CR0: Croy 5A **200**
Duppas Hill La.
CR0: Croy 6A **200** (1M **63**)
Duppas Hill Rd.
CR0: Wad 6A **200** (1L **63**)
Duppas Hill Ter.
CR0: Croy 5A **200** (9M **45**)
Duppas Rd. CR0: Wad 9L **45**
Durand Cl. SM5: Cars 7D **44**
Durban Rd. BR3: Beck 1J **47**
SE27 . . . . .5N **29**
Durbin Rd. KT9: Ches 1L **59**
Durfold Dr. RH2: Reig 3A **122**
Durfold Hill RH12: Warn 6H **179**
Durfold Rd. RH12: Hors 1K **197**
Durfold Wood RH14: Plais . . .2M **191**
Durford Cres. SW15 . . . . .2G **26**
Durham Av. TW5: Hest 1N **9**
Durham Cl. GU2: Guil 1J **113**
RH10: Craw 7C **182**
(not continuous)
SW20 . . . . .1G **43**
Durham Ct. TW11: Tedd 5E **24**
Durham Dr. GU16: Deep 5H **71**
Durham Rd. GU47: Owls 5K **49**
SW20 . . . . .9G **27**
TW14: Felt 1K **23**
Durham Wharf Dr.
TW8: Brent 3J **11**
Durkins Rd. RH19: E Grin 7N **165**
(not continuous)
Durleston Pk. Dr.
KT23: Book 3C **98**
Durley Mead RG12: Brac 4D **32**
Durlston Rd. KT2: K Tham 7L **25**
Durnford Ho. *SL4: Eton* *2G **4***
(off Slough Rd.)
Durning Pl. SL5: Asc 2M **33**
Durnsford Av. GU52: Fleet 6B **88**
SW19 . . . . .3M **27**
Durnsford Rd. SW19 . . . . .3M **27**
Durnsford Way GU6: Cranl . . .8A **156**
Durrant Way BR6: Farnb 2M **67**
Durrell Rd. SW6 . . . . .4L **13**
Durrell Way TW17: Shep 5E **38**
Durrington Av. SW20 . . . . .8H **27**
Durrington Pk. Rd.
SW20 . . . . .9H **27**
Dutch Barn Cl. TW19: Stan 9M **7**
Dutchells Copse
RH12: Hors 2L **197**
Dutch Elm Av. SL4: W'sor 3J **5**
Dutch Gdns. KT2: K Tham 7A **26**
Dutch Yd. SW18 . . . . .8M **13**
Duval Pl. GU19: Bag 4J **51**
Duxberry Av. TW13: Felt 4K **23**
Duxhurst La. RH2: Sid 5N **141**
Dwelly La. TN8: Eden 6D **126**
Dye Ho. Rd. GU8: Thur 6E **150**
Dyer Ho. TW12: Hamp 9B **24**
Dyer Rd. RG40: W'ham 1D **30**
Dyers Almhouses
RH10: Craw 2B **182**
Dyers Fld. RH6: Smal 8M **143**
Dyers La. SW15 . . . . .7G **13**
Dykes Path GU21: Wok 2E **74**
Dymchurch Cl. BR6: Orp 1N **67**
Dymes Path SW19 . . . . .3J **27**
Dymock St. SW6 . . . . .6N **13**
Dynevor Pl. GU3: Worp 8F **92**
Dynevor Rd. TW10: Rich 8L **11**
Dysart Av. KT2: K Tham 6J **25**
Dyson Cl. SL4: W'sor 6E **4**
Dyson Ct.
RH4: Dork 3J **201** (5G **119**)
Dyson Wlk. RH11: Craw 8N **181**

E

Eady Cl. RH13: Hors 6M **197**
Eagle Cl. RG45: Crow 1F **48**
SM6: W'ton 3J **63**
Eaglehurst Cotts. RG42: Bin 6H **15**
Eagle Rd.
GU1: Guil 3D **202** (3N **113**)
TW6: Lon A 6G **8**
Eagles Dr. TN16: Tats 5F **86**
Eagles Nest GU47: Sandh 6F **48**
Eagle Trad. Est. CR4: Mit 5D **44**
Ealing Pk. Gdns. W5 . . . . .1J **11**
Ealing Rd. TW8: Brent 1K **11**
Ealing Rd. Trad. Est.
TW8: Brent 1K **11**
Eardley Cres. SW5 . . . . .1M **13**
Eardley Rd. SW16 . . . . .6G **29**
Earhart Way
TW6: C'ford, Lon A 6H **9**
Earldom Rd. SW15 . . . . .7H **13**
Earle Cft. RG42: Warf 8A **16**
Earle Gdns. KT2: K Tham 8L **25**
Earle Ho. *RH19: E Grin 8B **166***
(off Badger's Way)
Earles Mdw. RH12: Hors 2N **197**
Earleswood KT11: Cob 8M **57**
Earleydene SL5: Asc 7M **33**
Earl of Chester Dr.
GU16: Deep 6H **71**
Earl Rd. SW14 . . . . .7B **12**
Earlsbourne GU52: C Cro 9C **88**
Earlsbrook Rd. RH1: Red 5D **122**
(not continuous)
EARL'S COURT 1N **13**
Earls Court Exhibition Building
. . . . .1M **13**
Earl's Ct. Gdns. SW5 . . . . .1N **13**
Earls Ct. Rd. SW5 . . . . .1M **13**
Earl's Ct. Sq. SW5 . . . . .1N **13**
Earl's Court Station (Tube) . . .1N **13**
EARLSFIELD 2A **28**
Earlsfield Ho.
KT2: K Tham 2H **203**
Earlsfield Rd. SW18 . . . . .2A **28**
Earlsfield Station (Rail) 2A **28**
Earls Gro. GU15: Camb 9C **50**
Earls Ho. TW9: Kew 3A **12**
Earlsthorpe M. SW12 . . . . .1E **28**
EARLSWOOD 5D **122**
Earlswood RG12: Brac 6N **31**
Earlswood Av. CR7: T Hea 4L **45**
Earlswood Cl. RH13: Hors . . .4M **197**
Earlswood Ct. RH1: Red 5D **122**
Earlswood Rd. RH1: Red 4D **122**
Earlswood Station (Rail) 5D **122**
Early Commons
RH10: Craw 2D **182**
(not continuous)
Easby Cres. SM4: Mord 5N **43**
Easedale Ho. TW7: Isle 8F **10**
EASHING 7C **132**
Eashing La. GU7: Eash 7C **132**
GU8: Mil 9C **132**
Eashing Point *SW15* *2G **26***
(off Wanborough Dr.)
Easington Pl. GU1: Guil 4B **114**
East Av. GU9: H End 6J **109**
KT12: Whit V 6G **56**
SM6: W'ton 2K **63**
Eastbank Rd. TW12: H Hill 6C **24**
EAST BEDFONT 1F **22**
Eastbourne Gdns.
SW14 . . . . .6B **12**
Eastbourne Rd.
RH7: Blin H, Newc, Ling
. . . . .1H **165**
RH9: Gods, S Gods 1F **124**
RH19: Fel 4J **165**
SW17 . . . . .7E **28**
TW8: Brent 1J **11**
TW13: Felt 3L **23**
W4 . . . . .2B **12**
Eastbrook Cl. GU21: Wok 3C **74**
Eastbury Ct. RG42: Brac 8L **15**
Eastbury Gro. W4 . . . . .1D **12**
Eastbury La. GU3: Comp 9D **112**
Eastbury Rd.
KT2: K Tham 1J **203** (8L **25**)
Eastchurch Rd.
TW6: Lon A 5F **8**
EAST CLANDON 9M **95**
Eastcote Av. KT8: W Mole 4N **39**
Eastcote Ho. KT17: Eps 8D **60**
Eastcote Pl. SL5: Asc 9H **17**
East Court 8B **166**
East Cres. SL4: W'sor 4C **4**
Eastcroft Ct. GU1: Guil 4C **114**
Eastcroft M. RH12: Hors 7F **196**
Eastcroft Rd. KT19: Ewe 4D **60**
East Croydon Station (Rail & CT)
. . . . .3E **200** (8A **46**)
Eastdean Av. KT18: Eps 9A **60**
East Dr. GU25: V Wat 6K **35**
SM5: Cars 5C **62**
Eastern Av. KT16: Chert 2J **37**
Eastern Bus. Pk.
TW6: Lon A 5F **8**
EASTERN INDUSTRIAL AREA
. . . . .1B **32**
Eastern La. RG45: Crow 3L **49**
Eastern Perimeter Rd.
TW6: Lon A 5G **8**
Eastern Rd. GU12: Alde 2B **110**
RG12: Brac 1B **32**
Eastern Vw. TN16: B Hil 4E **86**
Easter Way RH9: S Gods 6H **125**
EAST EWELL 6H **61**
Eastfield Rd. RH1: Red 4G **122**
Eastfields GU8: Wit 5C **152**
Eastfields Av. SW18 . . . . .7M **13**
Eastfields Rd. CR4: Mit 1E **44**
E. Flexford La. GU3: Wan 5C **112**
East Gdns. GU22: Wok 4E **74**
SW17 . . . . .7C **28**
Eastgate SM7: Ban 1L **81**
Eastgate Gdns.
GU1: Guil 4E **202** (4A **114**)
Eastgate M. RH13: Hors 7K **197**
East Grn. GU17: B'water 2H **69**
EAST GRINSTEAD 9A **166**
E. Grinstead Rd.
RH7: Ling 8N **145**
East Grinstead Sports & Country Club
. . . . .4L **185**
East Grinstead Station (Rail)
. . . . .9N **165**
East Grinstead Town Mus. . . .8B **166**
EASTHAMPSTEAD 4N **31**
Easthampstead Mobile Home Pk.
RG40: W'ham 8H **31**
Easthampstead Pk.
Crematorium & Cemetery
RG40: W'ham 7J **31**
Easthampstead Rd.
RG12: Brac 1M **31**
RG40: W'ham 3C **30**
Eastheath Av. RG41: W'ham . . .4A **30**
Eastheath Gdns.
RG41: W'ham 5A **30**
East Hill CR2: Sande 6B **64**
GU22: Wok 3E **74**
RH8: Oxt 7A **106**
RH19: D Pk 4A **166**
SW18 . . . . .8N **13**
TN16: B Hil 5D **86**
E. Hill Ct. RH8: Oxt 8A **106**
E. Hill La. RH10: Cop 4A **164**
E. Hill Rd. RH8: Oxt 7A **106**
EAST HORSLEY 7G **96**
E. India Way CR0: Croy 7C **46**
Eastlands Cl. RH8: Oxt 5N **105**
Eastlands Way RH8: Oxt 5N **105**
East La.
KT1: K Tham 5H **203** (2K **41**)
KT24: W Hors 4D **96**
Eastleigh Cl. SM2: Sut 4N **61**
Eastleigh Wlk. SW15 . . . . .1F **26**
Eastleigh Way TW14: Felt 2H **23**
EASTLY END 2G **36**
East Mall *TW18: Stain 5H **21***
(in Elmsleigh Shop. Cen.)
Eastman Ho. SW4 . . . . .1G **29**
Eastman Way KT19: Eps 6A **60**
Eastmead GU14: Farnb 1N **89**
GU21: Wok 4L **73**
East Meads GU2: Guil 4J **113**
Eastmearn Rd. SE21 . . . . .3N **29**
East M. RH12: Hors 6J **197**
EAST MOLESEY 3D **40**
Eastmont Rd.
KT10: H Wood 8E **40**
Eastney Rd.
CR0: Croy 1A **200** (7M **45**)
Eastnor Cl. RH2: Reig 5L **121**
Eastnor Pl. RH2: Reig 5M **121**
Eastnor Rd. RH2: Reig 6M **121**
East Pk. RH10: Craw 4B **182**
East Pk. La. RH7: Newc 2F **164**
East Parkside CR6: Warl 3K **85**
East Pl. SE27 . . . . .5N **29**
East Putney Station (Tube) . . .8K **13**
East Ramp TW6: Lon A 4C **8**
East Ring GU10: Tong 5E **110**
East Rd.
KT2: K Tham 1K **203** (9L **25**)
KT13: Weybr 4E **56**
RH2: Reig 2L **121**
SW19 . . . . .7A **28**
TW14: Bedf 1E **22**
EAST SHALFORD 9C **114**
E. Shalford La. GU4: Guil 8A **114**
EAST SHEEN 7B **12**
E. Sheen Av. SW14 . . . . .8C **12**
E. Station Rd. GU12: Alde . . .3N **109**
E. Stratton Cl. RG12: Brac 4D **32**
East St. GU9: Farnh 9H **109**
KT17: Eps 6L **201** (9D **60**)
KT23: Book 3B **98**
RH10: T Hil 5D **184**
RH12: Hors 7J **197**
RH12: Rusp 2C **180**
TW8: Brent 3J **11**
East Surrey Mus. 2C **104**
East Ter. SL4: W'sor 4H **5**
East Vw. Cotts.
GU6: Cranl 7L **155**
East Vw. La. GU6: Cranl 7L **155**
East Wlk. RH2: Reig 3N **121**
East Way CR0: Croy 8H **47**
GU2: Guil 3J **113**
Eastway KT19: Eps 7C **60**
RH6: Gat 3F **162**
SM4: Mord 4J **43**
SM6: W'ton 1G **62**
E. Whipley La.
GU5: Sha G 3H **155**
Eastwick Dr. KT23: Book 1A **98**
Eastwick Pk. Av.
KT23: Book 2B **98**
Eastwick Rd. KT12: Hers 3J **57**
KT23: Book 3B **98**
Eastwood KT13: Weybr 3E **56**
RH10: Craw 3D **182**
Eastwood Lodge
GU5: Braml 4B **134**
Eastwood Rd. GU5: Braml 4B **134**
Eastwood St. SW16 . . . . .7G **28**
EASTWORTH 7K **37**
Eastworth Rd. KT16: Chert 7J **37**
Eaton Ct. GU1: Guil 1C **114**
Eaton Dr. KT2: K Tham 8N **25**
Eaton Ho. *GU1: Guil 5B **114***
(off St Lukes Sq.)
Eaton Pk. KT11: Cob 1M **77**
Eaton Pk. Rd. KT11: Cob 1M **77**
Eaton Rd. GU15: Camb 2N **69**
SM2: Sut 3B **62**
TW3: Houn 7D **10**
Eatonville Rd. SW17 . . . . .3D **28**
Eatonville Vs. SW17 . . . . .3D **28**
Eaves Cl. KT15: Addl 3L **55**
Ebbage Ct. GU22: Wok 5A **74**
Ebbas Way KT18: Eps 2A **80**
Ebbisham Cen., The
KT19: Eps 6K **201** (9C **60**)
Ebbisham Cl.
RH4: Dork . . .3H **201** (5G **118**)
Ebbisham Ct. RH19: Fel 6J **165**
Ebbisham La.
KT20: Eps D, Wal H, Tad
. . . . .8E **80**
Ebbisham Rd. KT4: W Pk 8H **43**
KT18: Eps 1A **80**
Ebbisham Sports Club 7B **60**
Ebenezer Wlk. SW16 . . . . .9G **28**
Ebner St. SW18 . . . . .8N **13**
Ebor Cotts. SW15 . . . . .4D **26**
Ebury Cl. BR2: Kes 1G **67**
Ebury M. SE27 . . . . .4M **29**
Ecclesbourne Rd.
CR7: T Hea 4N **45**
Eccleshill RH5: Nth H 9J **119**
Echelforde Dr.
TW15: A'ford 5B **22**
Echo Barn La. GU10: Wrec . . .6D **128**
Echo Pit Rd.
GU1: Guil 8F **202** (7A **114**)
Eclipse, The KT10: Esh 8B **40**
Eclipse Ind. Est.
KT19: Eps 6H **201** (9B **60**)
Ecob Cl. GU3: Guil 8J **93**
Ecton Rd. KT15: Addl 1K **55**
Edar Ho. CR0: N Add 3L **65**
Eddeys Cl. GU35: H Dwn 3G **169**
Eddeys La. GU35: H Dwn 3G **168**
Eddington Cl. CR0: N Add 3M **65**
Eddington Hill
RH11: Craw 8M **181**
Eddington Rd. RG12: Brac 5K **31**
Eddiscombe Rd. SW6 . . . . .5L **13**
Eddy Rd. GU12: Alde 3A **110**
Eddystone Ct. GU10: Churt . . .9L **149**
Eddystone Wlk. TW19: Stan . . .1N **21**
Ede Cl. TW3: Houn 6N **9**
Ede Ct. KT17: Eps 8E **60**
EDENBRIDGE 2L **147**
Edenbridge Leisure Cen. 1L **147**
Edenbridge Station (Rail) . . .9K **127**
Edenbridge Town Station (Rail)
. . . . .1M **147**
Edenbridge Trad. Cen.
TN8: Eden 3M **147**
Eden Brook RH7: Ling 7A **146**
Edenbrook GU17: Haw 4L **69**
Eden Cl. KT15: N Haw 6K **55**
SL3: Lang 1C **6**
Edencourt Rd. SW16 . . . . .7F **28**
Edencroft GU5: Braml 4B **134**
Edenfield Gdns. KT4: W Pk 9E **42**
Eden Gro. Rd. KT14: Byf 9N **55**
Edenhurst Av. SW6 . . . . .6L **13**
Eden M. SW17 . . . . .4A **28**
EDEN PARK 4K **47**
Eden Pk. Av. BR3: Beck 3H **47**
(not continuous)
Eden Park Station (Rail) 4K **47**
Eden Pl. SL5: S'dale 6D **34**
Eden Rd. BR3: Beck 3H **47**
CR0: Croy 6D **200** (1A **64**)
RH11: Craw 5L **181**
SE27 . . . . .5M **29**
Edenside Rd. KT23: Book 2N **97**
Edensor Gdns. W4 . . . . .3D **12**
Edensor Rd. W4 . . . . .3D **12**
Eden St.
KT1: K Tham 4H **203** (1K **41**)
Eden Va. RH19: E Grin 7N **165**
(not continuous)
Edenvale Cl. CR4: Mit 8E **28**
Edenvale Rd. CR4: Mit 8E **28**
Edenvale St. SW6 . . . . .5N **13**
Eden Valley Mus., The 2L **147**
Eden Vs. TN8: Eden 4M **147**
Eden Wlk.
KT1: K Tham 4H **203** (1L **41**)
Eden Way BR3: Beck 4J **47**
CR6: Warl 5H **85**
Ederline Av. SW16 . . . . .2K **45**
Edes Fld. RH2: Reig 5K **121**
Edgar Cl. RH10: Wor 4J **183**
Edgar Ct. KT3: N Mal 1D **42**
Edgarley Ter. SW6 . . . . .4K **13**
Edgar Rd. CR2: Sande 5A **64**
TN16: Tats 8F **86**
TW4: Houn 1N **23**
Edgbarrow Ct. RG45: Crow 4F **48**
Edgbarrow Ri. GU47: Sandh . . .5F **48**
Edgbarrow Sports Cen. 4H **49**
Edgcumbe Pk. Dr.
RG45: Crow 2F **48**
Edge, The 9B **170**
Edgeborough Ct. GU1: Guil . . .4B **114**
Edge Cl. KT13: Weybr 4B **56**
Edgecombe Ho. SW19 . . . . . . .2K **27**
Edgecoombe CR2: Sels 4F **64**
Edgecoombe Cl.
KT2: K Tham 8C **26**
Edgedale Cl. RG45: Crow 3G **49**
Edgefield Cl. GU6: Cranl 6L **155**
RH1: Red 8E **122**
Edge Hill SW19 . . . . .8J **27**
Edgehill GU1: Guil 4B **114**
Edge Hill Ct. SW19 . . . . .8J **27**
Edgehill Ct. KT12: Wal T 7K **39**

A-Z Surrey 235

Fawcett Ct.—Fiske Ct.

Fawcett Ct. *SW10* *2N 13*
(off Fawcett St.)
Fawcett Rd.
CR0: Croy 5A 200 (9N 45)
SL4: W'sor 4E 4
Fawcett St. SW10 . . . . 2N 13
Fawcus Cl. KT10: Clay 3E 58
Fawe Pk. M. SW15 . . . . 7L 13
Fawe Pk. Rd. SW15 . . . . 7L 13
Fawler Mead RG12: Brac 3D 32
Fawley Cl. GU6: Cranl 8A 156
Fawn Dr. GU12: Alde 1C 110
Fawns Mnr. Cl. TW14: Bedf . . . 2E 22
Fawns Mnr. Rd. TW14: Bedf . . 2E 22
Fawsley Cl. SL3: Poy 3G 6
Fay Cotts. RH12: Fay 5D 180
FAYGATE 8E 180
Faygate Bus. Cen.
RH12: Fay 8E 180
Faygate La. RH9: S Gods 9H 125
RH12: Rusp, Fay 2D 180
Faygate Rd. SW2 . . . . 3K 29
Faygate Station (Rail) 8E 180
Fayland Av. SW16 . . . . 6G 28
Fay Rd. RH12: Hors 3J 197
Fays Pas.
GU1: Guil 5B 202 (4M 113)
Fearn Cl. KT24: E Hor 7F 96
Fearnley Cres.
TW12: Hamp 6M 23
Featherbed La. CR0: Sels 4J 65
CR6: Warl 4J 65
Feathercombe La.
GU8: Hamb 6G 153
Feathers La. TW19: Wray 3C 20
Featherstone RH7: Blin H . . . 3G 145
Fee Farm Rd. KT10: Clay 4F 58
FELBRIDGE 6K 165
Felbridge Av. RH10: Craw . . . 2H 183
Felbridge Cen., The
RH19: E Grin 7K 165
Felbridge Cl. GU16: Frim 4D 70
RH19: E Grin 7M 165
SM2: Sut 5N 61
SW16 . . . . 5L 29
Felbridge Ct. RH19: E Grin . . . 6K 165
TW13: Felt *2J 23*
(off High St.)
UB3: Harl 2E 8
Felbridge Rd. RH19: Fel 7G 164
Felcot Rd. RH19: Fel 7F 164
Felcott Cl. KT12: Hers 9K 39
Felcott Rd. KT12: Hers 9K 39
FELCOURT 2M 165
Felcourt La. RH7: Felc 1L 165
RH19: Felc 2L 165
Felcourt Rd.
RH7: Felc, Ling 3M 165
RH19: D Pk, Felc, E Grin
. . . . 3M 165
Feld, The RH19: E Grin 7K 165
FELDAY 6J 137
Felday Glade RH5: H Mary . . . 6J 137
Felday Ho's. RH5: H Mary . . . 4J 137
Felday Rd. RH5: A Ham 9G 116
FELDEMORE 5K 137
Feldemore Cotts.
RH5: H Mary 5K 137
Felden St. SW6 . . . . 4L 13
Felgate M. W6 . . . . 1G 12
Felix Dr. GU4: W Cla 6K 95
Felix La. TW17: Shep 5F 38
Felix Rd. KT12: Wal T 5H 39
Felland Way RH2: Reig 7B 122
Fellbrook TW10: Ham 4H 25
Fellcott Way RH12: Hors 7F 196
Fellmongers Yd.
CR0: Croy 4B 200
Fellowes Rd. SM5: Cars 9C 44
Fellow Grn. GU24: W End 9C 52
Fellow Grn. Rd.
GU24: W End 9C 52
Fellows Rd. GU14: Farnb 4B 90
Fell Rd.
CR0: Croy 4C 200 (9N 45)
(not continuous)
Felmingham Rd. SE20 . . . . . . 1F 46
Felnex Trad. Est.
SM6: W'ton 8E 44
Felsberg Rd. SW2 . . . . 1J 29
Felsham M. *SW15* *6J 13*
(off Felsham Rd.)
Felsham Rd. SW15 . . . . 6H 13
Felstead Rd. KT19: Eps 7C 60
FELTHAM 3H 23
Feltham Airparcs Leisure Cen.
. . . . 3L 23
Feltham Arenas 1H 23
Feltham Av. KT8: E Mol 3E 40
Felthambrook Ind. Est.
TW13: Felt 4J 23
Felthambrook Way
TW13: Felt 4J 23
Feltham Bus. Complex
TW13: Felt 3J 23
Feltham Corporate Cen.
TW13: Felt 4J 23
FELTHAMHILL 6G 23
Feltham Hill Rd.
TW15: A'ford 6B 22
Feltham Rd. CR4: Mit 1D 44
RH1: Red 8D 122
TW15: A'ford 5B 22
Feltham Station (Rail) 2J 23
Feltham Wlk. RH1: Red 8D 122
Felwater Ct. RH19: E Grin 7K 165
Fenby Cl. RH13: Hors 4A 198
Fenchurch Rd. RH10: Craw . . . 5F 182
Fencote RG12: Brac 5B 32
Fendall Rd. KT19: Ewe 2B 60
Fender Ho. RH12: Hors 6H 197
Fenelon Pl. W14 . . . . 1L 13
Fengates Rd. RH1: Red 3C 122
Fenhurst Cl. RH12: Hors 7F 196
Fen La. SW13 . . . . 4G 12
Fenmore Rd. CR8: Ken 7A 84
Fennel Cl. CR0: Croy 7G 47
GU1: Guil 9D 94
GU14: Cove 1G 89
SL5: Asc 4L 33
Fennel Cres. RH11: Craw 7N 181
Fennells Mead KT17: Ewe 5E 60
Fenner Ho. KT12: Hers 1H 57
Fenn Ho. TW7: Isle 4H 11
Fennscombe Ct.
GU24: W End 9B 52
Fenns La. GU24: W End 9B 52
Fenns Way GU21: Wok 2A 74
Fenn's Yd. GU9: Farnh 1G 128
Fenton Av. TW18: Stain 7L 21
Fenton Cl. RH1: Red 3E 122
Fenton Ho. TW5: Hest 2A 10
Fenton Rd. RH1: Red 3E 122
Fentum Rd. GU2: Guil 1K 113
Fenwick Cl. GU21: Wok 5L 73
Fenwick Pl. CR2: S Croy 4M 63
Ferbies GU52: Fleet 7B 88
Ferguson Av.
KT5: Surb 8M 203 (4M 41)
Ferguson Cl. BR2: Brom 2N 47
Fermandy La.
RH10: Craw D 9D 164
Fermor Dr. GU11: Alde 1L 109
Fern Av. CR4: Mit 3H 45
Fernbank Av. KT12: Wal T 6M 39
Fernbank Cres. SL5: Asc 9H 17
Fernbank Pl. SL5: Asc 9G 17
Fernbank Rd. KT15: Addl 2J 55
SL5: Asc 2G 33
Fernbrae Cl. GU10: Rowl 8G 128
Fern Cl. CR6: Warl 5H 85
GU16: Frim 3F 70
RG45: Crow 9G 30
Fern Cotts. RH5: A Ham 8F 116
Fern Ct. GU12: Ash 3D 110
Ferndale GU3: Guil 1H 113
Ferndale Av. KT16: Chert 9G 36
TW4: Houn 6M 9
Ferndale Rd. GU21: Wok 3B 74
GU52: C Cro 9A 88
SE25 . . . . 4E 46
SM7: Ban 3L 81
TW15: A'ford 6M 21
Ferndale Way BR6: Farnb 2M 67
Fernden Hgts. GU27: Hasl . . . 6F 188
Fernden La.
GU27: Hasl, Fern, K Grn
. . . . 5F 188
Fernden Ri. GU7: Goda 4H 133
Ferndown RH6: Horl 6E 142
RH10: Craw 8H 163
Ferndown Cl. GU1: Guil 4C 114
SM2: Sut 3B 62
Ferndown Ct.
GU1: Guil 1B 202 (2M 113)
Ferndown Gdns.
GU14: Cove 1K 89
KT11: Cob 9K 57
Fern Dr. GU51: C Cro 7A 88
Fernery, The TW18: Stain 6G 21
Ferney Ct. KT14: Byf 7M 55
Ferney Meade Way
TW7: Isle 5G 11
Ferney Rd. KT14: Byf 8M 55
Fern Gro. TW14: Felt 1J 23
Ferngrove Cl. KT22: Fetc 1E 98
Fernham Rd. CR7: T Hea 2N 45
FERNHILL 3J 163
Fernhill KT22: Oxs 1D 78
Fernhill Cl. GU9: U Hal 6G 109
GU17: Haw 5L 69
GU22: Wok 7M 73
RG42: Brac 8L 15
RH10: Craw D 9E 164
Fernhill Dr. GU9: U Hal 6G 109
Fernhill Gdns. KT2: K Tham . . . 6K 25
Fernhill La. GU9: U Hal 6G 109
GU17: Haw 5K 69
GU22: Wok 7M 73
(not continuous)
Fernhill Pk. GU22: Wok 7M 73
Fern Hill Pl. BR6: Farnb 2L 67
Fernhill Rd. GU14: Cove 9K 69
GU17: Haw 4K 69
RH6: Horl 3H 163
Fernhill Wlk. GU17: Haw 5L 69
Fernhurst Cl. RH11: Craw . . . 1N 181
Fernhurst Rd. CR0: Croy 6E 46
SW6 . . . . 4K 13
TW15: A'ford 5D 22
Ferniehurst GU15: Camb 2D 70
Fernihough Cl.
KT13: Weybr 6B 56
Fernlands Cl. KT16: Chert . . . 9G 37
Fern La. TW5: Hest 1N 9
Fernlea KT23: Book 2B 98
Fernlea Pl. KT11: Cob 7L 57
Fernlea Rd. CR4: Mit 1E 44
SW12 . . . . 2F 28
Fernleigh Cl. CR0: Wad 1L 63
KT12: Wal T 9J 39
Fernleigh Ri. GU16: Deep 7G 71
Fernley Ho. GU7: Goda 3H 133
Fern Rd. GU7: Goda 5J 133
Ferns, The GU9: U Hal 5H 109
GU14: Farnb 5B 90
Ferns Cl. CR2: Sande 6E 64
Fernshaw Rd. SW10 . . . . 2N 13
Fernside Av. TW13: Felt 5J 23
Fernside Rd. SW12 . . . . 2D 28
Ferns Mead GU9: Farnh 2F 128
Fernthorpe Rd. SW16 . . . . 7G 28
Fern Towers CR3: Cate 3D 104
Fern Wlk. TW15: A'ford 6M 21
Fern Way RH12: Hors 3K 197
Fernwood CR0: Sels 5H 65
SW19 . . . . 2L 27
Fernwood Av. SW16 . . . . 5H 29
Feroners Cl. RH10: Craw 5E 182
Feroners Ct. *RH10: Craw* *5E 182*
(off Feroners Cl.)
Ferrard Cl. SL5: Asc 9H 17
Ferraro Cl. TW5: Hest 2A 10
Ferrers Av. SM6: Bedd 1H 63
Ferrers Rd. SW16 . . . . 6H 29
Ferrier Ind. Est. *SW18* *7N 13*
(off Ferrier St.)
Ferrier St. SW18 . . . . 7N 13
Ferriers Way KT18: Tat C 5H 81
Ferring Cl. RH11: Craw 2N 181
Ferris Av. CR0: Croy 9J 47
Ferry Av. TW18: Stain 8G 21
Ferry La. GU2: Guil 7M 113
KT16: Chert 5J 37
SW13 . . . . 2E 12
TW8: Brent 2L 11
TW9: Kew 2M 11
TW17: Shep 7B 38
TW18: Lale 2L 37
TW19: Wray 3D 20
Ferrymoor TW10: Ham 4H 25
Ferry Quays *TW8: Brent* *3K 11*
(off Point Wharf La.)
TW8: Brent 2L 11
(Ferry La.)
Ferry Rd. KT7: T Dit 5H 41
KT8: W Mole 2A 40
SW13 . . . . 3F 12
TW1: Twick 2H 25
TW11: Tedd 6H 25
Ferry Sq. TW8: Brent 3L 11
Ferry Wharf TW8: Brent 3L 11
Festing Rd. SW15 . . . . 6J 13
Festival Ct. RH10: Craw 5G 183
SM1: Sut 6N 43
Festival Wlk. SM5: Cars 1D 62
FETCHAM 1D 98
Fetcham Comn. La.
KT22: Fetc 8B 78
FETCHAM DOWNS 4D 98
Fetcham Pk. Dr. KT22: Fetc . . . 1E 98
Fettes Rd. GU6: Cranl 7B 156
FICKLESHOLE 1N 85
Fiddicroft Av. SM7: Ban 1N 81
Field Cl. CR2: Sande 1E 84
GU4: Guil 1F 114
KT8: W Mole 4B 40
KT9: Ches 2J 59
TW4: C'ford 4J 9
UB3: Harl 3D 8
FIELDCOMMON 6N 39
Fieldcommon La.
KT12: Wal T 7M 39
Field Ct. RH8: Oxt 5A 106
SW19 . . . . 4M 27
Field Dr. TN8: Eden 9M 127
Field End CR5: Coul 1H 83
GU9: Farnh 8L 109
GU24: W End 9C 52
Fieldend RH12: Hors 3N 197
TW1: Twick 5F 24
Fieldend Rd. SW16 . . . . 9G 29
Fielden Pl. RG12: Brac 1B 32
Fielders Grn. GU1: Guil 3C 114
Fieldfare Av. GU46: Yate 9A 48
Fieldfare Dr. RG12: Brac 3J 31
Fieldgate Ct. KT11: Cob 1H 77
Fieldgate La. CR4: Mit 1C 44
Field Ho. Cl. SL5: Asc 7L 33
Fieldhouse Rd. SW12 . . . . 2G 29
Fieldhouse Vs. SM7: Ban 2C 82
Fieldhurst SL3: Lang 1B 6
Fieldhurst Cl. KT15: Addl 2K 55
Fielding Av. TW2: Twick 4C 24
Fielding Gdns. RG45: Crow . . . 3G 48
Fielding Ho. *W4* *2D 12*
(off Devonshire Rd.)
Fielding M. *SW13* *2G 12*
(off Jenner Pl.)
Fielding Rd. GU47: C Tow 9K 49
Fieldings, The GU21: Wok 3J 73
RH6: Horl 7F 142
SM7: Ban 4L 81
Field La. GU7: Goda 4J 133
GU16: Frim 5B 70
(not continuous)
TW8: Brent 3J 11
TW11: Tedd 6G 24
Field Pk. RG12: Brac 9B 16
Fieldpark Gdns. CR0: Croy 7H 47
Field Path GU14: Cove 5L 69
FIELD PLACE 3D 196
Field Pl. GU7: Goda 4H 133
KT3: N Mal 5E 42
Field Pl. Cotts.
RH12: Bro H 3D 196
Field Rd. GU14: Cove 5L 69
TW14: Felt 9J 9
W6 . . . . 1K 13
Fieldsend Rd. SM3: Chea 2K 61
Fieldside Cl. BR6: Farnb 1L 67
Field Stores App.
GU11: Alde 1A 110
Field Vw. TW13: Felt 5E 22
TW20: Egh 6E 20
Fieldview RH6: Horl 7F 142
SW18 . . . . 2B 28
Field Vw. Cotts.
GU7: Goda 7E 132
Fieldview Ct. TW18: Stain 6J 21
Field Wlk. *RH6: Horl* *8D 142*
(off Ct. Lodge Rd.)
RH6: Smal 7N 143
Field Way GU10: Tong 5D 110
GU12: Alde 1C 110
GU23: Rip 3H 95
Fieldway CR0: N Add 4L 65
GU27: Hasl 1G 189
Fieldway Stop (CT) 4L 65
Fifehead Cl. TW15: A'ford 7N 21
Fife Rd.
KT1: K Tham . . . 3J 203 (1L 41)
(not continuous)
SW14 . . . . 8B 12
Fife Way KT23: Book 3A 98
Fifield La. GU10: Fren 9H 129
Fifteenth Av. KT20: Lwr K 4L 101
Fifth Av. KT20: K'wood 3K 101
Fifth Cross Rd. TW2: Twick . . . 3D 24
Figges Rd. CR4: Mit 8E 28
Figgswood CR5: Coul 9G 83
Filbert Cres. RH11: Craw . . . 3M 181
Filby Rd. KT9: Ches 3M 59
Filey Cl. RH11: Craw 5L 181
SM2: Sut 4A 62
TN16: B Hil 6D 86
Filmer Chambers *SW6* *4K 13*
(off Filmer Rd.)
Filmer Gro. GU7: Goda 6H 133
Filmer Rd. SL4: W'sor 5A 4
SW6 . . . . 4K 13
Finborough Ho. *SW10* *2N 13*
(off Finborough Rd.)
Finborough Rd. SW10 . . . . 1N 13
SW17 . . . . 7D 28
Finborough Theatre, The *2N 13*
(off Finborough Rd.)
Fincham End Dr.
RG45: Crow 3E 48
Finchampstead Rd.
RG41: W'ham 6A 30
Finch Av. SE27 . . . . 5N 29
Finch Cl. GU21: Knap 4F 72
Finch Cres. RH10: T Hil 4F 184
Finchdean Ho. SW15 . . . . 1E 26
Finch Dr. TW14: Felt 1L 23
Finches Ri. GU1: Guil 1D 114
Finch Rd.
GU1: Guil 3D 202 (3N 113)
Findhorn Cl. GU47: C Tow 8J 49
Findings, The GU14: Cove 6K 69
Findlay Dr. GU3: Guil 8J 93
Findon Cl. SW18 . . . . 9M 13
Findon Ct. KT15: Addl 2H 55
Findon Rd. RH11: Craw 1N 181
Findon Way RH12: Bro H 5D 196
Finlat Ct. RH10: Craw 3D 182
Finlay Gdns. KT15: Addl 1L 55
Finlays Cl. KT9: Ches 2N 59
Finlay St. SW6 . . . . 4J 13
Finmere RG12: Brac 6A 32
Finnart Cl. KT13: Weybr 1D 56
Finnart Ho. Dr. KT13: Weybr . . 1D 56
Finney Dr. GU20: Windl 3A 52
Finney La. TW7: Isle 4G 11
Finsbury Cl. RH11: Craw 7A 182
Finstock Grn. RG12: Brac 3D 32
Fintry Pl. GU14: Cove 7K 69
Fintry Wlk. *GU14: Cove* *7K 69*
(off Pennine Way)
Finucane Ct. *TW9: Rich* *6M 11*
(off Lwr. Mortlake Rd.)
Fiona Cl. KT23: Book 2A 98
Fir Acre Rd. GU12: A Va 7D 90
Firbank Dr. GU21: Wok 6L 73
Firbank La. GU21: Wok 6L 73
Firbank Pl. TW20: Eng G 7L 19
Firbank Way RH19: E Grin . . . 9N 165
Fir Cl. GU51: Fleet 5A 88
KT12: Wal T 6H 39
Fircroft GU51: Fleet 4A 88
Fircroft Bus. Cen.
TN8: Eden 9L 127
Fircroft Cl. GU22: Wok 5B 74
Fircroft Ct. GU22: Wok 5B 74
Fircroft Rd. KT9: Ches 1M 59
SW17 . . . . 3D 28
TW20: Eng G 8M 19
Fircroft Way TN8: Eden 9L 127
Fir Dene BR6: Farnb 1H 67
Firdene KT5: Surb 7B 42
Fir Dr. GU17: Haw 3J 69
Fireball Hill SL5: S'dale 6A 34
Fire Bell All. KT6: Surb 5L 41
Fire Sta. M. BR3: Beck 1K 47
Fire Sta. Rd. GU11: Alde 1N 109
Fire Thorn Cl. GU52: Fleet 6B 88
Firfield Rd. GU9: Farnh 4F 128
KT15: Addl 1J 55
Firfields KT13: Weybr 3C 56
Firglen Dr. GU46: Yate 8C 48
Fir Grange Av. KT13: Weybr . . . 2C 56
Fir Gro. KT3: N Mal 5E 42
Firgrove GU21: Wok 6L 73
Firgrove Ct. GU9: Farnh 2G 129
GU14: Farnb 1N 89
Firgrove Hill GU9: Farnh 2H 129
Firgrove Pde. GU14: Farnb 1N 89
Firgrove Rd. GU14: Farnb 1N 89
GU46: Yate 9A 48
Firlands KT13: Weybr 3F 56
RG12: Brac 4A 32
RH6: Horl 7F 142
Firlands Av. GU15: Camb 1B 70
Firle Cl. RH10: Craw 1C 182
Firle Ct. KT17: Eps 8E 60
Fir Rd. SM3: Sut 7L 43
TW13: Hanw 6L 23
Firs, The CR3: Cate 9A 84
GU3: Art 7L 113
GU24: Bis 3D 72
KT14: Byf 8M 55
KT23: Book 2C 98
RG12: Brac 4D 32
Firs Av. GU5: Braml 5C 134
SL4: W'sor 6C 4
SW14 . . . . 7B 12
Firsby Av. CR0: Croy 7G 47
Firs Cl. CR4: Mit 9F 28
GU14: Farnb 3A 90
KT10: Clay 3E 58
RH4: Dork 7G 119
Firsdene Cl. KT16: Otter 3F 54
Firs Dr. TW5: C'ford 3J 9
Firs La. GU5: Sha G 7F 134
Firs Rd. CR8: Ken 2M 83
First Av. KT8: W Mole 3N 39
KT12: Wal T 5J 39
KT19: Ewe 5D 60
KT20: K'wood 3K 101
SW14 . . . . 6D 12
First Cl. KT8: W Mole 2C 40
First Cross Rd. TW2: Twick . . . 3E 24
First Quarter KT19: Eps 7D 60
First Slip KT22: Leat 5G 79
Firstway SW20 . . . . 1H 43
Firsway GU2: Guil 2J 113
Firswood Av. KT19: Ewe 2D 60
Firth Gdns. SW6 . . . . 4K 13
Fir Tree All. *GU11: Alde* *2M 109*
(off Heathland St.)
Fir Tree Av. GU27: Hasl 2B 188
Firtree Av. CR4: Mit 1E 44
Fir Tree Cl. KT10: Esh 2C 58
KT17: Eps D 2H 81
KT19: Ewe 1E 60
KT22: Leat 1J 99
RH11: Craw 9N 161
SL5: Asc 6L 33
Firtree Cl. GU47: Sandh 6E 48
SW16 . . . . 6G 29
Fir Tree Gdns. CR0: Croy 1K 65
Fir Tree Gro. SM5: Cars 4D 62
Fir Tree Pl. TW15: A'ford 6B 22
Fir Tree Rd. GU1: Guil 9M 93
KT17: Eps D 3G 80
KT22: Leat 1J 99
SM7: Ban 1H 81
TW4: Houn 7M 9
Fir Tree Wlk. RH2: Reig 3B 122
Fir Tree Way GU52: Fleet 5C 88
Fir Wlk. SM3: Chea 3J 61
Firway GU26: G'hott 4K 169
Firwood Cl. GU21: Wok 6H 73
Firwood Dr. GU15: Camb 1A 70
Firwood Rd. GU25: V Wat 5H 35
Fisher Cl. CR0: Croy 7C 46
KT12: Hers 1J 57
RH10: Craw 5C 182
Fisher Grn. RG42: Bin 7G 15
Fisher La.
GU8: Chid, Duns 1G 191
GU12: Alde 4A 110
Fisherman KT16: Chert 7L 37
Fisherman Cl. TW10: Ham 5H 25
Fisherman's Pl. W4 . . . . 2E 12
Fishermen's Cl. GU11: Alde . . . 8C 90
Fisher Rowe Cl.
GU5: Braml 5C 134
Fishers RH6: Horl 7G 142
Fisher's Cl. SW16 . . . . 4H 29
Fishers Ct. RH12: Hors 4J 197
Fishersdene KT10: Clay 4G 58
Fisher's La. W4 . . . . 1C 12
FISHERSTREET 5C 190
Fisher St. GU8: Chid 4C 190
GU28: Chid, North 4C 190
Fishers Wood SL5: S'dale 7F 34
Fishing Temple Pk. Homes
TW18: Stain 9H 21
Fishponds Rd. BR2: Kes 2F 66
SW17 . . . . 5C 28
Fisk Cl. TW16: Sunb 7G 23
Fiske Ct. GU46: Yate 9D 48
SM2: Sut 4A 62

Fitchet Cl.—Francis Ho.

Fitchet Cl. RH11: Craw 1N 181
Fitness First Health Club
Croydon 1A 200 (7M 45)
Epsom 6J 201 (9C 60)
Fleet 4A 88
Godalming 7H 133
(off High St.)
Mitcham 1D 44
Purley 8K 63
Tooting Bec 4E 28
Fitrooms 2L 13
Fitzalan Ho. KT17: Ewe 6E 60
Fitzalan Rd. KT10: Clay 4E 58
RH13: Hors 4N 197
Fitzgeorge Av. KT3: N Mal 9C 26
W14 . . . . .1K 13
Fitzgerald Av. SW14 . . . . .6D 12
Fitzgerald Rd. KT7: T Dit 5G 40
SW14 . . . . .6C 12
Fitzhugh Dr. GU51: Fleet 2A 88
Fitzhugh Gro. SW18 . . . . .1B 28
Fitzjames Av. CR0: Croy 8D 46
W14 . . . . .1K 13
Fitzjohn Cl. GU4: Guil 9E 94
Fitzrobert Pl. TW20: Egh 7C 20
Fitzroy Cl. RG12: Brac 5M 31
Fitzroy Ct. CR0: Croy 6A 46
Fitzroy Cres. W4 . . . . .3C 12
Fitzwilliam Av. TW9: Rich 5M 11
Fitzwilliam Ho. TW9: Rich 7K 11
Fitzwygram Cl.
TW12: H Hill 6C 24
Fiveacre Cl. CR7: T Hea 5L 45
Five Acres RH10: Craw 1C 182
Five Acres Cl. GU35: Lind 4A 168
Five Oaks Cl. GU21: Wok 6G 73
Five Oaks Rd.
RH13: Slin, Bro H, Itch . . .9J 195
Five Ways Bus. Cen.
TW13: Felt 4J 23
FIVEWAYS CORNER 1L 63
Flag Cl. CR0: Croy 7G 47
Flagon Ct. CR0: Croy 6C 200
(off St Andrew's Rd.)
Flambard Way GU7: Goda . . .7G 133
Flamborough Cl.
TN16: B Hil 6D 86
Flamsteed Hgts.
RH11: Craw 8M 181
Flanchford Ho.
RH2: Reig 2M 121
(off Somers Cl.)
Flanchford Rd. RH2: Leigh . . .9E 120
RH2: Reig 5H 121
Flanders Ct. TW20: Egh 6E 20
Flanders Cres. SW17 . . . . .8D 28
Flather Cl. SW16 . . . . .6G 29
Flats, The GU17: B'water 2G 69
Flaxley Rd. SM4: Mord 6N 43
Flaxman Ho. W4 . . . . .1D 12
(off Devonshire St.)
Fleece Rd. KT6: Surb 7J 41
FLEET 4B 88
Fleetbrook Ho. SL3: Dat 4N 5
Fleet Bus. Pk. GU52: C Cro 9C 88
Fleet Cl. KT8: W Mole 4N 39
Fleet La. KT8: W Mole 5N 39
Fleet Mill GU51: Fleet 1C 88
Fleet Pond (Nature Reserve)
. . . . .2C 88
Fleet Rd. GU11: Alde 6F 88
GU14: Cove 1G 89
GU51: Cove 1G 88
GU51: Fleet 2E 88
(Cove Rd.)
GU51: Fleet 5A 88
(Reading Rd. Nth.)
KT11: Cob 8B 56
Fleetside KT8: W Mole 4N 39
Fleet Station (Rail) 2C 88
Fleetway TW20: Thor 2E 36
Fleetwood Cl. CR0: Croy 9C 46
KT9: Ches 4K 59
KT20: Tad 7J 81
Fleetwood Ct. KT14: W By 9J 55
TW19: Stan 9M 7
Fleetwood Rd. KT1: K Tham . . .2A 42
Fleetwood Sq. KT1: K Tham . . .2A 42
Fleming Cen., The
RH10: Craw 8C 162
Fleming Cl. GU14: Farnb 8B 70
Fleming Ct. CR0: Wad 2L 63
Fleming Mead CR4: Mit 8C 28
Fleming Wlk.
RH19: E Grin 3B 186
Fleming Way RH10: Craw 8C 162
TW7: Isle 7F 10
Fleming Way Ind. Cen.
RH10: Craw 7D 162
Fleming Way Rdbt.
RH10: Craw 8B 162
Flemish Flds. KT16: Chert 6J 37
Flemish Pl. RG42: Warf 8B 16
Fletcher Cl. KT16: Otter 3G 54
RH10: Craw 5C 182
Fletcher Gdns. RG42: Brac 9J 15
Fletcher Rd. KT16: Otter 3F 54
Fletchers Cl. RH13: Hors 7L 197
Fleur Gates SW19 . . . . .1J 27
FLEXFORD 3M 111
Flexford Grn. RG12: Brac 5K 31
Flexford Rd. GU3: Flex 4M 111
(not continuous)
Flexlands La. GU24: Chob 6E 52
Flint Cl. BR6: Chels 3N 67
CR0: Croy 5K 45
KT23: Book 4C 98
RH1: Red 2D 122
RH10: Craw 6F 182
SM7: Ban 1N 81
Flint Cotts. KT22: Leat 8H 79
(off Gravel Hill)
Flintgrove RG12: Brac 9B 16
Flint Hill RH4: Dork 7H 119
Flint Hill Cl. RH4: Dork 8H 119
Flintlock Cl. TW19: Stan M 7J 7
Flitwick Grange GU8: Mil 1C 152
Flock Mill Pl. SW18 . . . . .2N 27
Flockton Ho. KT13: Weybr 8B 38
Flood La. TW1: Twick 2G 25
Flora Gdns. CR0: N Add 7M 65
Floral Ct. KT21: A'tead 5J 79
Floral Ho. KT16: Chert 7H 37
(off Fox La. Sth.)
Florence Av. KT15: N Haw 7J 55
SM4: Mord 4A 44
Florence Cl. GU46: Yate 9B 48
KT12: Wal T 6J 39
Florence Ct. GU21: Knap 5F 72
SW19 . . . . .7K 27
Florence Gdns.
TW18: Stain 8K 21
W4 . . . . .2B 12
Florence Ho. KT2: K Tham . . .1M 203
Florence Rd. BR3: Beck 1H 47
CR2: Sande 5A 64
GU47: C Tow 8J 49
GU52: Fleet 7B 88
KT2: K Tham . .1M 203 (8M 25)
KT12: Wal T 6J 39
SW19 . . . . .7N 27
TW13: Felt 2J 23
Florence Ter. SW15 . . . . .4D 26
Florence Way GU21: Knap 5F 72
SW12 . . . . .2D 28
Florian Av. SM1: Sut 1B 62
Florian Rd. SW15 . . . . .7K 13
Florida Ct. TW18: Stain 5J 21
Florida Rd. CR7: T Hea 9M 29
GU4: Chil 9A 114
Florys Ct. SW19 . . . . .2K 27
Floss St. SW15 . . . . .5H 13
Flower Cres. KT16: Otter 3D 54
Flower La. RH9: Gods 8G 105
Flowersmead SW17 . . . . .3E 28
Flower Wlk.
GU2: Guil 8B 202 (6M 113)
Floyd's La. GU22: Pyr 3J 75
Floyer Cl. TW10: Rich 8M 11
Flyers Way, The
TN16: Weste 4M 107
Foden Rd. GU11: Alde 3M 109
Folder's La. RG42: Brac 8A 16
Foley M. KT10: Clay 3E 58
Foley Rd. KT10: Clay 4E 58
TN16: B Hil 5F 86
Foley Wood KT10: Clay 4F 58
Folkestone Ct. SL3: Lang 1C 6
Follett Cl. SL4: O Win 9L 5
Folly, The GU18: Ligh 8M 51
Folly Cl. GU52: Fleet 6B 88
Follyfield Rd. SM7: Ban 1M 81
Follyhatch La. GU12: Ash 1J 111
Folly Hill
GU9: Farnh, U Hal 6F 108
Folly La. RH5: Holm 4H 139
Folly La. Nth. GU9: U Hal 5G 108
Folly La. Sth. GU9: U Hal 6F 108
Fontaine Rd. SW16 . . . . .8K 29
Fontana Cl. RH10: Wor 4H 183
Fontenoy Rd. SW12 . . . . .3F 28
Fonthill Cl. SE20 . . . . .1D 46
Fontley Way SW15 . . . . .1F 26
Fontmell Cl. TW15: A'ford 6B 22
Fontmell Pk. TW15: A'ford 6A 22
(not continuous)
Fontwell Cl. GU12: Alde 2B 110
Fontwell Rd. RH10: Craw 6E 182
Footpath, The SW15 . . . . .9F 12
Forbench Cl. GU23: Rip 9K 75
Forbes Chase
GU47: C Tow 8J 49
Forbes Cl. RH10: Craw 7F 182
Forbes Ho. W4 . . . . .1N 11
(off Stonehill Rd.)
Forbe's Ride SL4: Wink 1L 17
FORCE GREEN 2M 107
Force Grn. La.
TN16: Weste 2M 107
Fordbridge Cl. KT16: Chert 7K 37
Fordbridge Ct.
TW15: A'ford 7N 21
Fordbridge Pk. TW16: Sunb . . .5G 38
Fordbridge Rd.
TW15: A'ford 7N 21
TW16: Sunb 5F 38
TW17: Shep 5F 38
FORDBRIDGE RDBT. 7N 21
Ford Cl. CR7: T Hea 4M 45
TW15: A'ford 7N 21
TW17: Shep 3B 38
Fordham KT1: K Tham 4M 203
Fordham Cl. KT4: W Pk 7G 42
Fordingbridge Cl.
RH12: Hors 7J 197
Ford La. GU10: Wrec 5G 128
Ford Mnr. Cotts.
RH7: Dorm 1D 166
Ford Mnr. Rd.
RH7: Dorm 9D 146
Ford Rd. GU22: Wok 7D 74
GU24: Bis, W End 1B 72
GU24: Chob 6F 52
KT16: Chert 7K 37
TW15: A'ford 5A 22
Fordwater Rd. KT16: Chert 7K 37
Fordwater Trad. Est.
KT16: Chert 7L 37
Fordwells Dr. RG12: Brac 3D 32
Foreman Ct. TW1: Twick 2F 24
Foreman Pk. GU12: Ash 2F 110
Foreman Rd. GU12: A Grn . . .3F 110
Forest Cl. GU22: Pyr 2F 74
KT24: E Hor 3G 96
RH10: Craw D 1E 184
RH12: Hors 4A 198
SL5: Asc 2G 33
Forest Cres. KT21: A'tead 3N 79
FORESTDALE 5J 65
Forestdale GU26: Hind 6B 170
Forestdale Cen., The
CR0: Sels 4J 65
Forest Dean GU51: Fleet 1D 88
Forest Dene Ct. SM2: Sut 3A 62
Forest Dr. BR2: Kes 1G 66
GU10: L Bou 7H 129
KT20: K'wood 8L 81
TW16: Sunb 8G 22
Forest End GU47: Sandh 6E 48
GU52: Fleet 7A 88
Forest End Rd.
GU47: Sandh 6E 48
Forester Rd. RH10: Craw 5C 182
Foresters, The
RH13: Hors 7M 197
Foresters Cl. GU21: Wok 5J 73
SM6: W'ton 4H 63
Foresters Dr. SM6: W'ton 4H 63
Foresters Sq. RG12: Brac 2C 32
Foresters Way RG45: Crow 9K 31
Forestfield RH10: Craw 6E 182
RH13: Hors 5N 197
Forest Glade GU10: Rowl 8C 128
Forest Grange
RH13: Hors, Col 3C 198
Forest Grange Mnr.
RH13: Col 4D 198
FOREST GREEN 3M 157
Forest Grn. RG12: Brac 9B 16
Forest Grn. Rd. RH5: Ockl . . .3C 158
Forest Hills GU15: Camb 2N 69
Forest La. GU35: Lind 3B 168
KT24: E Hor 2G 97
Forest Lodge RH19: E Grin . . .1B 186
Forest M. RH12: Hors 3A 198
Forest Oaks RH13: Hors 4A 198
FOREST PARK 5D 32
Forest Recreational Cen. . . .7M 197
Forest Ridge BR2: Kes 1G 67
BR3: Beck 2K 47
Forest Rd. GU22: Pyr 2F 74
KT24: E Hor, E Jun 5G 96
RG40: W'ham 7A 14
RG42: Bin 7A 14
RG42: Warf, Wink R 6C 16
RG45: Crow 2H 49
RH11: P Pot 2K 199
RH12: Hors, Col 4A 198
RH12: P Pot 2K 199
RH18: F Row 8K 187
SL4: W'sor 5A 4
(Ash La.)
SL4: W'sor 2A 18
(Plain Ride)
SL5: Asc 6C 16
SM3: Sut 7M 43
TW9: Kew 3N 11
TW13: Felt 3K 23
FOREST ROW 6H 187
Forest Row Bus. Pk.
RH18: F Row 6H 187
Forestry Rd., The
RH14: Plais 5D 192
(not continuous)
Forest Side KT4: W Pk 7E 42
Forest Vw. RH10: Craw 6E 182
Forest Vw. Rd.
RH19: E Grin 3A 186
Forest Wlk. GU6: Cranl 8H 155
Forest Way KT21: A'tead 4M 79
RG42: Warf 8E 16
RH19: E Grin 1C 186
Forge, The RH6: Char 3K 161
RH12: Warn 9E 178
UB3: Harl 2E 8
Forge Av. CR5: Coul 7L 83
Forge Bri. La. CR5: Coul 9F 82
Forge Cl. GU9: Farnh 9J 109
RH12: Bro H 4D 196
Forge Cotts. RH12: Bro H 4D 196
(off Forge Cl.)
Forge Cft. TN8: Eden 2M 147
Forge Dr. KT10: Clay 4G 58
Forge End GU21: Wok 4A 74
Forgefield TN16: B Hil 3F 86
Forge La. GU11: Alde 7L 89
RH10: Craw 2E 182
RH12: Bro H 4D 196
SM3: Chea 4K 61
Forge La. TW10: Ham 2L 25
TW13: Hanw 6M 23
TW16: Sunb 2H 39
Forge M. CR0: A'ton 2K 65
Forge Pl. RH6: Hook 1C 162
Forge Rd. RH10: Craw 2E 182
Forge Steading SM7: Ban 2N 81
Forge Wood RH10: Craw 7H 163
Forge Wood Ind. Est.
RH10: Craw 8F 162
Forrest Gdns. SW16 . . . . .2K 45
Forster Rd. BR3: Beck 2H 47
GU2: Guil 8K 93
SW2 . . . . .1J 29
Forsythia Pl. GU1: Guil 1M 113
Forsyth Path GU21: Wok 9F 54
Forsyth Rd. GU21: Wok 2E 74
Fortescue Av. TW2: Twick 4C 24
Fortescue Rd.
KT13: Weybr 1A 56
SW19 . . . . .8B 28
Forth Cl. GU14: Cove 8J 69
Fort La. RH2: Reig 8N 101
Fort Narrien GU15: Camb 9K 49
Fort Rd.
GU1: Guil 8E 202 (6A 114)
KT20: Box H 9A 100
Fortrose Cl. GU47: C Tow 8J 49
Fortrose Gdns. SW2 . . . . .2J 29
Fortune Dr. GU6: Cranl 9N 155
Forty Footpath SW14 . . . . .6B 12
Forty Foot Rd. KT22: Leat 8J 79
(not continuous)
Forum, The KT8: W Mole 3B 40
RH12: Hors 6J 197
Forval Cl. CR4: Mit 4D 44
Foskett Rd. SW6 . . . . .5L 13
Foss Av. CR0: Wad 2L 63
Fosse Way KT14: W By 9H 55
Fosseway RG45: Crow 2E 48
Fossewood Dr. GU15: Camb . . .7B 50
Foss Rd. SW17 . . . . .5B 28
Foster Av. SL4: W'sor 6B 4
Fosterdown RH9: Gods 7E 104
Foster Rd. W4 . . . . .1C 12
Fosters Gro. GU20: Windl 1M 51
Fosters La. GU21: Knap 4F 72
Foster's Way SW18 . . . . .2N 27
Foulser Rd. SW17 . . . . .4D 28
Foulsham Rd. CR7: T Hea 2N 45
Foundation Units GU1: Guil . . .8A 94
Founders Gdns. SE19 . . . . .8N 29
Foundry Cl. RH13: Hors 4L 197
Foundry Ct. KT16: Chert 6J 37
RH13: Hors 5L 197
Foundry La. GU27: Hasl 2E 188
RH13: Hors 5L 197
SL3: Hort 6D 6
Foundry M. KT16: Chert 6J 37
(off Gogmore La.)
TW3: Houn 7B 10
Foundry Pl. SW18 . . . . .1N 27
Fountain Dr. SM5: Cars 4D 62
Fountain Gdns. SL4: W'sor 6G 4
Fountain Ho. CR4: Mit 1D 44
Fountain Rd. CR7: T Hea 2N 45
RH1: Red 5C 122
SW17 . . . . .6B 28
Fountain Rdbt. KT3: N Mal 3D 42
Fountains Av. TW13: Hanw 4N 23
Fountains Cl. RH11: Craw . . .5M 181
TW13: Hanw 3N 23
(not continuous)
Fountains Gth. RG12: Brac . . .2M 31
Four Acres GU1: Guil 1E 114
KT11: Cob 9M 57
Four Elms Rd. TN8: Eden 1L 147
Fourfield Cl. KT18: Head 9B 80
Four Oaks RH18: F Row 7H 187
Four Seasons Cres.
SM3: Sut 8L 43
Four Sq. Ct. TW3: Houn 9A 10
Fourteenth Av.
KT20: Lwr K 4K 101
Fourth Av. KT20: Lwr K 3K 101
Fourth Cross Rd.
TW2: Twick 3D 24
Fourth Dr. CR5: Coul 3G 83
Four Wents KT11: Cob 1K 77
Fowler Av. GU14: Farnb 3N 89
Fowler Cl. RH10: Craw 5G 182
Fowler Rd. CR4: Mit 1E 44
GU14: Cove 2L 89
Fowlerscroft GU3: Comp 1E 132
Fowlers La. RG42: Brac 9N 15
Fowlers Mead GU24: Chob 5H 53
Fowler's Rd. GU11: Alde 7A 90
Foxacre CR3: Cate 9B 84
Foxborough Cl. SL3: Lang 1C 6
Foxborough Hill
GU5: Braml 4N 133
Foxborough Hill Rd.
GU5: Braml 4N 133
(not continuous)
Foxbourne Rd. SW17 . . . . .3E 28
Foxbridge La.
RH14: Kird, Loxw 8D 192
Foxburrows Av. GU2: Guil 3J 113
Foxburrows Ct. GU2: Guil 2J 113
Fox Cl. GU12: Alde 1C 110
GU22: Pyr 2F 74
KT13: Weybr 2E 56
RH11: Craw 9N 161
Foxcombe CR0: N Add 3L 65
(not continuous)
Foxcombe Rd. SW15 . . . . .2F 26
FOX CORNER 3F 92
Fox Covert GU18: Ligh 7L 51
KT22: Fetc 2D 98
Fox Covert Cl. SL5: S'hill 4N 33
Foxcroft GU52: C Cro 8B 88
Fox Dene GU7: Goda 9F 132
Foxdown Cl. GU15: Camb 1A 70
Fox Dr. GU46: Yate 8C 48
Foxearth Cl. TN16: B Hil 5G 87
Foxearth Rd. CR2: Sels 6F 64
Foxearth Spur CR2: Sels 5F 64
Foxenden Rd.
GU1: Guil 4E 202 (4A 114)
Foxes Dale BR2: Brom 2N 47
Foxes Path GU4: Sut G 4B 94
Foxglove Av. RH12: Hors 2L 197
Foxglove Cl. RG42: Wink R 7E 16
TN8: Eden 9M 127
(off Wayside Dr.)
TW19: Stan 2M 21
Foxglove Gdns. CR8: Pur 7J 63
GU4: Guil 1E 114
Foxglove La. KT9: Ches 1N 59
Foxglove Wlk.
RH11: Craw 6N 181
Foxglove Way SM6: W'ton 7F 44
Fox Gro. KT12: Wal T 6J 39
Foxgrove Dr. GU21: Wok 2C 74
Foxhanger Gdns.
GU22: Wok 3C 74
Fox Heath GU14: Cove 2H 89
Foxheath RG12: Brac 4C 32
Fox Hill BR2: Kes 2E 66
Foxhill Cres. GU15: Camb 7F 50
Foxhills GU21: Wok 4M 73
Foxhills Cl. KT16: Otter 3D 54
Fox Hills La. GU12: Ash 1G 110
Foxhills M. KT16: L'cross 9D 36
Foxhills Rd. KT16: Otter 1C 54
Foxholes KT13: Weybr 2E 56
RH12: Rudg 9E 176
Foxhurst Rd. GU12: A Va 8E 90
Foxlake Rd. KT14: Byf 8A 56
FOX LANE 6K 69
Fox La. BR2: Kes 2D 66
CR3: Cate 8M 83
KT23: Book 2M 97
RH2: Reig 9N 101
RH5: Ran C 3B 118
Fox La. Nth. KT16: Chert 7H 37
Fox La. Sth. KT16: Chert 7H 37
Foxleigh Chase
RH12: Hors 4M 197
Foxley Cl. GU17: B'water 1H 69
RH1: Red 8E 122
Foxley Ct. SM2: Sut 4A 62
Foxley Gdns. CR8: Pur 9M 63
Foxley Hall CR8: Pur 9L 63
Foxley Hill Rd. CR8: Pur 8L 63
Foxley La. CR8: Pur 7G 63
RG42: Bin 7G 14
Foxley Rd. CR7: T Hea 3M 45
CR8: Ken 1M 83
Foxon Cl. CR3: Cate 8B 84
Foxon La. CR3: Cate 8A 84
Foxon La. Gdns.
CR3: Cate 8B 84
Fox Rd. GU10: L Bou 4H 129
GU27: Hasl 2C 188
Fox's Path CR4: Mit 1C 44
Foxton Gro. CR4: Mit 1B 44
Foxwarren KT10: Clay 5F 58
Fox Way GU10: Ews 5C 108
Fox Wood KT12: Whit V 4G 56
Foxwood GU51: Fleet 2D 88
RH12: K'fold 3H 179
Foxwood Cl. GU8: Worm 1C 172
TW13: Felt 4J 23
Fox Yd. GU9: Farnh 1G 128
Foye La. GU52: C Cro 8C 88
Frailey Cl. GU22: Wok 3D 74
Frailey Hill GU22: Wok 3D 74
Framfield Cl. RH11: Craw . . .1M 181
Framfield Rd. CR4: Mit 8E 28
Frampton Cl. SM2: Sut 4M 61
Frampton Rd. TW4: Houn 8M 9
France Hill Dr. GU15: Camb . . .1A 70
Frances Ct. SE25 . . . . .2D 46
Frances Rd. SL4: W'sor 6F 4
Franche Ct. Rd. SW17 . . . . . . .4A 28
Francis Av. TW13: Felt 4H 23
Francis Barber Cl.
SW16 . . . . .6K 29
Franciscan Rd.
SW17 . . . . .6D 28
Francis Chichester Cl.
SL5: Asc 4M 33
Francis Cl. KT19: Ewe 1C 60
TW17: Shep 3B 38
Francis Ct. GU2: Guil 1L 113
KT5: Surb 8K 203
Francis Crick Rd.
GU2: Guil 4G 113
Francis Edwards Way
RH11: Craw 7K 181
Francis Gdns. RG42: Warf 8B 16
Francis Gro. SW19 . . . . .7L 27
(not continuous)
Francis Ho. SW10 . . . . .3N 13
(off Coleridge Gdns.)

Francis Rd.—Garden Cl.

Francis Rd. CR0: Croy 6M 45
CR3: Cate 9A 84
SM6: W'ton 3G 63
TW4: Houn 5L 9
Francis Way GU15: Camb 2G 70
Frank Beswick Ho.
SW6 . . . .*2L 13*
(off Clem Attlee Ct.)
Franklands Dr. KT15: Addl 4H 55
Franklin Cl. KT1: K Tham 2N 41
SE27 . . . . .4M 29
Franklin Ct. *GU2: Guil* *3J 113*
(off Derby Rd.)
GU8: Worm 9C 152
GU14: Cove *1H 89*
(off Whetstone Rd.)
Franklin Cres. CR4: Mit 3G 45
Franklin Rd. RH10: Craw 4G 183
Franklin Sq. W14 . . . . .1L 13
Franklin Way CR0: Wad 6J 45
Franklyn Cres. SL4: W'sor 6A 4
Franklyn Rd. GU7: Goda 8E 132
KT12: Wal T 5H 39
Franks Av. KT3: N Mal 3B 42
Franksfield GU5: P'lake 4F 136
(not continuous)
Frank Soskice Ho.
SW6 . . . .*2L 13*
(off Clem Attlee Ct.)
Franks Rd. GU2: Guil 9K 93
Frank Towell Ct. TW14: Felt . . .1H 23
Frant Fld. TN8: Eden 2L 147
Frant Rd. CR7: T Hea 4M 45
Fraser Gdns. RH4: Dork 4G 118
Fraser Ho. TW8: Brent 1M 11
Fraser Mead GU47: C Tow 9K 49
Fraser Rd. RG42: Brac 9N 15
Fraser St. W4 . . . . .1D 12
Fraynes Cft. GU51: Fleet 5A 88
Frederick Cl. SM1: Sut 1L 61
Frederick Gdns. CR0: Croy 5M 45
SM1: Sut 2L 61
Frederick Rd. SM1: Sut 2L 61
Frederick Sanger Rd.
GU2: Guil 4G 113
Frederick St. GU11: Alde 2M 109
Fredley Pk. RH5: Mick 7J 99
Freeborn Way RG12: Brac 9C 16
Freedown La. SM2: Sut 9N 61
Freelands Av. CR2: Sels 5G 64
Freelands Rd. KT11: Cob 1J 77
Freeman Cl. TW17: Shep 3F 38
Freeman Ct. SW16 . . . . .1J 45
Freeman Dr. KT8: W Mole 2N 39
Freeman Rd. RH12: Warn 9F 178
SM4: Mord 4B 44
Freemantle Rd. GU19: Bag 3J 51
Freemasons Pl. *CR0: Croy* *7B 46*
(off Freemasons Rd.)
Freemasons Rd. CR0: Croy 7B 46
Free Prae Rd. KT16: Chert 7J 37
Freesia Dr. GU24: Bis 3D 72
Freestone Yd. *SL3: Coln* *3F 6*
(off Park St.)
French Apartments, The
CR8: Pur 8L 63
Frenchaye KT15: Addl 2L 55
Frenches, The RH1: Red 1E 122
Frenches Ct. RH1: Red 1E 122
Frenches Rd. RH1: Red 1E 122
French Gdns. GU17: Haw 2J 69
KT11: Cob 1K 77
Frenchlands Hatch
KT24: E Hor 5F 96
French La.
GU8: Bow G, Thur 6K 151
French St. TN16: Weste 6N 107
French's Wells GU21: Wok 4L 73
FRENSHAM 3H 149
Frensham RG12: Brac 5B 32
Frensham Av. GU51: Fleet 4D 88
Frensham Cl. GU46: Yate 9A 48
Frensham Common Country Pk.
. . . . .5K 149
Frensham Ct. SW19 . . . . .2B 44
Frensham Dr. CR0: N Add 4M 65
SW15 . . . . .4E 26
(not continuous)
FRENSHAM HEIGHTS 9F 128
Frensham Hgts. Rd.
GU10: Rowl 9F 128
Frensham La. GU10: Churt . . .7F 148
GU35: Head 1D 168
GU35: Head, Lind 3B 168
Frensham Pond Sailing Club
. . . . .5H 149
Frensham Rd. CR8: Ken 1M 83
GU9: Farnh 3H 129
GU10: Fren, L Bou 3H 129
RG45: Crow 1G 49
Frensham Va.
GU10: L Bou 7G 129
Frensham Way KT17: Eps D . . .3H 81
Freshborough Ct.
GU1: Guil 4B 114
Freshfield Bank
RH18: F Row 7G 186
Freshfield Cl. RH10: Craw . . .4E 182
Freshfield Flats
KT20: Lwr K 5L 101
Freshfields CR0: Croy 7J 47
Freshford St. SW18 . . . . .4A 28
Freshmount Gdns.
KT19: Eps 7A 60
Freshwater Cl. SW17 . . . . .7E 28
Freshwater Pde.
RH12: Hors *6H 197*
(off Bishopric)
Freshwater Rd. SW17 . . . . .7E 28
Freshwood Cl. BR3: Beck 1L 47
Freshwood Dr. GU46: Yate 2C 68
Freshwoods RH12: Rudg 9E 176
Freshwood Way
SM6: W'ton 5F 62
Frewin Rd. SW18 . . . . .2B 28
Friar M. SE27 . . . . .4M 29
Friars Av. SW15 . . . . .4E 26
Friars Ct. SM6: W'ton 1F 62
Friars Fld. GU9: Farnh 9G 108
Friar's Ga. GU2: Guil 5K 113
Friars Keep RG12: Brac 3N 31
Friars La. TW9: Rich 8K 11
Friars Orchard KT22: Fetc 8D 78
Friars Ri. GU22: Wok 5C 74
Friars Rd. GU25: V Wat 3N 35
Friars Rookery
RH10: Craw 3D 182
Friars Stile Pl. TW10: Rich 9L 11
Friars Stile Rd. TW10: Rich . . .9L 11
Friars Way KT16: Chert 5J 37
Friars Wood CR0: Sels 5H 65
Friary, The
GU1: Guil 5B 202 (4M 113)
SL4: O Win 9M 5
Friary Bri.
GU1: Guil 6B 202 (5M 113)
Friary Ct. GU21: Wok 5J 73
FRIARY ISLAND 9M 5
Friary Island TW19: Wray 9M 5
Friary Pas.
GU1: Guil 6B 202 (5M 113)
Friary Rd. SL5: Asc 5L 33
TW19: Wray 1M 19
(not continuous)
Friary St.
GU1: Guil 6B 202 (5N 113)
Friary Way RH10: Craw 4B 182
Friday Rd. CR4: Mit 8D 28
FRIDAYS HILL 9F 188
FRIDAY STREET 3N 137
Friday St. RH5: Ockl 6D 158
RH12: Rusp 4L 179
RH12: Warn 1E 196
Friday St. Rd.
RH5: A Com 3M 137
Friend Av. GU12: Alde 3B 110
Friends Cl. RH11: Craw 9B 162
Friendship Way RG12: Brac . . .2N 31
Friends Rd.
CR0: Croy 4D 200 (9A 46)
CR8: Pur 8M 63
Friends Wlk. TW18: Stain 6H 21
Friesian Cl. GU51: Fleet 1C 88
FRIMLEY 6A 70
Frimley Aqueduct 9E 70
Frimley Av. SM6: W'ton 2J 63
Frimley Bus. Pk.
GU16: Frim 6A 70
Frimley By-Pass
GU16: Frim 6A 70
Frimley Cl. CR0: N Add 4M 65
SW19 . . . . .3K 27
Frimley Cres. CR0: N Add 4M 65
Frimley Gdns. CR4: Mit 2C 44
FRIMLEY GREEN 8D 70
Frimley Grn. Rd.
GU16: Frim, Frim G 5B 70
Frimley Gro. Gdns.
GU16: Frim 5B 70
Frimley Hall Dr.
GU15: Camb 9D 50
Frimley High St.
GU16: Frim 6A 70
Frimley Lodge Pk.
GU16: Frim G 9D 70
FRIMLEY RIDGE 3F 70
Frimley Rd. GU12: A Va 4E 90
GU15: Camb 1M 69
GU16: Camb, Frim 5A 70
KT9: Ches 2K 59
Frimley Station (Rail) 6A 70
Frinton Rd. SW17 . . . . .7E 28
Friston St. SW6 . . . . .5N 13
Friston Wlk. RH11: Craw 1M 181
Fritham Cl. KT3: N Mal 5D 42
FRITHEND 6A 148
Frith End Rd. GU35: Slea 5A 148
FRITH HILL 5G 132
Frith Hill Rd. GU7: Goda 4G 133
GU16: Deep, Frim 5E 70
Frith Knowle KT12: Hers 2J 57
Frith Pk. RH19: E Grin 7A 166
Frith Rd.
CR0: Croy 3B 200 (8N 45)
Friths Dr. RH2: Reig 9N 101
Frithwald Rd. KT16: Chert 6H 37
Frobisher RG12: Brac 6A 32
Frobisher Cl. CR8: Ken 4N 83
Frobisher Ct. SM3: Chea 4K 61
Frobisher Cres. TW19: Stan 1N 21
Frobisher Gdns. GU1: Guil . . .2C 114
TW19: Stan 1N 21
Frodsham Way GU47: Owls 5K 49
Froggetts La.
RH5: W'wood 9K 157
Frog Gro. La.
GU3: Wood V 1C 112
Froghall Dr. RG40: W'ham 2D 30
FROGHOLE 1M 127
Froghole La. TN8: Weste 1M 127
TN16: Weste 1M 127
Frog La. GU4: Sut G 3A 94
RG12: Brac 2M 31
FROGMORE
GU17 . . . . .1H 69
SL4 . . . . .6J 5
Frogmore SW18 . . . . .8M 13
Frogmore Border SL4: W'sor . . .6H 5
Frogmore Cl. SM3: Chea 9J 43
Frogmore Ct.
GU17: B'water 2H 69
UB2: S'hall 1N 9
Frogmore Dr. SL4: W'sor 4H 5
Frogmore Gdns. SM3: Chea . . .1K 61
Frogmore Gro.
GU17: B'water 2H 69
Frogmore House 5J 5
Frogmore Leisure Cen. *1E 68*
(off Potley Hill Rd.)
Frogmore Pk. Dr.
GU17: B'water 2H 69
Frogmore Rd.
GU17: B'water 1G 69
Frome Cl. GU14: Cove 8J 69
Fromondes Rd. SM3: Chea 2K 61
Fromow Gdns. GU20: Windl . . .3A 52
Froxfield Down RG12: Brac . . .4D 32
Fruen Rd. TW14: Felt 1G 23
Fry Cl. RH11: Craw 8N 181
Fryday Gro. M. *SW12* *1G 29*
(off Weir Rd.)
Fryern Wood CR3: Cate 2N 103
Frylands Ct. CR0: N Add 7M 65
Fry La. GU19: Bag 5H 51
Frymley Vw. SL4: W'sor 4A 4
Fry's Acre GU12: A Va 1E 110
Fry's La. GU46: Yate 8D 48
Fryston Av. CR0: Croy 8D 46
CR5: Coul 1F 82
Fuchsia Way GU24: W End 9B 52
Fuel Farm Rd. RH6: Gat 1C 162
Fugelmere Rd. GU51: Fleet . . .3D 88
Fugelmere Wlk.
GU51: Fleet 3D 88
Fulbourn KT1: K Tham 4M 203
Fulbourne Cl. RH1: Red 1C 122
Fulbrook Av. KT15: N Haw 7J 55
Fulford Ho. KT19: Ewe 4C 60
Fulford Rd. CR3: Cate 8A 84
KT19: Ewe 4C 60
Fulfords Hill RH13: Itch 9A 196
Fulfords Rd. RH13: Itch 9B 196
FULHAM 5K 13
FULHAM BROADWAY 3M 13
Fulham B'way. SW6 . . . . .3M 13
Fulham B'way. Shop. Cen.
SW6 . . . .*3M 13*
(off Fulham B'way.)
Fulham Broadway Station (Tube)
. . . . .3M 13
Fulham Cl. RH11: Craw 7N 181
Fulham Ct. SW6 . . . . .4M 13
Fulham FC 4J 13
Fulham High St. SW6 . . . . .5K 13
Fulham Palace 5K 13
Fulham Pal. Rd. SW6 . . . . .1H 13
W6 . . . . .1H 13
Fulham Pk. Gdns.
SW6 . . . . .5L 13
Fulham Pk. Rd. SW6 . . . . .5L 13
Fulham Pools 2K 13
Fulham Rd. SW6 . . . . .5K 13
(Fulham High St.)
SW6 . . . . .3N 13
(King's Rd.)
SW10 . . . . .3N 13
Fullbrook La. GU8: Els 6G 130
Fullbrooks Av. KT4: W Pk 7E 42
Fullbrook School Sports Cen.
. . . . .8J 55
Fullers Av. KT6: Surb 8M 41
Fullers Farm Rd.
KT24: W Hors 2B 116
Fuller's Griffin Brewery & Vis. Cen.
. . . . .2E 12
Fullers Hill TN16: Weste 4M 107
Fullers Rd. GU10: Rowl 7B 128
Fullers Va. GU35: Head 4E 168
Fullers Way Nth. KT6: Surb . . .9M 41
Fullers Way Sth. KT9: Ches . . .1L 59
Fuller's Wood CR0: Croy 2K 65
Fullers Wood La.
RH1: Sth N 4G 123
Fullerton Cl. KT14: Byf 1A 76
Fullerton Ct. TW11: Tedd 7G 25
Fullerton Dr. KT14: Byf 1N 75
Fullerton Rd. CR0: Croy 6C 46
KT14: Byf 1N 75
SM5: Cars 5C 62
SW18 . . . . .8N 13
Fullerton Way KT14: Byf 1N 75
Fuller Way UB3: Harl 1G 8
Fullmer Way KT15: Wood 6H 55
Fulmar Cl. KT5: Surb 5M 41
RH11: Ifi 4J 181
Fulmar Dr. RH19: E Grin 7C 166
Fulmead St. SW6 . . . . .4N 13
Fulmer Cl. TW12: Hamp 6M 23
Fulstone Cl. TW4: Houn 7N 9
Fulvens GU5: P'lake 2F 136
FULWELL 5D 24
Fulwell Pk. Av. TW2: Twick 3B 24
Fulwell Rd. TW11: Tedd 5D 24
Fulwell Station (Rail) 5D 24
Fulwood Gdns. TW1: Twick 9F 10
Fulwood Wlk. SW19 . . . . .2K 27
Furlong Cl. SM6: W'ton 7F 44
Furlong Rd. RH4: Westc 6C 118
Furlongs, The KT10: Esh 9B 40
Furlong Way RH6: Gat 2D 162
Furlough, The GU22: Wok 3C 74
Furmage St. SW18 . . . . .1N 27
Furnace Dr. RH10: Craw 5D 182
Furnace Farm Rd.
RH10: Craw 5E 182
RH19: Fel 7E 164
FURNACE GREEN 5E 182
Furnace Pde. RH10: Craw 5E 182
Furnace Pl. RH10: Craw 5E 182
FURNACE WOOD 6F 164
Furneaux Av. SE27 . . . . .6M 29
Furness SL4: W'sor 5A 4
Furness Rd. SM4: Mord 5N 43
SW6 . . . . .5N 13
Furness Row SL4: W'sor 5A 4
Furniss Ct. GU6: Cranl 8H 155
Furnival Cl. GU25: V Wat 5N 35
Furrows, The KT12: Wal T 8K 39
Furrows Pl. CR3: Cate 1C 104
Furse Cl. GU15: Camb 2G 70
Furtherfield GU6: Cranl 6N 155
Furtherfield Cl. CR0: Croy 5L 45
Further Vell-Mead
GU52: C Cro 9A 88
Furzebank SL5: S'hill 3A 34
Furze Cl. GU12: A Va 5E 90
RH1: Red 2D 122
RH6: Horl 8H 143
FURZEDOWN 6F 28
Furzedown Cl. TW20: Egh 7A 20
Furzedown Dr. SW17 . . . . .6F 28
Furzedown Rd. SM2: Sut 7A 62
SW17 . . . . .6F 28
Furze Fld. KT22: Oxs 9D 58
Furzefield RH11: Craw 2N 181
Furzefield Chase
RH19: D Pk 4A 166
Furzefield Cres. RH2: Reig . . .5A 122
Furzefield Rd. RH2: Reig 5A 122
RH12: Hors 3A 198
RH19: E Grin 6N 165
Furze Gro. KT20: K'wood 8L 81
Furze Hall KT20: K'wood 8L 81
FURZE HILL 8L 81
Furze Hill CR8: Pur 7J 63
GU10: Run 9B 110
KT20: K'wood 7L 81
RH1: Red 2C 122
Furzehill Cotts. GU24: Pirb 9N 71
Furze Hill Cres.
RG45: Crow 3H 49
Furze Hill Rd.
GU35: H Dwn 5G 168
Furze La. CR8: Pur 7J 63
GU7: Goda 3J 133
RH19: E Grin 6L 165
Furzemoors RG12: Brac 4N 31
Furzen La. RH5: W'wood 6H 177
RH12: Rudg, W'wood 6H 177
Furze Pl. RH1: Red 2D 122
Furze Rd. CR7: T Hea 2N 45
KT15: Addl 3H 55
RH12: Rudg 9E 176
Furze Va. Rd.
GU35: H Dwn 5G 169
Furzewood TW16: Sunb 9H 23
Fuzzens Wlk. SL4: W'sor 5B 4
Fydler's Cl. SL4: Wink 7M 17
Fyfield Cl. BR2: Brom 3N 47
GU17: B'water 1J 69

G

Gable Ct. *RH1: Red* *2E 122*
(off St Anne's Mt.)
Gable End GU14: Farnb 1N 89
Gables, The GU2: Guil 9L 93
GU26: G'hott 6B 170
KT13: Weybr 2D 56
KT22: Oxs 8C 58
RH6: Horl 9E 142
RH10: Cop 7M 163
RH12: Hors 4K 197
SM7: Ban 4L 81
Gables Av. TW15: A'ford 6A 22
Gables Cl. GU12: A Va 8E 90
GU14: Cove 1M 89
GU22: Wok 7B 74
SL3: Dat 2K 5
Gables Ct. GU22: Wok 7B 74
Gables Rd. GU52: C Cro 9A 88
Gables Way SM7: Ban 4L 81
Gabriel Cl. TW13: Hanw 5M 23
Gabriel Dr. GU15: Camb 2F 70
Gabriel Rd. RH10: Craw 7G 183
Gadbridge La. GU6: Ewh 6F 156
Gadbrook Rd. RH3: Betch 9B 120
Gadd Cl. RG40: W'ham 1E 30
Gadesden Rd. KT19: Ewe 3B 60
(not continuous)
Gaffney Cl. GU11: Alde 6B 90
Gafton Bank SM7: Ban 4M 81
Gage Cl. RH10: Craw D 9F 164
Gage Ridge RH18: F Row 7G 187
Gaggle Wood
RH13: M Hea 9B 198
Gainsborough RG12: Brac 5A 32
Gainsborough Cl.
GU14: Farnb 3B 90
GU15: Camb 8D 50
KT10: Esh 7E 40
Gainsborough Ct.
GU51: Fleet 4B 88
KT12: Wal T 1H 57
KT19: Ewe 3E 60
W4 . . . .*1A 12*
(off Chaseley Dr.)
Gainsborough Dr.
CR2: Sande 9D 64
SL5: Asc 2H 33
Gainsborough Gdns.
TW7: Isle 8D 10
Gainsborough Mans.
W14 . . . .*2K 13*
(off Queen's Club Gdns.)
Gainsborough Pl.
KT11: Cob 2M 77
Gainsborough Rd.
KT3: N Mal 5C 42
KT19: Eps 6B 60
RH10: Craw 7D 182
TW9: Rich 5M 11
Gainsborough Ter. *SM2: Sut* . . .*4L 61*
(off Belmont Ri.)
Gaist Av. CR3: Cate 9E 84
Gala Bingo
Feltham 3J 23
Hounslow 7A 10
Kingston upon Thames
. . . . .2K 203 (9L 25)
Thornton Heath 4L 45
Tooting 6C 28
Woking *4B 74*
(in Big Apple)
Wokingham 2B 30
Galahad Rd. RH11: Ifi 3K 181
Galata Rd. SW13 . . . . .3F 12
Galba Ct. TW8: Brent 3K 11
Gale Cl. CR4: Mit 2B 44
TW12: Hamp 7M 23
Gale Cres. SM7: Ban 4M 81
Gale Dr. GU18: Ligh 6L 51
Galena Arches *W6* *1G 13*
(off Galena Rd.)
Galena Rd. W6 . . . . .1G 13
Galen Cl. KT19: Eps 7N 59
Galesbury Rd. SW18 . . . . .1A 28
Gales Cl. GU4: Guil 9F 94
GU27: Hasl 3C 188
Gales Dr. RH10: Craw 3D 182
Gales Pl. RH10: Craw 3D 182
Galgate Cl. SW19 . . . . .2J 27
Galileo Ct. RG12: Brac 1C 32
Galleries, The *GU11: Alde* . . .*2M 109*
(off High St.)
Gallery Ct. *SW10* *2N 13*
(off Gunter Gro.)
Gallery Rd. GU24: B'wood 6A 72
Galleymead Rd. SL3: Poy 4H 7
Gallica Ct. SM1: Sut 7N 43
Gallop, The CR2: Sels 4E 64
GU46: Yate 8C 48
SL4: W'sor 1F 18
SM2: Sut 5B 62
Gallops, The KT10: Esh 9B 40
Galloway Cl. GU51: Fleet 1D 88
Galloway Path
CR0: Croy 7D 200 (1A 64)
Gallwey Rd. GU11: Alde 1N 109
Gally Hill Rd. GU52: C Cro 8A 88
Gallys Rd. SL4: W'sor 5A 4
Galpins Rd. CR7: T Hea 4J 45
Galsworthy Rd.
KT2: K Tham 8A 26
KT16: Chert 6J 37
Galton Rd. SL5: S'dale 5C 34
Galvani Way CR0: Wad 7K 45
Galveston Rd. SW15 . . . . .8L 13
Galvins Cl. GU2: Guil 9K 93
Galway Rd. GU46: Yate 2B 68
Gambles La. GU23: Rip 2L 95
Gambole Rd. SW17 . . . . .5C 28
Gamlen Rd. SW15 . . . . .7J 13
Gander Grn. Cres.
TW12: Hamp 9A 24
Gander Grn. La. SM1: Sut 9L 43
SM3: Chea 8K 43
Gangers Hill CR3: Wold 6H 105
RH9: Gods 6H 105
Ganghill GU1: Guil 1C 114
Ganymede Ct. RH11: Craw 6K 181
Gapemouth Rd. GU24: Pirb 9H 71
Gap Rd. SW19 . . . . .6M 27
Garbetts Way GU10: Tong 6C 110
Garbrand Wlk. KT17: Ewe 5E 60
Garden Av. CR4: Mit 8F 28
Garden Cl. GU5: Sha G 7F 134
GU14: Cove 2K 89
KT15: Addl 1M 55
KT22: Leat 2J 99
RH19: E Grin 2B 186
SM6: W'ton 2J 63
SM7: Ban 2M 81

Garden Cl.—Glen Ct.

Garden Cl. SW15 1H 27
TW12: Hamp 6N 23
TW15: A'ford 7D 22
Garden Ct. CR0: Croy 8C 46
TW9: Kew 4M 11
TW12: Hamp 6N 23
Gardener Gro. TW13: Hanw 3N 23
Gardeners Cl. RH12: Warn 9E 178
Gardeners Ct. RH13: Hors 7K 197
GARDENERS GREEN 6D 30
Gardeners Grn.
RH12: Rusp 3B 180
Gardener's Hill Rd.
GU10: Fren, Wrec 6G 128
Gardeners Rd.
CR0: Croy 1A 200 (7M 45)
RG42: Wink R 7F 16
Gardener's Wlk.
KT23: Book 4B 98
Gardenfields KT20: Tad 6K 81
Garden Ho., The W6 2J 13
(off Bothwell St.)
Garden Ho. La.
RH19: E Grin 2B 186
Gardenia Dr. GU24: W End 9C 52
Garden La. SW2 2K 29
Garden Pl. RH12: Hors 4J 197
Garden Rd. KT12: Wal T 5J 39
SE20 1F 46
TW9: Rich 6N 11
Garden Royal SW15 9J 13
Gardens, The BR3: Beck 1M 47
GU10: Tong 5D 110
GU24: Pirb 9C 72
KT10: Esh 1A 58
KT11: Cob 6D 76
TW14: Felt 8E 8
Garden Wlk. BR3: Beck 1J 47
CR5: Coul 1F 102
RH11: Craw 3A 182
RH12: Hors 4J 197
Gardenwood Rd.
RH19: E Grin 9L 165
Gardiner Ct. CR2: S Croy 3N 63
Gardner Ho. TW13: Hanw 3N 23
Gardner La. RH10: Craw D 1D 184
Gardner Pl. TW14: Felt 9J 9
Gardner Rd.
GU1: Guil 2C 202 (3N 113)
Garendon Gdns.
SM4: Mord 6N 43
Garendon Rd. SM4: Mord 6N 43
Gareth Cl. KT4: W Pk 8J 43
Gareth Ct. SW16 4H 29
Garfield Pl. SL4: W'sor 5G 4
Garfield Rd. GU15: Camb 1A 70
KT15: Addl 2L 55
SW19 6A 28
TW1: Twick 2G 25
Garibaldi Rd. RH1: Red 4D 122
Garland Ct. RH19: E Grin 9N 165
(off Garland Rd.)
Garland Dr. TW3: Houn 5C 10
Garland Ho. KT2: K Tham 2J 203
Garland Rd. RH19: E Grin 8N 165
Garlands Ct. CR0: Croy 6E 200
TN8: Eden 1L 147
(off Minstrels Cl.)
Garlands Rd. KT22: Leat 8H 79
RH1: Red 4D 122
Garland Way CR3: Cate 9A 84
Garlichill Rd. KT18: Tat C 4G 81
Garner Ct. TW19: Stan 9M 7
(off Jeppesen Ct.)
Garnet Rd. CR7: T Hea 3N 45
Garrad's Rd. SW16 4H 29
Garrard Rd. SM7: Ban 3M 81
Garratt Cl. CR0: Bedd 1J 63
Garratt Ct. SW18 1N 27
Garratt La. SW17 4A 28
SW18 9N 13
Garratts La. SM7: Ban 3L 81
Garratt Ter. SW17 5C 28
Garraway Ct. SW13 3H 13
(off Wyatt Dr.)
Garrett Cl. RH10: Craw 5G 183
Garrett M. GU11: Alde 3M 109
Garrick Cl. KT12: Hers 1J 57
TW9: Rich 8K 11
TW18: Stain 8J 21
Garrick Cres.
CR0: Croy 3F 200 (8B 46)
Garrick Gdns. KT8: W Mole 2A 40
Garrick Ho. KT1: K Tham 8J 203
W4 2D 12
Garrick Rd. TW9: Rich 5N 11
Garricks Ho. KT1: K Tham 4H 203
Garrick Wlk. RH10: Craw 6C 182
Garrick Way GU16: Frim G 7C 70
Garrison Cl. TW4: Houn 8N 9
Garrison La. KT9: Ches 4K 59
Garrones, The
RH10: Craw 2H 183
Garsdale Ter. W14 1L 13
(off Aisgill Av.)
Garside Cl. TW12: Hamp 7B 24
Garson Cl. KT10: Esh 2N 57
Garson La. TW19: Wray 1N 19
Garson Rd. KT10: Esh 3N 57
Garson's La. RG42: Warf 2E 16
Garston Gdns. CR8: Ken 2A 84
Garston La. CR8: Ken 1A 84
Garstons, The KT23: Book 3A 98
Garswood RG12: Brac 5B 32
Garth, The GU12: Ash 3D 110
GU14: Farnb 1B 90
KT11: Cob 9M 57
TW12: H Hill 7B 24
Garth Cl. GU9: Farnh 4F 128
KT2: K Tham 6M 25
SM4: Mord 6J 43
Garth Ct. RH4: Dork 7H 119
W4 1C 12
Garth Hunt Cotts.
RG42: Brac 7N 15
Garth Rd. KT2: K Tham 6M 25
SM4: Mord 5H 43
W4 1C 12
Garth Rd. Ind. Est.
SM4: Mord 7J 43
Garthside TW10: Ham 6L 25
Garth Sq. RG42: Brac 8N 15
Gartmoor Gdns. SW19 2L 27
Garton Cl. RH11: Ifi 4K 181
Garton Pl. SW18 9N 13
Gascoigne Rd. CR0: N Add 6M 65
KT13: Weybr 9C 38
Gasden Copse GU8: Wit 5A 152
Gasden Dr. GU8: Wit 4A 152
Gasden La. GU8: Wit 4A 152
Gaskarth Rd. SW12 1F 28
Gaskyns Cl. RH12: Rudg 1E 194
Gassiot Rd. SW17 5D 28
Gassiot Way SM1: Sut 9B 44
Gasson Wood Rd.
RH11: Craw 5K 181
Gastein Rd. W6 2J 13
Gaston Bell Cl. TW9: Rich 6M 11
Gaston Bri. Rd.
TW17: Shep 5E 38
Gaston Rd. CR4: Mit 2E 44
Gaston Way TW17: Shep 4E 38
Gatcombe Cres. SL5: Asc 9K 17
Gate Cen., The TW8: Brent 3G 11
Gateford Dr. RH12: Hors 2M 197
Gatehouse Cl. KT2: K Tham 8B 26
SL4: W'sor 7E 4
Gates, The GU51: Fleet 1D 88
Gates Cl. RH10: Craw 7G 182
Gatesden Cl. KT22: Fetc 1C 98
Gatesden Rd. KT22: Fetc 9C 78
Gates Grn. Rd. BR2: Kes 1B 66
BR4: W Wick 1B 66
Gateside Rd. SW17 4D 28
Gate St. GU5: Braml 1C 154
(not continuous)
Gateway KT13: Weybr 9C 38
Gateway, The GU21: Wok 1D 74
Gateways GU1: Guil 3C 114
KT6: Surb 8K 203
Gateways, The TW9: Rich 7K 11
(off Park La.)
Gateways Ct. SM6: W'ton 2F 62
Gatfield Gro. TW13: Hanw 3A 24
Gatfield Ho. TW13: Hanw 3N 23
Gatley Av. KT19: Ewe 2A 60
Gatley Dr. GU4: B'ham 9B 94
GATTON 6D 102
GATTON BOTTOM 4F 102
Gatton Bottom RH1: Mers 5D 102
RH2: Reig 7A 102
Gatton Cl. RH2: Reig 9A 102
SM2: Sut 5N 61
Gatton Pk. Bus. Cen.
RH1: Mers 7F 102
Gatton Pk. Ct. RH1: Red 8D 102
Gatton Pk. Rd. RH1: Red 1B 122
RH2: Reig 1B 122
Gatton Rd. RH2: Reig 1A 122
SW17 5C 28
GATWICK 5K 131
GATWICK AIRPORT 3E 162
Gatwick Airport Beehive Area
RH6: Craw 5E 162
Gatwick Airport Skyview 3E 162
Gatwick Airport Station (Rail)
3F 162
Gatwick Aviation Mus. 4L 161
Gatwick Bus. Pk.
RH6: Craw 6F 162
Gatwick Ga. RH11: L Hea 5C 162
Gatwick Ga. Ind. Est.
RH11: L Hea 5C 162
Gatwick Intl. Distribution Cen.
RH10: Craw 6F 162
Gatwick Metro Cen.
RH6: Horl 8F 142
Gatwick Rd. RH6: Craw 5E 162
RH10: Craw 9E 162
SW18 1L 27
Gatwick Rd. Rdbt.
RH6: Craw 5E 162
Gatwick Way RH6: Gat 2D 162
Gauntlett Rd. SM1: Sut 2B 62
Gavell Rd. KT11: Cob 9H 57
Gaveston Cl. KT14: Byf 9A 56
Gaveston Rd. KT22: Leat 7G 78
Gavina Cl. SM4: Mord 4C 44
Gawton Cres. CR5: Coul 9G 83
Gayfere Rd. KT17: Ewe 2F 60
Gayhouse La. RH1: Out 3A 144
Gayler Cl. RH1: Blet 2C 124
Gaynesford Rd. SM5: Cars 4D 62
Gay St. SW15 6J 13
Gayton Cl. KT21: A'tead 5L 79
Gayton Ct. RH2: Reig 2M 121
Gayville Rd. SW11 1D 28
Gaywood Cl. SW2 2K 29
Gaywood Rd. KT21: A'tead 5M 79
Gearing Cl. SW17 5E 28
Geary Cl. RH6: Smal 1M 163
Geffers Ride SL5: Asc 2J 33
Gemini Cl. RH11: Craw 5K 181
Gemmell Cl. CR8: Pur 1K 83
Genesis Bus. Cen.
RH13: Hors 5M 197
Genesis Bus. Pk.
GU21: Wok 2E 74
Genesis Cl. TW19: Stan 2A 22
Geneva Cl. TW17: Shep 1F 38
Geneva Rd. CR7: T Hea 4N 45
KT1: K Tham 8K 203 (3L 41)
Genoa Av. SW15 8H 13
Genoa Rd. SE20 1F 46
Gentles La. GU30: Pass 8F 168
GU35: Head 6F 168
Genyn Rd.
GU2: Guil 5A 202 (4L 113)
George Denyer Cl.
GU27: Hasl 1G 189
George Eliot Cl. GU8: Wit 5C 152
George Gdns. GU11: Alde 5A 110
GU51: Fleet 4C 88
George Gro. Rd. SE20 1D 46
Georgeham Rd. GU47: Owls 5J 49
George Horley Pl.
RH5: Newd 1A 160
Georgelands GU23: Rip 8K 75
George Lindgren Ho.
SW6 3L 13
(off Clem Attlee Ct.)
George Pinion Ct.
RH12: Hors 5H 197
George Rd.
GU1: Guil 3C 202 (3N 113)
GU7: Goda 4H 133
GU8: Mil 9C 132
GU51: Fleet 4C 88
KT2: K Tham 8A 26
(not continuous)
KT3: N Mal 3E 42
George Sq. SW19 2M 43
George's Rd. TN16: Tats 7F 86
George's Sq. SW6 2L 13
(off North End Rd.)
Georges Ter. CR3: Cate 9A 84
George St.
CR0: Croy 3C 200 (8N 45)
GU24: B'wood 8L 71
TW3: Houn 5N 9
TW9: Rich 8K 11
TW18: Stain 5H 21
George Street Stop (CT)
3C 200 (8N 45)
George Wyver Cl. SW19 1K 27
Georgian Cl. GU15: Camb 8C 50
RH10: Craw 4H 183
TW18: Stain 5K 21
Georgian Ct. CR0: Croy 1E 200
SW16 5J 29
Georgia Rd. CR7: T Hea 9M 29
KT3: N Mal 3B 42
Georgina Ct. GU51: Fleet 4B 88
Gerald Ct. RH13: Hors 6L 197
Geraldine Rd. W4 2N 11
Gerald's Gro. SM7: Ban 1J 81
Geranium Cl. RG45: Crow 8G 30
Gerard Av. TW4: Houn 1A 24
Gerardes Lodge
GU27: Hasl 9H 171
Gerard Rd. SW13 4E 12
Germander Dr. GU24: Bis 2D 72
Gernigan Ho. SW18 1B 28
Gerrards Mead SM7: Ban 3L 81
Gervis Ct. TW7: Isle 3C 10
Ghyll Cres. RH13: Hors 8M 197
Giant Arches Rd. SE24 1N 29
Gibbet La. GU15: Camb 7E 50
Gibbins La. RG42: Warf 6B 16
Gibbon Rd.
KT2: K Tham 1K 203 (9L 25)
Gibbons Cl. GU47: Sandh 7H 49
RH10: Craw 6G 183
Gibbon Wlk. SW15 7F 12
Gibb's Acre GU24: Pirb 1C 92
Gibbs Brook La. RH8: Oxt 5N 125
Gibbs Grn. W14 1L 13
(not continuous)
Gibbs Grn. Cl. W14 1L 13
Gibbs Way GU46: Yate 2A 68
Giblets La. RH12: Hors 1M 197
Giblets Way RH12: Hors 1L 197
Gibraltar Cres. KT19: Ewe 6D 60
Gibson Cl. KT9: Ches 2J 59
TW7: Isle 6E 10
Gibson Ct. KT10: H Wood 8F 40
SL3: Lang 1B 6
Gibson Dr. RG12: Brac 2B 32
Gibson Ho. SM1: Sut 1M 61
Gibson M. TW1: Twick 9J 11
Gibson Pl. RH10: Craw 1C 182
TW19: Stan 9L 7
Gibson Rd. SM1: Sut 2N 61
Gibsons Hill SW16 8L 29
(not continuous)
Gidd Hill CR5: Coul 3E 82
Giffard Dr. GU14: Cove 9L 69
Giffards Cl. RH19: E Grin 9B 166
Giffards Mdw. GU9: Farnh 2K 129
Giffard Way GU2: Guil 9K 93
GIGGSHILL 6G 40
Giggs Hill Gdns. KT7: T Dit 7G 40
Giggs Hill Rd. KT7: T Dit 6G 40
Gilbert Cl. SW19 9N 27
(off High Path)
Gilbert Ho. SW13 3G 13
(off Trinity Chu. Rd.)
Gilbert Rd. GU16: Camb 5A 70
SW19 8A 28
Gilbert Scott SW18 9K 13
Gilberts Lodge KT17: Eps 8D 60
Gilbert St. TW3: Houn 6C 10
Gilbert Way CR0: Wad 8K 45
SL3: Lang 1B 6
Gilbey Rd. SW17 5C 28
Gilders Rd. KT9: Ches 4M 59
Gilesmead KT18: Eps 8L 201
Giles Travers Cl.
TW20: Thor 2E 36
Gilham La. RH18: F Row 7G 187
Gilhams Av. SM7: Ban 8J 61
Gill Av. GU2: Guil 4H 113
Gillespie Ho. GU25: V Wat 3A 36
(off Holloway Dr.)
Gillett Ct. RH13: Hors 4A 198
GILLETTE CORNER 3G 11
Gillett Rd. CR7: T Hea 3A 46
Gillham's La. GU27: Hasl 4A 188
Gilliam Gro. CR8: Pur 6L 63
Gillian Av. GU12: Alde 4A 110
Gillian Cl. GU12: Alde 4B 110
Gillian Pk. Rd. SM3: Sut 7L 43
Gilliat Dr. GU4: Guil 1F 114
Gilligan Cl. RH12: Hors 6H 197
Gill Ri. RG42: Warf 7A 16
Gilmais KT23: Book 3C 98
Gilman Cres. SL4: W'sor 6A 4
Gilmore Cres. TW15: A'ford 6B 22
Gilpin Av. SW14 7C 12
Gilpin Cl. CR4: Mit 1C 44
Gilpin Cres. TW2: Whitt 1B 24
Gilpin Way UB3: Harl 3E 8
Gilsland Rd. CR7: T Hea 3A 46
Gilstead Rd. SW6 5N 13
Gingers Cl. GU6: Cranl 8A 156
Ginhams Rd. RH11: Craw 3N 181
Gipsy La. RG12: Brac 1B 32
RG40: W'ham 3B 30
SW15 6G 12
Gipsy Rd. SE27 5N 29
Gipsy Rd. Gdns. SE27 5N 29
Girdlestoneites GU7: Goda 4F 132
Girdwood Rd. SW18 1K 27
Girling Way TW14: Felt 6H 9
Gironde Rd. SW6 3L 13
Girton Cl. GU47: Owls 6K 49
Girton Gdns. CR0: Croy 9K 47
Gisbourne Cl. SM6: Bedd 9H 45
GIVONS GROVE 4J 99
Givons Gro. KT22: Leat 3H 99
Givons Gro. Rdbt.
KT22: Leat 2H 99
Glade, The BR4: W Wick 9L 47
CR0: Croy 4G 46
CR5: Coul 6L 83
GU9: H End 5J 109
GU10: B Oak 1A 148
GU16: Mytc 3E 90
KT14: W By 9G 54
KT17: Ewe 3F 60
KT20: K'wood 8M 81
KT22: Fetc 9A 78
RH10: Craw 5E 182
RH13: Hors 5N 197
SL5: S'hill 4N 33
SM2: Chea 5K 61
TW18: Stain 7K 21
Glade Cl. KT6: Surb 8K 41
Glade Gdns. CR0: Croy 6H 47
Glade Ho. GU1: Guil 4B 114
Glades, The KT6: Surb 6L 41
RH19: E Grin 9D 166
Gladeside CR0: Croy 5G 46
Gladeside Cl. KT9: Ches 4K 59
Gladeside Ct. CR6: Warl 7E 84
Glade Spur KT20: K'wood 8N 81
Gladiator Way
GU14: Farnb 5M 89
Gladioli Cl. TW12: Hamp 7A 24
Gladsmuir Cl. KT12: Wal T 8K 39
Gladstone Av. TW2: Twick 2D 24
TW14: Felt 9H 9
Gladstone Gdns.
TW3: Houn 4C 10
Gladstone Ho. CR4: Mit 1D 44
Gladstone Pl. KT8: E Mol 4E 40
Gladstone Rd. BR6: Farnb 2L 67
CR0: Croy 6A 46
KT1: K Tham 2N 41
KT6: Surb 8K 41
KT21: A'tead 5K 79
RH12: Hors 5K 197
SW19 8M 27
Gladstone Ter. SE27 6N 29
(off Bentons La.)
Gladwyn Rd. SW15 6J 13
Glamis Cl. GU16: Frim 7D 70
Glamorgan Cl. CR4: Mit 2J 45
Glamorgan Rd. KT1: H Wic 8J 25
Glanfield Rd. BR3: Beck 3J 47
GLANTY 5E 20
Glanty, The TW20: Egh 5D 20
Glanville Wlk.
RH11: Craw 6M 181
Glasbrook Av. TW2: Whitt 2N 23
Glasford St. SW17 7D 28
Glassonby Wlk.
GU15: Camb 1G 70
(not continuous)
Glastonbury Rd.
SM4: Mord 6M 43
Glayshers Hill
GU35: H Dwn 3F 168
Glazbury Rd. W14 1K 13
Glazebrook Rd.
TW11: Tedd 8F 24
Glaziers La. GU3: Norm 1M 111
Gleave Cl. RH19: E Grin 8C 166
Glebe, The GU6: Ewh 4F 156
GU17: Haw 2K 69
KT4: W Pk 7E 42
RH2: Leigh 1F 140
RH6: Horl 8D 142
RH10: Cop 7M 163
RH19: Fel 6K 165
SW16 5H 29
Glebe Av. CR4: Mit 1C 44
Glebe Cl. CR2: Sande 7C 64
GU11: Alde 5M 109
GU18: Ligh 6N 51
KT23: Book 4A 98
RH10: Craw 2C 182
W4 1D 12
Glebe Cotts. GU4: W Cla 1K 115
TW13: Hanw 4A 24
(off Twickenham Rd.)
Glebe Ct. CR4: Mit 2D 44
GU1: Guil 3B 114
GU51: Fleet 4A 88
Glebe Gdns. KT3: N Mal 6D 42
KT14: Byf 1M 75
Glebe Hyrst CR2: Sande 8C 64
Glebeland Gdns.
TW17: Shep 5D 38
Glebeland Rd. GU15: Camb 2L 69
Glebelands KT8: W Mole 4B 40
KT10: Clay 5F 58
RH10: Craw D 2D 184
RH14: Loxw 4H 193
Glebelands Mdw. GU6: Alf 8H 175
Glebelands Rd.
RG40: W'ham 1B 30
TW14: Felt 2H 23
Glebe La. GU10: Rush 5A 150
RH5: A Com 3L 137
Glebe Path CR4: Mit 2D 44
Glebe Rd. CR6: Warl 4G 84
GU6: Cranl 7M 155
GU14: Cove 9L 69
GU35: Head 4D 168
KT21: A'tead 5K 79
RH1: Mers 2F 102
RH4: Dork 3G 201 (5F 118)
SL4: O Win 8L 5
SM2: Chea 5K 61
SM5: Cars 3D 62
SW13 5F 12
TW18: Stain 6K 21
TW20: Egh 6E 20
Glebe Side TW1: Twick 9F 10
Glebe Sq. CR4: Mit 2D 44
Glebe St. W4 1D 12
Glebe Ter. W4 1D 12
Glebe Way BR4: W Wick 8M 47
CR2: Sande 7C 64
TW13: Hanw 4A 24
Glebewood RG12: Brac 4A 32
Gledhow Gdns. SW5 1N 13
Gledhow Wood
KT20: K'wood 8N 81
Gledstanes Rd. W14 1K 13
Gleeson Dr. BR6: Chels 2N 67
Gleeson M. KT15: Addl 1L 55
Glegg Pl. SW15 7J 13
Glen, The CR0: Croy 9G 47
GU9: U Hal 6H 109
KT15: Addl 2H 55
RH1: Red 5D 122
SL5: S'hill 3A 34
UB2: S'hall 1N 9
Glen Albyn Rd. SW19 3J 27
Glenallan Ho. W14 1L 13
(off North End Cres.)
Glenalmond Ho.
TW15: A'ford 4N 21
Glena Mt. SM1: Sut 1A 62
Glen Av. TW15: A'ford 5B 22
Glenavon Cl. KT10: Clay 3G 58
Glenavon Ct. KT4: W Pk 8G 43
Glenavon Gdns. GU46: Yate 2C 68
Glenbuck Ct. KT6: Surb 5L 41
Glenbuck Rd. KT6: Surb 5K 41
Glenburnie Rd. SW17 4D 28
Glencairn Rd. SW16 9J 29
Glencar Ct. SE19 7M 29
Glen Cl. GU26: Hind 3A 170
KT20: K'wood 1K 101
TW17: Shep 3B 38
Glencoe Cl. GU16: Frim 6E 70
Glencoe Rd. KT13: Weybr 9B 38
Glen Ct. GU21: Wok 6K 73
GU26: Hind 3A 170
KT14: Byf 7M 55
KT15: Addl 2H 55
TW18: Stain 8H 21

Glendale Cl.—Grange, The

Glendale Cl. GU21: Wok 5M 73
RH12: Hors 2N 197
Glendale Dr. GU4: B'ham 9E 94
SW19 ....6L 27
Glendale M. BR3: Beck 1L 47
Glendale Ri. CR8: Ken 2M 83
Glendarvon St. SW15 ....6J 13
Glendene Av. KT24: E Hor 4F 96
Glendon Ho. RH10: Craw 4B 182
Glendower Gdns.
SW14 ....6C 12
Glendower Rd. SW14 ....6C 12
Glendyne Cl. RH19: E Grin ...1C 186
Glendyne Way
RH19: E Grin 1C 186
Gleneagle M. SW16 ....6H 29
Gleneagle Rd. SW16 ....6H 29
Gleneagles Cl.
TW19: Stan 9L 7
Gleneagles Ct.
RH10: Craw 4B 182
Gleneagles Dr. GU14: Cove ...2H 89
Gleneagles Ho. *RG12: Brac* ...*5K 31*
(off St Andrews)
Gleneldon M. SW16 ....5J 29
Gleneldon Rd. SW16 ....5J 29
Glenfield Cl. RH3: Brock 7A 120
Glenfield Cotts. RH6: Char ...3J 161
Glenfield Ho. RG12: Brac 3A 32
Glenfield Rd. RH3: Brock 6A 120
SM7: Ban 2N 81
SW12 ....2G 29
TW15: A'ford 7C 22
Glen Gdns. CR0: Wad 9L 45
Glenhaven Dr. TW19: Stan M ...8J 7
Glenheadon Cl. KT22: Leat 1K 99
Glenheadon Ri. KT22: Leat 1K 99
Glenhurst GU20: Windl 1L 51
Glenhurst Cl. GU17: Haw 2K 69
Glenhurst Ri. SE19 ....8N 29
Glenhurst Rd. TW8: Brent 2J 11
Glen Innes GU47: C Tow 6L 49
Glenister Pk. Rd.
SW16 ....8H 29
Glen Lea GU26: Hind 8C 170
Glenlea Hollow
GU26: Hind 9C 170
Glenmill TW12: Hamp 6N 23
Glenmore Cl. KT15: Addl 9K 37
Glenmount Rd. GU16: Mytc ...3E 90
Glenn Av. CR8: Pur 7M 63
Glennie Rd. SE27 ....4L 29
Glen Rd. GU26: G'hott 6B 170
GU26: Hind 3B 170
GU51: Fleet 5A 88
KT9: Ches 1M 59
Glen Rd. End SM6: W'ton 5F 62
Glenrosa St. SW6 ....5N 13
Glenside Cl. CR8: Ken 2A 84
Glentanner Way SW17 ....4B 28
Glentham Gdns. SW13 ....2G 12
Glentham Rd. SW13 ....2F 12
Glenthorne Av. CR0: Croy 7E 46
Glenthorne Cl. SM3: Sut 7M 43
Glenthorne Gdns. SM3: Sut ...7M 43
Glenthorne Rd.
KT1: K Tham ...7L 203 (3M 41)
Glenthorpe Av. SW15 ....7F 12
Glenthorpe Rd. SM4: Mord 4J 43
Glenvern Ct. *TW7: Isle* *5G 11*
(off White Lodge Cl.)
Glenview Cl. RH10: Craw 1D 182
Glenville Gdns.
GU26: Hind 5D 170
Glenville M. SW18 ....1N 27
Glenville M. Ind. Est.
SW18 ....1M 27
Glenville Rd.
KT2: K Tham ...1M 203 (9N 25)
Glen Vue RH19: E Grin 9A 166
Glen Wlk. TW7: Isle 8D 10
(not continuous)
Glenwood GU9: U Hal 6H 109
RG12: Brac 3B 32
RH5: Dork 7J 119
Glenwood Ct. GU14: Farnb 1M 89
Glenwood Rd. KT17: Ewe 3F 60
TW3: Houn 6D 10
Glenwood Way CR0: Croy 5G 47
Gliddon Rd. W14 ....1K 13
Globe Farm La.
GU17: B'water 1G 68
Glorney Mead GU9: B Lea ...6M 109
Glory Mead RH4: Dork 8H 119
Glossop Rd. CR2: Sande 5A 64
Gloster Cl. GU12: A Va 8D 90
Gloster Ct. *GU21: Wok* *3B 74*
(off Walton Rd.)
Gloster Rd. GU22: Wok 7C 74
KT3: N Mal 3D 42
Gloucester *W14* *1L 13*
(off Mornington Av.)
Gloucester Cl.
GU16: Frim G 8C 70
KT7: T Dit 7G 40
RH19: E Grin 1C 186
Gloucester Ct. CR4: Mit 4J 45
RH1: Red *2D 122*
(off Gloucester Rd.)
TW9: Kew 3N 11
Gloucester Cres.
TW18: Stain 7M 21
Gloucester Dr. TW18: Stain 4E 20
Gloucester Gdns.
GU19: Bag 4J 51
SM1: Sut 8N 43
Gloucester Ho. TW10: Rich ...8N 11
Gloucester Pl. SL4: W'sor 5G 5
Gloucester Rd. CR0: Croy 7A 46
GU2: Guil 1J 113
GU11: Alde 5A 110
GU19: Bag 4J 51
KT1: K Tham 1N 41
RH1: Red 2D 122
RH10: Craw 7C 182
TW2: Twick 2C 24
TW4: Houn 7M 9
TW9: Kew 3N 11
TW11: Tedd 6E 24
TW12: Hamp 8B 24
TW13: Felt 2K 23
Gloucestershire Lea
RG42: Warf 8D 16
Gloucester Sq. GU21: Wok 4A 74
Gloucester Wlk. GU21: Wok 4A 74
Glovers Cl. TN16: B Hil 3D 86
Glovers Fld. GU27: Hasl 2D 188
Glover's Rd. RH2: Reig 4N 121
RH6: Char 3J 161
Glover's Wood Nature Resrve
.....................3G 161
Gloxinia Wlk. TW12: Hamp 7A 24
Glyn Cl. KT17: Ewe 5F 60
SE25 ....1B 46
Glyn Ct. SW16 ....4L 29
Glyndale Grange SM2: Sut 3N 61
Glynde Ho. RH10: Craw 1C 182
Glynde Pl. *RH12: Hors* *6J 197*
(off South St.)
Glyn Rd. KT4: W Pk 8J 43
Glynswood GU10: Wrec 7F 128
GU15: Camb 3D 70
Goals Soccer Cen. 1D 8
Goater's All. *SW6* *3L 13*
(off Dawes Rd.)
GOATERS HILL 9G 17
Goaters Rd. SL5: Asc 1G 33
Goat Ho. Bri. SE25 ....2D 46
Goat Rd. CR4: Cars, Mit 6D 44
Goatsfield Rd. TN16: Tats 7E 86
Goat Wharf TW8: Brent 2L 11
GODALMING 7H 133
Godalming Av. SM6: W'ton 2J 63
Godalming Bus. Cen.
GU7: Goda 7J 133
Godalming Leisure Cen. 4K 133
Godalming Mus. 7G 133
Godalming Rd.
GU8: Hasc, Loxh 7A 154
Godalming Station (Rail) ...7G 132
Goddard Cl. GU2: Guil 8K 93
RH10: Craw 6F 182
TW17: Shep 2A 38
Goddard Rd. BR3: Beck 3G 47
Goddard's 4L 137
Goddards Cl. GU14: Cove 7J 69
Goddards La. GU15: Camb 3N 69
Goddard Way RG42: Brac 7B 16
(not continuous)
Godfrey Av. TW2: Whitt 1D 24
Godfrey Cl. GU47: C Tow 7J 49
Godfrey Way TW4: Houn 1M 23
Godley Rd. KT14: Byf 1A 76
SW18 ....2B 28
Godolphin Cl. SM2: Chea 7L 61
Godolphin Ct. RH10: Craw 5B 182
Godolphin Ho. *SL4: Eton* *2G 4*
(off Common La.)
Godolphin Rd. KT13: Weybr 3E 56
Godric Cres. CR0: N Add 6N 65
Godson Rd. CR0: Wad 9L 45
GODSTONE 9F 104
Godstone By-Pass
RH9: Gods 7F 104
Godstone Farm 1F 124
Godstone Grn. RH9: Gods 9E 104
Godstone Hill CR3: Gods 5E 104
RH9: Gods 5E 104
GODSTONE INTERCHANGE
......................7F 104
Godstone Mt. CR8: Pur 8M 63
Godstone Rd. CR3: Cate 2D 104
CR3: Ken 1A 84
CR8: Ken, Pur 8M 63
CR8: Pur 8M 63
RH1: Blet 2A 124
RH7: Ling 6M 145
RH8: Oxt 9K 105
SM1: Sut 1A 62
TW1: Twick 9H 11
Godstone Station (Rail) 7H 125
Godstone Vineyards 6F 104
Godwin Cl. KT19: Ewe 3B 60
Godwin Way RH13: Hors 4M 197
Goepel Ct. RH10: Craw 2E 182
Goffs Cl. RH11: Craw 4A 182
Goffs La. RH11: Craw 3N 181
(not continuous)
Goffs Pk. 4N 181
Goffs Pk. Rd. RH11: Craw 4A 182
Goffs Rd. TW15: A'ford 7E 22
Gogmore Farm Cl.
KT16: Chert 6H 37
Gogmore La. KT16: Chert 6J 37
Goidel Cl. SM6: Bedd 1H 63
Goldcliff Cl. SM4: Mord 6M 43
Goldcrest Cl. GU46: Yate 9A 48
RH6: Horl 7C 142
Goldcrest Way CR0: N Add 5N 65
CR8: Pur 6H 63
Gold Cup La. SL5: Asc 9H 17
Golden Ct. TW7: Isle 5D 10
TW9: Rich 8K 11
Golden Orb Wood
RG42: Bin 9J 15
Goldfinch Cl. GU11: Alde 4L 109
RH11: Craw 1B 182
RH12: Hors 1J 197
Goldfinch Gdns. GU4: Guil 2F 114
Goldfinch Rd. CR2: Sels 6H 65
Goldfort Wlk. GU21: Knap 3H 73
Goldhill GU10: L Bou 5H 129
Golding Cl. KT9: Ches 3J 59
RH10: Craw 4G 182
Golding La. RH13: M Hea 9C 198
Goldings, The GU21: Wok 3J 73
Golding's Hill RH13: M Hea ...9C 198
Gold La. GU11: Alde 9C 90
GU12: Alde 9C 90
Goldney Rd. GU15: Camb 2F 70
Goldrings Rd. KT22: Oxs 9B 58
Goldsmiths Cl. GU21: Wok 5M 73
Goldsmith Way RG45: Crow ...3G 48
Goldstone Farm Vw.
KT23: Book 5A 98
GOLDSWORTH 5N 73
Goldsworth Orchard
GU21: Wok 5K 73
GOLDSWORTH PARK 4K 73
Goldsworth Pk. Cen., The
GU21: Wok 4K 73
Goldsworth Pk. Trad. Est.
GU21: Wok 3K 73
Goldsworth Rd. GU21: Wok ...5M 73
Goldsworth Rd. Ind. Est.
GU21: Wok 4N 73
Goldvale Ho. *GU21: Wok* *4A 74*
(off Church St. W.)
Goldwell Rd. CR7: T Hea 3K 45
Gole Rd. GU24: Pirb 8N 71
Golf Cl. CR7: T Hea 9L 29
GU22: Pyr 1G 75
Golf Club Cotts. SL5: S'dale ...7F 34
Golf Club Dr. KT2: K Tham 8C 26
Golf Club Rd. GU22: Wok 7K 73
KT13: Weybr 5C 56
Golf Dr. GU15: Camb 2D 70
Golf House Rd. RH8: Limp 7E 106
Golf Links Av. GU26: Hind ...3N 169
Golf Rd. CR8: Ken 5A 84
Golf Side SM2: Chea 7K 61
TW2: Twick 4D 24
Golfside Cl. KT3: N Mal 1D 42
Gomer Gdns. TW11: Tedd 7G 24
Gomer Pl. TW11: Tedd 7G 24
GOMSHALL 8E 116
Gomshall Av. SM6: W'ton 2J 63
Gomshall Gdns. CR8: Ken 2B 84
Gomshall La. GU5: Shere 8B 116
Gomshall Mill & Gallery 8E 116
Gomshall Rd. SM2: Chea 6H 61
Gomshall Station (Rail) 8E 116
Gong Hill GU10: Fren 8J 129
Gong Hill Dr.
GU10: Fren, L Bou 7J 129
Gonston Cl. SW19 ....3K 27
Gonville Rd. CR7: T Hea 4K 45
Gonville St. SW6 ....6K 13
Gonville Works
RH6: Smal 9M 143
Goodchild Rd.
RG40: W'ham 2C 30
Goodden Cres. GU14: Cove 2L 89
Goodenough Cl. CR5: Coul 7L 83
Goodenough Rd.
SW19 ....8L 27
Goodenough Way
CR5: Coul 7K 83
Goodhart Ho. SM7: Ban 5A 82
Goodhart Way BR4: W Wick ...6N 47
Goodhew Rd. CR0: Croy 5D 46
Gooding Cl. KT3: N Mal 3B 42
Goodings Grn.
RG40: W'ham 2E 30
GOODLEY STOCK 8K 107
Goodley Stock Rd.
TN8: C Hil 9K 107
TN16: C Hil, Weste 9K 107
Goodman Ct. CR0: Croy 5M 45
Goodman Cres. SW2 ....3J 29
Goodman Pl. TW18: Stain 5H 21
Goodways Dr. RG12: Brac 1A 32
Goodwin Cl. CR4: Mit 2B 44
RH11: Craw 6L 181
TN8: Eden 1K 147
Goodwin Ct. SW19 ....8C 28
Goodwin Gdns. CR0: Wad 3M 63
Goodwin Rd.
CR0: Wad 8A 200 (2M 63)
Goodwins Cl.
RH19: E Grin 7N 165
Goodwood Cl. GU15: Camb ...7A 50
RH10: Craw 6E 182
SM4: Mord 3M 43
Goodwood Pde. BR3: Beck 3H 47
Goodwood Pl. GU14: Farnb 2C 90
Goodwood Rd. RH1: Red 1D 122
Goodwyns Pl. RH4: Dork 7H 119
Goodwyns Rd. RH4: Dork 8J 119
Goose Cnr. RG42: Warf 6D 16
GOOSE GREEN 2E 196
Goose Grn. GU5: Gorn 8D 116
KT11: Down 6H 77
Goosegreen Cl.
RH12: Hors 3K 197
Goose La. GU22: Wok 9L 73
Goosens Cl. SM1: Sut 2A 62
Goosepool KT16: Chert 6H 37
Goose Rye Rd. GU3: Worp 4G 93
Gordon Av. CR2: Sande 6N 63
GU15: Camb 2N 69
GU52: C Cro 7C 88
SW14 ....7D 12
TW1: Twick 8G 11
Gordon Cl. KT16: Chert 9G 37
TW18: Stain 6K 21
Gordon Ct. GU15: Camb 1A 70
RH1: Red *5D 122*
(off St John's Ter. Rd.)
Gordon Cres. CR0: Croy 7B 46
GU15: Camb 2A 70
Gordondale Rd. SW19 ....3M 27
Gordon Dr. KT16: Chert 9G 37
TW17: Shep 6E 38
Gordon Rd. BR3: Beck 2J 47
CR3: Cate 8A 84
GU11: Alde 3M 109
(not continuous)
GU14: Farnb 5B 90
(not continuous)
GU15: Camb 2A 70
KT2: K Tham ...2L 203 (9M 25)
KT5: Surb 6M 41
KT10: Clay 4E 58
RG45: Crow 4J 49
RH1: Red 9E 102
RH12: Hors 4K 197
SL4: W'sor 5C 4
SM5: Cars 3D 62
TW3: Houn 7C 10
TW9: Rich 5M 11
TW15: A'ford 4N 21
TW17: Shep 5E 38
TW18: Stain 5E 20
UB2: S'hall 1M 9
W4 ....2A 12
Gordons Way RH8: Oxt 6N 105
Gordon Wlk. GU46: Yate 1D 68
Gore Rd. SW20 ....1H 43
Goring Rd. TW18: Stain 6F 20
Goring's Mead RH13: Hors 7K 197
Gorings Sq. TW18: Stain 5G 21
Gorling Cl. RH11: Ifi 4K 181
GORRICK 7C 30
Gorrick Sq. RG41: W'ham 5A 30
Gorringe Pk. Av. CR4: Mit 8D 28
Gorringes Brook
RH12: Hors 2K 197
Gorse Bank GU18: Ligh 8L 51
Gorse Cl. GU10: Wrec 5F 128
KT20: Tad 7G 81
RH10: Cop 8M 163
RH11: Craw 9N 181
Gorse Cotts. GU10: Fren 1H 149
Gorse Ct. GU4: Guil 1E 114
Gorse Dr. RH6: Smal 8M 143
Gorse End RH12: Hors 3K 197
Gorse Hill GU22: Wok 8J 73
Gorse Hill La. GU25: V Wat ...3N 35
Gorse Hill Rd. GU25: V Wat ...3N 35
Gorselands GU9: U Hal 5H 109
GU46: Yate 2B 68
Gorselands Cl. GU12: A Va 8E 90
GU35: H Dwn 5H 169
KT14: W By 7L 55
Gorse La. GU10: Wrec 5G 128
GU24: Chob 4H 53
Gorse Path GU10: Wrec 5F 128
Gorse Pl. RG42: Wink R 8F 16
Gorse Ri. SW17 ....6E 28
Gorse Rd. CR0: Croy 1K 65
GU16: Frim 4C 70
Gorseway GU52: Fleet 6B 88
Gorsewood Rd. GU21: Wok 6G 73
Gort Cl. GU11: Alde 6C 90
Gosberton Rd. SW12 ....2D 28
Gosbury Hill KT9: Ches 1L 59
Gosden Cl. GU5: Braml 3B 134
RH10: Craw 4E 182
GOSDEN COMMON 3A 134
Gosden Comn. GU5: Braml 4A 134
Gosden Cotts. GU5: Braml 4B 134
Gosden Hill Rd.
GU4: B'ham 8E 94
Gosden Rd. GU24: W End 9C 52
Gosfield Rd.
KT19: Eps 5J 201 (8C 60)
Goslar Way SL4: W'sor 5E 4
Gosnell Cl. GU16: Frim 3H 71
GOSPEL GREEN 5B 190
Gossops Dr. RH11: Craw 4L 181
GOSSOPS GREEN 4L 181
Gossops Grn. La.
RH11: Craw 4M 181
Gossops Pde. *RH11: Craw* *4L 181*
(off Gossops Dr.)
Gostling Rd. TW2: Whitt 2A 24
Goston Gdns. CR7: T Hea 2L 45
Gostrode La. GU8: Chid 2D 190
Goswell Hill SL4: W'sor 4G 4
Goswell Rd. SL4: W'sor 4G 4
Gothic Ct. UB3: Harl 2E 8
Gothic Rd. TW2: Twick 3D 24
Gotwick Mnr.
RH19: Hamm 6H 167
Goudhurst Cl. RH10: Wor 3J 183
Goudhurst Keep
RH10: Wor 3J 183
Gough Ho. KT1: K Tham 3J 203
Gough Rd. GU51: Fleet 3A 88
Gough's Barn La.
RG42: Warf 1M 15
Gough's La. RG12: Brac 8B 16
Gough's Mdw. GU47: Sandh ...8G 48
Gould Ct. GU4: Guil 1F 114
Goulding Gdns. CR7: T Hea ...1M 45
Gould Rd. TW2: Twick 2E 24
TW14: Felt 1F 22
Government Ho. Rd.
GU11: Alde 5M 89
Government Rd.
GU11: Alde 9B 90
Governor's Rd. GU15: Camb ..9L 49
Govett Av. TW17: Shep 4D 38
Govett Gro. GU20: Windl 2A 52
Gowan Av. SW6 ....4K 13
Gower, The TW20: Thor 2D 36
Gower Lodge *KT13: Weybr* *3E 56*
(off St George's Rd.)
Gower Pk. GU47: C Tow 8J 49
Gower Rd. KT13: Weybr 3E 56
RH6: Horl 8C 142
TW7: Isle 2F 10
Gowland Pl. BR3: Beck 1J 47
Gowlland Cl. CR0: Croy 6D 46
Gownboys GU7: Goda 4F 132
Gowrie Pl. CR3: Cate 9N 83
Graburn Way KT8: E Mol 2D 40
Grace Bennett Cl.
GU14: Farnb 7M 69
Grace Bus. Cen. CR4: Mit 5D 44
Grace Ct. CR0: Croy 4A 200
RH12: Hors 4N 197
SM2: Sut 5N 61
Gracedale Rd. SW16 ....6F 28
Gracefield Gdns.
SW16 ....4J 29
Grace Gdns. GU51: Fleet 5A 88
Grace M. *SE20* *1F 46*
(off Marlow Rd.)
Grace Reynolds Wlk.
GU15: Camb 9A 50
Grace Rd. CR0: Croy 5N 45
RH11: Craw 8M 181
Gracious Pond Rd.
GU24: Chob 4K 53
Graemesdyke Av.
SW14 ....6A 12
Graffham Cl. RH11: Craw 1N 181
GRAFHAM 2E 154
Grafton Cl. KT4: W Pk 9D 42
KT14: W By 9H 55
TW4: Houn 2M 23
Grafton Ct. TW14: Bedf 2E 22
Grafton Pk. Rd. KT4: W Pk 8D 42
Grafton Rd. CR0: Croy 7L 45
KT3: N Mal 2D 42
KT4: W Pk 9C 42
Grafton Way KT8: W Mole 3N 39
Graham Av. CR4: Mit 9E 28
Graham Cl. CR0: Croy 8K 47
Grahame Ho. RH1: Red 1C 122
Graham Gdns. KT6: Surb 7L 41
Graham Ho. KT23: Book 2N 97
Graham Rd. CR4: Mit 9E 28
CR8: Pur 9L 63
GU20: Windl 3N 51
SW19 ....8L 27
TW12: H Hill 5A 24
Grainger Rd. TW7: Isle 5F 10
Grampian Cl. SM2: Sut 4A 62
UB3: Harl 3E 8
Grampian Rd. GU47: Sandh ...5E 48
Grampian Way SL3: Lang 1C 6
Granada St. SW17 ....6D 28
Granard Av. SW15 ....8G 13
Granard Rd. SW12 ....1D 28
Granary Cl. RH6: Horl 6E 142
RH12: Hors 7F 196
Granary Way RH12: Hors 7F 196
Grand Av. GU15: Camb 9A 50
KT5: Surb 4A 42
Grand Dr. SW20 ....1H 43
Granden Rd. SW16 ....1J 45
Grandfield Ct. W4 ....2C 12
Grandis Cotts. GU23: Rip 9K 75
Grandison Rd. KT4: W Pk 8H 43
Grand Pde. KT6: Surb 7N 41
RH10: Craw 3B 182
SW14 ....*7B 12*
(off Up. Richmond Rd. W.)
Grand Pde. M. SW15 ....8K 13
Grand Regency Hgts.
SL5: Asc 1J 33
Grandstand Rd.
KT17: Eps D 4E 80
Grand Vw. Av. TN16: B Hil 4E 86
Grange, The CR0: Croy 8J 47
GU10: Fren 3J 149
GU24: Chob 6H 53
GU25: V Wat *3A 36*
(off Holloway Dr.)
KT3: N Mal 4E 42
KT4: W Pk 1C 60
KT12: Wal T 8J 39

Grange, The—Green Mead

Grange, The RH6: Horl 5F 142
SL4: O Win 8L 5
SW19 . . . . .7J 27
W4 . . . . .1A 12
Grange Av. RG45: Crow 1G 48
SE25 . . . . .1B 46
TW2: Twick 3E 24
Grangecliffe Gdns.
SE25 . . . . .1B 46
Grange Cl. GU2: Guil 8L 93
GU7: Goda 6K 133
GU15: Camb 7F 50
KT8: W Mole 3B 40
KT22: Leat 7K 79
RH1: Blet 2A 124
RH1: Mers 6F 102
RH10: Craw 1E 182
TN8: Eden 2L 147
TN16: Weste 4L 107
TW5: Hest 2N 9
TW19: Wray 9A 6
Grange Ct. GU10: Tong 6C 110
KT12: Wal T 8H 39
RH1: Mers 6F 102
RH9: S Gods 7H 125
SM2: Sut 4N 61
SM6: W'ton 9F 44
TW17: Shep 3B 38
TW18: Stain 6J 21
TW20: Egh 6B 20
Grange Cres.
RH10: Craw D 2E 184
Grange Dr. GU21: Wok 2A 74
RH1: Mers 6F 102
Grange End RH6: Smal 8L 143
Grange Est. GU52: C Cro 8A 88
Grange Farm Rd.
GU12: Ash 1E 110
Grangefields Rd.
GU4: J Wel 6N 93
Grange Gdns. SE25 . . . . .1B 46
SM7: Ban 9N 61
Grange Hill SE25 . . . . .1B 46
Grange Lodge SW19 . . . . .7J 27
Grange Mans. KT17: Ewe 4E 60
Grange Mdw. SM7: Ban 9N 61
Grange M. TW13: Felt 5H 23
Grangemount KT22: Leat 7K 79
Grange Pk. GU6: Cranl 7A 156
GU21: Wok 2A 74
Grange Pk. Pl. SW20 . . . . .8G 26
Grange Pk. Rd.
CR7: T Hea 3A 46
Grange Pl. KT12: Wal T 8H 39
TW18: Lale 1L 37
Grange Rd. CR2: S Croy 6N 63
CR3: Cate 3D 104
CR7: T Hea 3A 46
GU2: Guil 7L 93
GU10: Til 2N 149
GU10: Tong 6C 110
GU12: Ash 2F 110
GU14: Farnb 7N 69
GU15: Camb 1C 70
GU21: Wok 1A 74
GU24: Pirb 9N 71
GU52: C Cro 8A 88
KT1: K Tham 5J 203 (2L 41)
KT8: W Mole 3B 40
KT9: Ches 1L 59
KT12: Hers 1M 57
KT15: N Haw 6J 55
KT22: Leat 7K 79
RG12: Brac 9A 16
RH10: Craw D 2D 184
SE19 . . . . .3A 46
SE25 . . . . .3A 46
SM2: Sut 4M 61
SW13 . . . . .4F 12
TW20: Egh 6B 20
(not continuous)
W4 . . . . .1A 12
Grange Va. SM2: Sut 4N 61
Grange Way RH6: Smal 8L 143
Grangewood Dr.
TW16: Sunb 8G 22
Grangewood Ter. SE25 . . . . . . .1A 46
Gransden Cl. GU6: Ewh 5F 156
Grantchester *KT1: K Tham 1N 41*
(off St Peters Rd.)
Grant Cl. TW17: Shep 5C 38
Grantham Cl. GU47: Owls 6K 49
Grantham Ct. KT2: K Tham 6K 25
Grantham Dr. GU14: Cove 9J 69
Grantham Ho. TW16: Sunb 8F 22
Grantham Rd. W4 . . . . .3D 12
Grantley Av. GU5: Wone 5D 134
Grantley Cl. GU4: Chil 1A 134
Grantley Ct. GU9: Farnh 5E 128
Grantley Dr. GU52: Fleet 6A 88
Grantley Gdns. GU2: Guil 2K 113
Grantley Pl. KT10: Esh 2B 58
Grantley Rd. GU2: Guil 2K 113
TW4: C'ford 5K 9
Granton Rd. SW16 . . . . .9G 29
Grant Pl. CR0: Croy 7C 46
Grant Rd. CR0: Croy 7C 46
RG45: Crow 4H 49
Grants La. RH8: Limp 1E 126
TN8: Eden, Limp 1E 126
Grant Wlk. SL5: S'dale 7B 34
Grant Way TW7: Isle 2G 10
Grantwood Cl. RH1: Red 8E 122
Granville Av. TW3: Houn 8A 10
TW13: Felt 3H 23
Granville Cl.
CR0: Croy 3F 200 (8B 46)
KT13: Weybr 3D 56
KT14: Byf 9A 56
Granville Gdns. SW16 . . . . . . .9K 29
Granville Pl. SW6 . . . . .3N 13
Granville Rd. GU22: Wok 7B 74
KT13: Weybr 4D 56
RH8: Oxt 7B 106
SW18 . . . . .1L 27
SW19 . . . . .8M 27
TN16: Weste 4L 107
Granwood Ct. TW7: Isle 4E 10
Grapsome Cl. KT9: Ches 4J 59
Grasholm Way SL3: Lang 1E 6
Grasmere SL4: W'sor 3B 4
Grasmere Av. SW15 . . . . .5C 26
SW19 . . . . .2M 43
TW3: Houn 9B 10
Grasmere Cl. GU1: Guil 2D 114
TW14: Felt 2G 22
TW20: Egh 8D 20
Grasmere Ct. SM2: Sut 3A 62
SW13 . . . . .2F 12
(off Verdun Rd.)
Grasmere Gdns.
RH12: Hors 2A 198
Grasmere Rd. CR8: Pur 7M 63
GU9: U Hal 6F 108
GU14: Cove 2K 89
GU18: Ligh 6M 51
SE25 . . . . .5E 46
SW16 . . . . .6K 29
Grasmere Way KT14: Byf 8A 56
Grassfield Cl. CR5: Coul 6F 82
Grasslands RH6: Smal 8L 143
Grassmere RH6: Horl 7G 142
Grassmount CR8: Pur 6G 63
Grass Way SM6: W'ton 1G 62
Gratton Dr. SL4: W'sor 7B 4
Grattons, The RH13: Slin 5M 195
Grattons Dr. RH10: Craw 9G 162
Gravel Hill CR0: A'ton 3G 64
KT22: Leat 8H 79
Gravel Hill Rd.
GU10: H Pou 8A 128
Gravel Hill Stop (CT) 3H 65
Gravelly Hill CR3: Cate 6B 104
Gravelpits Cotts.
GU5: Gorn 8D 116
Gravelpits La. GU5: Gorn 8D 116
Gravel Rd. GU9: U Hal 5G 108
GU14: Farnb 5B 90
GU52: C Cro 7C 88
TW2: Twick 2E 24
Gravenel Gdns. *SW17 . . . . .6C 28*
(off Nutwell St.)
Graveney Rd. RH10: Craw 4G 182
SW17 . . . . .5C 28
Gravetts La. GU3: Guil 8H 93
GRAVETYE 7J 185
Gravetye Cl. RH10: Craw 5E 182
Gray Cl. KT15: Addl 2K 55
RH7: Ling 7A 146
Grayham Cres. KT3: N Mal 3C 42
Grayham Rd. KT3: N Mal 3C 42
Graylands GU21: Wok 3A 74
Graylands Cl. GU21: Wok 3A 74
Graylands Ct. GU1: Guil 4B 114
Grayling KT16: Chert 7L 37
Gray Pl. KT16: Otter 3F 54
RG42: Brac 9K 15
Grays Cl. GU27: Hasl 9J 171
Grayscroft Rd. SW16 . . . . .8H 29
Grayshot Dr. GU17: B'water 1H 69
GRAYSHOTT 6A 170
Grayshott Laurels
GU35: Lind 4B 168
Grayshott Rd.
GU35: H Dwn 3G 169
Grays La. KT18: Eps D 6M 79
KT21: A'tead 6M 79
TW15: A'ford 5C 22
Grays Rd. GU7: Goda 4J 133
TN14: Weste 7M 87
TN16: Weste 8K 87
GRAYSWOOD 7K 171
Grays Wood RH6: Horl 8G 143
Grayswood Comn.
GU27: G'wood 8K 171
Grayswood Dr. GU16: Mytc 4E 90
Grayswood Gdns.
SW20 . . . . .1G 42
Grayswood M.
GU27: G'wood 7K 171
Grayswood Pl. GU27: Hasl 9J 171
Grayswood Point
SW15 . . . . .2F 26
Grayswood Rd.
GU27: Hasl, G'wood 1H 189
Great Austins GU9: Farnh 3J 129
Gt. Austins Ho. GU9: Farnh . . .3J 129
Great Benty UB7: W Dray 1N 7
GREAT BOOKHAM 4B 98
Great Bookham Common 8N 77
GREAT BURGH 4H 81
Gt. Chertsey Rd.
TW2: Twick 4N 23
TW13: Hanw, Twick 4N 23
W4 . . . . .5B 12
Gt. Church La. W6 . . . . .1J 13
Great Church Wood Nature Reserve
. . . . .3J 105
Great Cockcrow Railway 7F 36
Gt. Daux Rdbt.
RH12: Warn 1H 197
Great Ellshams SM7: Ban 3M 81
GREAT ENTON 6D 152
Greatfield Cl. GU14: Farnb 6N 69
Great Fld. Pl.
RH19: E Grin 7D 166
Greatfield Rd.
GU14: Farnb 6M 69
Greatford Dr. GU1: Guil 3F 114
Gt. Gatton Cl. CR0: Croy 6H 47
Gt. George St. GU7: Goda 7H 133
Gt. Goodwin Dr. GU1: Guil . . .1D 114
Greatham Rd. RH10: Craw 6G 182
Greatham Wlk. SW15 . . . . .2F 26
Greathead Manor 1E 166
GREAT HOLLANDS 5L 31
Gt. Hollands Rd.
RG12: Brac 5K 31
Gt. Hollands Sq.
RG12: Brac 5L 31
Great Ho. Ct. RH19: E Grin . . .1B 186
Greathurst End KT23: Book 2N 97
Greatlake Ct. *RH6: Horl 7F 142*
(off Tanyard Way)
Great Mead TN8: Eden 9L 127
Gt. Oaks Pk. GU4: B'ham 7D 94
Great Quarry
GU1: Guil 8D 202 (6N 113)
Great Sth. W. Rd.
TW4: Houn 1D 22
TW14: Bedf, Felt 1D 22
Great Tattenhams
KT18: Tat C 5G 81
Great W. Rd. TW5: Hest 5L 9
TW7: Brent, Isle 3E 10
TW8: Brent 3G 11
W4 . . . . .1E 12
(Cedars Rd.)
W4 . . . . .1A 12
(Harvard Rd.)
W6 . . . . .1E 12
Great W. Trad. Est.
TW8: Brent 2H 11
Greatwood Cl. KT16: Otter 5E 54
Gt. Woodcote Dr. CR8: Pur 6H 63
Gt. Woodcote Pk. CR8: Pur 6H 63
Greaves Pl. SW17 . . . . .5C 28
Grebe Ct. SM1: Sut 2L 61
Grebe Cres. RH13: Hors 7N 197
Grebe Ter.
KT1: K Tham 5J 203 (2L 41)
Grecian Cres. SE19 . . . . .7M 29
GREEN, THE 9C 72
Green, The CR0: Sels 5J 65
CR3: Wold 1K 105
CR6: Warl 4G 84
GU5: Sha G 6F 134
GU6: Ewh 5F 156
GU8: Chid 5F 172
GU8: Duns 3B 174
GU8: Els 7H 131
GU9: B Lea 7M 109
GU9: U Hal 6H 109
GU10: Seal 2C 130
GU16: Frim G 8D 70
GU17: B'water 2H 69
GU23: Rip 8L 75
GU28: North 8D 190
GU46: Yate 9A 48
KT3: N Mal 2C 42
KT10: Clay 3F 58
KT12: Hers 2L 57
KT12: Whit V 6F 56
KT17: Ewe 7F 60
KT20: Tad 1J 101
(Dorking Rd.)
KT20: Tad 6K 81
(Reigate Rd.)
KT22: Fetc 2D 98
RG12: Brac 3N 31
RH3: Buck 2F 120
RH5: Ockl 5D 158
RH9: Gods 1E 124
RH10: Cop 7M 163
RH11: Craw 2A 182
SL3: Dat 3L 5
SM1: Sut 9N 43
SM4: Mord 3K 43
SM5: Cars 1E 62
SW19 . . . . .6J 27
TN16: Weste 4M 107
TW2: Twick 2E 24
TW5: Hest 2A 10
TW9: Rich 8K 11
TW13: Felt 3J 23
TW15: A'ford 6M 21
TW17: Shep 3F 38
TW19: Wray 9A 6
TW20: Eng G 5M 19
Green Acre GU11: Alde 3L 109
GU21: Knap 3H 73
Greenacre SL4: W'sor 5B 4
Greenacre Ct.
TW20: Eng G 7M 19
Greenacre Pl. SM6: W'ton 8F 44
Green Acres CR0: Croy 9C 46
Greenacres GU10: Run 1A 130
GU35: Bor 5A 168
KT20: Lwr K 6L 101
Greenacres KT23: Book 2B 98
RH8: Oxt 5A 106
RH10: Craw 4E 182
RH12: Hors 4J 197
Greenacres Cl. BR6: Farnb 1L 67
Greenaway Ter. *TW19: Stan . . .2N 21*
(off Victory Cl.)
Green Bank Cotts.
RH5: For G 3M 157
Greenbank Way
GU15: Camb 4B 70
Greenbush La. GU6: Cranl . . .9A 156
Green Bus. Cen., The
TW18: Stain 5E 20
Green Cl. SM5: Cars 8D 44
TW13: Hanw 6M 23
Green Ct. TW16: Sunb 7G 23
Greencourt Av. CR0: Croy 8E 46
Greencourt Gdns.
CR0: Croy 7E 46
Green Cft. GU9: B Lea 6N 109
RG40: W'ham 9D 14
Greencroft GU1: Guil 3D 114
GU14: Farnb 1N 89
Greencroft Rd. TW5: Hest 4N 9
GREEN CROSS 9M 149
Green Cross La.
GU10: Churt 9M 149
Green Curve SM7: Ban 1L 81
Green Dene KT24: E Hor 4D 116
Green Dragon La.
TW8: Brent 1L 11
Green Dragons Airsports 7L 85
Green Dr. GU23: Rip 1H 95
RG40: W'ham 4D 30
SL3: Lang 1A 6
(not continuous)
Greene Fielde End
TW18: Stain 8M 21
Green End GU46: Yate 8C 48
KT9: Ches 1L 59
Greener Ct. *CR0: Croy 5M 45*
(off Goodman Ct.)
Green Farm Rd. GU19: Bag 4K 51
Greenfield GU9: Farnh 4F 128
TN8: Eden 2M 147
Greenfield Av. KT5: Surb 6A 42
Greenfield Ho. SW19 . . . . .2J 27
TW20: Eng G 7L 19
(off Kings La.)
Greenfield Link CR5: Coul 2J 83
Greenfield Rd. GU9: Farnh 4E 128
RH13: Slin 5L 195
Greenfields Cl. RH6: Horl 6C 142
RH12: Hors 2N 197
Greenfields Pl.
RH5: B Grn 7K 139
Greenfields Rd. RH6: Horl 6D 142
RH12: Hors 3N 197
Greenfields Way
RH12: Hors 2N 197
Greenfield Way RG45: Crow . . .9F 30
Green Finch Cl.
RG45: Crow 1E 48
Greenfinch Cl. GU47: Owls 7J 49
Greenfinch Way
RH12: Hors 1J 197
Greenford Rd. SM1: Sut 1N 61
(not continuous)
Green Gables GU14: Cove 6L 69
Green Gdns. BR6: Farnb 2L 67
Green Glades GU52: C Cro 8A 88
Greenham Ho. TW7: Isle 6D 10
Greenham Wlk. GU21: Wok 5M 73
Greenham Wood
RG12: Brac 5A 32
Greenhanger GU10: Churt . . .1M 169
Greenhaven GU46: Yate 1A 68
Greenhayes Av. SM7: Ban 1M 81
Greenhayes Cl. RH2: Reig . . .3A 122
Greenhayes Gdns.
SM7: Ban 2M 81
Green Hedges TW1: Twick 8J 11
Green Hedges Av.
RH19: E Grin 8N 165
Green Hedges Cl.
RH19: E Grin 8N 165
Greenheys Pl. GU22: Wok 5B 74
Green Hill BR6: Dow 8H 67
Greenhill SM1: Sut 8A 44
Greenhill Av. CR3: Cate 8E 84
Green Hill Cl. GU15: Camb 9G 51
Greenhill Cl. GU7: Goda 8G 133
GU9: Farnh 4F 128
Greenhill Gdns. GU4: Guil 1E 114
Green Hill La. CR6: Warl 4H 85
Green Hill Rd. GU15: Camb 9G 51
Greenhill Rd. GU9: Farnh 4J 129
Greenhills GU9: Farnh 3K 129
Greenhill Way GU9: Farnh 5F 128
Greenholme GU15: Camb 1H 71
Greenhow RG12: Brac 2M 31
Greenhurst La. RH8: Oxt 1B 126
Greenhurst Rd. SE27 . . . . .6L 29
Greening Wood
GU26: Hind 4D 170
Greenlake Ter. TW18: Stain 8J 21
Greenlands KT16: Chert 9E 36
KT19: Ewe 2A 60
Greenlands Rd.
GU15: Camb 5N 69
KT13: Weybr 9C 38
TW18: Stain 5J 21
Greenland Way CR0: Bedd 6H 45
Green La. CR3: Cate 9N 83
CR5: Coul 4L 101
CR6: Warl 3H 85
CR7: T Hea 8K 29
CR8: Pur 7G 63
GU1: Guil 3D 114
GU3: Wood V 1D 112
GU4: W Cla 5J 95
GU5: Sha G 5H 135
GU6: Alf 5H 175
GU7: Goda 2G 133
GU8: Mil 2B 152
GU9: B Lea, Weybo 6L 109
GU9: Farnh 3F 128
GU10: Churt 1L 169
GU10: Dock 4D 148
GU10: Til 5B 130
GU17: B'water 2G 69
GU17: Haw 2K 69
GU19: Bag 9F 32
(Bagshot Rd.)
GU19: Bag 5K 51
(Whitmoor Rd.)
GU22: Wok 8L 73
GU23: Ockh 2C 96
GU24: Chob 6J 53
GU27: Hasl 4F 188
GU46: Yate 9A 48
GU47: Sandh 8H 49
KT3: N Mal 4B 42
KT4: W Pk 7F 42
KT8: W Mole 4B 40
KT9: Ches 5K 59
KT11: Cob 8M 57
KT12: Hers 3J 57
KT14: Byf 8A 56
KT15: Addl 8G 36
KT16: Chert 8G 36
KT20: Lwr K 4L 101
KT21: A'tead 4J 79
KT22: Leat 8K 79
(not continuous)
RG40: W'ham 6F 14
RH1: Blet 9B 104
RH1: Out 1J 143
RH1: Red 1C 122
(Carlton Rd.)
RH1: Red 8E 122
(Spencer's Way)
RH2: Leigh 3D 140
RH2: Reig 3L 121
RH5: B Grn 1H 159
RH5: Newd 2C 160
RH5: Ockl 7M 157
RH6: S Bri 3K 163
RH7: Ling 8M 145
RH10: Craw 1C 182
RH10: Craw D 6C 164
RH10: Wor 3H 183
RH12: Hors 5L 179
SL3: Dat 4L 5
SL4: W'sor 5D 4
SL5: Asc 9B 18
SM4: Mord 5M 43
(Central Rd.)
SM4: Mord 6H 43
(Lwr. Morden La.)
SW16 . . . . .8K 29
TW4: Houn 6J 9
TW13: Hanw 6M 23
TW16: Sunb 8G 22
TW17: Shep 5D 38
TW18: Stain 9G 20
TW20: Egh 5D 20
(Avenue, The)
TW20: Egh 6D 20
(Vicarage Dr.)
TW20: Thor 1E 36
Green La. Av. KT12: Hers 2K 57
Green La. Cvn. Pk.
RH1: Salf 1J 143
Green La. Cl. GU15: Camb 8A 50
KT14: Byf 8A 56
KT16: Chert 8G 36
Green La. Cotts.
GU9: B Lea 7L 109
GU10: Churt 9L 149
Green La. E. GU3: Flex 4K 111
(not continuous)
Green La. Gdns.
CR7: T Hea 1N 45
Green Lanes KT19: Ewe 5D 60
(not continuous)
Green La. W. GU12: A Grn 4J 111
KT24: W Hors 3B 96
Greenlaw Gdns. KT3: N Mal 6E 42
Green Lawn La. TW8 . . . . .1K 11
Green Leaf Av. SM6: Bedd 1H 63
Greenleaf Cl. SW2 . . . . .1L 29
Greenlea Pk. SW19 . . . . .8B 28
Green Leas KT1: K Tham 5K 203
TW16: Sunb 7G 23
Greenleas GU16: Frim 4C 70
Green Leas Cl. TW16: Sunb 7G 23
Greenleas Cl. GU46: Yate 8B 48
Greenleaves Ct.
TW15: A'ford 7C 22
Green Leys GU52: C Cro 9A 88
Green Line Wlk. TW9: Kew 4A 12
Green Man La. TW14: Felt 7H 9
(not continuous)
Green Mead KT10: Esh 3N 57

Gurdon's La.—Harcourt Lodge

Gurdon's La. GU8: Worm 9B 152
(not continuous)
Gurney Cres. CR0: Croy 7K 45
Gurney Ho. UB3: Harl 1F 8
Gurney Rd. SM5: Cars 1E 62
Gurney's Cl. RH1: Red 4D 122
Guyatt Gdns. CR4: Mit 1E 44
Guy Rd. SM6: Bedd 9H 45
Gwalior Rd. SW15 7J 13
Gwendolen Av. SW15 7J 13
Gwendolen Cl. SW15 8J 13
Gwendolen Ho. *TW19: Stan 2N 21*
(off Yeoman Dr.)
Gwendwr Rd. W14 1K 13
Gwydor Rd. BR3: Beck 2G 47
Gwyn Cl. SW6 3N 13
Gwynne Av. CR0: Croy 6G 46
Gwynne Cl. SL4: W'sor 4B 4
W4 2E 12
Gwynne Ct. *GU2: Guil 8L 93*
(off Grange Rd.)
Gwynne Gdns.
RH19: E Grin 8M 165
Gwynne Rd. CR3: Cate 1A 104

H

Habershon Dr. GU16: Frim 4H 71
Haccombe Rd. SW19 7A 28
HACKBRIDGE 7E 44
Hackbridge Grn.
SM6: W'ton 8E 44
Hackbridge Pk. Gdns.
SM5: Cars 8D 44
Hackbridge Rd. SM6: W'ton 8E 44
Hackbridge Station (Rail) 8F 44
Hackenden Cl.
RH19: E Grin 7A 166
Hackenden Cotts.
RH19: E Grin 7A 166
Hackenden La.
RH19: E Grin 8A 166
Hacketts La. GU22: Pyr 1H 75
Hackhurst Down Nature Reserve
6F 116
Hackhurst La.
RH5: A Ham 8G 116
Haddenhurst Ct. RG42: Bin 7H 15
Haddon Cl. KT3: N Mal 4E 42
KT13: Weybr 9F 38
Haddon Rd. SM1: Sut 1N 61
(not continuous)
Hadfield Rd. TW19: Stan 9M 7
Hadleigh Cl. SW20 1L 43
Hadleigh Dr. SM2: Sut 5M 61
Hadleigh Gdns.
GU16: Frim G 8C 70
Hadley Ct. *SL3: Poy 4G 7*
(off Coleridge Cres.)
Hadley Gdns. UB2: S'hall 1N 9
W4 1C 12
Hadley Pl. KT13: Weybr 4B 56
Hadley Rd. CR4: Mit 3H 45
Hadleys GU10: Rowl 8D 128
Hadley Wood Ri. CR8: Ken 1M 83
Hadmans Cl. RH12: Hors 7J 197
Hadrian Cl. TW19: Stan 1N 21
Hadrian Ct. SM2: Sut 4N 61
Hadrians GU9: Farnh 8K 109
Hadrian Way TW19: Stan 1M 21
(not continuous)
Haggard Rd. TW1: Twick 1H 25
Haigh Cres. RH1: Red 5F 122
Haig La. GU52: C Cro 8C 88
Haig Pl. SM4: Mord 5M 43
Haig Rd. GU12: Alde 3A 110
GU15: Camb 9L 49
TN16: B Hil 4G 86
Hailes Cl. SW19 7A 28
Hailey Pl. GU6: Cranl 6A 156
Hailsham Av. SW2 3K 29
Hailsham Cl. GU47: Owls 6J 49
KT6: Surb 6K 41
Hailsham Rd. SW17 7E 28
Haines Ct. KT13: Weybr 2E 56
Haines Wlk. SM4: Mord 6N 43
Haining Cl. W4 1N 11
Haining Gdns. GU16: Mytc 2E 90
Hainthorpe Rd. SE27 4M 29
Halcyon *GU9: U Hal 5F 108*
(off Lawday Link)
Haldane Pl. SW18 2N 27
Haldane Rd. SW6 3L 13
Haldon Rd. SW18 9L 13
HALE 7J 109
Halebourne La.
GU24: Chob, W End 4D 52
Hale Cl. BR6: Farnb 1L 67
Hale End RG12: Brac 3D 32
Hale Ends GU22: Wok 8L 73
Hale Ho. Cl. GU10: Churt 9L 149
Hale Ho. La. GU10: Churt 9L 149
Hale Path SE27 5M 29
Hale Pit Rd. KT23: Book 4C 98
Hale Pl. GU9: Hale 7K 109
Hale Reeds GU9: H End 6J 109
Hale Rd. GU9: Farnh, Hale 7J 109
Hales Fld. GU27: Hasl 2G 189
Hales Oak KT23: Book 4C 98
Halesowen Rd. SM4: Mord 6N 43
Hale St. TW18: Stain 5G 21
Haleswood KT11: Cob 1J 77
Hale Way GU16: Frim 6B 70
Halewood RG12: Brac 5L 31
Half Acre TW8: Brent 2K 11
Halfacres RH10: Craw 2C 182
Half Moon Cotts.
GU23: Rip 8L 75
Half Moon Hill GU27: Hasl 2G 189
Half Moon St. GU19: Bag 4J 51
Halford Rd. SW6 2M 13
TW10: Rich 8L 11
Halfpenny Cl. GU4: Guil 9F 114
Halfpenny La. GU4: Guil 6E 114
SL5: S'dale 6D 34
Halfway Grn. KT12: Wal T 9J 39
Halfway La. GU7: Eash 7D 132
Haliburton Rd. TW1: Twick 8G 11
Halifax Cl. GU14: Cove 2L 89
RH10: Craw 9J 163
TW11: Tedd 7E 24
Halifax Rd. RG12: Brac 2A 32
Halimote Rd. GU11: Alde 3M 109
Haling Down Pas. CR8: Pur 6M 63
(not continuous)
Haling Gro. CR2: S Croy 4N 63
Haling Pk. Gdns.
CR2: S Croy 3M 63
Haling Pk. Rd.
CR2: S Croy 8A 200 (2M 63)
Haling Rd. CR2: S Croy 3A 64
Hallam Rd. GU7: Goda 5J 133
SW13 6G 13
Halland Cl. RH10: Craw 2E 182
Halland Ct. *TN8: Eden 2L 147*
(off Stangrove Rd.)
Hallane Ho. SE27 6N 29
Hallbrooke Gdns.
RG42: Bin 8K 15
Hall Cl. GU7: Goda 4H 133
GU15: Camb 9C 50
Hall Ct. SL3: Dat 3L 5
TW11: Tedd 6F 24
Hall Dene Cl. GU1: Guil 2E 114
Hall Dr. GU52: Fleet 7C 88
Halley Cl. RH11: Craw 8N 181
Halley Dr. SL5: Asc 1H 33
Halley's App. GU21: Wok 4K 73
Halley's Ct. GU21: Wok 5K 73
Halley's Wlk. KT15: Addl 4L 55
Hall Farm Cres. GU46: Yate 1C 68
Hall Farm Dr. TW2: Whitt 1D 24
Hallgrove Bottom
GU19: Bag 2K 51
Hall Gro. Farm Ind. Est.
GU19: Bag 2K 51
Hall Hill RH8: Oxt 9N 105
Halliards, The KT12: Wal T 5H 39
Halliford Cl. TW17: Shep 3E 38
Halliford Rd. TW16: Sunb 4F 38
TW17: Shep 4F 38
Halliloo Valley Rd.
CR3: Wold 7G 85
Hallington Cl. GU21: Wok 4L 73
Hall La. GU46: Yate 1B 68
UB3: Harl 3E 8
Hallmark Cl. GU47: C Tow 7K 49
Hallmead Rd. SM1: Sut 9N 43
Hallowell Av. CR0: Bedd 1J 63
Hallowell Cl. CR4: Mit 2E 44
Hallowes Cl. GU2: Guil 7L 93
Hallowfield Way CR4: Mit 2B 44
Hallows Gro. TW16: Sunb 6G 23
HALL PLACE 1G 175
Hall Pl. GU21: Wok 3C 74
Hall Pl. Dr. KT13: Weybr 2F 56
Hall Rd. GU5: Braml 5B 134
SM6: W'ton 5F 62
TW7: Isle 8D 10
Halls Dr. RH12: Fay 8E 180
Halls Farm Cl. GU21: Knap 4G 73
Hallsland RH10: Craw D 1F 184
Hallsland Way RH8: Oxt 2B 126
Hall Way CR8: Pur 9M 63
Halnaker Wlk. RH11: Craw 6L 181
Halsford Cft. RH19: E Grin 7L 165
Halsford Grn.
RH19: E Grin 7L 165
Halsford La. RH19: E Grin 8L 165
Halsford Pk. Rd.
RH19: E Grin 8M 165
Halstead Cl.
CR0: Croy 4B 200 (9N 45)
Halters End GU26: G'hott 6M 169
Halton Rd. CR3: Cate 7B 84
HAM 4J 25
Ham, The TW8: Brent 3J 11
Hamble Av. GU17: B'water 1J 69
Hamble Cl. GU21: Wok 4K 73
Hambleden Ct. RG12: Brac 3C 32
HAMBLEDON 9F 152
Hambledon Gdns.
SE25 2C 46
Hambledon Hill KT18: Eps 3B 80
Hambledon Pk.
GU8: Hamb 9E 152
Hambledon Pl. KT23: Book 1A 98
Hambledon Rd. CR3: Cate 1A 104
GU7: Bus 9J 133
(not continuous)
GU8: Bus, Hamb 7G 153
SW18 1L 27
Hambledon Va. KT18: Eps 3B 80
Hamblehyrst BR3: Beck 1L 47
Hamble St. SW6 6N 13
Hambleton Cl. GU16: Frim 3F 70
KT4: W Pk 8H 43
Hambleton Ct. RH11: Craw 5A 182
Hambleton Hill
RH11: Craw 5A 182
Hamble Wlk. GU21: Wok 5K 73
Hambridge Way SW2 1L 29
Hambrook Rd. SE25 2E 46
Hambro Rd. SW16 7H 29
Ham Cl. TW10: Ham 4J 25
(not continuous)
Ham Comn. TW10: Ham 4K 25
Ham Cft. Cl. TW13: Felt 4H 23
Hamesmoor Rd.
GU16: Mytc 1C 90
Hamesmoor Way
GU16: Mytc 1D 90
Ham Farm Rd.
TW10: Ham 5K 25
Hamfield Cl. RH8: Oxt 5M 105
Ham Ga. Av. TW10: Ham 4K 25
Hamhaugh Island
TW17: Shep 8B 38
Ham House 2J 25
Hamilton Av. GU22: Pyr 2G 75
KT6: Surb 8N 41
KT11: Cob 9H 57
SM3: Chea 8K 43
Hamilton Cl. CR8: Pur 8M 63
GU2: Guil 7K 93
GU19: Bag 4J 51
GU35: Bor 5A 168
KT16: Chert 7H 37
KT19: Eps 8B 60
TW11: Tedd 7H 25
TW13: Felt 6G 22
Hamilton Ct. CR0: Croy 7D 46
KT11: Cob 9H 57
KT23: Book 3B 98
SW15 6K 13
Hamilton Cres. TW3: Houn 8B 10
Hamilton Dr. GU2: Guil 7K 93
SL5: S'dale 6B 34
Hamilton Gdns.
GU14: Cove 9H 69
Hamilton Gordon Ct.
GU1: Guil 1B 202 (2M 113)
Hamilton Ho. W4 2D 12
Hamilton M. *KT13: Weybr 1B 56*
(off Holstein Av.)
SW18 2M 27
SW19 8M 27
Hamilton Pde. TW13: Felt 5G 23
Hamilton Pl. GU2: Guil 7K 93
GU11: Alde 3L 109
KT14: W By 9H 55
KT20: K'wood 9L 81
TW16: Sunb 8J 23
Hamilton Rd. CR7: T Hea 2A 46
GU52: C Cro 7C 88
RH12: Hors 5H 197
SW19 8N 27
TW2: Twick 2E 24
TW8: Brent 2K 11
TW13: Felt 5G 22
Hamilton Rd. M.
SW19 8N 27
Hamilton Way SM6: W'ton 5H 63
HAM ISLAND 7N 5
Ham Lands Nature Reserve
3G 25
Ham La. GU8: Els 7H 131
SL4: O Win 8M 5
TW20: Eng G 5L 19
Hamlash La. GU10: Fren 1H 149
Hamlet M. SE21 2N 29
Hamlet St. RG42: Warf 9C 16
Hamlyn Ho. TW13: Felt 2H 23
Hamm Ct. KT13: Weybr 8N 37
HAMMER 3B 188
HAMMER BOTTOM 2A 188
Hammerfield Dr.
RH5: A Ham 1G 136
Hammer Hill GU27: Hasl 4A 188
Hammer La. GU6: Cranl 3M 175
GU10: Churt 1K 169
GU26: G'hott 1K 169
GU26: Hasl 9A 170
GU27: Lip 2A 188
Hammer Pond Cotts.
GU8: Thur 4K 151
Hammerpond Rd.
RH13: Hors, M Hea, Col
7M 197
RH13: P Pla 9E 198
Hammersley Rd.
GU11: Alde 6N 89
HAMMERSMITH 1H 13
Hammersmith Bri. W6 1G 13
Hammersmith Bri. Rd.
W6 1H 13
HAMMERSMITH BROADWAY
1H 13
Hammersmith B'way.
W6 1H 13
Hammersmith Fitness &
Squash Cen. *1J 13*
(off Chalk Hill Rd.)
HAMMERSMITH FLYOVER 1H 13
Hammersmith Flyover
W6 1H 13
Hammersmith Ind. Est.
W6 2H 13
Hammersmith Rd. W6 1J 13
W14 1J 13
Hammersmith Station (Tube)
1H 13
Hammersmith Ter. W6 1F 12
Hammer Va. GU27: Lip 2A 188
HAMMERWOOD 7K 167
Hammerwood Copse
GU27: Hasl 3B 188
Hammerwood Pk. 8L 167
Hammerwood Rd.
RH19: Ash W 3F 186
Hammer Yd. RH10: Craw 4B 182
Hamm Moor La. KT15: Addl 2N 55
Hammond Av. CR4: Mit 1F 44
Hammond Cl. GU21: Wok 2M 73
TW12: Hamp 9A 24
Hammond Ct. *RG42: Brac 9M 15*
(off Crescent Rd.)
Hammond Rd. GU21: Wok 2M 73
RH11: Craw 9N 181
Hammond's Copse Nature Reserve
6D 140
Hammond Way GU18: Ligh 6M 51
HAM MOOR 1N 55
Hamond Cl. CR2: S Croy 5M 63
Hampden Av. BR3: Beck 1H 47
Hampden Cl. RH10: Craw 9J 163
Hampden Cres. RG12: Brac 2A 32
Hampden Rd. BR3: Beck 1H 47
KT1: K Tham 2N 41
Hampers Ct. RH13: Hors 6K 197
Hamper's La. RH13: Hors 6N 197
Hampshire Cl. GU12: Alde 5B 110
Hampshire Ct. KT15: Addl 2L 55
Hampshire Hog La.
W6 1G 12
Hampshire Ri. RG42: Warf 7D 16
Hampshire Rd.
GU15: Camb 7D 50
Hampstead La. RH4: Dork 6F 118
Hampstead Rd.
RG40: W'ham 6F 30
RH4: Dork 6G 118
Hampstead Wlk.
RH11: Craw 7A 182
HAMPTON 9B 24
Hampton & Richmond Borough FC
9B 24
Hampton Cl. GU21: Knap 6F 72
GU52: C Cro 9B 88
SW20 8H 27
HAMPTON COURT 3E 40
Hampton Court 1E 40
HAMPTON COURT 2E 40
Hampton Ct. Av. KT8: E Mol 5D 40
Hampton Ct. Bri.
KT8: E Mol 3E 40
Hampton Ct. Cres.
KT8: E Mol 2D 40
Hampton Ct. Est.
KT7: E Mol 3E 40
Hampton Ct. M. *KT8: E Mol 3E 40*
(off Feltham Av.)
Hampton Court Palace 3F 40
Hampton Ct. Pde.
KT8: E Mol 3E 40
Hampton Ct. Rd. KT1: H Wic 2F 40
KT8: E Mol 2F 40
TW12: Hamp 1C 40
Hampton Court Station (Rail)
3E 40
Hampton Ct. Way KT7: T Dit 8E 40
KT8: E Mol 8E 40
Hampton Farm Ind. Est.
TW13: Hanw 4M 23
Hampton Gro. KT17: Ewe 7E 60
HAMPTON HILL 6C 24
Hampton Hill Bus. Pk.
TW12: H Hill 6C 24
(off High St.)
Hampton Hill Playhouse Theatre
6C 24
Hampton La. TW13: Hanw 5M 23
Hampton Lodge RH6: Horl 9E 142
Hampton Open Air Pool 8C 24
Hampton Rd. CR0: Croy 5N 45
GU9: U Hal 6F 108
KT4: W Pk 8F 42
RH1: Red 8D 122
TW2: Twick 4D 24
TW11: Tedd 6D 24
TW12: Tedd 6D 24
Hampton Rd. E.
TW13: H Hill 5N 23
Hampton Rd. Ind. Pk.
CR0: Croy 5N 45
Hampton Rd. W.
TW13: Hanw 4M 23
Hampton Sport, Arts & Fitness Cen.
6A 24
Hampton Station (Rail) 9A 24
Hampton Way
RH19: E Grin 2B 186
HAMPTON WICK 2G 203 (9J 25)
Hampton Wick Station (Rail)
2G 203 (9J 25)
Hampton Youth Project (Sports Hall)
7N 23
Ham Ridings TW10: Ham 6M 25
HAMSEY GREEN 3E 84
Hamsey Grn. Gdns.
CR6: Warl 3E 84
Hamsey Way CR2: Sande 2E 84
Ham St. TW10: Ham 2H 25
Ham Vw. CR0: Croy 5H 47
Hanah Ct. SW19 8J 27
Hanbury Dr. TN16: B Hil 9D 66
Hanbury Path GU21: Wok 1F 74
Hanbury Rd. RH11: Ifi 4K 181
Hanbury Way
GU15: Camb 3A 70
Hancocks Mt. SL5: S'hill 5A 34
Hancombe Rd.
GU47: Sandh 6F 48
Handcroft Rd.
CR0: Croy 1A 200 (6M 45)
HANDCROSS 8N 199
Handel Mans. SW13 3H 13
Handford La. GU46: Yate 1C 68
Handinhand La.
KT20: Box H 8B 100
Handley Page Rd.
SM6: W'ton 4K 63
Handside Cl. KT4: W Pk 7J 43
Hanford Cl. SW18 2M 27
Hanford Row SW19 7H 27
Hanger, The GU35: Head 2D 168
Hanger Ct. GU21: Knap 4H 73
Hangerfield Cl. GU46: Yate 1B 68
Hanger Hill KT13: Weybr 3C 56
Hanging Wood Nature Reserve
6J 105
Hangrove Hill BR6: Dow 9K 67
Hankins Ct. GU52: Fleet 6B 88
Hanley Cl. SL4: W'sor 4A 4
Hannah Cl. BR3: Beck 2M 47
Hannah M. SM6: W'ton 4G 63
Hannah Peschar Sculpture Garden
8A 158
Hannay Wlk. SW16 3H 29
Hannell Rd. SW6 3K 13
Hannen Rd. SE27 4M 29
Hannibal Rd. TW19: Stan 1M 21
Hannibal Way CR0: Wad 2K 63
Hanover Av. TW13: Felt 2H 23
Hanover Cl. GU16: Frim 5C 70
GU46: Yate 8C 48
RH1: Mers 6G 102
RH10: Craw 5D 182
(not continuous)
SL4: W'sor 4C 4
SM3: Chea 1K 61
TW9: Kew 3N 11
TW20: Eng G 7L 19
Hanover Ct. GU1: Guil 1N 113
GU22: Wok 6A 74
RH4: Dork 2G 201 (5F 118)
RH13: Hors 5M 197
SW15 7E 12
Hanover Dr. GU51: Fleet 1D 88
Hanover Gdns. GU14: Cove 8K 69
RG12: Brac 6L 31
Hanover Pk. SL5: Asc 9K 17
Hanover Rd. SW19 8A 28
Hanover St.
CR0: Croy 4A 200 (9M 45)
Hanover Ter. TW7: Isle 4G 11
Hanover Wlk. KT13: Weybr 9E 38
Hanover Way SL4: W'sor 5C 4
Hansler Ct. *SW19 2K 27*
(off Princes Way)
Hansler Gro. KT8: E Mol 3D 40
Hanson Cl. GU4: B'ham 9B 94
GU15: Camb 8F 50
SW12 1F 28
SW14 6B 12
Hansworth Ho.
RH10: Craw 4B 182
(off Brighton Rd.)
HANWORTH
RG12 6M 31
TW13 5L 23
Hanworth Cl. RG12: Brac 5A 32
Hanworth La. KT16: Chert 7H 37
Hanworth Rd. RG12: Brac 7M 31
RH1: Red 8D 122
TW3: Houn 9A 10
TW4: Houn 2M 23
TW12: Hamp 5N 23
TW13: Felt 2J 23
TW16: Sunb 8H 23
(not continuous)
Hanworth Ter. TW3: Houn 7B 10
Hanworth Trad. Est.
KT16: Chert 7H 37
TW13: Hanw 4M 23
Harberson Rd. SW12 2F 28
Harbledown Rd.
CR2: Sande 7D 64
SW6 4M 13
Harbord St. SW6 4J 13
Harborough Rd.
SW16 5K 29
Harbour Cl. GU14: Farnb 6M 69
Harbourfield Rd. SM7: Ban 2N 81
Harbridge Av. SW15 1E 26
Harbury Rd. SM5: Cars 5C 62
Harcourt TW19: Wray 9A 6
Harcourt Av. SM6: W'ton 1F 62
Harcourt Cl. TW7: Isle 6G 11
TW20: Egh 7E 20
Harcourt Cotts. GU3: Put 8N 111
Harcourt Fld. SM6: W'ton 1F 62
Harcourt Lodge
SM6: W'ton 1F 62

Harcourt Rd.—Hawthorn Av.

Harcourt Rd. CR7: T Hea 5K 45
GU15: Camb 1M 69
RG12: Brac 5N 31
SL4: W'sor 4B 4
SM6: W'ton 1F 62
SW19 . . . . .8M 27
Harcourt Ter. SW10 . . . . .1N 13
Harcourt Way RH9: S Gods . . .6H 125
Hardcastle Cl. CR0: Croy 5D 46
Hardcourts Cl. BR4: W Wick . . .9L 47
Hardell Cl. TW20: Egh 6C 20
Hardel Ri. SW2 . . . . .2M 29
Hardel Wlk. SW2 . . . . .1L 29
Harden Farm Cl. CR5: Coul 8G 83
Hardham Cl. RH11: Craw 1M 181
Harding Cl. CR0: Croy 9C 46
Harding Ho. *SW13* *2G 13*
(off Wyatt Dr.)
Harding Rd. KT18: Eps D 6D 80
Harding's Cl.
KT2: K Tham . . .1L 203 (9M 25)
Harding Spur SL3: Lang 2B 6
Hardings Rd. GU10: B Oak . . .2A 148
Hardman Rd.
KT2: K Tham . . .3K 203 (1L 41)
Hardwell Way RG12: Brac 3C 32
Hardwick Cl. KT22: Oxs 2C 78
Hardwicke Av. TW5: Hest 4A 10
Hardwicke Rd. RH2: Reig 2M 121
TW10: Ham 5J 25
Hardwick La. KT16: Lyne 6E 36
Hardwick Pl. SW16 . . . . .8G 29
Hardwick Rd. RH1: Red 5B 122
Hardwicks Way SW18 . . . . . . .8M 13
Hardy Av. GU46: Yate 2B 68
Hardy Cl. RH5: Nth H 9H 119
RH6: Horl 8C 142
RH10: Craw 2G 182
RH12: Hors 4H 197
Hardy Grn. RG45: Crow 3G 49
Hardy Ho. SW4 . . . . .1G 29
SW18 . . . . .1N 27
Hardy Rd. SW19 . . . . .8N 27
Hardy's M. KT8: E Mol 3E 40
Harebell Hill KT11: Cob 1L 77
Harecroft KT22: Fetc 2B 98
RH4: Dork 8J 119
Harefield KT10: H Wood 9E 40
Harefield Av. SM2: Chea 5K 61
Harefield Rd. SW16 . . . . .8K 29
Hare Hill KT15: Addl 3G 55
Hare Hill Cl. GU22: Pyr 2J 75
Harelands Cl. GU21: Wok 4M 73
Harelands La. GU21: Wok 5M 73
(not continuous)
Hare La. GU7: Goda 5J 133
KT10: Clay 2D 58
RH7: Ling 7F 144
RH11: Craw 9N 161
Harendon KT20: Tad 8H 81
Hares Bank CR0: N Add 6N 65
Harestone Dr. CR3: Cate 2C 104
Harestone Hill CR3: Cate 4C 104
Harestone La. CR3: Cate 3B 104
(not continuous)
Harestone Valley Rd.
CR3: Cate 4B 104
Hareward Rd. GU4: Guil 1E 114
Harewood Cl. RH2: Reig 9A 102
RH10: Craw 9E 162
Harewood Gdns.
CR2: Sande 2E 84
Harewood Rd. CR2: S Croy 3B 64
SW19 . . . . .7C 28
TW7: Isle 3F 10
Harfield Rd. TW16: Sunb 1L 39
Harkness Cl. KT17: Eps D 3H 81
Harkness Ct. *SM1: Sut* *7N 43*
(off Cleeve Way)
Harland Av. CR0: Croy 9C 46
Harland Cl. SW19 . . . . .2N 43
Harlands Gro. BR6: Farnb 1K 67
Harlech Gdns. TW5: Hest 2K 9
Harlech Rd. GU17: Haw 2J 69
Harlequin Av. TW8: Brent 2G 11
Harlequin Cl. TW7: Isle 8E 10
Harlequin Rd. TW11: Tedd 8H 25
Harlequins RLFC 1E 24
Harlequins RUFC 1E 24
Harlequin Theatre & Cinema
. . . . .2D 122
Harley Gdns. BR6: Orp 1N 67
HARLINGTON 2E 8
Harlington Cen., The 4A 88
Harlington Cl. UB3: Harl 3D 8
HARLINGTON CORNER 4E 8
Harlington Rd. E.
TW13: Felt 1J 23
TW13: Hanw 5N 23
TW14: Felt 1J 23
Harlington Rd. W. TW14: Felt . . .9J 9
Harlington Way GU51: Fleet . . .4A 88
Harlow Ct. *RH2: Reig* *3B 122*
(off Wray Comn. Rd.)
Harman Pl. CR8: Pur 7M 63
Harmans Dr. RH19: E Grin . . .9D 166
Harmans Mead
RH19: E Grin 9D 166
HARMANS WATER 3C 32
Harman's Water Rd.
RG12: Brac 4A 32
Harmar Cl. RG40: W'ham 2D 30
Harmes Way GU11: Alde 6B 90
HARMONDSWORTH 2M 7
Harmondsworth La.
UB7: Harm, Sip 2N 7
Harmondsworth Moor Waterside
. . . . .2K 7
Harmondsworth Moor Waterside
Vis. Cen. 2K 7
Harmondsworth Rd.
UB7: W Dray 1N 7
Harmony Cl. RH11: Craw 5K 181
SM6: W'ton 5J 63
Harms Gro. GU4: Guil 9E 94
Harold Rd. RH10: Wor 4J 183
SM1: Sut 1B 62
Haroldslea RH6: Horl 1H 163
Haroldslea Cl. RH6: Horl 1G 163
Haroldslea Dr. RH6: Horl 1G 162
Harold Wilson Ho.
SW6 . . . .*2L 13*
(off Clem Attlee Ct.)
Harpenden Rd. SE27 . . . . .4M 29
Harper Dr. RH10: Craw 7G 182
Harper M. SW17 . . . . .4A 28
Harper's Rd. GU12: Ash 1G 111
Harpers Yd. *TW7: Isle* *5E 10*
(off Rennels Way)
Harpesford Av. GU25: V Wat . . .4L 35
Harps Oak La. RH1: Mers 3D 102
Harpswood Cl. CR5: Coul 9G 83
Harpton Cl. GU46: Yate 8C 48
Harpton Pde. GU46: Yate 8C 48
Harpurs KT20: Tad 9J 81
Harrier Cen., The 3C 60
Harrier Cl. GU6: Cranl 6N 155
Harrier Ct. *RH10: Craw* *9H 163*
(off Bristol Cl.)
TW4: Houn 6M 9
Harrier Rd. GU14: Farnb 4H 89
Harrier Way RG12: Brac 3J 31
Harriet Gdns. CR0: Croy 8D 46
Harriet Ho. *SW6* *3N 13*
(off Wandon Rd.)
Harriet Tubman Cl. SW2 . . . . . .1K 29
Harrington Cl. CR0: Bedd 8J 45
RH2: Leigh 1F 140
SL4: W'sor 7C 4
Harrington Ct.
CR0: Croy 3E 200 (8A 46)
Harrington Gdns. SW7 . . . . . . .1N 13
Harrington Rd. SE25 . . . . .3D 46
Harrington Road Stop (CT) . . .2F 46
Harriott's Cl. KT21: A'tead 7J 79
Harriott's La. KT21: A'tead 6J 79
Harris Cl. RH11: Craw 6N 181
TW3: Houn 4A 10
Harrison Cl. RH2: Reig 4N 121
Harrison's Ri.
CR0: Wad 4A 200 (9M 45)
Harrison Way TW17: Shep 4C 38
Harris Path RH11: Craw 6N 181
Harris Way TW16: Sunb 9F 22
Harrogate Ct. SL3: Lang 1C 6
Harroway Mnr. KT22: Fetc 9F 78
Harrow Bottom Rd.
GU25: V Wat 5B 36
Harrow Cl. KT9: Ches 4K 59
KT15: Addl 8K 37
RH4: Dork 6G 119
TN8: Eden 9M 127
Harrowdene GU6: Cranl 6N 155
Harrowdene Gdns.
TW11: Tedd 7G 25
Harrow Gdns. CR6: Warl 3J 85
Harrowgate Gdns.
RH4: Dork 7H 119
Harrowlands Pk.
RH4: Dork 6H 119
Harrow La. GU7: Goda 4H 133
Harrow Rd. CR6: Warl 2J 85
GU51: Fleet 2A 88
SM5: Cars 3C 62
TW14: Bedf 3B 22
Harrow Rd. E. RH4: Dork 7H 119
Harrow Rd. W. RH4: Dork 7G 118
Harrowsley Ct. RH6: Horl 7F 142
Harrowsley Grn. La.
RH6: Horl 9G 143
Harrow Way TW17: Shep 1D 38
Harry Cl. CR0: Croy 5N 45
Hart, The GU9: Farnh 1G 128
Hart Cen., The GU51: Fleet 4A 88
Hart Cl. GU14: Cove 6K 69
RG42: Brac 8N 15
RH1: Blet 2B 124
Hart Dene Ct. GU19: Bag 4J 51
Hart Dyke Cl. RG41: W'ham 6A 30
Harte Rd. TW3: Houn 5N 9
Hartfield Cres.
BR4: W Wick 1C 66
SW19 . . . . .8L 27
Hartfield Rd. BR4: W Wick 1C 66
KT9: Ches 2K 59
RH18: F Row 6H 187
SW19 . . . . .8L 27
TN8: Hev, M Grn 5M 147
Hartford Ri. GU15: Camb 9B 50
Hartford Rd. GU51: Fleet 2A 88
KT19: Ewe 3A 60
Hart Gdns.
RH4: Dork 1K 201 (4H 119)
Hartham Cl. TW7: Isle 4G 10
Hartham Rd. TW7: Isle 4F 10
Harting Ct. RH11: Craw 6L 181
Hartington Cl. BR6: Farnb 2L 67
RH2: Reig 1M 121
Hartington Ct. W4 . . . . .3A 12
Hartington Rd. TW1: Twick 1H 25
W4 . . . . .3A 12
Hartismere Rd. SW6 . . . . .3L 13
Hartland Cl. KT15: N Haw 6L 55
Hartland Pl. GU14: Farnb 8M 69
Hartland Rd. KT15: Addl 4J 55
SM4: Mord 6M 43
TW7: Isle 6G 11
TW12: H Hill 5B 24
Hartlands, The
TW5: C'ford 2J 9
Hartland Way CR0: Croy 9H 47
SM4: Mord 6L 43
Hartley Cl. GU17: B'water 1G 69
Hartley Copse SL4: O Win 9K 5
Hartley Down CR8: Pur 2K 83
Hartley Farm CR8: Pur 2K 83
Hartley Hill CR8: Pur 2K 83
Hartley Old Rd. CR8: Pur 2K 83
Hartley Rd. CR0: Croy 6N 45
TN16: Weste 3M 107
Hartley Way CR8: Pur 2K 83
Hart M. GU46: Yate 9A 48
Hartop Point *SW6* *3K 13*
(off Pellant Rd.)
Hart Rd. KT14: Byf 9N 55
RH4: Dork 1K 201 (4H 119)
Hartscroft CR0: Sels 5H 65
Harts Gdns. GU2: Guil 9L 93
Harts Gro. GU8: Chid 4E 172
Harts Hill GU2: Guil 2G 113
Hartshill Wlk. GU21: Wok 3L 73
Harts La. RH9: S Gods 5G 124
Hartsleaf Cl. GU51: Fleet 5A 88
Harts Leap Cl.
GU47: Sandh 6G 48
Harts Leap Rd.
GU47: Sandh 7F 48
Hartspiece Rd. RH1: Red 5E 122
Hartswood RH5: Nth H 8J 119
Hartswood Av. RH2: Reig 7M 121
Harts Yd. GU7: Goda 7H 133
GU9: Farnh 1G 129
Harvard Hill W4 . . . . .2A 12
Harvard La. W4 . . . . .1B 12
Harvard Rd. GU47: Owls 6K 49
TW7: Isle 4E 10
W4 . . . . .1A 12
Harvest Bank Rd.
BR4: W Wick 1B 66
Harvest Cl. GU46: Yate 2A 68
Harvest Ct. KT10: Esh 8A 40
TW17: Shep 3B 38
Harvest Cres. GU51: Fleet 9C 68
Harvester Rd. KT19: Eps 6C 60
Harvesters RH12: Hors 4K 197
Harvesters Cl. TW7: Isle 8D 10
Harvest Hill GU7: Goda 7G 132
RH19: E Grin 1A 186
Harvest La. KT7: T Dit 5G 40
Harvest Lea RG42: Warf 9E 16
Harvest Ride RG42: Warf 7M 15
Harvest Rd. RH10: Craw 5G 183
TW13: Felt 5H 23
TW20: Eng G 6N 19
Harvestside RH6: Horl 7G 142
Harvey Cl. RH11: Craw 8M 181
Harvey Ct. KT19: Eps 5A 60
Harvey Dr. TW12: Hamp 9B 24
Harvey Gdns. GU1: Guil 6F 202
Harvey Ho. TW8: Brent 1L 11
Harvey Lodge GU1: Guil 5F 202
Harvey Rd.
GU1: Guil 6E 202 (5A 114)
GU14: Cove 9H 69
KT12: Wal T 6G 39
TW4: Houn 1N 23
Harwood Av. CR4: Mit 2C 44
Harwood Ct. SW15 . . . . .7H 13
Harwood Gdns. SL4: O Win 1L 19
Harwood M. SW6 . . . . .3M 13
Harwood Pk. RH1: Salf 3E 142
Harwood Rd. RH13: Hors 5L 197
SW6 . . . . .3M 13
Harwoods Cl.
RH19: E Grin 2B 186
Harwoods La.
RH19: E Grin 2B 186
Harwood Ter. SW6 . . . . .4N 13
HASCOMBE 6N 153
Hascombe Cotts.
GU8: Bus 5M 153
Hascombe Ct. GU8: Hasc 6N 153
RH11: Craw 4M 181
Hascombe Rd. GU6: Cranl 9E 154
GU8: Bus 1K 153
Haslam Av. SM3: Sut 7K 43
Hasle Dr. GU27: Hasl 2F 188
HASLEMERE 2G 189
Haslemere and Heathrow Est., The
TW4: C'ford 5J 9
Haslemere Av. CR4: Mit 1B 44
SW18 . . . . .3N 27
TW5: C'ford 5K 9
Haslemere Cl. GU16: Frim 3G 70
SM6: W'ton 2J 63
TW12: Hamp 6N 23
Haslemere Educational Mus.
. . . . .1H 189
Haslemere Hall 1G 189
Haslemere Ind. Est.
GU27: Hasl 1F 188
SW18 . . . . .3N 27
Haslemere Rd. CR7: T Hea 4M 45
GU8: Brook, Wit 4M 171
GU8: Mil, Wit 6N 151
GU27: K Grn, Fern 7F 188
SL4: W'sor 4D 4
Haslemere Station (Rail) 2F 188
Haslett Av. E. RH10: Craw . . .3C 182
Haslett Av. W. RH10: Craw . . .4B 182
Haslett Rd. TW17: Shep 1F 38
Hassall Ct. GU22: Wok 8C 74
Hassocks Ct. RH11: Craw 6L 181
Hassocks Rd. SW16 . . . . .9H 29
Hassock Wood BR2: Kes 1F 66
Haste Hill GU27: Hasl 3H 189
Hastings Cl. GU16: Frim 7E 70
Hastings Ct. TW11: Tedd 6D 24
Hastings Dr. KT6: Surb 5J 41
Hastings Rd. CR0: Croy 7C 46
RH10: Craw 3G 182
Hastings Vw. RG12: Brac 3A 32
Hasty Cl. CR4: Mit 9F 28
Hatch Cl. GU6: Alf 6J 175
KT15: Addl 9K 37
Hatch End GU20: Windl 3N 51
RH18: F Row 7H 187
Hatches, The GU9: Farnh 3E 128
GU16: Frim G 8B 70
(not continuous)
Hatchet La. SL4: Wink 5L 17
SL5: Asc 6L 17
Hatchett Rd. TW14: Bedf 2D 22
Hatchetts Dr. GU27: Hasl 2A 188
Hatch Farm M. KT15: Addl 9L 37
HATCHFORD 6F 76
HATCHFORD END 6D 76
Hatchford Mnr. KT11: Cob 5F 76
Hatch Gdns. KT20: Tad 7J 81
Hatchgate RH6: Horl 9D 142
Hatchgate Copse
RG12: Brac 5K 31
Hatch Hill GU27: K Grn 7F 188
Hatchingtan, The
GU3: Worp 4M 93
HATCHLANDS 9A 96
Hatchlands RH5: Cap 5J 159
RH12: Hors 1N 197
Hatchlands Pk. 8A 96
Hatchlands Rd. RH1: Red 3C 122
Hatch La. CR5: Ban 2D 82
GU8: Worm 1A 172
GU23: Ockh 7C 76
GU27: K Grn 6F 188
KT11: Ockh 5C 76
RH1: Out, Sth N 2K 143
SL4: W'sor 6D 4
UB7: Harm 3M 7
Hatch Pl. KT2: K Tham 6M 25
Hatch Ride RG40: W'ham 8E 30
RG45: Crow 8F 30
Hatch Rd. SW16 . . . . .1J 45
Hatfeild Mead SM4: Mord 4M 43
Hatfield Cl. CR4: Mit 3B 44
KT14: W By 8K 55
SM2: Sut 5N 61
Hatfield Gdns. GU14: Farnb 2C 90
Hatfield Ho. GU12: A Va 8D 90
Hatfield Rd. KT21: A'tead 6M 79
Hatfield Wlk. RH11: Craw 6K 181
Hathaway Ct. *RH1: Red* *2E 122*
(off St Anne's Ri.)
Hathaway Rd. CR0: Croy 6M 45
Hatherleigh Cl. KT9: Ches 2K 59
SM4: Mord 3M 43
Hatherley Rd. TW9: Kew 4M 11
Hatherop Rd. TW12: Hamp 8N 23
Hathersham Cl. RH6: Smal 7L 143
Hathersham La.
RH6: Smal 4H 143
Hatherwood GU46: Yate 1E 68
KT22: Leat 8K 79
HATTON 7G 9
Hatton Ct. SL4: W'sor 5F 4
HATTON CROSS 7G 8
Hatton Cross Cen.
TW6: Lon A 6G 8
Hatton Cross Station (Tube) . . .7G 8
Hatton Gdns. CR4: Mit 4D 44
Hatton Grn. TW14: Felt 7H 9
HATTON HILL 2N 51
Hatton Hill GU20: Windl 1M 51
Hatton Ho. KT1: K Tham 4M 203
Hatton Rd. CR0: Croy 7L 45
TW14: Bedf, Felt 1D 22
Hatton Rd. Sth. TW14: Felt 7G 8
Haughton Ho. GU27: Hasl 2F 188
Havana Rd. SW19 . . . . .3M 27
Havelock Rd. CR0: Croy 8C 46
RG41: W'ham 2A 30
SW19 . . . . .6A 28
Havelock St. RG41: W'ham 2A 30
HAVEN, THE 6E 194
Haven, The TW9: Rich 6N 11
TW16: Sunb 8H 23
Havenbury Est.
RH4: Dork 1H 201 (4G 118)
Haven Cl. KT10: H Wood 8E 40
SW19 . . . . .4J 27
Haven Ct. BR3: Beck 1M 47
KT5: Surb 5M 41
KT10: H Wood 8E 40
Haven Dr. KT19: Ewe 7A 60
Haven Gdns.
RH10: Craw D 9E 164
Havengate RH12: Hors 3M 197
Haven Pl. KT10: H Wood 8E 40
Haven Rd. RH12: Rudg 2D 194
RH14: Slin, Have 7F 194
TW15: A'ford 5C 22
Haven Way GU9: Farnh 8J 109
KT19: Eps 7A 60
Haverfield Gdns. TW9: Kew 3N 11
Haverhill Rd. SW12 . . . . .2G 28
Havers Av. KT12: Hers 2L 57
Haversham Cl.
RH10: Craw 3D 182
TW1: Twick 9K 11
Haversham Dr. RG12: Brac 5N 31
Haversham Ho. RH6: Horl 6F 142
Havisham Pl. SE19 . . . . .8M 29
Hawarden Cl.
RH10: Craw D 1F 184
Hawarden Gro. SE24 . . . . .1N 29
Hawarden Rd. CR3: Cate 8N 83
Hawes La. BR4: W Wick 7M 47
Hawes Rd. KT20: Tad 7J 81
Haweswater Ct. *GU12: A Va* . . .*8D 90*
(off Lakeside Cl.)
Haweswater Ho. TW7: Isle 8F 10
Hawker Ct. KT1: K Tham 3M 203
Hawker Rd. CR0: Wad 3L 63
GU12: A Va 8D 90
Hawkesbourne Rd.
RH12: Hors 3M 197
Hawkesbury Rd. SW15 . . . . . . .8G 12
Hawkes Leap GU20: Windl 1M 51
Hawkesley Cl. TW1: Twick 5G 24
Hawkesmoor Rd.
RH11: Craw 5K 181
Hawkes Rd. CR4: Mit 9D 28
TW14: Felt 1H 23
Hawkesworth Dr.
GU19: Bag 6H 51
Hawkewood Rd.
TW16: Sunb 2H 39
Hawkfield Ct. TW7: Isle 5E 10
Hawkhirst Rd. CR3: Ken 4B 84
CR8: Ken 2A 84
Hawkhurst KT11: Cob 1A 78
Hawkhurst Gdns. KT9: Ches 1L 59
Hawkhurst Rd. SW16 . . . . .9H 29
Hawkhurst Wlk.
RH10: Craw 5F 182
Hawkhurst Way
BR4: W Wick 8L 47
KT3: N Mal 4C 42
Hawkins Cl. GU46: Yate 1A 68
RG12: Brac 1E 32
Hawkins Rd. RH10: Craw 6C 182
TW11: Tedd 7H 25
Hawkins Way GU52: Fleet 5D 88
RG40: W'ham 2D 30
Hawk La. RG12: Brac 3A 32
Hawkley Gdns. SE27 . . . . .3M 29
Hawkridge RH12: Rudg 8F 176
Hawkridge Ct. RG12: Brac 3C 32
Hawksbrook La. BR3: Beck 5L 47
(not continuous)
Hawkshaw Cl. SW2 . . . . .1J 29
Hawk's Hill KT22: Fetc 1F 98
Hawks Hill Cl. KT22: Fetc 1F 98
Hawkshill Cl. KT10: Esh 3A 58
Hawk's Hill Ct. KT22: Fetc 1F 98
Hawk's Hill Ho. KT22: Fetc 2F 98
Hawkshill Pl. KT10: Esh 3A 58
Hawkshill Way KT10: Esh 3N 57
Hawksmoore Dr.
RH5: B Grn 7J 139
Hawksmoor St. W6 . . . . .2J 13
Hawks Pas. KT1: K Tham 3L 203
Hawks Rd.
KT1: K Tham . . .4M 203 (1M 41)
Hawksview KT11: Cob 9N 57
Hawksway TW18: Stain 4H 21
Hawkswell Cl. GU21: Wok 4J 73
Hawkswell Wlk. GU21: Wok 4J 73
Hawkswood Av.
GU16: Frim 4D 70
Hawkswood Ho. *RG42: Brac* . . .*9K 15*
(off Moordale Av.)
Hawkwell GU52: C Cro 9C 88
Hawkwood Dell KT23: Book . . .4A 98
Hawkwood Ri. KT23: Book 4A 98
HAWLEY 3L 69
Hawley Cl. TW12: Hamp 7N 23
Hawley Ct. GU14: Cove 6K 69
Hawley Grn. GU17: Haw 3K 69
Hawley Gro. GU17: Haw 4K 69
HAWLEY LANE 7M 69
Hawley La. GU14: Farnb 5M 69
(not continuous)
Hawley La. Ind. Est.
GU14: Farnb 6N 69
Hawley Lodge GU17: Haw 4L 69
Hawley Rd. GU17: Haw 2J 69
HAWLEY'S CORNER 8K 87
Hawley Way
TW15: A'ford 6B 22
Hawmead RH10: Craw D 1F 184
Haworth Rd. RH10: Craw 4F 182
Haws La. TW19: Stan M 9J 7
Hawth Av. RH10: Craw 5C 182
Hawth Cl. RH10: Craw 5C 182
Hawthorn Av. CR7: T Hea 9M 29

Hawthorn Cl.—Heights Cl.

Hawthorn Cl. GU12: Alde 4C 110
GU22: Wok 7A 74
RG42: Brac 9M 15
RH1: Red 8E 122
RH11: Craw 9A 162
RH12: Hors 4J 197
SM7: Ban 1K 81
TN8: Eden 1L 147
TW5: C'ford 3J 9
TW12: Hamp 6A 24
Hawthorn Ct. GU14: Farnb 5A 90
TW9: Kew 4A 12
TW15: A'ford 8D 22
Hawthorn Cres. CR2: Sels 7F 64
SW17 6E 28
Hawthorn Dr. BR4: W Wick 1A 66
Hawthorne Av. CR4: Mit 1B 44
SL4: Wink 3M 17
SM5: Cars 4E 62
TN16: B Hil 2F 86
Hawthorne Cl. SM1: Sut 8A 44
Hawthorne Ct. KT12: Wal T 7L 39
TW19: Stan 1M 21
(off Hawthorne Way)
Hawthorne Cres.
GU17: Haw 2K 69
Hawthorne Dr. SL4: Wink 3M 17
Hawthorne Pl.
KT17: Eps 5M 201 (8D 60)
Hawthorne Rd. TW18: Stain 6E 20
Hawthorne Way
GU4: B'ham 8D 94
SL4: Wink 2M 17
TW19: Stan 1M 21
Hawthorn Hatch TW8: Brent 3H 11
HAWTHORN HILL 1B 16
Hawthorn La. GU10: Rowl 8E 128
RG42: Warf 1C 16
Hawthorn Pl. GU4: Guil 1F 114
Hawthorn Rd. GU7: Goda 9E 132
GU16: Frim 4D 70
GU22: Wok 7N 73
GU23: Rip 2J 95
SM1: Sut 3C 62
SM6: W'ton 4F 62
TW8: Brent 3H 11
TW13: Felt 2H 23
Hawthorns CR2: S Croy 7A 200
Hawthorns, The KT17: Ewe 4E 60
RH8: Oxt 2C 126
SL3: Poy 4H 7
Hawthorn Way GU24: Bis 3D 72
KT15: N Haw 6L 55
RH1: Red 5F 122
TW17: Shep 3E 38
Hawth Theatre 4D 182
Hawtrey Ho. *SL4: Eton 2G 4*
(off Slough Rd.)
Hawtrey Rd. SL4: W'sor 5F 4
HAXTED 3G 147
Haxted Mill & Mus. 3F 146
Haxted Rd. RH7: Ling 5A 146
TN8: Eden 5A 146
Haybarn Dr. RH12: Hors 1L 197
Haycroft Cl. CR5: Coul 5M 83
Haycroft Rd. KT6: Surb 8K 41
Hayden Ct. KT15: N Haw 7K 55
TW13: Felt 5F 22
Haydn Av. CR8: Pur 1L 83
Haydon Pk. Rd. SW19 6M 27
Haydon Pl.
GU1: Guil 4C 202 (4N 113)
GU14: Cove 6M 69
GU46: Yate 9D 48
Haydons Rd. SW19 6N 27
Haydons Road Station (Rail) 6A 28
Hayes, The KT18: Eps D 6D 80
Hayes Barton GU22: Pyr 3F 74
Hayes Chase BR4: W Wick 5N 47
Hayes Ct. SW2 2J 29
Hayes Cres. SM3: Chea 1J 61
Hayesens Ho. SW17 5A 28
Hayes La. BR3: Beck 2M 47
CR8: Ken 3M 83
RH13: Slin 8H 195
Hayes Wlk. RH6: Smal 7L 143
Hayes Way BR3: Beck 3M 47
Hayfields RH6: Horl 7F 142
Haygarth Pl. SW19 6J 27
Haygreen Cl. KT2: K Tham 7A 26
Haylett Gdns.
KT1: K Tham 8H 203 (3K 41)
Hayley Grn. RG42: Warf 6D 16
Hayling Av. TW13: Felt 4H 23
Hayling Ct. RH11: Craw 6A 182
SM3: Chea 1H 61
Haymeads Dr. KT10: Esh 3C 58
Haymer Gdns. KT4: W Pk 9F 42
Hayne Rd. BR3: Beck 1J 47
Haynes Cl. GU23: Rip 9K 75
SL3: Lang 1B 6
Haynt Wlk. SW20 2K 43
Hays Bri. Bus. Cen.
RH9: S Gods 5F 144
Hays Bri. Ho's.
RH9: S Gods 4E 144
Hayse Hill SL4: W'sor 4A 4
Haysleigh Gdns. SE20 1D 46
Hays Wlk. SM2: Chea 6J 61
Haywain RH8: Oxt 8N 105
Hayward Cl. SW19 8N 27
Haywardens RH7: Ling 6N 145
Hayward Gdns. SW15 9H 13
Hayward Rd. KT7: T Dit 7F 40
Haywards RH10: Craw 9H 163
Haywards Mead SL4: E Wic 1C 4
Haywood RG12: Brac 6A 32
Haywood Dr. GU52: Fleet 6B 88
Haywood Ri. BR6: Orp 2N 67
Hazel Av. GU1: Guil 8M 93
GU14: Cove 2L 89
(not continuous)
Hazel Bank SE25 1B 46
Hazelbank KT5: Surb 7B 42
Hazelbank Ct. KT16: Chert 7L 37
Hazelbank Rd. KT16: Chert 7L 37
Hazelbourne Rd.
SW12 1F 28
Hazelbury Cl. SW19 1M 43
Hazel Cl. CR0: Croy 6G 46
CR4: Mit 3H 45
RH2: Reig 5A 122
RH10: Craw D 1F 184
RH11: Craw 9A 162
TW2: Whitt 1C 24
TW8: Brent 3H 11
TW20: Eng G 7L 19
Hazel Ct. CR6: Warl 4H 85
GU1: Guil 8N 93
Hazeldene KT15: Addl 2L 55
Hazeldene Ct. CR8: Ken 2A 84
Hazel Dr. GU23: Rip 3H 95
Hazel Gro. GU26: Hind 8C 170
TW13: Felt 2H 23
TW18: Stain 7K 21
Hazelhurst BR3: Beck 1N 47
RH6: Horl 7G 143
Hazelhurst Cl. GU4: B'ham 7D 94
Hazelhurst Cres.
RH12: Hors 7F 196
Hazelhurst Dr. RH10: Wor 3J 183
Hazelhurst Rd. SW17 5A 28
Hazel La. TW10: Ham 3L 25
Hazell Hill RG12: Brac 2A 32
Hazell Rd. GU9: Farnh 1E 128
Hazel Mead KT17: Ewe 6F 60
Hazelmere Cl. KT22: Leat 6H 79
TW14: Felt 9F 8
Hazelmere Ct. SW2 2K 29
Hazel Pde. KT22: Fetc 9C 78
Hazel Rd. GU12: A Grn 5G 111
GU16: Mytc 3E 90
KT14: W By 1J 75
RH2: Reig 5A 122
Hazel Wlk. RH5: Nth H 8J 119
Hazel Way CR5: Chip 6D 82
KT22: Fetc 9C 78
RH10: Craw D 1F 184
Hazelway Cl. KT22: Fetc 1C 98
Hazelwick Av. RH10: Craw 1E 182
Hazelwick Ct. RH10: Craw 1E 182
Hazelwick Mill La.
RH10: Craw 1E 182
(not continuous)
Hazelwick Rd. RH10: Craw 2E 182
Hazelwick Rdbt.
RH10: Craw 1E 182
HAZELWOOD 7M 67
Hazelwood GU8: Els 7J 131
RH4: Dork 6H 119
RH11: Craw 3M 181
Hazelwood Av. SM4: Mord 3N 43
Hazelwood Cl.
RH10: Craw D 1C 184
Hazelwood Cotts.
GU6: Cranl 5M 175
GU7: Goda 7G 132
Hazelwood Ct. GU14: Cove 6K 69
KT6: Surb 5L 41
Hazelwood Gro. CR2: Sande 9E 64
Hazelwood Hgts. RH8: Oxt 9C 106
Hazelwood Ho's.
BR2: Brom 2N 47
Hazelwood La. CR5: Chip 5C 82
RG42: Bin, Warf 1M 15
Hazelwood Rd. GU21: Knap 5H 73
RH8: Oxt 1D 126
TN14: Cud 8M 67
Hazlebury Rd. SW6 5N 13
Hazledean Rd.
CR0: Croy 3E 200 (8A 46)
Hazledene Rd. W4 2B 12
Hazlemere Gdns.
KT4: W Pk 7F 42
Hazlewell Rd. SW15 8H 13
Hazlitt Cl. TW13: Hanw 5M 23
Hazon Way
KT19: Eps 5H 201 (8B 60)
Headcorn Pl. CR7: T Hea 3K 45
Headcorn Rd. CR7: T Hea 3K 45
Headington Cl.
RG40: W'ham 9C 14
Headington Ct. CR0: Croy 7B 200
Headington Dr.
RG40: W'ham 9C 14
Headington Rd. SW18 3A 28
Headlam Rd. SW4 1H 29
(not continuous)
Headland Way RH7: Ling 7M 145
HEADLEY
GU35 3C 168
KT18 4C 100
Headley Av. SM6: W'ton 2K 63
Headley Cl. KT19: Ewe 3N 59
RH10: Craw 9H 163
Headley Comn. Rd.
KT18: Head, Wal H 5C 100
Headley Ct. KT18: Head 1A 100
TN8: Eden 1M 147
HEADLEY DOWN 4G 169
Headley Dr. CR0: N Add 4L 65
KT18: Tat C 6G 81
Headley Flds. GU35: Head 4D 168
Headley Gro. KT20: Tad 7H 81
Headley Heath 6A 100
Headley Heath App.
KT20: Box H 8A 100
RH5: Mick 7N 99
Headley Hill Rd.
GU35: Head 4E 168
Headley La. GU30: Pass 8D 168
RH5: Mick 7J 99
Headley Mill 5B 168
Headley Pk. Cotts.
GU35: Head 9B 148
Headley Rd. GU26: G'hott 5K 169
GU35: Lind 4B 168
KT18: Eps D 7B 80
KT18: Eps D, Head 9N 79
KT18: Eps, Eps D 5A 80
KT22: Leat 9J 79
Headon Ct. GU9: Farnh 2J 129
Headway, The KT17: Ewe 5E 60
Headway Cl. TW10: Ham 5J 25
Hearmon Cl. GU46: Yate 9D 48
HEARN 2G 168
Hearne Rd. W4 2N 11
Hearn Va. GU35: H Dwn 2F 168
Hearnville Rd. SW12 2E 28
Hearn Wlk. RG12: Brac 9C 16
Hearsey Gdns.
GU17: B'water 9G 49
(not continuous)
Heart, The KT12: Wal T 7H 39
HEATH, THE 3C 56
Heath, The CR3: Cate 2N 103
GU3: Put 8A 112
Heathacre SL3: Coln 4G 6
Heatham Pk. TW2: Twick 1F 24
Heathbridge KT13: Weybr 4B 56
Heathbridge App.
KT13: Weybr 3B 56
Heath Bus. Cen. RH1: Salf 4F 142
TW3: Houn 7C 10
Heath Cl. CR2: S Croy 3M 63
GU9: U Hal 5H 109
GU12: Alde 3B 110
GU25: V Wat 3N 35
GU26: Hind 2A 170
RG41: W'ham 4A 30
RH12: Bro H 5E 196
SM7: Ban 1N 81
TW19: Stan 9L 7
UB3: Harl 3E 8
Heath Cnr. GU15: Camb 3E 70
Heathcote KT20: Tad 8J 81
Heathcote Cl. *GU12: A Va 1E 110*
(off Church Path)
Heathcote Ct. *SL4: W'sor 6G 4*
(off Osbourne Rd.)
Heathcote Dr.
RH19: E Grin 8L 165
Heathcote Rd. GU12: Ash 1F 110
GU15: Camb 1B 70
KT18: Eps 8K 201 (1C 80)
TW1: Twick 9H 11
Heathcotes RH10: Craw 5H 183
Heath Cotts. GU10: Fren 8J 129
GU26: Hind 3A 170
Heath Ct. CR0: Croy 7D 200
GU19: Bag 4J 51
RH12: Bro H 5E 196
TW4: Houn 7N 9
Heathcroft Av. TW16: Sunb 8G 22
Heathdale Av. TW4: Houn 6M 9
Heathdene KT20: Tad 5K 81
Heathdene Rd. SM6: W'ton 4F 62
SW16 8K 29
Heathdown Rd. GU22: Pyr 2F 74
Heath Dr. GU23: Send 9D 74
GU24: B'wood 7D 72
KT20: Wal H 3F 100
SM2: Sut 5A 62
SW20 3H 43
HEATH END 5H 109
Heatherbank Cl. KT11: Cob 7L 57
Heather Cl. GU2: Guil 2L 113
GU9: Farnh 5E 128
GU11: Alde 3K 109
GU12: A Va 8F 90
GU21: Wok 2M 73
KT15: N Haw 6K 55
KT20: K'wood 9K 81
RH1: Red 9F 102
RH10: Cop 8M 163
RH12: Hors 3K 197
TW7: Isle 8D 10
TW12: Hamp 9N 23
Heather Cotts. GU26: Hind 1B 170
Heather Ct. GU26: Hind 5E 170
Heatherdale Cl.
KT2: K Tham 7N 25
Heatherdale Rd.
GU15: Camb 2A 70
Heatherdene KT24: W Hors 3E 96
Heatherdene Av.
RG45: Crow 3D 48
Heatherdene Cl. CR4: Mit 3B 44
Heather Dr. GU35: Lind 4A 168
GU52: C Cro 8A 88
SL5: S'dale 6E 34
Heatherfield La.
KT13: Weybr 2F 56
Heatherfields KT15: N Haw 6K 55
Heather Gdns. GU14: Cove 3J 89
SM2: Sut 3M 61
Heatherlands RH6: Horl 7F 142
(not continuous)
TW16: Sunb 7H 23
Heatherlea Gro. KT4: W Pk 7G 43
Heatherleigh Ct.
RH12: Hors 4J 197
(off North Pde.)
Heatherley Cl. GU15: Camb 1N 69
Heatherley Rd. GU15: Camb 1N 69
Heather Mead GU16: Frim 4D 70
Heather Mead Ct.
GU16: Frim 4D 70
Heathermount RG12: Brac 3C 32
Heathermount Dr.
RG45: Crow 1E 48
Heathermount Gdns.
RG45: Crow 1E 48
Heather Pl. KT10: Esh 1B 58
Heather Ridge Arc.
GU15: Camb 2G 71
Heathers, The TW19: Stan 1A 22
Heatherset Cl. KT10: Esh 2C 58
Heatherset Gdns.
SW16 8K 29
HEATHERSIDE 2G 71
Heatherside Cl. KT23: Book 3N 97
Heatherside Dr.
GU25: V Wat 5K 35
Heatherside Rd. KT19: Ewe 4C 60
Heathersland RH4: Dork 8J 119
Heathervale Cvn. Pk.
KT15: N Haw 6L 55
Heathervale Rd.
KT15: N Haw 6K 55
Heathervale Way
KT15: N Haw 6L 55
Heather Vw. Cotts.
GU10: Fren 1H 149
Heather Wlk. GU24: B'wood 8A 72
KT12: Whit V 6F 56
RH6: Smal 8N 143
RH11: Craw 6N 181
TW2: Whitt 1A 24
(off Stephenson Rd.)
Heather Way CR2: Sels 5G 65
GU24: Chob 4H 53
GU26: Hind 5D 170
RH19: Fel 3J 165
Heatherway RG45: Crow 2F 48
Heathfield KT11: Cob 1A 78
RH10: Craw 9H 163
(not continuous)
Heathfield Av. SL5: S'dale 4B 34
SW18 1B 28
Heathfield Cl. BR2: Kes 2E 66
GU7: Goda 9H 133
GU22: Wok 5C 74
Heathfield Ct. W4 1C 12
Heathfield Dr. CR4: Mit 9C 28
RH1: Red 8C 122
Heathfield Gdns.
CR0: Croy 6C 200 (1A 64)
W4 1B 12
Heathfield Nth. TW2: Twick 1E 24
Heathfield Rd. BR2: Kes 2E 66
CR0: Croy 6D 200 (1A 64)
GU22: Wok 5C 74
KT12: Hers 1M 57
SW18 1B 28
Heathfields Cl. KT21: A'tead 5J 79
Heathfields Ct. TW4: Houn 8M 9
Heathfield Sth. TW2: Twick 1F 24
Heathfield Sq. SW18 1B 28
Heathfield Ter. W4 1B 12
Heathfield Va. CR2: Sels 5G 65
Heath Gdns. TW1: Twick 2F 24
Heath Gro. TW16: Sunb 8G 23
Heath Hill GU10: Dock 7D 148
RH4: Dork 2L 201 (5H 119)
Heath Hill Rd. Nth.
RG45: Crow 2G 48
Heath Hill Rd. Sth.
RG45: Crow 2G 49
Heath Ho. Rd. GU22: Wok 9F 72
Heathlands KT20: Tad 9J 81
RG12: Brac 3M 31
Heathlands Cl. GU21: Wok 1A 74
TW1: Twick 3F 24
TW16: Sunb 1H 39
Heathlands Ct. GU46: Yate 2D 68
RG40: W'ham 8E 30
Heathlands Rd.
RG40: W'ham 5E 30
Heathland St. GU11: Alde 2M 109
Heathlands Way TW4: Houn 8M 9
Heathland Vis. Cen. 6K 51
Heath La. GU5: Alb 1N 135
GU7: Bus 9K 133
GU9: U Hal 5H 109
GU10: Ews 6A 108
Heathmans Rd. SW6 4L 13
Heath Mead SW19 4J 27
Heath M. GU23: Rip 1K 95
Heath Mill La. GU3: Worp 3E 92
(not continuous)
Heathmoors RG12: Brac 4A 32
Heathpark Dr. GU20: Windl 3B 52
Heath Pl. GU19: Bag 4J 51
Heath Ride RG40: Finch 1A 48
RG45: Crow 2B 48
Heath Ridge Grn.
KT11: Cob 9A 58
Heath Ri. GU15: Camb 1B 70
GU23: Rip 1K 95
GU25: V Wat 3N 35
RH4: Westc 7C 118
SW15 9J 13
Heath Rd. CR3: Cate 1A 104
CR7: T Hea 2N 45
GU19: Bag 4J 51
GU21: Wok 2B 74
GU27: Hasl 3B 188
KT13: Weybr 1B 56
KT22: Oxs 8C 58
TW1: Twick 2F 24
TW2: Twick 2F 24
TW3: Houn, Isle 7B 10
Heathrow GU5: Gorn 8D 116
HEATHROW AIRPORT 6B 8
Heathrow Blvd. UB7: Sip 3A 8
(not continuous)
Heathrow C'way. Cen.
TW4: Houn 6J 9
Heathrow Central Station (Rail)
6B 8
Heathrow Cl. UB7: L'ford 4K 7
Heathrow Gateway
TW4: Houn 1M 23
Heathrow Intl. Trad. Est.
TW4: Houn 6J 9
Heathrow Terminals 1, 2 & 3 Station
(Tube) 6C 8
Heathrow Terminal 4 Station (Rail)
9D 8
Heathrow Terminal 4 Station (Tube)
8D 8
Heathrow Terminal 5 Station
(Rail & Tube, Open 2008)
6L 7
Heathrow Vis. Cen. 4D 8
Heath Royal SW15 9J 13
Heathside KT10: H Wood 9E 40
KT13: Weybr 2C 56
TW4: Houn 1N 23
Heathside Cl.
KT10: H Wood 9E 40
Heathside Ct. KT20: Tad 1G 101
Heathside Cres. GU22: Wok 4B 74
Heathside Gdns.
GU22: Wok 4C 74
Heathside La. GU26: Hind 3B 170
Heathside Pk. GU15: Camb 8G 50
Heathside Pk. Rd.
GU22: Wok 5B 74
Heathside Pl. KT18: Tat C 5J 81
Heathside Rd. GU22: Wok 5B 74
Heathurst Rd. CR2: Sande 5A 64
Heath Va. Bri. Rd.
GU12: A Va 7E 90
Heath Vw. KT24: E Hor 3G 97
Heathview Gdns. SW15 1H 27
Heathview Rd. CR7: T Hea 3L 45
GU8: Mil 3B 152
Heath Way RH12: Hors 3K 197
Heathway CR0: Croy 9J 47
CR3: Cate 3N 103
GU15: Camb 1B 70
KT24: E Hor 2G 97
SL5: Asc 9J 17
Heathway Cl. GU15: Camb 1B 70
Heathwood Cl. GU46: Yate 8C 48
Heathyfields Rd.
GU9: U Hal 6E 108
Heaton Rd. CR4: Mit 8E 28
Hebbecastle Down
RG42: Warf 7N 15
Hebdon Rd. SW17 4C 28
Heber Mans. *W14 2K 13*
(off Queen's Club Gdns.)
Heckets Ct. KT10: Esh 6C 58
Heckfield Pl. SW6 3M 13
Hectors La. RH19: E Grin 2E 186
Heddon Cl. TW7: Isle 7G 10
Heddon Wlk. GU14: Farnb 7M 69
Hedgecourt Pl. RH19: Fel 6H 165
Hedge Cft. GU46: Yate 9A 48
Hedgecroft Cotts. GU23: Rip 8K 75
Hedgehog La. GU27: Hasl 2F 188
Hedge La. RG42: Warf 7B 16
Hedgerley Ct. GU21: Wok 4M 73
Hedgers Almshouses
GU1: Guil 2F 114
(off Wykeham Rd.)
GU4: Guil 2F 114
(off Wykeham Rd.)
Hedgeside RH11: Craw 8A 182
Hedgeway GU2: Guil 5K 113
Hedingham Cl. RH6: Horl 7G 142
Hedingham Ho.
KT2: K Tham 2J 203
Hedley Rd. TW2: Whitt 1A 24
Heenan Cl. GU16: Frim G 7C 70
Heidegger Cres. SW13 3G 13
Heighton Gdns.
CR0: Wad 8A 200 (2M 63)
Heights, The KT13: Weybr 6B 56
Heights Cl. SM7: Ban 3K 81
SW20 8G 27

High St.—Holland

High St. GU10: Rowl 8D 128
GU11: Alde 2M 109
GU12: Alde 2N 109
GU14: Farnb 5B 90
GU15: Camb 9B 50
GU19: Bag 4J 51
GU21: Knap 4F 72
GU21: Wok 4B 74
(Broadmead Rd.)
GU21: Wok 2L 73
(Horsell Birch)
GU22: Wok 8C 74
GU23: Rip 8L 75
GU24: Chob 7H 53
GU24: W End 8C 52
GU27: Hasl 2H 189
GU35: Head 4D 168
GU47: Sandh 6E 48
(Church Rd.)
GU47: Sandh 6E 48
(Mountbatten Ri.)
KT1: H Wic 2G 203 (9J 25)
KT1: K Tham 5H 203 (2K 41)
KT3: N Mal 3D 42
KT7: T Dit 5G 40
KT8: W Mole 3A 40
KT10: Clay 3F 58
KT10: Esh 1B 58
KT11: Cob 1J 77
KT12: Wal T 7H 39
KT13: Weybr 1B 56
KT15: Addl 1K 55
KT17: Eps 9C 60
KT17: Ewe 6F 60
KT19: Eps 7J 201 (9C 60)
KT20: Tad 1H 101
KT22: Leat 9H 79
(not continuous)
KT22: Oxs 9D 58
KT23: Book 3B 98
RG12: Brac 1N 31
(not continuous)
RG45: Crow 3H 49
RH1: Blet 2N 123
RH1: Mers 6F 102
RH1: Nut 2K 123
RH1: Red 3D 122
RH2: Reig 3M 121
RH4: Dork 2K 201 (5H 119)
RH6: Horl 8F 142
RH7: Dorm 7N 145
RH8: Limp 6C 106
RH8: Oxt 8N 105
RH9: Gods 8F 104
RH10: Craw 3B 182
(not continuous)
RH12: Rusp 2B 180
RH14: Loxw 5H 193
RH19: E Grin 1B 186
SE25 . . . . .3C 46
SL3: Coln 3E 6
SL3: Dat 4L 5
SL3: Lang 1B 6
SL4: Eton 2G 4
SL4: W'sor 4G 5
SL5: Asc 2J 33
SL5: S'dale 4D 34
SL5: S'hill 4A 34
SM1: Sut 1N 61
SM3: Chea 3K 61
SM5: Cars 2E 62
SM7: Ban 2M 81
SW19 . . . . .6J 27
TN8: Eden 2L 147
TN16: Weste 5L 107
TW2: Whitt 1C 24
TW3: Houn 6B 10
(not continuous)
TW5: C'ford 4H 9
TW8: Brent 3J 11
TW11: Tedd 6F 24
TW12: Hamp, H Hill 9C 24
TW13: Felt 4G 23
TW17: Shep 5C 38
TW18: Stain 5G 21
TW19: Stan 9M 7
TW19: Wray 9B 6
TW20: Egh 6B 20
UB3: Harl 2E 8
UB7: Harm 2M 7
High St. Colliers Wood
SW19 . . . . .8B 28
HIGHSTREET GREEN 7K 173
High St. Grn. GU8: Chid 8H 173
High St. M. SW19 . . . . .6K 27
High Thicket Rd.
GU10: Dock 6C 148
High Tree Cl. KT15: Addl 2J 55
High Trees CR0: Croy 7H 47
SW2 . . . . .2L 29
High Trees Cl. CR3: Cate 9C 84
High Trees Ct. CR3: Cate 1C 104
RH6: Sid 7M 141
High Trees Rd. RH2: Reig 4A 122
High Vw. GU5: Gorn 8D 116
GU7: Goda 7H 133
(off Flambard Way)
Highview CR3: Cate 2B 104
GU21: Knap 4H 73
SM2: Chea 7L 61
Highview Av. SM6: W'ton 2K 63
High Vw. Cl. GU14: Farnb 1M 89
SE19 . . . . .1C 46
Highview Ct. RH2: Reig 3B 122
(off Wray Comn. Rd.)
Highview Cres.
GU15: Camb 6D 50
High Vw. Lodge
GU11: Alde 2M 109
Highview Path SM7: Ban 2M 81
High Vw. Rd. BR6: Dow 6J 67
GU2: Guil 6G 113
GU14: Farnb 1M 89
GU18: Ligh 7J 51
Highway RG45: Crow 2F 48
Highway, The SM2: Sut 5A 62
Highwayman's Ridge
GU20: Windl 1M 51
Highwold CR5: Chip 5E 82
Highwood BR2: Brom 2N 47
Highwood Cl. CR8: Ken 4N 83
GU46: Yate 2B 68
Highwood Pk.
RH11: Craw 7A 182
Highwoods CR3: Cate 3B 104
KT22: Leat 8J 79
Highworth RH13: Hors 7M 197
Hilary Av. CR4: Mit 2E 44
Hilary Cl. SW6 . . . . .3N 13
Hilbert Rd. SM3: Chea 9J 43
Hilborough Cl. SW19 . . . . .8A 28
Hilborough Way
BR6: Farnb 2M 67
Hilda Ct. KT6: Surb 6K 41
Hilda Va. Cl. BR6: Farnb 1K 67
Hilda Va. Rd. BR6: Farnb 1J 67
Hildenlea Pl. BR2: Brom 1N 47
Hildenley Cl. RH1: Mers 6H 103
Hildens, The RH4: Westc 7B 118
Hilder Gdns. GU14: Farnb 2B 90
Hilderley Ho. KT1: K Tham . . .5L 203
Hilders, The KT21: A'tead 4A 80
Hilders Cl. TN8: Eden 8K 127
Hilders La. TN8: Eden 8H 127
Hildreth St. SW12 . . . . .2F 28
Hildreth St. M. SW12 . . . . .2F 28
Hildyard Rd. SW6 . . . . .2M 13
Hilfield GU46: Yate 1E 68
Hilgay GU1: Guil 3B 114
Hilgay Cl. GU1: Guil 3B 114
Hilgay Ct. GU1: Guil 3B 114
Hill, The CR3: Cate 2C 104
Hillacre CR3: Cate 3B 104
Hilland Ri. GU35: Head 5E 168
Hillards Vw. GU6: Cranl 5N 155
Hillars Heath Rd. CR5: Coul . . .2J 83
Hillary Cl. GU9: Farnh 3G 129
RH19: E Grin 7C 166
Hillary Ct. TW19: Stan 2N 21
(off Explorer Av.)
Hillary Cres. KT12: Wal T 7K 39
Hillary Dr. RG45: Crow 1G 49
TW7: Isle 8F 10
Hillary Rd. GU9: Farnh 4G 128
Hill Barn CR2: Sande 7B 64
Hillberry RG12: Brac 6A 32
Hillborne Cl. UB3: Harl 1H 9
Hillbrook Gdns.
KT13: Weybr 4B 56
Hillbrook Ri. GU9: U Hal 6G 108
Hillbrook Rd. SW17 . . . . .4D 28
Hillbrow KT3: N Mal 2E 42
RH2: Reig 3A 122
Hillbrow Cl. GU3: Wood V 2E 112
Hillbrow Cotts. RH9: Gods 1F 124
Hillbrow Ct. RH9: Gods 1F 124
Hillbrow Rd. KT10: Esh 1C 58
Hillbury Cl. CR6: Warl 5F 84
Hillbury Gdns. CR6: Warl 5F 84
Hillbury Rd. CR3: Whyte 4D 84
CR6: Warl 4D 84
SW17 . . . . .4F 28
Hill Cl. CR8: Pur 9N 63
GU5: Wone 5D 134
GU21: Wok 3N 73
KT11: Cob 8A 58
Hill Copse Vw. RG12: Brac 9C 16
Hill Cnr. Farm Cvn. Pk.
GU14: Cove 7J 69
Hillcote Av. SW16 . . . . .8L 29
Hill Ct. GU7: Goda 4H 133
GU27: Hasl 2F 188
Hill Cres. KT4: W Pk 8H 43
KT5: Surb 8M 203 (4M 41)
Hill Crest GU8: Els 8H 131
(not continuous)
KT6: Surb 6L 41
Hillcrest GU9: H End 4J 109
(off Up. Weybourne La.)
GU51: Fleet 2B 88
KT13: Weybr 1C 56
RH19: D Pk 4A 166
Hillcrest Av. KT16: Chert 9G 36
Hillcrest Cl. BR3: Beck 5J 47
KT18: Eps 2E 80
RH10: Craw 3H 183
Hillcrest Ct. KT13: Weybr 1C 56
SM2: Sut 3B 62
(off Eaton Rd.)
Hill Crest Dr. GU10: Wrec 5E 128
Hillcrest Gdns.
KT10: H Wood 9F 40
Hillcrest Ho. GU4: Guil 1E 114
Hillcrest Mobile Home Pk.
KT20: Box H 9A 100
Hillcrest Pde. CR5: Coul 1F 82
Hillcrest Rd. CR3: Whyte 4C 84
CR8: Pur 6K 63
GU2: Guil 2J 113
GU15: Camb 8F 50
TN8: Eden 8L 127
TN16: B Hil 3F 86
Hillcrest Vw. BR3: Beck 5J 47
Hillcroft Av. CR8: Pur 9G 63
Hillcroft Ct. CR3: Cate 1B 104
Hillcroome Rd. SM2: Sut 3B 62
Hillcross Av. SM4: Mord 5J 43
Hilldale Rd. SM1: Sut 1L 61
Hilldeane Rd. CR8: Pur 5L 63
Hilldown Ct. SW16 . . . . .8J 29
Hilldown Rd. SW16 . . . . .8J 29
Hill Dr. SW16 . . . . .2K 45
Hillersdon Av. SW13 . . . . .5F 12
Hilley Fld. La. KT22: Fetc 9C 78
Hill Farm Cl. GU27: Hasl 3D 188
Hill Farm La. RG42: Bin 4K 15
Hillfield Av. SM4: Mord 5C 44
Hillfield Cl. GU1: Guil 1E 114
RH1: Red 3E 122
Hillfield Cotts. RH13: Itch 8B 196
Hillfield Ct. KT10: Esh 2B 58
Hill Fld. Rd. TW12: Hamp 8N 23
Hillfield Rd. RH1: Red 3E 122
Hillford Pl. RH1: Red 9E 122
Hillgarth GU26: Hind 4B 170
Hillgate Pl. SW12 . . . . .1F 28
Hill Gro. TW13: Hanw 3N 23
Hillhampton Pl. SL5: S'dale . . .6C 34
Hill Ho. Cl. RH10: T Hil 5D 184
Hill Ho. Dr. KT13: Weybr 7B 56
RH2: Reig 5N 121
TW12: Hamp 9A 24
Hillhouse La. RH12: Rudg . . .8N 175
Hill Ho. Rd. SW16 . . . . .6K 29
Hillhurst Gdns. CR3: Cate 7B 84
Hillier Gdns. CR0: Wad 2L 63
Hillier Ho. GU2: Guil 5L 113
Hillier Lodge TW11: Tedd 6D 24
Hillier Pl. KT9: Ches 3K 59
Hillier Rd. GU1: Guil 3C 114
SW11 . . . . .1D 28
Hilliers La. CR0: Bedd 9J 45
Hillingdale RH11: Craw 8A 182
TN16: B Hil 5D 86
Hillingdon Av. TW19: Stan 2N 21
Hill La. KT20: K'wood 8K 81
Hill Mead RH12: Hors 5G 197
Hillmead RH11: Craw 4L 181
Hillmont Rd. KT10: H Wood . . .9E 40
Hillmount GU22: Wok 5A 74
(off Constitution Hill)
HILL PARK 1K 107
Hill Pk. Ct. KT22: Leat 6F 78
Hill Pk. Dr. KT22: Leat 6F 78
Hill Pk. Sth. KT22: Leat 7F 78
Hill Path SW16 . . . . .6K 29
Hill Pl. RH11: Craw 5A 182
Hill Ri. KT10: H Wood 8H 41
RH4: Dork 3G 118
TW10: Rich 8K 11
Hillrise KT12: Wal T 6G 39
SL3: Lang 2C 6
Hill Ri. Ct. KT22: Leat 8H 79
(off Park Ri.)
Hill Rd. CR4: Mit 9F 28
CR8: Pur 8K 63
GU9: H End 5H 109
GU26: G'hott 6A 170
GU26: Hind 3A 170
GU27: Hasl 2G 188
KT22: Fetc 9B 78
SM1: Sut 2N 61
SM5: Cars 3C 62
Hillsborough Ct.
GU14: Cove 6K 69
Hillsborough Pk.
GU15: Camb 1G 70
Hills Farm La. RH12: Hors . . .7F 196
Hillside GU15: Camb 8L 49
GU22: Wok 7N 73
GU25: V Wat 5M 35
KT10: Esh 2B 58
RH10: Craw D 1E 184
RH12: Hors 6G 196
RH18: F Row 6H 187
SL5: S'hill 4N 33
SM7: Ban 2K 81
SW19 . . . . .7J 27
Hillside Av. CR8: Pur 9M 63
Hillside Cl. GU21: Knap 4G 72
GU35: H Dwn 3F 168
RH3: Brock 4N 119
RH11: Craw 5N 181
RH19: E Grin 7A 166
SM4: Mord 3K 43
SM7: Ban 3K 81
Hillside Ct.
GU1: Guil 5F 202 (4A 114)
Hillside Cres. GU16: Frim 7D 70
Hillside Dr. RG42: Bin 7H 15
Hillside Gdns. KT15: Addl 2H 55
RH3: Brock 3N 119
SM6: W'ton 4G 63
SW2 . . . . .3L 29
Hillside Ho. CR0: Wad 6A 200
Hillside La. GU9: H End 4J 109
Hillside Pk. SL5: S'dale 7C 34
Hillside Pas. SW16 . . . . .3K 29
Hillside Path CR5: Coul 5J 83
Hillside Rd.
CR0: Wad 8A 200 (2M 63)
CR3: Whyte 5D 84
CR5: Coul 5J 83
GU9: Weybo 5K 109
GU10: Fren 8H 129
GU11: Alde 4L 109
GU12: A Va 1F 110
GU27: Hasl 3D 188
KT5: Surb 8M 203 (3M 41)
KT17: Ewe 6H 61
KT21: A'tead 4M 79
SM2: Sut 4L 61
SW2 . . . . .3K 29
TN16: Tats 6G 87
Hillside Way GU7: Goda 4G 133
Hillsmead Way CR2: Sande . . .9D 64
Hills Pl. RH12: Hors 6G 197
Hillspur Cl. GU2: Guil 2J 113
Hillspur Rd. GU2: Guil 2J 113
Hill St. TW9: Rich 8K 11
Hill Sutton M.
RH19: E Grin 9B 166
Hillswood Dr. KT16: Chert 1D 54
Hillthorpe Cl. CR8: Pur 6K 63
Hill Top SM3: Sut 6L 43
SM4: Mord 5M 43
Hilltop Cl. GU3: Guil 8J 93
KT22: Leat 1J 99
SL5: Asc 1B 34
Hilltop La. CR3: Cate 4L 103
RH1: Cate, Mers 4L 103
Hilltop Ri. KT23: Book 4C 98
Hilltop Rd. CR3: Whyte 4B 84
RH2: Reig 5N 121
Hilltop Vw. GU46: Yate 1A 68
Hilltop Wlk. CR3: Wold 7H 85
Hill Vw.
RH4: Dork 1M 201 (4J 119)
RH18: F Row 8H 187
Hillview CR3: Whyte 4C 84
SW20 . . . . .8G 26
Hill Vw. Cl. KT20: Tad 8H 81
Hillview Cl. CR8: Pur 7M 63
Hillview Ct. GU22: Wok 5B 74
Hill Vw. Cres. GU2: Guil 1J 113
Hillview Dr. RH1: Red 4E 122
Hillview Gdns.
RH11: Craw 9A 182
Hill Vw. Pl. KT11: Cob 9N 57
Hill Vw. Rd. GU9: Farnh 1E 128
GU22: Wok 5B 74
KT10: Clay 4G 59
TW1: Twick 9G 10
TW19: Wray 9N 5
Hillview Rd. SM1: Sut 9A 44
Hillworth BR3: Beck 1L 47
Hillworth Rd. SW2 . . . . .1L 29
Hillybarn Rd. RH11: Ifi 9H 161
Hilsea Point SW15 . . . . .2G 26
Hilton Ct. RH6: Horl 7G 143
Hilton Way CR2: Sande 2E 84
Himley Rd. SW17 . . . . .6C 28
Hinchley Cl. KT10: H Wood 1F 58
Hinchley Dr. KT10: H Wood 9F 40
Hinchley Mnr.
KT10: H Wood 9F 40
Hinchley Way
KT10: H Wood 9G 40
HINCHLEY WOOD 9F 40
Hinchley Wood Station (Rail)
. . . . .9F 40
Hindell Cl. GU14: Farnb 6M 69
HINDHEAD 5D 170
Hindhead Cl. RH11: Craw 5A 182
Hindhead Common 4E 170
Hindhead Point SW15 . . . . .2G 26
Hindhead Rd. GU26: Hind 1C 188
GU27: Hasl 1C 188
Hindhead Way SM6: W'ton 2J 63
Hine Cl. CR5: Coul 9G 83
KT19: Eps 7A 60
Hinstock Cl. GU14: Cove 2M 89
Hinton Av. TW4: Houn 7L 9
Hinton Cl. RG45: Crow 9G 31
Hinton Dr. RG45: Crow 9G 31
Hinton Rd. SM6: W'ton 3G 63
Hipley Ct. GU1: Guil 4C 114
Hipley St. GU22: Wok 7D 74
Hippisley Ct. TW7: Isle 6F 10
Hitchcock Cl. TW17: Shep 2A 38
Hitchings Way RH2: Reig 7M 121
Hitherbury Cl.
GU2: Guil 8B 202 (6M 113)
Hitherfield Rd. SW16 . . . . .3K 29
Hitherhooks Hill RG42: Bin 9K 15
Hithermoor Rd.
TW19: Stan M 9H 7
Hitherwood GU6: Cranl 8N 155
Hitherwood Cl. RH2: Reig 1B 122
H Jones Cres. GU11: Alde 1A 110
HMP Brixton SW2 . . . . .1J 29
HMP Bronzefield
TW15: A'ford 5L 21
HMP Downview SM2: Sut 8A 62
HMP Highdown SM2: Sut 8A 62
HMP Wandsworth
SW18 . . . . .1B 28
HM Young Offenders Institution
Feltham TW13: Felt 4E 22
Hoadlands Cotts.
RH17: Hand 6N 199
Hoadly Rd. SW16 . . . . .4H 29
Hobart Ct. CR2: S Croy 8E 200
Hobart Gdns. CR7: T Hea 2A 46
Hobart Pl. TW10: Rich 1M 25
Hobart Rd. KT4: W Pk 9G 42
Hobbes Wlk. SW15 . . . . .8G 12
Hobbs Cl. KT14: W By 9K 55
Hobbs Ind. Est.
RH7: Newc 2H 165
Hobbs Rd. RH11: Craw 8M 181
SE27 . . . . .5N 29
Hobill Wlk. KT5: Surb 5M 41
Hocken Mead RH10: Craw . . .1H 183
Hockering Est.
GU22: Wok 5D 74
Hockering Gdns.
GU22: Wok 5C 74
Hockering Rd. GU22: Wok 5C 74
Hockford Cl. GU24: Pirb 4E 92
Hodge La. SL4: Wink 6L 17
(not continuous)
Hodges Cl. GU19: Bag 6H 51
Hodgkin Cl. RH10: Craw 4G 182
Hodgson Gdns. GU4: B'ham . . .9C 94
Hodgsonites GU7: Goda 4E 132
HOE 3F 136
Hoebrook Cl. GU22: Wok 8N 73
Hoe La. GU5: P'lake 3F 136
GU8: Hasc 6N 153
RH5: A Ham 3F 136
Hoffman Cl. RG42: Brac 7B 16
Hoffmann Gdns. CR2: Sels 4E 64
Hogan Bus. Cen.
GU21: Wok 4A 74
Hogarth Av. TW15: A'ford 7D 22
Hogarth Bus. Pk. W4 . . . . .2D 12
Hogarth Cl. GU47: C Tow 9K 49
Hogarth Ct. TW5: Hest 3M 9
Hogarth Cres. CR0: Croy 6N 45
SW19 . . . . .9B 28
Hogarth Gdns. TW5: Hest 3A 10
Hogarth La. W4 . . . . .2D 12
Hogarth Rd. RH10: Craw 6D 182
SW5 . . . . .1N 13
HOGARTH RDBT. 2D 12
Hogarth's House 2D 12
(off Hogarth La.)
Hogarth Ter. W4 . . . . .2D 12
Hogarth Way TW12: Hamp 9C 24
Hogden Cl. KT20: K'wood 3L 101
Hogden La. KT23: Book 7A 98
RH5: Ran C 9M 97
(not continuous)
HOG HATCH 6F 108
Hog Hatch GU9: U Hal 5F 108
(off Newmans Ct.)
Hoghatch La. GU9: U Hal 6F 108
Hog's Back
GU2: Guil 8A 202 (6H 113)
GU3: Guil, Put, Wan 7L 111
GU10: Seal 8B 110
(not continuous)
Hog's Back Brewery 7D 110
Hogscross La. CR5: Coul 1D 102
Hog's Hill RH10: Craw 6B 182
Hogshill La. KT11: Cob 1J 77
(not continuous)
Hogsmill Ho. KT1: K Tham 5L 203
Hogsmill La.
KT1: K Tham . . .6M 203 (2M 41)
Hogsmill Wlk.
KT1: K Tham 5J 203
Hogsmill Way KT19: Ewe 2B 60
Hogspudding La.
RH5: Newd 9B 140
Hogtrough La. RH1: Sth N 4G 123
RH8: Oxt 6L 105
RH9: Gods 5K 105
Hogwood Rd. RH14: Ifo 5E 192
Holbeach M. SW12 . . . . .2F 28
Holbeck RG12: Brac 5L 31
Holbein Rd. RH10: Craw 6D 182
Holborn Way CR4: Mit 1D 44
Holbreck Pl. GU22: Wok 5B 74
HOLBROOK 1L 197
Holbrook Cl. GU4: Chil 2A 134
GU9: Weybo 4L 109
Holbrook Club, The 2L 197
Holbrook Ct. TW20: Egh 6E 20
Holbrooke Pl. TW10: Rich 8K 11
Holbrook Mdw. TW20: Egh 7E 20
Holbrook School La.
RH12: Hors 1K 197
Holbrook Way GU11: Alde 5N 109
Holcombe Cl.
TN16: Weste 4M 107
Holcombe St. W6 . . . . .1G 13
Holcon Ct. RH1: Red 9E 102
Holcroft Ct. RH19: E Grin 6B 166
Holden Brook La.
RH5: Ockl 7M 157
Holden Pl. KT11: Cob 1J 77
Holdernesse Cl. TW7: Isle 4G 10
Holdernesse Rd.
SW17 . . . . .4D 28
Holderness Way SE27 . . . . . . .6M 29
Holder Rd. GU12: Alde 3C 110
RH10: Craw 6F 182
Holdfast La. GU27: Hasl 9K 171
HOLE HILL 5B 118
Holehill La. RH4: Westc 4A 118
Hole La. TN8: Eden 5H 127
Holford Rd. GU1: Guil 3C 114
HOLLAND 3C 126

Holland Av. SM2: Sut 5M 61
SW20 . . . . .9E 26
Holland Cl. GU9: Farnh 3K 129
KT19: Eps 7B 60
RH1: Red 3D 122
Holland Ct. KT6: Surb 6K 41
Holland Cres. RH8: Oxt 2C 126
Holland Gdns. GU51: Fleet 5B 88
TW8: Brent 2M 11
TW20: Thor 1H 37
Holland Ho. *SL4: Eton 2F 4*
(off Common La.)
Holland La. RH8: Oxt 2C 126
Holland Pines RG12: Brac 6L 31
Holland Rd. RH8: Oxt 2C 126
SE25 . . . . .4D 46
Hollands, The GU22: Wok 5A 74
KT4: W Pk 7E 42
TW13: Hanw 5L 23
Hollands Ct. RH19: E Grin 6C 166
Hollands Fld. RH12: Bro H . . .4E 196
Hollands Way RH12: Warn 9F 178
RH19: E Grin 6C 166
Hollerith Ri. RG12: Brac 5N 31
Holles Cl. TW12: Hamp 7A 24
Hollies, The GU17: Haw 5M 69
KT15: Addl 2L 55
(off Crockford Pk. Rd.)
RH8: Oxt 2D 126
Hollies Av. KT14: W By 9H 55
Hollies Cl. SW16 . . . . .7L 29
TW1: Twick 3F 24
Hollies Ct. KT15: Addl 2L 55
Hollies Way SW12 . . . . .1E 28
Hollin Ct. RH10: Craw 9C 162
Hollingbourne Cres.
RH11: Craw 9A 182
Hollingsworth Ct. KT6: Surb . . .6K 41
Hollingsworth Rd. CR0: Croy . . .3E 64
Hollington Cres. KT3: N Mal . . .5E 42
Hollingworth Cl.
KT8: W Mole 3N 39
Hollingworth Way
TN16: Weste 4M 107
Hollis Row RH1: Red 5D 122
Hollis Wood Dr.
GU10: Wrec 6D 128
Hollman Gdns. SW16 . . . . . . .7M 29
Hollow, The GU7: Eash 7C 132
GU10: Ews 5A 108
RH11: Craw 4L 181
Holloway Cl. UB7: Harm 1N 7
Holloway Dr. GU25: V Wat 3A 36
HOLLOWAY HILL 9H 133
Holloway Hill GU7: Goda 7G 133
KT16: Chert 9E 36
Holloway Ho. TW20: Egh 6B 20
Holloway La.
UB7: Harm, W Dray 2M 7
Holloway St. TW3: Houn 6B 10
Hollow Cl. GU2: Guil 4L 113
Hollow La. GU25: V Wat 2M 35
GU35: Head 3D 168
RH5: A Com, Wott 9L 117
RH7: Dorm 1D 166
RH19: E Grin 4F 166
Hollows, The TW8: Brent 2M 11
Hollow Way GU26: G'hott 5A 170
Holly Acre GU46: Yate 1C 68
Holly Av. GU16: Frim 3F 70
KT12: Wal T 7L 39
KT15: N Haw 6J 55
Hollybank GU24: W End 9C 52
Hollybank Cl. TW12: Hamp 6A 24
Holly Bank Rd. GU22: Wok 8L 73
Hollybank Rd. KT14: W By 1J 75
Hollybrook Pk. GU35: Bor 6A 168
Hollybush Bus. Cen.
RH10: S Bri 6K 163
Hollybush Cl. RH10: Craw . . .2C 182
Hollybush Ind. Est.
GU11: Alde 8C 90
Holly Bush La.
TW12: Hamp 8N 23
Hollybush La. GU10: Fren 1H 149
GU11: Alde 8C 90
GU23: Rip 6M 75
Hollybush Ride
GU20: Windl 9K 33
RG40: Finch 2B 48
RG45: Crow 3B 48
Hollybush Rd. KT2: K Tham . . .6L 25
RH10: Craw 2C 182
Holly Cl. BR3: Beck 3M 47
GU12: Alde 2A 110
GU14: Cove 1M 89
GU21: Wok 6L 73
GU35: H Dwn 4H 169
KT16: L'cross 9K 35
RH10: Craw 1E 182
RH12: Hors 3A 198
SM6: W'ton 5F 62
TW13: Hanw 6M 23
TW20: Eng G 7L 19
Hollycombe TW20: Eng G 5M 19
Holly Ct. *KT16: Chert 7H 37*
(off King St.)
KT22: Leat 9G 79
(off Belmont Rd.)
RG45: Crow 3D 48
SM2: Sut 4M 61
Holly Cres. BR3: Beck 4J 47
SL4: W'sor 5A 4
Hollycroft Cl.
CR2: S Croy . . .8F 200 (2B 64)
UB7: Sip 2B 8
Hollycroft Gdns. UB7: Sip 2B 8
Hollydale Dr. BR2: Brom 1H 67
Holly Dr. SL4: O Win 8H 5
Holly Farm Rd. UB2: S'hall 1M 9
Hollyfield Rd. KT5: Surb 6M 41
Hollyfields Cl. GU15: Camb 1N 69
Holly Ga. KT15: Addl 1K 55
Holly Grn. KT13: Weybr 1E 56
Hollygrove Cl. TW3: Houn 7N 9
Holly Hedge Cl. GU16: Frim . . .4C 70
Holly Hedge Rd. GU16: Frim . . .4C 70
Hollyhedge Rd. KT11: Cob 1J 77
HOLLY HILL 9N 187
Holly Hill Dr. SM7: Ban 3M 81
Holly Hill Pk. SM7: Ban 4M 81
Hollyhock Dr. GU24: Bis 2D 72
Hollyhook Cl. RG45: Crow 1F 48
Holly Ho. RG12: Brac 5N 31
TW8: Brent 2J 11
Holly La. GU3: Worp 7F 92
GU7: Goda 7F 132
SM7: Ban 3M 81
Holly La. E. SM7: Ban 3M 81
Holly La. W. SM7: Ban 4M 81
Holly Lea GU4: J Wel 6N 93
Holly Lodge *GU22: Wok 4B 74*
(off Heathside Cres.)
Holly Lodge Mobile Home Pk.
KT20: Lwr K 4K 101
Hollymead SM5: Cars 9D 44
Hollymead Rd. CR5: Chip 5E 82
Hollymeoak Rd. CR5: Coul 6F 82
Hollymoor La. KT19: Ewe 6C 60
Holly Pde. *KT11: Cob 1J 77*
(off High St.)
Hollyridge GU27: Hasl 2F 188
Holly Rd. GU12: Alde 2A 110
GU14: Cove 1L 89
RH2: Reig 5N 121
TW1: Twick 2F 24
TW3: Houn 7B 10
TW12: H Hill 7C 24
W4 . . . . .1C 12
Holly Spring Cotts.
RG12: Brac 8B 16
Holly Spring La. RG12: Brac . . .9A 16
Holly Tree Cl. SW19 . . . . .2J 27
Hollytree Gdns. GU16: Frim 6B 70
Holly Tree Rd. CR3: Cate 9B 84
Holly Wlk. SL4: W'sor 5B 18
HOLLYWATER 8A 168
Hollywater Rd. GU30: Pass . . .9A 168
GU35: Bor, White 8A 168
Holly Way CR4: Mit 3H 45
GU17: B'water 2J 69
Hollywood Bowl
Bracknell 1N 31
Crawley 2B 182
Hollywood Rd. SW10 . . . . .2N 13
Hollywoods CR0: Sels 5J 65
Holman Cl. RH11: Craw 9N 181
Holman Ct. KT17: Ewe 5F 60
Holman Hunt Ho. *W6 . . . . .1K 13*
(off Field Rd.)
Holman Rd. KT19: Ewe 2B 60
Holmbank Dr. TW17: Shep 3F 38
Holmbrook Cl. GU14: Cove 1H 89
Holmbrook Gdns.
GU14: Cove 1H 89
Holmbury Av. RG45: Crow 9F 30
Holmbury Cl. RH11: Craw 5A 182
Holmbury Ct. CR2: S Croy 2B 64
SW17 . . . . .4D 28
SW19 . . . . .8C 28
Holmbury Dr. RH5: Nth H 8J 119
Holmbury Gro. CR0: Sels 4J 65
Holmbury Hill Rd.
RH5: H Mary 9J 137
Holmbury Keep *RH6: Horl . . .7G 142*
(off Maize Cft.)
Holmbury La.
RH5: For G, H Mary 1L 157
Holmbury Rd.
GU5: H Mary 9H 137
GU6: Ewh 9H 137
RH5: H Mary 9H 137
HOLMBURY ST MARY 6K 137
Holmbush Cl. RH12: Hors 2K 197
Holmbush Ct. RH12: Fay 8G 181
Holmbush Farm World
RH12: Fay 8G 181
Holmbush Potteries Ind. Est.
RH12: Fay 8H 181
Holmbush Rd. SW15 . . . . .9K 13
Holm Cl. KT15: Wood 8G 55
Holm Ct. GU7: Goda 4G 132
Holmcroft KT20: Wal H 3G 101
RH10: Craw 4C 182
Holmdene Cl. BR3: Beck 1M 47
Holmead Rd. SW6 . . . . .3N 13
Holme Chase KT13: Weybr 3D 56
Holme Cl. RG45: Crow 9F 30
Holme Ct. TW7: Isle 6G 10
Holmefield Pl. KT15: N Haw . . .6K 55
HOLME GREEN 5E 30
Holmes Cl. CR8: Pur 9M 63
GU22: Wok 8B 74
SL5: S'hill 5N 33
Holmes Ct. *GU26: G'hott 6B 170*
(off Boundary Rd.)
Holmesdale *KT13: Weybr 3E 56*
(off Bridgewater Rd.)
Holmesdale Av.
RH1: Mers 9G 102
SW14 . . . . .6A 12
Holmesdale Cl. GU1: Guil 2D 114
SE25 . . . . .2C 46
Holmesdale Mnr.
RH1: Red 1E 122
Holmesdale Natural History Mus.
. . . . .3N 121
Holmesdale Pk. RH1: Nut 3K 123
Holmesdale Rd. CR0: Croy 4A 46
RH1: Sth N 5K 123
RH2: Reig 2M 121
RH5: Nth H 9H 119
SE25 . . . . .4A 46
TW9: Kew 4M 11
TW11: Tedd 8J 25
Holmesdale Ter.
RH5: Nth H 9H 119
Holmesdale Vs.
RH5: Mid H 2H 139
Holmes Place Health Club
Croydon 4C 200 (9N 45)
Hammersmith 1J 13
(off Hammersmith Rd.)
Merton 7A 28
Holmes Rd. SW19 . . . . .8A 28
TW1: Twick 3F 24
Holmeswood SM2: Sut 3N 61
HOLMETHORPE 9F 102
Holmethorpe Av. RH1: Red . . .9F 102
Holmethorpe Ind. Est.
RH1: Red 9F 102
Holmewood Gdns.
SW2 . . . . .1K 29
Holmewood Rd. SE25 . . . . . . .2B 46
SW2 . . . . .1J 29
Holmgrove Ho. CR8: Pur 8L 63
Holming End RH12: Hors 3A 198
Holmlea Ct. CR0: Croy 6E 200
Holmlea Rd. SL3: Dat 4N 5
Holmlea Wlk. SL3: Dat 4M 5
Holm Oak Cl. SW15 . . . . .9L 13
Holmoaks Ho. BR3: Beck 1M 47
Holmside Rd. SW12 . . . . .1E 28
Holmsley Cl. KT3: N Mal 5E 42
Holmsley Ho. *SW15 . . . . .1E 26*
(off Tangley Gro.)
Holm Ter. RH4: Dork 8H 119
Holmwood Av. CR2: Sande 9C 64
Holmwood Cl. KT15: Addl 2J 55
KT24: E Hor 6F 96
SM2: Chea 5J 61
HOLMWOOD CORNER 6K 139
Holmwood Gdns.
SM6: W'ton 3F 62
Holmwood Rd. KT9: Ches 2K 59
SM2: Chea 5H 61
Holmwood Station (Rail) 7J 139
Holmwood Vw. Rd.
RH5: Mid H 2H 139
Holne Chase SM4: Mord 5L 43
Holroyd Cl. KT10: Clay 5F 58
Holroyd Rd. KT10: Clay 5F 58
SW15 . . . . .7H 13
Holsart Cl. KT20: Tad 9G 81
Holstein Av. KT13: Weybr 1B 56
Holst Mans. SW13 . . . . .2H 13
Holsworthy Way KT9: Ches 2J 59
Holt, The SM4: Mord 3M 43
SM6: W'ton 1G 62
Holt Cl. GU14: Farnb 7A 70
Holt La. RG41: W'ham 1A 30
Holton Heath RG12: Brac 3D 32
HOLT POUND 7C 128
Holt Pound Cotts.
GU10: H Pou 7B 128
Holt Pound La.
GU10: H Pou 6B 128
Holtwood Rd. KT22: Oxs 9C 58
HOLTYE 7N 167
Holtye Av. RH19: E Grin 7B 166
HOLTYE COMMON 6N 167
Holtye Pl. RH19: E Grin 7C 166
Holtye Rd. RH19: E Grin 8B 166
RH19: Hamm 6L 167
TN8: Cow, Hamm 6L 167
Holtye Wlk. RH10: Craw 5E 182
Holwood Cl. KT12: Wal T 8K 39
Holwood Pk. Av.
BR6: Farnb 1H 67
Holybourne Av. SW15 . . . . .1F 26
Holyhead Ct. KT1: K Tham 8H 203
Holyoake Av. GU21: Wok 4M 73
Holyoake Cres. GU21: Wok . . .4M 73
Holyport Rd. SW6 . . . . .3J 13
Holyrood RH19: E Grin 12C 166
Holyrood Pl. RH11: Craw 7N 181
Holywell Cl. GU14: Farnb 7M 69
TW19: Stan 2N 21
Holywell Way TW19: Stan 2N 21
Hombrook Dr. RG42: Brac 9K 15
Hombrook Ho. RG42: Brac 9K 15
Homebeech Ho. *GU22: Wok . . .5A 74*
(off Mt. Hermon Rd.)
Home Cl. GU25: V Wat 5N 35
KT22: Fetc 8D 78
RH10: Craw 1G 183
SM5: Cars 8D 44
Home Ct.
KT6: K Tham 8H 203 (4K 41)
Home Farm Cl.
GU14: Farnb 8B 70
KT7: T Dit 6F 40
KT10: Esh 3B 58
KT16: Otter 4C 54
KT20: Tad 4J 81
RH3: Betch 4D 120
TW17: Shep 3F 38
Home Farm Cotts.
GU8: P Har 6N 131
Home Farm Gdns.
KT12: Wal T 8K 39
Home Farm Ho.
RH12: Hors 6J 197
(off Springfield Rd.)
Home Farm Rd. GU7: Bus . . .9H 133
Homefield GU8: Thur 7G 150
SM4: Mord 3M 43
Homefield Av. KT12: Hers 1L 57
Homefield Cl. KT15: Wood 8G 55
KT22: Leat 8J 79
RH6: Horl 7F 142
Homefield Gdns. CR4: Mit 1A 44
KT20: Tad 7H 81
Homefield Pk. SM1: Sut 3N 61
Homefield Rd. CR5: Coul 6M 83
CR6: Warl 6F 84
KT12: Wal T 6M 39
SW19 . . . . .7J 27
W4 . . . . .1E 12
Homegreen Ho.
GU27: Hasl 2E 188
Homeland Dr. SM2: Sut 5N 61
Homelands KT22: Leat 8J 79
Homelea Cl. GU14: Farnb 6N 69
Homeleigh Ct. SW16 . . . . .4J 29
Homeleigh Cres.
GU12: A Va 5E 90
Home Mdw. SM7: Ban 3M 81
Homemead Rd. CR0: Croy 5G 45
Home Pk. RH8: E Mol 4J 41
RH8: Oxt 9C 106
Home Pk. Cl. GU5: Braml 5B 134
Home Pk. Ct.
KT1: K Tham 8H 203
Homepark Ho. GU9: Farnh . . .1H 129
Home Pk. Pde.
KT1: H Wic 3G 203
Home Pk. Rd. GU46: Yate 9C 48
SW19 . . . . .5L 27
Home Pk. Ter. KT1: H Wic . . .3G 203
Home Pk. Wlk.
KT1: K Tham 8H 203 (3K 41)
Homer Rd. CR0: Croy 5G 47
Homersham Rd.
KT1: K Tham 1N 41
Homers Rd. SL4: W'sor 4A 4
Homesdale Rd. CR3: Cate . . .1A 104
Homestall GU2: Guil 3G 113
Homestall Rd.
RH19: Ash W 9G 166
Homestead GU6: Cranl 6A 156
Homestead & Middle Vw.
Mobile Home Pk.
GU3: Norm 9B 92
Homestead Dr. GU3: Norm 9A 92
Homestead Gdns.
KT10: Clay 2E 58
Homestead Rd. CR3: Cate . . .1A 104
SW6 . . . . .3L 13
TN8: Eden 7K 127
TW18: Stain 7K 21
Homestead Way
CR0: N Add 7M 65
Homestream Ho.
RH12: Hors 7H 197
Homethorne Ho.
RH11: Craw 4A 182
Home Vs. GU5: Alb 3L 135
Homewater Ho.
KT17: Eps 6M 201 (9D 60)
Homewaters Av.
TW16: Sunb 9G 23
Homewood GU6: Cranl 7B 156
Homewood Cl.
TW12: Hamp 7N 23
Homewoods SW12 . . . . .1G 28
Homeworth Ho. *GU22: Wok . . .5A 74*
(off Mt. Hermon Rd.)
Hone Hill GU47: Sandh 7G 48
Hones Yd. Bus. Pk.
GU9: Farnh 1J 129
Honeybrook Rd. SW12 . . . . . . .1G 28
Honeycrock Ct. RH1: Salf 1E 142
Honeycrock La. RH1: Salf 1E 142
Honeydown Cotts.
GU28: North 8E 190
HONEYHILL 7E 30
Honey Hill RG40: W'ham 6E 30
Honeyhill Rd. RG42: Brac 9M 15
Honey La.
RH12: Oak, Rowh 6M 177
Honey La. Ho. *SW10 . . . . .2N 13*
(off Finborough Rd.)
Honeypot La. TN8: Eden 8F 126
Honeypots Rd. GU22: Wok 9N 73
Honeysuckle Bottom
KT24: E Hor 3F 116
Honeysuckle Cl.
RG45: Crow 9F 30
RH6: Horl 7G 143
Honeysuckle Gdns.
CR0: Croy 6G 47
Honeysuckle La.
GU35: H Dwn 4G 168
RH5: Nth H 8J 119
RH11: Craw 9A 162
Honeysuckle Wlk.
RH12: Hors 3N 197
Honeywood Heritage Cen. . . .2D 62
Honeywood La. RH5: Oak . . .4M 177
Honeywood Rd.
RH13: Hors 4N 197
TW7: Isle 7G 10
Honeywood Wlk. SM5: Cars . . .1D 62
Honister Gdns. GU51: Fleet . . .3D 88
Honister Hgts. CR8: Pur 1A 84
Honister Wlk. GU15: Camb 2H 71
Honnor Gdns. TW7: Isle 5D 10
Honnor Rd. TW18: Stain 8M 21
Hood Av. SW14 . . . . .8B 12
Hood Cl.
CR0: Croy 1A 200 (7M 45)
Hood Rd. SW20 . . . . .8E 26
HOOK 2L 59
Hooke Rd. KT24: E Hor 3G 97
Hookfield
KT19: Eps 6G 201 (9B 60)
Hookfield M.
KT19: Eps 6G 201 (9B 60)
HOOK HEATH 7L 73
Hook Heath Av. GU22: Wok . . .6L 73
Hook Heath Gdns.
GU22: Wok 8J 73
Hook Heath Rd. GU22: Wok . . .8H 73
Hook Hill CR2: Sande 6B 64
Hook Hill La. GU22: Wok 8L 73
Hook Hill Pk. GU22: Wok 8L 73
Hook Ho. La. GU8: Duns 3M 173
Hookhouse La. GU8: Loxh . . .1N 173
Hookhouse Rd.
GU8: Duns, Loxh 1N 173
HOOK JUNC. 9L 41
Hook La. GU3: Put 8N 111
GU5: Shere 1B 136
GU24: W End 9N 51
Hookley Cl. GU8: Els 8J 131
Hookley La. GU8: Els 8J 131
Hook Mill La. GU18: Ligh 5A 52
Hook Ri. Nth. KT6: Surb 9L 41
Hook Ri. Sth. KT6: Surb 9L 41
Hook Ri. Sth. Ind. Pk.
KT6: Ches 9M 41
Hook Rd. KT6: Surb 8L 41
KT9: Ches 2K 59
KT19: Eps, Ewe
. . . . .5K 201 (4B 60)
Hookstile La. GU9: Farnh 2H 129
Hookstone La.
GU24: W End 7C 52
Hook St. GU6: Alf 8K 175
HOOKWOOD 9B 142
Hookwood Cnr. RH8: Limp . . .6D 106
Hookwood Cotts.
KT18: Head 2B 100
HOOKWOOD PARK 6D 106
Hookwood Pk. RH8: Limp 7D 106
HOOLEY 8F 82
Hooley La. RH1: Red 4D 122
Hope Av. RG12: Brac 6C 32
Hope Cl. SM1: Sut 2A 62
TW8: Brent 1L 11
Hope Cotts. RG12: Brac 2A 32
Hope Ct. RH11: Craw 8N 181
Hope Fountain GU15: Camb . . .2E 70
Hope Grant's Rd.
GU11: Alde 9M 89
(not continuous)
Hope Ho. CR0: Croy 6F 200
Hope La. GU9: U Hal 6G 108
Hopeman Cl. GU47: C Tow 7J 49
Hopes Cl. TW5: Hest 2A 10
Hope St. GU8: Els 7H 131
Hope Way GU11: Alde 1L 109
Hopfield GU21: Wok 3A 74
Hopfield Av. KT14: Byf 8N 55
Hopgarden Cl. TN8: Eden 9M 127
Hophurst Cl.
RH10: Craw D 1E 184
Hophurst Dr.
RH10: Craw D 1E 184
Hophurst Hill
RH10: Craw D 8G 164
Hophurst La.
RH10: Craw D 1E 184
Hopkin Cl. GU2: Guil 8L 93
Hopkins Ct. RH11: Craw 8N 181
Hopper Va. RG12: Brac 5M 31
Hoppety, The KT20: Tad 9J 81
Hoppingwood Av.
KT3: N Mal 2D 42
Hopton Ct. *GU2: Guil 3H 113*
(off Park Barn Dr.)
Hopton Gdns. KT3: N Mal 5F 42
Hopton Rd. SW16 . . . . .6J 29
Hopwood Cl. SW17 . . . . .4A 28
Horace Rd.
KT1: K Tham . . .6L 203 (2M 41)
Horatio Av. RG42: Warf 9C 16
Horatio Ho. *W6 . . . . .1J 13*
(off Fulham Pal. Rd.)
Horatio Pl. SW19 . . . . .9M 27
Horatius Way CR0: Wad 2K 63
Hordern Ho. RH12: Hors 7G 196
Horder Rd. SW6 . . . . .4K 13
Horewood Rd. RG12: Brac 5N 31

Jubilee Cl.—Kiln M.

Jubilee Cl. GU14: Cove 1J **89**
KT1: H Wic 9J **25**
SL5: Asc 9J **17**
TW19: Stan 1L **21**
Jubilee Cotts. SL3: Lang 1D **6**
Jubilee Ct. BR4: W Wick 7M **47**
RG12: Brac 2A **32**
SL5: Asc 8J **17**
*TW3: Houn 6B **10***
(off Bristow Rd.)
TW18: Stain 6J **21**
Jubilee Cres. KT15: Addl 2M **55**
Jubilee Dr. GU12: A Va 7E **90**
Jubilee Est. RH13: Hors 4L **197**
Jubilee Hall Rd.
GU14: Farnb 1A **90**
Jubilee La. GU10: Wrec 7F **128**
GU26: G'hott 6A **170**
Jubilee Rd. GU11: Alde 5N **109**
GU16: Mytc 3E **90**
RH12: Rudg 9E **176**
SM3: Chea 4J **61**
Jubilee Ter. RH3: Brock 7B **120**
RH4: Dork 1L **201** (4H **119**)
Jubilee Vs. KT10: Esh 7D **40**
Jubilee Wlk. RH10: Craw 3E **182**
*RH12: Hors 6J **197***
(off Albion Way)
Jubilee Way KT9: Ches 1N **59**
SL3: Dat 3M **5**
SW19 . . . . .9N **27**
TW14: Felt 2H **23**
Judge's Ter. RH19: E Grin 1A **186**
Judge Wlk. KT10: Clay 3E **58**
Judy's Pas. SL4: Eton 1F **4**
Jug Hill TN16: B Hil 3F **86**
Jugshill La. RH5: Oak 2B **178**
Julian Cl. GU21: Wok 5M **73**
Julian Hill KT13: Weybr 4B **56**
Julien Rd. CR5: Coul 2H **83**
Juliet Gdns. RG42: Warf 9D **16**
Julius Hill RG42: Warf 9D **16**
Jumps Rd. GU10: Churt 7K **149**
Junction Pl. GU27: Hasl 2D **188**
Junction Rd. CR2: S Croy 2A **64**
GU18: Ligh 6M **51**
RH4: Dork 2J **201** (5G **119**)
TW8: Brent 1K **11**
TW15: A'ford 6D **22**
W5 . . . . .1K **11**
June Cl. CR5: Coul 1F **82**
June La. RH1: Salf 1F **142**
Junewood Cl. KT15: Wood 7H **55**
Juniper RG12: Brac 7A **32**
Juniper Cl. GU1: Guil 7L **93**
KT9: Ches 2M **59**
RH2: Reig 5A **122**
RH8: Oxt 2D **126**
TN16: B Hil 4G **87**
Juniper Ct. KT8: W Mole 3B **40**
*TW3: Houn 7B **10***
(off Grove Rd.)
Juniper Dr. GU24: Bis 2D **72**
Juniper Gdns. SW16 . . . . .9G **28**
TW16: Sunb 7G **23**
Juniper Ho. TW9: Kew 4A **12**
Juniper Pl. GU4: Chil 1N **133**
Juniper Rd. GU14: Cove 9H **69**
RH2: Reig 5A **122**
RH11: Craw 9A **162**
Juniper Wlk. RH3: Brock 5B **120**
Jura Cl. RH11: Craw 6N **181**
Justin Cl. TW8: Brent 3K **11**
Justin Plaza CR4: Mit 3C **44**
Jutland Gdns. CR5: Coul 7K **83**
Jutland Ho. SL4: W'sor 5C **4**
Jutland Pl. TW20: Egh 6E **20**
Juxon Cl. RH11: Craw 5L **181**

K

K2 Leisure Cen. 7B **182**
Kalima Cvn. Site
GU24: Chob 6L **53**
Kamran Ct. *GU11: Alde 5M **109***
(off Boxhalls La.)
Karenza Ct. RH13: Hors 5L **197**
Kashmir Cl. KT15: N Haw 5M **55**
Kashmir Ct. GU14: Farnb 4A **90**
Katana *GU22: Wok 6A **74***
(off Brooklyn Rd.)
Katharine Ho. CR0: Croy 4C **200**
Katharine St.
CR0: Croy 4C **200** (9N **45**)
Katherine Cl. KT15: Addl 3J **55**
Katherine Ct. *GU15: Camb 1B **70***
(off Up. Gordon Rd.)
*GU21: Knap 6F **72***
(off Tudor Way)
Katherine M. CR3: Whyte 4C **84**
Katherine Rd. TN8: Eden 3L **147**
TW1: Twick 2G **24**
Kathleen Godfree Ct.
SW19 . . . . .7M **27**
Kay Av. KT15: Addl 9N **37**
Kay Cres. GU35: H Dwn 3F **168**
Kaye Ct. GU1: Guil 9M **93**
Kaye Don Way
KT13: Weybr 6B **56**
Kayemoor Rd. SM2: Sut 3B **62**
Kaynes Pk. SL5: Asc 9J **17**
Keable Rd. GU10: Wrec 4E **128**
Kean Ho. *TW1: Twick 9K **11***
(off Arosa Rd.)
Kearton Cl. CR8: Ken 4N **83**
Kearton Pl. CR3: Cate 9D **84**
Keate Ho. *SL4: Eton 2G **4***
(off Keates La.)
Keates Grn. RG42: Brac 9N **15**
Keates La. SL4: Eton 2F **4**
Keats Av. RH1: Red 1E **122**
Keats Cl. RH12: Hors 1M **197**
SW19 . . . . .7B **28**
Keats Gdns. GU51: Fleet 4C **88**
Keats Pl. RH19: E Grin 9N **165**
Keats Way CR0: Croy 5F **46**
GU46: Yate 2A **68**
RG45: Crow 9G **30**
UB7: W Dray 1A **8**
Keble Cl. KT4: W Pk 7E **42**
RH10: Craw 9H **163**
Keble Pl. SW13 . . . . .2G **13**
Keble St. SW17 . . . . .5A **28**
Keble Way GU47: Owls 5K **49**
Kedeston Ct. SM1: Sut 7N **43**
Keel KT16: Chert 7L **37**
Keeler Cl. SL4: W'sor 6B **4**
Keeley Rd.
CR0: Croy 3B **200** (8N **45**)
Keens Cl. SW16 . . . . .6H **29**
Keens La. GU3: Guil 8J **93**
Keens Pk. Rd. GU3: Guil 8J **93**
Keens Rd.
CR0: Croy 6C **200** (1N **63**)
Keep, The KT2: K Tham 7M **25**
Keepers Cl. GU4: Guil 9F **94**
Keepers Coombe
RG12: Brac 5B **32**
KEEPER'S CORNER 4N **163**
Keepers Ct. CR2: S Croy 8B **200**
Keepers Farm Cl. SL4: W'sor . . .5B **4**
(not continuous)
Keepers M. TW11: Tedd 7J **25**
Keepers Wlk. GU25: V Wat 4N **35**
Keephatch Rd.
RG40: W'ham 9D **14**
Keevil Dr. SW19 . . . . .1J **27**
Keir, The SW19 . . . . .6H **27**
Keir Hardie Ho.
RH11: Craw 8N **181**
*W6 . . . . .2J **13***
(off Fulham Pal. Rd.)
Keith Lucas Rd.
GU14: Cove 3L **89**
Keith Pk. Cres. TN16: B Hil . . .9D **66**
Keldholme RG12: Brac 2M **31**
Kelling Gdns. CR0: Croy 6M **45**
Kellino St. SW17 . . . . .5D **28**
Kelly Cl. TW17: Shep 1F **38**
Kelmscott Ri. RH11: Craw 9N **181**
Kelsall Pl. SL5: Asc 6M **33**
Kelsey Cl. RH6: Horl 8D **142**
Kelsey Ga. BR3: Beck 1L **47**
Kelsey Gro. GU46: Yate 1D **68**
Kelsey La. BR3: Beck 1K **47**
Kelsey Pk. Av. BR3: Beck 1L **47**
(not continuous)
Kelsey Pk. Rd. BR3: Beck 1K **47**
Kelsey Sq. BR3: Beck 1K **47**
Kelsey Way BR3: Beck 2K **47**
Kelso Cl. RH10: Craw 2J **183**
Kelso Rd. SM5: Cars 6A **44**
Kelvedon Av. KT12: Hers 4F **56**
Kelvedon Cl. KT2: K Tham 7N **25**
Kelvedon Rd. SW6 . . . . .3L **13**
Kelvin Av. KT22: Leat 6F **78**
TW11: Tedd 7E **24**
Kelvinbrook KT8: W Mole 2B **40**
Kelvin Bus. Cen.
RH10: Craw 9D **162**
Kelvin Cl. KT19: Ewe 3N **59**
Kelvin Ct. TW7: Isle 5E **10**
Kelvin Dr. TW1: Twick 9H **11**
Kelvin Gdns. CR0: Wad 6J **45**
Kelvin Ga. RG12: Brac 1B **32**
Kelvin Gro. KT9: Ches 9K **41**
Kelvington Cl. CR0: Croy 6H **47**
Kelvin La. RH10: Craw 8D **162**
Kelvin Way RH10: Craw 8D **162**
Kemble Cl. KT13: Weybr 1E **56**
Kemble Cotts. KT15: Addl 1J **55**
Kemble Rd. CR0: Wad 9M **45**
Kembleside Rd. TN16: B Hil . . .5E **86**
Kemerton Rd. BR3: Beck 1L **47**
CR0: Croy 6C **46**
Kemishford GU22: Wok 1K **93**
Kemnal Pk. GU27: Hasl 1H **189**
Kemp Ct. GU19: Bag 5K **51**
Kemp Gdns. CR0: Croy 5N **45**
Kempsford Gdns. SW5 . . . . . . .1M **13**
Kempshott M. RH12: Hors 4H **197**
Kempshott Rd.
RH12: Hors 4H **197**
SW16 . . . . .8H **29**
Kempson Rd. SW6 . . . . .4M **13**
Kempton Av. TW16: Sunb 9J **23**
Kempton Ct. GU14: Cove 3L **89**
TW16: Sunb 9J **23**
Kempton Pk. TW12: Hamp 9N **23**
Kempton Pk. Racecourse 8K **23**
Kempton Park Station (Rail)
. . . . .8J **23**
Kempton Rd. TW12: Hamp 1N **39**
(not continuous)
Kempton Wlk. CR0: Croy 5H **47**
Kemsing Cl. CR7: T Hea 3N **45**
Kemsley Rd. TN16: Tats 6F **86**
Kendal Cl. GU14: Cove 1K **89**
RH2: Reig 2B **122**
TW14: Felt 2G **22**
Kendale Cl. RH10: Craw 7G **183**
Kendal Gdns. SM1: Sut 8A **44**
Kendal Gro. GU15: Camb 2H **71**
Kendal Ho. *SE20 . . . . .1D **46***
(off Derwent Rd.)
Kendall Av. BR3: Beck 1H **47**
CR2: Sande 5A **64**
Kendall Av. Sth.
CR2: Sande 6N **63**
Kendall Ct. SW19 . . . . .7B **28**
Kendall Rd. BR3: Beck 1H **47**
TW7: Isle 5G **10**
Kendal Pl. SW15 . . . . .8L **13**
Kendor Av. KT19: Eps 7B **60**
Kendra Hall Rd.
CR2: S Croy 4M **63**
Kendrey Gdns. TW2: Whitt 1E **24**
Kendrick Cl. RG40: W'ham 3B **30**
Kenilford Rd. SW12 . . . . .1F **28**
Kenilworth Av. KT11: Sto D . . .1B **78**
RG12: Brac 9A **16**
SW19 . . . . .6M **27**
Kenilworth Cl.
RH11: Craw 7N **181**
SM7: Ban 3N **81**
Kenilworth Cres.
GU51: Fleet 3D **88**
Kenilworth Dr. KT12: Wal T 9L **39**
Kenilworth Gdns.
TW18: Stain 6L **21**
Kenilworth Rd. GU14: Cove 9H **69**
GU51: Fleet 4C **88**
(not continuous)
KT17: Ewe 2F **60**
TW15: A'ford 4M **21**
KENLEY 1N **83**
KENLEY AERODROME 6A **84**
Kenley Gdns. CR7: T Hea 3M **45**
Kenley La. CR8: Ken 1N **83**
Kenley Rd. GU35: H Dwn 4G **169**
KT1: K Tham 1A **42**
SW19 . . . . .1M **43**
TW1: Twick 9H **11**
Kenley Station (Rail) 1N **83**
Kenley Wlk. SM3: Chea 1J **61**
Kenlor Rd. SW17 . . . . .6B **28**
Kenmara Cl. RH10: Craw 9E **162**
Kenmara Ct. RH10: Craw 8E **162**
Kenmare Dr. CR4: Mit 8D **28**
Kenmare Rd. CR7: T Hea 5L **45**
Kenmore Cl. GU16: Frim 6B **70**
GU52: C Cro 8C **88**
TW9: Kew 3N **11**
Kenmore Rd. CR8: Ken 1M **83**
Kennard Ct. RH18: F Row 6G **187**
Kenneally SL4: W'sor 5A **4**
Kenneally Cl. SL4: W'sor 5A **4**
Kenneally Row *SL4: W'sor 5A **4***
(off Liddell Sq.)
Kenneally Wlk. *SL4: W'sor 5A **4***
(off Guards Rd.)
Kennedy Av. RH19: E Grin . . .7N **165**
Kennedy Cl. CR4: Mit 9E **28**
Kennedy Ct. TW15: A'ford 6D **22**
Kennedy Rd. RH13: Hors 7K **197**
Kennel Av. SL5: Asc 9K **17**
Kennel Cl. KT22: Fetc 2C **98**
SL5: Asc 7K **17**
Kennel Grn. SL5: Asc 9J **17**
Kennel La. GU10: Fren 9H **129**
GU20: Windl 2N **51**
KT22: Fetc 9B **78**
(not continuous)
RG42: Brac 8N **15**
RH6: Hook 9B **142**
Kennel Ride SL5: Asc 9K **17**
Kennels La. GU14: Cove 2G **88**
(not continuous)
Kennel Wood SL5: Asc 9K **17**
Kennelwood Cres.
CR0: N Add 7N **65**
Kennet Cl. GU12: Ash 3E **110**
GU14: Cove 8K **69**
RH11: Craw 4L **181**
Kenneth Rd. SM7: Ban 2B **82**
Kenneth Younger Ho.
*SW6 . . . . .2L **13***
(off Clem Attlee Ct.)
Kennet Rd. TW7: Isle 6F **10**
Kennet Sq. CR4: Mit 9C **28**
Kennett Ct. W4 . . . . .3A **12**
Kenny Dr. SM5: Cars 5E **62**
Kenrick Sq. RH1: Blet 2B **124**
Kensington Av. CR7: T Hea 9L **29**
Kensington Gdns.
KT1: K Tham 6H **203** (2K **41**)
(not continuous)
Kensington Hall Gdns.
W14 . . . . .1L **13**
Kensington Mans.
*SW5 . . . . .1M **13***
(off Trebovir Rd., not continuous)
Kensington Rd.
RH11: Craw 7N **181**
Kensington Ter.
CR2: S Croy 4A **64**
Kensington Village
W14 . . . . .1L **13**
Kent Cl. BR6: Chels 3N **67**
CR4: Mit 3J **45**
TW18: Stain 7M **21**
Kent Dr. TW11: Tedd 6E **24**
Kent Folly RG42: Warf 7D **16**
Kent Ga. Way CR0: A'ton 3J **65**
KENT HATCH 9K **107**
Kent Hatch Rd.
RH8: C Hil, Limp 7E **106**
TN8: C Hil 7E **106**
Kent Ho. *W4 . . . . .1D **12***
(off Devonshire St.)
Kentigern Dr. RG45: Crow 2J **49**
Kenton Av. TW16: Sunb 1L **39**
Kenton Cl. GU16: Frim 4D **70**
RG12: Brac 1B **32**
Kenton Ct. TW1: Twick 9K **11**
Kentone Ct. SE25 . . . . .3E **46**
Kentons La. SL4: W'sor 5B **4**
Kenton Way GU21: Wok 4J **73**
Kent Rd. BR4: W Wick 7L **47**
GU20: Windl 2A **52**
GU22: Wok 3D **74**
GU51: Fleet 4C **88**
KT1: K Tham 5H **203** (2K **41**)
KT8: E Mol 3C **40**
TW9: Kew 3N **11**
Kent's Pas. TW12: Hamp 9N **23**
Kent Way KT6: Surb 9L **41**
Kentwode Grn. SW13 . . . . .3F **12**
Kentwyns Dr. RH13: Hors 8L **197**
Kentwyns Pl. RH13: Hors 8L **197**
Kentwyns Ri. RH1: Sth N 4K **123**
Kenward Ct. RH3: Brock 7B **120**
Kenway Rd. SW5 . . . . .1N **13**
Kenwith Av. GU51: Fleet 4D **88**
Kenwood Cl. UB7: Sip 2B **8**
Kenwood Dr. BR3: Beck 2M **47**
KT12: Hers 3J **57**
Kenwood Pk. KT13: Weybr 3E **56**
Kenwood Ridge CR8: Ken 4M **83**
Kenworth Gro. GU18: Ligh 6L **51**
Kenwyn Rd. SW20 . . . . .9H **27**
Kenya Ct. RH6: Horl 7D **142**
Kenyngton Ct. TW16: Sunb . . .6H **23**
Kenyngton Dr. TW16: Sunb . . .6H **23**
Kenyon Mans. *W14 . . . . .2K **13***
(off Queen's Club Gdns.)
Kenyons KT24: W Hors 6C **96**
Kenyon St. SW6 . . . . .4J **13**
Keogh Cl. GU12: A Va 3F **90**
Keppel Rd. RH4: Dork 3H **119**
Keppel Spur SL4: O Win 1L **19**
Kepple Pl. GU19: Bag 4J **51**
Kepple St. SL4: W'sor 5G **5**
Kerria Way GU24: W End 9B **52**
Kerrill Av. CR5: Coul 6L **83**
Kerry Cl. GU51: Fleet 9C **68**
Kerry Ter. GU21: Wok 3D **74**
Kersey Dr. CR2: Sels 8F **64**
Kersfield Ho. SW15 . . . . .9J **13**
Kersfield Rd. SW15 . . . . .9J **13**
Kersland Cotts.
GU7: Hurt 4C **132**
Kerves La. RH13: Hors 9K **197**
KESTON 2E **66**
Keston Av. BR2: Kes 2E **66**
CR5: Coul 6L **83**
KT15: N Haw 7J **55**
Keston Ct. KT5: Surb 8L **203**
Keston Gdns. BR2: Kes 1E **66**
KESTON MARK 1G **67**
KESTON MARK 1G **66**
Keston Pk. Cl. BR2: Kes 1H **67**
Keston Rd. CR7: T Hea 5L **45**
Kestrel Av. TW18: Stain 4H **21**
Kestrel Cl. GU4: Guil 1F **114**
GU10: Ews 5C **108**
GU12: A Va 6E **90**
KT2: K Tham 5K **25**
KT19: Eps 8N **59**
RH11: Craw 1A **182**
RH12: Hors 3L **197**
TN8: Eden 9M **127**
Kestrel Ct. CR2: S Croy 3N **63**
SM6: W'ton 2G **63**
Kestrel Ho. GU9: Farnh 3F **128**
Kestrel Wlk. RH10: T Hil 4F **184**
Kestrel Way CR0: N Add 5N **65**
GU21: Wok 2L **73**
Keswick Av. SW15 . . . . .6D **26**
SW19 . . . . .1M **43**
TW17: Shep 2F **38**
Keswick B'way. *SW15 . . . . .8L **13***
(off Up. Richmond Rd.)
Keswick Cl. GU15: Camb 2H **71**
RH11: Ifi 5J **181**
SM1: Sut 1A **62**
Keswick Dr. GU18: Ligh 7M **51**
Keswick Rd. GU8: Wit 4A **152**
KT22: Fetc 2C **98**
KT23: Book 3B **98**
SW15 . . . . .8K **13**
TW2: Whitt 9C **10**
TW20: Egh 8D **20**
Ketcher Grn. RG42: Bin 5H **15**
Kettering Ct. CR7: T Hea 3N **45**
Kettering St. SW16 . . . . .7G **28**
Kettlewell Cl. GU21: Wok 1N **73**
Kettlewell Dr. GU21: Wok 1A **74**
Kettlewell Hill GU21: Wok 1A **74**
Ketton Grn. RH1: Mers 6H **103**
Kevan Dr. GU23: Send 3G **95**
Kevin Cl. TW4: Houn 5L **9**
Kevins Dr. GU46: Yate 8D **48**
Kevins Gro. GU51: Fleet 4C **88**
KEW 3N **11**
KEW BRIDGE 1M **11**
Kew Bri. TW8: Brent 2N **11**
TW9: Kew 2N **11**
Kew Bri. Arches TW9: Kew 2N **11**
Kew Bri. Ct. W4 . . . . .1N **11**
Kew Bri. Distribution Cen.
TW8: Brent 1M **11**
Kew Bri. Rd. TW8: Brent 2M **11**
Kew Bridge Station (Rail) . . .1M **11**
Kew Bridge Steam Mus. 1M **11**
Kew Ct.
KT2: K Tham 1J **203** (9L **25**)
Kew Cres. SM3: Chea 9K **43**
Kew Foot Rd. TW9: Rich 7L **11**
Kew Gdns. 3L **11**
Kew Gdns. Plants &
People Exhibition 3M **11**
Kew Gdns. Rd. TW9: Kew 3M **11**
Kew Gardens Station (Rail & Tube)
. . . . .4N **11**
Kew Gdns. Vis. Cen. 4M **11**
KEW GREEN 3N **11**
Kew Grn. TW9: Kew 2M **11**
Kew Mdw. Path TW9: Kew 4A **12**
TW9: Rich 5B **12**
Kew Palace 2M **11**
Kew Retail Pk. TW9: Kew 4A **12**
Kew Riverside Pk.
TW9: Kew 3A **12**
Kew Rd. TW9: Kew 2N **11**
TW9: Rich 7L **11**
Keymer Cl. TN16: B Hil 3E **86**
Keymer Rd. RH11: Craw 4A **182**
SW2 . . . . .3K **29**
Keynes Cl. GU52: C Cro 9C **88**
Keynsham Rd. SM4: Mord 7N **43**
Keynsham Wlk. SM4: Mord 7N **43**
Keynsham Way GU47: Owls 5J **49**
Keys Ct. CR0: Croy 5D **200**
Keysham Av. TW5: C'ford 4H **9**
Keywood Dr. TW16: Sunb 7H **23**
Khama Rd. SW17 . . . . .5C **28**
Khartoum Rd. GU8: Wit 4B **152**
SW17 . . . . .5B **28**
Kibble Grn. RG12: Brac 5A **32**
Kidborough Down
KT23: Book 5A **98**
Kidborough Rd.
RH11: Craw 4L **181**
KIDBROOKE PARK 8F **186**
Kidbrooke Ri.
RH18: F Row 7G **187**
Kidderminster Pl.
CR0: Croy 7M **45**
Kidderminster Rd.
CR0: Croy 7M **45**
Kidmans Cl. RH12: Hors 3M **197**
Kidworth Cl. RH6: Horl 6D **142**
Kielder Wlk. GU15: Camb 2G **71**
Kier Pk. SL5: Asc 2N **33**
Kilberry Cl. TW7: Isle 4D **10**
Kilburns Mill Cl.
SM6: W'ton 8F **44**
Kilcorral Cl. KT17: Eps 1F **80**
Kilkie St. SW6 . . . . .5N **13**
Killasser Ct. KT20: Tad 1H **101**
Killester Gdns. KT4: W Pk 1G **61**
Killick Ho. SM1: Sut 1N **61**
Killick M. SM3: Chea 3K **61**
Killicks GU6: Cranl 6A **156**
Killieser Av. SW2 . . . . .3J **29**
Killigrew Ho. TW16: Sunb 8F **22**
Killinghurst La. GU8: Chid 2N **189**
GU27: Hasl 2N **189**
KILLINGHURST PARK 9A **172**
Killy Hill GU24: Chob 4H **53**
Kilmaine Rd. SW6 . . . . .3K **13**
Kilmarnock Pk. RH2: Reig 2N **121**
Kilmartin Av. SW16 . . . . .2L **45**
Kilmartin Gdns. GU16: Frim 5D **70**
Kilmington Cl. RG12: Brac 6C **32**
Kilmington Rd. SW13 . . . . .2F **12**
Kilmiston Av. TW17: Shep 5D **38**
Kilmiston Ho. TW17: Shep 5D **38**
Kilmore Dr. GU15: Camb 2F **70**
Kilmorey Gdns. TW1: Twick 8H **11**
Kilmorey Rd. TW1: Twick 7H **11**
Kilmuir Cl. GU47: C Tow 8J **49**
Kiln Av. GU27: Hasl 9G **171**
Kiln Cl. RH10: Craw D 2E **184**
UB3: Harl 2E **8**
Kiln Copse GU6: Cranl 6N **155**
Kiln Cotts. RH5: Newd 7C **140**
Kilnfield Rd. RH12: Rudg 9E **176**
Kiln Heath Farm Bus. Cen.
RH6: S Bri 5L **163**
Kiln La. GU10: L Bou 5G **129**
GU23: Rip 2J **95**
GU24: Bis 4E **72**
KT17: Eps 7D **60**
RG12: Brac 1M **31**
RH3: Betch, Brock 4A **120**
RH6: Horl 6E **142**
SL4: Wink 7M **17**
SL5: S'dale 4D **34**
Kilnmead RH10: Craw 2B **182**
Kilnmead Cl. RH10: Craw 2C **182**
Kiln Mdws. GU3: Worp 8F **92**
Kiln M. SW17 . . . . .6B **28**

Kipings—Langhurst

Kipings KT20: Tad 8J 81
Kipling Cl. GU46: Yate 2B 68
RH10: Craw 1G 182
Kipling Ct. RH13: Hors 4N 197
SL4: W'sor 5E 4
Kipling Dr. SW19 7B 28
Kipling Hall RG45: Crow 2G 48
Kipling Way RH19: E Grin 9M 165
Kirby Cl. KT19: Ewe 2E 60
Kirby Rd. GU21: Wok 4M 73
Kirby Way KT12: Wal T 5K 39
Kirdford Cl. RH11: Craw 1M 181
Kirkby Ct. GU16: Frim 5C 70
Kirkefields GU2: Guil 9K 93
Kirkgate, The
KT17: Eps 6L 201 (9D 60)
Kirkham Cl. GU47: Owls 5J 49
Kirk Knoll GU35: Head 4E 168
Kirkland Av. GU21: Wok 3H 73
Kirkleas Rd. KT6: Surb 7L 41
Kirklees Rd. CR7: T Hea 4L 45
Kirkley Rd. SW19 9M 27
Kirkly Cl. CR2: Sande 5B 64
Kirk Ri. SM1: Sut 9N 43
Kirkstall Gdns. SW2 2J 29
Kirkstall Rd. SW2 2H 29
Kirksted Rd. SM4: Mord 7N 43
Kirkstone Cl. GU15: Camb 2H 71
Kirrane Cl. KT3: N Mal 4E 42
Kirriemuir Gdns.
GU12: Ash 1H 111
Kirsty Cl. RH5: Dork 7J 119
Kirton Lodge SW18 9N 13
Kitchener Rd. CR7: T Hea 2A 46
GU11: Alde 7B 90
Kites Cl. RH11: Craw 3A 182
Kithurst Cl. RH11: Craw 5B 182
Kitsmead RH10: Cop 8L 163
Kitsmead La. KT16: L'cross 7M 35
Kitson Rd. SW13 4F 12
Kittiwake Cl. CR2: Sels 6H 65
RH11: Ifi 5J 181
Kittiwake Pl. SM1: Sut 2L 61
Kitts La. GU10: Churt 9K 149
Klondyke Vs.
GU27: G'wood 8L 171
KNAPHILL 4G 72
Knapp Rd. TW15: A'ford 5A 22
Knapton M. SW17 7E 28
Knaresborough Dr.
SW18 2N 27
Kneller Gdns. TW7: Isle 9D 10
Kneller Rd. KT3: N Mal 6D 42
TW2: Whitt 9C 10
Knepp Cl. RH10: Craw 3G 182
Knevett Ter. TW3: Houn 7A 10
Knighton Cl. CR2: S Croy 5M 63
RH10: Craw 8H 163
Knighton Rd. RH1: Red 5E 122
Knightons La. GU8: Duns 5B 174
Knightsbridge Ct. *SL3: Lang* 1C 6
(off High St.)
Knightsbridge Cres.
TW18: Stain 7K 21
Knightsbridge Gro.
GU15: Camb 8C 50
Knightsbridge Ho.
GU1: Guil 4B 114
(off St Lukes Sq.)
Knightsbridge Rd.
GU15: Camb 8C 50
Knights Cl. KT8: W Mole 4N 39
SL4: W'sor 4A 4
TW20: Egh 7F 20
Knights Ct.
KT1: K Tham 5J 203 (2L 41)
Knights Hill SE27 6M 29
Knight's Hill Sq. SE27 5M 29
Knight's Pk.
KT1: K Tham 5K 203 (2L 41)
Knights Pl. RH1: Red 2E 122
SL4: W'sor 6F 4
TW2: Twick 2E 24
Knights Rd. GU9: H End 5K 109
Knights Way GU15: Camb 2G 70
Knightswood GU21: Wok 5J 73
RG12: Brac 7N 31
Knightwood Cl.
GU14: Farnb 3C 90
RH2: Reig 5M 121
Knightwood Cres.
KT3: N Mal 5D 42
Knipp Hill KT11: Cob 9N 57
Knivet Rd. SW6 2M 13
Knobfield RH5: A Ham 3G 136
Knob Hill RH12: Warn 9F 178
Knockholt Cl. SM2: Sut 6N 61
Knockholt Main Rd.
TN14: Knoc 6N 87
Knockhundred La.
GU26: Lip 9N 169
Knole Cl. CR0: Croy 5F 46
RH10: Craw 2H 183
Knole Gro. RH19: E Grin 7M 165
Knole Wood SL5: S'dale 7B 34
Knoll, The BR3: Beck 1L 47
KT11: Cob 9A 58
KT16: Chert 7H 37
KT22: Leat 8J 79
Knoll Cl. GU51: Fleet 3B 88
Knoll Ct. GU51: Fleet 2B 88
Knoll Farm Rd. RH5: Cap 7G 159
Knollmead KT5: Surb 7B 42
Knoll Pk. Rd. KT16: Chert 7H 37
Knoll Quarry GU7: Goda 5H 133
Knoll Rd. GU7: Goda 5G 133
GU15: Camb 9B 50
GU51: Fleet 3B 88
RH4: Dork 7G 118
SW18 8N 13
KNOLL RDBT. 8J 79
Knoll Rdbt. KT22: Leat 8J 79
Knolls, The KT17: Eps D 3H 81
Knolls Cl. KT4: W Pk 9G 42
Knoll Wlk. GU15: Camb 9B 50
Knoll Wood GU7: Goda 5G 133
Knollys Cl. SW16 4L 29
Knollys Rd. GU11: Alde 1L 109
SW16 4K 29
Knook, The GU47: C Tow 8J 49
Knowle, The GU35: Head 3G 168
KT20: Tad 8H 81
Knowle Cl. RH10: Cop 7N 163
Knowledge Ct. SW16 2K 45
Knowle Dr. RH10: Cop 7M 163
Knowle Gdns. KT14: W By 9H 55
KNOWLE GREEN 6K 21
Knowle Grn. TW18: Stain 6J 21
Knowle Gro. GU25: V Wat 6M 35
Knowle Gro. Cl.
GU25: V Wat 6M 35
KNOWLE HILL 6M 35
Knowle Hill GU25: V Wat 6L 35
Knowle La.
GU6: Cranl, Rudg 8M 155
RH12: Rudg 4M 175
Knowle Lodge CR3: Cate 1D 104
Knowle Pk. KT11: Cob 3M 77
Knowle Pk. Av. TW18: Stain 7K 21
Knowle Rd. TW2: Twick 2E 24
Knowles Av. RG45: Crow 2E 48
Knowles Ho. *SW18 9N 13*
(off Neville Gill Cl.)
Knowl Hill GU22: Wok 6D 74
Knox Grn. RG42: Bin 6H 15
Knox Rd. GU2: Guil 7K 93
Kohat Ct. GU11: Alde 2L 109
Kohat Rd. SW19 6N 27
Kohima Cl. GU11: Alde 1N 109
Koonowla Cl. TN16: B Hil 2F 86
Kooringa CR6: Warl 6E 84
Korda Cl. TW17: Shep 2A 38
Korea Cotts. KT11: Cob 3L 77
Kotan Dr. TW18: Stain 5E 20
Kramer M. SW5 1M 13
Kreisel Wlk. TW9: Kew 2M 11
Kristina Ct. *SM2: Sut 3M 61*
(off Overton Rd.)
Krooner Rd. GU15: Camb 3N 69
Kuala Gdns. SW16 9K 29
Kyle Cl. RG12: Brac 2N 31
Kynaston Av. CR7: T Hea 4N 45
Kynaston Ct. CR3: Cate 3B 104
Kynaston Cres. CR7: T Hea 4N 45
Kynaston Rd. CR7: T Hea 4N 45
Kyngeshene Gdns.
GU1: Guil 4D 114
Kynnersley Cl. SM5: Cars 9D 44

L

Laburnhum Rd. GU22: Wok 7N 73
Laburnum Av. SM1: Sut 9C 44
Laburnum Cl. GU1: Guil 9M 93
GU11: Alde 3M 109
Laburnum Ct. (Cvn. Pk.)
RH6: Smal 1N 163
Laburnum Cres.
TW16: Sunb 9J 23
Laburnum Gdns. CR0: Croy 6G 46
GU52: C Cro 8C 88
Laburnum Gro. KT3: N Mal 1C 42
SL3: Lang 2D 6
TW3: Houn 7N 9
Laburnum Ho. BR2: Brom 1N 47
Laburnum Pas.
GU11: Alde 2M 109
Laburnum Pl. TW20: Eng G 7L 19
Laburnum Rd. CR4: Mit 1E 44
GU9: Weybo 5K 109
GU11: Alde 3M 109
KT16: Chert 7J 37
KT18: Eps 7L 201 (9D 60)
SW19 8A 28
UB3: Harl 1H 9
Laburnums, The
GU17: B'water 1G 68
Laburnum Way TW19: Stan 2A 22
Lacey Av. CR5: Coul 7L 83
Lacey Cl. TW20: Egh 8F 20
Lacey Dr. CR5: Coul 7M 83
TW12: Hamp 9N 23
Lacey Grn. CR5: Coul 7L 83
Lackford Rd. CR5: Chip 5D 82
Lackland Ct. *GU51: Fleet 2A 88*
(off King John St.)
Lacock Cl. SW19 7A 28
Lacrosse Way SW16 9H 29
Lacy Rd. SW15 7J 13
(not continuous)
Ladas Rd. SE27 5N 29
Ladbroke Cotts. *RH1: Red 2E 122*
(off Ladbroke Rd.)
Ladbroke Ct. RH1: Red 1E 122
Ladbroke Gro. RH1: Red 2E 122
Ladbroke Hurst RH7: Dorm 1C 166
Ladbroke Rd.
KT18: Eps 8K 201 (1C 80)
RH1: Red 2E 122
RH6: Horl 6F 142
Ladbrook Rd. SE25 3A 46
Ladderstile Ride
TW10: Rich 6A 26
Ladybank RG12: Brac 7N 31
Lady Booth Rd.
KT1: K Tham 4J 203 (1L 41)
Ladycroft Gdns. BR6: Farnb 2L 67
Ladycroft Way BR6: Farnb 2L 67
Ladycross GU8: Mil 2B 152
Ladyegate Cl. RH5: Dork 4K 119
Ladyegate Rd. RH5: Dork 5J 119
Lady Elizabeth Ho.
SW14 6B 12
Lady Forsdyke Way
KT19: Eps 5N 59
Ladygate Dr. GU26: G'hott 6M 169
Ladygrove CR0: Sels 5N 65
Ladygrove Dr. GU4: B'ham 7C 94
Lady Harewood Way
KT19: Eps 5N 59
Lady Hay KT4: W Pk 8E 42
Lady Jane Ct.
KT2: K Tham 3M 203
Lady Margaret Rd.
RH11: Craw 2M 181
SL5: S'dale 7C 34
Lady Margaret Wlk.
RH11: Craw 2M 181
Ladymead
GU1: Guil 1B 202 (2M 113)
Ladymead Cl. RH10: Craw 6G 183
Ladymead Retail Cen.
GU1: Guil 1B 202 (2M 113)
Ladythorpe Cl. KT15: Addl 1K 55
Ladywood Av. GU14: Cove 1H 89
Ladywood Rd. KT6: Surb 8N 41
Laffan's Rd. GU11: Alde 7H 89
LA Fitness
Ewell 8H 61
Goldsworth 4N 73
Old Isleworth 6H 11
(off Swan St.)
Purley 6N 63
Lafone Av. TW13: Felt 3K 23
Lagham Pk. RH9: S Gods 6H 125
Lagham Rd. RH9: S Gods 7H 125
Laglands Cl. RH2: Reig 1A 122
Laings Av. CR4: Mit 1D 44
Lainlock Pl. TW3: Houn 4B 10
Lainson St. SW18 1M 27
Lairdale Cl. SE21 2N 29
Laird Ct. GU19: Bag 6J 51
Laitwood Rd. SW12 2F 28
Lake Cl. KT14: Byf 8M 55
SW19 6L 27
Lake End Way RG45: Crow 3F 48
Lake Gdns. SM6: W'ton 9F 44
TW10: Ham 3H 25
Lakehall Gdns. CR7: T Hea 4M 45
Lakehall Rd. CR7: T Hea 4M 45
Lakehurst Rd. KT19: Ewe 2D 60
Lakeland Dr. GU16: Frim 5C 70
Lake La. GU10: Dock 4D 148
RH6: Horl 6G 142
Laker Ct. RH10: Craw 3E 182
Lake Rd. CR0: Croy 8J 47
GU16: Deep 8E 70
GU25: V Wat 4L 35
SW19 6L 27
Laker Pl. SW15 9K 13
LAKER'S GREEN 5H 175
Lakers Lea RH14: Loxw 7H 193
Lakers Ri. SM7: Ban 3C 82
Lakes Cl. GU4: Guil 9D 114
Lakeside BR3: Beck 2L 47
GU21: Wok 6H 73
KT2: K Tham 8A 26
KT13: Weybr 8F 38
KT19: Ewe 3D 60
RG42: Brac 8A 16
RH1: Red 1E 122
RH12: Hors 3J 197
SM6: W'ton 1F 62
Lakeside, The
GU17: B'water 2J 69
Lakeside Bus. Pk.
GU47: Sandh 8F 48
Lakeside Cl. GU12: A Va 9D 90
GU21: Wok 6H 73
SE25 1D 46
Lakeside Ct. GU51: Fleet 2C 88
Lakeside Dr. KT10: Esh 3C 58
Lakeside Gdns. GU14: Cove 7J 69
Lakeside Grange
KT13: Weybr 9D 38
Lakeside Ind. Est. SL3: Coln 2H 7
Lakeside Pk. KT16: Chert 7L 37
Lakeside Rd. GU11: Alde 9C 90
GU14: Farnb 6M 89
SL0: R Pk 3H 7
SL3: Coln, R Pk 3H 7
Lakes La. GU8: Wit 5C 152
Lakes Rd. BR2: Kes 2E 66
Lakestreet Grn. RH8: Limp 7F 106
Lake Vw. RH5: Nth H 8J 119
RH19: D Pk 5B 166
Lakeview Pk. Cvn. Site
SL4: Wink 2J 17
Lake Vw. Rd. RH19: Fel 7E 164
Lakeview Rd. SE27 6L 29
LALEHAM 2L 37
Laleham Abbey TW18: Lale 3L 37
Laleham Cl. TW18: Stain 9K 21
Laleham Ct. GU21: Wok 3A 74
SM1: Sut 2A 62
LALEHAM REACH 2J 37
Laleham Reach KT16: Chert 2J 37
Laleham Rd. TW17: Shep 3A 38
TW18: Stain 6H 21
Lalor St. SW6 5K 13
Lamberhurst Rd.
SE27 5L 29
Lamberhurst Wlk.
RH10: Craw 4E 182
Lambert Av. TW9: Rich 6N 11
Lambert Cl. TN16: B Hil 3F 86
Lambert Cotts. RH1: Blet 2B 124
Lambert Cres.
GU17: B'water 2H 69
Lambert Lodge *TW8: Brent 1K 11*
(off Layton Rd.)
Lambert Rd. SM7: Ban 1M 81
Lambert's Pl.
CR0: Croy 1E 200 (7A 46)
Lamberts Rd. KT5: Surb 4L 41
Lambeth Cl. RH11: Craw 7N 181
Lambeth Crematorium
SW17 5A 28
Lambeth Rd. CR0: Croy 6L 45
Lambeth Wlk. RH11: Craw 7N 181
Lambly Hill GU25: V Wat 2A 36
Lamborne Cl. GU47: Sandh 6F 48
Lambourn Cl.
CR2: S Croy 5M 63
RH19: E Grin 7A 166
Lambourne Av. SW19 5L 27
Lambourne Cl.
RH10: Craw 5D 182
Lambourne Cres.
GU21: Wok 9F 54
Lambourne Dr. GU19: Bag 5H 51
KT11: Cob 2L 77
Lambourne Gro.
RG12: Brac 1C 32
Lambourne Way
GU10: Tong 5C 110
Lambourn Gro.
KT1: K Tham 1A 42
Lambrook Ter. SW6 4K 13
Lambs Bus. Pk.
RH9: S Gods 7E 124
Lambs Cres. RH12: Hors 3M 197
Lambs Farm Cl.
RH12: Hors 3N 197
Lambs Farm Rd.
RH12: Hors 3M 197
LAMBS GREEN 3E 180
Lambs Grn. RH12: Rusp 4E 180
Lambton Ho. SL4: W'sor 6D 4
Lambton Rd. SW20 9H 27
Lambyn Cft. RH6: Horl 7G 143
LAMDA 1J 13
(off Talgarth Rd.)
Lammas Av. CR4: Mit 1E 44
SL4: W'sor 5F 4
Lammas Cl. GU7: Goda 5K 133
TW18: Stain 4G 20
Lammas Ct. *GU7: Goda 6H 133*
(off Old Station Way)
SL4: W'sor 5F 4
TW19: Stain 3F 20
Lammas Dr. TW18: Stain 5F 20
Lammas Hill KT10: Esh 1B 58
Lammas La.
KT10: Esh, Hers 1N 57
Lammas Mead RG42: Bin 8K 15
Lammas Rd. GU7: Goda 6K 133
TW10: Ham 5J 25
Lammermoor Rd.
SW12 1F 28
Lampard La. GU10: Churt 8J 149
Lampeter Cl. GU22: Wok 5A 74
Lampeter Sq. W6 2K 13
Lamports Ct. *GU9: Farnh 2H 129*
(off Firgrove Hill)
Lampson Ct. RH10: Cop 7N 163
LAMPTON 4B 10
Lampton Av. TW3: Houn 4B 10
Lampton Ct. TW3: Houn 4B 10
Lampton Ho. Cl.
SW19 5J 27
Lampton Pk. Rd.
TW3: Houn 5B 10
Lampton Rd. TW3: Houn 5B 10
Lanark Cl. GU16: Frim 4C 70
RH13: Hors 6L 197
Lancashire Hill RG42: Warf 7D 16
Lancaster Av. CR4: Mit 4J 45
GU1: Guil 5B 114
GU9: Farnh 3H 129
SE27 3M 29
SW19 6J 27
Lancaster Cl. GU12: A Va 8D 90
GU21: Wok 3C 74
KT2: K Tham 6K 25
RH10: Craw 9H 163
TW15: A'ford 5N 21
TW19: Stan 9N 7
TW20: Eng G 6N 19
Lancaster Cotts.
TW10: Rich 9L 11
Lancaster Ct. KT12: Wal T 6H 39
KT19: Ewe 6C 60
SE27 3M 29
SM2: Sut 4M 61
(off Mulgrave Rd.)
SM7: Ban 1L 81
SW6 3L 13
TW19: Stan 2N 21
Lancaster Dr. GU15: Camb 9B 50
RH19: E Grin 7C 166
Lancaster Gdns.
KT2: K Tham 6K 25
RH7: Blin H 3H 145
SW19 6K 27
Lancaster Ho. RG12: Brac 4N 31
RH1: Red 6C 122
Lancaster M. SW18 8N 13
TW10: Rich 9L 11
Lancaster Pk. TW10: Rich 8L 11
Lancaster Pl. SW19 6J 27
TW1: Twick 9G 11
TW4: Houn 5K 9
Lancaster Rd. SE25 1C 46
SW19 6J 27
Lancaster Way GU14: Farnb 7A 70
KT4: W Pk 6G 43
Lancastrian Rd. SM6: W'ton 4J 63
Lancelot Cl. RH11: Ifi 3K 181
Lancer Ct. GU11: Alde 2K 109
Lanchester Dr. RG45: Crow 9H 31
Lancing Cl. RH11: Craw 1M 181
Lancing Ct. RH12: Hors 4N 197
Lancing Ho. CR0: Croy 6D 200
Lancing Rd. CR0: Croy 6K 45
TW13: Felt 3G 22
Landau Ct. CR2: S Croy 8B 200
Landen Ct. RG40: W'ham 4A 30
Landen Pk. RH6: Horl 6C 142
Landford Rd. SW15 6H 13
Landgrove Rd. SW19 6M 27
Landmark Arts Cen. 6H 25
Landmark Ho. *W6 1H 13*
(off Hammersmith Bri. Rd.)
Landon Way TW15: A'ford 7C 22
Landridge Rd. SW6 5L 13
Landscape Rd. CR6: Warl 6E 84
Landseer Cl. GU47: C Tow 9K 49
SW19 9A 28
Landseer Rd. KT3: N Mal 6C 42
SM1: Sut 3M 61
Lands End La. GU35: Lind 4A 168
Lane, The GU8: Thur 6G 150
GU25: V Wat 2A 36
KT16: Chert 2J 37
RH14: Ifo 4E 192
Lane Cl. KT15: Addl 2K 55
Lane End GU8: Hamb 1E 172
KT18: Eps 1A 80
RH7: Dorm 1C 166
SW15 9J 13
Lane End Dr. GU21: Knap 4F 72
Lane Gdns. KT10: Clay 4F 58
Lanehurst Gdns.
RH10: Craw 1G 182
Lanercost Cl. SW2 3L 29
Lanercost Rd. RH11: Craw 4A 182
SW2 3L 29
Laneway SW15 8G 12
Lanfrey Pl. W14 1L 13
Langaller La. KT22: Fetc 9B 78
Langborough Rd.
RG40: W'ham 3B 30
Langbourne Way
KT10: Clay 3G 58
Lang Cl. KT22: Fetc 1B 98
Langcroft Cl. SM5: Cars 9D 44
Langdale Av. CR4: Mit 2D 44
Langdale Cl. GU14: Cove 1K 89
GU21: Wok 3M 73
SW14 7A 12
Langdale Ct. *GU12: A Va 8D 90*
(off Lakeside Cl.)
Langdale Dr. SL5: Asc 1J 33
Langdale Pde. CR4: Mit 2D 44
Langdale Rd. CR7: T Hea 3L 45
RH11: Ifi 5J 181
Langdon Cl. GU15: Camb 2G 70
Langdon Pk. TW11: Tedd 8J 25
Langdon Pl. SW14 6B 12
Langdon Rd. SM4: Mord 4A 44
Langdon Wlk. SM4: Mord 4A 44
Langford Rd. SW6 5N 13
Langham Cl. GU7: Goda 6J 133
Langham Ct. GU9: Farnh 4H 129
SW20 1H 43
Langham Dene CR8: Ken 2M 83
Langham Gdns. TW10: Ham 5J 25
Langham Ho. Cl.
TW10: Ham 5K 25
Langham Mans. *SW5 1N 13*
(off Earl's Ct. Sq.)
Langham Pk. GU7: Goda 6J 133
Langham Pl. TW20: Egh 6B 20
W4 2D 12
Langham Rd. SW20 9H 27
TW11: Tedd 6H 25
Langholm Cl. SW12 1H 29
Langhorn Dr. TW2: Twick 1E 24
Lang Ho. TW19: Stan 2N 21
LANGHURST
RH12, Horsham 5L 179
RH12, Rusper 9F 160
TN8 5G 127

Langhurst Cl.—Leigh Ct.

Langhurst Cl. RH12: Hors 5K 179
Langhurst La. RH12: Rusp . . .1F 180
Langhurstwood Rd.
RH12: Hors 8J 179
Langland Gdns. CR0: Croy 8J 47
Langlands Ri.
KT19: Eps 6H 201 (9B 60)
Langley Av. KT4: W Pk 7J 43
KT6: Surb 7K 41
LANGLEY BOTTOM 6C 80
Langley Broom SL3: Lang 1B 6
Langley Cl.
GU1: Guil 1B 202 (2M 113)
GU52: C Cro 9A 88
KT18: Eps D 6C 80
Langley Ct. RH2: Reig 2N 121
Langley Cres. UB3: Harl 3G 9
Langley Dr. GU11: Alde 4M 109
GU15: Camb 9C 50
RH11: Craw 1A 182
LANGLEY GREEN 9A 162
Langley Gro. KT3: N Mal 1D 42
Langley La. KT18: Head 3A 100
RH11: Ifi 1M 181
Langley Oaks Av.
CR2: Sande 6D 64
Langley Pde. RH11: Craw 9A 162
Langley Pk. Girls School Sports Cen.
. . . . .5M 47
Langley Pk. Rd. SM1: Sut 2A 62
SM2: Sut 2A 62
Langley Pl. RH11: Craw 9A 162
Langley Rd. BR3: Beck 3H 47
CR2: Sels 5G 64
KT6: Surb 6L 41
SW19 . . . . .9L 27
TW7: Isle 5F 10
TW18: Stain 7H 21
LANGLEY RDBT. 1C 6
LANGLEY VALE 6D 80
Langley Va. Rd.
KT18: Eps D 7B 80
Langley Wlk. GU22: Wok 6A 74
RH11: Craw 9N 161
Langley Way BR4: W Wick 7N 47
Langmans La. GU21: Wok 5L 73
Langmans Way GU21: Wok 3H 73
Langmead St. SE27 . . . . .5M 29
Langport Ct. KT12: Wal T 7K 39
Langridge Dr.
RH19: E Grin 1A 186
Langridge Ho. RH12: Hors 6G 197
Langridge M. TW12: Hamp 7N 23
Langroyd Rd. SW17 . . . . .3D 28
LANGSHOTT 7G 143
Langshott RH6: Horl 6F 142
Langshott Cl. KT15: Wood 7G 55
Langshott La. RH6: Horl 8G 142
(not continuous)
Langside Av. SW15 . . . . .7F 12
Langsmead RH7: Blin H 3H 145
Langstone Cl. RH10: Craw 6G 183
Langthorne Ho. UB3: Harl 1F 8
Langthorne St. SW6 . . . . .3J 13
Langton Av. KT17: Ewe 7E 60
Langton Cl. GU21: Wok 4J 73
KT15: Addl 9K 37
Langton Dr. GU35: Head 2F 168
Langton Pl. SW18 . . . . .2M 27
Langton Rd. KT8: W Mole 3C 40
Langton Way CR0: Croy 9B 46
TW20: Egh 7E 20
Langtry Ho. KT2: K Tham 2M 203
(off London Rd.)
Langtry Pl. SW6 . . . . .2M 13
Langwood Chase
TW11: Tedd 7J 25
Langwood Cl. KT21: A'tead 4N 79
Lanigan Dr. TW3: Houn 8B 10
Lankester Sq. RH8: Oxt 6N 105
Lankton Cl. BR3: Beck 1M 47
Lannoy Point SW6 . . . . .3K 13
(off Pellant Rd.)
Lansbury Av. TW14: Felt 9J 9
Lansbury Est. GU21: Knap 5G 73
Lansbury Rd. RH11: Craw 7N 181
Lansdell Ho. SW2 . . . . .1L 29
(off Tulse Hill)
Lansdell Rd. CR4: Mit 1E 44
Lansdown GU1: Guil 3C 114
Lansdown Cl. GU21: Wok 6J 73
KT12: Wal T 7K 39
RH12: Hors 2A 198
Lansdowne Cl. KT6: Surb 8A 42
SW20 . . . . .8J 27
TW1: Twick 2F 24
Lansdowne Ct. CR8: Pur 6M 63
KT4: W Pk 8F 42
Lansdowne Hill SE27 . . . . .4M 29
Lansdowne Rd.
CR0: Croy 2C 200 (8A 46)
CR8: Pur 8L 63
GU11: Alde 3M 109
GU16: Frim 6E 70
KT19: Ewe 4B 60
SW20 . . . . .8H 27
TW3: Houn 6B 10
TW18: Stain 8K 21
Lansdowne Wood Cl.
SE27 . . . . .4M 29
Lantern Cl. SW15 . . . . .7F 12
Lantern Pl. BR6: Farnb 1K 67
Lanyon Cl. RH12: Hors 2N 197
Lanyon M. RH12: Hors 2N 197
Lapwing Cl. CR2: Sels 6H 65
RH13: Hors 5M 197
Lapwing Ct. KT6: Surb 9N 41
Lapwing Gro. GU4: Guil 1F 114
Lara Cl. KT9: Ches 4L 59
Larbert Rd. SW16 . . . . .8G 28
Larby Pl. KT17: Ewe 6D 60
Larch Av. GU1: Guil 1M 113
SL5: S'dale 4B 34
Larch Cl. CR6: Warl 6H 85
GU15: Camb 6C 50
KT20: K'wood 8A 82
RH1: Red 5A 122
SW12 . . . . .3F 28
Larch Cres. KT19: Ewe 3A 60
Larch Dr. W4 . . . . .1N 11
Larch End RH12: Hors 5H 197
Larches, The GU21: Wok 3A 74
RG42: Warf 8E 16
RH12: Hors 2B 198
RH19: E Grin 6D 166
Larches Av. SW14 . . . . .7C 12
Larches Ho. RH19: E Grin 6D 166
Larches Pl. RH19: E Grin 7C 166
Larches Way GU17: B'water . . .1G 68
RH10: Craw D 1E 184
Larchfield Rd. GU52: Fleet 6B 88
Larch Rd. GU35: H Dwn 3G 168
Larch Tree Way CR0: Croy 9K 47
Larchvale Ct. SM2: Sut 4N 61
Larch Way GU14: Cove 2H 89
Larchwood RG12: Brac 4D 32
Larchwood Cl. SM7: Ban 2K 81
Larchwood Dr.
TW20: Eng G 7L 19
Larchwood Glade
GU15: Camb 8E 50
Larchwood Rd. GU21: Wok 7G 73
Larcombe Cl. CR0: Croy 1C 64
Larcombe Ct. SM2: Sut 4N 61
(off Worcester Rd.)
Larges Bri. Dr. RG12: Brac 2A 32
Larges La. RG12: Brac 1A 32
Largewood Av. KT6: Surb 8N 41
Lark Av. TW18: Stain 4H 21
Larkfield GU6: Ewh 6F 156
KT11: Cob 9H 57
Larkfield Cl. GU9: Farnh 9E 108
Larkfield Ct. RH6: Smal 8L 143
Larkfield Rd. GU9: Farnh 1E 128
TW9: Rich 7L 11
Larkhall Cl. KT12: Hers 3K 57
(not continuous)
Larkham Cl. TW13: Felt 4F 22
Larkin Cl. CR5: Coul 4K 83
Larkins Rd. RH6: Gat 3B 162
Lark Ri. KT24: E Hor 9F 96
RH10: T Hil 4F 184
RH11: Craw 1A 182
Larksfield RH6: Horl 7F 142
TW20: Eng G 8L 19
Larkspur Cl. GU11: Alde 5M 109
Larkspur Way KT19: Ewe 2B 60
RH5: Nth H 8K 119
Larks Way GU21: Knap 3F 72
Larkswood Cl. GU47: Sandh 6F 48
Larkswood Dr. RG45: Crow 2G 49
Lark Way SM5: Cars 6C 44
Larnach Rd. W6 . . . . .2J 13
Larpent Av. SW15 . . . . .8H 13
Lascombe La. GU3: Put 8L 111
Lashmere GU6: Cranl 7J 155
RH10: Cop 7A 164
Laski Ct. RH11: Craw 8N 181
Lasswade Ct. KT16: Chert 6G 37
Lasswade Rd. KT16: Chert 6G 37
Lastingham Ct. TW18: Stain 7J 21
Latchmere Cl. TW10: Ham 6L 25
Latchmere La.
KT2: K Tham 7M 25
TW10: Ham 7M 25
Latchmere Rd.
KT2: K Tham 8L 25
Latchwood La.
GU10: L Bou 6J 129
Lateward Rd. TW8: Brent 2K 11
Latham Av. GU16: Frim 4C 70
Latham Cl. TN16: B Hil 3E 86
TW1: Twick 1G 24
Latham Ct. SW5 . . . . .1M 13
(off W. Cromwell Rd.)
Latham Rd. TW1: Twick 1F 24
Latham's Way CR0: Wad 7K 45
Lathkill Ct. BR3: Beck 1J 47
Latimer RG12: Brac 7N 31
Latimer Cl. GU22: Wok 3D 74
KT4: W Pk 1G 61
RH11: Craw 9B 162
Latimer Ct. RH1: Red 5D 122
Latimer Ho. GU51: Fleet 2A 88
Latimer Rd.
CR0: Croy 4A 200 (9M 45)
GU7: Goda 7H 133
RG41: W'ham 3A 30
SW19 . . . . .7N 27
TW11: Tedd 6F 24
Latitude KT16: Chert 7L 37
(off Bridge Wharf)
Lattimer Pl. W4 . . . . .3D 12
Latton Cl. KT10: Esh 1B 58
KT12: Wal T 6M 39
Latymer Cl. KT13: Weybr 1D 56
Latymer Upper School Sports Cen.
. . . . .1F 12
Laubin Pl. TW1: Twick 7H 11
Laud Dr. RH10: Craw 4H 183
Lauder Cl. GU16: Frim 4C 70
Lauderdale GU14: Cove 3J 89
Lauderdale Dr. TW10: Ham 4K 25
Lauderdale Ho.
TW18: Stain 6H 21
(off Gresham Rd.)
Laud St.
CR0: Croy 5B 200 (9N 45)
Laud Way RG40: W'ham 2D 30
Laughton Rd.
RH12: Hors 3M 197
Laundry Cotts.
RH11: Craw 7L 181
Laundry La. GU47: C Tow 9K 49
Laundry Rd.
GU1: Guil 4B 202 (4M 113)
W6 . . . . .2K 13
Laundry Way RH5: Cap 5J 159
Lauradale RG12: Brac 3M 31
Laurel Av. TW1: Twick 2F 24
TW20: Eng G 6L 19
Laurel Bank GU24: Chob 7H 53
(off Bagshot Rd.)
Laurel Bank Gdns.
SW6 . . . . .5L 13
Laurel Cl. GU14: Cove 2H 89
GU15: Camb 2B 70
RH10: Craw 6E 182
SL3: Poy 4H 7
SW17 . . . . .6C 28
Laurel Ct. CR2: S Croy 7F 200
RG12: Brac 3D 32
(off Wayland Clo.)
Laurel Cres. CR0: Croy 9K 47
GU21: Wok 9E 54
Laurel Dene RH19: E Grin 9B 166
Laureldene GU3: Flex 3M 111
Laurel Dr. RH8: Oxt 9B 106
Laurel Gdns. GU11: Alde 5M 109
KT15: N Haw 6K 55
TW4: Houn 7M 9
Laurel Gro. GU10: Wrec 6E 128
Laurel Ho. BR2: Brom 1N 47
Laurel Mnr. SM2: Sut 4A 62
Laurel Rd. SW13 . . . . .5F 12
SW20 . . . . .9G 26
TW12: H Hill 6D 24
Laurels, The GU9: Weybo 5L 109
GU51: Fleet 4B 88
KT11: Cob 2M 77
KT13: Weybr 9E 38
RH10: Craw 9E 162
SM7: Ban 4L 81
Laurel Wlk. RH13: Hors 7M 197
Laurier Rd. CR0: Croy 6C 46
Lauriston Cl. GU21: Knap 4G 72
Lauriston Rd. SW19 . . . . .7J 27
Lauser Rd. TW19: Stan 1L 21
Laustan Cl. GU1: Guil 3E 114
Lavant Cl. RH11: Craw 4L 181
Lavender Av. CR4: Mit 9C 28
KT4: W Pk 9H 43
Lavender Cl. CR3: Cate 3N 103
CR5: Coul 6G 82
KT22: Leat 9J 79
RH1: Red 8F 122
SM5: Cars 1F 62
Lavender Ct. KT8: W Mole 2B 40
KT22: Leat 9J 79
SM2: Sut 4A 62
TW14: Felt 9J 9
Lavender Ga. KT22: Oxs 1B 78
Lavender Gro. CR4: Mit 9C 28
Lavender Ho. TW9: Kew 4A 12
Lavender La. GU10: Rowl 7E 128
Lavender Pk. Rd.
KT14: W By 8J 55
Lavender Rd. CR0: Croy 5K 45
GU22: Wok 3D 74
KT19: Ewe 2A 60
SM1: Sut 1B 62
SM5: Cars 1E 62
Lavender Va. SM6: W'ton 3H 63
Lavender Wlk. CR4: Mit 2E 44
Lavender Way CR0: Croy 5G 47
Lavengro Rd. SE27 . . . . .3N 29
Lavenham Rd. SW18 . . . . .3L 27
Laverstoke Gdns.
SW15 . . . . .1E 26
Laverton Pl. SW5 . . . . .1N 13
Lavington Cl. RH11: Craw 2L 181
Lavington Rd. CR0: Bedd 9K 45
Lawbrook La.
GU5: Gorn, P'lake, Shere
. . . . .6D 136
Lawday Link GU9: U Hal 5F 108
Lawday Pl. GU9: U Hal 5F 108
Lawday Pl. La. GU9: U Hal . . .5F 108
Lawdons Gdns.
CR0: Wad 7A 200 (1M 63)
Lawford Cres. GU46: Yate 9C 48
Lawford Gdns. CR8: Ken 3N 83
Lawford Rd. W4 . . . . .3B 12
Lawford's Hill Cl.
GU3: Worp 2F 92
Lawford's Hill Rd.
GU3: Worp 2F 92
Lawley Ho. TW1: Twick 9K 11
Lawn, The UB2: S'hall 1A 10
Lawn Cl. KT3: N Mal 1D 42
SL3: Dat 3M 5
Lawn Cres. TW9: Kew 5N 11
Lawn Rd.
GU2: Guil 8B 202 (6M 113)
Lawns, The GU8: Mil 1C 152
GU14: Cove 2K 89
SE19 . . . . .1A 46
SL3: Poy 4G 7
SL5: Asc 2H 33
SM2: Chea 4K 61
SW19 . . . . .6L 27
Lawns Cotts.
RH12: Rudg 6B 176
Lawnsmead GU5: Wone 4D 134
Lawnsmead Cotts.
GU5: Wone 4D 134
Lawns Rd. RH12: Rudg 6B 176
Lawnwood Cotts.
GU7: Goda 6K 133
(off Catteshall La.)
Lawrence Av. KT3: N Mal 5C 42
Lawrence Cl. GU4: B'ham 7D 94
RG40: W'ham 2C 30
RH10: Craw 5H 183
Lawrence Ct. SL4: W'sor 5F 4
Lawrence Cres.
GU20: Windl 3A 52
Lawrence Est. TW4: Houn 7K 9
Lawrence Gro. RG42: Bin 9J 15
Lawrence La. RH3: Buck 1G 120
Lawrence Lodge
GU15: Camb 8B 50
Lawrence Pde. TW7: Isle 6H 11
(off Lower Sq.)
Lawrence Rd. BR4: W Wick . . .1C 66
GU52: Fleet 5A 88
SE25 . . . . .3C 46
TW4: Houn 7K 9
TW10: Ham 5J 25
TW12: Hamp 8N 23
Lawrence Way GU15: Camb 2L 69
Lawrence Weaver Cl.
SM4: Mord 5M 43
Laws Cl. RH11: Ifi 4K 181
SE25 . . . . .3A 46
Lawson Cl. SW19 . . . . .4J 27
Lawson Ct. KT6: Surb 6K 41
Lawson Hunt Ind. Pk.
RH12: Bro H 4D 196
Lawson Wlk. SM5: Cars 5E 62
Lawson Way SL5: S'dale 5E 34
Laws Ter. GU11: Alde 1A 110
Laxton Ct. CR7: T Hea 3N 45
Laxton Gdns. RH1: Mers 6H 103
Layard Rd. CR7: T Hea 1A 46
Layburn Cres. SL3: Lang 2D 6
Layhams Rd. BR2: Kes 1A 66
BR4: W Wick 1A 66
CR6: B Hil 8B 66
Layton Ct. KT13: Weybr 1C 56
TW8: Brent 1K 11
Layton Cres. CR0: Wad 2L 63
Layton Pl. TW9: Kew 4N 11
Layton Rd. TW3: Houn 7B 10
TW8: Brent 1K 11
Layton's La. TW16: Sunb 1G 38
Lazare Ct. TW18: Stain 6H 21
(off Gresham Rd.)
Lazell Gdns. RH3: Betch 9B 120
Lazenbys Est.
RH5: W'wood 9L 157
Lea, The TW20: Egh 8E 20
Leach Gro. KT22: Leat 9J 79
Lea Cl. GU9: B Lea 6M 109
GU12: Ash 3E 110
RH11: Craw 4L 181
TW2: Whitt 1N 23
Lea Coach Rd.
GU8: Thur, Wit 5L 151
Lea Ct. GU9: Weybo 5L 109
Lea Cft. RG45: Crow 1G 49
Leacroft RH19: E Grin 8N 165
SL5: S'dale 4D 34
TW18: Stain 6J 21
Leacroft Av. SW12 . . . . .1D 28
Leacroft Cl. CR8: Ken 3N 83
TW18: Stain 5K 21
Leaf Cl. KT7: T Dit 4E 40
Leafey La. GU26: G'hott 3K 169
Leaf Gro. SE27 . . . . .6L 29
Leafield Cl. GU21: Wok 5M 73
SW16 . . . . .7M 29
Leafield Copse RG12: Brac 3D 32
Leafield Rd. SM1: Sut 8M 43
SW20 . . . . .2L 43
Leafy Gro. BR2: Kes 2E 66
Leafy Way CR0: Croy 8C 46
Leamington Av. BR6: Orp 1N 67
SM4: Mord 3K 43
Leamington Cl. TW3: Houn 8C 10
Leamore St. W6 . . . . .1H 13
Leander Ct. KT6: Surb 6K 41
Leander Rd. CR7: T Hea 3K 45
SW2 . . . . .1K 29
Leapale La.
GU1: Guil 5C 202 (4N 113)
Leapale Rd.
GU1: Guil 5C 202 (4N 113)
Lea Rd. BR3: Beck 1K 47
GU15: Camb 4N 69
UB2: S'hall 1M 9
Leas Cl. KT9: Ches 4M 59
Leaside GU28: North 8D 190
KT23: Book 1A 98
Leas La. CR6: Warl 5G 84
Leas Rd. CR6: Warl 5G 84
GU1: Guil 4B 202 (4M 113)
Leather Cl. CR4: Mit 1E 44
TN8: Eden 3L 147
LEATHERHEAD 9H 79
Leatherhead Bus. Pk.
KT22: Leat 6F 78
Leatherhead By-Pass Rd.
KT22: Leat 7H 79
LEATHERHEAD COMMON 6G 79
Leatherhead Leisure Cen. . . .1G 98
Leatherhead Mus. of Local History
. . . . .9H 79
Leatherhead Rd. KT9: Ches 1H 79
KT21: A'tead 8K 79
KT22: Leat 8K 79
KT22: Oxs 1D 78
KT23: Book 4B 98
Leatherhead Station (Rail) . . .8G 79
Leatherhead Theatre & Cinema
. . . . .9H 79
Leatherhead Trade Pk.
KT22: Leat 8G 78
Leather La. GU5: Gorn 8D 116
Leaveland Cl. BR3: Beck 3K 47
Leavesden Rd.
KT13: Weybr 2C 56
LEAVES GREEN 7F 66
Leaves Grn. RG12: Brac 5B 32
Leaves Grn. Cres. BR2: Kes . . .7E 66
Leaves Grn. Rd. BR2: Kes 7F 66
Lea Way GU12: Alde 1D 110
Leaway GU9: B Lea 7M 109
Leazes Av. CR3: Cate 1L 103
Leazes La. CR3: Cate 1L 103
Lebanon Av. TW13: Hanw 6L 23
Lebanon Ct. TW1: Twick 1H 25
Lebanon Dr. KT11: Cob 9A 58
Lebanon Gdns. SW18 . . . . .9M 13
TN16: B Hil 4F 86
Lebanon Pk. TW1: Twick 1H 25
Lebanon Rd. CR0: Croy 7B 46
SW18 . . . . .8M 13
Lebanon Road Stop (CT) 8B 46
Le Chateau CR0: Croy 5E 200
Lechford Rd. RH6: Horl 9E 142
Leckford Rd. SW18 . . . . .3A 28
Leckhampton Pl. SW2 . . . . .1L 29
Leconfield Av. SW13 . . . . .6E 12
Ledbury Pl.
CR0: Croy 7C 200 (1N 63)
Ledbury Rd.
CR0: Croy 8C 200 (1A 64)
RH2: Reig 3M 121
Ledger Cl. GU1: Guil 1D 114
Ledger Dr. KT15: Addl 2H 55
Ledgers La. CR6: Warl 4L 85
Ledgers Rd. CR6: Warl 3K 85
Lee Acre RH4: Dork 7J 119
Leechcroft Rd. SM6: W'ton 9E 44
Leech La. KT18: Head 4A 100
Leechpool La. RH13: Hors 4N 197
Lee Ct. GU11: Alde 4A 110
Leegate Cl. GU21: Wok 3L 73
Lee Grn. La. KT18: Head 2A 100
Leehurst GU8: Mil 1B 152
Lee M. BR3: Beck 2H 47
Lee Rd. GU11: Alde 2K 109
SW19 . . . . .9N 27
Lees, The CR0: Croy 8J 47
Leeside RH12: Rusp 3B 180
Leeson Gdns. SL4: E Wic 1B 4
Leeson Ho. TW1: Twick 1H 25
Lee St. RH6: Horl 8C 142
Leeward Gdns. SW19 . . . . .6K 27
Leeways, The SM3: Chea 3K 61
Leewood Way KT24: Eff 5K 97
Le Freth Dr. GU51: Fleet 2A 88
Lefroy Pk. GU51: Fleet 4A 88
Legge Cres. GU11: Alde 3K 109
Leggyfield Ct. RH12: Hors 3H 197
Legion Ct. SM4: Mord 5M 43
Legoland 8A 4
Legrace Av. TW4: Houn 5L 9
Legsheath La.
RH19: F Row 8M 185
Leicester RG12: Brac 6C 32
Leicester Av. CR4: Mit 3J 45
Leicester Cl. KT4: W Pk 1H 61
Leicester Ct. RH10: Craw 3H 183
TW1: Twick 9K 11
(off Clevedon Rd.)
Leicester Rd. CR0: Croy 6B 46
LEIGH 1F 140
Leigh, The KT2: K Tham 8D 26
Leigham Av. SW16 . . . . .4J 29
Leigham Cl. SW16 . . . . .4K 29
Leigham Ct. Rd. SW16 . . . . . . .3J 29
Leigham Dr. TW7: Isle 3E 10
Leigham Hall Pde.
SW16 . . . . .4J 29
(off Streatham High Rd.)
Leigham Va. SW2 . . . . .4K 29
SW16 . . . . .4K 29
Leigh Cl. KT3: N Mal 3B 42
KT15: Addl 4H 55
Leigh Cl. Ind. Est.
KT3: N Mal 3C 42
Leigh Cnr. KT11: Cob 2K 77
Leigh Ct. KT11: Cob 1L 77

Leigh Ct. Cl.—Linnet Cl.

Leigh Ct. Cl. KT11: Cob 1K 77
Leigh Cres. CR0: N Add 4L 65
Leigh Hill Rd. KT11: Cob 2K 77
Leighlands RH10: Craw 1G 183
Leigh La. GU9: Farnh 3K 129
Leigh Orchard Cl.
SW16 4K 29
Leigh Pk. SL3: Dat 3L 5
Leigh Pl. KT11: Cob 2K 77
TW13: Felt 2K 23
Leigh Pl. Cotts.
RH2: Leigh 9F 120
Leigh Pl. La. RH9: Gods 1G 125
Leigh Pl. Rd. RH2: Leigh 9F 120
Leigh Rd. KT11: Cob 1J 77
RH3: Betch 9B 120
TW3: Houn 7D 10
Leigh Sq. SL4: W'sor 5A 4
Leighton Gdns. CR0: Croy 7M 45
CR2: Sande 9E 64
Leighton Mans. *W14* *2K 13*
(off Greyhound Rd.)
Leighton St.
CR0: Croy 1A 200 (7M 45)
Leighton Way
KT18: Eps 8K 201 (1C 80)
Leinster Av. SW14 6B 12
Leipzig Rd. GU52: C Cro 1C 108
Leisure La. KT14: W By 8K 55
Leisure Pursuits 3G 186
Leisure W. TW13: Felt 3J 23
Leith Cl. RG45: Crow 9F 30
Leithcote Gdns.
SW16 5K 29
Leithcote Path SW16 4K 29
Leith Dr. GU11: Alde 1L 109
Leith Gro. RH5: B Grn 7K 139
Leith Hill La.
RH5: A Com, H Mary 4M 137
Leith Hill Place (East) 9B 138
Leith Hill Place (West) 1N 157
Leith Hill Rd.
RH5: H Mary 9A 138
Leith Hill Tower 8B 138
Leith Lea RH5: B Grn 7K 139
Leith Rd. KT17: Eps 8D 60
RH5: B Grn 8J 139
Leith Towers SM2: Sut 4N 61
Leith Va. Cotts. RH5: Ockl 7A 158
Leith Vw. RH5: Nth H 9J 119
Leith Vw. Cotts.
RH12: K'fold 3H 179
Leith Vw. Rd. RH12: Hors 3N 197
Lela Av. TW4: Houn 5K 9
Le Marchant Rd.
GU15: Camb 3D 70
GU16: Frim 3D 70
Le May Cl. RH6: Horl 7E 142
Lemington Gro. RG12: Brac 5N 31
Lemmington Way
RH12: Hors 1M 197
Lemon Gro. TW13: Felt 2H 23
Lemon's Farm Rd.
RH5: A Com 5N 137
Lemuel St. SW18 9N 13
Lendore Rd. GU16: Frim 6B 70
Lenelby Rd. KT6: Surb 7N 41
Leney Cl. RG40: W'ham 9C 14
Len Freeman Pl. SW6 2L 13
Lenham Rd. CR7: T Hea 1A 46
SM1: Sut 1N 61
Lennard Rd.
CR0: Croy 1B 200 (7N 45)
Lennel Gdns. GU52: C Cro 7D 88
Lennox Ct. *RH1: Red* *2E 122*
(off St Anne's Ri.)
Lennox Gdns.
CR0: Wad 7A 200 (1M 63)
Lennox Ho. *TW1: Twick* *9K 11*
(off Clevedon Rd.)
Lenten Cl. GU5: P'lake 2E 136
Lenton Ri. TW9: Rich 6L 11
Leo Ct. TW8: Brent 3K 11
Leominster Rd. SM4: Mord 5A 44
Leominster Wlk.
SM4: Mord 5A 44
Leonard Av. SM4: Mord 4A 44
Leonard Cl. GU16: Frim 6B 70
Leonard Rd. SW16 9G 28
Leonardslee Ct.
RH10: Craw 5F 182
Leonard Way RH13: Hors 6M 197
Leopold Av. GU14: Farnb 9N 69
SW19 6L 27
Leopold Rd. RH11: Craw 3A 182
SW19 5L 27
Leopold Ter. SW19 6L 27
Le Personne Homes
CR3: Cate *9A 84*
(off Banstead Rd.)
Le Personne Rd. CR3: Cate 9A 84
Leppington RG12: Brac 7N 31
Leret Way KT22: Leat 8H 79
Lerry Cl. W14 2L 13
Lesbourne Rd. RH2: Reig 4N 121
Leslie Dunne Ho. SL4: W'sor 5B 4
Leslie Gdns. SM2: Sut 3M 61
Leslie Gro.
CR0: Croy 1F 200 (7B 46)
Leslie Gro. Pl.
CR0: Croy 1F 200 (7B 46)
Leslie Pk. Rd.
CR0: Croy 1F 200 (7B 46)
Leslie Rd. GU24: Chob 6H 53
RH4: Dork 3K 119
Lessingham Av. SW17 5D 28
Lessness Rd. SM4: Mord 5A 44
Lestock Cl. *SE25* *2D 46*
(off Manor Rd.)
Lestock Way GU51: Fleet 4D 88
Letchworth Av. TW14: Felt 1G 22
Letchworth Ct. RH11: Craw 6K 181
Letchworth St. SW17 5D 28
Letcombe Sq. RG12: Brac 3C 32
Letterstone Rd. SW6 3L 13
Lettice St. SW6 4L 13
Levana Cl. SW19 2K 27
Levehurst Ho. SE27 6N 29
Leveret Cl. CR0: N Add 7N 65
Leveret La. RH11: Craw 1N 181
Leverette Cl. GU12: Alde 1B 110
Leverkusen Rd.
RG12: Brac 2N 31
Levern Dr. GU9: U Hal 6H 109
Leverson St. SW16 7G 28
Levett Rd. KT22: Leat 7H 79
Levylsdene GU1: Guil 3E 114
Levylsdene Ct. GU1: Guil 3F 114
Lewes Cl. RH10: Craw 3G 183
Lewes Ct. *CR4: Mit* *2D 44*
(off Chatsworth Pl.)
Lewesdon Cl. SW19 2J 27
Lewes Rd.
RH18: F Row, W Cros 9F 186
RH19: Ash W, F Row, E Grin
1B 186
Lewin Rd. SW14 6C 12
SW16 7H 29
Lewins Rd. KT18: Eps 1A 80
Lewin Ter. TW14: Bedf 1E 22
Lewis Cl. KT15: Addl 1L 55
Lewis Ct. *KT22: Leat* *8G 78*
(off Highbury Dr.)
Lewisham Cl. RH11: Craw 7A 182
Lewisham Way GU47: Owls 6J 49
Lewis Ho. RG12: Brac 5N 31
Lewis Rd. CR4: Mit 1B 44
(not continuous)
SM1: Sut 1N 61
TW10: Rich 8K 11
Lewiston Cl. KT4: W Pk 6G 43
Leworth Pl. SL4: W'sor 4G 4
Lexden Rd. CR4: Mit 3H 45
Lexington Ct. CR8: Pur 6N 63
Lexton Gdns. SW12 2H 29
Leyborne Pk. TW9: Kew 4N 11
Leybourne Av. KT14: Byf 9A 56
Leybourne Cl. KT14: Byf 9A 56
RH11: Craw 8A 182
Leybourne Pl. RH19: Fel 7J 165
Leyburn Gdns. CR0: Croy 8B 46
Leycester Cl. GU20: Windl 1M 51
Leyfield KT4: W Pk 7D 42
Leylands SW18 9L 13
Leylands La. TW19: Stan M 7H 7
(not continuous)
Ley Rd. GU14: Farnb 6M 69
Leys, The KT12: Hers 1N 57
Leyside RG45: Crow 2F 48
Leys Rd. KT22: Oxs 8D 58
Leyton Rd. SW19 8A 28
Liberty Av. SW19 9B 28
Liberty Hall Rd. KT15: Addl 2J 55
Liberty La. KT15: Addl 2J 55
Liberty M. SW12 1F 28
Liberty Point *CR0: Croy* *6D 46*
(off Blackhorse La.)
Liberty Ri. KT15: Addl 3J 55
Library and Lifetime Mus.
4C 200
Library Way TW2: Whitt 1C 24
Lichfield Ct. KT6: Surb 8J 203
TW9: Rich 8L 11
Lichfield Gdns. TW9: Rich 7L 11
Lichfield Rd. TW4: Houn 6K 9
TW9: Kew 4M 11
Lichfields RG12: Brac 1C 32
Lichfield Ter. *TW9: Rich* *8L 11*
(off Sheen Rd.)
Lichfield Way CR2: Sels 6G 65
Lickey Ho. *W14* *2L 13*
(off North End Rd.)
Lickfolds Rd. GU10: Rowl 9D 128
Liddell SL4: W'sor 6A 4
Liddell Pl. SL4: W'sor 5A 4
Liddell Sq. SL4: W'sor 5A 4
Liddell Way SL4: W'sor 6A 4
SL5: Asc 4K 33
Liddington Hall Dr.
GU3: Guil 9H 93
Liddington New Rd.
GU3: Guil 9H 93
Lidiard Rd. SW18 3A 28
Lido Rd.
GU1: Guil 1D 202 (2N 113)
Lidsey Cl. RH10: Craw 5G 183
Lidstone Cl. GU21: Wok 4L 73
Liffords Pl. SW13 5E 12
Lifford St. SW15 7J 13
Lightermans Wlk.
SW18 7M 13
LIGHTWATER 6L 51
Lightwater By-Pass
GU18: Ligh 5L 51
Lightwater Country Pk. 7J 51
Lightwater Leisure Cen. 6K 51
Lightwater Mdw.
GU18: Ligh 7M 51
Lightwater Rd. GU18: Ligh 7M 51
Lightwood RG12: Brac 5B 32
Lilac Av. GU22: Wok 7N 73
Lilac Cl. GU1: Guil 8M 93
Lilac Ct. TW11: Tedd 5F 24
Lilac Gdns. CR0: Croy 9K 47
Lilian Rd. SW16 9G 28
Lilleshall Rd. SM4: Mord 5B 44
Lilley Ct. RG45: Crow 3G 49
Lilley Dr. KT20: K'wood 9N 81
Lillian Rd. SW13 2F 12
Lillie Mans. *SW6* *2K 13*
(off Lillie Rd.)
Lillie Rd. SW6 2K 13
TN16: B Hil 5F 86
Lillie Road Fitness Cen. 3J 13
Lillie Yd. SW6 2M 13
Lilliot's La. KT22: Leat 6G 79
Lillymead RH1: Mers 9G 102
Lily Cl. W14 1J 13
(not continuous)
Lily Ct. RG41: W'ham 2A 30
Lilyfields Chase GU6: Ewh 6F 156
Lily Hill Dr. RG12: Brac 1C 32
Lily Hill Rd. RG12: Brac 1C 32
Lilyville Rd. SW6 4L 13
Lime Av. GU15: Camb 9E 50
RH12: Hors 4N 197
SL4: W'sor 4J 5
(Adelaide Rd.)
SL4: W'sor 4C 18
(Sheet St. Rd.)
SL5: Asc 5F 32
Limebush Cl. KT15: N Haw 5L 55
Lime Cl. GU4: W Cla 6K 95
RH2: Reig 6N 121
RH10: Cop 7M 163
RH11: Craw 9A 162
SM5: Cars 8D 44
Lime Ct. CR4: Mit 1B 44
Lime Cres. GU12: Ash 2F 110
TW16: Sunb 1K 39
Limecroft GU46: Yate 1B 68
Limecroft Cl. KT19: Ewe 4C 60
Limecroft Rd. GU21: Knap 4E 72
Lime Dr. GU51: Fleet 1C 88
Lime Gro. CR6: Warl 5H 85
GU1: Guil 8L 93
GU4: W Cla 6J 95
GU22: Wok 8A 74
KT3: N Mal 3C 42
KT15: Addl 1J 55
TW1: Twick 9F 10
Lime Ho. TW9: Kew 4A 12
Lime Lodge *TW16: Sunb* *8G 22*
(off Forest Dr.)
Lime Mdw. Av. CR2: Sande 9D 64
Lime Quarry M. GU4: Guil 2F 114
Limerick Cl. RG42: Brac 9M 15
SW12 1G 28
Lime Rd. TW9: Rich 7M 11
Limes, The *GU21: Wok* *3C 74*
(off Maybury Rd.)
GU21: Wok 2N 73
(Ridgeway)
KT8: W Mole 3B 40
KT19: Eps 6A 60
KT22: Leat 1H 99
RG42: Warf 6D 16
RH12: Hors *4J 197*
(off Trafalgar Rd.)
RH19: Fel 5K 165
SL4: W'sor 4A 4
SW18 9M 13
TN8: Eden 2L 147
Limes Av. CR0: Wad 9L 45
RH6: Horl 9F 142
SM5: Cars 7D 44
SW13 5E 12
Limes Cl. TW15: A'ford 6B 22
Limes Fld. Rd. SW14 6D 12
Limes Gdns. SW18 9M 13
Limes M. TW20: Egh 6B 20
Limes Pl. CR0: Croy 6A 46
Limes Rd. BR3: Beck 1L 47
CR0: Croy 6A 46
GU14: Cove 9H 69
KT13: Weybr 1B 56
TW20: Egh 6B 20
Limes Row BR6: Farnb 2K 67
Lime St. GU11: Alde 2L 109
Lime Tree Av. KT7: T Dit 7E 40
KT10: Esh, T Dit 7D 40
Lime Tree Cl. KT23: Book 2A 98
Limetree Cl. SW2 2K 29
Lime Tree Copse
RG42: Warf 8E 16
Lime Tree Ct. CR2: S Croy 3N 63
KT21: A'tead 5L 79
Lime Tree Gro. CR0: Croy 9J 47
Lime Tree Pl. CR4: Mit 9F 28
Lime Tree Rd. TW5: Hest 4B 10
Lime Tree Wlk.
BR4: W Wick 1B 66
GU14: Farnb 5C 90
GU21: Wok 3N 73
GU25: V Wat 3A 36
Limetree Wlk. SW17 6E 28
Lime Wlk. GU5: Shere 8A 116
KT8: E Mol 3F 40
RG12: Brac 3A 32
Limeway Ter. RH4: Dork 3G 118
Limewood Cl. BR3: Beck 4M 47
GU21: Wok 7G 73
Lime Works Rd.
RH1: Mers 4G 102
LIMPSFIELD 7D 106
Limpsfield Av. CR7: T Hea 4K 45
SW19 3J 27
LIMPSFIELD CHART 8G 107
Limpsfield Rd. CR2: Sande 8D 64
CR6: Warl 3F 84
Linacre Ct. W6 1J 13
Linacre Dr. GU6: Cranl 7D 176
RH12: Cranl, Rudg 7D 176
Lince La. RH4: Westc 5D 118
Linchfield Rd. SL3: Dat 4M 5
LINCHMERE 6A 188
Linchmere Pl.
RH11: Craw 2M 181
Linchmere Ridge
GU27: Hasl 5B 188
Linchmere Rd.
GU27: Linch, Hasl 5A 188
Lincoln Av. SW19 4J 27
TW2: Twick 3C 24
Lincoln Cl. GU12: A Va 8D 90
GU15: Camb 2F 70
RH6: Horl 9E 142
RH10: Craw 6C 182
SE25 5D 46
Lincoln Ct. CR2: S Croy 8C 200
KT13: Weybr *3E 56*
(off Old Av.)
Lincoln Dr. GU22: Pyr 2G 74
Lincoln M. SE21 3N 29
Lincoln Rd. CR4: Mit 4J 45
GU2: Guil 1J 113
KT3: N Mal 2B 42
KT4: W Pk 7G 42
RH4: Dork 3J 119
SE25 2E 46
TW13: Hanw 4N 23
Lincolnshire Gdns.
RG42: Warf 8C 16
Lincolns Mead RH7: Ling 8M 145
Lincoln Wlk. KT19: Ewe 6C 60
(not continuous)
Lincoln Way TW16: Sunb 9F 22
Lincombe Ct. KT15: Addl 2K 55
Lindale Cl. GU25: V Wat 3J 35
Lindbergh Rd. SM6: W'ton 4J 63
Linden RG12: Brac 4D 32
SL3: Lang 1D 6
Linden Av. CR5: Coul 3F 82
CR7: T Hea 3M 45
RH19: E Grin 8M 165
TW3: Houn 8B 10
Linden Cl. KT7: T Dit 6F 40
KT15: N Haw 7J 55
KT20: Tad 7J 81
RH10: Craw 6E 182
RH12: Hors 4L 197
Linden Ct. GU15: Camb 8D 50
KT22: Leat 8H 79
TW20: Eng G 7L 19
Linden Cres.
KT1: K Tham 4M 203 (1M 41)
Linden Dr. CR3: Cate 2N 103
Linden Gdns. KT22: Leat 8J 79
W4 1D 12
Linden Gro. CR6: Warl 5H 85
KT3: N Mal 2D 42
KT12: Wal T 8G 39
TW11: Tedd 6F 24
Lindenhill Rd. RG42: Brac 9L 15
Linden Ho. TW12: Hamp 7A 24
Linden Lea RH4: Dork 7J 119
Linden Leas BR4: W Wick 8N 47
Linden Pit Path KT22: Leat 8H 79
(not continuous)
Linden Pl. CR4: Mit 3C 44
KT17: Eps 5M 201 (8D 60)
KT24: E Hor 4F 96
TW18: Stain 5J 21
Linden Rd.
GU1: Guil 2C 202 (3N 113)
GU35: H Dwn 4G 169
KT13: Weybr 5D 56
KT22: Leat 8H 79
TW12: Hamp 8A 24
Lindens, The CR0: N Add 3M 65
GU9: Farnh 2J 129
GU16: Mytc 2D 90
GU35: Lind 3B 168
RH10: Cop 7M 163
W4 4B 12
Lindens Cl. KT24: Eff 6M 97
Linden Way CR8: Pur 6G 63
GU22: Wok 8B 74
GU23: Rip 3H 95
TW17: Shep 4D 38
Lindfield Gdns. GU1: Guil 2B 114
Lindfield Rd. CR0: Croy 5C 46
LINDFORD 4A 168
Lindford Chase
GU35: Lind 4A 168
Lindford Rd.
GU35: Bor, Lind 3A 168
Lindford Wey GU35: Lind 4A 168
Lindgren Wlk. RH11: Craw 8N 181
Lindisfarne Rd. SW20 8F 26
Lindley Ct. KT1: H Wic 9J 25
Lindley Pl. TW9: Kew 4N 11
Lindley Rd. KT12: Wal T 9L 39
RH9: Gods 8F 104
Lindores Rd. SM5: Cars 6A 44
Lind Rd. SM1: Sut 2A 62
Lindrop St. SW6 5N 13
Lindsay Cl. KT9: Ches 4L 59
KT19: Eps 7G 201 (9B 60)
TW19: Stan 8M 7
Lindsay Ct. CR0: Croy 6D 200
Lindsay Dr. TW17: Shep 5E 38
Lindsay Rd. KT4: W Pk 8G 43
KT15: N Haw 6J 55
TW12: H Hill 5B 24
Lindsey Cl. CR4: Mit 3J 45
Lindsey Gdns. TW14: Bedf 1E 22
Lindum Cl. GU11: Alde 3M 109
Lindum Dene GU11: Alde 3M 109
Lindum Rd. TW11: Tedd 8J 25
Lindvale GU21: Wok 2A 74
Lindway SE27 6M 29
Linersh Dr. GU5: Braml 5C 134
Linersh Wood Cl.
GU5: Braml 6C 134
Linersh Wood Rd.
GU5: Braml 5C 134
Lines Rd. GU11: Alde 6B 90
Linfield Cl. KT12: Hers 2J 57
Ling Cres. GU35: H Dwn 3G 169
Ling Dr. GU18: Ligh 8K 51
LINGFIELD 7N 145
Lingfield Av.
KT1: K Tham 8K 203 (3L 41)
LINGFIELD COMMON 6M 145
Lingfield Comn. Rd.
RH7: Ling 6M 145
Lingfield Dr. RH10: Craw 2J 183
Lingfield Gdns. CR5: Coul 6M 83
Lingfield Pk. Racecourse 9A 146
Lingfield Rd. KT4: W Pk 9H 43
RH19: E Grin 6N 165
SW19 6J 27
TN8: Eden 3H 147
Lingfield Station (Rail) 7A 146
Lingmala Gro. GU52: C Cro 8C 88
Lings Coppice SE21 3N 29
Lingwell Rd. SW17 4C 28
Lingwood RG12: Brac 5A 32
Lingwood Gdns. TW7: Isle 3E 10
Link, The RH11: Craw 3B 182
(not continuous)
TW11: Tedd 7F 24
Link 10 RH10: Craw 9D 162
Link Av. GU22: Pyr 2F 74
Linkfield KT8: W Mole 2B 40
Linkfield Cnr. RH1: Red 3B 122
(Hatchlands Rd.)
RH1: Red 3C 122
(Linkfield St.)
Linkfield Gdns. RH1: Red 3C 122
Linkfield La. RH1: Red 2C 122
Linkfield Lodge RH1: Red 2C 122
Linkfield Rd. TW7: Isle 5F 10
Linkfield St. RH1: Red 3C 122
Link La. SM6: W'ton 3H 63
Link Rd. KT15: Addl 1N 55
SL3: Dat 4M 5
SM6: W'ton 7E 44
TW14: Felt 1G 23
Links, The KT12: Wal T 8H 39
SL5: Asc 1J 33
Links Av. SM4: Mord 3M 43
(not continuous)
Links Brow KT22: Fetc 2E 98
Links Bus. Cen. GU22: Wok 6E 74
Links Cl. GU6: Ewh 4F 156
KT21: A'tead 4J 79
Linkscroft Av. TW15: A'ford 7C 22
Links Gdns. SW16 8L 29
Links Grn. Way KT11: Cob 1A 78
LINKSIDE 2N 169
Linkside KT3: N Mal 1D 42
Linkside E. GU26: Hind 2A 170
Linkside Nth. GU26: Hind 2N 169
Linkside Sth. GU26: Hind 3A 170
Linkside W. GU26: Hind 2N 169
Links Pl. KT21: A'tead 4K 79
Links Rd. BR4: W Wick 7M 47
GU5: Braml 4A 134
KT17: Eps 9F 60
KT21: A'tead 5J 79
SW17 7E 28
TW15: A'ford 6N 21
Links Vw. Av. RH3: Brock 3N 119
Links Vw. Ct. TW12: H Hill 5D 24
Links Vw. Rd. CR0: Croy 9K 47
TW12: H Hill 6C 24
Links Way BR3: Beck 5K 47
GU14: Cove 2H 89
KT23: Book 6M 97
Link Way TW18: Stain 7K 21
Linkway GU2: Guil 2J 113
GU15: Camb 2A 70
GU22: Wok 4E 74
GU52: Fleet 7A 88
RG45: Crow 2E 48
SW20 2G 43
TW10: Ham 3H 25
Linkway, The SM2: Sut 5A 62
Linkway Pde. GU52: Fleet 7A 88
Linley Ct. SM1: Sut 1A 62
Linnell Cl. RH11: Craw 9N 181
Linnell Rd. RH1: Red 4E 122
Linnet Cl. CR2: Sels 6G 65

Linnet Gro.—Long Gdn. Wlk. W.

Linnet Gro. GU4: Guil 1F 114
Linnet M. SW12 ....1E 28
Linnett Cl. RH10: T Hil 4F 184
Linsford Bus. Pk.
GU16: Mytc 2C 90
Linsford La. GU16: Mytc 2D 90
Linslade Cl. TW4: Houn 8M 9
Linstead Rd. GU14: Cove 6K 69
Linstead Way SW18 ....1K 27
Linsted La. GU35: Head 2C 168
Lintaine Cl. W6 ....2K 13
Linters Ct. RH1: Red 1D 122
Linton Cl. CR4: Mit 6D 44
Linton Glade CR0: Sels 5H 65
(not continuous)
Linton Gro. SE27 ....6M 29
Lintons La. KT17: Eps 8D 60
Lintott Ct. TW19: Stan 9M 7
Lintott Gdns. RH13: Hors 5L 197
Linver Rd. SW6 ....5M 13
Lion & Lamb Way
GU9: Farnh 1G 128
Lion & Lamb Yd.
GU9: Farnh 1G 129
Lion Av. TW1: Twick 2F 24
Lion Cl. GU27: Hasl 1D 188
TW17: Shep 2N 37
Lionel Rd. Nth. TW8: Brent ...1L 11
Lionel Rd. Sth. TW8: Brent ...1M 11
Liongate Ent. Pk. CR4: Mit 3B 44
Lion Ga. Gdns. TW9: Rich 6M 11
Lion Ga. M. SW18 ....1M 27
Liongate M. KT8: E Mol 2K 40
Lion Grn. GU27: Hasl 2D 188
Lion Grn. Rd. CR5: Coul 3H 83
Lion Head Ct. CR0: Croy 6B 200
Lion La. GU27: Hasl 9D 170
RH1: Red 2D 122
RH10: T Hil 5D 184
Lion Mead GU27: Hasl 2D 188
Lion Pk. Av. KT9: Ches 1N 59
Lion Retail Pk. GU22: Wok ...3D 74
Lion Rd. CR0: Croy 4N 45
TW1: Twick 2F 24
Lion's La. GU6: Cranl 3K 175
(not continuous)
Lion Way GU52: C Cro 8C 88
TW8: Brent 3K 11
Lion Wharf Rd. TW7: Isle 6H 11
Lipcombe Cotts. GU5: Alb 3L 135
Liphook Rd. GU27: Hasl 2C 188
GU27: Hasl, Linch, Lip
.....................4A 188
GU30: Pass 6D 168
GU35: Head 6D 168
GU35: Lind 4A 168
GU35: White 9A 168
LIPSCOMB'S CORNER 2M 179
Lipsham Cl. SM7: Ban 9B 62
Lisbon Av. TW2: Twick 3C 24
Liscombe RG12: Brac 6N 31
Liscombe Ho. RG12: Brac 6N 31
Liskeard Dr. GU14: Farnb 8M 69
Liskeard Lodge CR3: Cate ...4D 104
Lisle Cl. SW17 ....5F 28
Lismore *SW19* *6L 27*
(off Woodside)
Lismore Cl. TW7: Isle 5G 10
Lismore Cres. RH11: Craw ...6N 181
Lismore Rd. CR2: S Croy 3B 64
Lismoyne Cl. GU51: Fleet 3A 88
Lissant Cl. KT6: Surb 6K 41
Lissoms Rd. CR5: Chip 5E 82
Lister Av. RH19: E Grin 3A 186
Lister Cl. CR4: Mit 9C 28
Listergate Ct. SW15 ....7H 13
Lister Ho. UB3: Harl 1F 8
Litchfield Av. SM4: Mord 6L 43
Litchfield Gdns. KT11: Cob 1J 77
Litchfield Rd. SM1: Sut 1A 62
Litchfield Way GU2: Guil 5J 113
Lithgow's Rd. TW6: Lon A 7F 8
Little Acre BR3: Beck 2K 47
Little All. TN8: M Grn 6K 147
Lit. Austins Rd.
GU9: Farnh 3J 129
Little Benty UB7: W Dray 1M 7
Lit. Birch Cl. KT15: N Haw 5M 55
LITTLE BIRKETTS 1L 157
Lit. Boltons, The SW5 ....1N 13
SW10 ....1N 13
LITTLE BOOKHAM 2N 97
LITTLE BOOKHAM COMMON
.....................9M 77
Lit. Bookham St.
KT23: Book 1N 97
Little Borough RH3: Brock ...4N 119
Littlebrook Cl. CR0: Croy 5G 47
Lit. Browns La. TN8: Eden ...8H 127
Little Buntings SL4: W'sor 6C 4
Little Chesters
KT20: Wal H 3F 100
Little Collins RH1: Out 4M 143
Littlecombe Cl. SW15 ....9J 13
Little Comn. La.
RH1: Blet 1M 123
Little Comptons
RH13: Hors 6M 197
Little Copse GU46: Yate 8C 48
GU52: Fleet 6A 88
Littlecote Cl. SW19 ....1K 27
Little Crabtree
RH11: Craw 2A 182
Lit. Cranmore La.
KT24: W Hors 6C 96
Little Cft. GU46: Yate 1C 68
Littlecroft Rd. TW20: Egh 6B 20
Littledale Cl. RG12: Brac 2C 32
Little Dimocks SW12 ....3F 28
Little E. Fld. CR5: Coul 8H 83
Little Elms UB3: Harl 3E 8
Lit. Ferry Rd. TW1: Twick 2H 25
Littlefield Cl. GU3: Worp 8G 92
GU12: Ash 3E 110
KT1: K Tham 4K 203 (1L 41)
LITTLEFIELD COMMON 7E 92
Littlefield Gdns.
GU12: Ash 3E 110
Littlefield Ho.
KT1: K Tham 4J 203
Littlefield Way GU3: Worp 8F 92
Littleford La. GU4: B'eath 2G 134
GU5: Sha G 2G 134
Little Fryth RG40: Finch 1B 48
Little Grebe RH12: Hors 3J 197
Little Green TW9: Rich 7K 11
Little Grn. La. GU9: Farnh 4F 128
KT16: Chert 9G 36
Little Gro. *RH4: Dork* *7J 119*
(off Stubs Hill)
Little Halliards
KT12: Wal T 5H 39
Little Hatch RH12: Hors 3M 197
LITTLE HAVEN 3L 197
Littlehaven Station (Rail) ...3M 197
Littleheath La.
KT11: Cob, Sto D 1A 78
Lit. Heath Rd. GU24: Chob 5H 53
Littleheath Rd. CR2: Sels 4E 64
Little Hide GU1: Guil 1D 114
Lit. Holland Bungs.
CR3: Cate 1A 104
Little Kiln GU7: Goda 3H 133
Lit. King St. RH19: E Grin 9A 166
LITTLE LONDON 1A 136
Little London GU5: Alb 1N 135
GU8: Wit 5B 152
Lit. London Hill
RH12: Warn 8G 179
Little Lullenden RH7: Ling ...6N 145
Lit. Manor Gdns.
GU6: Cranl 8M 155
Little Mead GU6: Cranl 8K 155
Littlemead GU21: Wok 3J 73
KT10: Esh 1D 58
Lit. Mead Ind. Est.
GU6: Cranl 7K 155
Little Moor GU47: Sandh 6H 49
Lit. Moreton Cl.
KT14: W By 8K 55
Little Oaks *RH19: E Grin* *7N 165*
(off Springfield)
Lit. Oaks Cl. TW17: Shep 3A 38
Little Orchard GU21: Wok 1C 74
KT15: Wood 7J 55
Little Orchards KT18: Eps 8L 201
Lit. Orchard Way
GU4: Chil 1A 134
Little Paddock GU15: Camb ...7E 50
Little Pk. Dr. TW13: Felt 3M 23
LITTLE PARROCK 7M 187
Little Platt GU2: Guil 2G 112
Lit. Queen's Rd.
TW11: Tedd 7F 24
Little Riding GU22: Wok 3D 74
Little Ringdale RG12: Brac 3C 32
Lit. Roke Av. CR8: Ken 1M 83
Lit. Roke Rd. CR8: Ken 1N 83
Littlers Cl. SW19 ....9B 28
Lit. St Leonard's
SW14 ....6B 12
LITTLE SANDHURST 5F 48
Little St. GU2: Guil 8L 93
Lit. Sutton La. SL3: Lang 2D 6
(Brands Hill)
SL3: Lang 1E 6
(Sutton)
Little Thatch GU7: Goda 5J 133
Lit. Thurbans Cl.
GU9: Farnh 5F 128
LITTLETON
GU3 ....8K 113
TW17 ....2B 38
LITTLETON COMMON 8D 22
Littleton Ho. *RH2: Reig* *2M 121*
(off Somers Cl.)
Littleton La. GU3: Art 8K 113
RH2: Reig 5J 121
TW17: Shep 6M 37
Littleton Rd. TW15: A'ford 8D 22
Littleton St. SW18 ....3A 28
Lit. Tumners Ct.
GU7: Goda 4H 133
Little Vigo GU46: Yate 2A 68
Lit. Warkworth Ho.
TW7: Isle 5H 11
Lit. Warren Cl. GU4: Guil 5D 114
Lit. Wellington St.
GU11: Alde 2M 109
LITTLEWICK 3H 73
Littlewick Rd.
GU21: Knap, Wok 3H 73
Littlewood GU6: Cranl 7A 156
LITTLE WOODCOTE 7F 62
Lit. Woodcote Est.
SM6: W'ton 7F 62
Lit. Woodcote La. CR8: Pur ...8F 62
SM5: Cars 8F 62
Little Woodlands SL4: W'sor ...6C 4
Lit. Wood St.
KT1: K Tham 3H 203 (1K 41)
Littleworth Av. KT10: Esh 2D 58
Littleworth Comn. Rd.
KT10: Esh 9D 40
Littleworth La. KT10: Esh 1D 58
Littleworth Pl. KT10: Esh 1D 58
Littleworth Rd. GU10: Seal ...2C 130
KT10: Esh 2D 58
Litttlehaven La.
RH12: Hors 3M 197
Liverpool Rd. CR7: T Hea 2N 45
KT2: K Tham 8N 25
Livesey Cl.
KT1: K Tham 5L 203 (2M 41)
Livingstone Cl. GU6: Cranl ...9A 156
Livingstone Ct. *TW19: Stan* ...*2N 21*
(off Explorer Av.)
Livingstone Mans.
W14 ....*2K 13*
(off Queen's Club Gdns.)
Livingstone Rd. CR3: Cate 9A 84
CR7: T Hea 1N 45
RH10: Craw 5C 182
RH13: Hors 7K 197
TW3: Houn 7C 10
Livingwell Health Club
Purley 3L 63
Llanaway Cl. GU7: Goda 5J 133
Llanaway Ho. *GU7: Goda* *5J 133*
(off Meadrow)
Llanaway Rd. GU7: Goda 5J 133
Llangar Gro. RG45: Crow 2F 48
Llanthony Rd. SM4: Mord 4B 44
Llanvair Cl. SL5: Asc 5L 33
Llanvair Dr. SL5: Asc 5K 33
Lloyd Av. CR5: Coul 1E 82
SW16 ....9J 29
Lloyd Pk. Av. CR0: Croy 1C 64
Lloyd Park Stop (CT) 1C 64
Lloyd Rd. KT4: W Pk 9H 43
Lloyds Ct. RH10: Craw 9C 162
Lloyds Lanes Raynes Pk. 2J 43
Lloyds Way BR3: Beck 4H 47
Lobelia Rd. GU24: Bis 2D 72
Locarno Ct. SW16 ....6G 29
Lochaline St. W6 ....2H 13
Lochinvar St. SW12 ....1F 28
Lochinver RG12: Brac 6N 31
Lock Cl. KT15: Wood 8G 55
Locke King Cl. KT13: Weybr ...4B 56
Locke King Rd.
KT13: Weybr 4B 56
Lockesley Sq. KT6: Surb 5K 41
Lockestone KT13: Weybr 3A 56
Lockestone Cl.
KT13: Weybr 3A 56
Lockets Cl. SL4: W'sor 4A 4
Locke Way GU21: Wok 4B 74
Lockfield Dr. GU21: Wok 3H 73
Lockhart Rd. KT11: Cob 9K 57
Lockhurst Hatch La.
GU5: Alb 5N 135
Lockie Pl. SE25 ....2D 46
Lockites *GU7: Goda* *4F 132*
(off Duke's Dr.)
Lock La. GU22: Pyr 3K 75
LOCKNER HOLT 9H 115
Lock Path SL4: Dorn, E Wic 2A 4
Lock Rd. GU1: Guil 9N 93
GU11: Alde 8B 90
TW10: Ham 5J 25
Locks La. CR4: Mit 9E 28
Locksley Dr. GU21: Wok 4J 73
Locksmeade Rd.
TW10: Ham 5J 25
Locks Mdw. RH7: Dorm 1C 166
Locks Ride SL5: Asc 9F 16
Lockswood GU24: B'wood 7E 72
Lockton Chase SL5: Asc 2H 33
Lockwood Cl. GU14: Cove 6K 69
RH12: Hors 3N 197
Lockwood Ct. RH10: Craw ...1D 182
Lockwood Path GU21: Wok 9F 54
Lockwood Way
KT9: Ches 2N 59
Lockyer Ho. SW15 ....6J 13
Locomotive Dr.
TW14: Felt 2H 23
Loddon Cl. GU15: Camb 9E 50
Loddon Rd. GU14: Cove 8J 69
Loddon Way GU12: Ash 3E 110
Loder Cl. GU21: Wok 9F 54
Lodge, The RH7: Newc 1H 165
SM7: Ban 4A 82
Lodge Av. CR0: Wad 9L 45
SW14 ....6D 12
Lodgebottom Rd.
KT18: Head 5N 99
RH5: Mick 5N 99
Lodge Cl. GU11: Alde 4A 110
KT11: Sto D 3N 77
KT17: Ewe 6H 61
KT22: Fetc 9D 78
RH5: Nth H 9J 119
RH11: Craw 3A 182
RH19: E Grin 9M 165
SM6: W'ton 7E 44
TW7: Isle 4H 11
TW20: Eng G 6N 19
Lodge Gdns. BR3: Beck 4J 47
Lodge Gro. GU46: Yate 9E 48
Lodge Hill CR8: Pur 2L 83
Lodge Hill Cl.
GU10: L Bou 5J 129
Lodge Hill Rd.
GU10: L Bou 5J 129
Lodge La. CR0: N Add 3K 65
RH1: Salf 3C 142
RH5: Holm 4L 139
TN16: Weste 5L 107
Lodge Pl. SM1: Sut 2N 61
Lodge Rd. CR0: Croy 5M 45
KT22: Fetc 9C 78
SM6: W'ton 2F 62
Lodge Wlk. CR6: Warl 3K 85
RH6: Horl *8D 142*
(off Thornton Pl.)
Lodge Way SL4: W'sor 6B 4
TW15: A'ford 3N 21
TW17: Shep 1D 38
Lodkin Hill GU8: Hasc 4N 153
Lodsworth GU14: Cove 2J 89
Loft Ho. Pl. KT9: Ches 3J 59
Lofts, The GU8: Worm 1C 172
Logan Cl. TW4: Houn 6N 9
Logmore La.
RH4: Dork, Westc 7B 118
Lois Dr. TW17: Shep 4C 38
Lollesworth La.
KT24: W Hors 4D 96
Loman Rd. GU16: Mytc 1E 90
Lomas Cl. CR0: N Add 4M 65
Lombard Bus. Pk.
CR0: Croy 6K 45
SW19 ....1N 43
Lombard Rd. SW19 ....1N 43
LOMBARD RDBT. 6K 45
Lombard St. GU8: S'ford 5K 131
Lombardy Cl. GU21: Wok 4J 73
Lomond Gdns. CR2: Sels 4H 65
Loncin Mead Av.
KT15: N Haw 5L 55
London Apollo 1H 13
LONDON - BIGGIN HILL AIRPORT
........................8F 66
London Butterfly House 4H 11
London Flds. Ho.
RH11: Craw 8A 182
LONDON GATWICK AIRPORT,
NORTH TERMINAL 2C 162
LONDON GATWICK AIRPORT,
SOUTH TERMINAL 3E 162
LONDON-HEATHROW AIRPORT
........................6B 8
London La. GU5: Shere 7B 116
KT24: E Hor 9G 97
London Rd.
CR0: Croy, T Hea
..............1A 200 (4L 45)
CR3: Cate 1A 104
CR4: Mit 4C 44
(Bishopsford Rd.)
CR4: Mit 6E 44
(Carshalton Rd.)
CR4: Mit 1D 44
(Holborn Way)
CR7: T Hea 9K 29
GU1: Guil 4E 202 (4A 114)
(not continuous)
GU4: B'ham 8D 94
(not continuous)
GU15: Camb 9A 50
GU17: B'water, Min 4D 68
GU19: Bag 6F 50
GU20: Windl 9M 33
GU23: Send 4G 94
(not continuous)
GU25: V Wat 2K 35
GU26: Hind 5D 170
KT2: K Tham ...3L 203 (1M 41)
(not continuous)
KT17: Ewe 5E 60
RG12: Bin 1G 31
RG12: Brac 1B 32
RG27: Min, B'water 4A 68
RG40: W'ham 2C 30
RG42: Bin 9H 15
RH1: Red 2D 122
RH2: Reig 3M 121
RH4: Dork 1L 201 (4H 119)
RH5: Dork 3H 119
RH10: Craw, L Hea 2B 182
RH12: Hors 6J 197
RH18: F Row 5G 186
RH19: E Grin 6K 165
SL3: Dat 3L 5
(not continuous)
SL3: Lang 1A 6
SL5: Asc 2E 32
SL5: Asc, S'hill 2M 33
SL5: S'dale 7B 34
SM3: Chea 9J 43
SM4: Mord 4M 43
SM6: W'ton 1F 62
SW16 ....9K 29
SW17 ....8D 28
TN16: Weste 1L 107
TW1: Twick 1G 24
TW3: Houn 6C 10
TW7: Brent, Isle 5F 10
TW7: Isle, Twick 8G 10
TW8: Brent 3H 11
London Rd. TW14: Bedf 4K 21
TW15: A'ford 4K 21
TW18: Stain 5J 21
TW20: Eng G 2K 35
London Rd. Nth.
RH1: Mers 4F 102
LONDON ROAD RDBT. 9G 10
London Rd. Sth.
RH1: Mers, Red 8E 102
London Road Station (Rail)
............3F 202 (3A 114)
London Scottish & Richmond RUFC
........................6K 11
London Sq.
GU1: Guil 3F 202 (3A 114)
London Stile W4 ....1N 11
London St. KT16: Chert 6J 37
London Welsh RUFC 6L 11
London Wetland Cen. 4G 13
Loneacre GU20: Windl 3B 52
Lone Oak RH6: Smal 1M 163
LONESOME 9G 28
Lonesome Cvn. Pk.
CR4: Mit 9F 28
Lonesome La.
RH2: Reig, Sid 7N 121
Lonesome Way SW16 ....9F 28
Long Acre RH10: Craw D 1D 184
Longacre GU12: Ash 2E 110
Longacre Pl. SM5: Cars 3E 62
Long Beech Dr. GU14: Cove ...2H 89
Longbourn SL4: W'sor 6D 4
Longbourne Grn.
GU7: Goda 3H 133
Longbourne Way
KT16: Chert 5H 37
Longboyds KT11: Cob 2J 77
Long Bri. GU9: Farnh 1H 129
Longbridge Ga. *RH6: Gat* *2C 162*
(off Gatwick Way)
Longbridge Rd. RH6: Horl 1D 162
Longbridge Rdbt.
RH6: Horl 9C 142
Longbridge Wlk.
RH6: Horl 1D 162
Longbridge Way RH6: Gat ...1D 162
Longchamp Cl. RH6: Horl ...8G 143
Long Cl. RH10: Craw 3H 183
Long Comn. GU5: Sha G 8E 134
Long Copse Cl. KT23: Book ...1B 98
Longcroft Av. SM7: Ban 1A 82
LONGCROSS 9K 35
Long Cross Hill
GU35: Head 4D 168
Longcross Rd. GU24: Chob 9J 35
KT16: L'cross 9A 36
Longcross Station (Rail) 7J 35
Longdene Rd. GU27: Hasl ...2F 188
LONG DITTON 7J 41
Longdon Wood BR2: Kes 1G 66
Longdown GU52: Fleet 7A 88
Longdown Chase Cotts.
GU26: Hind 6E 170
Longdown Cl.
GU10: L Bou 5H 129
Longdown La. Nth.
KT17: Eps 1F 80
Longdown La. Sth.
KT17: Eps, Eps D 1F 80
Longdown Lodge
GU47: Sandh 7G 48
Longdown Rd. GU4: Guil 6D 114
GU10: L Bou 6G 128
GU47: Sandh 6F 48
KT17: Eps 1F 80
Long Dyke GU1: Guil 1D 114
Longfellow Cl. RH12: Hors ...1L 197
Longfellow Rd. KT4: W Pk 8F 42
Longfield Av. SM6: W'ton 7E 44
Longfield Cl. GU14: Farnb 6M 69
Longfield Cres. KT20: Tad 7H 81
Longfield Dr. CR4: Mit 9C 28
SW14 ....8A 12
Longfield Rd. GU12: Ash 2E 110
RH4: Dork 6F 118
RH12: Hors 8G 196
Longfield St. SW18 ....1M 27
LONGFORD 4K 7
Longford Av. TW14: Felt 9F 8
TW19: Stan 2N 21
Longford Cir. UB7: L'ford 4K 7
Longford Cl. GU15: Camb 2B 70
TW12: H Hill 5A 24
TW13: Hanw 4M 23
Longford Ct. KT19: Ewe 1B 60
TW12: H Hill 7B 24
Longford Gdns. SM1: Sut 9A 44
Longford Ho. TW12: H Hill 5A 24
Longford Ind. Est.
TW12: Hamp 7B 24
LONGFORDMOOR 4J 7
Longford Rd. TW2: Whitt 2A 24
Longford Wlk. SW2 ....1L 29
Longford Way TW19: Stan 2N 21
Long Gdn. M. *GU9: Farnh* *1G 129*
(off Long Garden Wlk.)
Long Gdn. Pl. GU9: Farnh ...9G 109
Long Gdn. Wlk.
GU9: Farnh 1G 129
Long Gdn. Wlk. E.
GU9: Farnh 9G 109
Long Gdn. Wlk. W.
GU9: Farnh 9G 108

Long Gdn. Way—Lyndhurst Farm Cl.

Long Gdn. Way
GU9: Farnh 1G 128
Long Gore GU7: Goda 2H 133
Long Heath Dr. KT23: Book 2M 97
Longheath Gdns. CR0: Croy 4F 46
Long Hedges TW3: Houn 5A 10
Long Hill CR3: Wold 8G 85
GU10: Seal 2C 130
Long Hill Rd. SL5: Asc 1E 32
Longhope Dr. GU10: Wrec 5F 128
Long Ho's. GU24: Pirb 2A 92
Longhurst Rd. CR0: Croy 5E 46
KT24: E Hor 7F 96
RH11: Craw 8M 181
Longlands Av. CR5: Coul 1E 82
Longlands Ct. CR4: Mit 9E 28
Longlands Way
GU15: Camb 1H 71
Long La. CR0: Croy 5F 46
RG40: W'ham 7E 14
TW19: Stan 3A 22
Longleat Sq. GU14: Farnb 2C 90
Longleat Way TW14: Bedf 1E 22
Longley Rd. CR0: Croy 6M 45
GU9: Farnh 2J 129
SW17 7C 28
Long Lodge Dr. KT12: Wal T 9K 39
Longmead GU1: Guil 3E 114
GU52: Fleet 7B 88
SL4: W'sor 4B 4
Longmead Bus. Cen.
KT19: Eps 7C 60
Longmead Cl. CR3: Cate 9B 84
Longmead Ho. SE27 6N 29
Longmeadow GU16: Frim 3D 70
KT23: Book 3N 97
Long Mdw. Cl.
BR4: W Wick 6M 47
Long Mdw. Vs. RH6: Char 5K 161
Longmead Rd. KT7: T Dit 6E 40
KT19: Eps, Ewe 7C 60
SW17 6D 28
Longmere Gdns. KT20: Tad 6H 81
Longmere Rd. RH10: Craw 1B 182
Long Mickle GU47: Sandh 6F 48
Longmoor Point SW15 2G 26
(off Norley Vale)
Longmoors RG42: Brac 9K 15
Longmore Rd. KT12: Hers 1M 57
Long Orchards
KT20: K'wood 7K 81
Longpoles Rd. GU6: Cranl 8A 156
Long Reach GU23: Ockh 1B 96
KT24: W Hors 2C 96
Longridge Gro. GU22: Pyr 1H 75
Longridge Rd. SW5 1M 13
Longridge Vw. CR5: Chip 7D 82
Long Rd., The GU10: Rowl 8E 128
Longroyd KT24: E Hor 4F 96
(off Cobham Way)
Longs Cl. GU22: Pyr 3J 75
Longs Ct. TW9: Rich 7M 11
Longsdon Way CR3: Cate 2D 104
Longshaw KT22: Leat 7G 78
Longshot Ind. Est.
RG12: Brac 1K 31
Longshot La. RG12: Brac 2K 31
(not continuous)
Longside Cl. TW20: Egh 9E 20
Longstaff Cres. SW18 9M 13
Longstaff Rd. SW18 9M 13
Longstone Rd. SW17 6F 28
Long's Way RG40: W'ham 1D 30
Longthornton Rd.
SW16 1G 45
Long Wlk. GU4: E Cla 8N 95
KT3: N Mal 2B 42
KT14: W By 1L 75
KT18: Tat C 6H 81
SW13 5D 12
TN8: C Hil 9K 107
Long Wlk., The SL4: W'sor 2G 19
Longwater Ho.
KT1: K Tham 6H 203
Longwater Rd. RG12: Brac 5A 32
Longwood Av. SL3: Lang 1D 6
Longwood Bus. Pk.
TW16: Sunb 4G 38
Longwood Dr. SW15 9F 12
Longwood Rd. CR8: Ken 3A 84
(not continuous)
Longwood Vw.
RH10: Craw 6E 182
Longyard Ho. RH6: Horl 6F 142
Lonsdale Ct. KT6: Surb 6K 41
Lonsdale Gdns. CR7: T Hea 3K 45
Lonsdale M. TW9: Kew 4N 11
Lonsdale Pl. RH4: Dork 1L 201
Lonsdale Rd. KT13: Weybr 4B 56
RH4: Dork 1L 201 (4H 119)
SE25 3E 46
SW13 4E 12
Lonsdale Road Reservoir
Bird Sanctuary 3E 12
Look Out, The (Heritage Cen.)
7B 32
Loop Rd. GU22: Wok 7B 74
KT18: Eps 3B 80
Loppets Rd. RH10: Craw 5D 182
Lorac Ct. SM2: Sut 4M 61
Loraine Gdns. KT21: A'tead 4L 79
Loraine Ho. SM6: W'ton 1F 62
Loraine Rd. W4 2A 12
Lord Chancellor Wlk.
KT2: K Tham 9B 26
Lord Darby M. TN14: Cud 2M 87
Lordell Pl. SW19 7H 27
Lord Knyvett Cl.
TW19: Stan 9M 7
Lord Knyvetts Ct.
TW19: Stan 9M 7
Lord Napier Pl. W6 1F 12
Lord Raglan Ho. SL4: W'sor 6F 4
Lord Roberts M. SW6 3N 13
Lordsbury Fld. SM6: W'ton 6G 62
Lords Cl. SE21 3N 29
TW13: Hanw 3M 23
Lordsgrove Cl. KT20: Tad 7G 81
LORDSHILL COMMON 7F 134
Lords Hill Cotts.
GU5: Sha G 7E 134
Lordshill Rd. GU5: Sha G 6E 134
Lords Wood Ho. CR5: Coul 9H 83
Loretto Cl. GU6: Cranl 7A 156
Lorian Dr. RH2: Reig 2A 122
Loriners RH10: Craw 6B 182
Loriners Cl. KT11: Cob 1H 77
Loring Rd. SL4: W'sor 4C 4
TW7: Isle 5F 10
Lorne, The KT23: Book 4A 98
Lorne Av. CR0: Croy 6G 47
Lorne Gdns. CR0: Croy 6G 47
GU21: Knap 6G 72
Lorne Rd. TW10: Rich 8M 11
Lorraine Rd. GU15: Camb 7D 50
Lory Ridge GU19: Bag 3J 51
Loseberry Rd. KT10: Clay 2D 58
Loseley House 9H 113
LOSELEY PARK 9J 113
Loseley Rd. GU7: Goda 3H 133
Losfield Rd. SL4: W'sor 4B 4
Lothian Rd. GU24: B'wood 8L 71
Lothian Wood KT20: Tad 9G 80
Lots Rd. SW10 3N 13
Lotus Cl. SE21 4N 29
Lotus Pk. TW18: Stain 5F 20
Lotus Rd. TN16: B Hil 5H 87
Loubet St. SW17 7D 28
Loudwater Cl. TW16: Sunb 3H 39
Loudwater Rd. TW16: Sunb 3H 39
Loughborough RG12: Brac 5C 32
Louisa Ct. TW2: Twick 3E 24
Louise Margaret Rd.
GU11: Alde 1A 110
Louis Flds. GU3: Worp 8F 92
Louisville Rd. SW17 4E 28
Lovatt Ct. SW12 2F 28
Lovat Wlk. TW5: Hest 3M 9
Loveday Ho. GU6: Cranl 5L 155
Lovedean Ct. RG12: Brac 5C 32
Lovejoy La. SL4: W'sor 5A 4
Lovekyn Cl.
KT2: K Tham 3L 203 (1L 41)
Lovelace Cl. KT24: E Jun 1H 97
Lovelace Dr. GU22: Pyr 3G 75
Lovelace Gdns. KT6: Surb 6K 41
KT12: Hers 2K 57
Lovelace Rd. KT6: Surb 6J 41
RG12: Brac 3K 31
SE21 3N 29
Lovelace Vs. KT7: T Dit 6H 41
(off Portsmouth Rd.)
Lovelands La. GU24: Chob 9F 52
KT20: Lwr K 5N 101
Love La. CR4: Mit 2C 44
(not continuous)
GU12: Ash 2F 110
KT6: Surb 8J 41
KT20: Wal H 5E 100
RH5: Ockl 6D 158
RH9: Gods 1F 124
SE25 2E 46
(not continuous)
SM1: Sut 3L 61
SM3: Chea, Sut 3K 61
SM4: Mord 6M 43
Loveletts RH11: Craw 4M 181
Lovel La. SL4: Wink 5L 17
Lovell Path RH11: Ifi 4K 181
Lovell Rd. TW10: Ham 4J 25
Lovells Cl. GU18: Ligh 6M 51
Lovelock Cl. CR8: Ken 4N 83
Lovel Rd. SL4: Wink 5K 17
Lovers La. GU10: Fren 3H 149
RH13: Hors 9J 197
Lovett Dr. SM5: Cars 6A 44
Lovett Rd. TW18: Stain 5D 20
Lovibonds Av. BR6: Farnb 1K 67
Lowbury RG12: Brac 3C 32
Lowburys RH4: Dork 8H 119
Lowdell's Cl.
RH19: E Grin 6M 165
Lowdells Dr. RH19: E Grin 6M 165
Lowdell's La.
RH19: E Grin 6L 165
Lowe Cl. GU11: Alde 1L 109
RH11: Craw 9N 181
Lwr. Addiscombe Rd.
CR0: Croy 1F 200 (7B 46)
LOWER ASHTEAD 6K 79
Lwr. Barn Cl. RH12: Hors 3M 197
Lwr. Barn Rd. CR8: Pur 8N 63
LOWER BOURNE 4J 129
Lwr. Breache Rd.
GU6: Ewh 6H 157
Lower Bri. Rd. RH1: Red 3D 122
Lwr. Broadmoor Rd.
RG45: Crow 3H 49
Lwr. Charles St.
GU15: Camb 9A 50
Lwr. Church La.
GU9: Farnh 1G 129
Lwr. Church Rd.
GU47: Sandh 6D 48
Lwr. Church St.
CR0: Croy 3A 200 (8M 45)
Lower Comn. Sth.
SW15 6G 13
Lwr. Coombe St.
CR0: Croy 6B 200 (1N 63)
Lower Ct. Rd. KT19: Eps 7B 60
Lower Dene RH19: E Grin 9C 166
Lwr. Downs Rd.
SW20 9J 27
Lwr. Drayton Pl.
CR0: Croy 3A 200 (8M 45)
Lower Dunnymans
SM7: Ban 1L 81
LOWER EASHING 7C 132
Lower Eashing GU7: Eash 7B 132
Lwr. Edgeborough Rd.
GU1: Guil 4B 114
Lwr. Farm Rd. KT24: Eff 2J 97
Lwr. Farnham Rd.
GU11: Alde 5N 109
GU12: Alde 5N 109
LOWER FELTHAM 4G 23
Lwr. George St. TW9: Rich 8K 11
LOWER GREEN 8B 40
Lower Grn. Gdns.
KT4: W Pk 7F 42
Lower Grn. Rd. KT10: Esh 8B 40
Lower Grn. W. CR4: Mit 2C 44
Lower Gro. Rd.
TW10: Rich 9M 11
Lwr. Guildford Rd.
GU21: Knap 4G 72
LOWER HALLIFORD 5E 38
Lwr. Ham La. GU8: Els 7J 131
Lwr. Hampton Rd.
TW16: Sunb 2K 39
Lwr. Ham Rd.
KT2: K Tham 1J 203 (6K 25)
Lower Hanger GU27: Hasl 2A 188
Lwr. Hill Rd. KT19: Eps 8A 60
Lowerhouse La.
RH5: For G, W'wood 7K 157
Lwr. House Rd.
GU8: Bow G 9K 151
Lwr. King's Rd.
KT2: K Tham 1J 203 (9L 25)
LOWER KINGSWOOD 5L 101
Lower Lodge Shooting Grounds
6G 194
Lower Mall W6 1G 12
Lower Mnr. Rd.
GU7: Goda 5H 133
GU8: Mil 1B 152
Lwr. Marsh La.
KT1: K Tham 7L 203 (3M 41)
(not continuous)
Lower Mead RH1: Red 1D 122
Lower Mere RH19: E Grin 1B 186
Lower Mill KT17: Ewe 4E 60
Lwr. Mill Fld. GU19: Bag 5H 51
Lower Moor GU46: Yate 1C 68
Lwr. Morden La.
SM4: Mord 5H 43
Lwr. Mortlake Rd.
TW9: Rich 7L 11
Lwr. Moushill La.
GU8: Mil 1A 152
Lwr. Nelson St.
GU11: Alde 2M 109
Lwr. Newport Rd.
GU12: Alde 4B 110
Lower Northfield SM7: Ban 1L 81
Lower Nursery SL5: S'dale 4D 34
Lower Pk. Rd. CR5: Chip 5C 82
Lower Peryers KT24: E Hor 6F 96
Lwr. Pillory Down
CR5: Coul 9F 62
SM5: Cars 9F 62
Lwr. Pyrford Rd. GU22: Pyr 3K 75
Lwr. Richmond Rd.
SW14 6A 12
SW15 6G 13
TW9, Rich 6N 11
Lower Rd. CR8: Ken 9M 63
GU27: G'wood 7K 171
KT22: Fetc 1D 98
KT23: Book 3A 98
KT24: Eff 5L 97
RH1: Red 5B 122
RH18: F Row 6H 187
SM1: Sut 1A 62
Lower Sandfields
GU23: Send 2F 94
Lwr. Sand Hills KT6: Surb 6J 41
Lwr. Sandhurst Rd.
GU47: Sandh 5A 48
RG40: Finch 5A 48
Lower Sawleywood
SM7: Ban 1L 81
Lower Shott KT23: Book 4A 98
LOWER SOUTH PARK 9D 124
Lwr. South Pk.
RH9: S Gods 9D 124
Lwr. South St. GU7: Goda 7G 133
Lwr. South Vw.
GU9: Farnh 9H 109
Lower Sq. RH18: F Row 6H 187
TW7: Isle 6H 11
Lower Sq., The SM1: Sut 2N 61
Lower St. GU5: Shere 8B 116
GU27: Hasl 2F 188
Lwr. Sunbury Rd.
TW12: Hamp 1N 39
Lwr. Tanbridge Way
RH12: Hors 6H 197
Lwr. Teddington Rd.
KT1: H Wic 1G 203 (9K 25)
Lower Ter. SE27 6M 29
(off Woodcote Pl.)
Lwr. Village Rd. SL5: S'hill 4M 33
Lwr. Weybourne La.
GU9: B Lea, Weybo 6L 109
Lwr. Wokingham Rd.
RG40: Finch 1C 48
RG45: Crow 1C 48
Lwr. Wood Rd. KT10: Clay 3H 59
Lowestoft Wlk.
RH10: Craw 5F 182
Loweswater Wlk.
GU15: Camb 2H 71
Lowfield Cl. GU18: Ligh 7L 51
LOWFIELD HEATH 5C 162
Lowfield Heath Ind. Est.
RH11: L Hea 5C 162
Lowfield Heath Rd.
RH6: Char 4L 161
Lowfield Rd. RH13: Slin 5L 195
Lowfield Way RH11: L Hea 5C 162
Lowicks Rd. GU10: Rush 4N 149
Lowlands Dr. TW19: Stan 8M 7
Lowlands Rd.
GU17: B'water 2H 69
Low La. GU9: B Lea 6N 109
Lowndes Bldgs.
GU9: Farnh 9G 108
Lowry Cl. GU47: C Tow 9J 49
Lowry Cres. CR4: Mit 1C 44
Lowther Rd.
KT2: K Tham 1M 203 (9M 25)
SW13 4E 12
Lowthorpe GU21: Wok 5K 73
Loxford Ct. GU6: Cranl 8H 155
Loxford Ho.
KT17: Eps 5M 201 (8D 60)
Loxford Rd. CR3: Cate 3C 104
Loxford Way CR3: Cate 3C 104
LOXHILL 9A 154
Loxley Rd. SW18 2B 28
TW12: Hamp 5N 23
Loxmeadows Cl. RH14: Ifo 5F 192
LOXWOOD 4H 193
Loxwood KT13: Weybr 9F 38
Loxwood Cl. TW14: Bedf 2E 22
Loxwood Farm Pl.
RH14: Loxw 5H 193
Loxwood Rd. GU6: Alf 9H 175
RH12: Rudg 4N 193
RH14: Loxw 5J 193
RH14: Plais 6B 192
Loxwood Wlk. RH11: Craw 1L 181
(not continuous)
Lucan Dr. TW18: Stain 8M 21
Lucas Cl. GU46: Yate 1C 68
RH10: Craw 6F 182
RH19: E Grin 9C 166
Lucas Dr. GU46: Yate 1C 68
Lucas Fld. GU27: Hasl 2C 188
Lucas Grn. Rd.
GU24: W End 2A 72
Lucas Ho. SW10 3N 13
(off Coleridge Gdns.)
Lucas Rd. RH12: Warn 9E 178
Lucerne Cl. GU22: Wok 6A 74
Lucerne Dr. RH10: Craw 6H 183
Lucerne Rd. CR7: T Hea 4M 45
Lucie Av. TW15: A'ford 7C 22
Lucien Rd. SW17 5E 28
SW19 3N 27
Lucilina Dr. TN8: Eden 3L 147
Luckley Path RG40: W'ham 2B 30
Luckley Rd. RG41: W'ham 5A 30
Luckley Wood
RG41: W'ham 5A 30
Luddington Av.
GU25: V Wat 1B 36
Ludford Cl.
CR0: Wad 6A 200 (9M 45)
Ludgrove RG40: W'ham 5C 30
Ludlow RG12: Brac 6N 31
Ludlow Cl. GU16: Frim 7E 70
Ludlow Rd.
GU2: Guil 5A 202 (4L 113)
TW13: Felt 5H 23
Ludovick Wlk. SW15 7D 12
Ludshott Gro.
GU35: H Dwn 4G 169
Ludshott Mnr.
GU30: Brams 8H 169
Luff Cl. SL4: W'sor 6B 4
Luffs Mdw. GU28: North 9D 190
Luke Rd. GU11: Alde 4K 109
Luke Rd. E. GU11: Alde 4K 109
Lullarook Cl. TN16: B Hil 3E 86
LULLENDEN 5H 167
Lulworth Av. TW5: Hest 4B 10
Lulworth Cl. GU14: Farnb 7M 69
RH11: Craw 6M 181
Lulworth Cres. CR4: Mit 1C 44
Lumiere Ct. SW17 3E 28
Lumley Ct. RH6: Horl 7E 142
Lumley Gdns. SM3: Chea 2K 61
Lumley Rd. RH6: Horl 7E 142
SM3: Chea 2K 61
Lunar Cl. TN16: B Hil 3F 86
Luna Rd. CR7: T Hea 2N 45
Lundy Cl. RH11: Craw 6A 182
Lundy Dr. UB3: Harl 1F 8
Lunghurst Rd. CR3: Wold 7J 85
Lupin Cl. CR0: Croy 7G 46
GU19: Bag 6G 51
SW2 3M 29
UB7: W Dray 1M 7
Lupin Ride RG45: Crow 8G 30
Lurgan Av. W6 2J 13
Lushington Dr. KT11: Cob 1J 77
Lushington Ho.
KT12: Wal T 5K 39
Lusted Hall La.
TN16: B Hil, Tats 7E 86
Lusteds Cl. RH4: Dork 8J 119
Lutea Ho. SM2: Sut 4A 62
(off Walnut M.)
Luther M. TW11: Tedd 6F 24
Luther Rd. TW11: Tedd 6F 24
Lutterworth Cl. RG42: Brac 8A 16
Luttrell Av. SW15 8G 13
Lutyens Cl. RH11: Craw 5K 181
Luxford Cl. RH12: Hors 3M 197
Luxford's La.
RH19: E Grin 4D 186
LUXTED 1J 87
Luxted Rd. BR6: Dow 8J 67
Lyall Pl. GU9: U Hal 5G 108
Lychett Minster Cl.
RG12: Brac 4D 32
Lych Ga. Cl. GU47: Sandh 7E 48
Lych Way GU21: Wok 3N 73
Lyconby Gdns. CR0: Croy 6H 47
Lydbury RG12: Brac 2D 32
Lydden Gro. SW18 1N 27
Lydden Rd. SW18 1N 27
Lydele Cl. GU21: Wok 2B 74
Lydens La.
TN8: Eden, Hev 6N 147
Lydford Cl. GU14: Farnb 7M 69
GU16: Frim 7E 70
Lydger Rd. GU22: Wok 7D 74
Lydhurst Av. SW2 3K 29
Lydia Ct. KT1: K Tham 6J 203
(off Grove Cres.)
Lydney RG12: Brac 6N 31
Lydney Cl. SW19 3K 27
Lydon Ho. RH11: Craw 9B 162
Lye, The KT20: Tad 9H 81
Lye Copse Av.
GU14: Farnb 6N 69
Lyefield La. RH5: For G 4K 157
Lyell Rd. SL4: W'sor 6A 4
Lyfield KT22: Oxs 1B 78
Lyford Rd. SW18 1B 28
Lygon Ho. SW6 4K 13
(off Fulham Pal. Rd.)
Lyham Cl. SW2 1J 29
Lyham Rd. SW2 1J 29
Lyle Cl. CR4: Mit 6E 44
Lyle Ct. SM4: Mord 5B 44
Lymbourne Cl. SM2: Sut 6M 61
Lymden Gdns. RH2: Reig 4N 121
Lyme Regis Rd. SM7: Ban 4L 81
Lymescote Gdns. SM1: Sut 8M 43
Lyminge Gdns. SW18 2C 28
Lymington Av. GU46: Yate 1A 68
Lymington Cl. SW16 1H 45
Lymington Ct. SM1: Sut 9N 43
Lymington Gdns. KT19: Ewe 2E 60
Lynchborough Rd.
GU30: Pass 9C 168
Lynchen Cl. TW5: C'ford 4J 9
Lynchford La. GU14: Farnb 5C 90
Lynchford Rd. GU12: A Va 5D 90
GU14: Farnb 6N 89
(not continuous)
Lynchmere Pl. GU2: Guil 9K 93
Lynch Rd. GU9: Farnh 1J 129
Lyncroft Gdns. KT17: Ewe 5E 60
TW3: Houn 8C 10
Lyndale KT7: T Dit 6E 40
Lyndale Ct. KT14: W By 9J 55
RH1: Red 9E 102
Lyndale Dr. GU51: Fleet 4E 88
Lyndale Rd. RH1: Red 9D 102
Lynde Ho. KT12: Wal T 5K 39
Lynden Hyrst CR0: Croy 8C 46
Lyndford Ter. GU52: Fleet 6A 88
Lyndhurst Av. GU11: Alde 6A 110
GU17: B'water 9H 49
KT5: Surb 7A 42
SW16 1H 45
TW2: Whitt 2N 23
TW16: Sunb 2H 39
Lyndhurst Cl. BR6: Farnb 1K 67
CR0: Croy 9C 46
GU21: Wok 2N 73
RG12: Brac 2E 32
RH11: Craw 4B 182
Lyndhurst Ct. SM2: Sut 4M 61
(off Grange Rd.)
Lyndhurst Dr. KT3: N Mal 6D 42
Lyndhurst Farm Cl.
RH19: Fel 6G 165

Lyndhurst Rd.—Manor Ho.

Lyndhurst Rd. CR5: Coul 3E 82
CR7: T Hea 3L 45
RH2: Reig 6M 121
SL5: Asc 3L 33
Lyndhurst Vs. RH1: Red 9D 102
Lyndhurst Way KT16: Chert ...9G 36
SM2: Sut 5M 61
Lyndon Av. SM6: W'ton 9E 44
Lyndons, The GU30: Pass 9C 168
Lyndon Yd. SW17 ....5A 28
Lyndsey Cl. GU14: Cove 1G 88
Lyndum Pl. GU35: Lind 4A 168
Lyndwood Dr. SL4: O Win 9K 5
Lyndwood Pde. *SL4: O Win* *9K 5*
(off St Luke's Rd.)
LYNE 7C 36
Lyne Cl. GU25: V Wat 5B 36
Lyne Crossing Rd.
KT16: Lyne 5C 36
Lynegrove Av. TW15: A'ford ...6D 22
Lyneham Rd. RG45: Crow 2G 48
Lyne La. GU25: V Wat 5C 36
KT16: Lyne 5C 36
Lyne Rd. GU25: V Wat 5N 35
Lynford Ct. CR0: Croy 7F 200
Lynhurst KT13: Weybr 3C 56
Lynmead Cl. TN8: Eden 8K 127
Lynmouth Av. SM4: Mord 5J 43
Lynmouth Gdns. TW5: Hest 3L 9
Lynn Cl. TW15: A'ford 6E 22
Lynn Ct. CR3: Whyte 5C 84
Lynne Cl. BR6: Chels 3N 67
CR2: Sels 7F 64
Lynne Ct. CR2: S Croy 7F 200
Lynne Wlk. KT10: Esh 2C 58
Lynn Rd. SW12 ....1F 28
Lynn Wlk. RH2: Reig 6N 121
Lynn Way GU14: Cove 7L 69
Lynscott Way CR2: S Croy 5M 63
Lynstead Ct. BR3: Beck 1H 47
Lynton Cl. GU9: Farnh 4F 128
KT9: Ches 1L 59
RH19: E Grin 8B 166
TW7: Isle 7F 10
Lynton Ct. KT17: Ewe 7E 60
Lynton Pk. Av.
RH19: E Grin 8B 166
Lynton Rd. CR0: Croy 5L 45
KT3: N Mal 4C 42
LYNWICK 9B 176
Lynwick St. RH12: Rudg 1C 194
Lynwood GU2: Guil 4L 113
Lynwood Av. CR5: Coul 2F 82
KT17: Eps 1E 80
TW20: Egh 7A 20
Lynwood Chase RG12: Brac ...8A 16
Lynwood Cl. GU21: Wok 9F 54
GU35: Lind 4B 168
Lynwood Ct. KT1: K Tham 1A 42
KT17: Eps 9E 60
RH12: Hors 5J 197
Lynwood Cres. SL5: S'dale 5B 34
Lynwood Dr. GU16: Mytc 2E 90
KT4: W Pk 8F 42
Lynwood Gdns. CR0: Wad 1K 63
Lynwood Rd. KT7: T Dit 8F 40
KT17: Eps 1E 80
RH1: Red 1E 122
SW17 ....4D 28
Lynx Hill KT24: E Hor 6G 96
Lyon Cl. RH10: Craw 7G 183
Lyon Ct. RH13: Hors 6L 197
Lyon Oaks RG42: Warf 7N 15
Lyon Rd. KT12: Wal T 8M 39
RG45: Crow 1H 49
SW19 ....9A 28
Lyons Cl. RH13: Slin 5L 195
Lyons Ct.
RH4: Dork 2K 201 (5H 119)
Lyonsdene KT20: Lwr K 5L 101
Lyons Dr. GU2: Guil 7K 93
Lyons Farm Est.
RH13: Slin 6A 196
Lyons Rd. RH13: Slin 5L 195
Lyon Way GU16: Frim 5A 70
Lyon Way Ind. Est.
GU16: Frim 5A 70
Lyric Cl. RH10: Craw 5H 183
Lyric Rd. SW13 ....4E 12
Lyric Sq. *W6* *1H 13*
(off King St.)
Lyric Theatre
Hammersmith 1H 13
Lysander Dr. RG12: Brac 3A 32
Lysander Gdns. KT6: Surb 5M 41
Lysander Rd. CR0: Wad 3K 63
Lysia Ct. *SW6* *3J 13*
(off Lysia St.)
Lysias Rd. SW12 ....1F 28
Lysia St. SW6 ....3J 13
Lysons Av. GU12: A Va 5D 90
Lyson's Rd. GU11: Alde 3M 109
Lysons Wlk. SW15 ....7F 12
Lyster M. KT11: Cob 9K 57
Lytchgate Cl. CR2: S Croy 4B 64
Lytcott Dr. KT8: W Mole 2N 39
Lytham RG12: Brac 5K 31
Lytham Ct. SL5: S'hill 4N 33
LYTHE HILL 2L 189
Lythe Hill Pk. GU27: Hasl 3J 189
Lytton Dr. RH10: Craw 2H 183
Lytton Gdns. SM6: Bedd 1H 63
Lytton Gro. SW15 ....8J 13
Lytton Pk. KT11: Cob 8N 57
Lytton Rd. GU22: Wok 3D 74
Lyveden Rd. SW17 ....7D 28
Lywood Cl. KT20: Tad 9H 81

M

Mabbotts KT20: Tad 8J 81
Mabel St. GU21: Wok 5N 73
Maberley Rd. BR3: Beck 2G 46
Mablethorpe Rd. SW6 ....3K 13
Macadam Av. RG45: Crow 9H 31
McAlmont Ridge
GU7: Goda 4G 132
Macaulay Av. KT10: H Wood ...8F 40
Macaulay Rd. CR3: Cate 9B 84
Macbeth Ct. RG42: Warf 9C 16
Macbeth St. W6 ....1G 13
McCarthy Rd. TW13: Hanw 6L 23
McClaren Technology Cen.
GU21: Wok 7C 54
Macclesfield Rd.
SE25 ....4F 46
Macdonald Rd.
GU9: U Hal 5G 109
GU18: Ligh 8K 51
McDonalds Almshouses
GU9: Farnh 2F 128
McDonough Cl. KT9: Ches 1L 59
McDougall Ct. TW9: Rich 5N 11
Macdowall Rd. GU2: Guil 7L 93
Mace La. TN14: Cud 9M 67
Macfarlane La. TW7: Isle 2F 10
Machahon Cl. GU24: Chob 6H 53
McIndoe Rd. RH19: E Grin ...7N 165
McIntosh Cl. SM6: W'ton 4J 63
McIver Cl. RH19: Fel 6J 165
McKay Cl. GU11: Alde 1A 110
McKay Rd. SW20 ....8G 27
McKay Trad. Est. SL3: Poy 5G 7
Mackenzie Rd. BR3: Beck 1F 46
McKenzie Way KT19: Eps 5N 59
McKernan Ct. GU47: Sandh ...7E 48
Mackie Rd. SW2 ....1L 29
Mackies Hill GU5: P'lake 4E 136
Mackrells RH1: Red 6A 122
Maclaren Dr. RG42: Warf 9D 16
Maclaren M. SW15 ....7H 13
Macleod Rd. RH13: Hors 7L 197
(not continuous)
Macmillan Ho. *SM7: Ban* *1L 81*
(off Basing Rd.)
Macmillan Way SW17 ....5F 28
Macnaghten Woods
GU15: Camb 9C 50
McNaughton Cl.
GU14: Cove 2H 89
Macphail Cl.
RG40: W'ham 9D 14
McRae La. CR4: Mit 6D 44
Macrae Rd. GU46: Yate 9B 48
Madan Cl. TN16: Weste 3N 107
Madan Rd. TN16: Weste 3M 107
Madans Wlk.
KT18: Eps 8K 201 (2C 80)
(not continuous)
Maddison Cl. TW11: Tedd 7F 24
Maddox Dr. RH10: Wor 4H 183
Maddox La. KT23: Book 9M 77
Maddox Pk. KT23: Book 1M 97
Madehurst Ct.
RH11: Craw 6L 181
Madeira Av. RH12: Hors 6J 197
Madeira Cl. KT14: W By 9J 55
Madeira Cres. KT14: W By 9H 55
Madeira Rd. CR4: Mit 3D 44
KT14: W By 9H 55
SW16 ....6J 29
Madeira Wlk. RH2: Reig 2B 122
SL4: W'sor 4G 5
Madeley Rd. GU52: C Cro 7C 88
Madgehole La.
GU5: Sha G 7J 135
Madingley RG12: Brac 7N 31
Madison Cl. SM2: Sut 4B 62
Madox Brown End
GU47: C Tow 8K 49
Madrid Rd. GU2: Guil 4L 113
SW13 ....4F 12
Maesmaur Rd. TN16: Tats 8F 86
Mafeking Av. TW8: Brent 2L 11
Mafeking Rd. TW19: Wray 3D 20
Magazine Pl. KT22: Leat 9H 79
Magazine Rd. CR3: Cate 9M 83
Magdala Rd. CR2: S Croy 4A 64
TW7: Isle 6G 11
Magdalen Cl. KT14: Byf 1N 75
Magdalen Cres. KT14: Byf 1N 75
Magdalene Cl.
RH10: Craw 9G 162
Magdalene Rd.
GU47: Owls 5L 49
TW17: Shep 3A 38
Magdalen Rd. SW18 ....2A 28
Magellan Ter. RH10: Craw 8E 162
Magna Carta La.
TW19: Wray 2N 19
Magna Carta Monument 3N 19
Magna Rd. TW20: Eng G 7L 19
Magnolia Cl. GU47: Owls 6J 49
KT2: K Tham 7A 26
RG42: Warf 9E 16
Magnolia Ct. RH6: Horl 8E 142
SM2: Sut *4M 61*
(off Grange Rd.)
SM6: W'ton 2F 62
TW9: Kew 4A 12
TW13: Felt *2H 23*
(off Plum Cl.)
Magnolia Dr. TN16: B Hil 3F 86
Magnolia Pl. GU1: Guil 9M 93
Magnolia Rd. W4 ....2A 12
Magnolia St. UB7: W Dray 1M 7
Magnolia Way GU52: Fleet 6B 88
KT19: Ewe 2B 60
RH5: Nth H 8K 119
Magpie Cl. CR5: Coul 5G 83
GU10: Ews 4C 108
Magpie Grn. *TN8: Eden* *9M 127*
(off Woodland Dr.)
Magpie Wlk. RH10: Craw 1D 182
Maguire Dr. GU16: Frim 3G 71
TW10: Ham 5J 25
Mahonia Cl. GU24: W End 9C 52
Maida Rd. GU11: Alde 9N 89
MAIDENBOWER 5G 183
Maidenbower Bus. Pk.
RH10: Wor 5J 183
Maidenbower Community
Sports Cen. 5F 182
Maidenbower Dr.
RH10: Craw 5G 182
Maidenbower La.
RH10: Craw 4G 182
(Billinton Dr.)
RH10: Craw 5F 182
(St Leonard's Dr.)
Maidenbower Pl.
RH10: Craw 5G 183
Maidenbower Sq.
RH10: Craw 5G 183
Maidenhead Rd.
RG40: W'ham 6D 14
RG42: Warf 3N 15
SL4: W'sor 3A 4
Maiden La. RH11: Craw 1A 182
MAIDEN'S GREEN 3F 16
Maiden's Grn. SL4: Wink 3F 16
Maidenshaw Rd.
KT19: Eps 5J 201 (8C 60)
Maids of Honour Row
TW9: Rich 8K 11
Main Dr. RG42: Warf 8D 16
Mainprize Rd. RG12: Brac 9C 16
Main Rd. BR2: Kes 9E 66
GU10: B Oak 2A 148
SL4: W'sor 3A 4
TN8: C Hil, Eden 6K 127
TN16: B Hil, Weste 9E 66
Mainstone Cl. GU16: Deep 7G 71
Mainstone Cres.
GU24: B'wood 8A 72
Mainstone Rd. GU24: Bis 3C 72
Main St. KT15: Addl 9N 37
TW13: Hanw 6L 23
Mainwaring Ct. CR4: Mit 1E 44
Maisie Webster Cl.
TW19: Stan 1M 21
Maisonettes, The
SM1: Sut 2L 61
Maitland Cl. KT12: Wal T 8M 39
KT14: W By 9J 55
TW4: Houn 7N 9
Maitland Rd. GU14: Farnb 5N 89
Maitlands Cl. GU10: Tong 6C 110
Maize Cft. RH6: Horl 7G 142
Maize La. RG42: Warf 7B 16
Majestic Way CR4: Mit 1D 44
Majors Farm Rd. SL3: Dat 3N 5
Major's Hill RH10: Wor 4N 183
Makepiece Rd.
RG42: Brac 8N 15
Malacca Farm GU4: W Cla 5K 95
Malan Cl. TN16: B Hil 4G 87
Malbrook Rd. SW15 ....7G 13
Malcolm Dr. KT6: Surb 7L 41
Malcolm Gdns. RH6: Hook ...1B 162
Malcolm Rd. CR5: Coul 2H 83
SE25 ....5D 46
SW19 ....7K 27
Malden Av. SE25 ....3E 46
Malden Cen., The 3E 42
Malden Ct. SW20: N Mal 2G 42
MALDEN GREEN 7F 42
Malden Grn. Av.
KT4: W Pk 7E 42
Malden Grn. M. KT4: W Pk 7F 42
Malden Hill KT3: N Mal 2E 42
Malden Hill Gdns.
KT3: N Mal 2E 42
MALDEN JUNC. 4E 42
Malden Manor Station (Rail)
..........................6D 42
Malden Pk. KT3: N Mal 5E 42
Malden Rd. KT3: N Mal 4D 42
KT4: W Pk 6E 42
SM3: Chea 1J 61
MALDEN RUSHETT 7J 59
Malden Way KT3: N Mal 5C 42
Maldon Ct. SM6: W'ton 2G 62
Maldon Rd. SM6: W'ton 2F 62
Malet Cl. TW20: Egh 7F 20
Maley Av. SE27 ....3M 29
Malham Cl. RH10: Craw 6G 183
Malham Fell RG12: Brac 3M 31
Mall, The
CR0: Croy 2B 200 (8N 45)
KT6: Surb 4K 41
KT12: Hers *2L 57*
(off Hersham Grn. Shop. Cen.)
SW14 ....8B 12
TW8: Brent 2K 11
Mallard Cl. GU12: Ash 1D 110
GU27: Hasl 2C 188
RH1: Red 9E 102
RH6: Horl 6E 142
RH12: Hors 3J 197
TW2: Whitt 1A 24
Mallard Ct. *GU11: Alde* *5M 109*
(off Boxhalls La.)
RH4: Dork 1J 201
Mallard Pl. GU14: Cove 5M 69
RH19: E Grin 1B 186
TW1: Twick 4G 24
Mallard Rd. CR2: Sels 6G 65
Mallards, The GU16: Frim 4D 70
TW18: Lale 1K 37
Mallards Reach
KT13: Weybr 8E 38
Mallards Way GU18: Ligh 7L 51
Mallard Wlk. BR3: Beck 4G 47
Mallard Way GU46: Yate 9A 48
SM6: W'ton 5G 63
TN8: Eden 9L 127
Malling Cl. CR0: Croy 5F 46
Malling Gdns. SM4: Mord 5A 44
Mallinson Rd. CR0: Bedd 9H 45
Mallow Cl. CR0: Croy 7G 46
GU35: Lind 4B 168
KT20: Tad 7G 81
RH12: Hors 2L 197
Mallow Cres. GU4: B'ham 9D 94
Mallowdale Rd. RG12: Brac ...6C 32
Mall Rd. W6 ....1G 13
Mall Vs. *W6* *1G 13*
(off Mall Rd.)
Malmains Cl. BR3: Beck 3N 47
Malmains Way BR3: Beck 3M 47
Malmesbury Rd.
SM4: Mord 6A 44
Malmstone Av. RH1: Mers ...6G 103
Malory Cl. BR3: Beck 1H 47
Malta Rd. GU16: Deep 6J 71
Maltby Rd. KT9: Ches 3N 59
Malt Hill RG42: Warf 5C 16
TW20: Egh 6A 20
Malt Ho., The GU10: Til 8A 130
Malt Ho. Cl. SL4: O Win 1L 19
Malthouse Ct. GU24: W End ...8C 52
Malthouse Dr. TW13: Hanw ...6L 23
W4 ....2E 12
Malthouse La. GU3: Worp 2F 92
GU8: Hamb 9F 152
GU24: Pirb 1E 92
GU24: W End 9C 52
Malthouse Mead GU8: Wit ...5C 152
Malthouse Pas. *SW13* *5E 12*
(off Maltings Cl.)
Malthouse Rd.
RH10: Craw 5B 182
Malthouses, The
GU6: Cranl 7N 155
Maltings W4 ....1N 11
Maltings, The KT14: Byf 9A 56
RH8: Oxt 9B 106
TW18: Stain 5G 20
Maltings Cl. SW13 ....5E 12
Maltings Lodge *W4* *2D 12*
(off Corney Reach Way)
Maltings Pl. SW6 ....4N 13
Malting Way TW7: Isle 6F 10
Malus Cl. KT15: Addl 4H 55
Malus Dr. KT15: Addl 4H 55
Malva Cl. SW18 ....8N 13
Malvern Cl. CR4: Mit 2G 44
KT6: Surb 7L 41
KT16: Otter 3E 54
SE20 ....1D 46
Malvern Ct.
KT18: Eps 8K 201 (1C 80)
SL3: Lang 2C 6
SM2: Sut 4M 61
Malvern Dr. TW13: Hanw 6L 23
Malvern Rd. CR7: T Hea 3L 45
GU14: Cove 7J 69
GU17: Min 5E 68
KT6: Surb 8L 41
RH11: Craw 4A 182
TW12: Hamp 8A 24
UB3: Harl 3F 8
Malwood Rd. SW12 ....1F 28
Malyons, The TW17: Shep 5E 38
Manatee Pl. SM6: Bedd 9H 45
Manawey Bus. Units
GU12: Alde 3C 110
Manbre Rd. W6 ....2H 13
Manchester Rd. CR7: T Hea ...2N 45
Mandalay *GU9: U Hal* *5F 108*
(off Lawday Pl. La.)
Mandel Ho. SW18 ....7M 13
Mandeville Cl. GU2: Guil 9K 93
SW20 ....8K 27
Mandeville Ct. TW20: Egh 5C 20
Mandeville Dr. KT6: Surb 7K 41
Mandeville Rd. TW7: Isle 5G 10
TW17: Shep 4B 38
Mandora Rd. GU11: Alde 9N 89
Mandrake Rd. SW17 ....4D 28
Manfield Pk. GU6: Cranl 5K 155
Manfield Rd. GU12: Ash 2E 110
Manfred Rd. SW15 ....8L 13
Mangles Ct.
GU1: Guil 4B 202 (4M 113)
Mangles Rd. GU1: Guil 1N 113
Manitoba Gdns. BR6: Chels ...3N 67
Manley Bri. Rd.
GU10: Rowl, Wrec 6D 128
Mannamead KT18: Eps D 6D 80
Mannamead Cl.
KT18: Eps D 6D 80
Mann Cl.
CR0: Croy 4B 200 (9N 45)
RH11: Craw 9N 181
Manning Cl. RH19: E Grin ...7N 165
Manning Gdns. CR0: Croy 6E 46
Manning Pl. TW10: Rich 9M 11
Mannings Cl. RH10: Craw ...9H 163
MANNINGS HEATH 9B 198
Mannings Hill GU6: Cranl ...4M 155
Manningtree Cl. SW19 ....2K 27
Mann's Cl. TW7: Isle 8F 10
Manny Shinwell Ho.
SW6 ....*2L 13*
(off Clem Attlee Ct.)
Manoel Rd. TW2: Twick 4C 24
Manor, The GU8: Mil 1C 152
Manor Av. CR3: Cate 2B 104
TW4: Houn 6L 9
Manor Chase KT13: Weybr 2C 56
MANOR CIRCUS 6N 11
Manor Cl. CR6: Warl 4H 85
GU10: Tong 5D 110
GU22: Pyr 4H 75
GU27: Hasl 2C 188
KT4: W Pk 7D 42
KT24: E Hor 6F 96
RG42: Brac 8M 15
RH6: Horl 8D 142
RH9: S Gods 7J 125
Manor Ct. BR4: W Wick 7L 47
GU52: C Cro 9B 88
KT2: K Tham 9N 25
KT8: W Mole 3A 40
KT13: Weybr 1C 56
RH10: Craw 9D 162
RH12: Hors 3N 197
SM5: Cars 9E 44
SW6 ....4N 13
SW16 ....4J 29
TW2: Twick 3C 24
TW18: Stain 6F 20
Manor Cres. GU2: Guil 1L 113
GU24: B'wood 7A 72
GU27: Hasl 2C 188
KT5: Surb 5N 41
KT14: Byf 9A 56
KT19: Eps 8N 59
Manorcrofts Rd. TW20: Egh ...7C 20
Manordene Cl. KT7: T Dit 7G 40
Manor Dr. KT5: Surb 5M 41
KT10: H Wood 8F 40
KT15: N Haw 6J 55
KT19: Ewe 3D 60
RH6: Horl 8D 142
TW13: Hanw 6L 23
TW16: Sunb 1H 39
Manor Dr., The KT4: W Pk 7D 42
Manor Dr. Nth. KT3: N Mal 6C 42
KT4: W Pk 7D 42
Manor Farm GU3: Wan 6N 111
Mnr. Farm Av. TW17: Shep 5C 38
Mnr. Farm Bus. Cen.
GU10: Tong 7D 110
Mnr. Farm Cl. GU3: Norm ...1M 111
GU12: Ash 3D 110
KT4: W Pk 7D 42
SL4: W'sor 6C 4
Mnr. Farm Cotts.
GU3: Wan 6N 111
SL4: O Win 8K 5
Mnr. Farm Ct. TW20: Egh 6C 20
Manor Farm Craft Cen. 8F 110
MANOR FARM ESTATE 1M 19
Mnr. Farm Ho. SL4: W'sor 6C 4
Mnr. Farm La. TW20: Egh 6C 20
Mnr. Farm Rd. SW16 ....1L 45
Manor Flds. GU8: Mil 9B 132
GU10: Seal 7F 110
RH13: Hors 4N 197
SW15 ....9J 13
Manorfields RH11: Craw 7J 181
Manor Gdns. CR2: S Croy 3C 64
GU2: Guil 1L 113
GU7: Goda 4H 133
GU10: L Bou 6J 129
KT24: Eff 6L 97
SW20 ....1L 43
TW9: Rich 7M 11
TW12: Hamp 8B 24
TW16: Sunb 9H 23
W4 ....1D 12
Manor Ga. RH10: Craw 9D 162
Manorgate Rd.
KT2: K Tham 9N 25
Manor Grn. GU8: Mil 1B 152
Manor Grn. Rd. KT19: Eps 9A 60
Manor Gro. BR3: Beck 1L 47
TW9: Rich 7N 11
Manor Hill SM7: Ban 2D 82
Manor Ho. *SL4: Eton* *2G 4*
(off Common La.)

Manor Ho., The
GU15: Camb 9B 50
KT20: K'wood 1A 102
Manor Ho. Ct.
KT18: Eps 7H 201 (9B 60)
TW17: Shep 6C 38
Manor Ho. Dr. KT12: Hers 2G 57
SL5: Asc 8L 17
Manor Ho. Flats
GU10: Tong 6C 110
Manor Ho. Gdns.
TN8: Eden 2L 147
Manor Ho. La. KT23: Book . . .4M 97
SL3: Dat 3L 5
Manor Ho. Way TW7: Isle 6H 11
Manor La. GU5: Sha G 8G 134
KT20: Lwr K 7M 101
RH13: Hors 8A 198
SM1: Sut 2A 62
TW13: Felt 3H 23
TW16: Sunb 1H 39
UB3: Harl 2E 8
Manor Lea GU27: Hasl 2C 188
Manor Lea Cl. GU8: Mil 9B 132
Manor Lea Rd. GU8: Mil 9B 132
Manor Leaze TW20: Egh 6D 20
Manor Lodge GU2: Guil 1L 113
Manor Pk. TW9: Rich 7M 11
TW13: Felt 3H 23
TW18: Stain 4F 20
Manor Pk. Cl. BR4: W Wick . . .7L 47
Manor Pk. Dr. GU46: Yate 1C 68
Manor Pk. Ind. Est.
GU12: Alde 3A 110
Manor Pk. Rd.
BR4: W Wick 7L 47
SM1: Sut 2A 62
Manor Pk. Village
GU2: Guil 4H 113
Manor Pl. CR4: Mit 2G 45
KT12: Wal T 6G 39
(not continuous)
KT23: Book 4A 98
SM1: Sut 1N 61
TW14: Felt 2H 23
TW18: Stain 6K 21
Manor Rd. BR3: Beck 1L 47
BR4: W Wick 8L 47
CR4: Mit 3G 44
GU2: Guil 1L 113
GU9: Farnh 8K 109
GU10: Tong 4D 110
GU11: Alde 4L 109
GU12: Ash 4D 110
GU14: Farnb 1B 90
GU21: Wok 3M 73
GU23: Rip 1H 95
KT8: E Mol 3D 40
KT12: Wal T 6G 39
RH1: Mers 7G 102
RH2: Reig 1L 121
RH12: Hors 3N 197
RH19: E Grin 8M 165
SE25 . . . . .3D 46
SL4: W'sor 5B 4
SM2: Chea 4L 61
SM6: W'ton 1F 62
SW20 . . . . .1L 43
TN8: Eden 2K 147
TN16: Tats 7G 86
TW2: Twick 3C 24
TW9: Rich 7N 11
TW11: Tedd 6G 25
(not continuous)
TW15: A'ford 6A 22
Manor Rd. Nth. KT7: T Dit 9F 40
KT10: H Wood, T Dit 9F 40
SM6: W'ton 1F 62
Manor Rd. Sth.
KT10: H Wood 1E 58
Manor Royal RH10: Craw 9C 162
Mnr. Royal Ind. Est.
RH10: Craw 9C 162
Manor Ter. GU7: Goda 5J 133
Manor Va. TW8: Brent 1J 11
Manor Wlk. GU12: Alde 3N 109
(not continuous)
KT13: Weybr 2C 56
RH6: Horl 8D 142
(off Manor Dr.)
Manor Way BR3: Beck 1K 47
CR2: S Croy 3B 64
CR4: Mit 2G 44
CR8: Pur 8J 63
GU2: Guil 6H 113
GU19: Bag 5J 51
GU22: Wok 8D 74
KT4: W Pk 7D 42
KT22: Oxs 2C 78
SM7: Ban 3D 82
TW20: Egh 7B 20
Manor Way, The
SM6: W'ton 1F 62
Mnr. Wood Rd. CR8: Pur 9J 63
Mansard Beeches
SW17 . . . . .6E 28
Manse Cl. UB3: Harl 2E 8
Mansel Cl. GU2: Guil 7L 93
Mansell Cl. SL4: W'sor 4B 4
Mansell Way CR3: Cate 9A 84
Mansel Rd. SW19 . . . . .7K 27
Mansfield Cl. SL5: Asc 9H 17
Mansfield Cres. RG12: Brac . . .5N 31
Mansfield Dr. RH1: Mers 6H 103
Mansfield Pl. CR2: S Croy 3A 64
SL5: Asc 1H 33
Mansfield Rd. CR2: S Croy 3A 64
KT9: Ches 2J 59
Manship Rd. CR4: Mit 8E 28
Mansions, The SW5 . . . . .1N 13
Manston Av. UB2: S'hall 1A 10
Manston Cl. SE20 . . . . .1F 46
Manston Dr. RG12: Brac 5A 32
Manston Gro. KT2: K Tham 6K 25
Manston Rd. GU4: B'ham 8C 94
Mantilla Rd. SW17 . . . . .5E 28
Mantle Ct. *SW18 . . . . .9N 13*
(off Mapleton Rd.)
Mantlet Cl. SW16 . . . . .8G 29
Manville Ct. GU4: Chil 2A 134
Manville Gdns. SW17 . . . . .4F 28
Manville Rd. SW17 . . . . .3E 28
Manygate La. TW17: Shep 6D 38
Manygate Mobile Home Est.
TW17: Shep 5E 38
(off Mitre Cl.)
Manygates SW12 . . . . .3F 28
Maori Rd. GU1: Guil 3B 114
Maple Cl. CR3: Whyte 4C 84
CR4: Mit 9F 28
GU12: A Va 6D 90
GU17: B'water 1H 69
GU47: Sandh 6E 48
RH11: Craw 9A 162
RH12: Hors 3N 197
TW12: Hamp 7N 23
Maple Ct.
CR0: Croy 6C 200 (1N 63)
(Lwr. Coombe St.)
CR0: Croy 6B 200
(The Waldrons)
GU21: Wok 3M 73
KT3: N Mal 2C 42
KT22: Leat 7F 78
RG12: Brac 3D 32
SL4: W'sor 6F 4
TW15: A'ford 8E 22
TW20: Eng G 7L 19
Mapledale Av. CR0: Croy 8D 46
Mapledrakes Cl. GU6: Ewh . . .5F 156
Mapledrakes Rd.
GU6: Ewh 5F 156
Maple Dr. GU18: Ligh 7K 51
KT23: Book 3B 98
RG45: Crow 9H 31
RH1: Red 9D 122
RH19: E Grin 9C 166
Maple Gdns. GU46: Yate 1C 68
KT17: Eps 6L 201
TW19: Stan 3N 21
Maple Grn. RH11: Craw 4A 182
Maple Gro. GU1: Guil 1N 113
GU22: Wok 8A 74
KT23: Book 5A 98
TW8: Brent 3H 11
Maple Gro. Bus. Cen.
TW4: Houn 7K 9
Maplehatch Cl. GU7: Goda 9H 133
Maple Ho. KT1: K Tham 8J 203
RH1: Red 3D 122
(off Chapel Rd.)
TW9: Kew 4A 12
Maplehurst BR2: Brom 1N 47
KT22: Fetc 1D 98
Maplehurst Cl.
KT1: K Tham 8J 203 (3L 41)
Maple Ind. Est. TW13: Felt 4H 23
Maple Leaf Cl. GU14: Cove 2L 89
TN16: B Hil 3F 86
Mapleleaf Cl. CR2: Sels 7G 64
Maple Lodge GU27: Hasl 4J 189
Maple M. SW16 . . . . .6K 29
Maple Pl. SM7: Ban 1J 81
Maple Rd. CR3: Whyte 4C 84
GU23: Rip 2J 95
KT6: Surb 8J 203 (5K 41)
KT21: A'tead 6K 79
RH1: Red 7D 122
SE20 . . . . .1E 46
Maplers Dr. GU51: Fleet 2A 88
Maples, The KT1: Tedd 8J 25
KT10: Clay 4G 59
KT16: Otter 3D 54
SM7: Ban 1N 81
Maple Silver Birch
GU14: Cove 9J 69
Maplestead Rd. SW2 . . . . .1K 29
Maplethorpe Rd.
CR7: T Hea 3L 45
Mapleton Cres. SW18 . . . . .9N 13
Mapleton Rd. SW18 . . . . .9M 13
(not continuous)
TN16: Weste 8N 107
Maple Wlk. GU12: Alde 4B 110
SM2: Sut 6N 61
Maple Way CR5: Coul 8F 82
GU35: H Dwn 3G 169
TW13: Felt 4H 23
Marbeck Cl. SL4: W'sor 4A 4
Marble Hill Cl. TW1: Twick 1H 25
Marble Hill Gdns.
TW1: Twick 1H 25
Marble Hill House 1J 25
Marbles Way KT20: Tad 6J 81
Marbull Way RG42: Warf 7N 15
Marcellina Way BR6: Orp 1N 67
Marchant's Hill (Activity Cen.)
. . . . .2B 170
Marchbank Rd. W14 . . . . .2L 13
March Ct. SW15 . . . . .7G 12
Marcheria Cl.
RG12: Brac 5N 31
Marches, The
RH12: K'fold 4H 179
Marches Rd.
RH12: Warn, K'fold 5D 178
Marchmont Gdns.
TW10: Rich 8M 11
Marchmont Pl. RG12: Brac 2A 32
Marchmont Rd.
SM6: W'ton 4G 62
TW10: Rich 8M 11
March Rd. KT13: Weybr 2B 56
TW1: Twick 1G 24
Marchside Cl. TW5: Hest 4L 9
Marcus Ct. GU22: Wok 5B 74
Marcuse Rd. CR3: Cate 1A 104
Marcus St. SW18 . . . . .9N 13
Marcus Ter. SW18 . . . . .9N 13
Mardale GU15: Camb 2G 71
Mardell Rd. CR0: Croy 4G 46
Marden Cres. CR0: Croy 5K 45
MARDEN PARK 1H 105
Marden Rd. CR0: Croy 5K 45
Mardens, The RH11: Craw . . .2N 181
Mare La. GU8: Hasc 6L 153
RG42: Bin 1K 15
(not continuous)
Mareschal Rd.
GU2: Guil 7A 202 (5M 113)
Maresfield CR0: Croy 9B 46
Maresfield Ho. *GU1: Guil 2F 114*
(off Merrow St.)
Mareshall Av. RG42: Warf 7N 15
Mare St. GU8: Hasc 6N 153
Mareth Cl. GU11: Alde 2N 109
Marfleet Cl. SM5: Cars 8C 44
Margaret Cl. TW18: Stain 7M 21
Margaret Herbison Ho.
SW6 . . . . .2L 13
(off Clem Attlee Ct.)
Margaret Ho. *W6 . . . . .1H 13*
(off Queen Caroline St.)
Margaret Ingram Cl.
SW6 . . . . .2L 13
Margaret Lockwood Cl.
KT1: K Tham . . .7M 203 (3M 41)
Margaret Rd.
GU1: Guil 4B 202 (4M 113)
Margaret Rutherford Pl.
SW12 . . . . .2G 28
Margaret Way CR5: Coul 6M 83
MARGERY 7M 101
Margery Gro. KT20: Lwr K . . .7K 101
Margery La. KT20: Lwr K 7L 101
Margery Wood La.
KT20: Lwr K 7L 101
Margin Dr. SW19 . . . . .6J 27
Margravine Gdns. W6 . . . . .1J 13
Margravine Rd. W6 . . . . .1J 13
Marham Gdns. SM4: Mord 5A 44
SW18 . . . . .2C 28
Maria Ct. SE25 . . . . .1B 46
Marian Ct. SM1: Sut 2N 61
Marianne North Gallery 5M 11
Marian Rd. SW16 . . . . .9G 29
Maria Theresa Cl.
KT3: N Mal 4C 42
Mariette Way SM6: W'ton 5J 63
Marigold Cl. RG45: Crow 9E 30
Marigold Ct. GU1: Guil 9A 94
Marigold Dr. GU24: Bis 2D 72
Marigold Way CR0: Croy 7G 46
Marina Av. KT3: N Mal 4H 43
Marina Cl. KT16: Chert 7L 37
Marina Pl. *KT1: H Wic 1K 41*
(off Old Bri. St.)
Marina Way TW11: Tedd 8K 25
Marinefield Rd. SW6 . . . . .5N 13
Mariner Bus. Cen.
CR0: Wad 2L 63
Mariner Gdns.
TW10: Ham 4J 25
Mariners Dr. GU3: Norm 9M 91
GU14: Farnb 8A 70
Marion Av. TW17: Shep 4C 38
Marion M. SE21 . . . . .4N 29
Marion Rd. CR7: T Hea 4N 45
RH10: Craw 5F 182
Marius Mans. SW17 . . . . .3E 28
Marius Rd. SW17 . . . . .3E 28
Marjoram Cl. GU2: Guil 8K 93
GU14: Cove 1G 89
Marjorie Fosters Way
GU24: B'wood 6A 72
Marke Cl. BR2: Kes 1G 66
Markedge La. CR5: Coul 2D 102
RH1: Reig 2D 102
Markenfield Rd.
GU1: Guil 3C 202 (3N 113)
Markenhorn GU7: Goda 4G 132
Market, The SM5: Sut 7A 44
Market Cen., The
UB2: S'hall 1J 9
Market Dr. W4 . . . . .3D 12
Marketfield Rd. RH1: Red . . .3D 122
Marketfield Way RH1: Red . . .3D 122
Market Pde. SE25 . . . . .3D 46
TW13: Hanw 4M 23
Market Pl.
KT1: K Tham . . .3H 203 (1K 41)
RG12: Brac 1N 31
RG40: W'ham 2B 30
SL3: Coln 3E 6
TW8: Brent 3J 11
Market Rd. TW9: Rich 6N 11
Market Sq. GU21: Wok 4A 74
KT1: K Tham 4H 203
(off Market Pl.)
RH12: Hors 7J 197
TN16: Weste 4M 107
TW18: Stain 6G 21
Market St.
GU1: Guil 5C 202 (4N 113)
RG12: Brac 1N 31
SL4: W'sor 4G 5
Market Ter. *TW8: Brent 2L 11*
(off Albany Rd.)
Market Way TN16: Weste 4M 107
Markfield CR0: Sels 6J 65
(not continuous)
Markfield Rd. CR3: Cate 4E 104
Markham Ct. GU15: Camb 9B 50
Markham M.
RG40: W'ham 2A 30
Markham Rd. RH5: Cap 5J 159
Markhole Cl. TW12: Hamp 8N 23
Mark Oak La. KT22: Fetc 9A 78
Marksbury Av. TW9: Rich 6N 11
Marks Rd. CR6: Warl 5H 85
Marks St. RH2: Reig 2N 121
Markville Gdns. CR3: Cate . . .3D 104
Mark Way GU7: Hurt 3E 132
Markway TW16: Sunb 1K 39
Markwick La. GU8: Loxh 6L 153
Marlborough *SW19 . . . . .2J 27*
(off Inner Pk. Rd.)
Marlborough Bus. Cen.
KT16: Chert 8H 37
Marlborough Cl.
GU51: Fleet 5E 88
KT12: Hers 9L 39
RH11: Craw 7A 182
RH12: Hors 3K 197
SW19 . . . . .7C 28
Marlborough Ct.
CR2: S Croy 7F 200
RG40: W'ham 1C 30
RH4: Dork 3K 201 (5H 119)
SM6: W'ton 4G 62
TN16: Weste 4L 107
(off Croydon Rd.)
Marlborough Cres. UB3: Harl . . .3E 8
Marlborough Dr.
KT13: Weybr 9D 38
Marlborough Gdns.
KT6: Surb 6K 41
Marlborough Hill
RH4: Dork 3K 201 (5H 119)
Marlborough M. SM7: Ban 2M 81
Marlborough Pl.
RH12: Hors 5H 197
(off Rushams Rd.)
Marlborough Ri.
GU15: Camb 9C 50
Marlborough Rd.
CR2: S Croy 4N 63
GU21: Wok 3C 74
RH4: Dork 2K 201 (5H 119)
SL3: Lang 1A 6
SM1: Sut 9M 43
SW19 . . . . .7C 28
TW7: Isle 4H 11
TW10: Rich 9M 11
TW12: Hamp 7A 24
TW13: Felt 3L 23
TW15: A'ford 6M 21
W4 . . . . .1B 12
Marlborough Vw.
GU14: Cove 9H 69
Marld, The KT21: A'tead 5M 79
Marles La. RH14: Have 7D 194
Marley Av. GU27: Hasl 5C 188
Marley Cl. KT15: Addl 3H 55
Marley Combe Rd.
GU27: Hasl 3D 188
MARLEY COMMON 5D 188
Marley Hanger GU27: Hasl 5E 188
Marley Hgts. GU27: K Grn 8D 188
Marley La.
GU27: Hasl, K Grn 3C 188
Marley Ri. RH4: Dork 8G 119
Marlfield Cl. KT4: W Pk 7F 42
Marlhurst TN8: Eden 8K 127
Marlin Cl. TW16: Sunb 7F 22
Marling Ct. TW12: Hamp 7N 23
Marlingdene Cl.
TW12: Hamp 7A 24
MARLING PARK 8N 23
Marlings Cl. CR3: Whyte 4B 84
Marlins Cl. SM1: Sut 2A 62
Marlow Cl. SE20 . . . . .2E 46
Marlow Ct. RH10: Craw 2B 182
Marlow Cres. TW1: Twick 9F 10
Marlow Dr. SM3: Chea 8J 43
Marlowe Ho. KT1: K Tham . . .8H 203
Marlowe Sq. CR4: Mit 3G 44
Marlowe Way CR0: Bedd 8J 45
Marlow Ho. KT5: Surb 8K 203
TW11: Tedd 5G 25
Marlow Rd. SE20 . . . . .2E 46
Marlpit Av. CR5: Coul 4J 83
Marlpit Cl. RH19: E Grin 7A 166
TN8: Eden 8L 127
MARLPIT HILL 8K 127
Marlpit La. CR5: Coul 3H 83
Marl Rd. SW18 . . . . .7N 13
Marlyns Cl. GU4: B'ham 9C 94
Marlyns Dr. GU4: B'ham 8C 94
Marmot Rd. TW4: Houn 6L 9
Marncrest Ct. KT12: Hers 2J 57
Marnell Way TW4: Houn 6L 9
Marneys Cl. KT18: Eps 2N 79
Marnfield Cres. SW2 . . . . .2L 29
Marnham Pl. KT15: Addl 1L 55
Marqueen Towers
SW16 . . . . .8K 29
Marquis Ct. KT1: K Tham 8H 203
KT19: Eps 6J 201 (9C 60)
TW19: Stan 2N 21
Marrick Cl. SW15 . . . . .7F 12
Marriott Cl. TW14: Felt 9E 8
Marriott Lodge Cl.
KT15: Addl 1L 55
Marrowbrook Cl.
GU14: Cove 2M 89
Marrowbrook La.
GU14: Cove 3L 89
Marrowells KT13: Weybr 9G 38
Marrow Meade GU51: Fleet . . .2A 88
Marryat Cl. TW4: Houn 7N 9
Marryat Pl. SW19 . . . . .5K 27
Marryat Rd. SW19 . . . . .6J 27
Marryat Sq. SW6 . . . . .4K 13
Marsden Way BR6: Orp 1N 67
Marshall Cl. CR2: Sande 9D 64
GU14: Cove 7L 69
GU16: Frim 4H 71
TW4: Houn 8N 9
Marshall Hall *TW20: Eng G . . .4M 19*
(off Coopers Hill La.)
Marshall Pde. GU22: Pyr 2H 75
Marshall Pl. KT15: N Haw 5L 55
Marshall Rd. GU7: Goda 6H 133
GU47: C Tow 8J 49
RH10: Craw 5G 182
Marshalls Cl.
KT19: Eps 6H 201 (9B 60)
Marshall's Rd. SM1: Sut 1N 61
Marsham Ho. RG42: Brac 8N 15
Marsh Av. CR4: Mit 1D 44
KT19: Ewe 6D 60
Marsh Cl. GU35: Bor 6A 168
Marsh Ct. RH11: Craw 8N 181
SW19 . . . . .9A 28
Marsh Farm Rd. TW2: Twick . . .2F 24
Marshfield SL3: Dat 4M 5
MARSH GREEN 6K 147
Marsh Grn. Rd.
TN8: M Grn 7K 147
Marshlands Cotts.
RH5: Newd 7B 160
Marsh La. KT15: Addl 1K 55
Marshwood Rd. GU18: Ligh 7A 52
Marston KT19: Eps 7B 60
Marston Av. KT9: Ches 3L 59
Marston Ct. KT12: Wal T 7K 39
Marston Dr. CR6: Warl 5H 85
GU14: Farnb 7N 69
Marston Rd. GU9: Farnh 1E 128
GU21: Wok 4L 73
TW11: Tedd 6H 25
Marston Way SE19 . . . . .8M 29
SL5: Asc 1J 33
Martel Cl. GU15: Camb 8G 50
Martell Rd. SE21 . . . . .4N 29
Martens Pl. GU7: Goda 5H 133
Martin Cl. CR2: Sels 7G 64
CR6: Warl 3E 84
RH11: Craw 1B 182
SL4: W'sor 4A 4
Martin Ct. CR2: S Croy 8F 200
Martin Cres. CR0: Croy 7L 45
Martindale SW14 . . . . .8B 12
Martindale Av. GU15: Camb . . .2G 71
Martindale Cl. GU4: Guil 1F 114
Martindale Rd. GU21: Wok 5K 73
SW12 . . . . .1F 28
TW4: Houn 6M 9
Martineau Cl. KT10: Esh 1D 58
Martineau Dr. RH4: Dork 7H 119
TW1: Twick 7H 11
Martingale Cl. TW16: Sunb 3H 39
Martingale Ct. GU11: Alde 2K 109
Martingales Cl. TW10: Ham 4K 25
Martin Gro. SM4: Mord 2M 43
Martin Rd. GU2: Guil 1K 113
Martins, The
RH10: Craw D 1F 184
Martins Cl. BR4: W Wick 7N 47
GU1: Guil 2E 114
GU17: B'water 2J 69
Martin's Dr. RG41: W'ham 9A 14
MARTIN'S HERON 2D 32
Martin's Heron Station (Rail)
. . . . .3D 32
Martin's La. RG12: Brac 2C 32
Martins Pk. Cvn. Pk.
GU14: Cove 7J 69
Martins Wood GU8: Mil 3B 152
Martinsyde GU22: Wok 4E 74
Martin Way GU16: Frim 5C 70
GU21: Wok 5K 73
SM4: Mord 2K 43
SW20 . . . . .1J 43

Martlands Ind. Est.—Melfort Av.

Martlands Ind. Est.
GU22: Wok 1K 93
Martlets, The RH10: Craw 3C 182
Martlets Cl. RH12: Hors 3J 197
Martletts Cnr.
RH12: Rudg 1E 194
Marts, The RH12: Rudg 1E 194
Martyns Pl. RH19: E Grin 1B 186
Martyr Rd.
GU1: Guil 5C 202 (4N 113)
Martyrs Av. RH11: Craw 9A 162
MARTYR'S GREEN 7E 76
Martyr's La. GU21: Wok 8D 54
Marvell Cl. RH10: Craw 1G 182
Marville Rd. SW6 3L 13
Marwell TN16: Weste 4K 107
Mary Adelaide Cl.
SW15 5D 26
Mary Drew Almshouses
TW20: Eng G 7N 19
Mary Flowers Hall
SL5: S'hill 2C 34
(off Buckhurst Rd.)
Mary Flux Ct. *SW5* 1N 13
(off Bramham Gdns.)
Maryhill Cl. CR8: Ken 4N 83
Mary Holben Ho.
SW16 6G 28
Mary Ho. *W6* 1H 13
(off Queen Caroline St.)
Maryland Rd. CR7: T Hea 9M 29
Maryland Way
TW16: Sunb 1H 39
Marylebone Gdns.
TW9: Rich 7N 11
Mary Macarthur Ho.
W6 2K 13
Mary Mead RG42: Warf 7B 16
Mary Rd.
GU1: Guil 4B 202 (4M 113)
Mary Rose Cl. TW12: Hamp 9A 24
Mary Smith Ct. *SW5* 1M 13
(off Trebovir Rd.)
Mary's Ter. TW1: Twick 1G 24
(not continuous)
Mary Va. GU7: Goda 9G 133
Mary Wallace Theatre 2G 25
Marzell Ho. *W14* 1L 13
(off North End Rd.)
Marzena Ct. TW3: Houn 9C 10
Masault Ct. *TW9: Rich* 7L 11
(off Kew Foot Rd.)
Mascotte Rd. SW15 7J 13
Masefield Ct. KT6: Surb 6K 41
Masefield Gdns.
RG45: Crow 4G 48
Masefield Rd. RH11: Craw 6K 181
TW12: Hamp 5N 23
Masefield Way TW19: Stan 2A 22
Maskall Cl. SW2 2L 29
Maskani Wlk. SW16 8G 29
Maskell Rd. SW17 4A 28
Maskell Way GU14: Cove 2H 89
Mason Cl. GU46: Yate 1D 68
RH19: E Grin 8A 166
SW20 9J 27
TW12: Hamp 9N 23
Masonettes *KT19: Ewe* 6C 60
(off Sefton Rd.)
Masonic Hall Rd.
KT16: Chert 5H 37
Mason Pl. GU47: Sandh 7E 48
Mason Rd. GU14: Cove 8K 69
RH10: Craw 5C 182
SM1: Sut 2N 61
Mason's Av.
CR0: Croy 5C 200 (9N 45)
Mason's Bri. Rd.
RH1: Red, Salf 8F 122
Masons Fld. RH13: M Hea 9B 198
Masons Paddock
RH4: Dork 3G 118
Masons Pl. CR4: Mit 9D 28
Mason's Yd. SW19 6J 27
Mason Way GU11: Alde 5N 109
Massetts Rd. RH6: Horl 9D 142
Massingberd Way
SW17 5F 28
Master Cl. RH8: Oxt 7A 106
Masters Cl. SW16 7G 29
MASWELL PARK 8C 10
Maswell Pk. Cres.
TW3: Houn 8C 10
Maswell Pk. Rd.
TW3: Houn 8B 10
Matcham Ct. *TW1: Twick* 9K 11
(off Clevedon Rd.)
Matham Rd. KT8: E Mol 4D 40
Matheson Rd. W14 1L 13
Mathew Ter. GU11: Alde 2A 110
Mathias Cl.
KT18: Eps 7H 201 (9B 60)
Mathisen Way SL3: Poy 4G 7
Mathison Ho. *SW10* 3N 13
(off Coleridge Gdns.)
Mathon Ct. GU1: Guil 3B 114
Matlock Cres. SM3: Chea 1K 61
Matlock Gdns. SM3: Chea 1K 61
Matlock Pl. SM3: Chea 1K 61
Matlock Rd. CR3: Cate 8B 84
Matlock Way KT3: N Mal 9C 26
Maton Ho. *SW6* 3L 13
(off Estcourt Rd.)
Matthew Arnold Cl.
KT11: Cob 1H 77
TW18: Stain 7L 21
Matthew Arnold Sports Cen.
7L 21
Matthew Ct. CR4: Mit 4H 45
Matthew Rd. GU11: Alde 4K 109
Matthews Chase RG42: Bin 8L 15
Matthews Cl. GU14: Farnb 5B 90
Matthews Ct. SL5: S'hill 3A 34
Matthews Dr. RH10: Craw 7F 182
Matthews Gdns.
CR0: N Add 7N 65
Matthewsgreen Rd.
RG41: W'ham 9A 14
Matthews La. TW18: Stain 5H 21
Matthews Lodge
KT15: Addl 1M 55
Matthews Rd.
GU15: Camb 7A 50
Matthews St. RH2: Reig 7M 121
Matthews Way GU51: Fleet 3A 88
Matthews Yd. CR0: Croy 4B 200
Matthey Pl. RH10: Craw 9H 163
Maudit Ho. *GU51: Fleet* 2A 88
(off Rykmansford Rd.)
Maudsley Ho. TW8: Brent 1L 11
Maultway, The GU15: Camb 7F 50
Maultway Cl. GU15: Camb 7F 50
Maultway Cres.
GU15: Camb 7F 50
Maultway Nth. GU15: Camb 6E 50
Maunsell Pk. RH10: Craw 3F 182
Maureen Campbell Ct.
TW17: Shep 4C 38
(off Harrison Way)
Maureen Ct. BR3: Beck 1F 46
Maurice Av. CR3: Cate 9A 84
Maurice Ct. TW8: Brent 3K 11
Mausoleum 6J 5
Mauveine Gdns.
TW3: Houn 7A 10
Mavins Rd. GU9: Farnh 3J 129
Mavis Av. KT19: Ewe 2D 60
Mavis Cl. KT19: Ewe 2D 60
Mawbey Rd. KT16: Otter 3F 54
Mawson Cl. SW20 1K 43
Mawson La. W4 2E 12
Maxine Cl. GU47: Sandh 6G 48
Maxton Wlk. RH11: Craw 8N 181
Maxwell Cl. CR0: Wad 7J 45
Maxwell Dr. KT14: W By 7L 55
Maxwell Rd. SW6 3N 13
TW15: A'ford 7D 22
Maxwell Way RH10: Craw 9E 162
May Bate Av.
KT2: K Tham 1H 203 (9K 25)
Maybelle Cl. RH5: B Grn 8K 139
Mayberry Pl. KT5: Surb 6M 41
Maybourne Ri. GU22: Wok 2N 93
Maybrick Cl. GU47: Sandh 6E 48
MAYBURY 3E 74
Maybury Cl. GU16: Frim 6B 70
KT20: Tad 6K 81
Maybury Ct. CR2: S Croy 8A 200
Maybury Est. GU22: Wok 3E 74
Maybury Hill GU22: Wok 3D 74
Maybury Rd. GU21: Wok 4B 74
Maybury Rough
GU22: Wok 4D 74
Maybury St. SW17 6C 28
May Cl. GU7: Goda 9E 132
GU35: Head 5D 168
GU47: Owls 7J 49
KT9: Ches 3M 59
May Ct. *SW19* 9A 28
(off Pincott Rd.)
May Cres. GU12: Ash 3C 110
Maycross Av. SM4: Mord 3L 43
Mayday Rd. CR7: T Hea 5M 45
Maydwell Av. RH13: Slin 6J 195
Mayell Cl. KT22: Leat 1J 99
Mayes Cl. CR6: Warl 5G 85
RH10: Craw 4G 182
MAYES GREEN 7M 157
Mayes La. RH12: Warn 7E 178
Mayfair Av. KT4: W Pk 7F 42
TW2: Whitt 1C 24
Mayfair Cl. KT6: Surb 7L 41
Mayfield GU10: Rowl 8E 128
KT22: Leat 8J 79
RH7: Dorm 1C 166
RH10: Wor 3H 183
Mayfield Av. KT15: N Haw 6K 55
W4 1D 12
Mayfield Cl. GU9: B Lea 6N 109
KT7: T Dit 7H 41
KT12: Hers 1H 57
KT15: N Haw 6L 55
RH1: Red 9E 122
SE20 1E 46
TW15: A'ford 7C 22
Mayfield Ct. RH1: Red 8D 122
Mayfield Cres. CR7: T Hea 3K 45
Mayfield Dr. SL4: W'sor 6D 4
Mayfield Gdns. KT12: Hers 1H 57
KT15: N Haw 6K 55
TW18: Stain 7H 21
Mayfield Grn. KT23: Book 5A 98
Mayfield Light Ind. Est.
SL4: Wink 4M 17
Mayfield Mans.
SW15 8L 13
Mayfield Rd. CR2: Sande 5A 64
CR7: T Hea 3K 45
GU14: Cove, Farnb 7L 69
GU15: Camb 5N 69
KT12: Hers 1H 57
KT13: Weybr 2A 56
SM2: Sut 3B 62
SW19 9L 27
Mayflower Cl. RH10: Craw 4H 183
Mayflower Dr. GU46: Yate 8A 48
MAYFORD 9M 73
Mayford Cl. BR3: Beck 2G 47
GU22: Wok 9N 73
SW12 1D 28
Mayford Grn. GU22: Wok 9M 73
Mayford Rd. SW12 1D 28
Mayhurst Av. GU22: Wok 3E 74
Mayhurst Cl. GU22: Wok 3E 74
Mayhurst Cres. GU22: Wok 3E 74
Mayhurst M. GU22: Wok 3E 74
Maynard Cl. RH10: Cop 6N 163
SW6 3N 13
Maynard Ct. SL4: W'sor 4D 4
TW18: Stain 5J 21
Maynooth Gdns.
SM5: Cars 6D 44
Mayo Rd. CR0: Croy 4A 46
KT12: Wal T 6H 39
Maypole Rd.
RH19: Ash W 3G 186
RH19: E Grin 8N 165
May Rd. TW2: Twick 2E 24
Mayroyd Av. KT6: Surb 8N 41
Mays Cl. KT13: Weybr 6A 56
Mays Cft. RG12: Brac 3M 31
Maysfield Rd. GU23: Send 1F 94
MAY'S GREEN 7F 76
Mays Gro. GU23: Send 1F 94
Mays Rd. RG40: W'ham 2D 30
TW11: Tedd 6D 24
May St. W14 1L 13
(North End Rd.)
W14 1L 13
(Vereker Rd.)
Maytree Cl. GU1: Guil 8M 93
Maytree Ct. CR4: Mit 2E 44
Maytrees GU21: Knap 4F 72
Maytree Wlk. SW2 3L 29
Maywater Cl. CR2: Sande 7A 64
Maywood Dr. GU15: Camb 8F 50
Maze Rd. TW9: Kew 3N 11
Meachen Ct. RG40: W'ham 2B 30
Mead, The BR3: Beck 1M 47
BR4: W Wick 7N 47
GU14: Farnb 2N 89
KT21: A'tead 6L 79
RH4: Dork 8J 119
SM6: W'ton 3H 63
Mead Av. RH1: Salf 2E 142
Mead Cl. GU6: Cranl 8N 155
RH1: Red 9E 102
TW20: Egh 7D 20
Mead Ct. GU21: Knap 3H 73
TW20: Egh 7E 20
Mead Cres. KT23: Book 3A 98
SM1: Sut 9C 44
Meade Cl. W4 2N 11
Meade Ct. GU19: Bag 4K 51
KT20: Wal H 2F 100
Mead End KT21: A'tead 4M 79
Meades, The KT13: Weybr 3D 56
RH7: Dorm 1C 166
Meades Cl. RH7: Dorm 1D 166
Meadfoot Rd. SW16 8G 28
Meadhurst Pk. TW16: Sunb 7F 22
Meadhurst Rd. KT16: Chert 7K 37
Meadhurst Sports Club 6G 22
Meadlands Dr. TW10: Ham 3K 25
Mead La. GU9: Farnh 1G 128
KT16: Chert 6K 37
Meadow, The RH10: Cop 7L 163
Meadow App. RH10: Cop 7L 163
Meadow Av. CR0: Croy 5G 47
Meadow Bank GU1: Guil 1M 113
GU9: Farnh 1G 128
KT24: E Hor 5G 96
Meadowbank KT5: Surb 5M 41
Meadowbank Cl. SW6 3H 13
Meadowbank Gdns.
TW5: C'ford 4H 9
Meadowbank Rd.
GU18: Ligh 6N 51
Meadowbrook RH8: Oxt 8M 105
Meadowbrook Cl. SL3: Poy 4H 7
Meadowbrook Ct. TW7: Isle 6E 10
Meadow Brook Ind. Cen.
RH10: Craw 9E 162
Meadowbrook Rd.
RH4: Dork 1J 201 (4G 119)
Meadow Cl. CR8: Pur 9H 63
GU7: Goda 4H 133
GU8: Mil 1D 152
GU12: A Va 4D 90
GU17: Haw 2J 69
KT10: H Wood 9F 40
KT12: Hers 1N 57
RH10: Cop 7L 163
RH12: Hors 3N 197
SL4: O Win 8L 5
SM1: Sut 8A 44
SW20 3H 43
TW4: Houn 9A 10
TW10: Ham 2L 25
Meadow Cotts.
GU24: W End 8C 52
Meadow Ct. GU14: Cove 1L 89
GU51: Fleet 4A 88
KT18: Eps 7H 201 (9B 60)
RH1: Mers 8G 103
RH19: E Grin 8A 166
TW3: Houn 9B 10
TW18: Stain 4G 20
Meadowcroft *W4* 1N 11
(off Brooks Rd.)
Meadowcroft Cl.
RH6: Horl 2G 162
RH11: Craw 4L 181
RH19: E Grin 8M 165
Meadow Dr. GU23: Rip 1H 95
Meadow Farm La.
RH12: Hors 1M 197
Meadow Gdns.
TW18: Stain 6F 20
Meadow Ga.
KT21: A'tead 4L 79
Meadowgate *RH12: Hors* 1M 197
(off Giblets La.)
Meadow Ga. Av.
GU14: Farnb 3L 89
Meadow Hill CR5: Coul 1G 82
CR8: Pur 1G 82
KT3: N Mal 5D 42
Meadow Ho. *GU4: Guil* 2F 114
(off Merrow St.)
GU17: Haw 2K 69
Meadowlands
GU4: W Cla 8K 95
KT11: Cob 9H 57
RH8: Oxt 3C 126
RH11: Craw 3A 182
Meadowlands Pk.
KT15: Addl 9N 37
Meadow La. KT22: Fetc 9C 78
SL4: E Wic 2E 4
TN8: Eden 8K 127
Meadowlea Cl. UB7: Harm 2M 7
Meadow Pl. W4 3D 12
Meadow Ri. CR5: Coul 9H 63
GU21: Knap 4F 72
Meadow Rd. GU4: B'ham 8C 94
GU14: Farnb 7N 69
GU25: V Wat 4H 35
KT10: Clay 3E 58
KT21: A'tead 4L 79
SM1: Sut 1C 62
SW19 8A 28
TW13: Felt 3M 23
TW15: A'ford 6E 22
Meadows, The CR6: Warl 4G 85
GU2: Guil 8B 202 (6M 113)
GU10: Churt 9L 149
GU12: Ash 2F 110
(off Chester Rd.)
GU47: C Tow 1K 69
Meadows Bus. Pk., The
GU17: B'water 1K 69
Meadows End
TW16: Sunb 9H 23
Meadowside KT12: Wal T 8K 39
KT23: Book 1A 98
RH6: Horl 7F 142
TW1: Twick 1K 25
TW18: Stain 6J 21
Meadowside Pk.
RH7: Ling 5M 145
Meadowside Rd.
SM2: Chea 5K 61
Meadows Leigh Cl.
KT13: Weybr 9C 38
Meadow Stile
CR0: Croy 5C 200 (9N 45)
Meadowsweet Cl.
SW20 3H 43
Meadow Va. GU27: Hasl 2E 188
Meadow Vw. GU35: Bor 6A 168
KT16: Chert 7L 37
RH6: Smal 8N 143
TW19: Stan M 8H 7
Meadow Vw. Rd.
CR7: T Hea 4M 45
Meadowview Rd.
KT19: Ewe 5D 60
Meadow Wlk. KT17: Ewe 3D 60
KT19: Ewe 3D 60
(not continuous)
KT20: Wal H 2G 100
SM6: W'ton 9F 44
Meadow Way
GU10: Rowl 8E 128
GU12: Alde 1D 110
GU17: B'water 1H 69
GU24: W End 8C 52
KT9: Ches 2L 59
KT15: Addl 1K 55
KT20: Tad 4K 81
KT23: Book 1B 98
KT24: W Hors 3E 96
RG42: Brac 8M 15
RH2: Reig 7N 121
SL4: O Win 9L 5
Meadow Waye
TW5: Hest 2M 9
Mead Path SW17 5A 28
Mead Pl.
CR0: Croy 1A 200 (7N 45)
RH6: Smal 8N 143
Mead Rd. CR3: Cate 1C 104
GU6: Cranl 7N 155
GU26: Hind 5D 170
KT12: Hers 1M 57
RH10: Craw 2D 182
TN8: Eden 4M 147
TW10: Ham 4J 25
Meadrow GU7: Goda 6J 133
Meadrow Ct. GU7: Goda 5K 133
Meads, The GU27: Hasl 2D 188
RH19: E Grin 2A 186
SL4: W'sor 5D 4
SM3: Chea 9K 43
SM4: Mord 4C 44
Meadside *GU22: Wok* 5B 74
(off Park Dr.)
KT18: Eps 7J 201
Meads Rd. GU1: Guil 3D 114
MEAD VALE 5B 122
Meadvale RH12: Hors 6F 196
Meadvale Rd. CR0: Croy 6C 46
Mead Way CR0: Croy 8H 47
CR5: Coul 5J 83
GU4: B'ham 7E 94
Meadway BR3: Beck 1M 47
CR6: Warl 3F 84
GU16: Frim 4D 70
GU27: Hasl 2D 188
KT5: Surb 7B 42
KT10: Esh 5B 58
KT19: Eps 5G 201 (8B 60)
KT22: Oxs 1E 78
KT24: Eff 6M 97
SW20 3H 43
TW2: Twick 2D 24
TW15: A'ford 5B 22
TW18: Stain 8J 21
Meadway, The RH6: Horl 8G 142
Meadway Cl. TW18: Stain 8H 21
Meadway Ct. TW11: Tedd 6J 25
Meadway Dr. GU21: Wok 3M 73
KT15: Addl 4L 55
Mead Way Path CR5: Coul 5K 83
Meare Cl. KT20: Tad 1H 101
MEATH GREEN 6D 142
Meath Grn. Av. RH6: Horl 6D 142
Meath Grn. La. RH6: Horl 3C 142
Mecca Bingo
Croydon 2B 200
Earlsfield 2N 27
Fulham Broadway 3M 13
(off Vanston Pl.)
Hounslow 5C 10
Rosehill 6A 44
Medawar Rd. GU2: Guil 4G 113
Medcroft Gdns. SW14 7B 12
Mede Cl. TW19: Wray 2N 19
Mede Ct. TW18: Stain 4G 20
Mede Fld. KT22: Fetc 2D 98
Medfield St. SW15 1F 26
Medhurst Cl. GU24: Chob 5J 53
Medieval Undercroft 6C 202
Medina Av. KT10: H Wood 9E 40
Medina Sq. KT19: Eps 5N 59
Medlake Pl. TW20: Egh 8E 20
Medlake Rd. TW20: Egh 7E 20
Medland Cl. SM6: W'ton 7E 44
Medlar Cl. GU1: Guil 1M 113
RH11: Craw 9A 162
Medlar Dr. GU17: Haw 3L 69
Medlars Ct. RH5: Newd 1A 160
Medonte Cl. GU51: Fleet 5C 88
Medora Rd. SW2 1K 29
Medway RH10: Craw 4D 184
Medway Cl. CR0: Croy 5F 46
Medway Ct. RH12: Hors 3A 198
Medway Dr. GU14: Cove 8K 69
RH18: F Row 7J 187
RH19: E Grin 3N 185
Medway Ho.
KT2: K Tham 1H 203 (9K 25)
Medway Rd. RH11: Craw 4L 181
Medway Vw. RH18: F Row 7J 187
Medwin Wlk. RH12: Hors 6J 197
Megabowl
Croydon 8K 45
Feltham 3J 23
Kingston upon Thames
3K 203
(in The Rotunda Cen.)
Streatham Hill 3J 29
Melancholy Wlk.
TW10: Ham 3J 25
Melbourne Cl. SM6: W'ton 2G 62
Melbourne Mans. *W14* 2K 13
(off Musard Rd.)
Melbourne Rd. SM6: W'ton 2F 62
SW19 9M 27
TW11: Tedd 7J 25
Melbourne Ter. *SW6* 3N 13
(off Moore Pk. Rd.)
Melbourne Way
RH12: Hors 3M 197
Melbray M. SW6 5L 13
Melbury Cl. KT10: Clay 3H 59
KT14: W By 1J 75
KT16: Chert 6J 37
Melbury Gdns. SW20 9G 26
Meldone Cl. KT5: Surb 6A 42
Meldrum Cl. RH8: Oxt 1B 126
Melford Cl. KT9: Ches 2M 59
Melfort Av. CR7: T Hea 2M 45

Melfort Rd.—Mill La.

Melfort Rd. CR7: T Hea 2M 45
Melina Ct. SW15 . . . . .6F 12
Melksham Cl. GU47: Owls 6J 49
RH13: Hors 7L 197
Meller Cl. CR0: Bedd 9J 45
Mellersh Hill Rd.
GU5: Wone 4D 134
Mellifont Cl. SM5: Cars 6B 44
Mellison Rd. SW17 . . . . .6C 28
Melliss Av. TW9: Kew 4A 12
Mellor Cl. KT12: Wal T 6N 39
Mellor Wlk. SL4: W'sor 4G 4
(off Batchelors Acre)
Mellow Cl. SM7: Ban 1A 82
Mellows Rd. SM6: W'ton 2H 63
Melody Rd. TN16: B Hil 5E 86
Melrose RG12: Brac 7N 31
Melrose Av. CR4: Mit 8F 28
GU14: Cove 9H 69
SW16 . . . . .2K 45
SW19 . . . . .3L 27
TW2: Whitt 1B 24
Melrose Cl. GU14: Cove 9H 69
Melrose Cres. BR6: Orp 1M 67
Melrose Gdns. KT3: N Mal 2C 42
KT12: Hers 2K 57
Melrose Rd. CR5: Coul 2F 82
KT13: Weybr 2B 56
SW13 . . . . .5E 12
SW18 . . . . .9L 13
SW19 . . . . .1M 43
TN16: B Hil 3E 86
Melrose Tudor SM6: W'ton 2J 63
(off Plough La.)
Melsa Rd. SM4: Mord 5A 44
Melton Ct. SM2: Sut 4A 62
Melton Flds. KT19: Ewe 5C 60
Melton Pl. KT19: Ewe 5C 60
Melton Rd. RH1: Mers 8G 102
Melville Av. CR2: S Croy 2C 64
GU16: Frim 5D 70
SW20 . . . . .8F 26
Melville Ct.
GU2: Guil 8B 202 (6M 113)
W4 . . . . .1N 11
(off Haining Cl.)
Melville Rd. SW13 . . . . .4F 12
Melville Ter. GU9: Farnh 1G 128
Melvinshaw KT22: Leat 8J 79
Membury Cl. GU16: Frim 7E 70
Membury Wlk. RG12: Brac 3C 32
Memorial Cl. RH8: Oxt 5N 105
TW5: Hest 2N 9
Memorial Gdns. 3C 182
Mendip Cl. KT4: W Pk 7H 43
SL3: Lang 1C 6
UB3: Harl 3E 8
Mendip Rd. GU14: Cove 7K 69
RG12: Brac 4C 32
Mendip Wlk. RH11: Craw 3N 181
Mendora Rd. SW6 . . . . .3K 13
Menin Way GU9: Farnh 2J 129
Menlo Gdns. SE19 . . . . .8N 29
Mentone Mans. SW10 . . . . . . .3N 13
(off Fulham Rd.)
Meon Cl. GU14: Cove 8J 69
KT20: Tad 9G 80
Meon Ct. TW7: Isle 5E 10
Meopham Rd. CR4: Mit 9G 28
Merantun Way SW19 . . . . .9N 27
Mercedes-Benz World 5A 56
Mercer Cl. KT7: T Dit 6F 40
RH10: Craw 6G 182
Mercer Rd. RH12: Hors 9J 179
Mercers Country Pk. 9H 103
Merchants Cl. GU21: Knap 4F 72
SE25 . . . . .3D 46
Mercia Ho. TW15: A'ford 9D 22
Mercia Wlk. GU21: Wok 4B 74
Mercier Rd. SW15 . . . . .8K 13
Mercury Cen. TW14: Felt 8H 9
Mercury Cl. GU35: Bor 6A 168
RH11: Craw 6K 181
Mercury Ho. TW8: Brent 2J 11
(off Glenhurst Rd.)
Mercury Rd. TW8: Brent 2J 11
Merebank RH5: B Grn 7K 139
Merebank La. CR0: Wad 2K 63
Mere Cl. SW15 . . . . .1J 27
Meredyth Rd. SW13 . . . . .5F 12
Mere End CR0: Croy 6G 47
Merefield Gdns. KT20: Tad 6J 81
Mere Rd. KT13: Weybr 9E 38
KT20: Tad 2G 101
TW17: Shep 5C 38
Mereside Pk. TW15: A'ford 5D 22
Mereside Pl. GU25: V Wat 7K 35
Merevale Cres. SM4: Mord 5A 44
Mereway Rd. TW2: Twick 2D 24
Merewood Gdns. CR0: Croy 6G 46
Mereworth Dr.
RH10: Craw 1H 183
Merideth Ct.
KT1: K Tham . . .4M 203 (1M 41)
Meridian Cen. CR0: N Add 6A 66
Meridian Cl. RH11: Craw 6L 181
Meridian Ct. RH19: F Row 9A 186
SL5: Asc 7M 33
Meridian Gro. RH6: Horl 7G 143
Meridian Way
RH19: E Grin 7B 166
Merivale Rd. SW15 . . . . .7K 13
Merland Cl. KT20: Tad 7H 81
Merland Grn. KT20: Tad 7H 81
Merland Ri. KT18: Tat C 6H 81
KT20: Tad 6H 81
MERLE COMMON 5D 126
Merle Comn. Rd.
RH8: Oxt 4C 126
Merlewood RG12: Brac 4B 32
Merlewood Cl. CR3: Cate 7A 84
Merlin Cen. RH11: Craw 7B 162
Merlin Cl.
CR0: Croy 6F 200 (1B 64)
CR4: Mit 2C 44
RH11: Ifi 3K 181
SL3: Lang 2D 6
SM6: W'ton 3K 63
Merlin Clove RG42: Wink R 7F 16
Merlin Ct. GU16: Frim 5B 70
GU21: Wok 1E 74
Merling Cl. KT9: Ches 2J 59
Merlin Gro. BR3: Beck 3J 47
Merlins Cl. GU9: Farnh 2H 129
Merlin Way GU14: Cove 2J 89
RH19: E Grin 7C 166
Merredene St. SW2 . . . . .1K 29
Merrilands Rd. KT4: W Pk 7H 43
Merrilyn Cl. KT10: Clay 3G 58
Merrington Rd. SW6 . . . . .2M 13
Merrin Hill CR2: Sande 7B 64
Merritt Gdns. KT9: Ches 3J 59
(not continuous)
Merrivale Gdns.
GU21: Wok 4M 73
Merron Cl. GU46: Yate 1B 68
MERROW 2D 114
Merrow Bus. Pk. GU4: Guil 9F 94
Merrow Chase GU1: Guil 3E 114
Merrow Comn. Rd.
GU4: Guil 9E 94
Merrow Copse GU1: Guil 2D 114
Merrow Ct. CR4: Mit 1B 44
GU1: Guil 3F 114
Merrow Cft. GU1: Guil 2E 114
MERROW DOWNS 4F 114
Merrow La.
GU4: B'ham, Guil 7E 94
Merrow Pl. GU4: Guil 1F 114
Merrow Rd. SM2: Chea 5J 61
Merrow St. GU4: Guil 1F 114
Merrow Way CR0: N Add 3M 65
GU1: Guil 2F 114
Merrow Woods GU1: Guil 1D 114
Merryacres GU8: Wit 4B 152
Merrydene Ct. RG12: Bin 1H 31
Merryfield Dr. RH12: Hors . . .6G 197
Merryhill Rd. RG42: Brac 8M 15
Merryhills Cl. TN16: B Hil 3F 86
Merryhills La. RH14: Loxw 3J 193
Merrylands KT16: Chert 9G 37
Merrylands Rd.
KT23: Book 1N 97
Merryman Dr. RG45: Crow 1E 48
Merrymeet SM7: Ban 1D 82
Merryweather Ct.
KT3: N Mal 4D 42
Merrywood Gro.
KT20: Lwr K 8K 101
Merrywood Pk.
GU15: Camb 2D 70
RH2: Reig 1N 121
Merrywood Pk. Cvn. Site
KT20: Box H 8A 100
Merryworth Cl.
GU12: Ash 3D 110
Mersey Ct. KT2: K Tham 1H 203
Mersham Pl. CR7: T Hea 1A 46
(off Livingstone Rd.)
Mersham Rd. CR7: T Hea 2A 46
MERSTHAM 6G 102
Merstham Rd. RH1: Blet 7L 103
Merstham Station (Rail) 6G 102
Merthyr Ter. SW13 . . . . .2G 13
MERTON 8A 28
Merton Abbey Mills
SW19 . . . . .9A 28
Merton Av. W4 . . . . .1E 12
Merton Cl. GU47: Owls 5L 49
Merton Gdns. KT20: Tad 6J 81
Merton Hall Gdns.
SW20 . . . . .9K 27
Merton Hall Rd.
SW19 . . . . .8K 27
Merton High St. SW19 . . . . . . .8N 27
Merton Ind. Pk. SW19 . . . . . . .9N 27
Merton Mans. SW20 . . . . .1J 43
MERTON PARK 1M 43
Merton Pk. Pde.
SW19 . . . . .9L 27
Merton Park Stop (CT) 9M 27
Merton Pl. SW19 . . . . .9A 28
(off Nelson Gro. Rd.)
Merton Rd. RH11: Craw 9N 181
SE25 . . . . .4C 46
SW18 . . . . .9M 13
SW19 . . . . .8N 27
Merton Wlk. KT22: Leat 5G 79
Merton Way KT8: W Mole 3B 40
KT22: Leat 6G 79
Mervyn Rd. TW17: Shep 6D 38
Merwin Way SL4: W'sor 5A 4
Meryton Ho. SL4: W'sor 6D 4
Messenger Cl.
RH11: Craw 1M 181
Metana Ho. RH10: Craw 7E 162
Metcalf Rd. TW15: A'ford 6C 22
Metcalf Wlk. TW13: Hanw 5M 23
Metcalf Way RH11: Craw 8B 162
Meteor Way SM6: W'ton 4J 63
Metro Ind. Cen. TW7: Isle 5E 10
Metropolitan Club, The 1N 27
Metropolitan Sta. Bldgs.
W6 . . . . .1H 13
(off Beadon Rd.)
Meudon Av. GU14: Farnb 2N 89
Mews, The
GU1: Guil 4A 202 (4M 113)
GU8: Duns 4B 174
RH2: Reig 2N 121
RH12: Bro H 4D 196
(off Old Guildford Rd.)
TW1: Twick 9H 11
TW20: Eng G 5N 19
(off Coopers Hill La.)
Mews Ct. RH19: E Grin 3B 186
Mews End TN16: B Hil 5F 86
Mexfield Rd. SW15 . . . . .8L 13
Meyrick Cl. GU21: Knap 3H 73
Michael Cres. RH6: Horl 1E 162
Michael Flds.
RH18: F Row 7G 186
Michael La. GU2: Guil 7L 93
Michaelmas Cl.
GU46: Yate 2C 68
SW20 . . . . .2H 43
Michael Rd. SE25 . . . . .2B 46
SW6 . . . . .4N 13
Michael Stewart Ho.
SW6 . . . . .2L 13
(off Clem Attlee Ct.)
Micheldever Way
RG12: Brac 5D 32
Michelet Cl. GU18: Ligh 6M 51
Michelham Gdns.
KT20: Tad 7H 81
TW1: Twick 4F 24
Michell Cl. RH12: Hors 6G 197
Michelsdale Dr. TW9: Rich 7L 11
Michel's Row TW9: Rich 7L 11
(off Michelsdale Dr.)
MICKLEHAM 6J 99
Mickleham By-Pass
RH5: Mick 5H 99
MICKLEHAM DOWNS 4K 99
Mickleham Dr. RH5: Mick 4J 99
Mickleham Gdns.
SM3: Chea 3K 61
Mickleham Way
CR0: N Add 4N 65
Mickle Hill GU47: Sandh 6F 48
Micklethwaite Rd.
SW6 . . . . .2M 13
Mick Mill's Race
RH13: Col 4E 198
Midas Metropolitan Ind. Est.
SM4: Mord 6H 43
Mid City Lanes
Croydon 3L 63
Middle Av. GU9: Farnh 3J 129
MIDDLE BOURNE 4H 129
Middle Bourne La.
GU10: L Bou 5G 129
Middle Church La.
GU9: Farnh 1G 129
Middle Cl. CR5: Coul 7L 83
GU15: Camb 9F 50
KT17: Eps 8D 60
Middle Farm Cl. KT24: Eff 5L 97
Middle Farm Pl. KT24: Eff 5K 97
Middlefield GU9: Farnh 4F 128
(not continuous)
RH6: Horl 7G 143
Middlefield Cl. GU9: Farnh . . .3F 128
Middlefields CR0: Sels 5H 65
Middle Gordon Rd.
GU15: Camb 1A 70
Middle Grn. RH3: Brock 5A 120
TW18: Stain 8M 21
Middle Grn. Cl. KT5: Surb 5M 41
Middle Hill GU11: Alde 1M 109
TW20: Egh, Eng G 5M 19
Middle La. KT17: Eps 8D 60
TW11: Tedd 7F 24
Middlemarch GU8: Wit 5B 152
Middlemead Cl.
KT23: Book 3A 98
Middlemead Rd.
KT23: Book 3N 97
Middle Mill Halls of Residence
KT1: K Tham . . .6K 203 (2M 41)
Middlemoor Rd.
GU16: Frim 5C 70
Middle Old Pk. GU9: Farnh . . .8E 108
Middle Rd. KT22: Leat 8H 79
SW16 . . . . .1H 45
Middle Row RH19: E Grin 1B 186
Middlesex Ct. KT15: Addl 2L 55
(off Marnham Pl.)
W4 . . . . .1E 12
Middlesex Rd. CR4: Mit 4J 45
Middle St.
CR0: Croy 3C 200 (8N 45)
(not continuous)
GU5: Shere 8B 116
RH3: Betch, Brock 4A 120
RH12: Hors 6J 197
Middleton Gdns.
GU14: Cove 8K 69
Middleton Rd. GU15: Camb . . .9C 50
KT11: Down 6J 77
KT19: Ewe 6C 60
RH12: Hors 6G 197
SM4: Mord 5N 43
SM5: Cars 6B 44
Middleton Way RH11: Ifi 4K 181
Middle Vw. Dr. GU3: Norm 9A 92
Middle Wlk. GU21: Wok 4A 74
Middle Way SW16 . . . . .1H 45
Midgarth Cl. KT22: Oxs 1C 78
Midgeley Rd. RH10: Craw . . .1D 182
Midholm Rd. CR0: Croy 8H 47
MID HOLMWOOD 2H 139
Mid Holmwood La.
RH5: Mid H 2H 139
Midhope Cl. GU22: Wok 6A 74
Midhope Gdns.
GU22: Wok 6A 74
Midhope Rd. GU22: Wok 6A 74
Midhurst Av. CR0: Croy 6L 45
Midhurst Cl. RH11: Craw 2M 181
Midhurst Rd.
GU27: Fern, K Grn 7F 188
(not continuous)
GU27: Hasl 4E 188
Midleton Cl. GU8: Mil 9C 132
Midleton Ind. Est.
GU2: Guil 3L 113
Midleton Ind. Est. Rd.
GU2: Guil 1A 202 (2L 113)
Midleton Rd. GU2: Guil 2L 113
KT3: N Mal 2B 42
Midmoor Rd. SW12 . . . . .2G 29
SW19 . . . . .9J 27
Mid St. RH1: Sth N 6K 123
Midsummer Av. TW4: Houn 7N 9
Midsummer Wlk.
GU21: Wok 3N 73
Midway KT12: Wal T 8J 39
SM3: Sut 6L 43
Midway Av. KT16: Chert 2J 37
TW20: Thor 2D 36
Midway Cl. TW18: Stain 4K 21
Miena Way KT21: A'tead 4K 79
Mike Hawthorn Dr.
GU9: Farnh 9H 109
Milbanke Ct. RG12: Brac 1L 31
Milbanke Way RG12: Brac 1L 31
Milborne Rd. RH10: Craw 7G 182
Milbourne La. KT10: Esh 3C 58
Milbrook KT10: Esh 3C 58
Milburn Wlk. KT18: Eps 2D 80
Milbury Grn. CR6: Warl 5N 85
Milcombe Cl. GU21: Wok 5M 73
Milden Cl. GU16: Frim G 8E 70
Milden Gdns. GU16: Frim G . . .8D 70
Mildred Ct. CR0: Croy 7D 46
Mile Path GU22: Wok 8J 73
(not continuous)
Mile Rd. SM6: Bedd, W'ton 7F 44
(not continuous)
Miles Ct. CR0: Croy 3A 200
Miles La. KT11: Cob 9M 57
RH8: Tand 5J 125
RH9: Tand 5J 125
Miles Pl. GU18: Ligh 8K 51
KT5: Surb 8L 203 (3M 41)
Miles Rd. CR4: Mit 2C 44
GU12: Ash 1F 110
KT19: Eps 8C 60
Mile's Hill RH5: H Mary 8K 137
Milestone Cl. GU23: Rip 9J 75
SM2: Sut 3B 62
Milestone Dr. CR8: Pur 1K 83
MILESTONE GREEN 7B 12
Milestone Ho.
KT1: K Tham 6H 203
Mileswood Farm Ind. Est.
RG40: W'ham 7G 31
MILFORD 1C 152
Milford By-Pass Rd.
GU8: Mil 2A 152
Milford Gdns. CR0: Croy 4F 46
Milford Gro. SM1: Sut 1A 62
Milford Heath Rd.
GU8: Mil 2B 152
Milford Lodge GU8: Mil 2C 152
Milford M. SW16 . . . . .4K 29
Milford Rd. GU8: Els, Mil 7H 131
Milford Station (Rail) 3D 152
Milkhouse Ga.
GU1: Guil 6D 202 (5N 113)
Milking La. BR2: Kes 7F 66
BR6: Dow 8G 67
Mill, The KT13: Weybr 9B 38
Millais RH13: Hors 5N 197
Millais Cl. RH11: Craw 7L 181
Millais Ct. RH13: Hors 4N 197
Millais Cres. KT19: Ewe 2D 60
Millais Rd. KT3: N Mal 6D 42
Millais Way KT19: Ewe 1B 60
Millan Cl. KT15: N Haw 6K 55
Millbank SM6: W'ton 2H 63
Millbank, The
RH11: Craw 3L 181
Millbay La. RH12: Hors 7H 197
MILL BOTTOM 4K 139
Millbottom La. RH5: Holm . . .4K 139
Millbourne Rd.
TW13: Hanw 5M 23
MILLBRIDGE 9J 129
Millbridge Rd. GU46: Yate 7A 48
Millbrook
GU1: Guil 6B 202 (5N 113)
KT13: Weybr 1F 56
Millbrook Way SL3: Poy 5G 7
Mill Chase Leisure Cen. 6A 168
(off Mill Chase Rd.)
Mill Chase Rd. GU35: Bor . . .5A 168
Mill Cleave KT14: W By 8J 55
(off Claremont Rd.)
Mill Cl. GU19: Bag 4H 51
GU27: Hasl 2C 188
KT23: Book 2A 98
RH6: Horl 7C 142
RH19: E Grin 2A 186
SM5: Cars 8E 44
Mill Copse Rd.
GU27: Hasl 4F 188
Mill Cnr. GU51: Fleet 1D 88
Mill Cotts. RH12: Rudg 3E 194
RH19: E Grin 2A 186
Mill Ct. RH10: Craw 4D 182
Millennium Cen., The
GU9: Farnh 2F 128
Millennium Cotts.
GU5: Alb 8L 115
Millennium Ho.
RH11: Craw 6L 181
(off Meridian Cl.)
Millennium Way
RG12: Brac 9N 15
Miller Cen., The 2D 104
Miller Cl. CR4: Mit 6D 44
Miller Rd. CR0: Croy 7K 45
GU4: Guil 9E 94
SW19 . . . . .7B 28
Millers Cl. TW18: Stain 6K 21
Millers Copse KT18: Eps D 6C 80
RH1: Out 4M 143
Millers Ct. TW20: Egh 7F 20
Millers Ga. RH12: Hors 3K 197
Miller's La. RH1: Out 4M 143
SL4: O Win 9J 5
Millers Thumb RG12: Brac 9C 16
Mill Farm Av. TW16: Sunb 8F 22
Mill Farm Bus. Pk.
TW4: Houn 1M 23
Mill Farm Cres. TW4: Houn . . .2M 23
Mill Farm Rd. RH13: Hors . . .4N 197
MILLFIELD 7L 177
Mill Fld. GU19: Bag 4H 51
Millfield
KT1: K Tham . . .5L 203 (2M 41)
TW16: Sunb 9E 22
Millfield La. KT20: K'wood . . .3L 101
Millfield Rd. TW4: Houn 2M 23
Millfields Cres. RH6: Char . . .4J 161
Millford GU21: Wok 4L 73
Millgate Ct. GU9: Farnh 9J 109
Mill Grn. CR4: Mit 6E 44
RG42: Bin 8K 15
Mill Grn. Bus. Pk. CR4: Mit 6E 44
Mill Grn. Rd. CR4: Mit 6D 44
Millhedge Cl. KT11: Cob 3M 77
Mill Hill RH3: Brock 4B 120
SW13 . . . . .5F 12
TN8: Eden, M Grn 3L 147
Mill Hill La. RH3: Brock 3A 120
Mill Hill Rd. SW13 . . . . .5F 12
Millholme Wlk.
GU15: Camb 2G 71
Mill Ho. La. KT16: Chert 3D 36
TW20: Thor 3D 36
Millhouse Pl. SE27 . . . . .5M 29
Milliners Ho. SW18 . . . . .7M 13
Millins Cl. GU47: Owls 6K 49
Mill La. BR6: Dow 6J 67
CR0: Wad 9K 45
GU1: Guil 6C 202 (5N 113)
GU3: P'marsh 2M 133
GU4: Guil 8H 115
GU5: Braml 5B 134
GU7: Goda 7G 132
GU8: Chid 7D 172
GU8: Duns 4A 174
GU8: Wit 5C 152
GU10: Fren 3G 148
GU23: Rip 6M 75
GU24: Pirb 2A 92
GU27: Hasl 4G 188
GU30: Pass 8C 168
GU35: Lind 5B 168
GU46: Yate 7C 48
KT14: Byf 9A 56
KT17: Ewe 5E 60
KT22: Fetc 9G 78
RG12: Brac 3L 31
RH1: Mers 9G 103
RH4: Dork 1K 201 (4H 119)
RH5: For G 3L 157
RH5: Newd 7C 140
RH6: Hook 8B 142
RH7: Ling 1B 166
RH8: Limp 9H 107
RH8: Oxt 1B 126
RH11: Ifi 1M 181
RH13: Itch 8B 196
RH19: Fel 5H 165
SL3: Hort 6D 6
SL4: W'sor 3D 4
SL5: S'hill 1C 34
SM5: Cars 1D 62
TN16: Weste 5L 107
TW20: Thor 3E 36

Mill La. Trad. Est.—Moor Pk. Gdns.

Mill La. Trad. Est.
CR0: Wad 9K 45
Mill Mead TW18: Stain 5H 21
Millmead
GU2: Guil 6B 202 (5M 113)
KT10: Esh 8A 40
KT14: Byf 8A 56
Millmead Ct.
GU2: Guil 7B 202 (5M 113)
Millmead Ter.
GU2: Guil 7B 202 (5M 113)
Millmere GU46: Yate 8C 48
Mill Pl.
KT1: K Tham 5K 203 (2M 41)
SL3: Dat 5N 5
Mill Pl. Cvn. Pk. SL3: Dat 5M 5
Mill Plat TW7: Isle 5G 11
(not continuous)
Mill Plat Av. TW7: Isle 5G 10
Millpond Ct. KT15: Addl 2N 55
Millpond Pl. SM5: Cars 9E 44
Mill Pond Rd.
GU20: Windl 1M 51
Mill Reach GU4: Guil 7H 115
Mill Ride SL5: Asc 9G 17
Mill Rd. GU3: P'marsh 2M 133
KT10: Esh 8A 40
KT11: Cob 2K 77
KT17: Eps 5M 201 (8E 60)
KT20: Tad 1J 101
RH5: Holm 4J 139
RH10: Craw 2F 182
SW19 8A 28
TW2: Twick 3C 24
Mills Cl. RH13: Hors 7M 197
Mill Shaw RH8: Oxt 1B 126
Millshot Cl. SW6 4H 13
Millside SM5: Cars 8D 44
Millside Ct. KT23: Book 3A 98
Millside Pk. SL4: Wink 2K 17
Millside Pl. TW7: Isle 5H 11
Mills Rd. KT12: Hers 2K 57
Mills Row W4 1C 12
Mills Spur SL4: O Win 1L 19
Millstead Cl. KT20: Tad 9G 81
Mill Stream GU9: Weybo 6K 109
Millstream, The
GU27: Hasl 3C 188
Mill St.
KT1: K Tham 5K 203 (2L 41)
RH1: Red 4C 122
SL3: Coln 3F 6
TN16: Weste 5M 107
Millthorpe Rd.
RH12: Hors 4M 197
Mill Vw. Cl. KT17: Ewe 4E 60
Millview Cl. RH2: Reig 1B 122
Mill Vw. Gdns. CR0: Croy 9G 46
Mill Way KT18: Head, Leat 3N 99
KT22: Leat 2M 99
RH19: E Grin 2A 186
TW14: Felt 8J 9
Millway RH2: Reig 3B 122
Millwood RH10: T Hil 4H 185
Millwood Rd. TW3: Houn 8C 10
Milman Cl. RG12: Brac 1E 32
Milne Cl. RH11: Craw 6K 181
Milne Pk. E. CR0: N Add 7N 65
Milne Pk. W. CR0: N Add 7N 65
Milner App. CR3: Cate 8D 84
Milner Cl. CR3: Cate 9C 84
Milner Dr. KT11: Cob 8N 57
TW2: Whitt 1D 24
Milner Pl. SM5: Cars 1E 62
Milner Rd. CR3: Cate 9D 84
CR7: T Hea 2A 46
KT1: K Tham 6H 203 (2K 41)
SM4: Mord 4B 44
SW19 9N 27
Milnthorpe Rd. W4 2C 12
Milnwood Rd. RH12: Hors 5J 197
Milton Av. CR0: Croy 6A 46
RH4: Westc 6D 118
SM1: Sut 9B 44
Milton Cl. GU3: Norm 9M 91
RG12: Brac 5N 31
SL3: Hort 6C 6
SM1: Sut 9B 44
Milton Ct. RG40: W'ham 1A 30
RH4: Dork 5E 118
SW18 8M 13
TW2: Twick 4E 24
Milton Ct. La.
RH4: Dork 2G 201 (5E 118)
Milton Cres. RH19: E Grin 1M 185
Milton Dr. RG40: W'ham 1A 30
TW17: Shep 3N 37
Milton Gdns.
KT18: Eps 8L 201 (1D 80)
RG40: W'ham 2A 30
TW19: Stan 2A 22
Milton Grange GU12: A Va 8E 90
Milton Ho. SM1: Sut 9M 43
Milton Lodge TW2: Twick 1F 24
Milton Mans. *W14 2K 13*
(off Queen's Club Gdns.)
Milton Mt. RH10: Craw 9H 163
Milton Mt. Av.
RH10: Craw 1G 183
Milton Mount Gdns. 9H 163
Milton Rd. CR0: Croy 6A 46
CR3: Cate 8A 84
CR4: Mit 8E 28
Milton Rd. KT12: Wal T 9L 39
KT15: Addl 3J 55
RG40: W'ham 9A 14
RH10: Craw 2G 182
RH12: Hors 5J 197
SM1: Sut 9M 43
SM6: W'ton 3G 63
SW14 6C 12
SW19 7A 28
TW12: Hamp 8A 24
TW20: Egh 6B 20
Miltons Cres. GU7: Goda 9E 132
Milton St. RH4: Westc 6D 118
Miltons Yd. *GU8: Wit 6C 152*
(off Petworth Rd.)
Milton Way KT22: Fetc 3C 98
UB7: W Dray 1A 8
Milward Gdns. RG12: Bin 1H 31
MIMBRIDGE 9K 53
Mimosa Cl. GU35: Lind 4B 168
Mimosa St. SW6 4L 13
Mina Rd. SW19 9M 27
Minchin Cl. KT22: Leat 9G 79
Minchin Grn. RG42: Bin 6H 15
Mincing La. GU24: Chob 4J 53
Mindelheim Av.
RH19: E Grin 8D 166
Minden Rd. SM3: Sut 8K 43
Minehead Rd. SW16 6K 29
Minehurst Rd. GU16: Mytc 1D 90
Minerva Cl. TW19: Stan M 8J 7
Minerva Rd.
KT1: K Tham 3L 203 (1M 41)
Minimax Cl. TW14: Felt 9H 9
Mink Ct. TW4: Houn 5K 9
MINLEY 5C 68
Minley Cl. GU14: Cove 1K 89
Minley Ct. RH2: Reig 2M 121
Minley Gro. GU51: Fleet 2C 88
Minley La. GU17: Min 4C 68
Minley Link Rd.
GU14: Cove 1G 88
Minley Rd. GU14: Cove 8H 69
GU17: Min 6E 68
(Minley La.)
GU17: Min 7B 68
(Yateley Dr.)
GU51: Fleet 7B 68
Minniedale
KT5: Surb 8M 203 (4M 41)
Minorca Av. GU16: Deep 4J 71
Minorca Rd. GU16: Deep 5J 71
KT13: Weybr 1B 56
Minoru Pl. RG42: Bin 6J 15
Minstead Cl. RG12: Brac 2D 32
Minstead Dr. GU46: Yate 1B 68
Minstead Gdns. SW15 1E 26
Minstead Way KT3: N Mal 5D 42
Minster Av. SM1: Sut 8M 43
Minster Cl. GU14: Farnb 4B 90
Minster Ct. GU15: Camb 2L 69
(Tuscam Way)
GU15: Camb 8B 50
(York Rd.)
Minster Dr. CR0: Croy 1B 64
Minster Gdns. KT8: W Mole 3N 39
Minsterley Av. TW17: Shep 3F 38
Minster Rd. GU7: Goda 9H 133
Minstrel Gdns.
KT5: Surb 8M 203 (3M 41)
Minstrels Cl. TN8: Eden 1L 147
Mint, The GU7: Goda 7G 132
Mint Gdns.
RH4: Dork 1J 201 (4G 119)
Mint La. KT20: Lwr K 7M 101
Mint Rd. SM6: W'ton 1F 62
SM7: Ban 3A 82
Mint St. GU7: Goda 7G 133
Mint Wlk.
CR0: Croy 4C 200 (9N 45)
CR6: Warl 4G 85
GU21: Knap 4H 73
Mintwater Cl. KT17: Ewe 6F 60
Mirabel Rd. SW6 3L 13
Miranda Wlk. RH11: Craw 5K 181
Misbrooks Grn. Rd.
RH5: B Grn, Cap 1L 159
Missenden Cl. TW14: Felt 2G 23
Missenden Gdns.
SM4: Mord 5A 44
Mission Sq. TW8: Brent 2L 11
Mistletoe Cl. CR0: Croy 7G 46
Mistletoe Rd. GU46: Yate 2C 68
Mistley Ct. KT18: Eps 7K 201
Mistley Gdns. RH6: Hook 9B 142
Misty's Fld. KT12: Wal T 7K 39
MITCHAM 2D 44
Mitcham Ct. GU15: Camb 6F 50
Mitcham Gdn. Village
CR4: Mit 4E 44
Mitcham Ind. Est. CR4: Mit 9E 28
Mitcham Junction Station (Rail & CT)
4E 44
Mitcham La. SW16 7G 28
Mitcham Pk. CR4: Mit 3C 44
Mitcham Rd.
CR0: Croy 1A 200 (5J 45)
GU15: Camb 6E 50
SW17 6D 28
Mitcham Stop (CT) 3C 44
Mitchell Gdns. RH13: Slin 5L 195
Mitchell Pk. Farm Cotts.
GU28: North 8G 190
Mitchell Rd. BR6: Orp 1N 67
Mitchells Cl. GU4: Chil 9A 114
Mitchells Rd.
RH10: Craw 3D 182
Mitchells Row GU4: Chil 1A 134
Mitchener's La. RH1: Blet 3A 124
Mitchley Av. CR2: Sande 9N 63
CR8: Pur 9N 63
Mitchley Gro. CR2: Sande 9D 64
Mitchley Hill CR2: Sande 9C 64
Mitchley Vw. CR2: Sande 9D 64
Mitford Bldgs. *SW6 3M 13*
(off Dawes Rd.)
Mitford Cl. KT9: Ches 3J 59
Mitford Wlk. RH11: Craw 6M 181
Mitre Cl. SM2: Sut 4A 62
TW17: Shep 5E 38
Mitre Ct. RH12: Hors 6H 197
Mitre Pl. RG42: Warf 7N 15
Mixbury Gro. KT13: Weybr 3E 56
Mixnams La. KT16: Chert 2J 37
Mizen Cl. KT11: Cob 1L 77
Mizen Way KT11: Cob 2K 77
Moat, The KT3: N Mal 9D 26
Moat Ct. KT16: Otter 3E 54
KT21: A'tead 4L 79
Moated Farm Dr.
KT15: Addl, N Haw 4L 55
Moat La. KT8: E Mol 2F 40
Moat Lodge GU6: Cranl 7M 155
Moat Rd. RH19: E Grin 8A 166
Moat Side TW13: Hanw 5K 23
Moats La. RH1: Sth N 1J 143
Moat Wlk. RH10: Craw 2G 183
Moberly Rd. SW4 1H 29
Moberly Way CR8: Ken 7A 84
Mocatta M. RH1: Mers 9G 103
Mockford M. RH1: Mers 9G 102
Modder Pl. SW15 7J 13
Model Cotts. GU24: Pirb 8A 72
SW14 7B 12
Moffat Ct. SW19 6M 27
Moffat Rd. CR7: T Hea 1N 45
SW17 5D 28
Moffats Cl. GU47: Sandh 7F 48
MOGADOR 6K 101
Mogador Rd. KT20: Lwr K 6K 101
Mogden La. TW7: Isle 8F 10
Moir Cl. CR2: Sande 5D 64
Mole Abbey Gdns.
KT8: W Mole 2B 40
Mole Bus. Pk. KT22: Leat 8G 78
Mole Cl. GU14: Cove 8J 69
RH11: Craw 1N 181
Mole Ct. KT19: Ewe 1B 60
Molember Ct. KT8: E Mol 3E 40
Molember Rd. KT8: E Mol 4E 40
Mole Rd. KT12: Hers 2L 57
KT22: Fetc 8D 78
Moles Cl. RG40: W'ham 3C 30
Molesey Av. KT8: W Mole 4N 39
Molesey Cl. KT12: Hers 1M 57
Molesey Dr. SM3: Chea 8K 43
Molesey Pk. Av.
KT8: W Mole 4B 40
Molesey Pk. Cl. KT8: E Mol 4C 40
Molesey Pk. Rd.
KT8: W Mole, E Mol 4B 40
Molesey Rd. KT8: W Mole 6M 39
KT12: Hers, Wal T, W Mole
2L 57
Molesford Rd. SW6 4M 13
Molesham Cl. KT8: W Mole 2B 40
Molesham Way
KT8: W Mole 2B 40
Moles Hill KT22: Oxs 7D 58
Moles Mead TN8: Eden 1L 147
Mole St. RH5: Ockl 3A 158
Molesworth Rd. KT11: Cob 9H 57
Mole Valley Pl.
KT21: A'tead 6K 79
Molins Ct. *RH11: Craw 6M 181*
(off Brideake Cl.)
Mollison Dr. SM6: W'ton 4H 63
Mollison Sq. *SM6: W'ton 4H 63*
(off Mollison Dr.)
Molloy Ct. GU21: Wok 3C 74
Molly Huggins Cl.
SW12 1G 28
Molly Millars Bri.
RG41: W'ham 4A 30
Molly Millars Cl.
RG41: W'ham 4A 30
Molly Millars La.
RG41: W'ham 4A 30
Molyneux Dr. SW17 5F 28
Molyneux Rd. GU7: Goda 4J 133
GU20: Windl 3A 52
KT13: Weybr 2B 56
Monahan Av. CR8: Pur 8K 63
Monarch Cl. BR4: W Wick 1B 66
RH11: Craw 6M 181
TW14: Felt 1F 22
Monarch M. SW16 6L 29
Monarch Pde. CR4: Mit 1D 44
Monaveen Gdns.
KT8: W Mole 2B 40
Moncks Row SW18 9L 13
Mondial Way UB3: Harl 3D 8
Money Av. CR3: Cate 9B 84
Money Rd. CR3: Cate 9A 84
Mongers La. KT17: Ewe 6E 60
(not continuous)
Monkey Puzzle Rdbt.
GU14: Cove 2K 89
Monkleigh Rd. SM4: Mord 2K 43
Monks All. RG42: Bin 6G 14
Monks Av. KT8: W Mole 4N 39
Monks Cl. GU14: Farnb 1A 90
(not continuous)
SL5: Asc 5M 33
Monks Ct. RH2: Reig 3N 121
Monks Cres. KT12: Wal T 7J 39
KT15: Addl 2K 55
Monksdene Gdns.
SM1: Sut 9N 43
Monks Dr. SL5: Asc 5M 33
Monksfield RH10: Craw 3D 182
Monks Grn. KT22: Fetc 8C 78
Monks Gro. GU3: Comp 8B 112
Monkshanger GU9: Farnh 1K 129
Monks Hill Sports Cen. 4G 65
Monkshood Cl.
RG40: W'ham 1D 30
Monks La. RH5: Oak 4N 177
TN8: Eden 6F 126
MONKS ORCHARD 6H 47
Monks Orchard Rd.
BR3: Beck 7K 47
Monks Path GU14: Farnb 9B 70
Monks Pl. CR3: Cate 9E 84
Monks Rd. GU25: V Wat 3N 35
SL4: W'sor 5A 4
SM7: Ban 4M 81
Monks Wlk. GU9: Farnh 4L 129
KT16: Chert 3G 37
RH2: Reig 3N 121
SL5: Asc 5M 33
TW20: Thor 2F 36
Monks Way BR3: Beck 5K 47
TW18: Stain 8M 21
UB7: Harm 2N 7
Monks Well GU10: Farnh 2N 129
Monkswell La. CR5: Coul 2N 101
Monkton La.
GU9: Farnh, Hale 7K 109
Monkton Pk. GU9: Farnh 8L 109
Monmouth Av. KT1: H Wic 8J 25
Monmouth Cl. CR4: Mit 3J 45
Mono La. TW13: Felt 3J 23
Monro Dr. GU2: Guil 9K 93
Monroe Dr. SW14 8A 12
Monro Pl. KT19: Eps 5N 59
Mons Barracks GU11: Alde 8A 90
Mons Cl. GU11: Alde 6C 90
Monsell Gdns. TW18: Stain 6G 21
Monson Rd. RH1: Red 9D 102
Mons Wlk. TW20: Egh 6E 20
Montacute Cl. GU14: Farnb 1B 90
Montacute Rd. CR0: N Add 5M 65
SM4: Mord 5B 44
Montague Av. CR2: Sande 8B 64
Montague Cl. GU15: Camb 1N 69
GU18: Ligh 6L 51
KT12: Wal T 6J 39
RG40: W'ham 9D 14
Montague Dr. CR3: Cate 9N 83
Montague Rd.
CR0: Croy 1A 200 (7M 45)
SW19 8N 27
TW3: Houn 6B 10
TW10: Rich 9L 11
Montagu Gdns. SM6: W'ton 1G 62
Montagu Rd. SL3: Dat 4L 5
Montana Cl. CR2: Sande 6A 64
Montana Gdns. SM1: Sut 2A 62
Montana Rd. SW17 4E 28
SW20 9H 27
Monteagle La. GU46: Yate 1A 68
Montem Rd. KT3: N Mal 3D 42
Montford Rd. TW16: Sunb 3H 39
Montfort Pl. SW19 2J 27
Montfort Rd. RH1: Salf 2D 142
Montgomerie Dr. GU2: Guil 7K 93
Montgomery Av.
KT10: H Wood 8E 40
Montgomery Cl. CR4: Mit 3J 45
GU47: Sandh 7G 49
Montgomery Ct.
CR2: S Croy 8F 200
KT22: Leat 7H 79
(off Levett Rd.)
W4 3B 12
Montgomery Gdns.
SM2: Sut 4B 62
Montgomery of Alamein Ct.
RG12: Brac 9B 16
Montgomery Path
GU14: Cove 2L 89
Montgomery Rd.
GU14: Cove 2L 89
GU22: Wok 5A 74
Montgomery Way CR8: Ken 7A 84
Montholme Rd. SW11 1D 28
Montolieu Gdns.
SW15 8G 13
Montpelier Ct. SL4: W'sor 5F 4
Montpelier Rd. CR8: Pur 6M 63
SM1: Sut 1A 62
Montpelier Row TW1: Twick 1J 25
Montpellier Ct. KT12: Wal T 5H 39
Montreal Ct. GU11: Alde 3L 109
Montrell Rd. SW2 2J 29
Montreux Ct. RH11: Craw 3N 181
Montrose Av. SL3: Dat 3M 5
TW2: Whitt 1B 24
Montrose Cl. GU16: Frim 4C 70
GU51: Fleet 5C 88
TW15: A'ford 7D 22
Montrose Gdns. CR4: Mit 1D 44
KT22: Oxs 8D 58
SM1: Sut 8N 43
Montrose Rd. TW14: Bedf 9E 8
Montrose Wlk. KT13: Weybr 9C 38
Montrose Way SL3: Dat 4N 5
Montrouge Cres.
KT17: Eps D 3H 81
Mont St Aignan Way
TN8: Eden 2L 147
Montserrat Rd. SW15 7K 13
Monument Bri. Ind. Est. E.
GU21: Wok 2D 74
Monument Bri. Ind. Est. W.
GU21: Wok 2C 74
Monument Bus. Cen.
GU21: Wok 2D 74
Monument Grn.
KT13: Weybr 9C 38
Monument Hill
KT13: Weybr 1C 56
Monument Rd. GU21: Wok 1C 74
KT13: Weybr 1C 56
Monument Way E.
GU21: Wok 2D 74
Monument Way W.
GU21: Wok 2C 74
Moon Hall Rd. GU6: Ewh 1D 156
Moons, The RH1: Mers 9G 102
Moons Hill GU10: Fren 9G 129
Moons La. RH7: Dorm 3F 166
RH13: Hors 7L 197
MOOR, THE 3F 20
Moor Cl. GU47: Owls 6K 49
Moorcroft Cl. RH11: Craw 2N 181
Moorcroft Rd. SW16 4J 29
Moordale Av. RG42: Brac 9K 15
Moore Cl. CR4: Mit 1F 44
GU10: Tong 4D 110
GU52: C Cro 8B 88
KT15: Addl 2K 55
SW14 6B 12
Moore Ct. RH12: Hors 7G 196
Moore Gro. Cres.
TW20: Egh 7B 20
Moore Pk. Ct. *SW6 3N 13*
(off Fulham Rd.)
Moore Pk. Rd. SW6 3M 13
Moore Rd. GU24: B'wood 8M 71
GU52: C Cro 8B 88
SE19 7N 29
Moores Grn. RG40: W'ham 9D 14
Moores La. SL4: E Wic 1C 4
Moore's Rd.
RH4: Dork 1L 201 (4H 119)
Moore Way SM2: Sut 5M 61
Moorfield GU27: Hasl 3D 188
RH5: Holm 4K 139
Moorfield Cen., The
GU1: Guil 8N 93
Moorfield Point GU1: Guil 8A 94
Moorfield Rd. GU1: Guil 8N 93
KT9: Ches 2L 59
Moorfields Cl. TW18: Stain 9G 21
Moorhayes Dr. TW18: Lale 2L 37
Moorhead Rd. RH12: Hors 3A 198
Moorhead Rdbt.
RH12: Hors 1A 198
Moorholme GU22: Wok 6A 74
MOORHOUSE 5H 107
MOORHOUSE BANK 6J 107
Moorhouse Rd.
RH8: Limp, Weste 9H 107
TN16: Weste 9H 107
Moorhurst La. RH5: Holm 7G 138
Moorings, The GU26: Hind 6C 170
KT14: W By 8L 55
KT23: Book 3A 98
RH19: E Grin 7K 165
Moorings Ho. TW8: Brent 3J 11
MOOR JUNC. 3K 7
Moorland Cl. TW2: Whitt 1A 24
Moorland Rd. RH10: Craw 6G 183
UB7: Harm 2L 7
Moorlands *KT12: Wal T 9H 39*
(off Ashley Pk. Rd.)
Moorlands, The
GU22: Wok 8B 74
Moorlands Cl. GU26: Hind 5C 170
GU51: Fleet 5C 88
Moorlands Pl. GU15: Camb 1M 69
Moorlands Rd.
GU15: Camb 2M 69
Moor La. GU22: Wok 9A 74
KT9: Ches 1L 59
RG12: Bin 2H 31
RH7: Dorm 9D 146
TN8: Dorm, M Grn 9D 146
TW18: Stain 4G 20
TW19: Stain 2F 20
UB7: Harm 2L 7
Moormead Dr. KT19: Ewe 2D 60
Moor Mead Rd. TW1: Twick 9G 11
Moormede Cres.
TW18: Stain 5H 21
Moor Pk. *RH6: Horl 9F 142*
(off Aurum Cl.)
Moor Pk. Cres. RH11: Ifi 4J 181
Moor Pk. Gdns.
KT2: K Tham 8D 26

Moor Pk. Ho. RG12: Brac 5K 31
(off St Andrews)
Moor Pk. La. GU9: Farnh 9K 109
(not continuous)
GU10: Farnh 1M 129
Moor Pk. Way GU9: Farnh 1L 129
Moor Pl. GU20: Windl 2M 51
RH19: E Grin 8N 165
Moor Rd. GU14: Farnb 6M 69
GU16: Frim 6D 70
GU27: Hasl 3A 188
Moors, The GU10: Tong 5C 110
Moorside Cl. GU14: Cove 5M 69
Moors La. GU8: Els 8G 130
Moorsom Way CR5: Coul 4H 83
Moral Rd. GU17: Min 5E 68
Moray Av. GU47: C Tow 7J 49
(not continuous)
Moray Ct. CR2: S Croy 8B 200
Morcote Cl. GU4: Chil 1A 134
Mordaunt Dr. RG45: Crow 4G 48
MORDEN 2N 43
Morden Cl. KT20: Tad 7J 81
RG12: Brac 3D 32
Morden Ct. SM4: Mord 3N 43
Morden Ct. Pde.
SM4: Mord 3N 43
Morden Gdns. CR4: Mit 3B 44
Morden Hall Rd.
SM4: Mord 2N 43
Morden Ho. SM4: Mord 3M 43
MORDEN PARK 5K 43
Morden Pk. Pool 5L 43
Morden Rd. CR4: Mit 3A 44
SM4: Mord 3A 44
SW19 . . . . .9N 27
Morden Road Stop (CT) 1N 43
Morden South Station (Rail)
. . . . .4M 43
Morden Station (Tube) 2N 43
Morden Way SM3: Sut 6M 43
More Circ. GU7: Goda 4H 133
More Cl. CR8: Pur 7L 63
Morecombe Cl.
RH11: Craw 5L 181
Morecoombe Cl.
KT2: K Tham 8A 26
Moreland Av. SL3: Coln 3E 6
Moreland Cl. SL3: Coln 3E 6
More La. KT10: Esh 8B 40
Morella Cl. GU25: V Wat 3N 35
Morella Rd. SW12 . . . . .1D 28
More Rd. GU7: Goda 4H 133
Moresby Av. KT5: Surb 6A 42
Moretaine Rd.
TW15: A'ford 4M 21
Moreton Almshouses
TN16: Weste 4M 107
Moreton Av. TW7: Isle 4E 10
Moreton Cl. GU10: Churt 9K 149
GU52: C Cro 9A 88
Moreton Rd.
CR2: S Croy . . .8E 200 (2A 64)
KT4: W Pk 8F 42
Morgan Ct. GU14: Cove 1H 89
(off Whetstone Rd.)
SM5: Cars 1D 62
TW15: A'ford 6C 22
Morgan Ho. RH10: Craw 2F 182
(off Trafalgar Gdns.)
MORGAN'S GREEN 7D 194
Morgan Wlk. BR3: Beck 3L 47
Morie St. SW18 . . . . .8N 13
Moring Rd. SW17 . . . . .5E 28
Morland Av. CR0: Croy 7B 46
Morland Cl. CR4: Mit 2C 44
TW12: Hamp 6N 23
Morland Rd. CR0: Croy 7B 46
GU11: Alde 5N 109
SM1: Sut 2A 62
Morland's Rd. GU11: Alde 8B 90
Morley Cl. GU46: Yate 1A 68
Morley Ct. KT22: Fetc 8D 78
Morley Rd. CR2: Sande 6C 64
GU9: Farnh 2H 129
SM3: Sut 7L 43
TW1: Twick 9K 11
Morningside Rd. KT4: W Pk . . .8H 43
Mornington Av. W14 . . . . .1L 13
Mornington Av. Mans.
W14 . . . . .1L 13
(off Mornington Av.)
Mornington Cl. TN16: B Hil 4F 86
Mornington Cres.
TW5: C'ford 4J 9
Mornington Rd.
TW15: A'ford 6D 22
Mornington Wlk.
TW10: Ham 5J 25
Morrell Av. RH12: Hors 3M 197
Morris Cl. CR0: Croy 4H 47
Morris Ct. SL4: W'sor 4B 4
Morris Gdns. SW18 . . . . .1M 27
Morrish Rd. SW2 . . . . .1J 29
Morrison Ct. RH11: Craw 8N 181
Morrison Ho. SW2 . . . . .2L 29
(off High Trees)
Morris Rd. GU14: Farnb 5B 90
RH1: Sth N 5J 123
TW7: Isle 6F 10
Morston Cl. KT20: Tad 7G 81
Morth Gdns. RH12: Hors 7J 197
Mortimer Cl. SW16 . . . . .3H 29
Mortimer Cres. KT4: W Pk 9C 42
Mortimer Ho. W14 . . . . .1K 13
(off North End Rd.)
Mortimer Rd. CR4: Mit 9D 28
RH5: Cap 4K 159
TN16: B Hil 8E 66
MORTLAKE 6C 12
Mortlake Cl. CR0: Bedd 9J 45
Mortlake Crematorium
TW9: Rich 5A 12
Mortlake Dr. CR4: Mit 9C 28
Mortlake High St.
SW14 . . . . .6C 12
Mortlake Rd.
TW9: Kew, Rich 3N 11
Mortlake Station (Rail) 6B 12
Mortlake Ter. TW9: Kew 3N 11
(off Mortlake Rd.)
Morton KT20: Tad 8J 81
Morton Cl. GU16: Frim 7D 70
GU21: Wok 2M 73
RH11: Craw 9N 181
SM6: W'ton 4K 63
Morton Gdns. SM6: W'ton 2G 62
Morton M. SW5 . . . . .1N 13
Morton Rd. GU21: Wok 2N 73
RH19: E Grin 2A 186
SM4: Mord 4B 44
Morval Cl. GU14: Cove 1K 89
Morven Rd. SW17 . . . . .4D 28
Moselle Cl. GU14: Cove 9J 69
Moselle Rd. TN16: B Hil 5G 87
Mosford Cl. RH6: Horl 6D 142
Mospey Cres. KT17: Eps 2E 80
Mosquito Cl. SM6: W'ton 4J 63
(off Mollison Dr.)
MOSS END 3N 15
Mossfield KT11: Cob 9H 57
Moss Gdns. CR2: Sels 4G 64
TW13: Felt 3H 23
Moss La. GU7: Goda 7G 133
Mosslea Rd. CR3: Whyte 3C 84
Mossville Gdns. SM4: Mord 2L 43
Moston Cl. UB3: Harl 1G 8
Mostyn Ho. RG42: Brac 8N 15
(off Merryhill Rd.)
Mostyn Rd. SW19 . . . . .9L 27
Mostyn Ter. RH1: Red 4E 122
Moth Cl. SM6: W'ton 4J 63
MOTSPUR PARK 5F 42
Motspur Pk. KT3: N Mal 5E 42
Motspur Park Station (Rail)
. . . . .4G 42
Motts Hill La.
KT20: Tad, Wal H 1F 100
Mouchotte Cl. TN16: B Hil 8D 66
Moulsham Copse La.
GU46: Yate 8A 48
Moulsham Grn. GU46: Yate . . .8A 48
Moulsham La. GU46: Yate 8A 48
Moulton Av. TW3: Houn 5M 9
Mount, The CR2: S Croy 8C 200
CR5: Coul 2E 82
CR6: Warl 6D 84
GU2: Guil 8A 202 (5M 113)
GU6: Cranl 8N 155
GU6: Ewh 4F 156
GU21: Knap 6F 72
GU21: Wok 5N 73
(off Elm Rd.)
GU21: Wok 6K 73
(St Johns Ct.)
GU25: V Wat 5N 35
GU27: G'wood 7K 171
GU35: Head 3F 168
GU51: Fleet 3B 88
KT3: N Mal 2E 42
KT4: W Pk 1G 61
KT10: Esh 3A 58
KT13: Weybr 8F 38
KT17: Ewe 6E 60
KT20: Lwr K 4L 101
KT22: Fetc 1E 98
RH11: Ifi 1G 180
Mt. Angelus Rd. SW15 . . . . . .1E 26
Mt. Ararat Rd. TW10: Rich 8L 11
Mount Av. CR3: Cate 2N 103
Mountbatten Cl.
RH11: Craw 7A 182
Mountbatten Ct.
GU11: Alde 2M 109
(off Birchett Rd.)
Mountbatten Gdns.
BR3: Beck 3H 47
Mountbatten Lodge
GU9: Farnh 1G 128
(off The Hart)
Mountbatten M.
GU15: Camb 8A 50
SW18 . . . . .1A 28
Mountbatten Ri.
GU47: Sandh 6E 48
Mountbatten Sq. SL4: W'sor 4F 4
Mount Cl. CR8: Ken 3A 84
GU6: Ewh 5F 156
GU22: Wok 8M 73
KT22: Fetc 1E 98
RH10: Craw 2H 183
SM5: Cars 5E 62
Mount Cl., The
GU25: V Wat 5N 35
Mountcombe Cl. KT6: Surb 6L 41
Mount Cotts. RH11: Ifi 2H 181
Mount Ct. BR4: W Wick 8N 47
GU2: Guil 6B 202 (5M 113)
SW15 . . . . .6K 13
Mount Dr., The
RH2: Reig 1B 122
Mountearl Gdns.
SW16 . . . . .4K 29
Mt. Ephraim La.
SW16 . . . . .4H 29
Mt. Ephraim Rd.
SW16 . . . . .4H 29
Mount Felix KT12: Wal T 7G 38
MOUNT HERMON 6M 73
Mt. Hermon Cl. GU22: Wok . . .6N 73
Mt. Hermon Rd.
GU22: Wok 6N 73
Mount Holme KT7: T Dit 6H 41
Mount La. RG12: Brac 2A 32
RH10: T Hil 5D 184
Mount Lee TW20: Egh 6B 20
Mount M. TW12: Hamp 9B 24
Mount Noddy 8A 166
Mt. Nod Rd. SW16 . . . . .4K 29
Mount Pk. SM5: Cars 4E 62
Mount Pk. Av. CR2: S Croy . . .5M 63
Mount Pl.
GU2: Guil 6B 202 (5M 113)
Mt. Pleasant
GU2: Guil 7B 202 (5M 113)
GU9: Farnh 2F 128
GU47: Sandh 6F 48
KT13: Weybr 9B 38
KT17: Ewe 6E 60
KT24: Eff 6M 97
KT24: W Hors 7C 96
RG12: Brac 2A 32
RG41: W'ham 2A 30
RH5: A Ham 9G 116
SE27 . . . . .5N 29
TN16: B Hil 4F 86
Mt. Pleasant Cl. GU18: Ligh . . .6L 51
Mt. Pleasant Rd.
CR3: Cate 1D 104
GU12: Alde 2A 110
GU35: Lind 4A 168
KT3: N Mal 2B 42
RH7: Ling 7M 145
Mount Ri. RH1: Red 5B 122
Mount Rd. CR4: Mit 1B 44
GU6: Cranl 8N 155
GU22: Wok 8L 73
GU24: Chob 8L 53
KT3: N Mal 2C 42
KT9: Ches 2M 59
SW19 . . . . .3M 27
TW13: Hanw 4M 23
Mountsfield Cl.
TW19: Stan M 9J 7
Mounts Hill SL4: Wink 3N 17
Mountside CR3: Cate 2C 104
GU2: Guil 7A 202 (5L 113)
Mt. Side Pl. GU22: Wok 5B 74
Mount St.
RH4: Dork . . .2H 201 (5G 118)
Mount Vw. GU11: Alde 3M 109
Mountview Cl. RH1: Red 5C 122
Mountview Dr. RH1: Red 5C 122
Mount Vw. Rd. KT10: Clay 4H 59
Mount Vs. SE27 . . . . .4M 29
Mount Way SM5: Cars 5E 62
Mountwood KT8: W Mole 2B 40
Mountwood Cl. CR2: Sande . . .6E 64
Moushill La. GU8: Mil 2B 152
Mowat Ct. KT4: W Pk 8E 42
(off The Avenue)
Mowatt Rd. GU26: G'hott 7B 170
Mowbray Av. KT14: Byf 9N 55
Mowbray Cres. TW20: Egh 6C 20
Mowbray Dr. RH11: Craw 5L 181
Mowbray Gdns. RH4: Dork 3H 119
Mowbray Rd. TW10: Ham 4J 25
Mower Cl. RG40: W'ham 1E 30
Mower Pl. GU6: Cranl 6N 155
MOWSHURST 8N 127
Moxey Cl. TN16: B Hil 9E 66
Moylan Rd. W6 . . . . .2K 13
Moyne Ct. GU21: Wok 5J 73
Moyne Rd. RH11: Craw 7A 182
Moys Cl. CR0: Croy 5J 45
Moyser Rd. SW16 . . . . .6F 28
Muchelney Rd. SM4: Mord 5A 44
Muckhatch La. TW20: Thor 2D 36
Muggeridge Cl.
CR2: S Croy 8E 200 (2A 64)
Muggeridges Hill
RH12: Cap 1L 179
MUGSWELL 3N 101
Muirdown Av. SW14 . . . . .7C 12
Muirfield Cl. RH11: Ifi 4J 181
Muirfield Ho. RG12: Brac 5K 31
(off St Andrews)
Muirfield Rd. GU21: Wok 5K 73
Mulberries, The
GU9: Farnh 8L 109
Mulberry Av. SL4: W'sor 6J 5
TW19: Stan 2N 21
Mulberry Cl. GU12: A Va 9E 90
GU21: Wok 1A 74
GU47: Owls 7J 49
KT13: Weybr 9C 38
RG45: Crow 3H 49
RH12: Hors 3J 197
SW16 . . . . .5G 28
Mulberry Ct. GU4: Guil 1F 114
KT6: Surb 6K 41
RG12: Brac 4C 32
RG40: W'ham 2B 30
TW1: Twick 4F 24
Mulberry Cres. TW8: Brent 3H 11
Mulberry Dr. SL3: Lang 1A 6
Mulberry Gdns.
RH12: Bro H 5E 196
Mulberry Ga. SM7: Ban 3L 81
Mulberry Ho. BR2: Brom 1N 47
Mulberry La. CR0: Croy 7C 46
Mulberry M. SM6: W'ton 3G 62
Mulberry Pl. RH5: Newd 9B 140
W6 . . . . .1F 12
Mulberry Rd. RH11: Craw 9N 161
Mulberry Trees TW17: Shep . . .6E 38
Mulberry Way GU14: Cove 9J 69
Mulgrave Ct. SM2: Sut 3N 61
(off Mulgrave Rd.)
Mulgrave Rd.
CR0: Croy 5D 200 (9A 46)
GU16: Frim 4D 70
SM2: Sut 4L 61
SW6 . . . . .2L 13
Mulgrave Way GU21: Knap 5H 73
Mulholland Cl. CR4: Mit 1F 44
Mullards Cl. CR4: Mit 7D 44
Mullein Wlk. RH11: Craw . . .7M 181
Mullens Rd. TW20: Egh 6D 20
Muller Rd. SW4 . . . . .1H 29
Mullins Path SW14 . . . . .6C 12
Mulroy Dr. GU15: Camb 9E 50
Multon Rd. SW18 . . . . .1B 28
Muncaster Cl. TW15: A'ford . . .5B 22
Muncaster Rd.
TW15: A'ford 6C 22
Munday Ct. RG42: Bin 8K 15
Munday's Boro GU3: Put 8L 111
Munday's Boro Rd.
GU3: Put 8L 111
Mund St. W14 . . . . .1L 13
Mundy Ct. SL4: Eton 2G 4
Munnings Dr. GU47: C Tow 9J 49
Munnings Gdns. TW7: Isle 8D 10
Munro Ho. KT11: Cob 8L 57
Munro Way GU11: Alde 5B 90
Munslow Gdns. SM1: Sut 1B 62
Munstead Heath Rd.
GU5: Braml 9K 133
GU8: Bus 9K 133
Munstead Pk. GU8: Bus 8M 133
Munstead Vw. GU3: Art 7L 113
Munstead Vw. Rd.
GU5: Braml 6N 133
Munster Av. TW4: Houn 8M 9
Munster Ct. SW6 . . . . .5L 13
TW11: Tedd 7J 25
Munster M. SW6 . . . . .3K 13
Munster Rd. SW6 . . . . .3K 13
TW11: Tedd 7H 25
Murdoch Cl. TW18: Stain 6J 21
Murdoch Rd. RG40: W'ham 3B 30
Murfett Cl. SW19 . . . . .3K 27
Murray Av. TW3: Houn 8B 10
Murray Ct. RH11: Craw 8M 181
RH13: Hors 4A 198
SL5: S'hill 5N 33
TW2: Twick 3D 24
Murray Grn. GU21: Wok 1E 74
Murray Ho. KT16: Otter 3E 54
Murray Rd. GU14: Cove 2L 89
KT16: Otter 3E 54
SW19 . . . . .7J 27
TW10: Ham 3H 25
W5 . . . . .1J 11
Murray's La.
KT14: W By, Byf 1M 75
Murrays Rd. GU11: Alde 7B 90
Murrell Hill La. RG42: Bin 8H 15
Murrell Rd. GU12: Ash 1E 110
Murrells La. GU15: Camb 3N 69
Murrell's Wlk. KT23: Book 1A 98
Murreys, The KT21: A'tead 5J 79
Murreys Ct. KT21: A'tead 5K 79
Murtmead La. GU3: Put 9L 111
Musard Rd. W6 . . . . .2K 13
Muscal W6 . . . . .2K 13
(off Field Rd.)
Muschamp Rd. SM5: Cars 8C 44
Museum Hill GU27: Hasl 2H 189
Mus. of Eton Life 2G 5
Mus. of Richmond 8K 11
Mus. of Rugby, The 9E 10
Musgrave Av.
RH19: E Grin 2A 186
Musgrave Cres. SW6 . . . . .3M 13
Musgrave Rd. TW7: Isle 4F 10
Mushroom Castle
RG42: Wink R 7F 16
Musquash Way TW4: Houn 5K 9
Mustard Mill Rd.
TW18: Stain 5H 21
Mustians SL4: Eton 2F 4
(off Eton Wick Rd.)
Mustow Pl. SW6 . . . . .5L 13
Mutton Hill RG12: Bin 9H 15
RH7: Dorm 3C 166
Mutton Oaks RG12: Bin 9J 15
Muybridge Rd. KT3: N Mal 1B 42
Muybridge Yd. KT6: Surb 6M 41
Myers Way GU16: Frim 4H 71
Mylne Cl. W6 . . . . .1F 12
Mylne Sq. RG40: W'ham 2C 30
Mylor Cl. GU21: Wok 1A 74
Mynn's Cl. KT18: Eps 1A 80
MYNTHURST 4G 141
Mynthurst RH2: Leigh 4G 141
MYRKE 1J 5
Myrke, The SL3: Dat 1J 5
Myrna Cl. SW19 . . . . .8C 28
Myrtle Av. TW14: Felt 8F 8
Myrtle Cl. GU18: Ligh 7M 51
SL3: Poy 4G 6
Myrtle Dr. GU17: B'water 1J 69
Myrtle Gro. KT3: N Mal 1B 42
Myrtle Pas. RH4: Dork 2J 201
Myrtle Rd. CR0: Croy 9K 47
RH4: Dork 1J 201 (4G 119)
SM1: Sut 2A 62
TW3: Houn 5C 10
TW12: H Hill 7C 24
MYTCHETT 1D 90
Mytchett Farm Cvn. Pk.
GU16: Mytc 3D 90
Mytchett Heath GU16: Mytc . . .3E 90
Mytchett Lake Rd.
GU16: Mytc 4E 90
Mytchett Pl. Rd. GU12: A Va . . .4E 90
GU16: Mytc 2E 90
GU24: Pirb 4F 90
Mytchett Rd. GU16: Mytc 1D 90
Myton Rd. SE21 . . . . .4N 29

N

Naafi Rdbt. GU11: Alde 2N 109
Nadine Ct. SM6: W'ton 5G 62
Nailsworth Cres.
RH1: Mers 7H 103
Nairn Cl. GU16: Frim 4C 70
NALDERSWOOD 4H 141
Naldrett Cl. RH12: Hors 4M 197
Naldretts La. RH12: Rudg 3E 194
Nallhead Rd. TW13: Hanw 6K 23
Namba Roy Cl. SW16 . . . . . . .5K 29
Namton Dr. CR7: T Hea 3K 45
Napier Av. SW6 . . . . .6L 13
Napier Cl. GU11: Alde 6C 90
RG45: Crow 2H 49
Napier Ct. CR3: Cate 9B 84
GU21: Wok 3A 74
SW6 . . . . .6L 13
(off Ranelagh Gdns.)
Napier Dr. GU15: Camb 8E 50
Napier Gdns. GU1: Guil 2D 114
Napier La. GU12: A Va 9E 90
Napier Lodge TW15: A'ford 7E 22
Napier Rd. CR2: S Croy 4A 64
RG45: Crow 3H 49
SE25 . . . . .3E 46
TW7: Isle 7G 10
TW15: A'ford 8E 22
Napier Wlk. TW15: A'ford 8E 22
Napier Way RH10: Craw 9D 162
Napoleon Av. GU14: Farnb 8N 69
Napoleon Rd. TW1: Twick 1H 25
Napper Cl. SL5: Asc 1G 33
Napper Pl. GU6: Cranl 9N 155
Nappers Wood GU27: Fern . . .9E 188
Narborough St. SW6 . . . . .5N 13
Narrow La. CR6: Warl 6E 84
Narwhal Inuit Art Gallery 1C 12
Naseby RG12: Brac 7N 31
Naseby Cl. TW7: Isle 4E 10
Naseby Ct. KT12: Wal T 8K 39
NASH 3C 66
Nash Cl. GU14: Cove 1L 89
SM1: Sut 9B 44
Nash Dr. RH1: Red 1D 122
Nash Gdns. RH1: Red 1D 122
SL5: Asc 1J 33
Nashlands Cotts.
RH17: Hand 6N 199
Nash La. BR2: Kes 4C 66
Nash Pk. RG42: Bin 7G 15
Nash Rd. RH10: Craw 6C 182
SL3: Lang 1B 6
Nassau Rd. SW13 . . . . .4E 12
Nasturtium Dr. GU24: Bis 2D 72
Natalie Cl. TW14: Bedf 1E 22
Natalie M. TW2: H Hill 4D 24
Natal Rd. CR7: T Hea 2A 46
SW16 . . . . .7H 29
National Archives, The 3N 11
National Walks TW4: Houn 6N 9
Natural History Mus.
Eton 2G 4
Navigation Ho. KT15: Addl 1N 55
Navigator Pk. UB2: S'hall 1K 9
Neale Cl. RH19: E Grin 7L 165
Neath Gdns. SM4: Mord 5A 44
Neb La. RH8: Oxt 9M 105
Needham Cl. SL4: W'sor 4B 4
Needles Bank RH9: Gods 9E 104
(not continuous)
Needles Cl. RH12: Hors 7H 197
Neil Cl. TW15: A'ford 6D 22
Neil Wates Cres. SW2 . . . . . . .2L 29
Nella Rd. W6 . . . . .2J 13
Nell Ball RH14: Plais 6A 192
Nell Gwynne Av. SL5: S'hill . . .3A 34
TW17: Shep 5E 38
Nell Gwynne Cl. KT19: Eps . . .7N 59
SL5: S'hill 3A 34

Norman Av.—Oak Dell

Norman Av. CR2: Sande 6N 63
KT17: Eps 8E 60
TW1: Twick 1J 25
TW13: Hanw 3M 23
Normanby Cl. SW15 . . . . .8L 13
Norman Cl. GU35: Bor 6A 168
KT18: Tat C 6G 81
Norman Colyer Ct.
KT19: Eps 6C 60
Norman Ct. GU9: Farnh 2H 129
TN8: Eden 1K 147
Norman Cres. TW5: Hest 3L 9
Normand Gdns. W14 . . . . .2K 13
(off Greyhound Rd.)
Normand Mans. W14 . . . . .2K 13
(off Normand M.)
Normand M. W14 . . . . .2K 13
Normand Rd. W14 . . . . .2L 13
NORMANDY 9M 91
Normandy RH12: Hors 7J 197
Normandy Cl. GU16: Deep 6J 71
RH10: Craw 5F 182
RH19: E Grin 1B 186
NORMANDY COMMON 9L 91
Normandy Comn. La.
GU3: Norm 9M 91
Normandy Gdns.
RH12: Hors 7J 197
Normandy Wlk. TW20: Egh 6E 20
Norman Hay Trad. Est., The
UB7: Sip 3A 8
Norman Ho. TW13: Hanw 3N 23
(off Watermill Way)
Normanhurst TW15: A'ford 6B 22
Normanhurst Cl.
RH10: Craw 3D 182
Normanhurst Dr.
TW1: Twick 8G 11
Normanhurst Rd.
KT12: Wal T 8L 39
SW2 . . . . .3K 29
Norman Keep RG42: Warf 9D 16
Norman Rd. CR7: T Hea 4M 45
SM1: Sut 2M 61
SW19 . . . . .8A 28
TW15: A'ford 7E 22
Normansfield Av.
TW11: Tedd 8J 25
Normans Gdns.
RH19: E Grin 9A 166
Normans La. TN8: Eden 4G 147
Norman's Rd. RH1: Out 6N 143
RH6: Smal 6N 143
Normanton Av. SW19 . . . . .3M 27
Normanton Rd.
CR2: S Croy 8F 200 (2B 64)
Normington Cl. SW16 . . . . .6L 29
NORNEY 5B 132
Norney GU8: S'ford 5B 132
Norrels Dr. KT24: E Hor 4G 96
(not continuous)
Norrels Ride KT24: E Hor 3G 97
Norreys Av. RG40: W'ham 2C 30
Norris Cl. KT19: Eps 7A 60
Norris Hill Rd. GU51: Fleet 5D 88
GU52: Fleet 5D 88
Norris Rd. TW18: Stain 5H 21
Norroy Rd. SW15 . . . . .7J 13
Norstead Pl. SW15 . . . . .3F 26
North Acre SM7: Ban 3L 81
Northampton Cl.
RG12: Brac 2B 32
Northampton Rd. CR0: Croy . . .8D 46
Northanger Rd. SW16 . . . . .7J 29
NORTH ASCOT 9H 17
North Ash RH12: Hors 4J 197
North Av. GU9: H End 5J 109
KT12: Whit V 5F 56
SM5: Cars 4E 62
TW9: Kew 4N 11
Northborough Rd.
SW16 . . . . .2H 45
Northbourne GU7: Goda 3J 133
Nth. Breache Rd.
GU6: Ewh 4H 157
NORTH BRIDGE 3F 172
Northbrook Copse
RG12: Brac 5D 32
Northbrook Rd. CR0: Croy 4A 46
GU11: Alde 4N 109
NORTH CAMP 7A 90
North Camp Station (Rail) 5D 90
Nth. Camp Sta. Rdbt.
GU14: Farnb 5C 90
NORTHCHAPEL 9D 190
NORTH CHEAM 9H 43
North Cheam Sports Club 9J 43
Northcliffe Cl. KT4: W Pk 9D 42
North Cl. GU12: Alde 3C 110
GU14: Farnb 6M 69
RH5: Nth H 9J 119
RH10: Craw 2D 182
SL4: W'sor 4C 4
SM4: Mord 3K 43
TW14: Bedf 9E 8
North Comn. KT13: Weybr 1D 56
Northcote KT15: Addl 1M 55
Northcote Av. KT5: Surb 6A 42
TW7: Isle 8G 10
Northcote Cl. KT24: W Hors . . .3D 96
Northcote Cres.
KT24: W Hors 3D 96
Northcote La. GU5: Sha G 5F 134
Northcote Pk. KT22: Oxs 1C 78
Northcote Rd. CR0: Croy 5A 46
GU12: A Va 6D 90
GU14: Cove 8L 69
KT3: N Mal 2B 42
KT24: W Hors 3D 96
TW1: Twick 8G 11
Northcott RG12: Brac 7M 31
Northcott Gdns. GU14: Cove . . .9J 69
North Ct. GU7: Goda 4E 132
Northcroft Cl. TW20: Eng G 6L 19
Northcroft Gdns.
TW20: Eng G 6L 19
Northcroft Rd. KT19: Ewe 4D 60
TW20: Eng G 6L 19
Northcroft Vs. TW20: Eng G . . .6L 19
Northdale Ct. SE25 . . . . .2C 46
North Dene TW3: Houn 4B 10
North Down CR2: Sande 7B 64
Northdown Cl.
RH12: Hors 4M 197
Northdown La.
GU1: Guil 8F 202 (6A 114)
Northdown Rd. CR3: Wold . . .2K 105
SM2: Sut 6M 61
Northdowns GU6: Cranl 9N 155
Nth. Downs Cres.
CR0: N Add 5L 65
(not continuous)
Nth. Downs Rd. CR0: N Add . . .6L 65
Northdown Ter.
RH19: E Grin 7N 165
North Dr. BR3: Beck 3L 47
BR6: Orp 1N 67
GU24: B'wood 8N 71
GU25: V Wat 5H 35
SW16 . . . . .5G 28
TW3: Houn 5C 10
North E. Surrey Crematorium
SM4: Mord 5H 43
NORTH END 7L 165
North End
CR0: Croy 2B 200 (8N 45)
RH19: E Grin 7L 165
North End Cres. W14 . . . . .1L 13
North End Ho. W14 . . . . .1K 13
North End La. BR6: Dow 7J 67
SL5: S'dale 6E 34
North End Pde. W14 . . . . .1K 13
(off North End Rd.)
North End Rd. SW6 . . . . .2L 13
W14 . . . . .1K 13
Northerams Woods Nature Reserve
. . . . .3K 31
Northernhay Wlk.
SM4: Mord 3K 43
Northern Perimeter Rd.
TW6: Lon A 4C 8
Northern Perimeter Rd. (West)
TW6: Lon A 4M 7
Northey Av. SM2: Chea 6J 61
Nth. Eyot Gdns. W6 . . . . .1E 12
Nth. Farm Rd. GU14: Cove 6L 69
NORTH FARNBOROUGH 1N 89
NORTH FELTHAM 9J 9
Nth. Feltham Trad. Est.
TW14: Felt 8J 9
Northfield GU4: Chil 2A 134
GU8: Wit 6C 152
GU18: Ligh 7M 51
Northfield Cl. GU12: Alde 3B 110
GU52: C Cro 7D 88
Northfield Ct. TW18: Stain 9K 21
Northfield Cres. SM3: Chea . . .1K 61
Northfield Farm M.
KT11: Cob 9H 57
Northfield Pl. KT13: Weybr 4C 56
Northfield Rd. GU52: C Cro 7C 88
KT11: Cob 9H 57
TW5: Hest 2L 9
TW18: Stain 9K 21
Northfields KT17: Eps 7D 60
KT21: A'tead 5L 79
(not continuous)
SW18 . . . . .7M 13
Northfields Prospect Bus. Cen.
SW18 . . . . .7M 13
Northfleet Lodge
GU22: Wok 6A 74
North Fryerne GU46: Yate 7C 48
North Gdns. SW19 . . . . .8B 28
NORTHGATE 2C 182
Northgate Av. RH10: Craw . . .3C 182
Northgate Dr. GU15: Camb 8E 50
Northgate Pl. RH10: Craw . . .2C 182
Nth. Gate Rd. GU14: Farnb 3A 90
Northgate Rd. RH6: Gat 2D 162
(off Racecourse Rd.)
RH10: Craw 3B 182
North Grn. RG12: Brac 9B 16
North Gro. KT16: Chert 5H 37
Nth. Hatton Rd. TW6: Lon A 4E 8
Nth. Heath Cl. RH12: Hors . . .3K 197
Nth. Heath Est.
RH12: Hors 2K 197
Nth. Heath La.
RH12: Hors 4K 197
Nth. Holmes Cl.
RH12: Hors 3A 198
NORTH HOLMWOOD 9H 119
North Ho. GU6: Cranl 5L 155
Nth. Hyde La. TW5: Hest 1M 9
UB2: S'hall 1L 9
Northington Cl. RG12: Brac . . .5D 32
Northlands Av. BR6: Orp 1N 67
Northlands Bungs.
RH5: Newd 2A 160
Northlands Bus. Pk.
RH12: Warn 5C 178
Northlands Cotts.
RH12: Warn 5D 178
Northlands Rd.
RH12: Hors 1L 197
RH12: Warn 6D 178
North La. GU12: Alde 1B 110
TW11: Tedd 7F 24
Nth. Lodge Cl. SW15 . . . . .8J 13
Nth. Lodge Dr. SL5: Asc 1G 33
NORTH LOOE 9H 61
North Mall GU51: Fleet 4A 88
SW18 . . . . .8N 13
(off Buckhold Rd.)
TW18: Stain 5H 21
(in Elmsleigh Shop. Cen.)
North Mead RH1: Red 9D 102
RH10: Craw 1C 182
Northmead GU14: Farnb 1N 89
North Moors GU1: Guil 8A 94
NORTH MUNSTEAD 2L 153
Nth. Munstead La.
GU7: Bus 1K 153
GU8: Bus 1K 153
Northolt Rd. TW6: Lon A 4M 7
North Pde. KT9: Ches 2M 59
RH12: Hors 3J 197
North Pk. La. RH9: Gods 7D 104
North Pas. SW18 . . . . .8M 13
Nth. Perimeter Rd.
RH6: Gat 4B 162
(off Old Control Tower Rd.)
North Pl. CR4: Mit 8D 28
TW11: Tedd 7F 24
Northpoint Cl. SM1: Sut 9A 44
Nth. Pole La. BR2: Kes 3B 66
North Rd. BR4: W Wick 7L 47
GU2: Guil 9L 93
GU12: A Va 9D 90
GU21: Wok 3C 74
KT6: Surb 5K 41
KT12: Hers 2K 57
RH2: Reig 6L 121
RH10: Craw 1E 182
SL5: Asc 9F 16
SW19 . . . . .7A 28
TW5: Hest 2K 9
TW8: Brent 2L 11
TW9: Kew 4N 11
TW9: Rich 6N 11
TW14: Bedf 9E 8
Northrop Rd. TW6: Lon A 4F 8
NORTH SHEEN 6N 11
North Sheen Station (Rail) . . .7N 11
North Side GU10: Tong 5D 110
North Side Ct GU10: Tong 5E 110
Northspur Rd. SM1: Sut 9M 43
Nth. Station App.
RH1: Sth N 5K 123
Northstead Rd. SW2 . . . . .3L 29
North St.
GU1: Guil 5C 202 (4N 113)
GU7: Goda 4H 133
KT22: Leat 8G 79
RH1: Red 2D 122
RH4: Dork 2J 201 (5G 119)
RH10: T Hil 5D 184
RH12: Hors 6K 197
SL4: Wink 5K 17
SM5: Cars 9D 44
TW7: Isle 6G 11
TW20: Egh 6B 20
Nth. Terminal App.
RH6: Gat 2D 162
North Ter. SL4: W'sor 3G 5
NORTH TOWN 1C 110
Northtown Trad. Est.
GU12: Alde 2C 110
Northumberland Av.
TW7: Isle 4F 10
Northumberland Cl.
RG42: Warf 8D 16
TW19: Stan 9N 7
Northumberland Cres.
TW14: Felt 9F 8
Northumberland Gdns.
CR4: Mit 4H 45
TW7: Isle 3G 11
Northumberland Pl.
TW10: Rich 8K 11
Nth. Verbena Gdns.
W6 . . . . .1F 12
North Vw. RG12: Bin 2H 31
SW19 . . . . .6H 27
North Vw. Cres. KT18: Tat C . . .4H 81
North Wlk. CR0: N Add 3L 65
(not continuous)
Northway GU2: Guil 1K 113
GU7: Goda 4E 132
RH6: Gat 2D 162
(off Gatwick Way)
SM4: Mord 2K 43
SM6: W'ton 1G 63
Northway Rd. CR0: Croy 5C 46
Northweald La.
KT2: K Tham 6K 25
Nth. Weylands Ind. Est.
KT12: Wal T 8M 39
Northwood Av. CR8: Pur 8L 63
GU21: Knap 5G 72
Nth. Wood Ct. SE25 . . . . .2D 46
Northwood Ho.
KT2: K Tham 3M 203
Northwood Pk.
RH10: Craw 8E 162
Northwood Rd. SM5: Cars 3E 62
TW6: Lon A 4M 7
Nth. Worple Way
SW14 . . . . .6C 12
Norton Av. KT5: Surb 6A 42
Norton Cl. GU3: Worp 5G 93
Norton Ct. BR3: Beck 1J 47
Norton Gdns. SW16 . . . . .1J 45
Norton La. KT11: Cob 6G 77
Norton Pk. SL5: S'hill 4N 33
Norton Rd. GU15: Camb 2G 71
RG40: W'ham 3B 30
Norwich Av. GU15: Camb 3C 70
Norwich Rd. CR7: T Hea 2N 45
RH10: Craw 5E 182
Norwood Cl. KT24: Eff 6M 97
TW2: Twick 3D 24
UB2: S'hall 1A 10
Norwood Farm La.
KT11: Cob 7H 57
Norwood Grn. Rd.
UB2: S'hall 1A 10
Norwood High St.
SE27 . . . . .4M 29
NORWOOD HILL 7J 141
Norwood Hill RH6: N Hil 9H 141
Norwood Hill Rd.
RH6: Char, N Hil 8K 141
Norwood Junction Station (Rail)
. . . . .3D 46
NORWOOD NEW TOWN 7N 29
Norwood Pk. Rd. SE27 . . . . . . .6N 29
Norwood Rd. KT24: Eff 6M 97
SE24 . . . . .2M 29
SE27 . . . . .3M 29
UB2: S'hall 1A 10
Norwood Ter. UB2: S'hall 1B 10
Notley End TW20: Eng G 8M 19
Notson Rd. SE25 . . . . .3E 46
Nottingham Cl. GU21: Wok 5J 73
Nottingham Ct. GU21: Wok 5J 73
(off Nottingham Cl.)
Nottingham Rd.
CR2: S Croy 7B 200 (1N 63)
SW17 . . . . .2D 28
TW7: Isle 5F 10
Nova M. SM3: Sut 7K 43
Nova Rd. CR0: Croy 7M 45
Novello St. SW6 . . . . .4M 13
Novello Theatre 4A 34
Nowell Rd. SW13 . . . . .2F 12
Nower Cl. E. RH4: Dork 6F 118
Nower Cl. W. RH4: Dork 6F 118
Nower Rd.
RH4: Dork 3H 201 (5G 118)
Nowhurst Bus. Pk.
RH12: Bro H 2A 196
Nowhurst La.
RH12: Bro H 3N 195
Noyna Rd. SW17 . . . . .4D 28
Nuffield Ct. TW5: Hest 3N 9
Nuffield Dr. GU47: Owls 6L 49
Nugee Ct. RG45: Crow 2G 49
Nugent Cl. GU8: Duns 3B 174
Nugent Rd. GU2: Guil 3G 112
SE25 . . . . .2C 46
Numa Ct. TW8: Brent 3K 11
Nunappleton Way
RH8: Oxt 1C 126
Nuneaton RG12: Brac 5C 32
Nunns Fld. RH5: Cap 5J 159
Nuns Wlk. GU25: V Wat 4N 35
RH5: Ran C 8B 98
NUPTOWN 2D 16
Nuptown La. RG42: Warf 2D 16
Nursery Av. CR0: Croy 8G 46
Nursery Cl. CR0: Croy 8G 46
GU16: Frim G 7D 70
GU21: Wok 3M 73
GU51: Fleet 5E 88
KT15: Wood 6H 55
KT17: Ewe 6D 60
KT20: Wal H 3G 100
RH5: Cap 5J 159
SW15 . . . . .7J 13
TW14: Felt 1J 23
(not continuous)
Nursery Gdns. GU4: Guil 9D 114
TW4: Houn 8N 9
TW12: Hamp 5N 23
TW16: Sunb 1G 39
TW18: Stain 7K 21
Nursery Hill GU5: Sha G 6F 134
Nurserylands
RH11: Craw 3M 181
Nursery La. RH6: Hook 9B 142
SL5: Asc 9J 17
Nursery Pl. SL4: O Win 9L 5
Nursery Rd. CR4: Mit 2C 44
CR7: T Hea 3A 46
GU7: Goda 4J 133
GU21: Knap 4G 73
KT20: Wal H 3F 100
SM1: Sut 1A 62
SW19 . . . . .8K 27
(Elm Gro.)
Nursery Rd. SW19 . . . . .1N 43
(Parkleigh Rd.)
TW16: Sunb 1F 38
Nursery Way RH8: Oxt 7A 106
TW19: Wray 9N 5
Nutbourne GU9: Weybo 5K 109
Nutbourne Cotts.
GU8: Hamb 2H 173
Nutbourne Ct.
RH12: Hors 3K 197
(off Woodstock Cl.)
TW18: Stain 8H 21
NUTCOMBE 7C 170
Nutcombe La. GU26: Hind . . .9C 170
RH4: Dork 2G 201 (5F 118)
Nutcroft Gro. KT22: Fetc 8E 78
NUTFIELD 2K 123
Nutfield Cl. SM5: Cars 9C 44
Nutfield Ct. GU15: Camb 8B 50
RH1: Nut 1K 123
Nutfield Marsh Rd.
RH1: Nut 9H 103
NUTFIELD PARK 6L 123
Nutfield Pas. CR7: T Hea 3M 45
(off Nutfield Rd.)
Nutfield Priory 3H 123
Nutfield Rd. CR5: Coul 3E 82
CR7: T Hea 3M 45
RH1: Mers 7G 102
RH1: Red, Nut 3F 122
Nutfield Station (Rail) 5J 123
Nuthatch Cl. GU10: Ews 5C 108
TW19: Stan 2A 22
Nuthatch Gdns. RH2: Reig . . .7A 122
Nuthatch Way RH10: T Hil 4F 184
RH12: Hors 1K 197
Nuthurst RG12: Brac 4C 32
Nuthurst Av. GU6: Cranl 7N 155
SW2 . . . . .3K 29
Nuthurst Cl. RH11: Craw 2M 181
Nutley RG12: Brac 7M 31
Nutley Cl. GU46: Yate 1C 68
Nutley Ct. RH2: Reig 3L 121
(off Nutley La.)
Nutley Dean Bus. Pk.
RH6: N Hil 5K 141
Nutley Gro. RH2: Reig 3M 121
Nutley La. RH2: Reig 2L 121
Nutmeg Ct. GU14: Cove 9H 69
Nutshell La. GU9: U Hal 6H 109
Nuttall Gdns. GU6: Cranl 5N 155
Nutty La. TW17: Shep 2D 38
Nutwell St. SW17 . . . . .6C 28
Nutwood GU7: Goda 5G 133
(off Frith Hill Rd.)
Nutwood Av. RH3: Brock 4B 120
Nutwood Cl. RH3: Brock 4B 120
Nye Bevan Ho. SW6 . . . . .3L 13
(off St Thomas's Way)
Nyefield Pk. KT20: Wal H 4F 100
Nylands Av. TW9: Kew 4N 11
Nymans Cl. RH12: Hors 1N 197
Nymans Ct. RH10: Craw 6F 182
Nymans Gdns. SW20 . . . . .2G 42

O

Oakapple Cl. CR2: Sande 1E 84
RH11: Craw 8N 181
Oak Av. CR0: Croy 7K 47
GU47: Owls 6J 49
TW5: Hest 3L 9
TW12: Hamp 6M 23
TW20: Egh 8E 20
Oak Bank CR0: N Add 3M 65
Oakbank GU22: Wok 6A 74
KT22: Fetc 1C 98
Oakbank Av. KT12: Wal T 6N 39
Oakbark Ho. TW8: Brent 3J 11
(off High St.)
Oakbury Rd. SW6 . . . . .5N 13
Oak Cl. GU6: Ewh 4F 156
GU7: Goda 3H 133
GU8: Chid 5D 172
KT20: Box H 8A 100
RH10: Cop 7L 163
SM1: Sut 8A 44
Oakcombe Cl. KT3: N Mal 9D 26
Oak Cnr. RH5: B Grn 7J 139
Oak Cott. Cl. GU3: Wood V . . .2F 112
Oak Cotts. GU27: Hasl 2C 188
(not continuous)
RH17: Hand 5N 199
Oak Ct. GU9: Farnh 2G 129
GU14: Farnb 4C 90
RH10: Craw 8B 162
RH19: E Grin 8N 165
(off Newlands Cres.)
Oak Cft. RH19: E Grin 1C 186
Oakcroft Bus. Cen.
KT9: Ches 1M 59
Oakcroft Cl. KT14: W By 1H 75
Oakcroft Rd. KT9: Ches 1M 59
KT14: W By 1H 75
Oakcroft Vs. KT9: Ches 1M 59
Oakdale RG12: Brac 5B 32
Oakdale La. TN8: C Hil 2L 127
Oakdale Rd. KT13: Weybr 9B 38
KT19: Ewe 5C 60
SW16 . . . . .6J 29
Oakdale Way CR4: Mit 6E 44
Oak Dell RH10: Craw 2G 183

Old Epsom Rd.—Osborne Ct.

Old Epsom Rd. GU4: E Cla 9M 95
Old Esher Cl. KT12: Hers 2L 57
Old Esher Rd. KT12: Hers 2L 57
Old Farleigh Rd. CR2: Sels 6F 64
CR6: Warl 9H 65
Old Farm Cl. SW17 . . . . .3C 28
TW4: Houn 7N 9
Old Farm Dr. RG12: Brac 8A 16
Old Farm Ho. Dr. KT22: Oxs . . .2D 78
Old Farm Pas. TW12: Hamp . . .9C 24
Old Farm Pl. GU12: A Va 9D 90
Old Farm Rd. GU1: Guil 9N 93
TW12: Hamp 7N 23
(not continuous)
Old Farnham La.
GU9: Farnh 3H 129
GU10: Farnh 2A 128
Old Ferry Dr. TW19: Wray 9M 5
Oldfield Cl. RH6: Horl 1D 162
Oldfield Ct. KT5: Surb 8L 203
Oldfield Gdns. KT21: A'tead . . .6K 79
Oldfield Ho. *W4 . . . . .1D 12*
(off Devonshire Rd.)
Oldfield Rd. RH6: Horl 1D 162
SW19 . . . . .7K 27
TW12: Hamp 9N 23
Oldfields Rd. SM1: Sut 9L 43
Oldfields Trad. Est.
SM1: Sut 9M 43
Oldfield Wood GU22: Wok 4D 74
Old Forge, The RH13: Slin . . .5L 195
Old Forge Cl. RH12: Fay 8E 180
Old Forge Ct. GU4: Chil 9B 114
Old Forge Cres.
TW17: Shep 5C 38
Old Forge End GU47: Sandh . . .8G 49
Old Fox Cl. CR3: Cate 8M 83
Old Frensham Rd.
GU10: L Bou 5J 129
Old Glebe GU27: Fern 9F 188
Old Green La. GU15: Camb . . .8A 50
Old Guildford Rd.
GU16: Frim G 9F 70
GU24: Pirb 1H 91
RH12: Bro H 4D 196
Old Harrow La.
TN16: Weste 6L 87
Old Haslemere Rd.
GU27: Hasl 3G 189
Old Heath Rd. KT13: Weybr . . .3B 56
Old Heath Way GU9: U Hal . . .5H 109
Old Hill BR6: Dow 3M 67
GU22: Wok 7N 73
Old Hill Est. GU22: Wok 7N 73
Old Holbrook RH12: Hors 9L 179
Old Hollow
RH10: Craw, Wor 3K 183
Old Horsham Rd.
RH5: B Grn, Holm 6J 139
RH11: Craw 5N 181
Old Hospital Cl. SW12 . . . . . . .2D 28
Old Ho. Cl. KT17: Ewe 6E 60
SW19 . . . . .6K 27
Old Ho. Gdns. TW1: Twick 9J 11
Oldhouse La. GU20: Windl 4M 51
(not continuous)
GU24: Bis 1D 72
Old House M. RH12: Hors 6J 197
OLD ISLEWORTH 6H 11
Old Ively Rd. GU14: Farnb 5F 88
Old Kiln Cl. GU10: Churt 8L 149
Old Kiln La. GU10: Churt 7L 149
RH3: Brock 3B 120
Old Kiln Mus. & Rural Life Cen.
. . . . .8L 129
Old Kings Head Ct.
RH4: Dork 2K 201
Old Kingston Rd.
KT4: W Pk 8B 42
Old Lands Hill RG12: Brac 9B 16
Old La. GU10: Dock 5F 148
GU11: Alde 5M 109
GU12: Alde 1C 110
KT11: Cob 4C 76
RH8: Oxt 7B 106
(not continuous)
TN16: Tats 7F 86
Old La., The GU10: Churt 1L 169
Old La. Gdns. KT11: Cob 9H 77
Old Lodge Cl. GU7: Goda 8E 132
Old Lodge La.
CR8: Ken, Pur 4M 83
CR8: Pur 9K 63
Old Lodge Pl. TW1: Twick 9H 11
Old London Rd.
KT2: K Tham 3K 203 (1L 41)
KT18: Eps D 6F 80
(not continuous)
KT24: E Hor 4H 97
RH5: Mick 5J 99
OLD MALDEN 7D 42
Old Malden La. KT4: W Pk 8C 42
Old Malt Way GU21: Wok 4N 73
Old Manor Cl.
RH11: Craw 1M 181
Old Manor Ct.
RH11: Craw 1M 181
Old Manor Dr. TW7: Isle 9C 10
Old Manor Gdns.
GU4: Guil 9E 114
Old Manor Ho. M.
TW17: Shep 2B 38
Old Manor La. GU4: Guil 9E 114
Old Manor Yd. SW5 . . . . .1N 13
Old Market Ct. SM1: Sut 1N 61
Old Martyrs RH11: Craw 9B 162
Old Merrow St. GU4: Guil 9F 94
Old Mill La. RH1: Mers 6F 102
Old Millmeads
RH12: Hors 3J 197
Old Mill Pl. GU27: Hasl 1D 188
TW19: Wray 9D 6
Old Monteagle La.
GU46: Yate 9A 48
Old Mus. Ct. GU27: Hasl 2H 189
Old Nursery Pl.
TW15: A'ford 6C 22
Old Oak Av. CR5: Chip 6C 82
Old Oak Cl. KT9: Ches 1M 59
KT11: Cob 9J 57
Old Orchard KT14: Byf 8A 56
TW16: Sunb 1K 39
Old Orchard, The
GU9: Farnh 4E 128
Old Orchards RH10: Wor 3J 183
Old Overthorpe
RH6: Smal 1M 163
OLD OXTED 8N 105
Old Palace La. TW9: Rich 8J 11
Old Palace Rd.
CR0: Croy 4A 200 (9M 45)
GU2: Guil 4K 113
KT13: Weybr 9C 38
Old Palace Ter. TW9: Rich 8K 11
Old Palace Yd. TW9: Rich 8J 11
Old Park Av. SW12 . . . . .1E 28
Old Park Cl. GU9: U Hal 6F 108
Old Park La. GU9: Farnh 7F 108
GU10: U Hal 5E 108
(not continuous)
Old Park M. TW5: Hest 3N 9
Old Parvis Rd. KT14: W By 8L 55
Old Pasture Rd.
GU16: Frim 4D 70
Old Pharmacy Ct.
RG45: Crow 3G 49
Old Pond Cl. GU15: Camb 5A 70
Old Portsmouth Rd.
GU3: Art, P'marsh 3L 133
GU7: Art, Goda, P'marsh
. . . . .3L 133
GU8: Thur 6H 151
GU15: Camb 1E 70
Old Post Cotts.
RH12: Bro H 5E 196
(off Wickhurst La.)
Old Pottery Cl. RH2: Reig 5N 121
Old Pound Cl. TW7: Isle 4G 10
Old Pound Cotts. RH11: Ifi . . .2J 181
Old Priory La. RG42: Warf 7B 16
Old Pumphouse Cl.
GU51: Fleet 3C 88
Old Quarry, The
GU27: Hasl 4D 188
Old Rectory, The
KT23: Book 5N 97
Old Rectory Cl.
GU5: Braml 5B 134
KT20: Wal H 2F 100
Old Rectory Dr. GU12: Ash . . .2F 110
Old Rectory Gdns.
GU7: Bus 9J 133
GU14: Farnb 1B 90
Old Rectory La. KT24: E Hor . . .4F 96
Old Redstone Dr.
RH1: Red 4E 122
Old Reigate Rd.
RH3: Betch 3A 120
RH4: Dork 2M 119
Oldridge Rd. SW12 . . . . .1E 28
Old Rd. KT15: Addl 4H 55
RH3: Buck 3D 120
RH19: E Grin 9B 166
Old Rope Wlk. TW16: Sunb 2J 39
Old Row Ct. RG40: W'ham 2B 30
Old St Mary's KT24: W Hors . . .7C 96
Old Sawmill La.
RG45: Crow 1H 49
Old School Cl. BR3: Beck 1G 47
GU1: Guil 3C 202 (3N 113)
GU12: Ash 1E 110
(not continuous)
GU51: Fleet 4B 88
SW19 . . . . .1M 43
Old School Ct. KT22: Leat 9H 79
TW19: Wray 1A 20
Old School Ho. *TN8: Eden 2L 147*
(off Lingfield Rd.)
Old School La. GU46: Yate 9B 48
RH3: Brock 6A 120
Old School M. KT13: Weybr . . .1E 56
TW18: Stain 6F 20
Old School Pl. CR0: Wad 1L 63
GU22: Wok 8A 74
RH7: Ling 7N 145
Old Schools La. KT17: Ewe 5E 60
Old School Sq. KT7: T Dit 5F 40
Old School Ter. *GU51: Fleet 4B 88*
(off Old School Cl.)
SM3: Chea 4J 61
Old School Yd. RH1: Nut 2K 123
Old Slade La. SL0: R Pk 1H 7
SL3: Coln 1H 7
Old Station App. KT22: Leat . . .8G 78
Old Station Cl.
RH10: Craw D 2E 184
Old Station Gdns.
TW11: Tedd 7G 24
(off Victoria Rd.)
Old Station Way
GU7: Goda 6H 133
Oldstead RG12: Brac 4B 32
Old Stede Cl. KT21: A'tead 4M 79
Old St., The KT22: Fetc 1D 98
Old Studio Cl. CR0: Croy 6A 46
OLD SURREY HALL 5G 167
Old Swan Yd. SM5: Cars 1D 62
Old Tilburstow Rd.
RH9: S Gods 3F 124
Old Town
CR0: Croy 4A 200 (9M 45)
Old Tye Av. TN16: B Hil 3G 87
Old Water Yd.
RH4: Dork 1H 201 (4G 118)
Old Welmore GU46: Yate 1D 68
Old Westhall Cl. CR6: Warl 6F 84
Old Wharf Way
KT13: Weybr 1A 56
Old Wickhurst La.
RH12: Bro H 7D 196
OLD WINDSOR 9K 5
Old Windsor Lock
SL4: O Win 8M 5
OLD WOKING 8D 74
Old Wokingham Rd.
RG40: W'ham 6G 31
RG45: Crow 9H 31
Old Woking Rd.
GU22: Wok, Pyr 6D 74
KT14: W By 9H 55
Oldwood Chase
GU14: Cove 2G 89
Old Yard, The RH1: Blet 2N 123
Old York Rd. SW18 . . . . .8N 13
Oleander Cl. BR6: Farnb 2M 67
RG45: Crow 9E 30
Oliver Av. SE25 . . . . .2C 46
Oliver Cl. KT15: Addl 1J 55
W4 . . . . .2A 12
Oliver Gro. SE25 . . . . .3C 46
Olive Rd. SW19 . . . . .8A 28
Oliver Rd. KT3: N Mal 1B 42
RH12: Hors 7G 197
SL5: Asc 3L 33
SM1: Sut 1B 62
Olivette St. SW15 . . . . .6J 13
Olivia Ct. RG41: W'ham 2A 30
Olivia Dr. SL3: Lang 1B 6
Olivier Rd. RH10: Craw 4H 183
Ollerton RG12: Brac 7M 31
Olley Cl. SM6: W'ton 4J 63
Olveston Wlk. SM5: Cars 5B 44
O'Mahoney Ct. SW17 . . . . .4A 28
Omega Rd. GU21: Wok 3C 74
Omega Way TW20: Thor 9E 20
Omnibus Bldg.
RH2: Reig 4N 121
One Tree Hill Rd.
GU4: Guil 4D 114
Ongar Cl. KT15: Addl 3H 55
Ongar Hill KT15: Addl 3J 55
Ongar Pde. KT15: Addl 3J 55
Ongar Pl. KT15: Addl 3J 55
Ongar Rd. KT15: Addl 2J 55
SW6 . . . . .2M 13
Onslow Av. SM2: Chea 6L 61
TW10: Rich 8L 11
Onslow Cl. GU22: Wok 4C 74
KT7: T Dit 7E 40
Onslow Ct. RH10: Craw 9E 162
Onslow Cres. GU22: Wok 4C 74
Onslow Dr. SL5: Asc 8L 17
Onslow Gdns. CR2: Sande 8D 64
KT7: T Dit 7E 40
SM6: W'ton 3G 62
Onslow Ho. KT2: K Tham 1L 203
Onslow M. KT16: Chert 5H 37
Onslow Rd. CR0: Croy 6K 45
GU1: Guil 3D 202 (3N 113)
KT3: N Mal 3F 42
KT12: Hers 1G 57
SL5: S'dale 6E 34
TW10: Rich 8L 11
Onslow St.
GU1: Guil 5B 202 (4M 113)
ONSLOW VILLAGE 5J 113
Onslow Way GU22: Pyr 2H 75
KT7: T Dit 7E 40
Ontario Cl. RH6: Smal 9L 143
Openfields GU35: Head 4D 168
Openview SW18 . . . . .2A 28
Ophelia Ho. *W6 . . . . .1J 13*
(off Fulham Pal. Rd.)
Opladen Way RG12: Brac 4A 32
Opossum Way TW4: Houn 6K 9
Opus Pk. GU1: Guil 8N 93
Orange Ct. La. BR6: Dow 5J 67
Orangery, The TW10: Ham 3J 25
Orange Tree Theatre 7L 11
Orbain Rd. SW6 . . . . .3K 13
Orchard, The GU18: Ligh 7L 51
GU21: Wok 3L 73
GU22: Wok 9A 74
GU25: V Wat 4A 36
KT13: Weybr 1C 56
KT17: Ewe 4E 60
(Meadow Wlk.)
KT17: Ewe 6E 60
(Tayles Hill Dr.)
Orchard, The RH5: Nth H 9J 119
RH6: Horl 8E 142
RH12: Bro H 5D 196
RH13: Hors 4A 198
SM7: Ban 2M 81
TW3: Houn 5C 10
Orchard Av. CR0: Croy 8H 47
CR4: Mit 7E 44
KT3: N Mal 1D 42
KT7: T Dit 7G 41
KT15: Wood 7H 55
SL4: W'sor 4D 4
TW5: Hest 3M 9
TW14: Felt 8E 8
TW15: A'ford 7D 22
Orchard Bus. Cen.
RH1: Salf 3F 142
Orchard Cl. GU1: Guil 3D 114
GU3: Flex 3M 111
GU8: Els 7H 131
GU9: B Lea 6N 109
GU12: A Va 8E 90
GU17: Haw 5L 69
GU22: Wok 3D 74
GU24: W End 9A 52
GU27: Hasl 3D 188
KT7: T Dit 7H 41
KT12: Wal T 6J 39
KT19: Ewe 3A 60
KT22: Fetc 9D 78
KT22: Leat 6F 78
KT24: E Hor 2G 97
RG40: W'ham 2C 30
RH6: Horl 7D 142
SM7: Ban 1N 81
SW20 . . . . .3H 43
TN8: Eden 1K 147
TW15: A'ford 7D 22
TW20: Egh 6D 20
Orchard Cotts. GU4: Guil 9G 114
KT2: K Tham . . .2M 203 (9M 25)
RH6: Char 3L 161
Orchard Ct. CR3: Cate 2C 104
GU15: Camb 4N 69
(off Orchard Way)
KT4: W Pk 7F 42
KT12: Wal T 7G 39
(off Bridge St.)
RG12: Brac 1A 32
RH7: Ling 8N 145
SM6: W'ton 2F 62
TW2: Twick 3D 24
TW7: Isle 4D 10
UB7: L'ford 3L 7
Orchard Dene *KT14: W By 9J 55*
(off Madeira Rd.)
Orchard Dr. GU21: Wok 2A 74
GU35: Lind 5B 168
KT21: A'tead 7K 79
TN8: Eden 1K 147
TW17: Shep 2F 38
Orchard End CR3: Cate 9B 84
GU10: Rowl 8E 128
KT13: Weybr 8F 38
KT22: Fetc 2C 98
Orchard Fld. Rd.
GU7: Goda 4J 133
Orchard Flds. GU51: Fleet 4A 88
Orchard Gdns. GU6: Cranl 8A 156
GU12: Alde 4A 110
KT9: Ches 1L 59
KT18: Eps 1B 80
KT24: Eff 6M 97
RH12: Hors 4J 197
SM1: Sut 2M 61
Orchard Ga. GU47: Sandh 7G 49
KT10: Esh 7D 40
Orchard Gro. CR0: Croy 6H 47
Orchard Hill GU20: Windl 4A 52
RH12: Rudg 1D 194
SM5: Cars 2D 62
Orchard Ho. *GU4: Guil 2F 114*
(off Merrow St.)
GU10: Tong 5C 110
SW6 . . . . .3L 13
(off Varna Rd.)
Orchard La. KT8: E Mol 5D 40
SW20 . . . . .9G 27
Orchard Lea Cl. GU22: Pyr 2G 75
Orchardleigh KT22: Leat 9H 79
Orchard Mains GU22: Wok . . .6M 73
Orchard M. GU21: Knap 5E 72
SW17 . . . . .4A 28
Orchard Mobile Home Pk.
KT20: Box H 8A 100
Orchard Pk. Cvn. Site
RH1: Out 3K 143
Orchard Pl. BR2: Kes 5E 66
RG40: W'ham 2B 30
Orchard Ri. CR0: Croy 7H 47
KT2: K Tham 9B 26
TW10: Rich 7A 12
Orchard Rd. BR6: Farnb 2K 67
CR2: Sande 1E 84
CR4: Mit 8E 44
GU2: Guil 5J 113
GU4: B'ham 8D 94
GU4: Chil 9A 114
GU5: Shere 8B 116
GU9: B Lea 6M 109
GU14: Farnb 1M 89
KT1: K Tham 4J 203 (1L 41)
KT9: Ches 1L 59
Orchard Rd. RH2: Reig 3N 121
RH4: Dork 6H 119
RH6: Smal 8N 143
RH13: Hors 7L 197
SL4: O Win 9L 5
SM1: Sut 2M 61
TW1: Twick 8G 11
TW4: Houn 8N 9
TW8: Brent 2J 11
TW9: Rich 6N 11
TW12: Hamp 8N 23
TW13: Felt 2H 23
TW16: Sunb 8J 23
Orchards, The RH11: Ifi 4J 181
RH12: Hors 3M 197
Orchards Cl. KT14: W By 1J 75
Orchard Sq. W14 . . . . .1L 13
Orchard St. RH11: Craw 3B 182
Orchard Vw. KT16: Chert 5J 37
Orchard Wlk.
KT2: K Tham 2M 203
Orchard Way BR3: Beck 7H 47
CR0: Croy 7H 47
GU3: Flex 3M 111
GU3: Worp 2G 92
GU12: Alde 4A 110
GU15: Camb 4N 69
GU23: Send 3E 94
KT10: Esh 3C 58
KT15: Addl 2K 55
KT20: Lwr K 4L 101
RH2: Reig 6N 121
RH4: Dork 6H 119
RH8: Oxt 2C 126
RH19: E Grin 9A 166
SM1: Sut 1B 62
TW15: A'ford 3A 22
Orchid Cl. KT9: Ches 4J 59
Orchid Ct. TW20: Egh 5D 20
Orchid Dr. GU24: Bis 2D 72
Orchid Gdns. TW3: Houn 7N 9
Orchid Mead SM7: Ban 1N 81
Orde Cl. RH10: Craw 9H 163
Ordnance Cl. TW13: Felt 3H 23
Ordnance Rd.
GU11: Alde 2N 109
Ordnance Rdbt.
GU11: Alde 2N 109
Oregano Way GU2: Guil 7K 93
Oregon Cl. KT3: N Mal 3B 42
Orestan La. KT24: Eff 5J 97
Orewell Gdns. RH2: Reig 5N 121
Orford Ct. SE27 . . . . .3M 29
Orford Gdns. TW1: Twick 3F 24
ORGAN CROSSROADS 4F 60
Oriel, The RH6: Horl 9E 142
Oriel Cl. CR4: Mit 3H 45
RH10: Craw 9G 162
Oriel Ct.
CR0: Croy 1D 200 (7A 46)
Oriel Dr. SW13 . . . . .2H 13
Oriel Hill GU15: Camb 2B 70
Oriental Cl. GU22: Wok 4B 74
Oriental Rd. GU22: Wok 4B 74
SL5: S'hill 3A 34
Orion RG12: Brac 7M 31
Orion Cen., The CR0: Bedd 8J 45
Orion Ct. RH11: Craw 5J 181
Orlando Gdns. KT19: Ewe 6C 60
Orleans Cl. KT10: Esh 8D 40
Orleans Ct. KT12: Wal T 8K 39
TW1: Twick 1H 25
Orleans House Gallery 2H 25
Orleans Pk. School Sports Cen.
. . . . .1H 25
Orleans Rd. TW1: Twick 1H 25
Orltons La. RH12: Rusp 8E 160
Ormathwaites Cnr.
RG42: Warf 8C 16
Ormeley Rd. SW12 . . . . .2F 28
Orme Rd. KT1: K Tham 1A 42
SM1: Sut 3N 61
Ormerod Gdns. CR4: Mit 1E 44
Ormesby Wlk. RH10: Craw 5F 182
Ormond Av. TW10: Rich 8K 11
TW12: Hamp 9B 24
Ormond Cres. TW12: Hamp 9B 24
Ormond Dr. TW12: Hamp 8B 24
Ormonde Av. KT19: Ewe 6C 60
Ormonde Ct. SW15 . . . . .7H 13
Ormonde Pl. KT13: Weybr 3E 56
Ormonde Rd. GU7: Goda 5H 133
GU21: Wok 3M 73
RG41: W'ham 3A 30
SW14 . . . . .6B 12
Ormond Rd. TW10: Rich 8K 11
Ormsby SM2: Sut 4N 61
Ormside Way RH1: Red 8F 102
Orpen Ho. *SW5 . . . . .1M 13*
(off Trebovir Rd.)
Orpheus Cen., The 8D 104
Orpin Rd. RH1: Mers 8F 102
Orpwood Cl. TW12: Hamp 7N 23
Orwell Cl. GU14: Cove 8K 69
SL4: W'sor 6G 4
Osborne Av. TW19: Stan 2N 21
Osborne Cl. BR3: Beck 3H 47
GU16: Frim 6D 70
TW13: Hanw 6L 23
Osborne Ct. GU14: Farnb 5A 90
GU51: Fleet 5A 88
RH11: Craw 7N 181
SL4: W'sor 5F 4

Osborne Dr.—Park Ct.

Osborne Dr. GU18: Ligh 7L 51
GU52: Fleet 6C 88
Osborne Gdns. CR7: T Hea 1N 45
Osborne La. RG42: Warf 6A 16
Osborne M. SL4: W'sor 5F 4
Osborne Pl. SM1: Sut 2B 62
Osborne Rd. CR7: T Hea 1N 45
GU14: Farnb 4A 90
KT2: K Tham 8L 25
KT12: Wal T 7H 39
RG40: W'ham 2B 30
RH1: Red 9E 102
SL4: W'sor 5F 4
TW3: Houn 6N 9
TW20: Egh 7B 20
Osborne Ter. *SW17* *6D 28*
(off Church La.)
Osborne Way *KT9: Ches* *2M 59*
(off Bridge Rd.)
Osborn Rd. GU9: Farnh 8J 109
Osbourne Ho. TW2: Twick 3C 24
Oscar Cl. CR8: Pur 6L 63
Osgood Av. BR6: Chels 2N 67
Osier Ct. *TW8: Brent* *2L 11*
(off Ealing Rd.)
Osier M. W4 ....2D 12
Osier Pl. TW20: Egh 7E 20
Osiers Ct. KT1: K Tham 2H 203
Osiers Est., The
SW18 ....7M 13
Osiers Rd. SW18 ....7M 13
Osier Way CR4: Mit 4D 44
SM7: Ban 1K 81
Osman's Cl. RG42: Wink R 8F 16
Osmond Gdns. SM6: W'ton 2G 62
Osmunda Bank
RH19: D Pk 4A 166
Osmund Cl. RH10: Wor 3J 183
Osnaburgh Hill
GU15: Camb 1N 69
Osney Cl. RH11: Craw 4A 182
Osney Wlk. SM5: Cars 5B 44
Osprey Av. RG12: Brac 3J 31
Osprey Cl. KT22: Fetc 9C 78
SM1: Sut 2L 61
Osprey Gdns. CR2: Sels 6H 65
GU11: Alde 5M 109
Ostade Rd. SW2 ....1K 29
OSTERLEY 3D 10
Osterley Av. TW7: Isle 3D 10
Osterley Cl. RG40: W'ham 3E 30
Osterley Ct. TW7: Isle 4D 10
Osterley Cres. TW7: Isle 4E 10
Osterley Gdns. CR7: T Hea 1N 45
Osterley La. TW7: Isle 1C 10
UB2: S'hall 1A 10
(not continuous)
Osterley Lodge *TW7: Isle* *3E 10*
(off Church Rd.)
Osterley Pk. 2C 10
Osterley Pk. House (NT) 2C 10
Osterley Rd. TW7: Isle 3E 10
Osterley Station (Tube) 3D 10
Ostlers Dr. TW15: A'ford 6D 22
Oswald Cl. KT22: Fetc 9C 78
RG42: Warf 8C 16
Oswald Rd. KT22: Fetc 9C 78
Osward CR0: Sels 5J 65
(not continuous)
Osward Rd. SW17 ....3D 28
Otford Cl. RH11: Craw 9A 182
Othello Gro. RG42: Warf 9C 16
Otho Ct. TW8: Brent 3K 11
Otterbourne Pl.
RH19: E Grin 9L 165
Otterbourne Rd.
CR0: Croy 2B 200 (8N 45)
Otterburn Gdns.
TW7: Isle 3G 10
Otterburn St. SW17 ....7D 28
Otter Cl. GU12: Alde 1B 110
KT16: Otter 3D 54
RG45: Crow 9F 30
Otterden Cl. BR6: Orp 1N 67
Ottermead La. KT16: Otter 3E 54
Otter Mdw. KT22: Leat 6F 78
OTTERSHAW 3E 54
Ottershaw Pk. KT16: Otter 4C 54
(not continuous)
Ottway's Av. KT21: A'tead 6K 79
Ottways La. KT21: A'tead 7K 79
Otway Cl. RH11: Craw 5L 181
Oulton Wlk. RH10: Craw 5F 182
Ouseley Lodge
SL4: O Win *1M 19*
(off Ouseley Rd.)
Ouseley Rd. SL4: O Win 1M 19
(not continuous)
SW12 ....2D 28
TW19: Wray 1M 19
Outdowns KT24: Eff 8J 97
Outram Pl. KT13: Weybr 2D 56
Outram Rd. CR0: Croy 8C 46
OUTWOOD 3N 143
OUTWOOD COMMON 3N 143
Outwood Ho. *SW2* *1K 29*
(off Deepdene Gdns.)
Outwood La.
CR5: Chip, K'wood 7C 82
KT20: K'wood 9N 81
RH1: Blet, Sth N 2A 124
RH1: Out 3A 144
Outwood Post Windmill 3A 144
Oval, The GU2: Guil 4K 113
GU3: Wood V 2E 112
GU7: Goda 4J 133
SM7: Ban 1M 81
Oval Ho. CR0: Croy 1F 200
Oval Rd.
CR0: Croy 2E 200 (8A 46)
Overbrook GU7: Goda 6K 133
KT24: W Hors 7C 96
Overbury Av. BR3: Beck 2L 47
Overbury Cres. CR0: N Add 6M 65
Overdale KT21: A'tead 2L 79
RH1: Blet 2N 123
RH5: Dork 4J 119
Overdale Av. KT3: N Mal 1B 42
Overdale Ri. GU16: Frim 3C 70
Overdene Dr. RH11: Craw 3M 181
Overford Cl. GU6: Cranl 8M 155
Overford Dr. GU6: Cranl 8N 155
Overhill CR6: Warl 6F 84
Overhill Rd. CR8: Pur 5L 63
Overhill Way BR3: Beck 4N 47
Overlord Cl. GU15: Camb 7A 50
Overlord Ct. KT22: Fetc 8D 78
Overstand Cl. BR3: Beck 4K 47
Overstone Gdns. CR0: Croy 6J 47
Overthorpe Cl. GU21: Knap 4H 73
Overton Cl. GU11: Alde 6A 110
TW7: Isle 4F 10
Overton Ct. GU10: Tong 6D 110
RH19: E Grin 9A 166
SM2: Sut 4M 61
Overton Ho. *SW15* *1E 26*
(off Tangley Gro.)
Overton Rd. SM2: Sut 3M 61
Overton Shaw
RH19: E Grin 6A 166
Overton's Yd.
CR0: Croy 4B 200 (9N 45)
Oveton Way KT23: Book 4A 98
Ovington Ct. GU21: Wok 3J 73
Owen Cl. CR0: Croy 5A 46
SL3: Lang 1B 6
Owen Ho. TW1: Twick 1H 25
TW14: Felt 1H 23
Owen Mans. *W14* *2K 13*
(off Queen's Club Gdns.)
Owen Pl. KT22: Leat 9H 79
Owen Rd. GU7: Goda 5J 133
GU20: Windl 2A 52
Owers Cl. RH13: Hors 6L 197
Owlbeech Ct. RH13: Hors 4A 198
Owlbeech Pl. RH13: Hors 4A 198
Owlbeech Way
RH13: Hors 4A 198
Owl Cl. CR2: Sels 6G 65
Owletts RH10: Craw 2H 183
Owlscastle Cl. RH12: Hors 3K 197
OWLSMOOR 6K 49
Owlsmoor Rd.
GU47: C Tow, Owls 7J 49
(not continuous)
Ownstead Gdns.
CR2: Sande 7C 64
Ownsted Hill CR0: N Add 6M 65
Oxberry Av. SW6 ....5K 13
Oxdowne Cl. KT11: Sto D 1B 78
Oxenden Ct. GU10: Tong 4C 110
Oxenden Rd. GU10: Tong 4C 110
Oxenhope RG12: Brac 3M 31
Oxfield *TN8: Eden* *9M 127*
(off Rowfield)
Oxford Av. SW20 ....1K 43
TW5: Hest 1A 10
UB3: Harl 3G 8
Oxford Cl. CR4: Mit 2G 44
TW15: A'ford 8D 22
Oxford Ct.
KT18: Eps 8L 201 (1D 80)
TW13: Hanw 5L 23
W4 ....1A 12
Oxford Cres. KT3: N Mal 5C 42
Oxford Gdns. W4 ....1N 11
Oxford Rd.
GU1: Guil 6D 202 (5N 113)
GU14: Farnb 4A 90
GU47: Owls 5K 49
RG41: W'ham 2A 30
RH1: Red 2C 122
RH10: Craw 7C 182
RH13: Hors 6K 197
SL4: W'sor 4F 4
SM5: Cars 3C 62
SM6: W'ton 2G 62
SW15 ....7K 13
TW11: Tedd 6D 24
Oxford Rd. E. SL4: W'sor 4F 4
Oxford Rd. Nth. W4 ....1A 12
Oxford Rd. Sth. W4 ....1N 11
Oxfordshire Pl. RG42: Warf 8D 16
Oxford Ter.
GU1: Guil 6D 202 (5N 113)
Oxford Way TW13: Hanw 5L 23
Ox La. KT17: Ewe 5F 60
Oxleigh Cl. KT3: N Mal 4D 42
Oxlip Cl. CR0: Croy 7G 46
OXSHOTT 9D 58
Oxshott Ri. KT11: Cob 9L 57
Oxshott Rd. KT22: Leat 3E 78
Oxshott Station (Rail) 9C 58
Oxshott Village Sports Club
....1C 78
Oxshott Way KT11: Cob 2M 77
OXTED 7A 106
Oxted Cl. CR4: Mit 2B 44
Oxted Grn. GU8: Mil 3B 152
Oxted Rd. RH9: Gods 8F 104
Oxted Station (Rail) 7A 106
Oxtoby Way SW16 ....9H 29
Oyster La. KT14: Byf 6M 55
(not continuous)

P

Pachesham Dr. KT22: Leat 3F 78
PACHESHAM PARK 3F 78
Pachesham Pk. KT22: Leat 3G 78
Pacific Cl. TW14: Felt 2G 23
Packer Cl. RH19: E Grin 6C 166
Packham Ct. KT4: W Pk 9H 43
Packway GU9: Farnh 4K 129
Padbrook RH8: Limp 7C 106
(not continuous)
Padbrook Cl. RH8: Limp 7C 106
Padbury Cl. TW14: Bedf 2E 22
Padbury Oaks
UB7: L'ford 4K 7
Paddock, The GU1: Guil 2F 114
GU6: Cranl 7M 155
GU6: Ewh 6F 156
GU7: Goda 8H 133
GU18: Ligh 7M 51
GU26: G'hott 5M 169
GU27: Hasl 9E 170
GU35: Head 4D 168
RG45: Crow 1F 48
RH4: Westc 6B 118
RH10: Craw 2H 183
SL3: Dat 4L 5
SL4: Wink 1J 17
(Crouch La.)
SL4: Wink 2M 17
(Squirrel La.)
TN16: Weste 4L 107
Paddock Cl. BR6: Farnb 1K 67
GU8: Hamb 9F 152
GU15: Camb 9E 50
KT4: W Pk 7D 42
RH5: B Grn 7K 139
RH7: Ling 8M 145
RH8: Oxt 9B 106
TN8: Eden 9L 127
Paddock Gdns.
RH19: E Grin 2A 186
Paddock Gro. RH5: B Grn 7K 139
Paddock Ho. *GU4: Guil* *2F 114*
(off Merrow St.)
Paddockhurst Rd.
RH10: T Hil 9K 183
RH11: Craw 4M 181
Paddock Mobile Home Pk.
BR2: Kes 5G 67
Paddocks, The CR0: A'ton 3K 65
GU3: Flex 3N 111
GU25: V Wat 5A 36
KT13: Weybr 9F 38
KT15: N Haw 6K 55
KT23: Book 4B 98
Paddocks Cl. KT11: Cob 1K 77
KT21: A'tead 5L 79
Paddocks Mead GU21: Wok 3H 73
Paddocks Rd. GU4: B'ham 8C 94
Paddocks Way KT16: Chert 7K 37
KT21: A'tead 5L 79
Paddock Wlk. CR6: Warl 6E 84
Paddock Way GU21: Wok 1D 74
GU27: G'wood 7L 171
RH8: Oxt 9B 106
SW15 ....1H 27
Padley Cl. KT9: Ches 2M 59
Padstow Wlk. RH11: Craw 5K 181
TW14: Felt 2G 22
Padwick Rd. RH13: Hors 6N 197
Pageant Wlk.
CR0: Croy 4F 200 (9B 46)
Page Cl. TW12: Hamp 7M 23
Page Ct. RH10: Craw 4D 182
RH13: Hors 7K 197
Page Cres. CR0: Wad 2L 63
Page Cft. KT15: Addl 8K 37
Pagehurst Rd. CR0: Croy 6E 46
Pageites GU7: Goda 4E 132
Page Rd. TW14: Bedf 9E 8
Page's Cft. RG40: W'ham 3C 30
Pages Yd. W4 ....2E 12
Paget Av. SM1: Sut 9B 44
Paget Cl. GU15: Camb 8F 50
RH13: Hors 8L 197
TW12: H Hill 5D 24
Paget La. TW7: Isle 6D 10
Paget Pl. KT2: K Tham 7B 26
KT7: T Dit 7F 40
PAGEWOOD 3J 161
Pagewood Cl. RH10: Craw 5H 183
Pagoda Av. TW9: Rich 6M 11
Pagoda Gro. SE27 ....3N 29
Paice Grn. RG40: W'ham 1C 30
Painesfield Dr. KT16: Chert 7J 37
Pain's Cl. CR4: Mit 1F 44
PAINS HILL
KT11 ....1G 76
RH8 ....9E 106
PAINSHILL 9G 56
Pains Hill RH8: Limp 1E 126
Pains Hill Ho. KT11: Cob 1G 76
Painshill Pk. 1G 76
Paisley Rd. SM5: Cars 7B 44
Paisley Ter. SM5: Cars 6B 44
Pakenham Cl. SW12 ....2E 28
Pakenham Dr.
GU11: Alde 1L 109
Pakenham Rd. RG12: Brac 6B 32
Palace Ct. *GU21: Wok* *3C 74*
(off Maybury Rd.)
Palace Dr. KT13: Weybr 9C 38
Palace Grn. CR0: Sels 4J 65
Palace Mans.
KT1: K Tham 8H 203
Palace M. SW6 ....3M 13
Palace Rd.
KT1: K Tham 8H 203 (3K 41)
KT8: E Mol 2C 40
SW2 ....2K 29
TN16: Weste 8J 87
Palace Vw. CR0: Croy 1J 65
Palace Way GU22: Wok 7D 74
KT13: Weybr 9C 38
Palace Wharf *W6* *3H 13*
(off Rainville Rd.)
Palemead Cl. SW6 ....4J 13
Palestine Gro. SW19 ....9B 28
Palewell Comn. Dr.
SW14 ....8C 12
Palewell Pk. SW14 ....8C 12
Palgrave Ho. TW2: Whitt 1C 24
Palladino Ho. *SW17* *6C 28*
(off Laurel Cl.)
Pallant Way BR6: Farnb 1J 67
Pallingham Dr.
RH10: Craw 6G 182
Palliser Ct. *W14* *1K 13*
(off Palliser Rd.)
Palliser Rd. W14 ....1K 13
Palmer Av. SM3: Chea 1H 61
Palmer Cl. BR4: W Wick 9N 47
RG40: W'ham 8F 30
RH1: Red 4E 122
RH6: Horl 6D 142
TW5: Hest 4A 10
Palmer Ct. RG40: W'ham 2B 30
Palmer Cres.
KT1: K Tham 5J 203 (2L 41)
KT16: Otter 3F 54
Palmer Rd. RH10: Craw 6G 182
Palmer School Rd.
RG40: W'ham 2B 30
PALMERS CROSS 4F 154
Palmersfield Rd. SM7: Ban 1M 81
Palmers Gro. KT8: W Mole 3A 40
Palmers Lodge GU2: Guil 4K 113
Palmers Pas. *SW14* *6B 12*
(off Palmers Rd.)
Palmers Rd. SW14 ....6B 12
SW16 ....1K 45
Palmerston Cl. GU14: Cove 2J 89
GU21: Wok 1C 74
RH1: Red 6E 122
Palmerston Ct. KT6: Surb 6K 41
Palmerstone Ct.
GU25: V Wat *4A 36*
(off Sandhills La.)
Palmerston Gro.
SW19 ....8M 27
Palmerston Ho. *SM7: Ban* *2L 81*
(off Basing Rd.)
Palmerston Mans.
W14 ....*2K 13*
(off Queen's Club Gdns.)
Palmerston Rd. BR6: Farnb 1L 67
CR0: Croy 4A 46
SM1: Sut 2A 62
SM5: Cars 1D 62
SW14 ....7B 12
SW19 ....8M 27
TW2: Twick 9E 10
TW3: Houn 4C 10
Palm Gro. GU1: Guil 7M 93
Pampisford Rd.
CR2: S Croy 5M 63
CR8: Pur 7L 63
Pams Way KT19: Ewe 2C 60
Pankhurst Cl. TW7: Isle 6F 10
Pankhurst Ct. RH11: Craw 8N 181
Pankhurst Dr. RG12: Brac 4B 32
Pankhurst Rd. KT12: Wal T 6K 39
Panmuir Rd. SW20 ....9G 27
Pannell Cl. RH19: E Grin 1N 185
Pannells GU10: L Bou 6J 129
Pannells Ash RH14: Ifo 5E 192
Pannells Cl. KT16: Chert 7H 37
Pannells Ct.
GU1: Guil 5D 202 (4N 113)
Pan's Gdns. GU15: Camb 2D 70
Pantile Rd. KT13: Weybr 1E 56
Pantiles Cl. GU21: Wok 5L 73
Panton Cl.
CR0: Croy 1A 200 (7M 45)
Papercourt La. GU23: Rip 9H 75
Papercourt Sailing Club 9H 75
Paper M.
RH4: Dork 1L 201 (4H 119)
Papermill Cl. SM5: Cars 1E 62
Papworth Way SW2 ....1L 29
Parade, The CR0: Croy 5J 45
GU2: Guil *7L 93*
(off Burden Rd.)
GU12: A Va 9E 90
GU16: Frim 6B 70
Parade, The GU25: V Wat 5N 35
GU46: Yate 9D 48
KT2: K Tham 3K 203
KT4: W Pk 1E 60
KT10: Clay 3E 58
KT18: Eps *1N 79*
(off Spa Dr.)
KT18: Eps 7K 201 (9C 60)
(The Parade)
KT20: Tad 6K 81
KT22: Leat *7G 79*
(off Kingston Rd.)
RH1: Red 4E 122
RH10: Craw 2C 182
RH12: Hors *5G 197*
(off Caterways)
RH19: E Grin 7L 165
SL4: W'sor 4A 4
SM1: Sut 9L 43
SM5: Cars *2D 62*
(off Beynon Rd.)
TN16: Tats *8E 86*
(off Ship Hill)
TW12: Tedd 6D 24
TW16: Sunb 8G 23
TW18: Stain *6F 20*
(off Thorpe Rd.)
Parade Ct. KT24: E Hor 4F 96
Parade M. SE27 ....3M 29
Paradise Rd. TW9: Rich 8K 11
Paragon *TW8: Brent* *1J 11*
(off Boston Pk. Rd.)
Paragon Cotts. GU4: E Cla 9M 95
Paragon Gro. KT5: Surb 5M 41
Paragon Pl. KT5: Surb 5M 41
Parbury Ri. KT9: Ches 3L 59
Parchmore Rd.
CR7: T Hea 1M 45
Parchmore Way
CR7: T Hea 1M 45
Pares Cl. GU21: Wok 3N 73
Parfitts Cl. GU9: Farnh 1F 128
Parfour Dr. CR8: Ken 3N 83
Parfrey St. W6 ....2H 13
Parham Rd. RH11: Craw 2L 181
Parish Cl. GU9: U Hal 6F 108
GU12: Ash 3F 110
Parish Ct. KT6: Surb 4L 41
Parish Ho. RH11: Craw 4B 182
Parish Rd. GU14: Farnb 5A 90
Park, The KT23: Book 1A 98
RH4: Dork 7G 118
SM5: Cars 2D 62
Park & Ride
Artington 8M 113
Spectrum 1B 114
Hop Oast 9G 196
Kingston-upon-Thames
(November-mid. January)
....5J 59
Ladymead 1B 202 (2M 113)
University 3K 113
Windsor (Home Park) 2H 5
Windsor (Legoland) 8B 4
Park Av. BR4: W Wick 8M 47
CR3: Cate 2B 104
CR4: Mit 8F 28
GU8: P Har 6N 131
GU15: Camb 2A 70
RG40: W'ham 3A 30
(not continuous)
RH1: Salf 2D 142
SM5: Cars 3E 62
SW14 ....7C 12
TN8: Eden 1K 147
TW3: Houn 9B 10
TW17: Shep 2F 38
TW18: Stain 7H 21
TW19: Wray 8N 5
TW20: Egh 7E 20
Park Av. E. KT17: Ewe 3F 60
Park Av. M. CR4: Mit 8F 28
Park Av. W. KT17: Ewe 3F 60
PARK BARN 2H 113
Park Barn Dr. GU2: Guil 1H 113
Park Barn E. GU2: Guil 2J 113
Park Barn Way *GU2: Guil* *3H 113*
(off Southway)
Park Chase
GU1: Guil 3E 202 (3A 114)
GU7: Goda 9H 133
Park Cl. GU27: G'wood 8K 171
KT2: K Tham 1M 203 (9N 25)
KT10: Esh 3A 58
KT12: Wal T 8G 38
KT15: N Haw 6K 55
KT22: Fetc 2D 98
RH3: Brock 8A 120
RH8: Oxt 6B 106
SL4: W'sor 5G 5
SM5: Cars 3D 62
TW3: Houn 8C 10
TW12: Hamp 9C 24
W4 ....2C 12
Park Copse RH5: Dork 5K 119
Park Cnr. SL4: W'sor 6B 4
Park Cnr. Dr. KT24: E Hor 6F 96
Park Cotts. RH5: For G 2L 157
Park Ct. CR2: S Croy 8B 200
GU9: Farnh 9J 109
GU22: Wok 5B 74
KT1: H Wic 9J 25
KT3: N Mal 3C 42

Peascod St.—Pine Cl.

Peascod St. SL4: W'sor 4F 4
PEASE POTTAGE 2N 199
Pease Pottage Hill
RH11: Craw 8A 182
PEASE POTTAGE SERVICE AREA
..........9A 182
PEASLAKE 5E 136
Peaslake La. GU5: P'lake ...5E 136
Peaslake Rd. GU6: Ewh 2E 156
PEASMARSH 2M 133
Peat Comn. GU8: Els 9G 131
Peat Cotts. GU8: Els 9G 131
Peatmoor Cl. GU51: Fleet 3A 88
Peatmore Av. GU22: Pyr 3J 75
Peatmore Cl. GU22: Pyr 3J 75
Peatmore Dr.
GU24: B'wood 8N 71
Pebble Cl. KT20: Wal H 7D 100
Pebble Hill Rd.
RH3: Betch 7D 100
Pebble La. KT18: Eps D 9N 79
KT22: Leat 2M 99
(not continuous)
Pebworth Ct. RH1: Red 1E 122
Peddlars Gro. GU46: Yate 9D 48
Peeble Hill KT24: W Hors ...2D 116
Peek Cres. SW19 ....6J 27
Peeks Brook La.
RH6: S Bri, Horl 4J 163
Peel Av. GU16: Frim 7E 70
Peel Cen., The RG12: Brac ..1M 31
Peel Cl. SL4: W'sor 6E 4
Peel Ct. GU14: Farnb 5A 90
Peel Rd. BR6: Farnb 2L 67
Pegasus Av. GU12: Alde 1C 110
Pegasus Cl. GU27: Hasl 3B 188
Pegasus Ct. CR3: Cate 1C 104
GU12: Alde 3C 110
GU51: Fleet 3A 88
KT1: K Tham ...6H 203 (2K 41)
KT22: Leat 8J 79
(off Epsom Rd.)
RH11: Craw 5K 181
SM7: Ban 2M 81
TW8: Brent 1M 11
TW20: Egh 6D 20
Pegasus Pl. SW6 ....4M 13
Pegasus Rd. CR0: Wad 3L 63
GU14: Cove 7L 69
Pegasus Way
RH19: E Grin 7D 166
Peggotty Pl. GU47: Owls 5K 49
Pegg Rd. TW5: Hest 3J 9
Pegler Way RH11: Craw 3B 182
Pegwell Cl. RH11: Craw 5L 181
Peket Cl. TW18: Stain 9G 21
Pelabon Ho. *TW1: Twick 9K 11*
(off Clevedon Rd.)
Peldon Ct. TW9: Rich 7M 11
Peldon Pas. TW10: Rich 7M 11
Pelham Ct. RH11: Craw 7N 181
RH12: Hors 6H 197
TW18: Stain 6K 21
(off Kingston Rd.)
Pelham Dr. RH11: Craw 7M 181
Pelham Ho. CR3: Cate 2C 104
W14 ....1L 13
(off Mornington Av.)
Pelham Pl. GU10: Wrec 7F 128
RH11: Craw 7N 181
Pelham Rd. BR3: Beck 1F 46
SW19 ....8M 27
Pelham's Cl. KT10: Esh 1A 58
Pelham's Wlk. KT10: Esh 1A 58
Pelham Way KT23: Book 4B 98
Pellant Rd. SW6 ....3K 13
Pelling Hill SL4: O Win 1L 19
Pelman Way KT19: Eps 6A 60
Pelton Av. SM2: Sut 6N 61
Pemberley Chase
KT19: Ewe 2A 60
Pemberley Cl. KT19: Ewe 2A 60
Pemberley Ho. *KT19: Ewe 2A 60*
(off Pemberley Chase)
Pemberley Lodge SL4: W'sor ...6E 4
Pemberton Pl. KT10: Esh 9C 40
Pemberton Rd. KT8: E Mol ...3C 40
Pembley Grn. RH10: Cop 7A 164
Pembridge Av. TW2: Whitt ...2N 23
Pembridge Pl. SW15 ....8M 13
Pembroke RG12: Brac 6L 31
W14 ....1L 13
(off Mornington Av.)
Pembroke Av. KT5: Surb 4A 42
KT12: Hers 1L 57
Pembroke B'way.
GU15: Camb 1A 70
Pembroke Cl. SL5: S'hill 4A 34
SM7: Ban 4N 81
Pembroke Gdns.
GU22: Wok 5C 74
Pembroke M. SL5: S'hill 4A 34
Pembroke Pde. GU46: Yate ...8D 48
Pembroke Pl. TW7: Isle 5E 10
Pembroke Rd. CR4: Mit 1E 44
GU22: Wok 5C 74
RH10: Craw 9G 163
SE25 ....3B 46
Pembroke Vs. TW9: Rich 7K 11
Pembury Av. KT4: W Pk 7F 42
Pembury Cl. CR5: Coul 1E 82
Pembury Ct. UB3: Harl 2E 8
Pembury Pl. GU12: Alde 3A 110
Pembury Rd. SE25 ....3D 46
Pemdevon Rd. CR0: Croy 6L 45
Pemerich Cl. UB3: Harl 1G 8
Penart Ct. SM2: Sut 4A 62
Penates KT10: Esh 1D 58
Penbury Rd. UB2: S'hall 1N 9
Pendarves Rd. SW20 ....9H 27
Pendarvis Ct.
GU26: G'hott 6A 170
Pendell Av. UB3: Harl 3G 8
Pendell Rd. RH1: Blet 9M 103
Pendennis Cl. KT14: W By 1J 75
Pendennis Rd. SW16 ....5J 29
Pendenza KT11: Cob 3M 77
Penderel Rd. TW3: Houn 8A 10
Pendine Pl. RG12: Brac 4N 31
Pendlebury RG12: Brac 6M 31
Pendlebury Ct. KT5: Surb 8K 203
Pendle Rd. SW16 ....7F 28
Pendleton Cl. RH1: Red 4D 122
Pendleton Rd. RH1: Red 6A 122
RH2: Reig 6A 122
Pendragon Way
GU15: Camb 2H 71
Pendry's La. RG42: Warf 1M 15
Penfold Cl. CR0: Wad 9L 45
Penfold Cft. GU9: Farnh 8L 109
(not continuous)
Penfold Mnr. GU27: Hasl 2H 189
Penfold Rd. RH10: Craw 7F 182
Penfurzen La. RG42: Warf 1B 16
Penge Rd. SE20 ....2D 46
SE25 ....2D 46
Pengilly Ho. GU1: Guil 3E 114
Pengilly Rd. GU9: Farnh 1G 128
Penhurst GU21: Wok 1B 74
Peninsular Cl. GU15: Camb ...8F 50
TW14: Felt 9E 8
Peninsular Pl. RG45: Crow 3H 49
Penistone Rd. SW16 ....8J 29
Penlee Cl. TN8: Eden 1L 147
Pennards, The TW16: Sunb ...2K 39
Penn Cl. RH11: Craw 9B 162
Penn Ct. RH11: Craw 3L 181
Pennefather's Rd.
GU11: Alde 1L 109
Penner Cl. SW19 ....3K 27
Penners Gdns. KT6: Surb 6L 41
Penn Ho. *SL4: Eton 1G 4*
(off Common La.)
Pennine Cl. RH11: Craw 3N 181
Pennine Way GU14: Cove 7J 69
UB3: Harl 3E 8
Pennings Av. GU2: Guil 1J 113
Pennington Dr. KT13: Weybr ...9F 38
Pennington Lodge
KT5: Surb 8K 203
Penn Rd. SL3: Dat 4N 5
Penns Wood GU14: Farnb 4B 90
Pennycroft CR0: Sels 5H 65
Penny Dr. GU3: Wood V 2E 112
Pennyfield KT11: Cob 9H 57
Penny Hill Cvn. Pk.
GU17: Min 4B 68
PENNYHILL PARK 5F 50
Penny La. TW17: Shep 6F 38
Pennymead Dr. KT24: E Hor ...5G 96
Pennymead Pl. KT10: Esh 3N 57
Pennymead Ri.
KT24: E Hor 5G 96
Penny M. SW12 ....1F 28
PENNY POT 8F 52
Pennypot La. GU24: Chob 9E 52
Penny Royal SM6: W'ton 3H 63
Penrhyn Cl. CR3: Cate 7A 84
GU12: Alde 3N 109
Penrhyn Cres. SW14 ....7B 12
Penrhyn Gdns.
KT1: K Tham ...7H 203 (3K 41)
Penrhyn Rd.
KT1: K Tham 7J 203 (3L 41)
Penrith Cl. RH2: Reig 2C 122
SW15 ....8K 13
Penrith Pl. SE27 ....3M 29
Penrith Rd. CR7: T Hea 1N 45
KT3: N Mal 3C 42
Penrith St. SW16 ....7G 28
Penrose Ct. TW20: Eng G 7N 19
(not continuous)
Penrose Dr. KT19: Eps 7N 59
Penrose Gdns. GU12: A Va 7E 90
Penrose Rd. KT22: Fetc 9C 78
Penryn Dr. GU35: H Dwn 4H 169
Penryn Ho. *RH1: Red 1E 122*
(off London Rd.)
Pensfold La. RH12: Rudg 3F 194
Pensford Av. TW9: Kew 5N 11
Pensford Cl. RG45: Crow 9G 30
Penshurst Cl. RH10: Craw 2H 183
Penshurst Ri. GU16: Frim 6D 70
Penshurst Rd. CR7: T Hea 4M 45
Penshurst Way SM2: Sut 4M 61
Penstock M. GU7: Goda 6K 133
Pentelow Gdns. TW14: Felt 9H 9
Pentire Cl. GU21: Wok 1A 74
Pentland Av. TW17: Shep 4B 38
Pentland Gdns. SW18 ....9N 13
Pentland Pl. GU14: Cove 7K 69
Pentlands Cl. CR4: Mit 2F 44
Pentland St. SW18 ....9N 13
Pentlow St. SW15 ....6H 13
Pentney Rd. SW12 ....2G 28
SW19 ....9K 27
Penton Av. TW18: Stain 8H 21
Penton Ct. TW18: Stain 7H 21
Penton Hall TW18: Stain 9J 21
Penton Hall Dr. TW18: Stain ..9J 21
Penton Hook Marina 2J 37
Penton Hook Rd.
TW18: Stain 8J 21
Penton Pk. KT16: Chert 2K 37
Penton Rd. TW18: Stain 8H 21
Pentreath Av. GU2: Guil 4J 113
Penwerris Av. TW7: Isle 3C 10
Penwerris Ct. TW5: Hest 3C 10
Penwith Dr. GU27: Hasl 4B 188
Penwith Rd. SW18 ....3M 27
Penwith Wlk. GU22: Wok 6N 73
Penwood End GU22: Wok 8L 73
Penwood Gdns. RG12: Brac ...5J 31
Penwood Ho. SW15 ....9E 12
Penwortham Rd.
CR2: Sande 6N 63
SW16 ....7F 28
Pen-y-Bos Track
GU27: Hasl 5K 189
Penywern Rd. SW5 ....1M 13
Peperham Ho. GU27: Hasl ...1G 189
Peperham Rd. GU27: Hasl ...9G 171
PEPER HAROW 6N 131
Peper Harow La.
GU8: S'ford 5N 131
Peperharow Rd.
GU7: Goda 5E 132
Peppard Rd. RH10: Craw 5H 183
Pepperbox La. GU5: Braml 5F 154
Pepper Cl. CR3: Cate 3B 104
Peppercorn Cl. CR7: T Hea 1A 46
Peppermint Cl. CR0: Croy 6J 45
Peppers Yd. RH12: Hors 5K 197
Pepys Cl. KT21: A'tead 4N 79
SL3: Lang 2D 6
Pepys Rd. SW20 ....9H 27
Percheron Cl. TW7: Isle 6F 10
Percheron Dr. GU21: Knap 6F 72
Percival Cl. KT22: Oxs 7B 58
Percival Rd. SW14 ....7B 12
TW13: Felt 3G 22
Percival Way KT19: Ewe 1C 60
Percy Av. TW15: A'ford 6B 22
Percy Bryant Rd.
TW16: Sunb 8F 22
Percy Gdns. KT4: W Pk 7C 42
TW7: Isle 6G 11
Percy Laurie Ho.
SW15 ....7J 13
(off Nursery Cl.)
Percy Pl. SL3: Dat 4L 5
Percy Rd. CR4: Mit 6E 44
GU2: Guil 1L 113
RH12: Hors 5H 197
SE20 ....1G 46
SE25 ....4D 46
TW2: Whitt 2B 24
TW7: Isle 7G 11
TW12: Hamp 8A 24
Percy Way TW2: Whitt 2C 24
Peregrine Cl. GU6: Cranl 6N 155
RG12: Brac 4N 31
Peregrine Ct. SW16 ....5K 29
Peregrine Gdns. CR0: Croy 8H 47
Peregrine Rd. TW16: Sunb 1G 38
Peregrine Way SW19 ....8H 27
Perham Rd. W14 ....1K 13
Perifield SE21 ....2N 29
Perimeter Rd. RH6: Gat 3F 162
Perimeter Rd. E. RH6: Gat 5E 162
Perimeter Rd. Nth.
RH6: Gat 2B 162
Perimeter Rd. Sth.
RH6: Gat 5A 162
Periwinkle Cl. GU35: Lind 4B 168
Perkin Cl. TW3: Houn 7A 10
Perkins Ct. TW15: A'ford 6A 22
Perkstead Ct. *RH11: Craw 6M 181*
(off Waddington Cl.)
Perleybrooke La.
GU21: Wok 4K 73
Perotts Wood Nature Reserve
.............5A 82
Perowne St. GU11: Alde 2L 109
Perran Rd. SW2 ....2M 29
Perran Wlk. TW8: Brent 1L 11
Perrin Cl. TW15: A'ford 6A 22
Perrin Ct. GU21: Wok 2D 74
TW15: A'ford 5B 22
Perring Av. GU14: Cove 6K 69
Perring Rd. GU14: Farnb 4M 89
Perrior Rd. GU7: Goda 4H 133
Perry Av. RH19: E Grin 7A 166
Perry Cl. GU7: Goda 6K 133
Perry Ct. KT2: K Tham 3K 203
Perrycroft SL4: W'sor 6B 4
Perryfield Ho. *RH11: Craw 4B 182*
(off Perryfield Rd.)
Perryfield Rd. RH11: Craw 4A 182
Perryfield Way TW10: Ham 4H 25
Perry Hill GU3: Worp 5H 93
(not continuous)
Perryhill Dr. GU47: Sandh 6E 48
Perry How KT4: W Pk 7E 42
Perrylands RH6: Char 3L 161
Perrylands La. RH6: Horl 9K 143
Perrymead St. SW6 ....4M 13
Perryn Ct. TW1: Twick 9G 10
Perry Oaks RG12: Brac 1C 32
Perry Way GU9: U Hal 5G 109
GU18: Ligh 8K 51
GU35: Head 5E 168
RG12: Brac 1C 32
Perrywood Bus. Pk.
RH1: Salf 2F 142
Perseverance Cotts.
GU23: Rip 8L 75
Perseverance Pl. TW9: Rich ...7L 11
Persfield Cl. KT17: Ewe 6E 60
Persfield M. KT17: Ewe 6E 60
Pershore Gro. SM5: Cars 5B 44
Perth Cl. RH11: Craw 9B 162
SW20 ....1E 42
Perth Rd. BR3: Beck 1M 47
Perth Way RH12: Hors 4M 197
Petavel Rd. TW11: Tedd 7E 24
Peter Av. RH8: Oxt 7N 105
Peterborough M. SW6 ....5M 13
Peterborough Rd.
GU2: Guil 1J 113
RH10: Craw 7C 182
SM5: Cars 5C 44
SW6 ....5M 13
Peterborough Vs. SW6 ....4N 13
Peterhead M. SL3: Lang 1C 6
Peterhouse Cl. GU47: Owls 5L 49
Peterhouse Pde.
RH10: Craw 9G 162
Peter Kennedy Ct.
CR0: Croy 5J 47
Peterlee Wlk. RH11: Craw ...7K 181
Peter Scott Vis. Cen., The ...4G 12
Petersfield Av. TW18: Stain ...6L 21
Petersfield Cres. CR5: Coul ...2J 83
Petersfield Ri. SW15 ....2G 26
Petersfield Rd. TW18: Stain ...6L 21
PETERSHAM 2L 25
Petersham Av. KT14: Byf 8N 55
Petersham Cl. KT14: Byf 8N 55
SM1: Sut 2M 61
TW10: Ham 3K 25
Petersham Rd.
TW10: Rich, Ham 9K 11
Petersham Ter. *CR0: Bedd 9J 45*
(off Richmond Grn.)
Petersmead Cl. KT20: Tad 1H 101
Peterstow Cl. SW19 ....3K 27
Peters Wood RH5: Cap 5J 159
Peterwood Pk. CR0: Wad 8K 45
Peterwood Way CR0: Wad 8K 45
Petley Rd. W6 ....2J 13
Petridge Rd. RH1: Red 8D 122
PETRIDGE WOOD COMMON
.............8D 122
Petters Rd. KT21: A'tead 3M 79
Pettiward Cl. SW15 ....7H 13
Petts La. TW17: Shep 3B 38
Petworth Cl. CR5: Coul 6G 82
GU16: Frim 6D 70
Petworth Ct. *GU15: Camb 2D 70*
(off Portsmouth Rd.)
GU27: Hasl 2H 189
RH11: Craw 6L 181
SL4: W'sor 4D 4
Petworth Dr. RH12: Hors 1M 197
Petworth Gdns. SW20 ....2G 42
Petworth Rd. GU8: Chid 2C 190
(Cripplecrutch Hill)
GU8: Chid 4C 190
(Fisher St.)
GU8: Hasl 2H 189
GU8: Mil, Wit, Worm 3B 152
GU8: Worm 8C 152
GU27: Hasl 2H 189
Pevensey Cl. RH10: Craw 4G 182
TW7: Isle 3C 10
Pevensey Ct. SW16 ....4L 29
Pevensey Rd. SW17 ....5B 28
TW13: Felt 2M 23
Pevensey Way GU16: Frim 6D 70
Peverel Rd. RH11: Ifi 4K 181
Peveril Dr. TW11: Tedd 6D 24
Pewley Bank
GU1: Guil 6F 202 (5A 114)
Pewley Hill
GU1: Guil 6D 202 (5N 113)
Pewley Point
GU1: Guil 7F 202 (5A 114)
Pewley Way
GU1: Guil 6F 202 (5A 114)
Pewsey Va. RG12: Brac 4D 32
Peyton's Cotts. RH1: Nut 1K 123
Pharaoh Cl. CR4: Mit 6D 44
Pharaoh's Island
TW17: Shep 8A 38
Pheasant Cl. CR8: Pur 9M 63
Pheasant Vw. RG12: Brac 3J 31
Phelps Way UB3: Harl 1G 9
Philanthropic Rd.
RH1: Red 4E 122
Philbeach Gdns. SW5 ....1M 13
Philip Gdns. CR0: Croy 8J 47
Philip Rd. TW18: Stain 7M 21
Philips Cl. SM5: Cars 7E 44
Philips Ho. GU26: G'hott 6N 169
Phillip Copse RG12: Brac 6B 32
Phillippines Cl. TN8: Eden ...3M 147
Phillips Cl. GU7: Goda 9G 132
GU10: Tong 4C 110
GU35: Head 4E 168
RH10: Craw 8F 182
Phillips Cres. GU35: Head ...4E 168
Phillips Hatch GU5: Wone 3E 134
Phillip's Quad. GU22: Wok 5A 74
Philpot La. GU24: Chob 9L 53
Philpot Sq. SW6 ....6N 13
Phipps Bri. Rd. CR4: Mit 1A 44
SW19 ....1A 44
Phipps Bridge Stop (CT) 2B 44
Phoenix Bus. Pk.
RG12: Brac 1H 31
Phoenix Cen. 4J 63
Phoenix Cl. BR4: W Wick 8N 47
KT19: Eps 8N 59
Phoenix Ct. CR2: S Croy 2C 64
GU1: Guil 6C 202 (5N 113)
GU11: Alde 3M 109
KT3: N Mal 2E 42
KT17: Eps 6L 201
TW4: Houn 8L 9
TW8: Brent 1L 11
TW13: Felt 5F 22
Phoenix Dr. BR2: Kes 1F 66
Phoenix Ho. SM1: Sut 1N 61
Phoenix La. RH19: Ash W ...3G 186
Phoenix Trad. Pk.
TW8: Brent 1K 11
Phoenix Way TW5: Hest 2L 9
Phyllis Av. KT3: N Mal 4G 42
Phyllis Ho. CR0: Wad 7A 200
Piccards, The GU2: Guil 7M 113
Pickering RG12: Brac 3M 31
Pickering Gdns. CR0: Croy 5C 46
Pickering Pl. GU2: Guil 1K 113
Picket Post Cl. RG12: Brac 2D 32
Pickets St. SW12 ....1F 28
Picketts Hill
GU35: Head, Slea 9A 148
Picketts La. RH1: Salf 2G 142
RH6: Gat 4H 163
Pickford Ho. *GU11: Alde 2N 109*
(off Pickford St.)
Pickford St. GU11: Alde 2N 109
Pickhurst Ri. BR4: W Wick ...6M 47
Pickhurst Rd. GU8: Chid 6F 172
Pickins Piece SL3: Hort 5C 6
Pickwick Cl. TW4: Houn 8M 9
Pickwick Gdns. GU15: Camb ...2F 70
Picquets Way SM7: Ban 3K 81
Picton Cl. GU15: Camb 8G 50
Picton Mt. CR6: Warl 6D 84
Picton Pl. KT6: Surb 7N 41
Picts Hill RH13: Hors 9G 197
Picture Ho. SW16 ....3J 29
Pieris Ho. *TW13: Felt 3H 23*
(off Highfield Rd.)
Pierrefonde's Av.
GU14: Farnb 9M 69
Pier Rd. TW14: Felt 8J 9
Pierson Rd. SL4: W'sor 4A 4
Pier Ter. SW18 ....7N 13
Pigbush La. RH14: Loxw 1H 193
Pigeon Gro. RG12: Brac 3J 31
Pigeon Ho. La. CR5: Coul 3A 102
Pigeonhouse La. SL4: Wink ...4H 17
Pigeon La. TW12: Hamp 5A 24
Pigeon Pass RH10: T Hil 4F 184
Piggott Ct. RH13: Hors 7L 197
Pigott Rd. RG40: W'ham 9C 14
Pig Pound Wlk.
RH17: Hand 6N 199
Pike Cl. GU11: Alde 2A 110
KT10: H Wood 8F 40
Pikes Hill
KT17: Eps 6M 201 (9D 60)
Pikes La. RH7: Ling 2A 146
Pilgrim Cl. SM4: Mord 6N 43
Pilgrim Ct. GU8: Mil 2C 152
Pilgrim Hill SE27 ....5N 29
Pilgrims Cl. GU5: Shere 8B 116
GU9: Farnh 3F 128
RH5: Westh 9G 99
Pilgrims La. CR3: Cate 4K 103
RH8: T'sey 3D 106
TN16: Tats 1G 106
Pilgrims Pl. RH2: Reig 1M 121
Pilgrims Vw. GU12: A Grn ...4G 111
Pilgrims Way CR2: S Croy 3C 64
GU4: Guil 7N 113
(not continuous)
GU5: Alb 6H 115
GU5: Shere 8B 116
GU24: Bis 3D 72
GU35: Head 4D 168
RH2: Reig 1L 121
RH5: Westh 9H 99
TN16: Weste, Brast 1H 107
Pilgrims Way Cotts.
RH3: Betch 2B 120
Pilsden Cl. SW19 ....2J 27
Pilton Est., The
CR0: Croy 2A 200 (8M 45)
Pimms Cl. GU4: B'ham 8C 94
Pinckards GU8: Chid 4D 172
Pincott La. KT24: W Hors 7C 96
Pincott Rd. SW19 ....8A 28
Pine Av. BR4: W Wick 7L 47
GU15: Camb 2B 70
Pine Bank GU26: Hind 5C 170
Pine Cl. CR8: Ken 4A 84
GU12: A Va 7E 90
GU15: Camb 8K 49
GU21: Wok 3M 73
KT15: N Haw 7K 55
RH11: Craw 9A 162

Pine Coombe—Postford Farm Cotts.

Pine Coombe CR0: Croy 1G 64
Pinecote Dr. SL5: S'dale 6C 34
Pine Ct. GU11: Alde 2M 109
GU16: Mytc 2E 90
KT13: Weybr 2D 56
RG12: Brac 3C 32
Pine Cres. SM5: Cars 7B 62
Pinecrest Gdns. BR6: Farnb 1K 67
Pine Cft. *KT13: Weybr 3E 56*
(off St George's Rd.)
Pine Dean KT23: Book 3B 98
Pine Dr. GU17: Haw 3K 69
Pinefields *KT15: Addl 1K 55*
(off Church Rd.)
Pinefields Cl. RG45: Crow 2G 48
Pine Gdns. KT5: Surb 5N 41
RH6: Horl 9E 142
Pine Glade BR6: Farnb 1H 67
Pine Gro. GU10: L Bou 5K 129
GU20: Windl 3A 52
GU52: C Cro 8C 88
(not continuous)
KT13: Weybr 2C 56
RH19: E Grin 7L 165
SW19 6L 27
TN8: Eden 1K 147
Pine Gro. M. KT13: Weybr 2D 56
Pine Hill KT18: Eps 2C 80
Pinehill Ri. GU47: Sandh 7H 49
Pinehill Rd. RG45: Crow 3G 49
Pinehurst *GU22: Wok 5B 74*
(off Park Dr.)
RH12: Hors 4J 197
SL5: S'hill 4A 34
TW20: Eng G 8M 19
Pinehurst Av. GU14: Farnb 3N 89
Pinehurst Cl. KT20: K'wood 9M 81
Pinehurst Cotts.
GU14: Farnb 3N 89
Pinehurst Pas. GU14: Farnb 3N 89
Pinehurst Rd. GU14: Farnb 3M 89
Pinehurst Rdbt.
GU14: Farnb 2N 89
Pinel Cl. GU25: V Wat 3A 36
Pine Lodge *KT11: Cob 2K 77*
(off Leigh Cnr.)
Pinemount Rd.
GU15: Camb 2B 70
Pine Pk. GU3: Worp 7D 92
Pine Pl. SM7: Ban 1J 81
Piner Cotts. SL4: W'sor 6B 4
Pine Ridge SM5: Cars 4E 62
Pineridge Cl. KT13: Weybr 1F 56
Pine Ridge Dr.
GU10: L Bou 6G 129
Pine Ridge Mobile Home Pk.
RG40: W'ham 9D 30
Pine Rd. GU22: Wok 7M 73
Pines, The CR5: Coul 5F 82
CR8: Pur 9N 63
GU15: Camb 8D 50
GU21: Wok 1B 74
KT9: Ches 9L 41
RH4: Dork 6H 119
RH10: Wor 3H 183
RH12: Hors 3B 198
SE19 7M 29
TW16: Sunb 2H 39
Pine Shaw RH10: Craw 2H 183
Pines Rd. GU51: Fleet 3A 88
Pines Trad. Est., The
GU3: Guil 1H 113
Pinetops RH12: Hors 3B 198
Pine Tree Cl. TW5: C'ford 4J 9
Pine Tree Hill GU22: Pyr 3F 74
Pine Trees Bus. Pk.
TW18: Stain 6G 20
Pinetrees Cl. RH10: Cop 7M 163
Pine Vw. GU35: H Dwn 3H 169
Pine Vw. Cl. GU4: Guil 9H 115
GU9: B Lea 7M 109
GU27: Hasl 9G 170
Pine Wlk. CR3: Cate 9B 84
KT5: Surb 5N 41
KT11: Cob 1L 77
KT23: Book 3B 98
KT24: E Hor 6G 97
SM5: Cars 6B 62
SM7: Ban 4D 82
Pine Wlk. E. SM5: Cars 7B 62
Pine Wlk. W. SM5: Cars 6B 62
Pine Way TW20: Eng G 7L 19
Pine Way Cl. RH19: E Grin 2A 186
PINEWOOD 1G 48
Pine Wood TW16: Sunb 9H 23
Pinewood Av. KT15: N Haw 5L 55
RG45: Crow 1H 49
Pinewood Cvn. Pk.
RG40: W'ham 8H 31
Pinewood Cl. CR0: Croy 9H 47
GU21: Wok 2C 74
GU47: Sandh 7E 48
RH12: Bro H 5D 196
Pinewood Ct. GU51: Fleet 3B 88
KT15: Addl 1M 55
Pinewood Cres.
GU14: Cove 9H 69
Pinewood Dr. BR6: Orp 2N 67
TW18: Stain 6J 21
Pinewood Gdns. GU19: Bag 4G 50
Pinewood Gro.
KT15: N Haw 6K 55
Pinewood Hill GU51: Fleet 3B 88
Pinewood Leisure Cen. 8G 31
Pinewood M. TW19: Stan 9M 7
Pinewood Pk. GU14: Cove 7H 69
KT15: N Haw 7K 55
Pinewood Pl. KT19: Ewe 1C 60
Pinewood Rd. GU12: Ash 1H 111
GU25: V Wat 3K 35
TW13: Felt 4J 23
Pinfold Rd. SW16 5J 29
Pinglestone Cl. UB7: Harm 3N 7
Pinkcoat Cl. TW13: Felt 4J 23
Pinkerton Pl. SW16 5H 29
Pinkham Mans. W4 1N 11
Pinkhurst La. RH13: Slin 6A 196
PINKS HILL 2F 112
Pinova Cl. RH11: Ifi 9M 161
Pioneer Pl. CR0: Sels 5K 65
Pioneers Ind. Pk.
CR0: Bedd 7J 45
Piper Rd.
KT1: K Tham 5M 203 (2N 41)
Pipers Cl. KT11: Cob 2L 77
Pipers Cft. GU52: C Cro 9B 88
Pipers End GU25: V Wat 2N 35
RH13: Slin 5M 195
Piper's Gdns. CR0: Croy 6H 47
Pipers La. GU28: North 8D 190
Pipers Patch GU14: Farnb 1N 89
Pipewell Rd. SM5: Cars 5C 44
PIPPBROOK 1L 201 (4J 119)
Pippbrook Gdns.
RH4: Dork 1L 201 (4H 119)
Pippin Cl. CR0: Croy 7J 47
Pippin Link RH11: Ifi 9M 161
Pippins Ct. TW15: A'ford 7C 22
Pipson La. GU46: Yate 1C 68
Pipsons Cl. GU46: Yate 9C 48
Piquet Rd. SE20 1F 46
PIRBRIGHT 1C 92
PIRBRIGHT CAMP 8M 71
Pirbright Cres. CR0: N Add 3M 65
Pirbright Grn. GU24: Pirb 1C 92
Pirbright Rd. GU3: Norm 1J 111
GU14: Farnb 2A 90
SW18 2L 27
Pirbright Ter. GU24: Pirb 1C 92
Piries Pl. *RH12: Hors 6J 197*
(off East St.)
Pisley La. RH5: Ockl 6N 157
Pitcairn Rd. CR4: Mit 8D 28
Pitchfont La.
RH8: Limp, T'sey 3B 106
PITCH HILL 1D 156
PITCH PLACE
GU2 7K 93
GU8 7E 150
Pitch Pl. RG42: Bin 6J 15
Pit Farm Rd. GU1: Guil 3C 114
Pit Farm Tennis Club 3C 114
Pitfold Av. GU27: Hasl 2B 188
Pitfold Cl. GU27: Hasl 2C 188
Pitlake CR0: Croy 2A 200 (8M 45)
PITLAND STREET 6K 137
Pitland St. RH5: H Mary 6K 137
Pit La. TN8: Eden 8L 127
Pitson Cl. KT15: Addl 1M 55
Pitt Cres. SW19 5N 27
Pitt La. GU10: Fren 4F 148
Pitt Pl. KT17: Eps 8M 201 (1D 80)
Pitt Rd. BR6: Farnb 1L 67
CR0: Croy 4N 45
CR7: T Hea 4N 45
KT17: Eps 8M 201 (1D 80)
Pitts Cl. RG42: Bin 7J 15
Pitts Rd. GU11: Alde 9N 89
Pittville Gdns. SE25 2D 46
Pitt Way GU14: Cove 9L 69
Pitwood Grn. KT20: Tad 7H 81
Pitwood Pk. Ind. Est.
KT20: Tad 7G 81
PIXHAM 3K 119
Pixham End RH4: Dork 2J 119
Pixham La. RH4: Dork 2J 119
Pixholme Gro. RH4: Dork 3J 119
PIXTON HILL 5K 187
Pixton Way CR0: Sels 5H 65
Place Ct. GU11: Alde 5A 110
Place Farm Rd. RH1: Blet 8A 104
Placehouse La. CR5: Coul 6K 83
Plain Ride SL4: W'sor 2N 17
PLAISTOW 6A 192
Plaistow Rd. GU8: Chid 4C 190
GU8: Duns 1M 191
RH14: Kird 8D 192
RH14: Plais, Loxw 5D 192
Plaistow St. RH7: Ling 7N 145
Plane Ho. BR2: Brom 1N 47
Planes, The KT16: Chert 6L 37
Plane Tree Cres. TW13: Felt 4J 23
Plantagenet Cl. KT4: W Pk 1C 60
Plantagenet Pk.
RG42: Warf 9D 16
Plantain Cres.
RH11: Craw 7M 181
Plantation La.
CR3: Warl, Wold 6H 85
CR6: Warl 6H 85
Plantation Row
GU15: Camb 1N 69
Plas Newydd RH19: D Pk 4B 166
Plat, The RH12: Hors 5G 197
TN8: Eden 2M 147
Plateau, The RG42: Warf 8E 16
Platt, The RH7: Dorm 1C 166
SW15 6J 13
Platt Mdw. GU4: Guil 9F 94
Plaws Hill GU5: P'lake 5E 136
Playden Ct. RH11: Craw 6L 181
Playfair Mans. *W14 2K 13*
(off Queen's Club Gdns.)
Playfair St. W6 1H 13
Playground Cl. BR3: Beck 1G 47
Playhouse, The *7G 38*
(off Hurst Gro.)
Playing Fld. Cl.
GU27: Hasl 9G 171
Playscape Pro Racing Karting Track
6H 29
Plaza, The RG40: W'ham 3B 30
Pleasance, The SW15 7G 12
Pleasance Rd. SW15 8G 12
Pleasant Gro. CR0: Croy 9J 47
Pleasant Pl. KT12: Hers 3K 57
Pleasant Vw. Pl.
BR6: Farnb 2K 67
Pleasure Pit Rd.
KT21: A'tead 5A 80
Plesman Way SM6: W'ton 5J 63
Plevna Rd. TW12: Hamp 9B 24
Plough Cl. RH11: Ifi 1L 181
Plough Ind. Est. KT22: Leat 7G 79
Ploughlands RG42: Brac 9L 15
Plough La. CR8: Pur 5J 63
GU6: Ewh 6G 156
KT11: Cob 4H 77
RG40: W'ham 1E 30
RH12: Hors 3L 197
SM6: Bedd 1J 63
SW17 6N 27
SW19 6N 27
TW11: Tedd 6G 24
Plough La. Cl. SM6: Bedd 2J 63
Ploughmans End TW7: Isle 8D 10
Plough Rd. GU46: Yate 8D 48
KT19: Ewe 5C 60
RH6: Smal 8M 143
RH7: Dorm 9C 146
Plough Wlk. *TN8: Eden 9L 127*
(off Fircroft Way)
Plover Cl. RH11: Craw 1A 182
TN8: Eden 9M 127
TW18: Stain 4H 21
Plovers Ri. GU24: B'wood 7B 72
Plovers Rd. RH13: Hors 5M 197
Plum Cl. TW13: Felt 2H 23
Plum Gth. TW8: Brent 1K 11
Plummer La. CR4: Mit 1D 44
Plummer Rd. SW4 1H 29
Plumpton Way SM5: Cars 9C 44
Plumtree Cl. SM6: W'ton 4H 63
Plymen Ho. KT8: W Mole 4A 40
Plymouth Ct. KT5: Surb 8K 203
Pocket Cl. RG12: Bin 1J 31
Pockford Rd. GU8: Chid 5F 172
Pocklington Ct. SW15 2F 26
Pococks La. SL4: Eton 1H 5
Podmore Rd. SW18 7N 13
Poels Ct. RH19: E Grin 8A 166
Point, The *GU21: Wok 3B 74*
(off Chertsey Rd.)
Pointers, The KT21: A'tead 7L 79
Pointers Cotts. TW10: Ham 3J 25
POINTERS GREEN 5H 77
Pointers Hill RH4: Westc 7C 118
Pointers Rd. KT11: Cob 3D 76
Point Leisure Cen., The 1N 31
Point Pleasant SW18 7M 13
Point Wharf TW8: Brent 3L 11
Point Wharf La. TW8: Brent 3K 11
Polar Pk. UB7: Harm 3A 8
Polden Cl. GU14: Cove 7K 69
POLECAT 8D 170
Polecat Hill GU26: Hind 8D 170
GU27: Hasl 8D 170
Polecat Valley GU26: Hind 8D 170
Polehamptons, The
TW12: Hamp 8C 24
Polesden Gdns. SW20 1G 42
POLESDEN LACEY 8C 98
Polesden Lacey 8B 98
Polesden La. GU23: Rip 1H 95
Polesden Rd. KT23: Book 7B 98
Polesden Vw. KT23: Book 5B 98
Poles La. RH11: L Hea 6A 162
Polesteeple Hill TN16: B Hil 4F 86
Police Sta. Rd. KT12: Hers 3K 57
Polkerris Way GU52: C Cro 9C 88
Pollard Cl. SL4: O Win 8L 5
Pollard Gro. GU15: Camb 2G 71
Pollard Ho. KT4: W Pk 1H 61
Pollard Rd. GU22: Wok 3D 74
SM4: Mord 4B 44
Pollardrow Av. RG42: Brac 9L 15
(not continuous)
Pollards RH11: Craw 4M 181
Pollards Cres. SW16 2J 45
Pollards Dr. RH13: Hors 5L 197
Pollards Hill E. SW16 2K 45
Pollards Hill Nth.
SW16 2J 45
Pollards Hill Sth.
SW16 2J 45
Pollards Hill W. SW16 2K 45
Pollards Oak Cres.
RH8: Oxt 1C 126
Pollards Oak Rd. RH8: Oxt 1C 126
Pollards Wood Hill
RH8: Oxt 8D 106
Pollards Wood Rd.
RH8: Oxt 9D 106
SW16 2J 45
Pollocks Path GU26: Hind 7B 170
Polmear Cl. GU52: C Cro 9C 88
Polsted La. GU3: Comp 1E 132
Poltimore Rd. GU2: Guil 5K 113
Polworth Rd. SW16 6J 29
Polyanthus Way
RG45: Crow 8G 30
Polygon Bus. Cen. SL3: Poy 5H 7
Pomeroy Cl. TW1: Twick 7H 11
Pond Cl. KT12: Hers 3G 57
(not continuous)
RH14: Loxw 4H 193
Pond Copse La.
RH14: Loxw 3H 193
Pond Cott. La. BR4: Beck 7K 47
Pond Cft. GU46: Yate 9D 48
Pond Farm Cl.
KT20: Wal H 2G 100
Pondfield Ho. SE27 6N 29
Pondfield Rd. CR8: Ken 3M 83
GU7: Goda 4J 133
RH12: Rudg 9F 176
Pond Head La.
RH5: For G, Ockl 6L 157
Pond Hill Gdns. SM3: Chea 3K 61
Pond Ho. KT16: Chert 6K 37
Pond La. GU5: P'lake 4D 136
GU10: Churt 6H 149
Pond Mdw. GU2: Guil 3H 113
Pond Moor Rd. RG12: Brac 4N 31
Pond Piece KT22: Oxs 9B 58
Pond Pl. KT21: A'tead 4L 79
Pond Rd. GU22: Wok 7K 73
GU35: H Dwn 5F 168
TW20: Egh 7E 20
Ponds, The KT13: Weybr 3E 56
Pondside Cl. UB3: Harl 2E 8
Ponds La. GU5: Alb 2N 135
(not continuous)
PONDTAIL
GU51, Edenbridge 5M 167
GU51, Fleet 4D 88
Pondtail Cl. GU51: Fleet 5D 88
RH12: Hors 2K 197
Pondtail Copse
RH12: Hors 2K 197
Pondtail Dr. RH12: Hors 1K 197
Pondtail Gdns. GU51: Fleet 5D 88
Pondtail Pk. RH12: Hors 2K 197
Pondtail Rd. GU51: Fleet 5D 88
RH12: Hors 3J 197
Pondview Cl. GU51: Fleet 3C 88
Pond Way RH19: E Grin 9D 166
TW11: Tedd 7J 25
Pond Wood Rd.
RH10: Craw 1E 182
Ponsonby Rd. SW15 1G 26
Pony Chase KT11: Cob 9N 57
Pook Hill GU8: Chid, Hasl 5B 172
Pool Cl. KT8: W Mole 4N 39
Poole Ct. TW4: Houn 5M 9
Poole Ct. Rd. TW4: Houn 5M 9
POOL END 4B 38
Pool End Cl. TW17: Shep 4B 38
Poole Rd. GU21: Wok 5A 74
KT19: Ewe 3C 60
Pooles Cotts. TW10: Ham 3K 25
Pooley Av. TW20: Egh 6D 20
Pooley Dr. SW14 6B 12
POOLEY GREEN 6E 20
Pooley Grn. Cl. TW20: Egh 6E 20
Pooley Grn. Rd. TW20: Egh 6D 20
Pool in the Pk. 6B 74
Poolmans Rd. SL4: W'sor 6A 4
Pool Rd. GU11: Alde 5A 110
KT8: W Mole 4N 39
Pools on the Pk. 7K 11
POOTINGS 5N 127
Pootings Rd. TN8: C Hil 3M 127
Pope Cl. SW19 7B 28
TW14: Felt 2G 22
Popes Av. TW2: Twick 3E 24
Popes Cl. SL3: Coln 3D 6
Popes Ct. TW2: Twick 3E 24
Popes Gro. CR0: Croy 9J 47
TW1: Twick 3E 24
TW2: Twick 3F 24
Popes La. RH8: Oxt 3A 126
Popes Mead GU27: Hasl 1G 189
POPESWOOD 8J 15
Popeswood Rd. RG42: Bin 8J 15
Popeswood Rdbt. RG42: Bin 9J 15
Popham Cl. RG12: Brac 4D 32
TW13: Hanw 4N 23
Popham Gdns. TW9: Rich 6N 11
Popinjays Row *SM3: Chea 2J 61*
(off Netley Cl.)
Poplar Av. CR4: Mit 9D 28
GU20: Windl 1L 51
KT22: Leat 9H 79
Poplar Cl. GU14: Cove 9H 69
GU16: Mytc 2E 90
RG12: Brac 2B 32
RH11: Craw 9A 162
SL3: Poy 4G 7
Poplar Cotts. GU3: Guil 9H 93
Poplar Ct. SW19 6M 27
TW1: Twick 9J 11
Poplar Cres. KT19: Ewe 3B 60
Poplar Dr. SM7: Ban 1J 81
Poplar Farm Cl. KT19: Ewe 3B 60
Poplar Gdns. KT3: N Mal 1C 42
Poplar Gro. GU22: Wok 6A 74
KT3: N Mal 1C 42
Poplar Ho. SL3: Lang 1B 6
Poplar La. RH18: F Row 8G 187
Poplar Rd. GU4: Chil 1A 134
KT22: Leat 9H 79
SM3: Sut 7L 43
SW19 1M 43
TW15: A'ford 6D 22
Poplar Rd. Sth. SW19 2M 43
Poplars, The RH13: Hors 5L 197
SL5: Asc 4L 33
Poplar Vs. *GU16: Frim G 8D 70*
(off Beech Rd.)
Poplar Wlk.
CR0: Croy 1B 200 (8N 45)
CR3: Cate 1B 104
GU9: H End 5J 109
Poplar Way TW13: Felt 4H 23
Poppy Cl. SM6: W'ton 7E 44
Poppyhills Rd. GU15: Camb 7D 50
Poppy La. CR0: Croy 6F 46
Poppy Pl. RG40: W'ham 2A 30
Porchester SL5: Asc 3L 33
Porchester Rd.
KT1: K Tham 1A 42
Porchfield Cl. SM2: Sut 6N 61
Porridge Pot All.
GU1: Guil 7C 202 (5N 113)
GU2: Guil 7B 202 (5N 113)
Portal Cl. SE27 4L 29
Porters Lodge, The
SW10 3N 13
(off Coleridge Gdns.)
Portesbery Hill Dr.
GU15: Camb 9C 50
Portesbery Rd.
GU15: Camb 9B 50
Portia Gro. RG42: Warf 9C 16
Portinscale Rd. SW15 8K 13
Portland Av. KT3: N Mal 6E 42
Portland Bus. Cen. *SL3: Dat 4L 5*
(off Manor Ho. La.)
Portland Cl. KT4: W Pk 6G 42
Portland Cotts. CR0: Bedd 6H 45
Portland Cres. TW13: Felt 5E 22
Portland Dr. GU52: C Cro 9A 88
RH1: Mers 7H 103
Portland Ho. RH1: Mers 7G 103
Portland Pl. KT17: Eps 8D 60
SE25 3D 46
(off Sth. Norwood Hill)
Portland Rd. CR4: Mit 1C 44
KT1: K Tham 6K 203 (2L 41)
RH4: Dork 1J 201 (4G 119)
RH19: E Grin 1A 186
SE25 3D 46
TW15: A'ford 4N 21
Portland Ter. TW9: Rich 7K 11
Portley La. CR3: Cate 8B 84
Portley Wood Rd.
CR3: Whyte 7C 84
Portman Av. SW14 6C 12
Portman Cl. RG42: Brac 9M 15
Portman Rd.
KT1: K Tham 4M 203 (1M 41)
Portmore Pk. Rd.
KT13: Weybr 1B 56
Portmore Pl. *KT13: Weybr 9E 38*
(off Oatlands Dr.)
Portmore Quays
KT13: Weybr 1A 56
Portmore Way KT13: Weybr 9B 38
Portnall Dr. GU25: V Wat 4J 35
Portnall Ri. GU25: V Wat 4J 35
Portnall Rd. GU25: V Wat 4J 35
Portnalls Cl. CR5: Coul 3F 82
Portnalls Ri. CR5: Coul 3G 82
Portnalls Rd. CR5: Coul 5F 82
Porton Ct. KT6: Surb 5J 41
Portsmouth Av. KT7: T Dit 6G 40
Portsmouth Rd.
GU2: Guil 8B 202 (7M 113)
GU7: Goda 1D 152
GU8: Goda, Mil 1D 152
GU8: Mil, Thur 5E 170
GU15: Camb 9E 50
GU16: Frim 5B 70
GU23: Rip 8M 75
GU23: Send, Rip 3H 95
GU26: Brams, Lip 9M 169
KT1: K Tham 8G 203 (6G 41)
KT6: Surb 8G 203 (6G 41)
KT7: T Dit 8G 203 (6G 41)
KT10: Esh 3A 58
(Old Chestnut Av.)
KT10: Esh 1C 58
(Sandown Rd.)
KT11: Cob 9G 57
SW15 1G 27
Portswood Pl. SW15 9E 12
Portugal Gdns. TW2: Twick 3C 24
Portugal Rd. GU21: Wok 3B 74
Port Way GU24: Bis 3D 72
Portway KT17: Ewe 5F 60
Portway Cres. KT17: Ewe 5F 60
Post Boys Row KT11: Cob 1H 77
Postford Farm Cotts.
GU5: Alb 1J 135

Postford Mill Cotts.—Putney Bridge Station (Tube)

Postford Mill Cotts.
GU4: Guil 7H **115**
Post Horn Cl.
RH18: F Row 8K **187**
Post Horn La.
RH18: F Row 8J **187**
Post Ho. La. KT23: Book 3A **98**
Post La. TW2: Twick 2D **24**
Postmill Cl. CR0: Croy 9F **46**
Post Office All. *W4 . . . . 2A 12*
(off Thames Rd.)
Post Office Row
RH8: Limp 9G **107**
Potbury Cl. SL4: Wink 7M **17**
POT COMMON 8G **131**
Potkiln Ho. GU51: Fleet 1A **88**
Potley Hill Rd. GU46: Yate 9E **48**
Potter Cl. CR4: Mit 1F **44**
Potteries, The GU14: Cove 8J **69**
KT16: Otter 3G **54**
Potteries La. GU16: Mytc 2D **90**
Potterne Cl. SW19 . . . . 1J **27**
Potters Cl. CR0: Croy 7H **47**
GU8: Mil 9C **132**
Potters Ct. *SM1: Sut 3L 61*
(off Rosebery Rd.)
Potters Cres. GU12: Ash 1F **110**
Potter's Cft. RH13: Hors 6L **197**
Pottersfield RH10: Craw 2B **182**
Potters Ga. GU9: Farnh 1F **128**
Potters Gro. KT3: N Mal 3B **42**
Potter's Hill GU8: Ent G 5F **152**
Potters Ind. Pk.
GU52: C Cro 8D **88**
Potters La. GU23: Send 1D **94**
SW16 . . . . 7H **29**
Potters Pl. RH12: Hors 6J **197**
Potters Way RH2: Reig 7A **122**
Pottery Ct. GU10: Wrec 5E **128**
Pottery La. GU10: Wrec 5E **128**
Pottery Rd. TW8: Brent 2L **11**
Poulcott TW19: Wray 9A **6**
Poulett Gdns. TW1: Twick 2G **24**
Poulters Wood BR2: Kes 2F **66**
Poulton Av. SM1: Sut 9B **44**
Pound Cl. GU7: Goda 7H **133**
GU35: Head 4E **168**
KT6: Surb 7J **41**
KT19: Eps 7C **60**
RH14: Loxw 3H **193**
Pound Ct. GU3: Wood V 2E **112**
KT21: A'tead 5M **79**
Pound Cres. KT22: Fetc 8D **78**
Pound Farm Cl. KT10: Esh 7D **40**
Pound Farm La.
GU12: Ash, A Grn 2H **111**
Pound Fld.
GU1: Guil 2C **202** (2N **113**)
Poundfield Ct. GU22: Wok 8E **74**
Poundfield Gdns.
GU22: Wok 7E **74**
(not continuous)
Poundfield La.
RH14: Plais 4D **192**
POUND HILL 3G **183**
Pound Hill GU3: Wood V 2E **112**
Pound Hill Pde.
RH10: Craw 2G **183**
Pound Hill Pl. RH10: Craw 3G **183**
Pound La. GU3: Wood V 2E **112**
GU7: Goda 7H **133**
(not continuous)
GU20: Windl 3N **51**
KT19: Eps 5G **201** (8B **60**)
RG10: Hurst 4A **14**
Pound La. Cvn. Site
GU3: Wood V 2E **112**
Pound Pl. GU4: Chil 9B **114**
RG42: Bin 6H **15**
Pound Pl. Cl. GU4: Chil 9B **114**
Pound Rd. GU12: Alde 3A **110**
KT16: Chert 6K **37**
SM7: Ban 4L **81**
Pound St. SM5: Cars 2D **62**
POVEY CROSS 1B **162**
Povey Cross Rd.
RH6: Horl 1B **162**
Powderham Ct. GU21: Knap . . . 5G **72**
Powder Mill La. TW2: Whitt . . . 1N **23**
Powell Cl. GU2: Guil 5J **113**
KT9: Ches 2K **59**
RH6: Horl 7C **142**
SM6: W'ton 4J **63**
Powell Ct. CR2: S Croy 7A **200**
Powells Cl. RH4: Dork 8J **119**
Powell's Wlk. W4 . . . . 2D **12**
Power Cl.
GU1: Guil 1B **202** (2M **113**)
Powerleague Soccer Cen.
Norbury 9J **29**
Purley 3K **63**
Power Rd. W4 . . . . 1N **11**
Powers Ct. TW1: Twick 1K **25**
Pownall Gdns. TW3: Houn 7B **10**
Pownall Rd. TW3: Houn 7B **10**
POYLE 5G **7**
Poyle Cl. SL3: Poy 5G **6**
Poyle Gdns. RG12: Brac 9B **16**
Poyle Ho. *GU4: Guil 2F 114*
(off Merrow St.)
Poyle Ind. Est. SL3: Poy 6H **7**
Poyle New Cotts. SL3: Poy 5H **7**
Poyle Pk. SL3: Poy 6G **6**
Poyle Rd.
GU1: Guil 7E **202** (5A **114**)
GU10: Tong 6D **110**
SL3: Poy 6G **6**
Poyle Technical Cen.
SL3: Poy 5G **7**
Poyle Ter.
GU1: Guil 6D **202** (5N **113**)
Poyle Trad. Est. SL3: Poy 6G **7**
Poynders Ct. SW4 . . . . 1G **29**
Poynders Gdns. SW4 . . . . 1G **29**
Poynders Rd. SW4 . . . . 1G **28**
Poynes Rd. RH6: Horl 6C **142**
Poynings Rd. RH11: Ifi 4J **181**
Prairie Cl. KT15: Addl 9K **37**
Prairie Rd. KT15: Addl 9K **37**
Pratts La. KT12: Hers 1L **57**
Pratts Pas.
KT1: K Tham 4J **203** (1L **41**)
Prebend Gdns. W4 . . . . 1E **12**
Prebend Mans. *W4 . . . . 1E 12*
(off Chiswick High Rd.)
Precinct, The GU6: Cranl 6N **155**
TW20: Egh 6C **20**
Precincts, The SM4: Mord 5M **43**
Premier Ho.
RH10: Craw 8B **162**
Premier Pde. *RH6: Horl 8F 142*
(off High St.)
Premier Pl. SW15 . . . . 7K **13**
Prentice Cl. GU14: Farnb 6N **69**
Prentice Ct. SW19 . . . . 6L **27**
Prentis Rd. SW16 . . . . 5H **29**
Presburg Rd. KT3: N Mal 4D **42**
Presbury Ct. GU21: Wok 5K **73**
Prescott RG12: Brac 6L **31**
Prescott Cl. SW16 . . . . 8J **29**
Prescott Rd. SL3: Poy 5G **6**
Presentation M. SW2 . . . . 3K **29**
Preshaw Cres. CR4: Mit 2C **44**
Prestbury Cres. SM7: Ban 3D **82**
Preston Cl. TW2: Twick 4E **24**
Preston Ct. KT12: Wal T 7K **39**
Preston Dr. KT19: Ewe 3D **60**
Preston Gro. KT21: A'tead 4J **79**
Preston La. KT20: Tad 8G **81**
Preston Pl. TW10: Rich 8L **11**
Preston Rd. SE19 . . . . 7M **29**
SW20 . . . . 8E **26**
TW17: Shep 4B **38**
Prestwick Cl. RH11: Ifi 4J **181**
UB2: S'hall 1M **9**
Prestwick La. GU8: Chid 7L **171**
GU27: G'wood, Chid 7L **171**
Prestwood Cl. RH11: Craw . . . 9N **161**
Prestwood Gdns.
CR0: Croy 6N **45**
Prestwood La. RH11: Ifi 9H **161**
RH12: Rusp 9F **160**
Pretoria Rd. KT16: Chert 7H **37**
SW16 . . . . 7F **28**
Pretty La. CR5: Coul 8G **82**
Prewetts Mill RH12: Hors 7H **197**
Prey Heath Cl. GU22: Wok 2M **93**
Prey Heath Rd. GU22: Wok . . . 2L **93**
Preymead Ind. Est.
GU9: B Lea 5N **109**
Price Cl. SW17 . . . . 4D **28**
Price Gdns. RG42: Warf 7N **15**
Price Rd.
CR0: Wad 8A **200** (2M **63**)
Prices La. RH2: Reig 6M **121**
Price Way TW12: Hamp 7M **23**
Priddy Pl. RH1: Mers 9G **102**
Priddy's Yd.
CR0: Croy 3B **200** (8N **45**)
Prideaux Gdns. RH5: Ockl . . . 6D **158**
Prides Crossing SL5: Asc 8L **17**
Pridham Rd. CR7: T Hea 3A **46**
Priest Av. RG40: W'ham 3E **30**
Priestcroft Cl.
RH11: Craw 3M **181**
Priest Hill RH8: Limp 7D **106**
SL4: O Win 4M **19**
TW20: Eng G, O Win 4M **19**
Priestlands Cl. RH6: Horl 7D **142**
Priest La. GU24: W End 9N **51**
Priestley Gdns. GU22: Wok . . . 7C **74**
Priestley Rd. CR4: Mit 1E **44**
GU2: Guil 3G **112**
Priestley Way RH10: Craw . . . 8E **162**
Priest's Bri. SW14 . . . . 6D **12**
PRIESTWOOD 9M **15**
Priestwood Av. RG42: Brac . . . 9L **15**
Priestwood Ct. Rd.
RG42: Brac 9M **15**
Priestwood Sq. RG42: Brac . . . 9L **15**
Primrose Av. RH6: Horl 1F **162**
Primrose Cl. RH11: Craw 6N **181**
SM6: W'ton 6F **44**
Primrose Copse
RH12: Hors 1K **197**
Primrose Ct. GU12: Ash 2E **110**
SW12 . . . . 1H **29**
Primrose Dr. GU24: Bis 2D **72**
Primrose Gdns. GU14: Cove . . . 2K **89**
Primrose La. CR0: Croy 7F **46**
RH18: F Row 8J **187**
Primrose Pl. GU7: Goda 9E **132**
TW7: Isle 5F **10**
Primrose Ridge
GU7: Goda 9E **132**
Primrose Rd. KT12: Hers 2K **57**
Primrose Wlk. GU46: Yate 9A **48**
GU51: Fleet 3A **88**
KT17: Ewe 4E **60**
RG12: Brac 4A **32**
Primrose Way GU5: Braml . . . 6N **133**
GU47: Sandh 6G **49**
Primula Rd. GU35: Bor 6A **168**
Prince Albert Ct.
TW16: Sunb 8F **22**
Prince Albert Dr. SL5: Asc 3H **33**
Prince Albert Sq.
RH1: Red 8D **122**
Prince Albert's Wlk.
SL4: W'sor 4K **5**
Prince Andrew Way
SL5: Asc 1H **33**
Prince Charles Cres.
GU14: Farnb 6N **69**
Prince Charles Way
SM6: W'ton 9F **44**
Prince Consort Cotts.
SL4: W'sor 5G **4**
Prince Consort Dr. SL5: Asc . . . 3H **33**
Prince Consort's Dr.
SL4: W'sor 9C **4**
Prince Dr. GU47: Sandh 6F **48**
Prince George's Av.
SW20 . . . . 1H **43**
Prince George's Rd.
SW19 . . . . 9B **28**
Prince of Wales Ct.
GU11: Alde 2L 109
(off Queen Elizabeth Dr.)
Prince of Wales Rd.
RH1: Out 2L **143**
SM1: Sut 8B **44**
Prince of Wales Ter.
W4 . . . . 1D **12**
Prince of Wales Wlk.
GU15: Camb 9A **50**
Prince Regent Rd.
TW3: Houn 6C **10**
Prince Rd. SE25 . . . . 4B **46**
Princes Av. CR2: Sande 2E **84**
GU7: Goda 4F **132**
GU11: Alde 8N **89**
KT6: Surb 7N **41**
SM5: Cars 4D **62**
Princes Cl. CR2: Sande 2E **84**
SL4: E Wic 1C **4**
TW11: Tedd 5D **24**
Princes Ct. GU1: Guil 2C **202**
KT13: Weybr 2C 56
(off Princes Rd.)
Prince's Dr. KT22: Oxs 8E **58**
Princes Hall 2L **109**
Princes Mead (Shop. Cen.)
GU14: Farnb 1N **89**
Princes M. TW3: Houn 7A **10**
W6 . . . . 1G 13
(off Down Pl.)
Princes Rd. KT2: K Tham 8N **25**
KT13: Weybr 2C **56**
RH1: Red 5D **122**
SW14 . . . . 6C **12**
SW19 . . . . 7M **27**
TW9: Kew 4M **11**
TW10: Rich 8M **11**
TW11: Tedd 5D **24**
TW13: Felt 3G **22**
TW15: A'ford 6A **22**
TW20: Egh 7B **20**
Princess Anne Rd.
RH12: Rudg 1E **194**
Princess Av. SL4: W'sor 6E **4**
Princess Ct. KT1: K Tham 6L **203**
Princess Gdns. GU22: Wok 3D **74**
Princess Ho. RH1: Red 2E **122**
Princess Margaret Rd.
RH12: Rudg 1E **194**
Princess Mary Cl. GU2: Guil . . . 8K **93**
Princess Marys Rd.
KT15: Addl 1L **55**
Princess M.
KT1: K Tham . . . 6L **203** (2M **41**)
Princess Pde. BR6: Farnb 1J **67**
Princess Pct. *RH6: Horl 8E 142*
(off High St.)
Princess Rd. CR0: Croy 5N **45**
GU22: Wok 3D **74**
RH11: Craw 3A **182**
Princess Sq. RG12: Brac 1N **31**
Princes St. SM1: Sut 1B **62**
TW9: Rich 7L **11**
Princess Way GU15: Camb 9A **50**
RH1: Red 2E **122**
Princes Way BR4: W Wick 1B **66**
CR0: Wad 2K **63**
GU11: Alde 2M **109**
GU19: Bag 6J **51**
SW19 . . . . 1J **27**
Princeton Ct. SW15 . . . . 6J **13**
Princeton M.
KT2: K Tham . . . 2M **203** (9N **25**)
Prince William Ct.
TW15: A'ford 6A 22
(off Princes Rd.)
Pringle Gdns. CR8: Pur 6K **63**
SW16 . . . . 5G **28**
(not continuous)
Prior Av. SM2: Sut 4C **62**
Prior Cft. Cl. GU15: Camb 2E **70**
Prior End GU15: Camb 1E **70**
Prioress Rd. SE27 . . . . 4M **29**
Prior Rd. GU15: Camb 1E **70**
Priors, The KT21: A'tead 6K **79**
Priors Cl. GU14: Farnb 6M **69**
Priors Ct. GU12: Ash 3D **110**
GU21: Wok 5K **73**
Prior's Cft. GU22: Wok 7C **74**
Priorsfield Rd. GU3: Comp . . . 9C **112**
GU7: Hurt 9C **112**
Priors Hatch La.
GU7: Hurt 2C **132**
Priors Keep GU52: Fleet 5C **88**
Prior's La. GU17: B'water 1F **68**
Priors Mead KT23: Book 3C **98**
Priors Rd. SL4: W'sor 6A **4**
Priors Wlk. RH10: Craw 3C **182**
Priors Wood GU27: Hasl 2D **188**
KT10: H Wood 8F **40**
RG45: Crow 3C **48**
Priorswood GU3: Comp 1C **132**
Priory, The CR0: Wad 1L **63**
KT22: Leat 9H **79**
RH9: Gods 9E **104**
Priory Av. SM3: Chea 1J **61**
Priory Cl. BR3: Beck 2H **47**
GU21: Wok 9F **54**
KT12: Wal T 9H **39**
RH4: Dork 7G **119**
RH6: Horl 7D **142**
SL5: S'dale 6D **34**
SW19 . . . . 9N **27**
TW12: Hamp 9N **23**
TW16: Sunb 8H **23**
Priory Ct. GU2: Guil 7M **113**
GU15: Camb 1L **69**
KT1: K Tham 5J **203**
KT17: Ewe 5E **60**
RH4: Dork 7H **119**
SM3: Chea 1K **61**
TW3: Houn 6B **10**
TW20: Egh 7E **20**
Priory Cres. SE19 . . . . 8N **29**
SM3: Chea 1J **61**
Priory Dr. RH2: Reig 5M **121**
Priory Gdns. SE25 . . . . 3C **46**
SW13 . . . . 6E **12**
TW12: Hamp 8N **23**
TW15: A'ford 6E **22**
Priory Grn. TW18: Stain 6K **21**
Priory La. GU10: Fren 2K **149**
KT8: W Mole 3B **40**
RG42: Brac 8A **16**
SW15 . . . . 9D **12**
TW9: Kew 3N **11**
Priory Lodge *W4 . . . . 1N 11*
(off Kew Bri. Ct.)
Priory M. TW18: Stain 6K **21**
Priory Pl. KT12: Wal T 9H **39**
Priory Retail Pk.
SW19 . . . . 8B **28**
Priory Rd. CR0: Croy 6L **45**
KT9: Ches 9L **41**
RH2: Reig 5M **121**
RH18: F Row 9D **186**
SL5: Asc 9F **16**
SL5: S'dale 6D **34**
SM3: Chea 1J **61**
SW19 . . . . 8B **28**
TW3: Houn 8C **10**
TW9: Kew 2N **11**
TW12: Hamp 8N **23**
Priory St. GU14: Farnb 1B **90**
Priory Ter. TW16: Sunb 8H **23**
Priory Wlk. RG12: Brac 3D **32**
Priory Way SL3: Dat 3L **5**
UB7: Harm 2N **7**
Privet Rd. GU35: Lind 4B **168**
Probyn Rd. SW2 . . . . 3M **29**
Proctor Cl. CR4: Mit 9E **28**
RH10: Craw 5G **183**
Proctor Gdns. KT23: Book 3B **98**
Proctors Cl. TW14: Felt 2H **23**
Proctors Rd. RG40: W'ham 2E **30**
Proffits Cotts. KT20: Tad 9J **81**
Profumo Rd. KT12: Hers 2L **57**
Progress Bus. Pk.
CR0: Wad 8K **45**
Progress Way CR0: Wad 8K **45**
Prologis Pk. CR0: Bedd 6H **45**
TW4: Houn 7K **9**
Promenade, The W4 . . . . 5D **12**
Promenade App. Rd.
W4 . . . . 3D **12**
Promenade de Verdun
CR8: Pur 7H **63**
Prospect Av. GU14: Farnb 8N **69**
Prospect Cl. TW3: Houn 4N **9**
Prospect Cotts. GU12: A Va 9E **90**
SW18 . . . . 7M **13**
Prospect Cres. TW2: Whitt 9C **10**
Prospect Hill GU35: Head 1D **168**
Prospect Ho. KT19: Eps 5A **60**
SW19 . . . . 9B 28
(off Chapter Way)
Prospect La. TW20: Eng G 6K **19**
Prospect Pl.
KT17: Eps 6L **201** (8D **60**)
RH11: Craw 3A **182**
SL4: W'sor 6G 4
(off Osbourne Rd.)
SW20 . . . . 8G **27**
TW18: Stain 6H **21**
W4 . . . . 1C **12**
Prospect Quay *SW18 . . . . 7M 13*
(off Lightermans Wlk.)
Prospect Rd. GU10: Rowl 8D **128**
GU12: A Va 8E **90**
GU14: Cove, Farnb 1M **89**
KT6: Surb 5J **41**
Prossers KT20: Tad 8J **81**
Prothero Rd. SW6 . . . . 3K **13**
Providence La. UB3: Harl 3E **8**
Providence Pl. GU22: Pyr 1J **75**
KT17: Eps 5M **201** (8D **60**)
Providence Ter.
RH10: T Hil 5D **184**
Prudence La. BR6: Farnb 1J **67**
Prune Hill TW20: Egh, Eng G . . . 8N **19**
Prunus Cl. GU24: W End 9B **52**
Pryors Wood RH12: K'fold 3J **179**
Ptarmigan Hgts. RG12: Brac . . . 3J **31**
Puckridge Hill Rd.
GU11: Alde 7K **89**
Pucks Hill GU21: Knap 4G **73**
Puckshott Way GU27: Hasl . . . 9H **171**
Puddenhole Cotts.
RH3: Betch 2N **119**
Pudding La. RH6: Char 2K **161**
Puffin Cl. BR3: Beck 4G **46**
Puffin Hill RH10: T Hil 4F **184**
Puffin Rd. RH11: Ifi 4J **181**
Pulborough Rd. SW18 . . . . 1L **27**
Pulborough Way TW4: Houn . . . 7K **9**
Pullman Ct. SW2 . . . . 2J **29**
Pullman Gdns. SW15 . . . . 9H **13**
Pullman La. GU7: Goda 9F **132**
Pullman Pl. *RH1: Mers 6G 102*
(off Station Rd.)
Pullmans Pl. TW18: Stain 6J **21**
Pulteney Cl. TW7: Isle 6G **10**
Pulton Pl. SW6 . . . . 3M **13**
Pump All. TW8: Brent 3K **11**
Pumping Sta. Rd. W4 . . . . 3D **12**
Pump La. SL5: Asc 9B **18**
Pump Pail Nth.
CR0: Croy 5B **200** (9N **45**)
Pump Pail Sth.
CR0: Croy 5B **200** (9N **45**)
Punchbowl La. RH5: Dork 4K **119**
Punch Copse Rd.
RH10: Craw 2D **182**
Punnetts Ct. RH11: Craw 6L **181**
Purbeck Av. KT3: N Mal 5E **42**
Purbeck Cl. RH1: Mers 6H **103**
(not continuous)
Purbeck Ct. GU2: Guil 3H **113**
Purbeck Dr. GU21: Wok 1B **74**
Purberry Gro. KT17: Ewe 6E **60**
Purbrook Ct. RG12: Brac 5C **32**
Purcell Cl. CR8: Ken 1N **83**
Purcell Cres. SW6 . . . . 3J **13**
(not continuous)
Purcell Mans. *W14 . . . . 2K 13*
(off Queen's Club Gdns.)
Purcell Rd. RG45: Crow 9G **30**
RH11: Craw 6L **181**
Purcell's Cl. KT21: A'tead 5M **79**
Purdy Ct. KT4: W Pk 8F **42**
PURLEY 7L **63**
Purley Bury Av. CR8: Pur 7L **63**
Purley Bury Cl. CR8: Pur 7N **63**
Purley Cl. RH10: Craw 6H **183**
PURLEY CROSS 7L **63**
Purley Downs Rd.
CR2: Sande 6N **63**
CR8: Pur 6N **63**
Purley Hill CR8: Pur 8M **63**
Purley Knoll CR8: Pur 7K **63**
Purley Oaks Rd.
CR2: Sande 5A **64**
Purley Oaks Station (Rail) . . . 5A **64**
Purley Pde. CR8: Pur 7L **63**
Purley Pk. Rd. CR8: Pur 6M **63**
Purley Pool 7L **63**
Purley Ri. CR8: Pur 8K **63**
Purley Rd. CR2: S Croy 4A **64**
CR8: Pur 7L **63**
Purley Station (Rail) 7L **63**
Purley Va. CR8: Pur 9M **63**
Purley Vw. Ter. *CR2: S Croy . . . 4A 64*
(off Sanderstead Rd.)
Purley Way CR0: Croy, Wad . . . 6K **45**
CR8: Pur 7L **63**
GU16: Frim 6C **70**
Purley Way Cen., The
CR0: Wad 8L **45**
Purley Way Cnr. CR0: Croy . . . 6K **45**
Purmerend Cl. GU14: Cove . . . 9H **69**
Purser Ho. *SW2 . . . . 1L 29*
(off Tulse Hill)
Pursers Cross Rd. SW6 . . . . . . 4L **13**
(not continuous)
Pursers La. GU5: P'lake 2E **136**
Pursers Lea GU5: P'lake 4E **136**
Purslane RG40: W'ham 3C **30**
Purton Rd. RH12: Hors 4H **197**
Purvis Ho. CR0: Croy 6A **46**
PUTNEY 7J **13**
Putney Arts Theatre 7J **13**
Putney Bri. SW6 . . . . 6K **13**
SW15 . . . . 6K **13**
Putney Bri. App. SW6 . . . . 6K **13**
Putney Bri. Rd. SW15 . . . . 7K **13**
SW18 . . . . 7K **13**
Putney Bridge Station (Tube)
. . . . 6L **13**

Putney Comn.—Raleigh Gdns.

Putney Comn. SW15 6H 13
Putney Exchange Shop. Cen.
SW15 7J 13
PUTNEY HEATH 9H 13
Putney Heath SW15 1G 26
Putney Heath La.
SW15 9J 13
Putney High St. SW15 7J 13
Putney Hill SW15 1J 27
(not continuous)
Putney Leisure Cen. 7H 13
Putney Pk. Av. SW15 7F 12
Putney Pk. La. SW15 7G 12
(not continuous)
Putney Pier (Riverbus) 6K 13
Putney Station (Rail) 7K 13
PUTNEY VALE 4F 26
Putney Va. Crematorium
SW15 3F 26
Putney Wharf SW15 6K 13
PUTTENHAM 8N 111
Puttenham Heath Rd.
GU3: Comp, Put 8A 112
Puttenham Hill GU3: Put 7N 111
Puttenham La.
GU8: S'ford 2N 131
Puttenham Rd. GU10: Seal 8F 110
Puttocks Cl. GU27: Hasl 3B 188
Pye Cl. CR3: Cate 1A 104
Pyecombe Ct. RH11: Craw 6L 181
Pyegrove Chase RG12: Brac 6C 32
PYESTOCK 4G 88
Pyestock Cres. GU14: Cove 1H 89
Pyke Cl. RG40: W'ham 2C 30
Pylbrook Rd. SM1: Sut 9M 43
PYLE HILL 2N 93
Pyle Hill GU22: Wok 2N 93
Pylon Way CR0: Bedd 7J 45
Pymers Mead SE21 2N 29
Pyne Rd. KT6: Surb 7N 41
Pyramid Ct. *KT1: K Tham* 4M 203
(off Cambridge Rd.)
Pyramid Ho. TW4: Houn 5M 9
Pyrcroft La. KT13: Weybr 2C 56
Pyrcroft Rd. KT16: Chert 6G 36
PYRFORD 3J 75
Pyrford Comn. Rd.
GU22: Pyr 3F 74
Pyrford Ct. GU22: Pyr 4G 75
PYRFORD GREEN 4K 75
Pyrford Heath GU22: Pyr 3H 75
Pyrford Rd. GU22: Pyr 9J 55
KT14: W By 9J 55
PYRFORD VILLAGE 5J 75
Pyrford Wood Est.
GU22: Pyr 3H 75
Pyrford Woods GU22: Pyr 2G 75
Pyrford Woods Cl.
GU22: Pyr 2H 75
Pyrian Cl. GU22: Wok 3F 74
Pyrland Rd. TW10: Rich 9M 11
Pyrmont Gro. SE27 4M 29
Pyrmont Rd. W4 2N 11
Pytchley Cres. SE19 7N 29

Q

QUABROOK 8L 187
Quadrangle, The GU2: Guil 4K 113
GU16: Frim 6A 70
RH6: Horl 8E 142
SW6 3K 13
Quadrant, The GU1: Guil 5B 202
GU12: A Va 9E 90
KT13: Weybr 1B 56
(off Church St.)
KT17: Eps 6L 201 (9D 60)
SM2: Sut 3A 62
SW20 9K 27
TW9: Rich 7K 11
Quadrant Ct. RG12: Brac 2C 32
Quadrant Rd. CR7: T Hea 3M 45
TW9: Rich 7K 11
Quadrant Way KT13: Weybr 1B 56
Quadrum Pk.
GU3: P'marsh 1L 133
Quail Cl. RH12: Hors 1K 197
Quail Cnr. RG12: Brac 3K 31
Quail Gdns. CR2: Sels 6H 65
Quain Mans. *W14* 2K 13
(off Queen's Club Gdns.)
Quakers La. TW7: Isle 3G 10
(not continuous)
Quakers Way GU3: Worp 8F 92
Qualitas RG12: Brac 7L 31
Quality St. RH1: Mers 6F 102
Quantock Cl. RH11: Craw 3N 181
SL3: Lang 1C 6
UB3: Harl 3E 8
Quantock Dr. KT4: W Pk 8H 43
Quarrendon St. SW6 5M 13
Quarr Rd. SM5: Cars 5B 44
Quarry, The RH3: Betch 1C 120
Quarry Bank GU18: Ligh 7L 51
Quarry Cl. KT22: Leat 8K 79
RH8: Oxt 8A 106
RH12: Hors 2M 197
Quarry Cotts. RH2: Reig 9N 101
Quarry Gdns. KT22: Leat 8K 79
Quarry Hill GU7: Goda 8E 132
Quarry Hill Pk. RH2: Reig 9A 102
Quarry La. GU46: Yate 1D 68
Quarry Pk. Rd. SM1: Sut 3L 61
Quarry Path RH8: Oxt 9A 106
Quarry Ri. RH19: E Grin 7C 166
SM1: Sut 3L 61
Quarry Rd. GU7: Hurt 4D 132
RH8: Oxt 8A 106
RH9: Gods 6F 104
Quarryside Bus. Pk.
RH1: Red 9F 102
Quarry St.
GU1: Guil 6C 202 (5N 113)
Quarterbrass Farm Rd.
RH12: Hors 1K 197
Quartermaine Av.
GU22: Wok 9B 74
Quartermile Rd.
GU7: Goda 9H 133
Quarters Rd. GU14: Farnb 3N 89
Quayside Wlk.
KT1: K Tham 4H 203
(off Wadbrook St.)
Quebec Av. TN16: Weste 4M 107
Quebec Cl. RH6: Smal 8L 143
Quebec Cotts.
TN16: Weste 5M 107
Quebec Gdns. GU17: Haw 2J 69
Quebec House 4M 107
Quebec Sq. TN16: Weste 4M 107
Queen Adelaide's Ride
SL4: Wink 9A 4
Queen Alexandra's Ct.
SW19 6L 27
Queen Alexandra's Way
KT19: Eps 7N 59
Queen Anne Dr. KT10: Clay 4E 58
Queen Anne's Cl.
SL4: W'sor 4E 18
TW2: Twick 4D 24
Queen Anne's Gdns.
CR4: Mit 2D 44
KT22: Leat 8H 79
Queen Anne's Ga.
GU9: H End 5J 109
Queen Anne's Ride
SL4: W'sor 6D 18
Queen Anne's Rd.
SL4: W'sor 7F 4
(not continuous)
Queen Anne's Ter.
KT22: Leat 8H 79
Queen Ann's Ct. *SL4: W'sor* 4G 4
(off Peascod St.)
Queen Caroline St.
W6 1H 13
(not continuous)
Queen Catherine Ho.
SW6 3N 13
(off Wandon Rd.)
Queen Charlotte's Cottage 5K 11
Queen Charlotte St.
SL4: W'sor 4G 5
(off High St.)
Queendale Ct. GU21: Wok 3J 73
Queen Eleanor's Rd.
GU2: Guil 4J 113
Queen Elizabeth Cl.
GU12: Ash 2E 110
Queen Elizabeth Dr.
GU11: Alde 2L 109
Queen Elizabeth Gdns.
SM4: Mord 3M 43
Queen Elizabeth Ho.
SW12 1E 28
QUEEN ELIZABETH PARK 8K 93
Queen Elizabeth Rd.
GU15: Camb 6B 50
KT2: K Tham 3L 203 (1M 41)
RH12: Rudg 1E 194
Queen Elizabeth's Dr.
CR0: N Add 5N 65
Queen Elizabeth's Gdns.
CR0: N Add 6N 65
Queen Elizabeth's Wlk.
SL4: W'sor 5H 5
SM6: Bedd 1H 63
(off Croydon Rd.)
SM6: Bedd 1H 63
(Sandhills)
Queen Elizabeth Wlk.
SW13 4F 12
Queen Elizabeth Way
GU22: Wok 6B 74
Queenhill Rd. CR2: Sels 6E 64
Queenhythe Cres.
GU4: J Wel 6N 93
Queenhythe Rd. GU4: J Wel 6N 93
Queen Mary Av.
GU15: Camb 1M 69
SM4: Mord 4J 43
Queen Mary Cl. GU22: Wok 3E 74
GU51: Fleet 2A 88
KT6: Ches 9N 41
KT6: Surb 9A 42
Queen Mary Ct. TW19: Stan 2N 21
Queen Mary Rd. SE19 7M 29
TW17: Shep 1D 38
Queen Mary's Av.
SM5: Cars 4D 62
Queen Mary's Dr.
KT15: N Haw 6H 55
Queens Acre SL4: W'sor 7G 4
SM3: Chea 4J 61
Queens Acre Ho. SL4: W'sor 6G 4
Queens Av. GU11: Alde 1M 109
KT14: Byf 8M 55
TW13: Hanw 5K 23
Queensberry Ho. TW9: Rich 8J 11
Queensberry Pl. *TW9: Rich* 8K 11
(off Retreat Rd.)
Queensbridge Pk. TW7: Isle 8E 10
Queensbury Pl. GU17: Haw 3H 69
Queens Cl. GU14: Farnb 5N 89
GU24: Bis 3D 72
KT10: Esh 1B 58
KT20: Wal H 2F 100
SL4: O Win 8K 5
SL5: Asc 9J 17
SM6: W'ton 2F 62
Queen's Club Gdns.
W14 2K 13
Queen's Club, The (Tennis Courts)
1K 13
Queens Club Ter. *W14* 2L 13
(off Normand Rd.)
Queens Ct. CR2: S Croy 8C 200
CR7: T Hea 4L 45
GU1: Guil 3D 202 (3N 113)
GU9: U Hal 5G 109
GU14: Farnb 5A 90
GU22: Wok 5B 74
KT13: Weybr 2E 56
KT19: Ewe 6D 60
RH1: Red 2E 122
(off St Anne's Mt.)
RH6: Horl 8E 142
SM2: Sut 7M 61
TN8: Eden 2M 147
TW10: Rich 9M 11
TW18: Stain 7M 21
Queens Ct. Ride KT11: Cob 9H 57
Queen's Cres.
RH4: Dork 4J 201 (6G 119)
TW10: Rich 8M 11
Queens Dr. GU2: Guil 9K 93
GU7: Goda 4E 132
KT5: Surb 6N 41
KT7: T Dit 5G 41
KT22: Oxs 7C 58
Queensfield Ct. SM3: Chea 1H 61
Queen's Gdns. TW5: Hest 4M 9
Queens Ga. *GU7: Goda* 7H 133
(off Queen St.)
RH6: Gat 3E 162
Queensgate KT11: Cob 8L 57
Queens Ga. Cotts.
SL4: W'sor 7G 4
Queens Ga. Gdns.
SW15 7G 13
Queen's Ga. Rd.
GU14: Farnb 5N 89
Queens Hill Ri. SL5: Asc 2N 33
Queens Ho. TW11: Tedd 7F 24
Queen's Keep TW1: Twick 9J 11
Queensland Av. SW19 9N 27
Queens La. GU9: U Hal 5G 109
Queen's Mead GU8: Chid 5E 172
Queensmead GU14: Farnb 1N 89
KT22: Oxs 7C 58
SL3: Dat 3L 5
Queensmead Av.
KT17: Ewe 6G 61
Queensmere Cl. SW19 3J 27
Queensmere Ct. SW13 3E 12
Queensmere Rd.
SW19 3J 27
Queensmill Rd. SW6 3J 13
Queens Pde. *RH13: Hors* 7K 197
(off Queen St.)
Queen's Pde. Path
GU11: Alde 7N 89
Queen's Pk. Gdns.
TW13: Felt 4G 23
Queen's Pk. Rd. CR3: Cate 1B 104
Queens Pine RG12: Brac 5C 32
Queens Pl. SL5: Asc 2L 33
SM4: Mord 3M 43
Queen's Prom.
KT1: K Tham, Surb
8G 203 (3K 41)
Queens Reach
KT1: K Tham 4G 203 (1K 41)
KT8: E Mol 3E 40
Queens Ride RG45: Crow 9F 30
SW13 6F 12
SW15 6F 12
Queens Ri. TW10: Rich 9M 11
Queens Rd. BR3: Beck 1H 47
CR0: Croy 5M 45
CR4: Mit 2B 44
GU1: Guil 3D 202 (3N 113)
GU9: U Hal 6H 109
GU11: Alde 3L 109
GU14: Farnb 5A 90
GU15: Camb 2N 69
GU21: Knap 5F 72
GU24: Bis, B'wood 7B 72
GU52: Fleet 6B 88
KT2: K Tham 8N 25
KT3: N Mal 3E 42
KT7: T Dit 4F 40
KT12: Hers 1G 57
KT13: Weybr 1D 56
RH6: Horl 8E 142
RH19: E Grin 1A 186
SL3: Dat 3L 5
SL4: E Wic 1C 4
Queens Rd. SL4: W'sor 5F 4
SL5: S'hill 4A 34
SM2: Sut 6M 61
SM4: Mord 3M 43
SM6: W'ton 2F 62
SW14 6C 12
SW19 7L 27
TW1: Twick 2G 24
TW3: Houn 6B 10
TW10: Rich 1M 25
TW11: Tedd 7F 24
TW12: H Hill 5B 24
TW13: Felt 2J 23
TW20: Egh 6B 20
Queen's Rdbt. GU11: Alde 6N 89
Queen's Royal Surrey
Regiment Mus., The 1J 115
Queens Sports Cen. 4E 132
Queen's Sq. RH10: Craw 3B 182
Queens St. TW15: A'ford 5A 22
Queens Ter. *KT7: T Dit* 5G 41
(off Queens Dr.)
SL4: W'sor 6G 5
TW7: Isle 7G 11
Queen St.
CR0: Croy 6B 200 (1N 63)
GU5: Gorn 8D 116
GU12: Alde 2B 110
KT16: Chert 7J 37
RH13: Hors 7K 197
Queensville Rd. SW12 1H 29
Queens Wlk. RH19: E Grin 9A 166
TW15: A'ford 5M 21
Queens Way GU24: B'wood 6A 72
TW13: Hanw 5K 23
Queensway BR4: W Wick 1A 66
CR0: Wad 3K 63
GU6: Cranl 8A 156
GU16: Frim G 7E 70
RG42: Brac 9L 15
RH1: Red 2D 122
RH10: Craw 3C 182
RH13: Hors 7J 197
RH19: E Grin 9A 166
TW16: Sunb 1J 39
Queensway Nth. KT12: Hers 1K 57
(not continuous)
Queensway Sth. KT12: Hers 2K 57
(not continuous)
Queens Wharf W6 1H 13
Queenswood Av.
CR7: T Hea 4L 45
SM6: Bedd 1H 63
TW3: Houn 5N 9
TW12: Hamp 7B 24
Queenswood Rd.
GU21: Wok 6G 73
QUEEN VICTORIA 1H 61
Queen Victoria Ct.
GU14: Farnb 9N 69
Queen Victoria Rd.
GU24: B'wood 6A 72
Queen Victoria's Wlk.
GU15: Camb 9L 49
Queen Victoria Wlk.
SL4: W'sor 4H 5
Quell La. GU27: Hasl 9L 189
Quelmans Head Ride
SL4: W'sor 3A 18
Quelm La. RG42: Brac 8N 15
RG42: Warf 7N 15
Quennell Cl. KT21: A'tead 6M 79
Quennells Hill
GU10: Wrec 5D 128
Quentins Dr. TN16: B Hil 3K 87
Quentins Wlk. *TN16: B Hil* 3K 87
(off St Anns Way)
Quentin Way GU25: V Wat 3L 35
Querrin St. SW6 5N 13
Questen M. RH10: Craw 1H 183
Quetta Pk. GU52: C Cro 2C 108
Quiberon Ct. TW16: Sunb 2H 39
Quick Rd. W4 1D 12
Quicks Rd. SW19 8N 27
Quiet Cl. KT15: Addl 1J 55
Quiet Nook BR2: Kes 1F 66
Quill La. SW15 7J 13
Quillot, The KT12: Hers 2G 56
Quince Cl. SL5: S'hill 3N 33
Quince Dr. GU24: Bis 2E 72
Quincy Rd. TW20: Egh 6C 20
Quinney's GU14: Farnb 4A 90
Quintet, The KT12: Wal T 7H 39
Quintilis RG12: Brac 7L 31
(not continuous)
Quintin Av. SW20 9L 27
Quinton Cl. BR3: Beck 2M 47
SM6: W'ton 1F 62
TW5: C'ford 3J 9
Quinton Rd. KT7: T Dit 7G 41
Quinton St. SW18 3A 28
Quintrell Cl. GU21: Wok 4L 73

R

Rabbit La. KT12: Hers 4H 57
Rabies Heath Rd.
RH1: Blet 2B 124
Raby Rd. KT3: N Mal 3C 42
Raccoon Way TW4: Houn 5K 9
Racecourse Rd. RH6: Gat 2D 162
RH7: Dorm, Ling 8A 146
Racecourse Way *RH6: Gat* 2D 162
(off Nth. Terminal App.)
Rachael's Lake Vw.
RG42: Warf 8C 16
Rackfield GU27: Hasl 1B 188
Rackham Cl. RH11: Craw 5B 182
Rackham M. SW16 7G 29
Rack's Ct.
GU1: Guil 7D 202 (5N 113)
Rackstraw Rd.
GU47: C Tow, Owls 6H 49
Racquets & Fitness Spa, The
4A 24
Racquets Ct. Hill
GU7: Goda 5F 132
Racton Rd. SW6 2M 13
Radbourne Rd.
SW12 1G 29
Radcliffe Cl. GU16: Frim 7D 70
Radcliffe Gdns. SM5: Cars 5C 62
Radcliffe M. TW12: H Hill 6C 24
Radcliffe Rd. CR0: Croy 8C 46
Radcliffe Sq. SW15 9J 13
Radcliffe Way RG42: Brac 9K 15
Radford Cl. GU9: Hale 7K 109
Radford Rd. RH10: Craw 6F 162
Radipole Rd. SW6 4L 13
Radius Pk. TW14: Felt 7G 9
Rad La. GU5: P'lake 2E 136
(not continuous)
Radley Cl. TW14: Felt 2G 23
Radnor Cl. CR4: Mit 3J 45
Radnor Ct. RH1: Red 3C 122
Radnor Gdns. TW1: Twick 3F 24
Radnor Ho. SW16 1K 45
Radnor La. RH5: H Mary 9H 137
(Three Mile Rd.)
RH5: H Mary 4H 137
(Woodhouse La.)
Radnor Rd. GU5: P'lake 5E 136
KT13: Weybr 9B 38
RG12: Brac 2D 32
TW1: Twick 2F 24
Radnor Ter. SM2: Sut 4M 61
Radnor Wlk. CR0: Croy 5H 47
Radnor Way SL3: Lang 1A 6
Radolphs KT20: Tad 9J 81
Radstock Way RH1: Mers 6H 103
Radstone Ct. GU22: Wok 5B 74
Raeburn Av. KT5: Surb 7A 42
Raeburn Cl.
KT1: H Wic 1G 203 (8K 25)
Raeburn Ct. GU21: Wok 6K 73
Raeburn Gro. GU21: Wok 5K 73
Raeburn Way GU47: C Tow 9J 49
RAFBOROUGH 2K 89
Rafborough Footpath
GU14: Cove 2M 89
GU14: Farnb 2M 89
Rafdene Copse GU22: Wok 6M 73
Rag Hill Cl. TN16: Tats 8G 86
Rag Hill Rd. TN16: Tats 8F 86
Raglan Cl. GU12: Alde 3A 110
GU16: Frim 6E 70
RH2: Reig 1B 122
TW4: Houn 8N 9
Raglan Ct.
CR2: S Croy 8A 200 (2M 63)
Raglan Pct. CR3: Cate 9B 84
Raglan Rd. GU21: Knap 5H 73
RH2: Reig 9N 101
Raikes Hollow
RH5: A Ham 2J 137
Raikes La. RH5: A Ham 2J 137
Railey Rd. RH10: Craw 2C 182
Railpit La. CR6: Warl 2A 86
Railshead Rd. TW7: Isle 7H 11
Rails La. GU24: Pirb 3N 91
Railton Rd. GU2: Guil 8L 93
Railway App. KT16: Chert 7J 37
RH19: E Grin 9A 166
SM6: W'ton 2F 62
TW1: Twick 1G 24
Railway Cotts. GU19: Bag 3J 51
SW19 5N 27
Railway Pas. TW11: Tedd 7G 24
Railway Rd. TW11: Tedd 5E 24
Railway Side SW13 6D 12
(not continuous)
Railway Ter. *CR5: Coul* 2H 83
(off Station App.)
TN16: Weste 3M 107
TW13: Felt 2H 23
TW18: Stain 6F 20
Rainbow Ct. GU21: Wok 3H 73
Rainbow Ind. Est.
SW20 1G 43
Rainbow Leisure Cen.
5L 201 (8D 60)
Rainforest Wlk. *RG12: Brac* 4N 31
(off Pond Moor Rd.)
Rainville Rd. W6 2H 13
Rake La. GU8: Mil 3C 152
Rakers Ridge RH12: Hors 3K 197
Raleigh Av. SM6: Bedd 1H 63
Raleigh Ct. RH10: Craw 7E 162
SM6: W'ton 3F 62
TW18: Stain 5J 21
Raleigh Dr. KT5: Surb 7B 42
KT10: Clay 2D 58
RH6: Smal 8L 143
Raleigh Gdns. CR4: Mit 2D 44
(not continuous)

276 A-Z Surrey

Raleigh Rd.—Regents M.

Raleigh Rd. TW9: Rich ... 6M 11
TW13: Felt ... 4G 22
UB2: S'hall ... 1M 9
Raleigh Wlk. RH10: Craw ... 5C 182
Raleigh Way GU16: Frim ... 3D 70
TW13: Hanw ... 6K 23
Ralliwood Rd. KT21: A'tead ... 6N 79
Ralph Perring Ct.
BR3: Beck ... 3K 47
Ralph's Ride RG12: Brac ... 2C 32
(Broad La., not continuous)
RG12: Brac ... 4C 32
(Mendip Rd.)
Ralston Ct. SL4: W'sor ... 4G 4
(off Russell St.)
Rama Cl. SW16 ... 8J 29
Rambler Cl. SW16 ... 5G 28
Ramblers Way
RH11: Craw ... 9N 181
Rame Cl. SW17 ... 6E 28
Ramillies Cl. GU11: Alde ... 6C 90
RAMILLIES PARK ... 7B 90
Ramin Ct. GU1: Guil ... 9M 93
Ramones Ter. CR4: Mit ... 3J 45
(off Yorkshire Rd.)
Ramornie Cl. KT12: Hers ... 1N 57
Ram Pas.
KT1: K Tham ... 4H 203 (1K 41)
Rampling Ct. RH10: Craw ... 4D 182
Ramsay Cl. GU15: Camb ... 8F 50
Ramsay Ct. RH11: Craw ... 8N 181
Ramsay Rd. GU20: Windl ... 2B 52
Ramsbury Cl. RG12: Brac ... 5K 31
Ramsdale Rd. SW17 ... 6E 28
Ramsden Rd. GU7: Goda ... 8G 133
SW12 ... 1E 28
Ramsey Cl. RH6: Horl ... 8D 142
RH12: Hors ... 3K 197
Ramsey Ct. CR0: Croy ... 3A 200
Ramsey Pl. CR3: Cate ... 9N 83
Ramsey Rd. CR7: T Hea ... 5K 45
Ramslade Cotts.
RG12: Brac ... 2A 32
Rams La. GU8: Duns ... 7C 174
RAMSNEST COMMON ... 1D 190
Ramster Cotts.
GU8: Chid ... 1C 190
Ram St. SW18 ... 8N 13
Ramuswood Av. BR6: Chels ... 2N 67
Ranald Ct. SL5: Asc ... 7K 17
Rances La. RG40: W'ham ... 2D 30
Randal Cres. RH2: Reig ... 5M 121
Randall Cl. SL3: Lang ... 1B 6
Randall Ct. SL4: O Win ... 9K 5
(off Lyndwood Dr.)
Randall Mead RG42: Bin ... 7G 15
Randall Scholfield Ct.
RH10: Craw ... 2E 182
Randalls Cres. KT22: Leat ... 7G 78
Randalls Pk. Av. KT22: Leat ... 7G 78
Randalls Pk. Crematorium
KT22: Leat ... 7E 78
Randalls Pk. Dr. KT22: Leat ... 8G 78
Randalls Rd. KT22: Leat ... 6E 78
Randalls Way KT22: Leat ... 8G 78
Randell Cl. GU17: Haw ... 5K 69
Randell Ho. GU17: Haw ... 5K 69
Randle Rd. TW10: Ham ... 5J 25
Randolph Cl. GU21: Knap ... 4H 73
KT2: K Tham ... 6B 26
KT11: Sto D ... 2A 78
Randolph Dr. GU14: Cove ... 2H 89
Randolph Rd.
KT17: Eps ... 8M 201 (1E 80)
SL3: Lang ... 1B 6
Randolph's La.
TN16: Weste ... 4K 107
Ranelagh SL4: Wink ... 3M 17
Ranelagh Av. SW6 ... 6L 13
SW13 ... 5F 12
Ranelagh Cres. SL5: Asc ... 9G 17
Ranelagh Dr. RG12: Brac ... 2A 32
TW1: Twick ... 7H 11
Ranelagh Gdns. SW6 ... 6K 13
(not continuous)
W4 ... 3B 12
Ranelagh Gdns. Mans.
SW6 ... 6K 13
(off Ranelagh Gdns.)
Ranelagh Pl. KT3: N Mal ... 4D 42
Ranelagh Rd. RH1: Red ... 3C 122
Ranfurly Rd. SM1: Sut ... 8M 43
Range, The GU5: Braml ... 7C 134
Range Ride GU15: Camb ... 8L 49
Range Rd. GU14: Farnb ... 5J 89
RG40: Finch ... 9A 30
Ranger Wlk. KT15: Addl ... 2K 55
Range Vw. GU47: C Tow ... 7K 49
Range Way TW17: Shep ... 6B 38
Rankine Cl. GU9: B Lea ... 6M 109
Ranmere St. SW12 ... 2F 28
Ranmore Av. CR0: Croy ... 9C 46
Ranmore Cl. RH1: Red ... 9E 102
RH11: Craw ... 9A 182
RANMORE COMMON ... 3D 118
Ranmore Comn. Rd.
RH5: Ran C, Westh ... 3M 117
Ranmore Pk. RH4: Dork ... 3G 118
Ranmore Pl. KT13: Weybr ... 2D 56
Ranmore Rd.
RH4: Dork ... 1H 201 (3C 118)
SM2: Chea ... 5J 61
Rannoch Rd. W6 ... 2H 13
Ransome Cl. RH11: Craw ... 6K 181
Ranyard Cl. KT9: Ches ... 9M 41
Rapallo Cl. GU14: Farnb ... 1A 90
Rapeland Hill RH12: Hors ... 7M 179
Raphael Dr. KT7: T Dit ... 6F 40
Rapley Cl. GU15: Camb ... 7D 50
Rapley Grn. RG12: Brac ... 5A 32
Rapley's Fld. GU24: Pirb ... 1B 92
Rapsley La. GU21: Knap ... 5E 72
Rashleigh Ct. GU52: C Cro ... 9C 88
Rastell Av. SW2 ... 3H 29
Ratcliffe Rd. GU14: Cove ... 6L 69
Rathbone Ho. RH11: Craw ... 8N 181
Rathbone Sq.
CR0: Croy ... 6B 200 (1N 63)
Rathgar Cl. RH1: Red ... 8E 122
Rathlin Rd. RH11: Craw ... 6N 181
Rathmell Dr. SW4 ... 1H 29
Ravelin Cl. GU51: Fleet ... 1A 88
Raven Cl. GU46: Yate ... 9A 48
RH10: T Hil ... 4F 184
RH12: Hors ... 2L 197
Ravendale Rd. TW16: Sunb ... 1G 38
Ravendene Ct.
RH11: Craw ... 4B 182
Ravenfield TW20: Eng G ... 7M 19
Ravenfield Rd. SW17 ... 4D 28
Raven La. RH11: Craw ... 1A 182
Ravenna Rd. SW15 ... 8J 13
Ravensbourne Av.
TW19: Stan ... 2N 21
Ravensbourne Rd.
TW1: Twick ... 9J 11
Ravensbourne Ter.
TW19: Stan ... 2N 21
Ravensbury Av. SM4: Mord ... 4A 44
Ravensbury Ct. CR4: Mit ... 3B 44
(off Ravensbury Gro.)
Ravensbury Gro. CR4: Mit ... 3B 44
Ravensbury La. CR4: Mit ... 3B 44
Ravensbury Path CR4: Mit ... 3B 44
Ravensbury Rd.
SW18 ... 3M 27
Ravensbury Ter. SW18 ... 3N 27
Ravenscar Rd. KT6: Surb ... 8M 41
Ravens Cl. GU21: Knap ... 3F 72
KT6: Surb ... 5K 41
RH1: Red ... 2D 122
Ravens Ct. KT1: K Tham ... 8H 203
Ravenscourt TW16: Sunb ... 9G 23
Ravenscourt Av. W6 ... 1F 12
Ravenscourt Pl. W6 ... 1G 12
Ravenscroft Cl. GU12: Ash ... 1G 111
Ravenscroft Ct.
RH12: Hors ... 5J 197
Ravenscroft Rd. BR3: Beck ... 1F 46
KT13: Weybr ... 7D 56
Ravensdale Cotts.
GU26: Hind ... 9A 170
Ravensdale Gdns.
TW4: Houn ... 6M 9
Ravensdale M. TW18: Stain ... 7K 21
Ravensdale Rd. SL5: Asc ... 4L 33
TW4: Houn ... 6M 9
Ravensfield Gdns.
KT19: Ewe ... 2D 60
Ravenshead Cl. CR2: Sels ... 7F 64
Ravenside KT1: K Tham ... 8G 203
Ravenslea Rd. SW12 ... 1D 28
Ravensmede Way W4 ... 1E 12
Ravenstone Rd.
GU15: Camb ... 1H 71
Ravenstone St. SW12 ... 2E 28
Ravenswold CR8: Ken ... 2N 83
Ravenswood Av.
BR4: W Wick ... 7M 47
KT6: Surb ... 8M 41
RG45: Crow ... 2D 48
Ravenswood Cl. KT11: Cob ... 2L 77
Ravenswood Ct.
GU22: Wok ... 5B 74
KT2: K Tham ... 7A 26
Ravenswood Cres.
BR4: W Wick ... 7M 47
Ravenswood Dr.
GU15: Camb ... 1E 70
Ravenswood Gdns.
TW7: Isle ... 4E 10
Ravenswood Rd.
CR0: Wad ... 5A 200 (9M 45)
SW12 ... 1F 28
Ravensworth Ct. SW6 ... 3M 13
(off Fulham Rd.)
Rawchester Cl. SW18 ... 2L 27
Rawdon Ri. GU15: Camb ... 1F 70
Rawlings Cl. BR3: Beck ... 4M 47
Rawlins Cl. CR2: Sels ... 4H 65
Rawlinson Rd. GU11: Alde ... 8A 90
GU15: Camb ... 9L 49
RH10: Craw ... 5H 183
Rawnsley Av. CR4: Mit ... 4B 44
Raworth Cl. RH10: Craw ... 5F 182
Rawsthorne Ct. TW4: Houn ... 7N 9
Raybell Ct. TW7: Isle ... 5F 10
Ray Cl. KT9: Ches ... 3J 59
RH7: Ling ... 6M 145
Ray La. RH7: Blin H, Ling ... 4J 145
Rayleigh Av. TW11: Tedd ... 7E 24
Rayleigh Ct.
KT1: K Tham ... 3M 203 (1N 41)
Rayleigh Ri. CR2: S Croy ... 3B 64
Rayleigh Rd. SW19 ... 9L 27
Raymead Av. CR7: T Hea ... 4L 45
Raymead Cl. KT22: Fetc ... 9E 78
Raymead Pas. CR7: T Hea ... 4L 45
(off Raymead Av.)
Raymead Way KT22: Fetc ... 9E 78
Raymer Wlk. RH6: Horl ... 7G 142
Raymond Cl. SL3: Poy ... 4G 7
Raymond Cres. GU2: Guil ... 4J 113
Raymond Rd. BR3: Beck ... 3H 47
SW19 ... 7K 27
Raymond Way KT10: Clay ... 3G 59
Raynald Ho. SW16 ... 4J 29
Rayne Ho. SW12 ... 1E 28
Rayners Cl. SL3: Coln ... 3E 6
Rayners Rd. SW15 ... 8K 13
RAYNES PARK ... 3H 43
Raynes Pk. Bri. SW20 ... 1H 43
Raynes Pk. School Sports Cen. ... 2G 42
Raynes Park Station (Rail) ... 1H 43
Ray Rd. KT8: W Mole ... 4B 40
Ray's Av. SL4: W'sor ... 3C 4
Rays Rd. BR4: W Wick ... 6M 47
Raywood Cl. UB3: Harl ... 3D 8
Read Cl. KT7: T Dit ... 6G 40
Readens, The SM7: Ban ... 3C 82
Reading Arch Rd.
RH1: Red ... 3D 122
Reading Rd. GU14: Farnb ... 4A 90
GU17: B'water ... 8A 48
GU46: Yate ... 8A 48
RG41: Win ... 1A 30
SM1: Sut ... 2A 62
Reading Rd. Nth.
GU51: Fleet ... 4A 88
Reading Rd. Sth.
GU51: Fleet ... 5A 88
GU52: C Cro, Fleet ... 5A 88
Read Rd. KT21: A'tead ... 4K 79
Reads Rest La. KT20: Tad ... 7M 81
Reapers Cl. RH12: Hors ... 3K 197
Reapers Way TW7: Isle ... 8D 10
Reckitt Rd. W4 ... 1D 12
Recovery St. SW17 ... 6C 28
Recreation Cl. GU14: Cove ... 5L 69
Recreation Rd.
GU1: Guil ... 2B 202 (3N 113)
GU10: Rowl ... 8D 128
Recreation Way CR4: Mit ... 2H 45
Rectory Cl. GU4: Guil ... 1F 114
GU6: Ewh ... 5F 156
GU7: Bus ... 9J 133
GU47: Sandh ... 7E 48
KT6: Surb ... 7J 41
KT14: Byf ... 9M 55
KT21: A'tead ... 6M 79
RG12: Brac ... 3A 32
RG40: W'ham ... 2B 30
RH5: Ockl ... 7C 158
SL4: W'sor ... 4D 4
SW20 ... 2H 43
TW17: Shep ... 2B 38
Rectory Ct. SM6: W'ton ... 1G 63
TW13: Felt ... 5K 23
Rectory Flats RH11: Ifi ... 1L 181
Rectory Gdn. GU6: Cranl ... 7M 155
Rectory Grn. BR3: Beck ... 1J 47
Rectory Gro.
CR0: Croy ... 3A 200 (8M 45)
TW12: Hamp ... 5N 23
Rectory La. GU5: Shere ... 8B 116
GU20: Windl ... 3N 51
KT6: Surb ... 7H 41
KT14: Byf ... 9N 55
KT21: A'tead ... 6M 79
KT23: Book ... 4N 97
RG12: Brac ... 4N 31
RH3: Buck ... 9E 100
RH6: Char ... 3J 161
RH11: Ifi ... 1L 181
SM6: W'ton ... 1G 63
SM7: Ban ... 1D 82
SW17 ... 7E 28
TN16: Tats ... 1G 106
Rectory Orchard SW19 ... 5K 27
Rectory Pk. CR2: Sande ... 9B 64
Rectory Rd. BR2: Kes ... 4F 66
BR3: Beck ... 1K 47
CR5: Coul ... 3A 102
GU14: Farnb ... 1A 90
RG40: W'ham ... 2B 30
SM1: Sut ... 9M 43
SW13 ... 5F 12
TW4: C'ford ... 5K 9
Rectory Row RG12: Brac ... 3N 31
Red Admiral St.
RH12: Hors ... 2L 197
Redan Gdns. GU12: Alde ... 2A 110
REDAN HILL ... 2B 110
Redan Hill Ind. Est.
GU12: Alde ... 2A 110
Redan Rd. GU12: Alde ... 2A 110
Redbarn Cl. CR8: Pur ... 7M 63
Redcliffe Cl. SW5 ... 1N 13
(off Old Brompton Rd.)
Redcliffe Gdns. SW10 ... 1N 13
W4 ... 3A 12
Redcliffe M. SW10 ... 1N 13
Redcliffe Sq. SW10 ... 1N 13
Redcliffe St. SW10 ... 2N 13
Redclose Av. SM4: Mord ... 4M 43
Redcote Pl. RH4: Dork ... 3K 119
Red Cotts. GU27: G'wood ... 7J 171
Redcourt
CR0: Croy ... 5F 200 (9B 46)
GU22: Pyr ... 2F 74
Redcrest Gdns.
GU15: Camb ... 1D 70
Redcroft Wlk. GU6: Cranl ... 8N 155
Red Deer Cl. RH13: Hors ... 5A 198
Reddington Cl.
CR2: Sande ... 5A 64
Redding Way GU21: Knap ... 6E 72
Redditch RG12: Brac ... 6B 32
Redditch Cl. RH11: Craw ... 7K 181
Reddown Rd. CR5: Coul ... 5H 83
Rede Ct. GU14: Farnb ... 4A 90
KT13: Weybr ... 9C 38
(off Old Palace Rd.)
Redehall Rd. RH6: Smal ... 8M 143
Redenham Ho. SW15 ... 1F 26
(off Ellisfield Dr.)
Redesdale Gdns. TW7: Isle ... 3G 10
Redfern Av. TW4: Houn ... 1A 24
Redfields La. GU52: C Cro ... 1A 108
Redfields Pk. GU52: C Cro ... 1A 108
Redford Av. CR5: Coul ... 2F 82
CR7: T Hea ... 3K 45
RH12: Hors ... 4H 197
SM6: W'ton ... 3J 63
Redford Cl. TW13: Felt ... 3G 22
Redford Rd. SL4: W'sor ... 4A 4
Redgarth Ct. RH19: E Grin ... 7L 165
Redgate Ter. SW15 ... 9J 13
Redgrave Cl. CR0: Croy ... 5C 46
Redgrave Ct. GU12: Ash ... 2D 110
Redgrave Dr. RH10: Craw ... 4H 183
Redgrave Rd. SW15 ... 6J 13
Redhall Ct. CR3: Cate ... 1A 104
Redhearn Flds.
GU10: Churt ... 8K 149
Redhearn Grn.
GU10: Churt ... 8K 149
RED HILL ... 1L 109
REDHILL ... 2D 122
Redhill Aerodrome and Heliport ... 8H 123
Redhill Ct. SW2 ... 3L 29
Redhill Distribution Cen.
RH1: Salf ... 2E 142
Redhill Ho. RH1: Red ... 1D 122
Redhill Rd. KT11: Cob ... 8C 56
Redhill Station (Rail) ... 2E 122
Redhill Tennis Club ... 1D 122
Red Ho. La. GU8: Els ... 8G 131
KT12: Wal T ... 8H 39
Redhouse Rd. CR0: Croy ... 5H 45
TN16: Tats ... 7E 86
Redkiln Cl. RH13: Hors ... 5M 197
Redkiln Cl. Ind. Est.
RH13: Hors ... 4M 197
Redkiln Way RH13: Hors ... 4M 197
Redknap Ho. TW10: Ham ... 4J 25
Redlake La. RG40: W'ham ... 6E 30
Redland Gdns.
KT8: W Mole ... 3N 39
REDLANDS
GU10 ... 5A 108
RH5 ... 5G 139
Redlands CR5: Coul ... 3J 83
TW11: Tedd ... 7G 25
Redlands, The BR3: Beck ... 1L 47
Redlands Cotts.
RH5: Mid H ... 2H 139
Redlands La.
GU10: Cron, Ews ... 5A 108
RH5: Mid H ... 2G 139
Redlands Way SW2 ... 1K 29
Red La. GU35: H Dwn ... 2G 168
KT10: Clay ... 3G 58
RH5: Holm ... 1L 139
RH8: Oxt ... 3D 126
Redleaf Cl. KT22: Fetc ... 2D 98
Redleaves Av. TW15: A'ford ... 7C 22
Redlees Cl. TW7: Isle ... 7G 10
Redlin Ct. RH1: Red ... 1D 122
Red Lion Bus. Pk.
KT6: Surb ... 9M 41
Red Lion La. GU9: Farnh ... 2G 129
GU24: Chob ... 5H 53
Red Lion Rd. GU24: Chob ... 5H 53
KT6: Surb ... 8M 41
Red Lion Sq. SW18 ... 8M 13
Red Lion St. TW9: Rich ... 8K 11
Red Lodge BR4: W Wick ... 7M 47
Red Lodge Rd.
BR4: W Wick ... 7M 47
Redmayne Cl. GU15: Camb ... 2G 71
Red River Ct. RH12: Hors ... 3H 197
Red Rd. GU15: Ligh ... 9H 51
GU18: Ligh ... 9H 51
KT20: Betch, Box H ... 1A 120
Red Rose RG42: Bin ... 6H 15
RED ROVER ... 7F 12
Redruth Gdns. KT10: Clay ... 4F 58
Redruth Ho. SM2: Sut ... 4N 61
Redshank Ct. RH11: Ifi ... 4J 181
(off Stoneycroft Wlk.)
Redstart Cl. CR0: N Add ... 6N 65
Redstone Hill RH1: Red ... 3E 122
Redstone Hollow
RH1: Red ... 4E 122
Redstone Mnr. RH1: Red ... 3E 122
Redstone Pk. RH1: Red ... 3E 122
Redstone Rd. RH1: Red ... 4E 122
Red Tiles Gdns. CR8: Ken ... 2M 83
Redvers Buller Rd.
GU11: Alde ... 6A 90
Redvers Ct. CR6: Warl ... 5G 84
(off Redvers Rd.)
Redvers Rd. CR6: Warl ... 5G 84
RG12: Brac ... 4N 31
Redway Dr. TW2: Whitt ... 1C 24
Redwing Av. GU7: Goda ... 2G 133
Redwing Cl. CR2: Sels ... 7G 64
RH13: Hors ... 5M 197
Redwing Gdns. KT14: W By ... 8K 55
Redwing Ri. GU4: Guil ... 1F 114
Redwing Rd. SM6: W'ton ... 4J 63
Redwood TW20: Thor ... 1G 37
Redwood Cl. CR8: Ken ... 1N 83
RH10: Craw ... 1C 182
Redwood Ct. KT6: Surb ... 6K 41
KT17: Ewe ... 7E 60
KT22: Leat ... 7F 78
(off Park Vw. Rd.)
Redwood Dr. GU15: Camb ... 2H 71
SL5: S'dale ... 5E 34
Redwood Est. TW5: C'ford ... 2J 9
Redwood Gro. GU4: Guil ... 9E 114
Redwood Ho. TN16: Weste ... 1K 107
Redwood Mnr. GU27: Hasl ... 1G 188
Redwood M. TW15: A'ford ... 8E 22
(off Staines Rd. W.)
Redwood Mt. RH2: Reig ... 9M 101
Redwoods KT15: Addl ... 3J 55
SW15 ... 2F 26
Redwoods, The SL4: W'sor ... 6G 4
Redwoods Way
GU52: C Cro ... 8C 88
Redwood Wlk. KT6: Surb ... 7K 41
Reed Cl. GU11: Alde ... 7B 90
Reed Dr. RH1: Red ... 6E 122
Reed Hall TW20: Eng G ... 4M 19
(off Coopers Hill La.)
Reedham Dr. CR8: Pur ... 9K 63
Reedham Pk. Av. CR8: Pur ... 3L 83
Reedham Station (Rail) ... 9K 63
Reedings RH11: Ifi ... 5J 181
Reed Pl. KT14: W By ... 9G 54
TW17: Shep ... 7A 38
REEDS, THE ... 8L 129
Reedsfield Cl. TW15: A'ford ... 4C 22
Reedsfield Rd.
TW15: A'ford ... 5C 22
Reed's Hill RG12: Brac ... 4N 31
Reeds Mdw. RH1: Mers ... 8G 102
Reeds Rd., The
GU10: Fren, Til ... 1J 149
Rees Gdns. CR0: Croy ... 5C 46
Reeve Ct. GU2: Guil ... 8K 93
(off Tarragon Rd.)
Reeve Rd. RH2: Reig ... 7A 122
Reeves Cnr.
CR0: Croy ... 3A 200 (8M 45)
Reeves Corner Stop (CT)
... 3A 200 (8M 45)
Reeves Ho. RH10: Craw ... 3F 182
(off Trafalgar Gdns.)
Reeves Rd. GU12: Alde ... 3A 110
Refectory Hall
TW20: Eng G ... 4M 19
(off Coopers Hill La.)
Regal Ct. GU1: Guil ... 2D 202
Regal Cres. SM6: W'ton ... 9F 44
Regal Dr. RH19: E Grin ... 1B 186
Regalfield Cl. GU2: Guil ... 8J 93
Regal Pl. SW6 ... 3N 13
Regan Cl. GU2: Guil ... 7L 93
Regatta Ho. TW11: Tedd ... 5G 25
Regatta Point TW8: Brent ... 2M 11
Regency Cl. TW12: Hamp ... 6N 23
Regency Ct. KT15: Addl ... 9M 37
(off Albert Rd.)
SM1: Sut ... 1A 62
TW11: Tedd ... 7H 25
Regency Dr. KT14: W By ... 9H 55
Regency Gdns. KT12: Wal T ... 7K 39
Regency Lodge
KT13: Weybr ... 9F 38
(off Oatlands Chase)
Regency M. TW7: Isle ... 8E 10
Regency Wlk. CR0: Croy ... 5J 47
TW10: Rich ... 8L 11
(off Grosvenor Av.)
TW10: Rich ... 8L 11
(off The Vineyard)
Regent Cl. GU51: Fleet ... 5B 88
KT15: N Haw ... 5M 55
RH1: Mers ... 7G 102
TW4: C'ford ... 4J 9
Regent Ct. GU2: Guil ... 1L 113
GU19: Bag ... 5K 51
SL4: W'sor ... 4G 5
Regent Cres. RH1: Red ... 1D 122
Regent Ho. KT17: Eps ... 7D 60
RH1: Red ... 2D 122
Regent Pde. SM2: Sut ... 3A 62
Regent Pk. KT22: Leat ... 5G 78
Regent Pl. CR0: Croy ... 7C 46
SW19 ... 6A 28
Regent Rd. KT5: Surb ... 4M 41
Regents Cl. CR2: S Croy ... 3B 64
CR3: Whyte ... 5B 84
RH11: Craw ... 7A 182
Regents Ct. KT2: K Tham ... 2J 203
KT13: Weybr ... 3C 56
Regents Dr. BR2: Kes ... 2F 66
Regents M. RH6: Horl ... 8E 142

Riverside Av.—Rosevine Rd.

Riverside Av. GU18: Ligh ... 7N 51
KT8: E Mol ... 4D 40
Riverside Bus. Cen.
GU1: Guil ... 3A 202 (3M 113)
SW18 ... 2N 27
Riverside Bus. Pk.
GU9: Farnh ... 9J 109
SW19 ... 9A 28
Riverside Cl. GU14: Cove ... 9L 69
GU24: B'wood ... 7C 72
KT1: K Tham ... 7H 203 (3K 41)
SM6: W'ton ... 9F 44
TW18: Stain ... 9H 21
Riverside Ct. GU9: Farnh ... 9H 109
KT22: Fetc ... 9G 78
RH4: Dork ... 3K 119
TN8: Eden ... 2M 147
TW7: Isle ... 5F 10
(off Woodlands Rd.)
TW14: Felt ... 1F 22
Riverside Dr. CR4: Mit ... 4C 44
GU5: Braml ... 4C 134
KT10: Esh ... 1A 58
TW10: Ham ... 4H 25
TW18: Stain ... 6G 21
W4 ... 3C 12
Riverside Gdns.
GU22: Wok ... 8D 74
W6 ... 1G 13
Riverside Health & Raquets Club ... 4D 12
Riverside Ind. Pk.
GU9: Farnh ... 9J 109
Riverside M. CR0: Bedd ... 9J 45
Riverside Pk. GU9: Farnh ... 9J 109
KT13: Addl ... 2N 55
SL3: Poy ... 5G 6
Riverside Pk. (Watchmoor Pk.)
GU15: Camb ... 3M 69
Riverside Pl. TW19: Stan ... 9M 7
Riverside Rd. KT12: Hers ... 1L 57
SW17 ... 5N 27
TW18: Stain ... 8H 21
TW19: Stan ... 8M 7
(not continuous)
Riverside Studios ... 1H 13
Riverside Vs. KT6: Surb ... 5J 41
Riverside Wlk.
BR4: W Wick ... 7L 47
GU7: Goda ... 6G 133
KT1: K Tham ... 3G 203 (2K 41)
SL4: W'sor ... 3G 5
(off Thames Side)
SW6 ... 6K 13
TW7: Isle ... 6E 10
W4 ... 2E 12
(off Chiswick Wharf)
Riverside Way
GU15: Camb ... 3M 69
Riverside Yd. SW17 ... 5A 28
Riverstone Ct.
KT2: K Tham ... 2L 203 (9M 25)
River St. SL4: W'sor ... 3G 4
River Ter. W6 ... 1H 13
River Thames Vis. Cen. ... 8K 11
(within Mus. of Richmond)
River Vw. KT15: Addl ... 2L 55
Riverview
GU1: Guil ... 2A 202 (3M 113)
River Vw. Gdns. TW1: Twick ... 3F 24
Riverview Gdns. KT11: Cob ... 9H 57
SW13 ... 2G 13
Riverview Gro. W4 ... 2A 12
Riverview Rd. KT19: Ewe ... 1B 60
W4 ... 3A 12
River Wlk. KT12: Wal T ... 5H 39
W6 ... 3H 13
River Way KT19: Ewe ... 2C 60
TW2: Twick ... 3B 24
Riverway TW18: Stain ... 9K 21
Riverway Est.
GU3: P'marsh ... 3M 133
Riverwood Ct. GU1: Guil ... 1M 113
Rivett Drake Cl. GU2: Guil ... 8L 93
Rivey Cl. KT14: W By ... 1H 75
RLC Mus. ... 6H 71
Road Ho. Est. GU22: Wok ... 8C 74
Roakes Av. KT15: Addl ... 8J 37
Roan Ind. Est. CR4: Mit ... 9D 28
(off Lavender Av.)
Roasthill La. SL4: Dorn ... 2A 4
Robert Cl. KT12: Hers ... 2J 57
Robert Gentry Ho.
W14 ... 1K 13
(off Gledstanes Rd.)
Robert Owen Ho. SW6 ... 4J 13
Robertsbridge Rd.
SM5: Cars ... 7A 44
Roberts Cl. CR7: T Hea ... 2A 46
SM3: Chea ... 4J 61
TW19: Stan ... 9L 7
Roberts Ct. KT9: Ches ... 2K 59
Robertson Ct. GU21: Wok ... 5H 73
Robertson Gro. SW17 ... 6C 28
Robertson Way GU12: Ash ... 3D 110
Roberts Rd. GU12: Alde ... 3A 110
GU15: Camb ... 9M 49
Robert St.
CR0: Croy ... 4C 200 (9N 45)
Roberts Way GU6: Cranl ... 6N 155
TW20: Eng G ... 8M 19
Robert Way GU16: Mytc ... 2D 90
RH12: Hors ... 1M 197
Robin Cl. GU12: A Va ... 7E 90
KT15: Addl ... 2M 55
RH11: Craw ... 1A 182
RH19: E Grin ... 8B 166
TW12: Hamp ... 6M 23
Robin Ct. SM6: W'ton ... 2G 63
Robin Gdns. RH1: Red ... 1E 122
Robin Gro. TW8: Brent ... 2J 11
Robin Hill GU7: Goda ... 4G 133
Robin Hill Dr. GU15: Camb ... 3E 70
ROBIN HOOD ... 4D 26
Robin Hood Cl.
GU14: Farnb ... 7M 69
GU21: Wok ... 5J 73
Robinhood Cl. CR4: Mit ... 2G 45
Robin Hood Cres.
GU21: Knap ... 4H 73
Robin Hood La.
GU4: Sut G ... 2B 94
RH12: Warn ... 3E 196
SM1: Sut ... 2M 61
SW15 ... 4D 26
Robinhood La. CR4: Mit ... 2G 45
Robin Hood Rd.
GU21: Knap, Wok ... 4G 73
(not continuous)
SW19 ... 6F 26
Robin Hood Rdbt.
RH12: Warn ... 3H 197
Robin Hood Way
SW15 ... 4D 26
SW20 ... 4D 26
Robin Hood Works
GU21: Knap ... 4H 73
Robinites GU7: Goda ... 4E 132
Robin La. GU47: Sandh ... 7G 49
(not continuous)
Robin Row RH10: T Hil ... 4F 184
Robin's Bow GU15: Camb ... 2N 69
Robins Ct. BR3: Beck ... 1N 47
CR2: S Croy ... 7F 200
Robins Dale GU21: Knap ... 4F 72
Robins Gro. Cres.
GU46: Yate ... 9A 48
Robinson Cl. GU22: Wok ... 7E 74
Robinson Ct. CR7: T Hea ... 5M 45
TW9: Rich ... 7M 11
Robinson Ho. RH11: Craw ... 4B 182
Robinson Rd. SW17 ... 7C 28
Robinsway KT12: Hers ... 1K 57
Robinswood Ct.
RH12: Hors ... 4M 197
Robin Way GU2: Guil ... 8L 93
TW18: Stain ... 4H 21
Robin Willis Way
SL4: O Win ... 9K 5
Robinwood Pl. SW15 ... 5C 26
Robson Rd. SE27 ... 4M 29
Roby Dr. RG12: Brac ... 6B 32
Robyns Way TN8: Eden ... 3M 147
Roche Rd. SW16 ... 9K 29
Rochester Av. TW13: Felt ... 3G 23
Rochester Cl. SW16 ... 8J 29
Rochester Gdns. CR0: Croy ... 9B 46
CR3: Cate ... 9B 84
Rochester Gro. GU51: Fleet ... 5B 88
Rochester Pde. TW13: Felt ... 3H 23
Rochester Rd. SM5: Cars ... 1D 62
TW18: Stain ... 7F 20
Rochester Wlk. RH2: Reig ... 8N 121
Roche Wlk. SM5: Cars ... 5B 44
Rochford Way CR0: Croy ... 5J 45
Rock Av. SW14 ... 6C 12
Rock Cl. CR4: Mit ... 1B 44
Rockdale Dr. GU26: G'hott ... 6B 170
Rockdale Ho.
GU26: G'hott ... 6B 170
Rockdene Cl.
RH19: E Grin ... 9C 166
Rockery, The GU14: Cove ... 2J 89
Rockfield Cl. RH8: Oxt ... 9B 106
Rockfield Rd. RH8: Oxt ... 7B 106
Rockfield Way
GU47: C Tow ... 7J 49
Rock Gdns. GU11: Alde ... 3L 109
Rockhampton Cl. SE27 ... 5L 29
Rockhampton Rd.
CR2: S Croy ... 3B 64
SE27 ... 5L 29
Rock Hill GU8: Hamb ... 8G 152
Rock Ho. La. GU10: Farnh ... 9L 109
Rockingham Cl. SW15 ... 7E 12
Rockland Rd. SW15 ... 7K 13
Rock La. GU10: Wrec ... 6F 128
Rocks, The RH19: Ash W ... 3E 186
Rockshaw Rd. RH1: Mers ... 5G 102
Rocks La. SW13 ... 5F 12
ROCKWOOD PARK ... 4M 185
Rocky La. RH2: Reig ... 6D 102
Rocque Ho. SW6 ... 3L 13
(off Estcourt Rd.)
Rodale Mans. SW18 ... 9N 13
Rodborough Hill Cotts.
GU8: Mil ... 3N 151
Rodd Est. TW17: Shep ... 4D 38
Roden Gdns. CR0: Croy ... 5B 46
Rodenhurst Rd. SW4 ... 1G 29
Rodgate La. GU27: Hasl ... 3A 190
Rodgers Ho. SW4 ... 1H 29
(off Clapham Pk. Est.)
Roding Cl. GU6: Cranl ... 8H 155
Rodmel Ct. GU14: Farnb ... 4C 90
Rodmill La. SW2 ... 1J 29
Rodney Cl.
CR0: Croy ... 1A 200 (7M 45)
KT3: N Mal ... 4D 42
KT12: Wal T ... 7K 39
Rodney Gdns. BR4: W Wick ... 1C 66
Rodney Grn. KT12: Wal T ... 8K 39
Rodney Pl. SW19 ... 9A 28
Rodney Rd. CR4: Mit ... 2C 44
KT3: N Mal ... 4D 42
KT12: Wal T ... 8K 39
TW2: Whitt ... 9A 10
Rodney Way GU1: Guil ... 2C 114
SL3: Poy ... 4G 7
Rodona Rd. KT13: Weybr ... 7E 56
Rodsall La. GU3: Put ... 3K 131
Rodway Rd. SW15 ... 1F 26
Rodwell Ct. KT12: Wal T ... 9J 39
KT15: Addl ... 1L 55
Roebuck Cl. KT21: A'tead ... 7L 79
RH2: Reig ... 3M 121
RH13: Hors ... 4A 198
TW13: Felt ... 5J 23
Roebuck Est. RG42: Bin ... 8H 15
Roebuck Rd. KT9: Ches ... 2N 59
Roedean Cres. SW15 ... 9D 12
Roedeer Copse
GU27: Hasl ... 2C 188
ROEHAMPTON ... 1F 26
Roehampton Cl. SW15 ... 7F 12
Roehampton Ga.
SW15 ... 9D 12
Roehampton High St.
SW15 ... 1F 26
ROEHAMPTON LANE ... 2G 27
Roehampton La. SW15 ... 7F 12
Roehampton Recreation Cen. ... 1F 26
Roehampton Va. SW15 ... 4E 26
Roe Way SM6: W'ton ... 3J 63
Roffe's La. CR3: Cate ... 2A 104
ROFFEY ... 4N 197
Roffey Cl. CR8: Pur ... 3M 83
RH6: Horl ... 8D 142
ROFFEY PARK ... 2E 198
Roffey Pk. RH12: Col ... 2D 198
Roffey's Cl. RH10: Cop ... 6L 163
Roffey Social and Sports Club ... 3N 197
(off Spooners Rd.)
Roffords GU21: Wok ... 4L 73
Roffye Ct. RH12: Hors ... 4N 197
Rogers Cl. CR3: Cate ... 9E 84
CR5: Coul ... 5M 83
Roger Simmons Ct.
KT23: Book ... 2N 97
Rogers La. CR6: Warl ... 5J 85
Rogers Mead RH9: Gods ... 1E 124
Rogers Rd. SW17 ... 6B 28
ROGER'S TOWN ... 6N 167
Rokeby Cl. RG12: Brac ... 9B 16
Rokeby Ct. GU21: Wok ... 4J 73
Rokeby Ho. SW12 ... 1F 28
(off Lochinvar St.)
Rokeby Pl. SW20 ... 8G 27
Roke Cl. CR8: Ken ... 1N 83
GU8: Wit ... 5B 152
Roke La. GU8: Wit ... 6N 151
Roke Lodge Rd. CR8: Pur ... 9M 63
Roke Rd. CR8: Ken ... 2N 83
Rokers La. GU8: S'ford ... 4A 132
(not continuous)
Rokewood Dr. RH11: Ifi ... 9M 161
Roland Way KT4: W Pk ... 8E 42
Rolinsden Way BR2: Kes ... 1F 66
Rollesby Rd. KT9: Ches ... 3N 59
Rolleston Rd. CR2: S Croy ... 4A 64
Rollit Cres. TW3: Houn ... 8A 10
Rolls Royce Cl. SM6: W'ton ... 4J 63
Rolston Ho. GU27: Hasl ... 2D 188
Romana Ct. TW18: Stain ... 5J 21
Romanby Ct. RH1: Red ... 4D 122
Roman Cl. TW14: Felt ... 8K 9
Roman Ct. TN8: Eden ... 2L 147
Roman Farm Way
GU2: Guil ... 2G 113
Romanfield Rd. SW2 ... 1K 29
Romanhurst Gdns.
BR2: Brom ... 3N 47
Roman Ind. Est. CR0: Croy ... 6B 46
Roman Ride RG45: Crow ... 2C 48
Roman Rd. RH4: Dork ... 7G 119
TN8: M Grn ... 5M 147
Romans Bus. Pk.
GU9: Farnh ... 9J 109
Romans Way GU22: Pyr ... 2J 75
Roman Way
CR0: Croy ... 2A 200 (8M 45)
GU9: Farnh ... 8K 109
RG42: Warf ... 9D 16
SM5: Cars ... 5D 62
Romany, The GU14: Farnb ... 4F 88
Romany Gdns. SM3: Sut ... 6M 43
Romany Rd. GU21: Knap ... 2F 72
Roma Read Cl. SW15 ... 1G 26
Romayne Cl. GU14: Cove ... 9M 69
Romberg Rd. SW17 ... 4E 28
Romeo Hill RG42: Warf ... 9D 16
Romeyn Rd. SW16 ... 4K 29
Romily Ct. SW6 ... 5L 13
Romley Ct. GU9: Farnh ... 2J 129
Romney Cl. KT9: Ches ... 1L 59
TW15: A'ford ... 6D 22
Romney Ho. RG12: Brac ... 3C 32
Romney Lock SL4: W'sor ... 2H 5
Romney Lock Rd.
SL4: W'sor ... 3G 5
Romney Rd. KT3: N Mal ... 5C 42
Romney Wlk. SL4: W'sor ... 3G 5
Romola Rd. SE24 ... 2M 29
Romsey Cl. BR6: Farnb ... 1K 67
GU11: Alde ... 6A 110
GU17: B'water ... 9H 49
Romulus Ct. TW8: Brent ... 3K 11
Rona Cl. RH11: Craw ... 6N 181
Ronald Cl. BR3: Beck ... 3J 47
Ronald Ross Rd.
GU2: Guil ... 4H 113
Ronelean Rd. KT6: Surb ... 8M 41
Ronneby Cl. KT13: Weybr ... 9F 38
Ronson Way KT22: Leat ... 8G 78
Roof of the World Cvn. Pk.
KT20: Box H ... 9A 100
Rookeries Cl. TW13: Felt ... 4J 23
Rookery, The RH4: Westc ... 7A 118
Rookery Cl. KT22: Fetc ... 2E 98
Rookery Dr. RH4: Westc ... 7A 118
Rookery Hill KT21: A'tead ... 5N 79
RH1: Out ... 4L 143
RH6: Out ... 4L 143
Rookery La.
RH6: Out, Smal ... 6L 143
Rookery Mead CR5: Coul ... 9H 83
Rookery Rd. BR6: Dow ... 6H 67
TW18: Stain ... 6K 21
Rookery Way KT20: Lwr K ... 5L 101
Rook La. CR3: Cate ... 3K 103
Rookley Cl. SM2: Sut ... 5N 61
Rooks Hill GU5: Braml ... 9D 134
Rooksmead Rd.
TW16: Sunb ... 1G 39
ROOKS NEST ... 8H 105
Rookstone Rd. SW17 ... 6D 28
Rookswood RG42: Brac ... 8N 15
Rook Way RH12: Hors ... 2M 197
Rookwood Av. GU47: Owls ... 5K 49
KT3: N Mal ... 3F 42
SM6: Bedd ... 1H 63
Rookwood Cl. RH1: Mers ... 7F 102
Rookwood Ct.
GU2: Guil ... 8A 202 (6M 113)
Rookwood Pk. RH12: Hors ... 5F 196
Rookwood Pl. RH1: Mers ... 6F 102
(off London Rd. Sth.)
Roosthole Hill RH13: Col ... 8C 198
Roothill La. RH3: Betch ... 1N 139
Ropeland Way RH12: Hors ... 1L 197
Ropers Wlk. SW2 ... 1L 29
Roper Way CR4: Mit ... 1E 44
Rope Wlk. TW16: Sunb ... 2K 39
Rorkes Drift GU16: Mytc ... 1D 90
Rosa Av. TW15: A'ford ... 5B 22
Rosalind Franklin Cl.
GU2: Guil ... 4H 113
Rosaline Rd. SW6 ... 3K 13
Rosaline Ter. SW6 ... 3K 13
(off Rosaline Rd.)
Rosamund Cl.
CR2: S Croy ... 7E 200 (1A 64)
Rosamund Rd.
RH10: Craw ... 5F 182
Rosamun St. UB2: S'hall ... 1M 9
Rosary Cl. TW3: Houn ... 5M 9
Rosary Gdns. GU46: Yate ... 9C 48
TW15: A'ford ... 5C 22
Rosaville Rd. SW6 ... 3L 13
Roseacre RH8: Oxt ... 3C 126
Roseacre Cl. SM1: Sut ... 8A 44
TW17: Shep ... 4B 38
Roseacre Gdns. GU4: Guil ... 9H 115
Rose & Crown Pas.
TW7: Isle ... 4G 11
Rose Av. CR4: Mit ... 9D 28
SM4: Mord ... 4A 44
Rosebank
KT18: Eps ... 8H 201 (1B 80)
SW6 ... 3H 13
Rosebank Cl. TW11: Tedd ... 7G 25
Rose Bank Cotts.
GU22: Wok ... 9A 74
Rosebay RG40: W'ham ... 9D 14
Roseberry Gdns. BR6: Orp ... 1N 67
Rosebery Av. CR7: T Hea ... 1N 45
KT3: N Mal ... 1E 42
KT17: Eps ... 8M 201 (1D 80)
Rosebery Cl. SM4: Mord ... 5J 43
Rosebery Cres. GU22: Wok ... 7B 74
Rosebery Gdns. SM1: Sut ... 1N 61
Rosebery Rd. KT1: K Tham ... 1A 42
KT18: Eps D ... 6C 80
SM1: Sut ... 3L 61
TW3: Houn ... 8C 10
Roseberys, The KT18: Eps ... 1D 80
Rosebery Sq. KT1: K Tham ... 1A 42
Rosebine Av. TW2: Twick ... 1D 24
Rosebriar Cl. GU22: Pyr ... 3J 75
Rosebriars CR3: Cate ... 7B 84
KT10: Esh ... 2C 58
(not continuous)
Rosebury Dr. GU24: Bis ... 2D 72
Rosebury Rd. SW6 ... 5N 13
Rose Bushes KT17: Eps D ... 3G 81
Rose Cotts. BR2: Kes ... 7E 66
GU8: Worm ... 8D 152
RH12: Fay ... 9H 181
RH18: F Row ... 6G 187
Rose Ct. RG40: W'ham ... 2B 30
Rosecourt Rd. CR0: Croy ... 5K 45
Rosecroft Cl. TN16: B Hil ... 5H 87
Rosecroft Gdns.
TW2: Twick ... 2D 24
Rosedale CR3: Cate ... 1B 104
GU12: Alde ... 2A 110
KT21: A'tead ... 5J 79
RG42: Bin ... 6H 15
Rosedale Cl. RH11: Craw ... 5M 181
Rosedale Gdns.
RG12: Brac ... 4M 31
Rosedale Pl. CR0: Croy ... 6G 47
Rosedale Rd. KT17: Ewe ... 2F 60
TW9: Rich ... 6L 11
Rosedene Av. CR0: Croy ... 6J 45
SM4: Mord ... 4M 43
SW16 ... 4K 29
Rosedene Gdns.
GU51: Fleet ... 3A 88
Rosedene La.
GU47: C Tow ... 9J 49
Rosedew Rd. W6 ... 2J 13
Rose End KT4: W Pk ... 7J 43
Rosefield Cl. SM5: Cars ... 2C 62
Rosefield Gdns.
KT16: Otter ... 3F 54
Rosefield Rd. TW18: Stain ... 5J 21
Rose Gdns. GU14: Cove ... 2K 89
RG40: W'ham ... 2B 30
TW13: Felt ... 3H 23
TW19: Stan ... 1M 21
Roseheath Rd. TW4: Houn ... 8N 9
ROSE HILL ... 3K 201 (5G 119)
ROSEHILL ... 6A 44
Rose Hill RG42: Bin ... 6H 15
RH4: Dork ... 3J 201 (5G 119)
SM1: Sut ... 8N 43
Rosehill KT10: Clay ... 3G 58
RH2: Reig ... 2B 122
TW12: Hamp ... 9A 24
Rose Hill Arch M.
RH4: Dork ... 2K 201
Rose Hill Av. SM5: Sut ... 7A 44
Rosehill Av. GU21: Wok ... 3M 73
Rosehill Ct. SM4: Mord ... 6A 44
(off St Helier Av.)
Rosehill Ct. Pde.
SM4: Mord ... 6A 44
(off St Helier Av.)
Rosehill Farm Mdw.
SM7: Ban ... 2N 81
Rosehill Gdns. SM1: Sut ... 8N 43
Rose Hill Pk. W. SM1: Sut ... 7A 44
Rosehill Rd. SW18 ... 9N 13
TN16: B Hil ... 4E 86
ROSE HILL RDBT. ... 6A 44
Rose La. GU23: Rip ... 8L 75
Roseleigh Cl. TW1: Twick ... 9K 11
Rosemary Av. GU12: A Va ... 5E 90
KT8: W Mole ... 2A 40
TW4: Houn ... 5L 9
Rosemary Cl. CR0: Croy ... 5J 45
GU14: Cove ... 9J 69
RH8: Oxt ... 2C 126
Rosemary Ct. GU27: Hasl ... 1G 188
RH6: Horl ... 7C 142
Rosemary Cres. GU2: Guil ... 8J 93
Rosemary Gdns.
GU17: B'water ... 1H 69
KT9: Ches ... 1L 59
SW14 ... 6B 12
Rosemary Ga. KT10: Esh ... 2C 58
Rosemary La. GU6: Alf ... 9E 174
GU10: Rowl ... 7D 128
GU17: B'water ... 9H 49
RH6: Char ... 3K 161
RH6: Horl ... 9F 142
SW14 ... 6B 12
TW20: Thor ... 2D 36
Rosemary Rd. SW17 ... 4A 28
Rosemead KT16: Chert ... 6K 37
Rosemead Av. CR4: Mit ... 2G 45
TW13: Felt ... 3G 22
Rosemead Cl. RH1: Red ... 5B 122
Rosemead Gdns.
RH10: Craw ... 4C 182
(off Richmond Ct.)
Rose Mdw. GU24: W End ... 9D 52
Rosemont Rd. KT3: N Mal ... 2B 42
TW10: Rich ... 9L 11
Rosemount SM6: W'ton ... 3G 62
(off Clarendon Rd.)
Rosemount Av.
KT14: W By ... 9J 55
Rosendale Rd. SE21 ... 4N 29
SE24 ... 1N 29
Roseneath Ct. CR3: Cate ... 3D 104
Roseneath Dr. GU8: Chid ... 5E 172
Roseneath Pl. SW16 ... 5K 29
(off Curtis Fld. Rd.)
Rose Pk. KT15: Otter ... 5G 54
Rosery, The CR0: Croy ... 5G 46
TW20: Thor ... 5D 36
Rose's Cotts. RH4: Dork ... 2J 201
(off Junction Rd.)
Roses La. SL4: W'sor ... 5A 4
Rose St. RG40: W'ham ... 2B 30
Rosethorn Cl. SW12 ... 1H 29
Rosetrees GU1: Guil ... 4C 114
Rose Vw. KT15: Addl ... 2L 55
Roseville Av. TW3: Houn ... 8A 10
Roseville Rd. UB3: Harl ... 1H 9
Rosevine Rd. SW20 ... 9H 27

Rose Wlk.—Ruxley Cl.

Rose Wlk. BR4: W Wick 8M **47**
CR8: Pur 7H **63**
GU51: Fleet 3A **88**
KT5: Surb 4A **42**
RH11: Craw 5N **181**
Rosewarne Cl. GU21: Wok 5K **73**
Rosewood GU22: Wok 6C **74**
KT7: T Dit 8G **40**
SM2: Sut 6A **62**
Rosewood Ct. KT2: K Tham . . .8N **25**
Rosewood Dr. TW17: Shep 4A **38**
Rosewood Gro. SM1: Sut 8A **44**
Rosewood Rd. GU35: Lind . . .4B **168**
Rosewood Way
GU24: W End 9B **52**
Roshni Ho. SW17 . . . . .7C **28**
Roskell Rd. SW15 . . . . .6J **13**
Roslan Ct. RH6: Horl 9F **142**
Roslyn Cl. CR4: Mit 1B **44**
Roslyn Ct. GU21: Wok 5K **73**
Ross Cl. RH10: Craw 6D **182**
Ross Ct. RH6: Horl 8F **142**
SW15 . . . . .1J **27**
Rossdale SM1: Sut 2C **62**
Rossdale Rd. SW15 . . . . .7H **13**
Rossett Cl. RG12: Brac 3N **31**
Rossetti Gdns. CR5: Coul 5K **83**
Rossignol Gdns. SM5: Cars . . .8E **44**
Rossindel Rd. TW3: Houn 8A **10**
Rossiter Lodge GU1: Guil 4C **114**
Rossiter Rd. SW12 . . . . .2F **28**
Rosslare Cl. TN16: Weste . . .3M **107**
Rosslea GU20: Windl 1L **51**
Rosslyn Av. SW13 . . . . .6D **12**
TW14: Felt 9H **9**
Rosslyn Cl. TW16: Sunb 7F **22**
Rosslyn Pk. KT13: Weybr 1E **56**
Rosslyn Pk. RUFC 7E **12**
Rosslyn Rd. TW1: Twick 9J **11**
Rossmore Cl. RH10: Craw 8H **163**
Rossmore Gdns.
GU11: Alde 3K **109**
Ross Pde. SM6: W'ton 3F **62**
Ross Rd. KT11: Cob 9K **57**
SE25 . . . . .2A **46**
SM6: W'ton 2G **62**
TW2: Whitt 2B **24**
Rosswood Gdns.
SM6: W'ton 3G **62**
Rostella Rd. SW17 . . . . .5B **28**
Rostrevor Gdns. UB2: S'hall 1M **9**
Rostrevor M. SW6 . . . . .4L **13**
Rostrevor Rd. SW6 . . . . .4L **13**
SW19 . . . . .6M **27**
Rothbury Gdns. TW7: Isle 3G **10**
Rothbury Wlk. GU15: Camb 2G **71**
Rother Cl. GU47: Sandh 7H **49**
Rother Cres. RH11: Craw 4L **181**
Rotherfield Rd. SM5: Cars 1E **62**
Rotherhill Av. SW16 . . . . .7H **29**
Rother Rd. GU14: Cove 8K **69**
Rothervale RH6: Horl 5E **142**
Rotherwick Ct. GU14: Farnb . . .5A **90**
Rotherwood Cl. SW20 . . . . . . .9K **27**
Rotherwood Rd. SW15 . . . . . . .6J **13**
Rothesay Av. SW20 . . . . .1K **43**
TW10: Rich 7A **12**
Rothesay Rd. SE25 . . . . .3A **46**
Rothes Rd.
RH4: Dork 1K **201** (4H **119**)
Rothsay Ct. KT13: Weybr 3E **56**
Rothschild St. SE27 . . . . .5M **29**
Rothwell Ho. RG45: Crow 3H **49**
TW5: Hest 2A **10**
Rotunda Cen., The
. . . . .3K **203** (1L **41**)
Rotunda Est. GU11: Alde 2N **109**
Rougemont Av. SM4: Mord 5M **43**
Rough, The GU22: Wok 4F **74**
ROUGHETS, THE 7C **104**
Roughets La. RH1: Blet 7B **104**
Rough Fld. RH19: E Grin 6N **165**
Roughgrove Copse
RG42: Bin 7G **15**
Roughlands GU22: Pyr 2G **75**
Rough Rew RH4: Dork 8H **119**
Rough Rd. GU22: Wok 9F **72**
Rough Way RH12: Hors 3M **197**
Rounce La. GU24: W End 9A **52**
Roundabout Rd.
RH10: Cop 6A **164**
Roundacre SW19 . . . . .3J **27**
Roundals La. GU8: Hamb 1H **173**
Round Cl. GU46: Yate 1E **68**
Round Gro. CR0: Croy 6G **47**
ROUND HILL 1K **109**
Roundhill GU22: Wok 6D **74**
Roundhill Dr. GU22: Wok 5D **74**
Roundhill Way GU2: Guil 3J **113**
KT11: Cob 7B **58**
ROUNDHURST 7M **189**
Round Oak Rd.
KT13: Weybr 1A **56**
ROUNDSHAW 4J **63**
Roundshead Dr.
RG42: Warf 9B **16**
ROUNDS HILL 9L **15**
Rounds Hill RG12: Brac 9K **15**
Roundthorn Way
GU21: Wok 3J **73**
Roundway GU15: Camb 9G **50**
TN16: B Hil 3E **86**
TW20: Egh 6E **20**
Roundway, The KT10: Clay 3F **58**
Roundway Cl. GU15: Camb . . .9G **50**
Roundway Ct. RH10: Craw . . .1B **182**
Roundwood Vw. SM7: Ban 2J **81**
Roundwood Way SM7: Ban 2J **81**
Rounton Rd. GU52: C Cro 7B **88**
Roupell Ho. KT2: K Tham . . .1M **203**
Roupell Rd. SW2 . . . . .2K **29**
Routh Ct. TW14: Bedf 2E **22**
Routh Rd. SW18 . . . . .1C **28**
Row, The TN8: Eden 8K **127**
Rowallan Rd. SW6 . . . . .3K **13**
Rowan RG12: Brac 4D **32**
Rowan Av. TW20: Egh 6E **20**
Rowan Chase GU10: Wrec . . .6F **128**
Rowan Cl. GU1: Guil 9L **93**
GU15: Camb 7D **50**
GU51: Fleet 4D **88**
KT3: N Mal 1D **42**
RH2: Reig 5A **122**
RH10: Craw 3D **182**
RH12: Hors 3A **198**
SW16 . . . . .9G **29**
TW15: A'ford 5M **21**
Rowan Ct. SW11 . . . . .1D **28**
Rowan Cres. SW16 . . . . .9G **29**
Rowan Dale GU52: C Cro 8A **88**
Rowan Dr. RG45: Crow 9H **31**
Rowan Gdns. CR0: Croy 9C **46**
Rowan Grn. KT13: Weybr 1E **56**
Rowan Gro. CR5: Coul 8F **82**
Rowan Hall *TW20: Eng G 4M 19*
(off Coopers Hill La.)
Rowan Mead KT20: Tad 6G **81**
Rowan Rd. SW16 . . . . .1G **45**
TW8: Brent 3H **11**
UB7: W Dray 1M **7**
Rowans, The GU22: Wok 5A **74**
GU26: Hind 7B **170**
TW16: Sunb 6G **23**
Rowans Cl. GU14: Cove 5K **69**
Rowanside Cl.
GU35: H Dwn 5H **169**
Rowan Wlk. RH10: Craw D 1F **184**
Rowan Way RH12: Hors 3A **198**
Rowbarns Way KT24: E Hor . . .8G **97**
Rowberry Cl. SW6 . . . . .3H **13**
Rowbury GU7: Goda 3K **133**
Rowcliffe Springs
GU8: Hasc 6A **154**
Rowcroft Cl. GU12: A Va 7E **90**
Rowden Rd. KT19: Ewe 1A **60**
Rowdown Cres. CR0: N Add 5N **65**
Rowe La. GU24: Pirb 2D **92**
Rowena Ho. *RH11: Craw 9B 162*
(off Dobson Rd.)
ROWFANT 2A **184**
Rowfant Bus. Cen.
RH10: Row 3A **184**
Rowfant Cl. RH10: Wor 3J **183**
Rowfant Rd. SW17 . . . . .2E **28**
Rowfield TN8: Eden 9M **127**
ROWHILL 3H **55**
Rowhill KT15: Addl 3H **55**
Rowhill Av. GU11: Alde 3L **109**
Rowhill Cl. GU14: Cove 9H **69**
Rowhill Cres. GU11: Alde 4L **109**
Rowhill Nature Reserve 4K **109**
Rowhills GU9: H End 4J **109**
Rowhills Cl. GU9: Weybo 5L **109**
ROWHOOK 8M **177**
Rowhook Hill
RH12: Rowh 8M **177**
Rowhook Rd.
RH12: Rowh, Bro H 9N **177**
(not continuous)
Rowhurst Av. KT15: Addl 3K **55**
KT22: Leat 4F **78**
Rowland Cl. RH10: Cop 5B **164**
SL4: W'sor 6A **4**
Rowland Hill Almshouses
TW15: A'ford 6B 22
(off Feltham Hill Rd.)
Rowland Ho. GU6: Cranl 7M **155**
Rowland Rd. GU6: Cranl 7M **155**
Rowlands Rd. RH12: Hors . . .2N **197**
Rowland Way SW19 . . . . .9N **27**
TW15: A'ford 8E **22**
Row La. GU5: Alb 8N **135**
(not continuous)
ROWLEDGE 8D **128**
ROWLEY 4K **155**
Rowley Cl. GU22: Pyr 3K **75**
RG12: Brac 2C **32**
Rowley Ct. CR3: Cate 9A **84**
Rowlls Rd.
KT1: K Tham . . .5M **203** (2M **41**)
Rowly Dr. GU6: Cranl 5J **155**
Rowly Edge GU6: Cranl 4J **155**
Rowntree Rd. TW2: Twick 2E **24**
Rowplatt Cl. RH19: Fel 6H **165**
Rowplatt La. RH19: Fel 7H **165**
ROW TOWN 3J **55**
Row Town KT15: Addl 4H **55**
Roxbee Cox Rd.
GU14: Farnb 3E **88**
Roxborough Av. TW7: Isle 3F **10**
Roxburgh Cl. GU15: Camb 2G **71**
Roxburgh Rd. SE27 . . . . .6M **29**
Roxby Pl. SW6 . . . . .2M **13**
Roxeth Ct. TW15: A'ford 6B **22**
Roxford Cl. TW17: Shep 4F **38**
Roxton Gdns. CR0: A'ton 2K **65**
Royal Aerospace Establishment Rd.
GU14: Farnb 4N **89**
Royal Army Medical Corps Mus.
. . . . .4F **90**
Royal Ascot Golf Course 1L **33**
Royal Av. KT4: W Pk 8D **42**
Royal Botanic Gdns. 4L **11**
Royal Cir. SE27 . . . . .4L **29**
Royal Cl. BR6: Farnb 1K **67**
KT4: W Pk 8D **42**
SW19 . . . . .4J **27**
Royal County of Berkshire
Racquets and Health Club, The
. . . . .7B **32**
Royal Dr. KT18: Tat C 5G **80**
Royal Duchess M.
SW12 . . . . .1F **28**
Royal Earlswood Pk.
RH1: Red 6E **122**
Royale Cl. GU11: Alde 4A **110**
Royal Free Ct. *SL4: W'sor 4G 4*
(off Batchelors Acre)
Royal Holloway
University of London 7N **19**
Royal Holloway University
Sports Cen. 8A **20**
Royal Horticultural Society Cotts.
GU23: Wis 3N **75**
Royal Horticultural Society
Gardens, The (Wisley)
. . . . .5N **75**
Royal Huts Av. GU26: Hind . . .5D **170**
Royal Mausoleum 6H **5**
Royal M. KT8: E Mol 2E **40**
SL4: W'sor 4G **5**
Royal Mid Surrey Golf Course
. . . . .6K **11**
Royal Military Academy Sandhurst
. . . . .8M **49**
Royal Oak Cl. GU46: Yate 9D **48**
Royal Oak Dr. RG45: Crow 8G **30**
Royal Oak Ho.
RH10: Craw D 2E **184**
Royal Oak M. TW11: Tedd 6G **25**
Royal Oak Rd. GU21: Wok 5M **73**
Royal Orchard Cl.
SW18 . . . . .1K **27**
Royal Pde. GU26: Hind 5D **170**
SW6 . . . . .3K **13**
TW9: Kew 4N 11
(off Station App.)
Royal Quarter
KT2: K Tham 2H **203** (9L **25**)
Royal Rd. TW11: Tedd 6D **24**
Royals, The
GU1: Guil 5E **202** (4N **113**)
Royal Victoria Gdns.
SL5: Asc 4L **33**
Royal Wlk. SM6: W'ton 8F **44**
Royal Windsor Racecourse 2B **4**
Royce Rd. RH10: Craw 7E **162**
Roycroft Cl. SW2 . . . . .2L **29**
Roydon Ct. KT12: Hers 1H **57**
TW20: Egh 7F **20**
Roy Gro. TW12: Hamp 7B **24**
Roymount Ct. TW2: Twick 4E **24**
Royston Av. KT14: Byf 8N **55**
SM1: Sut 9B **44**
SM6: Bedd 1H **63**
Royston Cen., The
GU12: A Va 5D **90**
Royston Cl. KT12: Wal T 7H **39**
RH10: Craw 8E **162**
TW5: C'ford 4J **9**
Royston Ct. KT10: H Wood 8F **40**
SE24 . . . . .1N **29**
TW9: Kew 4M **11**
Royston Pk. KT14: Byf 8N **55**
Royston Rd. KT14: Byf 8N **55**
TW10: Rich 8L **11**
Roystons, The KT5: Surb 4A **42**
Rozeldene GU26: Hind 6C **170**
Rozel Ter. CR0: Croy 4B **200**
RQ33 SW18 . . . . .7M **13**
RSPB Great Bramshot Reserve
. . . . .1G **88**
Rubus Cl. GU24: W End 9B **52**
Ruckmans La. RH5: Oak 3A **178**
Rudd Hall Ri. GU15: Camb 3B **70**
Ruddlesway SL4: W'sor 5A **4**
(not continuous)
Ruden Way KT17: Eps D 3G **80**
Rudge Ri. KT15: Addl 2H **55**
RUDGWICK 9E **176**
Rudgwick Keep *RH6: Horl . . .7C 142*
(off Langshott La.)
Rudgwick Rd. RH11: Ifi 2L **181**
Rudloe Rd. SW12 . . . . .1G **28**
Rudsworth Cl. SL3: Coln 4F **6**
Ruffetts, The CR2: Sels 4E **64**
Ruffetts Cl. CR2: Sels 4E **64**
Ruffetts Way KT20: Tad 5K **81**
Rufford Cl. GU52: Fleet 7B **88**
Rufus Bus. Cen. SW18 . . . . . . .3N **27**
Rufwood RH10: Craw D 1D **184**
Rugby Cl. GU47: Owls 6K **49**
Rugby La. SM2: Chea 5J **61**
Rugby Rd. TW1: Twick 8E **10**
Ruggles-Brise Rd.
TW15: A'ford 6M **21**
Rugosa Rd. GU24: W End 9B **52**
Ruislip St. SW17 . . . . .5D **28**
Rumbold Rd. SW6 . . . . .3N **13**
Rumsey Cl. TW12: Hamp 7N **23**
RUN COMMON 1G **155**
Runcorn Cl. RH11: Craw 7K **181**
Runes Cl. CR4: Mit 3B **44**
RUNFOLD 8A **110**
Runfold St George
GU10: B Lea 7N **109**
Runnemede Rd. TW20: Egh . . .5B **20**
Running Horse Yd.
TW8: Brent 2L **11**
RUNNYMEDE 3N **19**
Runnymede 3N **19**
Runnymede SW19 . . . . .9A **28**
Runnymede Cl. TW2: Whitt . . .9B **10**
Runnymede Ct.
GU14: Farnb 7M **69**
SM6: W'ton 3F **62**
SW15 . . . . .2F **26**
TW20: Egh 5C **20**
Runnymede Cres.
SW16 . . . . .9H **29**
Runnymede Gdns.
TW2: Whitt 9B **10**
Runnymede Ho.
KT16: Chert 6J 37
(off Heriot Rd.)
Runnymede Rd. TW2: Whitt . . .9B **10**
Runnymede Rdbt.
TW20: Egh 5D **20**
Runshooke Ct.
RH11: Craw 6M **181**
Runtley Wood La.
GU4: Sut G 3B **94**
Runwick La. GU10: Farnh 3A **128**
Rupert Ct. *KT8: W Mole 3A 40*
(off St Peters Rd.)
Rupert Ho. *SW5 . . . . .1M 13*
(off Nevern Sq.)
Rupert Rd.
GU2: Guil 5A **202** (4M **113**)
Rural Cl. GU9: Farnh 5E **128**
Rural Way RH1: Red 3E **122**
SW16 . . . . .8F **28**
Ruscoe Dr. GU22: Wok 4C **74**
Ruscombe Gdns. SL3: Dat 3K **5**
Ruscombe Way TW14: Felt 1G **22**
Rush, The *SW19 . . . . .9L 27*
(off Kingston Rd.)
Rusham Ct. TW20: Egh 7C **20**
Rusham Pk. Av. TW20: Egh 7B **20**
Rusham Rd. SW12 . . . . .1D **28**
TW20: Egh 7B **20**
Rushams Rd. RH12: Hors 6H **197**
Rushbury Ct. TW12: Hamp 9A **24**
Rush Comn. M. SW2 . . . . .1K **29**
(Cotherstone Rd.)
SW2 . . . . .1J **29**
(New Pk. Rd.)
Rush Cft. GU7: Goda 3K **133**
Rushdene Wlk. TN16: B Hil 4F **86**
Rushden Way GU9: H End 5J **109**
Rushen Wlk. SM5: Cars 7B **44**
RUSHETT 5K **127**
Rushett Cl. KT7: T Dit 7H **41**
RUSHETT COMMON 1E **154**
Rushett Dr. RH4: Dork 8H **119**
Rushett La. KT9: Ches 7J **59**
Rushett Rd. KT7: T Dit 6H **41**
RUSHETTS FARM 7A **122**
Rushetts Pl. RH11: Craw 9A **162**
Rushetts Rd. RH2: Reig 7A **122**
RH11: Craw 9N **161**
Rushey Cl. KT3: N Mal 3C **42**
Rushfords RH7: Ling 6A **146**
Rushley Cl. BR2: Kes 1F **66**
Rushmead TW10: Ham 4H **25**
Rushmead Cl. CR0: Croy 1C **64**
Rushmere Ct. KT4: W Pk 8F **42**
Rushmere Pl. SW19 . . . . .6J **27**
TW20: Eng G 6A **20**
Rushmon Gdns.
KT12: Wal T 9J **39**
Rushmon Pl. SM3: Chea 3K **61**
Rushmon Vs. KT3: N Mal 3E **42**
RUSHMOOR 4A **150**
Rushmoor Arena 9K **89**
Rushmoor Cl. GU2: Guil 9J **93**
GU52: Fleet 6B **88**
Rushmoor Ct. GU14: Farnb 5A **90**
Rushmoor Gym 5A **110**
Rushmoor Rd. GU11: Alde 8J **89**
Rushmore Ho. SW15 . . . . .1F **26**
Rusholme Rd. SW15 . . . . .9J **13**
Rushton Av. RH9: S Gods 7F **124**
Rushworth Rd. RH2: Reig 2M **121**
Rushy Mdw. La. SM5: Cars . . .8C **44**
Ruskin Av. TW9: Kew 3N **11**
(not continuous)
TW14: Felt 9G **9**
Ruskin Cl. RH10: Craw 9G **163**
Ruskin Ct. RG45: Crow 3E **48**
Ruskin Dr. KT4: W Pk 8G **43**
Ruskin Ho. CR2: S Croy 8D **200**
Ruskin Mans. *W14 . . . . .2K 13*
(off Queen's Club Gdns.)
Ruskin Pde. CR2: S Croy 8D **200**
Ruskin Rd.
CR0: Croy 2A **200** (8M **45**)
SM5: Cars 2D **62**
TW7: Isle 6F **10**
TW18: Stain 7H **21**
Ruskin Way SW19 . . . . .9B **28**
Rusmon Ct. KT16: Chert 6H **37**
RUSPER 2C **180**
Rusper Ct. Cotts.
RH12: Rusp 3D **180**
Rusper Rd. RH5: Cap 6J **159**
RH5: Newd 2A **160**
RH11: Ifi 2H **181**
RH12: Hors 4M **197**
RH12: Ifi 2F **180**
RH12: Newd, Rusp 9C **160**
Rusper Rd. Rdbt.
RH12: Hors 1M **197**
Euspers Keep RH11: Ifi 2L **181**
Russell Cl. BR3: Beck 2L **47**
GU21: Wok 2M **73**
KT20: Wal H 3F **100**
RG12: Brac 7B **32**
W4 .2E **12**
Russell Ct. CR8: Pur 6L **63**
GU1: Guil 9M **93**
GU17: B'water 1J **69**
GU26: Hind 5D **170**
KT22: Leat 9H **79**
SM6: W'ton 2G 63
(off Ross Rd.)
SW16 . . . . .6K **29**
Russell Dr. TW19: Stan 9M **7**
Russell Gdns. TW10: Ham 3J **25**
UB7: Sip 1B **8**
Russell Grn. Cl. CR8: Pur 6L **63**
Russell Hill CR8: Pur 6K **63**
Russell Hill Pl. CR8: Pur 7L **63**
Russell Hill Rd. CR8: Pur 7L **63**
Russell Kerr Cl. W4 . . . . .3B **12**
Russell Pl. SM2: Sut 4N **61**
Russell Rd. CR4: Mit 2C **44**
GU21: Wok 2M **73**
KT12: Wal T 5H **39**
SW19 . . . . .8M **27**
TW2: Twick 9F **10**
TW17: Shep 6D **38**
Russells KT20: Tad 9J **81**
Russells Cres. RH6: Horl 9E **142**
Russell's Footpath
SW16 . . . . .6J **29**
Russell St. SL4: W'sor 4G **4**
Russell Wlk. TW10: Rich 9M **11**
Russell Way RH10: Craw 4E **182**
SM1: Sut 2N **61**
Russell Yd. SW15 . . . . .7K **13**
Russet Av. TW17: Shep 2F **38**
Russet Cl. GU10: Tong 5C **110**
KT12: Hers 9L **39**
RH6: Horl 8G **143**
TW19: Stan M 9H **7**
Russet Ct. RH13: Hors 4N **197**
Russet Dr. CR0: Croy 7H **47**
Russet Gdns. GU15: Camb 3B **70**
Russet Glade GU11: Alde 4J **109**
Russets KT20: Tad 1H **101**
Russett Ct. CR3: Cate 3D **104**
Russetts Cl. GU21: Wok 2B **74**
Russetts Dr. GU51: Fleet 5B **88**
Russet Way RH5: Nth H 8K **119**
RUSS HILL 5G **161**
Russ Hill RH6: Char 5F **160**
Russ Hill Rd. RH6: Char 4J **161**
Russington Rd. TW17: Shep 5E **38**
Russhall Cl. CR0: Croy 5F **46**
Rustic Av. SW16 . . . . .8F **28**
Rustic Glen GU52: C Cro 8A **88**
Rustington Wlk. SM4: Mord . . .6L **43**
Ruston Av. KT5: Surb 6A **42**
Ruston Cl. RH10: Craw 6G **182**
Ruston Way SL5: Asc 1H **33**
Rutford Rd. SW16 . . . . .6J **29**
Ruth Cl. GU14: Cove 9H **69**
Ruthen Cl. KT18: Eps 1A **80**
Rutherford Cl. SL4: W'sor 4C **4**
SM2: Sut 3B **62**
Rutherford Way
RH10: Craw 7E **162**
Rutherford Way Ind. Est.
RH10: Craw 7E **162**
Rutherwick Cl. RH6: Horl 8D **142**
Rutherwick Ri. CR5: Coul 4J **83**
Rutherwick Twr. RH6: Horl . . .8D **142**
Rutherwyke Cl. KT17: Ewe 3F **60**
Ruthyrfyrk Rd. KT16: Chert 6G **36**
Rutland Cl. GU11: Alde 1M **109**
KT9: Ches 3M **59**
KT19: Ewe 6C **60**
KT21: A'tead 4L **79**
RH1: Red 2D **122**
SW14 . . . . .6A **12**
SW19 . . . . .8C **28**
Rutland Ct. KT1: K Tham 8H **203**
Rutland Dr. SM4: Mord 5L **43**
TW10: Ham 2K **25**
Rutland Gdns. CR0: Croy 1B **64**
Rutland Gro. W6 . . . . .1G **13**
Rutland Rd. SW19 . . . . .8C **28**
TW2: Twick 3D **24**
UB3: Harl 1E **8**
Rutland Ter. GU11: Alde 1M **109**
Rutlish Rd. SW19 . . . . .9M **27**
Rutson Rd. KT14: Byf 1A **76**
Rutter Gdns. CR4: Mit 3A **44**
Rutton Hill Rd.
GU8: Bow G 2H **171**
Ruvigny Gdns. SW15 . . . . .6J **13**
Ruxbury Ct. TW15: A'ford 4N **21**
Ruxbury Rd. KT16: Chert 5E **36**
Ruxley Cl. KT19: Ewe 2A **60**

280 A-Z Surrey

St Johns Dr. KT12: Wal T ... 7K 39
SL4: W'sor ... 5D 4
SW18 ... 2N 27
St John's Gdns. *GU21: Wok ... 5K 73*
(off St John's Rd.)
St Johns Gro. GU9: Farnh ... 3G 129
SW13 ... 5E 12
TW9: Rich ... 7L 11
St John's Hill CR5: Coul ... 4L 83
St John's Hill Rd.
GU21: Wok ... 6K 73
St Johns Lodge GU21: Wok ... 6K 73
St John's Lye GU21: Wok ... 6J 73
St John's Mdw.
RH7: Blin H ... 3G 145
St John's M. GU21: Wok ... 6K 73
KT1: H Wic ... 1J 41
St John's Pas. SW19 ... 7K 27
St Johns Ri. GU21: Wok ... 6L 73
TN16: B Hil ... 3K 87
St John's Rd.
CR0: Croy ... 4A 200 (9M 45)
GU2: Guil ... 4J 113
GU9: Farnh ... 3G 129
GU14: Cove ... 1J 89
GU21: Wok ... 6J 73
GU47: Sandh ... 8G 49
KT1: H Wic ... 1J 41
KT3: N Mal ... 2B 42
KT8: E Mol ... 3D 40
KT22: Leat ... 8J 79
RH1: Red ... 5D 122
RH4: Westc ... 6C 118
RH11: Craw ... 3A 182
RH19: E Grin ... 8A 166
SL4: W'sor ... 5D 4
SL5: Asc ... 8K 17
(not continuous)
SM1: Sut ... 8N 43
SM5: Cars ... 9C 44
SW19 ... 8K 27
TW7: Isle ... 5F 10
TW9: Rich ... 7L 11
TW13: Hanw ... 5M 23
St Johns St. GU7: Goda ... 5J 133
RG45: Crow ... 2G 49
St John's Ter. *SW15 ... 4D 26*
(off Kingston Va.)
St John's Ter. Rd.
RH1: Red ... 5D 122
St Johns Waterside
GU21: Wok ... 5J 73
(off Copse Rd.)
St Johns Way KT16: Chert ... 7J 37
TN8: Eden ... 9K 127
St Joseph's Cl. BR6: Orp ... 1N 67
St Joseph's College Sports Cen.
... 7M 29
St Joseph's Rd.
GU12: Alde ... 3M 109
St Jude's Cl. TW20: Eng G ... 6M 19
St Jude's Cotts.
TW20: Eng G ... 6M 19
St Judes Rd. TW20: Eng G ... 4M 19
St Julian's Cl. SW16 ... 5L 29
St Julian's Farm Rd.
SE27 ... 5L 29
St Katherines Rd.
CR3: Cate ... 3D 104
St Lawrence Bus. Cen.
TW13: Felt ... 3J 23
St Lawrence Ct.
GU24: Chob ... 7H 53
St Lawrence Ho.
GU24: Chob ... 7H 53
(off Bagshot Rd.)
St Lawrence's Way
RH2: Reig ... 3M 121
St Lawrence Way
CR3: Cate ... 1N 103
St Leonard's Av. SL4: W'sor ... 5F 4
St Leonards Ct. SW14 ... 6B 12
St Leonard's Dr.
RH10: Craw ... 5E 182
ST LEONARDS FOREST ... 3C 198
St Leonard's Gdns.
TW5: Hest ... 3M 9
St Leonard's Hill SL4: W'sor ... 7A 4
ST LEONARD'S PARK ... 5A 198
St Leonards Pk.
RH19: E Grin ... 9A 166
St Leonard's Ri. BR6: Orp ... 1N 67
St Leonard's Rd. CR0: Wad ... 9M 45
KT6: Surb ... 4K 41
KT7: T Dit ... 5G 40
KT10: Clay ... 3F 58
KT18: Tat C ... 6H 81
RH13: Hors ... 8L 197
SL4: Wink ... 9A 4
SL4: W'sor ... 6D 4
SW14 ... 6A 12
St Leonards Sq. KT6: Surb ... 4K 41
St Leonard's Wlk. SW16 ... 8K 29
St Louis Rd. SE27 ... 5N 29
St Luke's Cl. SE25 ... 5E 46
St Lukes Ct. GU21: Wok ... 1E 74
St Luke's Pas.
KT2: K Tham ... 1L 203 (9M 25)
St Luke's Rd. CR3: Whyte ... 5C 84
SL4: O Win ... 9K 5
St Lukes Sq. GU1: Guil ... 4B 114
St Margaret Dr.
KT18: Eps ... 8H 201 (1B 80)

ST MARGARETS ... 9H 11
St Margarets GU1: Guil ... 3B 114
St Margarets Av.
RH19: D Pk ... 4A 166
SM3: Chea ... 9K 43
TN16: B Hil ... 3K 87
TW15: A'ford ... 6C 22
St Margarets Bus. Cen.
TW1: Twick ... 9H 11
St Margarets Cotts.
GU27: Fern ... 9F 188
St Margarets Ct.
SW15 ... 7G 12
St Margaret's Cres.
SW15 ... 8G 13
St Margaret's Dr.
TW1: Twick ... 8H 11
St Margaret's Gro.
TW1: Twick ... 9G 11
St Margarets Rd. CR5: Coul ... 8F 82
RH19: E Grin ... 7B 166
TW1: Twick ... 9H 11
TW7: Isle ... 7H 11
ST MARGARETS RDBT. ... 9H 11
St Margrets Ct. RH4: Dork ... 4J 201
St Marks Cl. GU14: Farnb ... 4A 90
SW6 ... 4M 13
St Mark's Ct. *GU22: Wok ... 6A 74*
(off Brooklyn Rd.)
St Mark's Gro. SW10 ... 3N 13
St Mark's Hill KT6: Surb ... 5L 41
St Mark's La. RH12: Hors ... 2L 197
St Marks Pl. GU9: U Hal ... 5G 109
SL4: W'sor ... 5F 4
SW19 ... 7L 27
St Marks Rd. CR4: Mit ... 1D 44
KT18: Tat C ... 5H 81
RG42: Bin ... 8H 15
SE25 ... 3D 46
SL4: W'sor ... 5F 4
TW11: Tedd ... 8H 25
St Martha's Av. GU22: Wok ... 8B 74
St Marthas Ct. GU4: Guil ... 9D 114
St Martin Cl. RH17: Hand ... 9N 199
St Martin's Av.
KT18: Eps ... 8L 201 (1D 80)
St Martins Cl.
KT17: Eps ... 7M 201 (9E 60)
KT24: E Hor ... 7F 96
St Martin's Ct. KT24: E Hor ... 7F 96
TW15: A'ford ... 6L 21
St Martins Dr. KT12: Wal T ... 9K 39
St Martins Est. SW2 ... 2L 29
St Martin's La. BR3: Beck ... 4L 47
St Martins M. GU22: Pyr ... 3J 75
RH4: Dork ... 2J 201 (5G 119)
St Martin's Wlk.
RH4: Dork ... 1K 201 (4H 119)
St Martins Way SW17 ... 4A 28
St Mary Av. SM6: W'ton ... 9E 44
St Marys KT13: Weybr ... 9E 38
St Mary's Av. TW11: Tedd ... 7F 24
TW19: Stan ... 1M 21
St Mary's Av. Central
UB2: S'hall ... 1B 10
St Mary's Av. Sth.
UB2: S'hall ... 1B 10
St Mary's Cl. GU47: Sandh ... 7H 49
KT9: Ches ... 4M 59
KT17: Ewe ... 4E 60
KT22: Fetc ... 1D 98
RH8: Oxt ... 7A 106
TW16: Sunb ... 3H 39
TW19: Stan ... 1M 21
St Mary's Copse KT4: W Pk ... 8D 42
St Mary's Ct. SM6: W'ton ... 1G 62
TN16: Weste ... 4M 107
St Mary's Cres. TW7: Isle ... 3D 10
TW19: Stan ... 1M 21
St Mary's Dr. RH10: Craw ... 1F 182
TW14: Bedf ... 1D 22
St Marys Gdn. GU23: Worp ... 5H 93
St Mary's Gdns. GU19: Bag ... 4J 51
RH12: Hors ... 7J 197
St Mary's Grn. TN16: B Hil ... 5E 86
St Mary's Gro. SW13 ... 6G 12
TN16: B Hil ... 5E 86
TW9: Rich ... 7M 11
W4 ... 2A 12
St Mary's Hill SL5: S'hill ... 5N 33
St Mary's Ho. *RH12: Hors ... 7J 197*
(off Normandy)
St Mary's La. SL4: Wink ... 4H 17
St Marys M. TW10: Ham ... 3J 25
St Marys Mill GU8: Chid ... 6E 172
St Mary's Mt. CR3: Cate ... 2C 104
St Marys Pl. GU9: Farnh ... 9H 109
St Mary's Rd. CR2: Sande ... 6A 64
GU12: A Va ... 8E 90
GU15: Camb ... 9A 50
GU21: Wok ... 4M 73
KT4: W Pk ... 8D 42
KT6: Surb ... 6J 41
(St Chads Cl.)
KT6: Surb ... 5K 41
(Victoria Rd.)
KT8: E Mol ... 4D 40
KT13: Weybr ... 1E 56
KT22: Leat ... 9H 79
RH2: Reig ... 4N 121
SE25 ... 2B 46
SL5: Asc ... 6M 33
SW19 ... 6K 27

St Mary's Ter. GU1: Guil ... 6C 202
St Mary's University College
Sports Cen. ... 5F 24
St Mary's Wlk. RH1: Blet ... 2A 124
RH12: Hors ... 7J 197
St Marys Way GU2: Guil ... 1H 113
St Matthew's Av.
KT6: Surb ... 7L 41
St Matthew's Ct.
TW15: A'ford ... 5B 22
(off Feltham Rd.)
St Matthew's Rd.
RH1: Red ... 2D 122
St Maur Rd. SW6 ... 4L 13
St Michael's RH8: Limp ... 8C 106
St Michaels Av. GU3: Worp ... 7F 92
St Michaels Cl.
GU28: North ... 9D 190
GU51: Fleet ... 5D 88
KT4: W Pk ... 8E 42
KT12: Wal T ... 8K 39
St Michaels Cotts.
RG40: W'ham ... 8H 31
St Michael's Ct. CR0: Croy ... 1B 200
KT13: Weybr ... 2D 56
(off Pine Gro.)
St Michaels Rd.
CR0: Croy ... 1C 200 (7N 45)
CR3: Cate ... 9A 84
GU12: Alde ... 3N 109
GU14: Farnb ... 8N 69
GU15: Camb ... 1N 69
GU21: Wok ... 1F 74
GU47: Sandh ... 7E 48
RH19: E Grin ... 8A 166
SM6: W'ton ... 3G 62
TW15: A'ford ... 6B 22
St Mildred's Rd.
GU1: Guil ... 2B 114
St Monica's Rd.
KT20: K'wood ... 8L 81
St Nazaire Cl. TW20: Egh ... 6E 20
St Nicholas Av. KT23: Book ... 3B 98
St Nicholas Cen. SM1: Sut ... 2N 61
St Nicholas Cl. GU51: Fleet ... 4A 88
St Nicholas Ct.
KT1: K Tham ... 8J 203
RH10: Craw ... 2G 182
St Nicholas Cres. GU22: Pyr ... 3J 75
St Nicholas Dr. TW17: Shep ... 6B 38
St Nicholas Glebe
SW17 ... 6E 28
St Nicholas Hill KT22: Leat ... 9H 79
St Nicholas M. KT7: T Dit ... 5F 40
St Nicholas Rd. KT7: T Dit ... 5F 40
SM1: Sut ... 2N 61
St Nicholas Way SM1: Sut ... 1N 61
St Nicolas Av. GU6: Cranl ... 7N 155
St Nicolas Cl. GU6: Cranl ... 7N 155
St Normans Way KT17: Ewe ... 6F 60
St Olaf's Rd. SW6 ... 3K 13
St Olaves Cl. TW18: Stain ... 8H 21
St Olaves Wlk. SW16 ... 1G 45
St Omer Ridge GU1: Guil ... 4C 114
St Omer Rd. GU1: Guil ... 4C 114
St Oswald's Rd.
SW16 ... 9M 29
St Oswalds Studios
SW6 ... 2M 13
(off Sedlescombe Rd.)
St Pauls Cl. GU10: Tong ... 5D 110
KT9: Ches ... 1K 59
KT15: Addl ... 2J 55
SM5: Cars ... 7C 44
TW3: Houn ... 5M 9
TW15: A'ford ... 6D 22
UB3: Harl ... 1E 8
St Paul's Ct. TW4: Houn ... 6M 9
St Paul's Ga. RG41: W'ham ... 2A 30
St Pauls M.
RH4: Dork ... 4L 201 (6H 119)
St Paul's Rd. CR7: T Hea ... 2N 45
GU22: Wok ... 4C 74
TW8: Brent ... 2K 11
TW9: Rich ... 6M 11
TW18: Stain ... 6F 20
St Paul's Rd. E.
RH4: Dork ... 3L 201 (5H 119)
St Paul's Rd. W.
RH4: Dork ... 4J 201 (6G 119)
St Paul's Studios *W14 ... 1K 13*
(off Talgarth Rd.)
St Paul's Wlk. KT2: K Tham ... 8N 25
St Peters KT16: Chert ... 9E 36
St Peters Av. TN16: B Hil ... 3K 87
St Peter's Cl. GU22: Wok ... 7E 74
SL4: O Win ... 8K 5
SW17 ... 3C 28
TW18: Stain ... 7H 21
St Peters Ct. KT8: W Mole ... 3A 40
St Peters Gdns.
GU10: Wrec ... 5E 128
GU46: Yate ... 9C 48
SE27 ... 4L 29
St Peter's Gro. W6 ... 1F 12
St Peters Mead GU12: Ash ... 2F 110
St Peters Pk. GU11: Alde ... 4K 109
St Peters Rd.
CR0: Croy ... 6D 200 (1A 64)
GU22: Wok ... 8D 74
KT1: K Tham ... 1N 41
KT8: W Mole ... 3A 40
RH11: Craw ... 3A 182

St Peters Rd. SL4: O Win ... 8K 5
TW1: Twick ... 8H 11
W6 ... 1F 12
St Peter's Sq. W6 ... 1E 12
St Peter's St.
CR2: S Croy ... 8E 200 (2A 64)
St Peter's Ter. SW6 ... 3L 13
St Peter's Vs. W6 ... 1F 12
St Peters Way GU16: Frim ... 7D 70
KT15: Addl ... 1F 54
KT16: Chert ... 1F 54
UB3: Harl ... 1E 8
St Peter's Wharf W4 ... 1F 12
St Philip's Av. KT4: W Pk ... 8G 42
St Philip's Ga. KT4: W Pk ... 8G 43
St Philips Rd. KT6: Surb ... 5K 41
St Phillips Ct. GU51: Fleet ... 4B 88
St Pier's La. RH7: Ling ... 8B 146
TN8: Ling ... 8B 146
St Pinnock Av. TW18: Stain ... 9J 21
St Richard's M.
RH10: Craw ... 3D 182
(off Broomdashers Rd.)
St Sampson Rd.
RH11: Craw ... 7L 181
St Saviour's Ct. *CR8: Pur ... 9K 63*
(off Lodge La.)
St Saviours Pl.
GU1: Guil ... 3B 202 (3M 113)
St Saviour's Rd. CR0: Croy ... 5M 45
Saints Cl. SE27 ... 5M 29
St Sebastian's Cl.
RG40: W'ham ... 9D 30
St Simon's Av. SW15 ... 8H 13
Saints M. CR4: Mit ... 2C 44
St Stephen Cl.
RH11: Craw ... 9B 162
St Stephen's Av.
KT21: A'tead ... 3L 79
St Stephens Cl.
GU27: Hasl ... 2D 188
St Stephens Ct.
RH9: S Gods ... 7H 125
(off Oaklands)
St Stephen's Cres.
CR7: T Hea ... 2L 45
St Stephen's Gdns.
SW15 ... 8L 13
TW1: Twick ... 9J 11
St Stephen's Pas.
TW1: Twick ... 9J 11
St Stephen's Rd.
TW3: Houn ... 9A 10
St Swithun's Cl.
RH19: E Grin ... 9B 166
St Theresa Cl.
KT18: Eps ... 8H 201 (1B 80)
St Theresa's Rd. TW14: Felt ... 7G 9
St Thomas Cl. GU4: Guil ... 9E 114
GU21: Wok ... 4M 73
KT6: Surb ... 7M 41
St Thomas Dr. GU4: E Cla ... 9N 95
St Thomas Rd. W4 ... 2B 12
St Thomas's M. GU1: Guil ... 5B 114
St Thomas's Way SW6 ... 3L 13
St Thomas Wlk. SL3: Coln ... 3F 6
St Vincent Cl. RH10: Craw ... 4H 183
SE27 ... 6M 29
St Vincent Rd. KT12: Wal T ... 9J 39
TW2: Whitt ... 9C 10
St Winifreds CR8: Ken ... 2N 83
St Winifred's Rd.
TN16: B Hil ... 5H 87
TW11: Tedd ... 7H 25
Salamanca RG45: Crow ... 2D 48
Salamander Cl.
KT2: K Tham ... 6J 25
Salamander Quay
KT1: H Wic ... 2G 203 (9K 25)
Salbrook Rd. RH1: Salf ... 2E 142
Salcombe Dr. SM4: Mord ... 7J 43
Salcombe Rd. TW15: A'ford ... 4N 21
Salcombe Vs. TW10: Rich ... 8L 11
Salcot Cres. CR0: N Add ... 6M 65
Salcott Rd. CR0: Bedd ... 9J 45
Sale Gdn. Cotts.
RG40: W'ham ... 3B 30
Salehurst Rd. RH10: Wor ... 3J 183
Salem Pl.
CR0: Croy ... 5B 200 (9N 45)
Salerno Cl. GU11: Alde ... 1M 109
Sales Ct. GU11: Alde ... 3L 109
Salesian Gdns. KT16: Chert ... 7J 37
Salesian Vw. GU14: Farnb ... 5C 90
Salford Rd. SW2 ... 2H 29
SALFORDS ... 2E 142
Salfords Ind. Est.
RH1: Salf ... 3E 142
Salfords Station (Rail) ... 2F 142
Salisbury Av. SM1: Sut ... 3L 61
Salisbury Cl. KT4: W Pk ... 9E 42
Salisbury Ct. SM5: Cars ... 2D 62
Salisbury Gdns.
SW19 ... 8K 27
Salisbury Gro. GU16: Mytc ... 1D 90
Salisbury Ho. SM6: W'ton ... 2F 62
Salisbury M. SW6 ... 3L 13
Salisbury Pas. *SW6 ... 3L 13*
(off Dawes Rd.)
Salisbury Pavement
SW6 ... 3L 13
(off Dawes Rd.)
Salisbury Pl. KT14: W By ... 7L 55

Salisbury Rd. GU12: Ash ... 1E 110
GU14: Farnb ... 1A 90
GU17: B'water ... 1H 69
GU22: Wok ... 6A 74
KT3: N Mal ... 2C 42
KT4: W Pk ... 1C 60
RH9: Gods ... 9F 104
RH10: Craw ... 7C 182
(not continuous)
RH13: Hors ... 8G 196
SE25 ... 5D 46
SM5: Cars ... 3D 62
SM7: Ban ... 1N 81
SW19 ... 8K 27
TW4: Houn ... 6K 9
TW6: Lon A ... 9D 8
(not continuous)
TW9: Rich ... 7L 11
TW13: Felt ... 2K 23
Salisbury Ter. GU16: Mytc ... 2E 90
Salix Cl. KT22: Fetc ... 1B 98
TW16: Sunb ... 8J 23
Salliesfield TW2: Whitt ... 9D 10
Salmons La. CR3: Whyte ... 7B 84
CR3: Whyte, Cate ... 7B 84
Salmons La. W. CR3: Cate ... 7B 84
Salmons Rd. KT9: Ches ... 3L 59
KT24: Eff ... 7J 97
Saltash Cl. SM1: Sut ... 1L 61
Saltbox Hill TN16: B Hil ... 9D 66
Salt Box Rd. GU3: Guil ... 7J 93
GU4: Guil ... 7J 93
Saltdean Cl. RH10: Craw ... 6B 182
Salterford Rd. SW17 ... 7E 28
Salterns Rd. RH10: Craw ... 6G 182
Salter's Hill SE19 ... 6N 29
Saltire Gdns. RG42: Brac ... 9M 15
Salt La. GU8: Hamb ... 4G 153
Saltram Rd. GU14: Farnb ... 3C 90
Salvador SW17 ... 6D 28
Salvation Pl. KT22: Fetc ... 2G 98
Salvia Ct. GU24: Bis ... 3D 72
Salvington Rd.
RH11: Craw ... 6L 181
Salvin Rd. SW15 ... 6J 13
Salwey Cl. RG12: Brac ... 5N 31
Samaritan Cl. RH11: Craw ... 5K 181
Samarkand Cl. GU15: Camb ... 2F 70
Samels Ct. W6 ... 1F 12
Samian Pl. RG42: Bin ... 8K 15
Sammi Ct. CR7: T Hea ... 3N 45
Samos Rd. SE20 ... 1E 46
Samphire Cl. RH11: Craw ... 6M 181
Sampleoak La.
GU4: B'eath, Guil ... 9G 114
Sampson Ct. TW17: Shep ... 4D 38
Sampson Pk. RG42: Bin ... 9J 15
Sampson's Almshouses
GU9: Farnh ... 2E 128
Samuel Gray Gdns.
KT2: K Tham ... 1H 203 (9K 25)
Samuel Johnson Cl.
SW16 ... 5K 29
Samuel Lewis Trust Dwellings
SW6 ... 3M 13
(off Vanston Pl.)
Samuel Richardson Ho.
W14 ... 1L 13
(off North End Cres.)
San Carlos App.
GU11: Alde ... 2A 110
Sanctuary, The SM4: Mord ... 5M 43
Sanctuary Rd. TW6: Lon A ... 9B 8
Sandal Rd. KT3: N Mal ... 4C 42
Sandalwood GU2: Guil ... 4L 113
Sandalwood Av.
KT16: Chert ... 9G 36
Sandalwood Rd. TW13: Felt ... 4J 23
Sandbanks TW14: Felt ... 2F 22
Sandbourne Av. SW19 ... 1N 43
Sandcross La. RH2: Reig ... 6L 121
Sandell's Av. TW15: A'ford ... 5D 22
Sandeman Way
RH13: Hors ... 8L 197
Sanders Cl. TW12: H Hill ... 6C 24
Sandersfield Gdns.
SM7: Ban ... 2M 81
Sandersfield Rd. SM7: Ban ... 2N 81
SANDERSTEAD ... 8D 64
Sanderstead Cl. SW12 ... 1G 29
Sanderstead Ct. Av.
CR2: Sande ... 9D 64
Sanderstead Hill
CR2: Sande ... 7B 64
Sanderstead Rd.
CR2: Sande, S Croy ... 4A 64
Sanderstead Station (Rail) ... 5A 64
Sandes Pl. KT22: Leat ... 5G 79
Sandfield Ct. GU1: Guil ... 4C 202
Sandfield Gdns.
CR7: T Hea ... 2M 45
Sandfield Pas. CR7: T Hea ... 2N 45
Sandfield Pl. CR7: T Hea ... 2N 45
Sandfield Rd. CR7: T Hea ... 2M 45
Sandfields GU23: Send ... 2F 94
Sandfield Ter.
GU1: Guil ... 4C 202 (4N 113)
Sandford Ct. GU11: Alde ... 3L 109
Sandford Down RG12: Brac ... 4D 32
Sandford Rd. GU9: U Hal ... 5G 109
GU11: Alde ... 3L 109
Sandford St. SW6 ... 3N 13
Sandgate La. SW18 ... 2C 28

Selwyn Dr.—Shirley Pl.

Selwyn Dr. GU46: Yate 9A 48
Selwyn Rd. KT3: N Mal 4C 42
Semaphore Rd.
GU1: Guil 7E 202 (5A 114)
Semley Rd. SW16 . . . . .1J 45
Semper Cl. GU21: Knap 4H 73
Sen Cl. RG42: Warf 7A 16
SEND 2F 94
Send Barns La.
GU23: Send 2F 94
Send Cl. GU23: Send 1E 94
Send Hill GU23: Send 3E 94
SEND MARSH 1H 95
Send Marsh Grn. GU23: Rip . . .1H 95
Send Marsh Rd.
GU23: Rip, Send 2F 94
Send Pde. Cl. GU23: Send 1E 94
Send Rd. GU23: Send 1D 94
Seneca Rd. CR7: T Hea 3N 45
Sener Ct. CR2: S Croy 3N 63
Senga Rd. SM6: W'ton 7E 44
Senhouse Rd. SM3: Chea 9J 43
Sentamu Cl. SE24 . . . . .2M 29
Sepen Meade GU52: C Cro 9A 88
Sequoia Pk. RH11: Craw 5B 182
Sergeant Ind. Est.
SW18 . . . . .9N 13
Sergeants Pl. CR3: Cate 9N 83
Serpentine Grn.
RH1: Mers 7H 103
Serrin Way RH12: Hors 3L 197
Servite Ho. BR3: Beck 1J 47
GU21: Knap 4G 73
KT4: W Pk 8E 42
(off The Avenue)
RH4: Dork 7G 119
(off Harrow Rd. W.)
Servius Ct. TW8: Brent 3K 11
Setley Way RG12: Brac 2D 32
Sett, The GU46: Yate 1A 68
Setter Combe RG42: Warf 7B 16
Settrington Rd. SW6 . . . . .5N 13
Seven Acres SM5: Cars 8C 44
Seven Arches App.
KT13: Weybr 4A 56
Seven Hills Cl.
KT12: Whit V 5F 56
Seven Hills Rd. KT11: Cob 6F 56
KT12: Hers, Whit V 6F 56
Seven Hills Rd. Sth.
KT11: Cob 9F 56
Seven Kings Way
KT2: K Tham 1J 203 (9L 25)
Sevenoaks Cl. SM2: Sut 6M 61
Sevenoaks Rd.
BR6: Chels, Orp 2N 67
BR6: P Bot 4N 67
Sevenseas Rd. TW6: Lon A 9D 8
Seventh Av. KT20: Lwr K 3K 101
Severells Copse 4N 137
Severn Cl. GU47: Sandh 7H 49
Severn Ct. KT2: K Tham 1H 203
Severn Cres. SL3: Lang 1D 6
Severn Dr. KT10: H Wood 8G 41
KT12: Wal T 8L 39
Severn Rd. GU14: Cove 8K 69
RH10: Craw 4G 182
Seward Rd. BR3: Beck 1G 47
Sewell Av. RG41: W'ham 9A 14
Sewer's Farm Rd.
RH5: A Com 5N 137
Sewill Cl. RH6: Char 3L 161
Seymour Av. CR3: Cate 1N 103
KT17: Ewe 5G 61
SM4: Mord 6J 43
Seymour Cl. KT8: E Mol 4C 40
Seymour Ct. GU51: Fleet 3B 88
KT11: Cob 9G 57
KT19: Ewe 5D 60
RG45: Crow 3D 48
Seymour Dr. GU15: Camb 7F 50
Seymour Gdns. KT5: Surb 4M 41
TW1: Twick 1H 25
TW13: Hanw 5K 23
Seymour Ho. SM2: Sut 3N 61
(off Mulgrave Rd.)
Seymour M. KT17: Ewe 6F 60
Seymour Pl. GU22: Wok 7L 73
SE25 . . . . .3E 46
Seymour Rd. CR4: Mit 6E 44
GU7: Goda 8E 132
GU35: H Dwn 5H 169
KT1: H Wic 2G 203 (9K 25)
KT8: W Mole, E Mol 4C 40
RH11: Craw 7M 181
SM5: Cars 2E 62
SW18 . . . . .1L 27
SW19 . . . . .4J 27
TW12: H Hill 6C 24
Seymour Ter. SE20 . . . . .1E 46
Seymour Vs. SE20 . . . . .1E 46
Seymour Way TW16: Sunb 8G 22
Shabden Cotts. CR5: Chip 8D 82
SHACKLEFORD 4A 132
Shackleford Rd.
GU8: Els, S'ford 7L 131
GU8: S'ford 4A 132
GU22: Wok 7C 74
Shacklegate La.
TW11: Tedd 5E 24
Shackleton Cl. GU12: A Va 8D 90
Shackleton Ct. TW19: Stan 9N 7
(off Whitley Cl.)
Shackleton Rd.
RH10: Craw 6C 182
Shackleton Wlk. GU2: Guil . . .3H 113
(off Chapelhouse Cl.)
Shackstead La. GU7: Goda 8F 132
Shadbolt Cl. KT4: W Pk 8E 42
Shadyhanger GU7: Goda 5H 133
Shady Nook GU9: U Hal 6G 108
Shaef Way TW11: Tedd 8G 25
Shaftesbury Av. TW14: Felt 9H 9
Shaftesbury Cl. RG12: Brac . . .4B 32
Shaftesbury Ct.
GU14: Farnb 5A 90
RG40: W'ham 1C 30
SW6 . . . . .4N 13
(off Maltings Pl.)
SW16 . . . . .4H 29
Shaftesbury Cres.
TW18: Stain 8M 21
Shaftesbury Ho. CR5: Coul 9H 83
Shaftesbury Mt. GU17: Haw . . .3H 69
Shaftesbury Rd. BR3: Beck 1J 47
GU22: Wok 4D 74
GU24: Bis 3C 72
RH10: Craw 5H 183
SM5: Cars 6B 44
TW9: Rich 6L 11
Shaftesbury Way
TW2: Twick 4D 24
Shakespeare Av. TW14: Felt 9H 9
Shakespeare Gdns.
GU14: Cove 9J 69
Shakespeare Rd.
KT15: Addl 1M 55
Shakespeare Way
RG42: Warf 8C 16
TW13: Hanw 5K 23
Shalbourne Ri.
GU15: Camb 1B 70
Shalden Ho. SW15 . . . . .9E 12
Shalden Rd. GU12: Alde 4B 110
Shaldon Dr. SM4: Mord 4K 43
Shaldon Way KT12: Wal T 9K 39
Shale Grn. RH1: Mers 7H 103
Shalesbrook La.
RH18: F Row 8H 187
SHALFORD 9A 114
Shalford Cl. BR6: Farnb 1L 67
Shalford Hill GU27: K Grn 8G 189
Shalford Mill 8A 114
Shalford Rd.
GU1: Guil 8D 202 (6N 113)
GU4: Guil 6N 113
Shalford Station (Rail) 9A 114
Shalstone Rd. SW14 . . . . .6A 12
Shalston Vs. KT6: Surb 5M 41
Shambles, The
GU1: Guil 6C 202 (5N 113)
SHAMLEY GREEN 7G 134
Shamrock Cl. GU16: Frim 6B 70
KT22: Fetc 8D 78
Shamrock Cotts. GU3: Worp . . .6K 93
Shamrock Rd. CR0: Croy 5K 45
Shandys Cl. RH12: Hors 7G 196
Shanklin Ct. GU12: Alde 3A 110
Shannon Cl. UB2: S'hall 1L 9
Shannon Commercial Cen.
KT3: N Mal 3F 42
SHANNON CORNER 3F 42
Shannon Cnr. Retail Pk.
KT3: N Mal 3F 42
Shannon Ct. CR0: Croy 1C 200
Shanti Ct. SW18 . . . . .2M 27
Shap Cres. SM5: Cars 7D 44
Sharland Cl. CR7: T Hea 5L 45
Sharman Row SL3: Lang 1B 6
Sharnbrook Ho. W14 . . . . .2M 13
Sharon Cl. KT6: Surb 7J 41
KT19: Eps 6H 201 (9B 60)
KT23: Book 2A 98
RH10: Craw 6E 182
Sharon Ct. CR2: S Croy 8C 200
Sharon Rd. W4 . . . . .1C 12
Sharp Ho. TW1: Twick 9K 11
Sharpthorne Cl. RH11: Ifi 3L 181
Shaw Cl. CR2: Sande 8C 64
KT16: Otter 3E 54
KT17: Ewe 7E 60
Shaw Ct. CR3: Cate 8A 84
SL4: O Win 8K 5
SM4: Mord 6A 44
Shaw Cres. CR2: Sande 6C 64
Shaw Dr. KT12: Wal T 6K 39
SHAW FARM 7H 5
Shawfield Cotts.
GU12: Ash 2D 110
Shawfield La. GU12: Ash 2D 110
Shawfield Rd. GU12: Ash 3D 110
Shawford Ct. SW15 . . . . .1F 26
Shawford Rd. KT19: Ewe 3C 60
Shaw Gdns. SL3: Lang 1B 6
Shaw Ho. SM7: Ban 6A 82
Shawley Cres. KT18: Tat C 5H 81
Shawley Way KT18: Tat C 5G 81
Shaw Pk. RG45: Crow 4G 48
Shaw Rd. TN16: Tats 7E 86
Shaws Cotts. GU2: Guil 7J 93
(off Worplesdon Rd.)
Shaws Path KT1: H Wic 9J 25
(off Bennett Cl.)
Shaws Rd. RH10: Craw 2D 182
Shaw Way SM6: W'ton 4J 63
Shaxton Cres. CR0: N Add 5M 65
Sheaf Cotts. KT7: T Dit 7E 40
(off Weston Grn.)
Shearing Dr. SM5: Cars 6A 44
SHEARS, THE 8F 22
Shears Ct. TW16: Sunb 8F 22
Shears Way TW16: Sunb 9F 22
Shearwater Ct. RH11: Ifi 4J 181
(off Stoneycroft Wlk.)
Shearwater Rd. SM1: Sut 2L 61
Sheath Cotts. KT7: T Dit 5H 41
(off Ferry Rd.)
Sheath's La. KT22: Oxs 9B 58
Sheen Comn. Dr.
TW10: Rich 7N 11
Sheen Ct. TW10: Rich 7N 11
Sheen Ct. Rd. TW10: Rich 7N 11
Sheendale Rd. TW9: Rich 7M 11
Sheen Ga. Gdns.
SW14 . . . . .7B 12
Sheengate Mans.
SW14 . . . . .7C 12
Sheen La. SW14 . . . . .8B 12
Sheen Pk. TW9: Rich 7M 11
Sheen Rd. TW9: Rich 8L 11
TW10: Rich 8L 11
Sheen Sports & Fitness Cen.
. . . . .7D 12
Sheen Way SM6: W'ton 2K 63
Sheen Wood SW14 . . . . .8B 12
Sheepbarn La. CR6: B Hil 8B 66
Sheepcote Cl. TW5: C'ford 3H 9
Sheepcote Rd. SL4: E Wic 1D 4
SL4: W'sor 5B 4
Sheepfold Rd. GU2: Guil 9J 93
SHEEP GREEN 3C 158
Sheephatch La.
GU10: Til 6N 129
Sheep Ho. GU9: Farnh 3H 129
Sheephouse Grn.
RH5: Wott 9N 117
Sheephouse La.
RH5: A Com, Wott 8N 117
(not continuous)
Sheephouse Way
KT3: N Mal 7C 42
Sheeplands Av. GU1: Guil 1E 114
Sheepmoor Dr. GU51: Fleet 2A 88
Sheep Wlk. KT18: Eps D 8C 80
RH2: Reig 9L 101
TW17: Shep 6A 38
Sheep Wlk., The
GU22: Wok 5F 74
Sheepwalk La.
KT24: E Hor 3G 116
RH5: Ran C 3H 117
Sheep Wlk. M. SW19 . . . . .7J 27
SHEERWATER 1F 74
Sheerwater Av.
KT15: Wood 8G 55
Sheerwater Bus. Cen.
GU21: Wok 2E 74
Sheerwater Rd. GU21: Wok 8G 54
KT14: W By 9G 55
KT15: Wood 8G 54
Sheet's Heath La.
GU24: B'wood 6D 72
Sheet St. SL4: W'sor 5G 5
Sheet St. Rd. SL4: W'sor 5A 18
Sheffield Cl. GU14: Cove 1L 89
RH10: Craw 5F 182
Sheffield Rd. TW6: Lon A 9D 8
Sheffield Way TW6: Lon A 8E 8
Shefford Cres.
RG40: W'ham 9C 14
Shelburne Dr. TW4: Houn 9A 10
Sheldon Cl. RH2: Reig 4N 121
RH10: Craw 4H 183
Sheldon Ct. GU1: Guil 4B 114
Sheldon St.
CR0: Croy 5B 200 (9N 45)
Sheldrick Cl. SW19 . . . . .1B 44
Shelford KT1: K Tham 1N 41
Shelley Av. RG12: Brac 1C 32
Shelley Cl. CR5: Coul 4K 83
GU51: Fleet 5B 88
RH10: Craw 1G 182
SL3: Lang 1B 6
SM7: Ban 2J 81
Shelley Ct. GU15: Camb 1A 70
Shelley Cres. TW5: Hest 4L 9
Shelley Dr. RH12: Bro H 5C 196
Shelley Ri. GU14: Farnb 8L 69
Shelley Rd. RH12: Hors 5H 197
RH19: E Grin 9M 165
Shelleys Ct. RH13: Hors 4N 197
Shelley Wlk. GU46: Yate 1A 68
Shelley Way SW19 . . . . .6B 28
Shellfield Cl. TW19: Stan M 8J 7
SHELLWOOD CROSS 4D 140
Shellwood Dr. RH5: Nth H 9J 119
Shellwood Rd. RH2: Leigh 1B 140
Shelson Av. TW13: Felt 4G 22
Shelton Av. CR6: Warl 4F 84
Shelton Cl. CR6: Warl 4F 84
GU2: Guil 7K 93
Shelton Rd. SW19 . . . . .9M 27
Shelvers Grn. KT20: Tad 8H 81
Shelvers Hill KT20: Tad 8G 81
Shelvers Spur KT20: Tad 8H 81
Shelvers Way KT20: Tad 8H 81
Shenfield Cl. CR5: Coul 6G 82
Shenley Cl. CR2: Sande 6C 64
Shenley Rd. TW5: Hest 4M 9
Shenston Ct. SL4: W'sor 4G 4
(off James St.)
Shenstone Ho. SW16 . . . . .6G 29
Shenstone Pk. SL5: S'hill 3B 34
Shepherd & Flock Rdbt.
GU9: Farnh 9K 109
Shepherd Cl. RH10: Craw 6C 182
TW13: Hanw 5M 23
Shepherds Chase
GU19: Bag 5J 51
Shepherds Cl. TW17: Shep 5C 38
Shepherds Ct. GU9: Farnh . . .3H 129
SL4: W'sor 5B 4
Shepherds Gro. La.
RH19: E Grin 5H 167
Shepherds Hill GU2: Guil 1K 113
GU27: Hasl 2G 188
RG12: Brac 9A 16
RH1: Mers 4G 102
TN7: C Hat 8M 187
Shepherd's Hill Bungs.
GU27: Hasl 2G 189
(off Shepherd's Hill)
Shepherds La. GU2: Guil 9J 93
GU20: Windl 2C 52
RG42: Brac 8M 15
Shepherds Wlk.
GU14: Cove 7K 69
KT18: Eps D 8A 80
Shepherds Way CR2: Sels 4G 64
GU4: Guil 7A 114
(not continuous)
GU10: Til 7A 130
RG45: Crow 3D 48
RH12: Hors 3N 197
Shepiston La. UB3: Harl 1C 8
Shepley Cl. SM5: Cars 9E 44
Shepley Dr. SL5: S'dale 5F 34
Shepley End SL5: S'dale 4F 34
Sheppard Cl.
KT1: K Tham 8K 203 (3L 41)
Sheppard Ho. SW2 . . . . .2L 29
SHEPPERTON 5C 38
Shepperton Bus. Pk.
TW17: Shep 4D 38
Shepperton Ct. TW17: Shep . . .5C 38
Shepperton Ct. Dr.
TW17: Shep 4C 38
Shepperton Film Studios 2A 38
SHEPPERTON GREEN 3B 38
Shepperton Rd.
TW18: Lale, Shep 2L 37
Shepperton Station (Rail) 4D 38
Sheppey Cl. RH11: Craw 6N 181
Sheraton Cl. GU17: Haw 2K 69
Sheraton Dr.
KT19: Eps 6H 201 (9B 60)
Sheraton Wlk.
RH11: Craw 8N 181
Sherborne Cl. KT18: Tat C 4H 81
SL3: Poy 4G 7
Sherborne Ct.
GU2: Guil 6B 202 (5M 113)
Sherborne Cres. SM5: Cars . . .6C 44
Sherborne Gdns.
TW17: Shep 6F 38
Sherborne La. GU5: Ewh 1G 157
RH5: H Mary 1G 157
Sherborne Rd. GU14: Farnb 4B 90
KT9: Ches 2L 59
SM3: Sut 8M 43
TW14: Bedf 2E 22
(not continuous)
Sherborne Wlk. KT22: Leat 8J 79
Sherbourne GU5: Alb 8M 115
Sherbourne Cotts.
GU5: Alb 7N 115
Sherbourne Ct. SM2: Sut 3A 62
Sherbourne Dr. SL4: W'sor 7C 4
SL5: S'dale 4G 34
Sherbrooke Rd. SW6 . . . . .3K 13
Sherbrooke Ter. SW6 . . . . .3K 13
(off Sherbrook Rd.)
Sherbrooke Way KT4: W Pk 6G 42
SHERE 8B 116
Shere Av. SM2: Chea 6H 61
Shere Cl. KT9: Ches 2K 59
RH5: Nth H 9J 119
Shere La. GU5: Shere 8B 116
Shere Mus. 8B 116
Shere Rd.
GU4: Guil, W Cla 4J 115
GU5: Alb, Gorn, Shere . . .7N 115
GU6: Ewh 2E 156
KT24: W Hors 8C 96
(not continuous)
Sherfield Cl. KT3: N Mal 3A 42
Sherfield Gdns. SW15 . . . . . . .9E 12
Sheridan Cl. GU11: Alde 4M 109
Sheridan Ct. CR0: Croy 6F 200
SW5 . . . . .1N 13
(off Barkston Gdns.)
TW4: Houn 8M 9
Sheridan Dr. RH2: Reig 1N 121
Sheridan Grange
SL5: S'dale 5D 34
Sheridan Ho. KT22: Leat 8G 78
Sheridan Pl. RH19: E Grin 9M 165
SW13 . . . . .6E 12
Sheridan Rd. GU16: Frim 6B 70
SW19 . . . . .9L 27
TW10: Ham 4J 25
Sheridans Rd. KT23: Book 4C 98
Sheridan Wlk. SM5: Cars 2D 62
Sheridan Way BR3: Beck 1J 47
Sheriden Pl. TW12: Hamp 9B 24
Sheringham Av. TW2: Whitt . . .2N 23
TW13: Felt 4H 23
Sheringham Ct. TW13: Felt 4H 23
(off Sheringham Av.)
Sheringham Rd. SE20 . . . . .2F 46
Sherington Cl. GU14: Farnb 8N 69
Sherland Rd. TW1: Twick 2F 24
Sherlocks Ct RH4: Dork 1J 201
Shermanbury Ct.
RH12: Hors 4K 197
(off Blenheim Rd.)
Shernden La. TN8: M Grn 5L 147
Sherriff Cl. KT10: Esh 8B 40
Sherring Cl. RG42: Brac 8A 16
Sherrydon GU6: Cranl 6A 156
Sherwin Cres. GU14: Farnb 6N 69
Sherwood KT6: Surb 8K 41
Sherwood Av. SW16 . . . . .8H 29
Sherwood Cl. KT22: Fetc 1C 98
RG12: Brac 1E 32
SW13 . . . . .6G 13
Sherwood Ct. CR2: S Croy . . .8B 200
SL3: Lang 1B 6
Sherwood Cres. RH2: Reig . . .7N 121
Sherwood Pk. Rd. CR4: Mit 3G 44
SM1: Sut 2M 61
Sherwood Rd. CR0: Croy 6E 46
CR5: Coul 3G 82
GU21: Knap 4H 73
SW19 . . . . .8L 27
TW12: H Hill 6C 24
Sherwood Wlk.
RH10: Craw 6D 182
Sherwood Way
BR4: W Wick 8M 47
Shetland Cl. GU4: B'ham 7D 94
RH10: Craw 2J 183
Shetland Rd. TW6: Lon A 9D 8
Shetland Way GU51: Fleet 1C 88
Shewens Rd. KT13: Weybr 1E 56
Shey Copse GU22: Wok 4E 74
Shield Dr. TW8: Brent 2G 11
Shield Rd. TW15: A'ford 5D 22
Shilburn Way GU21: Wok 5K 73
Shildon Cl. GU15: Camb 3H 71
SHILLINGLEE 3G 190
Shillinglee Rd.
GU8: Chid, Plais 4G 190
RH14: Plais 4G 190
Shimmings, The GU1: Guil 2C 114
Shinners Cl. SE25 . . . . .4D 46
Shinwell Wlk. RH11: Craw . . .8N 181
Ship All. GU14: Farnb 8A 70
W4 . . . . .2N 11
Shipfield Cl. TN16: Tats 8E 86
Ship Hill TN16: Tats 8E 86
Shipka Rd. SW12 . . . . .2F 28
Shiplake Ho. RG12: Brac 3D 32
Ship La. GU14: Farnb 8A 70
SW14 . . . . .6B 12
SHIPLEY BRIDGE 4K 163
Shipley Bri. La.
RH6: S Bri 5K 163
RH10: S Bri 5K 163
Shipley Rd. RH11: Craw 2M 181
Ship St. RH19: E Grin 1A 186
Ship Yd. KT13: Weybr 9C 38
Shire Av. GU51: Fleet 1D 88
Shire Cl. GU19: Bag 5J 51
RG42: Warf 8D 16
Shire Ct. GU11: Alde 2K 109
KT17: Ewe 4E 60
Shire Horse Way TW7: Isle 6F 10
Shire La. BR2: Kes 5G 67
BR6: Chels, Dow 4K 67
(not continuous)
Shire M. TW2: Whitt 9C 10
Shire Pde. RH10: Craw 2H 183
Shire Pl. RH1: Red 5D 122
RH10: Craw 2H 183
(off The Ridings)
SW18 . . . . .1A 28
TW8: Brent 3K 11
Shires, The TW10: Ham 5L 25
Shires Cl. KT21: A'tead 6K 79
Shires Ho. KT14: Byf 9N 55
Shires Wlk. TN8: Eden 9K 127
Shires Way GU46: Yate 8C 48
SHIRLEY 8F 46
Shirley Av. CR0: Croy 7F 46
CR5: Coul 6M 83
RH1: Red 8D 122
SL4: W'sor 4C 4
SM1: Sut 1B 62
SM2: Chea 5L 61
Shirley Chu. Rd. CR0: Croy . . .9G 46
Shirley Cl. RH11: Craw 7J 181
TW3: Houn 8C 10
Shirley Ct. GU1: Guil 4D 202
SW16 . . . . .8J 29
Shirley Cres. BR3: Beck 3H 47
Shirley Dr. TW3: Houn 8C 10
Shirley Hgts. SM6: W'ton 5G 62
Shirley Hills Rd. CR0: Croy 2F 64
Shirleyhyrst KT13: Weybr 3E 56
SHIRLEY OAKS 7G 46
Shirley Oaks Rd. CR0: Croy 7G 46
Shirley Pk. CR0: Croy 8F 46
Shirley Pk. Rd. CR0: Croy 7E 46
Shirley Pl. GU21: Knap 4F 72

Springbok Cotts.—Station App.

Springbok Cotts. GU6: Alf 7F 174
Springbok Est. GU6: Alf 7F 174
Springbottom La.
RH1: Blet 5L 103
Spring Cl. GU7: Goda 3H 133
RH11: Craw 4B 182
Springclose La.
SM3: Chea 3K 61
Spring Copse RH10: Cop . . .7N 163
RH19: E Grin 7B 166
Spring Copse Bus. Pk.
RH13: Slin 5K 195
Springcopse Rd.
RH2: Reig 5A 122
Spring Cnr. TW13: Felt 4H 23
Spring Cotts. KT6: Surb 4K 41
RH5: Holm 6J 139
Spring Ct. GU2: Guil 8L 93
KT17: Ewe 5E 60
Springcross Av. GU17: Haw . . .3J 69
Springfarm Rd.
GU27: Hasl 3C 188
Springfield GU8: Els 7H 131
GU18: Ligh 7A 52
RH8: Oxt 8N 105
RH19: E Grin 6N 165
SE25 . . . . .2D 46
Springfield Av. SW20 . . . . .2L 43
TW12: Hamp 7B 24
Springfield Cl. GU21: Knap . . .5H 73
SL4: W'sor 5E 4
Springfield Ct.
KT1: K Tham 6J 203
RH11: Craw 4B 182
RH12: Hors 6J 197
SM6: W'ton 2F 62
Springfield Cres.
RH12: Hors 6H 197
Springfield Dr. KT22: Leat 6E 78
Springfield Gdns.
BR4: W Wick 8L 47
Springfield Gro.
TW16: Sunb 9G 23
Springfield La. GU51: Fleet 4A 88
KT13: Weybr 1C 56
RH12: Col 5F 198
Springfield Mdws.
KT13: Weybr 1C 56
Springfield Pk.
RH12: Hors 5J 197
Springfield Pk. Rd.
RH12: Hors 6H 197
Springfield Pl. KT3: N Mal 3B 42
Springfield Rd. CR7: T Hea . . .9N 29
GU1: Guil 4E 202 (4A 114)
GU12: A Va 8E 90
GU15: Camb 1E 70
KT1: K Tham 6K 203 (2L 41)
KT17: Ewe 6H 61
KT22: Leat 6F 78
RG12: Bin 1H 31
RH4: Westc 6B 118
RH11: Craw 4A 182
RH12: Hors 6H 197
(not continuous)
SL3: Lang 3D 6
SL4: W'sor 5E 4
SM6: W'ton 2F 62
SW19 . . . . .6L 27
TN8: Eden 2K 147
TW2: Whitt 2A 24
TW11: Tedd 6G 24
TW15: A'ford 6A 22
Springfields Cl. KT16: Chert . . .7K 37
Springfield Way GU8: Els 8J 131
Springflower Cotts.
GU3: Worp 9F 92
Spring Gdns. GU14: Farnb . . .7M 69
GU15: Camb 1E 70
KT8: W Mole 4B 40
RH4: Dork 2H 201 (5G 118)
RH10: Cop 7N 163
RH12: Hors 5J 197
SL5: Asc 8J 17
(New Rd.)
SL5: Asc 3M 33
(Ringwood Cl.)
SM6: W'ton 2G 62
TN16: B Hil 5E 86
SPRING GROVE 4E 10
Spring Gro. CR4: Mit 9E 28
GU7: Goda 3H 133
KT22: Fetc 1B 98
TW12: Hamp 9B 24
W4 . . . . .1N 11
Spring Gro. Cres.
TW3: Houn 4C 10
Spring Gro. Rd.
TW3: Houn, Isle 4B 10
TW7: Isle 4B 10
TW10: Rich 8M 11
Springhaven GU8: Els 8J 131
(off Up. Springfield)
Springhaven Cl. GU1: Guil . . .3C 114
Spring Health Leisure Club
Richmond 7K 11
(in Pools on the Pk.)
Springhill GU8: Els 8J 131
Springhill Ct. RG12: Brac 3N 31
Springholm Cl.
GU9: B Lea 6N 109
TN16: B Hil 5E 86
Springhurst Cl. CR0: Croy 1J 65
Springlakes Ind. Est.
GU12: Alde 1C 110
Spring La. GU9: U Hal 5F 108
RH8: Oxt 9N 105
RH13: Slin 5K 195
SE25 . . . . .5E 46
Spring La. W. GU9: U Hal 6F 108
Springmead Ct.
GU27: Hasl 3B 188
(off Copse Rd.)
GU47: Owls 6K 49
Spring Mdw. RG12: Brac 9B 16
RH18: F Row 8H 187
Spring M. KT17: Ewe 5E 60
SPRING PARK 9K 47
Spring Pk. Av. CR0: Croy 8G 47
Springpark Dr. BR3: Beck 2M 47
Spring Pk. Rd. CR0: Croy 8G 47
Spring Pas. SW15 . . . . .6J 13
Spring Plat RH10: Craw 3G 183
Spring Plat Ct.
RH10: Craw 3G 183
Spring Ri. TW20: Egh 7A 20
Spring Rd. TW13: Felt 4G 23
Springside Ct.
GU1: Guil 1B 202 (2M 113)
Spring St. KT17: Ewe 5E 60
Spring Ter. TW9: Rich 8L 11
Springvale Av. TW8: Brent 1K 11
Springvale Cl. KT23: Book 3B 98
Spring Wlk. RH6: Horl 8D 142
Spring Way RH19: E Grin 6C 166
Springwell Cl. SW16 . . . . .5K 29
Springwell Rd.
RH5: B Grn 8K 139
SW16 . . . . .5L 29
TW4: Houn 5L 9
TW5: Hest 5L 9
Springwood GU8: Mil 1D 152
Springwood Ct.
CR2: S Croy 7F 200
(off Birdhurst Rd.)
Springwood Pl.
KT13: Weybr 4C 56
Spring Woods GU25: V Wat . . .3L 35
GU47: Sandh 6H 49
GU52: Fleet 6A 88
Sprint Ind. Est. KT14: Byf 7M 55
Sproggit Ind. Est.
TW19: Stan 9A 8
Spruce Cl. RH1: Red 2D 122
Sprucedale Gdns.
CR0: Croy 1G 64
SM6: W'ton 5J 63
Spruce Dr. GU18: Ligh 8L 51
Spruce Rd. TN16: B Hil 3F 86
Spruce Way GU51: Fleet 4E 88
Spur, The GU21: Knap 5E 72
KT12: Wal T 8K 39
Spurfield KT8: W Mole 2B 40
Spurgeon Cl. RH11: Craw . . .2A 182
Spurgeon Rd. SE19 . . . . .9N 29
Spur Rd. TW7: Isle 3G 11
TW14: Felt 7J 9
Spurs Ct. GU11: Alde 2K 109
Spy La. RH14: Loxw 3H 193
Square, The CR3: Cate 2D 104
GU2: Guil 5J 113
GU5: Shere 8B 116
GU10: Rowl 8D 128
GU14: Farnb 3N 89
GU18: Ligh 6N 51
GU19: Bag 4J 51
GU23: Wis 3N 75
GU26: G'hott 6B 170
KT13: Weybr 1D 56
RG12: Brac 3C 32
RH7: Ling 7M 145
RH10: Craw 3B 182
SM5: Cars 2E 62
TN16: Tats 7E 86
TW9: Rich 8K 11
UB7: L'ford 4K 7
W6 . . . . .1H 13
Square Dr. GU27: K Grn 7F 188
Squarey St. SW17 . . . . .4A 28
Squerryes TN16: Weste 6L 107
Squerryes, The CR3: Cate 8B 84
Squerryes Court Manor House &
Garden 6L 107
Squerryes Mede
TN16: Weste 5L 107
Squerryes Pk. Cotts.
TN16: Weste 5L 107
Squire's Bri. Rd.
TW17: Shep 3A 38
Squires Cl. RH10: Craw D . . .1D 184
Squires Ct. KT16: Chert 7K 37
SW19 . . . . .5M 27
Squires Hill La. GU10: Til 6A 130
Squire's Rd. TW17: Shep 3A 38
Squires Wlk. TW15: A'ford 8E 22
(not continuous)
Squirrel Cl. GU47: Sandh 7G 48
RH11: Craw 9N 161
TW4: Houn 6K 9
Squirrel Ct. GU12: Alde 1C 110
Squirrel Dr. SL4: Wink 2M 17
Squirrel Keep KT14: W By 8K 55
Squirrel La. GU14: Cove 9M 69
SL4: Wink 2M 17
Squirrel Ridge
RH10: Craw D 2E 184
Squirrel's Cl. GU7: Goda 2G 133
Squirrels Ct. KT4: W Pk 8E 42
(off The Avenue)
Squirrels Drey BR2: Brom 1N 47
(off Park Hill Rd.)
RG45: Crow 2E 48
Squirrels Grn. KT4: W Pk 8E 42
KT23: Book 1A 98
RH1: Red 2D 122
Squirrels Way KT18: Eps 1C 80
Squirrel Wood KT14: W By 8K 55
Stable Cl. KT2: K Tham 7M 25
KT18: Eps D 6D 80
RH10: Craw 6H 183
Stable Cotts. GU7: Goda 4K 133
RH11: P Pot 9M 181
Stable Ct. CR3: Cate 9D 84
SM6: W'ton 9E 44
Stable Cft. GU19: Bag 5H 51
Stable Flats RH11: P Pot 9M 181
Stable M. RH2: Reig 3M 121
Stables, The GU1: Guil 9N 93
KT11: Cob 1N 77
Stables M. SE27 . . . . .6N 29
Stables Yd. SW18 . . . . .9M 13
Stable Vw. GU46: Yate 8C 48
Stable Yd. SW15 . . . . .6H 13
Stableyard M. TW11: Tedd 7F 24
Stace Way RH10: Craw 1J 183
Stacey Ct. RH1: Mers 7G 102
Stacey's Farm Rd.
GU8: Els 8H 131
Staceys Mdw. GU8: Els 7H 131
Stackfield TN8: Eden 9M 127
Stackfield Rd. RH11: Ifi 4K 181
Stack Ho. RH8: Oxt 8A 106
Staddon Cl. BR3: Beck 3H 47
Staff College Rd.
GU15: Camb 9M 49
Staffhurst Wood Nature Reserve
. . . . .6E 126
Staffhurst Wood Rd.
TN8: Limp 6E 126
Stafford Cl. CR3: Cate 1C 104
SM3: Chea 3K 61
Stafford Cripps Ho.
SW6 . . . . .2L 13
(off Clem Attlee Ct.)
Stafford Cross Bus. Pk.
CR0: Wad 2K 63
Stafford Gdns. CR0: Wad 2K 63
Stafford Ho. GU11: Alde 2N 109
STAFFORDLAKE 5C 72
Stafford Lake GU21: Knap 5C 72
Stafford Pl. TW10: Rich 1M 25
Stafford Rd. CR0: Wad 1L 63
CR3: Cate 1C 104
KT3: N Mal 2B 42
RH11: Craw 9M 161
SM6: W'ton 3G 62
Staffordshire Cft.
RG42: Warf 7D 16
Staffords Pl. RH6: Horl 1F 162
Stafford Sq. KT13: Weybr 1E 56
Staff Rd. GU12: Alde 2A 110
Stagbury Av. CR5: Chip 5C 82
Stagbury Cl. CR5: Chip 6C 82
Stagbury Ho. CR5: Chip 6C 82
Stag Ct. KT2: K Tham 2M 203
Stagelands RH11: Craw 1N 181
Stagelands Ct.
RH11: Craw 1A 182
Stag Hill GU2: Guil 4K 113
Stag Hill Ct. GU2: Guil 3L 113
STAG LANE 3E 26
Stag La. SW15 . . . . .4E 26
Stag Leys KT21: A'tead 7L 79
Stag Leys Cl. SM7: Ban 2C 82
Stag Meadow 7E 4
Stags Way TW7: Isle 2F 10
Stainash Cres. TW18: Stain . . .6K 21
Stainash Pde. TW18: Stain 6K 21
(off Kingston Rd.)
Stainbank Rd. CR4: Mit 2F 44
STAINES 5H 21
Staines Av. SM3: Chea 8J 43
Staines Bri. TW18: Stain 6G 20
Staines By-Pass
TW15: A'ford 5K 21
TW18: Stain 5K 21
TW19: Stain 3E 20
Staines La. KT16: Chert 5H 37
Staines La. Cl. KT16: Chert . . .5H 37
Staines Moor Nature Reserve
. . . . .2G 21
Staines Reservoirs (Bird Sanctuary)
. . . . .3L 21
Staines Rd. KT16: Chert 1H 37
TW2: Twick 4A 24
TW3: Houn 9J 9
TW4: Houn 9J 9
TW14: Bedf, Felt 2B 22
(not continuous)
TW18: Lale, Stain 9K 21
TW19: Wray 1A 20
Staines Rd. E. TW16: Sunb . . .8H 23
Staines Rd. W.
TW15: A'ford 7C 22
TW16: Sunb 7C 22
Staines Station (Rail) 6J 21
Staines Town FC 8J 21
Stainford Cl. TW15: A'ford 6E 22
Stainton Wlk. GU21: Wok 5M 73
Staiths Way KT20: Tad 7G 81
Stake La. GU14: Cove 1M 89
Stakescorner Rd. GU3: Art . . .2K 133
Stalisfield Pl. BR6: Dow 6J 67
Stambourne Way
BR4: W Wick 8M 47
Stamford Av. GU16: Frim 5D 70
Stamford Bridge 3N 13
Stamford Bri. Studios
SW6 . . . . .3N 13
(off Wandon Rd.)
Stamford Cotts. SW6 . . . . .3N 13
(off Billing St.)
Stamford Ga. SW6 . . . . .3N 13
STAMFORD GREEN 9A 60
Stamford Grn. Rd.
KT18: Eps 9A 60
Stamford Ho. GU24: Chob 7H 53
(off Bagshot Rd.)
Stamford Rd. KT12: Wal T 9L 39
Stammerham Bus. Cen.
RH12: Rusp 2L 179
Stanacre Ct. KT20: K'wood 8L 81
Stanborough Cl.
TW12: Hamp 7N 23
Stanborough Rd.
TW3: Houn 6D 10
Stanbridge Cl. RH11: Ifi 3K 181
Stanbridge Rd. SW15 . . . . .6H 13
TN8: Eden 1K 147
Standard Rd. BR6: Dow 6J 67
TW4: Houn 6M 9
Standen 5N 185
Standen Cl. RH19: E Grin 7K 165
Standen Pl. RH12: Hors 1N 197
Standen Rd. SW18 . . . . .1L 27
Standford Hill
GU35: Stand 8B 168
Standford La. GU30: Pass 8B 168
GU35: Head, Stand 5B 168
GU35: Stand 8B 168
STANDFROD 8B 168
Standinghall La.
RH10: T Hil 6L 183
Standish Ho. W6 . . . . .1F 12
(off St Peter's Gro.)
Standish Rd. W6 . . . . .1F 12
Standon Cotts. RH5: Ockl 7B 158
Standon La. RH5: Ockl 8M 157
Stane Cl. SW19 . . . . .8N 27
Stane St. RH5: Ockl 9B 158
RH13: Slin 9H 195
RH14: Bill 9H 195
Stane St. Cotts.
RH12: Rowh 8M 177
Stane Way KT17: Ewe 6F 60
Stanford Cl. TW12: Hamp 7N 23
STANFORD COMMON 4B 92
Stanford Cotts. GU24: Pirb 4B 92
Stanford Ct. RH10: Craw 5G 183
(off Maidenbower Pl.)
SW6 . . . . .4N 13
Stanford Orchard
RH12: Warn 9F 178
Stanford Rd. SW16 . . . . .1H 45
Stanfords, The KT17: Eps 8E 60
(off East St.)
Stanfords Pl. RH7: Ling 8N 145
Stanford Way RH12: Bro H . . .5D 196
SW16 . . . . .1H 45
Stanger Rd. SE25 . . . . .3D 46
Stangrove Lodge
TN8: Eden 2L 147
Stangrove Pde. TN8: Eden . . .2L 147
(off Stangrove Rd.)
Stangrove Rd. TN8: Eden 2L 147
(not continuous)
Stan Hill RH6: Char 1H 161
Stanhope Ga. GU15: Camb 1M 69
Stanhope Gro. BR3: Beck 4J 47
Stanhope Heath TW19: Stan 9L 7
Stanhope Rd.
CR0: Croy 4F 200 (9B 46)
GU15: Camb 2L 69
SM5: Cars 4E 62
Stanhopes RH8: Limp 6D 106
Stanhope Ter. TW2: Twick 1F 24
Stanhope Way TW19: Stan 9L 7
Stanier Cl. RH10: Craw 4F 182
W14 . . . . .1L 13
Staniland Dr. KT13: Weybr 7A 56
Stanley Av. BR3: Beck 1M 47
KT3: N Mal 4F 42
Stanley Bri. Studios
SW6 . . . . .3N 13
(off King's Rd.)
Stanley Cen. RH10: Craw 9D 162
Stanley Cl. CR5: Coul 4K 83
RH10: Craw 5C 182
Stanley Ct. SM2: Sut 4N 61
SM5: Cars 4E 62
Stanleycroft Cl. TW7: Isle 4E 10
Stanley Dr. GU14: Cove 2H 89
Stanley Gdns. CR2: Sande 8D 64
CR4: Mit 7E 28
KT12: Hers 3K 57
SM6: W'ton 3G 62
Stanley Gdns. Rd.
TW11: Tedd 6E 24
Stanley Gro. CR0: Croy 5L 45
Stanley Hill GU24: Pirb 9N 71
Stanley Ho. SW10 . . . . .3N 13
(off Coleridge Gdns.)
Stanley M. SW10 . . . . .3N 13
(off Coleridge Gdns.)
Stanley Pk. Rd. SM5: Cars 4C 62
SM6: W'ton 3F 62
Stanley Picker Gallery 6K 203
(within Kingston University)
Stanley Rd. CR0: Croy 6L 45
CR4: Mit 8E 28
GU21: Wok 3B 74
RG40: W'ham 2D 30
SM2: Sut 3N 61
SM4: Mord 3M 43
SM5: Cars 4E 62
SW14 . . . . .7A 12
SW19 . . . . .7M 27
TW2: Twick 4D 24
TW3: Houn 7C 10
TW11: Tedd 5E 24
TW15: A'ford 6N 21
Stanley Sq. SM5: Cars 5D 62
Stanley St. CR3: Cate 9N 83
Stanley Wlk. RG12: Brac 1A 32
RH13: Hors 6K 197
Stanmore Cl. SL5: Asc 3L 33
Stanmore Gdns. SM1: Sut 9A 44
TW9: Rich 6M 11
Stanmore Rd. TW9: Rich 6M 11
Stanmore Ter. BR3: Beck 1K 47
STANNERS HILL 4N 53
Stannet Way SM6: W'ton 1G 62
Stansfield Rd. TW4: C'ford 5J 9
Stanstead Mnr. SM1: Sut 3M 61
Stanstead Rd. CR3: Cate 5A 104
Stansted Rd. TW6: Lon A 9A 8
Stan's Way RH12: Hors 6J 197
Stanthorpe Cl. SW16 . . . . .6J 29
Stanthorpe Rd. SW16 . . . . .6J 29
Stanton Av. TW11: Tedd 7E 24
Stanton Cl. GU6: Cranl 7J 155
KT4: W Pk 7J 43
KT19: Ewe 2A 60
Stanton Ct. CR2: S Croy 8F 200
Stanton Dr. GU51: Fleet 5A 88
Stanton Rd. CR0: Croy 6N 45
SW13 . . . . .5E 12
SW20 . . . . .9J 27
Stantons Wharf
GU5: Braml 4C 134
Stanton Way SL3: Lang 1A 6
STANWELL 9M 7
Stanwell Cl. TW19: Stan 9M 7
Stanwell Gdns. TW19: Stan 9M 7
STANWELL MOOR 8J 7
Stanwell Moor Rd.
TW18: Stain 4J 21
TW19: L'ford, Stan M 7K 7
TW19: Stain, Stan M 4K 21
UB7: L'ford 7K 7
Stanwell New Rd.
TW18: Stain 4J 21
Stanwell Rd. SL3: Hort 6C 6
TW14: Bedf 1C 22
TW15: A'ford 3N 21
Stanwick Rd. W14 . . . . .1L 13
Stanworth Ct. TW5: Hest 3N 9
Staplecross Ct.
RH11: Craw 6M 181
Staplefield Cl. SW2 . . . . .2J 29
Stapleford Cl. KT1: K Tham . . .1N 41
SW19 . . . . .1K 27
Staple Hill Rd. GU24: Chob . . .3G 53
Staplehurst RG12: Brac 6K 31
Staplehurst Cl. RH2: Reig 7A 122
Staplehurst Rd. RH2: Reig 7A 122
SM5: Cars 4C 62
Staple La. GU4: E Cla 1M 115
GU5: Shere 3A 116
Stapleton Gdns. CR0: Wad 2L 63
Stapleton Rd. SW17 . . . . .4E 28
Star & Garter Hill
TW10: Rich 2L 25
Starborough Rd.
TN8: Eden, M Grn 5F 146
Star Cl. RH13: Hors 4N 197
Star Hill GU10: Churt 8J 149
Star Hill Dr. GU10: Churt 7J 149
Star La. CR5: Coul 8E 82
GU12: Ash 2D 110
Starling Cl. CR0: Croy 5H 47
Starlings, The KT22: Oxs 9C 58
Starling Wlk. TW12: Hamp 6M 23
Starmead Dr. RG40: W'ham 3C 30
Star Post Rd. GU15: Camb 7C 50
Star Rd. TW7: Isle 5D 10
W14 . . . . .2L 13
Starrock La. CR5: Chip 7D 82
Starrock Rd. CR5: Coul 6F 82
Starts Hill Av. BR6: Farnb 1K 67
Starts Hill Rd. BR6: Farnb 1K 67
Starwood Cl. KT14: W By 7L 55
State Farm Av. BR6: Farnb 1K 67
Staten Gdns. TW1: Twick 2F 24
Statham Ct. RG42: Brac 9K 15
Station App. BR4: W Wick 6M 47
CR0: Croy 3E 200
CR2: Sande 5A 64
CR3: Whyte 4D 84
CR5: Chip 5D 82
CR5: Coul 3H 83
CR8: Pur 7L 63
GU1: Guil 4E 202 (4A 114)
GU3: Flex 3M 111
GU4: Chil 9A 114

Station App.—Stratton Ct.

Station App. GU5: Gorn 8E **116**
GU7: Goda 7G **132**
GU8: Worm 1C **172**
GU12: A Va 6E **90**
GU14: Farnb 9N **69**
GU16: Frim 6B **70**
GU17: B'water 2K **69**
GU22: Wok 5B **74**
GU25: V Wat 3N **35**
GU51: Fleet 2C **88**
KT1: K Tham 9N **25**
KT4: W Pk 7F **42**
KT10: H Wood 9F **40**
KT13: Weybr 3B **56**
KT14: W By 8J **55**
KT17: Ewe 6G **60**
(Cheam Rd.)
KT17: Ewe 5E **60**
(Fennels Mead)
KT19: Eps 6J **201** (9C **60**)
KT19: Ewe 2F **60**
KT20: Tad 9H **81**
KT22: Leat 8G **78**
(not continuous)
KT22: Oxs 8C **58**
KT24: E Hor 4F **96**
RG40: W'ham 2A **30**
RH1: Red 2E 122
(off Redstone Hill)
RH4: Dork 3J **119**
RH5: Ockl 5H **159**
RH6: Horl 8F **142**
RH8: Oxt 7A **106**
SM2: Chea 4K **61**
SM2: Sut 6N **61**
SM5: Cars 1D **62**
SW6 . . . . .6K **13**
SW14 . . . . .6B **12**
SW16 . . . . .7H **29**
(Estreham Rd.)
SW16 . . . . .6H **29**
(Gleneagle Rd.)
SW20 . . . . .1G **43**
TN8: Eden 1L **147**
TW8: Brent 2J 11
(off Sidney Gdns.)
TW9: Kew 4N **11**
TW12: Hamp 9A **24**
TW15: A'ford 5A **22**
TW16: Sunb 9H **23**
TW17: Shep 4D **38**
TW18: Stain 6J **21**
Station App. E. RH1: Red 5D **122**
Station App. Rd. CR5: Coul . . .2H **83**
RH6: Gat 2F **162**
W4 . . . . .3B **12**
Station App. W. RH1: Red . . .5D **122**
Station Av. CR3: Cate 2D **104**
KT3: N Mal 2D **42**
KT12: Wal T 1H **57**
KT19: Ewe 5D **60**
TW9: Kew 4N **11**
Station Bldgs.
KT1: K Tham 3J **203**
Station Cl. RH13: Hors 6K **197**
TW12: Hamp 9B **24**
Station Cotts. RH13: Hors . . .9D **196**
Station Cres. TW15: A'ford 4M **21**
Station Est. BR3: Beck 2G **47**
Station Est. Rd. TW14: Felt 2J **23**
Station Garage M.
SW16 . . . . .7H **29**
Station Gdns. W4 . . . . .3B **12**
Station Hill GU9: Farnh 1H **129**
RH10: Craw 2F **182**
SL5: Asc 2L **33**
Station Ind. Est.
RG41: W'ham 2A **30**
Station La.
GU8: Ent G, Hamb, Mil
. . . . .1D **152**
GU8: Worm 9B **152**
Station Pde. GU25: V Wat 3N **35**
KT24: E Hor 4F **96**
(not continuous)
SL5: S'dale 6D **34**
SM2: Sut 3A 62
(off High St.)
SW12 . . . . .2E **28**
TW9: Kew 4N **11**
TW14: Felt 2J **23**
TW15: A'ford 5A **22**
W4 . . . . .3B **12**
Station Path SW6 . . . . .6L **13**
TW18: Stain 5H **21**
Station Pl. GU7: Goda 4J **133**
Station Ri. SE27 . . . . .3M **29**
Station Rd. BR4: W Wick 7M **47**
CR0: Croy 1B **200** (7N **45**)
CR3: Whyte 5C **84**
CR3: Wold 9H **85**
CR8: Ken 1N **83**
GU4: Chil 9A **114**
GU5: Braml 5B **134**
GU5: Gorn 8D **116**
GU7: Goda 4J **133**
(Grays Rd.)
GU7: Goda 7G **132**
(Station App.)
GU11: Alde 2N **109**
GU14: Farnb 1N **89**
GU16: Frim 5A **70**
GU19: Bag 3J **51**
Station Rd. GU24: Chob 7J **53**
KT1: H Wic 1G **203** (9J **25**)
KT2: K Tham 9N **25**
KT3: N Mal 4G **42**
KT7: T Dit 6F **40**
KT9: Ches 2L **59**
KT10: Clay 3E **58**
KT10: Esh 8D **40**
KT11: Sto D 4M **77**
KT14: W By 8J **55**
KT15: Addl 1L **55**
KT16: Chert 7H **37**
KT22: Leat 8G **79**
RG12: Brac 1N **31**
RG40: W'ham 2A **30**
RH1: Mers 6G **102**
RH1: Red 2C **122**
(not continuous)
RH3: Betch 9D **100**
(not continuous)
RH4: Dork 1H **201** (4G **118**)
RH6: Horl 8F **142**
RH7: Ling 6A **146**
RH9: S Gods 7H **125**
RH10: Craw 4B **182**
RH10: Craw D 1E **184**
RH12: Cranl, Rudg 6C **176**
RH12: Rudg 1E **194**
RH12: Warn 9G **179**
RH13: Hors 9D **196**
(Christs Hospital Rd.)
RH13: Hors 6K **197**
(Station Cl.)
RH14: Loxw 5H **193**
RH18: F Row 6H **187**
RH19: E Grin 9N **165**
SE25 . . . . .3C **46**
SL5: S'dale 5D **34**
SM2: Sut 6M **61**
SM5: Cars 1D **62**
SW13 . . . . .5E **12**
SW19 . . . . .9A **28**
TN8: Eden 9L **127**
TW1: Twick 2F **24**
TW3: Houn 7B **10**
TW11: Tedd 7G **24**
TW12: Hamp 9A **24**
TW15: A'ford 5A **22**
TW16: Sunb 8H **23**
TW17: Shep 4D **38**
TW19: Wray 9B **6**
TW20: Egh 6C **20**
Station Rd. E. GU12: A Va 6D **90**
RH8: Oxt 7A **106**
Station Rd. Nth.
RH1: Mers 6G **102**
TW20: Egh 6C **20**
Station Rd. Sth.
RH1: Mers 6G **102**
Station Rd. W. GU12: A Va 5D **90**
RH8: Oxt 7A **106**
Station Row GU4: Chil 9A **114**
Station Ter.
RH4: Dork 1H **201** (4G **118**)
Station Vw.
GU1: Guil 4A **202** (4M **113**)
GU12: A Va 5E **90**
Station Way KT10: Clay 3E **58**
KT19: Eps 6J **201** (9C **60**)
RG12: Brac 1A **32**
RH10: Craw 4B **182**
SM3: Chea 3K **61**
Station Yd. CR8: Pur 8M **63**
TW1: Twick 1G **24**
Staunton Rd. KT2: K Tham 7L **25**
Staveley Gdns. W4 . . . . .4C **12**
Staveley Rd. TW15: A'ford 7E **22**
W4 . . . . .2B **12**
Staveley Way GU21: Knap 4H **73**
Staverton Cl. RG40: W'ham 2E **30**
RG42: Brac 8N **15**
Stavordale Rd. SM5: Cars 6A **44**
Stayne End GU25: V Wat 3K **35**
Stayton Rd. SM1: Sut 9M **43**
Stbale M. TW1: Twick 2F **24**
Steadfast Rd.
KT1: K Tham . . .2H **203** (9K **25**)
Steam Farm La. TW14: Felt 7G **8**
Steele Rd. TW7: Isle 7G **11**
Steele's Rd. GU11: Alde 9N **89**
(not continuous)
Steel's La. KT22: Oxs 1B **78**
Steep Hill
CR0: Croy 6F **200** (1B **64**)
GU24: Chob 4F **52**
SW16 . . . . .4H **29**
Steeple Cl. SW6 . . . . .5K **13**
SW19 . . . . .6K **27**
Steeple Gdns. KT15: Addl 2K **55**
Steeple Hgts. Dr.
TN16: B Hil 4F **86**
Steeple Point SL5: Asc 2M **33**
Steepways GU26: Hind 3N **169**
Steeres Hill RH12: Rusp 3B **180**
Steerforth Copse
GU47: Owls 5K **49**
Steerforth St. SW18 . . . . .3A **28**
Steer Pl. RH1: Salf 3E **142**
Steers La. RH10: Craw 6G **162**
Steers Mead CR4: Mit 9D **28**
Stella Rd. SW17 . . . . .7D **28**
Stembridge Rd. SE20 . . . . .1E **46**
Stem Ct. KT16: Chert 7L **37**
Stennings, The
RH19: E Grin 8M **165**
Stents La. KT11: Sto D 7N **77**
Stepbridge Path
GU21: Wok 4N **73**
Stepgates KT16: Chert 6K **37**
Stepgates Cl. KT16: Chert 6K **37**
Stephanie Chase Ct.
RG40: W'ham 1C **30**
Stephen Cl. BR6: Orp 1N **67**
TW20: Egh 7E **20**
Stephendale Rd.
GU9: Farnh 8J **109**
SW6 . . . . .6N **13**
Stephen Fox Ho. *W4 . . . . .1D 12*
(off Chiswick La.)
Stephenson Ct. *SM2: Chea 4K 61*
(off Station App.)
Stephenson Dr.
RH19: E Grin 2B **186**
SL4: W'sor 3E **4**
Stephenson Pl. *RH1: Mers . . .6G 102*
(off Station Rd. Nth.)
RH10: Craw 3F **182**
Stephenson Rd. GU2: Guil . . .3G **112**
TW2: Whitt 1A **24**
Stephenson Way
RH10: Craw 3E **182**
Stephenson Way Ind. Est.
RH10: Craw 3F **182**
Stephyns Dr. GU51: Fleet 1A **88**
Stepney Cl. CR4: Mit 9E **28**
RH10: Craw 5G **182**
Sterling Bldgs.
RH12: Hors 6J 197
(off Carfax)
Sterling Cen. RG12: Brac 1B **32**
Sterling Ct. KT16: Chert 6J **37**
Sterling Gdns. GU47: C Tow . . .7K **49**
Sterling Pk. RH10: Craw 7F **162**
Sterling Pl. KT13: Weybr 1F **56**
W5 . . . . .1L **11**
Sternhold Av. SW2 . . . . .3H **29**
Sterry Dr. KT7: T Dit 5E **40**
KT19: Ewe 1D **60**
Steve Biko Way TW3: Houn 6A **10**
Stevenage Rd.
RH11: Craw 6K **181**
SW6 . . . . .3J **13**
Stevens Cl.
KT17: Eps 6M **201** (8D **60**)
TW12: Hamp 7N **23**
Stevens Hill GU46: Yate 1D **68**
Stevens La. KT10: Clay 4G **59**
Stevenson Dr. RG42: Bin 6H **15**
Stevens Pl. CR8: Pur 9M **63**
Stewards Ri. GU10: Wrec 4E **128**
Stewart KT20: Tad 8J **81**
Stewart Av. TW17: Shep 3B **38**
Stewart Cl. GU21: Wok 4J **73**
TW12: Hamp 7M **23**
Stewart Ho.
KT1: K Tham . . .6L **203** (2M **41**)
Steyning Cl. CR8: Ken 3M **83**
RH10: Craw 1C **182**
Steyning Way TW4: Houn 7K **9**
St Helier Station (Rail) 5M **43**
Stickle Down GU16: Deep 6H **71**
Stile Footpath RH1: Red 3D **122**
Stile Gdns. GU27: Hasl 2D **188**
Stile Hall Gdns. W4 . . . . .1N **11**
Stile Hall Pde. W4: Brent 1N **11**
Stile Ho. *GU1: Guil 2F 114*
(off Merrow St.)
Stile Path TW16: Sunb 2H **39**
Stillers GU8: Chid 5E **172**
Stillingfleet Rd. SW13 . . . . . . .2F **12**
Stilwell Cl. GU46: Yate 9D **48**
Stirling Av. SM6: W'ton 4J **63**
TW17: Shep 2F **38**
Stirling Cl. GU12: A Va 8D **90**
GU14: Cove 2M **89**
GU16: Frim 4C **70**
RH10: Craw 4F **182**
SL4: W'sor 5A **4**
SM7: Ban 4L **81**
SW16 . . . . .9H **29**
Stirling Dr. CR3: Cate 8N **83**
Stirling Gro. TW3: Houn 5C **10**
Stirling Ho. RH1: Red 3D **122**
Stirling Pl. RH12: Bro H 5D **196**
Stirling Rd. GU2: Guil 3G **113**
TW2: Whitt 1A **24**
TW6: Lon A 9A **8**
Stirling Wlk. KT5: Surb 6L **51**
Stirling Way CR0: Bedd 6J **45**
RH13: Hors 6L **197**
RH19: E Grin 7D **166**
Stirrup Way RH10: Craw 2H **183**
Stites Hill Rd. CR5: Coul 7M **83**
St Margarets Station (Rail) . . .9H **11**
Stoatley Hollow
GU27: Hasl 9E **170**
Stoatley Ri. GU27: Hasl 9E **170**
Stoats Nest Rd. CR5: Coul 1J **83**
Stoats Nest Village
CR5: Coul 2J **83**
Stockbridge Dr.
GU11: Alde 6A **110**
Stockbridge Way
GU46: Yate 2C **68**
Stockbury Rd. CR0: Croy 5F **46**
Stockdales Rd. SL4: E Wic 1C **4**
Stockers La. GU22: Wok 7B **74**
(not continuous)
Stockfield RH6: Horl 7F **142**
Stockfield Rd. KT10: Clay 2E **58**
SW16 . . . . .4K **29**
Stockham's Cl.
CR2: Sande 6A **64**
Stock Hill TN16: B Hil 3F **86**
Stockhurst Cl. SW15 . . . . .5H **13**
Stocklund Sq. GU6: Cranl 7L **155**
Stockport Rd. SW16 . . . . .9H **29**
Stocks Cl. RH6: Horl 9F **142**
Stockton Av. GU51: Fleet 2A **88**
Stockton Pk. GU51: Fleet 3A **88**
Stockton Rd. RH2: Reig 6M **121**
Stockwell Cen.
RH10: Craw 3E **182**
Stockwell Rd.
RH19: E Grin 3A **186**
Stockwood Ri. GU15: Camb . . .1D **70**
Stockwood Way
GU9: Weybo 5L **109**
Stocton Cl.
GU1: Guil 1B **202** (2M **113**)
Stocton Rd.
GU1: Guil 1B **202** (2N **113**)
Stoford Cl. SW19 . . . . .1K **27**
Stoke Cl. KT11: Sto D 3N **77**
STOKE D'ABERNON 4M **77**
Stoke Flds.
GU1: Guil 4C **202** (3N **113**)
(Church Rd.)
GU1: Guil 3C **202**
(Drummond Rd.)
Stokeford Cl. RG12: Brac 4D **32**
Stoke Gro.
GU1: Guil 3D **202** (3N **113**)
Stoke Hills GU9: Farnh 9H **109**
Stoke Hospital GU1: Guil 3D **202**
Stoke M.
GU1: Guil 4D **202** (4N **113**)
Stoke Mill Cl. GU1: Guil 1N **113**
Stokenchurch St. SW6 . . . . . . .4N **13**
Stoke Pk. Ct.
GU1: Guil 3D **202** (3N **113**)
Stoke Rd.
GU1: Guil 1D **202** (2N **113**)
KT2: K Tham 8B **26**
KT11: Cob, Sto D 2K **77**
KT12: Wal T 9K **39**
Stoke Rd. Cotts. KT22: Fetc . . .8D **78**
Stokers Cl. RH6: Gat 2C **162**
Stokesby Rd. KT9: Ches 3M **59**
Stokes Cl. RH10: Craw 5G **183**
Stokesheath Rd. KT22: Oxs 7C **58**
Stoke Sq. GU1: Guil 3C **202**
Stokes Ridings KT20: Tad 1J **101**
Stokes Rd. CR0: Croy 5G **47**
Stompond La. KT12: Wal T 8H **39**
Stonards Brow GU5: Sha G 7E **134**
Stonebanks KT12: Wal T 6H **39**
STONEBRIDGE 8K **119**
Stonebridge Ct.
RH11: Craw 7A **182**
RH12: Hors 6G **197**
Stonebridge Fld. SL4: Eton 1E **4**
Stonebridge Flds.
GU4: Chil 1N **133**
Stonebridge Wharf
GU4: Chil 1N **133**
Stonecot Cl. SM3: Sut 7K **43**
Stonecot Hill SM3: Sut 7K **43**
Stone Ct. CR3: Cate 3B **104**
RH10: Craw 3H **183**
Stonecourt Cl. RH6: Horl 8G **143**
Stone Cres. TW14: Felt 1G **22**
Stonecroft Way CR0: Croy 6J **45**
Stonecrop Cl. RH11: Craw 6N **181**
Stonecrop Rd. GU4: Guil 1E **114**
Stonedene Cl.
GU35: H Dwn 5G **169**
RH18: F Row 7K **187**
Stonefield Cl. RH10: Craw 4B **182**
Stonegate GU15: Camb 9G **50**
Stone Hatch GU6: Alf 6J **175**
STONEHILL 3A **54**
Stone Hill RH19: E Grin 7M **185**
Stonehill Cl. KT23: Book 3A **98**
SW14 . . . . .8C **12**
Stonehill Cres. KT16: Otter 3A **54**
Stonehill Ga. SL5: S'hill 5A **34**
Stonehill Pk.
GU35: H Dwn 5G **169**
Stone Hill Rd. W4 . . . . .1N **11**
Stonehill Rd. GU18: Ligh 6L **51**
GU24: Chob 6M **53**
GU35: H Dwn 5H **169**
KT16: Otter 2B **54**
SW14 . . . . .8B **12**
Stone Ho. Gdns.
CR3: Cate 3B **104**
Stonehouse Ri. GU16: Frim 5C **70**
STONELEIGH 2F **60**
Stoneleigh Av. KT4: W Pk 1F **60**
Stoneleigh B'way.
KT17: Ewe 2F **60**
Stoneleigh Cl.
RH19: E Grin 9B **166**
Stoneleigh Ct. GU16: Frim 5D **70**
KT11: Sto D 4M **77**
Stoneleigh Cres. KT19: Ewe . . .2E **60**
Stoneleigh Pk.
KT13: Weybr 2D **56**
Stoneleigh Pk. Av.
CR0: Croy 5G **47**
Stoneleigh Pk. Rd.
KT19: Ewe 3E **60**
Stoneleigh Rd. RH8: Limp 8G **107**
SM5: Cars 6C **44**
Stoneleigh Station (Rail) 2F **60**
Stone Pk. Av. BR3: Beck 3K **47**
Stonepark Dr.
RH18: F Row 7J **187**
Stonepit Cl. GU7: Goda 2E **132**
Stone Pl. KT4: W Pk 8F **42**
STONEQUARRY 6C **166**
Stones La. RH4: Westc 6C **118**
(not continuous)
Stone's Rd. KT17: Eps 8D **60**
Stone St. GU12: Alde 4B **110**
Stoneswood Rd.
RH8: Limp 8D **106**
Stoney Bottom
GU26: G'hott 6A **170**
Stoney Brook GU2: Guil 2H **113**
Stoneybrook RH12: Hors 7F **196**
Stoney Cl. GU46: Yate 2C **68**
Stoney Cft. CR5: Coul 9G **83**
Stoneycroft Wlk. RH11: Ifi 4J **181**
Stoneydeep TW11: Tedd 5G **25**
Stoneyfield Rd. CR5: Coul 4K **83**
Stoneyfields GU9: Farnh 2K **129**
Stoneylands Ct. TW20: Egh 6B **20**
Stoneylands Rd. TW20: Egh 6B **20**
Stoney Rd. RG42: Brac 9M **15**
Stonny Cft. KT21: A'tead 4M **79**
Stonor Rd. W14 . . . . .1L **13**
Stonyfield TN8: Eden 9M **127**
Stony Hill KT10: Esh 4N **57**
Stookes Way GU46: Yate 2A **68**
Stoop Ct. KT14: W By 8K **55**
Stoop Memorial Ground 1E **24**
Stopham Rd. RH10: Craw 6G **182**
Stormont Way KT9: Ches 2J **59**
Storrington Ct.
RH11: Craw 2M **181**
Storrington Rd. CR0: Croy 7C **46**
Storr's La. GU3: Worp 2F **92**
STOUGHTON 9K **93**
Stoughton Av. SM3: Chea 2J **61**
Stoughton Cl. SW15 . . . . .2F **26**
Stoughton Rd. GU1: Guil 9K **93**
GU2: Guil 9K **93**
Stour Cl. BR2: Kes 1E **66**
Stourhead Cl. GU14: Farnb 1B **90**
SW19 . . . . .1J **27**
Stourhead Gdns.
SW20 . . . . .2F **42**
Stourton Av. TW13: Hanw 5N **23**
Stovell Rd. SL4: W'sor 3E **4**
Stovolds Hill GU6: Cranl 9E **154**
Stovold's Way GU11: Alde 4L **109**
Stowell Av. CR0: N Add 6N **65**
Stowting Rd. BR6: Orp 1N **67**
Strachan Pl. SW19 . . . . .7H **27**
Strachey Ct. RH11: Craw 8N **181**
Stradella Rd. SE24 . . . . .1N **29**
Strafford Rd. TW1: Twick 1G **25**
TW3: Houn 6N **9**
Straight Mile, The
RG10: S Row, Twy 1C **14**
RG40: W'ham 1C **14**
Straight Rd. SL4: O Win 8K **5**
Strand Cl. KT18: Eps D 6C **80**
RH10: Craw 5H **183**
Strand Dr. TW9: Kew 3A **12**
STRAND ON THE GREEN 2N **11**
Strand on the Grn. W4 . . . . . . .2N **11**
Strand School App.
W4 . . . . .2N **11**
Strata Ct. KT12: Wal T 7G **39**
Stratfield RG12: Brac 7K **31**
Stratford Ct. GU9: Farnh 2H **129**
KT3: N Mal 3C **42**
Stratford Gro. SW15 . . . . .7J **13**
Stratford Rd. CR7: T Hea 3L **45**
GU12: A Va 5D **90**
TW6: Lon A 9C **8**
Strathan Cl. SW18 . . . . .9K **13**
Strathavon Cl. GU6: Cranl 3K **155**
Strathbrook Rd. SW16 . . . . . . .8K **29**
Strathcona Av. KT23: Book 6M **97**
Strathcona Gdns.
GU21: Knap 5G **72**
(not continuous)
Strathdale SW16 . . . . .6K **29**
Strathdon Dr. SW17 . . . . .4B **28**
Strathearn Av. TW2: Whitt 2B **24**
UB3: Harl 3G **9**
Strathearn Rd. SM1: Sut 2M **61**
SW19 . . . . .6M **27**
Strathmore Cl. CR3: Cate 8B **84**
Strathmore Ct. GU15: Camb 9B **50**
Strathmore Rd. CR0: Croy 6A **46**
RH11: Ifi 9M **161**
SW19 . . . . .4M **27**
TW11: Tedd 5E **24**
Strathville Rd. SW18 . . . . .3M **27**
(not continuous)
Strathyre Av. SW16 . . . . .2L **45**
STRATTON 1F **124**
Stratton Av. SM6: W'ton 5H **63**
Stratton Cl. KT12: Wal T 7K **39**
SW19 . . . . .1M **43**
TW3: Houn 4A **10**
Stratton Ct. GU2: Guil 1K **113**

Stratton Rd.—Sutherland Dr.

Stratton Rd. SW19 1M 43
TW16: Sunb 1G 38
Stratton Ter. TN16: Weste 5L 107
Stratton Wlk. GU14: Farnb 7M 69
Strawberry Cl.
GU24: B'wood 8A 72
Strawberry Ct. GU16: Deep 6H 71
Strawberry Flds.
BR6: Farnb 2K 67
GU24: Bis 2D 72
STRAWBERRY HILL 4F 24
Strawberry Hill RG42: Warf 7C 16
TW1: Twick 4F 24
Strawberry Hill Cl.
TW1: Twick 4F 24
Strawberry Hill House 4F 24
(within St Mary's College)
Strawberry Hill Rd.
TW1: Twick 4F 24
Strawberry Hill Station (Rail) 4F 24
Strawberry La. SM5: Cars 9E 44
Strawberry Ri. GU24: Bis 2D 72
Strawberry Va. TW1: Twick 4G 24
(not continuous)
Straw Cl. CR3: Cate 1N 103
Strawson Ct. RH6: Horl 7D 142
Stream Banks
GU3: Wood V 2E 112
(off Pound Ct.)
Stream Cl. KT14: Byf 8M 55
Stream Cotts. *GU16: Frim 5B 70*
(off Grove Cross Rd.)
Stream Farm Cl.
GU10: L Bou 4J 129
Stream Pk. RH19: E Grin 7K 165
Streamside GU51: Fleet 5B 88
Stream Valley Rd.
GU10: L Bou 5H 129
Streatfield TN8: Eden 2M 147
STREATHAM 6J 29
Streatham Cl. SW16 3J 29
STREATHAM COMMON 7J 29
Streatham Comn. Nth.
SW16 6J 29
Streatham Comn. Sth.
SW16 7J 29
Streatham Common Station (Rail) 7H 29
Streatham Ct. SW16 4J 29
Streatham High Rd.
SW16 5J 29
STREATHAM HILL 3J 29
Streatham Hill SW2 3J 29
Streatham Hill Station (Rail) 3J 29
Streatham Ice Arena 6H 29
Streatham Leisure Cen. 6J 29
STREATHAM PARK 6G 29
Streatham Pl. SW2 1J 29
Streatham Rd. CR4: Mit 9E 28
SW16 9E 28
Streatham Station (Rail) 6H 29
STREATHAM VALE 8G 29
Streatham Va. SW16 9G 29
Streathbourne Rd.
SW17 3E 28
Street, The GU3: Comp 9D 112
GU3: Put 8M 111
GU4: Chil 8N 113
GU4: E Cla 9M 95
GU4: W Cla 6J 95
GU5: Alb 8K 115
GU5: Wone 4C 134
GU6: Ewh 4F 156
(not continuous)
GU8: Hasc 4N 153
GU8: S'ford 3N 131
GU8: Thur 7G 150
GU10: Dock 4D 148
GU10: Fren 3H 149
GU10: Tong 5D 110
GU10: Wrec 5D 128
KT21: A'tead 6L 79
KT22: Fetc 9D 78
KT24: Eff 5L 97
KT24: W Hors 7C 96
RH3: Betch 4D 120
RH5: Cap 5J 159
RH6: Char 3K 161
RH13: Slin 5K 195
RH14: Plais 6A 192
Streeters Cl. GU7: Goda 5K 133
Streeters La. SM6: Bedd 9H 45
Streetfield RH13: Slin 5L 195
Street Hill RH10: Wor 4J 183
Streets Heath GU24: W End 8C 52
(not continuous)
Stretton Rd. CR0: Croy 6B 46
TW10: Ham 3J 25
Strickland Cl. RH11: Ifi 4K 181
Strickland Row SW18 1B 28
Strides Ct. *KT16: Otter 3E 54*
(off Brox Rd.)
Stringer's Av. GU4: J Wel 6N 93
STRINGERS COMMON 7M 93
Stringhams Copse
GU23: Rip 2H 95
Strode Rd. SW6 3K 13
Strode's Coll. La.
TW20: Egh 6B 20
(off High St.)
Strode's Cres. TW18: Stain 6L 21
Strode St. TW20: Egh 5C 20
Stronsay Cl. GU26: Hind 4C 170
STROOD GREEN
RH3 7B 120
RH12 2B 196
Strood La.
RH12: Bro H, Warn 1B 196
SL4: Wink 7N 17
STROUD 6L 171
Stroud Cl. SL4: W'sor 6A 4
STROUD COMMON 9H 135
Stroud Comn. GU5: Sha G 8H 135
Stroud Cres. SW15 4F 26
STROUDE 2A 36
Stroude Rd. GU25: V Wat 4A 36
TW20: Egh 7C 20
Stroudes Cl. KT4: W Pk 6D 42
Stroud Grn. Gdns.
CR0: Croy 6F 46
Stroud Grn. Way CR0: Croy 6E 46
Stroud La. GU5: Sha G 9J 135
GU17: B'water 2F 68
Stroudley Cl. RH10: Craw 4F 182
Stroudley Ct. *RH19: E Grin 8B 166*
(off Badger's Way)
Stroud Rd. SE25 5D 46
SW19 4M 27
Stroudwater Pk.
KT13: Weybr 3C 56
Stroud Way TW15: A'ford 7C 22
Struan Gdns. GU21: Wok 2A 74
Strudgate Cl. RH10: Craw 5F 182
Strudwicks Fld.
GU6: Cranl 6A 156
Stuart Av. KT12: Wal T 7J 39
Stuart Cl. GU14: Cove 9M 69
RH10: Craw 4G 183
SL4: W'sor 5C 4
Stuart Ct. CR0: Croy 4A 200
GU7: Goda 7H 133
RH1: Red 2E 122
(off St Anne's Ri.)
Stuart Cres. CR0: Croy 9J 47
RH2: Reig 6M 121
Stuart Gro. TW11: Tedd 6E 24
Stuart Ho. *RG42: Brac 9L 15*
(off Windlesham Rd.)
Stuart Lodge KT18: Eps 7K 201
Stuart Pl. CR4: Mit 9D 28
Stuart Rd. CR6: Warl 7E 84
CR7: T Hea 3N 45
RH2: Reig 6M 121
SW19 4M 27
TW10: Ham 3H 25
Stuart Way GU25: V Wat 3K 35
RH19: E Grin 2B 186
SL4: W'sor 5B 4
TW18: Stain 7K 21
Stubbs Ct. *W4 1A 12*
(off Chaseley Dr.)
Stubbs Folly GU47: C Tow 8J 49
Stubbs Hill RG42: Bin 5K 15
Stubbs La. KT20: Lwr K 6L 101
Stubbs Moor Rd.
GU14: Cove 9L 69
Stubbs Way SW19 9B 28
Stubfield RH12: Hors 5G 196
Stubpond La. RH7: Newc 2F 164
(not continuous)
RH19: Fel 2F 164
Stubs Cl. RH4: Dork 7J 119
Stubs Hill RH4: Dork 7J 119
Stucley Rd. TW5: Hest 3C 10
Studdridge St. SW6 5M 13
(not continuous)
Studio Arts & Media Cen., The 1H 47
Studio Plaza KT12: Wal T 7H 39
Studios Rd. TW17: Shep 2A 38
Studio Theatre 1E 62
Studland Rd. KT2: K Tham 7L 25
KT14: Byf 9A 56
Studland St. W6 1G 12
Stumblets RH10: Craw 2G 183
Stumps La. CR3: Whyte 4C 84
(not continuous)
Sturdee Cl. GU16: Frim 5C 70
Sturges Rd. RG40: W'ham 3B 30
Sturney Dr. GU51: Fleet 1A 88
Sturt Av. GU27: Hasl 3D 188
Sturt Ct. GU4: Guil 1D 114
Sturt Mdw. Cotts.
GU27: Hasl 3D 188
Sturt Rd. GU9: U Hal 5G 109
GU16: Frim G 9D 70
GU27: Hasl 2D 188
Sturt's La. KT20: Wal H 5E 100
Stychens Cl. RH1: Blet 2N 123
Stychens La. RH1: Blet 9N 103
Styles End KT23: Book 5B 98
Styles Way BR3: Beck 3M 47
Styventon Pl. KT16: Chert 6H 37
Subrosa Cvn. Site
RH1: Mers 8F 102
Subrosa Dr. RH1: Mers 8F 102
Succombs Hill CR3: Warl 7E 84
CR6: Warl 7E 84
Succombs Pl. CR6: Warl 6E 84
Sudbrooke Rd. SW12 1D 28
Sudbrook Gdns.
TW10: Ham 4K 25
Sudbrook La. TW10: Ham 2L 25
Sudbury Gdns. CR0: Croy 1B 64
Sudbury Ho. SW18 8N 13
Sudlow Rd. SW18 8M 13
Suffield Cl. CR2: Sels 8G 64
Suffield La.
GU8: Els, Put, S'ford 4H 131
Suffield Rd. SE20 1F 46
Suffolk Cl. GU19: Bag 5J 51
RH6: Horl 9E 142
Suffolk Combe RG42: Warf 8D 16
Suffolk Ct. GU16: Deep 6H 71
Suffolk Dr. GU4: B'ham 7D 94
Suffolk Ho. CR0: Croy 3D 200
Suffolk Rd. KT4: W Pk 8E 42
SE25 3C 46
SW13 3E 12
Sugden Rd. KT7: T Dit 7H 41
Sulina Rd. SW2 1J 29
Sulivan Ct. SW6 5M 13
Sulivan Ent. Cen. SW6 6N 13
Sulivan Rd. SW6 6M 13
Sullington Hill
RH11: Craw 5B 182
Sullington Mead
RH12: Bro H 5E 196
Sullivan Cl. GU14: Farnb 1N 89
KT8: W Mole 2B 40
Sullivan Dr. RH11: Craw 6K 181
Sullivan Rd. GU15: Camb 1M 69
Sullivans Reach
KT12: Wal T 6G 39
Sultan St. BR3: Beck 1G 47
Sulzers Rdbt. GU14: Farnb 2N 89
Summer Av. KT8: E Mol 4E 40
Summer Crossing
KT7: E Mol 4E 40
Summerene Cl. SW16 8G 29
Summerfield KT21: A'tead 6K 79
Summerfield Cl.
KT15: Addl 2H 55
Summerfield La.
GU10: Fren 9F 128
KT6: Surb 8K 41
Summerfield Pl.
KT16: Otter 3F 54
Summerfold RH12: Rudg 9F 176
Summer Gdns.
GU15: Camb 1G 71
KT8: E Mol 4E 40
Summerhayes Cl.
GU21: Wok 1A 74
Summerhays KT11: Cob 9L 57
Summerhill GU7: Goda 5G 132
Summerhill Cl. BR6: Orp 1N 67
Summerhill Way CR4: Mit 9E 28
Summer Ho. *RH11: Craw 4A 182*
(off Oak Rd.)
Summerhouse Av.
TW5: Hest 4M 9
Summerhouse Cl.
GU7: Goda 8G 133
Summerhouse Ct.
GU26: G'hott 6B 170
Summerhouse La.
UB7: Harm 2M 7
Summerhouse Rd.
GU7: Goda 8G 133
Summerlands GU6: Cranl 6N 155
Summerlands Lodge
BR6: Farnb 1J 67
Summerlay Cl. KT20: Tad 7K 81
Summerleigh *KT13: Weybr 3E 56*
(off Gower Rd.)
Summerley St. SW18 3N 27
Summerly Av. RH2: Reig 2M 121
Summer Pl. RG12: Brac 9M 15
Summer Rd. KT7: T Dit 4E 40
KT8: E Mol 4D 40
(not continuous)
Summersbury Dr.
GU4: Chil 2A 134
Summersbury Hall
GU4: Chil 2A 134
Summersby Cl. GU7: Goda 4J 133
Summers Cl. KT13: Weybr 7B 56
SM2: Sut 4M 61
Summers La. GU7: Hurt 3D 132
Summer's Rd. GU7: Goda 4J 133
SUMMERSTOWN 4A 28
Summerstown SW17 4A 28
Summersvere Cl.
RH10: Craw 9E 162
Summerswood Cl.
CR8: Ken 3A 84
Summer Trees TW16: Sunb 9J 23
Summerville Gdns.
SM1: Sut 3L 61
Summerwood Rd. TW7: Isle 8F 10
Summit Av. GU14: Cove 1G 88
Summit Bus. Pk.
TW16: Sunb 8H 23
Summit Pl. KT13: Weybr 4B 56
Sumner Cl. BR6: Farnb 1L 67
KT22: Fetc 2D 98
Sumner Ct. GU9: Farnh 9H 109
Sumner Gdns. CR0: Croy 7L 45
Sumner Pl. KT15: Addl 2J 55
Sumner Rd. CR0: Croy 7L 45
GU9: Farnh 9H 109
Sumner Rd. Sth. CR0: Croy 7L 45
Sun All. TW9: Rich 7L 11
Sun Brow GU27: Hasl 3D 188
SUNBURY 2K 39
Sunbury Av. SW14 7C 12
Sunbury Av. Pas.
SW14 7D 12
Sunbury Bus. Cen.
TW16: Sunb 9G 22
Sunbury Cl. KT12: Wal T 5H 39
SUNBURY COMMON 8G 23
Sunbury Ct. SL4: Eton 2G 4
Sunbury Ct. Island
TW16: Sunb 2L 39
Sunbury Ct. M. TW16: Sunb 1L 39
Sunbury Ct. Rd.
TW16: Sunb 1K 39
Sunbury Cres. TW13: Felt 5G 23
SUNBURY CROSS 8H 23
Sunbury Cross Cen.
TW16: Sunb 8G 23
Sunbury Ho. *TW16: Sunb 9F 22*
(off Windmill Rd. W.)
Sunbury La. KT12: Wal T 5H 39
Sunbury Leisure Cen. 9G 23
Sunburylock Ait KT12: Sunb 3J 39
Sunbury Pk. Walled Garden 2J 39
Sunbury Rd. SL4: Eton 2G 4
SM3: Chea 9J 43
TW13: Felt 4G 23
Sunbury Station (Rail) 9H 23
Sunbury Way TW13: Hanw 6K 23
Sun Cl. SL4: Eton 2G 4
Sundale Av. CR2: Sels 6F 64
Sundeala Cl. TW16: Sunb 8H 23
Sunderland Ct. *TW19: Stan 9N 7*
(off Whitley Cl.)
Sundew Cl. GU18: Ligh 7A 52
RG40: W'ham 1D 30
RH11: Craw 7M 181
Sundial Av. SE25 2C 46
Sundials Cvn. Site
RH6: Hook 9B 142
Sundon Cres. GU25: V Wat 4L 35
Sundown Av. CR2: Sande 7C 64
Sundown Rd. TW15: A'ford 6D 22
Sundridge Pl. CR0: Croy 7D 46
Sundridge Rd. CR0: Croy 6C 46
GU22: Wok 6C 74
Sun Hill GU22: Wok 8K 73
Sun Inn Rd. GU8: Duns 4B 174
Sunken Rd. CR0: Croy 2F 64
Sunkist Way SM6: W'ton 5J 63
Sun Life Trad. Est.
TW14: Felt 6H 9
Sunlight Cl. SW19 7A 28
Sunmead Cl. KT22: Fetc 9F 78
Sunmead Rd. TW16: Sunb 2H 39
Sunna Gdns. TW16: Sunb 1J 39
Sunna Lodge TW16: Sunb 8G 22
Sunniholme Ct.
CR2: S Croy 8B 200
Sunning Av. SL5: S'dale 6B 34
SUNNINGDALE 6D 34
Sunningdale Av.
TW13: Hanw 3M 23
Sunningdale Cl. KT6: Surb 8L 41
Sunningdale Ct.
RH10: Craw 5B 182
TW7: Isle 9D 10
(off Whitton Dene)
Sunningdale Golf Course 8E 34
Sunningdale Pk. 4C 34
Sunningdale Rd. SM1: Sut 9L 43
Sunningdale Station (Rail) 6D 34
SUNNINGHILL 4A 34
Sunninghill Cl. SL5: S'hill 3A 34
Sunninghill Ct. SL5: S'hill 3A 34
SUNNINGHILL PARK 8A 18
Sunninghill Rd.
GU20: Windl 9L 33
SL4: Wink 6A 18
SL5: Asc 6A 18
SL5: S'hill 4A 34
Sunningvale Av. TN16: B Hil 2E 86
Sunningvale Cl. TN16: B Hil 3F 86
Sunny Av. RH10: Craw D 1D 184
Sunny Bank CR6: Warl 4H 85
SE25 2D 46
Sunnybank KT18: Eps 3B 80
SL5: Asc 3L 33
Sunnybank Rd. GU14: Cove 8J 69
(not continuous)
Sunnybank Vs. RH1: Blet 1C 124
Sunnycroft Rd. SE25 2D 46
TW3: Houn 5B 10
Sunnydell La. GU10: Wrec 5F 128
(not continuous)
Sunnydene Rd. CR8: Pur 9M 63
Sunnydown GU8: Wit 5B 152
Sunnyhill GU8: Wit 5B 152
Sunnyhill Cl.
RH10: Craw D 1D 184
Sunny Hill Rd. GU11: Alde 2J 109
Sunnyhill Rd. SW16 5J 29
Sunnyhurst Cl. SM1: Sut 9M 43
Sunnymead RH10: Craw D 1E 184
(not continuous)
RH11: Craw 3B 182
Sunnymead Av. CR4: Mit 2H 45
Sunnymead Rd. SW15 8G 12
SUNNYMEADS 7A 6
Sunnymeads Station (Rail) 6A 6
Sunnymede Av. KT19: Ewe 5D 60
SM5: Cars 7B 62
Sunny Nook Gdns.
CR2: S Croy 3A 64
Sunny Ri. CR3: Cate 2A 104
SUNNYSIDE 2A 186
Sunnyside GU21: Knap 6E 72
GU51: Fleet 3A 88
KT12: Wal T 4K 39
SW19 7K 27
TN8: Eden 9K 127
Sunnyside Cotts.
RH5: H Mary 6K 137
Sunnyside Pas. SW19 7K 27
Sunnyside Pl. SW19 7K 27
Sunnyside Rd.
GU35: H Dwn 5H 169
TW11: Tedd 5D 24
Sunnyview Cl. GU12: Alde 3A 110
Sunoak Rd. RH13: Hors 6B 198
Sun Pas. SL4: W'sor 4G 4
Sunray Av. KT5: Surb 8A 42
Sunray Est. GU47: Sandh 7F 48
Sunrise Cl. TW13: Hanw 4N 23
Sun Rd. W14 1L 13
Sunset Gdns. SE25 1C 46
Sunset Rd. SW19 6G 26
Sunshine Way CR4: Mit 1D 44
Sunstone Gro. RH1: Mers 7H 103
Sunvale Av. GU27: Hasl 2B 188
Sunvale Cl. GU27: Hasl 2B 188
Superior Dr. BR6: Chels 3N 67
SURBITON 5K 41
Surbiton Ct. KT6: Surb 5J 41
Surbiton Cres.
KT1: K Tham 8J 203 (3L 41)
Surbiton Hall Cl.
KT1: K Tham 8J 203 (3L 41)
Surbiton Hill Pk. KT5: Surb 4M 41
Surbiton Hill Rd.
KT6: Surb 8J 203 (3L 41)
Surbiton Pde. KT6: Surb 5L 41
Surbiton Rd. GU15: Camb 6E 50
KT1: K Tham 7H 203 (3K 41)
Surbiton Station (Rail) 5L 41
Surly Hall Wlk. SL4: W'sor 4C 4
Surrenden Ri. RH11: Craw 9A 182
Surrey & Sussex Crematorium
RH10: Craw 8H 163
Surrey Av. GU15: Camb 2M 69
Surrey Cloisters
GU7: Goda 5J 133
Surrey County Council
Smallholdings Rd.
KT17: Eps 8H 61
(not continuous)
Surrey County Cricket Cen. 1C 114
Surrey Ct. GU2: Guil 3L 113
RG42: Warf 8D 16
Surrey Cres. W4 1N 11
Surrey Gdns. KT24: E Jun 9H 77
Surrey Golf & Fitness 4L 55
Surrey Gro. SM1: Sut 9B 44
Surrey Guild Craft Gallery 2B 152
Surrey Heath Mus. 9B 50
Surrey Hills Av.
KT20: Box H 8B 100
Surrey Hills Bus. Pk.
RH5: Wott 8A 118
Surrey Hills Pk. GU3: Norm 9B 92
Surrey Hills Res. Pk.
KT20: Box H 8B 100
Surrey History Cen. 5N 73
Surrey Lodge *KT12: Hers 2J 57*
(off Queens Rd.)
Surrey Research Pk., The
GU2: Guil 3G 112
Surrey Rd. BR4: W Wick 7L 47
Surrey St.
CR0: Croy 3B 200 (8N 45)
Surrey Technology Cen.
GU2: Guil 4G 113
Surrey Towers *KT15: Addl 2L 55*
(off Garfield Rd.)
Surrey Way GU2: Guil 2L 113
Surridge Ct. GU19: Bag 5J 51
Sury Basin
KT2: K Tham 1H 203 (9L 25)
Sussex Av. TW7: Isle 6E 10
Sussex Cl. GU21: Knap 5F 72
KT3: N Mal 3D 42
RH2: Reig 4B 122
TW1: Twick 9H 11
Sussex Ct. GU21: Knap 4F 72
KT15: Addl 2L 55
RH13: Hors 7K 197
Sussex Gdns. GU51: Fleet 1C 88
KT9: Ches 3K 59
Sussex Lodge RH12: Hors 4J 197
Sussex Mnr. Bus. Pk.
RH10: Craw 8E 162
Sussex Pl. GU21: Knap 5F 72
KT3: N Mal 3D 42
W6 1H 13
Sussex Rd. BR4: W Wick 7L 47
CR2: S Croy 3A 64
CR4: Mit 4J 45
GU21: Knap 5F 72
KT3: N Mal 3D 42
SM5: Cars 3D 62
Sutherland Av. GU4: J Wel 6A 94
TN16: B Hil 4F 86
TW16: Sunb 1G 39
Sutherland Chase SL5: Asc 9J 17
Sutherland Dr. GU4: B'ham 9B 94
SW19 9B 28

A-Z Surrey 289

Sutherland Gdns.—Teddington Bus. Pk.

Sutherland Gdns.
KT4: W Pk 7G **42**
SW14 . . . . .6D **12**
TW16: Sunb 1G **39**
Sutherland Grange
SL4: W'sor 3A **4**
Sutherland Gro. SW18 . . . . . . .9K **13**
TW11: Tedd 6E **24**
Sutherland Rd. CR0: Croy 6L **45**
W4 . . . . .2D **12**
SUTTON
SL3 . . . .**1E 6**
SM1 . . . .**2N 61**
SUTTON ABINGER **3H 137**
Sutton Arena Leisure Cen. . . .6A **44**
Sutton Av. GU21: Wok 6H **73**
Sutton Comn. Rd. SM1: Sut . . .6L **43**
SM3: Sut 6L **43**
Sutton Common Station (Rail)
. . . . .8N **43**
Sutton Ct. KT8: W Mole 4N **39**
SM2: Sut 3A **62**
W4 . . . . .2B **12**
Sutton Ct. Rd. SM1: Sut 3A **62**
W4 . . . . .3B **12**
Sutton Dene TW3: Houn 4B **10**
Sutton Ecology Cen. 1D **62**
Sutton Gdns. CR0: Croy 4C **46**
RH1: Mers 7H **103**
SUTTON GREEN **4B 94**
Sutton Grn. Rd. GU4: Sut G . . .4A **94**
Sutton Gro. SM1: Sut 1B **62**
Sutton Hall Rd. TW5: Hest 3A **10**
Sutton Hgts. SM2: Sut 4B **62**
Sutton Hill GU4: B'ham 7E **94**
Sutton Junior Tennis Cen. 7N **43**
Sutton La.
RH5: A Com, A Ham 3J **137**
SL3: Lang 2D **6**
SM2: Sut 7N **61**
SM7: Ban 7N **61**
TW3: Houn 6N **9**
Sutton La. Nth. W4 . . . . .1B **12**
Sutton La. Sth. W4 . . . . .2B **12**
Sutton Lodge GU1: Guil 3F **202**
SUTTON PARK **4B 94**
Sutton Pk. Rd. SM1: Sut 3N **61**
Sutton Pl. RH5: A Ham 3G **136**
SL3: Lang 2D **6**
Sutton Rd. GU15: Camb 6E **50**
TW5: Hest 4A **10**
Sutton Sq. TW5: Hest 4N **9**
Sutton Station (Rail) 3A **62**
Sutton Superbowl 2N **61**
Sutton United FC 1M **61**
Sutton Way TW5: Hest 4N **9**
Swaby Rd. SW18 . . . . .2A **28**
Swaffield Rd. SW18 . . . . .1N **27**
Swail Ho.
KT18: Eps 7K **201** (9C **60**)
Swain Cl. SW16 . . . . .7F **28**
Swain Rd. CR7: T Hea 4N **45**
Swains Rd. SW17 . . . . .8D **28**
Swaledale RG12: Brac 4M **31**
Swaledale Cl. RH11: Craw . . .6A **182**
Swaledale Gdns.
GU51: Fleet 1C **88**
Swale Rd. GU14: Cove 8K **69**
Swallow Cl. GU8: Mil 3B **152**
GU46: Yate 9A **48**
TW18: Stain 5H **21**
Swallowdale CR2: Sels 5G **65**
Swallowfield RH7: Dorm 1C **166**
TW20: Eng G 7L **19**
Swallowfields *RH6: Horl 8F 142*
(off Rosemary La.)
Swallow Gdns. SW16 . . . . .6H **29**
Swallow La. RH5: Mid H 2H **139**
Swallow Pk. KT6: Surb 9M **41**
Swallow Ri. GU21: Knap 4F **72**
Swallow Rd. RH11: Craw 1A **182**
Swallow St. RH10: T Hil 4F **184**
Swallowtail Rd.
RH12: Hors 2L **197**
SWAN, THE **8M 47**
Swanage Rd. SW18 . . . . .1A **28**
Swan Barn Rd.
GU27: Hasl 2H **189**
Swan Cen., The KT22: Leat . . .8H **79**
SW17 . . . . .4N **27**
Swan Cl. CR0: Croy 6B **46**
TW13: Hanw 5M **23**
Swancote Grn. RG12: Brac 4N **31**
Swan Ct. GU1: Guil 1N **113**
GU17: Haw 2K 69
(off Toad La.)
KT22: Leat 9H **79**
SW6 . . . . .3M 13
(off Fulham Rd.)
TW7: Isle 6H 11
(off Swan St.)
Swandon Way SW18 . . . . .8N **13**
Swandrift TW18: Stain 8H **21**
Swan Island TW1: Twick 4G **24**
Swan La.
GU1: Guil 5C **202** (4N **113**)
GU47: Sandh 8G **48**
RH6: Char 3L **161**
TN8: Eden 8L **127**
Swan M. CR4: Mit 9D **28**
SW6 . . . . .4L **13**
Swan Mill Gdns.
RH4: Dork 3J **119**
Swann Ct. *TW7: Isle 6G 11*
(off South St.)
Swanns Mdw. KT23: Book 4A **98**
Swann Way RH12: Bro H 5E **196**
Swan Pl. SW13 . . . . .5E **12**
Swan Ridge TN8: Eden 8M **127**
Swan Rd. TW13: Hanw 6M **23**
Swan Sanctuary, The 5F **38**
Swanscombe Rd. W4 . . . . .1D **12**
Swansea Rd. TW14: Felt 9D **8**
Swans Ghyll
RH18: F Row 6G **187**
Swan Sq. RH12: Hors 6J **197**
Swan St. TW7: Isle 6H **11**
Swansway, The
KT13: Weybr 9B **38**
Swan Ter. SL4: W'sor 3E **4**
Swanton Gdns. SW19 . . . . .2J **27**
Swan Wlk. RH12: Hors 6J **197**
TW17: Shep 6F **38**
Swanwick Cl. SW15 . . . . .1E **26**
Swanworth La. RH5: Mick 6G **99**
Swathling Ho. *SW15 . . . . .9E 12*
(off Tunworth Cres.)
Swaynesland Rd.
TN8: C Hil 3H **127**
Swayne's La. GU1: Guil 3G **114**
Sweeps Ditch Cl.
TW18: Stain 8J **21**
Sweeps La. TW20: Egh 6B **20**
Sweetbriar RG45: Crow 9F **30**
Sweet Briar La.
KT18: Eps 8J **201** (1C **80**)
Sweet La. GU5: P'lake 3F **136**
Sweetwater Cl.
GU5: Sha G 7F **134**
Sweetwater La.
GU5: Sha G 7F **134**
GU8: Worm 7D **152**
Sweetwell Rd. RG12: Brac 1K **31**
Swievelands Rd.
TN16: B Hil 6D **86**
Swift Cen. CR0: Wad 4K **63**
Swift Ct. GU51: Fleet 4B **88**
SM2: Sut 4N **61**
Swift La. GU19: Bag 4K **51**
RH11: Craw 1A **182**
Swift La. Cvn. Site
GU19: Bag 4L **51**
Swift La. Ind. Est.
GU19: Bag 4L **51**
Swift Rd. GU9: U Hal 5H **109**
TW13: Hanw 4M **23**
Swift's Cl. GU10: Farnh 2N **129**
Swift St. SW6 . . . . .4L **13**
Swinburne Cres. CR0: Croy 5F **46**
Swinburne Rd. SW15 . . . . .7F **12**
Swindon Rd. RH12: Hors 4H **197**
TW6: Lon A 8D **8**
Swinfield Cl. TW13: Hanw 4M **23**
Swingate Rd. GU9: Farnh 3J **129**
Swinley Rd. GU19: Bag 1H **51**
SL5: Asc 2G **32**
Swires Shaw BR2: Kes 1F **66**
Swiss Cl. GU10: Wrec 7F **128**
Swissland Hill RH19: D Pk . . .4N **165**
Switchback La.
GU10: Rowl 7E **128**
(not continuous)
Swithin Chase RG42: Warf 8C **16**
Swithins Rd. GU51: Fleet 1A **88**
Swordsmans Rd.
GU16: Deep 5H **71**
Swyncombe Av. W5 . . . . .1H **11**
Sybil Thorndike Casson Ho.
SW5 . . . . .1M 13
(off Kramer M.)
Sycamore Av. RH12: Hors . . .2B **198**
Sycamore Cl.
CR2: S Croy 8F **200** (2B **64**)
GU16: Frim 5C **70**
GU47: Sandh 8G **48**
KT22: Fetc 1F **98**
RH11: Craw 9A **162**
SM5: Cars 1D **62**
TW13: Felt 4H **23**
Sycamore Cotts.
GU15: Camb 3N 69
(off Frimley Rd.)
Sycamore Ct. *GU1: Guil 5F 202*
(off Harvey Rd.)
GU7: Goda 5J **133**
KT3: N Mal 2D **42**
KT13: Weybr 9G **38**
RH8: Oxt 7A **106**
SL4: W'sor 6F **4**
TW4: Houn 7M **9**
Sycamore Dr. GU10: Wrec 5F **128**
GU12: A Va 6E **90**
GU16: Frim 4C **70**
RH19: E Grin 9C **166**
Sycamore Gdns. CR4: Mit 1B **44**
Sycamore Gro. KT3: N Mal 2C **42**
Sycamore Ho. CR6: Warl 2L **85**
Sycamore Lodge
TW16: Sunb 8G **22**
Sycamore Ri. RG12: Brac 2B **32**
SM7: Ban 1J **81**
Sycamore Rd.
GU1: Guil 2C **202** (3N **113**)
GU14: Farnb 3A **90**
(not continuous)
SW19 . . . . .7H **27**
Sycamores, The
GU14: Farnb 2B **90**
GU17: B'water 1G **68**
KT23: Book 2C **98**
Sycamore Wlk. RH2: Reig . . .6A **122**
TW20: Eng G 7L **19**
Sycamore Way CR7: T Hea 4L **45**
TW11: Tedd 7J **25**
Sydcote SE21 . . . . .2N **29**
Sydenham Ct. CR0: Croy 1D **200**
Sydenham Pl. SE27 . . . . .4M **29**
Sydenham Rd.
CR0: Croy 2C **200** (7N **45**)
GU1: Guil 6D **202** (5N **113**)
Sydney Av. CR8: Pur 8K **63**
Sydney Cl. RG45: Crow 9H **31**
Sydney Cres.
TW15: A'ford 7C **22**
Sydney Loader Pl.
GU17: B'water 9F **48**
Sydney Pl. GU1: Guil 4B **114**
Sydney Rd. GU1: Guil 4B **114**
SM1: Sut 1M **61**
SW20 . . . . .1J **43**
TW9: Rich 7L **11**
TW11: Tedd 6F **24**
TW14: Felt 2H **23**
Sydney Ter. *KT10: Clay 3F 58*
(off The Green)
Sykes Dr. TW18: Stain 6K **21**
Sylvan Cl. CR2: Sels 6E **64**
GU22: Wok 4D **74**
RH8: Limp 7D **106**
Sylvan Ct. GU14: Farnb 4B **90**
Sylvan Est. SE19 . . . . .1C **46**
Sylvan Gdns. KT6: Surb 6K **41**
Sylvan Ridge GU47: Sandh 6F **48**
Sylvan Rd. RH10: Craw 5E **182**
Sylvanus RG12: Brac 6L **31**
Sylvan Way BR4: W Wick 1A **66**
GU52: C Cro 8A **88**
RH1: Red 4E **122**
(not continuous)
Sylvaways Cl. GU6: Cranl . . .7B **156**
Sylverdale Rd.
CR0: Croy 4A **200** (9M **45**)
CR8: Pur 9M **63**
Sylverns Ct. RG42: Warf 8B **16**
Sylvestrus Cl. KT1: K Tham . . .9N **25**
Symonds Ho. RH11: Ifi 9M **161**
Symondson M. RG42: Bin 5H **15**
Syon Ga. Way TW8: Brent 3G **11**
Syon House 4J **11**
Syon La. TW7: Isle 2E **10**
Syon Lane Station (Rail) 3G **11**
Syon Pk. 4H **11**
Syon Pk. Gdns. TW7: Isle 3F **10**
Syon Pl. GU14: Farnb 1B **90**
Sythwood GU21: Wok 4L **73**
Szabo Cres. GU3: Flex 3M **111**

T

Tabarin Way KT17: Eps D 3H **81**
Tabor Ct. SM3: Chea 3K **61**
Tabor Gdns. SM3: Chea 3L **61**
Tabor Gro. SW19 . . . . .8L **27**
Tachbrook Rd. TW14: Felt 1G **23**
Tadlow KT1: K Tham 5M **203**
Tadmor Cl. TW16: Sunb 3G **39**
Tadorne Rd. KT20: Tad 8H **81**
Tadpole La. GU10: Ews 3C **108**
TADWORTH **9H 81**
Tadworth Av. KT3: N Mal 3E **42**
Tadworth Cl. KT20: Tad 9J **81**
Tadworth Ct. KT20: Tad 8J **81**
TADWORTH PARK **8J 81**
Tadworth Station (Rail) 9H **81**
Tadworth St. KT20: Tad 1H **101**
Taff Ho. *KT2: K Tham 1H 203*
(off Henry Macaulay Av.)
Taffy's Row CR4: Mit 2C **44**
Taggs Ho. *KT1: K Tham 4H 203*
(off Wadbrook St.)
Taggs Island TW12: Hamp 1D **40**
Tait Rd. CR0: Croy 6B **46**
Tait Rd. Ind. Est. *CR0: Croy . . .6B 46*
(off Tait Rd.)
Talavera Cl. RG45: Crow 3E **48**
Talavera Pk. GU11: Alde 1M **109**
Talbot Cl. GU16: Mytc 1E **90**
RH2: Reig 4N **121**
Talbot Ct. SL4: W'sor 6E **4**
Talbot La. RH12: Hors 7J **197**
Talbot Lodge KT10: Esh 2A **58**
Talbot Pl. GU19: Bag 3J **51**
SL3: Dat 4M **5**
Talbot Rd. CR7: T Hea 3A **46**
GU9: Farnh 3G **128**
RH7: Ling 8N **145**
SM5: Cars 2E **62**
TW2: Twick 2E **24**
TW7: Isle 7G **11**
TW15: A'ford 6N **21**
Talcott Path SW2 . . . . .2L **29**
Taleworth Cl. KT21: A'tead 7K **79**
Taleworth Pk. KT21: A'tead 7K **79**
Taleworth Rd. KT21: A'tead 7K **79**
Talfourd Way RH1: Red 6D **122**
Talgarth Dr. GU14: Farnb 3B **90**
Talgarth Mans. *W14 . . . . .1K 13*
(off Talgarth Rd.)
Talgarth Rd. W6 . . . . .1J **13**
W14 . . . . .1J **13**
Talina Cen. SW6 . . . . .4N **13**
Talisman Cl. RG45: Crow 2C **48**
Talisman Way KT17: Eps D 3H **81**
Tallis Cl. RH11: Craw 6L **181**
Tallow Rd. TW8: Brent 2J **11**
Tall Pines KT17: Eps 7E **60**
Tall Trees RH19: E Grin 1B **186**
SL3: Coln 4G **7**
SW16 . . . . .2K **45**
Tally Rd. RH8: Limp 9G **107**
Talma Gdns. TW2: Twick 9E **10**
Talman Cl. RH11: Ifi 4K **181**
Tamar Cl. RH10: Craw 4G **182**
Tamarind Cl. GU2: Guil 7K **93**
Tamarind Ct. TW20: Egh 6B **20**
Tamarisk Ri. RG40: W'ham 1B **30**
Tamar Way SL3: Lang 1D **6**
Tamerton Sq. GU22: Wok 6A **74**
Tamesis Gdns. KT4: W Pk 8D **42**
Tamian Ind. Est. TW4: Houn . . .7K **9**
Tamian Way TW4: Houn 7K **9**
Tamworth RG12: Brac 6B **32**
Tamworth Dr. GU51: Fleet 1C **88**
Tamworth La. CR4: Mit 1F **44**
Tamworth Pk. CR4: Mit 3F **44**
Tamworth Pl.
CR0: Croy 3B **200** (8N **45**)
Tamworth Rd.
CR0: Croy 3A **200** (8M **45**)
Tamworth St. SW6 . . . . .2M **13**
Tamworth Vs. CR4: Mit 3F **44**
Tanbridge Ho. RH12: Hors 7H **197**
Tanbridge Pk. RH12: Hors 7G **197**
Tanbridge Pl. RH12: Hors 7H **197**
Tanbridge Retail Pk.
RH12: Hors 7H **197**
Tandem Cen. SW19 . . . . .9B **28**
Tandem Way SW19 . . . . .9B **28**
TANDRIDGE **2K 125**
Tandridge Ct. CR3: Cate 9D **84**
Tandridge Gdns.
CR2: Sande 9C **64**
Tandridge Golf Course 9M **105**
Tandridge Hill La.
RH9: Gods 6J **105**
Tandridge La. RH7: Ling 4K **145**
RH8: Tand 1K **125**
Tandridge Leisure Cen. 7A **106**
Tandridge Rd. CR6: Warl 6G **84**
Tanfield Ct. RH12: Hors 6H **197**
Tanfield Rd.
CR0: Croy 6B **200** (1N **63**)
Tangier Ct. GU11: Alde 2L **109**
SL4: Eton 2G **5**
Tangier La. SL4: Eton 2G **4**
Tangier Rd. GU1: Guil 4C **114**
TW10: Rich 7N **11**
Tangier Way KT20: Tad 4K **81**
Tangier Wood KT20: Tad 5K **81**
Tangle Oak RH19: Fel 6H **165**
Tanglewood Cl. CR0: Croy 9F **46**
GU22: Pyr 3F **74**
KT16: L'cross 9L **35**
Tanglewood Ride
GU24: W End 8A **52**
Tanglewood Way TW13: Felt . . .4J **23**
Tangley Dr. RG41: W'ham 4A **30**
Tangley Gro. SW15 . . . . .9E **12**
Tangley La. GU3: Guil 8J **93**
Tangley Pk. Rd.
TW12: Hamp 6N **23**
Tanglyn Av. TW17: Shep 4C **38**
Tangmere Gro.
KT2: K Tham 6K **25**
Tangmere Rd. RH11: Craw . . .3L **181**
Tanhouse Rd. RH8: Oxt 1N **125**
Tanhurst Ho. *SW2 . . . . .1K 29*
(off Redlands Way)
Tanhurst La. RH5: H Mary . . .2M **157**
Tankerton Rd. KT6: Surb 8M **41**
Tankerton Ter. CR0: Croy 5K **45**
Tankerville Ct. TW3: Houn 6C **10**
Tankerville Rd. SW16 . . . . .8H **29**
Tank Rd. GU47: C Tow 1L **69**
Tanners Cl. KT12: Wal T 5J **39**
Tanners Ct. RH3: Brock 4A **120**
(Middle St.)
RH3: Brock 7B **120**
(Tanners Mdw.)
Tanners Dean KT22: Leat 9J **79**
Tannersfield GU4: Chil 2A **134**
Tanner's Hill RH3: Brock 5A **120**
Tanners La. GU27: Hasl 1G **188**
Tanners Mdw. RH3: Brock 7A **120**
Tanners M. TN8: Eden 2L **147**
Tanners Yd. GU19: Bag 4H **51**
Tannery, The RH1: Red 3D **122**
Tannery Cl. BR3: Beck 4G **46**
RH13: Slin 5L **195**
Tannery Ct. *RH13: Hors 7K 197*
(off Boxall Wlk.)
Tannery La. GU5: Braml 3B **134**
GU23: Send 1F **94**
Tansy Cl. GU4: Guil 1E **114**
Tantallon Rd. SW12 . . . . .2E **28**
Tanyard Av. RH19: E Grin 1C **186**
Tanyard Cl. RH10: Craw 6G **182**
RH13: Hors 7L **197**
Tanyard Ho. *TW8: Brent 3J 11*
(off High St.)
Tanyard Way RH6: Horl 6F **142**
Tapestries Hall SL4: O Win 8K **5**
Tapestry Cl. SM2: Sut 4N **61**
Taplow Ct. CR4: Mit 3C **44**
Tapner's Rd. RH2: Leigh 9E **120**
RH3: Betch 8E **120**
Tapping Cl. KT2: K Tham 8N **25**
Tara Arts Cen. 2N 27
(off Garratt La.)
Tara Ct. BR3: Beck 1L **47**
Tarbat Ct. GU47: C Tow 7J **49**
Target Cl. TW14: Felt 9F **8**
Target Hill RG42: Warf 8B **16**
Tarham Cl. RH6: Horl 6C **142**
Tarmac Way UB7: Harm 3K **7**
Tarnbrook Way RG12: Brac 6C **32**
Tarn Cl. GU14: Cove 3K **89**
Tarn Rd. GU26: Hind 6B **170**
Tarragon Cl. GU14: Cove 1H **89**
RG12: Brac 8B **16**
Tarragon Ct. GU2: Guil 8K **93**
Tarragon Dr. GU2: Guil 7K **93**
Tarragon Rd. GU2: Guil 8K **93**
Tarrant Grn. RG42: Warf 8A **16**
Tarrington Cl. SW16 . . . . .4H **29**
Tartar Hill KT11: Cob 9K **57**
Tartar Rd. KT11: Cob 9K **57**
Tasker Cl. UB3: Harl 3D **8**
Tasman Ct. TW16: Sunb 8F **22**
Tasso Rd. W6 . . . . .2K **13**
Tasso Yd. *W6 . . . . .2K 13*
(off Tasso Rd.)
Tatchbury Ho. *SW15 . . . . .9E 12*
(off Tunworth Cres.)
Tate Cl. KT22: Leat 1J **99**
Tate Rd. SM1: Sut 2M **61**
Tates Way RH12: Rudg 1E **194**
Tatham Ct. RH11: Craw 8N **181**
TATSFIELD **8E 86**
TATSFIELD GREEN **8G 86**
Tatsfield La. TN16: Tats 8H **87**
TATTENHAM CORNER **5G 80**
Tattenham Cnr. Rd.
KT18: Eps D, Tat C 4E **80**
Tattenham Corner Station (Rail)
. . . . .5G **80**
Tattenham Cres.
KT18: Tat C 5F **80**
Tattenham Gro. KT18: Tat C . . .5G **80**
Tattenham Way KT20: Tad 5J **81**
Tattersall Cl. RG40: W'ham 3D **30**
Taunton Av. CR3: Cate 1C **104**
SW20 . . . . .1G **42**
TW3: Houn 5C **10**
Taunton Cl. RH10: Craw 2H **183**
SM3: Sut 7M **43**
Taunton La. CR5: Coul 6L **83**
Tavern Cl. SM5: Cars 6C **44**
Tavistock Cl. TW18: Stain 8M **21**
Tavistock Ct. *CR0: Croy 7A 46*
(off Tavistock Rd.)
Tavistock Cres. CR4: Mit 3J **45**
Tavistock Gdns.
GU14: Farnb 7N **69**
Tavistock Ga.
CR0: Croy 1D **200** (7A **46**)
Tavistock Gro. CR0: Croy 6A **46**
Tavistock Rd.
CR0: Croy 1D **200** (7A **46**)
SM5: Cars 7B **44**
Tavistock Wlk. SM5: Cars 7B **44**
Tawfield RG12: Brac 6K **31**
Tawny Cl. TW13: Felt 4H **23**
Tawny Cft. GU47: C Tow 7K **49**
Tayben Av. TW2: Twick 9E **10**
Tay Cl. GU14: Cove 8K **69**
Tayles Hill Dr. KT17: Ewe 6E **60**
Taylor Av. TW9: Kew 5A **12**
Taylor Cl. KT19: Eps 7N **59**
TW3: Houn 4C **10**
TW12: H Hill 6C **24**
Taylor Ct. *SE20 . . . . .1F 46*
(off Elmers End Rd.)
Taylor Rd. CR4: Mit 8C **28**
GU11: Alde 6B **90**
KT21: A'tead 4K **79**
SM6: W'ton 2F **62**
Taylor's Bushes Ride
SL4: W'sor 3N **17**
Taylors Cl. GU35: Lind 4A **168**
Taylors Ct. TW13: Felt 3H **23**
Taylors Cres. GU6: Cranl 7A **156**
Taylors La. GU35: Lind 4A **168**
Taylor Wlk. RH11: Craw 3A **182**
Taymans Track
RH17: Hand 8L **199**
Taynton Dr. RH1: Mers 8H **103**
Teal Cl. CR2: Sels 7G **64**
RH12: Hors 3J **197**
Teal Ct. RH4: Dork 1J **201**
SM6: W'ton 2G **63**
Tealing Dr. KT19: Ewe 1C **60**
Teal Pl. SM1: Sut 2L **61**
Teasel Cl. CR0: Croy 7G **46**
RH11: Craw 6N **181**
Teazlewood Pk. KT22: Leat 4G **78**
Tebbit Cl. RG12: Brac 1B **32**
Teck Cl. TW7: Isle 5G **11**
Tedder Cl. KT9: Ches 2J **59**
Tedder Rd. CR2: Sels 4F **64**
TEDDINGTON **6G 24**
Teddington Bus. Pk.
TW11: Tedd 7F 24
(off Station Rd.)

Triangle, The—Up. Hale Rd.

Triangle, The GU21: Wok 5M 73
KT1: K Tham 1A 42
Trickett Ho. SM2: Sut 5N 61
Trident Bus. Cen.
SW17 . . . . .6D 28
Trident Ho. *TW19: Stan 1N 21*
(off Clare Rd.)
Trident Ind. Est. SL3: Poy 6G 7
Triffins Girls Community Sports Cen. 7L 25
Trigg's Cl. GU22: Wok 6N 73
Trigg's La. GU21: Wok 6M 73
GU22: Wok 6M 73
Trigo Ct. KT19: Eps 7C 60
Trig St. RH5: B Grn, Newd 1L 159
Trilakes Country Pk. 7E 48
Trimmers GU9: Farnh 2F 128
Trimmers Cl. GU9: U Hal 5G 109
Trimmers Fld. GU9: Farnh . . .2K 129
Trimmers Wood
GU26: Hind 3B 170
Trimmer Wlk. TW8: Brent 2L 11
Trinder M. TW11: Tedd 6G 25
Trindledown RG42: Brac 7M 15
Trindles Rd. RH1: Sth N 5K 123
Tring Ct. TW1: Twick 5G 24
Tringham Cl. GU21: Knap 5F 72
KT16: Otter 2E 54
Tringham Cotts.
GU24: W End 8C 52
Trinity GU47: Owls 5K 49
Trinity Chu. Pas.
SW13 . . . . .2G 13
Trinity Chu. Rd. SW13 . . . . . . .2G 13
Trinity Chyd.
GU1: Guil 6D 202 (5N 113)
Trinity Cl. CR2: Sande 5B 64
RH10: Craw 1G 183
TW4: Houn 7M 9
TW19: Stan 9L 7
Trinity Cotts. TW9: Rich 6M 11
Trinity Ct.
CR0: Croy 2C 200 (8N 45)
RG12: Brac 1L 31
RH12: Hors 5J 197
SE25 . . . . .5B 46
Trinity Cres. SL5: S'dale 4D 34
SW17 . . . . .3D 28
Trinity Flds. GU9: U Hal 5F 108
Trinity Ga. GU1: Guil 5E 202
Trinity Hill GU9: U Hal 5F 108
Trinity M. SE20 . . . . .1E 46
Trinity Pl. SL4: W'sor 5F 4
Trinity Ri. SW2 . . . . .2L 29
Trinity Rd. GU21: Knap 5E 72
SW17 . . . . .2C 28
SW18 . . . . .1B 28
SW19 . . . . .7M 27
TW9: Rich 6M 11
Trinity Sq. RH13: Hors 6K 197
Trist Way RH11: Craw 1M 181
Tritton Av. CR0: Bedd 1J 63
Trittons KT20: Tad 8J 81
Triumph Cl. UB3: Harl 4D 8
Trodd's La. GU1: Guil 2F 114
GU4: Guil 2F 114
Trojan Way CR0: Wad 9K 45
Troon Cl. RH11: Ifi 4J 181
Troon Ct. SL5: S'hill 4N 33
Troston Ct. TW18: Stain 6H 21
Trotsford Mdw.
GU17: B'water 2H 69
Trotsworth Av. GU25: V Wat . . .3A 36
Trotsworth Ct. GU25: V Wat . . .3N 35
Trotters La. GU24: Chob 8L 53
Trotter Way KT19: Eps 8N 59
Trotton Cl. RH10: Craw 6G 182
Trotts La. TN16: Weste 5L 107
Trotwood Cl. GU47: Owls 5K 49
Troutbeck Wlk.
GU15: Camb 3H 71
Trout Rd. GU27: Hasl 2C 188
Trouville Rd. SW4 . . . . .1G 29
Trowers Way RH1: Red 9F 102
Trowlock Av. TW11: Tedd 7J 25
Trowlock Island TW11: Tedd . . .7K 25
Trowlock Way TW11: Tedd 7K 25
Troy Cl. KT20: Tad 7G 81
Troy La. TN8: Eden 8H 127
TROY TOWN 8H 127
Trueman Rd. CR8: Ken 7A 84
Truggers RH17: Hand 8N 199
Trumble Gdns. CR7: T Hea 3M 45
Trumbull Rd. RG42: Brac 8M 15
Trumpets Hill Rd.
RH2: Reig 4G 120
TRUMPS GREEN 5N 35
Trumpsgreen Av.
GU25: V Wat 5N 35
Trumps Grn. Cl.
GU25: V Wat 4A 36
Trumpsgreen Rd.
GU25: V Wat 7M 35
Trumps Mill La.
GU25: V Wat 5B 36
Trundle Mead RH12: Hors 3J 197
Trunk Rd. GU14: Cove 1H 89
Trunley Heath Rd.
GU5: Braml 4M 133
Truslove Rd. SE27 . . . . .6L 29
Truss Hill Rd. SL5: S'hill 4N 33
Trust Wlk. SE21 . . . . .2M 29
Trystings Cl. KT10: Clay 3G 59
Tubbenden Dr. BR6: Orp 1M 67
Tubbenden La. BR6: Orp 1M 67
Tubbenden La. Sth.
BR6: Farnb 2M 67
Tucker Rd. KT16: Otter 3F 54
Tuckers Cnr. GU6: Cranl 7K 155
Tuckers Dr. GU6: Cranl 7K 155
Tuckey Gro. GU23: Rip 1H 95
Tucklow Wlk. SW15 . . . . .1E 26
Tudor Av. KT4: W Pk 9G 42
TW12: Hamp 7A 24
Tudor Circ. GU7: Goda 4H 133
Tudor Cl. CR2: Sande 2E 84
CR5: Coul 5L 83
GU22: Wok 4C 74
GU26: G'hott 7B 170
KT9: Ches 2L 59
KT11: Cob 9N 57
KT17: Ewe 6E 60
KT23: Book 2N 97
(not continuous)
RG40: W'ham 3E 30
RH6: Smal 8M 143
RH10: Craw 4H 183
RH19: E Grin 1B 186
SM3: Chea 2J 61
SM6: W'ton 4G 63
SM7: Ban 2K 81
SW2 . . . . .1K 29
TW12: H Hill 6C 24
TW15: A'ford 5N 21
Tudor Ct. GU12: Ash 3D 110
GU21: Knap 4G 72
RH1: Red 2E 122
(off St Anne's Ri.)
TN16: B Hil 5G 86
TW11: Tedd 7F 24
TW13: Hanw 5K 23
TW19: Stan 9N 7
TW20: Egh 6C 20
Tudor Dr. GU46: Yate 2C 68
KT2: K Tham 6K 25
KT12: Wal T 7L 39
SM4: Mord 5J 43
Tudor Gdns. BR4: W Wick 9M 47
SW13 . . . . .6D 12
TW1: Twick 2F 24
Tudor Grange KT13: Weybr 8F 38
Tudor Hall GU15: Camb 9D 50
Tudor Ho. KT13: Weybr 3B 56
RG12: Brac 4N 31
Tudor La. SL4: O Win 1M 19
Tudor Lodge KT20: K'wood 8L 81
Tudor Pl. CR4: Mit 8C 28
Tudor Rd. BR3: Beck 2M 47
GU7: Goda 4H 133
KT2: K Tham 8N 25
SE25 . . . . .4E 46
TW3: Houn 7D 10
TW12: Hamp 8A 24
TW15: A'ford 7E 22
Tudors, The RH2: Reig 9A 102
Tudor Wlk. KT13: Weybr 9C 38
KT22: Leat 7F 78
Tudor Way GU21: Knap 6F 72
GU52: C Cro 9B 88
SL4: W'sor 4B 4
TUESLEY 1F 152
Tuesley Cnr. GU7: Goda 8G 132
Tuesley La. GU7: Goda 8G 133
Tufton Gdns. KT8: W Mole 1B 40
Tugela Rd. CR0: Croy 5A 46
Tuggles Plat RH12: Warn 1E 196
Tugmutton Cl. BR6: Farnb 1K 67
Tugwood Cl. CR5: Coul 8H 83
Tulip Cl. CR0: Croy 7G 46
TW12: Hamp 7N 23
Tulip Ct. RH12: Hors 4J 197
Tulip Tree Ct. SM2: Sut 7M 61
Tulk Ho. KT16: Otter 4D 54
Tullett Rd. RH10: Craw 7F 182
Tulleys Farm 5A 184
Tulls La. GU35: Stand 7C 168
Tull St. CR4: Mit 6D 44
Tulse Cl. BR3: Beck 2M 47
TULSE HILL 2M 29
Tulse Hill SW2 . . . . .1L 29
Tulse Hill Est. SW2 . . . . .1L 29
Tulse Hill Station (Rail) 3M 29
Tulse Ho. SW2 . . . . .1L 29
Tulsemere Rd. SE27 . . . . .3N 29
Tulyar Cl. KT20: Tad 7G 81
Tumber Cl. GU12: Ash 2E 110
Tumber St. KT18: Head 3B 100
Tumblewood Rd. SM7: Ban 3K 81
Tumbling Bay KT12: Wal T 5H 39
Tummons Gdns. SE25 . . . . . . .1B 46
Tunbridge La.
GU30: Brams 8F 168
Tunley Rd. SW17 . . . . .2E 28
Tunnel Link Rd. TW6: Lon A 8B 8
Tunnel Rd. RH2: Reig 3M 121
RH6: Gat 2C 162
Tunnel Rd. E. TW6: Lon A 4C 8
Tunnel Rd. W. TW6: Lon A 4B 8
Tunnmeade RH11: Ifi 4K 181
Tunsgate
GU1: Guil 6D 202 (5N 113)
Tunsgate Sq. GU1: Guil 6C 202
Tunstall Cl. BR6: Orp 1N 67
Tunstall Rd. CR0: Croy 7B 46
Tunstall Wlk. TW8: Brent 2L 11
Tunworth Cres. SW15 . . . . .9E 12
Tupwood Ct. CR3: Cate 2D 104
Tupwood La. CR3: Cate 4D 104
Tupwood Scrubbs Rd.
CR3: Cate 6D 104
Turbary St. GU51: Fleet 1A 88
Turf Hill Rd. GU15: Camb 7D 50
Turfhouse La. GU24: Chob 5H 53
Turing Dr. RG12: Brac 5M 31
Turks Boatyard
KT1: K Tham 2H 203 (9K 25)
Turks Head Ct. SL4: Eton 3G 4
Turle Rd. SW16 . . . . .1J 45
Turnberry RG12: Brac 5K 31
Turner Av. CR4: Mit 9D 28
TN16: B Hil 8E 66
TW2: Twick 4C 24
Turner Cl. GU4: B'ham 9B 94
Turner Ct. *KT22: Leat 8G 78*
(off Highbury Dr.)
RH19: E Grin 7C 166
Turner Ho. RH5: B Grn 7J 139
TW1: Twick 9K 11
(off Clevedon Rd.)
Turner M. SM2: Sut 4N 61
Turner Pl. GU47: C Tow 9J 49
Turner Rd. KT3: N Mal 6C 42
Turners Cl. TW18: Stain 6K 21
TURNERS HILL 5D 184
Turners Hill Pk.
RH10: T Hil 4F 184
Turners Hill Rd.
RH10: Craw D 7B 164
RH10: Craw, Wor 3H 183
RH10: T Hil 4C 184
RH19: E Grin 4J 185
Turners La. KT12: Hers 3J 57
Turners Mead GU8: Chid 6F 172
Turners Mdw. Way
BR3: Beck 1J 47
Turner's Way CR0: Wad 8L 45
Turner Wlk. RH10: Craw 6D 182
Turneville Rd. W14 . . . . .2L 13
Turney Rd. SE21 . . . . .1N 29
Turnham Cl. GU2: Guil 7M 113
Turnham Grn. Ter. W4 . . . . . . .1D 12
Turnham Grn. Ter. M.
W4 . . . . .1D 12
Turnoak Av. GU22: Wok 7A 74
Turnoak La. GU22: Wok 7A 74
Turnoak Pk. SL4: W'sor 7B 4
Turnpike La. SM1: Sut 2A 62
Turnpike Link
CR0: Croy 3F 200 (8B 46)
Turnpike Pl. RH11: Craw 1B 182
Turnpike Rd. RG42: Brac 1J 31
Turnpike Way TW7: Isle 4G 10
Turnstone Cl. CR2: Sels 6H 65
Turnstone End GU46: Yate 9A 48
Turnville Cl. GU18: Ligh 6L 51
Turpin Rd. TW14: Felt 9G 9
Turpins Ri. GU20: Windl 1M 51
Turpin Way SM6: W'ton 4F 62
Turret Ct. RH19: E Grin 7M 165
Turtledove Av. RH10: T Hil . . .4F 184
Turville Ct. KT23: Book 3B 98
Tuscam Way GU15: Camb 2L 69
Tuscany Gdns.
RH10: Craw 9C 162
Tuscany Way GU46: Yate 2B 68
Tushmore Av. RH10: Craw 9C 162
Tushmore Ct. RH10: Craw 1C 182
Tushmore Cres.
RH10: Craw 9B 162
Tushmore La. RH10: Craw 1C 182
Tushmore Rdbt.
RH10: Craw 1B 182
Tussock Cl. RH11: Craw 5M 181
Tuxford Cl. RH10: Craw 5G 182
Tweed Cl. GU14: Cove 8K 69
Tweeddale Rd. SM5: Cars 7B 44
Tweed La. RH3: Brock 7N 119
RH11: Ifi 9L 161
Tweed Rd. SL3: Lang 2D 6
Tweedsmuir Cl. GU14: Cove . . .2J 89
Twelfth Av. KT20: Lwr K 4K 101
Twelve Acre Cl. KT23: Book . . .2N 97
Twelve Acre Cres.
GU14: Cove 9J 69
Twelve Trees Ho.
RG45: Crow 3H 49
(off Cambridge Rd.)
Tweseldown Race Course 8D 88
Tweseldown Rd.
GU52: C Cro 9C 88
TWICKENHAM 2G 25
Twickenham Baths 2G 25
Twickenham Bri.
TW1: Twick 8J 11
TW9: Rich 8J 11
Twickenham Cl. CR0: Bedd 9K 45
Twickenham Pl. *KT7: T Dit 8F 40*
(off Woodfield Rd.)
Twickenham Rd. TW7: Isle 8G 10
TW9: Rich 7J 11
TW11: Tedd 5G 24
(not continuous)
TW13: Hanw 4N 23
Twickenham Rugby Union Football Ground 9E 10
Twickenham Station (Rail) . . .1G 24
Twickenham Trad. Est.
TW1: Twick 9F 10
Twilley St. SW18 . . . . .1N 27
Twin Bridges Bus. Pk.
CR2: S Croy 3A 64
Twining Av. TW2: Twick 4C 24
Twinoaks KT11: Cob 9A 58
Twitten, The RH11: Craw 3A 182
Twitten La. RH19: Fel 6H 165
Two Rivers Retail Pk.
TW18: Stain 5G 21
Two Ways RH14: Loxw 4J 193
Twycross Rd. GU7: Goda 4G 132
RG40: W'ham 1D 30
Twyford Ct. GU2: Guil 3K 113
Twyford La. GU10: Wrec 5G 128
Twyford Rd. RG40: W'ham 9A 14
RG42: Bin 1H 15
SM5: Cars 7B 44
Twyhurst Ct. RH19: E Grin . . .7N 165
Twyne Cl. RH11: Craw 5L 181
Twyner Cl. RH6: Horl 7H 143
Twynersh Av. KT16: Chert 5H 37
Twynholm Mans. *SW6 . . . . . . .3K 13*
(off Lillie Rd.)
Tybenham Rd. SW19 . . . . .2M 43
Tychbourne Dr. GU4: Guil 9E 94
Tydcombe Rd. CR6: Warl 6F 84
Tye La. BR6: Farnb 2L 67
KT18: Head 5D 100
Tylden Way RH12: Hors 2M 197
Tylecroft Rd. SW16 . . . . .1J 45
Tylehost GU2: Guil 8K 93
Tylehurst Dr. RH1: Red 4D 122
Tyle Pl. SL4: O Win 8K 5
Tyler Gdns. KT15: Addl 1L 55
Tyler Rd. RH10: Craw 6B 182
Tylers Cl. RH9: Gods 8E 104
Tylers Ct. *GU6: Cranl 7M 155*
(off Rowland Rd.)
TYLER'S GREEN 7E 104
Tylers Path SM5: Cars 1D 62
Tyler Wlk. SL3: Lang 1B 6
Tymperley Ct. *RH13: Hors . . .5L 197*
(off King's Rd.)
Tynamara KT1: K Tham 7H 203
Tynan Cl. TW14: Felt 2H 23
Tyndalls GU26: Hind 5D 170
Tyne Cl. GU14: Cove 8K 69
RH10: Craw 4G 183
Tynedale Rd. RH3: Brock 7A 120
Tyne Ho.
KT2: K Tham 1H 203 (9K 25)
Tynemouth Rd. CR4: Mit 8E 28
Tynemouth St. SW6 . . . . .5N 13
Tynley Gro. GU4: J Wel 6N 93
Typhoon Cl. RG12: Brac 2B 32
Typhoon Way SM6: W'ton 4J 63
Tyrawley Rd. SW6 . . . . .4N 13
Tyrell Ct. SM5: Cars 1D 62
Tyrell Gdns. SL4: W'sor 6C 4
Tyrells Pl. GU1: Guil 4B 114
Tyrrell Sq. CR4: Mit 9C 28
TYRRELL'S WOOD 2N 99
Tyrwhitt Ct. *GU2: Guil 8L 93*
(off Grange Rd.)
Tythebarn Cl. GU4: B'ham 7D 94
Tytherton RG12: Brac 1A 32
Tyting Cotts. GU4: Guil 6E 114

U

Uckfield Gro. CR4: Mit 8E 28
Udney Pk. Rd. TW11: Tedd 7G 25
Uffington Dr. RG12: Brac 3C 32
Uffington Rd. SE27 . . . . .5L 29
Ujima Ct. SW16 . . . . .5J 29
Ullathorne Rd. SW16 . . . . .5G 28
Ullswater RG12: Brac 6K 31
Ullswater Av. GU14: Cove 2K 89
Ullswater Bus. Pk. CR5: Coul . . .3J 83
Ullswater Cl. GU9: U Hal 6F 108
GU18: Ligh 6M 51
SW15 . . . . .5C 26
Ullswater Ct. *GU12: A Va 8D 90*
(off Lakeside Cl.)
Ullswater Cres. CR5: Coul 3H 83
SW15 . . . . .5C 26
Ullswater Rd. GU18: Ligh 6M 51
SE27 . . . . .3M 29
SW13 . . . . .3F 12
Ulric Ho. GU51: Fleet 9A 68
Ulstan Cl. CR3: Wold 1K 105
Ulva Rd. SW15 . . . . .8J 13
Ulverstone Rd. SE27 . . . . .3M 29
Ulwin Av. KT14: Byf 9N 55
Umberstones GU25: V Wat 5N 35
Umbria St. SW15 . . . . .9F 12
Underhill Cl. GU7: Goda 8H 133
Underhill La. GU10: L Bou 4G 129
Underhill Pk. Rd.
RH2: Reig 9M 101
Underhill Rd. RH5: Newd 1A 160
Underwood CR0: N Add 2M 65
RG12: Brac 5K 31
Underwood Av. GU12: Ash . . .3C 110
Underwood Cl.
RH10: Craw D 1E 184
Underwood Ct. CR3: Cate 3B 104
RG42: Bin 7H 15
Underwood Ho.
KT8: W Mole 4A 40
(off Approach Rd.)
Underwood Rd. CR3: Cate 4B 104
GU27: Hasl 1D 188
Undine St. SW17 . . . . .6D 28
Unicorn Trad. Est.
GU27: Hasl 1F 188
Union Cl. GU47: Owls 5K 49
Union Ct. TW9: Rich 8L 11
Union Rd. CR0: Croy 6N 45
GU9: Farnh 1H 129
GU16: Deep 6H 71
Union St. GU11: Alde 2M 109
GU14: Farnb 1M 89
GU24: B'wood 8L 71
KT1: K Tham 3H 203 (1K 41)
Union Ter. GU11: Alde 2M 109
Unisport 3K 113
Unitair Cen. TW14: Bedf 9D 8
Unity Cl. CR0: N Add 5L 65
SE19 . . . . .6N 29
University College for the Creative Arts Epsom Campus 8K 201 (1D 80)
University Ct.
GU2: Guil 3A 202 (3L 113)
University of Surrey
Austin Pearce Building 3A 202 (3K 113)
St Mary's College 4F 24
University of Surrey Gallery *3K 113*
(in University of Surrey)
University Rd. SW19 . . . . .7B 28
Unstead La. GU5: Braml 4M 133
Unstead Wood
GU3: P'marsh 2M 133
UNSTED 6N 133
Unwin Av. TW14: Felt 8E 8
Unwin Mans. *W14 . . . . .2L 13*
(off Queen's Club Gdns.)
Unwin Rd. TW7: Isle 6E 10
Upavon Gdns. RG12: Brac 4D 32
Upcroft SL4: W'sor 6E 4
Updown Hill GU20: Windl 3A 52
Upfield CR0: Croy 9E 46
RH6: Horl 9E 142
Upfield Cl. RH6: Horl 1E 162
Upfold Cl. GU6: Cranl 4K 155
Upfold La. GU6: Cranl 5K 155
Upfolds Grn. GU4: B'ham 8E 94
Upgrove Mnr. Way
SW2 . . . . .1L 29
Upham Pk. Rd. W4 . . . . .1D 12
Upland Rd.
CR2: S Croy 8D 200 (2A 64)
CR3: Warl, Wold 7K 85
GU15: Camb 8B 50
SM2: Sut 4B 62
Uplands BR3: Beck 1K 47
CR6: Warl 5J 85
KT21: A'tead 7K 79
Uplands Cl. GU27: Hasl 9H 171
GU47: Sandh 7G 48
SW14 . . . . .8A 12
Uplands Dr. KT22: Oxs 1D 78
Uplands Rd. CR8: Ken 3N 83
GU9: Farnh 2K 129
Upland Way KT18: Tat C 5H 81
Uppark Gdns. RH12: Hors . . .2M 197
Up. Bourne La.
GU10: Wrec 6F 128
Up. Bourne Va.
GU10: Wrec 6F 128
Upper Bri. Rd. RH1: Red 3C 122
Up. Brighton Rd. KT6: Surb . . .5K 41
Up. Broadmoor Rd.
RG45: Crow 2H 49
Upper Butts TW8: Brent 2J 11
Up. Charles St.
GU15: Camb 9A 50
Up. Chobham Rd.
GU15: Camb 3E 70
Up. Church La.
GU9: Farnh 1G 129
Upper Cl. RH18: F Row 7H 187
Up. College Ride
GU15: Camb 7C 50
Upper Ct. Rd. CR3: Wold 1K 105
KT19: Eps 7B 60
Upper Dr. TN16: B Hil 5E 86
Upper Dunnymans
SM7: Ban 1L 81
UPPER EASHING 7D 132
Up. Edgeborough Rd.
GU1: Guil 4B 114
UPPER ELMERS END 4J 47
Up. Elmers End Rd.
BR3: Beck 3H 47
Up. Elms Rd. GU11: Alde 3M 109
Up. Fairfield Rd.
KT22: Leat 8H 79
Up. Farm Rd. KT8: W Mole 3N 39
UPPER GATTON 5B 102
Up. Gordon Rd.
GU15: Camb 1B 70
Upper Grn. E. CR4: Mit 2D 44
Upper Grn. W. CR4: Mit 1D 44
(not continuous)
Up. Grotto Rd. TW1: Twick 3F 24
Upper Gro. SE25 . . . . .3B 46
Up. Guildown Rd.
GU2: Guil 8A 202 (6L 113)
UPPER HALE 6H 109
Up. Hale Rd.
GU9: Hale, U Hal 5F 108

A-Z Surrey 293

Upper Halliford—Vincent Av.

UPPER HALLIFORD 3F 38
Up. Halliford By-Pass
TW17: Shep 4F 38
Up. Halliford Grn.
TW17: Shep 3F 38
Up. Halliford Rd.
TW17: Shep 2F 38
Upper Halliford Station (Rail)
. . . . .1F 38
Up. Ham Rd. TW10: Ham 5K 25
Upper Harestone
CR3: Cate 5D 104
Up. High St.
KT17: Eps 6L 201 (9D 60)
Up. House La.
GU5: Sha G 1H 155
UPPER IFOLD 1B 192
Upper Kiln RH4: Dork 7J 119
(off Stubs Hill)
Up. Lodge Way CR5: Coul 9H 83
Upper Mall W6 . . . . .1F 12
(not continuous)
Up. Manor Rd. GU7: Goda . . .4H 133
GU8: Mil 1B 152
Upper Mt. GU27: G'wood 8K 171
Up. Mulgrave Rd.
SM2: Chea 4K 61
UPPER NORWOOD 1A 46
Upper Nursery SL5: S'dale 4D 34
Up. Old Pk. La.
GU9: Farnh 7E 108
Upper Pk. Rd. GU15: Camb . . .1B 70
KT2: K Tham 7N 25
UPPER PARROCK 7N 187
Upper Path RH4: Dork 7H 119
Up. Pillory Down SM5: Cars . . .9E 62
Upper Pines SM7: Ban 4D 82
Up. Pinewood Rd.
GU12: Ash 1H 111
Up. Queen St. GU7: Goda 7H 133
(not continuous)
Up. Richmond Rd.
SW15 . . . . .7E 12
Up. Richmond Rd. W.
SW14 . . . . .7N 11
TW10, Rich 7N 11
Upper Rd. SM6: W'ton 2H 63
Up. Rose Hill
RH4: Dork 4K 201 (6H 119)
Up. St Michael's Rd.
GU11: Alde 4N 109
Upper Sawleywood
SM7: Ban 1L 81
Up. School Dr. GU27: Hasl . . .3D 188
Up. Selsdon Rd.
CR2: Sande, Sels 4C 64
UPPER SHIRLEY 1G 64
Up. Shirley Rd. CR0: Croy 8F 46
Up. South Vw. GU9: Farnh . . .9H 109
Upper Springfield GU8: Els . . .8J 131
Upper Sq. RH18: F Row 6H 187
TW7: Isle 6G 11
Upper Stanford GU24: Pirb . . .3C 92
Up. Star Post Ride
RG12: Brac 9N 31
Upper St. GU5: Shere 7A 116
(not continuous)
GU51: Fleet 4A 88
Up. Sunbury Rd.
TW12: Hamp 9M 23
Up. Sutton La. TW5: Hest 3A 10
Up. Teddington Rd.
KT1: H Wic 8J 25
Upperton Rd.
GU2: Guil 6A 202 (4M 113)
UPPER TOOTING 5D 28
Up. Tooting Pk. SW17 . . . . . .3D 28
Up. Tooting Rd. SW17 . . . . . .5D 28
Up. Tulse Hill SW2 . . . . .1K 29
Up. Union St.
GU11: Alde 2M 109
Up. Union Ter.
GU11: Alde 2M 109
UPPER VANN 8J 153
Up. Vann La. GU8: Hamb 9K 153
Up. Vernon Rd. SM1: Sut 2B 62
Up. Verran Rd.
GU15: Camb 3B 70
Up. Village Rd. SL5: S'hill 4N 33
Upper Wlk. GU25: V Wat 3A 36
Upper Warlingham Station (Rail)
. . . . .5D 84
Upper Way GU9: Farnh 4F 128
Up. West St. RH2: Reig 3L 121
Up. Weybourne La.
GU9: H End 4J 109
Up. Woodcote Village
CR8: Pur 8H 63
Upshire Gdns. RG12: Brac 3D 32
Upshot La. GU22: Pyr 4H 75
Upton GU21: Wok 4L 73
Upton Cl. GU14: Farnb 2B 90
Upton Dene SM2: Sut 4N 61
Upton Rd. CR7: T Hea 1A 46
TW3: Houn 6A 10
Upwood Rd. SW16 . . . . .9J 29
Urmston Dr. SW19 . . . . .2K 27
Usherwood Cl.
KT20: Box H 9A 100
Uvedale Cl. CR0: N Add 7N 65
Uvedale Cres. CR0: N Add 7N 65
Uvedale Rd. RH8: Oxt 8B 106
Uxbridge Ct. KT1: K Tham 8H 203
Uxbridge Rd.
KT1: K Tham 8G 203 (3K 41)
TW12: Hamp, H Hill 5A 24
TW13: Felt 3K 23

V

Vachery La. GU6: Cranl 2N 175
Vaillant Rd. KT13: Weybr 1D 56
Vale, The CR0: Croy 8G 47
CR5: Coul 1H 83
TW5: Hest 2M 9
TW14: Felt 9J 9
TW16: Sunb 7H 23
Vale Border CR0: Sels 7G 65
CR2: Sels 7G 65
Vale Cl. BR6: Farnb 1J 67
CR5: Coul 1J 83
GU10: L Bou 7H 129
GU21: Wok 3A 74
KT13: Weybr 9E 38
TW1: Twick 4G 24
Vale Cotts. SW15 . . . . .4D 26
Vale Ct. GU12: A Va 6E 90
KT13: Weybr 9E 38
Vale Cres. SW15 . . . . .5D 26
Vale Cft. KT10: Clay 5F 58
Vale Dr. RH12: Hors 6H 197
Vale Farm Rd. GU21: Wok 4A 74
Vale Ho. GU21: Wok 4A 74
Valentines RH14: Plais 3N 191
Valentines Lea
GU28: North 8D 190
Valentyne Cl. CR0: N Add 7A 66
Vale Pde. SW15 . . . . .4D 26
Valerie Ct. SM2: Sut 4N 61
Vale Rd. CR4: Mit 2H 45
GU12: A Va 6E 90
GU15: Camb 2M 69
(not continuous)
KT4: W Pk 9E 42
KT10: Clay 5E 58
KT13: Weybr 9E 38
KT19: Ewe 1E 60
SL4: W'sor 3C 4
SM1: Sut 1N 61
Vale Rd. Nth. KT6: Surb 8L 41
Vale Rd. Sth. KT6: Surb 8L 41
Valery Pl. TW12: Hamp 8A 24
Vale St. SE27 . . . . .4N 29
Vale Wood Dr. GU10: L Bou . . .7J 129
Vale Wood La.
GU26: G'hott 5A 170
(not continuous)
Valewood Rd. GU27: Hasl 4G 188
Valiant Pl. RG12: Brac 2A 32
Vallance By-Ways Gatwick
RH6: Char 4L 161
Valley, The GU2: Guil 7M 113
Valley Ct. CR3: Cate 9D 84
VALLEY END 3D 52
Valley End Rd. GU24: Chob . . .3D 52
Valleyfield Rd. SW16 . . . . . . .6K 29
Valley Gdns., The 1H 35
Valley Gdns. SW19 . . . . .8B 28
Valley La. GU10: L Bou 5H 129
Valley Leisure Pk. CR0: Wad . . .7J 45
Valley M. TW1: Twick 3F 24
Valley Point Ind. Est.
CR0: Bedd 6J 45
Valley Rd. CR8: Ken 2A 84
GU16: Deep, Frim 6E 70
SW16 . . . . .6K 29
Valley Trade Pk. CR0: Bedd 6J 45
(off Therapia La.)
Valley Vw. GU7: Goda 7G 132
GU47: Sandh 8F 48
TN16: B Hil 5E 86
Valley Vw. Gdns. CR8: Ken 2B 84
Valley Wlk. CR0: Croy 8F 46
Vallis Way KT9: Ches 1K 59
Valnay St. SW17 . . . . .6D 28
Valonia Gdns. SW18 . . . . .9L 13
Valroy Cl. GU15: Camb 9B 50
Vanbrugh Cl. RH11: Craw 6K 181
Vanbrugh Dr. KT12: Wal T 6K 39
Vanbrugh M. KT12: Wal T 6K 39
Vancouver Cl. KT19: Eps 7B 60
Vancouver Ct. RH6: Smal 8L 143
Vancouver Dr. RH11: Craw . . .9B 162
Vancouver Rd. TW10: Ham 5J 25
Vanderbilt Rd. SW18 . . . . . . .2N 27
Van Dyck Av. KT3: N Mal 6C 42
Vandyke RG12: Brac 5K 31
Vandyke Cl. RH1: Red 9D 102
SW15 . . . . .1J 27
Van Gogh Cl. TW7: Isle 6G 10
Vanguard Cl.
CR0: Croy 1A 200 (7M 45)
Vanguard Way SM6: W'ton 4J 63
TW6: Lon A 5F 8
VANN COMMON 9E 188
Vanneck Sq. SW15 . . . . .8F 12
Vanners RH10: Craw 2C 182
Vanners Pde. KT14: Byf 9N 55
Vann Farm Rd. RH5: Ockl 6E 158
Vann Lake RH5: Ockl 6F 158
Vann Lake Rd. RH5: Ockl 7F 158
Vann La. GU8: Chid, Hamb . . .9G 152
Vann Rd. GU27: Fern 9E 188
Vanquish Cl. TW2: Whitt 1A 24
Vansittart Est. SL4: W'sor 3F 4
Vansittart Rd. SL4: W'sor 4E 4
Vanston Pl. SW6 . . . . .3M 13
Vantage Ct. GU21: Wok 4N 73
Vantage Pl. TW14: Felt 9H 9
Vantage Point CR2: Sande 5A 64
Vantage W. TW8: Brent 1M 11
Vant Rd. SW17 . . . . .6D 28
Vapery La. GU24: Pirb 8A 72
Varley Way CR4: Mit 1B 44
Varna Rd. SW6 . . . . .3K 13
TW12: Hamp 9B 24
Varney Cl. GU14: Cove 9K 69
Varsity Dr. TW1: Twick 8E 10
Varsity Row SW14 . . . . .5B 12
Vaughan Almshouses
TW15: A'ford 6C 22
(off Feltham Hill Rd.)
Vaughan Cl. TW12: Hamp 7M 23
Vaughan Copse SL4: Eton 1G 4
Vaughan Ct. GU2: Guil 8L 93
(off Grange Rd.)
Vaughan Gdns. SL4: E Wic 1C 4
Vaughan Ho. SW4 . . . . .1G 29
Vaughan Rd. KT7: T Dit 6H 41
Vaughan Way
RH4: Dork 2H 201 (5G 118)
Vaux Cres. KT12: Hers 3J 57
Vauxhall Gdns.
CR2: S Croy 3N 63
Veals Mead CR4: Mit 9C 28
Vectis Gdns. SW17 . . . . .7F 28
Vectis Rd. SW17 . . . . .7F 28
Vector Point RH10: Craw 8D 162
Vegal Cres. TW20: Eng G 6L 19
Veitch Cl. TW14: Felt 1G 23
Vellum Dr. SM5: Cars 9E 44
Velmead Cl. GU52: Fleet 6C 88
Velmead Rd. GU52: Fleet 6B 88
Vencourt Pl. W6 . . . . .1F 12
Ventnor Rd. SM2: Sut 4N 61
Ventnor Ter. GU12: Alde 3A 110
Venton Cl. GU21: Wok 4L 73
Venus M. CR4: Mit 2C 44
Vera Rd. SW6 . . . . .4K 13
Verbania Way
RH19: E Grin 9D 166
Verbena Cl. UB7: W Dray 1M 7
Verbena Gdns. W6 . . . . .1F 12
Verdayne Av. CR0: Croy 8G 47
Verdayne Gdns.
CR6: Warl 3F 84
Verdun Rd. SW13 . . . . .2F 12
Vereker Dr. TW16: Sunb 2H 39
Vereker Rd. W14 . . . . .1K 13
Verge Wlk. GU11: Alde 5M 109
Verites GU7: Goda 4F 132
Vermont Rd. SM1: Sut 9N 43
SW18 . . . . .9N 13
Verne, The GU52: C Cro 8B 88
Verner Cl. GU35: Head 5D 168
Vernon Av. SW20 . . . . .1J 43
Vernon Cl. KT16: Otter 3F 54
KT19: Ewe 3B 60
RH12: Hors 4N 197
TW19: Stan 2N 21
Vernon Ct. GU9: Farnh 1F 128
SL5: Asc 2H 33
Vernon Dr. CR3: Cate 9N 83
SL5: Asc 1H 33
Vernon Mans. W14 . . . . .2L 13
(off Queen's Club Mans.)
Vernon Rd. SM1: Sut 2A 62
SW14 . . . . .6C 12
TW13: Felt 3G 22
Vernon Wlk. KT20: Tad 7J 81
Vernon Way GU2: Guil 2J 113
Vern Pl. TN16: Tats 8E 86
Verona Ct. TW15: A'ford 5C 22
W4 . . . . .1D 12
Verona Dr. KT6: Surb 8L 41
Veronica Gdns. SW16 . . . . . . .9G 28
Veronica Rd. SW17 . . . . .3F 28
Verralls GU22: Wok 4D 74
(not continuous)
Verran Rd. GU15: Camb 3B 70
SW12 . . . . .1F 28
Verulam Av. CR8: Pur 8G 63
Veryan GU21: Wok 4K 73
Vesey Cl. GU14: Farnb 9M 69
Vevers Rd. RH2: Reig 6A 122
Vibart Gdns. SW2 . . . . .1K 29
Vibia Cl. TW19: Stan 1M 21
Viburnum Ct. GU24: W End 9B 52
Vicarage Av. TW20: Egh 6D 20
Vicarage Cl. GU9: Farnh 4J 129
KT4: W Pk 8D 42
KT20: K'wood 2K 101
KT23: Book 3A 98
RH7: Ling 7N 145
RH12: Col 2H 199
Vicarage Ct. BR3: Beck 2H 47
TW14: Bedf 1D 22
TW20: Egh 7D 20
Vicarage Cres. TW20: Egh 6D 20
Vicarage Dr. BR3: Beck 1K 47
SW14 . . . . .8C 12
Vicarage Farm Ct.
TW5: Hest 3N 9
Vicarage Farm Rd.
TW3: Houn 5M 9
TW4: Houn 5M 9
TW5: Hest 4M 9
Vicarage Flds. KT12: Wal T 5K 39
Vicarage Gdns. CR4: Mit 2C 44
GU26: G'hott 6A 170
GU52: C Cro 9A 88
SL5: Asc 4L 33
SW14 . . . . .8B 12
Vicarage Ga. GU2: Guil 5K 113
Vicarage Ga. M.
KT20: K'wood 2K 101
Vicarage Hill GU9: Farnh 4J 129
GU10: L Bou 4J 129
RH14: Loxw 5J 193
TN16: Weste 4M 107
Vicarage Ho.
KT1: K Tham 3M 203
Vicarage La. GU9: Farnh 1G 129
(Lwr. Church La.)
GU9: Farnh 4J 129
(Vicarage Hill)
GU9: U Hal 5H 109
GU19: Bag 2E 50
GU23: Send 4E 94
GU27: Hasl 2D 188
GU46: Yate 8B 48
KT17: Ewe 5F 60
(not continuous)
KT20: K'wood 1K 101
KT22: Leat 9H 79
RH5: Cap 4K 159
RH6: Horl 7D 142
TW18: Lale 2L 37
TW19: Wray 2A 20
Vicarage Rd. CR0: Wad 9L 45
GU17: Haw 2K 69
GU19: Bag 3G 50
GU22: Wok 8B 74
GU24: Chob 7G 53
GU46: Yate 8A 48
KT1: H Wic 9J 25
KT1: K Tham . . .3H 203 (1K 41)
RH7: Ling 7N 145
RH10: Craw D 2D 184
SM1: Sut 9N 43
SW14 . . . . .8B 12
TW2: Twick 3E 24
TW2: Whitt 9C 10
TW11: Tedd 6G 24
TW16: Sunb 6G 23
TW18: Stain 4G 20
TW20: Egh 6C 20
Vicarage Wlk. GU7: Goda 6G 132
(off Borough Rd.)
KT12: Wal T 6H 39
RH19: E Grin 9B 166
Vicarage Way SL3: Coln 3E 6
Viceroy Ct.
CR0: Croy 1D 200 (7A 46)
Vickers Cl. SM6: W'ton 4K 63
Vickers Ct. TW19: Stan 9N 7
(off Whitley Cl.)
Vickers Dr. Nth.
KT13: Weybr 6N 55
Vickers Dr. Sth.
KT13: Weybr 7N 55
Vickers Rd. GU12: A Va 8D 90
Vickers Way TW4: Houn 8M 9
Victor Ct. RH10: Craw 9H 163
Victoria Almshouses
RH1: Red 9E 102
RH2: Reig 3A 122
Victoria Av. CR2: Sande 6N 63
GU15: Camb 1M 69
KT6: Surb 5K 41
KT8: W Mole 2B 40
SM6: W'ton 9E 44
TW3: Houn 8A 10
Victoria Cl. KT8: W Mole 2A 40
KT13: Weybr 9E 38
RH6: Horl 8E 142
TN8: Eden 3L 147
Victoria Cotts. TW9: Kew 4M 11
Victoria Ct. GU1: Guil 4C 202
GU4: Chil 9A 114
(off Station Row)
GU19: Bag 6J 51
GU51: Fleet 4A 88
RH1: Red 6E 122
RH13: Hors 6K 197
Victoria Cres. SW19 . . . . .8L 27
Victoria Dr. GU17: B'water 2H 69
SW19 . . . . .1J 27
Victoria Gdns. GU14: Cove 1J 89
GU51: Fleet 4A 88
RG40: W'ham 9D 14
TN16: B Hil 2E 86
TW5: Hest 4M 9
Victoria Ho. KT22: Leat 8J 79
Victoria La. UB3: Harl 1E 8
Victoria Mans. W14 . . . . .2L 13
(off Queen's Club Mans.)
Victoria M. KT13: Weybr 1B 56
(off Balfour Rd.)
RH11: Craw 3B 182
SW18 . . . . .2A 28
TW20: Eng G 7M 19
Victoria Pde. TW9: Kew 4N 11
(off Sandycombe Rd.)
Victoria Pl. GU21: Wok 3C 74
(off North Rd.)
KT10: Esh 1B 58
(off Esher Pk. Av.)
KT11: Cob 1J 77
KT17: Eps 5M 201 (8D 60)
TW9: Rich 8K 11
Victoria Rd. CR4: Mit 8C 28
CR5: Coul 2H 83
GU1: Guil 3E 202 (3A 114)
GU6: Cranl 7M 155
GU7: Goda 7H 133
GU9: Farnh 1H 129
GU11: Alde 2M 109
GU14: Farnb 1M 89
GU21: Knap 4G 72
GU22: Wok 4A 74
GU47: Owls 6K 49
GU51: Fleet 4A 88
KT1: K Tham . . .4L 203 (1M 41)
KT6: Surb 5K 41
KT13: Weybr 9E 38
KT15: Addl 1M 55
RH1: Red 4E 122
RH6: Horl 8E 142
RH11: Craw 3A 182
SL4: E Wic 1B 4
SL5: Asc 4L 33
SM1: Sut 2B 62
SW14 . . . . .6C 12
TN8: Eden 3L 147
TW1: Twick 1H 25
TW11: Tedd 7G 24
TW13: Felt 2J 23
TW18: Stain 4G 20
Victoria Sq. RH6: Horl 8E 142
(off Consort Way)
Victoria St. RH13: Hors 6K 197
SL4: W'sor 4G 4
TW20: Eng G 7M 19
Victoria Ter. GU26: G'hott 6A 170
(off Crossways Rd.)
RH4: Dork 3J 201 (5G 119)
RH19: E Grin 7A 166
Victoria Vs. TW9: Rich 6M 11
Victoria Wlk.
RG40: W'ham 9D 14
Victoria Way GU21: Wok 4A 74
KT13: Weybr 9E 38
RH19: E Grin 2B 186
Victor Rd. SL4: W'sor 6F 4
TW11: Tedd 5E 24
Victors Dr. TW12: Hamp 7M 23
Victor Wlk. RG12: Brac 2B 32
Victor Way GU14: Farnb 5J 89
Victory Av. SM4: Mord 4A 44
Victory Bus. Cen. TW7: Isle 7F 10
Victory Cl. TW19: Stan 2N 21
Victory Cotts. KT24: Eff 6M 97
Victory Pk. Rd. KT15: Addl 9L 37
(not continuous)
Victory Rd. KT16: Chert 7J 37
RH12: Hors 5H 197
SW19 . . . . .8A 28
Victory Rd. M. SW19 . . . . . . .8A 28
(off Victory Rd.)
Victory Way TW5: C'ford 1K 9
Vidler Cl. KT9: Ches 3J 59
View Cl. TN16: B Hil 3E 86
Viewfield Rd. SW18 . . . . .9L 13
Viewlands Av. TN16: Weste . . .7N 87
View Ter. RH7: Dorm 2C 166
Viggory La. GU21: Wok 2M 73
Vigo La. GU46: Yate 2B 68
Viking RG12: Brac 4K 31
Viking Ct. SW6 . . . . .2M 13
Viking Ho. RH6: L Hea 5B 162
VILLAGE, THE 4D 18
Village, The GU6: Ewh 4E 156
Village Cl. KT13: Weybr 9E 38
Village Ct. KT13: Weybr 1E 56
(off Oatlands Dr.)
Village Gdns. KT17: Ewe 6E 60
Village Ga. TW17: Shep 4C 38
Village Grn. Av.
TN16: B Hil 4G 87
Village Grn. Way
TN16: B Hil 4G 87
Village Health Club, The 9N 83
Village Rd. TW20: Thor 2E 36
Village Row SM2: Sut 4M 61
Village Sq., The
CR5: Coul 9H 83
Village St. RH5: Newd 1A 160
Village Way BR3: Beck 1K 47
CR2: Sande 9D 64
GU6: Cranl 7M 155
GU46: Yate 8C 48
TW15: A'ford 5A 22
Villas, The RH7: Blin H 3H 145
Villiers, The
KT13: Weybr 3E 56
Villiers Av.
KT5: Surb 8L 203 (4M 41)
TW2: Whitt 2N 23
Villiers Cl.
KT5: Surb 8M 203 (3M 41)
Villiers Ct. SL4: W'sor 3D 4
Villiers Gro. SM2: Chea 5J 61
Villiers Ho. SL4: Eton 1F 4
(off Common La.)
Villiers Path KT6: Surb 4L 41
Villiers Rd. BR3: Beck 1G 47
KT1: K Tham . . .7L 203 (3M 41)
TW7: Isle 5E 10
Vimy Cl. TW4: Houn 8N 9
Vinall Gdns. RH12: Bro H 4D 196
Vincam Cl. TW2: Whitt 1A 24
Vincent Av. KT5: Surb 8B 42
SM5: Cars 7B 62

Vincent Cl.—Warltersville Way

Vincent Cl. CR5: Chip 7D 82
KT10: Esh 9B 40
KT16: Chert 6G 37
KT22: Fetc 1B 98
RH13: Hors 6M 197
UB7: Sip 2B 8
Vincent Ct. GU51: Fleet 4B 88
Vincent Dr.
RH4: Dork 4H 201 (6G 118)
TW17: Shep 2F 38
Vincent La.
RH4: Dork 2H 201 (5G 118)
Vincent Ri. RG12: Brac 2C 32
Vincent Rd. CR0: Croy 6B 46
CR5: Coul 3G 82
KT1: K Tham 2N 41
KT11: Sto D 3M 77
KT16: Chert 6G 37
RH4: Dork 3H 201 (5G 118)
TW4: Houn 5L 9
TW7: Isle 4D 10
Vincent Row TW12: H Hill 7C 24
Vincent Sq. TN16: B Hil 9E 66
Vincent Wlk. *RH4: Dork 2J 201*
(off South St.)
Vincent Works
RH4: Dork 3H 201 (5G 118)
Vine Cl. GU3: Worp 4G 93
GU10: Wrec 7F 128
GU11: Alde 7M 89
KT5: Surb 5M 41
RH5: Holm 4J 139
SM1: Sut 9A 44
TW19: Stan M 8J 7
UB7: W Dray 1B 8
Vine Cotts. GU6: Cranl 7K 155
GU28: North 8D 190
Vine Ct. KT12: Hers 3K 57
Vine Ho. Cl. GU16: Mytc 2E 90
Vine La. GU10: Wrec 6F 128
Vine Pl. TW3: Houn 7B 10
Viner Cl. KT12: Wal T 5K 39
Vineries Cl. UB7: Sip 2B 8
Vine Rd. KT8: E Mol 3C 40
SW13 . . . . .6E 12
Vine Sq. *W14 . . . . .1L 13*
(off Star Rd.)
Vine St. GU11: Alde 3M 109
Vine Way GU10: Wrec 6F 128
Vineyard, The TW10: Rich 8L 11
Vineyard Cl.
KT1: K Tham . . .5L 203 (2M 41)
Vineyard Hill Rd.
SW19 . . . . .5L 27
Vineyard M. TW10: Rich 8L 11
Vineyard Pas. TW10: Rich 8L 11
Vineyard Path *SW14 . . . . .6C 12*
(off Church Path)
SW14 . . . . .6C 12
(Sheen La.)
Vineyard Rd. TW13: Felt 4H 23
Vineyard Row KT1: H Wic 9J 25
Vineyards, The *TW13: Felt 4H 23*
(off High St.)
TW16: Sunb 2H 39
Viney Bank CR0: Sels 5J 65
Vinter Ct. TW17: Shep 4B 38
Viola Av. TW14: Felt 9K 9
TW19: Stan 2M 21
Viola Cft. RG42: Warf 9D 16
Violet Cl. SM3: Sut 7K 43
SM6: W'ton 7E 44
Violet Gdns.
CR0: Wad 8A 200 (2M 63)
Violet La.
CR0: Wad 8A 200 (3M 63)
Virgin Active 2B 182
Virgin Active TW16: Sunb 9H 23
Virginia Av. GU25: V Wat 4M 35
Virginia Beeches
GU25: V Wat 2L 35
Virginia Cl. KT3: N Mal 3B 42
KT13: Weybr 3D 56
KT21: A'tead 5K 79
TW18: Lale 2L 37
Virginia Ct. GU25: V Wat 3N 35
Virginia Dr. GU25: V Wat 4M 35
Virginia Gdns. GU14: Farnb 3A 90
Virginia Ho. TW11: Tedd 6H 25
Virginia Pk. GU25: V Wat 3A 36
Virginia Pl. KT11: Cob 1H 77
Virginia Rd. CR7: T Hea 9M 29
Virginia Wlk. SW2 . . . . .1K 29
VIRGINIA WATER 4A 36
Virginia Water 2H 35
Virginia Water Station (Rail)
. . . . .4A 36
Viscount Cl. GU12: A Va 8D 90
Viscount Ct. SL4: W'sor 4F 4
Viscount Gdns. KT14: Byf 8N 55
Viscount Ind. Est. SL3: Poy 6G 6
Viscount Rd. TW19: Stan 2N 21
Viscount Way TW6: Lon A 7F 8
Vista Ho. *SW19 . . . . .9B 28*
(off Chapter Way)
Vivenne Ho. TW18: Stain 6J 21
Vivian Cl. GU52: C Cro 7C 88
Vivien Cl. KT9: Ches 4L 59
Vivienne Cl. RH11: Craw 9B 162
TW1: Twick 9K 11
Vixen Dr. GU12: Alde 1C 110
Voewood Cl. KT3: N Mal 5E 42
Vogan Cl. RH2: Reig 6N 121
Volta Way CR0: Wad 7K 45
Voss Ct. SW16 . . . . .7J 29
Vowels La. RH19: E Grin 8F 184
Vue Cinema
Croydon, Hesterman Way
. . . . .7K 45
Croydon, High St.
. . . . .4C 200 (9N 45)
Fulham Broadway 3M 13
Staines 5G 21
Vulcan Bus. Cen.
CR0: N Add 5A 66
Vulcan Cl. GU47: Sandh 8F 48
RH11: Craw 7A 182
Vulcan Ct. GU47: Sandh 8F 48
Vulcan Dr. RG12: Brac 2A 32
Vulcan Way CR0: N Add 6A 66
GU47: Sandh 8F 48
SM6: W'ton 5J 63

W

Wadbrook St.
KT1: K Tham 4H 203 (1K 41)
Waddington Av. CR5: Coul 7L 83
Waddington Cl. CR5: Coul 6M 83
RH11: Craw 6M 181
Waddington Way SE19 . . . . . . .8N 29
WADDON 9L 45
Waddon Cl. CR0: Wad 9L 45
Waddon Ct. Rd. CR0: Wad 9L 45
Waddon Marsh Stop (CT) 8L 45
Waddon Marsh Way
CR0: Wad 7K 45
Waddon New Rd.
CR0: Croy 4A 200 (9M 45)
Waddon Pk. Av. CR0: Wad 1L 63
Waddon Rd.
CR0: Croy, Wad
. . . . .4A 200 (9L 45)
Waddon Station (Rail) 1L 63
Waddon Way CR0: Wad 3L 63
Wades La. TW11: Tedd 6G 24
Wadham GU47: Owls 6L 49
Wadham Cl. RH10: Craw 9G 162
TW17: Shep 6D 38
Wadham Rd. SW15 . . . . .7K 13
Wadhurst Cl. SE20 . . . . .1E 46
Wadlands Brook Rd.
RH19: E Grin 5N 165
Wagbullock Ri. RG12: Brac 5A 32
Wagg Cl. RH19: E Grin 9C 166
Waggon Cl. GU2: Guil 2H 113
Waggoners Hollow
GU19: Bag 5J 51
WAGGONERS RDBT. 4J 9
Waggoners Way
GU26: G'hott 6M 169
Waggoners Wells La.
GU26: G'hott 6M 169
Wagner M. *KT6: Surb 4L 41*
(off Avenue Elmers)
Wagon Yd. GU9: Farnh 1G 129
Wagtail Cl. RH12: Hors 1K 197
Wagtail Gdns. CR2: Sels 6H 65
Wagtail Wlk. BR3: Beck 4M 47
Waight's Ct.
KT2: K Tham 1K 203 (9L 25)
Wain End RH12: Hors 3K 197
Wainford Cl. SW19 . . . . .2J 27
Wainhouse Cl. TN8: Eden 9M 127
Wainscot SL5: S'dale 5C 34
Wainwright Cl.
RG40: W'ham 2F 30
Wainwright Gro. TW7: Isle 7D 10
Wainwrights RH10: Craw 6B 182
Wait Ct. *CR0: Croy 5M 45*
(off Goodman Ct.)
Wake Cl. GU2: Guil 7L 93
Wake Ct. GU2: Guil 9L 93
Wakefield Cl. KT14: Byf 8N 55
Wakefield Ct. RH12: Hors 6H 197
Wakefield Rd. TW10: Rich 8K 11
Wakefords Cl. GU11: Alde 7B 90
Wakefords Copse
GU52: C Cro 1C 108
Wakefords Pk. GU52: C Cro . . .1C 108
(not continuous)
Wakehams Grn. Dr.
RH10: Craw 9H 163
Wakehurst Dr. RH10: Craw . . .6B 182
Wakehurst M. RH12: Hors 7F 196
Wakehurst Path GU21: Wok . . .1E 74
Wakely Cl. TN16: B Hil 5E 86
Walburton Rd. CR8: Pur 9G 63
Walbury RG12: Brac 3C 32
Waldby Ct. RH11: Craw 6M 181
Waldeck Gro. SE27 . . . . .4M 29
Waldeck Rd. SW14 . . . . .6B 12
W4 . . . . .2N 11
Waldeck Ter. *SW14 . . . . .6B 12*
(off Waldeck Rd.)
Waldegrave Gdns.
TW1: Twick 3F 24
Waldegrave Pk. TW1: Twick . . .5F 24
Waldegrave Rd. TW1: Twick . . .5F 24
TW11: Tedd 5F 24
Waldegrove CR0: Croy 9C 46
Waldemar Av. SW6 . . . . .4K 13
Waldemar Rd. SW19 . . . . .6M 27
Walden Cotts. GU3: Norm 1L 111
Walden Gdns. CR7: T Hea 2K 45
Waldens Pk. Rd.
GU21: Wok 3M 73
Waldens Rd. GU21: Wok 4N 73
Waldo Pl. CR4: Mit 8C 28
Waldorf Cl. CR2: S Croy 5M 63
Waldorf Hgts. GU17: Haw 3J 69
Waldron Gdns. BR2: Brom 2N 47
Waldron Hill RG12: Brac 9D 16
Waldronhyrst
CR2: S Croy . . .7A 200 (1M 63)
Waldron Rd. SW18 . . . . .4A 28
Waldrons, The
CR0: Croy 7A 200 (1M 63)
RH8: Oxt 9B 106
Waldron's Path
CR2: S Croy . . .7B 200 (1N 63)
Waldy Ri. GU6: Cranl 6N 155
Waleron Rd. GU51: Fleet 1A 88
Wales Av. SM5: Cars 2C 62
Walesbeech RH10: Craw 4E 182
Waleton Acres
SM6: W'ton 3G 63
Waley's La. RH5: Ockl 8C 158
Walford Rd. RH5: Nth H 9H 119
WALHAM GREEN 4M 13
Walham Grn. Ct. *SW6 . . . . .3N 13*
(off Waterford Rd.)
Walham Gro. SW6 . . . . .3M 13
Walham Ri. SW19 . . . . .7K 27
Walham Yd. SW6 . . . . .3M 13
Walhatch Cl. RH18: F Row 7H 187
Walk, The RH8: Tand 2K 125
SL4: E Wic 1D 4
TW16: Sunb 8G 22
Walker Cl. TW12: Hamp 7N 23
TW14: Felt 1G 22
Walker Cres. SL3: Lang 1B 6
Walker Rd. RH10: Craw 5F 182
Walkerscroft Mead
SE21 . . . . .2N 29
Walkers Pl. SW15 . . . . .7K 13
Walker's Ridge
GU15: Camb 2C 70
Walkfield Dr. KT18: Tat C 4G 81
Walking Bottom
GU5: P'lake 5D 136
Wallace Cl. GU3: Worp 9F 92
TW17: Shep 3E 38
Wallace Cres. SM5: Cars 2D 62
Wallace Flds. KT17: Eps 9F 60
Wallace Sq. CR5: Coul 9H 83
Wallace Wlk. KT15: Addl 1L 55
SL4: Eton 1J 5
Wallace Way GU11: Alde 1L 109
Wallage La. RH10: Row 3N 183
Wallbrook Bus. Cen.
TW4: Houn 6J 9
Wallcroft Cl. RG42: Bin 8K 15
Walldown Rd.
GU35: White 8A 168
Walled Gdn., The KT20: Tad . . .9J 81
RH3: Betch 4C 120
RH14: Loxw 1H 193
Walled Gdn. Cl. BR3: Beck 3L 47
Waller La. CR3: Cate 1C 104
WALL HILL 5G 186
Wall Hill Rd.
RH19: Ash W, F Row 4F 186
Wallingford Cl. RG12: Brac 3C 32
WALLINGTON 3F 62
Wallington Cnr. *SM6: W'ton 1F 62*
(off Manor Rd. Nth.)
Wallington Ct. *SM6: W'ton 3F 62*
(off Stanley Pk. Rd.)
WALLINGTON GREEN 1F 62
Wallington Rd.
GU15: Camb 6E 50
Wallington Sq. SM6: W'ton 3F 62
Wallington Station (Rail) 3F 62
Wallis Ct. RH10: Craw 8D 162
Wallis Ho. *RH19: E Grin 9A 166*
(off Orchard Way)
Wallis M. KT22: Leat 9G 78
Wallis's Cotts. SW2 . . . . .1J 29
Wallis Way RH13: Hors 4N 197
WALLISWOOD 9L 157
Wallis Wood Nature Reserve
. . . . .8M 157
Wallner Way RG40: W'ham 3D 30
Wallorton Gdns. SW14 . . . . . . .7C 12
Walls Ct. GU16: Frim 6C 70
Walmer Cl. BR6: Farnb 1M 67
GU16: Frim 7E 70
RG45: Crow 2H 49
Walmer Ct. KT5: Surb 8K 203
Walnut Cl. GU11: Alde 4M 109
GU46: Yate 2C 68
KT18: Eps 2E 80
SM5: Cars 2D 62
Walnut Ct. RH13: Hors 7L 197
Walnut Dr. KT20: K'wood 2K 101
Walnut Flds. KT17: Ewe 5E 60
Walnut Gro. SM7: Ban 1J 81
Walnut Ho. RH2: Reig 5A 122
Walnut La. RH11: Craw 9N 161
Walnut M. SM2: Sut 4A 62
Walnuts, The RH12: Hors 4J 197
Walnut Tree Av. *CR4: Mit 2C 44*
(off Dearn Gdns.)
Walnut Tree Cl.
GU1: Guil 2A 202 (3M 113)
SM7: Ban 8K 61
SW13 . . . . .4E 12
Walnut Tree Cl.
TN16: Weste 4M 107
TW17: Shep 2D 38
Walnut Tree Cotts.
SW19 . . . . .6K 27
Walnut Tree Gdns.
GU7: Goda 4H 133
Walnut Tree Ho. *SW10 . . . . . . .2N 13*
(off Tregunter Rd.)
Walnut Tree La. KT14: Byf 8M 55
Walnut Tree Pk.
GU1: Guil 2A 202 (3M 113)
Walnut Tree Pl.
GU23: Send 1F 94
Walnut Tree Rd. TW5: Hest 2N 9
TW8: Brent 2L 11
TW17: Shep 1D 38
Walpole Av. CR5: Chip 6D 82
TW9: Kew 5M 11
Walpole Ct. TW2: Twick 3E 24
Walpole Cres. TW11: Tedd 6F 24
Walpole Gdns. TW2: Twick 3E 24
W4 . . . . .1B 12
Walpole Ho. *KT8: W Mole 4A 40*
(off Approach Rd.)
SL4: Eton 2F 4
(off Eton Wick Rd.)
Walpole M. SW19 . . . . .7B 28
Walpole Pk. KT13: Weybr 4B 56
Walpole Pl. TW11: Tedd 6F 24
Walpole Rd.
CR0: Croy 2D 200 (8A 46)
KT6: Surb 6L 41
SL4: O Win 1L 19
SW19 . . . . .7B 28
TW2: Twick 3E 24
TW11: Tedd 6F 24
Walsham Rd. TW14: Felt 1J 23
Walsh Av. RG42: Warf 8C 16
Walsh Cres. CR0: N Add 8A 66
Walsingham Gdns.
KT19: Ewe 1D 60
Walsingham Lodge
SW13 . . . . .4F 12
Walsingham Mans.
SW6 . . . . .3N 13
(off Fulham Rd.)
Walsingham Rd.
CR0: N Add 6M 65
CR4: Mit 4D 44
Walstead Ct. RH10: Craw 4B 182
Walstead Ho. RH10: Craw 4B 182
Walters Mead KT21: A'tead 4L 79
Walters Rd. SE25 . . . . .3B 46
Walter St.
KT2: K Tham 2J 203 (9L 25)
Waltham Av. GU2: Guil 8L 93
Waltham Cl. GU47: Owls 6J 49
Waltham Rd. CR3: Cate 9E 84
SM5: Cars 6B 44
Walton & Hersham FC 8H 39
Walton Av. KT3: N Mal 3E 42
SM3: Chea 9L 43
Walton Bri. KT12: Wal T 6F 38
TW17: Shep 6F 38
Walton Bri. Rd.
TW17: Shep 6F 38
Walton Cl. GU51: Fleet 5A 88
Walton Ct. CR2: S Croy 8C 200
GU21: Wok 3C 74
Walton Dr. RH13: Hors 4A 198
SL5: Asc 9K 17
Walton Gdns. TW13: Felt 5G 22
Walton Grn. CR0: N Add 5L 65
WALTON HEATH 5E 100
Walton Heath RH10: Craw 1H 183
Walton Heath Golf Course
. . . . .4G 101
Walton La. KT13: Weybr 8C 38
TW17: Shep 6E 38
WALTON-ON-THAMES 7H 39
Walton-on-Thames Station (Rail)
. . . . .1H 57
WALTON ON THE HILL 2F 100
Walton Pk. KT12: Wal T 8L 39
Walton Pk. La. KT12: Wal T . . .8L 39
Walton Rd. GU21: Wok 3B 74
KT8: W Mole, E Mol 3N 39
KT12: Wal T 4K 39
KT18: Eps D 4E 80
KT18: Eps D, Head 8B 80
Walton Screen Cinema 7H 39
Walton St. KT20: Wal H 2F 100
Walton Ter. GU21: Wok 2D 74
Walton Way CR4: Mit 3G 44
WANBOROUGH 6N 111
Wanborough Bus. Cen.
GU3: Flex 4B 112
WANBOROUGH COMMON . . .9C 112
Wanborough Dr.
SW15 . . . . .2G 26
Wanborough Hill
GU3: Wan 6N 111
Wanborough La.
GU6: Cranl 6B 156
Wanborough Station (Rail)
. . . . .3N 111
Wandle Bank CR0: Bedd 9J 45
SW19 . . . . .8B 28
Wandle Cl. GU12: Ash 3E 110
RH10: Craw 4G 182
Wandle Ct. CR0: Bedd 9J 45
KT19: Ewe 1B 60
Wandle Ct. Gdns.
CR0: Bedd 9J 45
Wandle Industrial Mus.
(within The Vestry Hall Annexe)
. . . . .2D 44
Wandle Meadow Nature Pk.
. . . . .6A 28
Wandle Park Stop (CT) 8L 45
Wandle Pk. Trad. Est., The
CR0: Croy 7M 45
Wandle Recreation Cen. 9N 13
Wandle Rd. CR0: Bedd 9J 45
CR0: Croy 5C 200 (9N 45)
SM4: Mord 3A 44
SM6: W'ton 9F 44
SW17 . . . . .3C 28
Wandle Side CR0: Wad 9K 45
SM6: W'ton 9F 44
Wandle Technology Pk.
CR4: Mit 6D 44
Wandle Trad. Est. CR4: Mit . . .6D 44
Wandle Way CR4: Mit 4D 44
SW18 . . . . .2N 27
Wandon Rd. SW6 . . . . .3N 13
(not continuous)
Wandsdown Pl. SW6 . . . . .3N 13
WANDSWORTH 8N 13
Wandsworth Bri. SW6 . . . . . . .6N 13
Wandsworth Bri. Rd.
SW6 . . . . .4N 13
WANDSWORTH COMMON 2D 28
Wandsworth Common Station (Rail)
. . . . .2D 28
WANDSWORTH GYRATORY
. . . . .8N 13
Wandsworth High St.
SW18 . . . . .8M 13
Wandsworth Mus. 8N 13
Wandsworth Plain
SW18 . . . . .8N 13
Wandsworth Town Station (Rail)
. . . . .7N 13
Wanmer Ct. *RH2: Reig 2M 121*
(off Birkheads Rd.)
Wansdyke Cl. GU16: Frim 6D 70
Wansford Grn. GU21: Wok 4J 73
Wanstraw Gro. RG12: Brac 6C 32
Wantage Cl. RG12: Brac 4C 32
RH10: Craw 6G 182
Wantage Rd. GU47: C Tow 7J 49
Waplings, The
KT20: Wal H 2G 100
Wapses Lodge CR3: Wold 7E 84
WAPSES LODGE RDBT. 7E 84
Wapshott Rd. TW18: Stain 7G 20
Warbank Cl. CR0: N Add 6A 66
Warbank Cres. CR0: N Add 6A 66
Warbank La. KT2: K Tham 8E 26
Warbeck Ho. *KT13: Weybr 2E 56*
(off Queens Rd.)
Warbler's Grn. KT11: Cob 1N 77
Warbleton Ho.
RH11: Craw 6L 181
(off Salvington Rd.)
Warboys App. KT2: K Tham 7A 26
Warboys Rd. KT2: K Tham 7A 26
Warburton Cl.
RH19: E Grin 9C 166
Warburton Rd. TW2: Whitt 2B 24
Warbury La. GU21: Knap 2E 72
War Coppice Rd. CR3: Cate . . .5A 104
Ward Cl. CR2: S Croy 3B 64
RG40: W'ham 9C 14
Wardens Fld. Cl.
BR6: Chels 3N 67
Ward La. CR6: Warl 3F 84
Wardle Cl. GU19: Bag 4J 51
Wardley St. SW18 . . . . .1N 27
Wardo Av. SW6 . . . . .4K 13
Ward Rd. SW19 . . . . .9A 28
Wardrobe, The *TW9: Rich 8K 11*
(off Old Palace Rd.)
Ward Royal SL4: W'sor 4F 4
Ward Royal Pde. *SL4: W'sor 4F 4*
(off Alma Rd.)
Ward's Pl. TW20: Egh 7E 20
Wards Stone Pk.
RG12: Brac 6C 32
Ward St.
GU1: Guil 5D 202 (4N 113)
Ware Ct. SM1: Sut 1L 61
Wareham Cl. TW3: Houn 7B 10
Wareham Rd. RG12: Brac 4D 32
Warehouse Theatre
. . . . .2E 200 (8A 46)
Warenne Rd. KT22: Fetc 9C 78
WARFIELD 4C 16
WARFIELD PARK 8E 16
Warfield Rd. RG12: Brac 7A 16
RG42: Brac 7A 16
TW12: Hamp 9B 24
TW14: Felt 1F 22
Warfield St. RG42: Warf 6A 16
Wargrove Dr. GU47: C Tow 7J 49
Warham Rd.
CR2: S Croy 8A 200 (2M 63)
Waring St. SE27 . . . . .5N 29
Warkworth Gdns. TW7: Isle 3G 10
WARLINGHAM 5G 84
Warlingham Rd.
CR7: T Hea 3M 45
Warltersville Way
RH6: Horl 1G 162

Warminster Gdns.—Wellesley Dr.

Warminster Gdns.
SE25 . . . 1D 46
Warminster Rd. SE25 . . . 1C 46
Warminster Sq. SE25 . . . 1D 46
Warminster Way CR4: Mit . . . 9F 28
Warner Av. SM3: Chea . . . 8K 43
Warner Cl. RH10: Craw . . . 7G 182
TW12: Hamp . . . 6N 23
UB3: Harl . . . 3E 8
Warner Ct. GU47: C Tow . . . 8K 49
Warners La. GU5: Alb . . . 1N 135
KT2: K Tham . . . 5K 25
Warnford Ho. *SW15* . . . *9D 12*
(off Tunworth Cres.)
WARNHAM . . . 9F 178
Warnham Ct. RH12: Warn . . . 1F 196
Warnham Ct. M.
RH12: Warn . . . 1F 196
Warnham Ct. Rd.
SM5: Cars . . . 4D 62
Warnham Ho. *SW2* . . . *1K 29*
(off Up. Tulse Hill)
Warnham Mnr.
RH12: Warn . . . 1C 196
Warnham Nature Reserve . . . 3H 197
Warnham Pk. . . . 2F 196
Warnham Rd. RH10: Craw . . . 5E 182
RH12: Bro H . . . 4D 196
RH12: Warn, Hors . . . 3H 197
Warnham Station (Rail) . . . 9J 179
Warramill Rd. GU7: Goda . . . 6K 133
Warre Ho. *SL4: Eton* . . . *1F 4*
(off Common La.)
WARREN, THE
GU6 . . . 1C 156
RG12 . . . 3D 32
Warren, The GU9: H End . . . 4K 109
GU11: Alde . . . 3L 109
GU30: Pass . . . 9D 168
KT4: W Pk . . . 1C 60
KT20: K'wood . . . 1K 101
KT21: A'tead . . . 6L 79
KT22: Oxs . . . 8C 58
KT24: E Hor . . . 8G 96
RG12: Brac . . . 3D 32
SM5: Cars . . . 5B 62
TW5: Hest . . . 3N 9
Warren Av. BR6: Chels . . . 2N 67
CR2: Sels . . . 4G 64
SM2: Chea . . . 6L 61
TW10: Rich . . . 7A 12
Warren Cl. GU47: Sandh . . . 7F 48
GU52: Fleet . . . 6C 88
KT10: Esh . . . 1B 58
RH19: Fel . . . 7H 165
SE21 . . . 1N 29
WARREN CORNER . . . 5C 108
Warren Cnr. GU10: Ews . . . 5B 108
Warren Cotts. RH17: Hand . . . 8N 199
Warren Ct. CR0: Croy . . . 7B 46
KT13: Weybr . . . 2B 56
Warren Cutting
KT2: K Tham . . . 8C 26
Warren Down RG42: Brac . . . 9K 15
Warren Dr. KT20: K'wood . . . 9L 81
RH11: Craw . . . 2M 181
Warren Dr. Nth. KT5: Surb . . . 7A 42
Warren Dr. Sth. KT5: Surb . . . 7B 42
Warreners La. KT13: Weybr . . . 4E 56
Warren Farm Mobile Home Pk.
GU22: Pyr . . . 6K 75
Warren Footpath
TW1: Twick . . . 2J 25
Warren Hill KT18: Eps . . . 3C 80
Warren Ho. Rd.
RG40: W'ham . . . 9B 14
Warrenhyrst GU1: Guil . . . 4C 114
Warren La. GU5: Alb . . . 8L 115
GU22: Pyr . . . 5J 75
KT22: Oxs . . . 7C 58
RH8: Oxt . . . 3C 126
Warren Lodge
KT20: K'wood . . . 2K 101
Warren Lodge Dr.
KT20: K'wood . . . 2K 101
Warren Mead SM7: Ban . . . 2H 81
Warrenne Hgts. RH1: Red . . . 5B 122
Warrenne Rd. RH3: Brock . . . 5B 120
Warrenne Way RH2: Reig . . . 3M 121
Warren Pk. CR6: Warl . . . 5G 84
GU8: Thur . . . 5K 151
KT2: K Tham . . . 7B 26
KT20: Box H . . . 9B 100
Warren Pk. Rd. SM1: Sut . . . 3B 62
Warren Ri. GU16: Frim . . . 4C 70
KT3: N Mal . . . 9C 26
Warren Rd. BR6: Chels . . . 2N 67
CR0: Croy . . . 7C 46
CR8: Pur . . . 8M 63
GU1: Guil . . . 4B 114
GU7: Goda . . . 4H 133
KT2: K Tham . . . 7B 26
KT15: N Haw . . . 6J 55
RH2: Reig . . . 2N 121
SM7: Ban . . . 1H 81
SW19 . . . 7C 28
TW2: Whitt . . . 9C 10
TW15: A'ford . . . 8F 22
Warren Row SL5: Asc . . . 1H 33
Warren Way KT13: Weybr . . . 2D 56
Warrington Cl.
RH11: Craw . . . 7K 181
Warrington Ct. CR0: Wad . . . 5A 200
Warrington M. GU11: Alde . . . 4K 109
Warrington Rd.
CR0: Wad . . . 5A 200 (9M 45)
TW10: Rich . . . 8K 11
Warrington Spur
SL4: O Win . . . 1L 19
Warsop Trad. Est.
TN8: Eden . . . 3M 147
Warwark Ct. KT6: Surb . . . 8L 41
Warwick RG12: Brac . . . 5C 32
W14 . . . *1L 13*
(off Kensington Village)
Warwick Av. TW18: Stain . . . 7L 21
TW20: Egh . . . 9E 20
Warwick Cl. GU11: Alde . . . 4A 110
GU15: Camb . . . 3F 70
RH5: Holm . . . 4H 139
TW12: Hamp . . . 8C 24
Warwick Ct. BR2: Brom . . . 1N 47
KT13: Weybr . . . 2B 56
SL4: W'sor . . . *5F 4*
(off Alma Rd.)
Warwick Deeping
KT16: Otter . . . 2E 54
Warwick Dr. SW15 . . . 6G 12
Warwick Gdns. CR7: T Hea . . . 2L 45
KT7: T Dit . . . 4F 40
KT21: A'tead . . . 4J 79
Warwick Gro. KT5: Surb . . . 6M 41
Warwick Ho. KT2: K Tham . . . 1K 203
Warwick La. GU21: Wok . . . 6K 73
Warwick Lodge TW2: Twick . . . 4B 24
Warwick Pl. KT7: T Dit . . . 5G 40
Warwick Quad. RH1: Red . . . 2E 122
Warwick Rd. CR5: Coul . . . 1G 83
CR7: T Hea . . . 2L 45
GU12: A Va . . . 5E 90
KT1: H Wic . . . 9J 25
KT3: N Mal . . . 2B 42
KT7: T Dit . . . 4F 40
RH1: Red . . . 2D 122
RH5: Holm . . . 5J 139
SE20 . . . 2E 46
SM1: Sut . . . 1A 62
SW5 . . . 1M 13
TW2: Twick . . . 2E 24
TW4: Houn . . . 6J 9
TW15: A'ford . . . 6N 21
Warwicks Bench
GU1: Guil . . . 7D 202 (5N 113)
Warwick's Bench La.
GU1: Guil . . . 6B 114
Warwick's Bench Rd.
GU1: Guil . . . 8E 202 (6A 114)
Warwick Vs. TW20: Egh . . . 9E 20
WARWICK WOLD . . . 7L 103
Warwick Wold Rd.
RH1: Mers . . . 7L 103
Wasdale Cl. GU47: Owls . . . 5J 49
Washford Cl. GU35: Bor . . . 5A 168
Washford La. GU35: Lind . . . 4A 168
Washington Cl. RH2: Reig . . . 1M 121
Washington Dr. SL4: W'sor . . . 6B 4
Washington Rd.
KT1: K Tham . . . 4M 203 (1N 41)
KT4: W Pk . . . 8G 42
RH11: Craw . . . 6K 181
SW13 . . . 3F 12
Washpond La. CR6: Warl . . . 5M 85
WASP GREEN . . . 3N 143
Wasp Grn. La. RH1: Out . . . 3N 143
Wassand Cl. RH10: Craw . . . 3E 182
Watchetts Dr. GU15: Camb . . . 4A 70
Watchetts Lake Cl.
GU15: Camb . . . 3B 70
Watchetts Rd. GU15: Camb . . . 2N 69
Watchfield Ct. W4 . . . 1B 12
Watchmoor Point
GU15: Camb . . . 2M 69
Watchmoor Rd.
GU15: Camb . . . 3M 69
Watchmoor Trade Cen.
GU15: Camb . . . 2M 69
Watcombe Cotts. TW9: Kew . . . 2N 11
Watcombe Pl. SE25 . . . 4E 46
Watcombe Rd. SE25 . . . 4E 46
Waterbourne Way CR8: Ken . . . 1A 84
Watercress Pl.
RH13: Hors . . . 5M 197
Watercress Way GU21: Wok . . . 4L 73
Waterden Cl. GU1: Guil . . . 4B 114
Waterden Rd.
GU1: Guil . . . 4F 202 (4A 114)
Waterer Gdns. KT20: Tad . . . 5J 81
Waterer Ri. SM6: W'ton . . . 3H 63
Waterers Ri. GU21: Knap . . . 4G 72
Waterfall Cl. GU25: V Wat . . . 2K 35
Waterfall Cotts. SW19 . . . 7B 28
Waterfall Rd. SW19 . . . 7B 28
Waterfall Ter. SW17 . . . 7C 28
Waterfield KT20: Tad . . . 7G 81
(Campion Dr.)
KT20: Tad . . . 7G 81
(Watermead)
Waterfield Cl. RH13: Hors . . . 5L 197
Waterfield Dr. CR6: Warl . . . 6F 84
KT18: Tat C . . . 6G 81
KT20: Tad . . . 6G 81
Waterfield Gdns.
RH11: Craw . . . 5K 181
SE25 . . . 3A 46
Waterfield Grn. KT20: Tad . . . 7G 81
Waterfields KT22: Leat . . . 6H 79
Waterford Cl. KT11: Cob . . . 7M 57
Waterford Rd. SW6 . . . 3N 13
(not continuous)
Waterford Way
RG40: W'ham . . . 2B 30
Waterfront Bus. Pk.
GU51: Fleet . . . 2C 88
Watergardens, The
KT2: K Tham . . . 7B 26
Waterham Rd. RG12: Brac . . . 5N 31
Waterhouse Ct. W6 . . . 1J 13
Waterhouse La. CR8: Ken . . . 6N 83
KT20: K'wood . . . 8K 81
RH1: Blet . . . 1C 124
Waterhouse Mead
GU47: C Tow . . . 8J 49
Waterlakes TN8: Eden . . . 3L 147
Waterlands La.
RH12: Rowh . . . 9M 177
Water La. GU5: Alb . . . 6K 115
GU8: Ent G . . . 7D 152
GU9: Farnh . . . 8K 109
GU14: Farnb . . . 7M 69
GU24: Bis . . . 6B 72
GU24: Chob . . . 5E 52
KT1: K Tham . . . 2H 203 (9K 25)
KT11: Cob . . . 2M 77
KT23: Book . . . 3L 97
RH1: Blet . . . 8M 103
RH5: A Ham . . . 3J 137
RH8: Limp . . . 4C 106
RH9: S Gods . . . 7G 124
TN8: Eden . . . 4F 146
TN16: Weste . . . 5M 107
TW1: Twick . . . 2G 25
TW9: Rich . . . 8K 11
Water Lea RH10: Craw . . . 4E 182
Waterloo Cl. GU15: Camb . . . 8F 50
RG40: W'ham . . . 3D 30
TW14: Felt . . . 2G 23
Waterloo Cres.
RG40: W'ham . . . 3D 30
WATERLOO PARK . . . 1N 109
Waterloo Pl. RG45: Crow . . . 3G 49
SM5: Cars . . . *9D 44*
(off Wrythe La.)
TW9: Kew . . . 2N 11
TW9: Rich . . . 7L 11
Waterloo Rd. GU12: Alde . . . 3A 110
KT19: Eps . . . 5K 201 (8C 60)
RG40: W'ham . . . 3D 30
RG45: Crow . . . 3F 48
SM1: Sut . . . 2B 62
Waterloo Ter. *KT13: Weybr* . . . *1C 56*
(off Baker St.)
Waterlow Rd. RH2: Reig . . . 4A 122
Waterman Cl. GU35: Bor . . . 7A 168
Watermans Art Cen.,
Cinema & Theatre . . . 2L 11
Watermans Bus. Pk.
TW18: Stain . . . 5G 20
Watermans Cl.
KT2: K Tham . . . 8L 25
Watermans Ct. *TW8: Brent* . . . *2K 11*
(off High St.)
Waterman St. SW15 . . . 6J 13
Water Mead CR5: Chip . . . 4D 82
Watermead GU21: Wok . . . 3J 73
KT20: Tad . . . 8G 81
TW14: Felt . . . 2F 22
Watermead La. SM5: Cars . . . 6D 44
Watermill Cl. TW10: Ham . . . 4J 25
Water Mill Ho. TW13: Hanw . . . 3A 24
Watermill Way SW19 . . . 9A 28
TW13: Hanw . . . 3N 23
Waterperry La. GU24: Chob . . . 6J 53
Water Rede GU52: C Cro . . . 1A 108
Waters Dr. TW18: Stain . . . 4H 21
Water's Edge *SW6* . . . *4H 13*
(off Palemead Cl.)
Watersedge KT19: Ewe . . . 1B 60
WATERSIDE . . . 4A 146
Waterside KT20: Tad . . . 7G 81
RH6: Horl . . . 6E 142
RH19: E Grin . . . 9D 166
UB7: Harm . . . 3L 7
Waterside Av. *BR3: Beck* . . . *4M 47*
(off Adamson Way)
Waterside Bus. Cen.
TW7: Isle . . . 7H 11
Waterside Cen., The . . . 1M 113
Waterside Cl. GU7: Goda . . . 6K 133
GU35: Bor . . . 5A 168
KT6: Surb . . . 8L 41
RH11: Craw . . . 5K 181
Waterside Ct. GU51: Fleet . . . 2C 88
SM5: Cars . . . *9E 44*
(off Millpond Pl.)
Waterside Dr. KT12: Wal T . . . 4H 39
Waterside La. GU7: Goda . . . 8F 132
Waterside M. GU1: Guil . . . 1M 113
GU51: Fleet . . . 2C 88
Waterside Pk. Ind. Est.
RG12: Brac . . . 9L 15
(not continuous)
Waterside Rd. GU1: Guil . . . 9N 93
Waterside Trad. Est.
KT15: Addl . . . 1N 55
Waterside Way GU21: Wok . . . 5L 73
SW17 . . . 5A 28
Waterslade RH1: Red . . . 3C 122
Watersmeet Cl.
GU4: B'ham . . . 7C 94
Waters Pl. SW15 . . . 5H 13
Watersplash Cl.
KT1: K Tham . . . 5J 203 (2L 41)
Watersplash La.
RG42: Warf . . . 7N 15
SL5: Asc . . . 9A 18
TW5: C'ford . . . 1J 9
UB3: Harl . . . 1H 9
Watersplash Rd.
TW17: Shep . . . 4B 38
Waters Rd. KT1: K Tham . . . 1A 42
Waters Sq. KT1: K Tham . . . 2A 42
Water Twr. Hill
CR0: Croy . . . 6E 200 (1A 64)
Water Vw. RH6: Horl . . . 8H 143
Waterway Rd. KT22: Leat . . . 9G 78
Waterworks Cl.
RH18: F Row . . . 5H 187
Waterworks Yd. *CR0: Croy* . . . *4B 200*
(off Surrey St.)
Watery La. GU24: Chob . . . 6G 52
KT16: Lyne . . . 6F 36
SW20 . . . 1L 43
UB3: Harl . . . 1F 8
Wates Way CR4: Mit . . . 5D 44
Watford Cl. GU1: Guil . . . 3B 114
Wathen Rd.
RH4: Dork . . . 1L 201 (4H 119)
Watlings Cl. CR0: Croy . . . 5H 47
Watney Cl. CR8: Pur . . . 9K 63
Watney Cotts. SW14 . . . 6B 12
Watney Rd. SW14 . . . 6B 12
Watney's Rd. CR4: Mit . . . 4H 45
Watson Av. SM3: Chea . . . 8K 43
Watson Cl. RH10: Craw . . . 5G 182
SW19 . . . 7C 28
Watson Ho. RH2: Reig . . . 2M 121
Watson Rd. RH4: Westc . . . 6C 118
Wattendon Rd. CR8: Ken . . . 3M 83
Wattlehurst Farm . . . 2H 179
Watt's Cl. KT20: Tad . . . 9J 81
Watts Farm Pde.
GU24: Chob . . . *6J 53*
(off Barnmead)
Watts Gallery, The . . . 8E 112
Watts La. KT20: Tad . . . 9J 81
TW11: Tedd . . . 6G 24
Watts Lea GU21: Wok . . . 2K 73
Watt's Mead KT20: Tad . . . 9J 81
Watts Rd. GU14: Cove . . . 9L 69
KT7: T Dit . . . 6G 40
Wavel Ct. CR0: Croy . . . 8E 200
Wavell-Cody Community Campus
(Leisure Cen.) . . . 6N 89
Wavendene Av. TW20: Egh . . . 8D 20
Wavendon Av. W4 . . . 1C 12
Waveney Wlk. RH10: Craw . . . 5F 182
Waverleigh Rd.
GU6: Cranl . . . 9N 155
Waverley RG12: Brac . . . 4K 31
Waverley Av. CR8: Ken . . . 3B 84
GU51: Fleet . . . 2A 88
KT5: Surb . . . 5A 42
SM1: Sut . . . 8N 43
TW2: Whitt . . . 2N 23
Waverley Cl. GU9: Farnh . . . 1J 129
GU15: Camb . . . 2D 70
KT8: W Mole . . . 4A 40
Waverley Cotts. GU10: Til . . . 3B 130
Waverley Ct. GU22: Wok . . . 5A 74
RH12: Hors . . . 6H 197
Waverley Dr. GU12: A Va . . . 7E 90
GU15: Camb . . . 1C 70
GU25: V Wat . . . 2K 35
KT16: Chert . . . 9F 36
Waverley Gdns. GU12: A Va . . . 7E 90
Waverley Hgts.
GU9: Farnh . . . 2K 129
Waverley La. GU9: Farnh . . . 1J 129
GU10: Farnh, Til . . . 1J 129
Waverley Pl. KT22: Leat . . . 9H 79
Waverley Rd. GU14: Farnb . . . 2B 90
GU19: Bag . . . 4J 51
KT11: Sto D, Oxs . . . 1B 78
KT13: Weybr . . . 2B 56
KT17: Ewe . . . 2G 60
KT22: Oxs . . . 1B 78
SE25 . . . 3E 46
Waverley Way SM5: Cars . . . 3C 62
Waverton Rd. SW18 . . . 1A 28
Wavertree Ct. *RH6: Horl* . . . *9D 142*
(off Massetts Rd.)
SW2 . . . 2J 29
Wavertree Rd. SW2 . . . 2K 29
Way, The RH2: Reig . . . 2B 122
Waye Av. TW5: C'ford . . . 4H 9
Wayland Cl. RG12: Brac . . . 3D 32
Waylands TW19: Wray . . . 9A 6
Waylands Mead
BR3: Beck . . . 1L 47
Waylett Pl. SE27 . . . 4M 29
Wayman Rd. GU14: Cove . . . 6K 69
Wayneflete Pl. KT10: Esh . . . 9A 40
Wayneflete Twr. Av.
KT10: Esh . . . 9A 40
Waynflete *SL4: Eton* . . . *2F 4*
(off Common La.)
Waynflete Av.
CR0: Wad . . . 5A 200 (9M 45)
Waynflete Ho. *KT10: Esh* . . . *1B 58*
(off High St.)
Waynflete La. GU9: Farnh . . . 1E 128
Waynflete St. SW18 . . . 3A 28
Ways End GU15: Camb . . . 2C 70
Wayside CR0: N Add . . . 3L 65
RH5: Cap . . . 4K 159
RH11: Ifi . . . 5K 181
SW14 . . . 8B 12
Wayside Cotts.
GU10: Churt . . . 7J 149
RH5: H Mary . . . 5K 137
RH12: Rudg . . . 5G 177
Wayside Ct. GU21: Wok . . . 3H 73
TW1: Twick . . . 9J 11
Wayside Dr. TN8: Eden . . . 9M 127
Weald, The RH19: E Grin . . . 6B 166
Weald Cl. GU4: Chil . . . 9A 114
RH13: Hors . . . 8L 197
Weald Dr. RH10: Craw . . . 4E 182
Wealden Ho.
RH19: E Grin . . . 3E 186
Wealdon Ct. GU2: Guil . . . 3J 113
Wealdstone Rd. SM3: Sut . . . 8L 43
Weald Way CR3: Cate . . . 6B 104
RH2: Reig . . . 7A 122
Weall Cl. CR8: Pur . . . 8K 63
Weare St. RH5: Cap, Ockl . . . 5G 158
RH5: Ockl . . . 2C 178
Weasdale Ct. GU21: Wok . . . 3J 73
Weatherall Cl. KT15: Addl . . . 2K 55
WEATHERHILL . . . 8L 143
Weatherhill Cl. RH6: Horl . . . 8K 143
Weatherhill Rd.
RH6: Horl, Smal . . . 8K 143
Weather Way RG12: Brac . . . 1A 32
Weaver Cl. CR0: Croy . . . 1C 64
RH11: Ifi . . . 4K 181
Weaver Moss GU47: Sandh . . . 8G 49
Weavers Cl. TW7: Isle . . . 7E 10
Weavers Gdns.
GU9: Farnh . . . 4E 128
Weavers Ter. *SW6* . . . *2M 13*
(off Micklethwaite Rd.)
Weavers Yd. GU9: Farnh . . . 1G 129
Weaver Wlk. SE27 . . . 5N 29
Webb Cl. GU19: Bag . . . 6J 51
RG42: Bin . . . 8K 15
RH11: Craw . . . 8N 181
Webb Ct. RG40: W'ham . . . 9D 14
Webb Ho. TW13: Hanw . . . 4M 23
Webb Rd. GU8: Mil, Wit . . . 3N 151
Webster Cl. KT22: Oxs . . . 1B 78
Webster Ct. *GU5: Braml* . . . *4B 134*
(off Horsham Rd.)
Websters Cl. GU22: Wok . . . 7L 73
Weddell Rd. RH10: Craw . . . 6D 182
Wedgwood Pl. KT11: Cob . . . 9H 57
Wedgwoods TN16: Tats . . . 8E 86
Wedgwood Way SE19 . . . 8N 29
Weighton M. SE20 . . . 1E 46
Weighton Rd. SE20 . . . 1E 46
Weihurst Ct. SM1: Sut . . . 2C 62
Weihurst Gdns. SM1: Sut . . . 2B 62
Weimar St. SW15 . . . 6K 13
Weint, The SL3: Coln . . . 3E 6
Weir Av. GU14: Cove . . . 2M 89
Weirbrook RH10: Craw . . . 6E 182
Weir Cl. GU14: Cove . . . 2M 89
Weir Ct. KT13: Weybr . . . 8C 38
Weir Pl. TW18: Stain . . . 9G 21
Weir Rd. KT12: Wal T . . . 5H 39
KT16: Chert . . . 6K 37
SW12 . . . 1G 28
SW19 . . . 4N 27
WEIR WOOD . . . 7D 186
Weir Wood Reservoir . . . 7B 186
Weiss Rd. SW15 . . . 6J 13
Welbeck RG12: Brac . . . 4K 31
Welbeck Cl. GU14: Cove . . . 2L 89
KT3: N Mal . . . 4E 42
KT17: Ewe . . . 4F 60
Welbeck Rd. SM1: Sut . . . 8B 44
SM5: Cars . . . 8B 44
Welbeck Wlk. SM5: Cars . . . 7B 44
Welcomes Cotts.
CR3: Wold . . . 1K 105
Welcomes Rd. CR8: Ken . . . 4A 84
Welcomes Ter. CR3: Ken . . . 3C 84
Weldon Cl. GU52: C Cro . . . 8C 88
Weldon Dr. KT8: W Mole . . . 3N 39
Weldon Way RH1: Mers . . . 7H 103
Welford Pl. SW19 . . . 5K 27
Welham Rd. SW16 . . . 7F 28
SW17 . . . 6E 28
Welhouse Rd. SM5: Cars . . . 7C 44
Welland Cl. SL3: Lang . . . 2D 6
Wellbrook Rd. BR6: Farnb . . . 1J 67
Wellburn Cl. GU47: Sandh . . . 8G 49
Well Cl. GU15: Camb . . . 2N 69
GU21: Wok . . . 4M 73
SW16 . . . 5K 29
Weller Cl. RH10: Wor . . . 4H 183
Weller Dr. GU15: Camb . . . 3A 70
Weller Pl. BR6: Dow . . . 7J 67
Wellers Ct. TN16: Weste . . . 5L 107
Wellers Ct. GU5: Shere . . . 8B 116
Weller's La. RG42: Warf . . . 3A 16
Wellesford Cl. SM7: Ban . . . 4L 81
Wellesley Cl. GU12: A Va . . . 6D 90
GU19: Bag . . . 4G 51
Wellesley Ct. RG45: Crow . . . 3E 48
SM3: Sut . . . 7K 43
Wellesley Ct. Rd.
CR0: Croy . . . 3D 200 (8A 46)
Wellesley Cres. TW2: Twick . . . 3E 24
Wellesley Dr. RG45: Crow . . . 2D 48

296 A-Z Surrey

Wellesley Gdn.—W. Norwood Crematorium

Wellesley Gdn.
GU9: U Hal . . . 5H 109
Wellesley Ga.
GU12: Alde . . . 3N 109
Wellesley Gro.
CR0: Croy . . . 3D 200 (8A 46)
Wellesley Ho. *SL4: W'sor* . . . *4E 4*
(off Vansittart Rd.)
Wellesley Mans. *W14* . . . *1L 13*
(off Edith Vs.)
Wellesley Pde. TW2: Twick . . . 4E 24
Wellesley Pas.
CR0: Croy . . . 2C 200 (8N 45)
Wellesley Rd.
CR0: Croy . . . 1C 200 (7N 45)
GU10: Rush . . . 4N 149
GU11: Alde . . . 1J 109
(not continuous)
GU12: A Va . . . 6D 90
(not continuous)
SM2: Sut . . . 3A 62
(not continuous)
TW2: Twick . . . 4D 24
W4 . . . 1N 11
Wellesley Road Stop (CT)
. . . 2D 200 (8A 46)
Welley Av. TW19: Wray . . . 7A 6
Welley Rd. SL3: Hort . . . 9A 6
TW19: Wray . . . 9A 6
Well Farm Rd. CR6: Warl . . . 6D 84
Wellfield RH19: E Grin . . . 2E 186
Wellfield Gdns. SM5: Cars . . . 5C 62
Wellfield Rd. SW16 . . . 5J 29
Wellfield Wlk. SW16 . . . 6K 29
(not continuous)
Well Ho. SM7: Ban . . . 2N 81
Wellhouse La. RH3: Betch . . . 7B 120
Wellhouse Rd. BR3: Beck . . . 3K 47
Wellingham Way
RH12: Fay . . . 7H 181
Wellington Av.
GU11: Alde . . . 2K 109
GU25: V Wat . . . 4L 35
GU51: Fleet . . . 3C 88
KT4: W Pk . . . 9H 43
TW3: Houn . . . 8A 10
Wellington Bus. Pk.
RG45: Crow . . . 3D 48
Wellington Cen., The
GU11: Alde . . . 2M 109
Wellington Cl.
GU47: Sandh . . . 7H 49
KT12: Wal T . . . 7G 39
RH10: Craw . . . 9J 163
Wellington College Sports Club, The
. . . 3E 48
Wellington Cotts.
KT24: E Hor . . . 7F 96
Wellington Ct. *SW6* . . . *4N 13*
(off Maltings Pl.)
TW12: Tedd . . . 6D 24
TW15: A'ford . . . 6N 21
TW19: Stan . . . 1N 21
Wellington Cres.
KT3: N Mal . . . 2B 42
Wellington Dr. CR8: Pur . . . 6K 63
RG12: Brac . . . 4B 32
Wellington Gdns.
GU11: Alde . . . 3L 109
TW2: Twick . . . 5D 24
Wellingtonia Av.
GU15: Camb . . . 1H 71
RG45: Crow . . . 3A 48
Wellingtonia Ho.
KT15: Addl . . . 2J 55
Wellingtonia Pl.
RH2: Reig . . . 2M 121
Wellingtonia Rdbt.
RG45: Crow . . . 3D 48
Wellingtonias RG42: Warf . . . 8E 16
Wellingtonia Way
TN8: Eden . . . 1L 147
Wellington La. GU9: H End . . . 5J 109
Wellington Lodge
SL4: Wink . . . 3M 17
Wellington Mans. *W14* . . . *2L 13*
(off Queen's Club Mans.)
Wellington M. SW16 . . . 4H 29
Wellington Monument . . . 1K 109
Wellington Pl. GU12: A Va . . . 9D 90
KT11: Cob . . . 8A 58
Wellington Rd. CR0: Croy . . . 6M 45
CR3: Cate . . . 9N 83
GU47: Sandh . . . 7G 48
RG40: W'ham . . . 2A 30
RG45: Crow . . . 3H 49
RH12: Hors . . . 6K 197
SW19 . . . 3M 27
TW2: Twick . . . 6D 24
TW12: H Hill . . . 6D 24
TW14: Felt . . . 8F 8
TW15: A'ford . . . 6N 21
Wellington Rd. Nth.
TW4: Houn . . . 6N 9
Wellington Rd. Sth.
TW4: Houn . . . 7N 9
Wellington Rdbt.
GU11: Alde . . . 2K 109
Wellington St. GU11: Alde . . . 2M 109
Wellington Ter. GU21: Knap . . . 5H 73
GU47: Sandh . . . 7H 49
Wellington Town Rd.
RH19: E Grin . . . 8N 165
Wellington Way
KT13: Weybr . . . 6A 56
RH6: Horl . . . 6D 142
Well La. GU8: Worm . . . 1A 172
GU21: Wok . . . 4M 73
GU27: Hasl . . . 2H 189
SW14 . . . 8B 12
Wellow Wlk. SM5: Cars . . . 7B 44
Well Path GU21: Wok . . . 4M 73
WELLS, THE . . . 1N 79
Wells Cl. CR2: S Croy . . . 2B 64
KT23: Book . . . 2C 98
RH12: Hors . . . 6F 196
SL4: W'sor . . . 4D 4
Wells Cotts. GU9: Farnh . . . 4F 128
Wells Ct. BR2: Brom . . . 1N 47
Wells Ho. KT18: Eps . . . 1N 79
Wellside Gdns. SW14 . . . 7B 12
Wells La. GU3: Norm . . . 9N 91
SL5: Asc . . . 2M 33
Wells Lea RH19: E Grin . . . 7N 165
Wells Mdw. RH19: E Grin . . . 7N 165
Wells Pl. RH1: Mers . . . 8F 102
SW18 . . . 1A 28
TN16: Weste . . . 5L 107
Wells Pl. Ind. Est.
RH1: Mers . . . 7F 102
Wells Rd. GU4: Guil . . . 9E 94
KT18: Eps . . . 1N 79
RH10: Craw . . . 7C 182
Wellswood SL5: Asc . . . 2M 33
Well Way KT18: Eps . . . 2N 79
Wellwood Cl. CR5: Coul . . . 1J 83
RH13: Hors . . . 4A 198
Wellwynds Rd. GU6: Cranl . . . 8N 155
Weltje Rd. W6 . . . 1F 12
Welwyn Av. TW14: Felt . . . 9G 8
Welwyn Cl. RH11: Craw . . . 7K 181
Wembley Rd. TW12: Hamp . . . 9A 24
Wembury Pk. RH7: Newc . . . 1H 165
Wend, The CR5: Coul . . . 1H 83
Wendela Cl. GU22: Wok . . . 5B 74
Wenderholme CR2: S Croy . . . 8E 200
Wendley Dr. KT15: N Haw . . . 6H 55
Wendling Rd. SM1: Sut . . . 7B 44
Wendover Dr. GU16: Frim . . . 3G 70
KT3: N Mal . . . 5E 42
Wendover Pl. TW18: Stain . . . 6F 20
Wendover Rd. TW18: Stain . . . 6E 20
Wendron Cl. GU21: Wok . . . 5K 73
Wendy Cres. GU2: Guil . . . 1K 113
Wenlock Cl. RH11: Craw . . . 5M 181
Wenlock Edge RH4: Dork . . . 7J 119
Wensleydale RH11: Craw . . . 6A 182
Wensleydale Dr.
GU15: Camb . . . 1H 71
Wensleydale Gdns.
TW12: Hamp . . . 8B 24
Wensleydale Pas.
TW12: Hamp . . . 9A 24
Wensleydale Rd.
TW12: Hamp . . . 7A 24
Wensley Dr. GU51: Fleet . . . 2B 88
WENTWORTH . . . 4H 35
Wentworth Av. SL5: Asc . . . 1G 33
Wentworth Cl. BR6: Farnb . . . 2N 67
GU9: Weybo . . . 6L 109
GU12: A Va . . . 6E 90
GU23: Rip . . . 8K 75
GU46: Yate . . . 1C 68
KT6: Surb . . . 8K 41
RG45: Crow . . . 1E 48
SM4: Mord . . . 6M 43
TW15: A'ford . . . 5C 22
Wentworth Ct. *SW18* . . . *9N 13*
(off Garratt La.)
TW2: Twick . . . 4E 24
W6 . . . *2K 13*
(off Paynes Wlk.)
Wentworth Cres.
GU12: A Va . . . 7E 90
(not continuous)
Wentworth Dene
KT13: Weybr . . . 2C 56
Wentworth Dr. GU25: V Wat . . . 3J 35
RH10: Craw . . . 2H 183
Wentworth Golf Course
(East Course) . . . 4K 35
Wentworth Golf Course
(West Course) . . . 4K 35
Wentworth Ho. KT15: Addl . . . 1K 55
Wentworth Pl. *GU15: Camb* . . . *2M 69*
(off Vale Rd.)
Wentworth Rd. CR0: Croy . . . 6L 45
UB2: S'hall . . . 1L 9
Wentworth Tennis &
Health Club, The . . . 4K 35
Wentworth Way CR2: Sande . . . 1D 84
SL5: Asc . . . 1G 33
Werndee Rd. SE25 . . . 3D 46
Werter Rd. SW15 . . . 7K 13
Wesco Ct. GU21: Wok . . . 3C 74
Wescott Rd. RG40: W'ham . . . 2C 30
Wesley Av. TW3: Houn . . . 5M 9
Wesley Cl. RH2: Reig . . . 4L 121
RH6: Horl . . . 6E 142
RH11: Craw . . . 6K 181
Wesley Dr. TW20: Egh . . . 7C 20
Wesley Pl. SL4: Wink . . . 3M 17
Wessels KT20: Tad . . . 8J 81
Wessex Av. SW19 . . . 2M 43
Wessex Cl. KT1: K Tham . . . 9A 26
KT7: T Dit . . . 8F 40
Wessex Ct. TW19: Stan . . . 9N 7
Wessex Pl. GU9: Farnh . . . 2H 129
West Acres KT10: Esh . . . 4N 57
West Av. GU9: H End . . . 6J 109
KT12: Whit V . . . 6F 56
RH1: Red . . . 9E 122
RH10: Craw . . . 1E 182
SM6: W'ton . . . 2J 63
West Bank
RH4: Dork . . . 4G 201 (6F 118)
Westbank Rd. TW12: H Hill . . . 7C 24
WEST BARNES . . . 4G 42
W. Barnes La. KT3: N Mal . . . 3G 43
SW20: N Mal . . . 2G 42
WEST BEDFONT . . . 9A 8
WESTBOROUGH . . . 2J 113
Westbourne Av. SM3: Chea . . . 8K 43
Westbourne Ho. TW5: Hest . . . 2A 10
Westbourne Rd. CR0: Croy . . . 5C 46
GU47: C Tow . . . 8K 49
TW13: Felt . . . 4G 22
TW18: Stain . . . 8K 21
West Brompton Station (Rail & Tube)
. . . 2M 13
WESTBROOK . . . 6F 132
Westbrook RH18: F Row . . . 6G 187
Westbrook Av. TW12: Hamp . . . 8N 23
Westbrook Gdns.
RG12: Brac . . . 9A 16
Westbrook Hill GU8: Els . . . 7F 130
Westbrook Rd. CR7: T Hea . . . 1A 46
GU7: Goda . . . 6F 132
TW5: Hest . . . 3N 9
TW18: Stain . . . 6H 21
Westbury *SL4: Eton* . . . *2F 4*
(off Eton Wick Rd.)
Westbury Av. GU51: Fleet . . . 5E 88
KT10: Clay . . . 3F 58
Westbury Cl. CR3: Whyte . . . 5C 84
GU51: Fleet . . . 5D 88
RG45: Crow . . . 1G 48
TW17: Shep . . . 5C 38
Westbury Gdns.
GU9: Farnh . . . 8K 109
GU51: Fleet . . . 5E 88
Westbury Pl. TW8: Brent . . . 2K 11
Westbury Rd. BR3: Beck . . . 2H 47
CR0: Croy . . . 5A 46
KT3: N Mal . . . 3C 42
SE20 . . . 1G 46
TW13: Felt . . . 2L 23
Westbury Ter.
TN16: Weste . . . 5L 107
Westbury Way GU12: Alde . . . 2B 110
WEST BYFLEET . . . 9J 55
West Byfleet Station (Rail) . . . 8J 55
Westcar La. KT12: Hers . . . 3J 57
WEST CLANDON . . . 6K 95
West Cl. GU9: H End . . . 5J 109
GU27: Fern . . . 9F 188
TW12: Hamp . . . 7M 23
TW15: A'ford . . . 5N 21
Westcombe Av. CR0: Croy . . . 6J 45
Westcombe Cl. RG12: Brac . . . 6C 32
West Comn. Rd. BR2: Hay . . . 1D 66
BR2: Kes . . . 1D 66
Westcoombe Av.
SW20 . . . 9E 26
Westcote Rd. KT19: Eps . . . 7A 60
SW16 . . . 6G 29
WESTCOTT . . . 6C 118
Westcott Cl. CR0: N Add . . . 5L 65
RH11: Craw . . . 9A 182
WESTCOTT COMMON . . . 7B 118
Westcott Keep *RH6: Horl* . . . *7G 142*
(off Langshott La.)
Westcott Rd.
RH4: Dork . . . 3G 201 (6D 118)
Westcotts Grn. RG42: Warf . . . 7B 16
Westcott St. RH4: Westc . . . 6B 118
Westcott Way SM2: Chea . . . 6H 61
West Ct. GU4: B'ham . . . 8C 94
TW7: Isle . . . 3C 10
West Cres. SL4: W'sor . . . 4C 4
Westcroft Gdns. SM4: Mord . . . 2L 43
Westcroft Leisure Cen. . . . 1E 62
Westcroft Rd. SM5: Cars . . . 1E 62
SM6: W'ton . . . 1E 62
W. Cromwell Rd. SW5 . . . 1M 13
W14 . . . 1L 13
W. Cross Cen. TW8: Brent . . . 2G 11
W. Cross Way TW8: Brent . . . 2H 11
West Croydon Station (Rail & CT)
. . . 1B 200 (7N 45)
Westdean Cl. SW18 . . . 9N 13
West Dene SM3: Chea . . . 3K 61
Westdene KT12: Hers . . . 1J 57
Westdene Mdws.
GU6: Cranl . . . 7J 155
Westdene Way KT13: Weybr . . . 9F 38
West Down KT23: Book . . . 5B 98
West Dr. GU25: V Wat . . . 6H 35
KT15: N Haw . . . 6K 55
KT20: Tad . . . 5J 81
SL5: S'dale, V Wat . . . 4G 34
SM2: Chea . . . 5J 61
SM5: Cars . . . 6B 62
SW16 . . . 5G 28
WEST DULWICH . . . 3N 29
WEST END
GU24 . . . 8C 52
KT10 . . . 2N 57
RG42 . . . 6N 15
W. End Cen. *GU11: Alde* . . . *2L 109*
(off Queen's Rd.)
West End Gdns. KT10: Esh . . . 2N 57
West End Gro. GU9: Farnh . . . 1F 128
West End La. GU10: Fren . . . 1D 148
GU27: Hasl . . . 9A 172
KT10: Esh . . . 4N 57
RG42: Warf . . . 6N 15
UB3: Harl . . . 3D 8
Westerdale Dr. GU16: Frim . . . 3F 70
Westerfolds Cl. GU22: Wok . . . 4E 74
Westergate Ho.
KT1: K Tham . . . 8H 203
WESTERHAM . . . 4M 107
Westerham Cl. KT15: Addl . . . 3L 55
SM2: Sut . . . 6M 61
WESTERHAM HILL . . . 7J 87
Westerham Hill
TN16: Weste . . . 8K 87
Westerham Rd. BR2: Kes . . . 3F 66
RH8: Limp, Weste, Oxt
. . . 7B 106
TN16: Weste . . . 7B 106
Westerham Trade Cen.
TN16: Weste . . . 3M 107
Westerley Ware *TW9: Kew* . . . *2N 11*
(off Waterloo Pl.)
Westermain KT15: N Haw . . . 6L 55
Western Av. KT16: Chert . . . 2J 37
TW20: Thor . . . 2D 36
Western Cen., The
RG12: Brac . . . 1L 31
Western Cl. KT16: Chert . . . 2J 37
Western Dr. TW17: Shep . . . 5E 38
WESTERN INDUSTRIAL AREA
. . . 1L 31
Western Intl. Mkt.
UB2: S'hall . . . 1J 9
Western La. SW12 . . . 1E 28
Western Pde. RH2: Reig . . . 6N 121
Western Perimeter Rd.
TW6: Lon A . . . 5K 7
TW6: Lon A, L'ford . . . 5K 7
UB7: L'ford . . . 5K 7
Western Pl. RH4: Dork . . . 3J 201
Western Rd. CR4: Mit . . . 9B 28
GU11: Alde . . . 3K 109
RG12: Brac . . . 9K 15
SM1: Sut . . . 2M 61
SW19 . . . 9B 28
Western Ter. *W6* . . . *1F 12*
(off Chiswick Mall)
WEST EWELL . . . 5C 60
W. Farm Av. KT21: A'tead . . . 5J 79
W. Farm Cl. KT21: A'tead . . . 6K 79
W. Farm Dr. KT21: A'tead . . . 6K 79
WESTFIELD . . . 8A 74
Westfield KT21: A'tead . . . 5M 79
RH2: Reig . . . 9N 101
RH5: A Ham . . . 3G 136
Westfield Av. CR2: Sande . . . 9A 64
GU22: Wok . . . 8A 74
Westfield Cl. SM1: Sut . . . 1L 61
SW10 . . . 3N 13
Westfield Comn.
GU22: Wok . . . 9A 74
Westfield Ct. GU51: Fleet . . . 4A 88
KT6: Surb . . . *8H 203*
(off Portsmouth Rd)
Westfield Dr. KT23: Book . . . 9A 78
Westfield Gdns.
RH4: Dork . . . 2H 201 (5G 118)
Westfield Gro. GU22: Wok . . . 7A 74
Westfield Ho. SW18 . . . 2N 27
Westfield La. GU10: Wrec . . . 5D 128
Westfield Pde.
KT15: N Haw . . . 6M 55
Westfield Rd. BR3: Beck . . . 1J 47
CR0: Croy . . . 2A 200 (8M 45)
CR4: Mit . . . 1C 44
GU1: Guil . . . 8A 94
GU15: Camb . . . 4N 69
GU22: Wok . . . 9N 73
KT6: Surb . . . 4K 41
KT12: Wal T . . . 6M 39
RH11: Craw . . . 3N 181
SM1: Sut . . . 1L 61
Westfields GU8: Wit . . . 5C 152
SW13 . . . 6E 12
Westfields Av. SW13 . . . 6D 12
Westfield Sq. GU22: Wok . . . 9A 74
Westfield Way GU22: Wok . . . 9A 74
W. Flexford La.
GU3: Flex, Wan . . . 3N 111
West Fryerne GU46: Yate . . . 7C 48
West Gdns. KT17: Ewe . . . 6D 60
SW17 . . . 7C 28
Westgate Cl. KT18: Eps . . . 2C 80
Westgate Est. TW14: Bedf . . . 2C 22
Westgate Ho. *KT18: Eps* . . . *2C 80*
(off Chalk La.)
TW7: Isle . . . 5D 10
Westgate Rd. BR3: Beck . . . 1M 47
SE25 . . . 3E 46
Westgate Ter. SW10 . . . 2N 13
West Glade GU14: Cove . . . 1J 89
WEST GREEN . . . 2A 182
West Grn. GU46: Yate . . . 8A 48
West Grn. Dr. RH11: Craw . . . 2A 182
West Green Pk. . . . 2A 182
West Gro. KT12: Hers . . . 2J 57
Westhall Pk. CR6: Warl . . . 6F 84
W. Hall Rd. TW9: Kew . . . 4A 12
Westhall Rd. CR6: Warl . . . 5D 84
Westhatch La. RG42: Warf . . . 5N 15
Westhay Gdns. SW14 . . . 8A 12
WEST HEATH
GU14 . . . 9L 69
RH8 . . . 8C 106
West Heath GU24: Pirb . . . 1A 92
(not continuous)
W. Heath Rd. GU14: Cove . . . 1L 89
WEST HILL . . . 9L 13
West Hill BR6: Dow . . . 8H 67
CR2: Sande . . . 6B 64
GU8: Els . . . 8G 131
KT19: Eps . . . 6G 201 (9A 60)
RH8: Oxt . . . 8N 105
RH19: D Pk . . . 4A 166
RH19: E Grin . . . 1N 185
SW15 . . . 1J 27
SW18 . . . 1J 27
W. Hill Av.
KT19: Eps . . . 5G 201 (9A 60)
W. Hill Bank RH8: Oxt . . . 8N 105
W. Hill Cl. GU8: Els . . . 8G 131
GU24: B'wood . . . 7E 72
W. Hill Ct. KT19: Eps . . . 6H 201
W. Hill Rd. GU22: Wok . . . 6N 73
SW18 . . . 9L 13
W. Hoathly Rd.
RH19: E Grin . . . 5M 185
(not continuous)
Westhorpe Rd. SW15 . . . 6H 13
WEST HORSLEY . . . 7C 96
West Ho. GU6: Cranl . . . 5L 155
West Ho. Cl. SW19 . . . 2K 27
WESTHUMBLE . . . 9H 99
Westhumble St.
RH5: Westh . . . 9H 99
W. Kensington Ct.
W14 . . . *1L 13*
(off Edith Vs.)
W. Kensington Mans.
W14 . . . *1L 13*
(off Beaumont Cres.)
West Kensington Station (Tube)
. . . 1L 13
Westland Cl. TW19: Stan . . . 9N 7
Westland Ct. GU14: Cove . . . 1J 89
Westlands RH13: Hors . . . 5L 197
Westlands Ct. KT8: E Mol . . . 3D 40
KT18: Eps . . . 2B 80
Westlands Way RH8: Oxt . . . 5N 105
West La. RH5: Wott . . . 8L 117
RH19: E Grin . . . 1N 185
Westleas RH6: Horl . . . 6C 142
Westlees Cl. RH5: N Holm . . . 8K 119
West Leigh RH19: E Grin . . . 2A 186
Westleigh Av. CR5: Coul . . . 3E 82
SW15 . . . 8G 13
Westleigh Ct. CR2: S Croy . . . 7F 200
Westley Mill RG42: Bin . . . 1K 15
Westmacott Dr. TW14: Felt . . . 2G 22
Westmark Point *SW15* . . . *2G 26*
(off Norley Vale)
West Mead KT19: Ewe . . . 3D 60
Westmead GU9: Farnh . . . 1G 128
GU14: Farnb . . . 2N 89
GU21: Wok . . . 4L 73
SL4: W'sor . . . 6E 4
SW15 . . . 9G 12
Westmead Cnr. SM5: Cars . . . 1C 62
Westmead Dr. RH1: Salf . . . 2E 142
Westmead Ho. SM1: Sut . . . 1B 62
Westmead Rd. SM1: Sut . . . 1B 62
West Meads GU2: Guil . . . 4J 113
RH6: Horl . . . 8G 143
Westminster Av.
CR7: T Hea . . . 1M 45
Westminster Cl.
GU51: Fleet . . . 3B 88
TW11: Tedd . . . 6G 24
TW14: Felt . . . 2H 23
Westminster Ct.
GU1: Guil . . . 5E 202 (4A 114)
GU22: Wok . . . 8D 74
Westminster Rd.
RH10: Craw . . . 4G 182
SM1: Sut . . . 8B 44
WEST MOLESEY . . . 3A 40
Westmont Rd.
KT10: H Wood . . . 8E 40
Westmore Ct. SW15 . . . 8K 13
Westmore Grn. TN16: Tats . . . 7E 86
Westmoreland Dr.
SM2: Sut . . . 4N 61
Westmoreland Rd.
SW13 . . . 4E 12
Westmore Rd. TN16: Tats . . . 8E 86
Westmorland Cl.
KT19: Ewe . . . 6D 60
TW1: Twick . . . 9H 11
Westmorland Ct. KT6: Surb . . . 6K 41
Westmorland Dr.
GU15: Camb . . . 3F 70
RG42: Warf . . . 7D 16
Westmorland Sq. *CR4: Mit* . . . *4J 45*
(off Westmorland Way)
Westmorland Way CR4: Mit . . . 3H 45
West Mt.
GU2: Guil . . . 7A 202 (5M 113)
(not continuous)
WEST NORWOOD . . . 5N 29
W. Norwood Crematorium
SE27 . . . 4N 29

West Norwood Station (Rail)—Whittingham Ct.

West Norwood Station (Rail) 5M 29
Weston Av. KT7: T Dit 6E 40
KT8: W Mole 2M 39
KT15: Addl 1K 55
Weston Cl. CR5: Coul 7K 83
GU7: Goda 5H 133
Weston Ct. GU7: Goda 5H 133
KT1: K Tham 6J 203
Weston Dr. CR3: Cate 9N 83
Weston Farm Cotts.
GU5: Alb 8K 115
Westonfields GU5: Alb 8L 115
Weston Gdns. GU22: Pyr 3G 75
TW7: Isle 4E 10
WESTON GREEN 7E 40
Weston Grn. KT7: T Dit 8E 40
(Hampton Ct. Way)
KT7: T Dit 7E 40
(Weston Grn. Rd.)
Weston Grn. Rd.
KT7: T Dit 7E 40
KT10: Esh 7D 40
Weston Gro. GU19: Bag 5K 51
Weston Lea KT24: W Hors 3E 96
Weston Pk.
KT1: K Tham 3J 203 (1L 41)
KT7: T Dit 7E 40
Weston Pk. Cl. KT7: T Dit 7E 40
Weston Rd. GU2: Guil 2K 113
(not continuous)
KT7: T Dit 7E 40
KT17: Eps 7D 60
Westons Cl. RH12: Hors 1K 197
Westons Yd. SL4: Eton 2G 4
Weston Way GU22: Pyr 3G 75
Weston Yd. GU5: Alb 8L 115
Westover Cl. SM2: Sut 5N 61
Westover Rd. GU51: Fleet 4C 88
SW18 1A 28
West Pal. Gdns.
KT13: Weybr 9C 38
West Pde. RH12: Hors 4J 197
West Pk. Av. TW9: Kew 4N 11
West Pk. Cl. TW5: Hest 2N 9
West Pk. Rd. KT19: Eps 8M 59
RH7: Newc 6C 164
RH10: Cop, Newc 6C 164
(not continuous)
RH17: Hand 9N 199
TW9: Kew 4N 11
West Parkside CR6: Warl 2K 85
West Pl. SW19 6H 27
W. Point Cl. *TW4: Houn* 6N 9
(off Grosvenor Rd.)
West Ramp TW6: Lon A 4B 8
West Ridge GU10: Seal 7C 110
West Ring GU10: Tong 5D 110
West Rd.
GU1: Guil 4F 202 (4A 114)
GU14: Farnb 6N 69
GU15: Camb 1B 70
KT2: K Tham 9B 26
KT9: Ches 8J 59
KT13: Weybr 5C 56
RG40: W'ham 6G 31
RH2: Reig 4N 121
TW14: Bedf 9E 8
Westrow SW15 9H 13
W. Sheen Va. TW9: Rich 7M 11
W. Side Comn. SW19 6H 27
Westside Ct. GU24: W End 9B 52
Westside Ho. RH1: Salf 1F 142
West St.
CR0: Croy 6C 200 (1N 63)
GU9: Farnh 2E 128
GU21: Wok 4B 74
GU27: Hasl 1G 189
KT17: Ewe 5E 60
KT18: Eps 7H 201 (9B 60)
(not continuous)
RH2: Reig 3K 121
RH4: Dork 2J 201 (5G 119)
RH7: Dorm 1C 166
RH11: Craw 4B 182
RH12: Hors 6J 197
RH19: E Grin 1A 186
SM1: Sut 2N 61
SM5: Cars 9D 44
TW8: Brent 2J 11
West St. La. SM5: Cars 1D 62
(not continuous)
West St. Pl. CR0: Croy 6C 200
West Sutton Station (Rail) 1M 61
W. Temple Sheen
SW14 8A 12
West Vw. KT21: A'tead 6J 79
TW14: Bedf 1D 22
Westview *GU22: Wok* 5B 74
(off Park Dr.)
West Vw. Av.
CR3: Whyte 5C 84
Westview Cl. RH1: Red 5C 122
West Vw. Cotts.
RH5: Newd 2A 160
West Vw. Gdns.
RH19: E Grin 1A 186
West Vw. Rd.
GU35: H Dwn 5H 169
Westview Rd. CR6: Warl 6E 84
Westville Rd. KT7: T Dit 7G 41
Westward Ho. GU1: Guil 1B 114
Westwates Cl. RG12: Brac 9B 16
West Way BR4: W Wick 5N 47
CR0: Croy 8H 47
RH10: Craw 2E 182
RH13: Slin 5L 195
SM5: Cars 6B 62
TW5: Hest 4N 9
TW17: Shep 5E 38
Westway CR3: Cate 9A 84
GU2: Guil 1J 113
GU8: Worm 1C 172
RH6: Gat 3F 162
RH10: Cop 7K 163
SW20 2G 43
Westway Cl. SW20 2G 43
Westway Ct. CR3: Cate 1A 104
W. Way Gdns. CR0: Croy 8G 47
Westway Gdns.
RH1: Red 9E 102
Westways KT19: Ewe 1E 60
TN8: Eden 1L 147
TN16: Weste 4L 107
Westwell M. SW16 7J 29
Westwell Rd. SW16 7J 29
Westwell Rd. App.
SW16 7J 29
Westwick *KT1: K Tham* 4M 203
(off Chesterton Ter.)
Westwick Gdns. TW4: C'ford 5J 9
WEST WICKHAM 7M 47
West Wickham Pools 7M 47
West Wickham Station (Rail) 6M 47
Westwood Av. KT15: Wood 8H 55
SE19 9N 29
Westwood Cl. KT10: Esh 9D 40
Westwood Ct. GU2: Guil 2J 113
Westwood Gdns.
SW13 6E 12
Westwood La. GU3: Norm 1L 111
Westwood Rd. CR5: Coul 5H 83
GU20: Windl 8B 34
SW13 6E 12
Wetherby Gdns.
GU14: Farnb 5A 90
SW5 1N 13
Wetherby Mans. *SW5* 1N 13
(off Earls Ct. Sq.)
Wetherby M. SW5 1N 13
Wetherby Way KT9: Ches 4L 59
Wettern Cl. CR2: Sande 6B 64
Wetton Pl. TW20: Egh 6B 20
Wexfenne Gdns.
GU22: Pyr 3K 75
Wexford Rd. SW12 1D 28
Wey and Arun Junction Canal 7D 134
Wey Av. KT16: Chert 2J 37
Weybank GU23: Wis 3N 75
Weybank Cl. GU9: Farnh 1H 129
Wey Barton KT14: Byf 9A 56
WEYBOURNE 6K 109
Weybourne Pl. CR2: Sande 6A 64
Weybourne Rd.
GU9: Farnh 7K 109
Weybourne St. SW18 3A 28
WEYBRIDGE 1B 56
Weybridge Bus. Pk.
KT15: Addl 1N 55
Weybridge Ho.
KT13: Weybr 2E 56
Weybridge Mead
GU46: Yate 8D 48
Weybridge Pk. KT13: Weybr 2B 56
Weybridge Rd. CR7: T Hea 3L 45
KT13: Weybr 1N 55
KT15: Addl 1N 55
Weybridge Station (Rail) 3B 56
Weybrook Dr. GU4: B'ham 7D 94
Wey Cl. GU12: Ash 3E 110
GU15: Camb 1N 69
KT14: W By 9K 55
Weycombe Rd.
GU27: Hasl 1G 189
(not continuous)
Wey Ct.
GU1: Guil 4B 202 (4M 113)
GU7: Goda 5K 133
KT15: N Haw 5M 55
KT19: Ewe 1B 60
Wey Ct. Cl. GU7: Goda 5J 133
Weycrofts RG42: Brac 8L 15
Weydon Farm La.
GU9: Farnh 3G 128
Weydon Hill Cl.
GU9: Farnh 3G 129
Weydon Hill Rd.
GU9: Farnh 3G 129
Weydon La. GU9: Farnh 4E 128
Weydon Mill La.
GU9: Farnh 2G 128
Weydown Cl. GU2: Guil 7K 93
SW19 2K 27
Weydown Cotts.
GU27: Hasl 8G 170
Weydown Ct. GU27: Hasl 1F 188
Weydown Ind. Est.
GU27: Hasl 1F 188
(not continuous)
Weydown La. GU2: Guil 7K 93
Weydown Rd. GU27: Hasl 2F 188
Wey Gdns. GU27: Hasl 3D 188
Wey Hill GU27: Hasl 2E 188
Weylands Cl. KT12: Wal T 7N 39
Weylands Ct. *KT15: Addl* 1M 55
(off Corrie Rd.)
Weylands Pk. KT13: Weybr 3E 56
Weylea Av. GU4: B'ham 9C 94
Wey Mnr. Rd. KT15: N Haw 5M 55
Weymead Cl. KT16: Chert 7L 37
Wey Mdws. KT13: Addl 2N 55
Weymede KT14: Byf 8A 56
Weymouth Ct. SM2: Sut 4M 61
Wey Retail Pk. KT14: Byf 8N 55
Wey Rd. GU7: Goda 6K 133
KT13: Weybr 9A 38
Weyside GU9: Farnh 1H 129
Weyside Cl. KT14: Byf 8A 56
Weyside Gdns. GU1: Guil 1M 113
Weyside Pk. GU7: Goda 6K 133
Weyside Rd. GU1: Guil 1L 113
Weysprings GU27: Hasl 1D 188
Weystone Rd. KT13: Addl 1A 56
Weyvern Pk. GU3: P'marsh 2L 133
Weyvern Pl. GU3: P'marsh 2L 133
Weyview Cl. GU1: Guil 1M 113
Wey Vw. Ct.
GU1: Guil 4A 202 (4M 113)
Weywood Cl. GU9: Weybo 5L 109
Weywood La. GU9: Weybo 5K 109
Whaley Rd. RG40: W'ham 9C 14
Wharf, The GU7: Goda 6H 133
KT13: Weybr 8B 38
Wharfedale Gdns.
CR7: T Hea 3K 45
Wharfedale St. SW10 1N 13
Wharfenden Way
GU16: Frim G 8D 70
Wharf La. GU23: Rip 5M 75
GU23: Send 1E 94
TW1: Twick 2G 24
Wharf Rd.
GU1: Guil 3B 202 (3M 113)
GU12: A Va 9E 90
GU16: Frim G 8D 70
TW19: Wray 1M 19
Wharf St. GU7: Goda 7H 133
Wharf Way GU16: Frim G 8E 70
Wharncliffe Gdns.
SE25 1B 46
Wharncliffe Rd. SE25 1B 46
Whateley Cl. GU2: Guil 7L 93
Whatley Av. SW20 2J 43
Whatley Grn. RG12: Brac 5N 31
Whatmore Cl. TW19: Stan M 9J 7
Wheatash Rd. KT15: Addl 8K 37
Wheatbutts, The SL4: E Wic 1C 4
Wheatcroft Ct. *SM1: Sut* 7N 43
(off Cleeve Way)
Wheatfield Way
KT1: K Tham 5J 203 (1L 41)
RH6: Horl 6F 142
Wheathill Ho. *SE20* 1E 46
(off Croydon Rd.)
Wheathill Rd. SE20 2E 46
Wheat Knoll CR8: Ken 3N 83
Wheatlands TW5: Hest 2A 10
Wheatlands Rd. SW17 4E 28
Wheatley RG12: Brac 4K 31
Wheatley Ho. *SW15* 1F 26
(off Ellisfield Dr.)
Wheatley Rd. GU11: Alde 1L 109
TW7: Isle 6F 10
Wheatley's Eyot
TW16: Sunb 4H 39
Wheatsheaf Cl. GU21: Wok 3A 74
KT16: Otter 3F 54
RH12: Hors 3L 197
Wheatsheaf Ct.
GU35: Head 3E 168
Wheatsheaf La. SW6 3H 13
TW18: Stain 8H 21
Wheatsheaf Pde. *SL4: O Win* 8K 5
(off St Luke's Rd.)
Wheatsheaf Pk. 9J 21
Wheatsheaf Ter. SW6 3L 13
Wheatstone Cl. CR4: Mit 9C 28
RH10: Craw 7F 162
Wheeler Av. RH8: Oxt 7N 105
Wheeler La. GU8: Wit 4B 152
Wheeler Rd. RH10: Craw 5F 182
Wheelers La.
KT18: Eps 8G 201 (1A 80)
RH3: Brock 5A 120
RH6: Smal 9L 143
Wheeler's St. SM1: Sut 9M 43
WHEELERSTREET 4C 152
Wheelerstreet GU8: Wit 4C 152
Wheelers Way RH19: Fel 7H 165
Wheelwright Ct.
RH5: Ockl 5D 158
Wheelwrights La.
GU26: G'hott 5M 169
Wheelwrights Pl. SL3: Coln 3E 6
Whelan Way SM6: Bedd 9H 45
Wherwell Rd.
GU2: Guil 6A 202 (5M 113)
Whetstone Rd. GU14: Cove 1H 89
Whimbrel Cl. CR2: Sande 7A 64
Whinfell Cl. SW16 6H 29
Whin Holt GU52: Fleet 7B 88
Whins Cl. GU15: Camb 2N 69
Whins Dr. GU15: Camb 2N 69
Whinshill Ct. SL5: S'dale 7D 34
Whipley Cl. GU4: B'ham 7D 94
Whistler Cl. RH10: Craw 6D 182
Whistler Gro. GU47: C Tow 9J 49
Whistley Cl. RG12: Brac 2C 32
Whitby Cl. GU14: Farnb 4C 90
TN16: B Hil 6D 86
Whitby Gdns. SM1: Sut 8B 44
Whitby Rd. SM1: Sut 8B 44
Whitchurch Cl.
GU11: Alde 6B 110
Whitcombe M. TW9: Kew 4A 12
Whitcome M. TW9: Kew 4A 12
White Acres Rd.
GU16: Mytc 1D 90
Whitebeam Dr. RH2: Reig 6N 121
Whitebeam Gdns.
GU14: Cove 2H 89
White Beam Way
KT20: Tad 8F 80
White Beech La.
GU8: Chid 4K 173
Whiteberry Rd.
RH5: A Com, Cold 3B 138
Whitebines GU9: Farnh 1J 129
White Bri. Av. CR4: Mit 2B 44
Whitebridge Cl. TW14: Felt 9G 9
WHITE BUSHES 8E 122
Whitebushes RH1: Red 7E 122
White City RG45: Crow 2J 49
(not continuous)
White Cott. Cl. GU9: Hale 6J 109
White Ct. GU2: Guil 9K 93
Whitecroft RH6: Horl 7F 142
Whitecroft Cl. BR3: Beck 3N 47
Whitecroft Way BR3: Beck 4M 47
White Down La.
RH5: Ran C 4K 117
Whitefield Av. CR8: Pur 3L 83
Whitefield Cl. SW15 9K 13
White Ga. GU22: Wok 7B 74
White Gates KT7: T Dit 6G 40
Whitegates CR3: Warl 6D 84
Whitegate Way KT20: Tad 7G 81
WHITEGROVE 7B 16
Whitehall 3K 61
Whitehall Cres. KT9: Ches 2K 59
Whitehall Dr. RH11: Ifi 3K 181
Whitehall Farm La.
GU25: V Wat 1A 36
(not continuous)
Whitehall Gdns. W4 2A 12
Whitehall La. RH2: Reig 7L 121
TW19: Wray 9C 6
TW20: Egh 8B 20
Whitehall Pde.
RH19: E Grin 9A 166
(off London Rd.)
Whitehall Pk. Rd. W4 2A 12
Whitehall Pl. SM6: W'ton 1F 62
Whitehall Rd. CR7: T Hea 4L 45
White Hart Cl. UB3: Harl 2E 8
White Hart Ct. GU23: Rip 8L 75
RH12: Hors 4J 197
White Hart Ind. Est.
GU17: B'water 2K 69
White Hart La.
GU3: Wood V 2D 112
SW13 6D 12
White Hart Mdws.
GU23: Rip 8L 75
White Hart Row KT16: Chert 6J 37
Whitehead Cl. SW18 1A 28
White Hermitage
SL4: O Win 8M 5
White Heron M.
TW11: Tedd 7F 24
White Hill CR2: Sande 6A 64
CR5: Chip 1C 102
GU20: Windl 1M 51
Whitehill Cl. GU15: Camb 8B 50
White Hill La. RH1: Blet 5A 104
Whitehill La. KT11: Cob 1D 96
Whitehill Pk.
GU35: White 9A 168
Whitehill Pl. GU25: V Wat 4A 36
Whitehill Rd. GU35: Stand 8A 168
White Horse Dr.
KT18: Eps 8G 201 (1B 80)
White Horse La. GU23: Rip 8L 75
Whitehorse La. SE25 3A 46
White Horse Rd.
SL4: W'sor 6A 4
Whitehorse Rd. CR0: Croy 6N 45
CR7: T Hea 6N 45
RH12: Hors 2A 198
White Ho. KT15: Addl 1L 55
SW4 1H 29
(off Clapham Pk. Est.)
White Ho., The
RH10: Craw 7B 162
Whitehouse Cl.
GU14: Farnb 8N 69
White Ho. Dr. GU1: Guil 3D 114
White Ho. Gdns.
GU46: Yate 8B 48
White Ho. La. GU4: J Wel 7N 93
(not continuous)
White Ho. Wlk.
GU9: H End 5J 109
White Knights Rd.
KT13: Weybr 4D 56
White Knobs Way
CR3: Cate 3D 104
Whitelands Cres.
SW18 1K 27
Whitelands Dr. SL5: Asc 9H 17
White La. GU4: Guil 5E 114
GU5: Alb 5E 114
GU10: Tong 7G 110
GU12: A Grn 3G 110
RH8: T'sey 1D 106
TN16: Tats, T'sey 1D 106
Whiteley SL4: W'sor 3B 4
Whiteley's Way
TW13: Hanw 4A 24
WHITELEY VILLAGE 5F 56
White Lillies Island
SL4: W'sor 3D 4
White Lion Ct. TW7: Isle 6H 11
White Lion Ga. KT11: Cob 1H 77
White Lion Wlk.
GU1: Guil 6C 202 (4N 113)
White Lion Way GU46: Yate 8C 48
White Lodge KT21: A'tead 7L 79
SE19 8M 29
White Lodge Cl. SM2: Sut 4A 62
TW7: Isle 5G 11
White Lodge Ct.
TW16: Sunb 9K 23
White Lodge Gdns.
RH1: Salf 2E 142
WHITELY HILL 8K 183
Whitely Hill RH10: Wor 8K 183
Whitemore Rd. GU1: Guil 8N 93
White Oak Dr. BR3: Beck 1M 47
Whiteoaks SM7: Ban 9N 61
White Pillars GU22: Wok 7L 73
WHITE POST 2B 124
Whitepost Hill RH1: Red 3C 122
(not continuous)
White Post La.
GU10: Wrec 7F 128
White Rd. GU15: Camb 9L 49
KT20: Betch, Box H 2N 119
RH3: Betch 2N 119
White Rose La.
GU10: L Bou 4G 129
GU22: Wok 5B 74
Whites La. GU24: Pirb 2D 92
SL3: Dat 2L 5
Whites Rd. GU14: Farnb 4C 90
Whitestile Rd. TW8: Brent 1J 11
White Swan M. W4 1D 12
Whitethorn Av. CR5: Coul 2E 82
Whitethorn Cl. GU12: Ash 3F 110
Whitethorn Cotts.
GU6: Cranl 5K 155
Whitethorn Gdns.
CR0: Croy 8E 46
Whitethorns *GU9: H End* 4J 109
(off Lwr. Weybourne La.)
Whitewalls *RH11: Craw* 3L 181
(off Rusper Rd.)
Whitewater Rd. GU51: Fleet 1A 88
Whiteway KT23: Book 4B 98
Whiteways Ct. TW18: Stain 8K 21
WHITEWOOD 5D 144
Whitewood Cotts.
TN16: Tats 7E 86
Whitewood La. RH6: Horn 5D 144
RH9: S Gods 5D 144
Whitfield Cl. GU2: Guil 9K 93
GU27: Hasl 8G 171
Whitfield Rd. GU27: Hasl 9G 171
Whitford Gdns. CR4: Mit 2D 44
Whitgift Av.
CR2: S Croy 8A 200 (2M 63)
Whitgift Cen.
CR0: Croy 2C 200 (8N 45)
Whitgift Ct. CR2: S Croy 8C 200
Whitgift Sq.
CR0: Croy 3C 200 (8N 45)
Whitgift St.
CR0: Croy 5B 200 (9N 45)
Whitgift Wlk. RH10: Craw 6B 182
Whitland Rd. SM5: Cars 7B 44
Whitlet Cl. GU9: Farnh 2G 128
Whitley Cl. TW19: Stan 9N 7
Whitley Rd. GU46: Yate 2C 68
Whitlock Dr. SW19 1K 27
Whitmead Cl. CR2: S Croy 3B 64
Whitmead La. GU10: Til 6C 130
Whitmoor La. GU4: Sut G 4N 93
Whitmoor Rd. GU19: Bag 4K 51
Whitmoor Va.
GU26: G'hott 2K 169
Whitmoor Va. Rd.
GU26: G'hott, Hind 2L 169
Whitmore Cl. GU47: Owls 7J 49
Whitmore Grn.
GU9: H End 6K 109
Whitmore La.
SL5: S'dale, S'hill 4D 34
Whitmore Rd. BR3: Beck 2J 47
Whitmores Cl. KT18: Eps 2B 80
Whitmore Vale Rd.
GU26: G'hott 5M 169
Whitmore Way RH6: Horl 7C 142
Whitnell Way SW15 8H 13
Whitstable Cl. BR3: Beck 1J 47
Whitstable Pl.
CR0: Croy 7C 200 (1N 63)
Whitstone La. BR3: Beck 4L 47
Whittaker Av. TW9: Rich 8K 11
Whittaker Ct. KT21: A'tead 4K 79
Whittaker Pl. *TW9: Rich* 8K 11
(off Whittaker Av.)
Whittaker Rd. SM3: Sut 9L 43
Whittingham Ct. W4 3D 12

Whittingstall Rd.—Windermere Ho.

Whittingstall Rd. SW6 ... 4L 13
Whittington Rd.
RH10: Craw ... 6B 182
Whittlebury Cl. SM5: Cars ... 4D 62
Whittle Cl. GU12: A Va ... 8D 90
GU47: Sandh ... 6F 48
Whittle Cres. GU14: Cove ... 7L 69
Whittle Rd. TW5: Hest ... 3K 9
Whittle Way RH10: Craw ... 6E 162
WHITTON ... 1C 24
Whitton Dene TW3: Houn ... 8C 10
TW7: Isle ... 9D 10
Whitton Mnr. Rd. TW7: Isle ... 9C 10
Whitton Rd. RG12: Brac ... 2D 32
TW1: Twick ... 9F 10
TW2: Twick ... 9E 10
TW3: Houn ... 7B 10
WHITTON ROAD RDBT. ... 9F 10
Whitton Sports & Fitness Cen. ... 3B 24
Whitton Station (Rail) ... 1C 24
Whitton Waye TW3: Houn ... 9A 10
Whitwell Hatch
GU27: Hasl ... 3H 189
Whitworth Rd.
RH11: Craw ... 8B 162
SE25 ... 2B 46
Whopshott Av. GU21: Wok ... 3M 73
Whopshott Cl. GU21: Wok ... 3M 73
Whopshott Dr. GU21: Wok ... 3M 73
Whynstones Rd. SL5: Asc ... 5L 33
Whyteacre CR3: Warl ... 7E 84
Whyte Av. GU12: Alde ... 4B 110
Whytebeam Vw.
CR3: Whyte ... 5C 84
Whytecliffe Rd. Nth.
CR8: Pur ... 7M 63
Whytecliffe Rd. Sth.
CR8: Pur ... 7L 63
Whytecroft TW5: Hest ... 3L 9
WHYTELEAFE ... 5C 84
Whyteleafe Bus. Village
CR3: Whyte ... 4C 84
Whyteleafe Hill CR3: Whyte ... 7B 84
(not continuous)
Whyteleafe Rd. CR3: Cate ... 7B 84
Whyteleafe South Station (Rail) ... 6D 84
Whyteleafe Station (Rail) ... 4C 84
Whyte M. SM3: Chea ... 4K 61
Wicket, The CR0: A'ton ... 2K 65
Wicket Hill GU10: Wrec ... 5F 128
Wickets, The TW15: A'ford ... 5N 21
Wickham Av. CR0: Croy ... 8H 47
SM3: Chea ... 2H 61
Wickham Chase
BR4: W Wick ... 7N 47
Wickham Cl. GU52: C Cro ... 7A 88
KT3: N Mal ... 5E 42
RH6: Horl ... 7D 142
Wickham Ct. KT5: Surb ... 8L 203
Wickham Ct. Rd.
BR4: W Wick ... 8M 47
Wickham Cres.
BR4: W Wick ... 8M 47
Wickham La. TW20: Egh ... 8C 20
Wickham Pl. GU52: C Cro ... 7A 88
Wickham Rd. BR3: Beck ... 1L 47
CR0: Croy ... 8G 46
GU15: Camb ... 7C 50
GU52: C Cro ... 7A 88
Wickham Theatre Cen. ... 8N 47
Wickham Va. RG12: Brac ... 5K 31
Wickham Way BR3: Beck ... 3M 47
WICK HILL ... 8B 16
Wick Hill La. RG40: Finch ... 1A 48
Wick Ho. KT1: H Wic ... 1G 203
Wickhurst Gdns.
RH12: Bro H ... 5E 196
Wickhurst La.
RH12: Bro H ... 5E 196
Wickland Ct. RH10: Craw ... 6B 182
Wick La. TW20: Eng G ... 7J 19
Wick Rd. TW11: Tedd ... 8H 25
TW20: Eng G ... 9K 19
Wick's Grn. RG42: Bin ... 5H 15
Wicks La. RG10: S Row ... 1D 14
Wicksteed Ho. TW8: Brent ... 1M 11
Wide Way CR4: Mit ... 2H 45
Widewing Cl. TW11: Tedd ... 8H 25
Widgeon Way RH12: Hors ... 3J 197
Widmer Ct. TW3: Houn ... 5M 9
Wiggett Gro. RG42: Bin ... 7H 15
Wiggie La. RH1: Red ... 1E 122
Wiggington Ho. SL4: Eton ... 3G 4
(off High St.)
Wiggins La. TW10: Ham ... 3J 25
Wiggins Yd. GU7: Goda ... 7H 133
Wight Ho. KT1: K Tham ... 6H 203
Wighton M. TW7: Isle ... 5E 10
Wigley Rd. TW13: Felt ... 3L 23
Wigmore La. RH5: B Grn ... 9J 139
Wigmore Rd. SM5: Cars ... 8B 44
Wigmore Wlk. SM5: Cars ... 8B 44
Wilberforce Cl.
RH11: Craw ... 9A 182
Wilberforce Ct. BR2: Kes ... 4F 66
KT18: Eps ... 8K 201
Wilberforce Way
RG12: Brac ... 4B 32
SW19 ... 7J 27
Wilbury Av. SM2: Chea ... 6L 61
Wilbury Rd. GU21: Wok ... 4N 73
Wilcot Cl. GU24: Bis ... 3D 72
Wilcot Gdns. GU24: Bis ... 3D 72
Wilcox Gdns. TW17: Shep ... 2N 37
Wilcox Rd. SM1: Sut ... 1N 61
TW11: Tedd ... 5D 24
Wildacre Cl. RH14: Ifo ... 5F 192
Wild Acres KT14: W By ... 7L 55
Wildbank Ct. GU22: Wok ... 5B 74
Wildcroft Dr. RH5: Nth H ... 8K 119
Wildcroft Mnr. SW15 ... 1H 27
Wildcroft Rd. SW15 ... 1H 27
Wildcroft Wood GU8: Wit ... 4A 152
Wilde Pl. SW18 ... 1B 28
Wilderness, The
KT8: W Mole, E Mol ... 4C 40
TW12: H Hill ... 5B 24
Wilderness Ct. GU2: Guil ... 5J 113
Wilderness Island Nature Reserve ... 8E 44
Wilderness Ri.
RH19: D Pk ... 5C 166
Wilderness Rd. GU2: Guil ... 5J 113
GU16: Frim ... 4C 70
RH8: Oxt ... 8N 105
Wilders Cl. GU16: Frim ... 3C 70
GU21: Wok ... 5M 73
RG42: Brac ... 8M 15
Wilderwick Rd.
RH7: E Grin ... 3C 166
RH19: E Grin ... 3C 166
Wilde Theatre ... 6A 32
Wildfield Cl. GU3: Wood V ... 2E 112
Wildgoose Dr. RH12: Hors ... 5F 196
Wildmoor Heath Local Nature Reserve ... 5H 49
WILDRIDINGS ... 3M 31
Wildridings Rd. RG12: Brac ... 3L 31
Wildridings Sq.
RG12: Brac ... 3M 31
Wild Wood RH12: Hors ... 5F 196
Wildwood Cl. GU6: Cranl ... 9A 156
GU22: Pyr ... 2H 75
KT24: E Hor ... 3G 96
Wildwood Ct. CR8: Ken ... 2A 84
Wildwood Gdns.
GU46: Yate ... 2B 68
Wildwood La.
GU6: Alf, Cranl ... 4J 175
Wilford Rd. CR0: Croy ... 5N 45
Wilfred Owen Cl.
SW19 ... 7A 28
Wilfred St. GU21: Wok ... 5N 73
Wilhelmina Av. CR5: Coul ... 6G 83
Wilkes Rd. TW8: Brent ... 2L 11
Wilkins Cl. CR4: Mit ... 9C 28
UB3: Harl ... 1G 9
Wilkinson Ct. RH11: Craw ... 8N 181
SW17 ... 5B 28
Wilkinson Gdns. SE25 ... 1B 46
Wilks Gdns. CR0: Croy ... 7H 47
Willard Way RH19: E Grin ... 7K 165
Willats Cl. KT16: Chert ... 5H 37
Willcocks Cl. KT9: Ches ... 9L 41
Willems Av. GU11: Alde ... 2L 109
Willems Rdbt. GU11: Alde ... 2L 109
Willerton Lodge
KT13: Weybr ... 3E 56
Willett Pl. CR7: T Hea ... 4L 45
Willett Rd. CR7: T Hea ... 4L 45
Willetts Way RH14: Loxw ... 5H 193
Willey Broom La.
CR3: Cate ... 3L 103
Willey Farm La. CR3: Cate ... 4N 103
WILLEY GREEN ... 9A 92
Willey La. CR3: Cate ... 3A 104
William Banfield Ho.
SW6 ... 5L 13
(off Munster Rd.)
William Ct. GU14: Farnb ... 4A 90
(off Cambridge Rd. W.)
William Dyce M.
SW16 ... 5H 29
William Ellis Cl. SL4: O Win ... 8K 5
William Evans Rd.
KT19: Eps ... 7N 59
William Evelyn Ct.
RH5: Wott ... 8N 117
William Farm La.
SW15 ... 6G 13
William Farthing Cl.
GU11: Alde ... 2M 109
William Gdns. SW15 ... 8G 13
William Harvey Ho.
SW19 ... 2K 27
(off Whitlock Dr.)
William Hitchcock Ho.
GU14: Farnb ... 7N 69
William Hunt Mans.
SW13 ... 2H 13
William Morris Ho.
W6 ... 2J 13
William Morris Way
RH11: Craw ... 9N 181
SW6 ... 6N 13
William Penney Hall
SL5: S'hill ... 2C 34
(off Buckhurst Rd.)
William Rd. CR3: Cate ... 9A 84
GU1: Guil ... 3B 202 (3M 113)
SM1: Sut ... 2A 62
SW19 ... 8K 27
William Russell Ct.
GU21: Wok ... 5H 73
Williams Cl. KT15: Addl ... 2K 55
SW6 ... 3K 13
Williams Dr. TW3: Houn ... 7A 10
Williams Gro. KT6: Surb ... 5J 41
Williams Hall TW20: Eng G ... 4M 19
(off Coopers Hill La.)
William Sim Wood
RG42: Wink R ... 7F 16
Williams La. SM4: Mord ... 4A 44
SW14 ... 6B 12
Williamson Cl.
GU27: G'wood ... 8K 171
Williams Pl. GU6: Ewh ... 5F 156
Williams Rd. UB2: S'hall ... 1M 9
Williams Ter. CR0: Wad ... 3L 63
William St. SL4: W'sor ... 4G 4
SM5: Cars ... 9C 44
William's Wlk. GU2: Guil ... 8L 93
Williams Way GU51: Fleet ... 4D 88
RH10: Craw ... 3F 182
Willian Pl. GU26: Hind ... 3C 170
Willingham Way
KT1: K Tham ... 2N 41
Willington Cl. GU15: Camb ... 9N 49
Willis Av. SM2: Sut ... 3C 62
Willis Cl. KT18: Eps ... 1A 80
Willis Ct. BR4: W Wick ... 8N 47
CR7: T Hea ... 5L 45
Willis Rd. CR0: Croy ... 6N 45
Will Miles Ct. SW19 ... 8A 28
Willmore End SW19 ... 9N 27
Willoughby Av. CR0: Bedd ... 1K 63
Willoughby Rd.
KT2: K Tham ... 1M 203 (9M 25)
RG12: Brac ... 2L 31
TW1: Twick ... 8J 11
(not continuous)
Willoughbys, The
SW14 ... 6D 12
Willow Av. SW13 ... 5E 12
Willow Bank GU22: Wok ... 9A 74
SW6 ... 6K 13
TW10: Ham ... 4H 25
Willowbank CR5: Coul ... 1J 83
Willowbank Gdns.
KT20: Tad ... 9G 81
Willowbank Pl.
CR8: S Croy ... 5M 63
Willow Brean RH6: Horl ... 7C 142
Willowbrook SL4: Eton ... 1G 5
TW12: H Hill ... 6B 24
Willowbrook Rd.
TW19: Stan ... 3N 21
Willow Bus. Cen., The
CR4: Mit ... 5D 44
Willow Cl. GU16: Mytc ... 1C 90
KT15: Wood ... 7H 55
KT16: Chert ... 8G 36
RH5: B Grn ... 7J 139
RH10: Craw ... 1C 182
RH19: E Grin ... 7N 165
SL3: Coln ... 3E 6
TW8: Brent ... 2J 11
Willow Cnr. RH6: Char ... 3L 161
Willow Cotts. TW9: Kew ... 2N 11
TW13: Hanw ... 4M 23
Willow Ct. GU12: A Va ... 6E 90
GU16: Frim ... 5B 70
(off Grove Cross Rd.)
RH6: Horl ... 5F 142
TW16: Sunb ... 8F 22
(off Staines Rd. W.)
W4 ... 3D 12
(off Corney Reach Way)
Willow Cres. GU14: Farnb ... 7N 69
Willowdene Cl. TW2: Whitt ... 1C 24
Willow Dr. GU3: Flex ... 3N 111
GU23: Rip ... 2J 95
RG12: Brac ... 9A 16
Willow End KT6: Surb ... 7L 41
Willowfield RH11: Craw ... 4A 182
Willow Flds. GU12: A Grn ... 3F 110
Willowford GU46: Yate ... 9C 48
Willow Gdns. TW3: Houn ... 4A 10
Willow Glade RH2: Reig ... 6A 122
Willow Grn. GU24: W End ... 9C 52
RH5: Nth H ... 9H 119
Willowhayne Ct.
KT12: Wal T ... 6J 39
(off Willowhayne Dr.)
Willowhayne Dr.
KT12: Wal T ... 6J 39
Willowhayne Gdns.
KT4: W Pk ... 9H 43
Willowherb Cl.
RG40: W'ham ... 1D 30
Willow Ho. CR6: Warl ... 2L 85
Willow La. CR4: Mit ... 4D 44
GU1: Guil ... 2C 114
GU17: Haw ... 2J 69
Willow Lodge SW6 ... 4J 13
TW16: Sunb ... 8G 23
(off Forest Dr.)
Willow Mead GU8: Wit ... 5B 152
RH4: Dork ... 1J 201 (4G 119)
RH19: E Grin ... 1B 186
Willowmead TW18: Stain ... 9K 21
Willowmead Cl. GU21: Wok ... 3K 73
Willowmere KT10: Esh ... 1C 58
Willow M. GU8: Wit ... 5C 152
Willow Mt. CR0: Croy ... 9B 46
Willow Pk. GU12: Ash ... 2D 110
Willow Pl. SL4: Eton ... 2F 4
Willow Ridge RH10: T Hil ... 6D 184
Willow Rd. GU7: Goda ... 3J 133
KT3: N Mal ... 3B 42
RH1: Red ... 6A 122
RH12: Hors ... 3A 198
SL3: Poy ... 5G 7
SM6: W'ton ... 4F 62
Willows, The GU2: Guil ... 7K 93
(off Worplesdon Rd.)
GU4: Guil ... 1E 114
GU8: Chid ... 5D 172
GU10: Run ... 8A 110
GU18: Ligh ... 6A 52
KT10: Clay ... 3E 58
KT13: Weybr ... 9B 38
KT14: Byf ... 9N 55
RG12: Brac ... 3D 32
RH1: Red ... 4D 122
RH12: Hors ... 3K 197
SL4: W'sor ... 3A 4
Willows Av. SM4: Mord ... 4N 43
Willows End GU47: Sandh ... 7G 48
Willows Lodge SL4: W'sor ... 3A 4
Willows Mobile Home Pk., The
GU3: Norm ... 9A 92
Willows Path KT18: Eps ... 1A 80
SL4: W'sor ... 4A 4
Willow Tree Cl. SW18 ... 2N 27
Willowtree Way CR7: T Hea ... 9L 29
Willow Va. KT22: Fetc ... 1B 98
(not continuous)
Willow Vw. SW19 ... 9B 28
Willow Wlk. BR6: Farnb ... 1K 67
GU5: Shere ... 8B 116
KT16: Chert ... 6J 37
KT20: Box H ... 8A 100
RH1: Red ... 5F 122
SM3: Sut ... 9L 43
TW20: Eng G ... 6M 19
Willow Way GU1: Guil ... 8L 93
GU9: Hale ... 6J 109
GU12: Alde ... 4C 110
GU22: Wok ... 8A 74
GU47: Sandh ... 6E 48
KT14: W By ... 7L 55
KT19: Ewe ... 3C 60
RH9: Gods ... 1E 124
TW2: Twick ... 3B 24
TW16: Sunb ... 3H 39
Willow Wood Cres.
SE25 ... 5B 46
Wills Cres. TW3: Houn ... 9B 10
Willson Rd. TW20: Eng G ... 6L 19
Wilmar Gdns. BR4: W Wick ... 7L 47
Wilmer Cl. KT2: K Tham ... 6M 25
Wilmer Cres. KT2: K Tham ... 6M 25
Wilmerhatch La. KT18: Eps ... 5A 80
Wilmington Av. W4 ... 3C 12
Wilmington Cl.
RH11: Craw ... 8N 181
Wilmington Ct. SW16 ... 8J 29
Wilmot Cl. RG42: Bin ... 7H 15
Wilmot Cotts. SM7: Ban ... 2N 81
Wilmot Rd. CR8: Pur ... 8L 63
SM5: Cars ... 2D 62
Wilmots Cl. RH2: Reig ... 2A 122
Wilmot's La. RH1: Horn ... 4A 144
RH6: Horn ... 4A 144
Wilmot Way GU15: Camb ... 3D 70
SM7: Ban ... 1M 81
Wilna Rd. SW18 ... 1A 28
Wilson Av. CR4: Mit ... 8C 28
Wilson Cl.
CR2: S Croy ... 8D 200 (2A 64)
RH10: Craw ... 6H 183
Wilson Dr. KT16: Otter ... 2D 54
Wilson Rd. GU12: Alde ... 3B 110
GU14: Cove ... 2L 89
KT9: Ches ... 3M 59
Wilsons KT20: Tad ... 8J 81
Wilsons Rd. GU35: H Dwn ... 4G 169
W6 ... 1J 13
Wilson Way GU21: Wok ... 3N 73
Wilstrode Av. RG42: Bin ... 8L 15
Wilton Av. W4 ... 1D 12
Wilton Cl. UB7: Harm ... 2M 7
Wilton Ct. GU14: Farnb ... 2B 90
Wilton Cres. SL4: W'sor ... 7A 4
SW19 ... 8L 27
Wilton Gdns. KT8: W Mole ... 2A 40
KT12: Wal T ... 7L 39
Wilton Gro. KT3: N Mal ... 5E 42
SW19 ... 9L 27
Wilton Ho. CR2: S Croy ... 8B 200
RH11: Craw ... 3A 182
Wilton Pde. TW13: Felt ... 3H 23
Wilton Pl. KT15: N Haw ... 5M 55
Wilton Rd. GU15: Camb ... 3N 69
RH1: Red ... 4D 122
SW19 ... 8C 28
TW4: Houn ... 6L 9
Wiltshire Av. RG45: Crow ... 1G 48
Wiltshire Ct.
CR2: S Croy ... 8C 200 (2N 63)
Wiltshire Dr. RG40: W'ham ... 1C 30
Wiltshire Gdns. TW2: Twick ... 2C 24
Wiltshire Gro. RG42: Warf ... 7D 16
Wiltshire Rd. CR7: T Hea ... 2L 45
RG40: W'ham ... 9B 14
Wilverley Cres. KT3: N Mal ... 5D 42
Wilwood Rd. RG42: Brac ... 9K 15
Wimbart Rd. SW2 ... 1K 29
WIMBLEDON ... 6J 27
Wimbledon
All England Lawn Tennis & Croquet Club ... 5K 27
Wimbledon Bri. SW19 ... 7L 27
Wimbledon Chase Station (Rail) ... 1K 43
Wimbledon Cl. GU15: Camb ... 6D 50
SW20 ... 8J 27
Wimbledon Common ... 5E 26
Wimbledon Greyhound & Speedway Stadium ... 5A 28
Wimbledon Hill Rd.
SW19 ... 7K 27
Wimbledon Lawn Tennis Mus. ... 4K 27
Wimbledon Leisure Cen. ... 7N 27
Wimbledon Mus. of Local History ... 7K 27
WIMBLEDON PARK ... 4M 27
Wimbledon Pk. Ct.
SW19 ... 2L 27
Wimbledon Pk. Rd.
SW18 ... 3K 27
SW19 ... 3K 27
Wimbledon Pk. Side
SW19 ... 4J 27
Wimbledon Park Station (Tube) ... 4M 27
Wimbledon Rd.
GU15: Camb ... 6D 50
SW17 ... 5A 28
Wimbledon Stadium Bus. Cen.
SW17 ... 4N 27
Wimbledon Station (Rail, Tube & CT) ... 7L 27
Wimbledon Theatre ... 8M 27
Wimbledon Windmill Mus. ... 3G 27
WIMBLE HILL ... 1A 128
Wimblehurst Ct.
RH12: Hors ... 4J 197
Wimblehurst Rd.
RH12: Hors ... 4J 197
Wimborne Av. RH1: Red ... 8D 122
Wimborne Cl. KT4: W Pk ... 7H 43
KT17: Eps ... 7M 201 (9D 60)
Wimborne Ct. SW12 ... 4G 28
Wimborne Ho. GU14: Farnb ... 3B 90
SW12 ... 4G 28
Wimborne Way BR3: Beck ... 2G 47
Wimbourne Ho.
RH11: Craw ... 3A 182
Wimland Hill RH12: Fay ... 7C 180
Wimland Rd.
RH12: Rusp, Fay ... 4A 180
Wimlands La. RH12: Fay ... 7C 180
Wimpole Cl.
KT1: K Tham ... 4M 203 (1M 41)
Wimshurst Cl. CR0: Wad ... 7J 45
Wincanton Cl. RH10: Craw ... 2H 183
Wincanton Rd. SW18 ... 1L 27
Winch Cl. RG42: Bin ... 6H 15
Winchcombe Cl.
GU51: Fleet ... 5B 88
Winchcombe Rd.
SM5: Cars ... 6B 44
Winchelsea Cl. SW15 ... 8J 13
Winchelsey Ri. CR2: S Croy ... 3C 64
Winchendon Rd. SW6 ... 4L 13
TW11: Tedd ... 5D 24
Winches, The RH13: Col ... 2H 199
Winchester Av. TW5: Hest ... 2N 9
Winchester Cl.
KT2: K Tham ... 8A 26
KT10: Esh ... 1A 58
SL3: Poy ... 4G 7
Winchester Ho. KT19: Eps ... 8N 59
(off Phoenix Cl.)
Winchester M. KT4: W Pk ... 8J 43
Winchester Rd.
GU10: Rush ... 3N 149
GU12: Ash ... 1E 110
KT12: Wal T ... 7H 39
RH10: Craw ... 7C 182
TW1: Twick ... 9H 11
TW13: Hanw ... 4N 23
UB3: Harl ... 3F 8
Winchester St.
GU14: Farnb ... 5A 90
Winchester Way
GU17: B'water ... 9H 49
Winchet Wlk. CR0: Croy ... 5F 46
Winchfield Ho. SW15 ... 9E 12
Winchgrove Rd.
RG42: Brac ... 8M 15
Winchilsea Cres.
KT8: W Mole ... 1C 40
Winchstone Cl. TW17: Shep ... 3A 38
Windborough Rd.
SM5: Cars ... 4E 62
Windermere Av. SW19 ... 2N 43
Windermere Cl.
GU14: Cove ... 2K 89
TW14: Felt ... 2G 22
TW19: Stan ... 2N 21
TW20: Egh ... 8D 20
Windermere Ct. CR8: Ken ... 2M 83
GU12: A Va ... 9D 90
(off Lakeside Cl.)
GU21: Wok ... 5K 73
(off St John's Rd.)
SM5: Cars ... 9E 44
SW13 ... 2E 12
Windermere Ho. TW7: Isle ... 8F 10

Woodcroft Rd.—Worple Rd.

Woodcroft Rd. CR7: T Hea 4M **45**
RH11: Ifi 5J **181**
Woodcut Rd. GU10: Wrec 5E **128**
WOOD END 7M **17**
Wood End GU14: Farnb 2B **90**
RH12: Hors 3B **198**
Wood End, The SM6: W'ton . . .5F **62**
Woodend KT10: Esh 8C **40**
KT22: Leat 3J **99**
SE19 . . . . .7N **29**
SM1: Sut 8A **44**
Woodend Cl. GU21: Wok 6K **73**
RH10: Craw 1E **182**
SL5: Asc 9J **17**
Woodend Dr. SL5: S'hill 4M **33**
Woodend Pk. KT11: Cob 2L **77**
Woodend Ride SL4: Wink 8M **17**
SL5: Asc 8M **17**
Woodend Rd. GU16: Deep 7G **71**
Woodenhill RG12: Brac 6K **31**
Wooderson Cl. SE25 . . . . .3B **46**
Woodfield KT21: A'tead 4K **79**
Woodfield Av. SM5: Cars 3E **62**
SW16 . . . . .4H **29**
Woodfield Cl. CR5: Coul 6G **82**
KT21: A'tead 4K **79**
RH1: Red 1C **122**
RH10: Craw 2C **182**
SE19 . . . . .8N **29**
Woodfield Gdns.
KT3: N Mal 4E **42**
Woodfield Gro. SW16 . . . . .4H **29**
Woodfield Hill CR5: Coul 6F **82**
Woodfield Ho. *KT7: T Dit 8F 40*
(off Woodfield Rd.)
Woodfield La. KT21: A'tead 4L **79**
SW16 . . . . .4H **29**
Woodfield Lodge
RH10: Craw 1E **182**
Woodfield Rd. KT7: T Dit 8F **40**
KT21: A'tead 4K **79**
RH10: Craw 2C **182**
RH12: Rudg 1E **194**
TW4: C'ford 5J **9**
Woodfields, The
CR2: Sande 7C **64**
Woodfield Way RH1: Red 1C **122**
Woodforde Ct. UB3: Harl 1E **8**
Woodford Grn. RG12: Brac 3D **32**
Woodgate GU51: Fleet 2D **88**
Woodgate Av. KT9: Ches 2K **59**
Woodgate Cl. KT11: Cob 9J **57**
Woodgates Dr. SW16 . . . . .8H **29**
Woodgates Cl.
RH13: Hors 5M **197**
Woodgavil SM7: Ban 3L **81**
Woodger Cl. GU4: Guil 1E **114**
Woodhall La. SL5: S'dale 8B **34**
WOODHAM 6J **55**
Woodham Hall Farm
GU21: Wok 1D **74**
Woodham La. GU21: Wok 1D **74**
KT15: Wok 1D **74**
KT15: Wood, N Haw 8G **55**
Woodham Lock KT14: W By . . .8H **55**
Woodham Pk. Rd.
KT15: Wood 5H **55**
Woodham Pk. Way
KT15: Wood 7H **55**
Woodham Pl. GU21: Wok 1B **74**
Woodham Ri. GU21: Wok 1B **74**
Woodham Rd. GU21: Wok 2A **74**
Woodham Waye
GU21: Wok 9D **54**
WOODHATCH 6N **121**
Woodhatch Rd. RH1: Red 6N **121**
RH2: Reig 6N **121**
Woodhatch Spinney
CR5: Coul 3J **83**
Woodhaven M. KT12: Wal T . . .1H **57**
Woodhaw TW20: Egh 5D **20**
Woodhayes RH6: Horl 7F **142**
Woodhayes Rd. SW19 . . . . .8H **27**
Woodhill GU23: Send 4F **94**
Woodhill Ct. GU23: Send 3F **94**
Woodhill La. GU5: Sha G 7G **135**
GU10: Fren 2D **148**
Woodhouse La.
RH5: H Mary 3H **137**
Woodhouse St. RG42: Bin 8K **15**
Woodhurst La. RH8: Oxt 8A **106**
Woodhurst Pk. RH8: Oxt 8A **106**
Woodhyrst Gdns. CR8: Ken 2M **83**
Woodies Cl. RG42: Bin 8H **15**
Wooding Gro. RH11: Craw . . .8N **181**
Woodland Av. GU6: Cranl 7A **156**
SL4: W'sor 7C **4**
Woodland Cl. KT13: Weybr 1E **56**
KT19: Ewe 3D **60**
KT24: E Hor 5G **97**
RH13: Hors 4A **198**
Woodland Ct. GU52: C Cro 9A **88**
KT17: Eps 8E **60**
RH8: Oxt 6N **105**
Woodland Craft Cen. 8C **62**
Woodland Cres.
GU14: Farnb 8A **70**
RG42: Brac 8A **16**
Woodland Dr. GU10: Wrec 5G **128**
KT24: E Hor 5G **96**
RH5: Ockl 5G **159**
RH10: Craw D 1E **184**
TN8: Eden 9M **127**
Woodland Gdns. CR2: Sels 7F **64**
TW7: Isle 6E **10**
Woodland Gro.
KT13: Weybr 1E **56**
Woodland La. RH13: Col 6G **198**
Woodland M. SW16 . . . . .4J **29**
Woodland Ri.
GU52: C Cro 8A **88**
RH8: Oxt 8A **106**
Woodland Rd. CR7: T Hea 3L **45**
WOODLANDS 5E **10**
Woodlands GU22: Wok 5B **74**
GU23: Send 3H **95**
GU46: Yate 3C **68**
GU51: Fleet 3A **88**
KT15: Addl 9N **37**
KT21: A'tead 5L **79**
RH6: Horl 7G **143**
RH10: Craw 1H **183**
SW20 . . . . .3H **43**
Woodlands, The GU1: Guil . . .2E **114**
KT10: Esh 8C **40**
RH6: Smal 8M **143**
SE19 . . . . .8N **29**
SM6: W'ton 5F **62**
TW7: Isle 5F **10**
Woodlands Av.
GU9: Weybo 5L **109**
KT3: N Mal 9B **26**
KT4: W Pk 8E **42**
KT14: W By 9H **55**
RH1: Red 4D **122**
Woodlands Cvn. Pk.
GU12: Ash 3D **110**
Woodlands Cl. GU1: Guil 8A **94**
GU6: Cranl 7A **156**
GU12: A Va 8E **90**
GU17: Haw 5K **69**
KT10: Clay 4F **58**
KT16: Otter 6D **54**
RH10: Craw D 2E **184**
SL5: Asc 5K **33**
Woodlands Copse
KT21: A'tead 3K **79**
Woodlands Cotts.
RH5: Newd 7B **160**
Woodlands Ct. GU21: Wok 5K **73**
GU22: Wok 6A **74**
GU47: Owls 6L **49**
RH1: Red 5D **122**
Woodlands Dr.
RH9: S Gods 6H **125**
TW16: Sunb 1K **39**
Woodlands Gdns.
KT18: Tat C 4H **81**
Woodlands Ga. *SW15 . . . . .8L 13*
(off Woodlands Way)
Woodlands Gro. CR5: Coul 4E **82**
TW7: Isle 5E **10**
Woodlands Ho. GU21: Wok 1E **74**
Woodlands La.
GU20: Windl 3A **52**
GU27: Hasl 1D **188**
KT11: Leat, Sto D 4A **78**
Woodlands Pde.
TW15: A'ford 7D **22**
Woodlands Pk. GU1: Guil 2D **114**
GU21: Wok 1E **74**
KT15: Addl 2H **55**
KT20: Box H 9A **100**
Woodlands Ride SL5: Asc 5K **33**
Woodlands Rd. GU1: Guil 8N **93**
GU8: Hamb 9G **152**
GU14: Cove 8J **69**
GU15: Camb 1N **69**
GU25: V Wat 3M **35**
KT6: Surb 6K **41**
KT14: W By 1H **75**
KT18: Eps 2N **79**
KT22: Leat 4D **78**
KT23: Book 6M **97**
RH1: Red 5D **122**
RH19: E Grin 6C **166**
SW13 . . . . .6E **12**
TW7: Isle 6D **10**
Woodlands Rd. E.
GU25: V Wat 3M **35**
Woodlands Rd. W.
GU25: V Wat 3M **35**
Woodlands Vw.
RH5: Mid H 2H **139**
Woodlands Wlk.
GU17: Haw 5K **69**
Woodlands Way
KT21: A'tead 3N **79**
SW15 . . . . .8L **13**
Woodland Vw.
GU7: Goda 2H **133**
Woodland Wlk.
GU12: Alde 1B **110**
KT19: Ewe 3N **59**
Woodland Way
BR4: W Wick 1L **65**
CR0: Croy 7H **47**
CR3: Cate 6B **104**
CR4: Mit 8E **28**
CR8: Pur 9L **63**
KT5: Surb 8A **42**
KT13: Weybr 2E **56**
KT20: Box H 8B **100**
KT20: K'wood 9K **81**
RH13: Hors 4N **197**
SM4: Mord 3L **43**
Wood La. CR3: Cate 2A **104**
GU10: Seal 8F **110**
GU14: Cove 2M **89**
GU21: Knap 5G **72**
GU51: Fleet 4D **88**
KT13: Weybr 5D **56**
KT20: Tad 4L **81**
RG42: Bin 6J **15**
TW7: Isle 2E **10**
Woodlark Glade
GU15: Camb 8B **50**
Woodlawn Cl. SW15 . . . . .8L **13**
Woodlawn Cres.
TW2: Whitt 3B **24**
Woodlawn Dr. TW13: Felt 3L **23**
Woodlawn Gro.
GU21: Wok 2B **74**
Woodlawn Rd. SW6 . . . . .3J **13**
Woodlawns KT19: Ewe 4C **60**
Wood Lea Cotts.
RH12: Bro H 1N **195**
Woodlee Cl. GU25: V Wat 1M **35**
Woodleigh GU51: Fleet 5B **88**
Woodleigh Gdns.
SW16 . . . . .4J **29**
Woodley Cl. SW17 . . . . .8D **28**
Woodley Ho. GU7: Goda 3H **133**
Woodley La. SM5: Cars 9C **44**
Woodlodge KT21: A'tead 4L **79**
Wood Lodge La.
BR4: W Wick 9M **47**
Woodmancote Ct.
RH12: Hors 3K 197
(off Blenheim Rd.)
Woodmancote Gdns.
KT14: W By 9J **55**
Woodmancott Cl.
RG12: Brac 5D **32**
Woodman Ct. GU51: Fleet 5A **88**
Woodmancourt
GU7: Goda 3F **132**
Woodman M. TW9: Kew 4A **12**
Woodman Rd. CR5: Coul 2G **83**
Woodmans Hill
RH11: Craw 8A **182**
WOODMANSTERNE 2D **82**
Woodmansterne La.
SM5: Cars 8D **62**
SM6: W'ton 8D **62**
SM7: Ban 2N **81**
Woodmansterne Rd.
CR5: Coul 2G **83**
SM5: Cars 8D **62**
SW16 . . . . .8G **29**
Woodmansterne Station (Rail)
. . . . .3F **82**
Woodmansterne St.
SM7: Ban 2C **82**
Woodmere RG12: Brac 3C **32**
Woodmere Av. CR0: Croy 6F **46**
Woodmere Cl. CR0: Croy 6G **47**
Woodmere Gdns.
CR0: Croy 6G **46**
Woodmere Way BR3: Beck 4N **47**
Woodmill Ct. SL5: Asc 2H **33**
Woodnook Rd. SW16 . . . . .6F **28**
Woodpecker Cl.
GU10: Ews 4C **108**
KT11: Cob 8M **57**
TN8: Eden 9M **127**
Woodpecker La.
RH5: Newd 9B **140**
Woodpecker Mt. CR0: Sels 5H **65**
Woodpeckers GU8: Mil 3B **152**
RG12: Brac 3N 31
(off Crowthorne Rd.)
Woodpecker Way
GU22: Wok 2N **93**
RH10: T Hil 4F **184**
Woodplace Cl. CR5: Coul 6G **83**
Woodplace La. CR5: Coul 5G **83**
Woodridge Cl. RG12: Brac 2A **32**
Wood Riding GU22: Pyr 2G **75**
Woodridings KT13: Weybr 3B **56**
Wood Ri. GU3: Guil 1H **113**
Wood Rd. GU7: Goda 4J **133**
GU9: U Hal 5H **109**
GU15: Camb 5N **69**
GU26: Hind 3B **170**
TN16: B Hil 5E **86**
TW17: Shep 3B **38**
Woodroffe Benton Ho.
RH11: Craw 3L 181
(off Rusper Rd.)
Woodrough Copse
GU5: Braml 6C **134**
Woodrough La. *GU5: Braml . . .5B 134*
(off High St.)
Woodrow Dr.
RG40: W'ham 2D **30**
Woodroyd Av. RH6: Horl 9D **142**
Woodroyd Gdns.
RH6: Horl 1D **162**
Woodruff Av. GU1: Guil 9C **94**
Woods Hill Cl.
RH19: Ash W 3F **186**
Woods Hill La.
RH19: Ash W 3F **186**
Woodshore Cl.
GU25: V Wat 5L **35**
WOODSIDE
SE25 . . . . .5D **46**
SL4 . . . . .6N **17**
Woodside GU14: Farnb 7N **69**
GU15: Camb 8L **49**
GU17: Haw 4H **69**
KT12: Wal T 7H **39**
KT20: Lwr K 6L **101**
KT22: Fetc 9B **78**
KT24: W Hors 4D **96**
RH13: Hors 4A **198**
SW19 . . . . .7L **27**
Woodside Av. KT10: Esh 6E **40**
KT12: Hers 1J **57**
SE25 . . . . .5E **46**
Woodside Cl. CR3: Cate 2B **104**
GU8: Chid 5E **172**
GU21: Knap 4G **73**
KT5: Surb 6B **42**
Woodside Cotts.
CR3: Wold 1K **105**
GU8: Els 8G **131**
Woodside Ct. *GU14: Cove 9J 69*
(off Guillemont Flds.)
Woodside Ct. Rd.
CR0: Croy 6D **46**
Woodside Cres.
RH6: Smal 8L **143**
Woodside Gdns.
GU51: Fleet 4D **88**
Woodside Grn. SE25 . . . . .5D **46**
(not continuous)
Woodside Ho. SW19 . . . . .7L **27**
Woodside La. SL4: Wink 6N **17**
Woodside Pk. SE25 . . . . .5E **46**
Woodside Pk. Est.
GU7: Goda 7J **133**
Woodside Rd. CR8: Pur 9H **63**
GU2: Guil 2J **113**
GU8: Chid 4C **172**
GU9: Weybo 5K **109**
GU14: Farnb 6L **89**
KT2: K Tham 8L **25**
KT3: N Mal 1C **42**
KT11: Cob 9A **58**
RH5: B Grn 8K **139**
RH10: Craw 1D **182**
SE25 . . . . .5E **46**
SL4: Wink 6M **17**
SM1: Sut 9A **44**
Woodside Rd. Flats
GU8: Chid 5E 172
(off Woodside Rd.)
Woodside Stop (CT) 5E **46**
Woodside Way CR0: Croy 5F **46**
CR4: Mit 9F **28**
GU25: V Wat 2L **35**
RH1: Red 4E **122**
(Redstone Hollow)
RH1: Red 9E **122**
(West Av.)
Woodsome Lodge
KT13: Weybr 3D **56**
Woodspring Rd. SW19 . . . . . . .3K **27**
WOODSTOCK, THE 6L **43**
Woodstock GU4: W Cla 6K **95**
RH19: E Grin 8M **165**
Woodstock Av. SL3: Lang 1N **5**
SM3: Sut 6L **43**
TW7: Isle 8G **10**
Woodstock Cl. GU6: Cranl 9A **156**
GU21: Wok 3A **74**
RH12: Hors 3K **197**
Woodstock Ct.
KT19: Eps 5K **201** (9C **60**)
Woodstock Gro.
GU7: Goda 4G **133**
Woodstock La. KT9: Ches 1H **59**
Woodstock La. Nth.
KT6: Surb 8J **41**
Woodstock La. Sth.
KT9: Ches 2H **59**
KT10: Clay 2H **59**
Woodstock Ri. SM3: Sut 6L **43**
Woodstock Rd.
CR0: Croy 5D **200** (9A **46**)
CR5: Coul 3F **82**
SM5: Cars 2E **62**
Woodstocks GU14: Farnb 8A **70**
Woodstock Way CR4: Mit 1F **44**
Woodstone Av. KT17: Ewe 2F **60**
Wood St. CR4: Mit 6E **44**
GU12: A Va 7E **90**
KT1: K Tham 3H **203** (1K **41**)
(not continuous)
RH1: Mers 7G **103**
RH19: E Grin 9N **165**
W4 . . . . .1D **12**
Wood St. Grn.
GU3: Wood V 1D **112**
WOOD STREET VILLAGE 1E **112**
Woodsway KT22: Oxs 1E **78**
Woodthorpe Rd.
SW15 . . . . .7G **13**
TW15: A'ford 7M **21**
Woodvale Av. SE25 . . . . .2C **46**
Woodvale Wlk. SE27 . . . . .6N **29**
Woodview KT9: Ches 7J **59**
Woodview Cl. CR2: Sande 1E **84**
KT21: A'tead 3N **79**
SW15 . . . . .5C **26**
Woodview Ct. KT13: Weybr 2D **56**
Woodville Cl.
GU17: B'water 1G **68**
TW11: Tedd 5G **24**
Woodville Ct. KT22: Leat 7H **79**
Woodville Gdns. KT6: Surb 6K **41**
Woodville Rd. CR7: T Hea 3N **45**
SM4: Mord 3M **43**
TW10: Ham 4H **25**
Woodvill Rd. KT22: Leat 7H **79**
Woodward Cl. KT10: Clay 3F **58**
Woodwards RH11: Craw 8N **181**
Woodward's Footpath
TW2: Whitt 9C **10**
Woodway GU1: Guil 2D **114**
GU15: Camb 1N **69**
Woodyers Cl. GU5: Wone 4D **134**
Woolacombe Way UB3: Harl 1G **8**
Woolborough Cl.
RH10: Craw 2C **182**
Woolborough La. RH1: Out . . .3K **143**
RH10: Craw 9D **162**
Woolborough Rd.
RH10: Craw 2B **182**
Wooldridge Cl. TW14: Bedf 2D **22**
Woolf Dr. RG40: W'ham 1A **30**
Woolford Cl. RG42: Wink R 8F **16**
Woolfords La. GU8: Els 3E **150**
Woolhampton Way
RG12: Brac 4B **32**
Woolhams CR3: Cate 4D **104**
Woollards Rd. GU12: A Va 9F **90**
Woolmead, The
GU9: Farnh 9H **109**
Woolmead Rd. GU9: Farnh . . .9H **109**
Woolmead Wlk.
GU9: Farnh 9H 109
(off Woolmead Rd.)
WOOLMER HILL 1A **188**
Woolmer Hill Rd.
GU27: Hasl 9A **170**
Woolmer La. GU30: Brams . . .8F **168**
(not continuous)
Woolmer Vw. GU26: G'hott . . .6B **170**
Woolneigh St. SW6 . . . . .6N **13**
Wool Rd. SW20 . . . . .7G **27**
Woolsack Ct. GU2: Guil 9K **93**
Woolsack Way GU7: Goda 7H **133**
Wootton KT10: Esh 1C **58**
Wootton Cl. KT18: Eps 3E **80**
Wootton Grange *GU22: Wok . . .6A 74*
(off Langley Wlk.)
Worbeck Rd. SE20 . . . . .1E **46**
Worcester Cl. CR0: Croy 8K **47**
CR4: Mit 1E **44**
GU14: Farnb 7N **69**
Worcester Ct. *GU51: Fleet 2A 88*
(off King John St.)
KT4: W Pk 9D **42**
KT12: Wal T 8K **39**
RH1: Red 1C 122
(off Timperley Gdns.)
Worcester Dr. TW15: A'ford . . .6C **22**
Worcester Gdns. KT4: W Pk . . .9D **42**
WORCESTER PARK 7F **42**
Worcester Pk. Rd.
KT4: W Pk 9C **42**
Worcester Park Station (Rail)
. . . . .7F **42**
Worcester Rd. GU2: Guil 1J **113**
RH2: Reig 2L **121**
RH10: Craw 7C **182**
SM2: Sut 4M **61**
SW19 . . . . .6L **27**
Worcestershire Lea
RG42: Warf 8D **16**
Wordsworth RG12: Brac 4K **31**
Wordsworth Av. CR8: Ken 2A **84**
GU46: Yate 1A **68**
Wordsworth Cl.
RH10: Craw 1F **182**
Wordsworth Dr. SM3: Chea 1H **61**
Wordsworth Mans.
W14 . . . . .2L 13
(off Queens Club Gdns.)
Wordsworth Mead
RH1: Red 1E **122**
Wordsworth Pl.
RH12: Hors 1L **197**
Wordsworth Ri.
RH19: E Grin 9M **165**
Wordsworth Rd.
KT15: Addl 1M **55**
SM6: W'ton 3G **63**
TW12: Hamp 5N **23**
Wordsworth Way
UB7: W Dray 1N **7**
Workshop Gym, The
. . . . .1D **202** (2N **113**)
World Bus. Cen. TW6: Lon A . . .4D **8**
World's End KT11: Cob 1H **77**
Worlds End Hill RG12: Brac 5D **32**
Worleys Dr. BR6: Orp 1M **67**
Worlidge St. W6 . . . . .1H **13**
WORMLEY 9C **152**
Wormley La. GU8: Worm 9D **152**
Worple, The TW19: Wray 9B **6**
Worple Av. SW19 . . . . .8J **27**
TW7: Isle 8G **10**
TW18: Stain 7K **21**
Worple Rd.
KT18: Eps 8K **201** (2C **80**)
KT22: Leat 9H **79**
(Orchard Leigh, not continuous)
KT22: Leat 1H **99**
(The Driftway, not continuous)
SW19 . . . . .1H **43**
SW20 . . . . .1H **43**

HOSPITALS and HOSPICES
covered by this atlas.

N.B. Where Hospitals and Hospices are not named on the map, the reference given is for the road in which they are situated.

ABRAHAM COWLEY UNIT 9F **36**
Holloway Hill
Lyne
CHERTSEY
KT16 0AE
Tel: 01932 872010

ALPHA HOSPITAL, WOKING 5G **72**
Redding Way
Knaphill
WOKING
GU21 2QS
Tel: 01483 795100

ASHFORD HOSPITAL 3N **21**
London Road
ASHFORD
TW15 3AA
Tel: 01784 884488

ASHTEAD CAPIO HOSPITAL 6L **79**
The Warren
ASHTEAD
KT21 2SB
Tel: 01372 221400

BARNES HOSPITAL 6D **12**
South Worple Way
LONDON
SW14 8SU
Tel: 020 88784981

BECKENHAM HOSPITAL 1J **47**
379 Croydon Road
BECKENHAM
BR3 3QL
Tel: 01689 863000

BETHLEM ROYAL HOSPITAL 6K **47**
Monks Orchard Road
BECKENHAM
BR3 3BX
Tel: 020 32286000

BRITISH HOME, THE 6M **29**
Crown Lane
LONDON
SW16 3JB
Tel: 020 8670 8261

BROADMOOR HOSPITAL 2K **49**
Kentigern Drive
CROWTHORNE
RG45 7EG
Tel: 01344 754520

CANE HILL FORENSIC MENTAL HEALTH UNIT
..........................5G **82**
Brighton Road
COULSDON
CR5 3YL
Tel: 01737 758300

CARSHALTON WAR MEMORIAL HOSPITAL
..........................3D **62**
The Park
CARSHALTON
SM5 3DB
Tel: 020 8647 5534

CASSEL HOSPITAL, THE 5K **25**
1 Ham Common
RICHMOND
TW10 7JF
Tel: 020 8940 8181

CASUALTY PLUS WALK-IN CENTRE
(BRENTFORD) 1J **11**
1010 Great West Road
BRENTFORD
TW8 9BA
Tel: 0845 677 7999

CATERHAM DENE HOSPITAL 1C **104**
Church Road
CATERHAM
CR3 5RA
Tel: 01883 837500

CHARING CROSS HOSPITAL 2J **13**
Fulham Palace Road
LONDON
W6 8RF
Tel: 020 88461234

CHASE CHILDREN'S HOSPICE
(CHRISTOPHER'S) 8M **113**
Old Portsmouth Road
Artington
GUILDFORD
GU3 1LP
Tel: 01483 230960

CHILDREN'S TRUST, THE 8J **81**
Tadworth Court
TADWORTH
KT20 5RU
Tel: 01737 365000

CLARE PARK CLASSIC HOSPITAL 8A **108**
Crondall Lane
FARNHAM
GU10 5XX
Tel: 01252 850216

COBHAM COMMUNITY HOSPITAL 9J **57**
Portsmouth Road
COBHAM
KT11 1HT
Tel: 020 8296 2000

CRANLEIGH VILLAGE HOSPITAL 8M **155**
6 High Street
CRANLEIGH
GU6 8AE
Tel: 01483 782000

CRAWLEY HOSPITAL 3A **182**
West Green Drive
CRAWLEY
RH11 7DH
Tel: 01293 600300

DORKING COMMUNITY HOSPITAL 6H **119**
Horsham Road
DORKING
RH4 2AA
Tel: 01306 887150

EAST SURREY HOSPITAL 7E **122**
Canada Avenue
REDHILL
RH1 5RH
Tel: 01737 768511

EDENBRIDGE & DISTRICT WAR
MEMORIAL HOSPITAL 4L **147**
Mill Hill
EDENBRIDGE
TN8 5DA
Tel: 01732 863164 / 862137

EPSOM DAY SURGERY UNIT 9E **60**
The Old Cottage Hospital
Alexandra Road
EPSOM
KT17 4BL
Tel: 01372 739002

EPSOM GENERAL HOSPITAL 2B **80**
Dorking Road
EPSOM
KT18 7EG
Tel: 01372 735735

FARMFIELD 1N **161**
Farmfield Drive
Charlwood
HORLEY
RH6 0BN
Tel: 01293 787500

FARM PLACE 2C **178**
Stane Street
Ockley
DORKING
RH5 5NG
Tel: 01306 627742

FARNHAM HOSPITAL & CENTRE FOR HEALTH
..........................9K **109**
Hale Road
FARNHAM
GU9 9QL
Tel: 01483 782000

FARNHAM ROAD HOSPITAL
..................6A **202** (5L **113**)
Farnham Road
GUILDFORD
GU2 7LX
Tel: 01483 443535

FLEET COMMUNITY HOSPITAL 3A **88**
Church Road
FLEET
GU51 4LZ
Tel: 01483 782700

FRIMLEY PARK HOSPITAL 4B **70**
Portsmouth Road
Frimley
CAMBERLEY
GU16 7UJ
Tel: 01276 604604

GATWICK PARK BUPA HOSPITAL 9C **142**
Povey Cross Road
HORLEY
RH6 0BB
Tel: 01293 785511

GUILDFORD NUFFIELD HOSPITAL 3H **113**
Stirling Road
GUILDFORD
GU2 7RF
Tel: 01483 555800

HARLINGTON HOSPICE
(THE REG HOPKINS DAY CARE HOSPICE)
..........................1E **8**
St Peters Way
HAYES
UB3 5AB
Tel: 020 8759 0453 / 1700

HASLEMERE COMMUNITY HOSPITAL ...1H **189**
Church Lane
HASLEMERE
GU27 2BJ
Tel: 01483 782000

HEATHERWOOD HOSPITAL 2J **33**
London Road
ASCOT
SL5 8AA
Tel: 01344 623333

HENDERSON HOSPITAL 5N **61**
2 Homeland Drive
SUTTON
SM2 5LY
Tel: 020 86611611

HOLY CROSS HOSPITAL 1D **188**
Hindhead Road
HASLEMERE
GU27 1NQ
Tel: 01428 643311

HORSHAM HOSPITAL 5J **197**
Hurst Road
HORSHAM
RH12 2DR
Tel: 01403 227000

KING EDWARD VII HOSPITAL 6F **4**
St Leonard's Road
WINDSOR
SL4 3DP
Tel: 01753 860 441

KINGSTON HOSPITAL 9A **26**
Galsworthy Road
KINGSTON UPON THAMES
KT2 7QB
Tel: 020 8546 7711

LEATHERHEAD HOSPITAL 9J **79**
Poplar Road
LEATHERHEAD
KT22 8SD
Tel: 01372 384384

MACMILLAN HOUSE DAY THERAPY UNIT
(HOSPICE) 3A **30**
Wokingham Community Hospital,
Barkham Road
WOKINGHAM
RG41 2RE
Tel: 0118 949 5030

MARIE CURIE HOSPICE, CATERHAM, THE
..........................3C **104**
Harestone Drive
CATERHAM
CR3 6YQ
Tel: 01883 832600

MAYDAY UNIVERSITY HOSPITAL 5M **45**
530 London Road
THORNTON HEATH
CR7 7YE
Tel: 020 8401 3000

MCINDOE SURGICAL CENTRE 7B **166**
Holtye Road
EAST GRINSTEAD
RH19 3EB
Tel: 01342 330300

MEDICAL RECEPTION STATION (SANDHURST)
..........................7M **49**
Royal Military Academy Sandhurst
Egerton Road
CAMBERLEY
GU15 4PQ
Tel: 01276 412234

MILFORD HOSPITAL 2F **152**
Tuesley Lane
GODALMING
GU7 1UF
Tel: 01483 782000

MOLESEY HOSPITAL 4A **40**
High Street
WEST MOLESEY
KT8 2LU
Tel: 020 8941 4481

MOUNT ALVERNIA BMI HOSPITAL
..................6F **202** (5A **114**)
46 Harvey Road
GUILDFORD
GU1 3LX
Tel: 01483 570122

NELSON HOSPITAL 1L **43**
Kingston Road
LONDON
SW20 8DB
Tel: 020 8251 1111

NEW EPSOM & EWELL COMMUNITY HOSPITAL
..........................7L **59**
West Park
Horton Lane
EPSOM
KT19 8PB
Tel: 01372 734834

NEW VICTORIA HOSPITAL 9D **26**
184 Coombe Lane West
KINGSTON UPON THAMES
KT2 7EG
Tel: 020 8949 9000

NHS WALK-IN CENTRE (ASHFORD) 3N **21**
Ashford Hospital
London Road
ASHFORD
TW15 3AA
Tel: 01784 884488

NHS WALK-IN CENTRE (CHARING CROSS)
..........................1J **13**
Charing Cross Hospital
Fulham Palace Road
LONDON
W6 8RF
Tel: 020 8846 1234

NHS WALK-IN CENTRE (CRAWLEY) 3A **182**
Crawley Hospital
West Green Drive
CRAWLEY
RH11 7DH
Tel: 01293 600300

NHS WALK-IN CENTRE (CROYDON)
..................4C **200** (9N **45**)
45 High Street
CROYDON
CR0 1QD
Tel: 020 8666 0555

NHS WALK-IN CENTRE (PARSONS GREEN)
..........................4M **13**
5-7 Parsons Green
LONDON
SW6 4UL
Tel: 020 8846 6758

NHS WALK-IN CENTRE (TEDDINGTON) ...7E **24**
Teddington Memorial Hospital
Hampton Road
TEDDINGTON
TW11 0JL
Tel: 020 8714 4004

NHS WALK-IN CENTRE (TOOTING) 6C **28**
St. George's Hospital
Blackshaw Road
LONDON
SW17 0QT
Tel: 020 8700 0505

NHS WALK-IN CENTRE (WEYBRIDGE)
..........................1B **56**
Weybridge Community Hospital
22 Church Street
WEYBRIDGE
KT13 8DY
Tel: 01932 826013

NHS WALK-IN CENTRE (WOKING) 5B **74**
Woking Community Hospital
Heathside Road
WOKING
GU22 7HS
Tel: 01483 776080

NORTH DOWNS CAPIO HOSPITAL ...3C **104**
46 Tupwood Lane
CATERHAM
CR3 6DP
Tel: 01883 348981

PARKSIDE HOSPITAL 4J **27**
53 Parkside
LONDON
SW19 5NX
Tel: 020 8971 8000

PHYLLIS TUCKWELL HOSPICE 2K **129**
Waverley Lane
FARNHAM
GU9 8BL
Tel: 01252 729400

PRINCESS ALICE HOSPICE, THE 2A **58**
West End Lane
ESHER
KT10 8NA
Tel: 01372 468811

PRINCESS MARGARET BMI HOSPITAL ...5G **4**
Osborne Road
WINDSOR
SL4 3SJ
Tel: 01753 743434

PRINCESS ROYAL UNIVERSITY HOSPITAL, THE
......................................1J **67**
Farnborough Common
ORPINGTON
BR6 8ND
Tel: 01689 863000

PURLEY WAR MEMORIAL HOSPITAL ...7L **63**
856 Brighton Road
PURLEY
CR8 2YL
Tel: 020 8401 3000

QUEEN MARY'S HOSPITAL FOR CHILDREN
......................................7A **44**
Wrythe Lane
CARSHALTON
SM5 1AA
Tel: 020 8296 2000

QUEEN MARY'S HOSPITAL, ROEHAMPTON
......................................9F **12**
Roehampton Lane
LONDON
SW15 5PN
Tel: 020 8487 6000

QUEEN VICTORIA HOSPITAL 7B **166**
Holtye Road
EAST GRINSTEAD
RH19 3DZ
Tel: 01342 414000

REDWOOD BUPA DIAGNOSIS &
TREATMENT CENTRE 7F **122**
Canada Drive
REDHILL
RH1 5BY
Tel: 01737 277277

RICHMOND ROYAL HOSPITAL 6L **11**
Kew Foot Road
RICHMOND
TW9 2TE
Tel: 020 8940 3331

RIDGEWOOD CENTRE, THE 3G **71**
Old Bisley Road
CAMBERLEY
GU16 9QE
Tel: 01276 692919

ROEHAMPTON HUNTERCOMBE HOSPITAL
......................................1F **26**
Holybourne Avenue
LONDON
SW15 4JL
Tel: 020 8780 6155

ROEHAMPTON PRIORY HOSPITAL 7E **12**
Priory Lane
LONDON
SW15 5JJ
Tel: 020 8876 8261

ROYAL HOSPITAL FOR NEURO-DISABILITY
......................................9K **13**
West Hill
LONDON
SW15 3SW
Tel: 020 8780 4500

ROYAL MARSDEN HOSPITAL (SUTTON), THE
......................................6A **62**
Downs Road
SUTTON
SM2 5PT
Tel: 020 8642 6011

ROYAL SURREY COUNTY HOSPITAL ...3H **113**
Egerton Road
GUILDFORD
GU2 7XX
Tel: 01483 571122

RUNNYMEDE BMI HOSPITAL 9F **36**
Guildford Road
Ottershaw
CHERTSEY
KT16 0RQ
Tel: 01932 877800

ST ANTHONY'S HOSPITAL 7J **43**
London Road
SUTTON
SM3 9DW
Tel: 020 8337 6691

ST CATHERINE'S HOSPICE 5B **182**
Malthouse Road
CRAWLEY
RH10 6BH
Tel: 01293 447333

ST EBBA'S 5B **60**
Hook Road
EPSOM
KT19 8QJ
Tel: 01883 388300

ST GEORGE'S HOSPITAL (TOOTING) ...6C **28**
Blackshaw Road
LONDON
SW17 0QT
Tel: 020 8672 1255

ST HELIER HOSPITAL 7A **44**
Wrythe Lane
CARSHALTON
SM5 1AA
Tel: 020 8296 2000

ST JOHN'S AND AMYAND HOUSE 1G **25**
Strafford Road
TWICKENHAM
TW1 3AD
Tel: 020 8744 9943

ST PETER'S HOSPITAL 9F **36**
Guildford Road
CHERTSEY
KT16 0PZ
Tel: 01932 872000

ST RAPHAEL'S HOSPICE 8J **43**
St. Anthony's Hospital
London Road
SUTTON
SM3 9DX
Tel: 020 8335 4575

SAM BEARE HOSPICE 1B **56**
in Weybridge Hospital
22 Church Street
WEYBRIDGE
KT13 8DY
Tel: 01932 826095

SHIRLEY OAKS BMI HOSPITAL 6F **46**
Poppy Lane
CROYDON
CR9 8AB
Tel: 020 8655 5500

SHOOTING STAR HOUSE, CHILDREN'S
HOSPICE 7N **23**
The Avenue
HAMPTON
TW12 3RA
Tel: 020 8783 2000

SLOANE BMI HOSPITAL, THE 1N **47**
125 Albemarle Road
BECKENHAM
BR3 5HS
Tel: 020 8466 4000

SPRINGFIELD UNIVERSITY HOSPITAL ..4C **28**
61 Glenburnie Road
LONDON
SW17 7DJ
Tel: 020 8682 6000

STURT HOUSE PRIORY HOSPITAL 5F **100**
Sturts Lane
Walton on the Hill
TADWORTH
KT20 7RQ
Tel: 01737 817610

SURBITON HOSPITAL 5L **41**
Ewell Road
SURBITON
KT6 6EZ
Tel: 020 8399 7111

SUTTON HOSPITAL 6N **61**
Cotswold Road
SUTTON
SM2 5NF
Tel: 020 8296 2000

TEDDINGTON MEMORIAL HOSPITAL ...7E **24**
Hampton Road
TEDDINGTON
TW11 0JL
Tel: 020 8714 4000

THAMES HOSPICECARE (ASCOT) 2J **33**
Paul Bevan House
King's Ride
ASCOT
SL5 7RD
Tel: 08456 128812

THAMES HOSPICECARE (WINDSOR) ...6D **4**
Hatch Lane
WINDSOR
SL4 3RW
Tel: 08456 128812

TOLWORTH HOSPITAL 8N **41**
Red Lion Road
SURBITON
KT6 7QU
Tel: 020 8390 0102

UNSTED PARK NEURO REHABILITATION
CENTRE 6M **133**
Munstead Heath Road
GODALMING
GU7 1UW
Tel: 01483 892061

WALTON COMMUNITY HOSPITAL 8J **39**
Rodney Road
WALTON-ON-THAMES
KT12 3LD
Tel: 01932 220060

WEALD DAY HOSPITAL 3A **182**
Crawley Hospital
West Green Drive
CRAWLEY
RH11 7DH
Tel: 01293 600300

WEST MIDDLESEX UNIVERSITY HOSPITAL
......................................5G **11**
Twickenham Road
ISLEWORTH
TW7 6AF
Tel: 020 8560 2121

WEST PARK HOSPITAL SITE 8L **59**
Horton Lane
EPSOM
KT19 8PB
Tel: 01883 388300

WEYBRIDGE COMMUNITY HOSPITAL ...1B **56**
22 Church Street
WEYBRIDGE
KT13 8DY
Tel: 01932 852931

WOKING COMMUNITY HOSPITAL 5B **74**
Heathside Road
WOKING
GU22 7HS
Tel: 01483 715911

WOKINGHAM COMMUNITY HOSPITAL
......................................2A **30**
41 Barkham Road
WOKINGHAM
RG41 2RE
Tel: 0118 949 5000

WOKING HOSPICE 5B **74**
5 Hill View Road
WOKING
GU22 7HW
Tel: 01483 881750

WOKING NUFFIELD HOSPITAL 1A **74**
Shores Road
WOKING
GU21 4BY
Tel: 01483 227800

WOKING PRIORY HOSPITAL 3F **72**
Chobham Road
Knaphill
WOKING
GU21 2QF
Tel: 01483 489211